海上货物保险

MARINE CARGO INSURANCE

杨良宜 | 著

法律出版社
LAW PRESS · CHINA

序

通过写书来传播知识是我本人三十年以来一直坚信的理念,也是支持自己笔耕不辍的原因。本书是近四年来我出版的第八本书(独著及合著)。其中既有对较早期作品的更新,也有对于某些领域进行更深入研究后的作品。通过这些工作,我本人目前的系列作品已达到十八本。

促使我以海上货物保险为课题来写本书的原因主要有四个方面:一是本人之前的作品多集中在仲裁法律以及航运法律方面,所以我希望将研究的范围进一步扩大到与航运及贸易关系密切的领域,而保险这一与整个商业社会中各项活动都息息相关的领域无疑十分合适;二是我本人之前关于海上保险的作品已经跟不上法律的发展与变化了;三是英国协会货物保险条文在2009年有了新版本,研究这一重要改版具有很大的现实意义;四是在我日常的业务中也会有很多朋友向我咨询有关保险的问题,说明该方面的知识在中国还是非常需要的。另外考虑到中国目前居于世界前列的巨大贸易量,了解海上货物保险方面的知识也是非常必要的。

众所周知,1982年版的英国协会货物保险条文在生效后的二十多年里取得了巨大成功,几乎所有国际海上货物运输保险的标准条文都或多或少地借鉴了此标准条文。所以很有必要通过研究该改版后的条文而关注整个货物保险领域法律的发展与变化。本书也正是本着此目标,以2009年版的英国协会货物保险条文为基础,着重分析该条文的改变以及涉及的相关法律的改变。本书也同时介绍了英国目前针对岸上保险法正在酝酿的一些重大改革,包括绝对善意理论下受保人的披露责任与误述、承诺性保证、保险人延误赔付的责任或不合理要求损失的证明等内容。

由于保险法律十分复杂且内容丰富,即使在本书最后的审阅与校对阶段,我仍然不断找到新的内容加入,但为了能够使本书与大家见面,不得不暂时告一段落。另外,很多方面在书中也只是浅尝辄止,希望能引起一些喜爱保险的朋友的研究兴趣。

我接下来的研究目标都会更加偏重于基础的合约法与贸易法领域,如已经在筹划与进行中的同属一系列丛书的《国际货物买卖》(杨大明律师著)以及《信用证与见索即付的保函》(本人与本人助手司嘉女士合著)。

最后，要在此感谢为此书出版做了大量工作的司嘉、陈淑玲、袁凯与周琳琳。另外，也要感谢法律出版社吴昉女士对于本书出版所做的大量工作。

杨良宜
2010年8月

目　录

第一章　海上货物保险简介

1. 序言

简单说，海上货物保险的历史十分悠久，早在意大利的《Florentine Ordinance 1523》就已经有记录。在英国，首次有关货物的保单出现在 1555 年。到了 1601 年，英国议院就第一次通过了，针对海上保险的立法，名为《An Act Concerning Matters of Assurances Used Among Merchants》。19 世纪，海上贸易大增，这带来有关法律的大发展。在英国法院，如 Mansfield 勋爵等著名法官以及陪审团（当时英国法院的民商事案件有关事实的争议也是由陪审团来审理）等，累积了 2000 个判例，慢慢建立了海上保险的法律体系。这些判例给 Mackenzie Chalmers 大法官编成成文法，这就是 1906 年《英国海上保险法》。

针对货物保险，早在 1795 年，英国议院就把保单标准化并收取印花税。在该规定下，船舶与货物保险是分开，船舶是"S" Form（S 显然是代表 Ship），货物是"G" Form（G 显然是代表 Goods）。到了 1779 年，劳合社保险人同意把保单合并为 S. G. 保单，毕竟两种保单所承保的海上风险都很接近。S. G. 保单使用了近两百年，而且 1906 年《英国海上保险法》是被列为 First Schedule，可以说地位崇高。但也开始有了批评，如在先例 Middows Ltd. v. Robertson（1940）68 Lloyd's Rep. 45 中就被批评为是"clumsy, imperfect and obscure"。在 The "Anita"（1970）2 Lloyd's Rep. 365，Mocatta 大法官批评说"It cannot be beyond the writ of underwriters and those who advise them in this age of law reform to devise more straightforward and easily comprehended terms of cover"。

在先例 The "Salem"（1982）1 Lloyd's Rep. 369，Kerr 大法官批评说："marine policies are notoriously ill - drawn."。而最关键性的就是联合国贸易发展委员会（UNCTAD）于 1975 年发表的报告，其中对 S. G. 保单有十分尖锐的批评，并建议联合国拟定新的保单作为替代。有关这方面在笔者与汪鹏南教授所著的《英国海上保险条款详论》第 3 ~ 5 页有详论，请参阅。

英国保险市场为了比 UNCTAD 先一步，于 1982 年由著名的海事律师 Donald O'May先生拟定了一份新的海上保险保单，以及合并相关的协会条文，完全替代劳合社标准 S. G. 保单。这种保单的格式是名为 MAR Form（Lloyd's Marine Policy），它的内容相对简单,不像 S. G. 保单包括了许多内容(如列明承保风险,救助费用等)。这些内容都是在附加的协会条文内。MAR Form 只是针对一些主要的事项,如受保人的名字(name of assured),船舶名字(vessel),承保航次或保险期间(voyage or period of insurance),保险标的(subject – matter insured),约定保险价值(agreed value),投保金额(amount insured hereunder),保费(premium)以及有关的条文,特别条件与承诺性保证条文(clause, endorsements, special conditions and warranties)。MAR 基本上就是一个框架协议(framework agreement),共有四页纸,其中一页主要内容包括上述所讲的主要事项。另外还有一页是填写"Definitive numbers of the Syndicates and proportions",该页的备注是"The List of Underwriting Members of Lloyd's mentioned in the above Table shows their respective Syndicates and Shares therein, and is deemed to be incorporated in and to form part of this Policy. It is available for inspection at Lloyd's Policy Signing Office by the Assured or his or their representatives and at true copy of the material parts of it certified by the General Manager of Lloyd's Policy Signing Office will be furnished to the Assured on application."如果投保的是海上货物运输的一切险,就会在"Clauses endorsements special conditions and warranties"中合并协会货物条文。在同一个地方也会加上其他承保的条文(如协会战争条文或协会罢工条文)。上述简单的内容介绍就显示了 MAR 与劳合社标准 S. G. 保单不同之处,后者的前身就是份完整的保单,所以有不少内容是针对承保的风险,然后附上协会货物条文,只为了增加一些承保的风险或者排除在 S. G. 保单中本来承保的风险。这一来,S. G. 保单变得有点不伦不类。但在 MAR,由于它只是个框架协议,所以不针对承保风险,只需要合并协会货物条文(一切险)就已经足够。

也可以说 MAR Form 只是一件"外衣"(jacket),真正保险合约的内容是在合并的协会条文。而针对货物保险,这些合并的条文包括了"协会货物条文(一切险)"(Institute Cargo Clauses [A] 1/1/82,这在 2009 年有更新);"协会战争条文(货物)"(Institute War Clauses [Cargo] 1/1/82);"协会罢工条文(货物)"(Institute Strikes Clause [Cargo] 1/1/82);"协会战争条文(空运货物)"(Institute War Clauses [Air Cargo]);"协会战争条文(邮寄)"(Institute War Clauses [Sending by Post])等。这些条文会稍后介绍。

在海上货物保险,由于越来越多的大批量的生意(volume business),做法上也有了改变,即伦敦市场越来越少以 MAR Form 的保单承保个别航次的付运。替代的做法是承保一段较长的时间,如半年或一年不等,甚至是没有期限(但有条文允许保险人或者受保人给一个通知终止保险合约)的开口/预约保单,承保所有或是大部分受保人在这一个期间做出的付运以及相关商业活动。伦敦市场包括劳合社的开口/预约保单的标准格式名为 Market Reform Contract 或简称 MRC,在本章第 4 段会有进一步介绍。这种保险合约会更加全面针对受保人在保险期间遇到的所有风险,而涉及海上货物运输的开口/预约保单都会合并有关的协会货物条文、协会战争险条文(货物)、协会罢工条文(货物)等。

2. 开口/预约保单的做法(Open Cover)

开口/预约保单在订约自由下可以各种形式出现。第一种是“选择性的开口保单”(facultative open cover),这一种是对双方都没有约束力,受保人可以选择是否宣告某次货物的付运,而保险人也是可以选择是否接受该次宣告货物的承保。这种开口保单没有约束力,好像一般商业合约中的无约束力意向书。

第二种是“受保人选择宣告保险人必须接受的开口保单”(facultative/obligatory open cover)。这种保单允许受保人选择性地作出宣告,而保险人必须接受,只要有关的付运是在开口保单的保险范围内。从保险人角度看,这种安排显然会有危险,即受保人选择性的宣告一些风险大的付运。也有开口保单把这两种形式合并在一起,如有关货物的海上运输或它的付运属于必须宣告与接受,不存在任何一方有选择权。但如果涉及了储存(这会是受保人由于各种原因突然有这样的需要,如一批货物到了卸港卖不出去而需要长期储存,但也会不需要),就可以让受保人有权选择是否投保/加保。在先例 Glencore International v. Alpina Insurance (2004) 1 Lloyd's Rep. 111 中针对货物的储存,有关的规定是“Including, **if required**, storage and blending prior to shipment or after final discharge in Land Tankers, Refineries, and storage in barge (s)...”

第三种是“标准/必须接受的开口保单”(standard/obligatory open cover),这是最常见的做法,就是保险人与受保人一达成开口保单,受保人必须宣告每次的付运并作出保费的支付,而保险人也必须接受承保,只要有关的付运是在开口保单的保险范围内。

以上三种主要不同的开口保单,最关键之处在于它们何时达成对双方都有约束力的保险合约有很大的不同之处。上文介绍的第一种是要到受保人宣告与保险人接受后才会有保险合约;第二种开口保单会是直到受保人宣告才会有保险合约,但在约定这种开口保单时还不能算是达成个别付运的保险合约;第三种开口保单则不一样,开口保单达成时双方就有了保险合约,任何一方都无法脱身。这达成保险合约不同的时间会在很大程度上影响受保人的披露责任,其中第二种开口保单更加是存在争议。这方面的影响在第二章第 4.1.7 段与本章第 2.2 段有提到,不再重复。

在今天的国际货物买卖,业务量达到一定规模的卖方与买方都会有开口保单的安排,也可以让他们随意以 CIF、FOB、CFR、Ex - Work 等方式进行买卖。事实上,他们在谈判买卖时,谁比较更容易安排海上货物运输保险也是其中一个考虑。甚至会有 CIF 买卖,但卖方是要求买方在他的开口保单中投保。

在一些涉及集装箱运输的承运人,他们也会有海上货物保险的开口保单,可为一些小的货方作出投保,真正是提供“一条龙”服务。

2.1　第一种：选择性的开口保单

前已述及，这种开口保单只是像一般商业合约中的无约束力意向书或框架协议（framework agreement），根本不是有约束力与最终的保险合约。受保人与保险人所同意的也只是程序上的机制（procedural mechanism）为将来个别付运的保险合约达成奠定基础。而事后每次受保人的宣告，保险人接不接受还是要看他每次的表态。如果接受的话，双方在那时才算是订立了保险合约。反正是大家都有权选择：Societe Anonyme d' Intermediaries Luxembourgeois v. Farex Gie (1995) Lloyd's Rep IR 116。在这种开口保单下，受保人在每次宣告时有自动作出全面批露的责任：Berger and Light Diffusesrs Pty Ltd. v. Pollock (1973) 2 Lloyd's Rep. 442。

在这里也可以提另一种相同的做法，就是劳合社的保险人或伦敦保险公司授权给一家保险公司或是保险经纪人接受某些风险，如海上货物保险。这种做法可称为是 line slip。它的定义可见先例 Balfour v. Beaumont (1982) 2 Lloyd's Rep. 493，Webster 大法官这样说："A line slip is an authority (known in the London market as a facility) given in writing by a number of underwriters which enables the leading underwriter (or writers) to agree to proposals for insurance of risks within a prescribed class on behalf of all underwriters subscribing to the line slip provided that the proposed insurance is within the scope of the terms of the authority."

另在先例 American Airlines v. Hope (1974) 2 Lloyd's Rep. 301，304，Diplock 勋爵关于授权保险经纪人这样说："[The broker] takes the slip in the first instance to an underwriter whom he has selected to deal with as leading underwriter, i. e. , one who has a reputation in the market as an expert in the kind of cover required and whose lead is likely to be followed by other insurers in the market. If it is the first contract of insurance covering that risk in which a particular underwriter has acted as leading underwriter it is treated as an original insurance. The broker and the leading underwriter go through the slip together. They agree on any amendments to the broker's draft and fix the premium. When agreement has been reached the leading underwriter initials the slip for this proportion of the cover and the broker then takes the initialed slip round the market to other insurers who initial it for such proportion of the cover as each is willing to accept. For practical purposes all the negotiations about the terms of the insurance and the rate of premium are carried on between the broker and the leading underwriter alone."

2.2　第二种：受保人选择宣告保险人必须接受的开口保单

这种形式的保单已经较早时简单介绍过，在这里给一些权威的定义。在先例 Ionides v. The Pacific Fire & Marine Insurance Company (1871) LR 6 QB 674，Blackburn 大法官说："The contract of an underwriter who subscribes a policy on goods by ship or ships to be declared is, that he will insure any goods of the description specified which may be shipped on any vessel answering the description, if any there be, in the policy, on the voyages specified in the policy, to which the assured elects to apply the policy. The object of the declaration is to earmark and identify the particular adventure to which the assured elects to apply the policy. The assent of the insurer is not required to this, for he has no option to reject any vessel which the assured may select; nor is it necessary that the declaration should do more than identify the adventure, and so prevent the possible dishonesty of a party insured, who might intend to apply the policy to particular goods, so that they should be at the risk of the assurers, and he could come on them if there was a loss; and then, when those goods had arrived safely, to pretend that he intended to apply the policy to another set of goods still subject to risks..."

与稍后介绍的标准/必须接受的开口保单相比,其缺点可以贵族院先例 Aneco v. J & H (2002) 1 Lloyd's Rep. 157 显示(内容虽然针对再保险,但道理一样),如下:"Fac/Oblig treaties are naturally less attractive to reinsurers than quota share treaties. They are subject to the obvious risk that the insurer will retain good business for his own account and cede poor business to the treaty. There is, or at least is assumed to be, no obligation of good faith on the part of the ceding party when exercising his discretion whether to cede or retain a risk. The only constraint upon him is that he must exercise some restraint if he wishes to maintain a good reputation in the market and any hope of doing future business with existing and prospective reinsurers."

该种开口保单只要是受保人选择为某些付运的货物作出了宣告,保险人都必须承保,所以在受保人每次宣告时就产生独立与有约束力的保险合约。因此,就有观点认为在受保人每次宣告时他就有相应的披露义务。但法律地位并非这样,正如本书第二章介绍,受保人之所以有很重的披露责任,是想让保险人有机会评估风险以决定是否要承保以及保费是多少。而该种开口保单下,受保人每次作出宣告,保险人都必须承保,即他已经没有任何选择的余地,所有披露的作用实现不了,披露也就没有必要了。

这可节录 Bennett 教授所著的《The Law of Marine Insurance》第 2 版之 2.42 段所说的话:"Since the assured owes the insurer no counter - obligation, a facultative/obligatory cover must be regarded as a unilateral offer, albeit one that is regarded by market custom as irrevocable, accepted each time the assured makes a declaration within the terms of the cover and giving rise to a separate contract on each occasion. In consequence, since the doctrine of utmost good faith is designed to ensure that the insurer makes an informed decision on the acceptability of the risk and the terms of cover, the doctrine attaches to the cover itself, but it has no function to perform in respect of and does not attach to individual declarations: Ionides v. Pacific Fire & Marine (1871) L. R. 6 Q. B. 674; Law Guarantee Trust & Accident Society v. Munich Reinsurance (1915) 31 TLR 572; Citadel Insurance v. Atlantic Union (1982) 2 Lloyd's Rep. 543; The 'La Pointe' (1986) 2 Lloyd's Rep.

513 (Supreme Court of British Columbia)."

2.3　第三种:标准/必须接受的开口保单

海上货物保险通常是以开口保单形式投保,很少会单独为一票货物与一个航次作出投保。开口保单是投保受保人在某个期间所有会购买、生产、出售的货物。在受保人一有货物需要付运时,他可以向保险人作出宣告。而该宣告会被视为仅具有行政意义,目的是让双方根据开口保单所同意的保费费率计算有关航次与该票货物的保费,而与保险合约是否生效无关,因为开口保单已经达成,后面每次付运的宣告已经不存在需要重新达成任何协议。这种是最常见的开口保单,也被称为双方必须接受的开口保单(obligatory open cover)或标准开口保单(standard open cover)。在这种开口保单下,受保人所有的付运都必须宣告,而且受保人的定义会特别广泛(在本章2.5段会介绍),而保险人也必须接受承保每次宣告的付运。这完全是来自标准开口保单,以文字清楚写明,没有其他的巧妙。如协会标准开口保单所用的措辞是:"It is a condition of this contract that the Assured are **bound to** declare hereunder every consignment without exception, Underwriters being **bound to** accept up to but not exceeding the amount specified in Clause 3 below."这种开口保单的定义也可节录R. H. Brown先生所著的《Dictionary of Marine Insurance Terms》,如下:"A form of long - term insurance contract whereby the insurer guarantees to accept risks when they are put forward by the assured as they arise during the period of the contract. The assured agrees to declare every item that falls within the scope of the cover and does not have the option to place such risks elsewhere should he consider it an obligatory contract binding both parties to its terms."

这种标准开口保单受欢迎是可以理解的,因为如果每次的付运都需要重新谈判保险合约,会给保险人与受保人带来许多麻烦与不必要的工作量。而且还会有其他的问题,如时间上晚了、受保人漏了或错误投保、保险人没有办法约束一家可能是庞大与信誉良好的贸易商成为他的长期客户等。对保险人还有另外的好处是,在谈判开口保单时,受保人通常需要告诉保险人在保险期间,如一年内估计的保费收入(estimated premium income,简称EPI)。这就令保险人可以正确预期与该客户的业务量。EPI的估计必须是绝对善意,不得有误述,因为该信息显然有实质性重要。

2.4　标准/必须接受的开口保单的前身:浮动保单

开口保单之前的做法是浮动保单(floating policy),这是最早的一种提供较长期的保险安排的做法。1906年《英国海上保险法》在Section 29针对浮动保单这样规定:"(1)A floating policy is a policy which describes the insurance in general terms, and leaves the name of the ship or ships and other particulars to be defined by subsequent declaration. (2)The subsequent declaration or declarations may be made by indorsement on the policy, or in other customary manner. (3) Unless the policy otherwise provides, the declarations **must** be made in the order of dispatch or shipment. They must, in the case of goods, comprise all consignments within the terms of the policy, and the value of the goods or other property must be honestly stated, but an omission or erroneous declaration may be rectified even after loss or arrival, provided the omission or declaration was made in good faith.(加黑部分是笔者的强调,它要求受保人每次付运必须宣告。)(4) Unless the policy otherwise provides, where a declaration of value is not made until after notice of loss or arrival, the policy must be treated as an unvalued policy as regards the subject - matter of that declaration."

这种在19世纪就已经开始有的做法,保险人与受保人是同意一个总的保险金额。然后在每次付运并作出宣告后,总金额就会因为每次付运所宣告的保险价值而减少,直到总金额变为零为止。在这种做法下,可以看到受保人在每次宣告时,要特别小心剩下的保险金额。此外,宣告的次序也要准确,因为每次的宣告都会使总的保险金额发生改变。

相比现在的标准开口保单,受保人就不用担心这方面的问题,反正在开口保单有效的期间每次付运的宣告保险人都必须接受。更会有安排是在只需要受保人按时(如每个月)把所有付运的货物与航次一次性地进行宣告与支付保费。而针对保险金额的限制,再也没有一个总的金额。但反而会有一条限制每次付运或者货物集中地点(如装港、卸港或其他的储存地点)的货物总金额,如500万美元。原因是为了避免风险太集中,保险人吃不消。这表示受保人要小心,如有几次不同的付运,每艘船舶的货物价值都不超过500万美元。但由于卸港十分拥挤,结果前后在装港开航的5艘船舶都堵在卸港等候泊位。结果发生了一场重大的天灾,如台风。5艘船舶中的3艘受到了严重损坏,这也包括船上的货物。这一来,受保人向保险人的索赔就会有所限制而赔不足。

因为在Section 29(3)中是规定了在浮动保单,受保人必须(must)在每次的付运都需要宣告,这在一定程度上与现在的标准开口保单有相似之处。但另一方面,Section 29(3)规定了宣告必须是"in the order of dispatch or shipment",这就缺少了现在的标准开口保单的一些灵活性(该灵活性可以从下文要介绍的先例The "Beursgracht" (2002) 1 Lloyd's Rep. 574中看出来)。但在受保人每次付运都必须宣告与保险人必须接受每次的宣告,这在现在的标准开口保单与以前的浮动保单是在本质上一致的。正如Tuckey大法官在先例The "Beursgracht"中所说:"So this is not a cover of the facultative/obligatory type, but one which is more like a floating policy."

2.5　开口/预约保单中受保人的定义与范围

开口/预约保单由于是针对将来的贸易活动中存在的风险,但在投保时也不确定将来有什么贸易活动以及所涉及的风险,所以订立的条文都会尽量广泛,其中就是受保人的定义与范围,以避免在千变万化的贸易活动中会有遗漏。例如,将来有一次或多次的付运是分公司或联营公司作出,主要的受保人出了事故之后才知道,去向保险人宣告。如果受保人的定义是否包括出事故的分公司或联营公司并不明确,就会受到保险人的拒赔。在国际货物买卖中,主要受保人还会经常被对方的买方/卖方要求以某些条件投保,如 CIF 卖方要求有一个开口保单让 CIF 买方为他投保。

在 MRC,对受保人的定义就包括了主要受保人、他的代理人、分公司、联营公司与任何希望他代为投保的人士(A Limited, and/or as agents and/or subsidiaries and/or associated companies an/or for whom they may have instructions to insure)。至于在协会货物条文第 15.1 条更是加上了受让人(assignee),这显然是想包括如 CIF 买方或分买方。有关这一方面,在本书第十三章第 9.2 段会有更详尽的解释。

有关是否被包括在受保人的定义而成为是共同受保人(co – assured),有一些案例可以介绍。第一个是 National Oil Well Ltd. v. Davy Offshore Ltd. (1993) 2 Lloyd's Rep. 582,Colman 大法官说:

"(1) Where at the time when the contract of insurance was made the principal assured or other contracting party had express or implied actual authority to enter into that contract so as to bind some other party as co – assured and intended to bind that party, the latter may sue on the policy as the undisclosed principal and co – assured regardless of whether the policy described a class of co – assured of which he was or became a member.(这种情况在海上货物保险应该不多,就是主要受保人投保时已经有了其他第三人明示或者默示的授权作为共同受保人。)

(2) Where at the time when the contract of insurance was made the principal assured or other contracting party had no actual authority to bind the other party to the contract of insurance, but the policy is expressed to insure not only the principal assured but also a class of others who are not identified in that policy, a party who at the time when the policy was effected could have been ascertained to qualify as a member of that class can ratify and sue on the policy as a co – assured if at the time it was intended by the principal assured or other contracting party to create privity of contract with the insurers on behalf of that particular party.(这种情况在海上货物保险最常见,就是在投保时主要受保人没有其他第三人的授权,开口保单只是在受保人的定义包括了其他的类别,但没有讲明是谁。这一来,将来只要是属于这一个类别的人士就可以通过追认授权作为该保单的共同受保人。唯一的要求就是主要受保人有意图使该类别人士与保险人产生合约的相互关系。简单说,就是将来该类别人士出现时,主要受保人希望他是作为共同受保人被包括在保险合约内。)

(3) Evidence as to whether in any particular case the principal assured or other contracting party did have the requisite intention may be provided by the terms of the policy itself, by the terms of any contract between the principals assured or other contracting party and the alleged co – assured, or by any other admissible material showing what was subjectively intended by the principal assured.(这里是针对怎样证明主要受保人有关上述所讲的投保时的意图。)"

另一个有关的先例涉及受保人不够广泛的危险,该先例并不是海上货物保险,但道理一样。该先例 The "Jascon 5" (2006) 2 Lloyd's Rep. 195 的案情涉及一艘部分在中国建造的船舶(是一艘非常昂贵的用于海上管道铺设的驳船),被拖去新加坡以完成建造工程。船东指令保险经纪人为他与船厂(新加坡的 Sembawang 船厂)对该船舶的可保利益投保造船风险保险(Builder's Risk Policy),这在笔者所著的《造船合约》一书第十三章第 3.3 段有介绍。结果在该保单,受保人除了船东外,也包括了"Subsidiary, Affiliate, Associated and Interrelated Companies and/or Joint Ventures as may be required as their respective rights and interests may appear",但没有把 Sembawang 船厂加入作为共同受保人,也没有告诉保险人。结果发生了船舶在船厂完成建造时被损坏,这就涉及船厂是否是共同受保人的争议。上诉庭判是 Sembawang 船厂不是一个共同受保人,也不包括在"Subsidiary, Affiliate, Associated and Interrelated Companies and/or Joint Ventures"的范围内。另针对 Sembawang 船厂是否可以以未公开的委托人身份作为共同受保人,上诉庭认为在该先例的案情下是不可以,因为投保时是有机会披露并加入 Sembawang 船厂为共同受保人。Moore - Bick 大法官指出这种情况下委托人应该在投保时就被披露出来,因为会影响风险,即保险人会考虑如果在船厂出事时涉及船厂有疏忽也不会有代位求偿权向船厂索赔,把赔付给船东的钱要回来,说:

"The mere identification, whether by name or description, of certain persons as assureds cannot be sufficient of itself to demonstrate an unwillingness on the part of the insurer to contract with any other person. If it were otherwise, the principles under discussion would have no application at all to contracts of insurance. Each case must therefore be decided by reference to the terms of the contract under consideration and the circumstances in which it came to be made, though no doubt due regard should be had to the warning of Lord Lloyd in Siu Yin Kwan v Eastern Insurance Co. Ltd. (1994) 2 AC 199 that if the courts are too ready to construe written contracts as contradicting the right of an undisclosed principal to intervene it would go far to destroy the beneficial assumption in commercial cases to which Diplock L. J. referred in Teheran - Europe Co. Ltd. v S. T. Belton (Tractors) Ltd. (1968) 2 QB 545...

Having regard to the circumstances of the present case I think the judge was right to attach particular significance to the omission of Sembawang from the categories of assureds set out in the slip. When a vessel enters a shipyard for completion and fitting out the persons most immediately interested in her safety are the owner and the shipyard. Other parties with commercial interests in her may also be adversely affected if she suffers loss or damage and it is not surprising, therefore, to find that the assureds in the present policy include other companies within the same group as the owner and even joint venturers. In this context the absence of any reference to the shipyard and its sub - contractors is striking, particularly when it is borne in mind that their inclusion as co - assureds would have a significant effect on the insurers' rights of subrogation and therefore on the risk.

Bearing in mind the context in which this policy was issued, I have come to the conclusion that the omission of any reference to the yard or its sub – contractors is not neutral but must be regarded as a positive indication that the insurers were not willing to contract with them. I am satisfied that this is a case, therefore, in which the terms of the contract by implication exclude any right on the part of Sembawang to sue on it as an undisclosed principal."

3. 延误宣告

延误宣告在三种开口保单下都会发生。在第一种选择性的开口保单(Facultative Open Cover),每次付运只有在受保人宣告与保险人接受的情况下才会有独立的保险合约产生,所以如果是受保人延误宣告(特别是在已经发生货损货差时,而且这是必须作出披露的),保险人也就不可能接受,也就不会有相应的保险合约产生,自然保险人也就没有任何的赔付责任。至于其他的两种开口保单下的延误宣告,会在以下段节作出详细介绍。

3.1　标准/必须接受的开口保单下的延误宣告(late declaration under Standard/Obligatory Open Cover)

3.1.1　善意的延误宣告(late declaration in utmost good faith)

在这种开口保单,由于承保人必须接受受保人的宣告,所以除非在保险合约中另有规定,法律默示地位对受保人延误的宣告(但必须是在绝对善意的大精神下)也特别宽松。在合约中另有规定的例子可见先例:Union Insurance of Canton v. George Wills & Co.,(P. C.)(1916) 1 A. C 281,该浮动保单中有一条明示条文要求受保人在开航后尽快(as soon as possible after sailing of vessel)作出宣告。法院判这是一条承诺性保证条文,一旦违反,保险人就自动解除保险合约下的赔付责任。在该先例,保险人提供证据证明延误宣告的违反对他的严重后果,因为他在每次准时宣告后都要作出再保安排。

但在先例 The "Beursgracht" (2002) 1 Lloyd's Rep. 574,受保人 Glencore 与保险人签订了标准开口保单,有次风险(该开口保单是承保受保人 Glencore 对租赁船舶的责任保险)的宣告延误7年,法院还是判保险人需要对船东的责任(涉及一个装卸小工的死亡)作出赔付。在该先例,高院与上诉庭比较详尽地探讨了受保人延误宣告的后果。由于在该标准开口保单没有特别的字样要求受保人尽快作出宣告,加上宣告在这种形式的开口保单被视为只是有行政与计算保费的意义,所以高院与上诉庭都判延误宣告不是违反承诺性保证,也不是违反赔付的先决条件。它只是该标准开口保单中的中间条文,而在该先例延误了7年才宣告产生的后果被认定是并不严重。延误宣告的风险所涉及的保费只是该月份的1%,保费金额只是250美元,而且保险人也没有提供任何有关再保险会带来何种影响的证据。所以即使受保人违反,这也是局限在金钱的赔偿而不可以让保险人逃避赔付责任。上诉庭的 Tuckey 大法官这样说:"For the purpose of analyzing the seriousness and effect of the admitted breach one must bear in mind that despite the absence of a declaration underwriters were at all material times on risk and that the failure to make a declaration of this one risk was due to a good faith mistake. The mistake may not have been formally rectified for some time, but by mid -1992 at the latest underwriters were aware that the assured were saying that they were on risk. The Lloyd's brokers' fax of Aug. 2, 1994, to which I have referred, makes this perfectly clear. In terms of this risk, which would have yielded a premium of U. S. MYM250, the commercial consequences for underwriters of not having the declaration on their file were negligible, as the Judge said. Underwriters called no evidence to the contrary and one would not expect them to have been able to do so. I do not ignore the extent of the potential exposure, but this could not possibly have affected their reinsurance program or reinsurance to close."

另 Tuckey 大法官也提到了受保人善意的延误宣告,即使是属于违反中间条文,损失也会只局限在赔付迟延计算与支付保费带来的利息损失,说:"This is not the time or the place to consider whether as a matter of law underwriters could have recovered lost interest as damages for the breach of the obligation to make a timely declaration. In this case the liability to do so was conceded and in practice I would expect an assured who had made a late declaration by mistake to offer to pay interest on his late payment of premium. In any event I do not think that the fact that underwriters' legal right to recover interest is, or may be, doubtful is a good reason for saying that underwriters should be entitled to avoid liability for the risk."

针对海上货物保险,迟延宣告的付运货物被视为是非定值保单(unvalued policy)。原因是如果标准开口保单是定值保险(valued policy),在作出宣告并同时已经发生了事故,岂非保险人还要赔付保险价值(insured value),而这个保险价值是来自受保人延误的宣告,受保人也无需证明?但如果是被视为是非定值保单,就会需要受保人证明保险标的的可保价值(insurable value)。这方面请看本书第十二章第 3 段,这也是在 1906 年《英国海上保险法》Section 29(4)的规定。

3.1.2　恶意的延误宣告(late declaration in bad faith)

恶意的延误宣告或选择性宣告在先例 Rivaz v. Gerussi Bros & Co. (1880) 6 QBD 222 有出现过。这带来的后果显然就是违反在第二章所针对的绝对善意大原则,有关保险人可以有的救济就是作出令保险合约无效(avoid the contract)的选择。这也是 1906 年《英国海上保险法》的法律地位:"A contract of marine insurance is a contract based upon the utmost good faith, and, if the utmost good faith be not observed by either party, the contract may be avoided by the other party."

3.2 受保人选择宣告保险人必须接受的开口保单下的延误宣告(late declaration under Facultative/ Obligatory open cover)

在这种形式的开口保单下,显然是提供了给受保人伸缩性与取巧的机会。其中一种取巧的机会就会在宣告,或是宣告的内容尽量含糊,或是在知道损失发生后才宣告。看来,英国法律对这种开口保单的宣告比较严格,不像标准开口保单的延误7年作出宣告仍然可以被视为是有效:The "Beursgracht" (2002) 1 Lloyd's Rep. 574。

首先针对内容含糊的宣告,不明确说明是什么航次或付运,这在先例 Ionides v. Pacific Fire & Marine (1871) L. R. 6 Q. B. 674 中有针对宣告的内容。即宣告的内容必须明确,为了避免不诚实的受保人在他本来宣告针对的那票货物安全到达目的地后假装本来的宣告其实是针对另外一票尚在运输途中的货物。这在本章第2.2段有提到。现将 Blackburn 大法官说过的比较重要与相关的话重新节录如下:"The contract of an underwriter who subscribes a policy on goods by ship or ships to be declared is, that he will insure any goods of the description specified which may be shipped on any vessel answering the description, if any there be, in the policy, to which the assured elects to apply the policy. The object of the declaration is to earmark and identify the particular adventure to which the assured elects to apply the policy..."

至于在损失发生后才作出宣告,这在 Glencore International v. Alpina Insurance (2004) 1 Lloyd's Rep. 111 先例中有涉及,有关的部分判决可以节录如下:

"Under a contract of this kind (这是指标准开口保单) making declarations in arrears does not give rise to any difficulty in relation to transits because the insurance is obligatory on both sides. Accordingly, even if the insured fails to declare a shipment it is covered: see The 'Beursgracht' [2002] 1 Lloyd's Rep. 574. Declarations simply provide the insurer with information about the risks that have already attached to the cover in accordance with its terms. Under this cover (这是指受保人可以选择宣告保险人必须接受的开口保单), however, the position in relation to storage risks is different because in respect of them the insurance is facultative on the part of the insured, but obligatory on the part of the insurers. Without a declaration of some kind, therefore, there is no means of telling whether the insured wishes to invoke his right to obtain cover. I think Mr. Rainey Q. C. (保险人的代表大律师) was right, therefore, in saying that in that situation the declaration performs a quite different function.

Mr. Rainey submitted that in principle under a facultative/obligatory cover on goods such as this the insured must communicate his intention to attach the particular goods to the cover before the insurers can come on risk. That is certainly a good starting point, but it is necessary to have regard to the particular terms of the contract, the nature of the business insured and any established course of dealing between the parties. In the present case it would have been difficult in practical terms for Glencore (受保人) to have declared storage risks in advance. Transit risks were declared some months in arrears because, as Alpina (保险人) recognised, it took time for an organisation such as Glencore to collate the information necessary to enable that to be done, but in most cases the storage risk arose when the relevant transit risk ended and it would have been equally difficult therefore for Glencore to collate the necessary information to enable it to declare goods for storage cover more promptly. Moreover, if declarations with retrospective effect could never be made, the storage cover would have lost much of its commercial value in a situation where risks were routinely being declared three months or more in arrears because in many cases the goods are likely to remain in store for a much shorter period than that. That appears to have been recognised by Alpina which consistently accepted declarations of storage risks in arrears in the same way as transit risks without ever suggesting that cover attached only from the date the declaration was received. Mr. Rainey submitted that those declarations did not make it clear whether cover was being sought retrospectively or only prospectively, but the natural inference in the absence of any indication to the contrary is that Glencore was seeking cover from the moment the goods were put into store rather than from some later and largely arbitrary date and expected to be charged a premium on that basis (as indeed it was). In those circumstances, whatever might otherwise have been the position, I do not think that Alpina can now say that declarations of storage risks were effective only from the date at which it received the relevant declarations and that the goods were therefore covered only from that time."

虽然如上述节录判词的第2段中所讲,Moore - Bick大法官说可以理解像Glencore这样庞大的贸易商是需要时间收集资料后(如明确货物要储存多久)才能向保险人作出选择性宣告,所以免不了有些延误。而且保险人在过往的做法中,也都接受了Glencore作出的延误宣告。但接下来的判决中显示了在Facultative/Obligatory的保险安排下,还是不像标准/必须接受的开口保单(在这个先例必须接受的开口保单是只适用在付运风险[transit risks]而不适用在储存风险[storage risk])。道理是受保人可以有选择宣告或者不宣告的权利,这就表示了受保人可以随时改变主意,而且是没有违反绝对善意。所以,虽然两种形式的保单都可以延误宣告,但针对Facultative/Obligatory的保险安排,在知道发生损失后就不能再作出有效的宣告了。而标准/必须接受的开口保单,就没有这个限制,正如1906年《英国海上保险法》Section 29(3)所说的情况,在浮动保单下(这是标准/必须接受的开口保单的前身,在本章第2.4段有介绍),漏掉或错误宣告是可以在损失发生后再作出或者修正,只要是善意。Moore - Bick大法官接着这样说:"I can see the commercial force of that argument in a case where it can be shown that there was a fixed intention to declare the risk in question to the cover, but it does face very substantial difficulties. The element of risk is fundamental to a contract of insurance and for that reason it is essential where the cover is facultative/obligatory in nature that an unequivocal step of some kind attaching the risk to the cover has been taken before the insured knows of the loss. If, whatever may have been its original intention, Glencore remained free to change its mind at any time before making a formal declaration, it would have been able to declare a risk when a loss had been suffered and free not to declare it if there had been no loss."

所以 Moore - Bick 大法官在最后判是受保人在知道货物或保险标的有了损失后不能作出有效的宣告,也就是判保险人不必赔付,说:"In these circumstances I am unable to accept that Glencore was entitled to declare to the cover with retrospective effect goods which it already knew had been subject to a loss."

这样看来,也可以说是 facultative/obligatory 的保险安排对受保人或保险人都会有不利,比不上标准/必须要接受(standard/obligatory)的开口保单,就是受保人在发生损失后作出宣告已经为时太晚。

4.　标准开口保单的有关条文

以下是一个标准开口保单格式(contract of insurance),在伦敦市场通常就是一份 Market Reform Contract 或简称 MRC 的样本,并加上相关的内容解释让读者知道涉及的内容。

RISK DETAILS(承保风险细节)

REFERENCE:　(档案号)

TYPE:　Marine Cargo Insurance (风险类别:海上货物保险)

ASSURED:　[A Limited, and/or as agents and/or subsidiaries and/or associated companies an/or for whom they may have instructions to insure]

(**受保人:**A 公司或/与它的代理人或/与他的分公司或/是与它们的联营公司或/与它们被要求投保的第三人。受保人通常是尽量广泛以避免在千变万化的贸易活动中会有遗漏,如有一次的付运是分公司所作出,A 公司是出了事之后才知道。或是在国际货物买卖中被对方的买方/卖方要求以某些条件投保。)

PRINCIPAL ADDRESS:　(这里是指 A 公司的地址)

PERIOD:　Risk attaching from ____ to ____ both days inclusive, local standard time.

(**保险期间:**风险从哪一天开始到哪一天为止,如为期一年。也会有情况是约定更精确的时间,如写明是从某天的几点开始与到某天的几点终止。也会是一条常青条文[evergreen clause],说明保单每年自动更新,只在受保人或保险人提前3个月给通知的情况下才终止保险合约。)

CANCELLATION CLAUSE:　[For example: This insurance may be cancelled either by the Assured or by the Underwriters by one party giving the other 7 days notice in respect of War and Strikes Risks except in respect of sendings to or from the United States when Strikes Risks will be subject to 48 hours notice of cancellation.]

(**终止条文**:这也是针对终止保险合约的权利。但针对的是有关战争与罢工的风险可以作出7天的终止通知,除了美国是只有48小时。这方面所涉及的 Waterborne Agreement 在本书第八章第9.2段有介绍。)

CONVEYANCE:　[For example: Any land water or air conveyance, ... Ocean going vessels in accordance with the Institute Classification Clause 01/01/2001 (CL. 354) ...]

(**运输工具**:这里可以规定是什么运输工具,如航空、火车、公路加上船舶。如果是船舶,由于无法确定将来会租用什么船舶,所以在这里加上协会船级条文,以保证作出运输的船舶不会太差。有关协会船级条文在本书第八章第8.4段有详细介绍。)

INTEREST:　[For example: Goods and/or merchandise of every description consisting principally of crude oil, petroleum products...]

(**保险利益**:如所有不同类别的货物或/与商品,主要包括原油、石油产品等。受保人也通常会尽量广泛以避免在千变万化的贸易活动或者在保险期间有新的业务中会产生遗漏。在先例 Glencore International A. G. v. Alpina Insurance Company Limited [2004] 1 Lloyd's Rep. 111,它包括的是"crude oil, kerosene, gas oil, naphtha, liquid petroleum gases and all products incidental to Glencore's business or otherwise as might be declared.")

VOYAGE:　[For example: At and from ports or places anywhere in the world...]

(**航次**:如从或去世界的任何港口或地点。受保人也是通常会尽量广泛以避免在千变万化的贸易活动或者在保险期间有新的业务中有遗漏。)

LIMIT:　[For example: USMYM 10,000,000 any one sending and/or shipment and/or location...]

(**保险金额的限制**:如1000万美元在每次付运或/与地点。这方面在较早前已经解释过,就是保险人加上这一条文限制每次的付运或者一个地点[如装港、卸港或其他的储存地点]的保险金额,避免风险太集中。)

Contract Leader Initial(首席保险人签署)

Basis of Valuation Clause:[[For example:Cost insurance and freight plus 10%...]

(**货物保险价值**:这是针对每次宣告时计算货物保险价值的基础,就是 CIF 价格加上 10% 不等的估计利润。根据这样计算出来的保险价值,再根据保费率算的出每次付运要交的保费。另在发生赔付时,也可以作为定值保单赔付。这方面在本书第十二章第 3.5 与 3.6 段有介绍。

该条文有时也会变得很复杂,因为承保风险广泛的开口保单不一定只有 CIF 买卖,而会涉及千变万化的不同贸易活动。如在先例 Glencore International A. G. v. Alpina Insurance Company Limited [2004] 1 Lloyd's Rep. 111 的开口保单中,Basis of Valuation Clause 规定如下:

"1. Shipments which are sold by the Assured prior to attachment of risk are valued at:

1.1 The sum declared if such declaration is made prior to known or reported loss but in no event shall such declaration be less than the Assured's Sale Price.

1.2 In the event of no declaration having been made prior to loss, valued at Assured's Sale Price plus, if applicable, additional charges.

2. Shipments which are not sold at the time of attachment of risk are valued at:

2.1 The sum declared if such declaration is made prior to loss;

2.2 If no declaration is made prior to loss valued at the higher of either the Assured's cost plus expenses plus 10% or replacement cost.

3. Shipments insured on instruction of third parties:...

4. Interests in store which are not sold at time of attachment are valued at 'replacement cost'.")

CONDITIONS: All terms and conditions as LPO62A Lloyd's Marine Policy (MAR 91)

(**开口保单的条文**:通常情况下由两部分组成,标准印本条文与保险经纪人根据特定的情况/要求自己草拟的附加条文。前者像协会货物条文[Institute Cargo Clauses],而后者像由 Joint Cargo Committee 根据某些特定的情况草拟的附加条文。以下举一些例子:

Institute Cargo Clauses [A] 01/01/2009 协会货物条文[一切险]

Institute War Clauses [Cargo] 01/01/2009 协会战争条文[货物]

Institute Strikes Clause [Cargo] 01/01/2009 协会罢工条文[货物]

Institute War Clauses [Air Cargo] 协会战争条文[空运货物]
Institute War Clauses [Sending by Post] 协会战争条文[邮寄])

LOSS PAYEE(S): Loss, if any, payable to Assured and/or order. [This heading is deleted if there are no loss payee instructions agreed.]

(**接受保险赔付的人士:**赔付给受保人或/与根据受保人的指令赔付给相关的人士,[如果没有赔付指令是要把本条文删除]。在涉及银行融资中,会是在保险合约中接受保险赔付的就是有关的银行,也会是受保人不只是一家公司或个别人士,就有必要说明接受保险赔付的是谁。)

EXPRESS WARRANTIES: [If none, this is stated]

(**明示承诺性保证:**根据保险人与受保人之间有约定的明示承诺性保证就需要在此列出。但如果没有明示承诺性保证约定,也要在此说明是没有。有关在保险法律中承诺性保证条文的特殊性与严格,请看本书第四章有针对,另在本书许多其他地方也有涉及,如第八章第8.1段有关船舶适航的默示保证。)

CONDITIONS PRECEDENT: [If none, this is stated]

(**先决条件:**根据保险人与受保人之间有约定的先决条件就需要在此列出。但如果没有明示先决条件,也要在此说明是没有。有关保险合约的先决条件也请看本书第四章。)

SUBJECTIVITIES: [Any subjectivities are stated in full, with the timeframe for compliance and consequence of non – compliance: if none, this is stated]

(**保险经纪人的自拟条文:**在本格式内介绍"开口保单的条文"时就提到说"开口保单的条文通常情况下由两部分组成:标准印本条文与保险经纪人根据特定的情况自己草拟的附加条文。"而这里 subjectivities 实际上就是属于保险经纪人根据特定的情况自己草拟的附加条文。它有可能是保证条文或是条件条文。)

CHOICE OF LAW AND JURISDICTION: [For example: This insurance shall be governed by and construed in accordance with the law of England and Wales and each party agrees to submit to the exclusive jurisdiction of the Courts of England and Wales, except as may be expressly provided herein to the contrary.]

(**适用法与管辖权:**除非有其他相反规定,保险合约要根据英国法解释并且英国法院有排外管辖权。这个问题在本书第五章有详论,请参阅。)

PREMIUM: [For example: Minimum and deposit premium of... payable in equal quarterly/half - yearly installments on the following dates... adjustable at expiry...]

(**保险费:**这里也是订约自由,可以根据双方的约定有不同的规定。例如,最低金额的保险费的支付、保险费的押金必须是要每季度/半年一次在以下日期支付,承保期间结束或其他时间作出实际保费的计算等。)

PREMIUM PAYMENT TERMS: [For example: if the premium due under this policy has not been paid to Underwriters by the 60th day from the inception of this policy... Underwriters shall have the right to cancel this policy by notification to the Insured...]

(**保险费支付条文:**例如,如果到期的保险费在保单签发后60天还没有支付给保险人,保险人有权给予受保人通知并取消保险合约。)

TAXES PAYABLE BY INSURED AND ADMINISTERED BY INSURERS: [This specifies country and tax applicable; e. g. x% UK Insurance Premium Tax]

(**受保人要支付的印花税并由保险人管理:**这是关于英国政府对印花税的征收。)

Contract Leader Initial(首席保险人签署)

RECORDING TRANSMITTING AND STORING INFORMATION: Where [the broker] maintains risk and claim data/information / documents [the broker] may hold data / information / documents electronically.

(**记录传输与信息储存:**保险经纪人可以以电子形式储存数据、信息等。)

INSURER CONTRACT DOCUMENTATION: This contract document details the contract terms entered into by the Insurer(s) and constitutes the contract document.

(**保险合约:**这份合约文件代表了保险合约的所有具体内容。)

[**Broker's Wording and Clause appear here as well as any amendments to**

standard Market Referenced/ Registered Wording and Clauses.]

INFORMATION

Underwriting Information:

[This includes source and date of any information provided.]

(**承保信息:**这将包括所有受保人提供的数据与信息。)

Loss Experience:

[This includes source and date of the loss experience]

(**过往索赔记录:**这会是包括受保人所有过往的索赔信息。)

SECURITY DETAILS

INSURERS LIABILITY: Insurer's liability several not joint [This section provides that the liability of insurers is several not joint and is not re-produced.]

PROPORTION OF LIABILITY: [This section deals with insurer's proportion of liability in case of adjustment to the 'signed' lines and is not re-produced.]

(**保险人责任:**英国法律针对保险人的责任是按份额而并非是连带,每一个保险人的责任只限于自己承保的份额。)

ORDER HEREON: 100% of 100% [This identifies the percentage amount of the order placed with the broker concerned. This may be less than 100% where the assured bears part of the risk himself or where, for example, part of the risk is placed in overseas markets.]

(**承保份额**)

Contract Leader Initial(首席保险人签署)

BASIS OF WRITTEN LINES: [This will specify one of the following]
Percentage of Order
Percentage of Whole
Part of Whole

SIGNING PROVISIONS: [This section deals with adjustment of lines, particularly by signing down and is not re – produced.]

Written Lines

(这是针对不同保险人愿意承保的份额。)

This section of the contract is for insurers to evidence their agreement to enter into their stated participation to the contract.

Written %	Singed and Dated Stamp` Incorporation Underwriting Reference

[The insurer's lines, e. g. 10%, appear here adjacent to their "box" stamps which, as indicated, give their market reference and are then signed and dated by the insurers to indicate acceptance of the insurance contract for their own percentage of the risk.]

CONTRACT ADMINISTRATION AND ADVISORY SECTIONS

[The Market Reform Contract also includes Contract Administration and Advisory Sections which are not re – produced here.]

5. 开口保单内容

5.1 开口保单内容例子之一:Glencore International v. Alpina Insurance

开口保单作为保险合约的内容千变万化,主要是在订约自由下满足贸易商作为受保人的需求。而贸易商的业务也不断在改变,所以开口保单的内容也会在每年或其他保险期间作出改变。这一做法的介绍可节录 Moore – Bick 大法官在 Glencore International v. Alpina Insurance (2004) 1 Lloyd's Rep. 111 中所说:

"For many years Glencore has made use of open covers in connection with its commodity trading activities for the purposes of insuring goods in transit. This form of policy, under which goods in transit falling within the terms of the cover are automatically insured as soon as the policyholder acquires an interest in them, provides the flexibility and continuity of cover which are essential to enable a large trading organisation to carry on business in the modern world. Commerce could not function efficiently if traders handling any significant volume of business had to negotiate separate terms for each individual shipment. Open covers also provide benefits for underwriters because they enable large numbers of similar risks to be underwritten without the need for individual presentations.

From the early 1980's Glencore's open cover in respect of oil and oil products was placed in the London market through the brokers Lloyd Thompson (now Jardine Lloyd

Thompson). Over the years the policy wording developed in response to changes in the nature of Glencore 's business but the underlying philosophy throughout was to procure a broad and flexible contract providing cover against all risks of loss and damage to oil in which Glencore acquired an interest wherever it was situated. As the insurers were aware, Glencore's involvement in the purchase and sale of crude oil and products was solely as a trader; it did not participate either in the production of crude oil or in the final distribution of products.

As might be expected in these circumstances, the contract was worded in very broad terms. It took the form of a marine open cover in favour of Glencore and its associated and subsidiary companies and other interested parties for whom they might receive orders to insure. It covered transit by land, water, air and pipeline from any ports or places in the world to any other ports or places in the world. It covered crude oil, kerosene, gasoil, naphtha, liquid petroleum gases and all products incidental to Glencore's business or otherwise as might be declared. It provided cover on four different bases at the insured's option, that which was most commonly used being based on the American Institute Cargo Clauses. To these basic conditions was added a large number of general conditions dealing with various aspects of the business insured. It will be necessary to refer to some of those in detail at a later stage. Subject to the insured's right to choose the basis of cover, the contract was obligatory on both sides as regards transit risks. There was also a separate section providing cover, if required by the insured, against political risks (confiscation etc., usually known as 'CNED' risks) at a rate to be agreed by underwriters. The policy ran for 12 months from 1st April each year. In the year 1994 – 95 approximately 79. 75 million tons of crude oil and products with a total value of USMYM4. 9 billion were declared to the open cover generating a gross premium of about USMYM5. 5 million."。

上述针对的 Glencore 是跨国的贸易商,尤其是在石油贸易。为了让他庞大业务的每次货物(主要是原油)付运或涉及有利益的货物都在一开始有风险就自动获得承保,所以在伦敦市场投保了一个非常广泛的开口保单。这开口保单的内容随着 Glencore 业务的改变也不断有修改。该广泛的开口保单对受保人的定义非常广泛,包括了 Glencore 与他的联营公司或分公司或其他相关人士(如在买卖合约中要求 Glencore 为货物投保等)。付运的方式包括陆上的公路与火车、海上、空中与管道,不论是从世界上哪一个港口去其他任何港口。针对货物,包括了原油以及所有其他石油产品,只要是与 Glencore 的业务有关或 Glencore 作出宣告。该开口保单还允许 Glencore 通过选择 CNED 条文去加保政治风险(这方面不属于针对货物运输的必须接受的开口保单,而只是 facultative/obligatory 的保险安排)。这开口保单的保险期间是 12 个月,而在 1994 到 1995 年,大约有 7975 万吨的原油与其他石油产品被 Glencore 宣告而获得承保,保险人收到的保费是 550 万美元。

政治风险的部分是属于 facultative/obligatory 保险安排,就是让 Glencore 可以选择是否要投保,但保险人不得拒绝接受承保,另一个部分也属于这种保险安排的是储存风险,这在该先例中的开口保单是第 1.18 条:"Including, **if required**, storage and blending prior to shipment or after final discharge in Land Tanks, Refineries, and storage in barge(s), irrespective of whether transit covered hereunder subject to Policy terms and conditions but excluding loss and/or damage caused by faulty blending on amount at risk at particular location involved at Additional premium of 0.015% each 30 days or pro – rata in excess of first 30 days if transit covered hereunder, otherwise, 0.015% each 15 days or part thereof."

5.2 开口保单内容例子之二:WISE (Underwriting Agency) Ltd. v. Grupo Nacional Provincial S. A

有关 WISE (Underwriting Agency) Ltd. v. Grupo Nacional Provincial S. A (2004) 2 Lloyd's Rep. 483 先例的介绍在第二章第 4.4.5 段对案情有详细介绍,这里可以节录有关再保险纸条(reinsurance slip)内容的部分如下:

"There was no policy. The reinsurance contract was made on about 28 December 2000 on the basis of a slip presentation, which, unusually, was not even initialled by the reinsurers' underwriter. The slip provided as follows:

Cedant: Grupo Nacional Provincial, S. A.

Insured: Perfumeria Ultra S. A. De C. V.

Locations:

1) Classical Gift Inc

9431 S. W. 65 Street

Miami...

2) Fragrances of the Word [sic] Inc.

10840 S. W. Street

Miami

3) Jewelry Time Inc

13228 N. W. Street

Miami...

Period: From December 31st, 2000 to December 31st, 2001

Type: Facultative cargo reinsurance. With monthly declarations

Interest: All real and personal property of any kind and description, including property but not limited to property of other in care, custody or control of the insured or for which the insured has assumed responsibility. All the shipments done by the insured consistent in but not limited to, cosmetics, perfumery, gifts, jewelery, Lladró, (kind of porcelain) accessories, and in general on any type of supplies related to the Insured's activity and in which it has an insurable interest.

Coverage:
Ordinary Transit Risk terrestrial, maritime and air
Total and/or partial theft.
Wetting
Spots
Pollution
All risk of cargo as per GNP wording
Warehouse to warehouse
Theft by bulk by hole [sic]
Breakage, bump, bend or crack
Oxidation
Contact with other charges [cargoes?]
Spillage
Strikes and civil commotion
Loading and unloading manoeuvres.
Damage for derailed. [sic]
Lay up for 15 fifteen days
Activity: Commercialisation of Perfumes, gifts Lladro, and jewelery.
Transportation: Any kind of usual transportation, terrestrial, maritime and air.
Geographic Limit: From Miami Florida US to Cancun Q. R. Mexico
From warehouse to any store in Cancun city.
Maximum Limit of USMYM 1,500,000.00 per shipment
Responsibility: USMYM 50,000.00 per vehicle inside Cancun
Annual Estimated: USMYM 17,000,000.00 of Shipments:
Conditions: ...
Cancellation clause (60 days)
Cooperation clause as per GNP wording"
The slip contained an Information clause as follows:
Information: Loss Record:
Nil for the last 12 Twelve years
Maximum amount and rate of the merchandise:

- Perfumes and cosmetics: USMYM700,000 USMYM250,000
- Gifts (crystals, porcelain, leather bags, clothes, silverware): USMYM250,000 USMYM150,000
- Clocks: USMYM1,000,000 USMYM200,000
- Jewelry (gold, diamonds, stones, precious pearls and semi-precious and over

and lose [sic]: USMYM350,000 USMYM200,000.

– Clocks: less expensive piece: USMYM40. Most expensive piece USMYM18,000 and average cost USMYM1,500.

– Jewelry: more expensive piece (rare circulation); more expensive piece: USMYM30,000; Most expensive set USMYM50,000 average cost

– Maximum Transport: USMYM1,500,000 (high season).

– Average: USMYM500,000

– Average Transport USMYM500,000 per trip

– During the month: Three trips..."

6. 保险证明(certificate of insurance)

保险证明是一份确认有关的付运货物已经有了承保,并列明有关保险合约(通常指开口保单)的条文(主要是与有关的付运或者航次有关系)的文件。保险证明的使用通常在 CIF 买卖,因为卖方或者发货人需要为这票付运的货物投保,并需要一份保险证明才能向买方收取货款或向银行的信用证结汇。通常,卖方如果是大的贸易商,他会有广泛的标准开口保单。而该标准开口保单往往也包括了这票货物的付运。但问题是卖方不可能把整个可能长达一年或更久的开口保单交出给买方作为投保的证明,以利将来发生货损货差时让买方向保险人索赔。而且,开口保单也无法显示该票付运的货物是什么根据买卖合约要去的目的地,所以就有了保险人针对每次付运或航次签发保险证明的做法。在保险证明中,如劳合社的标准格式,[1]它是有一句说明劳合社保险人承诺签发保单,承保在保险证明中所列明的风险/货物(underwriters at Lloyd's have undertaken to issue policy)。劳合社的标准格式也有关于索赔的重要指示,如要求买方提供这份正本的保险证明或者保单,正本提单或其他运输合约、检验报告等。

在法律的角度,CIF 买方是一定要提供一份海上货物保险的保单(policy)而不能是一份保险证明。这可节录《Benjamin's Sale of Goods》第 6 版第 19－041 段所说:

---

〔1〕 该标准格式当然是有针对不同的付运内容填写,如有关的船舶名字、从哪里到哪里、保险价值、货物标记与数量等。另是在劳合社标准格式的两页纸,第二页是一些标准条文与有关发生损失需要索赔的重要指示,如即时向承运人或托管人或其他第三人保留索赔的权利,向保险人提供索赔所需要的文件等。其他标准条文包括:Own Vehicle Theft Exclusion Clause, Pairs and Sets Clause, Accumulation Clause, Brands Clause, Cargo ISM Endorsement, Cargo ISM Forwarding Charges Clause, Increased Value (Duty and/or Taxes) Clause, Labels Clause, Process Clause, Secondhand Replacement Clause, Exhibition Risks Extension Clause, Contracts (Rights of Third Parties) Act 1999 Exclusion Clause (Cargo), Concealed Damage Clause, Debris Removal Clause, Insolvency Exclusion Clause, Termination of Transit Clause (Terrorism)。

"The seller is *prima facie* bound to tender a policy of insurance. He does not perform his obligations by tendering some other document such as a certificate of insurance or a broker's cover note or a written statement that he holds the buyer 'covered by insurance.': Diamond Alkali Export Corporation v. FL. Bougreois (1921) 8 Lloyd's 282."此外,根据1906年《英国海上保险法》Section 50(3),法律也要求保单可以转让。还有要求保单只针对买卖合约的货物,而不是把其他无关的货物扯在一起:Manbre Saccharine Export Corp v. Corn Products Ltd. (1919) 1 KB 198。法律还要求保单必须包括全程直到买卖合约中约定的交货目的地:Lindon Tricotagefabrik v. White & Meacham (1975) 1 Lloyd's Rep. 384。

但在今天的国际贸易中,通过大家的做法与明示条文规定,保险证明的接受性可以说已经没有太大的问题。这包括在 Incoterms 2000 第 A3 段要求 CIF 卖方提供给买方保单或其他投保证明(provide the buyer with the insurance policy or other evidence of insurance cover)。另在 UCP 600, Article 28 说:"An insurance document, such as an insurance policy, an insurance certificate or a declaration under an open cover"。在今天的海上货物保险中,在英国的做法很少会有一份保单(policy),所以普遍使用的文件还是一份保险证明。这一做法的改变,也因为海上货物运输的保险普遍是以开口保单而不是以个别的保单承保。而在开口保单,只能是为个别的货物付运出一份保险证明。稍后在本章第6.3段,会进一步分析保险证明与保单的区别。

6.1　保险证明的有关条文或内容

以下也给一个样本看看保险证明的有关条文或内容,是在先例 The "Surf City" (1995) 2 Lloyd's Rep. 242,保险人作出的保险证明主要内容如下:

"This is to certify that this Company has insured under Open Policy No. MOP/454 issued on behalf of Kuwait Petroleum Corporation and/or Kuwait Petroleum Corporation (UK) Ltd, as their respective interest may appear. (这说明是哪一份开口保单与受保人。)

US MYM 5,115,000/ - - (US Dollars Five Million One Hundred Fifteen Thousand Only). (保险价值/金额,这是根据稍后计算货物保险价值的基础得出的,通常也就是实际付运的货量乘以 CIF 价格加10%。)

On Goods as specified below, valued at sum insured.

Per 'SURF CITY' B/L dd. 18.2.1990. (承保货物是装在 Surf City 轮并且有关货物的提单是在1990年2月18日签发)

Voyage: Mina Abdullah Kuwait to 1/2 Italian ports. (航次)

Claims to be adjusted according to the conditions of the policy which contains, inter alia, the following clause: (承保风险与索赔理算如下)

Bulk Oil Clause (SP 13C) extended to include shortage and/or leakage and/or contamination howsoever arising subject deductible 0.5% of the insured value of the whole shipment (other than claims for contamination), total loss, constructive total loss, general average and salvage charges which shall be payable in full irrespective of percentage).

Including war and strike clauses.（包括战争与罢工险）

Special Conditions as attached.

The validity of this insurance coverage attaches from the date of the Bill of Lading.（本保险在提单日期也就是货物装船的一天生效）

Then a little further down, the goods are described as: Naphtha for ENIMONT SUPPLY SA, LUGANO.（稍后重复该批货物详述）

QUANTITY as per Bill of Lading dated 18. 2. 1990.（货物重量根据提单记载的数据）

Valued for US MYM 4,650,000/ - +10%（计算货物保险价值的基础）

There is a printed note at the bottom which reads: This Certificate represents and takes the place of the original Stamped Policy and conveys, subject to the terms of that Policy, all the rights of the original Policy – Holder (for the purpose of collecting claims) as fully as if the property insured was covered by a Special Policy direct to the holder of this Certificate."

6.2 保险证明与开口保单是属于两份不同的保险合约

保险证明是在一份开口保单下由保险人(例如劳合社)或保险经纪人所签发,但往往保险证明只是引进了开口保单部分的内容(显然最重要的就是承保的风险,如协会货物条文[一切险]),它甚至会有不同的条文。它也不像租约提单,会在提单中明确引进租约的条文。保险证明只会提到有关的开口保单,而反过来开口保单也不会引进保险证明。看来,英国法律下保险证明与开口保单应该是属于两份不同的保险合约,可以理解为保险人在开口保单中允许受保人将来作为代理人为 CIF 买方/分买方的利益作出投保。而不是原来的受保人把只有一份合约的开口保单下的索赔利益转让给 CIF 买方,也就是保险证明的持有人。这可以节录 John Dunt 所著的《Marine Cargo Insurance》第 3. 54 段所说:"The position, which is explored further below, appears to be that the certificate holder becomes party to a new and separate contract. It may be said, therefore, that he is not an assignee in the usual sense that A (CIF 卖方) passes all his own rights and obligations under a contract to B (CIF 买方). What happens is that the underwriters 'open' the contract made with the original assured so as to enable the original assured, as agent, to insure for the benefit of his c. i. f buyers."

这一说法,也符合劳合社标准开口保单的 Market Reform Contract 中要求明确受保人的规定,而受保人通常非常广泛,也会包括这种 CIF 卖方代替买方投保的情况,说:"ASSURED: ABC Limited, and/or as agents and/or subsidiaries and/or associated companies and/or **for whom they may have instructions to insure**."。另在协会货物条文(一切险)1/1/09 第 15.1 条文,也十分广泛地包括了受让人,说:"covers the Assured which **includes the person claiming indemnity either as the person by or on whose behalf the contract of insurance was effected or as an assignee.**"

保险证明与开口保单是前后两份不同的保险合约，也可以节录有关的先例，第一个是 Denning 大法官在先例 Macleod Ross & Co. , Ltd. v. Cie d' Assurances Generales I' Helvetia（1952）1 Lloyd's Rep. 12 是说：

"It was argued on behalf of the insurance company that there was only one contract between the insurance company and the forwarding agents, namely, that contained in the policy No. 648. I do not think that argument is correct. In my opinion, in respect of each of these parcels of goods, there were two of these parcels of goods, there were two contracts between the Swiss insurance company and the forwarding agents:

1. The open cover, whereby the insurance company agreed to insure all goods of which the forwarding agents took charge, provided that their customers had asked them to effect insurance of them. In order that the goods should be covered the forwarding agents, on taking charge of them, had to enter details in a book and send corresponding declarations to the insurance company.

2. The open cover, or 'certificate of insurance', whereby the insurance company implemented the contract contained in the open cover. Each of these certificates was, I think, **a new contract** in respect of the goods covered by it. That is shown by the fact that the certificate covered strike risks and war risks on conditions which are not to be found in the open cover at all. It also contained a special provision to the effect that: 'Every indemnity for the goods mentioned above will only be paid to the holder of this certificate of insurance indorsed by the forwarding agents and against presentation of this certificate. This certificate will be of no value if the duplicate is presented before it.'

Now, that provision did not appear in the open cover at all. Indeed, the open cover contained no reference whatever to certificates of insurance. This provision—that the indemnity was only payable to the holder of the certificate—was obviously intended to facilitate the transfer of the certificate and to make it freely assignable. It was a new provision of **a new contract** which was intended to be acted upon, not only by the forwarding agents, but also by the customer on whose behalf they were acting and any holder to whom it was duly indorsed."

另外，Denning 大法官也在上述的先例讲到保险人是怎样拟定保险证明的条文，说："When the insurance company printed conditions on the back [of the certificate] they presumably printed all those which concerned the holder, and omitted those which did not concern him. I do not think it would be right to hold him bound by other conditions which were not drawn to his attention, especially procedural conditions which do not affect the insurance itself but only the way of enforcing it."

另在先例 National Oilwell (UK) Limited v. Davy Offshore Limited (1993) 2 Lloyd's Rep. 582,Colman 大法官这样说:

"(1) Where at the time when the contract of insurance was made the principal assured or other contracting party has express or implied actual authority to enter into that contract so as to bind some other party as co-assured and intended so to bind party, the latter may sue on the policy as the undisclosed principal and co-assured regardless of whether the policy described a class of co-assured of which he was or become a member.

Where at the time when the contract of insurance was made the principal assured or other contracting party had no actual authority to bind the other party to the contract of insurance, but the policy is expressed to insure not only the principal assured but also a class of others who are not identified in that policy, a party who at the time when the policy was effected could have been ascertained to qualify as a member of that class can ratify and sue on policy as co-assured if at that time it was intended by the principal assured or other contracting party to create privity of contract with the insurers on behalf of that particular party."

6.3 保险证明不是一份保单

在 1906 年《英国海上保险法》,有不少条文是针对保单(insurance policy)的定义,但没有针对保险证明。如 1906 年的立法提到了一份保单必须有三个要求:(1)在 Section 23(1)要求保单明确谁是受保人或者他的代理人;(2)在 Section 24(1) 要求保单是由保险人或者在他的授权下签发;(3)Section 26(1) 要求保险标的必须在保单下合理明确的说明。

在 1906 年的立法,也说明海上保险合约不被接受为证据,除非是在一份保单内(a contract of marine insurance is inadmissible in evidence unless it is embodied in a marine policy in accordance with this Act. The policy may be executed and issued either at the time when the contract is concluded, or afterwards.)估计这样的立法都有它的历史背景,如保单涉及缴付印花税,到了现在就已经没有关系(海上保险的印花税是在 1970 年的《财政法》[Finance Act]被取消),但 1906 年的立法还是改不了。

一份保险证明不一定能够同时满足保单的三个要求,例如保险证明通常只会针对开口保单受保人,以及很多由保险经纪人作出的保险证明是没有保险人签字的。而最重要的或明显的就是劳合社的标准海上保单(Lloyd's Marine Policy)与劳合社的标准保险证明(Lloyd's Certificate of Insurance),在保险证明中的第一大段说明是保险人承诺签发保单以承保有关的货物(the said Underwriters have undertaken to issue to [开口保单的受保人] policy/policies of insurance at Lloyd's to cover, up to [每次付运的保险金额限制] in all by any one steamer and/or conveyances...)。在这样的明确写法下,保险证明应该不是一份保单。

这会带来一些争议,例如在先例 Diamond Alkali Export Corporation v. FL.

Bougreois (1921) 8 Lloyd's 282,就是涉及了 CIF 买卖,文件的要求包括了一份保单,但卖方提供的是一份保险证明。这被法院判是不符合要求,买方可以拒绝该文件买卖。

这一来,1906 年《英国海上保险法》的其他有关保单的条文也不适用在一份保险证明,其中就是有关转让。该立法的 Section 50(3)是这样说:"海上保单是可以通过背书或者其他的习惯性方式转让。"(A marine policy may be assigned by indorsement thereon or in other customary manner)。事实上,以前针对海上货物的保单,通常或习惯性做法就是交出这份保单(连同提单与发票) 给 CIF 买方/分买方。正如先例 Safadi v. Westrn Assurance Company (1933) 46 Lloyd's Rep. 140 中 Roche 大法官所说:"I have no doubt myself that policies often are assigned otherwise than by indorsement. In the case of c. i. f. contracts they are so often handed over without any indorsement being made upon them that I should be surprised if it could not be proved that that is a customary manner of assigning policies."

这样看来,一份保险证明就不一定能够根据 1906 年的立法转让,虽然它能够转让还是有必要,因为 CIF 买卖经常涉及在海上运输时转售(以文件买卖的方式)。但还是有不同的看法例如在 John Dunt 所著的《Marine Cargo Insurance》之 53 页之注脚 168 就提到了 Clarke 大法官在先例 The "Surf City" (1995) 2 Lloyd's Rep. 242 所说:"... treated a certificate that purported to represent and take the place of the original stamped policy as entitling the assignee to sue the insurer in his own name under s. 50(2) of the Act of 1906."

虽然这份保险证明不一定能够根据 1906 年的立法去转让(因为它严格意义说不上是保单),它还是可以根据一般合约利益(保险证明下就是向保险人索赔货损货差的利益)作出转让。它可以根据 1925 年《财产法》(Law of Property Act)之 Section 136 作出立法转让(legal assignment),或是根据衡平法进行衡平转让(equitable assignment)。有关这一方面,在本书第十三章第 7 段有更详细的介绍,请参阅。在立法转让下,是要求转让方以文书作出通知给债务人(保险人)。但这不应该是一个困难,在损失发生后,转让的通知会给保险人。正如 John Dunt 在所著的《Marine Cargo Insurance》第 3. 53 段所说:"Neither of these requirements present insuperable problems even if, as may commonly be the case, assignment will not take place by way of written notice to the insurers, until after loss. The notice of assignment will normally take the form in practice of the presentation of the claim by the assignee to the insurers or their agents as, for example, where a loss is notified to Lloyd's agents."

这样看来,把一份保险证明在一连串的 CIF 买卖中转让应该是不成问题的,也经常是这样做,甚至好像保单一样不必去背书(除非保险证明有规定需要背书),只交给受让人或下一个 CIF 买方。另也可以把保险证明视为是持有人与保险人之间的合约,不论他是 CIF 买方还是分买方,因为在开口保单中对受保人广泛的定义就有可能包括他们。

7. 开口/预约保单与保险证明之间的矛盾

由于开口保单与保险证明是两份不同的保险合约，所以有了争议，也必须是根据它们自己的条文作出解释。但无可否认，它们之间还是有密切关系的，会在有些情况下两份文件是需要相互参考。显然，有不少开口保单中的条文，只是保险人与原受保人之间有关，与保险证明无关。这包括是开口保单中的保费计算与结算、受保人可能有的选择在不同层次被承保（different levels of cover）、选择终止开口保单、保险金额的限制（保险证明会有每次付运的限制，但通常不会有开口保单中的地点限制）、开口保单的绝对免赔额等。

有关这两份不同保险合约的解释，也有说法是保险证明中的明示或默示条文应该有较多的分量，因为它有针对性。Andrew Smith 大法官在先例 Evialis v. S. I. A. T (2003) 2 Lloyd's Rep. 377 这样说："I consider that the proper approach to identifying the contract of insurance is to consider both documents as potentially expressing the parties' intention as to the terms upon which the insurance was effected. I do not consider that, in the absence of express words so providing, it is proper to approach the question on the basis that the certificate is the only contractual document determining the terms of the insurance and to have regard to the terms of the open cover only to the extent that they have been incorporated into the certificate. However, in determining the terms of the insurance contract by interpreting the two documents, **it is likely that the certificate will be given more weight, since, being directed to the specific risk, it is likely to prevail over more general terms.** As Visc Dunedin put it in De Monchy v Phoenix Insurance Co. of Hartford (1929) 34 201, it 'clinches the bargain as to the particular shipment' and as such is 'the determinative of the two instruments'. It is true that there are references in the judgments to the terms of the cover being 'incorporated' into the certificate, but this does not, in my judgment, require express reference to them in the certificate. On analysis, I do not consider that that requires more than that the parties evinced an intention that a term in the open cover should be of contractual effect in relation to the insurance of the particular risk, which they might do despite it not being referred to in the document that was specifically directed to that risk."。

开口保单与保险证明也可以由不同国家的法院管辖：Tradigrain SA v. S. I. A. T (2002) 2 Lloyd's Rep. 553，Craft Enterprises (International) v. Axa Insurance Co. (2005) Lloyd's Rep. IR 14。

如果保险证明的承保范围比开口保单更广泛，看来也应该是分别解释：Silver

Dolphin Product Limited v. Parcels & General Assurance Association (1984) 2 Lloyd's Rep. 404。在该先例,涉及的航次是从纽约到 Felixstowe,装有肥皂与香水的集装箱因为坏天气的原因被冲落入大海。保险证明是在这次事故发生后才签发,不过在签发的时候保险人与受保人都不知道该事故的发生。开口保单中的运输条款(transit clause)是很广泛,规定保险人的责任是要从货物离开供货商的工厂时开始。保险证明中是规定如果签发该证明时货物是在海上,则承保的风险是从保险证明签发之日开始。受保人争辩说,综合考虑开口保单与保险证明中的条文,并考虑开口保单的通常做法,该份保险合约是意图去承保货物离开工厂后的整个运输过程。但是 Neill 大法官判风险是从保险证明签发之日起才开始被承保,本案中也就是在损失已经发生后。所以受保人不能够索赔成功。由此可见保险证明中条文的效力是高于开口保单中的。

第二章　绝对善意

1. 序言

在所有的合约关系中，都会涉及签约方是否有善意（good faith）的疑问。这一精神也有很多其他不同的叫法，如"绝对善意"（utmost/absolute good faith）、"最大善意"（greatest good faith）、"最完美的善意"（most perfect good faith）、"荣誉"（honor）等。部分说法看起来有一点感情化，但很难给它们一个法律上肯定的定义。

这方面不同国家的法律有不同的看法，而本书所要针对的英国法律与做法下是没有善意的要求，但这不表示在合约关系中允许恶意（bad faith）。针对恶意，英国法律还是作出保护。这在订立合约的时候，主要表现在大家不能相互欺骗或误导，这就是不能误述（misrepresentation）。至于在合约的履行中不允许恶意，英国法律主要就是通过一些假设，如假设订约方不能从他自己错误的行为中获利以及有默示条件是合约双方必须给予协助/合作以让对方顺利履行合约。通常合约方在履行的时候有恶意，往往是会违反这些默示条文。

但英国法律对某些合约关系因为情况的不同而在善意方面有更严格的要求，其中最典型的是保险合约。但也会与其他合约关系有不同程度的善意要求，如合伙人之间的协议（partnerships agreement）：R C l'Anson Banks, Lindley & Banks on Partnership, 17th ed (2002), para 16－01－16－11；信托关系（fiduciary duty）：Davies v. London and Provincial Marine Insurance Company (1878) 8 Ch D 469, 474 (per Fry, J)；Bell v. Lever Brothers Limited (1932) AC 161, 232 (per Lord Thankerton)；股票上市买卖合约（contract for the share's sale and purchase publicly）：New Brunswick & Canada Railway v. Muggeridge (1860) 1 Dr & Sm 363, Possfund Custodian Trustee Ltd. v. Diamond (1996) 2 BCLC 665，另有关针对股票上市的善意要求与披露已经有立法针对《Financial Services and Market Act 2000》s. 90(1)等。

善意的要求在订立合约的时候主要体现在"披露"（disclosure）与不能"误述"（misrepresentation）两个方面。已经提到过，一般的合约没有善意的要求但也不允许恶意，主要是显示在误述，但就不存在自动作出披露的责任，这是与要求善意的合约最大的不同之处。比较接近的就是两种合约都不允许误述，而误述就是合约一方如果提出了一些问题，甚至他没有主动提出，另一方不能作出错误的陈述，而误述通常的目的就是诱使(induce)对方达成合约。如果作出错误的陈述,另一方就可以根据相关法律向法院请求救济,这包括终断合约与/或索赔损失。在一般的合约关系,误述是需要有一个明确的陈述,只是对合约另一方的误解不表态或不主动纠正也不代表是误述(《Chitty on Contracts》29th edition, 2004, 6 - 013:Tacit acquiescence in another's self - deception does not itself amount to a misrepresentation, provide that it has not previously been caused by a positive misrepresentation)。

这表示一般的合约由于不要求披露,它的大精神就是货物买卖合约的"让买方自己小心"(let the buyers be aware 或 caveat emptor)一样。每位订约方都要自己小心,不确定的地方就要向对方提问,因为对方没有自动披露的责任。如果对方拒绝回答,订约方就要考虑是否订立合约。如果对方回答但答案是错误的这就是误述,可以有法律的救济。这方面可节录《Good faith and insurance contracts》(第二版)第 1.08 段:"In short, the principle of *caveat emptor* applies to all contracting parties, not just buyers and sellers under a contract of sale. That is not to say that parties to normal commercial contracts are permitted to deceive the other: they are not. The law of misrepresentation has been developed to protect a contracting party against lies and misstatement which may induce him to enter into the contract. Further, the doctrine of mistake and estoppel provide further relief, where there has been a misunderstanding as to the nature or subject - matter of the contract or as to the parties' rights or position."

但如果合约有善意的要求如保险合约,除了在误述与其他的合约有比较接近的地位外,还多加了一个就是双方都必须主动作出有关的全面披露。如果不主动披露,通常是不能以自己忘了或对方没有问作为抗辩的理由。而它给受害人带来的救济也是可以终断合约。

可以简单的总结说,一般合约只有不能误述的责任,但要求善意的合约就有不能误述与必须作出披露两个责任。法律对这两个责任的要求也有不同之处。针对误述,不论是欺诈性、疏忽或无辜,受害人都可以终断合约。换言之,即使误述方是完全无辜(也就是说他根本不知道,也不可能知道)也不能逃避这一个可能是很严重的后果。但针对披露,不披露的一方如果是完全无辜就不存在没有尽责任。这种情况往往是被指称未披露一方根本不知道有关的事实/情况,变得是无从披露。这就谈不上他有这个责任了:Hearts of Oak Building Society v. Law Union (1908) 2 KB 863; Whitwell v. Autocar Fire and Accident Insurance Co. (1927) 27 Lloyd's Rep. 418; Crane v. Hannover Ruckversicherungs - Aktiengesellschaft (2008) EWHC 3165 (Comm)。

本章会在以下对个别针对合约善意的课题详细解释。

2. 英国法律对一般合约没有善意（good faith）要求的原因

英国法律（中国香港地区法律也一样）对一般合约没有善意（good faith）的要求，但这地位就与很大部分的大陆法国家甚至同样是普通法国家的美国（美国的《统一商法典》有了改变）有所不同。在这一方面笔者可以节录 Bingham 大法官在 Interfoto Picture Library Ltd. v. Stiletto Visual Programs Ltd.（1989）QB 433 中说的："In many civil law systems, and perhaps in most legal systems outside the common law world, the law of obligations recognizes and enforces an overriding principle that in making and carrying out contracts parties should act in good faith. This does not simply mean that they should not deceive each other ... its effect is perhaps most aptly conveyed by such metaphorical colloquialisms as 'playing fair;' 'coming clean' or 'putting one's cards face upwards on the table.' It is in essence a principle of fair and open dealing ... English law has, characteristically, committed itself to no such overriding principle but has developed piecemeal solutions in response to demonstrated problems of unfairness."

这与中国大陆合同法的规定也非常不同，中国大陆合同法的第 6 条、第 42 条与第 60 条均有对诚实信用的规定，应该与善意的说法是一回事。另在欧盟合约法《Lando Commission's Principles of European Contract Law》的 Article 1.106 也规定了善意，而且不准试图以合约条文对这善意的要求作出改变："（i）In exercising his rights and performing his duties each party must act in accordance with good faith and fair dealing.（ii）The parties may not exclude or limit this duty."

这也是反映了几个重要欧盟国家的有关这方面的法律，如德国的 BGB 民法典的 Section 242，法国民法典的 Article 1134 与意大利民法典的 Article 1377、1366 与 1375。在这些国家，善意延伸至合约的履行与执行。而在美国，虽然是属于普通法体系，而普通法也是这一个地位，但也已经立法包括了这一个善意的要求：《Uniform Commercial Code》s 1－203 和 1981 年《Restatement（Second）of Contracts》s 205。

英国在最早有关善意的先例 Carter v. Boehm（1766）3 Burr 1905 中，Mansfield 勋爵是希望所有的合约关系都符合善意的要求。但事后普通法的发展显示了这一想法并不可行，其中反对把善意引入合约的谈判与履行，尤其是涉及商业的合约，有几个重要的原因。例如，在 Harrison 所著的《Good Faith in Sales 1997》就提到了四个反对理由：（1）善意是欧洲的说法，现在还加上了欧盟官僚的想法。（2）管制公平合理的交易是议会立法的工作，不属于法院的工作。而议会立法只会针对一些特殊情况，如 1977 年《不公平合约法》为了保护消费者，而且善意也只是单向的。（3）引入善意就表示大家长期以来熟悉的合约有关法律与做法从此死亡。（4）引入善意将令商业人士失去肯定，再也不知道他们的地位。

2.1　原因之一：与合约方各自为己谋利的根本地位相矛盾

以下对其中一些反对理由比较详细地谈谈。第一就是善意与英国合约法下承认每个人为他自己谋取合约利益与谈判双方处于敌对地位有了基本矛盾。这很容易举一个例子说明，如果一般买卖合约有善意的要求，这等于强加给了双方自动披露的责任。这表示一个商店卖汽水给买方，就会有披露的责任说：你往前走 10 米就会有另一个商店汽水便宜 1 毛钱。这显然是不现实，也是与自己谋利相矛盾。

以下介绍贵族院在 1992 年的先例，名为 Walford v. Miles (1992) 2 AC 128。有关的案情是有一个互锁合约(lock – out agreement)，内容是说明在一个收购一家公司及其办公楼的交易中有独享的谈判权利。互锁合约对这种交易非常重要，因为买方要投入资金与精力，如作出尽职的调查。所以不以互锁合约约束卖方，就会被卖方在背后与其他买方谈判，最后价高者得，导致第一个买方被卖方利用作为与其他卖方谈判的筹码。

在有关先例的互锁合约，是没有谈判的期限。买方在谈判的时候出价 200 万英镑，但卖方以同样的价格卖给了第三方。买方跳起来，因为他私下有内幕消息知道该收购的标的值 300 万英镑，但卖方自己却不知道。所以“走了宝”的买方向卖方索赔 100 万英镑的损失，因为卖方违反了互锁合约。买方也指责卖方在该合约下，应该有默示要善意(good faith)与他谈判，而不应该背后找第三方。但贵族院判是英国法律对谈判没有善意的要求，因为这是与潜在的谈判地位相矛盾(inherently inconsistent with the position of a negotiating party)。这是人性，谈判双方为了各自的巨大的经济利益都只为自己考虑，只要这是合法。在本案例，贵族院质疑如果有谈判必需是善意的默示要求，买方自己就有问题了，因为他应该把私下有的内幕消息告诉卖方，毕竟善意应该是双向的。

其中贵族院的 Ackner 勋爵这样说：“The concept of a duty to carry on negotiations in good faith is inherently repugnant to the adversarial position of the parties when involved in negotiations. Each party to the negotiations is entitled to pursue his (or her) own interest, so long as he avoids making misrepresentations ... A duty to negotiate in good faith is as unworkable in practice as it is inherently inconsistent with the position of a negotiating party.”

2.2　原因之二：善意的说法空泛

第二个原因是善意的说法非常空泛，很难说它在各谋其利的一个商业合约中应该受限制达到什么程度。善意是针对一个道德标准，但说不清楚的就是这个道德标准是什么。如果没有一个最低标准作出衡量，将来就会有很大的不稳定与无数争议。例如，善意是针对订约方自己主观的看法(自己凭自己的良心)或者是有一个客观的标准(不理会订约方自己主观的看法)。还有是善意是否包括不能利用机会(non – opportunities)，不占对方便宜，不论合约条文怎么写都不应该剥削对方(non – exploitation)或不推卸责任(non - shirking)等。

2.3 原因之三:善意难以定下标准/准则与难以证明主观的思维是否善意

第三个原因与第二个原因十分接近,就是即使是善意有了最低标准或准则,如根据订约方自己主观的看法,问题是怎样认定他想些什么。一些有关善意的文章强调善意是要看某一个行动的原因是什么。但问题是这一原因是任由被质疑缺乏善意的订约方自己提供,而对方往往是没有办法否定或质疑,因为他怎么想的只有他自己知道。如在 Walford v. Miles (1992) 2 AC 128 先例,卖方不理会互锁协议中断谈判,可以是因为经济利益,因为市场有了变化,或是卖方认为他与买方的谈判成功机会很低,对继续谈判不乐观。这一来,如果第一个原因是不善意,但第二个原因是善意,法院或仲裁庭怎样才能区分?如果任由卖方提供证据,他肯定会坚持是因为第二个原因或其他善意的原因才中断谈判。在现实中,更加会是一个重要的行动如中断谈判,会有太多的原因,很难作出区分,而内中是包括了善意的或不善意的。

2.4 原因之四:善意与订约自由有矛盾/冲突

第四个原因是善意的说法与订约自由有严重冲突。在订约自由下,订约方会各自争取对自己有利的条文,并会在谈判时作出各种让步或坚持。如果最后争取到的条文,虽然是写得清清楚楚,但因为善意的说法而得不到严格的承认与执行,就会导致它们之间的严重冲突。这里可举一个香港地产买卖的先例,它一直上诉到英国枢密院。案件名为 Union Eagle Ltd. v. Golden Achievement Ltd. (1997) 2 All ER 215。在该先例,涉及一幢房产,根据买卖合约,买方给了 10% 的订金存在卖方的律师那里作为保管人。合约规定了一个时间,就是在 1991 年 9 月 30 日下午 5 时前完成交易。另在合约第 12 条文说明如果买方有任何违约,卖方就可以没收订金并中断合约。结果,买方在完成交易的时间上比规定晚了 10 分钟,卖方就宣告中断合约并没收了 10% 的巨额订金。显然,买方不会想违约,因为当时楼市上涨,他不会不想完成交易。这一案件一路上诉到枢密院,枢密院拒绝给予买方救济。Hoffmann 勋爵这样说:"The principle that equity will restrain the enforcement of legal rights when it would be unconscionable to insist upon them has an attractive breadth. But the reasons why the courts have rejected such generalizations are founded not merely upon authority ... but also upon practical considerations of business. These are, in summary, that in many forms of transaction it is of great importance that if something happens for which the contract has made express provision, the parties should know with certainty that the terms of the contract will be enforced. The existence of an undefined discretion to refuse to enforce the contract on the ground that this would be 'unconscionable' is sufficient to create uncertainty. Even if it is most unlikely that a discretion to grant relief will be exercised, its mere existence enables litigation to be employed as a negotiating tactic. The realities of commercial life are that this may cause injustice which cannot be fully compensated by the ultimate decision in the case."

在上述先例,并不存在10%订金是惩罚性条文的争议。这也是地产买卖通常被视为合理的数字。所以,不存在这方面的救济。另外,也不涉及卖方有任何误导买方而导致他比规定的时间晚了10分钟,否则也会有另外的救济。上述先例纯粹涉及了买方自己晚了10分钟,而如果由于这是一个轻微的违约,但卖方却利用这个机会占了很大便宜(包括没收订金与估计转售可以卖更高价钱),虽然表面看来觉得卖方并不善意,但如果作出救济,将来存在一个问题就是10分钟只是轻微的延误可以作出救济的话,那要到什么程度才算是太长的延误(how late is much too late)的争议,分界线应该在哪里。而如果有了这些不稳定,就会带来其他问题,如卖方虽然取巧中断了买卖合约,但也不敢把这房产转售等问题。所以,枢密院最后决定坚持肯定性,按合约条文作出严格的解释,而不理会公平合理。

同样的精神也出现在租船合约,纽约土产期租合约就规定了如果承租人没有准时或足数支付租金(punctual and regular payment of hire),船东有权撤回该船舶(withdrawal)。这里的"准时"与"足数"都是要严格遵守,一分钟、一分钱都不能差。这方面可见杨大明律师所著的《期租合约》一书第十八篇。

2.5 原因之五:善意与订约方努力进行谈判以达致对己方有利的结果相矛盾

第五个原因是每一份合约内容都会不一样,如买卖合约有时对卖方有利,但有时对买方有利。反正市场的波动加上谈判水平的差异,会有千变万化的不同内容。这一来,就很难以一套善意的说法适用在这些完全不同内容的合约条文。否则,双方努力进行谈判,寸土必争,也变成枉然了。Michael Bridge教授在1999年的文章《Good Faith in Commercial Contracts》这样说:"It is a fair reproach to English contract law that it unthinkingly treats the rules and principles of commodity sales, time and voyage charterparties and so on as though they could be applied without modification in very different contractual settings. Good faith theorists should avoid making the same sort of mistake. In my view, what is needed is an informed treatment of different areas of commercial contract and market activity."

2.6 总结的看法

总结而言,笔者对以上针对英国法律在一般商业合约不支持引进善意的反对原因是有一定的认同。虽然,引进善意的说法也有一定的好处,如让英国法律与国际上的法律更加接近,提升商业道德等。但根据笔者这些年来在商业中的经验,特别是在国际航运与外贸,笔者觉得要求一些唯利是图、自私自利与精明狡猾的商人在谈判与履行合约中善意(不论是主观或客观的准则),恐怕最终会是纸上谈兵。而即使引进了善意的要求,如保险合约,也带来了其他更大的问题。在保险合约,披露的要求主要是加在受保人的头上,因为他通常比保险人更了解投保风险。但这也带来不断有保险人取巧的情况,如经常以不披露为由拒绝赔付。正如Sumner勋爵在先例Commercial Union Assurance v. The Niger (1922) 13 Lloyd's Rep. 75, 82所说"what is an indispensable shield for the underwriter into an engine of oppression against the assured."

这方面稍后会更详尽地探讨。

3. 保险合约要求善意的原因

在英国法律,除了少数类别的合约,如保险合约、合伙人合约与信托关系的合约有这方面明示或默示条文的要求外,其他一般的合约都没有这方面的要求。例如,货物买卖合约针对现货的买卖就有著名的“买方自己小心”(caveat emptor)原则,就等于否定了善意的要求,因为它没有要求卖方主动作出披露。如针对现货(present goods)买卖,不要求卖方自动披露有关货物所有的缺点与局限。英国法律一般要求订约方自己要照顾自己的合约利益,而主要的原因是为了简单与肯定,加上合约涉及了双方不同的利益,很难要求他们向对方推心置腹。但这不表示英国法律在早期没有尝试过在所有的合约中引入善意的要求。已经提到过 Mansfield 勋爵就曾经希望这样做,但接下去的英国商法发展的方向并没有跟从。这里可以节录 Atkin 勋爵在 Bell v. Lever Brother (1932) AC 161 中第 227 页所说的:“Ordinarily the failure to disclose a material fact which might influence the mind of a prudent contractor does not give the right to avoid the contract. The principle of *caveat emptor* applies outside contracts of sale. There are certain contracts expressed by the law to be contracts of the utmost good faith, where material facts must be disclosed; if not, the contract is voidable. Apart from special fiduciary relationships, contracts for partnership and contracts of insurance are the leading instances. In such cases the duty does not arise out of contract; the duty of a person proposing an insurance arises before a contract is made, so of an intending partner.”

在保险合约,早在 Carter v. Boehm (1766) 3 Burr 1905 中,Mansfield 勋爵就已经判被保险人有这样一个善意责任,主要的原因是在双方对有关资料与消息的了解并不对等。加上那个年代通讯十分困难,伦敦保险人想查任何东西也查不到。保险人在被保险人没有善意地告诉他有关的风险的情况下,贸然承诺承保,根本没有能力定下准确与适当的保费,甚至是接不接受投保也难以确定。Mansfield 勋爵这样说:“Insurance is a contract upon speculation. (保险合约是一个根据预测与估计订立的合约。) The special facts, upon which the contingent chance is to be computed, lie most commonly in the knowledge of the insured only: the underwriter trusts to his representation, and proceeds upon confidence that he does not keep back any circumstance in his knowledge, to mislead the underwriter into a belief that the circumstance does not exist, and to induce him to estimate the risk, as if it did not exist. The keeping back of such circumstance is a fraud, and therefore the policy is void. Although the suppression should happen through mistake, without any fraudulent intention; yet still the underwriter is deceived, and the policy is void; because the risk run is really different from the risk understood and intended to be run, at the time of the agreement."（第二段还提到了普通法对这种保险合约不披露的敌意，就是认为不披露是等同欺诈。就算不披露没有涉及欺诈意图，仅仅是错漏，实际造成的结果是保险人最终还是被欺骗，因为他同意承担的风险根本不是他实际上承担的风险，故保险合约无效。）

这一个对善意的要求，也从普通法搬到1906年《英国海上保险法》section 17："A contract of marine insurance is a contract based upon the utmost good faith, and, if the utmost good faith be not observed by either party, the contract may be avoided by the other party."（海上保险合约是一个绝对善意原则的合约，如果有违反，无辜的一方可以令该合约无效。）

可以说，1906年《英国海上保险法》Section 17差不多就是依照了Mansfield勋爵在Carter v. Boehm（1766）3 Burr 1905中的判法，只有一点不同。这就是可撤销（voidable）与无效（void）的分别。1766年英国法律还没有发展到把合约分为可撤销与无效两种，但1906年就已经有了这个分别。而违反绝对善意，保险合约只是属于可撤销，而不像非法的合约，一定是无效。可撤销也表示受害方的保险人是有选择权去决定是否令保险合约无效（whether to avoid the insurance contract）。

1906年《英国海上保险法》用的词是"绝对善意"（utmost good faith），事实上绝对善意与"善意"（good faith）是同样的意思，仅在这里作出澄清，避免引起疑惑。而显示绝对善意表现在受保人或者他的保险经纪人在投保时要自动作出披露与不得误述。

4. 披露

在1906年的《海上货物保险法》之Section 18对受保人的披露责任这样规定："Subject to the provisions of this section, the assured must disclose to the insurer, before the contract is concluded, every material circumstance which is known to the assured, and the assured is deemed to know every circumstance which, in the ordinary course of business, ought to be known by him. If the assured fails to make such disclosure, the insurer may avoid the contract."

从该条文可以看出受保人是否履行了披露责任主要是看四个方面：披露时间、受保人知情、是否实质性重要、可撤销保险合约的救济。

4.1　履行披露责任的时间（time of disclosure）

根据第18条的规定，受保人的披露责任在保险合约订立后就已经结束。所以有必要就保险合约何时订立给一个明确的说明。1906年《英国海上保险法》Section 21规定："A contract of marine insurance is deemed to be concluded when the proposal of the assured is accepted by the insurer, whether the policy be then issued or not; for the purpose of showing when the proposal was accepted, reference may be made to the slip or covering note or other customary memorandum of the contract..."

在实务当中,劳合社以及伦敦的保险市场,通常是保险人在保险纸条(slip)上签字之后就认为保险合约成立,尽管合约上有"to be agreed 或简写为 TBA"或者是用铅笔书写。

4.1.1 披露责任的持续性疑问

这带来了一个疑问,就是 1906 年《英国海上保险法》没有针对绝对善意以及披露的持续性。而普通法也是到了贵族院先例 The "Star Sea" (2001) 1 Lloyd's Rep. 399 (HL)才有了比较稳定的说法。这说法就是绝对善意(也就是披露责任与不得误述的责任),根据第 18~20 条是针对订立保险合约之前,该立法根本没有针对保险合约订立后提出这方面的要求。如果在保险合约的履行期间也适用绝对善意,就带来违反的时候允许保险人使保险合约无效。这显然对受保人太不公平且太危险,这是法院不愿意见到的,正如 Hobhouse 勋爵在 The "Star Sea"所说:"It is not right to reason... from the existence of an extensive duty pre-contract positively to disclose all material facts to the conclusion that post-contract there is a similarly extensive obligation to disclose all facts which the insurer has an interest in knowing and which might affect his conduct. The courts have consistently set their face against allowing the assured's duty of good faith to be used by the insurer as an instrument for enabling the insurer himself to act in bad faith. An inevitable consequence in the post-contract situation is that the remedy of avoidance of the contract is in practical terms wholly one-sided. It is a remedy of value to the insurer and of disproportionate benefit to him; it enables him to escape, retrospectively the liability to indemnify which he has previously and validly undertaken..."

4.1.2 有关披露责任与绝对善意在保险合约订立前后不同对待的先例:Pan Atlantic Insurance Co. Ltd. v. Pine Top Insurance Co. Ltd.

在较早的先例 The "Litsion Pride" (1985) 1 Lloyd's Rep. 437 中,Hirst 大法官根据一些不是太有说服力的理由认为绝对善意也适用在保险合约订立后,即使在 1906 年的立法是没有这样的明确规定。但问题是 1906 年的立法仅仅是把以前判例的判法立法,而以前没有先例涉及保险合约订立后的绝对善意问题。如果说这是保险合约的默示条件要求持续的绝对善意,问题是绝对善意的原则在 Pan Atlantic Insurance Co. Ltd. v. Pine Top Insurance Co. Ltd. (1994) 2 Lloyd's Rep. 427 (HL)被认为不是根据合约,而是根据法律特别是衡平法,这表示默示条文的说法站不住脚(本章第 7.1 段有详论)。这到了先例 The "Star Sea" (2001) 1 Lloyd's Rep. 399 (HL)才明确,主要就是:(1)只在证明有欺诈的情况下才适用。否则,在保险期间发生了令风险增加的非欺诈性情况,受保人无须自动披露。(2)双方在诉讼时没有任何善意可言,受保人的披露与否完全是依据法律程序,与保险合约无关。Hobhouse 勋爵的说法显示了保险合约订立之前要适用法律规定的绝对善意原则,但有了保险合约之后基本上就应该适用普通合约法，他这样说："A coherent scheme can be achieved by distinguishing a lack of good faith which is limited to the making of the contract itself (or some variation of it) and a lack of good faith during the performance of the contract which may prejudice the other party or cause him loss or destroy the continuing contractual relationship. The former derives from requirements of the law which pre – exist the contract and are not created by it, although they only become material because a contract has been entered into. The remedy is the right elect to avoid the contract. The latter can derive from express or implied terms of the contract: it would be a contractual obligation arising from the contract and the remedies are the contractual remedies provided by the law of contract."

其中 Clyde 勋爵是说在保险人与受保人之间的绝对善意与坦率(openness)在订立保险合约之前是很高的要求，但之后就没有必要要求同样的标准，双方的善意应该是在不同的阶段程度要求是不同，并非是一个绝对不变的标准。Clyde 勋爵这样说："Since even after the contract is entered into the relationship between the parties should in any event be colored by considerations of good faith, the point is in some respects academic. But once it is recognised that in a contract of insurance, and indeed in certain other contracts, an element of good faith is to be observed, and that that element may impose certain duties particularly of disclosure between one party and the other, duties which may vary in their content and substance according to the circumstances, then a question may arise as to the utility of the concept of an utmost good faith or an *uberrima fides*. In my view the idea of good faith in the context of insurance contracts reflects the degrees of openness required of the parties in the various stages of their relationship. It is not an absolute. The substance of the obligation which is entailed can vary according to the context in which the matter comes to be judged. **It is reasonable to expect a very high degree of openness at the stage of the formation of the contract, but there is no justification for requiring that degree necessarily to continue once the contract has been made.**"

该判法被之后的先例所遵从，如 The "Mercandian Continent" (2001) 2 Lloyd's Rep. 563 与 The "Aegeon"(2002) 2 Lloyd's Rep. 42。接下来进一步探讨保险合约成立后对绝对善意的不同程度上的要求。

4.1.3 进一步明确保险合约订立后善意的要求是以合约关系为准的先例：The "Mercandian Continent"

在先例 The "Mercandian Continent" (2001) 2 Lloyd's Rep. 563 中，案情是涉及了受保人的修船厂为了想帮助保险人，主动伪造了一份文件提供给保险人，结果反而被保险人反咬一口，说是违反了绝对善意。上诉庭判该欺诈是没有实质性重要，也没有损害保险人的利益，所以保险人不能取巧。而整个分析是以合约关系针对，而不是像保险合约订立前的绝对善意是合约以外的法律。其中 Longmore 大法官这样说："It is, in my judgment, only appropriate to invoke the remedy of avoidance in a post – contractual context in situations analogous to situations where the insurer has a right to terminate for breach. For this purpose (A) the fraud must be material in the sense that the fraud would have an effect on underwriters' ultimate liability as Mr. Justice Rix held in *Royal Boskalis* [1997] L. R. L. R. and (B) the gravity of the fraud or its consequences must be such as would enable the underwriters, if they wished to do so, **to terminate for breach of contract**... the giving of information, pursuant to an express or implied obligation to do so in the contract of insurance, is an occasion when good faith should be exercised. Since, however, the giving of information is essentially an obligation stemming from contract, **the remedy for the insured fraudulently misinforming the insurer must be commensurate with the insurer's remedies for breach of contract**. The insurer will not, therefore, be able to avoid the contract of insurance with retrospective effect unless he can show that the fraud was relevant to his ultimate liability under the policy and was such as would entitle him to terminate the insurance contract."

4.1.4 情况之一:保单更改(variation)的绝对善意

这里涉及保险人与受保人需要对已经订立的保险合约进行某一些内容的更改。已经有不少的先例说明绝对善意原则如果不被遵守,保险人可以令保险合约无效的只是更改的部分,而不是原来整个保险合约。这里的先例包括 Cory v. Patton (1872) LR 7 QB 304;Lishman v. North Maritime Insurance Co. (1875) LR 10 CP 179;Niger Co. Ltd. v. Guardian Assurance Co. (1922) 13 Lloyd's Rep. 75;Bank of Nova Scotia v. Hellenic War Risks Mutual Insurance Assurance Ltd. (1988) 1 Lloyd's Rep. 514;Iron Trades Mutual Insurance Co. Ltd. v. Cie de Seguros Imperio (1991) 1 Re. L. R. 213;New Hampshire Insurance Co. v. Mirror Group Newspapers Ltd. (1997) LRLR 24 等。

其中可以介绍 Niger Co. Ltd. v. Guardian Assurance Co. 的案情,虽然它也将在本书第十三章代位求偿权第 16.6.4 段提到。该案涉及一份长达好几年的保险合约或开口保单(open cover),该保险合约是尼日利亚一间名为 Niger Co. Ltd. 的贸易/出口公司为其需要收集、储藏与出售到欧洲的货物向 Guardian Assurance Co. 保险公司进行投保。货物是从尼日利亚各地集中到 Niger 河一个名为 Burutu 的货物集散地,这有点类似长江流域的货物集中到上海再进行出口的情况。Niger 河在一年中的 8 月至 11 月期间由于河水上涨适合河道运输,导致有大批的货物储存在 Burutu 等待付运,令保险人的风险大大增加与集中。结果一次发生火灾,大批货物被烧毁,Niger 公司向保险公司索赔高达 100 万英镑的损失。碰巧在发生火灾不久以前 Niger 公司与保险公司对保险合约中的某些事项进行过更改,保险公司以此为理由抗辩说 Niger 公司没有在对保险合约更改时对大批货物都集中在 Burutu 付运的事实进行披露,不符合绝对善意原则,从而保险公司可以令保险合约无效。贵族院的 Buckmaster 勋爵判在保险合约进行更改时仅需要对更改的事项进行披露,但这不包括一些与更改事项无关的披露,更加不存在可让保险人趁机令一个可能是他起初保费订得较低的亏本保险合约无效。

另在 The "Shakir III" (1997) 1 Lloyd's Rep. 586 案例中,涉及该船被拖带至上海拆废船。但中途,中国买方根据买卖合约在 1993 年 5 月 25 日指定了黄埔港作为目的地,结果船舶开航去黄埔港,并在 1993 年 6 月 24 日抵达。卖方的船东是在 1993 年 6 月 25 日才告诉保险人有关的改变航线计划,即从上海改去黄埔港,保险人也接受。当时黄埔港口拥挤,船舶在锚地等待,但受到台风的威胁,导致该失去动力的船舶在 6 月 27 日被拖离锚地去避风。但船舶最后搁浅在五株州而变成推定全损。保险人的抗辩之一就是在更改保单前应该把重要的风险都披露出来。有些减少风险或不重要的事实应该可以披露,如船舶拖带去黄埔港比拖带去上海距离更近。但有关台风威胁的风险就没有在更改保单的时候披露,而这明显是重要的事实。Potter 大法官说:"The evidence disclosed that there were Royal Observatory of Hong Kong High Seas Forecasts on June 24/25 to the effect that the typhoon would pass close to Huang Pu. I also heard evidence, which I accepted, that the path in fact followed by the typhoon was not untypical of the track and speed of typhoons of similar type and origin in the area. Further, the belief that the vessel would be alongside a berth by the onset of the typhoon was, on the evidence as it emerged, at best highly doubtful and at worst wholly unrealistic. None of these considerations, let alone the master's mounting concern about the approach of the typhoon and his proper course of action, were brought to the attention of the underwriters. They were plainly matters on which any prudent underwriter would have wishes to form his own views. Further, so far as the meteorological developments were concerned, it was common ground that Lloyd's List, which was available to the underwriters, is typically 24 hours behind local information in such matters. No one was in a better position to form a view than the tug master on the spot. However, none of his concerns was brought to the attention of the underwriters."

Potter 大法官也判保险人接受更改保单并不构成弃权,因为弃权一方必须了解有关的事实与他的权利才存在放弃与否。

4.1.5 情况之二:续保(held covered)的绝对善意

有关续保的课题在本书第九章第 7 段有介绍,而涉及海上货物运输保险,在协会货物条文第 9 条有关航次的终止与第 10.1 条有关航次的改变就涉及了续保,这也是在第九章第 7 与 8 段有介绍。另在第六章第 8.4 段介绍协会船级条文时也有涉及续保的问题。

保险合约有许多情况下需要续保,在很大的程度上,这情况与更改保险合约十分接近,所以道理也是一致,就是绝对善意原则只是针对续保后的合约期间,如果在续保时违反该义务并不会影响续保前的保险合约,保险人不可以令续保前的保险合约无效。在 The "Mercandian Continent" (2001) 2 Lloyd's Rep. 563 案中,上诉庭的 Longmore 大法官说:"The requirement that an insurer hold the insured covered in certain circumstances has been held to require the exercise of good faith by the insured ... but, although it is settled that good faith must be observed, it is never suggested that lack of good faith in relation to a matter held covered by the policy avoids the whole contract of the insurance."

这一判法是被先例 Groupama Insurance Co. Ltd. v. Overseas Partners Re Limited (2003) EWHC 34 (Comm) 跟从。较早的先例 Overseas Commodities Limited v. Style (1958) 1 Lloyd's Rep. 546 与 Liberian Insurance Agency Inc v. Mosse (1977) 2 Lloyd's Rep. 560 也是判绝对善意为一项延续性的义务。

4.1.6 情况之三:向保险人要求赔付

受保人向保险人提出要求赔付的时候,是需要绝对善意。如果有违反,保险人是有权利令保险合约无效,也就是拒绝赔付。在要求赔付的时候,受保人违反绝对善意,最常见的就是作出欺诈性索赔(fraudulent claim)。这在本书第十二章第10段有详细介绍。

4.1.7 情况之四:开口/预约保单下受保人的绝对善意

在开口/预约保单(open cover)的情况下,涉及在最开始向保险人要求签发开口/预约保单时,受保人就有绝对善意的披露责任。但是否之后每个航次或付运的宣告也有责任披露?这方面的法律地位与再保协议(reinsurance treaty)基本上一样。

根据 Berger and Light Diffusesrs Pty Ltd. v. Pollock (1973) 2 Lloyd's Rep. 442,要求受保人每次宣告时都要履行披露的义务。该先例的案情是原告是4个用于生产塑胶荧光扩散器的巨大铁制注坯模具的所有人。这批模具本来是在香港生产,但有兴趣的潜在买家测试后结果是质量不合格。所以原告就想将当时在澳大利亚的这批模具运往英国进行再切割。1966年10月24日,原告将模具装上了 Paparoa 轮,并收到了船长签发的提单。提单上面的批注是"unprotected, secondhand, insufficiently packed"。1966年11月1日,原告的保险经纪人在他自己与保险人之间的开口保单下向保险人宣告这批模具的付运与保险价值是2万英镑。船舶抵达英国卸港时,由于船舱漏水而导致模具生锈,受损严重。受保人向保险人提出全损索赔共2万英镑,但保险人拒绝赔付指称受保人没有在宣告的时候作出披露,其中有:(1)提单有批注;(2)模具的质量不合格的历史;(3)模具不值钱,不应该超额投保。但受保人抗辩说是开口保单在宣告时没有责任披露,因为保险人没有权利选择保或不保,必须接受宣告的风险。Kerr 大法官认为受保人在开口保单下是有披露的责任,并提到有关浮动保单(floating policy)在1906年《英国海上保险法》Section 29(3)有明确规定受保人必须诚实宣告与善意的要求,而浮动保单就是开口保单的以前做法,Kerr 大法官这样说:"Apart from this, I do not think that the existence of an open cover, even in cases of direct contractual nexus, automatically relieves the assured from the obligation to disclose material circumstance. This also appears to have been the view of Mr. Justice Pickford (as he then was) in Republic of Bolivia v. Indemnity Mutual Marien Assurance Co. reported on this point in (1908) 14 Com. Cas. 156, at pp. 167,168. It is clear that in the case of floating policies sect. 29(3) of the Act has modified the duty of disclosure as laid down in Section 18. But this was not a case of a floating policy."

另有关的先例 Ionides v. The Pacific Fire & Marine Insurance Company (1871) LR 6 QB 674, (1872) LR 7 QB 517 (CA)也是针对浮动保单。看来针对开口保单,到底每次的宣告是否需要作出主动的披露还是要看不同形式与不同措辞的开口保单。在一种标准的开口保单,也就是最常见的,保险人是必须接受承保受保人的所有宣告的付运,只要是在承保范围内的风险。这种可被称为是必须接受的开口保单(Obligatory Open Cover)。这一来,既然保险人必须接受承保,而且也不存在可以单方面改变同意了的保费费率,即使还是有善意的要求,也不应该存在受保人需要作出主动披露,也不会有实质性重要的披露。因为 1906 年《英国海上保险法》Section 18 (2)规定,只会对一个谨慎的保险人核定保险费率或者是是否承保时的判断的任何情况才是有实质性重要的影响。

另有说法是在这种开口保单,每次的宣告只是一种行政上的操作(administration machinery),主要为了让保险人计算与收取这次付运的保费。正如 John Dunt 在所著的《Marine Cargo Insurance》第 3.9 段所说:"In The 'BeurS. G. racht' (2002) Lloyd's Rep. 335 there was an open cover for declarations in respect of the assured's liability as charterer under which the assured had to declare all vessels chartered and the underwriters had to 'accept' all declarations. It was held that this was like a floating policy and that the underwriters were bound when the goods were shipped and not when the declaration was made. The declaration was not consensual in nature but was a part of the administrative machinery of the contract since it informed the underwriter what risks had attached to the cover and enabled him as necessary to collect the premium due. It is apparent therefore that a declaration under such an obligatory open cover has no part to play in any contractual offer and acceptance."

但也有其他形式的开口保单,如一种属于是框架安排(framework arrangement)的开口保单,被称为是"facilities"或者"line slips",这就涉及每次的宣告都要保险人同意才算是接受承保并有了保险合约。如此,显然每次付运都会需要受保人作出实质性披露的宣告。

所以总结而言,可节录 John Dunt 在所著的《Marine Cargo Insurance》第 3.10 段说:"It should be added that in Berger v. Pollock (1973) 2 Lloyd's Rep. 442 Kerr J. said that the existence of an open cover, even in cases of direct contractual nexus between the assured and the underwriters, did not automatically relieve the assured from the obligation to disclose material circumstances. He added that even if open covers on goods can at common law be assimilated to floating policies on goods, as opposed to the carrying ship, need not be disclosed. It must, as Kerr J. recognised, depend upon the existence and terms of the particular open cover together with any particular course of dealing thereunder. Where the cover is obligatory and the goods and shipments fall within the cover, and must therefore be ‘accepted’ by the underwriters, the declaration is no more than an administrative arrangement for identifying risks which the underwriters have already agreed to accept.”

另也可以节录《Good faith and insurance contracts》(第二版)第1.47段:“Whether the duty of the utmost good faith applies to such instruments depends on when the contract of insurance is made. It may be that one or both of the parties (assured, insurer; reassured, reinsurer) is obliged to declare or accept the risk under the open cover or treaty; or it may be that either or both parties retain a discretion to utilize the facility. If, for example, the parties agree to an obligatory open cover, so that both are obliged to declare and accept risks under the open cover, while the insurance is not effected until the declaration, the contract of insurance may be said to be made when the open cover or treaty was agreed. It is at that point of time that the duty of disclosure is owed and comes to an end, unless the declaration exceeds the scope of the cover, in which case a new contract of insurance is being made. If, however, both parties are allowed to choose whether they will declare or accept the risk, the open cover is not binding as a contract, and the declaration itself, once it is agreed, will constitute the insurance contract. Logically enough, in this case, the duty of disclosure attached to the declaration, rather than the open cover or the treaty. Where the open cover is obligatory (as far as the insurer is concerned), it has been described as an irrevocable standing offer to accept liability for declarations which fall within the terms of the open cover. In such cases, the insurer will be entitled to full disclosure at the time the open cover is agreed. However, where the open cover (or standing offer) may be revoked, the insurer will be entitled to full disclosure at the time of the declaration. The corollary is that the insurer will not be entitled to full disclosure when the revocable cover is agreed.”

至于还有一种开口保单,名为受保人可以选择宣告保险人必须接受的开口保单(facultative/ obligatory open cover),这是在本书第一章第2.2段有详细的介绍。简单地说,这种开口保单下,受保人在每次披露时就会成立独立的保险合约,但是受保人在每次宣告时是没有披露责任。

4.1.8 总结履行披露责任的时间

看来,履行披露责任的时间虽然在程度上不一样,但基本上是一直不能违反,即使是在保险合约履行期间。唯一的例外情况就是受保人与保险人在诉讼(法院或者仲裁)时,这在本章第4.1.2段有介绍。

这例外的情况也配合早在18世纪发展出来的做法,就是法院可以下命令在要求保险人作出抗辩请求之前,先要受保人通常是船东要先交出所有有关的船舶文件。而一天没有交出,法院诉讼的程序就暂停。这种命令是不适用于岸上的保险:Tannenbaum & Co. v. Heath (1908) 13 Com Cas 264。这一个历史长远而且受到了局限以防止保险人以此作为延误与刁难受保人的做法,还存在于英国目前的民事诉讼法(CPR 58.14[2])。有关这种做法的原因以及演变在笔者与汪鹏南教授所著的《英国海上保险条款详论》第 402 ~ 404 页有介绍。贵族院在 The "Star Sea" (2001) 1 Lloyd's Rep. 399 (HL)也有针对这种做法说这是法院程序上的一种做法,与绝对善意的精神是无关。在该先例的上诉庭 Leggatt 大法官也提到从来没有先例就是在法院作出这种命令,但受保人的船东有违反,这就可以让保险人有选择权令保险合约无效的做法。这显示了法院程序的违反并非是等同绝对善意的违反,印证了诉讼期间不适用绝对善意原则。Leggatt 大法官这样说:"If orders for an affidavit of ship's papers were made in direct implementation of the duty of utmost good faith, they could as well be made against insurers, since the obligation is mutual. Yet there is no recorded instance of an order having been made against an insurer. Such orders in our judgment constitute no more than examples of Court's procedure for handling cases of this kind. It has never been suggested that a failure to disclose ship's papers, either without an order of the Court or after such an order, would entitle underwriters to avoid the policy."

但针对某些保险合约履行期间的情况是否有严格遵守绝对善意的责任(即使是不同程度)还是不断有新的疑问。举例说,受保人与保险人针对某项损失的赔付达成和解协议,该和解协议是否有绝对善意的责任?如果有的话,岂非是大家都需要作出正确与全面的披露,包括他们在谈判时的底线。或者,这和解协议也只是一般的合约,想终止只能是在一些合约法的说法下如一方的误述导致了和解协议的达成,或是和解协议有一个基本性的共同错误等。涉及这个问题的先例包括 Magee v. Pennine Insurance (1969) 2 QB 507 和 The "Shakir III" (1997) 1 Lloyd's Rep. 586,笔者不再多介绍。

4.2 受保人知情(the knowledge of the assured)

1906 年的《英国海上保险法》Section 18 有关应该披露的事实或者情况(facts or circumstances)涉及了两个方面:一是某些可能应该披露的事实或者情况,如对投保的风险是有些不正常与特殊的方面。二是该事实或情况是否有实质性的重要与是从谁的角度看待。这些方面会做进一步的介绍,值得一提的是第 19 条也是针对披露,不过针对的是受保人的保险经纪人,这主要在英国保险市场(特别是劳合社)的做法。

4.2.1 对事实或情况的披露

在 1906 年《英国海上保险法》生效前,曾经有先例判是保险人只能在受保人欺诈性隐瞒实质性重要的事实才可以使保险合约无效:Mayne v. Walter (1787) 3 Dougl 79。但这在 1906 年的立法中有了改变,可以说目前针对受保人披露的责任是在上诉庭的先例 Joel v. Law Union and Crown Insurance Co. (1908) 2 KB 863 中,就是受保人有披露实质性重要事实的责任,只要这些事实是他在正常的商业活动中应该知道的事实或情况。而保险人是否可以使保险合约无效不再与受保人的不披露是否有欺诈有关,而只是看保险人是否因此受到误导。

这一法律地位也是在之后无数的先例被依从,如在先例 Container Transport International Inc v. Oceanus (1984) 1 Lloyds Rep. 476, Kerr 大法官说:"The principle is that if a certain fact is material... so that a failure to draw the underwriter's attention to it distorts the fairness of the broker's presentation of the risk, then it is not sufficient that this fact could have been extracted by the underwriter in the material to which he had access or which was cursorily shown to him. On the other hand, if the disclosed facts give a fair presentation of the risk, then the underwriter must enquire if he wishes to have more information... Provided that the presentation of the material facts in summarised form is given fairly there is no need for more."

接下来可以介绍一个也是依从了上述法律地位的有趣先例,有关根据事实找出受保人有否作出公平的陈述(fair presentation)以及保险人是否受到误导(mislead):Newbury v. Reliance (1994) 1 Lloyd's Rep. 83。案情涉及投保方程式赛车奖金的保险,这种保险在很多有很高奖金的国际赛事中都有,如高尔夫球赛中一杆就打进洞的巨额奖金,以增加比赛的吸引力。但组织者都会为这些高额奖金投保,而由于奖金可能会颁发,也可能不会颁发,纯粹是一个风险的问题。这一风险是可以作出投保的,显然其中一个必须作出披露的重要的事实或情况就是谁是参赛者。例如,打高尔夫球,Tiger Wood 有否参与比赛对保险人承保的风险是有很大的影响,也会对保费费率的高低有很大的影响,甚至是因为他的参与,会令部分保险人拒绝承保。在先例 Newbury v. Reliance,涉及新西兰的方程式赛车比赛中有一位赛车手名为 Russell Ingall,他在过去几年的方程式赛车比赛中都创造了辉煌的成绩。而有关的争议就涉及了保险经纪人有否对保险人作出披露,或只作出误导性的披露。在双方的口头证据中,有很多互相矛盾的指控,如保险人说是听到 Russell Ingall 过去几年在比赛中都没有什么成绩,但保险经纪人则否认这样说过。这导致了 Hobhouse 大法官不重视口头证据,而看有关的文件证据。其中一份是在向保险人询问保险费率时提供给他的重要文件,措辞如下(其中提到了 Russell Ingall 与其他的赛车手):

"GRAHAM LORIMER RACING

Wants to add to his team a driver by the name of Russell Ingall.

The sum insured is 400,000 pounds payable to the driver in the event he achieved a Top 3 Championship position by the end of the 12th Race Series.

Russell Ingall this season has raced in the German Formula 3 season. His highest position was a 2nd place in the penultimate race of the season. However he was not in the top 6 of the Championship. He had no other top 3 finishes.

He contested the Formula Ford Festival this year, and finished a creditable second after a few leading drivers had fallen away.

Other contenders for the New Zealand Championship are likely to be :
Gary Croft - Swift 92
Andy Stitchbury—Walter Leihner—Van Diemen 92
Andrew Masquarado—92 Swift
2 other Swift 92 have been entered (drivers tbn)
Jonathon Clus—Swift (will be driving)
Can we receive a quote on 400,000 pounds sum insured?"

在这份文件中可以马上看到的是没有提供 Russell Ingall 非常辉煌的成绩,而只是提到 1992 年在德国举办的方程式赛车第三赛季中,他在倒数第二场比赛中是名列第二。这被 Hobhouse 大法官认为是误导性的披露,因为保险人会认为 Russell Ingall 得奖的机会只是中等(modest)。但事实上在承保的新西兰赛事中,Russell Ingall 在全部 13 场比赛中是有 12 场排第一,而另外的一场也是因为犯规被取消比赛资格才没有成绩。所以 Hobhouse 大法官判受保人没有尽到披露的责任,说:"The result of the presentation both written and oral to these two underwriters was that they were both left in ignorance of Mr. Russell Ingall's previous performance and given a wrong impression of this performance in 1992 and in fact one piece of unequivocally inaccurate information—that he had not achieved a top 3 place in any other race in the German Formula 3 Championship."

当然涉及这种争议的案件还有其他复杂的地方,如受保人会说保险人应该进一步询问,否则就是弃权(waiver)。这里还会涉及保险人承保这些风险的话,自己应该有的有关知识。例如,Russell Ingall 是非常有名,只要在这方面有涉及业务的保险人都应该知道他。这些都是事实的认定,反正 Hobhouse 大法官认为受保人根本没有在开始时做到公平的陈述,就不存在有第二步的保险人需要进一步的主动询问(put on enquiry)。Hobhouse 大法官说:"The question therefore is whether Mr. Woods (保险经纪人) made a fair presentation of this risk to Miss Clay (保险人). In my judgment he clearly did not. A fair presentation must have involved some disclosure of the performance of Russell Ingall in Formula Ford championships in previous years. The presentation made in respect of 1992 was designed to disarm further enquiry and play down his achievements. It is clear that the presentation succeeded in misleading both Miss Clay and Mr. Paschen. The obligation of an underwriter to make further enquiries only arises after a fair presentation has been made to him. He is entitled to assume that the risk has been presented to him in a fair fashion."

在这里顺便一提的是,不涉及商业活动的保险,就不存在有正常的商业活动中应该知道的事实或情况。这一来,披露只局限在非商业性受保人实际上知道(actually knew)或应该知道(imputed to know)的事实与情况。如某人向保险人投保人寿或医疗保险,他需要披露的也就是年龄、自己的过往病史等非常有限与不涉及专业知识的一般性信息。但如果延伸到披露正常的商业活动中应该知道的事实或情况，而且涉及的是较复杂的商业活动，受保人应该知道的事实与情况就会非常多。但是如果受保人业务水平不行，他应该知道的却不知道，显然就会在披露的责任上有更大的危险。

在这里也可以探讨什么是受保人应该知道的事实与情况，这可在许多的案件中列举 London General Insurance Co. v. General Marine Underwriters Association (1921) K. B. 104。案情涉及再保险，保险人（在本案是受保人）为他承保的一批货物，装运在一艘名为 Vigo 的船舶上去投保再保险。在投保的一天，实际上已经有劳合社的事故报告广泛报道了该船舶与货物已经遭受损失。但受保人没有向再保险人披露这一个情况与事实，再保险人事后以这一理由拒赔。受保人说是他当天工作非常繁忙，根本没有时间看该份事故报告，但这不被法院接受，并认为是受保人即使是不知道，也属于他应该知道的。至于说再保险人也应该看到这一份事故报告，可以说是他在业务中应该知道的事实与情况，所以不必披露。法院认为再保险人在还没有接受再保之前对该船舶与货物没有任何利益关系，所以看了这些事故报告也会是漫不经心，可以理解，即使是一个谨慎的再保险人也会是如此。看来，这种争议是根据每一个不同案件的情况而定。

4.2.2 从谁的角度看是实质性重要

有关实质重要性的课题主要在下一段会介绍，在这里只是针对一项事实或情况的实质性是从谁的角度看待。因为受保人对某项事实有否实质性重要的看法可能与保险人的看法不同。这是因为披露的责任只是限于具有实质性重要的事实或情况，否则要求事无大小都要全面披露就会是不现实。可以说在目前的法律是从保险人的角度看某项事实或情况是否是实质性重要。这表示受保人的知情也包括需要了解保险人在承保某种业务时会考虑什么因素，才可以向保险人就有关的风险作出充分的公平陈述（fair presentation）。

在 Robert Merkin 教授所著的《Colinvaux's Law of Insurance in Hong Kong》第 6.005 段，他这样说："There are dicta [in Anglo - African Merchants Ltd. v. Barley (1970) 1 QB 311, 319] which indicate that the assured's duty extends only to disclosing those facts which a reasonable assured ought to have realized would be material to a prudent insurer, so that the proper test of materiality is some sort of hybrid based on the prudence of both parties, but it may be that what is being said is that a reasonable assured ought to know what is material to a prudent insurer. However, later cases emphasise that the prudence or otherwise of the assured's conduct plays no part. The law is thus settled, but it was nevertheless commented by Staughton LJ in Kausar v. Eagle Star Insurance Co. Ltd. (2000) Lloyd's Rep. IR 154 that, if the assured has acted innocently, the insurer's right to avoid liability should be confined to 'plain' cases, which presumably means cases in which the evidence of materiality is overwhelming."

即使是一个完全合理与无意瞒骗的受保人,对某项事实有否实质性重要的看法与一个谨慎的保险人看法不同的情况很多,也在法院提到过:Reynolds v. Phoenix Assurance Co. Ltd. (1978) 2 Lloyd's Rep. 440, 457。但目前的英国法律是对受保人不利,所以有说法是在某些种类的保险合约,如针对消费者保险合约,法律应该改过来:实质性重要是从合理受保人的角度来看。这方面在本章最后第10段有进一步的探讨。

4.3 什么是对一个谨慎保险人有实质性重要(the test for "materiality")

根据1906年的立法 Section 18(2),只要是会影响"一个谨慎的保险人"厘定保险费率或者是是否承保时的判断,可以说任何事实与情况都是有实质性重要(every circumstance is material which would influence the judgement of a prudent insurer in fixing the premium, or determining whether he will take the risk)。这句话就蕴涵了几个需要进一步解释的问题,如下。

4.3.1 谁是谨慎保险人

"一个谨慎的保险人"(a prudent insurer)一词并没有提到真正承保风险的保险人(假设他是一个谨慎保险人)在个别案件对没有披露的事实与情况会否受影响。毕竟真正承保风险的保险人的谨慎程度可能比一般保险人高,也可能比一般保险人低,这种说法是谨慎保险人应该是当时市场上的一般保险人。在先例 Associated Oil Carriers Ltd. v. Union Insurance Society of Canton Ltd. (1917) 2 KB 184, Atkin 大法官这样说:"I think that [the alleged] standard of prudence indicates an underwriter much too bright and too good for human nature's daily food. There seems no good reason to impute to the insurer a higher degree of knowledge and foresight than that possessed by the more experienced and intelligent insurers carrying on business at that time... [If] the standard of prudence is the ideal one contended for... there were in July 1914, no prudent insurers in London, or if there were, they were not to be found in the usual places where one would seek for them."

这样一来,保险人就可以很容易令保险合约无效,因为他是可以去伦敦保险市场随便找一个有一定知名度或经验的从业保险人让他提供给法院专家意见说"这些未披露的事实与情况会影响我是否决定接受承保与保险费率的厘定"去证明未披露的事实与情况是实质性重要。想令合约无效的保险人反而是不必出庭举证他自己是否是会受到未披露信息的影响。这导致有一些案件中,认为1906年的立法中"谨慎保险人"是应该包括了市场上一般的保险人与实际承保的保险人,Kerr 大法官在先例 Berger v. Pollock (1973) 2 Lloyd's Rep. 442 中说:"Thus, Section 18(3) refers throughout to 'the insurer'. If one looks at the authorities one finds many references both to the judgment of prudent insurers in general and to the insurers in the particular cases. I do not think that such expressions give any guidance one way or the other. The historical development of the admissibility of evidence concerning the materiality of undisclosed circumstances is also of little assistance. For over 100 years it has been the practice to admit independent evidence for this purpose: see, for instance, the review of the position by Mr. Justice McNair in Roselodge Ltd. v. Castle (1966) 2 Lloyd's Rep. 113, at p. 129. But the admissibility of evidence on this question by the insurer concerned has never been in doubt since the time when the parties to the action before the Court could be examined as witnesses, and there are a number of references in reported decisions in which Judges have stressed the desirability for the underwriter concerned to go into the witness – box, at any rate in cases of doubt. It seems to me, as a matter of principle, that the Court's task in deciding whether or not the defendant insurer can avoid the policy for non – disclosure must be to determine as a question of fact whether, by applying the standard of the judgment of a prudent insurer, the insurer in question would have been influenced in fixing the premium or determining whether to take the risk if he had been informed of the undisclosed circumstances before entering into the contract. Otherwise one could in theory reach the absurd position where the Court might be satisfied that the insurer in question would in fact not have been so influenced but that other prudent insurers would have been. It would then be a very odd result if the defendant insurer could nevertheless avoid the policy. I do not think that this is the correct interpretation of Section 18 despite the generality of the language used in sub – s. 2."

这在 Pan Atlantic Insurance Co. Ltd. v. Pine Top Insurance Co. Ltd. (1994) 2 Lloyd's Rep. 427 (HL)带来了一点重要的改变,就是对谁是谨慎保险人多增加了一个"诱使"(inducement)的条件。这实际上就是把有关承保的保险人也加入进来,要他证明没有披露的事实与情况的确是诱使他,等于是证明实际上他确实也是受到了影响。这里可以节录 Mustill 勋爵在该先例中所说的两个条件如下:"I propose the following short answers: 1. A circumstance may be material even though a full and accurate disclosure of it would not itself have had a decisive effect on the prudent underwriter's decision whether to accept the risk and if so at what premium. But, 2. If the misrepresentation or non – disclosure of a material fact did not in fact induce the making of the contract (in the sense in which that expression is used in the general law of misrepresentation) the underwriter is not entitled to rely on it as a ground for avoiding the contract."

也可节录 Goff 勋爵在该先例中对 Mustill 勋爵观点认同的说法,认为是应该有一个"真正诱使的考验"看承保的保险人是否是受到影响,说:"I accept that the actual inducement test accurately represents the law. I do so for the reasons given by my noble and learned friend Lord Mustill. Like him, and for the reasons he gives, I conclude that there is to be implied in the Marine Insurance Act, 1906 a requirement that a material misrepresentation will only entitle the insurer to avoid the policy if it induced the making of the contract; and that a similar conclusion must be reached in the case of a material non – disclosure. This conclusion is, as I understand it, consistent with the opinion expressed by my noble and learned friend Lord Lloyd that Parliament, by enacting the law as it did in s. 20 of the 1906 Act must have intended to codify the common law on materiality, without touching the common law on inducement."

最后节录 John Dunt 在所著的《Marine Cargo Insurance》第 5.14 段有关这一点的论述："The leniency of this standard of 'materiality'［这是指以前对保险人非常宽松的举证责任］is tempered by the additional requirement of 'inducement' where the actual underwriter must show that, 'but for the relevant non - disclosure... he would not have entered into the contract on those terms'. In other words the missing information must have effectively induced the contract and prompted a different decision on the risk or the premium."

4.3.2 受影响要到什么程度

4.3.2.1 三种不同程度的考验

1906 年的立法 Section 18(2)是指任何情况会"影响"(influence)一个谨慎保险人决定是否接受承保与厘定保费费率就是实质性重要。但它没有对影响的程度作出明确的规定,所以就带来了三种不同的说法或考验(test)如下:(1)决定性影响(decisive influence test)。这是要求想令保险合约无效的保险人满足法院就是一个谨慎保险人会有不同的反应(如拒绝承保或多收保费),如果某一项事实与情况有作出披露或没有误述的话。(2)增加风险考验(increase risk test)。这是要求想令保险合约无效的保险人满足法院,即如果某一项事实与情况有作出披露或没有误述,会导致一个谨慎保险人认为这很可能增加风险,但不一定会导致他拒绝承保或多收保费。(3)纯粹会影响考验(mere influence test)或是有兴趣知道考验(would be interested test)。这是要求想令保险合约无效的保险人满足法院,即如果某一项事实与情况有作出披露或没有误述,一个谨慎保险人会认为他希望知道该事实与情况,虽然他不一定因此而拒绝承保或多收保费。

这三种不同程度的考验会带来很不一样的结果,如 Templeman 勋爵在 Pan Atlantic Insurance Co. Ltd. v. Pine Top Insurance Co. Ltd. (1994) 2 Lloyd's Rep. 427 (HL)中所说:"If an expert says, 'if I had known I would not have accepted the risk or I would have demanded a higher premium', his evidence can be evaluated against other insurances accepted by him and against other insurances accepted by other insurers. But if the expert says, 'I would have wanted to know but the knowledge would not have made any difference' then there are no objective or rational grounds upon which this statement of belief can be tested'."(如果专家证人说是我不会接受承保或者我会要求更高的保费,法院就可以根据他在其他保险的做法或保险市场的一般做法考虑这个证据是否被接纳。但如果专家证人只是说我有兴趣知道,这完全是一个主观的说法,没有一个客观的办法作出考验。)

4.3.2.2 第一种与第三种考验的取舍

这里实际是就提到了第一种考验与第三种考验的分别与审理的难处。第一种考验就是证人或专家证人说是我如果知道某项事实/情况我就会多收多少保费，这一个证人证言是可以反驳如证人的其他承保业务并非是收取这样的保费，或者伦敦市场上的其他保险人并非是收取这样的保费。这些反驳的证据显然就是由受保人提供给法院的。但第三种考验就是证人或专家证人说我会希望知道某项事实或情况，虽然知道了也不一定真的会影响，这就根本没有客观的标准或提供证据去反驳，因为这纯粹是他自己的想法。

结果是在 Pan Atlantic Insurance Co. Ltd. v. Pine Top Insurance Co. Ltd. (1994) 2 Lloyd's Rep. 427 (HL)中，多数的判决认为是以第三种考验为准，主要第三种考验才符合 1906 年的立法 Section 18(2)中的"influence a prudent insurer"的措辞，因为这样的措辞只能解释为"an effect on the mind of the insurer in weighting up the risk."，而不能解释为一定要拒绝承保或多收保费。但少数意见还是认为应以第一个考验为准，而第三个考验对保险人会是太优待或宽松，虽然在同一个贵族院先例中也有针对保险人就是需要实际承保的保险人证明他是受到实际的影响，可以说该先例对保险人与受保人都是有好有坏的。Robert Merkin 教授所著的《Colinvaux's Law of Insurance in Hong Kong》第 6.023 段是这样总结："This reasoning was confirmed by a majority of the House of Lords in Pan Atlantic Insurance Co. Ltd. v. Pine Top Insurance Co. Ltd. (1994) 2 Lloyd's Rep. 427 (HL), it being laid down that the phrase 'influence the judgment of a prudent insurer' meant no more than 'an effect on the mind of the insurer in weighing up the risk'. The minority's view was that the insurer should not be able to deny liability unless it could be shown that a prudent underwriter would have regarded the information as increasing the risk and would have altered the premium or rejected the risk accordingly."

4.3.2.3 第二种与第三种考验取舍的可能性

剩下还有一点不明确的地方就是第二种考验与第三种考验的取舍，这在 St Paul Fire & Marine Co. (UK) Ltd. v. McConnell Dowell Constructors Ltd. (1995) 2 Lloyd's Rep. 116 被明确为第三种的考验为准。其中上诉庭的 Evans 大法官这样说："Now that inducement of the actual underwriter must also be proved, there is no reason why 'material' should be limited to factors which are seen as increasing the risk, and in my judgment there are good reasons for not doing so. First many factors may not be 'clear-cut' in this way; the risk may be increased in some respects but decreased in others. The present case provides an example of this, as will appear below. Secondly, the duty of disclosure operates both ways because the duty of good faith is reciprocal, so the definition of 'material' is not concerned with the proposer of insurance alone. For these reasons alone, I would reject Mr. Phillips'（受保人大律师）submission that the fact cannot be material unless the risk is thereby increased, and I would support this conclusion on the wider ground that 'material' like 'relevant' denotes a relationship with the subject - matter rather than a prediction of its effect."

有关第二种与第三种考验，在《Good faith and insurance contracts》(第二版)一书也有很详细的涉及。第二种在该书被称为是"客观看是与承保风险有关系"(objective connection to the risk 或 material to the risk)，第三种可被称为是与"诱使达成保险合约有关系"(material to inducement)。与承保风险有关系的实质性重要事实与情况显然是包括了可能会令有关风险增加的事实，或影响赔付金额与频率的事实等。它也包括了道德风险会增加的事实，如投保金额过高等。至于与第三种考验可举先例 The "Dora" (1989) 1 Lloyd's Rep. 69 为例，案情涉及受保人对保险人作出误述(虽然这不是披露但针对实质性重要的道理是一样)令保险人以为将来会有更多的生意。为此保险人除了接受承保外还将保费打了折扣。这被判是误述，而且有实质性重要。但明显这是与承保的风险没有关系，针对的只是将来的生意。

事实上，也有不少判例是认为第三种考验才是正确的，如在较早提到的先例 St Paul Fire & Marine Insurance Co. (UK) Ltd. v. McConnell Dowell Contractor Ltd.。另在先例 The "Moonacre" (1992) 2 Lloyd's Rep. 501，Colman 大法官说"Given the width of the general principle of the utmost good faith, there can be no justification for confining material circumstances to those which are directly relevant to the assessment of the risk."

但也有先例持不同的看法，如在先例 Glicksman v. Lancashire (1925) 2 KB 593, Scrutton 大法官这样说："it is generally accepted that the material facts are those relating to the nature of the risk."

这方面看来还没有先例直接针对，但可节录《Good faith and insurance contracts》(第二版)第 14.70 段，说是第二种考验应该受到支持以及理由："It is submitted that it would be rendering the duty of disclosure unacceptably wide if the facts to be disclosed need have no connection with the risk. As Lord Sumner said in Yorkshire Insurance Company v. Campbell (1917) AC 218,221, the material fact must be one which is both material to the risk and material to be known to the prudent underwriter. This is consistent with the supposed purpose of the duty of disclosure which binds the assured when the insurance contract is agreed, namely to enable the insurer to adjudge the character of the risk and determine its extent so that he may decide whether to accept the engagement and the level of premium. If the contrary were true, materiality as a concept would give up any meaning to the mere application of the prudent underwriter test. (It has also been said that the materiality must be 'direct' so that if a fact, if disclosed, would merely lead the insurer to discover a more material fact, then the first fact is not material; it is too indirect. Such a distinction will be of little practical use, since the assured would be obliged to disclose the latter fact, being material. Nevertheless, such an approach is suggestive of a need to provide some limitation to the notion of materiality other than the attitude of the prudent underwriter.)”

4.3.3 实质性重要在不同的保险类别有所不同

必须要披露实质性重要的事实与情况也在其他保险的类别有要求,虽然1906年《英国海上保险法》只是针对海上保险。在19世纪早期,曾经在英国法院有过争议就是自动披露的责任只是局限在海上保险:Fowkes v. Manchester & London Life Assurance & Loan Association (1863) 3 B & S 917,929。但在一连串的案例中,披露的责任也延伸至其他类别的保险,包括像人寿险:Anderson v. Gitzgerald (1853) 4 HLC 484, 504; Hambrough v. Mutual Life Insurance of New York (1895) 72 LT 140, 141;财产险与火险:Lindenau v. Desborough (1828) 8 B&C 586, London Assurance v. Mansel (1879) LR 11 QB 363,367 等。

但怎样才是有实质性重要的披露就因为保险类别的不同而不一致,毕竟一个谨慎保险人在不同保险类别会有不同的考虑。例如,受保人有否被其他保险公司或保险人曾经拒绝承保。在人寿保险先例 London Assurance v. Mansel (1879) LR 11 QB 363,Jessel 大法官认为这是有实质性重要说:“The question is whether this is a material fact. I should say, no human being acquainted with the practice of companies or of insurance societies or underwriters could doubt for a moment that it is a fact of great materiality, a fact upon which the offices place great reliance. They always want to know what other offices have done with respect to the lives.”

但在水险或者船舶险,这种做法并不现实,因为受保人或者他的保险经纪人所接触过的保险人会是很多。所以在先例 Hamilton & Co. v. Eagle Star (1924) 19 Lloyd's Rep. 242,Bailhache 大法官是这样说:“It is not the business of a broker who submits a risk to an underwriter to tell him what other underwriters have done about it, whether they have refused it, or whether they have refused to renew, or whether they have cancelled. It is not his business to say anything about that, always provided that he says nothing about it. Of course, if he begins to talk about it then the matter becomes quite different.”

4.3.4 对实质性重要的总结

英国法律发展到目前的情况可以总结说在 Pan Atlantic Insurance Co. Ltd. v. Pine Top Insurance Co. Ltd. (1994) 2 Lloyd's Rep. 427 (HL)先例中,对保险人与受保人各有利弊。已经提到过,在该先例贵族院比较第一种与第三种考验是采纳了后者,也就是纯粹会影响考验(mere influence test)或是有兴趣知道考验(would be interested test),这明显对保险人有利。这带来的问题是在这个考验下,如果一项事实与情况即使作出披露,一个谨慎保险人也不一定会因为知道了而拒绝承保或/与多收保费,这会否是该事实与情况更接近或属于是本章第6.1段的会减少承保风险,所以在1906年《英国海上保险法》Section 18(3)(a)说明是不必要披露?看来这就要受保人以这一理由提出与争辩,另外也要依赖审理法官的良好商业常识了。

最后一提的是,实质性并不需要是增加风险,只要是对保险人而言所要承保的风险是有所不同就已经足够:St Paul Fire and Marine Insurance Co. Ltd. v. McConnell Dowell Construction Ltd. (1996) 1 All E. R. 96。

Pan Atlantic Insurance Co. Ltd. v. Pine Top Insurance Co. Ltd 先例对受保人有利的是,在谨慎保险人的基础上又多增加了一个"诱使"(inducement)的条件,这实际上就是把有关承保的保险人也加入进来,要求他提供证据。如果有关保险人不出庭举证,而只是提供其他保险人的专家意见证据,这被认为不足够,或是无关:Lewis v. Norwich Union Healthcare Ltd. (2009) EW Misc 2 (EWCC)。这变成想使保险合约无效的保险人的举证责任加重。这里的举证责任与步骤,在先例 Assicurazioni Generali SpA v. Arab Insurance Group (BSC) (2003) Lloyd's Rep. IR 131,Clarke 大法官这样说:"(1) In order to be entitled to avoid a contract of insurance or reinsurance, an insurer or reinsurer must prove on the balance of probabilities that he was induced to enter into the contract by a material non – disclosure or by a material misrepresentation. (2) There is no presumption of law that an insurer or reinsurer is induced to enter into the contract by a material non – disclosure or misrepresentation. (3) The facts may, however, be such that it is to be inferred that the particular insurer or reinsurer was so induced even in the absence from evidence from him. (4) In order to prove inducement the insurer or reinsurer must show that the non – disclosure or misrepresentation was an effective cause of his entering into the contract on the terms on which he did. He must therefore show at least that, but for the relevant non – disclosure or misrepresentation, he would not have entered into the contract on those terms. On the other hand, he does not have to show that it was the sole effective cause of his doing so."

4.4　保险人选择让合约无效与重新确认合约的有效性(avoidance and affirmation)

在有需要披露而受保人没有披露的情况,保险人在知道这一情况后是有选择的权利令保险合约无效,这在 1906 年《英国海上保险法》Section 18(1)的用词是"the insurer may avoid the contract"。即是保险人可以这样做,但也可以不选择这样做。如果保险人是以行动或者语言显示了他不这样做,就等于是确认(affirm)保险合约的继续有效,而如果涉及保险合约的所有赔付也必须作出。确认本身就是一种弃权,就是保险人放弃了他的权利令保险合约无效。Langley 大法官在先例 Sphere Drake Insurance plc v. Orion Insurance plc (1999) All ER (D) 133 说:"Affirmation is one form of the general doctrine of waiver."

所以保险人在这种受保人违反绝对善意下所能够有的救济就是所谓的"all or nothing":Pan Atlantic Insurance Co. Ltd. and Another v. Pine Top Insurance Co. Ltd. (1993) 1 Lloyd's Rep. 496,508,The Star Sea (1995) 1 Lloyd's Rep. 651,667。曾经有过争议就是保险人可否采取或被局限在比较中庸的救济,如只对有关违反绝对善

意的损失拒绝赔偿,但可以不必选择令保险合约无效。这种情况会出现在保险人希望继续一个赚钱的开口保单(open cover)或是其他的原因不想终止保险合约。但这已经是被法院否定:Brewtnall v. Cornhill Insurance Company (1931) 40 Lloyd's Rep. 166,168; West v. National Motor and Accident Union (1955) 1 Lloyd's Rep. 207,210。

另针对合约一方如果有明示或默示的选择权,法律地位怎样针对。类似的明示或者默示选择权终止合约在一般的合约中也普遍存在,如在期租合约下承租人没有准时支付租金,通常有一个明示选择权给船东撤船(请参阅杨大明律师著《期租合约》第18篇),就有好几个先例船东知道了他有这一个权利后,被要求在作出选择时必须是明确且不能托泥带水,时间上必须是尽快,否则都会构成对这一选择权的放弃。

4.4.1 令保险合约无效的弃权的大原则

在保险合约中,保险人在知道他有令保险合约无效的选择权后,如果不在合理时间内行使,就会构成弃权,也就是说保险合约继续有效。这里的公平之处是如果保险人在合理时间内行使选择权,令保险合约无效后,受保人就可以与其他保险人尽早再另外安排保险作为替代。而如果超出合理时间保险人没有作出这样的选择,或者是保险人作出一些拖泥带水的行为或是含糊的行为,会令受保人有错觉。如果期间发生损失,保险人才选择令保险合约无效,这对受保人明显是不公平。所以这种情况下就会视为是保险人弃权。

总结而言,根据先例 WISE (Underwriting Agency) Limited v. Grupo Nacional Provincial SA (2004) 2 Lloyd's Rep. 483,构成弃权是要满足以下的条件:"(1) The insurer or his authorised agent must have actual knowledge of the facts not disclosed prior to the contract. Constructive knowledge is insufficient. (这是指保险人或者他的代理人/经理人必须知道因为受保人没有作出实质性的披露,他有权利可以令保险合约无效。) (2) The insurer must also know that the breach of duty gives rise to the right to avoid. (这与上面一致。) (3) The insurer has a reasonable time in which to decide what to do. (保险人有一个合理时间决定是令保险合约无效或者是弃权让保险合约继续生效。) (4) There must be an unequivocal communication to the assured by words or conduct that the insurer has made an informed choice to affirm the contract and to pay the claim. (保险人必须是通过语言或者行为清楚明白的告诉受保人,他经过深思熟虑的决定是令保险合约继续有效。看来这一法律地位比较向着保险人,因为受保人需要证明保险人有这样意思的清楚明白的表示,而不是指保险人讲了些含糊的话就足够了。例如,如果保险人告诉受保人在发生损失后采取一些行动,并说明是"无损害"[without prejudice],就已经有先例判是保险人没有对令合约无效弃权:Callaghan & Hedges v. Thompson [2000] Lloyd's Rep. IR 125。) (5) Whether such a communication is found depends upon how a reasonable person in the position of the assured would interpret the insurer's words or conduct. (保险人给受保人的语言或者行为是否足够是弃权或者令保

险合约继续有效是从一个合理受保人的角度看待，这合理受保人也表示一般在保险市场的受保人会怎样看待。）

上述所讲的一些弃权的大原则，也可以节录先例 Liberian Insurance Agency Inc v. Mosse（1977）2 Lloyd's Rep. 560，其中 Donaldson 大法官这样说："Full knowledge of the facts is essential before there can be any question of affirmation—being put upon inquiry is insufficient. And even when the underwriter has full knowledge of the facts, he is still entitled to a reasonable time in which to decide whether to affirm the contract: McCormick v. National Motor & Accident Insurance Union Ltd. [1934] 49 Lloyd Rep. 361 at 365. In a situation in which the underwriter has taken no action to affirm or repudiate the contract and a reasonable time for making up his mind has elapsed, he will be deemed to have affirmed the contract if either so much time has elapsed that the necessary inference is one of affirmation or the assured has been prejudiced by the delay in making an election or rights of third parties have intervened."

有关保险人的弃权令保险合约继续生效，最明确不过的就是保险人明示说明他愿意继续承保。如在先例 Morrison v. The Universal Marine Insurance Co.（1873）LR 8 Ex 197 中，在保险人知道受保人没有披露的事实后，他重新确认说他愿意继续承保，那么他之后将失去令合约无效的权利。但比较容易起争议的就是保险人在知道发生损失与他可以令合约无效的权利后，作出一些比较含糊的语言与行动，如要求受保人如何处理受损害的货物，但之后又以没有履行披露责任拒赔。针对这种争议如何解决稍后介绍。

4.4.2　何谓保险人知道他的权利

在上述先例 WISE（Underwriting Agency）Ltd. v. Grupo Nacional Provincial S. A（2004）2 Lloyd's Rep. 483，节录判词的第一项就已经说明是保险人必须知道他有令保险合约无效的权利是弃权的先决条件之一。但不是有很多先例针对保险人必须知道他有这个权利的程度，直到先例 Insurance Co. of the Channel Islands v. Royal Hotel（No. 2）（1998）Lloyd's Rep. IR 151。在该先例 Mance 大法官判是保险人必须有真正的了解（actual knowledge of the facts），而不需要 100% 肯定的程度。但只是一个推定的了解（constructive knowledge）是并不足够。Mance 大法官这样说："For practical purposes, knowledge presupposes the truth of the matters known, and a firm belief in their truth, as well as sufficient justification for that belief in terms of experience, information and/or reasoning."（现实中什么算是"知道"，前提就是知道事实的真相，也相信这一真相，以及有一个根据有关经验、信息与理由足够证明对这一真相的信任是有道理。例如，保险人如果从他的代表律师或者合资格的理算师知道事实的真相，就应该可以被视为是足够证明。相反，保险人如果只是道听途说，或者是信息来源说明还没有经过调查证实，保险人就不能被视为是"知道"。）

另外，Mance 大法官也讲到如果保险人故意或为了其他原因不掌握事实的真相，他还是会被视为是“知道”,说:“a person who deliberately and for tactical reasons decides not to acquire definite knowledge of a matter which he believes it likely that he could confirm must be treated as having knowledge of that matter.”

在这里还可以顺便一提其他的变数,如保险人在之前知道了他的权利,但选择不令保险合约无效。但之后,保险人又知道了进一步的事实真相与严重性,而选择令保险合约无效,这是可以的。因为,保险人的选择是依据了新的进一步事实真相。这方面可节录 Robert Merkin 教授所著的《Colinvaux's Law of Insurance in Hong Kong》的第6.095 段:“waiver of the right to avoid on a limited matter does not preclude a subsequent decision to avoid on the basis of after – acquired information. This point was made in Spriggs v. Wessington Court School Ltd. (2005) Lloyd's Rep. IR 474, where liability insurers affirmed a policy taken out by a school despite non – disclosure of allegations of abuse against pupils by its headmaster, but were subsequently permitted to avoid the policy on discovering that there were many more undisclosed instances of abuse than had previously been thought.”

4.4.3 何谓合理时间以及保险人保持沉默的后果

在 Liberian Insurance Agency Inc v. Mosse (1977) 2 Lloyd's Rep. 560 中,Donaldson 大法官的判词可以看到在保险人知道了受保人没有披露的内容后,在选择令保险合约无效或是重新确认保险合约的有效性之前,他是可以有合理的时间进行调查。但何谓合理时间呢? 本来“合理”一词很难有固定的定义,任何事情合理或不合理都要看个别情况。在该先例的事实,我们可以看看 Donaldson 大法官是怎么说的。

该先例中,保险人是正在利比亚就一票搪瓷(enamelware)所提出的索赔进行调查。调查结果还没有出来,保险人通知受保人说在调查报告作出前不要将被承保的货物出售。之后,受保人就争辩说他的利益被损害,因为保险人的指示导致他不能将货物以更好的价钱及时出售。受保人还争辩说,在保险人作出先不要出售承保货物的通知时,决定是否令保险合约无效或重新确认保险合约有效性的合理时间已经过去(reasonable time has expired)。但 Donaldson 大法官不买受保人的账,他说:“Avoidance on these grounds [non – disclosure] is a very serious matter requiring careful consideration and consultation between those who had subscribed to the risk.”

另可节录 Robert Merkin 教授所著的《Colinvaux's Law of Insurance in Hong Kong》的第6.092 段:“Perhaps the most difficult cases arise where the insurer has not acted at all, but has delayed in communicating any form of decision to the assured, particularly where this is coupled with action which might be construed as evidencing a willingness to pay. Delay may give rise to waiver by affirmation where the assured has been given reason for believing that the claim will be met: Simner v. New India Assurance Co. Ltd. (1995) LRLR 240. In this type of case, unless the insurer takes the obvious step of reserving his rights: Nicholson v. Power (1869) 20 LT 580, the court may infer an intention to waive, on the principle that 'a businessman knows how to reserve his rights': Barber v. Imperio Reinsurance Co. (UK) Ltd. (unrep, 1993). Nevertheless, it is clear that not every delay will be construed as waiver, whether or not there is a reservation of rights. Insurers are entitled to a reasonable time to reach their decision: Callaghan & Hedges v. Thompson (2000) Lloyd's Rep. IR 125. It has thus been held that inaction for a period of five days, without prejudice being caused to the assured, is not an act of implicit waiver: McCormick v. National Motor & Accident Insurance Union (1934) 40 Com Cas 76."

正如上述所讲,保险人如果保持沉默会是一种比较困难的情况,因为通常保持沉默是不构成弃权。在先例 HIH Casualty & General Insurance v. Axa Corporation Solutions (2003) Lloyd's Rep. IR 1, [26],Tuckey 大法官引述了《Chitty on Contract》说:"Although a promise or representation may be made by conduct, mere inactivity will not normally suffice for the present purpose since 'it is difficult to imagine how silence and inaction can be anything but equivocal.' Unless the law took this view mere failure to assert a contractual right could lead to its loss; and the Courts have on a number of occasions rejected this clearly undesirable conclusion."

在该先例,Tuckey 大法官也有提到有些情况下法律会强加"必须讲话或采取积极行动的责任"(a duty to speak or to act)。所以在《Good faith and insurance contracts》(第二版)第 17.155 段有这样的论述:"In such circumstances, the courts might be prepared to view the failure to speak as amounting to a promise that the insurer would not exercise his legal rights."另在该书也讲到如果保险人不讲话与不行动之余,但有其他的相关行动(如承诺或表示愿意赔付,对发生的损失作出一些要求或建议等),这也会被视为是作出了决定,如确认(affirm)保险合约而不令它无效。这是在第 17.147 段:"The suggestion has been made that silence or inactivity, combined with other conduct on the part of the representor, could amount to unequivocal conduct. This view found favor with Potter, LJ in The 'Happy Day' (2002) 2 Lloyd's Rep. 487 [66]."

4.4.4 保险人作出无损害保留(reservation)

在上一段 Merkin 教授著作的节录中多次提到保留保险人的权利(reserve the right),这在实践中体现为保险人为了更好地保护自己的地位,在给出像"暂不要出售承保货物"的指示时,会说明"our actions are without prejudice to the right to avoid"。这也是保险人通常的做法,以避免他的讲话或行动(如支付赔付或接受保险费)被视为是确认保险合约的继续有效:Morrison v. The Universal Marine Insurance (1872) LR 8 Ex 40,57; Iron Trades Mutual Insurance v. Companhia De Seguros Imperio (1991) 1 Re LR 213,224; Clarence Roy Hilll v. Citadel Insurance (1995) LRLR 218,239, Callaghan v. Thompson (2000) Lloyd's Rep. IR 125。

但是这种保留在受保人的利益真的被损害时,有效性不清楚。特别是,保险人已经知道了有关的不披露或误述,以及他所有的法律权利选择令保险合约无效。这可以节录《Good faith and insurance contracts》(第二版)第17.163段:“It has been suggested that a reservation of rights would not protect the insurer after he has acquired relevant knowledge of the right to avoid or a breach of warranty if he then commits acts which are consistent with the continued existence of the contract or of the cover. It is submitted that whether this would be the case will depend on the facts. If the insurer has reserved his rights and then acted in such a way that the reservation of rights has plainly been superseded, the insurer may well then have difficulty in persuading the court that the reservation remained intact.”

这种情况可以是货物仍在运输途中,风险仍然存在,如果保险人早点告知他选择令保险合约无效,受保人可以尽早安排另外的保险。但如果保险人迟迟不作出选择,而期间给受保人的指示或要求都作出无损害保留,结果发生货物全损的新事故后才宣布保险合约无效,这看来会有很大问题。根据1906年《英国海上保险法》Section 17,保险人对受保人也具有善意的义务,如果过了合理时间,保险人尚未作出是否令保险合约无效或重新确认保险合约有效的通知,将会视为保险合约被重新确认有效。

4.4.5 有关什么是确认保险合约之一:继续有效的通知

根据先例Insurance Corporation of the Channel Islands v. Royal Hotel Ltd. (1998) Lloyd's Rep. IR 151,通知会否造成保险合约继续有效的后果要客观来看,保险人是否是有意或只是无意中造成受保人的误解并没有关系,关键是保险人的行为或这一通知是否让一个正常理智与合理的人士(从受保人的角度)觉得保险人是在掌握了全部的信息后有意作出的。这也完全合理,因为受保人才是需要作出相应行动的一方。

在先例WISE (Underwriting Agency) Limited v. Grupo Nacional Provincial SA (2004) 2 Lloyd's Rep. 483,案情涉及一批劳力士手表被盗窃,损失高达80万美元。有关的开口保单所承保的货物是“钟表”(clock),保险人试图令保险合约无效理由就是受保人误述。有关案情在本章第5.4段与第6.3段都有介绍,在这里只针对有关保险人作出确认保险合约继续有效的通知。这部分有关的案情是在保险人知道了劳力士手表被盗窃后的两天(这表示在那个时候他已经知道了自己有令保险合约无效的权利),保险人在与受保人的保险经纪人的谈话中,被指称口头作出一个销约通知(Notice of Cancellation),根据保险合约中有条文允许提前两个月通知中断开口保单。之后,该保险经纪人随即给受保人一个电邮,说:“Owing to this very recent loss of USMYM 800,000 approx, we have received 60 days notice effective today to cancel this cover...”

该电邮的内容,在该先例中被双方都接受为等同是确认了保险合约继续有效,至少是在接下来的60天。由于双方都同意这样的解释(只是保险人否认在口头曾经讲过类似的内容),判决中就没有就此有太多解释。但不难推断为什么双方都不进一步争议,因为从该销约通知客观的来看,应该是意味着保险人对因为受保人误述而令保险合约无效权利的放弃。毕竟在销约通知,说明是保险合约在接下来的60天继续有效,受保人当然不会安排马上再投保。试想,如果在这60天内另一票劳力士表也被盗窃,保险人对两批劳力士表都以受保人误述拒绝赔付,对受保人非常不公平。

这导致了在该先例的争议主要还是在保险人是否口头作出了销约通知,而针对这一点保险人是否认的。而保险经纪人作为重要的证人之一,在法院被盘问时承认他可能会听错。这种争议可以说也是口头证据不可靠的地方,等于说如果销约通知是直接以文书形式来自保险人,根本就无可争议。现在可以有一个争论是,保险人可能跟经纪人提过这方面的事情,只是经纪人误解了才给了受保人这样一封电邮。从某种程度上来讲,保险人显然是想终断需要面对很大赔付的开口保单,也没必要给这样一个销约通知,因为他是直接可根据误述令保险合约无效。估计是保险人那个时候应该知道但事实上不是很清楚自己有这方面的权利,为了保险一点给了销约通知(如果真的是口头做出),但这却带来了弃权的争议。至于这方面事实的认定,可以说高院与上诉庭的多数意见也不同,可见口头证据的不稳定与危险。

4.4.6 有关什么是确认保险合约之二:作出赔付或承诺赔付

作出赔付会是最明显与经常会发生的确认保险合约的行动:Container Transport International Inc v. Oceanus (1984) 1 Lloyds Rep. 476,518; Svenska Handelsbanken v. Sun Alliance and London Insurance (1996) 1 Lloyd's Rep. 619,569。除非在作出赔付时同时明示作出无损害保留:Callaghan v. Thompson (2000) Lloyd's Rep. IR 125。承诺赔付也被视为是确认保险合约的讲话或行动:Irish National Insurance v. Oman Insurance (1983) 2 Lloyd's Rep. 453,462; Baghbadrani v. Commercial Union Assurance (2000) Lloyd's Rep. IR 94, 123。

4.4.7 弃权与禁止翻供

弃权与禁止翻供是经常一起出现的说法,这在笔者《国际商务游戏规则——英国合约法》第十一章有详细介绍,请参阅。它们之间实际上有一点区别。首先,弃权涉及弃权方本来有一个明示或者默示的权利,但在弃权方知道了他的权利后,不在合理时间内或规定的时间内行使他的权利或者作出某些明确的行为可被视为是放弃权利。但禁止翻供是不必存在有一个权利,只是由于对方作出了某种表示、行为或者承诺,导致了另一方因为依赖而采取相应的行动。例如,一方的A本来在某一天根据双方合约必须支付一笔钱给对方的B,合约并且规定如果不准时支付,B可以中断合约。如果B对A在支付前的一两天说:"我会给你一个新的账户让你作出支付",但结果并没有及时通知A新账户是什么。这导致A没有准时作出支付,显然如果B想取消合约是完全不公平,A可以根据禁止翻供出抗辩,因为A是依赖了B的表示或行为不作出支付,而带来的损害就是现在的被指称是违约。在这种情况下,不存在A有什么权利被放弃,也不存在A必须知道什么是事实真相,所以不是弃权的说法。

在保险的法律中,也会有这两种一起的说法。涉及弃权,就是保险人作出明示或者默示的确认保险合约继续有效,这可被称为"waiver by affirmation"。涉及禁止翻供,可被称为"waiver by estoppel",而这种禁止翻供的情况出现在保险合约机会应该不多,而且也不容易与弃权分开,毕竟禁止翻供是衡平法的说法。这方面可节录Robert Merkin 教授所著的《Colinvaux's Law of Insurance in Hong Kong》的第6.097段:

"Waiver by estoppel arises where a person conducts himself in such a way that it is inequitable for him to rely upon his contractual rights, normally by reason of the other party's detrimental reliance. As is the case with waiver by affirmation, an unequivocal representation on the part of the allegedly waiving party is required, but waiver by estoppel differs from waiver by affirmation in two respects: waiver by affirmation does not rest upon equitable principles and in particular does not require detrimental reliance; and a finding of waiver by estoppel is not precluded by the absence of knowledge on the part of the representor of his legal rights. Estoppel is, in principle, applicable to insurance, where the insurer has stated that it intends to pay and causes the assured to incur expenditure.

This form of estoppel has yet to be pleaded successfully in an insurance case, although in Callaghan & Hedges v. Thompson (2000) Lloyd's Rep. IR 125, David Steel J expressed the view that an insurer would be estopped from denying a claim if the insurer decided not to avoid the policy for breach of the duty of utmost good faith and wrote to the assured in terms that the policy was still alive: such conduct is not waiver as it is a prerequisite of waiver that the manner of such indication makes it clear to the assured that the insurer was aware of the assured's breach of duty and had made an informed choice to pay. The absence of the need to convey informed choice, coupled with the lack of any need for reliance, at first sight appears to render estoppel a serious threat to insurers. However, it is to be borne in mind that the form of estoppel in question, promissory estoppel, based on the insurer's promise as to his future behavior operates, only in equity. In accordance with the general principle applicable to equitable remedies, promissory estoppel can be relied upon only by an assured who has acted equitably. Accordingly, if the assured has sought to mislead the insurer; and in particular if there has been deliberate fraud in the presentation of the risk, a plea of equitable promissory estoppel against the insurer will not be available to him."

5. 海上货物保险需要被披露的情况

1906年《英国海上保险法》Section 18需要受保人以绝对善意披露的事实与情况需要具备两个特征:实质性重要(materiality)与诱使(inducement),这包括承保货物的所有权、价值以及对货物的描述等。但什么样的事实与情况才算得上实质性重要会根据个案的不同而不同,而怎样的情况才算得上是诱使也是要看实际承保的保险人能够提供什么样的证据。

5.1 所有权或者其他形式的可保利益

1906年《英国海上保险法》Section 26针对保险合约中对承保货物的描述，节录如下："26. Designation of subject – matter (1) The subject – matter insured must be designated in a marine policy with reasonable certainty. (2) The nature and extent of the interest of the assured in the subject – matter insured need not be specified in the policy. (3) Where the policy designates the subject – matter insured in general terms, it shall be construed to apply to the interest intended by the assured to be covered. (4) In the application of this section regard shall be had to any usage regulating the designation of the subject – matter insured."

与本小段介绍内容最相关的是Section 26(3)，因为"intended"一词的存在，受保人的争辩"我只需要对承保货物有可保利益就足够了，至于是哪一种可保利益我可以不告诉保险人"倒也可以成立。例如，在先例MacKenzie v. Whitworth (1875) 3 Asp MLC 81，案情涉及受保人（他实际上是再保险人想为他所承保的棉花投保）在投保的时候没有披露他不是棉花的所有人，而只是棉花的再保险人。按说，货物所有人与再保险人对此票棉花都具有可保利益，该先例是判受保人不必要披露他的可保利益仅仅是他作为再保险人，这一事实与情况并非实质性重要。在海上货物运输保险中，其实承运人以及仓库保管人对处于他们托管之下的货物都具有可保利益，也都可以为被托管的货物进行投保。同样道理，抵押权人与典押权人也对抵押物/典押物享有可保利益，是可以为它们进行投保。在这种情况下，承运人、仓库保管人、抵押权人与典押权人都没有必要自动披露他们的可保利益是哪一种类。

5.2 估值过高（over – valuation）

如果货物的估计价值与它的实际价值之间有很大差距，受保人是否必须将这样的差距披露给保险人呢？毕竟，这可能会影响一位谨慎的保险人，如对来历不明的受保人害怕会有道德风险。如果没有披露，在定值保险（valued policy）与非定值保险（unvalued policy）的情况下，保险人仍可以主张受保人没有履行他的披露责任，但差别就是在定值保险的情况下，这样的主张更容易成立。因为根据先例Williams v. Atlantic Insurance Co. Ltd. (1932) 42 Lloyd's Rep. 206；(1932) 43 Lloyd's Rep. 177 (CA)，如果是非定值保险，保险人也仅仅是根据承保货物的实际价值给受保人一个比较低的赔偿金额。但针对海上货物运输，通常都是定值保险，保险价值是货物的CIF价格另加10%。如果货物的估值是在没有任何合理依据的基础上作出，以至于纯粹是一种猜测（a purely speculative nature），这样的估值可以说是超过很多。这里可举一个古老的先例名为：Ionides v. Pender (1874) LR 9 QB 531，投保的货物（洋酒）价值是973英镑，但投保的定值保险是2800英镑。Blackburn大法官认为受保人有披露的责任，因为估值过高令风险变的纯粹是一种猜测（the overvaluation is so great as to make the risk speculative）。

到底是否构成估值过高而要作出披露，根据先例 Berger v. Pollock (1973) 2 Lloyd's Rep. 442，标准就是看正常理智与合理的人士客观看来是否会这样认为。此外，保险人如果以估值过高拒赔，他还要证明估值过高如果作出披露是会对一个谨慎保险人有影响。Kerr 大法官说："It must always be borne in mind that, in the absence of fraud, an excessive over - valuation is not in itself a ground for repudiating a contract of insurance. Over - valuation is only one illustration of the general principle that insurers are entitled to avoid policies on the ground of non - disclosure of material circumstances. It must, therefore, always be shown that the over - valuation was such that, if it had been disclosed, it would have entitled the insurer to avoid the policy because it would have affected his judgment as a prudent insurer in fixing the premium or determining whether or not to take the risk."

在现实当中，法院不会轻易因为估值过高的幅度太大就认定货物估值过高的信息对保险人来说是实质性的重要。在先例 Berger v. Pollock (1973) 2 Lloyd's Rep. 442，案情涉及的货物是机器，投保的是非定值保险，保险人的最大的赔偿责任是20000英镑。最终法院判是虽然机器的价值仅仅是 5000 英镑，因为机器被估值过高也是完全的善意，所以这不能被算作是具有实质性的重要。在先例 Liberian Insurance Agency Inc v. Mosse (1977) 2 Lloyd's Rep. 560，承保货物是用很便宜的价格买来的仓底货(an end of stock or job lot purchase)。Donaldson 大法官说："price of itself is not material... it is what it may indicate as to the quality of the goods that matters."大意也就是说货物价格本身并非是实质性重要，货物的质量才是关键。

在近期先例 North Star Shipping Limited v. Sphere Drake Insurance plc (2006) 2 Lloyd's Rep. 183 中，涉及的是 North Star 投保了船壳战争险，保险价值是 400 万美元。而该船舶的市场价格是 135 万美元。一审的时候，法院判是因为该艘船舶的管理比较到位，所以将该船舶的保险价值说是在 300 万美元的范围内是合理，但超过 300 万美元的那部分保险价值就是具有实质性的重要。但这种判法在上诉庭被 Waller 大法官质疑，他是这样说："the underwriter may prefer to take the extra premium rather than investigate whether good management reasons establish USMYM 4 m as opposed to some lesser figure."同样的道理，这也就是为什么货物保险的保险人会愿意接受一个比较高的保险价值以收取一笔比较高的保费。

然而如果承保货物估值过高到一种程度以至于会带来保险骗局与道德风险，根据先例 Mathie v. The Argonaut Marine Insurance Co. Ltd. (1924) 18 Lloyd's Rep. 118, (1925) 21 Lloyd's Rep. 145，这种估值过高对保险人承保的风险就会有实质性的重要。

最后要一提的就是估值过高还会涉及不同的险种。以海上保险为例，一般的船舶保险涉及了懂业务的保险人是应该知道投保船舶的市场价格，这种资料也是很容易获得的。所以，可能法院对船舶保险人提出类似的理由拒绝赔付会感到难以接受。

但针对海上货物运输保险，会有不少的货物保险人没有办法从其他渠道知道投保货物的实际价值，毕竟有不少货物是不会有市场，或者即使是有，市场也会很狭窄。这一来，保险人提出估值过高的理由拒绝赔付，就会有可能比较容易被法院接受。

5.3　双重保险(double insurance)

这一问题在本书第十三章代位求偿权第16段将有详细讨论，不再重复。只说是这一问题表面上看来是与估值过高很接近，受保人都会在发生事故时得利，导致在这种事实与情况下会有严重的道德风险。但在英国法律，受保人对于是否投保了双重保险是没有披露的责任，这里可节录Robert Merkin教授所著的《Colinvaux's Law of Insurance in Hong Kong》第6.056段："The fact that the assured has insured the subject matter elsewhere, with the result that it has been in the aggregate over - insured, would prima facie seem to be indistinguishable from over - valuation in terms of materiality, in that in both cases the risk of fraud is enhanced. However, the common law position is seemingly that other policies are not always treated as material facts, possibly because the assured's right to insure his property with as many insurers as he wishes—in order to guard against the insolvency of any of them—was recognised at common law and preserved in s 32 of the Marine Insurance Ordinance."

这也解释了为什么在有些岸上保险合约，会有一些明示条文禁止受保人投保双重保险，除非得到保险人的批准。这是因为英国法律的默示地位下，受保人是没有披露的责任。

5.4　承保货物是价值很高的名牌的情况

如果承保货物是价值很高的名牌，受保人是否必须确切地披露相关的事实与情况？如要投保的货物是"劳力士手表"或者是"香奈儿手袋"，受保人是否在投保时必须自动告诉保险人说"这是劳力士手表"或者"这是香奈儿手袋"，而不可以只是对保险人说"这是手表"或者"这是手袋"？

在先例WISE（Underwriting Agency）Limited v. Grupo Nacional Provincial SA（2004）2 Lloyd's Rep. 483，保单是写明承保"all real and personal property of any kind and description, for transit from Miami Florida to Cancun in Mexico."承保货物包括香水、化妆品、小礼品、珠宝与"钟表"，而实际的货物涉及手表并且绝大部分都是劳力士牌的。后来损失真的发生，法院判"劳力士手表"这一信息对保险人承担的风险是具有实质性重要的意义，Simon大法官这样说："In my view Mr. Gooding［被告保险人聘请的专家证人］was right in saying that high value watches are regarded as attractive targets for thieves and that Rolex watches are particularly attractive targets in view of the cachet that the brand name carries. They are portable, high value and relatively easily disposable goods. The failure to disclose the fact that such goods were being shipped deprived the prudent underwriter of information as to the true nature of the risk and the opportunity to consider whether to cover the risk and, if so, on what terms."（大意是说劳力士手表

便于携带又容易出手,所以备受盗贼的青睐,也就是说,这个牌子本身让手表被盗的风险大大增加。)

而本案中真正承保风险的保险人(尽管被法院视为不是特别可信的证人),他还是给证据说如果他知道承保货物中是包括了劳力士手表,他是不会答应承保。这一证据也不能是太可信,因为在一定程度上说不通,这是因为该开口保单也明确说承保了珠宝,而珠宝被盗的几率也不见得比劳力士手表被盗的几率低太多。

由此可见,构成"诱使"的两个要素("谨慎保险人"与"诱使")都被满足了,也就是未被披露的事实与情况会影响保险人决定是否接受承保以及用什么样的合约条文来接受承保。最终判未被披露的信息诱使保险人答应承保该批货物。(该案件后来去了上诉庭,关于劳力士手表是实质性重要的信息,这一争议没有被挑战,而针对"诱使"这一争议的挑战失败,上诉庭的三位大法官一致认定"诱使"成立。)

5.5 承保货物的历史:二手货或者是旧物品

在先例 Liberian Insurance Agency Inc. v. Mosse (1977) 2 Lloyd's Rep. 560,承保货物是被描述成"装于木箱内的搪瓷器",法院是判保险人是应该被告知这些货物是仓底货,因为这样意味着该批货物当中肯定是有一定比例的次品。如果保险人在承保当时不知道这些情况,在发生货损后,判断货损到底是原来就存在还是后来在运输过程中造成的就会有困难。

大的原则是如果货物的某一种性质会对将来核定货损的多少造成影响,该性质就对保险人具有实质性重要的意义。因为这样的事实与情况在披露后,保险人可能将承保的范围局限在仅仅是列明风险而不是承保一切险,如协会货物条文(平安险)。即使仅仅是对货物的质量有怀疑,保险人也都会希望事前安排检测。根据 Berger v. Pollock (1973) 2 Lloyd's Rep. 442,如果货物的过往历史对保险人承保的风险不会有影响,这些事实与情况在正常情况下不需要披露。

5.6 包装

货物的包装通常会在保险合约的"描述"(description of cargo)栏里写明。在先例 Liberian Insurance Agency Inc v. Mosse (1977) 2 Lloyd's Rep. 560,保险合约中注明了是"装在木箱内"(in wooden cases),而事实上部分货物是被装进了纸箱,这会让箱内的货物更容易被水损坏,这被判是受保人有实质性重要的事实与情况没有对保险人披露。

在先例 Wilson Holgate & Co. Ltd. v. Lancashire & Cheshire Insurance Corp. Ltd. (1922) 13 Lloyd's Rep. 486,法院判是受保人不需要告诉保险人装橄榄油的木箱是新的还是旧的,除非保险人特别问到这一点。Bailhache 大法官之所以这样判,是因为根据提供的证据,告诉保险人油装在什么种类的木桶中并非是通常的做法。但如果货物用的是不同于该类贸易惯常情况下的包装以至于会增加货物受损风险,这类信息将非常有可能被法院认定是对保险人有实质性重要的意义。

“包装不足/不当”是协会货物条文之4.3条规定的列明除外风险。这种除外只适用于：货损是由任何时候受保人自己对货物的包装不足/不当造成；以及在风险开始/生效前，独立承包商对货物的包装不足/不当造成。对于在风险开始到风险结束整个期间发生的货物包装，保险人是愿意承担货物包装不足/不当的风险，就像他们愿意承担运输过程中不良堆装、坏天气导致货损的风险一样。但有说法是，如果受保人在明知的情况下仍然雇用服务质量很差的独立承包商对货物进行包装以致让货物遭受损失的风险增加，这样的信息将会是实质性重要的。如果这样的信息在订立保险合约时没有被披露给保险人，这会让事后发现的保险人有权选择令保险合约无效。

在开口/预约保单(open cover)的情况下，通常受保人并不是对于每票货物都有披露的义务。但如果是一次性(one - off)的保单，受保人是有意向使用不足够的包装，而这样的意向是没有被披露，保险人在知道后是有权选择令保险合约无效。同样的道理，如果在开口/预约保单最初的谈判阶段，或在保单的续约期间受保人没有将使用不足够包装的意向告诉保险人，保险人在知道后也是会有权选择令保险合约无效。

5.7　之前有被其他的保险人拒绝承保与以前的索赔记录

在先例 Glasgow Insurance Corp. Ltd. v. William Symondson and Co. (1911) 16 Com Cas 109，Scrutton 大法官说：“[It is] elementary marine insurance law that such refusals need not be disclosed.”不过要注意的是，即使之前有被其他的保险人拒绝承保的事实是不需要披露，但之前被其他的保险人拒绝承保的原因是需要披露的。

在非海上保险，如人寿保险、盗窃险、火险，该方面的法律地位有所不同，这在本章第4.3.3段有介绍。根据先例 Glicksman v. Lancashire & General Assurance (1925) 2 Lloyd's Rep. 179(CA)，(1926) 26 Lloyd's Rep. 69 (HL)，在非海上保险中保险人几乎无一例外地会在他的表格里问询受保人是否曾经被其他的保险人拒绝承保。这其实是间接的传递给受保人一个意思，就是之前有被其他的保险人拒绝承保这类信息对保险人具有实质性重要意义，并且受保人是有义务披露，如(如果是给建筑物投保)建筑物的方位与状况。

在海上保险中，其他的保险人可能因为与风险增加毫无关系的原因而拒绝承保，如风险太大或者太小，超出保险人的承受范围或者是不值得做这笔生意、所要承保的风险与他公司专业承保的风险不符合。因此，在伦敦市场，之前有被其他的保险人拒绝的事实与情况本身对下一个保险人来讲并不具有实质性重要意义。即便是 Scrutton 大法官在先例 Glasgow Insurance Corp. Ltd. v. William Symondson and Co 曾说过这是非常基本的海上保险法规则，但最终是不是像 Scrutton 大法官说的那样还是要看某个特定市场的惯例，因为是否是实质性重要还要看这个市场内部的谨慎保险人会提供怎样的证据。

与这方面相关的还有受保人的索赔记录(claim record or experience)，这方面的争议在 Pan Atlantic Insurance Co. v. Pine Top Insurance Co. Ltd. (1992) 1 Lloyd's Rep.

101中出现。案情是有关再保险人试图令再保险合约无效,抗辩称受保人(第一层的保险人)没有披露1977~1979年之间的索赔记录与1980~1981年的额外损失记录。对于第一项的抗辩,高院的Waller大法官判是受保人已经有了足够的披露,是再保险人自己不看。他这样说:"An underwriter knows, as well as anybody, or should know, that the earlier years are the only real guide to assessing a rate. The broker has brought along for the underwriter the history in relation to the earlier years and that history, if the underwriter had bothered to study it, was a perfectly fair presentation of those earlier years. As I see it the negotiation is a commercial one, the broker does not have an obligation to tell the underwriter how to do his job."

但是对于第二项没有披露的抗辩,主要针对的是受保人的经纪人在作出披露的时候,将计算1981年的索赔额的期限截止至9月30日,而9月30日至12月31日的索赔额是没有包括在内。恰恰这第四季度的索赔数额是相当大的,并且使整个1981年的损失率(索赔额占保费的比率)由计算至9月30日的30%升高至60%。而也正是这1981年第四季度的没有披露与整个做法有点转移再保险人的注意力,被Waller大法官判是有误述/不披露而违反绝对善意。

该先例最后被贵族院维持高院的判决,并且不接受在本章第4.3.2.1段的第一种考验的决定性影响(decisive influence test)。

5.8 代位求偿权

在本书第十三章介绍过通常情况下,保险人在赔付受保人之后都会有代位求偿权向第三者追偿,可以说这对保险人而言是很重要的一项权利。根据先例Tate & Sons v. Hyslop (1885) LR 15 QBD 368,如果受保人与承运人有特别不寻常的协议可以限制或者豁免承运人的责任,受保人是必须将此披露给保险人。在该先例中,受保人在签订运输合约时,为了获得比较优惠的运费,他就接受了驳船承运人的要求答应豁免他作为公共承运人所应该承担的责任。法院判是运输合约中这样的条文是应该在订立保险合约时披露给保险人。因为有证据证明如果驳船承运人仅仅是承担疏忽责任而不承担作为公共承运人通常应当承担的较宽泛的责任时,保险人在承保此类风险时会收取更高的保费。

不过从先例Tate & Sons v. Hyslop延伸出来的这条规则还是会受到限制,这就是如果保险人在有关这种业务的承保中应该知道的事实/信息就不需要受保人披露。这在本章第6.2段有详细介绍。

在先例Glencore International A. G. v. Alpina Insurance Company Limited (2004) 1 Lloyd's Rep. 111,保险合约是合并了协会货物条文,其中第14条明确规定允许为承保货物的增加价值投保(increased value insurance may be taken out on the cargo)。在先例Boag v. Standard Marine Insurance Co. Ltd. (1937) 57 Lloyd's Law Rep. 83 (CA),上诉庭判是增值保险的保险人不可以从向第三人追偿回来的款项中分一杯羹,否则主保险人的代位求偿权会受到损害。并且上诉庭不准备在主保险合约中认

定是有默示条文存在，允许受保人为承保货物的增加价值投保。伦敦保险市场对该Boag先例的判法不是很满意，为了回避该先例，他们在协会货物条文中加入了第14条意图通过明示条文来改变普通法的默示地位（这方面请参阅本书第十三章第14段）。这样一来，在Glencore先例中判是因为主合约中保险人已经明示承认增值保险人的权利，受保人是不需要披露增值保险合约的存在。

不过要注意的是，不管是伦敦保险市场还是外国保险市场都已经成为一种习惯做法，就是如果承运人或者托管人都与受保人有关联关系的公司，代位求偿权不适用，因为包括承运人或者托管人在内的公司都会在保险合约内被包括在受保人的定义内。这种习惯做法会是在开口/预约保单约定给受保人广泛的定义包括有关联关系的公司（associated and/or affiliated companies），针对这些关联公司，保险公司是不可以行使代位求偿权的：National Oilwell（UK）Limited v. Davy Offshore Limited（1993）2 Lloyd's Rep. 582。这种情况下的受保人不必在投保时向保险人披露代位求偿权会受到限制也就理所当然。

5.9 道德风险

道德风险（Moral Hazard）与上面已经讨论过的不披露事项有所不同，因为它可能就是隐藏在上面已经讨论过的各项事由中，特别是在进行关于货物描述或性质的披露时，受保人会有意无意的避重就轻。

5.9.1 货物估值过高中蕴涵的道德风险

最常见出现道德风险的情况还是在对承保货物的估值过高方面，这一方面在本章第5.2段已经提到过，不过这里再从道德风险的角度讨论一下。在先例Ionides & Another v. Pender（1874）LR 9 QBD 531，Blackburn大法官在他的判词中这样说："It is to be observed that the excessive valuation not only may lead to suspicion of foul play, but that it has a direct tendency to make the assured less careful in selecting the ship and captain, and to diminish the efforts which in case of disaster he ought to make to diminish the loss as far as possible, and cannot therefore properly be called altogether extraneous to the risks; but we would scarcely base our judgment on so special a ground."

上诉庭在该先例还认为过分估值过高（excessive over - valuation）是一项具有实质性意义的信息，因为它会影响谨慎保险人的决定是否接受承保以及保费高低。上面所讲的各种事项本身可能并不会毫无疑问地成为影响谨慎保险人决定的因素，不过在货物保险中，如果估值过高，会诱使受保人在为承保货物安排包装时不怎么上心，或者是受保人会雇佣经济状况不好的承运人，只因为他们的运费费率更低，所以由于过分估值过高而引发的道德风险会成为保险人在接受承保风险时比较关心的一点。

同样是估值过高的情况下，针对一般的船舶保险就可能比较宽松。在先例North Shipping Ltd. v. Sphere Drake Insurance plc（2006）2 Lloyd's Rep. 183（CA），涉及了市场价格是135万美元的船舶，投保价值是400万美元，表面看来是估值过高。但上诉庭的 Waller 大法官不认为需要船东主动作出披露的实质性事实,说:"the test of materiality was whether the disparity between the insured value and the market value was consistent with prudent ship management... An underwriter knowing the market value roughly would appreciate the difference between USMYM4 million and USMYM1. 35 million, and ask questions if he were interested in finding out what the reasons were for the differential. The sale logically added nothing to the knowledge that the underwriter had of the market. If the sale had no relevance the underwriter could see for himself that the difference between USMYM4 million and the vessel's market value would raise questions. The underwriter might prefer to take the extra premium rather than investigate whether the good management reasons established USMYM4 million as opposed to some lesser figure."

看来,保险标的估值过高是否需要受保人自动作出披露在船舶保险与货物保险会有些不同,因为这里与1906 年《英国海上保险法》Section 18(3)(b)有一定的冲突,这方面在本章第6.3 段有详细介绍。在船舶保险,由于船舶的种类相对比较少,而且大部分的船舶都有市场,这变成是船舶保险人是应该知道有关的市场价格以及船东很多时候需要估值较高(如因为船舶融资的需要)。这变成是有疑问应该是保险人提出询问而不是受保人的船东自动披露。但货物的种类多不胜数,很多也是没有市场存在或者即使存在也是很狭窄,货物保险人就不能视为应该知道货物的市场或实际价值与受保人是否估值过高,想询问也无从问起。

5.9.2 受保人面对欺诈指控蕴涵的道德风险

有关受保人过往的欺诈指控(不论是否成立)是否需要披露在先例 North Star Shipping Limited v. Sphere Drake Insurance plc (2006) 2 Lloyd's Rep. 183 有涉及,虽然它实际是属于船舶保险的先例。这是因为在保险人的专家证人在面对对方律师盘问的时候,承认与船舶保险相比,货物的战争险合约的道德风险会小得多。在承认之后,该专家证人又说:"I can only reiterate ... that any moral hazard is moral hazard and, as such, a consideration for any prudent underwriter, whether it be under a Hull policy, War policy, as I said earlier, Cargo policy or any other policy."

因此,上诉庭认为道德风险适用于船舶保险,并且也同样适用于货物保险,尽管在海上货物运输,受保人故意造成货物损失的机会会小得多,但也不是不可能。如在 The "Lady Gwendolen" (1965) 1 Lloyd's Rep. 335,船东与货物所有人是一家公司,如果涉及道德风险也就会涉及货物保险人。另在先例 The "Salem" (1983) 1 Lloyd's Rep. 342,原来的受保人(但后来保单转让给了 Shell 石油公司)也就是货物的卖方(虽然这票货是不诚实侵占得来)就是不诚实的船东。

显然,受保人之前成立的欺诈指控是需要自动披露的。但以前的指控最终被证明是不成立(false allegations of dishonesty)以及无关承保风险的欺诈指控是否也需要披露,这点法律不是太明确。毕竟,这些如果要作出披露就会是很繁重与苛求,如一个60 岁的船东是否需要披露他在20 来岁大学毕业考试当中不诚实的指控。这方面可节录 Waller 大法官在 North Star Shipping 先例所说如下：

"Courts have previously wrestled with this problem, recognising first that there is something unjust in the notion that insurers can avoid a policy on the grounds of a suspicion as to the insured's probity flowing from an allegation which is in fact false, but second that it is difficult to gainsay an underwriter who gives evidence that an allegation of fraud would have an influence on his underwriting judgment if it was unknown at that time whether that allegation was true or false.

Different judges have come to different conclusions. Forbes J in Reynolds and Anderson v. Phoenix Assurance Co. Ltd. [1978] 2 Lloyd's Rep. 440 at 460 recognised that the odd feature of a rule that required allegations to be disclosed was that it was in fact only false allegations to which such a rule had any relevance. If the allegation was true then the insured was bound to disclose that he had committed the fraud, and disclosure of the allegation as such added nothing. As he put it 'the only occasion on which the allegation as an allegation must be disclosed is when it is not true' – 'a conclusion so devoid of any merit that I do not consider that a responsible insurer would adopt it and nor do I.' However, May J had expressed a contrary view in March Cabaret Club & Casino Ltd. v. The London Assurance [1975] 1 Lloyd's Rep. 169, and Phillips J in The "Dora" [1989] 1 Lloyd's Rep. 69 said that he preferred the view of May J. Colman J then in The "Grecia Express" [2002] Lloyd's Rep. IR 669 at 718 supported Phillips J, saying 'if an allegation of criminal conduct has been made against an assured but is as yet unresolved at the time of placing the risk and the evidence is that the allegation would have influenced the judgment of a prudent insurer, the fact the allegation is unfounded cannot divest the circumstances of the allegation of the attribute of materiality.' But Colman J, having found that the allegation was material, mitigated that finding by holding that for the insurers to persist at a trial in taking the point, in the face of evidence before the court that the suggested facts never existed, would be contrary to their obligation of good faith. In his words 'Such a course would be so starkly unjust that I would hold that in such a case it would be unconscionable for the Court to permit the insurers to avoid the policy on the grounds of non – disclosure.'"

在先例 North Star Shipping，也涉及这方面的问题，因为该先例中的受保人（是希腊船东），在投保前与订立保险合约当时在希腊法院有针对受保人的刑事诉讼程序，虽然该刑事指控在船舶爆炸发生后被撤销。一审 Colman 大法官是判该刑事指控是应该被披露的实质性事实与情况。二审上诉庭判："The judge's conclusion that the charges in the Greek criminal proceedings were material was unimpeachable."Waller 大法官在他的判词中这样说：

"He（受保人的代表大律师）suggested that there might be a distinction between allegations which related to the risk and allegations which bore no relation to the risk. He submitted that the court ought somehow to limit the extent to which allegations which ultimately turned out to be false should be held to be material to the risk and disclosable. His suggestion was that allegations that related to the risk itself were one thing but allegations of dishonesty, which had nothing to do with the risk and nothing to do with either the particular insurance or with insurance at all, were another. In relation to fact (1), the Greek criminal proceedings, the allegations of dishonesty had nothing to do with the risks being insured and nothing to do with claims under an insurance policy...

All that said, it does not seem to me that what must be disclosed can be defined as a matter of law in the way that Mr. Goldstone（受保人的代表大律师）would have us do and in a way which I might have been tempted to follow. It is a matter of evidence what is a material circumstance and, as the head note in Pan Atlantic v. Pinetop accurately records, a 'material circumstance' is one that would have an effect on the mind of a prudent insurer in estimating the risk and it is not necessary that it should have a decisive effect on his acceptance of the risk or the amount of premium to be paid.

Expert evidence is called to guide the court as to what would influence the judgment of an underwriter. The only way that, under the present state of the law, the obligation of disclosure in this area of moral hazard can be confined is either by underwriters giving evidence that they would not be influenced and would not take into account an allegation of dishonesty, or by a robust judge rejecting an underwriter's evidence that he would take it into account. Spent convictions no longer have to be disclosed, and old allegations of dishonesty or allegations of not very serious dishonesty, one would hope, expert underwriters would not suggest would influence the judgement of prudent underwriters. But it is unreal to contemplate as a general proposition that underwriters as expert witnesses would ever give evidence that a prudent underwriter would not take into account in assessing the risk or the terms of the insurance a recent allegation of serious dishonesty the truth or falsity of which has yet to be determined, even if it is quite unconnected with insurance or the risk being insured. Furthermore it is difficult to see a judge not accepting that evidence."

从最后一段看来，如果指控不成立而且年代很久远的指控是不会影响谨慎保险人的判断的。但对一个非常近期的严重指控（无论是成立、不成立或者还在审理），就完全不同了。看来关键还是以谨慎保险人的判断为准。

6. 不需要被披露的情况

6.1 会减少承保风险的情况

减少承保风险的情况可以不必披露，这是规定在1906年《英国海上保险法》Section 18(3)(a):"In the absence of inquiry the following circumstances need not be disclosed, namely:(a) Any circumstance which diminishes the risk."

这一方面是很容易理解,因为可以减少承保风险的情况受保人没有理由不作出披露,因为很有可能保费会减少。所以,有关的先例不多。估计即使有这一方面的争议也是受保人与保险人之间针对某一项没有披露的事实或者情况到底是否能减少承保风险。在不多的先例中,也可以举一些。第一个就是 The "Dora" (1989) 1 Lloyd's Rep. 69,Phillips 大法官判是该投保的游艇在保单订立时还在台湾造船厂的事实没有披露是可以接受的,因为它是减少风险而不是增加风险。第二个先例 The "Zeus V" (2000) 2 Lloyd's Rep. 587,上诉庭判受保人没有把投保游艇的检验报告自动披露给保险人是可以接受,因为检验报告中的内容根本没有什么针对该游艇不妥的地方,所以保险人不得因此拒绝赔付游艇的全损索赔。另在先例 The "Elena G" (2002) Lloyd's Rep. IR 450,判是未被披露的事实有关投保的游艇在锚地没有实质性重要。

6.2　保险人应该知道的情况

这是规定在 1906 年《英国海上保险法》Section 18(3)(b):"In the absence of inquiry the following circumstances need not be disclosed, namely:(b) Any circumstance which is known or presumed to be known to the insurer. The insurer is presumed to know matters of common notoriety or knowledge, and matters which an insurer in the ordinary course of his business, as such, ought to know."

有关这一课题就是保险人承保某一种投保的风险知道或应该知道的事实或行业信息,就不需要受保人作出披露。这也是有实际的需要,因为像不少开口/预约保单的承保范围非常广泛(例如针对所有种类的商品与货物,以及针对全球的运输以任何形式的运输方法如陆上/航空/海上运输等,只是包含了有限的豁免),如果要事无巨细都披露根本做不到或不现实。所以,披露主要想针对的还是一些不寻常与特殊(unusual and special)的情况,这种情况是熟悉有关业务的保险人也不会知道的。相反如果是一般谨慎的保险人应该知道的情况,就不必强加披露责任在受保人身上。发生争议后关键就是怎样找出不寻常与寻常(usual)的分水线。在一些极端的情况,总是很容易给一些例子。比如海上货物运输承保的保险人应该知道大西洋在冬季有 8、9 级的大风是司空见惯的,或是船舶去亚丁湾途经非洲东岸会遇上索马里海盗是正常的。当然作为懂业务的保险人不能仅是知道这些路人都知道的信息,对他的要求会是更高。而且法律也好像是这样在发展,这在下一小段会再提到。

现在再举个例子是懂业务的保险人应该知道的行业信息。就是在本书第十三章第 6 段提到离岸石油保险中的 Knock - for - Knock 是行业做法。所以,该行业的保险人是不应该对代位求偿权在合约中被剥夺感觉到大惊小怪,更不应该以这个理由指责受保人没有在投保的时候作出披露。其他的例子包括 Tennant v. Henderson (1813) 1 Dow 324,判是保险人应该知道承保的有关港口怎么样习惯性装卸货物。

另在先例 Da Costa v. Edmonds (1815) 4 Camp 142,判是保险人应该知道某些货物是习惯性装在船舶甲板上(这样装是会增加风险)。在这里可以推理出某些货物不是习惯性被装在甲板上,而受保人的货方在投保的时候是知道这一可能性,显然他是必须要披露了。

这里也有一些比较近期的先例判是保险人不能假设应该知道的事实,换言之受保人是需要作出披露。这包括 Strive Shipping Corp v. Hellenic Mutual War Risks Association (2002) Lloyd's Rep. IR 669,判是保险人忘记以前发生过事故的细节是可以接受的。另在先例 Brotherton v. Aseguradora Colseguros SA (No 3) (2003) Lloyd's Rep. IR 774,判是英国保险人对在哥伦比亚被广泛报道的事实不知情是可以接受。

但要找出一个分水线就是什么是某一种保险的合理谨慎保险人应该知道的事实或行业消息也不是一件容易的事情。接下去介绍近期的重要有关货物保险的先例,名为 Glencore International A. G. v. Alpina Insurance Company Limited (2004) 1 Lloyd's Rep. 111。Glencore 是一家世界著名的原油贸易商,保险公司向受保人 Glencore 签发了一个承保范围十分广泛、有弹性长达 12 个月的开口/预约保单(open cover),针对的承保货物就是 Glencore 有保险利益的石油与石油产品(包括原油、火水、柴油、石脑油、液态汽油与其他相关的石油产品),而承保的风险就是海上运输风险的一切险。开口/预约保单对石油产品来自哪里与最终运往哪里也没有限制,只说明是承保岸上、海上、空中与管道的运输,从世界任何港口/地点去其他任何港口/地点。

此外保险人也知道受保人 Glencore 是一家世界著名的原油贸易商,但不涉及原油的生产与石油产品最终的分销。

在先例中是 Glencore 向 MTI 的炼油厂提供原油,所提供的原油会储存在 MTI 在阿拉伯联合酋长国的富吉拉(Fujairah)港外的的浮动油库。该浮动油库实际上是一艘改装了的超级油轮,名为"Metrotank"。MTI 会不断提供原油给集团内的另一家拥有炼油厂的姐妹公司,名为 MOC。浮动油库也储存了属于其他石油公司的石油,但 Glencore 占的份额是最大。实际上的合约是 Glencore 与 MOC 签订,就是由 MOC 去提炼 Glencore 的原油,然后再将炼好后的石油产品归还给 Glencore。

1998 年 2 月 Metro Group 倒闭,MTI 与 MOC 是该集团的成员也随之倒闭。Glencore(与其他石油公司)发现储存在 MTI 浮动油库中的石油质量与储量是远远低于预期。Glencore 认为是 MTI 以及 Metro Group 的其他公司盗用了他们的油,而盗用的价值高达 2.5 亿美元。Glencore 因此向他的保险人索赔,毕竟这是属于一切险的损失。保险人提出的抗辩是鉴于 Glencore 与 MTI 之间关系的特殊情况,不管是单独考虑这些特殊情况还是综合考虑,都会将承保的风险非比寻常的提高,这些特殊情况都包括:(1) the high volume of oil traded between the parties (双方的石油贸易量是很大);(2) the fact that the oil was to be sold to MTI as end - user for its business of blending and selling fuel oil (石油最终是卖给 MTI);(3) the absence of independent inspectors to monitor discharge of cargoes carried into the facility (没有指定独立检验员监督将石油卸到浮动油库);(4) the failure of Glencore to instruct independent inspectors to measure the quantity of oil held in storage (没有指定独立检验员定期测量浮动油库中的数量);(5) the fact that MTI, rather than Glencore, chose the vessels that made up the floating storage facility (不是 Glencore 而是由 MTI 选择以什么船舶作为浮动油库)。

双方争议的焦点就是在承保范围非常广泛的开口/预约保单下,受保人是否有义务在他所制定的计划中有一定风险存在时,必须将该具体计划详尽的披露给保险人。Moore - Bick 大法官首先参考了先例 Harrower v. Hutchinson (1870) LR 5 QB 584,得出的结论是:"... when an insurer is asked to write an open cover in favor of a commodity trader, he must be taken to be aware of the whole range of circumstances that might arise in the course of carrying on a business of that kind. In the context of worldwide trading the range of circumstances likely to be encountered is inevitably very wide. That does not mean that the insured is under no duty of disclosure, of course, but it does mean that the range of circumstances that the prudent underwriter can be presumed to have in mind is very broad and that the insured's duty of disclosure, which extends only to matters which are unusual in the sense that they fall outside the contemplation of the reasonable underwriter familiar with the business of oil trading, is correspondingly limited. It also means that the insured is not bound to disclose matters which tend to increase the risk unless they are unusual in the sense just described."(这里主要强调受保人要披露一些不寻常的事实与情况,是一个熟悉国际石油贸易业务的保险人也不会想到的。)

Moore - Bick 大法官又说:"Two aspects of the risk that was presented to Alpina (保险人) are particularly significant for present purposes. The first is the extremely broad scope of the proposed cover which extends to transit by land, water, air and pipeline from any place in the world to any place in the world. Similarly, cover against risks of loss of or damage to goods in store is worldwide with no restrictions as to location. It is difficult to imagine a policy on goods being written in wider terms than these. The second is the nature of the insured's business. Glencore is, and was known by Alpina to be, one of the largest independent traders in crude oil and products with interests all over the world. A successful commodity trader must take advantage of market opportunities as and when they arise; he must also be prepared to be innovative in the ways he does business. An insurer who is asked by a commodity trader to provide an open cover on goods must in my view be taken to know that. As Lord Mansfield said in Carter v. Boehm (1766) 3 Burr. 1905 at page 1911 'every underwriter is presumed to be acquainted with the practice of the trade he insures; if he does not know, he ought to inform himself'. A similar statement of principle is to be found in Noble v. Kennoway (1780) 2 Doug. K. B. 510, 513."(这里提到必须考虑两方面:一是保险人签发开口保单承保的风险十分广泛;二是保险人知道受保人 Glencore 是世界最大的石油贸易商,而一个成功的贸易商必须灵活掌握市场上会出现的

机会与做生意必须有创意。这是承保世界著名的石油贸易商有关他的所有贸易风险的保险人必须知道的情况。)

也就是说,Moore - Bick 大法官认为在该先例中,在该开口/预约保单下,受保人的披露责任是非常有限的。值得一提的是,针对保险人所提到的比较重要的特殊情况的(c)与(d)项是可以多做一些解释。通常情况下,在石油贸易中在卸港安排独立检验人作出测量是习惯做法,否则到底卸下了多少石油,根本没有任何数字可言。保险人也会要求这样做,特别是保险合约是采用“保证卸货量”(guaranteed outturn)的措辞时。对该习惯做法的存在,双方的代表大律师以及大法官都是认同的。而在 Glencore 与 MTI 交易最开始的时候也确实是这样做的,但是从 1995 年 4 月之后,双方就达成协议不需要安排独立检验人在卸港检验。原因如下:(1)将油运往 MTI 仓库的那些船舶绝大部分都是 MTI 期租的船舶,也就是说 MTI 同时是承运人与收货人,而即使检验出石油在运输的过程中发生了短少或是短卸,还是 MTI 自己要负责任。与 Glencore 达成协议说提单上的数字是装船石油数量及质量的最终证据并不会给 MTI 带来实质上的影响。(2)双方都可以省下指定独立检验员的费用。(3)这海上运输的路程是很短,这样运输过程中石油损耗的几率是相对很小,并且所用的都是同一批船舶,这次没有卸光在船上的石油下次还可以卸下来,反正都是 MTI 的。这样看来,Glencore 与 MTI 达成这样的安排也完全是合情合理的。Moore - Bick 大法官是这样说:“Not surprisingly, both Mr. Rambaud and Miss Bossley (双方的专家证人) considered it normal to appoint independent discharge inspectors when a cargo of oil is put into store and I am satisfied that that is the case. However, Mr. Rambaud (Glencore 专家证人) was certainly not surprised at the idea that parties in the position of Glencore and MTI should agree to be bound by bill of lading figures and both he and Miss Bossley (保险人专家证人) recognised that it favoured Glencore. Miss Bossley was at pains to emphasise at various points in her evidence that it was necessary to view the picture as a whole and that is a matter to which I shall return, but she did not go so far as to say that this particular aspect of the arrangements between Glencore and MTI was extraordinary and I do not think it was. Two major international oil companies (另一家是 Shell) that were doing business with MTI at that time also agreed to dispense with discharge inspectors in circumstances where cargoes were carried into Fujairah on ships time - chartered to MTI. That is not conclusive, of course, but it does provide further support for Mr. Rambaud's view that it is not uncommon in certain circumstances to accept bill of lading figures as binding. I am not persuaded that an arrangement of this kind is so unusual that it ought to be disclosed in connection with a policy of the kind under consideration.”(内容大致是保险人专家证人也不敢说 Glencore 与 MTI 之间的安排是不寻常。事实上,另一家大的石油公司也与 MTI 达成相同的安排,就是在卸货时不用指定独立检验人。这虽然不是结论性,但支持 Glencore 的专家证人的说法,接受提单上的数字来约束双方并非不寻常。Moore -

Bick 大法官认为这种并非不寻常的安排是不需要向一份十分广泛的开口保单的保险人披露的。)

最终 Moore－Bick 大法官判是保险人不可以通过指责受保人未履行披露责任而让保险合约无效。

笔者最后简单介绍针对海上货物保险,会有哪些事实与情况是保险人应该被假设知道的,不需要受保人再作出主动与全面的披露。这包括:(1)承保货物(以及装运船舶)所要去的港口涉及的地理环境、特征、习惯性操作与特有的风险:Stewart v. Bell (1821) 5B & Ald 238; Commercial Union Assurance v. The Niger Company (1922) 13 Lloyd's Rep. 75,77; The "Shakir III" (1997) 1 Lloyd's Rep. 586。但针对一些不知名的港口,受保人最好还是披露:Marc Rich v. Portman (1996) 1 Lloyd's Rep. 430, 439。(2)承保货物的开口保单会涉及的一般性情况与市场,特别是承保十分广泛。在先例 Glencore v. Alphia Insurance (2004) 1 Lloyd's Rep. 111, Moore－Bick 大法官说:"In the context of worldwide trading the range of circumstances likely to be encountered is inevitably very wide. That does not mean that the insured is under no duty of disclosure, of course, but it does mean that the range of circumstances that the prudent underwriter can be presumed to have in mind is very broad and that the insured's duty of disclosure, which extends only to matters which are unusual in the sense that they fall outside the contemplation of the reasonable underwriter familiar with the business of oil trading, is correspondingly limited. It also means that the insured is not bound to disclose matters which tend to increase the risk unless they are unusual in the sense just described."(3)一些行内人士应该知道的情况,如货物装在甲板上就容易受到某种损害:British and Foreign Marine Insurance v. Sturge (1897) 77 LT 208。

6.3　保险人弃权(waive)的信息

这是规定在 1906 年《英国海上保险法》Section 18(3)(c):"In the absence of inquiry the following circumstances need not be disclosed, namely: Any circumstance as to which information is waived by the insurer."

弃权理论这一重要的课题在笔者《国际商务游戏规则—英国合约法》第十一章有介绍。弃权是可以口头、书面的形式作出,也可以从行为推断出来。弃权也必须是在弃权方知道自己的权利的前提下作出明确的行为放弃。另说明它是属于一种衡平法的救济,所以在个别案件的适用中最重要的还是看公平与否。这表示每个案件的案情都不一样,公平与否也就会因为个案的不同而不同,所以只能就大原则进行介绍。

就保险的披露而言,保险人对某些信息弃权是一个不容易掌握的事情。对一些受保人而言,他就不会把所有的事情讲得清清楚楚,这可能是为了避免麻烦,或是受保人除非进一步调查自己也不知道太多,又或是担心讲多错多或多讲后保费会受影响(不论担心是对是错)。但对懂业务与谨慎的受保人而言,一般应该披露的事实只要他知道都不会隐瞒，顶多就是避重就轻，会造成一些内容不是很详细的披露。出了事情后，希望拒赔的保险人就会说受保人没有披露或是披露不足。而受保人的反驳可能就是有关的事实已经有披露，虽然讲得不多，但保险人如果需要进一步的信息，是需要自己主动询问的。如举一个简单的例子，如果投保人身伤亡的受保人向保险人披露说，我身体很健康，但最近去医院检查发现心脏有一点毛病。这样看来，受保人已经作出了公平合理的披露。估计多数合理谨慎的保险人如果想进一步知道涉及的风险会向受保人索取一份心电图或其他的检查报告。而针对货物保险，可另举一个例子是受保人在投保时说："这票货在付运前的一程船运输途中遇到一些意外"，如果保险人想知道多一些信息这就应该轮到他主动提问"是什么意外?"如果保险人不问，将来发生货损保险人以此理由拒赔就会有弃权的争议了。

但即使在这简单的例子中也会有很多变数，举例说，如果遇到的意外是"非常严重，不正常与特殊的事故"，从公平的角度就可能会认为受保人轻描淡写一句话"遇到意外"不足够。但反过来，如果遇到的意外并非是"非常严重，不正常与特殊的事故"，而且这种意外也不太罕见(如在装卸时有个别包装刮花)，从公平的角度会认为是保险人自己不问就是弃权。这种争议在先例 Greenhill v. Federal Insurance Co. Ltd. (CA) (1926) 24 Lloyd's Rep. 383 中有出现。还有一个更严重的变数是公平与否在不同的法官或在仲裁员看来也不完全是一致：WISE (Underwriting Agency) Ltd. v. Grupo Nacional Provincial SA (2004) 2 Lloyd's Rep. 483。

以下先介绍这方面的大原则，这可节录《MacGillivray on Insurance Law》(2003 年第10 版)第 17 – 83 段："'The test appears to be as follows: The assured must perform his duty of disclosure properly by making a fair presentation of the risk proposed for insurance. If the insurers thereby receive information from the assured or his agent which, taken on its own or in conjunction with other facts known to them or which they are presumed to know, would naturally prompt a reasonably careful insurer to make further inquiries, then, if they omit to make the appropriate check or inquiry, assuming it can be made simply, they would be held to have waived disclosure of the material fact which that inquiry would necessarily have revealed. Waiver is not established by showing merely that the insurers were aware of the possibility of the existence of other material facts; they must be put fairly on inquiry about them."(从大原则看来，是受保人必须履行他的披露责任，公平合理地陈述有关投保的风险。如果保险人收到了有关的陈述与信息，加上他自己知道的或应该知道的有关风险，会像任何一个合理谨慎的保险人自然提出其他询问跟进。这样一来，如果某一位保险人不这样做，这才会构成对披露的弃权。只是指责一位保险人应该警觉一些实质性事实存在的可能性，应该主动向受保人询问，而不这样做就构成弃权的说法是不对的。)

所以如果想让保险人的弃权成立，受保人必须首先披露足够的信息让保险人知道他能够、可以、应该继续询问下去，即他知道自己权利的存在。而且，继续询问下去的是一些其他合理谨慎保险人也会跟进的问题(obvious question)。其实保险合约下,是非常强调受保人是有主动披露的义务,反过来说是保险人弃权因为他不主动向受保人询问有一点本末倒置,所以认定保险人弃权成立的情况是很少见的,正如Hobhouse大法官在先例Iron Trades Mutual Insurance Co. Ltd. v. Companhia de Seguros Imperio (1991) 1 Re LR 213 中说:"It is possible for an insurer to waive information... However it will only be very rarely that such a situation arises. If a proposer has made a fair presentation of the risk, he has discharged his duty; if he has not, then a failure by an insurer to inquire will not relieve the proposer of his duty to make proper disclosure."

所以针对这种争议,第一步与最主要的一步就是根据事实找出受保人有否向保险人对有关的投保风险作出了公平合理的陈述(fair presentation)。如果没有,这就是受保人没有作出实质性事实的披露。如果答案是有,就把责任转移到保险人,就是他如果想知道多一点有关的风险,为什么他自己不提出询问。在先例WISE (Underwriting Agency) Ltd. v. Grupo Nacional Provincial SA (2004) 2 Lloyd's Rep. 483, Longmore大法官是这样说:"On this basis one merely inquires whether there has been a fair presentation. If the answer is no, that is the end of the matter; the assured cannot assert that if only the underwriter had asked an obvious question he would have discovered something which should have been disclosed. If the answer is that there was a fair presentation, that is also the end of the matter; the underwriter cannot say that he ought to have been told more because his remedy was to make further enquiry of the assured or his broker about anything about which he wanted to know more. There will be no room for expert evidence on the question whether a prudent underwriter would have asked further questions so as to achieve the result that the actual underwriter who did not ask such questions will be deemed to have waived disclosure of any material fact revealed by the answers to the questions. That, as Kerr LJ pointed out on page 497 (referred to case Container Transport International Inc v. Oceanus [1984] 1 Lloyds Rep. 476), would be akin to the doctrine of constructive notice."

在实务当中,代表受保人利益的保险经纪人(如劳合社的做法)就会在向保险人披露有关投保风险信息的时候,有意无意地将很重要的信息以口头方式向保险人轻描淡写地提起,同时也会提供一份书面的材料(由不太重要的信息组成)给保险人,但是通过对这些书面材料的发掘也可以找出隐藏在里面的重要信息。可以说保险经纪人/受保人是希望通过已经提交的书面材料的"掩护"可以让保险人构成"弃权",而且书面材料也能够在诉讼的时候用作优质的文件证据,并为增加口头证据的分量提供支持。为了保持双方的平衡,怎样结合事实解释并运用弃权理论就显得尤为重要。而这个问题在先例WISE (Underwriting Agency) Limited v. Grupo Nacional Provincial SA (2004) 2 Lloyd's Rep. 483 中经验丰富的英国商事法院上诉庭的法官们也有了分歧。这是保险人与伦敦再保险人之间的诉讼。争议的出现并不是因为再保险合约条文用词的精明,而仅仅是因为翻译的错误引起。受保人是奢侈品的经销商,他将包括了瑞士名表(劳力士表)的一批货物向保险人投保,保险人在伦敦再保险市场进行再保。而伦敦再保险人签发的保险合约上是有如下信息:

"Information: Loss Record: Nil for the last 12 Twelve years

Maximum amount and rate of the merchandise: ...

- Clocks: USMYM1,000,000 USMYM200,000

- Clocks: less expensive piece: USMYM40. Most expensive piece USMYM18,000 and average cost USMYM1,500."

结果运输途中货物被盗,总共损失了 USMYM817,797,而劳力士名表就占了 USMYM700,390。再保险人举证是他之前从未承保过"手表"(watches),虽然这是保险人不知道的事实。照理说,"钟表"是否包括了"手表"是很容易通过询问搞清楚的,毕竟有文书说明每只会高达 USMYM18,000 的钟表应该引起再保险人的注意:什么样的钟表会这么昂贵呢?保险人也指称再保险人针对再保的航次是从迈阿密运到 Cancun,而 Cancun 是一个高级旅游与免税的圣地,通常零售的都是名贵的奢侈品,保险人并非以英语作为母语(所以把名贵手表笼统的称为是钟表)等。

关于弃权最主要的先例是 CTI v. Oceanus (1984) 1 Lloyd's Rep. 476 (CA), Rix 大法官引述了 Kerr 大法官在该先例中所说:"The principle is that if a certain fact is material for the purposes of ss. 18(2) and 20(2), so that a failure to draw the underwriter's attention to it distorts the fairness of the broker's presentation of the risk, then it is not sufficient that this fact could have been extracted by the underwriter from material to which he had access or which was cursorily shown to him. On the other hand, if the disclosed facts give a fair presentation of the risk, then the underwriter must enquire if the wishes to have more information. This is borne out by the authorities."

接着 Rix 大法官又引述了 Lord Esher 勋爵在 Asfar v. Blundell (1896) 1 QB 123 中所说:"But it is not necessary to disclose minutely every material fact; assuming that there is a material fact which he is bound to disclose, the rule is satisfied if he discloses sufficient to call the attention of the underwriters in such a manner that they can see that if they require further information they should ask for it."

后来 Rix 大法官又提到了 Parker 大法官在先例 CTI v. Oceanus (1984) 1 Lloyd's Rep. 476 (CA)中所说:"If the assured seeks to rely on a waiver he must in my view show a clear case. What he seeks to show is that the insurer dispensed with information which would influence the judgment of a prudent underwriter albeit he, the insurer, was unaware of the existence of such information... in order to establish waiver by implication from non-enquiry the insurer must be put on enquiry by the disclosure of facts which would raise in the mind of a reasonable insurer at least a suspicion that there were other circumstances which would or might vitiate the presentation made to him..."

但最终是以多数意见(Rix 大法官是少数意见)认为再保险人有权根据再保险合约条文的规定接受承保货物中的"clocks"就是"clocks",仅仅说为"钟表"是不构成足够的原因引起再保险人的怀疑再继续询问,也不是一个公平的陈述(fair presentation)。本章第5.4段就介绍过同一先例中,法院判"劳力士手表"这一信息对再保险人承担的风险具有实质性的重要意义。同时,也判再保险人不进一步继续询问是没有弃权,这加起来直接的结论就是再保险人可以选择令再保险无效,即再保险人胜诉。

不过在该先例中,Rix 大法官也发表了他强而有力的不同意见(dissenting opinion),总结说,他并没有好像持多数意见的大法官把"实质性重要"与"弃权"分开讨论。他是这样说:"where the section 18(3)(c) doctrine of waiver applies, there is no need for disclosure and it is impossible to talk of non – disclosure or even of materiality."也就是说,1906 年的立法 Section 18(3)(c)规定的是"不需要披露的事实与情况",而并非那些"需要披露但因为弃权的原因变得无关的情况"。Rix 大法官说:

"In my judgment, the issue of fairness cannot be resolved without considering the matter in the round. Where a proposer for insurance makes an error in the translation of his presentation, but the error, against the background of the trade, begs a simple question (and I would say an obvious one), and does so in circumstances where the insurer knows (but the proposer does not) that he would never be prepared to insure the goods in question (here, watches) but keeps that information to himself, I think it is unfair of the insurer to say that he has been dealt with unfairly and is entitled to treat his contract as something he can avoid...

Ultimately, it seems, the question is: Has the insurer been put fairly on inquiry about the existence of other material facts, which such inquiry would necessarily have revealed? The test has to be applied by reference to a reasonably careful insurer rather than the actual insurer, and not merely by reference to what such an insurer is told in the assured's actual presentation but also by reference to what he knows or ought to know, i. e. his section 18(3)(b) knowledge. The reasonably careful underwriter is neither a detective on the one hand nor lacking in common – sense on the other hand. Mere possibilities will not put him on inquiry, and very little if anything can make up for non – disclosure of the unusual or special. Overriding all, however, is the notion of fairness, and that applies mutually to both parties, even if the presentation starts with the would – be assured."

由此可见,在 Rix 大法官看来,弃权理论的适用并不需要是在"a clear case"或是一种很特殊/罕见的情况。Rix 大法官也提到了善意责任是双方都有的责任。John Dunt 在所著的《Marine Cargo Insurance》中认为 Rix 大法官的这种说法是预示了弃权理论将来的发展方向。加上了对保险人承保业务的专业水平要求提高,则他是更需要小心与警觉特别是针对潜在受保人（would - be insured）作出的有关投保风险的口头或书面陈述。这可节录 John Dunt 在所著的《Marine Cargo Insurance》第 5. 47 - 5. 48 段所讲：

"This passage, with a stress on the mutuality of the duty of good faith, acknowledges that non - disclosure of the unusual or special is not to be excused, but does not suggest that waiver will only apply in exceptional cases or that it will be necessary to show 'a clear case'.

In so far as the judgment of Rix L. J. may indicate the way in which the law will develop, a cargo underwriter should be alert to any untoward matters suggested by the slip, or the oral presentation made to him, and if he fails to enquire he will find himself bound by the duty of good faith not to avoid the contract. As to what amounts to 'untoward matters' one must anticipate that the courts will expect an increasingly high standard of expertise, consistent with the views of Moore - Bick J. in Glencore v. Alpina [2004] 1 Lloyd's Rep. 111. It would be unwise, in today's climate, for a cargo underwriter to assume that the law is that waiver will only apply in exceptional cases where he should have been alerted to an obvious problem, at least to the extent that what is 'obvious' will be judged by the highest standards of expertise and professionalism."

总结说本段不再进一步介绍好像 CTI v. Oceanus（1984）1 Lloyd's Rep. 476（CA）等著名的有关先例，许多这些先例在较早时候都有提到，有兴趣研究的人士可以继续"询问"，这里就无意再介绍案件的具体案情，因为每个案件都会根据不同的案情来判，关键就是掌握大原则。

另一提的是保险人对披露的弃权还可以以其他的形式出现，不过这些比较多是发生在岸上的保险，海上货物运输保险反而是很少出现，所以不多谈。其中一种比较简单的形式就是以明示条文同意或规定受保人需要提供信息的一份列表，这里就会有争议是对其他没有在列表上写明的信息是否是对披露弃权。正如 Simon Brown 大法官在先例 Economides v. Commercial Union Assurance Co. Plc（1997）3 All ER 635 中是说："Where... material facts are dealt with by specific questions in the proposal form and no sustainable case of misrepresentation arises, it would be remarkable indeed if the policy could then be avoided on grounds of non - disclosure."

这种明示条文也可以以其他的方式出现，如不允许保险人以不披露或误述使保险合约无效：HIH Casualty & General Insurance Ltd. v. Chase Manhattan Bank（2001）Lloyd's Rep. IR 191。这方面会在稍后第 6. 5 段进一步探讨。

最后一提的是，据说在中国有这种情况，部分保险公司在受保人提出索赔的时候，倾向于以受保人没有履行披露责任为由令保险合约无效从而拒赔。而且部分保险公司为了达到这一个出了事情可以拒赔的目的，在签订保险合约前还尽量不主动询问受保人有关风险的事实与情况。这种做法如果在国际层面，只要是受保人已经给了一个公平的陈述(fair presentation),而保险人自己不主动询问,将会被视为是弃权,不可以逃脱赔付责任。此外,从宏观上来讲,保险公司这种只收保费而不想赔付的心态与做法已经让保险公司失去了分散社会风险的能力。从微观上来讲,部分保险公司的这种做法只显示出他们与伦敦保险公司水平上的差距。

6.4 因为保险合约中明示或默示保证条文的存在而变得多余的信息

这是规定在1906年《英国海上保险法》Section 18(3)(d):"In the absence of inquiry the following circumstances need not be disclosed, namely: Any circumstance which it is superfluous to disclose by reason of any express or implied warranty."

首先要说明(这一问题将会在本书第四章第2段详细介绍)保险合约中的承诺性保证条文与一般合约中的保证条文是两码事,因为1906年《英国海上保险法》Section 33规定如下:"(1) A warranty, in the following sections relating to warranties, means a promissory warranty, that is to say, a warranty by which the assured undertakes that some particular thing shall or shall not be done, or that some condition shall be fulfilled, or whereby he affirms or negates the existence of a particular state of facts. (2) A warranty may be express or implied. (3) A warranty, as above defined, is a condition which must be exactly complied with, whether it be material to the risk or not. If it be not so complied with, then, subject to any express provision in the policy, the insurer is discharged from liability as from the date of the breach of warranty, but without prejudice to any liability incurred by him before that date."

上述就是说明如果保险合约中规定了一个保证条文,它必须被切实的遵守,无论该条文对后来发生的损失是否有关系。如果该保证条文没有被遵守,保险人可以从违反之日起解除保险合约下的责任,除非其他的明示条文有相反的约定。不过在违反保证条文前发生的损失,保险人还是有赔偿责任。

保险合约的保证条文可以是默示或者明示,重要默示的保证条文相关规定是在1906年《英国海上保险法》Section 36(针对保证的中立性,这在发生战争的时候,船舶与货物的中立性是十分重要),Section 39(航次保险的船舶必须绝对适航)与Section 41(有关的航次是合法,如有关货物不是违禁品)。

但明示保证条文在订约自由下可以说是千变万化,因为本书在第四章第2.3.1段有介绍,所以也不多讲。

通常情况下,如果就某一事项在保险合约中有明示或默示的保证条文时,如果受保人有违反,保险人可以根据受保人违反了保证条文拒绝受保人的索赔。换句话说,保险人应该不需要从受保人没有披露的角度入手令保险合约无效。也有一个说法就是在保险合约加入一条明示保证条文,就等于保险人对这一方面作出进一步披露的弃权。

有关这方面的先例不太多,但可以举一些先例:(1) The "Dora" [1989] 1 Lloyd's Rep. 69中保险人指受保人没有披露他把承保货物的游艇作为示范品的意图,但法院判保险合约中有一条保证条文限制了该游艇只能是用于休闲娱乐的用途,所以没有必要再披露其他用途。(2) Gan Insurance Co. Ltd. v. Tai Ping Insurance Co. Ltd. (No. 2) (2001) Lloyd's Rep. IR 291,判是保险合约有一条明示的保证条文针对防火设备,就没有必要再披露防火方面的事实与情况。

违反保证条文与没有披露也有其他比较微妙的区别,如:(1)时间性方面受保人的披露责任仅仅是局限在保险合约签订之前,也局限在受保人所知道与应该知道的事实与情况。而保证条文的遵守义务是在保险合约整个生效期间,相比之下保证条文的遵守期间是会更长一些。(2)违反两者的后果有所不同。在违反保证条文前发生的损失,保险人还是有赔付责任;而如果是违反披露责任,保险人可以选择令保险合约无效,相当于整个保险合约从一开始就不存在,也就是不会再负任何的赔付责任,不论是前后发生的损失。

另外可以一提的是,根据1906年《英国海上保险法》Section 39,受保人是有默示保证义务令船舶适航,有如此严格的保证义务,受保人是不再有关于船舶适航的披露责任,他的义务就是使船舶适航。这在《Good faith and insurance contracts》(第二版)第15.70段:"Where a policy is issued on a cargo against transit risks, the identity and condition of the vessel on which the goods have been shipped, is so far as it is known, generally are treated as material. However, where there is a voyage policy on goods, there is an implied warranty in the policy that the vessel is seaworthy and reasonably fit to carry the cargo; this warranty renders the disclosure of the condition of the carrying vessel superfluous."

不过在本书第八章第8.2段就提到协会货物条文中第5.2条的"Seaworthiness Admitted Clause"(承认适航条文),原因就是受保人的货方对船舶的适航没有控制权。这样一来,如果受保人知道有关船舶不适航的某些迹象或信息,他是否就有披露责任了呢?如在前一个的航次中,受保人是发现船舱的舱盖渗水,虽然在该前一航次中天气一直很好没有造成货损,他是否有义务在为下一个航次(计划是以同一船舶运输)投保的时候向保险人披露呢?这个问题到现在还是没有答案,仅仅是笔者的一点思考。

6.5　保险合约内减轻或排除受保人披露义务条文的效力

已经提到过对于岸上的保险合约,会是由保险人提供一份信息的列表,让受保人填写,这可能会被视为是保险人对受保人要进一步自动披露的弃权。该份列表有时会进一步说明是只要提供的信息是正确,保险人就不能再以没有披露或误述去令保险合约无效。反正,该列表的后果最后还是看它的内容,就是万事不离订约自由。这种列表的例子可看先例 HIH Casualty & General Insurance Ltd. v. Chase Manhattan Bank (2003) Lloyd's Rep. IR 61,列表是名为真实陈述(statement of truth),并作为保险合约的一个条文,如下:"[1] It is a condition precedent to this policy that: Elmood Films Inc. has truthfully completed Section 1 of the Questionnaire to the best of its knowledge... [2] Provided that Elmwood Films Inc. completes the sections of the Questionnaire required to be completed by it and delivers the same to the Lead Insurers. [3] (it being acknowledged that any mis – statement in any part of the Questionnaire... shall not be the responsibility of the insured or constitute a ground for avoidance of the insurers' obligations under the Policy...)... [5] Subject to the obligations of the Insured under 'General Conditions—Due Diligence Clause'... [6] the insured will not have any duty or obligation to make any representations, warranty of disclosure of any nature express or implied... [7] and shall have no liability of any nature to the insurers for any information provided by any other parties and [8] any such information provided by or non – disclosure by other parties... shall not be a ground or grounds for avoidance of the insurers' obligations under the Policy..."

这里首先涉及一个基本的问题,就是可否以合约条文减轻受保人的披露责任,这些责任毕竟是来自绝对善意的原则。而在本章第 7.1 段,是有详细的解释保险合约的绝对善意原则是源自法律而不是来自合约。这表示如果违反了绝对善意,根据法律地位是可以让保险人令保险合约无效,就再也不存在保险合约里条文的解释了。但看来,英国法院还是在原则上可以接受合约条文减轻受保人的绝对善意责任。这可以节录 Aiken 大法官在先例 HIH Casualty & General Insurance Ltd. v. Chase Manhattan Bank (2001) 1 Lloyd's Rep. 30 中所说:

"The difficulty with the effectiveness of clauses in an insurance contract that either purport to exclude or reduce the duty of utmost good faith or the consequences of its breach is that the clauses only exist and can only be enforced if the contract itself continues to exist. The whole point about the duty of utmost good faith is that it arises outside the contract, but if there is a breach it gives the right to avoid the contract and when that right is exercised the whole contract ceases to exist, including the clause that purports to restrict the duty or the consequences of its breach. This problem was emphasized by Lord Justice Steyn in the Court of Appeal in Pan Atlantic Insurance Co. Ltd. v. Pine Top Insurance Co. Ltd.

However Lord Justice Steyn was prepared to accept that conceptually it is possible to draft a clause in an insurance contract which excluded the other party's right to avoid for non – disclosure 'except in the case of fraud, even though the clause excluding rescission forms part of a contract which upon rescission would be rendered retrospectively null and void'. In Toomey v. Eagle Star Insurance Co. Ltd. (No. 2) (1995) 2 Lloyd's Rep. 88, Mr. Justice Colman, following the statements of Lord Justice Steyn in the Pan Atlantic case, accepted the principle that a clause in a contract of insurance could exclude the right to rescind the contract for non – disclosure and also misrepresentation. But he held that the drafting in that case did not exclude the right to avoid for negligent non – disclosure. I will consider that issue and the question of fraud presently. But, subject to those points, I accept that it is possible in principle to limit or exclude by contractual wording the right to avoid for a breach of the duty of utmost good faith."

在先例 HIH Casualty & General Insurance Ltd. v. Chase Manhattan Bank 就涉及了法律加在受保人身上的绝对善意披露责任是否可以被合约中的特定条文减轻或者排除。不过因为受保人违反绝对善意披露责任可能是无辜性违反,也可能是由于疏忽性违反,更有可能是欺诈性违反,所以用来减轻或排除受保人披露责任的保险合约条文可以起到的作用到底是到什么程度还有争议。在该先例,贵族院判是本案中的该条文只能针对无辜性违反,但因为用词不够明确,所以不足够针对疏忽性违反与欺诈性违反。贵族院根据一连串的先例如 Canadian Steamship v. The King (1952) A. C. 192 与 Gillespie Brothers v. Roy Bowles Transport (1973) Q. B. 400 等,在后者 Buckley 大法官是这样说:"... inherently improbable that one party to the contract should intend to absolve the other party from the consequences of the latter's own negligence. The intention to do so must therefore by made perfectly clear..."

换言之,保险合约这一种减轻或排除披露责任的条文实际上有局限性。如果不明确说明包括了疏忽,是不会包括的。同样道理适用在欺诈,现实中难以想象保险人会接受一条条文减轻或排除对欺诈性违反绝对善意义务的责任。

7. 受保人未能完全履行披露责任时保险人的救济

在 1906 年《英国海上保险法》Section 18(1)就很简单与明确说明了如果受保人没有能够履行披露责任,保险人可以使保险合约无效。从这一表面看来,简单与明确的救济有几个方面需要加以探讨。

7.1 绝对善意下要求披露的责任是否是合约以外的责任

这一点所涉及的影响就是如果受保人没有作出披露,保险人除了使保险合约无效的救济之外可否向受保人索赔,如把没有披露(或违反绝对善意)作为受保人违反了保险合约的默示条文。这违反合约条文的损失可以是不同保费之间的差额,但估计不会有太多其他损失。这一问题已经在贵族院的 Pan Atlantic Insurance Co. Ltd. and Another v. Pine Top Insurance Co. Ltd. (1994) 2 Lloyd's Rep. 427 与 The "Star Sea" (2001) 1 Lloyd's Rep. 399 (HL)被明确认定为是合约以外的责任。这方面可节录 Robert Merkin 教授所著的《Colinvaux's Law of Insurance in Hong Kong》第 6.001 段:"There has long been dispute as to whether the duty of utmost good faith has extra contractual effect, whether the duty is an implied term in all contracts of insurance or whether it constitutes a tortuous duty. In La Banque Financiere de la Cite SA v. Westgate Insurance Co. Ltd. (1989) 2 All ER 952 the Court of Appeal held that the duty is extra-contractual. The House of Lords has confirmed this on two separate subsequent occasions..."

另外，没有披露（或违反绝对善意）也与侵权无关，因为在先例 HIH Casualty & General Insurance Ltd. v. Chase Manhattan Bank（2001）Lloyd's Rep. IR 191 判是受保人对保险人是没有一个谨慎的责任（duty of care）主动作出披露。可以说只有在受保人有欺诈性或疏忽性误述的时候才会有侵权的可能。

这表示披露与绝对善意只能说是一个英国法律的地位，这里包括了衡平法以及 1906 年《英国海上保险法》Section 17 的规定。这也带来了一些微妙的问题，如适用于一般合约或侵权的 6 年时效（规定在《Limitation Act》）不适用在没有披露或违反绝对善意的争议。

而绝对善意的误述也与一般合约的误述不尽相同，也不适用 1967 年的《误述法》。有关一般合约下的误述理论在笔者的《国际商务游戏规则——英国合约法》一书第五章有详论，请参阅。其中不相同的地方就是保险合约对误述，只要是有实质性重要，唯一的救济是使合约无效。

另针对可否索赔损失的问题会在下一段介绍。

7.2　违反披露责任的唯一救济是令保险合约无效

根据 1906 年《英国海上保险法》以及相关的法律，受保人违反披露责任，保险人的唯一救济就是令保险合约无效。也就是在本章第 4.4 段提到过的"all or nothing"，即要不是保险人确认保险合约的有效（这一来，他就必须严格履行包括赔付所有的承保风险造成的损失），要不就是令合约无效。这里是不存在向受保人索赔损失或是只拒绝赔付已经产生了的损失，正如上一段所说。例如，保险人很希望继续做这个生意，令保险合约继续有效，而只希望向受保人索赔因为后者没有全面披露所导致的保费差额。或是即使令保险合约无效，保险人也产生了一些费用，如作出原来承保的安排，花钱进行了调查工作等。

这里可以节录《Chitty on Contracts》（2008 年第 30 版）第 6 - 142 段关于这一个问题是这样说："However, even if the non - disclosure is negligent, it does not give rise to liability in damages under Misrepresentation Act 1967 s. 2(1) or, without more, at common law."

另可以节录 Robert Merkin 教授所著的《Colinvaux's Law of Insurance in Hong Kong》第 6.002 段："The remedy is all or nothing. The courts have no power to apply proportional recovery and to allow the assured to recover that proportion of his loss represented by the premium actually paid; neither may the assured make full recovery by proferring the balance of the premium that would have been charged had full disclosure been made. If the insurer purports to avoid the policy but has no justification for doing so, the insurer's conduct amounts to a repudiation of the contract which the assured can either accept, in which case he may bring proceedings immediately; or reject, in which case the repudiation has no legal effects."

上述节录所提到的就是受保人可以补加保费费率的差额而获得赔付，因为保险人根据没有披露而拒绝赔付通常总要说得出,如果某项事实与情况被披露的话,他作为合理谨慎的保险人所厘定的保费会增加多少。这的确是某些欧洲国家保险法的规定(也是欧盟在 1979 年对保险合约所作的指令中的规定,这在本章第 10 段有详述),但不是英国法律的地位。这一欧盟的指示是希望统一这方面的保险法律地位,但没有成功。这方面在 Container Transport International Inc v. Oceanus (1984) 1 Lloyds Rep. 476, Kerr 大法官也有提到说:

"I must shortly deal with what he said at the end of that page, since this clearly influenced his (一审的 Lloyd 大法官) approach throughout. He said: '... In other jurisdictions, the assured could enforce the claim, by tendering the additional premium. But not so in England.'

This is a brief reference to what is sometimes called the 'principle of proportionality' which applies in some, but by no means all, civil law jurisdictions to a limited extent in lieu of a right to avoid the insurance for non-disclosure. In the present context this reference to the law of some other countries is of no assistance. The introduction of 'proportionality', to harmonize the law of insurance throughout the E. E. C., was proposed by the European Commission in a Draft Directive some years ago, but this appears to have made little progress and has so far not been accepted in this country, if indeed it ever will be."

可以看出上述部分所讲欧洲国家的做法会对保险人很不公平,因为如果没有发生承保的风险,保险人只能是收偏低的保费但是承保可能是很大的风险,而只有在发生了事故的情况下(但不一定会发生),才可以补收额外的保费,而往往额外的保费与实际的保险赔付是完全不相称的。这显然是传统上相对偏袒保险人的英国法律不会肯接受的。

8. 受保人的误述

这里重复本章序言里所讲,受保人误述与受保人没有履行披露责任都是违反绝对善意,两者的法律地位基本上是一样。事实上有说法是在保险合约因为受保人有披露的责任,所以不作出实质性的披露本质上就好像保险人误述说:"没有进一步的事实/信息需要提供"。

8.1　1906 年《英国海上保险法》与一般合约法有关误述的差异

关于受保人误述的相关条文是在 1906 年《英国海上保险法》Section 20: "(1) Every material representation made by the assured or his agent to the insurer during the negotiations for the contract, and before the contract is concluded, must be true. If it be untrue the insurer may avoid the contract. (2) A representation is material which would influence the judgment of a prudent insurer in fixing the premium, or determining whether he will take the risk."

误述中的两个核心概念是"实质性重要"(material)与"诱使"(influence),这是与没有履行披露责任中的两个概念的意思完全相同。所以现实中,没有履行披露责任争议的焦点会集中在什么是实质性重要,当然相关的判断标准也适用于误述。而对于误述,争议的焦点更会倾向于到底受保人在签订保险合约之前说了什么,或者是提供的书面材料中的某一项内容到底是什么意思。而不论是说了什么或者书面材料中怎么表述,最终都要判断表述的内容到底是否是真实与全面,才能认定是否存在误述。

上文已经提到说没有履行披露责任对保险人有的唯一救济就是令保险合约无效而不可以索赔损失。而对误述,根据1906年的立法Section 20(1),令保险合约无效应该也是唯一的救济。但是这与一般合约的误述有一点差异,特别是根据1967年《英国误述法》。有关一般合约的误述在笔者《国际商务游戏规则——英国合约法》一书第五章有介绍,其中误述分为欺诈性、疏忽性与无辜三种,其中后两种是来自1967年《英国误述法》。在因误述而导致合约产生的情况,法律对无辜方的救济就是允许他取消合约(除了在一些特殊的情况,如不可能恢复原状、伤害无辜第三方、对合约追认、时隔太久)。此外,在欺诈性误述,无辜方还可以向误述方提出索赔。该书也介绍了1967年《英国误述法》是把以前区分为欺诈性与非欺诈性误述两者之中的后者,进一步区分为疏忽性与无辜性欺诈。换言之,1967年的立法不适用于欺诈性误述。其中重要的条文包括像Section 2(1),误述方如果证明他有合理根据相信他的陈述是正确,他可免除赔偿责任。另在Section 2(2),他的目的是减少无辜方借误述取巧,取消不利于他的合约。

8.2 1906年《英国海上保险法》与1967年《英国误述法》差异的先例

现在把一般性合约的误述的法律救济适用到保险合约,就会有一定的疑问。首先是1967年《英国误述法》是否适用与适用到何种程度,毕竟这是比1906年《英国海上保险法》更晚的立法,如果没有说明,是有可能比1906年立法的效力更大。而在有关的立法中也没有加以说明,毕竟是一贯以来,在海上保险中法院不大可能给保险人经济赔偿方面的救济,救济只是让保险人有权令保险合约无效。这方面在先例Highlands Insurance Co. v. Continental Insurance Co. (1987) 1 Lloyd's Rep. 109中有针对,案情是有关一个在以色列(在Hollon,是以色列首都附近的一个地方)几栋商业房屋的火灾险再保险合约。在投保时,受保人向分保险人提供的文书材料是说明:"Top location Hollon with non - combustible construction and sprinklered(喷水装置)..." ,但发生火灾后分保人得到消息说发生火灾的第66号大楼并没有喷水装置,这就带来一个误述的争议,并且被Steyn大法官接受,判分保险人可以令分保险合约无效。但受保人根据1967年《英国误述法》Section 2(2)要求法院不批准分保险人取消合约,毕竟受保人本身也是保险人,他所提供的资料有误述也只是无辜的误述。但Steyn大法官最终是判保险合约的恰当救济还是令保险合约无效,而不是向保险人作

出金钱上的赔偿,其中有关的判词可节录如下:

"Given a finding that Highlands (分保险人) validly avoided the reinsurance contract, Continental (保险人) now seeks an order under s. 2(2) of the Misrepresentation Act, 1967, declaring that the reinsurance contract is still subsisting. Section 2(2) reads as follows:

'2(2) Where a person has entered into a contract after a misrepresentation has been made to him otherwise than fraudulently, and he would be entitled, by reason of the misrepresentation, to rescind the contract, then, if it is claimed, in any proceedings arising out of the contract, that the contract ought to be or has been rescinded, the court or arbitrator may declare the contract subsisting and award damages in lieu of rescission, if of opinion that it would be equitable to do so, having regard to the nature of the misrepresentation and the loss that would be caused by it if the contract were upheld, as well as to the loss that rescission would cause to the other party.'

Mr. Thomas (保险人的代表大律师) submitted that it would be equitable in this case to declare the reinsurance contract subsisting. The main planks of the submission were as follows:

(a) He emphasized the substantial sum (U. S. MYM1,000,000 or thereabouts) which Continental would lose if no relief is granted under s. 2(2) in respect of Highlands and those represented by Highland.

(b) He submitted that the fire occurred at Building No. 66, and that no misrepresentation was made about that building.

(c) In any event, he submitted the actual underwriter was not induced to enter into the reinsurance contract.

(d) Finally, he submitted that the nature of the misrepresentation is important: it was not culpable.

The submission was that the cumulative effect of these matters renders it equitable to grant relief under s. 2(2). Consideration (a) is, of course, relevant and I take it into account. It was, however, not suggested that by itself it could warrant an order under s. 2(2). Considerations (b), (c) and (d) have not been established on the evidence. On the contrary, I have found that the misrepresentation covered Building No. 66; that the actual underwriter was induced by the misrepresentation; and that the cause of the misrepresentation was a mistake by Continental's underwriter which, I would add, I regard as culpable. The factual basis of the argument has therefore collapsed. I did not understand Mr. Thomas to suggest that the argument can survive the adverse findings of facts which I have made. Plainly, it must fail. I ought, however, to make clear that even if I had made findings of fact favorable to the Continental on each of the above matters, I would still have declined to grant relief under s. 2(2). Where a contract of reinsurance has been validly avoided on the grounds of a material misrepresentation, it is difficult to conceive of circumstances in which it would be equitable within the meaning of s. 2(2) to grant relief from such avoidance. Avoidance is the appropriate remedy for material misrepresentation in relation to marine and non – marine contracts of insurance. See Arnould, Law of Marine Insurance and Average, 16th edition, vol 2, p. 626. The rules governing material misrepresentation fulfil an important 'policing' function in ensuing that the brokers make a fair representation to underwriters. If s. 2(2) were to be regarded as conferring a discretion to grant relief from avoidance on the grounds of material misrepresentation the efficacy of those rules will be eroded. This policy consideration must militate against granting relief under s. 2(2) from an avoidance on the grounds of material misrepresentation in the case of commercial contracts of insurance."

最后可以一提《Chitty on Contracts》(2008 年第 30 版)第 6 – 152 段也有提到了这一个 1967 年的立法适用在保险合约中的不明朗地位,特别是在受保人在投保时的不披露往往通过一条明示条文加在保险合约内变为一个误述的问题。但总之还是说英国法院在保险合约出现误述的情况下,是不大可能会阻止保险人令保险合约无效,毕竟这是 1906 年《英国海上保险法》明确赋予保险人的权利。第 6 – 152 段节录如下:"Effect of Misrepresentation Act on insurance contracts. It has been seen above that the Act of 1967 has no application to cases of pure non – disclosure: Stone v. Reliance Mutual Insurance Society Ltd. (1972) 1 Lloyd's Rep. 469. But most insurance contracts in effect convert what would be a non – disclosure into a positive misrepresentation constituting a term of the contract. It has also been seen above that it is not clear whether s. 2(2) of the Misrepresentation Act enables a court to refuse to allow rescission for misrepresentation where the statement in question was later incorporated as a term of the contract. If it did have this effect, the totally unexpected result might follow, that an insurer might no longer be able to repudiate liability for an immaterial misrepresentation, or even for a material misrepresentation which had no bearing in the risk which has occurred. But this is not generally thought to be the result of the 1967 Act; and in any event it is very unlikely that the court would exercise its jurisdiction to prevent an insurer rescinding on the ground of misrepresentation by the insured."

8.3 事实误述与意见误述的区别

误述通常是针对过去或者现在的事实(facts),这也相对容易证明陈述的事实实际上是不正确的,构成一个误述。但针对意见(opinion),传统的说法是不存在误述,毕竟有不同意见正常不过。现实中,对意见是完全可以误述,等于是中国人讲的"口是心非"。但问题是证明误述方心里想的是什么几乎不大可能,所以证明不了误述。这种困难也可以反映在其他方面,如法院或者仲裁的程序中,事实证人(factual witness)就有危险给别人查出来是做伪证,而专家证人(expert witness)几乎不可能被指控是做伪证,除非是他自己承认"口是心非"。这表示对陈述方而言,陈述事实相对危险,但陈述或者发表意见就安全得多。所以有建议说,要作出陈述的一方针对事实是必须严谨与尽量准确,但发表意见就可以宽松得多,事实上吹捧性的卖花赞花香或者向对方诱导性的游说在现实生活中大量存在。在谈判任何合约包括保险合约时,无可避免是受保人会向保险人作出有关投保风险的各种意见,以下谈谈与这方面有关的问题。

8.3.1 一般合约对事实误述与意见误述的法律地位

这方面可节录《Chitty on Contracts》(2008 年第 30 版)第 6 – 006 段如下:"The traditional rule is that a misrepresentation must be a false statement of fact, past or present, as distinct from a statement of opinion, or of intention or mere commendatory statements. Mere 'puffs' do not amount to representation. A mere statement of opinion which proves to have been unfounded, will not be treated as a misrepresentation, nor will a simple statement of intention which is not put into effect; for as a general rule these cannot be regarded as representation of fact, except in so far as they show that the opinion or intention is held by the person expressing it. Moreover, statements must be construed as they would reasonably be understood by the recipient in the context in which the statement was made. Thus a statement as to the nature of a policy made to an experienced loss adjuster who had a copy of the policy schedule that described it correctly, and was thought to have a copy of the policy itself, was regarded as 'a contention, not as a representation'—in other words, it was merely an expression of opinion."

但一旦能够证明一个意见是"口是心非",表达并不诚实,这可以变为对事实的误述。这方面可以继续节录《Chitty on Contracts》(2008 年第 30 版)第 6 – 007 & 6 – 008 段如下:"However, in certain circumstances a statement of opinion or of intention may be regarded as a statement of fact, and therefore as a ground for avoiding a contract if the statement is false. Thus, if it can be proved that the person who expressed the opinion did not hold it, or could not, as a reasonable man having his knowledge of the facts, honestly have held it, the statement may be regarded as a statement of fact. If a person states as his opinion something which he does not in fact believe, or which given the facts known to him, he could not honestly hold, he makes a false statement of fact. So where, at a sale of property, the vendor described the occupier as 'a most desirable tenant', while in fact he knew that the rent was considerably in arrear, this was held to entitle the purchaser to rescind the contract."

在上述的节录里,最后的一句是针对了著名的先例 Smith v. Land and House Property Corp (1884) 28 Ch D 7。案情是有关卖方在出售他的一间酒店时向买方说:"该酒店出租给弗莱克先生,他应是'一个称心如意的租客'(a most desirable tenant),

一年租金400英镑,租期27年半,是一项一流投资。”事实上,讲这话时弗莱克先生从未按时交租,而且当时有债务未清,这些事实都是事后可以找到证据证明。表面看来,指弗莱克先生称心如意只是卖方的一个意见,但法院判是误述,买方可取消合约。法院认为只有卖方才了解他的租客,买方不了解,在双方对事实的了解程度并非等量齐观,那么知道得更多的一方的意见表述就通常会被认为是事实的陈述。

另举多一个著名先例 Edgington v. Fitzmaurice (1885) 29 Ch D. 459,案情是某公司出了一份邀请认购债券的说明书,声称公司意图将募集的金钱改建公司大楼,买马和车辆,以及发展公司业务。但后来实际上这些金钱被用在还债,显然该公司在邀请认购的时候已经欠债并要马上清还。法院判是公司董事要负上侵权的欺诈误述责任,上诉庭的 Bowen 大法官讲了几句名言如下:“This is an action for deceit, in which the plaintiff complains that he was induced to take certain debentures by the misrepresentations of the defendants, and that he sustained damage thereby... A mere suggestion of possible purposes to which a portion of the money might be applied would not have formed a basis for an action of deceit. There must be a misstatement of an existing fact: but the state of a man's mind is as much a fact as the state of his digestion... A misrepresentation as to the state of a man's mind is, therefore, a misstatement of fact.”

换言之,在表述此意图或愿望时,陈述方或表述方已是在讲假话,他在当时根本没有愿望或能力把这意图将来转化为事实,这就是事实的误述。但证明意见的误述比证明事实误述要困难得多。

8.3.2　《英国海上保险法》对事实误述与意见误述的相关规定

关于事实误述与意见误述的区别在1906年《英国海上保险法》Section 20规定如下:“...(3) A representation may be either a representation as to a matter of fact, or as to a matter of expectation or belief. (4) A representation as to matter of fact is true, if it be substantially correct, that is to say, if the difference between what is represented and what is actually correct would not be considered material by a prudent insurer. (5) A representation as to a matter of expectation or belief is true if it be made in good faith.”

从上述的规定来看,针对这方面,保险合约与一般合约的法律基本上相同。Section 20(4)是说如果对事实的陈述大致上准确就已经算是准确,不存在误述。这表示陈述的事实与真正的事实是相差不远,不构成实质性重要,就不存在误述。而实质性重要是被解释为会影响谨慎保险人决定是否承保以及厘定保费高低。例如,投保的一艘船舶实际船龄是10年3个月,而受保人船东对保险人的陈述是10年,则3个月的差别会被视为非实质性重要,所以不存在误述,保险人不能够因为这些错误而令保险合约无效。

如果陈述的内容是受保人的意见或想法,它们本身是否正确并不重要(正如在一早提到过大家可以有不同的意见),根据 Section 20(5),除非是受保人怀着恶意给予或表达,也就是较早时所讲的“口是心非”,否则不会被视为误述。当然,要证明受保人并非是善意在表达他的意见是有一定的困难,也不能客观判断该意见是否误述。通常的途径就是证明受保人在表达意见的时候,他的意见是没有任何合理依据可以支持。这在先例 Economides v. Commercial Union Assurance Co. plc (1998) Lloyd's Rep. IR 9 (CA), Gibson 大法官说:"Once statute deems and honest representation as to a matter of belief to be true, I cannot see that there is scope for inquiry as to whether there were objectively reasonable grounds for that belief. Of course the absence of reasonable grounds for belief may point to the absence of good faith for that belief. But in a case such as the present where the bad faith of the [assured] is not alleged, I can see no basis for the implication of a representation of reasonable grounds for belief."

8.3.3 实质性重要先例介绍之一:The "Game Boy"

以下介绍先例 The "Game Boy" (2004) 1 Lloyd's Rep. 238,案件涉及了受保人对保险标的的实际价值提供了错误的意见,事后被法院认定受保人并非是善意的表达,最后判保险人有权令保险合约无效。案情是 Game Boy 这艘船舶在希腊港口内因为附近发生爆炸事件导致船舶损坏而沉没,但船东的受保人向保险人索赔的时候,保险人以误述为由令保险合约无效。有关的实质性误述是受保人估值过高,该船舶实际的价值只在 10 万~15 万美元,但约定的保险价值与投保金额高达 180 万美元。船东指称 180 万美元的保险价值是他所认为的船舶价值,是一个意见。船东也提供了其他的证明,如一份二手船买卖合约(MOA)约定的船价是 180 万美元与光船租约等。但高院判是二手船买卖与光船租约都是不可信的文件(被保险人挑出来是漏洞百出),所以认定是船东并非是善意的表达有关船价的意见,等同于误述,所以保险人可以令保险合约无效。Simon 大法官这样说:"In the light of the findings of fact set out above, I have concluded that the Assureds had no genuine belief that the value of the vessel was MYM1,800,000. My reasons can be stated shortly: the documents which were said to form the basis for the Assureds' stated belief were, to their knowledge, not genuine. They were not created to support a genuine belief in the value of MYM1,800,000; they were created because the Assureds knew very well that the valuation of MYM1,800,000 could not be justified without them. In my judgment the true value of the vessel (at the time of the contract of insurance) was the value estimated by the experts without the benefit of what I find to have been the fictitious Charterparty: approximately MYM100 - 150,000; and I further find that the Assureds knew this. I specifically reject Mr Ghiolman's (受保人的证人) evidence that he believed that the vessel's value was MYM1,800,000 and that he had good grounds for that belief."

这一先例也针对了在上一小段提到的 1906 年《英国海上保险法》Section 20(4)所规定的受保人陈述的事实(或是一个意见被视为是事实)与真正的事实是相差不远,不构成实质性重要,就不存在误述。案例中,Game Boy 轮的实际价值是 10 万~15 万美元,即使有误差,双方的专家证人接受船东所提供的船舶价值要求作出投保可以是在 50 万美元的范围内。但本案例中却是 180 万美元,显然构成实质性重要,所以可构成误述。Simon 大法官这样说:"The underwriting experts (Mr Hart for the Assureds and Mr Outhwaite for the Insurer) did not significantly disagree. Both experts agreed that an insurer relies on the assured being honest. In Mr Hart's view an over – valuation was only material if extreme. Mr Outhwaite thought it was material if the over – valuation was in multiples. In view of my finding that the vessel was only worth (and was known to be worth) in the order MYM100 – 150,000, I have concluded that the misrepresentation was material. Mr Outhwaite also said that if the value had been up to MYM500,000 the over – valuation would have been material."

8.3.4 实质性重要先例介绍之二:Glencore v. Alpina

另一个上文已经提到的先例 Glencore International A. G. v. Alpina Insurance Co. Ltd. (2004) 1 Lloyd's Rep. 111(具体案情在本章第 6.2 段有介绍),涉及保险人是给受保人签发了一份承保范围非常广泛的开口保单。承保标的是石油以及相关的产品。在投保的时候,受保人向保险人说明承保的风险是包括浮动油库的石油时,受保人作出如下的陈述:"This is purely a storage risk exposure and there are no blending risks involved."也就是说,该保单是不承保在混合不同的石油产品时产生的风险如产品受到污染,承保的范围仅仅是限于石油的实际短量(这是库存最大的承保风险)。不过后来是把石油进行混合作业。法院判这种误述可能是具有实质性重要,因为这种混合作业的过程会提高石油实际损失的风险。不过最终法院也没有就该误述是否具有实质性重要下结论,因为法院判,无论如何,该误述都没有影响到保险人。也就是接受投保当时,保险人知道了真正的情况,他仍是愿意以相同的保险合约条件与保费接受承保,即"诱使"(inducement)是不成立。Moore – Bick 大法官说:"I turn, therefore, to the question of inducement. There was a tendency... to approach the question of inducement by considering how the underwriter would have responded if told the true position. That may be appropriate when the issue before the court is one of non – disclosure but it is not appropriate in the case of misrepresentation because the court is then concerned only with the effect the false statement had on the underwriter's mind."

8.3.5 实质性重要先例介绍之三:Hamilton & Co. v. Eagle Star

本章第 5.7 段已提到过说,针对海上保险,受保人在投保时,之前被其他保险人拒绝承保的事实本身是不具有实质性重要,所以不必披露。我们现在来考虑一下误述的问题,简单地说就是投保的时候保险人向受保人询问是否曾被其他保险人拒绝承保,受保人也就必须准确作出陈述。这里也不存在是否有实质性重要的问题,因为是保险人主动提出询问。但在不同的案件还是会有千变万化的情况会出现,如在投保的时候受保人在一个现存的保险合约(current policy)与该保险合约的保险人因为某些合约条文发生问题,这会否需要披露或作出准确的陈述?

在先例 Hamilton & Co. v. Eagle Star & British Dominion Insurance Co. Limited

(1924) 19 Lloyd's Rep. 242,Hamilton 是一家苹果经销商,他为运输中的苹果向 New Zealand Insurance Co. 投保一年期的开口保单,保险合约中是有一条"延长航次条文"(Prolongation of Voyage Clause),内容相对复杂,并有针对不同船舶的航速规定了航次多久。在 1922 年 4 月,被承保的其中一个航次的船舶 Nessian 轮本来的目的地是曼切斯特,但却挂靠了利物浦港,使得航程大大增加,并因此导致了苹果的腐烂,Hamilton 向 New Zealand 索赔。虽然 New Zealand 给予了赔付,但是却引起了他的强烈不满,认为船舶会挂靠利物浦是事先根本没有想到的风险。随即,到 New Zealand 根据保险合约条文中规定保险人是可以提前 30 天给通知说是期满之后就不再承保。在 1922 年 4 月 20 日,New Zealand 根据保险合约作出了提前 30 天的通知。但之后双方又把原来的保险合约重新约定(reinstate),但删除有关的延长航次条文。几个月后开口保单快要届满的时候,Hamilton 就需要去市场上看看有没有其他的保险人愿意为他承保苹果运输的风险。于是他找到了保险经纪人,保险经纪人就与另一家保险人 Eagle Star 接触,并呈递给了 Eagle Star 一份保险合约条文,其中也包括了延长航次条文。但是 Eagle Star 从未见过该保险条文,保险经纪人告诉 Eagle Star 说呈递给他的保险条文与现在 Hamilton 还没有履行完毕的保险合约,也就是与 New Zealand 承保的内容是一样的。当时 New Zealand 是一家非常著名的保险公司,显然这句话会令 Eagle Star 感觉到安心。Eagle Star 询问过去的索赔经历,保险经纪人就告诉他说只有一笔 221 英镑的索赔。事实上也就是导致 New Zealand 向 Hamilton 作出终止保险合约通知的索赔。但 Hamilton 并没有告诉保险经纪人他与 New Zealand 之间是因为延长航次条文发生了很大的问题,以致 New Zealand 不愿意继续承保的事实。所以保险经纪人告诉 Eagle Star 的是不全面的事实陈述。法院判由于该条文的重要性以及它可能带来的困难,该条文是具有实质性重要,所以保险人 Eagle Star 是有权以 Hamilton 没有全面对事实作出陈述,令合约无效。

8.3.6　有关事实与意见之间的不同的先例介绍:Kamidian v. Holt and Others

上文 8.3.1 节录了《Chitty on Contracts》(2008 年第 30 版)第 6 – 006 段,其中最后一句提到了区分事实误述与意见误述的困难的先例:IFE Fund SA v. Goldman Sachs International (2007) 2 Lloyd's Rep. 449 与 Kyle Bay Ltd. v. Underwriters Subscribing under Policy No. 019057/08/01 (2007) EWCA Civ 57。以下介绍一个货物保险的雷同先例,就是 Kamidian v. Holt and Others (2009) Lloyd's Rep. IR 242。该先例中,受保人是为一个古董钟表投保。受保人在日内瓦的苏特比拍卖行买进了这个古董钟表,虽然他是以远远低于真品的价格买进的,但是他以为是一件历史上的真品(而实际上是赝品)。而受保人为该钟表投保的保险金额是 250 万美元。该钟表在运输的过程中被损坏,之后保险人就以受保人误述而选择令保险合约无效。Tomlinson 大法官判是受保人的关于承保货物是属于真品的陈述(这陈述如果属于事实就不正确)并非是事实的陈述,因为这是受保人在投保时无法证明,并且受保人也不大可能作出事实的陈述,毕竟该古董钟表是真是假已经是历史。他最终是判受保人的陈述是"艺术界的人普遍接受这是真品",但因为艺术界的人没有这样的普遍接受,所以受保人还是构成了对事实的误述,保险人是可以令保险合约无效。

9. 保险人针对受保人没有披露或误述的举证责任总结与保险人自己的披露责任

以下分两部分谈谈保险人在这方面的一些责任,首先是有关他对受保人没有披露或误述的举证责任。这在 Robert Merkin 教授所著的《Colinvaux's Law of Insurance in Hong Kong》第 6.029 段,他这样说:

"A number of different matters have to be proved in a non – disclosure or misrepresentation case.

(1) The insurer must prove that there has been a false statement made to him, or that the assured has failed to disclose material facts to him. This burden of proving the fact of the absence or presence of a statement rests squarely on the insurer. (保险人需要证明未被披露的实质性重要事实/错误披露的存在。)

(2) Proof of the absence or falsity of the information provided by the assured rests equally on the insurer. (保险人需要证明未被披露的事实到底是什么/披露的信息到底错在哪里。)

(3) The insurer must prove the materiality of the information withheld or misstated, generally by adducing expert evidence. Subject to that principle, there is a presumption of materiality in respect of express question put to the assured by the insurer, so that it will be difficult for an assured who has misrepresented the true position to deny the materiality of his answer, even though, in the absence of an express question, disclosure would not have been required. In such a case the parties are considered to have agreed the difficult question as to which facts are material. By contrast, there is no presumption of immateriality in respect of information which is not specifically requested by an insurer. Thus where the assured's answers are literally true, the insurer is nevertheless not prevented from relying on non – disclosure in respect of an answer which is misleading, incomplete or evasive. Proof of materiality is possible only by expert evidence. In some situations such evidence may be given by experts in the field: evidence relating to the assured's state of health may thus be given by doctors. Evidence may also be received from other insurers, from brokers and from the insurer himself acting as a prudent insurer. The admissibility of the evidence of other insurers as to materiality clearly puts the assured under some difficulty, as it will be virtually impossible to rebut unanimous statements from insurers as to the materiality of a given fact. This indeed appears to have been recognised by Lord Mansfield in the root decision on

the duty of utmost good faith, Carter v. Boehm (1766) 3 Burr 1905, which the evidence of other underwriters was described by him as: ' mere opinion; which is not evidence. ' It is opinion without the least foundation from any previous precedent or usage. This view has not, however, prevailed. A substantial part of the protection for an assured in relation to materiality is, therefore, the commercial sense of the trial judge in assessing the weight to be given to such testimony. There are few cases in which the evidence of other insurers has been rejected or criticised by a court, although Colman J warned in Strive Shipping Corp v. Hellenic Mutual War Risks Association (2002) Lloyd's Rep. IR 669 that expert evidence would not be uncritically accepted by the courts. "。(保险人需要证明未被披露实质性重要的事实或错误披露信息具有实质性。保险人曾经问过受保人的问题原则上是会被视为是具有实质性。对于保险人没有问过的问题,受保人作出的陈述只要表面上看是真实的,即使是由于披露不全面而具有误导性,保险人也是不可以依赖未履行披露义务而令合约无效。某种信息实质性重要的证明往往是通过专家意见。其他保险人提供的专家意见很多情况下是与涉案保险人的说法一致,让受保人无法辩驳。Mansfield 勋爵在先例 Carter v. Boehm (1766) 3 Burr 1905 就认为其他保险人提供的专家证言顶多只算是"意见而非证据"。不过这种观点并没有被后来的先例普遍采纳。现在什么信息是具有实质性重要往往由法官们根据他们的商业常识来判断。也曾经有先例是其他保险人的证人证言被法院拒绝。)

(4) Fourth, the insurer must prove that he was induced to enter into the contract by the assusred's failure to make a fair presentation of the risk. (保险人必须证明恰恰就是没有披露的信息/错误披露的信息诱使他签订了该保险合约)。"

第二部分是针对保险人对受保人作出披露与不得误述的责任,因为在 1906 年《英国海上保险法》下的绝对善意(utmost good faith)责任已经明确下来双方都有的。保险人对受保人的披露责任以前没有这种先例,现实中也不大会发生。但现在已经在贵族院的先例被确认保险人也是有这一责任:La Banque Financiere de la Cite SA v. Skandia (UK) Insurance Co. Ltd. (1990) 2 Lloyd's Rep. 377。在该先例,涉及四家银行贷款给一个珠宝商,并以该珠宝商所提供的红宝石、绿宝石和蓝宝石作为质押。这批宝石均经过专家鉴定价值,表面看来,该巨额贷款应该是有足够的担保。四家银行通过一家保险经纪人与被告保险人作出投保,投保的风险就是该贷款人无法足额还清债务,如贷款人倒闭而质押的宝石在期间贬值。这个约定的保险合约中的一条是"诈骗除外"条文(fraud exception clause),即保险人不愿意承担四家银行面对被诈骗的风险。结果这四家银行遇上的正是贷款人的诈骗,而后发现被质押的宝石其实是不值钱的。这导致了四家银行作为受保人与被告保险人之间的诉讼。保险人显然是以该条诈骗除外条文作为抗辩,而受保人争辩说保险人事前已经知道他的保险经纪人不诚实,应该对这个事实作出披露责任。但最后在贵族院,判的是受保人的损失与保险人未作出披露之间没有直接的因果关系。只要受保人愿意接受一条诈骗除外条文,就已经注定了这四家银行的损失是无法从保险人那里得到赔付。Templeman 勋爵这样说:“the advance would have been lost whether it had been insured or not because the banks (受保人) had accepted and paid a premium for insurance which contained a fraud exception clause; the fraud of Mr. Ballestero (贷款人/骗子) which caused the loss of the advance and the rejection of claims under the insurance policies was not foreseeable; Mr. Lee's (受保人的保险经纪人) fraud which caused the advance to be made did not affect the rights of the banks to recover their loss and did not cause the loss of advance; the policies of insurance did not or would not have protected the banks against the fraud of Mr. Ballestero and his fraud was causative of the loss of the advance; the failure by Mr. Dungate (保险人的经纪人) to inform the banks of the fraud of Mr. Lee was not causative of the bank's loss.”

贵族院是认同高院及上诉庭认为保险人对受保人也是有绝对善意的责任,包括披露。而这就带来后来一连串的同类争议,包括:Searle v. A R Hales & Co. Ltd. (1996) LRLR 68 (QB), Norwich Union Life Insurance Society v. Qureshi (1999) Lloyd's Rep. IR 263。

然而在现实中保险人仍是安全的,第一就是他们必须作出实质性披露(会影响受保人是否投保与怎样投保),估计情况是非常罕见。可以想得到的会是在 Carter v. Boehm (1766) 3 Burr 1905 的古老先例中,Mansfield 勋爵所举的例子,一个是船舶已经安全抵达了英国,而且保险人比受保人早一步知道,但还是接受受保人的投保与他支付的保费。另一个例子就是保险人明知道一栋房子被火烧,但还是接受火险的投保。但这种例子在今天通讯发达的时候很少出现。还有可以让保险人安心的是他的救济,因为受保人即使成功地证明保险人没有作出实质性披露,这一方面的救济在 1906 年《英国海上保险法》也有规定,即是受保人可以令保险合约无效,顶多再加上一个权力把已经支付了的保费取回。这种救济比起保险人可以令保险合约无效的救济就差得远了。

10. 法律改革

在英国有关绝对善意的法律地位是受保人必须作出全面的披露,否则保险人可以令合约无效,这就已经带来了很多反对的意见,认为法律没有在保险人与受保人之间达成平衡。虽然在某些情况也已经有立法作出改变,如机动车辆的第三人强制保险。交通意外的受害人根据 1930 年《Third Parties (Rights against Insurers) Act》是不必向肇事的机动车司机索赔(他可能会在该意外中死亡),而可以直接向有关保险人索赔。但问题是如果该保险人根据受保人没有作出披露或误述而令保险合约无效,无辜的受害人还是得不到赔偿。所以就同时有 1934 年《Road Traffic Act》,其中 section 10 强制有关保险人必须作出赔付就算受保人是有实质性重要信息未披露或误述,除非保险人在无辜受害人提起诉讼的 7 天内作出通知。这接下去还有其他的发展,如 1988 年《Road Traffic Act》section 152(2),但由于这不是本书的重点,所以略过不讲。

10.1 欧盟有关保险合约的指令

以下针对的是整体有关保险合约的绝对善意的法律地位,这里首先要介绍的在 1979 年欧盟曾经作出指令(European Council Directive relating to insurance contracts 31/12/79 OJ C355)。针对披露责任,它是 Article 3 规定了以下的责任与权利:

"1. The policyholder shall declare to the insurer 'any circumstances of which he ought reasonably to be aware and which he ought to expect to influence a prudent insurer's assessment or acceptance of the risk'. Such circumstances include those which are the subject of specific questions put to the policyholder in writing.

2. There is no obligation to disclose information already known to the insurer or matters of common knowledge.

3. If the policyholder fails to disclose circumstances of which he was aware but which he did not expect to influence a prudent insurer's assessment of the risk, or if further circumstances of which both parties were unaware come to light after the contract is made, the insurer or the policyholder may propose an amendment to or termination of the contract. The other party may choose to accept or reject the amendment proposed and, if he rejects it, the party proposing the amendment may elect to terminate the cover with prospective effect so that any claim which arises prior to the termination will be honored by the insurer.

4. If the policyholder fails to discharge his duty of disclosure as set out in para. 1 above, the insurer may terminate the contract or propose an amendment to it. In the latter case, the assured may accept or reject the proposed amendment. If he rejects it, the insurer may terminate the contract. If the contract is terminated, the insurer will be obliged to pay any otherwise recoverable claim which arose prior to termination in proportion to the 'ration between the agreed premium and the premium which a prudent insurer would have fixed if the policyholder had fulfilled his obligations under para. 1'. However, if the insurer can demonstrate that the prudent insurer would not have accepted the risk on the terms proposed, then the insurer will not have to pay any claim.

5. If the policyholder fails to discharge his duty of disclosure 'with the intention of deceiving the insurer', the insurer may terminate the cover and, in that event, will not be obliged to pay any claim arising for cover before the termination.

6. If the contract is terminated, the insurer will be obliged to return to the policyholder the proportion of the premium in respect of the period of the insurance not covered, unless the policyholder breached his duty with the intention of deceiving the insurer, in which case the in-

surer will be entitled to retain the premium paid ‘by way of damage’ and claim further damages.

7. The insurer will bear the burden of proving that the policyholder has failed to discharge his duty or acted fraudulently. ”

以上只是欧盟有关保险合约立法的部分内容,但显然在有些重要的地方是很难被英国接受的。如在上述节录的(4)就有提到解决的办法是要求保险人收取保费的差额作为受保人没有作出披露的损失,但不能令合约无效与拒赔。这方面的问题与不足之处在本章第7.2段有涉及。总而言之,欧盟的指令已经被英国的法律委员会(Law Commission)拒绝立法。

10.2　英国法律改革委员会的1957年与1980年报告

早在1957年,英国法律改革委员会作出了第五份报告(Fifth Report: Cmnd 62),针对保险合约披露的问题。委员会建议了两方面的有关改变:(1)实质性的重要是从一位合理受保人的角度看待;(2)如果受保人能够证明他的陈述即使是错误,也是他最好的理解与相信(to the best of his knowledge and believe)。

另在1980年,法律委员会在Kerr大法官作为主席作出了一份有关保险法的报告,名为Insurance Law: Non－disclosure and Breach of Warranty, No 104, Cmnd 8064。这一报告其实是针对了第10.1段中提到的欧盟1979年的指令作出分析与建议。在该报告中,他断然拒绝了欧盟指令,但同意英国的法律需要尽快作出改革。报告中是作出了以下的一些建议:

“1. A fact should be disclosed if:

(a) it is material in the sense that it would influence a prudent insurer in deciding whether to offer cover, and if so, on what terms and at what premium; and

(b) it is known to the assured or may be assumed to be known to the assured (for this purpose, an assured would be assumed to know a fact if it was reasonable for him to have made reasonable enquiry); and

(c) a reasonable assured in the position of the assured would have disclosed it.

2. Questions in proposal forms should be answered by the assured to the best of his information and belief, after making reasonable enquiry; proposal forms should contain prominent warnings as to the nature of the duty upon the assured and of the consequences of failure to discharge the duty. If the insurer failed to comply with the proposed requirements as regards proposal forms, the insurer should not be permitted to set aside the contract, unless he could show that no prejudice was suffered by the assured in respect of his obligation of disclosure. Renewal notices should be treated in a similar fashion.

3. If the insurer asked a question, it is presumed to be concerned with a material fact, but the assured should not be obliged to answer any immaterial question. If the insurer did not ask a question, it is assumed that the required no further information in respect of the subject of the question.

4. Basis clauses (clauses which render the truth of stated facts the basis of the contract) should be ineffective, unless they are the subject of a specific warranty.

5. If there has been a breach of the assured's duty of disclosure, the insurer should not be able to rely on any non-fraudulent misrepresentation; the insurer's rights and remedies should be limited to remedies for breach of the duty of disclosure."

但要说明的是,该报告不适用在再保险或专业性的保险,如海上保险。该报告认为在这种专业性的保险中,保险行业自己会作出调整以减轻绝对善意原则的严格性,不需要立法干预。

10.3 澳大利亚法律改革委员会的报告

2001年4月,澳大利亚法律改革委员会也作出了针对1909年《Marine Insurance Act》的第91号报告。而该澳大利亚立法是以1906年《英国海上保险法》为蓝本的。其中关于绝对善意是这样建议的:

"1. The implication of a provision in the contract of marine insurance to the effect that each party should act towards the other with the utmost good faith. Further, the duty of utmost good faith will continue for the duration of the insurance relationship, except in so far as any claim or other aspect of that relationship is the subject of litigation. (海上保险的默示地位还是要求受保人与保险人之间双向的绝对善意。而该义务是持续在整个保险期间,并不局限在订约前,但是在诉讼开始后就不再有这样的义务[这与目前英国的法律地位是相同:见本章第4.1.2段]。)

2. The test of materiality is to be applied by reference to the position of a reasonable person in the position of the assured (not the insurer). (注意是实质性重要的判定是以合理受保人的判断为准,而非是英国目前法律下的谨慎保险人的标准。)

3. Avoidance should no longer be the automatic and inflexible remedy (most often available to the insurer) for a breach of the duty of good faith. (令保险合约无效的救济不再是自动与唯一的救济。)

4. In the event of a fraudulent breach of the duty of utmost good faith, the innocent party should be entitled to avoid the insurance contract with no return of premium. (如果受保人欺诈性违反绝对善意义务,保险人可以令合约无效并不退还保费。)

5. In the event of a non-fraudulent breach of duty, the insurer should be entitled to avoid the insurance contract, but with a return of premium, provided that he can prove that he would not have entered into the contract has there been full and accurate disclosure. (如果受保人并非是欺诈性违反绝对善意义务,在保险人能够证明如果披露全面与正确的话他不会接受承保的情况下,保险人可以选择令合约无效,但需要退还保费。)

6. In the event of a not-fraudulent breach of duty, if the insurer would still have entered into the contract had there been full and accurate disclosure, the insurer will have three remedies available to him: (a) he will not be liable for any loss proximately caused

by the undisclosed or misrepresented circumstance; (b) he will be entitled to vary his liability to reflect the variation in the terms of the contract (as to premium, excess or deductible) which he would have imposed had there been full and accurate disclosure; and (c) he will have a right to cancel the policy (prospectively) in accordance with the provisions of the Act.(如果受保人并非是欺诈性违反绝对善意义务,且保险人即使在披露全面与正确的情况下也会接受承保,则保险人有三种救济:[a]他是不必为直接因未披露信息而导致的损失向受保人作出赔付;[b]在知悉了有关披露并非是全面与正确的情况后,保险人有权就保险合约的具体条文进行修改[特别是针对保费率或绝对免赔额];[c]保险人也可以根据法律的规定取消保险合约。)

7. The duty of pre – contractual disclosure will be regulated by sections 24 – 26 of the Act. These will be amended, but largely retaining the structure of sections 18 – 20 of the Marine Insurance Act 1906. The most significant suggested changes relate to the broker's duty of disclosure; further, the exception of superfluity is to be amended so that it will be determined by reference to the 'express terms' of the insurance contract, instead of the 'warranties'. (订约前的披露责任是要根据澳大利亚立法 1909 年《Marine Insurance Act》第 24 ~26 条来确定,1906 年《英国海上保险法》Section 18 – 20。建议的最大改变是与保险经纪人的披露责任有关;多余信息是属于不需披露的一种例外,这可以是根据保险合约中的明示条文而非保证条文来确定。)

8. The parties will not be permitted to agree to a contractual duty or remedies which are more burdensome to the assured than that provided for in the Act. (合约双方是不允许通过合约条文使受保人的义务比法律规定更重,这是为了禁止订约自由以明示条文把默示地位作出改变而保护不了受保人。)

9. A following insurer will be deemed to have been induced by the misrepresentation or non – disclosure if all of the leading insurers were so induced. (如果可以证明一份保单中的首席保险人因为误述或者是不披露而被诱使订立合约,则可以认定其他的随从保险人也被视为是同样诱使。这是由于一些保险合约如海上保险,经常会有一份保单分别由多位不同的保险人分别作出部分承保。而个别保险人所占的份额是被视为与受保人独立的一个保险合约。这样建议,就是避免一份保单的每个保险人都为同样的误述或者是不披露的争议打一场官司。)"

10.4　英国法律目前的改革

笔者在与汪鹏南教授合著的《英国海上保险条款详论》一书中曾对此进行了探讨。[1] 最新的消息是英国法律委员会在目前已经作出了 7 份报告针对保险法律需要改革的地方,而最近的一份报告是在 2010 年 7 月 9 日,针对的是欺诈性索赔(fraudulent claim)。此外,法律委员会也在 2006 年草拟了一部立法,如果被议院通过

[1] 杨良宜、汪鹏南:《英国海上保险条款详论》,大连海事大学出版社 2009 年版,第 425 页。

就会豁免所有涉及消费者保险合约的披露责任。该草拟立法并不针对商业的保险合约,包括海上保险。由于英国目前的政治环境(政府是由两个政党联合组成),所以立法看来也不是会很快完成。另是,法律委员会承诺在2010年年底会做出另一个草拟立法针对商业与海上保险合约。但在将来会出现的草拟立法,到底会怎么样针对海上保险合约的披露责任,目前还没有决定。看来本章所讲的英国法律地位针对绝对善意原则的精神还会适用很长一段时间。

第三章　可保利益(insurable interest)

1. 有关可保利益的历史演变

可保利益与其他许多本书要针对的课题如代位求偿权与双重保险等都是与补偿损失原则(principle of indemnity)有紧密关系。目前可保利益在英国的保险法是属于一个强制性的要求,即受保人必须拥有可保利益,否则保险合约不被承认。可保利益的说法在18世纪前是不被理会,曾经有好几个先例涉及普通法执行一些完全是赌博性质的保险合约,只要它不违反当时英国的公共政策:Jones v. Randall (1774) 1 Cowp 37;Micklefield v. Hepgin (1793) 1 Anst 133。接下来普通法的发展是法院开始要求赌博性质的保险合约有必要在保单中明示说明是不要求受保人拥有或证明他的可保利益:Lucena v. Craufurd (1802) 3 Bos & Pul 75。在该先例,Lawrence J 大法官也给了一个被视为是可保利益的经典与非常广泛的解释。这些明示规定不要求受保人拥有或证明他的可保利益有不同的写法,包括像"interest or not interest"、"policy proof of interest"、"without benefit of salvage"等。

18世纪开始,法律逐渐发展要求受保人必须有可保利益,是为了防止受保人以保险的形式去赌博。所以在1745年就有了《海上保险法》的立法要求针对英国船舶与该船上的货物的保险合约中必须说明谁是有可保利益,否则该保险合约无效。1745年的立法在序言中说明了赌博性保险合约的三种坏处:(1)造成一个后果是无限度地在同一个风险上投保,引发保险欺诈;(2)以赌博性保险对被英国法律所禁止的航次投保,并遮盖了其非法性;(3)对本来是用作保障合法商人利益的做法带来不良影响与坏名声。

到了1774年,又通过了另外一个针对岸上保险的《人寿保险法》(Life Assurance Act),[1]作用也是令受保人没有可保利益的保险合约无效,如一般的民众为英国国

[1] 1774年《人寿保险法》Section 1 说:"From and after the passing of this Act no insurance shall be made by any person or persons bodies politick or corporate, on the life or lives of any person or persons, or on any other event or events whatsoever, wherein the person or persons for whose use, benefit, or on whose account such policy or policies shall be made, shall have no interest, or by way of gaming or wagering; and that every assurance made contrary to the true intent and meaning hereof shall be null and void to all intents and purposes whatsoever."

王的寿命投保。到了1845年通过了《赌博法》(Gambling Act),这是进一步把以保险形式的赌博变为是无效。接下来就是取代了1745年立法的1906年《英国海上保险法》,其中Section 5针对可保利益,并在Section 5(1)明确说明任何人(不再是只针对英国船舶,而只要是英国法院有管辖权的都包括在内)以海上保险作为赌博有关的保险合约都是无效。接下来在Section 5(2)就说明受保人没有可保利益的情况下,该合约就被视为是赌博的合约。在1909年更进一步通过了《海上保险(有关赌博性保单)法》(Marine Insurance [Gambling Policies] Act 1909)令没有可保利益的受保人会犯法,[1]但在善意的情况下没有可保利益,对受保人的后果只是局限在保险合约是无效。到了2005年《赌博法》Section 335更是明确允许一个赌博合约可以被法院执行。所以到了今天探讨可保利益,再也不是赌博与否的问题,而是保险法下的一个强制性要求。而除了商业与社会的复杂化,可保利益也变成有很多种形式与法律不断在放宽,再也不是以前比较强调的财产所有权或占有权。至于不涉及财产险的其他类别的保险,如责任险,更是随着商业与社会的发展而带来千变万化的各种责任,可保利益更是在大幅度放宽。总结以上所介绍的,可节录Colman大法官在The "Moonacre" (1992) 2 Lloyd's Rep. 501先例中所讲的这方面的历史发展与演变:

"By the beginning of the 18th century a contract of marine insurance could be enforced at common law by the assured notwithstanding he had no personal interest in the subject matter of the insurance, that is to say even if he stood neither to lose nor to gain from the success or failure of the adventure or the contracts were in substance wagering contracts. It was only by a 1745 Act (19 Geo. 2c. 37) that such contracts were declared to be null and void in respect of British ships and their cargoes. It provided that no assurances should be made on any goods on board any British ships—

... interest or no interest, or with or without further proof of interest than the policy, or by way of gaming or wagering... and that every such assurance shall be null and void to all intents and purposes.

The Life Assurance Act, 1774, applied the same principle to other contracts of insur-

---

[1] 1909年《海上保险有关赌博性保单法》Section 1说:"If -(a) any person effects a contract of marine insurance without having any bona fide interest, direct or indirect, either in the safe arrival of the ship in relation to which the contract is made or in the safety or preservation of the subject - matter insured or a bona fide expectation of acquiring such an interest; or (b) any person in the employment of the owner of a ship, not being a part owner of the ship, effects a contract of marine insurance in relation to the ship, and the contract is made 'interest or no interest,' or 'without further proof of interest than the policy itself,' or 'without benefit of salvage to the insurer,' or subject to any other like term, the contract shall be deemed to be a contract by way of gambling on loss by maritime perils, and the person effecting it shall be guilty of an offence, and shall be liable, on summary conviction, to imprisonment ... for a term not exceeding six months or to a fine not exceeding [level 3 on the standard scale], and in either case to forfeit to the Crown any money he may receive under the contract."

ance except non – marine policies on goods. The Gaming Act, 1845, s. 18, had the effect of making void all contracts of insurance which were wagers by reason of the assured's lack of interest in the subject matter of the policy. Eventually by s. 4 of the Marine Insurance Act, 1906 it was provided:

(1) Every contract of marine insurance by way of gaming or wagering is void.

(2) A contract of marine insurance is deemed to be a gaming or wagering contract—(a) Where the assured has not an insurable interest as defined by this Act, and the contract is entered into with no expectation of acquiring such an interest; or (b) Where the policy is made 'interest or no interest', or without further proof of interest than the policy itself, or 'without benefit of salvage to the insurer', or subject to any other like term...

Accordingly the essential question to be investigated in those cases which since 1745 have been concerned to test the existence of an insurable interest has been whether the relationship between the assured and the subject matter of the insurance was sufficiently close to justify his being paid in the event of its loss or damage, having regard to the fact that, if there were no or no sufficiently close relationship, the contract would be a wagering contract. The typical wagering contract was defined by Mr. Justice Hawkins in Carlill v. Carbolic Smoke Ball Co., [1892] 2 QB 484 at p 490:

'A wagering contract is one by which two persons, professing to hold opposite views touching the issue of a future uncertain event, mutually agree that, dependent upon the determination of that event, one shall win from the other, and that other shall pay or hand over to him, a sum of money or other stake; *neither of the contracting parties having any other interest in that contract than the sum or stake he will so win or lose, there being no other real consideration for the making of such contract either of the parties.* '

There is thus in a wagering contract the essential feature that neither party has any interest in the outcome of the future uncertain event save for that amount which will be won or lost under the contract. Conversely, if the outcome of the future uncertain event upon the happening of which one party is entitled to be paid by the other would or might but for the contract cause loss or damage to the payee, then one essential characteristic of a wagering contract has gone and there is nothing in the Gaming Act, 1845 or in subsequent betting and gaming legislation which renders that contract void and unenforceable. Neither the words of any statute since 1845 nor any judicial pronouncement suggest that there should be a category of contracts of insurance which were not wagering contracts but which on account of the absence of an 'insurable interest' should not be enforceable. Accordingly, in approaching the construction and application of s. 5 of the Marine Insurance Act it is, in my judgment, right to proceed on the assumption that, provided the assured has sufficient interest in the subject matter of the insurance to prevent his contract being a wagering contract, he is entitled to enforce that contract."

最后一提的是在协会货物条文(Institute Cargo Clauses)中,也有一条明示的"赔付或保险人要负责任的先决条件"(condition precedent to liability),说明受保人必须在发生损失的时候对保险标的有可保利益,保险人才会赔付。该条文是"11.1 In order to recover under this insurance the Assured must have an insurable interest in the subject - matter insured at the time of the loss."

所以,在英国法律的默示地位以及针对海上货物保险的保险合约的明示条文都离不开可保利益。

2. 可保利益的定义与类别

2.1 可保利益在1906年《英国海上保险法》下的定义

1906年《英国海上保险法》有好几个章节是针对受保人的可保利益。其中针对它的定义是在Section 5:"(1) Subject to the provisions of this Act, every person has an insurable interest who is interested in a marine adventure. (2) In particular a person is interested in a marine adventure where he stands in any legal or equitable relation to the adventure or to any insurable property at risk therein, in consequence of which he may benefit by the safety or due arrival of insurable property, or may be prejudiced by its loss, or by damage thereto, or by the detention thereof, or may incur liability in respect thereof."

Section 5(1)规定了受保人必须有可保利益,而什么是可保利益就是在Section 5(2)中有规定。这立法规定包括一些什么可节录Colman大法官在The "Moonacre" (1992) 2 Lloyd's Rep. 第501~510页所说如下:"The starting point for consideration of the meaning of 'insurable interest' under s. 5(1) is clearly sub - s (2). This does not provide an exhaustive definition, but it does identify three characteristics which the presence of an insurable interest would normally require: - (a) The assured may benefit by the safety or due arrival of insurable property or be prejudiced by its loss or damage or detention or in respect of which he may incur liability. (b) The assured stands in a legal or equitable relation to the adventure or to any insurable property at risk in such adventure. (c) The benefit, prejudice or incurring of liability referred to at (a) must arise in consequence of the legal or equitable relation referred to at (b)."

在上述所讲,可保利益就是主要针对受保人会因为海上航程(marine adventure)或受保财产(insurable property)的安全到达而受益,或者也会因为它们的灭失、损坏、被滞留而受损,也或者因为受保财产而招致责任。但仅是这一个定义就会令可保利益变得太广泛,所以1906年的立法还加上了另一个要求,即受保人需要对受保财产有"合法或公平的关系"(legal or equitable relation)。

这里的区别可举简单的例子来说明,就是在人流很多的大厦外的街道上有一个熟食档的小贩。显然,如果该大厦发生火灾或者因地震而坍塌,该小贩会受到影响。这就符合对可保利益的定义,即他会因为该大厦的损坏或灭失而利益受损,那岂非是他可以有可保利益为该大厦投保财产险?但加上了要求该小贩要与该大厦有合法或公平的关系,情况就变得很清楚,就是他不能为该大厦投保财产险。相反,如果是大厦的所有人、住户或者融资银行则是与该大厦有合法或公平的关系,可以为该大厦投保财产险。固然小贩对他的每天收入有可保利益,这是可以投保,而且对他自己的收入显然是有合法或公平的关系。但这不是对大厦的财产险,而且能够投保的价值(insurable value)恐怕也相差很远。但这正是符合可保利益与补偿损失原则(principle of indemnity)的大精神,就是不让受保人通过保险合约赚钱,而只能是补偿他的损失。

这一点也可以一个年代很久远的先例进一步解释,它是 Knox v. Wood (1808) 1 Camp 543。案情涉及受保人为一艘船舶回程去英国的航次估计货物会赚取的利润投保,但船舶因为事故根本没有这一个回程的航次,所以也没有这个货物。贵族院判是受保人没有可保利益,因为这一个估计的利润纯粹是"希望"(hope),没有任何其他东西支持如合约。这种在期望上的期望(expectation upon expectation)太间接与遥远,Ellenborough 勋爵说:"This case carries us into the land of dreams; and, if supported, would introduce the practice of insuring a 20,000 pounds prize in the lottery without purchasing a ticket!"

2.2　什么是合法或公平的关系

合法或公平的关系(legal or equitable relation)可以包括许多不同的所有权(proprietary)、合约(contractual)或风险(risk)的关系。例如,与对受保财产的关系是托管人(bailee)、信托人(trustee)、无担保债权人(unsecured creditor)(Waterkeyn v. Eagle, Star & British Dominions Insurance Co. Ltd. (1920) 5 Lloyd's Rep. 42)、担保持有人(这包括了各式各样的担保,如质押、抵押与留置权等)、租赁人等。针对船壳保险,可以有可保利益的除了船东外还包括了许多其他会有合法或公平关系的人士,如光船承租人、期租或程租承租人(其中一项可保利益是承租人责任)、抵押银行、船舶经纪人(The "Martin P" [2004] 1 Lloyd's Rep. 389)等。

针对合法或公平的关系的解释,最重要的是来自贵族院的先例:Macaura v. Northern Assurance Co. (1925) 21 Lloyd's Rep. 333。案情涉及受保人为一批木材投保,该木材是存放在爱尔兰一个仓库。但后来受保人成立了一家公司并把所有的木材出售给了该公司以交换公司股份。事实上,受保人是该公司唯一的股东,也是该公司的债权人。通俗一点的说法受保人就是老板。但由于一直以来的做法,受保人还是以个人名义为该批木材投保,没有把它变为是该公司是受保人。结果发生火灾,该批木材大部分烧毁。保险人以受保人没有可保利益作出拒赔,这被贵族院确认,说:"He stood in no 'legal or equitable relation' to the timber at all. He had no 'concern in' the subject insured. His relation was to the company, not to its goods..."

看来该受保人投保错误的风险,他可以为他的债务或股票持有人风险投保,但他不能为一家独立公司的财产投保财产险,因为公司的财产并不属于股东。但该先例 Macaura v. Northern Assurance Co 在今天看来是被视为是太技术性与没有弹性。这也被其他一些普通法体系的国家法院拒绝,如加拿大法院:Constitution Insurance Company of Canada v. Kosmopolous (1987) 34 DLR (4th) 208。

在近期的先例有放松的迹象。首先在先例 The "Moonacre" (1992) 2 Lloyd's Rep. 501,是与先例 Macaura v. Northern Assurance Co. (1925) 21 Lloyd's Rep. 333 有相同的地方,有关的保险标的是属于一家公司,并非是受保人拥有。但结果 Colman 大法官去与 Macaura v. Northern Assurance Co. 作出了一些区分而判受保人是有可保利益。案情涉及一艘游艇发生大火而变得推定全损。该游艇是原告(Sharp 先生)在"背后"拥有,并且是住在船上。"背后"是因为税务的考虑,该游艇是注册在直布罗陀一家名为 Roarer 公司的名下。但 Sharp 先生在保险合约中却是受保人。在发生推定全损并向保险人提出了索赔后,受到了保险人的拒赔,指 Sharp 先生对该游艇没有合法或公平关系,他只不过是一位被准许使用该游艇的人士(licensee)。但 Colman 大法官不同意,认为 Roarer 以授权书让 Sharp 先生全权使用该游艇,而该游艇的损坏或灭失显然会使 Sharp 先生受损,这就是足够的合法或公平关系。Colman 大法官这样说:"Let it be assumed that Mr. Sharp was indeed no more than a licensee and further that he was subject to no duty of care in relation to the vessel, can it be said that he is in no materially different relation to the vessel from that of Mr. Macaura to the timber? I do not consider that it can. Such a submission entirely overlooks the fact that by the two powers of attorney Roarer had conferred on Mr. Sharp authority to enjoy the use of the vessel exclusively for his own purposes. That was a valuable benefit which would be lost if the vessel were lost. The legal relation in which he stood to the vessel was that for as long as the powers of attorney remained he was entitled to use it for his own purposes and to exercise over it such control as he saw fit. His powers were such that he could even abandon it to the insurers in the event of constructive total loss; a relation to the goods sometimes considered decisive on the issue of title to sue."

在接下来的一个先例 National Oilwell (UK) Limited v. Davy Offshore Limited (1993) 2 Lloyd's Rep. 582,案情是有关北海的钻油平台的建造,NOW 作为一个分承包商是要提供一些设备。而有关可保利益的争议就是 NOW 是否有可保利益为整个工程投保。又是 Colman 大法官审理,他认为 NOW 是有可保利益,因为整个工程发生事故也会是影响他要提供的设备。Colman 大法官认为可保利益不应该只狭隘地限制在对受保财产享有占有权或者所有权。他这样说:

"I remain firmly of the view that the analysis of principle... be applicable to a supplier of equipment who takes no part in construction at the project site. There is, in my judgment, in particular no reason in principle why such a supplier should not, and every commercial reason why he should, be able to insure against loss of or damage to property involved in the common project not owned by him and not in his possession. The argument that because he has no possessory or proprietary interest in the property he can have no insurable interest in it and that his potential liability in respect of loss of or damage to it is insufficient to found such an insurable interest is in my judgment misconceived. That the presence of such an interest in the property insured is unnecessary to found an insurable interest was a point which arose in The Moonacre, [1992] 2 Lloyd's Rep. 501, where the issue was whether the plaintiff had an insurable interest in a yacht of which he was not the Registered owner, or the bailee or the charterer, but which he merely sailed under a power of attorney from the Registered owner. I rejected the submission on behalf of underwriters that he had no insurable interest and I endeavoured to explain that in order to establish a sufficient relationship to the property in question, having regard to the decisions in Lucena v. Crawford [1806] 2 B. & PNR 269, John Anderson v. James Farquhar Morice (1876) 1 App. Cas. 713 and Macaura v. Northern Assurance (1925) 21 Lloyd's Rep. 333; [1925] AC 619, it might in some cases be unnecessary to establish that the assured had any proprietary legal or equitable interest in the goods: see pp. 510 – 513.

The suggestion that there cannot as a matter of law be an insurable interest based merely on potential liability arising from the existence of a contract between the assured and the owner of property or from the assured's proximate physical relationship to the property in question, is in my judgment, to confine far too narrowly the requirements of insurable interest. There is nothing in the authorities which prevents such a relationship to the property from giving rise to an insurable interest in the property of the purposes of an insurance on property."

另在先例 Deepak v. ICI (1999) 1 Lloyd's Rep. 387,上诉庭也有同样的判法。Stuart – Smith 大法官这样说:"In our judgment Davy undoubtedly had an insurable interest in the plant under construction and on which they were working because they might lose the opportunity to do the work and to be remunerated for it if the property or structure were damaged or destroyed by any of the 'all risks', such as fire or flood. Thereafter Davy would only suffer disadvantage if the damage to or destruction of the property or structure was the result of their breach of contract or duty of care. In order to protect the contractor and sub – contractors against this risk of disadvantage by reason of damage or destruction of the property or structure resulting from their breach or contract or duty they would, in accordance with normal practice, take out liability insurance or, in the case of architects, professional indemnity insurance."

该先例涉及了原告 Deepak 在印度建造的一个甲醇厂,由于需要被告 ICI 的技术协助,所以双方达成了协议。但实际作出协助的不是 ICI,而是 ICI 授权许可使用该技术的 Davy。但后来该工厂出现问题并发生事故,而双方的争议其中涉及了 Davy 的可保利益。上诉庭认为 Davy 虽然与建造中的工厂没有直接关系,但如果工厂在建造中受到损坏或灭失,Davy 也会因此而失去他的工作与相关的收费。

以上两个先例放宽的地方就是受保人即使与投保财产没有直接合法或公平的关系,如果因为风险的发生会导致受保人失去他的合法使用权或损失经济上的利益(economic benefit),那么该受保人也被视为是有可保利益。也是同样的理念,所以在 The "Martin P" (2004) 1 Lloyd's Rep. 389 先例,判船舶经理人(ship manager)对他管理的船舶也有可保利益,因为船舶的灭失会导致他失去工作与赚取管理费的机会。这一来,似乎就开始接近上一小段所举熟食档小贩的例子,即他应该可以为旁边的大厦投保了,恐怕欠缺的会是一张文件如合约——把他与大厦扯上点合法或公平的关系。

2.3 可保利益变得宽松与不明确之处

总的来说,宽松对待可保利益是早有这一说法了,可节录 Brett 大法官早在先例 Inglis v. Stock (1884) 12 QBD 564 中所说:"... it is the duty of a court always to lean in favour of an insurable interest, if possible, for it seems to me that after underwriters have received the premium, the objection that there was no insurable interest is often, as nearly as possible, a technical objection, and one which has no real merit, certainly not as between the assured and the underwriter."

近期一点的说法可举:The "Capricorn" (1995) 1 Lloyd's Rep. 622,Mance 大法官是说:"... the present policy is not on its face one which the parties made for other than ordinary business reasons; it does not bear the hallmarks of wagering or the like. If underwriters make a contract in deliberate terms which covers their assured in respect of a specific situation, a Court is likely to hesitate before accepting a defence of lack of insurable interest."

由于商业与社会环境的复杂化,越来越多有关系的人士会有财产与责任风险或其他经济上的利益需要保险的保障。所以,可保利益也在很大程度上被放宽。但还是很难在法律上给可保利益比较肯定的定义,正如 Waller 大法官在先例 Feasey v. Sun Life Assurance Co. of Canada (2003) Lloyd's Rep. IR 637 中所说:"[it is] difficult to define insurable interest in words which will apply in all situations."

其中一个很大的原因难做出定义是法官之间对此也有不同的看法,大家松紧掌握不一致。以 Feasey v. Sun Life Assurance Co. of Canada 为例,上诉庭的 Ward 大法官认为可保利益还是必须涉及受保人对保险标的有一定的合法或公平关系或利益,仅是有预期利益或损害并不足够。他是说:"legal or equitable interest between the assured and the subject - matter insured, expectation of harm or benefit, not being enough."。但 Waller 大法官却表达了一个更宽松的看法,说:"It is not a requirement of property insurance that the assured must have a legal or equitable interest in the property as those terms might normally be understood... It is sufficient under Section 5 of the Marine Insurance Act for a person interested in a marine adventure to stand in a legal or equitable relation to the adventure. That is intended to be a broad concept."

2.4 目前对可保利益范围的权威说法

这是在 The "Martin P" (2004) 1 Lloyd's Rep. 389 先例中,Siberry 大法官在考虑了所有有关的先例后,对可保利益包括些什么作出了以下总结:"(1) Ownership or possession (or the right to possession) of the property insured is not a necessary requirement of an insurable interest therein(可保利益并不要求对投保财产的所有权或占有权);(2) Commercial convenience can be a relevant factor in determining the existence of an insurable interest(商业上的便利做法是考虑有否可保利益的一个因素,这一点会在本段稍后进一步解释);(3) A person exposed to liability in respect of the custody or care of property may, as an alternative to taking out liability insurance to protect his exposure, insure the property itself, and in the event of loss or damage thereto by a peril insured against may recover in respect thereof up to the full sum insured, even if that exceeds the amount for which he is liable and even if the loss or damage has occurred without any actionable fault on his part. If and to the extent that he has suffered no personal loss he will be liable to account to the owner of the goods who has suffered the loss (托管或负责照顾受保财产并因此会有责任的人士对投保财产有可保利益,即使他不需要对投保财产的损坏或灭失负责);(4) A legal right to the use of goods, the benefit of which would be lost by their damage or destruction, may be sufficient to constitute an insurable interest therein (有权使用投保财产的人士对投保财产的损坏或灭失有可保利益);(5) A person may also have an insurable interest in property if loss of or damage to that property would deprive him of the opportunity of carrying out work in relation to that property and being remunerated for such work... (工作或赚取费用的机会会因为受保财产的损坏或灭失被剥夺的人士有可保利益)"

对以上所讲,许多在本章其他地方已有涉及,在此只进一步针对(2)中的商业上便利做法。这里的说法就是英国的商业法律很大程度上要考虑商业上是怎样做的,建立商业法律是要尽量配合而不是妨碍商业上的做法。举一个例子说明法院考虑有否可保利益,很大程度是看商业上的做法然后宽松对待,这可见 National Oilwell (UK) Limited v. Davy Offshore Limited (1993) 2 Lloyd's Rep. 582。在该先例,Colman 大法官提到了在本章第 3.3 段所针对的货物托管人可以为托管给他的货物投保一切险(即使托管人对托管货物并不负任何责任也不享有所有权)的例外与独特情况,就是来自商业上便利做法的考虑。Colman 大法官接下去针对另一种情况就是在一个工程合约内,主要的承建商可以为整个工程投保并把其他分承建商加入为受保人,而主要的承建商被视为有可保利益。Colman 大法官是判主要的原因就是考虑到

商业上的便利做法,说:

"In the case of a building or engineering contract , where numerous different sub – contractors may be engaged, there can be no doubt about the convenience from everybody's point of view, including, I would think, the insurers, of allowing the head contractor to take out a single policy covering the whole risk, that is to say covering all contractors and sub – contractors in respect of loss of or damage to the entire contract works. Otherwise each sub – contractor would be compelled to take out his own separate policy. This would mean, at the very least, extra paperwork: at worst it could lead to overlapping claims and cross – claims in the event of an accident. Furthermore, as Mr Wignall pointed out in the course of his evidence, the cost of a small sub – contractor, be uneconomic. The premium might be out of all proportion to the value of the sub – contract. If the sub – contractor had to insure his liability in respect of the entire works, he might well have to decline the contract.

For all these reasons I would hold that a head contractor ought to be able to insure the entire contract works in his own name and the name of all his sub – contractors, just like a bailee or mortgagee, and that a sub – contractor ought to be able to recover the whole of the loss insured, holding the excess over his own interest in trust for the others."

3. 海上货物保险所涉及的不同可保利益

本书所针对的是海上货物保险,以下可以分别看看受保人的货方会涉及哪些可保利益。

3.1 海上航程的终止(loss of marine adventure)

1906年《英国海上保险法》Section 5(2)就说明海上航程可以投保。这一风险事实上在协会货物条文中是有承保的,就是在第12条:"Where, as a result of the operation of a risk covered by this insurance, the insured transit is terminated at a port or place other than that to which the subject – matter insured is covered under this insurance, the insurers will reimburse the Assured for any extra charges properly and reasonably incurred in unloading storing and forwarding the subject – matter insured to the destination to which it is insured."

有关这一方面这在本书第七章第5段有关续运费用(forwarding charges)部分有详细介绍,不去重复。受保人的货方除了投保货物的灭失或损坏的财产险外,还可以加保这一海上航程终止的风险。这两种不同的风险可举先例 Wilson v. Jones (1867) LR 2 Ex 139,它涉及了当年很重要的工程就是在英国与美国之间铺设海底电缆,让两国之间首次可以通过电报进行通讯。这些海底电缆先是放在一艘名为 Great Eastern

轮上,不过最终铺设因为电缆断裂而没有能够成功进行。受保人不是电缆的所有人,而只是工程承包商的大西洋电报公司(Atlantic Telegraph Company)的一位股东。该保险合约是海上货物保险(S. G. Policy),但加保了电缆铺设失败的风险。Wills 大法官判是该保险合约并非针对货物(电缆)的投保,而是针对受保人对该项工程顺利完工(the success of adventure)可得利益的投保。

3.2 利润损失(loss of profit)以及货物增值(increased value)

大原则是受保人的货方针对商品市场涨跌而造成的利润损失,受保人应该分开投保,而不应该与海上货物保险的货物保险价值(insured value)混在一起:Anderson v. Morice (1875) 10 CB 609 (CA); Mackenzie v. Whitworth (1875) 1 Ex D 36; Maurice v. Goldborough Mort (1939) AC 542。这是因为在 1906 年《英国海上保险法》Section 16(3),对货物的可保价值(insurable value)的规定没有包括利润,是"In insurance on goods or merchandise, the insurable value is the prime cost of the property insured, plus the expenses of and incidental to shipping and the charges of insurance upon the whole."

但实际上,正常的估计利润是经常加在货物的可保价值,把它视为是货物价值的一部分。这就是在 CIF 买卖经常会加上 10% 的估计利润,以保障买方。这在本书第十二章第 3.6 段提到。这一普遍性的做法并没有受到法院的质疑,也估计难以质疑:请参阅《Marine Insurance: The Law in Transition》, 2006, Informa, Chapter 2 "Insurable Interest - Accelerating the Liberal Spirit" by D. Rhidian Thomas at p. 248 para. 29。

会有情况是买方分开投保额外的利润,其中一个原因是买方不希望让 CIF 卖方知道他在这个买卖中实际赚取的利润。也会是因为市场的上涨,导致了在运输途中这票货物的价值大增,如果遇到了灭失或者损坏,买方就会在原来的 CIF 加 10% 的保险价值是不足够补偿。这些情况都会导致买方分开投保额外利润损失或/与货物增值的保险。显然在这种情况下有一个可保利益,另根据 Blackburn 大法官在 Anderson v. Morice (1875) 10 CB 609 (CA)中所说,海上货物保险并不反对受保人投保预计的利润与市场波动带来的增值,只要是一个"合理拟定的保险合约"(properly framed policy)。而事实上,协会货物条文第 14 条就是针对分开投保增加价值如果发生代位求偿权下向第三人成功索赔是要怎么样分配(有关该条文的详细解释是在第十三章第 14 段),规定是:

"**Increased Value**

14.1 If any increased Value insurance is effected by the Assured on the subject - matter insured under this insurance the agreed value of the subject - matter insured shall be deemed to be increased to the total amount insured under this insurance and all Increased Value insurances covering the loss, and liability under this insurance shall be in such proportion as the sum insured under this insurance bears to such total amount insured.

In the event of claim the Assured shall provide the Insurers with evidence of the amounts insured under all other insurances.

14.2 Where this insurance is on Increased Value the following clause shall apply:

The agreed value of the subject matter insured shall be deemed to be equal to the total amount insured under the primary insurance and all Increased Value insurances covering the loss and effected on the subject - matter insured by the Assured, and liability under this insurance shall be in such proportion as the sum insured under this insurance bears to such total amount insured. In the event of claim the Assured shall provide the Insurers with evidence of the amounts insured under all other insurances."

针对货物价值,货方还可以投保其他金钱的损失而不仅是货物的市场价值。在先例 The "Joint Frost" (1998) 1 Lloyd's Rep. 310,受保人为他从爱尔兰出口至中东的肉食投保。除了水险外,也包括了肉食被拒绝进口(这种情况经常会发生)。另在肉食的保险价值,也包括了根据欧盟法规可以取得的出口退税、可以退还的罚款以及其他适当的补贴。这看来是没有问题,Tuckey 大法官这样说:"It will be apparent from what I have so far said that in this case, unlike The Frio Chile, [1995] 1 Lloyd's Rep. 182 (about which more later), the policy insured both the meat itself and the export refund (seen for insurance purposes as profit beyond market value). Both interests were insured in the terms of cl. 1 of the I. M. T. A Frozen Meat Extension Clause..."

3.3 货物的托管人

3.3.1 货物托管人可以为托管货物投保一切险的独特情况

海上货物运输经常会涉及货物的托管人,这包括了仓库保管人(warehouse keeper)、公路或铁路承运人(haulier)等。他们都可以为处于他们托管之下的货物投保一切险,可保价值就是货物的全部价值:Waters v. Monarch Fire & Life Assurance Co. (1856) 5 E & B 870; Hepburn v. A Tomlinson (Hauliers) Ltd. (1966) 1 Lloyd's Rep. 309。保险合约会是根据协会货物条文,或如果货物是金属会以 Institute Metals Storage Clauses (A)与(B)投保。托管人这样做也并不是作为货物所有人或货方的代理人,这完全取决于托管人的决定,也不必告诉货方。

作为货物的托管人,他对这批货物有"可保利益"投保财产险,早在先例 Waters v. Monarch Fire & Life Assurance Co. 已经是被承认,也在 Hepburn v. A Tomlinson (Hauliers) Ltd. 的贵族院先例中被 Reid 勋爵强调说:"A bailee can, if he chooses, merely insure to cover his own loss or personal liability to the owner of the goods either at common law or under contract and if he does that of course he can recover no more under the policy than sufficient to make good his own personal loss or liability. But equally he can if he chooses insure up to his full insurable interest—up to the full value of the goods entrusted to him. And if he does that he can recover the value of the goods though he has suffered no personal loss at all. But in that case the laws will require him to account to the owner of the goods who has suffered the loss... **The fact that a bailee has an insurable**

interest beyond his own personal loss if the goods are destroyed has never been regarded as in any way inconsistent with the overriding principle that insurance of goods is a contract of indemnity."

上述加黑的部分是显示了海上货物运输的托管人可为货物投保(指的是财产险而不仅是托管人有的责任险)是补偿损失原则(principle of indemnity)的一种独特与例外的情况。就是在发生货物灭失或损坏的时候,即使托管人没有任何个人的损失,加上不必为发生损失的事故对货方负任何责任,托管人还是可以向保险人索赔货物的价值。同样的原则也适用在岸上的托管人,这可以节录上诉庭 Waller 大法官在先例 Ramco (UK) Ltd. v. International Insurance Company of Hannover Ltd. (2004) 2 Lloyd's Rep. 596 中所说:"It was common ground that bailees in the position of Ramco and RIL (该先例中的托管人) could insure goods in their possession for their full value regardless of whether or not they were liable or potentially liable in respect of the goods. If a contract could be framed so as to allow a bailee to recover for goods held as bailee even if the bailee had no liability and had suffered no loss himself, it was equally possible for a contract to be framed so as to make it clear that the cover was restricted to covering damage to goods for which the bailee was liable or 'responsible' in that sense. The question whether the bailee had insured the goods of others, and which goods, depended on the wording of the policy."

托管人在这种独特与例外的情况可节录 John Dunt 2009 年所著的《Marine Cargo Insurance》第 63 页的一段话:"These principles are well established, though to say that they do not offend against the rule that an insurance on goods is a contract of indemnity, appears to be a somewhat technical approach as the bailee has suffered no loss either in terms of property owned or liability to the owners of the property, such as a loss of income to be earned from them. The insurable interest thus recognised is, it is submitted, in reality an anomaly or exception to the indemnity principle."

至于托管人看来是没有什么可保利益也不会受到损害的情况下,还是可以对托管货物作出投保的背后原因在 Petrofina (U. K.) Ltd. v. Magnaload Ltd. (1983) 2 Lloyd's Rep. 91,Lloyd 大法官有提到说:"What are the reasons why it has been held ever since Waters v. Monarch Fire and Life Assurance Co. (1856) 5 E. & B. 870 that a bailee is entitled to insure and recover the full value of goods bailed? Do those reasons apply in the case of the sub – contractor? One reason is historical. The bailee could always sue a wrongdoer in trover. If his possessory interest in the goods was sufficient to enable him to recover the full value of the goods in trover, why should he not be able to insure that interest? Another reason was that, as bailee, he was 'responsible' for the goods. Responsibility is here used in a different sense from legal liability. A bailee might by contract exclude his legal liability for loss of or damage to the goods in particular circumstances, e. g.

by fire. But he would still be ‘responsible’ for the goods in a more general sense, sufficient, at any rate, to entitle him to insure the full value... There is a third reason which is frequently mentioned in connection with a bailee's right to insure the full value of the goods. From a commercial point of view it was always regarded as highly convenient."

3.3.2 托管人投保是责任险或是财产险的区分

托管人作出的投保会有情况是不清楚到底投保的是货物的一切险(insurance of the goods)或只是他的责任险(insurance on liability)。这会影响赔付多少,因为托管人可能在有关的托管合约内对损失是没有责任或有条文把赔偿责任局限在一个金额,所以保险合约如果只针对责任就可能不必赔付或赔付很少。如果有争议,这是涉及看有关的保险合约并作出解释。其中有一些先例是针对保险合约内的"for which the bailee is responsible"一词,认为这样的写法是表示针对托管人的责任,所以是责任险:North British & Mercantile Insurance Co. v. Moffatt (1871) LR 7 CP 25 Court of Common Pleas; Engel v. Lancashire & General Assurance Co. Ltd. (1925) Com Cas 202; Ramco (UK) Ltd. v. International Insurance Company of Hannover Ltd. (2004) 2 Lloyd's Rep. 596。

在先例 Ramco (UK) Ltd. v. International Insurance Company of Hannover Ltd,案情涉及了仓库发生火灾,存放在其中的货物也因火灾而灭失。损失的货物中部分是属于原告 Ramco 所有,但也有部分是英国国防部交给原告托管,而原告是为所有这些存货(也包括了托管的货物)投保了一切险,包括火灾险。有关存货,在保险合约内是包括了受保人的货物或处于受保人托管下并且他要负责的货物(Contents therein and thereon the property of the insured or held by the insured in trust for which the insured **is responsible**)(加黑部分是笔者的强调)。

上诉庭是认为该保险合约针对托管货物的损失赔付责任只是局限在托管人要负责的金额,而不是货物损失的全部金额,因为有"is responsible"一词。但针对受保人自己的存货,就可以获得保险金额的全数赔付。Waller 大法官这样说:"Thus there has been a clear authority from at least 1925 when North British & Mercantile Insurance Co. v. Moffatt, was fully considered by Mr. Justice Roche in Engel v. Lancashire & General Assurance Co. Ltd. and very probably a common understanding in the insurance world before that following North British & Mercantile Insurance Co. v. Moffatt, that the addition of words such as ‘for which he is responsible’ restricts liability for damage to goods held by a bailee for third parties, to circumstances when the insured bailee is liable for the damage."

另一提的是如果海上货物运输,托管人是以协会货物条文作出投保,这会被视为是投保货物的财产险。这里可以节录 John Dunt 2009 年所著的《Marine Cargo Insurance》第 63 页的一段话:"It is submitted, therefore, that contracts of marine insurance on the terms of the Institute Cargo Clauses, or the Institute Metals Storage Clauses, are likely to be construed as insurances on the goods rather than as liability policies."至于托管人的责任险,船东作为托管人的责任险很明确就是通常向互保协会投保。至于岸上的仓库所有人或公路承运人,他们投保的责任险会是一种名为货物运输险(Goods in Transit 或 GIT)的保险。

3.3.3 托管人对货物的保险与货方自己投保一切险的关系

最后是讲讲托管人对货物的保险与货方通常会自己也作出投保的一切险之间的关系。显然,在多数情况下,他们是向不同保险人投保。在托管人投保责任险的情况下,显然保险人的赔付也就是货方可向托管人索赔的金额。如果货方已经获得他自己保险人的赔付,这笔金额也就是可以由货方保险人根据代为求偿权可向托管人索赔。

但如果托管人对货物的保险是财产险,加上托管人对货方的损失没有责任,这就会构成双重保险(double insurance)。这方面的问题在本书第十三章16.1段有详细介绍,不再重复。

3.4 可取消(defeasible)与可能发生的(contingent)可保利益

针对这两种可保利益在1906年《英国海上保险法》的Section 7规定如下:"7 Defeasible or contingent interest (1) A defeasible interest is insurable, as also is a contingent interest. (2) In particular, where the buyer of goods has insured them, he has an insurable interest, notwithstanding that he might, at his election, have rejected the goods, or have treated them as at the seller's risk, by reason of the latter's delay in making delivery or otherwise."

这种不稳定的可保利益在海上货物保险会出现,而且也经常被货方(卖方或者买方)投保。货方作出这种保险是不会在1909年《赌博法》之下被视为非法,也不会把保险合约视为无效。要了解这种保险针对的风险,需要简单了解国际货物买卖经常会发生的争议,这就是货物到了卸港的时候被买方拒货。拒货的理由往往是由于货物不符合买卖合约中对货物的描述或货物的质量有问题。也会是由于货物付运的日期有了延误,如提单被倒签(back dated),这被CIF买方在船舶抵达卸港前发觉并拒货。针对国际货物买卖,涉及的都是将来的货物(future goods),也就是买卖双方在订合约时是看不见货物也没有办法作出检查的。这导致双方在订买卖合约时只能规定将来供应的货物是需要符合哪些描述与质量。这一来,卖方到了规定的时间(付运期)提供的货物如果被买方在最早有机会进行检查的时候发觉不符合买卖合约的描述与质量,买方就可以拒货,原因是"货不对版"。而通常买方最早有机会进行检查就是货物抵达卸港或是交货地点。这是英国法律默示的地位,在1979年《货物销售法》里有明确的规定,可部分节录有关的一些条文。首先是有关买方有权对卖方提供的货物作出检查,在Section 34:"Unless otherwise agreed, when the seller tenders delivery of goods to the buyer, he is bound on request to afford the buyer a reasonable opportunity of examining the goods for the purpose of ascertaining whether they are in conformity with the contract."

接下去的 Section 35 是针对买方是否接受或拒绝该批货物,以下节录部分内容:"(2) Where goods are delivered to the buyer, and he has not previously examined them, he is not deemed to have accepted them ... until he has had a reasonable opportunity of examining them for the purpose - (a) of ascertaining whether they are in conformity with the contract, and ..."

再接下来是 Section 35A 针对如果买方不接受该批货物(即拒货)是可以部分拒货等方面。

该法律默示地位对国际货物买卖有很大的影响,因为在这种买卖可以说是一定涉及将来的货物而不是现货(present goods)买卖,现货买卖只会发生在岸上的超级市场或者百货商店。而能够让买方对货物作出全面检查的最早机会,就是船舶在卸港交货后的合理时间内,表示在非常昂贵的航次后才会发生。如果买方在这个时候才拒货,卖方就会非常困难与被动。而在现实中,即使是"货不对版",买方会不会拒货很多时候还是根据当时的市场。如果有关的货物市场下跌,买方有合法理由或借口拒货就肯定不会放过了。这种问题会大量发生在 CIF 与 CFR 的买卖,但即使是 FOB 买卖,由买方派船,也不代表在装港买方有机会对卖方提供的货物有合理检查的机会。为了避免货物到了卸港或交货地点被拒绝接受,卖方会试图以明示条文超越英国法律默示地位。其中最普遍的做法就是在买卖合约中加上一条"货物的描述与质量以装港检查证书为准"或其他的一些"不容许拒货条文"(non - rejection clauses)。有关这些方面的详细内容,可参阅杨大明律师正在进行更新修订的笔者的《国际货物买卖》一书。

以下介绍有关可保利益在以上介绍的国际货物买卖中产生的问题。首先,是可取消(defeasible)的可保利益,这是在 1906 年《英国海上保险法》Section 7(2) 有写明是针对什么情况。这就是买方会有权拒货,但他不一定会行使这个权利,并且会等到最后的一刻才下决定(如看商品市场的走势),但他还是可以为这票货物投保并且有合法的可保利益。但如果真要向保险人索赔,买方还是需要证明在发生货损货差的时候他是有可保利益。

而针对卖方而言,如果发生拒货的情况或是信用证无法结汇的情况就会十分困难与被动,因为卖方被迫要重新拥有与占有(repossess)该批在一个遥远港口/地点的货物而必须要尽快处理。如果是 CIF 或 CFR 买卖,卖方租用的船舶会一直产生滞期费直到货物全部卸下。而如果卖方无法与买方谈妥新的条件让买方接受货物,就会赶紧要找其他买方买下这票"跳楼货"(distress cargo),这往往表示该票货物还要转运至其他地方才能成功出售。这一来,卖方的风险会很大而且没有保障。在原来只是计划去卸港的海上运输,在 CFR、FOB 或 Ex - work 的买卖下,是由买方投保,卖方可能根本没有任何的保险保障。如果货物在卸港/交货地点顺利被买方接受,加上运输风险是在买方,卖方的确是不需要有任何保险的保障。而即使在 CIF 买卖,卖方本来是有投保运输风险,有关的保单或保险证明也会转让与交出给买方,自己没有保障或认为不需要。但由于有可能将来被拒货的危险,即使是CIF卖方或其他贸易术语下的卖方都会要事先投保万一货物被拒后把货物转卖甚至把该票货物运回装港处置的多出来的风险。CIF卖方即使还有原来投保的保单或保险证明在手,也要知道在协会货物条文中有第9条规定了承保风险的终止,这在本书第十一章第4与5段有详细介绍。

这就带来了一种可能发生的(contingent)可保利益,就是卖方根据一种名为"Seller's contingency risk"可投保货物如果给买方拒绝而对有关货物继续有可保利益的情况。这种做法今天在开口保单往往就是加上一条名为"卖方利益条文"(seller's interest clause)。这方面可节录John Dunt 2009年所著的《Marine Cargo Insurance》第67页的一段话:"London market open covers commonly include a Seller's Interest Clause which applies to shipments sold on f. o. b or c. f. r terms and protects the seller as holder of the open cover. The contingency is the failure of the buyer to comply with his contractual obligations, but, for a claim under the Institute Cargo Clauses, there must also be loss of or damage to the goods. Such clauses apply where the goods have been lost or damaged and the buyer, who would generally be responsible for arranging the marine insurance (i. e. , the insurance from the time the goods had passed the ship's rail), fails to take up the documents or to pay for the goods. On the modern approach to insurable interest, these clauses are almost certainly valid and effective as the seller has an economic interest in the adventure to protect and the effect of the clause is to extend the insurance to embrace the category of insurable interest. It should be stressed that the insurance provides cover where there has been loss or damage to the goods and is not triggered merely by the buyer's default. In the usual case the existence of the cover is confidential as between the seller and his insurer who, in addition to his usual subrogation rights against the carrier, will also be entitled to exercise subrogation rights against the buyer under the sale contract."

除了拒货,卖方还会有危险被买方拒付,特别是在托收的情况下。这一来,卖方也可以在保险合约中加保有关的损失,条文会是针对如果受保人没有办法向买方取得货款,保险人会先作出支付:"underwriters shall advance the amount of such loss pending collection from the buyer."

笔者见过好几次是中国的出口商或卖方不加保"Seller's contingency risk"而带来的不良后果。记得多年前中国一家公司以CFR买卖出口价值较高的设备去印度尼西亚,所以给这票货物投保一切险的是印尼买方。但由于某种原因印尼买方突然不想要这票设备,结果在信用证上挑出毛病而拒付。但中国卖方还没有想到办法如何处置这票在航程中的设备,就发生沉船事件导致货物全损。这一来,中国卖方才发现自己根本没有任何保险的保障。结果在与印尼买方谈判后,印尼买方同意把他手中的一切险保单背书并转让给中国卖方向外国保险公司索赔,但最终是失败。原因也不难明白,就是因为印尼买方对保险标的根本没有任何利益的情况下(因为该票设备已经全损)是不能转让。这是1906年《英国海上保险法》Section 51的规定,并在本章第4.2段有详细介绍,不再重复。

3.5 对有关船舶优先权的可保利益

受保人的货方或是行使代位求偿权的保险人向承运人/船东索赔货损货差,很多情况下会需要扣船取得诉前保全。这通常是非常关键的一步,因为在今天的航运市场中大部分都是单船船东。如果在诉讼期间,被告的承运人/船东把有关的船舶出售,或者是船舶因为事故沉没,货方或保险人即使是胜诉也是枉然。如果想直接向背后的船东互保协会,这已经在贵族院的先例 The "Fanti" and The "Padre Island" (1990) 2 Lloyd's Rep. 191 判是此路行不通。[1] 所以,货方或保险人在一个金额比较大的货损货差,特别是责任明确(如明显是船舶不适航),就千万不要忘了尽快扣船取得诉前保全。这一步成功的话,往往可以迫使船东互保协会前来谈判和解。但由于不一定很快会有扣船的机会(如船舶在一个不愿意扣船的小港口或法律不完善的港口长期停留),为了防止在扣船之前发生船舶因为各种海上风险而毁灭,就可以作出投保,而保险金额就是估计的索赔金额或债务。这种情况下,货方是有可保利益在 Moran, Galloway & Co. v. Uzielli (1905) 2 K. B. 555 得到承认。

3.6 对货物的财产险

这应该是海上货物保险最重要的险种,保险金额恐怕也是最大即为CIF价格再加10% 。这在以前的先例 Anderson v. Morice (1875) 10 CB 609 (CA),显示了对有关货物所有权与风险会涉及对有关买卖合约的分析。该先例涉及投保人的买方为一批在缅甸仰光装的大米作出投保。而支付货价的条文是"payment by seller's draft on purchaser at six months' sight, with documents attached."该船舶在装了大部分的货后由于船舶沉没而导致部分货物全损。法院判是根据对有关买卖合约的分析,该批货物的所有权与风险都没有转移给受保人的买方。该买卖合约规定整船的大米都需要装完风险才会转移(这明示条文超越了普通法货物越过船舷即风险也随之转移的默示地位)。买方对这票货物既没有所有权也没有风险,所以不具有可保利益。否则是买方只要承担风险,不必要有货物所有权就也已经有可保利益:Inglis v. Stock

---

[1] 在该先例,由于互保协会的规则通常十分具有保护性,如著名的"paid to be paid",要求承运人的船东先作出支付后,互保协会才作出补偿。这条文被贵族院在该先例中被判是有效,它不违反1930年的《Third Parties (Rights against Insurer) Act》。但注意是英国在2011年4月6日,会有一个新的立法替代1930年的立法,该立法是2010年的《Third Parties (Rights against Insurer) Act》。新的立法主要是允许第三人的受害方直接向责任保险人提出索赔,不必先向有责任的被告提出索赔并要将其清盘之后才能向责任保险人索赔。可以说是对第三人的受害方开了方便之门。至于在新的立法下,船东互保协会的地位会是怎样笔者还没有研究。但对于在货损货差的受害方,也就是货方或是代位求偿权的保险人,他向部分责任保险人如GIT保险人(仓库所有人或公路承运人承保的责任险),肯定是大开方便之门。

(1885) 10 App Cas 263。该先例曾经上诉至贵族院,虽然是不成功,但贵族院的4位大法官是2:2的各执一词。

随着英国法院对受保人可保利益的宽松,这一方面也有了变化。法院不会再分析与挑剔在买卖合约中有关所有权与风险的转移。这在 Wunsche v. Tai Ping Insce (1998) 2 Lloyd's Rep. 8(案情将会在本章4.1段介绍),由于德国CIF买方是以受让人的身份向太平保险提出索赔,而有关的损失是发生在付运前的岸上运输,所以中国卖方自己是否在损失发生的时候有可保利益是非常重要以及是争议的焦点之一。显然,卖方如果自己没有可保利益,就不存在可以转让他自己也无法索赔的权利转让给受让人的CIF买方,让后者有更大的权利。卖方提供的证据显示他支付了货价的30%,而且他非要向供应商/生产商购买这票货物不可。但被告的保险人也提供了证据说明是该批货物(罐头蘑菇与芦笋)是要安全运到深圳之后,中国CIF卖方才会有责任作出支付给供应商/生产商。换言之,在没有安全抵达深圳之前的货损货差,CIF卖方是没有风险与责任,也没有可保利益,所以也不能转让给德国CIF买方任何的保险利益。但英国法院最后还是根据很不齐全的证据判中国CIF卖方在货物发生损失时是有可保利益。

针对这方面,John Dunt 2009年所著的《Marine Cargo Insurance》第4.3段说:"Unlike the approach of the court in Anderson v. Morice (1875) 10 CB 609 (CA), the English courts today are less likely to enquire too deeply as to whether the assured was contractually obliged to pay for the goods where the assured has in fact paid for them, has clearly suffered a loss, and there are no potential competing claimants for indemnity under the policy."

3.7　卖方对货物运输中发生腐烂的风险投保

最后一提的是卖方会需要针对容易腐烂的货物投保在航次中会发生腐烂的风险。这种风险是来自普通法要求卖方提供的货物必须能够承受一般航程的时间能够安全抵达目的地港并预留些时间让买方处置。这是在先例 Mash & Murrell Ltd. v. Joseph I. Emanuel Ltd. (1961) 2 Lloyd's Rep. 326, Diplock大法官是说:"When goods are sold under a contract such as a c. i. f contract, or f. o. b contract, which involves transit before use, there is an implied warranty not merely that they shall be merchantable at the time they are put on the vessel, but that they shall be in such a state that they can endure the normal journey and be in a merchantable condition on arrival; and for a reasonable time thereafter to allow for disposal, or use, as the case may be."

3.8　卖方对易腐货物会被拒绝进口与其他风险的投保

有关易腐货物被拒绝进口的投保在本书第九章1.2段有详细介绍,不再重复。其他货方还会面对风险而要作出投保会是在责任方面,如货方对危险品货物在海上运输期间造成第三人与承运人的损失所带来的责任就会是非常严格与重大。

另对某一些出口商品/货物,会在外国有严格的产品责任,如英国就会面对普通法或是立法(1987 年《Consumer Protection Act》)的责任。这也有保险可以投保,标准的产品责任保险条文是:"Indemnity for all sums which the insured shall be legally liable to pay as damages/compensation in respect of accidental bodily injury (including death, decease, or illness) of any person other than an employee and/or accidental loss of or damage to material property arising out of an in the course of the business occurring during the period of insurance within the territorial limits caused by or arising from products/goods."

可见在国际贸易,各式各样的风险很多,都会需要投保。但这不是一般探讨海上货物运输保险的范畴,所以笔者不多讲。

4. 受保人何时需要有可保利益

1906 年《英国海上保险法》Section 6(1)规定受保人在货物发生损失或损坏的时候是必须有保险利益,规定如下:"The assured must be interested in the subject - matter insured at the time of the loss though he need not be interested when the insurance is effected..."

同样要求可保利益作为是赔付的先决条件也在协会货物条文的第 11.1 条有规定,条文是:"11.1 In order to recover under this insurance the Assured must have an insurable interest in the subject - matter insured at the time of the loss."

这表示了海上货物(或船舶)保险,在投保的时候是不必对保险标的有可保利益,只要是有一个善意的期望。所以在投保开口保单,会是要针对的保险标的如货物根本还没有存在,更谈不上已经面对风险。但在发生损失或者损坏的时候,向保险人要求赔付的话受保人必须证明在那个时候他是有可保利益。这在国际货物买卖尤其是重要,因为货物的所有权是在承保风险期间也就是在航次中不断会转手。

4.1 CIF 买卖在船舶付运前发生的货损货差买方有否可保利益

首先针对的是海上运输中的货物风险,众所周知,国际贸易中最常见的 CIF 买卖都会把货物在越过船舷时作为风险转移的分水线,从卖方转移给买方。这方面可看 Incoterms 2000, c. i. f., Rule B5 或许多有关的先例,如 Fragano v. Long (1825) 4 B. & C 219。换言之,买方即使还没有取得货物的所有权(这会是在稍后卖方交出了代表货物所有权的提单给买方的时候才会转移),买方就已经要承担海上运输的风险。这显然表示了 CIF/CFR 买方在海上运输这段时间,即使他还没有取得货物的所有权,也因为要承担风险而对货物有可保利益。比较困难的是,如果货物在装船之前,也就是在岸上运输的期间就已经因为承保风险发生货损,而在这种情况下发生损失的时间,买方是既没有所有权也没有风险。这种情况在传统的运输方式会比较少地发生问题,因为货物在装船的时候有困难取得一套清洁提单。这在今天的散货运输仍然会是一样,在岸上运输的货损货差会是无法在装船的时候取得清洁提单。但在集装箱运输,这种问题就会有可能发生,在岸上运输的货损货差在装船的时候没发觉。这一来,CIF 买方的利益就会受影响,因为在损失的时候他显然是没有可保利益。

这种情况在先例 Wunsche v. Tai Ping Insce (1998) 2 Lloyd's Rep. 8 发生。其中的案情是涉及罐头蘑菇与竹笋从中国几个不同的产区包括福建与四川用火车、卡车与驳船运往深圳,并在深圳进行贴牌包装后装进集装箱出口去德国。当货物到了汉堡,被发觉罐头是严重生锈、变形与短缺。估计绝大部分损坏都是在福建与四川运往深圳途中发生。例如,是淡水而不是咸水造成生锈。货物短缺估计是被盗窃,因为在岸上运输是散装,而集装箱运输中的封条是没有被动过,所以是不大可能发生在集装箱运输途中。原告 Wunsche 是该票货物的 CIF 买方,他向被告的太平保险公司提出索赔就是以保单受让人(assignee)的身份,这就解决了发生在岸上运输的货损货差的时候,Wunsche 本人是没有可保利益,但作为受让人,转让给他的权利也就是转让人(assignor)的权利。转让人在 CIF 买卖就应该是卖方,显然在岸上发生的货损货差,该卖方应是有所有权或/与占有或/与风险,肯定有可保利益。在《Arnould's Law of Marine Insurance and Average》, 15 edn, Vol. 3,288 与 291 段有说明 CIF 买方通常是以受让人而非买方的身份向保险人索赔。

4.2　CIF 买方以受让人的身份向保险公司索赔存在的问题与补救

但 CIF 买方以受让人的身份向保险公司索赔也会在理论上有另一个问题。这就是在货物运输的后期,CIF 卖方已经把所有权以及风险全部转移给了买方,就不存在转让的权利。这是在 1906 年《英国海上保险法》Section 51:

"Assured who has no interest cannot assign

Where the assured has parted with or lost his interest in the subject - matter insured, and has not, before or at the time of so doing, expressly or impliedly agreed to assign the policy, any subsequent assignment of the policy is inoperative:

Provided that nothing in this section affects the assignment of a policy after loss."

这一危险在 John Dunt 2009 年所著的《Marine Cargo Insurance》第 64 页的脚注 53 也有提到说:"Where loss of or damage to cargo has occurred after transfer of risk and property, the seller will have neither risk nor property and therefore no insurable interest to assign to the buyer. In theory it is open to the insurers to argue that as the assignor had no interest at the time of the loss the assignee has no claim wearing the assignor's hat and therefore has no claim at all unless he is also an 'Assured' in his own right."

笔者还经历过其他千变万化的情况,如在 CIF 买卖合约中有条文明确规定货物一装上船舶,所有权与风险都转让给买方。但实际的做法是卖方事后通过信用证的结汇把装船提单与保单背书转让给买方。但考虑到卖方已经根据合约明示条文把所有权与风险转移给买方,他就不能够有效转让保险权益。

这一个问题可以扩大在保险合约中受保人的定义解决。这在开口保单就已经介绍过受保人的定义是非常广泛的。更明确的是在协会货物条文 1/1/09 第 15.1 条是把受让人也加进来作为共同受保人说:"covers the Assured which includes the person claiming indemnity either as the person by or on whose behalf the contract of insurance was effected or as an assignee"。注意该条文在 1/1/82 的版本中是没有。有了这第 15.1 条,CIF 买方是可以受让人与受保人的身份向保险人索赔货损货差,不论是在运输过程的哪一段发生。

4.3 CFR/FOB 买卖在船舶付运前发生的货损货差买方有否可保利益

在 CFR/FOB 的买卖中,货损货差发生在付运之前的岸上运输问题会是更大。这是因为在这种买卖保险是由买方投保,而不是来自卖方通过背书保单或是保险证明转让有关保险利益。这种问题也是在集装箱运输里特别严重,因为传统运输方式下,货物在装船前如果已经发生货损货差就通常取不到清洁提单,但集装箱运输在装船前发生的货损货差就有可能不被发现。在澳大利亚的先例 New South Wales Leather Pty Ltd. v. Vanguard Insurance Co. Ltd. (1991) 105 FLR 381, Supreme Court of New South Wales, Court of Appeal,案情涉及一票装在集装箱内的皮具,以 FOB 买卖从巴西运至澳大利亚,而付款的办法是付款交单(cash against documents)并且 FOB 的买方也已经是付了钱。集装箱到了目的地,被发现装在其中的皮具在装船前被盗,而集装箱的封条是被一个新的封条遮盖而没有被发觉。

对这种付运前发生的货损货差,FOB 或者是 CFR 买方会有可能根据买卖合约向卖方索赔,因为这是卖方的风险。但由于买卖合约条文有订约自由,不知道会有什么规定。加上还有其他的困难,如卖方倒闭或是扯皮。所以,买方还是会希望知道他能否向他的保险人提出索赔。这就有了问题,因为在发生货损货差时,FOB 买方没有可保利益。有关这一个可能是严重的问题,在接下去的段节,特别是第 4.5 段与第 4.7 段会介绍。

4.4 保险合约中"是否已经有损失"(lost or not lost)的解释

保险合约中"lost or not lost"的规定是来自先例 Sutherland v. Pratt (1843) 11 M&W 296。案情涉及一批货物从印度孟买去伦敦,并且质押(pledged)给了受保人。质押人为了保障他的担保,为这批货物投保了 2000 英镑,并且规定了"lost or not lost"。但在作出质押与投保的当时,大家都不知道货物已经发生了严重的全损。这种情况也可以想象得到,因为在那个年代通讯是非常困难与缓慢的。保险人以受保人在投保时与在发生损失时都没有可保利益,因为货物已经是全损。但由于明示的规定"lost or not lost",法院判保险人败诉,说:"The simple question is, whether it is any answer to an action on a policy on goods (lost or not lost), that the interest in them was not acquired until after the loss. We are of the opinion that it is not. Such a policy is clearly a contract of indemnity against all past, as well as future losses, sustained by the assured, in respect of the interest insured."

这可以说是明确了"lost or not lost"的作用。而且在当时通讯困难的年代,可以说是起到很大的作用。主要是在受保人投保或者在浮动保单(floating policy)或开口保单宣告时,不受到保险标的(海上货物或船舶)可能已经发生损失或损坏的影响。

针对这个规定或术语,也在1906年《英国海上保险法》Section 6(1)有说:"The assured must be interested in the subject – matter insured at the time of the loss though he need not be interested when the insurance is effected: Provided that where the subject – matter is insured "lost or not lost," the assured may recover although he may not have acquired his interest until after the loss, unless at the time of effecting the contract of insurance the assured was aware of the loss, and the insurer was not."

另在该立法的附表针对保险术语解释,也有说:"rule 1 Where the subject – matter is insured 'lost or not lost,' and the loss has occurred before the contract is concluded, the risk attaches unless, at such time the assured was aware of the loss, and the insurer was not."

在1982年前200年一直使用的SG保单就在第一段说明是保险人是承保,不论是该保险标的是否已经有损失(lost or not lost)。

4.5 "lost or not lost"保护FOB/CFR买方在装船前货损货差的先例

看来,"lost or not lost",加上FOB/CFR买方投保的风险的期限是包括了装船前岸上运输的风险,买方是可以获得保障的。这可以以Reinhart Company v. Joshua Hoyle & Sons, Ltd. (1961) 1 Lloyd's Rep. 346为例,该先例的案情涉及一批300捆棉花CFR买卖,从墨西哥运至英国利物浦。货物到了卸港的利物浦,被发现其中50捆有水湿的损坏,由于是淡水所造成,所以被认定是岸上运输阶段发生的损坏,是所谓的"country damage"。这导致了CFR买方向卖方索赔损失,因为是在装船之前就已经存在的损坏,这是卖方的风险。

卖方抗拒赔偿责任,认为在买卖合约中第8条有限制卖方的责任,只是在买方无法从保险获得赔付的损失才需要负责:"... the Seller shall repay to the Buyer any loss not covered by insurance due to such damage in accordance with the cost of the Survey."而卖方认为买方应该投保的保险合约是包括了"lost or not lost",也应该包括船舶付运前的岸上运输风险,正如在CIF买卖的话卖方自己会这样投保。

事实上,买方是在他的开口保单宣告了。在该开口保单,是针对CFR买卖的棉花。而承保的规定或条文除了有"lost or not lost"外,保险期是类似仓至仓运输,显然是包括船舶付运前的岸上运输风险,说:"at and from (including risk of craft) PORT OR PORTS, PLACE OR PLACES IN THE COUNTRIES OF ORIGIN TO PORT OR PORTS, PLACE OR PLACES IN THE UNITED KINGDOM, or held covered at a premium to be arranged, and until delivered into mill or warehouse at final destination at port and/or in the interior."

在一审的高院,卖方的抗辩获得支持,判是"country damage"应该可以向买方的保险人要求赔付,根据买卖合约第8条是卖方不必负责。Pearson大法官的判决主要内容是:"(1) that the damage to the cotton was country damage; (2) that the words 'lost or not lost' covered partial as well as total loss; (3) that it was reasonable and according to the presumed intention of the parties that, if the contract was made c. & f. and buyers had under the contract expressly the duty of effecting insurance, they should effect a proper marine insurance, as defined in the incorporated Rules, covering country damage, and their insurance should be such as to protect, if necessary, sellers as well as buyers."

败诉的买方不服上诉,但被上诉庭驳回。其中 Sellers 大法官这样说:

"The judgment (这是指一审判决) states, I think accurately, (1) that a policy of insurance may be effected in respect of a loss which may have already occurred and (2) which happened before the assured acquired an insurable interest and (3) that the words 'lost or not lost' cover partial loss as well as total loss. See Marine Insurance Act, 1906, Section 6(1) and the First Schedule, Rule 1.

The policy provides that the insurance 'shall be and is an Insurance (lost or not lost) upon... 50 bales Mexican cotton.' No doubt the bales were damaged before shipment but as the insurance was against the risk of country damage and there was partial damage, unknown to the policy holder at the time the goods came under cover, it was a risk the underwriters had agreed to cover as an extension of an ordinary marine policy. I think the learned Judge's quotation from Baron Parke in Sutherland v. Pratt and Others, (1843) 11 M. & W. 296, is apt."

4.6 保险合约中"是否已经有损失"(lost or not lost)的作用

总结而言,"lost or not lost"的主要作用是保障受保人的货方,并体现在以下几种情况:(1)在货方投保(facultative)或是在一个开口保单(facultative/obligatory)宣告等的时候,而风险已经开始,甚至在货方不知道的情况下货物已经发生了货损货差(所以也不存在自动披露的问题),保险的赔付也不会因为发生损失的时候货方没有可保利益而受到影响。(2)允许受保人的买方可以在货损货差后才取得货物所有权,依然对以前发生的货损货差获得赔付。这种情况在国际货物买卖经常会有,如货物在还有一天才到卸港的时候才被转卖给最后的收货人。(3)在货物付运前岸上运输发生货损货差,但 CFR/FOB 买方不能或不想拒绝货物如卖方倒闭或索赔有困难。(4)在卸港或交货地点才发觉的货损货差,如果买方在保险合约有举证的责任,其中包括证明在损失的时候他有可保利益,会在货损货差难证明发生在运输期间的哪一个时段面对困难。但如果有了"lost or not lost"的规定就可以避免。

对以上四种情况,前两种在 John Dunt 2009 年所著的《Marine Cargo Insurance》第 4.18 段有提到说:"It should be stressed that there were two quite distinct issues in this case giving rise to the two meanings of the phrase 'lost or not lost.' First the policy was entered into retrospectively after the loss had occurred without either party being aware of the loss. We have seen a modern example of this in relation to the Wunsche v. Tai Ping Insce (1998) 2 Lloyd's Rep. 8 case. We might call that the first meaning of 'lost or not lost' (the '***late or retrospective declaration***' meaning). The second meaning allows the assured to acquire his interest in the goods after the loss. We shall call this the 'retrospective insurable interest' provision."

至于后两种情况,在 Bennett 教授所著的《The Law of Marine Insurance》第二版之 3.14 段有针对说:"'lost or not lost' wording provides the solution to a problem that may confront a buyer of goods on FOB terms. Such a buyer acquires an insurable interest in the goods on their loading on board the carrying vessel. However, in two situations the buyers may wish to claim on a cargo policy even though no loss can be proved to have occurred at a time when the buyer had an insurable interest. First, where it is established that the loss occurred before loading, the buyer may wish to claim on insurance cover either because the loss does not justify rejection of the goods or the buyer has paid in advance and the seller is now insolvent. Secondly, it may be impossible to determine when the loss occurred so that the buyer cannot prove a breach of contract by the seller. In either case, provided it can be established that the loss occurred during the contractual period of cover, the buyer can recover if the policy contained a 'lost or not lost' clause and the proviso to section 6(1) is satisfied."

4.7 1982 年与 2009 年协会货物条文没有"lost or not lost"的规定

已经提到在 SG 保单中有明示规定"lost or not lost",另在 1963 年协会货物条文(这是合并在 SG 保单)中的第 1 条,就是著名的"仓到仓"条文,名为"Transit Clause (incorporating Warehouse to Warehouse Clause)"。这一来,根据先例 Reinhart Company v. Joshua Hoyle & Sons, Ltd. (1961) 1 Lloyd's Rep. 346,CFR/FOB 的买方就应该在整个仓到仓运输期间发生货损货差都是可以得到赔付而不管他是否在发生损失的时候有否可保利益。

但到了 1982 年有了新的协会货物条文并且以 Lloyd's Marine Policy 替代了 SG 保单后,再也没有"lost or not lost"的规定。这一情况在 2009 年协会货物条文也没有变化。而代取"lost or not lost"规定的是第 11 条:

"11.1 In order to recover under this insurance the Assured must have an insurable interest in the subject – matter insured at the time of the loss.

11.2 Subject to Clause 11.1 above, the Assured shall be entitled to recover for insured loss occurring during the period covered by this insurance, notwithstanding that the loss occurred before the contract of insurance was concluded, unless the Assured were aware of the loss and the insurers were not..."

表面看来,11.2 条是"lost or not lost"的规定,但其实不是。它只是提供给了受保人一半的保障。这保障就是在保险合约还没有约定与生效前,如果投保的货物已经发生了货损货差,这是会保障受保人的。但这只是针对本章 4.6 段所提到的第一种保障,也就是在 John Dunt 2009 年所著的《Marine Cargo Insurance》第 4. 18 段有提到“late or retrospective declaration”的保障。但它却不能保障第二种的“retrospective insurable interest”,特别在第 11. 2 条前面的加黑部分就说明是“取决于”(subject to)第 11. 1 条,也就是说,在发生损失的时候,受保人除了第一种保障是必须有可保利益才可以索赔。看来,伦敦市场的保险人对先例 Reinhart Company v. Joshua Hoyle & Sons, Ltd. (1961) 1 Lloyd's Rep. 346 是不满意,所以在 1982 年与 2009 年的协会货物条文通过明示规定改变了 SG 保单加 1963 年协会货物条文所提供的保障。显然这会是影响 CFR/FOB 买方在装船前发生的损失,特别在集装箱的运输。

这方面的危险在 John Dunt 2009 年所著的《Marine Cargo Insurance》第 4. 19 段有提出说:“It is clear from the above (协会货物条文第 11 条) that it is only the first meaning of ‘lost or not lost’ (the ‘late or retrospective declaration’ meaning) that is available to the assured. Clause 11. 2 is ‘subject to’ the overriding requirement in clause 11. 1 that the assured must have an insurable interest at the time of the loss. Accordingly, the Institute Cargo Clauses do not allow for the retrospective acquisition of an insurable interest. As we have seen, this cover was previously provided under the SG Form ‘lost or not lost’ provision and the provision to section 6(1) of the Marine Insurance Act 1906. It was also provided under the Institute Cargo Clause (All Risks) 1/1/63, but was withdrawn in the 1/1/82 Clauses and was not reinstated when the Clauses were revised and reissued in 2009.”

另在 Bennett 教授所著的《The Law of Marine Insurance》第二版之 3. 15 段也有同样的说法针对 1982 年的协会货物条文(它没有针对 2009 年的协会货物条文是因为该书在 2008 年出版的时候新的条文还没有出现,但反正是没有任何改变):“The now obsolete SG policy, used by the London market until the early 1980s, included ‘lost or not lost’ wording. The modern Institute cargo clauses do not. Instead, clause 11. 2 provides as follows: ‘Subject to 11. 1 above, the Assured shall be entitled to recover for insured loss occurring during the period covered by this insurance, notwithstanding that the loss occurred before the contract of insurance was concluded, unless the Assured were aware of the loss and the Underwriters were not.’ This sub – clause is not a ‘lost or not lost’ clause. Although it resembles the proviso to section 6(1) (1906 年《英国海上保险法》) to some extent, it provides exclusively for a conditional, retrospective attachment of risk. The policy covers pre – formation loss sustained during the contractual period of cover, provided the assured did not possess an information advantage at the time the contract was concluded. However, the opening words to clause 11. 2 state specifically that it is subject to clause 11. 1, which is. As noted above, expressly requires the assured to have an insurable interest at the time of loss.”

最后可举澳大利亚的先例 New South Wales Leather Pty Ltd. v. Vanguard Insurance Co. Ltd. (1991) 105 FLR 381, Supreme Court of New South Wales, Court of Appeal,案情在本章4.3段有介绍,最终被澳大利亚法院判是FOB买方对付运之前的货物损失是没有所有权或风险,是没有可保利益的,除非保险合约条文是给予更广泛的保障,但这只是在以前的SG保单与1963年的协会货物条文才有的。

第四章　保险合约的解释

1. 序言

保险合约与所有其他的合约一样，保险人与受保人之间有了争议，最重要的就是怎么解释保险合约的有关条文或协调所有有关但看来有矛盾的条文给出整体的解释。涉及协会货物条文（Institute Cargo Clauses），由于它是由精通业务的专业人士在深思熟虑后拟定出来的，所以估计会比较少争议。这等于是很著名商会或者机构（如国际商会或 BIMCO）拟定的格式合约。但不表示这种协会货物条文或标准条文不会产生争议并导致诉讼，而经过诉讼被发觉或被法院判定是标准条文有缺陷后，拟定条文的机构有可能会相应的作出改善。此外是随着业务的发展与改变，协会货物条文与标准格式合约本来是十分完善也会变的有欠缺，因此也是需要随着时代改进的。

即使是拟定得比较好的协会货物条文，毕竟只是一个保险合约中部分合并的内容。而在一个货物保险合约，在今天的做法就是在第一章介绍的开口/预约保单（open cover）。这里就会有很多千变万化的条文针对受保人的业务要求与保险人愿意承担的风险。这些条文都没有标准格式或文字，通常只是由双方当事人自己拟定或在涉及保险经纪人时，由保险经纪人作出建议。这一来，一份货物保险合约本质上与租约的拟定就十分接近。而显然这种条文更加容易产生争议，需要法院或者仲裁庭作出解释，这种案例实际上有不少。

解释合约，大家是可以参阅笔者于 2007 年所著的《合约的解释》一书。在这里只一提该书有提到法院或仲裁庭解释合约条文，主要的目的是客观找出双方订约的意图。这一个做法以前主要从双方所选择的措辞与文字中找出它们所能表达出来的意图（contractual intention as expressed）。换言之，合约怎么样写就怎么样解释，而且是比较严格的解释。但最近的三四十年来，英国法院在这方面有了改变。现在解释商业合约的侧重点是在尽量找出商业上看来是合理的解释，而且尽量考虑订约时双方都了解的背景（surrounding circumstances）与语境（factual matrix）。这种解释合约的做法，可称为是“目的解释”（purposive construction）、“本质解释”（contextual construction）、“商业解释”（commercial construction）或“自由解释”（liberal construction）。

在该书中也介绍了这一改变或趋势被明确下来的几个最主要贵族院先例以及有

关的案情:Charter Reinsurance Co. Ltd. v. Fagan (1997) AC 313, HL; Mannai Investments Co. Ltd. v. Eagle Star Life Assurance (1997) AC 749; Investors Compensation Scheme v. West Bromwich Building Society (1998) 1 WLR 897; BCCI v. Ali (2001) 1 UKHL 8 与 The "Starsin" (2003) 1 Lloyd's Rep. 571。

当然在这种做法下,还是要注意客观合理的解释仍要与双方约定的合约措辞与文字套得上。换言之,法官与仲裁员并非是订约方,不能自说自话更改双方同意的合约条文。所以现在解释合约条文,在强调客观合理之余,还是要与合约的措辞与文字之间找到平衡点。

显示保险合约的解释也是同样道理,可举近期的先例 The "Resolute" (2009) 1 Lloyd's Rep. 225,它不是关于海上货物保险而是船壳保险,但道理是一样的。该保险合约中,保险标的是一艘名为"Resolute"的渔船,它投保了 12 个月的定期风险。在该保险合约中有一条保证条文如下:"Warranted Owner and/or Owner's experienced skipper on board and in charge at all times and one experienced crew member."(保证船东[也就是本案的原告]或有经验船长在所有时间内在船上负责,与另有一位有经验的船员。)

从字面上看,保证条文是需要在任何时间渔船上必须有两位船员(其中一位是船东或有经验船长)。事实上该渔船上共有 4 个人,就是船东作为船长,另加上 3 位船员。在 2006 年 12 月 10 日,该渔船出海捕虾后回到 Fleetwood 港口基地把捕获的虾从渔船上卸下。期间,船东去了岸上的渔业办公室办事,但船上的 3 位船员也陆续离开该渔船。其中一位是回家,另一位去 200 码(yards)以外的酒吧喝啤酒,而最后一位船员在不久后也去了同一家酒吧。稍后时间,船东接到电话说该渔船发生火灾,这导致了船东与其他的船员赶紧赶回去。而消防员最后将火全部熄灭,但这已经导致了该渔船的推定全损,因为估计修理费用比保险金额更高。该火灾应该是发生在渔船的厨房,实际起火地点与原因没有办法肯定。能够肯定的是起火的时候船上是没有人的,从表面看来船东是违反了保证条文。

保险人的解释显然就是指有关的保证条文说明必须在所有时间内有船长在船上负责(on board and in charge at all times)。但船东的抗辩就是这样的解释不合理与不符合渔船的做法,比较合理的解释是渔船在出海与航行时才是有关保证条文所要针对的情况。而在该先例中,涉及有关的保证条文怎么样作出解释,上诉庭的 Clarke 大法官介绍法院对该保险合约条文的解释就是采用了上文提到的"目的解释"与"商业解释"说:

"It is to my mind possible to over-elaborate the relevant principles. Indeed there was a tendency to do so during the argument in this appeal. They are the principles relevant to the construction of contracts in general and of warranties in insurance contracts in particular. As I see it, any clause in a contract must be construed having regard to its context within the contract, which must in turn be set in its surrounding circumstances or factual matrix. The general principles are to be found in a number of comparatively recent cases, notably Investors Compensation Scheme Ltd. v. West Bromwich Building Society [1998] 1 WLR 897, where they were summarised by Lord Hoffmann at pages 912H to 913E as follows:

'(1) Interpretation is the ascertainment of the meaning which the document would convey to a reasonable person having all the background knowledge which would reasonably have been available to the parties in the situation in which they were at the time of the contract.

(2) The background was famously referred to by Lord Wilberforce as the 'matrix of fact', but this phrase is, if anything, an understated description of what the background may include. Subject to the requirement that it should have been reasonably available to the parties and to the exception to be mentioned next, it includes absolutely anything which would have affected the way in which the language of the document would have been understood by a reasonable man.

(3) The law excludes from the admissible background the previous negotiations of the parties and their declarations of subjective intent. They are admissible only in an action for rectification. The law makes this distinction for reasons of practical policy and, in this respect only, legal interpretation differs from the way we would interpret utterances in ordinary life. The boundaries of this exception are in some respects unclear. But this is not the occasion on which to explore them.

(4) The meaning which a document (or any other utterance) would convey to a reasonable man is not the same thing as the meaning of its words. The meaning of words is a matter of dictionaries and grammars; the meaning of the document is what the parties using those words against the relevant background would reasonably have been understood to mean. The background may not merely enable the reasonable man to choose between the possible meanings of words which are ambiguous but even (as occasionally happens in ordinary life) to conclude that the parties must, for whatever reason, have used the wrong words or syntax. (See Mannai Investments Co. Ltd. v. Eagle Star Life Assurance Co. Ltd. [1997] AC 749)

(5) The 'rule' that words should be given their 'natural and ordinary meaning' reflects the common sense proposition that we do not easily accept that people have made linguistic mistakes, particularly in formal documents. On the other hand, if one would nevertheless conclude from the background that something must have gone wrong with the language, the law does not require judges to attribute to the parties an intention which they plainly could not have had. Lord Diplock made this point more vigorously when he said in Antaios Compania Neviera SA v. Salen Rederierna AB [1985] 1 AC 191, 201:

'... if detailed semantic and syntactical analysis of words in a commercial contract is going to lead to a conclusion that flouts business commonsense, it must be made to yield to business commonsense.'

I should add that in BCCI v Ali [2001] UKHL 8, [2002] 1 AC 251, at [39] Lord Hoffmann said that, in referring to "absolutely anything" in his proposition (2) he meant anything which a reasonable man would have regarded as relevant. He added that there is no conceptual limit to what can be regard as relevant and then said:

'But the primary source for understanding what the parties meant is their language interpreted in accordance with conventional usage: 'we do not easily accept that people make linguistic mistakes, particularly in formal documents'. I was certainly not encouraging a trawl through 'background' which could not have made a reasonable person think that the parties must have departed from conventional usage.'

Lord Steyn put the general position thus in Sirius Insurance Co. v. FAI Insurance [2004] UKHL 54, [2004] 1 WLR 3251 at [19]:

'There has been a shift from literal methods of interpretation towards a more commercial approach.'

He then referred to the well - known passage from Lord Diplock's speech in the Antaios case quoted by Lord Hoffmann as part of his proposition (5) and to a statement of his own from the Mannai Investment case, which was also referred to by Lord Hoffmann, and concluded that '[t]he tendency should therefore be against literalism'.

As Lord Hoffmann expressly noted in BCCI v. Ali, none of this is to say that the language is not important. As Lord Mustill put it in Charter Reinsurance v. Fagan [1997] AC 313 at page 384C - D:

'Subject to [the use of a specialist vocabulary] the inquiry will start, and usually finish, by asking what is the ordinary meaning of the words used.'

I should also refer to this further proposition, which was relied upon by the judge at [26], which is stated by Lord Mustill at page 388C, after referring to Lord Reid's well - known statement in Wickman Machine Tool Sales Ltd. v. Schuler AG [1974] AC 235, 251 that the more unreasonable the result, the more unlikely it is that the parties can have intended it, and if they do intend it the more necessary it is that they should make their meaning clear:

'This practical rule of thumb ... must however have its limits. There comes a point at which the court should remind itself that the task is to discover what the parties meant from what they have said, and that to force upon the words a meaning which they cannot fairly bear is to substitute for the bargain actually made one which the court believes could better have been made. This is an illegitimate role for the court.'"

在进一步探讨英国高院与上诉庭怎么样解释 The "Resolute"（2009）1 Lloyd's Rep. 225 先例中的保证条文前，可以介绍另一个案情看来十分接近的先例：The "Newfoundland Explorer"（2006）Lloyd's Rep. IR 704。该先例涉及的是一艘游艇，有关的保证条文是"Warranted vessel fully crewed at all times"。由于是一艘游艇，停泊的时候根本不涉及任何工作，所以游艇上工作人员需要更少，只有1位船长。但该船长暂时离开该游艇回他15公里外的家里，就在此期间，游艇因为发电机发热而发生火灾。Gross 大法官判是所有时间或24小时都需要至少1位船员在游艇上是不合理与不实际的解释，否则该船员或者船长非常短暂离开游艇检查船舶的缆绳也会变成是违反保证。结果判是该保证条文的解释不适用在该船员暂时离开游艇，如由于紧急事故需要他离开，或是暂时离开为了履行他的职务（如为游艇购买必需品）或相关活动，说："The warranty obliged the defendant to keep at least one crew member on board the vessel 24 hours a day, subject to: (i) emergencies rendering his departure necessary; or (ii) necessary temporary departures for the purpose of performing his crewing duties or other related activities."

现在回到先例 The "Resolute"（2009）1 Lloyd's Rep. 225，在一审 Mackie 大法官判是该渔船船东破坏了保证条文。相比 The "Newfoundland Explorer"，首先就是两条保证条文在文字上并不相同。更重要的是大家的背景也不一样，一艘是游艇，另一艘是有工作人员的渔船。反正，在上诉庭的判决，Clarke 大法官是以以下做法作出介绍：

"In the present case the judge（指 Mackie 大法官）held at [24]（保险合约中的保证条文）that the natural and literal meaning of the words is that the owner or owner's experienced skipper must be on board at all times and that there is no ambiguity except, perhaps, as to whether the 'one experienced crew member' must also be on board and in charge at all times, which he said was a consideration irrelevant to this dispute. As to context, he focused at [25] on the parties' awareness that the insured vessel was a trawler with a small crew, spartan living accommodation and the ability to fish at sea for only a limited number of days a year. However, he held that those considerations did not shift the natural meaning of 'wording as explicit as this', save to the extent that they bear on the extent of the qualification to the literal meaning of 'on board ... at all times' which he correctly said that both sides accept is required.

The judge identified Mr Nolan's（渔船船东代表大律师）argument as being that the clause should be read to include 'but only while the vessel is underway or working' and Mr Bailey's（保险人代表大律师）argument as being that the limitations should only be those recognised by Gross J in The Newfoundland Explorer, namely limitations restricted to emergencies requiring departure from the vessel or for the purpose of carrying out other crewing duties. He also noted Mr Bailey's alternative argument that if working was accepted as a limitation, the vessel was working because at the time of the fire the generator was in operation. The judge held at [26] that the qualification to the literal wording should only be that required by commercial common – sense and not a means to arrive at what might be thought to be a more advantageous bargain. In that regard he quoted the extract from Lord Mustill's speech in the Charter Reinsurance case at page 388C which I have quoted above. The judge limited the qualification to the circumstances suggested by Gross J and held that, although the owner and crew were reasonably ashore when the fire broke out, their absence was due neither to emergency nor a requirement of crewing duties. He further held that the clause was not ambiguous and, although he thought that the clause was in a sense inconsistent with some of the standard terms of the contract, that was of little weight. For these reasons he held that the claim failed. "

但该案例去了上诉庭,第一审的判决被推翻。上诉庭对有关保证条文的解释作出了截然不同的结论,认为渔船船东没有违反。其中是 Clarke 大法官认为保证条文主要是针对航行的风险才会需要一位有经验的船长(Owner and/or Owner's experienced skipper)。Clarke 大法官是这样说:

"The critical aspect of the language of this clause is to my mind 'Warranted Owner and/or Owner's skipper on board and in charge'. It was no doubt contemplated that the owner would be capable of acting as skipper, as was indeed the case. Moreover, I note in passing that the proposal form makes it clear that Mr Lee Pratt (这是渔船船东的儿子), the appellant's son, is an experienced skipper. However that may be, the warranty requires that the owner or his skipper be on board and in charge. The natural inference from that is that an experienced skipper was to be on board and that the reason for that is that underwriters wanted protection from risks which a skipper would be needed to guard against. That suggests to me that the primary purpose of the warranty was to protect the vessel against navigational hazards.

That is I think underlined by the reference to 'and one experienced crew member' because, as I see it, the warranty was for the owner or skipper to be on board and in charge and for a second person to be on board at the same time but not of course in charge. That second person was to be an experienced crew member. Thus the underlying purpose of the warranty, read as a whole, was to protect the vessel in circumstances in which at least two members of the crew, ie the skipper and one other, could be expected to be on board. The judge disregarded the last part of the warranty on the basis that its meaning was irrelevant to this dispute. For my part, I would not accept that that is so. For the reasons I have given, the existence and meaning of the last part of the warranty help to construe the warranty as a whole.

As I see it, the principal time when at least two members of the crew including the skipper would be required was when the vessel was being navigated, including when she was manoeuvring. I can see that it would probably be held to apply when the vessel was, say, landing her catch, when again there might well be a need to have the skipper and a crew member on board. The question is how far the expression 'at all times' should be qualified. As the judge recognised and, as Mr Bailey correctly concedes, the expression cannot be given its ordinary and natural (or literal) meaning. In this case the clause seems to me to be ambiguous because it does not make clear or give any indication as to what the extent of the qualification should be."

最后,Clarke 大法官也根据另外一个著名的解释合约原则"越不合理的约定就越要写清楚",这在笔者所著的《合约的解释》第 22 页有详细介绍,包括节录了 Reid 勋爵在先例 Schuler v. Wickman (1974) A. C. 235 名言:"The fact that a particular construction leads to a very unreasonable result must be a relevant consideration. The more unreasonable the result the more unlikely it is that the parties can have intended it, and if they do intend it the more necessary it is that they shall make that intention abundantly clear."

Clarke 大法官认为保险人如果要求该渔船在不航行时还必须有两位船员在船上(一位是有经验的船长),就必须明确写明如"at all times"加上批注是"即使船舶不在航行中,而只是靠挂在泊位,是一艘没有动力的船"以使得对该保证条文再也找不出另外一种解释的措辞或文字。Clarke 大法官这样说:"In these circumstances, in accordance with the principles summarised above, the clause should be construed contra proferentem, that is against the insurer. At the time the crew left, the vessel was safely tied up alongside, as must happen very often. Sometimes, no doubt, the generator was left running and sometimes it was not. If the insurer wanted the owner or skipper and an experienced crew member on board whenever the vessel was left with the generator still running it should clearly have so provided. So too, if the insurer wanted them on board whenever the vessel was left, it should clearly have so stipulated. It did not."

希望通过上述先例,大家可以明白解释合约的困难。另外,还有在合约条文的意思起争议时,怎么样正确运用解释规则作出希望是正确的解释。可以说,准确解释保险合约的重要性在本书多处地方都有提到,如在第六章第 4.5.3 段。

1906 年《英国海上保险法》附表一的"解释保单规则"(Rules for Construction of Policy)与今天的保险合约条文的解释关系不大。这些解释规则是针对已经过时的 S. G. 保单内的文字。但由于这是立法的一部分,所以有关一些目前保险合约还是有的措辞或文字,这些解释仍然适用。如针对海上风险(perils of the seas)、海盗(pirates)、暴力盗窃(thieves)、船员的蓄意恶行(barratry)等。

2. 承诺性保证条文(promissory warranty)

2.1　一般合约条文的分类

保险合约中的保证条文或保证与一般合约的保证条文,虽然在名称上相同,但违反的后果却是有很大不同。针对一般的合约解释,普通法在先例 Hong Kong Fir Shipping v. Kawasaki (1961) 2 Lloyd's Rep. 478 之后是将合约条文分为三大类:(1)条件条文(condition);(2)中间条文(intermediate 或 innominate terms);(3)保证条文(warranty)。条件条文的违反(即使是轻微的违反)可以导致受害方有权终断合约并索赔损失,而保证条文的违反,受害方只能索赔金钱上的损失。至于中间条文就要看个案的不同本质与事实,如果违反的后果严重,它的救济与违反条件条文一样。今天的合约条文绝大部分是属于中间条文而不会归类为条件条文。这里有一个重要原因,如英国法律尽量支持合约的履行而不支持合约的终断。另在现实中有许多合约条文的违反可轻可重,必须在每次事件中看它会造成的后果严重性才能决定恰当的救济。

类似的分类(但没有针对中间条文)也在针对货物买卖的 1979 年《货物销售法》的 Section 11(3)说:"Whether a stipulation in a contract of sale is a condition, the breach of which may give rise to a right to treat the contract as repudiated, or a warranty, the breach of which may give rise to a claim for damages but not to a right to reject the goods and treat the contract as repudiated, depends in each case on the construction of the contract; and a stipulation may be a condition, though called a warranty in the contract."

2.2　1906 年《英国海上保险法》对"保证"的定义

可以说违反一般合约的保证条文的后果应该比较轻微,救济也仅仅限于金钱上的赔偿。但针对保险合约,地位就很不一样了,因为它的重要性十分显著,在 1906 年《英国海上保险法》中有明确规定。首先,是保证的定义在 Section 33:"A warranty.. means a promissory warranty, that is to say, a warranty by which the assured undertake that some particular thing shall or shall not be done, or that some condition shall be fulfilled, or whereby he affirms or negatives the existence of a particular state of facts."

为了与一般合约的保证条文能够更明确地作出区分,在本段的标题与接下去的内容会把保险有关的保证条文称为是"承诺性保证条文"(promissory warranty)。承诺性保证条文在保险合约内的作用是受保人向保险人作出承诺会或者不会在保险期间内做某些事情,或是承诺在保险期间会或不会发生或者出现某些事情,或是承诺会进行一些保险人要求的事情等。在订约自由下,这种承诺性保证可以是以各种不同的措辞与文字出现,根据保险人的要求与受保人愿意作出的承诺而定。针对海上货物保险,这种明示与默示的承诺性保证不是太多,也没有很多的先例。其中在先例 Overseas Commodities v. Style (1958) 1 Lloyd's Rep. 546,保单中有一条明示承诺性保证说："marked by manufacturers with a code for verification of date of manufacture."

2.3 两种承诺性保证：明示与默示

2.3.1 明示承诺性保证

有关明示承诺性保证，其实就是指保险合约中以条文明确规定受保人承诺一些什么保证与保证什么的内容。这在订约自由下，明示承诺性保证可以是千变万化。在1906年《英国海上保险法》的Section 35，针对明示承诺性保证是规定如下："(1) An express warranty may be in any form of words from which the intention to warrant is to be inferred. (2) An express warranty must be included in, or written upon, the policy, or must be contained in some document incorporated by reference into the policy. (3) An express warranty does not exclude an implied warranty, unless it be inconsistent therewith."

2.3.1.1 明示承诺性保证的写法与解释

伦敦保险市场一直以来喜欢用"保证"(warranted)的措辞作为该条文的开始，而且"保证"一词还经常用大字/黑体字强调重要性。随便举一个例子，在先例Vaughan Motors v. Scottish General (1960) 1 Lloyd's Rep. 479，承保的是一个车库每天收入的盗窃险，有关的保证条文是："**WARRANTED** (a) that a complete record shall be kept of the Money in transit and on the premises (b) that such record shall be deposited in some place other than in the safe(s) containing the Money (c) that in the case of unoccupied premises the keys of the safe(s) shall not be left in the premises after business hours and in the case of occupied premises that the keys of the safe(s) shall not be left after business hours in or about that particular portion of the premises in which the safe(s) is /are kept and (d) all money on the premises after business hours shall be secured in a locked safe."

2.3.1.2 明示承诺性保证对受保人的承诺写得不够明确的先例

但条文有保证一词也不代表一定是一个承诺性保证，特别是在受保人到底承诺或保证些什么的内容写得并不够明确的情况。毕竟解释合约还要考虑有关的背景/语境以及合理性(除非写了十分明确只能有一个不合理的解释)，而且是会针对保险人解释(contra proferentem)。在一个新加坡上诉庭的先例Marina Offshore v. China Insurance (2007) 1 Lloyd's Rep. 66，承保的一艘在日本神户抛了锚的老龄小拖轮，准备在购买后开往新加坡作为新加坡与印尼近岸水域的用途。在日本去新加坡的航次，船东以定期保险(time policy)为该航次投保了船舶险。但船舶在中途遇到坏天气而沉没，保险人以船东破坏了承诺性保证(其中包括有关航线)作为拒赔的抗辩。有关的条文是："Warranted satisfactory vessel seaworthiness/condition survey for her safe voyage to Singapore by appointed surveyor – TG Marine and all recommendations to be complied [sic] at owner's expenses [sic] before her sailing from Kobe to Singapore."上述TG Marine的验船师其中的一个建议是有关航线(route)。在新加坡上诉庭，认为该承诺性保证条文内容不够明确。有关航线，上诉庭是这样说："There was no express warranty on the route of the vessel. The written warranty did not expressly mention the route or contain any language relating or referring to the course of the voyage. Further, its terms, by providing that the surveyor's recommendations had to be complied with before the vessel left Kobe, made it clear that any recommendations that the surveyor had as to what had to be done once the vessel was en route would not be part of the warranty requirements."

受保人的承诺或保证写得不够明确,带来对保险人的挑剔与针对也显示在另一个先例 De Maurier (Jewels) v. Bastion Insurance (1967) 2 Lloyd's Rep. 550,投保的风险是珠宝店的存货。其中有承诺性保证条文要求珠宝运输的车辆必须是装有锁与警报装置:"[Warranted] road vehicles (whether owned by assured or otherwise) fitted with locks and alarm system (approved by underwriters) and in operation... Locks and alarms fitted to cars owned by assured by Hartwood Alarms Limited or other approved alarm systems."之后发生了价值高达4万英镑的珠宝在受保人的车辆内被盗,但保险人以各种理由拒赔。双方其中一个争议是该车辆被发现警报装置其中有两个开关间断性出现故障。Donaldson大法官判是受保人没有违反承诺性保证,因为警报装置有启动,而两个开关的间断性故障并没有违反承诺性保证,说:"the plaintiffs say that it means 'switched on' and, so far as the person using it know, fully operative. The warranty requires that the system – I stress the word system – is in operation and it is sufficient for the purposes of this case to hold, and I do hold, that the system was in operation, notwithstanding that two of the contact switches were, unknown to the plaintiffs, their servants or agents, subject to a fault of an intermittent character."

2.3.1.3　违反明示承诺性保证严厉结果的安全写法

有关违反承诺性保证条文会带来的严厉结果,最安全的写法是明示规定说如果受保人作出的保证不正确或者将来某些事情受保人承诺了不去做,承保的风险就自动终断或保险人再也没有赔付的责任。如果把这种救济写得这么清楚,通常法院就没有办法作出另外的解释。如在先例 Hales v. Reliance Fire (1960) 2 Lloyd's Rep. 391,保单中就有条文是"Every Warranty to which the Policy is, or may be, made subject, shall from the time the Warranty attached apply and continue to be in force during the whole currency of the Policy, and non – compliance with any such Warranty, **whether it increases the risk or not shall be a bar to any claim hereunder**..."

2.3.1.4　没有写明是"保证"但被解释为承诺性保证的先例

但是在某些情况下,即使是没有用"保证"(Warranted)的措辞,如果订约双方被解释为有真实的意图去把该条文视为是承诺性保证,也是会被解释为是"保证"。在先例 J. Kirkaldy v. Walker (1999) Lloyd's IR 410,保险人要求受保人提供一份拖带检验(Towage Approval Survey)与一份状况检验(Condition Survey)。这两项要求是出现在保单中的"条件"(Conditions)的标题下,而不是"承诺性保证"(Warranties)的标题下。但是这两项要求只有在被解释为 Warranties 的情况下才是合理的。加上这也是承保拖带风险的一贯做法。

较早期的先例 Allen v. Universal Automobile Insurance (45) Lloyd's Rep. 55，它的有关条文是"The truth of the statements and answers in the proposal shall be conditions precedent to any liability of the company to make payments under this policy."，条文中虽然没有"保证"(warranty)一词，而只说明是一个保险人赔付责任的"先决条件"(conditions precedent)，这被判是等同一个承诺性保证。

在先例 HIH Casualty and General v. New Hampshire (2001) Lloyd's Rep. IR 596，案件是针对一条名为利益条文(Interests Clause)，这被判是一条承诺性保证，保证多少部电视片集会被拍摄。Rix 大法官提出了三个方面看某一条条文是否属于承诺性保证："(1) Did the term go to the root of the contract? (2) Was it descriptive of the risk or did it bear materially on the risk? (3) Would damages be an inadequate or unsatisfactory remedy for breach?"（第一方面，看条文是否对保险合约的基础性重要；第二方面，看条文是否是描述/局限承保的风险范围或者对承保的风险有实质性重要[参见下一段的进一步解释]；第三方面，看金钱赔偿是否足够或者是满意的救济。）

2.3.1.5 承诺性保证条文与描述或局限承保风险范围条文的区别

在上一小段 Rix 大法官所提出的三个方面，第一与第三方面是类似一般合约区分条件条文(condition)与保证条文(warranty)的考验，只有第二个是针对保险合约需要进一步解释它的区别。这可节录先例 De Maurier (Jewels) v. Bastion Insurance (1967) 2 Lloyd's Rep. 550 中 Donaldson 大法官所说："I also hold... that the warranty delimits and is part of the description of the risk and is not of a promissory character. By a warranty of a promissory character I mean a warranty by the assured that a particular state of affairs will exist, breach of which destroys a substratum of the contract and entitles the underwriter to decline to come on risk or, as the case may be, to terminate the risk as from the date of breach. In the marine field 'warranted free from capture and seizure' is a warranty of the former character leaving the contract effective in respect of loss by other perils. 'Warranted to sail on or before a particular date' is, however, of a promissory character, breach of which renders the contract voidable. The commercial reasoning behind this legal distinction is clear, namely, that breach of the former type of warranty does not affect the nature or extent of the risks falling outside the terms of the warranty; breach of a promissory warranty may, however, materially affect such risks."

以上 Donaldson 大法官是以船壳险经常会见到的"保证"为例描述或是局限承保的风险范围或者与一个真正的承诺性保证之间的不同。船壳险以前经常有一条"warranted free from capture and seizure"附在 SG 保单，目的是把 SG 保单中的战争险排除在承保的范围外，只承保水险。虽然有"保证"一词，但它与受保人的承诺性保证毫无关系，也不存在受保人的违反。将来如果发生损失是来自战争险，承保水险的保险人只是不必赔付。但在另一个例子，就是在航次保险中经常会要求受保人的船东承诺与保证在哪一天之前必须开航(Warranted to sail on or before a particular date)，这是对承保风险会有实质性重大的影响。如在哪一天之前不开航就会有天气变坏或冰封的危险，而承保的时间也因为迟迟不开航而延长。显然，两种情况都是用"保证"一词，但只有后者才是承诺性保证。

区分这两种条文有时候并不容易，这在 Robert Merkin 教授所著的《Colinvaux's Law of Insurance in Hong Kong》的 7.033 段："The distinction between a warranty and a clause delimiting the insurer's risk is necessarily fine, for the same wording may be equally app[illegible]ate to the creation of either: Thus a clause by which an assured householder is required to [illegible] failing to do so, [illegible] assured is in breach of a continuing [illegible], or that the insurer is not to be liable for any loss occur[illegible]ile window locks are not fitted. It is perhaps not unreasonable to comment that the courts, in most cases, have construed clause as risk delimitation provisions in order to protect the assured against the frequently harsh consequences of a continuing warranty."

区分这两种条文还是十分重要的，这可举一个先例说明：Provincial Insurance v. Morgan (1933) AC 240。有关的保险标的是一辆卡车，保险合约中有一条说明是"保证"的条文，内容是该卡车的用途只是运输煤炭。但事实上，该卡车间断地被用来运输木材，即违反了该"保证"（如果被解释为承诺性保证的话）。在卡车发生事故前不久，刚把车上的木材卸下。贵族院判有关的条文并不是一个明示承诺性保证，只是局限承保的风险范围。所以不存在保险人可以在违反后自动解除赔付责任，相反是由于该卡车在发生事故受到损失的时候，并没有运输木材，所以属于承保风险范围内，保险人必须作出赔付。

同样有这类争议的案例还有：De Maurier (Jewels) Ltd. v. Bastion Insurance Co. Ltd. & Coronet Insurance Co. Ltd. (1967) 2 Lloyd's Rep. 550, CTN Cash & Carry v. General Accident Fire & Life Assurance Corp (1989) 1 Lloyd's Rep. 299, Kler Knitwear Ltd. v. Lombard General Insurance Co. Ltd. (2000) Lloyd's Rep. IR 47。

另外在其他国家如在加拿大最高院也有过同样的先例：The "Bamcell II" (1983) 2 SCR 47。案情涉及保单里面有一条条文，表面看来明确是一个承诺性保证条文，说"Warranted that a watchman is stationed on board The Bamcell II each night from 2200 hours to 0600 hours with instructions for shutting down all equipment in an emergency"。但加拿大法院判这个条文只是属于一条局限承保风险范围的条文，而不是一条承诺性保证条文，说双方不可能同意即使一个晚上没有护卫员或护卫员在一个晚上迟到了，过了 22 时才上班，保险人在整个保单以后都可以解除赔付责任（The Parties cannot have intended that, if the watchman was late one night, or even missed a night, then the insurers should be discharged from liability for the remainder of the term of the policy.）。这样判也是至关重要的，因为这个先例中虽然在出事故之前的那个晚上，碰巧是没有护卫员当值。但事故发生是在第二天的早上，该条条文是没有要求需要护卫员在船上的。

这些案例把看来是承诺性保证条文解释为局限承保风险，也是反映了法院对承诺性保证的严厉性不满，所以作出看来是扭曲的解释。但这样做会带来不良的后果，正如在 Baris Soyer 所著的《Warranties in Marine Insurance》一书中有关上述加拿大先例说："Thus, it can be concluded that the justice instinct of the judges, in The Bamcell II, motivated them to alter the legal character of the clause in question. However, by doing this they have, unintentionally, harmed the fine distinction between express warranties and other terms of a marine insurance contract. Identifying the legal status of certain clauses in marine insurance policies has [illegible] to the assured by The Bancell II to challenge the warranty status of certain cla[illegible] Without a doubt, this situation creates an uncertainty in law and the unfairness in question [illegible] dy afforded by s 33(3), in case of breach of a warranty, in an accessory to crime [illegible] forced the judges to pull the trigger."

2.3.1.6 对明示承诺性保证写法与解释的小结

由于历史悠久，针对什么才算是一条明示承诺性保证条文的先例还有很多，但笔者不准备多探讨，只希望把一些重点的考虑或精神在上述的介绍挑出来。它的解释就涉及怎么样对保险人与受保人同意的措辞与文字作出解释。也已经在 The "Resolute" (2009) 1 Lloyd's Rep. 225 说明了，由于承诺性保证的严格性，所以解释是要 contra proferentem，也就是说，如果有多于一种的解释是要选对保险人不利的解释。这种敌意的解释也在其他段节涉及，例如在本章 2.3.1.5 段，就提到了 Merkin 教授的一句话："It is perhaps not unreasonable to comment that the courts, in most cases, have construed clause as risk delimitation provisions in order to protect the assured against the frequently harsh consequences of a continuing warranty."

2.3.1.7 现在与持续的明示承诺性保证

其中一种经常会要解释与会带来不肯定的情况就是保险合约中没有把承诺性保证写明是只适用在保单承保风险开始之前（present promissory warranty）或是承诺性保证持续适用在整个保险合约履行的期间（continuous promissory warranty），这到底会是哪一种。它们的区别是显然可见的，因为后者的持续性保证对受保人来讲比较严厉与苛刻。简单的举例就是防盗险，如果有承诺性保证是受保人的相关地点有防盗设施，而且状况良好。如果是后者的持续性承诺保证，这就可能在漫长的承保期间该防盗设施都是状况良好，换言之，就是要求受保人不断维修保养作出检查与有效地使用。但如果只是前者的在风险开始前的承诺性保证，受保人只需要在那一个短时间内符合要求就已经是满足了条文的要求。之后受保人在防盗设施变坏的情况下也不维修保养或置之不理，也算不上是违反了承诺性保证。

现在承诺性保证与持续承诺性保证的区别还包括在其他方面，如保费的支付。在现在承诺性保证的违反由于是在承保风险开始之前，所以，保险人实际上没有承担过任何风险，等于是没有支付任何对价。所以，根据 1906 年《英国海上保险法》之 Section 84(1):"Where the consideration for the payment of the premium totally fails, and there has been no fraud or illegality on the part of the assured or his agents, the premium is thereupon returnable to the assured",保险人是不能收取保费或需要退还已经支付了的保费。但在持续承诺性保证中,由于保险人还是要对违反之前的赔付负责,等于是有付出对价,所以就不存在保险人需要退还保费。

解释到底是哪一种的承诺性保证做法上还是看有关的措辞与写法,会有条文明确说明有关的承诺性保证是持续性。在 Hales v. Reliance Fire and Accident (1960) 2 Lloyd's Rep. 391,有关的条文是 Every Warranty to which the Policy is, or may be, made subject, shall from the time **the Warranty attached apply and continue to be in force during the whole currency of the Policy**, and non - compliance with any such Warranty, whether it increases the risk or not shall be a bar to any claim hereunder..."(加黑部分是强调有关的内容)

但如果有关的条文没有写清楚,就要看承诺性保证在本质上是否更合理是属于或不属于一个持续的承诺性保证。这可介绍先例 Hales v. Reliance Fire and Accident (1960) 2 Lloyd's Rep. 391,McNair 大法官曾经引用了 Macgillivray on Insurance Law 中的说法:"Doubts frequently arise as to whether a warranty applies only to the present or to the future as well as the present. It may be clear that the warranty applies only to the commencement of the risk, as in all warranties as to health in life insurance. Any warranty as to the insured's habits, such as a warranty that he is sober and temperate, would prima facie apply to the past and present, and not to the future. But, in fire and burglary insurance, warranties as to the nature of the premises and precautions taken against loss will prima facie be read as applicable to the whole duration of the policy. It would obviously be of little value to have a warranty that a building contained no artificial heating apparatus, or that a night watchman was kept on the premises, unless the warranty was effective to ensure the subsistence of those conditions throughout the duration of the risk..."(这里是说在人寿保险合约中,有关的保证如受保人身体健康,显然只能是针对投保的时候而不是一个持续的承诺性保证,因为受保人没有能力对将来作出这种承诺或保证。在火灾险与盗窃险,关于建筑物性质以及所采取预防措施的承诺性保证是表面看来要适用于保险合约的整个期间,否则就没有意义。)

但在先例 Hussain v. Brown (1996) 1 Lloyd's Rep. 627,上诉庭的 Saville 大法官不同意,认为最终还是解释有关的承诺性保证条文,说:"In my judgment, despite these authorities and the passage from Macgillivray approved by Mr. Justice McNair, there is no special principle of insurance law requiring answers in proposal forms to be read, prima facie or otherwise, as importing promises as to the future. Whether or not they do depends upon ordinary rules of construction, namely consideration of the words the parties have used in the light of the context in which they have used them and (where the words admit of more than one meaning) selection of that meaning which seems most closely to correspond with the presumed intentions of the parties."

在该先例,Saville 大法官也提到了一个持续的承诺性保证对受保人极度危险与苛刻,不应该轻易作出这样的解释,说:"It must be remembered that a continuing warranty is a draconian term. As I have noted, the breach of such a warranty produces an automatic cancellation of the cover, and the fact that a loss may have no connection at all with that breach is simply irrelevant. In my view, if underwriters want such protection, then it is up to them to stipulate for it in clear terms. A good example of the way this can be done is in fact to be found in the standard printed terms incorporated into the certificate itself when dealing with theft risks, though, of course, these are not directly relevant to the insurance under discussion which was limited to fire risks. The fact that such a warranty would be likely to give underwriters more protection than a warranty as to the existing state of affairs is not in itself a reason for construing a question which on its face is only directed to that sate of affairs, as importing warranties as to the future."

在该先例案情涉及了一个火险,在投保的时候,针对问卷的其中一个问题问投保的建筑是否装有不明人士潜入报警装置(Are the premises fitted with any system of intruder alarm?),受保人的回答为"是"。而事实上,的确是有这样的装置。该保险提供给保险人要求他接受承保的表格(proposal form)是有一条文说明受保人保证以上的陈述是正确,并作为双方之间合约的基础(I/We the Proposer warrant that the above statements are true and that they shall be the basis of the contract between me/us and the Underwriters and will be incorporated into such contract)。结果该房子发生火灾,但被发觉在火灾之前该警报装置是失效的,保险人因此拒绝赔付,也就是说,受保人违反承诺性保证条文。而违反承诺性保证的严厉之处就是自动解除保险人以后的赔付责任,即使发生的事故是与承诺性保证扯不上关系。但在高院与上诉庭,保险人都败诉。原因就是该保证并非是持续性的承诺性保证,所以,不存在警报装置在后来失效有任何违反。

2.3.2 默示承诺性保证

默示承诺性保证是指一些在立法或普通法下强加在所有有关类别的保险合约,即使没有明示条文另去针对,默示承诺性保证还是适用。如果保险人与受保人不想适用,就要以十分清楚且明确的明示条文排除,因为明示条文是超越默示条文的,在订约自由下前者更能代表双方的订约意愿。

默示的承诺性保证条文,与海上货物运输有关的是在 1906 年《英国海上保险法》之 Section 36(承保货物必须保持政治性中立)、Section 39(保证运载的船舶适航)、Section 41(承保货物必须合法)。至于岸上保险,由于没有立法针对,是没有默示的承诺性保证,只有明示的形式。虽然是根据案例法,也曾经试图对岸上保险作出一些默示承诺性保证。如由于海上保险有对船舶适航的默示承诺性保证,所以有判例认为公路上的卡车在运输货物的时候也有一个默示承诺性保证就是适合公路的行驶(roadworthy):Barrett v. London General Insurance (1935) 1 KB 238。但在先例 Trickett v. Queensland Insurance (1936) AC 159,Privy Council 是不同意这种说法的。不过在先例 Clarke v. National Insurance and Guarantee Corp (1964) 1 QB 199 是判超载的汽车不适合公路运输(unroadworthy),也就是说,违反了默示承诺性保证。

针对海上货物保险,上述提到的 Section 36 的默示承诺性保证在今天的和平环境下关系不大。但如果在战争的时候,特别是英国宣布是敌国的情况下,承保的货物如果涉及了敌国就会是违反了政治中立(neutrality)与合法(legal)的默示承诺性保证。

上述提到的 Section 39 是有关运载船舶适航的默示承诺性保证,由于它强加在受保人的货方身上不现实,所以在海上货物运输的保险合约内,都有明示条文排除该默示承诺性保证。这方面在本书中有很详细地探讨,包括在本章的最后一段与第八章第 8.2 段。

比较最有关海上货物运输的是 Section 41 承保货物必须合法的默示承诺性保证,而且这一个保证不像 Section 39 中有关运载船舶适航的默示承诺性保证可以排除,因为这涉及公共政策。为了方便阅读,Section 41 是如下:"There is an implied warranty that the adventure is a lawful one, and that, so far as the assured can control the matter, the adventure shall be carried out in a lawful manner."

涉及货物运输的合法性,已经说过在和平时期很少会出现。但也并非是没有这回事了。如涉及联合国的禁令,就往往会导致有关的货物运输从合法变得非法了。在海湾战争,联合国就禁止了所有国家与伊拉克的贸易,这包括了英国,有关的联合国决议是《UN Resolution 1990/66》。另在英国也通过欧共体的《Council Regulation (EC) 97/338》,引入了 1973 年通过的《Convention on International Trade in Endangered Species of Wild Fauna and Flora》,该公约是为了保护濒危的野生动植物。这表示公约针对的货物的出口除非有海关的批文,否则就会是非法。

1906 年《英国海上保险法》的默示承诺性保证条文只是局限于英国法下的非法,毕竟世界上其他国家(友好或者不友好)的不同法律太多,在 1906 年立法时根本不会理会。这方面也有判决是 Royal Boskalis Westminster NV v. Mountain (1997) LRLR 523,该高院判决是因为其他理由被上诉庭推翻。但高院的 Rix 大法官与上诉庭的 Phillips 大法官都认为 Section 41 的默示承诺性保证只是针对英国法。

这方面有些先例可介绍。首先是先例 Parkin v. Dick (1809) 11 East 502,案情涉及一票货物要从伦敦运往巴西。但其中的部分货物是海军的军火,而当时的英国法是禁止军火的出口。法院判,该整票货物都是通过同一份保单承保,所以整个航程都是非法。结果是受保人的索赔完全失败,而原因就是该票货物的运输违反了英国法,也就是说违反了"合法"的默示承诺保证(虽然当时还没有 1906 年《英国海上保险法》)。

在比较近期的先例 Euro Diam v. Bathurst (1987) 1 Lloyd's Rep. 178,运往德国

的钻石投保了一切险,其中有一条明示承诺保证条文是:“3A Warranted that the Assured comply in all aspects with the laws (local or otherwise) of any country within whose jurisdiction the property may be . . . Should failure to comply with the above warranties prejudice this insurance to the extent of a loss no liability shall attach hereunder”,看来它的作用是把英国的“合法”的默示承诺保证延伸至其他有关的国家法律而不是仅限制在英国法。

该批货物(钻石)的发票上少报了价值意图欺骗德国海关减少税收,这违反了德国的税法,所以判是违反明示承诺保证条文。但是法院在随口说说的判词部分是说明 1906 年立法的 Section 41 是仅仅要求该航程(adventure)不能违反英国法,而没有延伸到外国法下的违法。Staughton 大法官说:“I can thus find no support for an implied term such as the insurers rely on in relation to foreign law. As I have said, even if I had held that there was such an implied term so far as concerns compliance with English law, I would have considerable doubt whether it extended to foreign law as well.”

另在新加坡高院的先例 Everbright Commercial v. Axa Insurance Singapore (2000) 4 SLR 226 也是有涉及这个问题。有关的保单规定是适用新加坡法律,而新加坡的法律基本上是与英国一致,包括 1906 年《英国海上保险法》。案情涉及一票木材要从 Soloman 群岛出口去印度。而这被指称说违反了 Soloman 群岛的《Customs and Excise Act》以及其他的一些法规,原因是该票木材的价值为了少缴税而被少报。保险人是不能够证明他的这些指控。而 Judith Prakash 大法官却针对这个问题,说“the weight of authority in England therefore appears to be that the implied warranty given under s. 41 by the assured is that the adventure shall be lawful under English law.”所以最终她是判即便木材的出口违反了 Soloman 群岛的立法,Section 41 的默示承诺保证也没有被违反。因为在这种情况下,只有违反新加坡的法律(因为 1906 年英国的立法下 Section 41 也只是针对英国法律的非法而不理会其他国家法律下的非法,而新加坡的保险法是移植英国的法律),才构成对“合法”默示承诺保证的违反。所以,违反 Soloman 群岛的立法不构成违反新加坡立法的默示承诺保证。

日本东京区法院(Tokyo District Court)在 1998 年 5 月 13 日也是有相关的先例:Connor v. Nippon Fire and Marine Insurance。该判决也是采用了类似的解释方法,就是说在货物保险中对外国法的违反是不构成对“合法”默示承诺保证的违反。该案件中涉及的保单是 Institute Cargo Clause (All Risks) 1/1/63,其中写明适用英国法。受保人是美国人,他要将自己的私人物品从日本运往美国,其中包括了许多伊朗的地毯。后来这些地毯在运输途中丢失,在进行索赔调查时保险人发觉美国法律是禁止伊朗货物的进口。受保人曾经向美国海关当局披露了这一事实,海关当局也同意不追究此事。但保险人还是想依赖非法拒绝赔付。在一审日本法院是判保险人可以因此而拒赔,并认为美国海关的不追究并没有改变此事的非法性质(it being said that the disclosure statement and lack of measures by the US Customs Authorities did not eliminate any illegality of the past acts of the assured)。但是日本法院的上诉庭以及最高院(Supreme Court)却持相反的意见,认为该运输是无论如何不违反日本的法律(笔者看来也不是违反英国法),所以是不违反1906年《英国海上保险法》的Section 41,所以受保人是没有违反任何承诺性保证。

除了海上保险,其他的一般保险也都是有“合法”的默示承诺性保证,即使这是不属于1906年《英国海上保险法》Section 41针对的范围,但应该是英国的公共政策。

3. 违反承诺性保证条文的后果

违反承诺性保证的严重后果不像一般合约违反保证可以作出金钱上的赔偿就足够。保险合约下违反的后果是十分严重的,就是从违反的一天起就让保险人自动解除保险合约下的责任,而这责任主要指对违反后所有损失的赔付。而且,法律不要求违反与后来的损失有任何因果关系(causation)。换言之,在违反的一刻起受保人是完全失去了保险合约给他的保障。但是对于承诺性保证被违反之前发生的损失,保险人还是有赔付责任的。这是在1906年《英国海上保险法》Section 33(3):“A warranty... is a condition which must be exactly complied with, whether it be material to the risk or not. If it be not so complied with, then, subject to any express provision in the policy, the insurer is discharged from liability as from the date of the breach of warranty, but without prejudice to any liability incurred by him before that date.”

3.1 违反后果的严重性

这一严重的后果可节录一直以来的一些权威性说法,这是在笔者与汪鹏南教授所著的《英国海上保险条款详论》的第325~326页:“承诺性保证的严格性也包括它的违反是不需要与真正的损失有任何的因果关系[参见Christin v. Ditchell (1797) Peake Add Cas 141;Vesta v Butcher (1989) 1 Lloyd's Rep. 331 (HL)]。它不考虑因果关系的原因是把承诺性的保证视为保险人承保的前提或基础,所以一有违反,风险就再也不是保险人所同意去承保的了。”

另一个严格性就是它不考虑违反到底是轻微的还是重要的(Material),在Newcastle Fire Insurance Co. v. Macmorran & Co. (1815) 3 Dow 255一案中,Eldon勋爵说:“... it is a first principle of the law of insurance, on all occasions, that where a representation is material it must be complied with—if immaterial, that immateriality may be inquired into and shown; but that if there is a warranty it is part of the contract that the matter is such as it is represented to be. Therefore the materiality or immateriality signifies nothing. The only question is as to the mere fact.”

再一个严格性就是在违反后也不能作出补救,这在1906年《英国海上保险法》第34(2)条里有如下说明:“Where a warranty is broken, the assured cannot avail himself of the defence that the breach has been remedied, and the warranty complied with, before loss."

这方面的先例可举 De Hahn v. Hartley (1786) 1 TR 343,该船壳保险合约中有一个明示承诺性保证是"船上至少要有50个船员"。在开航时,船上只有46个船员,这显然是违反了承诺性保证。但后来在事故发生前不久,由于该船舶从海里救上来6位船员,所以船上的船员在事故发生时总数变成是52个。但是最终法院判承诺性保证已经是被违反,这是不能事后补救,所以之后发生事故的索赔不能成功。

3.2 违反承诺性保证与违反绝对善意后果的不同

可以多补充有关承诺性保证的严格性是在 The "Good Luck" (1991) 2 Lloyd's Rep. 191,Goff 勋爵所说:"... if a promissory warranty is not complied with, the insurer is discharged from liability as from the date of the breach of warranty, for the simple reason that fulfilment of the warranty is a condition precedent to the liability or further liability of the insurer. This moreover reflects the fact that the rationale of warranties in insurance law is that the insurer only accepts the risk provided that the warranty is fulfilled. This is entirely understandable; and it follows that the immediate effect of a breach of a promissory warranty is to discharge the insurer from liability as from the date of the breach. In the case of conditions precedent, the word 'condition' is being used in its classical sense in English law, under which the coming into existence of (for example) an obligation, or the duty or further duty to perform an obligation, is dependent upon the fulfilment of the specified condition. Here, where we are concerned with a promissory warranty, i. e. a promissory condition precedent, contained in an existing contract of insurance, non-fulfilment of the condition does not prevent the contract from coming into existence. What it does (as s. 33 [3] makes plain) is to discharge the insurer from liability as from the date of the breach. Certainly, it does not have the effect of avoiding the contract ab initio. Nor, strictly speaking, does it have the effect of bringing the contract to an end. It is possible that there may be obligations of the assured under the contract which will survive the discharge of the insurer from liability, as for example, a continuing liability to pay premium. Even if in the result no further obligations rest on either parties, it is not correct to speak of the contract being avoided; and it is, strictly speaking, more accurate to keep to the carefully chosen words in s. 33(3) of the Act, rather than to speak of the contract being brought to an end, though that may be the practical effect."

Goff 勋爵的这段话至少说明了两个问题:(1)违反第二章介绍的受保人是有披露责任或不得误述,否则会导致保险合约的无效(voidable)。承诺性保证的违反表面看来的救济也是差不多,但实际上是有些区别。这些区别是违反披露责任可以令保险合约从一开始或从头至尾变为无效。但违反承诺性保证,只是令保险人以后的赔付责任可以解除(the insurer is discharged from liability),但在违反承诺性保证之前的损失还是需要赔付。这区别就会涉及其他方面,如退还保费。如果违反披露责任,会有可能是在完全没有对价下(total failure of consideration)保险人需要退还保费,但违反承诺性保证就不一样。(2)从承诺性保证违反之日起,保险人的责任就自动全部被解除。这自动解除是不需要保险人的书面或行动作出选择,这带来一个说法就是一旦违反,就不能由单方面令保险合约有效,如通过保险人的弃权或禁止反供,这方面稍后会在本章第3.3.3.3段中详谈。但违反披露责任就不一样,因为它只是给保险人一个选择的权利令保险合约无效。但保险人完全是可以通过语言或者行动确认这个保险合约的有效性。

3.3 可以合法违反承诺性保证的三种情况

在某些局限的情况下,承诺性保证是可以不需要严格遵守的。这是在1906年《英国海上保险法》的Section 34:"(1) Non - compliance with a warranty is excused when, by reason of a change of circumstances, the warranty ceases to be applicable to the circumstances of the contract, or when compliance with the warranty is rendered unlawful by any subsequent law... (3) A breach of warranty may be waived by the insurer."

3.3.1 情况之一:状况的改变(change of circumstances)

简单的举例就是,针对船壳保险,如果从船舶安全考虑如因为紧急情况要去一个避难港口,而该避难港口会导致船舶违反航区保证(trading warranty),这是可以不遵守该承诺性保证。否则,船长为了避免违反承诺性保证的严格性,要与船舶安全作出平衡,这就不是好事了。再举一个例子,也是船壳保险中的航区保证禁止去索马里的港口,但有关的船舶在印度洋被索马里海岛袭击,被挟持开去索马里的港口,这也是受保人可以合法违反承诺性保证的情形。船舶在袭击的半途中因为承保风险沉没,保险人不得以违反承诺性保证为由拒赔。

而针对海上货物保险,可举一个例子就是在1906年《英国海上保险法》,Section 41是有要求航次必须合法的默示承诺性保证。这一来,如果付运的货物是要去一个联合国通过决议要制裁的国家或地区(并得到英国的承认),这就会是个典型的非法,并违反了默示的承诺性保证。但如果是联合国突然撤销制裁,这就是情况的改变导致了不必再遵守这个变得多余或无关的承诺性保证。

在先例Agapitos v. Agnew (No. 2) (2003) Lloyd's Rep. IR 54,涉及的也是船壳保险,其中有一条承诺性保证是不进行烧焊工作,因为烧焊是船舶在修理改装的时候会导致火灾的最危险因素,措辞是"Warranted London Salvage Association approval of location, fire fighting and mooring arrangements and all recommendations complied with. **Warranted no hot work**."事故发生是在1996年2月,船舶在锚地停泊,船上正在进行工程要把这艘滚装船改装成游船。在装汽车的甲板上是要安装很多的座椅,所以需要焊接工作,而焊接产生的火花让附近的家具起火。港口当局命令该船从泊位被拖带去一个附近的小岛。而在这个过程中,船舶碰到了之前出事的另一艘船舶的残骸,以致倾覆并沉没。受保人争辩说由于事故发生时,船舶是在改装的过程中,所以是环境发生了改变,所以根据1906年立法Section 34(1),保证条文要停止适用。Moore - Bick大法官拒绝了这争辩,判是没有状况的改变,说:"the circumstances to which the warranty was directed remained unchanged."法院在解释"环境的变化"时是要结合商业与实务,标准就是看环境的变化是否让保证的内容变得多余或者无关。

3.3.2 情况之二:遵守承诺性保证因为后来法律的改变而变成违法

这种情况很少会在海上货物保险出现,即英国法律改变导致了原来的承诺性保证变的是违法。但它所针对的情况是可以想像。笔者随手假设一个例子,会有保险合约如火险或防盗险经常要求受保人承诺保证安装与维持一些装置,但如果以后有了立法必须在某一天之前替换这些装备而以其他的装置或办法所替代,受保人也就没有办法遵守承诺性保证了。在很大的程度情况之一也适用在这种法律的改变。

3.3.3 情况之三:对违反承诺性保证的弃权

3.3.3.1 允许违反承诺性保证的弃权类别

根据《Chitty on Contract》22 - 040段,弃权分为两种:(1)选择弃权(waiver by election);(2)禁止反供弃权(waiver by estoppel)。看来,第一种的选择弃权可以适用在违反承诺性保证发生之前。但针对违反承诺性保证后不应选择弃权,因为受保人一违反承诺性保证就自动解除保险人以后的赔付责任,这是不存在可以通过保险人单方面的选择改变。所以不存在"选择弃权"的说法。在先例The"Good Luck"(1991) 2 Lloyd's Rep. 191,Goff勋爵说:"When as s. 34(3) contemplates, the insurer waives a breach of a promissory warranty, the effect is that, to the extent of the waiver, the insurer cannot rely upon the breach as having discharged him from liability. This is a very different thing from saying that discharge of the insurer from liability is dependent upon a decision by the insurer."

在J. Kirkaldy & Sons Ltd. v. Walker (1999) Lloyd's Rep. IR 410,Longmore大法官说:"Section 33 of the MIA 1906 provides for the insurer to be discharged from liability as from the date of breach of warranty. It is, therefore apparent that no question of election arises although by Section 34(3) the insurer may waive the breach. Since the breach of warranty does not give rise to any election by the insurer, eg, to choose to keep the contract on foot, the doctrine of waiver by election has no application."

另在The"Milasan" (2000) 2 Lloyd's Rep. 458,Aikens大法官也认为是违反承诺性保证后没有选择弃权(waiver by election)。以下进一步探讨这方面的问题。

3.3.3.2 违反前的保险人选择弃权

保险人是可以在非常有限的情况下构成对违反承诺性保证的弃权,这是在1906年《英国海上保险法》之Section 34(3):"A breach of warranty may be waived by the insurer."但这是要求保险人在违反承诺性保证之前作出十分明确无误的语言或行为来表示这一点,很难成立保险人的禁止反供的弃权可以在较近期的一个案例看到,就是Kirkaldy & Sons Ltd. v. Walker (1999) Lloyd's Rep. IR 410。案情是有关一个拖带的保险合约中有一个承诺性保证,就是需要在拖带前进行一个拖带检验(Towage Survey)与一个状况检验(Condition Survey)。但受保人只执行了一个拖带检验,并把报告交给保险人。保险人去度假,他的助手文书确认说"收到并且同意"(Noted and Agreed)。Longmore 大法官判这不构成对违反承诺性保证的弃权:"... no insurer (let alone his deputy) can be expected to carry in his mind all the terms of all the insurances currently operative. It will only be if the insurer (or his deputy) addressed his mind to the question of the absence of a condition survey that any unequivocal representation could begin to arise."

也就是说,因为"noted and agreed"并不是足够的清楚与明确(clear and unequivocal),并不等于是"保险人接受没有状况检验报告也没有关系"(we accept that the absence of a condition survey doesn't matter.)。如果保险人或有他表面授权可代表他的人士作出了后者表示,则这会是十分明确无误构成禁止反供的弃权。

另一个显示同样理念的先例是在 Sleigh v. Tyser (1900) 2 QB 333,案情涉及受保人的船舶因为不适航而沉没,开航前不适航是违反了默示承诺性保证。但受保人争辩说在开航前保险人曾经安排代理人上船检查并认为没有问题,这是对船舶不适航的弃权。但法院判这一检查只是保险人的额外小心的做法,并不代表对承诺性保证的弃权。

当然成功依赖弃权的先例也不是没有,在加拿大法院的先例 Fellas v. Continental Insurance Co. (1973) ILR 558,案件涉及一艘小船要开出航区限制以外的地点,而航区限制是明示承诺性保证。在要开出之前,船东向保险人的代理人查问并被告知没有问题。结果船舶在航区限制以外受到了风浪的损坏,保险人拒赔。但法院判是保险人授权的代理人已经弃权,说:"... the [assured] was led to believe that [the agent] had the power to waive the warranty. The policy itself said it was not valid 'unless countersigned by the duly Authorised Representative of the company'. Facsimiles of the signatures of the president of the company and the secretary appear. Then it says, 'Countersigned at Vancouver BC this 28th day of April, 1970'. Over the words, 'Authorised Representative', [the agent's] stamp has been imprinted... In my view, the company cannot issue a policy to an applicant which on its face declares [the agent] to be its authorised representative, which depends for its validity upon [his] signature, and then turn around and say: [He] was not our agent..."

3.3.3.3 违反后的保险人禁止反供弃权

通常在受保人违反了承诺性保证条文,最安全的办法还是告诉保险人有关这一违反并要求保险人明确同意(最好是以书面)继续有关的保险合约:Weir v. Aberdein (1819) 2 B& Ald 320;Kin Yuen v. Lombard Insurance (1994) 2 SLR 887。这是因为1906 年《英国海上保险法》之 Section 33(3)明确说明在违反的一天就自动令保险人解除责任。如果这一说法是把这个保险合约视为是终断,就表示要重新令保险合约有效必须是通过双方的协议重新订立(reinstate)。

但也有其他的先例说明保险人的表示构成禁止反供的弃权,这包括了保险人明知道受保人违反承诺性保证,但还是收取保费:Holdsworth v. Lancashire and Yorkshire Insurance (1907) 23 TLR 521; Handler v. Mutual Reserve Fund Life Association (1904) 90 LT 192; Acey v. Fernie (1840) 7 M&W 151; West v. National Motor and Accident Insurance Union (1955) 1 All ER 800;(但在 The "Milasan" (2000) 2 Lloyd's Rep. 458,有不同的判法,请看稍后详细介绍)。保险人知道受保人违反承诺性保证,但还是接受一个保单的批注(endorsement),如为了加保:American International Marine Agency of New York v. Dandridge (2005) Lloyd's Rep. IR 643; M J Harrington Syndicate 2000 v. Axa Oyak Sigorta AS (2007) Lloyd's Rep. IR 60。

此外保险人知道受保人违反承诺性保证条文,但还是表示愿意对发生的损失给予保险赔付:Yorkshire Insurance v. Craine (1922) 2 AC 541;Compagnia Tirrena di Assicurazioni SpA v. Grand Union Insurance (1991) 2 Lloyd's Rep. 143。

另是保险人知道受保人的违反后,不作出任何表示,这不会构成禁止反供的弃权:Melik v. Norwich Union Fire Insurance Society Ltd. (1980) 1 Lloyd's Rep. 523;The "Milasan" (2000) 2 Lloyd's Rep. 458;Bhopal v. Sphere Drake Insurance (2002) Lloyd's Rep. IR 413;HIH Casualty and General v. Axa Corporate Solutions (2003) Lloyd's Rep. IR 1;Philips & Co. v. Whatley (2008) Lloyd's Rep. IR 111。

但在本章第 3.3.3.1 段已经提到过在违反了承诺性保证之后,第一种的选择弃权应该不适用,而能够适用的应该就是第二种。第二种虽然被称为是禁止反供弃权,它本质上就是禁止反供(estoppel)。禁止反供与弃权(waiver)虽然有很大差别,但因为在 1906 年《英国海上保险法》之 Section 34(3)只提到"a breach of warranty may be waived by the insurer",所以即使本质上是适用禁止反供(estoppel)但也不得不与弃权(waiver)扯上关系。在禁止反供里首先就是保险人对承诺性保证的违反或知悉并不像弃权那么重要,但是正如《Warranties in Marine Insurance》一书中 footnote 117 里所说的:"There must be some concern with the insurer's knowledge, however, for if the assured believes that the insurer is unaware of his breach of warranty, he will find it difficult to convince a court that he, justifiably, relied on the insurer's not pleading a breach, of which the insurer was unaware, and that the insurer had been estopped."。

禁止反供通常需要符合三个要求:第一,构成禁止反供的一方有某些言行举止并导致另一方产生信任或者加强了另一方对他的相信(belief);第二,另一方在相信的基础上依赖该言行举止并作出某些改变(reliance and change of position);第三,该改变给另一方带来了损害(detriment)。

针对第一个要求,已经在本小段较早的时候举了不少的先例,现在可节录 Baris Soyer 所著的《Warranties in Marine Insurance》一书第 218 页的一段话作为总结:"Accordingly, issuing or renewing the policy after the breach of warranty, or in some cases, advice given by the insurer to the assured about loss prevention in future (after the warranty is breached), may amount to an unequivocal representation from the insurer's point of view."

至于第二与第三个要求也可以节录 Baris Soyer 所著的《Warranties in Marine Insurance》一书第 218 ~219 页所说如下:"Secondly, in order to establish the existence of promissory estoppel, it is essential to show that the assured acted in reliance on the promise of the insurer that the legal rights arising from the breach of the warranty would not be enforced. The reliance must also be reasonable. For example, reliance would not be reasonable in cases where the alleged representation was made by an agent of the insurer who lacked both ostensible and actual authority to make it. Whether the reliance is so reasonable will depend on the circumstances of the case. Pure reliance is not sufficient, as a final element, the assured must prove that he has suffered detriment as result of the insurer's representation. For instance, not seeking alternative cover was held to be sufficient to establish detriment in Hargett v. Gulf Insurance Co. 55 P 2d 12."

另在 The "Milasan" (2000) 2 Lloyd's Rep. 458,涉及一艘游艇的保单中有一条承诺性保证是要求有专业的船长与船员在所有的时间都在船上负责(warranted a professional skippers and crew in charge at all times),而该保证指是被违反。但受保人的抗辩是指保险人一早就知道没有一个专业的船长在游艇上,可是保险人一直也没有任何表示,直到多年后才在抗辩的时候提出来,并且在期间收取保费,这构成弃权。但 Aikens 大法官说是违反承诺性保证后适用的是禁止反供的弃权,而这是需要保险人作出清楚与无可争辩的言行举止,并且该言行举止使受保人产生依赖。但在该先例,受保人根本没有指出保险人什么言行举止,只能说他早就知道这一违反,这不足以构成禁止反供。Aikens 大法官这样说:

"That leaves the argument of the claimants that the insurers have waived compliance with the warranty by (i) accepting the second instalment of the premium for the policy in November, 1995 despite their knowledge that there had been no professional skipper on board from May 1 to July 1, 1995; and (ii) not repudiating liability for breach of the warranty until the point was taken in the re – re – amended points of defence in October, 1999.

As I understand pars. 96 to 100 of the claimants' closing submissions, they accept that the doctrine of 'waiver by election' is not applicable to a breach of a warranty in a marine insurance contract. But they do argue that there has been a waiver by estoppel ... Waiver by estoppel requires proof of a clear and unequivocal representation by the representor and reliance by the person to whom the representation was made. There is no plea of an express representation in the re – re – amended points of reply... The only points taken are that the insurers knew of the lack of a professional skipper by July 27, 1995 at the latest, yet they did not rely on the breach of warranty until five years later in their re – re – amended points of defence. No particulars of reliance by the claimants are pleaded. There is nothing in the witness statement of Sheikh Khalid(受保人的证人,也就是游艇的主人)to suggest that he relied on the defendants' demand for the second instalment of the premium as a representation that they were waiving compliance with the warranty. Nor is there any statement from him that he regarded the failure of the insurers to take the 'warranty point' as a representation that they waived compliance with it, or that he relied upon this failure. Even if it had been pleaded, it is very difficult to see what 'reliance' there could have been in fact by Sheikh Khalid. In those circumstances the waiver argument must fail. "

3.4 保险合约的承诺性保证条文与免责条文

保险合约里需要有承诺性保证是因为保险人只是靠受保人在接受承保前作出全面披露与不误述是不足够保障的,因为所能针对的只是当时的情况。如一个盗窃险(burglar)的承保,受保人披露或作出正确的陈述是在投保的当时,有一套完善的防盗设施。但之后的保险期间,英国保险法律是不反对受保人增加承保的风险,只要承保风险的本质没有改变。笔者不妨先讲讲这个重要的方面。

3.4.1 英国法律不反对受保人增加承保风险,只要不改变风险本质

这一法律地位可先举一个很古老的先例 Baxendale v. Harvey (1859) K&N 445,涉及了火灾险,Frederick Pollock 大法官是说受保人可以在家里燃点任何他喜欢数目的蜡烛,也不会影响保险合约,即使每支蜡烛都增加了一点火灾的风险:"The insurer when it has had notice of the risk is not entitled to any notice by reason of the increase in danger. A person who insures may light as many candles as he pleases in his house, though each additional candle increases the danger of setting the house on fire. "

在同样的道理下,很容易推想如果在人寿险或意外险,是不存在受保人有默示保证在生活不健康或喜欢做冒险的事情时导致他的保险合约无效或者违约。也可以推想在盗窃险中受保人在保险合约生效后的履行期间可以让防盗设施失效,不维修保养,甚至作出改装。

只要受保人没有到蓄意恶行(wilful misconduct)的程度,因为这在 1906 年《英国海上保险法》Section 55(2)(a)是保险人不必赔付的损失,盗窃险的赔付还是保险人没有办法赖掉的。而仅是对该防盗设施不维修保养或作出些改装,这些行动恐怕与受保人构成蓄意恶行还差得很远。明显的蓄意恶行会是受保人在火险去放火或盗窃险去监守自盗等。也可以从另一个角度看,受保人是违反了本书第二章的绝对善意(utmost good faith)。

但英国法院反对的是受保人在履行合约时改变风险本质,所以在这方面的争议法院通常会问:"这是否是一个与原来双方同意的保险合约本质上不同的合约?"(Is it a different contract than the one originally entered into?)

但在现实的做法中找出什么是增加风险与什么是改变风险本质的分水线不容易

确定。一个方面是针对财产保险,受保人长期作出了有关的用途改变。如在先例 Farnham v. Royal Insurance (1976) 2 Lloyd's Rep. 437,本来说明的用途是储存货物,但结果是变成用来修理集装箱并涉及烧焊。针对船壳险,本来是一条油船被改装为矿砂船,即使承保的风险不会因此有所增加,但本质上的改变还是明显。

而针对海上货物保险,在本书第十一章会举一些有关改变风险本质的例子,如在 6.3 小段的船舶不合理绕航,9 小段的开航前不准备走承保航次的"鬼船"。

3.4.2 以承诺性保证、先决条件与免责条文避免受保人增加承保风险

由于法律默示地位对什么是增加风险与什么是改变风险本质的分水线不明确,加上保险人也不想受保人任意增加承保风险,所以最妥善的办法就是以明示条文不让受保人增加承保风险。这种明示条文可以是以承诺性保证(promissory warranty)、先决条件(condition precedent)与免责条文(exclusion clause)达到这个目的。

举一些例子,在先例 Exchange Theatre Ltd. v. Iron Trades Mutual Insurance Co. Ltd. (1984) 1 Lloyd's Rep. 149,针对的是一个娱乐场所的财产险,有条件条文是:"This policy shall be avoided with respect to any item thereof in regard to which there be any alteration after the commencement of this insurance whereby the risk of destruction is increased."

针对岸上财产险如工厂或者娱乐场所,笔者还见过另一条细致与苛刻的承诺性保证:"The insured warrants that in the event of the nature of insured property, or its use or the nature of its occupation, being altered in any manner, whether permanent or temporary, so as to increase risk of loss or damage, he will notify the insurer prior to or within 24 hours subsequent to the increased risk, and, in any event, cover shall be suspended from the date of increase. The insurer shall have the option of continuing the cover upon the same or different terms (to be agreed) or canceling the policy."

在先例 Morley v. United Friendly (1993) 1 Lloyd's Rep. 490,涉及的是人身意外保险,它就有一条类似免责条文说明受保人如果故意冒不必要的风险,保单是不赔付:"No accident shall be payable if death, injury... shall result directly or indirectly from or be accelerated by... (iii) wilful exposure to needless peril..."

在先例 Hussain v. Brown (1996) 1 Lloyd's Rep. 627 (CA),条文是没有明确讲明违反带来什么后果(会被视为是合约条文中的中间条文):"The assured shall as soon as possible give notice in writing to the underwriters of any alteration likely to increase the risk of loss or of damage to the property insured or underwriters' liability and shall pay such reasonable premium if any as may be required by the underwriters."

最后针对火灾险,笔者也见过一条细致与苛刻的承诺性保证与先决条件条文:"(a) The insured warrants that it will maintain the sprinkler system on a regular basis. (b) It is a condition precedent to the insurers liability that the insured will notify the insurer immediately (and within no more than 24 hours) of the sprinkler system becoming inoperative as a result of mechanical failure or other unexpected event. (c) The insured further warrants that, following the failure, he will immediately carry out all remedial and protective steps necessary to protect the insured property to include but not limited to action recommended by the insurer. (d) In any circumstances other than those specified in (b) above, if the insured intends to shut off the sprinklers he must give seven days notice of such intention to insurers seeking their written consent. Such notice shall be a condition precedent to the insurers being liable under this policy. Insurers shall provided a response within seven days and such consent may be subject to conditions but not unreasonably withheld."

针对海上货物保险,显然就没有必要加上太苛刻的条文,毕竟一位受保人把货物交给承运人运输就再也管不了,也没有能力增加或减少承保风险。所以在协会货物条文中只有一条比较接近这方面要求的合约条文(也应该是条中间条文),就是16.1条:"to take such measures as may be reasonable for the purpose of averting or minimizing such loss."

显然,在保险合约或保单中加上一个承诺性保证或先决条件条文是十分严厉的做法,因为一旦违反,保险人就可以完全解除保险合约下的赔付责任。特别严厉的地方是,它根本不会看这种违反与实际损失之间是否有因果关系(causation)。这导致保险人以这种理由拒赔时,受保人总会觉得保险人是故意找借口。

3.5 承诺性保证条文的发展与展望

承诺性保证的严重后果普遍被视为是过分严厉(harsh)、不可原谅(unforgiving)、不成比例(disproportionate)、僵化(inflexible)与过时(over due)。这一理念本来就是与本书第二章受保人的绝对善意的义务是一致,就是为了保护保险人。其中不可以接受的就是违反与事故造成的损失根本不要求因果关系(causation),这与其他的违约截然不同。这里只介绍其中一个批评就是过时,对承诺性的严厉是Mansfield勋爵在18世纪建立起来的,在当时的环境下,伦敦的保险人完全依赖受保人的披露与陈述,以及对现状与将来的所作所为所作出的保证。保险人没有任何其他渠道可以调查或确保自己所愿意承担的风险,所以Mansfield勋爵对承诺性保证认为需要严格执行,否则必须要有严厉的后果,这也是1906年《英国海上保险法》立法的基础。但到了现在的环境就有了很大的变化,一是通讯越来越简单与快捷,受保人自己要取得信息与资料一点也不困难,要依赖受保人单方面作出的保证再也不是那么重要。保险人现在谈判的力量比以前也强得多。此外,保险人还有其他的保障,如本书第二章要求受保人在保险合约履行的期间要有绝对善意(utmost good faith),所以就没有必要再多加一个看来不成比例严厉的承诺性保证。

但对受保人而言,这被视为是一种过度的保护,经常被保险人的取巧。据闻在部分保险合约下发生事故后,保险人派遣的事故调查员会是关心保险合约中的承诺性保证是否被严格遵守与能否挑出毛病远大于关心事故造成的损失,即使是明显看得出承诺性保证与事故是扯不上关系的。如此一来,针对岸上保险会给消费者带来很大的不公平与反感,尤其是考虑到一般消费者没有保险的法律知识,如充分了解承诺性保证的严厉性。这导致了曾经有一个针对岸上保险的草案希望在议院通过,但最终英国法律委员会(Law Commission)与保险协会(Association of British Insurers)达成协议,同意保险行业通过自律来解决这个问题,而没有立法。这一自律就反映在1986年《The Statement of General Insurance Practice》之Section 2(b)(iii):"... on the grounds of breach of warranty or condition where circumstances of the loss are unconnected with the breach unless fraud is involved."

所以在岸上的保险,针对承诺性保证条文已经与海上保险有很不同的解释与做法。针对海上保险,因为有1906年《英国海上保险法》,所以要改变就比较困难,除非根本性的改变法律。在1980年,英国的法律委员会在研究过该问题后曾经作出一份报告,结论是不想作出改变。理由是包括了海上保险是由专业人士操作,不需要像岸上消费者的保险一样作出保护。还有是伦敦在国际海上保险占主导地位,法律的肯定很重要,最好不要改来改去。还有一些业内人士的说法是尤其是在复杂的商业保险合约下,当然这也包括了在保险经纪辅助下由伦敦保险市场承保的海上保险合约,在一些专门性的商业保险合约如海上拖带或是海上钻油台,如果立法禁止保险合约中加入明示承诺性保证(或类似的条文),会有危险是没有保险人愿意承保。

海上保险也并非都是专业人士在操作,如游艇。针对游艇的船东,大部分人就是一般的消费者,好像汽车的车主一样。所以西方也有好几个国家专门立法针对游艇,而这些立法就是直接照搬1906年《英国海上保险法》。例如在澳大利亚,1984年通过保险法修正案,把游艇保险视为是岸上的一般保险,受保人如果破坏承诺性保证不会导致保险人自动解除以后的赔付责任。

但也有很多支持法律作出改变的理由,除了上述已经讲过的过分严厉、不可原谅、不成比例、僵化与过时,还有一个国际竞争的考虑。这就是据统计英国在海上保险的保费收入在近年大跌,1996年的一个报告就指出了英国在海上保险的保费收入从1992年开始(当年的保费收入是12.78亿英镑)在四年间下降了超过50%。这方面的原因有很多,海上保险法律过度保护保险人就是其中一个原因。相比国际保险市场上英国的一些主要竞争者,如挪威、德国、美国(包括华盛顿州、夏威夷州、德州、佛罗里达州等)等,它们的保险法针对承诺性保证的违反都是要求与损失要有直接关系,这对受保人而言就公平得多了。

英国海上保险合约的承诺性保证条文将来的发展还不是很确定。根据LC Consultation Paper 2007第8.45段,法律改革委员会是建议说,如果平衡起来较大可能(on the balance of probabilities)受保人对承诺性保证条文的违反对损失的发生并没有影响,受保人是可以得到保险赔偿。该建议的实用性还是有疑问的。

在这样的大环境之下,英国海上保险市场的本身也在作出改变,如海上保险已经是尽量避免在保险合约中加入承诺性保证条文。相反,为了改变1906年《英国海上保险法》的默示地位,已经是用明确的文字说明违反一些以前被视为是承诺性的保证,会带来的后果只在违反期间遭受损失才可以拒赔,原因是在这种情况下损失通常是与违反承诺性保证有关,就不能获得赔付。但在违约过后所发生的损失,可以说是再与违反承诺性保证无关,保险人还是必须作出赔付。而合约也不会因为较早时候违反而让保险人可以终断之后的赔付责任(这本来是1906年《英国海上保险法》Section 33(3)的默示地位)。举例说,涉及船壳保险,是会有不少的明示与默示承诺性保证,其中著名的是航区保证(trading warranty)。2003年《国际船壳保险条文》把以前的航区保证以文字改为是一条中止条文(suspensive condition),说明在受保人的船东如果违反航区的限制(如船舶去了一个被限制的航区,如北极),保险合约就会处于休眠状态。保险人对违反期间发生的损失不负赔付责任,因为损失会与违反航区限制有关。但之后如果船舶回来保险合约中允许的航区,该船舶重新获得承保。

针对这方面可参见笔者与汪鹏南教授所著的《英国海上保险条款详论》。[1] 反正是在2003年《国际船壳保险条文》,可以被列为是承诺性保证的不多。有的话也只是针对十分重要的方面以及如果这一承诺被保险人违反,涉及的损失通常扯不上关系。这就是在2003年《国际船壳保险条文》中的"营运费用保证"(disbursements warranty)。这是为了防止受保人的船东超额投保不要求他证明受保利益的船舶营运费用,所以限制在船舶投保船壳保险价值的25%。如果受保人超额投保,特别是找不同的保险人,就会带来道德风险。这是船壳保险人不愿意见到的,所以以严格的承诺性保证条文针对与阻吓船东动歪脑筋。由于本书不是针对船壳保险,所以有兴趣的读者可看笔者与汪鹏南教授所著的《英国海上保险条款详论》。

同样的发展与改变也出现在海上货物保险。与1982年协会货物条文相比,2009年协会货物条文中的5.1~5.3条针对船舶适航就有了明显改变。针对船舶适航,起点就是1906年《英国海上保险法》之Section39(1),规定了一个默示承诺性保证就是船舶必须严格或绝对适航。这一承诺性保证也适用在海上货物运输保险。但这并不现实,因为受保人的货方是控制不了船舶的适航,所以涉及海上货物保险,一直有明示条文否定这一默示承诺性保证。在1982年的协会货物条文,这是在5.2条:"The Underwriters waive any breach of the implied warranties of seaworthiness of the ship and fitness of the ship to carry the subject - matter insured to destination, unless the Assured or their servants are privy to such unseaworthiness or unfitness."。但这只是一种有条件的否定,因为如果货方的受保人或者他的雇员对船舶的不适航是有私谋,这默示承诺性保证就否定不了。但问题是它的违反会造成的情况是一个损失(如货物被盗)与船舶不适航(如第一舱进水)完全没有关系也会被拒赔。这是在今天的保险市场中认为不公平与应该避免的。所以在2009年的5.3条文就无条件否定了这一默示的承

---

[1] 杨良宜、汪鹏南:《英国海上保险条款详论》(第2版),大连海事大学出版社2009年版,第274页。

诺性保证。但在5.1条加上一些情况所带来的货物损失或损坏,保险人是不必赔付的。如货方的受保人或者他的雇员明知道有关的船舶是不适航或明知道一个集装箱是不适合安全运输,但还是堆货或/与作出付运,这就会导致由于这个原因带来的货物损失或损坏保险人是不必赔付的。这样的规定显然再也不是属于承诺性保证的范畴。有关这方面的内容可参阅本书的第八章第8.2段。

4. 条件条文(condition)

保险合约经常会有各式各样的条件条文,要求受保人履行合约。如支付保费的日期,受保人在受保期间不能向其他人投保或者加保,不能增加承保风险,索赔通知,协助保险人调查与处理索赔,协助保险人行使代位求偿权向第三人索赔等。

正如一般性的合约一样,"condition"可以有不同的解释,这一个词本身不表示条文的严重性,一经违反对方就可以有权终止合约并提出索赔。在一般性合约,"condition"可以指该合约的所有条件(terms)。如许多标准格式合约会印上许多的条件,其中针对很轻微的问题,在抬头也会印上"合约条件"(Conditions of Contract)。许多小买卖的订货单与发票也会印上一句"条件请看背面"(for Conditions see back)。看来,"condition"就是指合约的条文。所以在先例 Schuler AG v. Wickman Machine Tool Sales (1973) 2 Lloyd's Rep. 53,它的一条条文说明是"合约的条件条文"(condition of this agreement)就被贵族院否定是合约法中的条件条文,一经违反就可以让无辜方终断合约。原因之一是它针对的事项非常繁重与琐碎,在履行的时候很难避免有轻微的违反。双方在订约时的意图不会是接受一有轻微的违反就可以终断一个长期的合约。

在保险合约,"condition"也可以分为三大类:第一种是"保单生效的先决条件"(condition precedent to policy)或是稍有不同的"承保风险开始的先决条件"(condition precedent to the attachment of risk);第二种是"赔付或保险人要负责任的先决条件"(condition precedent to liability);第三种是与一般性合约一致的"条件条文"(condition)。这些"condition"的产生与分类完全是看保险合约的措辞以及解释起来的背景与语境。

4.1　第一种:保单生效或承保风险开始的先决条件

第一种是要求受保人必须满足先决条件才会有保单或是承保风险的开始(后一种情况是假设已经有了有效保险合约的存在)。可以说,只要这一先决条件还没有满足,保险人就不必负责任。这些先决条件可以是:(1)要求受保人必须提供进一步的资料:Mulchrone v. Swiss Life (UK) Plc (2006) Lloyd's Rep. IR 339; Bonner v. Cox Dedicated Corporate Member Ltd. (2006) Lloyd's Rep. IR 385。(2)要求保险标的必须先作出检查与遵守检查后的建议:The "Zeus V" (2000) 2 Lloyd's Rep. 587; M J

Harrington Syndicate 2000 v. Axa Oyak Sigorta AS (2007) Lloyd's Rep. IR 60。(3)支付保费:Aspen Insurance UK Ltd. v. Pectel Ltd. (2009) Lloyd's Rep. IR 440。(4)安全措施的执行:M J Harrington Syndicate 2000 v. Axa Oyak Sigorta AS (2007) Lloyd's Rep. IR 60 等。

在文字上可举 The "Zeus V" (2000) Lloyd's Rep. 587 先例,在该保险合约中的先决条件条文是"Subject to survey including valuation by independent qualified surveyor prior to commencement of in commission period." 另在 Aspen Insurance UK Ltd. v. Pectel Ltd. (2009) Lloyd's Rep. IR 440,相关的文字是"cover is conditional on the Assured paying in full the premium demanded"。

再举一个写得比较明确的先决条件就是船东互保协会(Britannia P& I)的保险合约条文如下:"All particulars and information given in the course of applying for insurance shall, if the entry of the relevant Ship be accepted, be deemed to form part of the contract of insurance between the Member and the Association and it shall be **a condition of precedent of such insurance** that all such particulars and information were true so far as was within the Member's knowledge or could with reasonable diligence have been ascertained."

先决条件通常都是以"取决于"(subject to)作为句子的开始,然后是要明确说明受保人如果没有满足有关的先决条件,后果就是承保风险还没有开始等的字样。

在很大程度上这种的先决条件是与受保人作出的承诺性保证带来的后果十分接近。但它们之间还是有一些微妙的区别:(1)承诺性保证并不影响保险合约的生效,但先决条件会导致保险合约不能生效。这一点区别会影响保费的退还,这是根据1906年《英国海上保险法》之 Section 84(1),只会在先决条件的情况下才会有保费的退还,除非涉及了欺诈。(2)可能更重要的区别是,先决条件不会像承诺性保证一样,一般的写法就是一旦在一个先决条件有了满足(如满足一个检验或支付欠下的保费),保险合约就会生效。但违反了承诺性保证就会是永远解除了保险人的赔付责任,除非是涉及了双方重新谈判并达成协议或保险人弃权。(3)先决条件条文会被法院针对性作出对保险人不利的解释,所以效力还是要看该条文的文字与措辞。针对承诺性保证,虽然法院也是针对保险人去解释,但只要一定性为承诺性保证条文,法院所能做的就非常有限了。因为针对违反承诺性保证条文的严厉后果已经在1906年《英国海上保险法》讲得非常清楚了,没有什么余地留下给法院作出不同的解释。

4.2 第二种:赔付或保险人要负责任的先决条件

第二种是要求受保人必须满足先决条件保险人才会有赔付的责任。这种条文的内容也可以是千变万化,在措辞上也会是采用"取决于"(subject to)。但在没有满足先决条件的后果会是与第一种不一样。这种针对后果的写法可以是"no claim shall attach to this policy":Richardson v. Roylance (1933) 47 Lloyd's Rep. 173;"the insurer will not be liable to pay any claim": Eagle Star v. Cresswell (2004) Lloyd's Rep. IR 437;"no claim under this policy shall be payable unless the terms of this condition have been complied with": Welch v. Royal Exchange Assurance (1939) 1 KB 294;"the insurer is liable provided that (某些条件是被遵守)": Millichap v. Pontrilas Timber & Builders' Merchants Ltd. (unrep, 1992); Den Danske Bank A/S v. Skipton Building Society (unrep, 1997); Colonial Fire & General Insurance v. Chung (unrep 2002)等。反正这是订约自由,但怎么样写也必须清楚明确无误,因为法院对有一些赔付责任的先决条件是有很大的敌意,如不得延误作出发生事故的通知,这方面稍后会介绍。

最后介绍一个香港先例 Hang Seng Goldsmith v. American International Assurance (1985) 1 HKC 146 所涉及的完整一条赔付责任的先决条件条文是:"**It is a condition precedent to the liability** of the company under this policy that: (a) the insured's premises containing the property insured are fitted with burglary/ robbery alarm system(s) stated in the said written proposal and declaration and approved by the company and that no withdrawal, alteration or variation of the system (s), or any structural alterations to the insured's premises which might affect the system, shall be made without the consent of the company; (b) the burglary/robbery alarm system(s) and all locks and padlocks shall have been put into full and effective operation at all times when the insured's premises are closed for business and at all other appropriate times."

4.3 与一般性合约一致的"条件条文"

第三种就是与一般性合约一致的"条件条文"(condition)。也就是说,在这种情况下,"条件条文"的意思是与本章 2.1 段提到的一般性合约三种条文(条件条文[condition]、中间条文[intermediate 或 innominate terms]、保证条文[warranty])中的条件条文是一致的。由于保险合约的履行责任主要是在受保人,所以受保人违反一些条文,但条文没有明确规定是先决条件的话,就有必要看这一条文是属于哪一种才能决定对保险人的救济。显然如果是属于一条条件条文,它的违反被视为是损害了保险合约的根本(go to the root of the contract),保险人作为无辜方就有权终断保险合约并索赔违约带来损失。保险人也可以确认保险合约的继续存在而只索赔有关的损失: West v. National Motor Insurance (1955) 1 WLR 343。

但大体上看来,保险合约或保单中很少会有条文可以被视为对保险人有根本性重要(fundamentally important going to the root of the contract)。一种可能的对象是支付保费,但这里已经是有不少先例认为晚了支付保费并非是违反条件条文: Fenton Insurance v. Gothaer Versicherungsbank WaG (1991) 1 Lloyd's Rep. 172; Figre Ltd. v. Mander (1999) Lloyd's Rep. IR 193; The "Beursgracht" (2002) Lloyd's Rep. IR 335; Limit No. 2 Ltd. v. Axa Versicherung (2008) Lloyd's Rep. IR 330。除非是受保人明确向保险人表示不会再支付保费,这就构成了违约(repudiation),保险人可以接受并终断保险合约: Pacific & General Insurance v. Hazell (1996) LRLR 65。这些道理

都是在一般的合约法范畴内。另一提的就是在开口保单中，准时作出宣告条文也不被视为是条件条文：The "Beursgracht" (2002) 1 Lloyd's Rep. 574。

保险合约通常都会有关于受保人索赔的条件(claim condition)，如发生承保的损失应该在一个时限内通知保险人，作用明显就是让保险人尽早派出调查员调查事故、保存证据(不论是否为了将来拒赔或代位求偿权)，减少损失，参与修理或补救行动等。如果受保人违反(这可以是很轻微的违反)，有先例是法院不会接受保险人可以因此而终断合约。这表示针对这种违反(甚至是保险合约其他条文的违反)，保险人唯一的救济就是索赔损失。但问题是在保险合约下，保险人很难证明违约会带来什么损失。就算是受保人晚了通知保险人有关承保的损失，保险人也没有办法证明这违约带来了什么损失。除非是在一些极端的情况，如在 Diab v. Regent Insurance Co. Ltd. (2006) Lloyd's Rep. IR 779，保单中有条文说明损失通知必须是在发生后的 15 天内，但受保人晚了 9 年才给通知。笔者估计在这种情况下受保人会可能能够证明损失，如一个本来很有成功机会的代位求偿权向第三人索赔，但由于时效已经届满而失去。

在 Porter v. Zurich Insurance (2009) 2 All ER (Comm) 658，保险人指受保人不合作，但法院判这不能自动说明保险人可以索赔损失，而损失就是索赔的金额。根据 Robert Merkin 教授所著的《Colinvaux's Law of Insurance in Hong Kong》的 7.008 段所说，甚至还没有先例判保险人可以成功索赔金钱上的损失，除了唯一的先例 Hussain v. Brown (No 2) (Unrep, 1996)。其中的内容是如下："In ordinary contract law the remedy for breach of an ancillary term, or for inconsequential breach of an innominate term, is damages. That said, there are no reported cases in which an insurer has been awarded damages for non-repudiatory breach of condition. The reason is simply that it is difficult for the insurers to prove any loss as a result of the assured's breach. This is particularly so where the breach consists of a late claim: the insurers' subrogation rights against third parties may have been prejudiced or, in the case of a liability policy, the ability to defend the claim against the assured may have been hampered. If the loss was the result of the assured's own conduct, then absent fraud or a deliberate intention to cause loss, there is no third party who can be pursued for a subrogation recovery and the insurer's only real prospect of showing loss flowing from breach of a claims or similar provisions is that an investigation might have shown that the sums claimed by the insured were inflated."

4.4 索赔条件(claims conditions)之损失通知

保险合约通常都会有索赔条件，内容是针对尽快作出通知以及怎样的通知，采取行动减少损失以及向第三人保留将来索赔的权利，与保险人充分合作，只要保险人提出就要提供证明与文件等。其中，最常见也是引起了最多争议的就是损失的通知(notice of claim or loss)。这一条通知条文可以有不同的写法，因为这也是涉及了订约自由。大致上可以分两类：第一类就是规定了一个时限，如 48 小时或 3 天不等。

第二类是不规定时间,但要求受保人"马上"(immediately 或 forthwith)作出损失通知。也会是写为"合理的尽快"(as soon as reasonably practical)。

除了时间外,损失通知还会涉及形式。在形式方面,如果保险合约与保单内没有规定,就是什么形式都可以,包括了口头。但会有条文说明是必须以文书作出通知,这一来口头就不足够:Wong Wink Tak v. Euro – America Insurance Ltd. (1995) 1 HKC 88。

至于损失通知的内容,会是只需要让保险人知道要作出赔付就已经是足够。如果损失通知实在是太含糊,法院也可以看保险人与受保人之前的通信往来以确定保险人获得通知:Forrest v. Glasser (2006) 2 Lloyd's Re 392。在先例 Merrill Lynch International Bank Ltd. v. Winterthur Swiss Insurance Co. (2007) Lloyd's Rep. IR 532, Gloster 大法官不认为通知需要给所有的细节说:"no reason why the insurer should escape liability to indemnify, simply because details which it claims should have been originally provided to it were not."

另在先例 HLB Kidsons v. Lloyd's Underwriters (2008) Lloyd's Rep. IR 237, Gloster 大法官说是损失通知必须是足够清楚与不含糊,必须让保险人没有合理怀疑知道受保人的通知(sufficient clear and unambiguous that it leaves the reasonable recipient in no reasonable doubt that the assured is by the communication purporting to give notice...)。但上诉庭的判决 HLB Kidsons v. Lloyd's Underwriters (2009) Lloyd's Rep. IR 178 不同意,认为一份通讯文件主要在客观看来是足够被视为是一份通知就已经足够,没有必要要求该通讯文件必须是让保险人"没有合理怀疑"(beyond reasonable doubt)。除非是有保险合约明示规定了更苛刻的索赔通知,如在内容是要求把所有的细节加上。

4.5 索赔条件是先决条件还是一般合约条文

在以上简单的解释中,就可以看到索赔条件如索赔或损失通知会很容易被挑出毛病,不是在时间上稍微晚了一点,就是内容不足够等。这一来,该条文被解释为先决条件或一般合约条文就变得非常关键。因为如果是属于后者,也就是一般合约条文与违约,这已经解释过去索赔金钱损失作为唯一的救济是很难证明有什么损失。这表示受保人如果晚了作出损失通知,或是通知内容不足够,这是受保人的违约。但不会给保险人有实质性的救济,因为保险人通常是证明不了损失。这一方面可节录 Colman 大法官在先例 McAlpine v. BAI (1998) 2 Lloyd's Rep. 694 中所说如下:"If an assured who has put forward a claim under the policy, he acts in so doing in breach of contract. The remedy for that breach depends crucially on the proper construction of the policy. If it provides that compliance is a pre – condition to the bringing of a valid claim, any non – compliance will provide the insurers with a complete defence to that claim. If it does not so provide, the insurers will have a claim for damages for the assured's breach in advancing a claim without first complying with the specified claims conditions. In that event the insurer will be able to set off his losses against the amount due to the assured. In cases where the omission to comply with the claims conditions has seriously prejudiced the insurers' defence to the claim, their cross – claim in damages may be equivalent to a substantial part of the assured's claim."

但如果该条文被解释为是赔付或保险人要负责任的先决条件,就代表受保人一违反,保险人就可以不赔付了。所以在这方面也引起了不少的争议,因为对保险人而言这是会有很大不同的结果。在先例 McAlpine v. BAI (1998) 2 Lloyd's Rep. 694,案情涉及一个承包商责任的保单,其中承保的风险包括意外人身伤亡的赔偿。有关的工程涉及了英国桥梁的建造,发生的不幸事故是一个工人从高处坠下。反正是在该保单内有一"**Claims Conditions**"条文是:"In the event of any occurrence which may give rise to a claim under this Policy, this insured shall, as soon as possible, give notice thereof to the Company, in writing, with full details and as far as practicable there shall not be any alteration or repair until the Company have had an opportunity of inspecting."

但事实上,受保人并没有"尽快"(as soon as possible)与提供"全面细节"(full details)作出索赔通知,但针对这一索赔条件条文,到底是先决条件还是一般合约条文是双方主要的争议,因为两种情况下受保人的违约带来的后果是很不一样。Colman 大法官判是上述节录的索赔通知(Claims Conditions)并非是先决条件。他也说到法院对这种条文怀有敌意,因为受保人轻微的违反就会让保险人合法赖掉庞大金额的索赔,这对受保人十分不公平。除非是有关的条文写了是明确无误,不能有其他合理的解释,属于"赔付或保险人要负责任的先决条件"。Colman 大法官这样说:

"In recent times the Courts have not construed notice of claim or occurrence clauses as imposing conditions precedent to the insurers' liability unless either the clause itself was expressed to be a condition precedent or the policy contained a general provision to the effect of that in Farrell v. Federated Employers, sup. Thus in Re Williams and the Lancashire and Yorkshire Accident Insurance Co's Arbitration (1903) W. R. 222 time was expressly made of the essence of the notice condition. In Allen v. Robles (1969) 1 W. L. R 1193, the occurrence notification clause was expressed to be 'at the risk of forfeiture'.

In the cases where compliance with the claims notification clause has not been specifically stated to be a condition precedent to the insurers' liability but where other particular policy terms have been so expressed it has been held that the omission to include such express provision in the claim notification clause is a strong indication that it was not the mutual intention that it should be a condition precedent: see Stonehouse v. Ocean Railway and General Accident Insurance (1887) 19 QBD 237.

In the present case there is no term of general application the effect of which is to make the performance of cl. 1(a) a condition precedent to underwriters' liability. There is, however, another condition—cl. 4—which expressly states that in case of a difference as to quantification of the loss in cases where liability is admitted the matter must be referred to arbitration and an award is to be 'condition precedent to any right of action against the company'. It is a strong indication that the occurrence notification clause is not intended to be a condition precedent that where a term was intended so to operate the policy expressly said so."

只说 Colman 大法官的一审判决被上诉庭确认：McAlpine v. BAI (2000) Lloyd's Rep. IR 352。

5. 协会货物条文的条件条文

在海上货物保险中，协会货物条文（Institute Cargo Clauses）也有先决条件与一般合约条文。

5.1 协会货物条文的先决条件

首先，很可能被视为先决条件的条文是第 18 条："**Avoidance of delay** – It is a condition of this insurance that the Assured shall act with reasonable dispatch in all circumstances within their control."

这一条文看来反映 1906 年《英国海上保险法》的 Section 48，要求受保人尽力合理速遣，否则保险人就解除责任："**Delay in voyage** – In the case of a voyage policy, the adventure insured must be prosecuted throughout its course with reasonable despatch, and, if without lawful excuse it is not so prosecuted, the insurer is discharged from liability as from the time when the delay became unreasonable."

这一条文首先是在 1942 年出现，主要是针对"二战"时期的延误特别是船舶需要等待护航。但航次时间的延长对收固定保费的保险人而言是不公平的，所以加上了这一条明示条文。到了 1952 年的协会货物条文，这条明示条文也加进来，之后就变成是协会货物条文的一条标准条文。

这一条文在南非法院曾经被判是保险合约的先决条件，如果受保人有违反，保险人就可以解除责任：Verna Trading Pty Ltd. v. New India Assurance (1991) 1 VR 129。在该先例 Ormiston 大法官这样说："Clause 18 is expressed clearly in terms of a condition of liability under the policy... the onus rests on the assured."。在 John Dunt 2009 年所著的《Marine Cargo Insurance》，认为南非的判决也会被英国法院采纳，并在 6.26 段说："this clause has been approached by the South African courts as one which discharges insurers from liability in case of breach. The goods come off risk if the assured fails to act with reasonable despatch. In so far as the Clause delineates the risk it appears to act as a condition precedent to insurers' liability or a promissory warranty whereby the assured promises to act with reasonable despatch. Accordingly, a failure to honor that promise by the assured discharges the insurers from liability."

5.2 协会货物条文中的合约条文

协会货物条文中也有合约条文(contractual terms),违反的话只能让保险人提出金钱上损失的索赔,并需要证明损失与违反该条文是有因果关系。换言之,这不是赔付或保险人要负责任的先决条件。该条文是协会货物条文的第16条,它本质上是"施救责任"(sue and labor):

"Duty of Assured – It is the duty of the Assured and their employees and agents in respect of loss recoverable hereunder

16.1 to take such measures as may be reasonable for the purpose of averting or minimising such loss, and

16.2 to ensure that all rights against carriers, bailees or other third parties are properly preserved and exercised and the Insurers will, in addition to any loss recoverable hereunder, reimburse the Assured for any charges properly and reasonably incurred in pursuance of these duties."

在The "Vasso" (1993) 2 Lloyd's Rep. 309,受保人的货方被保险人指称没有采取行动保障他对承运人/船东的索赔权利,因为他没有申请一个Mareva禁令把船东的保险赔付冻结起来。有关的船舶在该事故中沉没,由于船东只有这一艘船,所以船东获得船壳保险人赔付后很快会变得一无所有,令货方或代位求偿的保险人将来的索赔变得是毫无意义。此外,保险人也指称协会货物条文的第16条是承诺性保证。

但在高院,Hobhouse大法官首先不认为受保人没有申请一个Mareva禁令是违反第16条,说:"On the facts, the mere failure to apply for a Mareva injunction did not, without more, establish any failure to perform the duty imposed by cl. 16; the assured acted reasonably and properly; on the correct construction of the clause more had to be shown than merely that some step had not been taken and underwriters had to show that the step was a proper one which a reasonable assured, having regard to the interests of himself and the insurers and to the provisions of the policy should have taken."

但与本段有关系的主要还是Hobhouse用明确的判词说明第16条并不是一条承诺性保证,即使是违反了也只能索赔金钱上的损失,说:"The duty is essentially a duty to sue and labour. The breach of that duty may cause loss to the insurer in which case the insurer will have a claim for damages against the assured in respect of such breach of duty insofar as the insurer has been caused loss. Where the failure of the assured is a failure to exercise or preserve some right against a third party to which the insurer is entitled to be subrogated, the loss to the insurer will be equivalent to the value of the lost right against the third party... The duty is a contractual duty, breach of which gives rise to liability in damages. In certain circumstances those damages may be equivalent to the full amount of the assured's claim. Where the subrogated right against the third party would have provided the insurer with a full reimbursement, the damages for the breach of the duty would, when set-off against the liability of the insurer to the assured, eliminate that liability and provide the insurer with a defence to the claim upon the policy. More usually, though, the defence will at best be a partial defence."

第五章　适用法与管辖权

1. 适用法概述

由于历史的传承与发展,英国的保险业在世界都处于领先地位。伦敦保险业界拟定的保险标准条文是在世界范围内都被跟从与借用,另与之相配合的英国保险法的优越性也是显著。根据联合国贸易发展委员会(UNCTAD)于1975年的报告,世界范围内大约有三分之二是用英国的保单与相关条款,这样一来,用英国的保险法来配合解释相应的保险合约也更准确,能够找出拟定合约条文的订约意图。英国法院一贯以来也是这样的看法,特别海上保险(船舶与海上货物运输)两百多年来以劳合社标准 S. G. 保单作为保险合约。The "Al Wahab" (1983) 2 Lloyd's Rep. 365 先例就显示了这点,贵族院一致支持上诉庭的多数意见,就是英国法适用,因为有关的保险合约是劳合社 S. G. 保单(只有英国法律才对 S. G 保单有全面的解释)。其中 Bingham 大法官的一审提出这一因素的重要性,如下:"The use of a English standard form may be powerful, even a conclusive indication that the parties intended to contract with reference to English law. See, for example, The Industries (1894) p. 58. But there is, in my judgment, a factor which cannot be ignored in assessing whether and, if so, how strongly, that inference should be drawn. The evidence in this case plainly establishes that this form of marine policy, produced and developed in the London insurance market, has achieved a world-wide currency. Partly this is due to the long history, the great experience, the professional expertise and the high standing of that market, combined with the traditional dominance of London as a commercial centre. Partly it is due to the process of imperial fertilisation which has led to reproduction of the Marine Insurance Act, 1906, in far corners of the globe. The result is that in Western Europe, Australia and New Zealand, South Africa, Singapore, North Yemen, Israel, various parts of black Africa, Indonesia, China, and elsewhere, the standard form of English marine policy is in regular use. In Kuwait (该先例涉及科威特) itself the form has been used since insurance companies were first set up 20 years ago. Similar use is made in other parts of the Gulf and the Middle East. Sometimes there is an express choice of jurisdiction. Often the reference to Lombard Street, the Royal Exchange, or elsewhere in London, is deleted. But frequently there is no express choice of jurisdiction and subject to that deletion the policy wording substantially remains as in the Schedule to the Act, often with the Institute clauses added. Sometimes the text is translated (as it is into Chinese) sometimes, as here, it is not. But it seems fair to conclude on the evidence that this form is part of the lingua franca of international marine insurance."

但在上诉庭属于少数意见的Goff大法官是强烈支持科威特法律适用,因为与该先例有关的所有事情都是在科威特而与英国无关,说:"the policy was issued in Kuwait, by a Kuwait insurance company carrying on business in Kuwait, and ... it provided for performance in Kuwait."但要注意的是科威特根本没有一套完整的保险法。

这一个先例也不再管用,因为在1983年劳合社标准S. G. 保单已经被MAR Form (Lloyd's Marine Policy)所替代。此外,英国针对适用法的法律也有了改变,主要就是因为加入了欧共体而导致了普通法在这一方面已经不再重要。而欧共体的法律,也就是英国的法律,适用在海上货物运输保险的有两个立法:一个就是2000年《Financial Services and Markets Act》与根据该立法制定的法例2001年《Insurance Law Regulations》;另一个就是根据《Rome Convention》而立法的1990年《Contracts (Applicable Law) Act》。前一个立法或法例是适用在承保风险是在EEA国家(这包括了欧共体的所有国家与冰岛、挪威与列支敦士登的所谓EFTA或欧洲自由贸易区[European Free Trade Association,简称EFTA]国家)。后一个立法是适用在承保风险是在EEA国家以外的所有其他国家,这显然是包括了中国。而"承保风险所在地"(risk is situated)通常就是指受保人的所在地。针对海上货物运输保险,这两个不同的立法都允许保险合约的订约双方选择明示适用法条文,只要它是"合理的肯定"(with reasonable certainty)。

针对海上货物运输保险中会需要在岸上储存货物,而且是适用《Insurance Law Regulations》,情况有一点复杂。这是由于欧共体法律为了保护保险合约下的消费者,就强制规定受保人所在地的法律是唯一适用的法律。除非受保人是一家很大的机构(substantial concern),才会有订约自由可以选择明示适用法条文。

再进一步探讨,可以一提的是适用法就是解释保险合约的实体法。这显然至关重要,因为在出现争议决定谁是谁非时,这有决定性的因素。很不幸但也是可以理解的就是,世界上不同国家由于历史、文化、国情等原因导致法律针对同一个问题可能会有不同的规定,甚至有时候规定完全相反。例如,普通法系与大陆法系就有很多不同的地方,其中一个就是在本书第二章探讨在保险合约的绝对善意要求。就算是大陆法系,不同的国家也可能就同一个问题有非常不一样的规定。

2. 不同国家法律作为保险合约适用法会带来的后果

不同国家的法律所带来的差异有时候会有天渊之别,随便挑几个有关保险合约的案例,可介绍如下。

2.1 Ace Insce v. Zurich (2000) 2 Lloyd's Rep. 423

这一先例涉及了一家瑞士的再保险公司,也就是本案的被告。而作为受保人是美国德州的一家保险公司,它作为第一线的保险人承保了一些油井的风险。在有关的保险合约中,有一个承诺性保证名为“blowout preventer warranty”,条文部分内容如下:“A blowout preventer of standard make will be set on the surface casing per usual industry practice same to be installed and tested in accordance with the usual practices.”。

这是一个防止油井喷气(blowout)的很重要的设施,喷气就是原油或天然气从地底喷涌而出,如果这种喷涌不能够被马上控制是会带来极大的危险,其中包括了爆炸与火灾。如果这发生在海上的钻油台,一个活生生的例子就是2010年4月20日发生在美国墨西哥湾“深水地平线”(Deepwater Horizon)钻井平台的严重事故。可以说,每个在生产石油的油井都会有喷气的危险,特别是在钻探与开采的早期。为了防止油井喷气,就有了这一所谓“blowout preventer”的设施,它是在发生油井喷气的时候能够在很短的时间(如30秒内)把油井喷气的管道封死。操作可以是自动,也可以是手动。在“深水地平线”钻井平台的事故中,据说就是因为这个“blowout preventer”失灵,而失灵的原因至今也没弄明白。加上这是发生在深达5000米的海底,由于水压很高,蛙人无法潜到,只能靠一种无人的潜水艇与机器人(名为remotely - operated vehicle)操作。所以“blowout preventer”失灵,另外采取措施将油井封死是很难做到的,以至于给美国墨西哥湾带来了空前的环境灾难。据说,该“blowout preventer”的生产商Cameron会面对BP以及其他的产品责任控诉与索赔,它虽然投保了5亿美元的责任保险,估计对这种事故的最后赔偿也仅仅是杯水车薪。现在再回来谈本案例就可以明白为什么保险合约中要放一条“blowout preventer warranty”的条文,因为对承保油井损失的保险人实在是太重要。

在本案例,承保的沙特阿拉伯的一个岸上油井最终发生了无法控制的喷气并造成了损失,但保险人是拒绝赔付。发生事故的时候“blowout preventer”装置还没有安装妥,而“blowout preventer warranty”的条文只是要求它将会被安装。本来它的安装与这一事故没有关系,但再保险人找出了蛛丝马迹证明该“blowout preventer”装置并没有根据业内习惯做法安装,所以是违反“blowout preventer warranty”。这里根据1906年《英国海上保险法》Section 33(3),对保险合约的承诺性保证是非常严格。只要承诺性保证没有被严格遵守,不论违约与之后发生的事故是否有关系,都可以让再保险人有权否认所有的赔付责任。

但在另外一个有关国家的法律,也就是美国的德州,法律显然对再保险人不利。美国德州的法律认为破坏保险合约的承诺性保证/先决条件还是必须要与后来发生的损失有关系,换言之,是再保险人因为受保人(第一线的保险人)违反承诺性保证而受到损害。这方面在本书第四章第3.5段有详论。这导致了双方的争议重点是到底英国法还是美国德州的法律才是适用法。Longmore大法官认为德州法律才是适用法,说:

"(3) the proper law of the reinsurance policy was that of Texas, since it was the law of the underlying policy; or, if pursuant to Forsikringsaktieselskapet Vesta v. Bucher (1989) 1 Lloyd's Rep. 331; [1989] A. C. 852, it was preferable to say that the reinsurance policy had to be interpreted so as to give indemnity for risks for which Zurich were liable under Texan law, Texan law was critical for the claim. This was important because the law of Texas did not allow an insurer or reinsurer to rely on a failure to comply with a condition precedent, unless they were prejudiced by such failure;

(4) Texas was more appropriate on the facts since (a) Texas was the place where the claim was settled and paid; (b) the evidence whether such settlement was reasonable, or (in the absence of any follow settlement provision) whether Zurich were in fact liable, was all or mostly in Texas or Saudi Arabia and not in London; (c) the evidence about breach of the obligation to notify was mainly in the hands of the brokers whose chain of communication started in Texas; (d) witnesses of fact in relation to the blowout preventer and standard Industry practice in relation to its installation were not in London."

2.2　The "Mount I" (2000) 2 Lloyd's Rep. 684

这一先例涉及了保险合约的转让(assignment),但针对转让不同国家的法律有不同的说法。在该先例涉及的是法国与英国的法律,在英国法律保险合约可以自由转让是已经在1906年《英国海上保险法》Section 50被确认。但根据法国法律,保险合约的转让通知必须要通过法国法院的执达吏(bailiff)送达才是有效。所以在该先例决定英国法还是法国法才是适用法又是一个至关重要的例子。Longmore大法官判英国法律才是适用法,说:"The insurer and the insured have agreed that the law of the contract of insurance is English law and English law is thus the law which is to determine whether RZB, as assignee, has a good claim against the insurers. Under English law there is no doubt that RZB do have a good claim. By s. 50(2) of the Marine Insurance Act, 1906 a policy of marine insurance is freely assignable. Even if (as in this case) the policy is assigned by way of security rather than absolutely and even if notice of assignment has to be given to the insurers because, for that reason, the assignment is to be treated as an assignment in equity rather than an assignment at law (see The 'Evelpidis Era' [1981] 1 Lloyd's Rep. 54) English law does not require that notice to be given in any formal manner. Any notice required by English law was, in fact, given to the insurers."

2.3　CGU International v. AstraZeneca Ins (2007) 1 Lloyd's Rep. 142

在这一先例中涉及是再保险合约(reinsurance contract),投保的风险是一家跨国生物科技(bioscience)集团的人命伤亡与财产损失(property damage)。但第一线的保险人(也就是受保人)与再保险人对财产损失的定义或解释有了争议,就是是否包括该集团旗下的一家美国Iowa公司(Garst)所作出的赔偿损失。Garst生产与销售一种基因改造的农产品,带来了来自农民、食物生产商、消费者、出口商等人士大量的索赔,总金额高达20亿美元。到了2003年1月,Garst向部分索赔人士赔付了8000万美元,并向保险人(实际上是集团下的一家保险公司)索赔并获得赔付。而该保险人再向再保险人要求赔付时就产生了这个争议,因为再保险人指这些损失并非是财产损失。这就带来一个重要之处,就是再保险合约到底适用什么法?如果根据英国法,对财产的定义是比较狭窄。但根据Iowa的法律,对财产的定义是比较宽松。显然,再保险合约是没有一条明示的适用法条文,但由于针对美国的受保人,有一条名为"接受美国诉讼条文"(USA Service of Suit clause),所以会带来争议,因为如果在Iowa法院审理是不会考虑英国法。结果在仲裁中(再保险合约是有一条仲裁条文),是以2:1的多数意见判是适用Iowa法律,而有关的案例是根据1996年《英国仲裁法》的Section 69的上诉法律观点条文。以下可简单节录仲裁员之间的不同看法:"As regards the ELP(再保险合约的excess loss policy) it was common ground that the original law applicable to the ELP was English law. The majority ruled that it was not the intention from inception that the ELP was to be subject to the law of Iowa, but that Garst's interest was insured separately and the Exercise of Suit clause showed that it was contemplated that any claim by Garst would be governed by US law. The dissenting arbitrator, Mr. Rokison QC, held that there was no intention that the ELP should, in respect of Garst, be governed by the law of Iowa. While it was the case that, had Garst brought proceedings against AZICL (保险人) in Iowa it was likely that the Iowa court would have applied the law of Iowa to the ELP, that was not a sufficient ground to conclude that the question of AZICL's liability to Garst should be determined by Iowa law."

3. 保险合约内的明示适用法条文

在本章第1段有提到在2001年《Insurance Law Regulations》与1990年《Contracts (Applicable Law) Act》,针对海上货物运输保险,这两个立法都允许保险合约的订约双方选择明示适用法条文,只要它是合理的肯定。以下探讨怎么样才算是合理肯定的明示适用法条文,毕竟在协会货物条文(Institute Cargo Clause)的第19条就是这样的条文。

3.1 合理肯定的明示适用法条文会受到尊重

在英国法律下,如果是有一条合理肯定的明示适用法条文,是肯定会受到尊重。即使是明示适用法与保险合约没有实际的关系,也一样受到尊重:Anderson v. Equitable Assurance Co. of the United States (1926) All ER 93。这也可以随手节录先例Akai v. People's Insurance Co. Ltd. (1998) 1 Lloyd's Rep. 90,Thomas大法官这样说:

"It is clear that the parties to the insurance policy bargained for English law. This

Court should therefore give effect to that intention, unless it would be contrary to English public policy (which includes international public policy) to give effect to the enforcement of the jurisdiction clause which is otherwise valid...

In this case, however, the Court is concerned with the enforceability of the parties' freely chosen choice of law and jurisdiction in a credit insurance policy. In contracts of this kind between commercial enterprises, there is no equivalent restriction in English law or Community law on the party's choice of law. Nor, in my judgment, are the provisions of Australian law which operated to restrict the parties' choice of law and jurisdiction within the type of stipulation referred to by Lord Halsbury in Re Missouri Steamship Co. (1889) 42 Ch. D 321. It cannot be said that they are of a character that is anywhere near the ambit of the type of stipulation to which he referred.

In my judgement therefore this Court should give effect to the bargain of the parties and their freely negotiated choice of law and jurisdiction. It should not, as a matter of comity, give effect to the decision of the High Court that overrode that bargain and that choice."

在协会货物条文(Institute Cargo Clause A/B/C),不论是1982年版本还是2009年版本都有了一条英国法律作为适用法的明示条文。在2009年版本,它是在第19条:" This insurance is subject to English law and practice."如果保险合约的MAR 91(它只有一条英国法院管辖权条文)合并协会货物条文(包括适用法条文),这在英国法院是足够明确与肯定的条文说明英国法与做法适用。在The "Prestrioka" (2003) 2 Lloyd's Rep. 327,法院是支持协会货物条文这一条适用法条文,虽然它在保单中也加了一条:"Notwithstanding anything contained herein or attached hereto to the country, it is understood and agreed that this insurance is subject to English law and practice only as to all questions of liability for and settlement of any and all claims arising under this Policy."

另在美国的先例Javed v. British Airways plc (1993) 980 F. 2d 1407,美国上诉庭也认为协会货物条文的适用法条文是不含糊与可以执行。在日本的海上货物运输保险合约,通常合并协会货物条文,其中有适用法条文"subject to English law and usage as to liability for the adjustment and settlement of all and any claims"。在日本的先例Connor v. Nippon Fire and Marine Insurance Co. Ltd., Tokyo High Court Judgment of 9 February 2000,判解释协会货物条文是要根据英国法。

所以在船舶保险,由于投保的有关条文是协会船壳条文(Institute Hull Clause),有了类似的适用法条文,船壳保险人与船东有了争议,通常适用法就是英国法。但针对海上货物运输的保险,就比较复杂。首先是在订约自由下,双方当事人即使是使用协会货物条文,也可以对适用法条文作出改变,如把英国法改为中国法。虽然,这在现实中很少会出现。但另一个现实中的变数就是今天的海上货物保险往往不会是一个单独航次的保险(facultative insurance),而经常是通过开口/预约保单为每次付运的货物单独签发一张保险证明(certificate of insurance),这一来,协会货物条文充其量只是被合并解释有关保险合约的承保范围等方面,较难解释被合并的协会货物条文中的适用法条文适用在开口/预约保单与所有在开口保单下签发的保险证明。接下来的段节就看看这方面的复杂情况。

3.2 含糊不清与浮动适用法条文不被承认

适用法条文只有在非常罕见的情况下才会被否定,如写得含糊不清。在先例 Cie. Tunisienne de Nav. v. Cie d'Armement Maritime (1970) 2 Lloyd's Rep. 99,有关的明示条文是:"This Contract shall be governed by the laws of the Flag of the Vessel carrying the goods..."(船旗国家的法律是适用法)。但有关的合约关于争议的解决另有一条伦敦仲裁条文。合约实际上是一个 COA,以多个航次运输35 万吨的原油。由于承租人是法国公司,所以计划中是想使用悬挂法国旗的船舶。但可以想到,如果该 COA 要租用其他的船舶运输,如希腊旗与利比里亚旗,这适用法就会更加混乱了。反正在该先例所争议的就是有关合约的适用法到底是英国法还是法国法。结果在该先例中,贵族院虽然最终是判法国法律是适用法,但有两位贵族院大法官认为该明示适用法条文因为太含糊而无效,同意法国法律默示适用是因为它是与该合约有最密切的关系。

除了明示条文含糊不清之外,也会因其他原因被否定,如一条浮动适用法条文(floating proper law clause)。这就是一条约定了不止一个国家的法律适用的条文,而最终哪个适用会是根据事后的变化或是其中一个当事人的选择。这会导致一个合约在履行开始时说不清楚到底是哪个国家的法律适用,这种情况在英国法律下不被接受,认为一个合约必须从头到尾有明示或者默示的稳定法律适用而不能停留在真空内。在先例 The "Iran Vojdan" (1984) 2 Lloyd's Rep. 380,相关的条文是规定承运人可以选择伊朗的法律与伊朗自己版本的《海牙规则》或者是德国法律与它自己版本的《海牙规则》,并且是选了哪个国家的法律就等于是选了哪个国家的管辖权。Bingham 大法官描述该条文是"非常令人不满意"(extremely unattractive),说:"The proper law is something so fundamental to questions relating to the formation, validity, interpretation and performance of a contract that it must in my judgment, be built into the fabric of the contract from the start and cannot float in an indeterminate way until finally determined at the option of one party. As I say, it is, as I understand, common ground that as a matter of English law effect cannot be given to that part of this clause."

在保险合约中也有这种浮动适用法条文并且不被接受。例如在先例 Heath Lambert v. Sociedad De Corretaje De Seguros (2004) 1 Lloyd's Rep. 495,案情是涉及了第一线保险人通过伦敦保险经纪人向伦敦劳合社与保险公司投保再保险。这通常被视为是适用英国法律,也等同适用 1906 年《英国海上保险法》。但它有一条明示条文说是"Subject to Venezuelan Law and/or Venezuelan Jurisdiction if required."表面看来,如果有一方事后提出要求,就会令适用法从英国法律变为委内瑞拉的法律。这条文被 Hirst 大法官否定，认为是一条浮动适用法条文令合约的适用法无法肯定，说：

"I consider that it is an unnatural construction of the policy to confine the effect of 'if required' as he suggested. In my judgment, the clause gave the Venezuelan principal the option to demand Venezuelan law and/or jurisdiction. It was a so – called floating choice of law clause: see Dicey & Morris on the Conflict of Laws (13th ed) at §32 – 084. I do not accept that just because the underlying insurance policy contained a Venezuelan arbitration clause or was, implicitly, governed by Venezuelan law (if it was), that meant that Venezuelan law and/or jurisdiction had been required. It by no means follows, for instance, that Banesco as reassured would prefer to have the case decided by a Venezuelan judge, rather than by the Commercial Court in London, or that it would prefer Venezuelan law to English law.

This was an option to be exercised by Banesco. No such option was exercised during the currency of the policy or afterwards. Mr. Millett（委内瑞拉被告的代表大律师）contended that, if necessary, he could exercise it in argument before me. I am very doubtful whether this option is still open so many years after the policy has expired, but if it were, the election would have to be communicated to underwriters. They were not before the Court."

这方面的先例另有 King v. Brandywine Reinsurance Co. (UK) Ltd. (2004) Lloyd's Rep. IR 554 与 Craft Enterprises (International) v. Axa Insurance Co. (2005) Lloyd's Rep. IR 14。

最后是一条明示适用法条文也会有受阻的争议，如在双方约定之后有关的法律作出重大与根本性的改变。这种争议在先例 Perry v. Equitable Life Assurance Society of the United States (1929) 45 TLR 468 也曾经出现过。至于一条适用法条文由于公共政策的原因而被否定的话，这也仅仅是停留在理论的层面，英国至今也没有针对这方面的先例。

3.3　合并另一个合约通常不包括该合约的适用法条文

一个合约合并另一个合约，在商业中是经常见的情况，这包括在海上货物保险。正如在第一章详细介绍过有关的做法，就是通常在一个开口/预约保单中，去为个别的付运签发一份保险证明(certificate of insurance)。在保险证明中会提到开口/预约保单，甚至会合并部分条文。关于条文合并其他合约的法律/理论及具体情况的应用，在笔者所著《装卸时间与滞期费》第二章与《提单及其付运单证》第四章等都有介绍，其中一条重要原则就是泛泛的合并不包括被合并合约中的附属性条文(ancillary clause)。能够合并的必须是直接有关联的内容或是属于主要内容(subject – matter)的部分。如租约提单经常会合并租约，泛泛的一条合并条文就把整份租约引进来适用在提单中。可以说，看到这份提单的人通常不会知道合并进来的租约内容是什么，所以有必要对合并条文作出比较局限的解释，否则会对提单的持有人或买方来说很不公道。所以,合并条文只能引进提单合约主体或主要内容的事项,如涉及货物运输、装卸与交付。因为如果不引进来,提单合约由于欠缺这方面的条文也没有办法顺利履行,如船东还是货方负责装卸?但租约内的仲裁条文、管辖权条文、时效条文等并非是必要而且是被视为附属性的条文就不包括在合并的范围内。合约的适用法条文也是属于附属性条文,不会给一条泛泛的合并条文引进来。有关的保险案例有 GAN Insurance Co. v. Tai Ping Insurance Co. (1999) Lloyd's Rep. IR 472 与 Burrows v. Jamaica Private Power Co. Ltd. (2002) Lloyd's Rep. IR 466。

另是被合并进来的条文不能与该合约的明示条文有冲突,否则以后者优先。

上述所讲对海上货物保险的关系可以协会货物条文有一条明示的英国法适用条文(第 19 条)为例,它是不会因为开口/预约保单合并了协会货物条文而一并把英国法适用条文也引进。毕竟,开口/预约保单会是像 Evialis v. S. I. A. T (2003) 2 Lloyd's Rep. 377 先例一样,所有有关人士都是意大利公司,开口保单是意大利文(是一份名为 Polizza Italiana 的意大利标准格式),保险合约的履行也主要是在意大利等。可以说整个保险合约的重心(centre of gravity)全都是在意大利,只是合并了协会货物条文。如果这样合并就可以引进英国法适用条文,导致开口保单也等于有一条合理肯定的明示适用法条文,这恐怕不会是有关人士订约的意愿。

事实上,在该开口/预约保单,它本身就有一条意大利适用法条文(在 Article 1 的 General Condition),令这一方面的问题更加明确。但问题是在该开口保单所签发的一份保险证明,它并没有明示适用法条文,只合并了协会货物条文。这一来,在英国法院,原告的法国受保人(他是该批损坏货物的 CIF 买方,也是保险证明的持有人)争议说是英国法适用,但意大利的保险人说是意大利法适用。而适用英国法或意大利法会对索赔时效有很大关系,因为受保人的索赔如果根据《意大利航海法》之 Article 1457 只有 1 年时效,而该时效已过。他们之间的争议可节录该先例判决的有关部分:"Mr Morris (受保人代表大律师) seeks to establish the position under English law because he submits that English law is the governing law of the contract (and, no doubt, because he would say that, if the contract is governed by Italian law, English law should be applied in the absence of satisfactory evidence that Italian law differs from it). I shall have to consider in due course whether Mr Morris is correct in his submission as to the proper law. However, the insurers dispute the position under English law, arguing that the proper approach is to look at the open cover and the certificate together, both being contractual documents between the insurers and their insured, Ametra (意大利 CIF 卖方)."

在该先例,Smith 大法官针对这一点说:

"However, this argument assumes that the clauses in type of the certificate (as well as those in print) are governed by the words 'integrated as follows', and are not governed directly by the words, 'the following conditions, known to the parties.' Mr. Morris (受保人代表大律师) disputes this, and so does not accept that insurers' contention that the Institute Clauses（协会货物条文）are introduced into the certificate as part and parcel of the ‘integration’ of the Polizza Italiana（意大利标准格式的开口/预约保单）... and the words ‘integrated as follows’ cannot govern that typed provision, and that the certificate does not refer to the same versions of the Institute Clauses as the open cover.

I accept Mr. Morris’ argument thus far. However, it does not follow that the reference in the certificate（开口/预约保单下签发的保险证明）to Institute Clauses expresses a choice by the parties that the contract of insurance should be governed by English law. I do not understand Mr. Morris to dispute that the open cover itself is governed by Italian law, and so the choice of English law as the governing law of one particular cover declared under it and recorded in the certificate would, on the face of it, be rather surprising, particularly the certificate was issued by Italian insurers（被告的意大利保险人）through an Italian broker to an Italian assured（意大利 CIF 卖方 Ametra). The law and practice provisions were not specifically referred to in the certificate. **It might be that the effect of the provisions was that the interpretation of the Institute Clauses themselves was governed by English law and practice – that does not call for consideration on these applications. However that may be, I do not consider that the reference to the Institute Clauses in the certificate evinces the parties’ intention to choose an English governing clause for the contract of insurance as a whole, still less does it express or demonstrate a choice ‘with reasonable certainty’.**”（加黑部分是说有可能光在解释协会货物条文,是要根据英国法律与做法,但这不是本案所要考虑。反正 Smith 大法官不认为保险证明中合并协会货物条文显示了双方选择英国法律作为保险合约的适用法,也谈不上这样是“合理肯定”的。）

4. 保险合约没有明示适用法条文：风险所在地在非 EEA 国家

如果保险合约没有明示条文,风险所在地在非 EEA 国家时,也就是在欧共体或欧洲自由贸易区外的国家,如中国,所根据的就是 1990 年《Contracts（Applicable Law）Act》,它是在 Schedule 1 合并了《Rome Convention》。如较早时所讲,《Rome Convention》之 Article 3 是允许订约自由,双方可以约定一条明示的适用法条文。但如果没有明示条文,Article 4 就适用,其中 Article 4(2) 是这样说:“... it shall be presumed that the contract is most closely connected with the country where the party who is to effect the performance which is characteristic of the contract has, at the time of conclusion of the contract, his habitual residence, or, in the case of a body corporate or unincorporate, its central administration...”

这表示英国针对适用法的默示地位是找出与合约有最密切关系(closest connection)的法律作为适用法。《Rome Convention》如上述的节录是假设一方当事人要作出"主要履行"(characteristic performance)的所在地就是有最密切关系,除非从整体看是有关合约有另一个更密切关系的国家。这与英国普通法的默示地位在大原则是一致,普通法也是找出与合约有最密切关系的法律。它们之间主要的区别是在它们所用的方法上,普通法考虑的因素是无限制的。举例说 The "Komninos S" (1991) 1 Lloyd's Rep. 370,双方争议的是该案例的默示适用法到底应该是英国法还是希腊法,其中,提到的部分考虑因素是:"That the system of law with which the transaction has its closest and most real connection was that of Greece. That was the place where the contracts were made, where the vessel was managed, where the cargo came from, where the cargo was shipped. That was the nationality of the managers and the shippers. There was provision in the booking note that freight should be paid in Greek currency in Greece at the rates of exchange prevailing in Greece... This features heavily outweighed the non - Greek features of the transaction: the Cypriot nationality of the shipowners, the Panamanian flag of the vessel, the Italian port of discharge, the provision for general average adjustment in London, the reference to sterling, U. S. dollars and Deutschmarks in the bills of lading and the choice of British court to resolve disputes."

而针对海上货物运输保险或者其他保险合约,以前在普通法在许多考虑的因素中非常重要的一个,比起其他因素有更大的分量,就是保险人所在的地点与国家。例如,向劳合社投保就会有很大的考虑默示适用法是英国法。这可节录 Robert Merkin 教授所著的《Colinvaux's Law of Insurance in Hong Kong》的 2.011 段:"In the few cases where the courts have had to determine the proper law of an insurance policy at common law, the location of the head office of the insurers has tended to be a significant factor. There may well be sound reasons for this conclusion, as it is in the interests of an insurer to have all of its agreements governed by the law, and particularly principles applicable to placement, rather than to have law determined by arbitrary factors such as the situation of the risk or the place of the assured's residence."

针对海上保险首先是先例 Armadora Occidental SA v. Horace Mann Insurance Co. (1977) 2 Lloyd's Rep. 406,如果不是保险合约中有一条说是"跟从伦敦条文"(follow London clause),英国上诉庭会选择美国法律,因为这是被告保险人的所在地的法律。但在先例 Atlantic Underwriting Agencies Ltd. and David Gale (Underwriting) Ltd. v. Compagnia di Assicurazioni di Milano SpA (1979) 2 Lloyd's Rep. 240,Lloyd 大法官认为有关保险合约与英国法律的关系并不像先例 Armadora Occidental SA v. Horace Mann Insurance Co 中的关系那么密切,相反被告的保险人是一家意大利公司,所以选择意大利法律是适用法说:"On reflection, it seems to me clear that the balance must come down in favor of Italian Law. The factor which weighs most strongly with me is that the defendants are resident in Italy and that is where they both negotiated and signed the contract. ”

说到底保险人所在地也只是确定保险合约适用法的重要考虑因素之一,大趋势还是非常重视整个保险案件所有因素的重心(centre of gravity)找出保险合约的默示适用法。这方面的先例有 Cantieri Navali Riumiti SpA v. NV Omne Justitia (1985) 2 Lloyd's Rep. 428,这种趋势在再保险合约看来,普通法对保险人(再保险中的受保人)与再保险人在不同所在地不大重视,重视的反而是整个再保险合约考虑所有因素后才确定重心所在。在先例 Citadel Insurance Co. v. Atlantic Union Insurance Co. SA (1982) 2 Lloyd's Rep. 543,再保险合约(是关于船舶的开口/预约保单)涉及的是一个加拿大的保险人,而再保险人是一家希腊的保险公司,他们通过伦敦的保险经纪人达成了再保安排。在一审,Bingham 大法官认为再保险合约的适用法不是英国法,说:“had no connection with the English system of law other than the mechanics of the transaction. ”但这不被上诉庭所认同,认为 Bingham 大法官没有充分考虑英国保险经纪人的角色,保险合约的格式与保险合约的履行地点。其中 Kerr 大法官关于该先例的重心为什么是在伦敦解释的很详细,说:

“In all of these circumstances it seems to me that there is no candidate other than London and English law as the centres of gravity with which this business had its closest connection . International Excess could have stipulated for the law of New York, but they did not do so. Like the defendants they wished to operate on the London market and left the governing law open. The whole of the business, both from the point of view of the defendants as reinsurers and of the reinsured plaintiffs, was run by Austen(保险经纪人)in London. All the documents are here, and it is only by an examination of those documents that is possible to determine the rights and wrongs of the dispute...

But what [the learned judge] (指一审的 Bingham 大法官) calls the ‘mechanisms’ were in fact the substance of the whole business; and London is in effect the only place where these transactions between the plaintiffs and the defendants can be said to be located. There is no other candidate. ”

但上述所介绍的案例都不是针对《Rome Convention》,而在《Rome Convention》考虑的因素就相对局限,即“主要履行当事人”(characteristic performer)的所在地。这就带来一个疑问,在一个保险合约中到底谁是主要履行当事人?是保险人(或涉及多位就是首席保险人)或是受保人?在 Article 4 与其他的条文,是没有针对“主要履行”(characteristic performance)的定义。但根据权威性解释《Rome Convention》的 The Giuliano and Lagarde Report, n. 12,认为主要履行当事人是保险人,因为他提供保险的服务(insurance services)。另在 Dornoch Ltd. v Mauritius Union Assurance Co. Ltd. (2006) Lloyd's Rep. I. R. 127,涉及再保险合约,再保险人肯定在伦敦。法院判主要履行当事人是英国的再保险人,所以英国法律是有最密切关系的,说:“... The proper law of the excess policy had not been chosen in accordance with the Rome Convention 1980 Art. 3(1), Gan Insurance Co. Ltd. v Tai Ping Insurance Co. Ltd. (No. 1) [1999] 2 All E. R. (Comm) 54 considered. Thus, applying Art. 4(2), England was the country with which the contract was most closely connected as the leading reinsurers were based in England and the characteristic performance of the excess reinsurance would be performed in England. The conclusion that the excess policy was governed by English law..."

从上述所讲,看来普通法与《Rome Convention》的默示地位相差也不远,就是把保险人所在地国家的法律视为一个重要的考虑因素。

5. 保险合约没有明示适用法条文:风险所在地在 EEA 国家

针对保险合约,由于英国是欧共体的成员之一,所以另有立法针对欧共体成员之间的适用法默示地位。虽然这不适用在中国大陆,但由于欧共体的重要性,也可以一提该有关的立法,这就是《Financial Services and Markets Act 2000》。根据该立法制定的法例 2001 年《Insurance Law Regulations》之 6(1) 条是有如下的规定:"1. If the policyholder resides in the EEA State in which the risk is situated, then the starting point is that the law of that state applies. However: (i) if the risk covered by the insurance is a 'large risk', defined so as to include a risk to goods in transit, the parties may choose any law as the applicable law, and (ii) if the state of residence of establishment permits a choice of law, the parties may validly choose the law of another country. 2. A choice made by the parties under (i) or (ii) must be expressed or demonstrated with reasonable certainty by the terms of the contract or the circumstances of the case."

该条文的第一句是说明受保人或保单持有人的所在地是在 EEA 国家,起点就是所在地国家法律适用。但接下去提供了一种例外情况可以订约自由选择其他国家的法律适用。这就是保险合约所承保的风险是一个"大风险"(large risk),而这一大风险也包括了海上货物的运输。另外是受保人所在地国家的法律也必须允许去自由约定其他国家的法律适用。

5.1 海上货物运输是属于大风险,允许选择其他国家法律

在法例《Insurance Law Regulations》之 6(1) 条中是把欧共体的保险合约分为两大类:一类属于大风险;另一类不属于大风险。如果属于大风险,才允许受保人与保险人明示约定适用法。而与本书非常有关的海上货物运输(但会除了岸上的储存),它属于大风险,换言之是可以有明示适用法条文。这里可以节录 John Dunt 在所著的《Marine Cargo Insurance》之 2.10 段所说:"The definition of 'large risks' includes goods 'in transit' but there may be restriction on choice for storage risks as discussed below. For goods in transit there is freedom of choice though the choice must be exercised or demonstrated with reasonable certainty in accordance with regulation 6(1). In particular that choice must be demonstrated with sufficient certainty to oust the default choice of the law of the assured's residence or place of establishment."

5.2 岸上储存不属于大风险

但大风险并不包括储存的风险,而货物在不持续运输时,越来越多是涉及了投保储存的风险以针对货物会被盗窃、火灾与爆炸等风险,例如,以 Institute Metals Storage Clauses (A)作为承保的条文。储存风险不属于大风险,除非受保人是一家"很大机构"(substantial concern),才会被视为是"大风险"(large risk)。而一家很大机构必须要平均雇佣至少250个雇员或公司机构的资产负债表(a balance sheet)是不少于620万欧元或每年的纯营业额不低于1280万欧元。反正属于大风险就有订约自由可以通过明示条文选择适用法。

当然,这还要看该很大机构的所在地国家法律。有关保险合约能否有订约自由选择适用法,欧共体成员各自的立法,可以说,有一些国家允许订约自由(如英国),但有一些国家不允许。

6. 管辖权概述

管辖权(jurisdiction)与适用法(proper/governing law)经常会出现在同一个合约条文,但它们并非同一码事。而管辖权的重要性在于确定双方如果有了争议去哪里打官司。去哪里打官司就像在战争时所讲"天时、地利与人和"中的"地利与人和"。

也是因为英国加入了欧共体或欧盟(European Community 或 EC)而导致了普通法在这一方面的重要性减少,但针对非欧盟国家如中国,在管辖权方面还是普通法地位最重要。而针对欧盟国家,《Council Regulation [EC] 44/2001》已经通过《Civil Jurisdiction and Judgments Order 2001》在英国成为立法。

普通法或《Council Regulation [EC] 44/2001》是完全可以在合约里有明示的适用法条文,但如果没有明示的管辖权条文,就要根据英国普通法或《Council Regulation [EC] 44/2001》看管辖权应该是哪个国家的法院。

6.1 明示排外管辖权条文的好处与做法

好像明示适用法条文一样,保险合约中有一条明示管辖权条文也是会带来肯定与避免将来择地行诉(forum shopping)的麻烦。而一条明示管辖权条文最常见的做法就是在合约中约定一条排外管辖权条文(exclusive jurisdiction clause)。在英国法院,一贯以来都是尊重这条排外管辖权条文,不论约定的管辖权是否在英国。如果由一方当事人漠视一条外国法院的排外管辖权条文,在英国法院起诉,英国法院只会在很少情况下才会支持原告的"违约行为",并拒绝中止(stay)英国法院的程序:The

"Eleftheria" (1969) 1 Lloyd's Rep. 237。如果合约的双方明示约定一条英国法院的排外管辖权条文,英国法院是绝少会拒绝管辖:S&W Berisford plc and NGI International Precious Metals Inc. v. New Hampshire Insurance Co. Ltd. (1990) 2 QB 621, 638; Bouygues Offshore SA v. Caspian Shipping Co. (1998) 2 Lloyd's Rep. 461;Donohue v. Armco Inc (2002) 1 All ER 749 (HL)。如果双方同意了英国法院的管辖,但没有同意怎样送达(mode of service),英国法院在涉及外国被告的案件中允许把原告开始诉讼的告票(writ of summons)向外国送达。

针对英国海上货物保险,在有关的标准格式中都有印上一条排外性管辖权条文。伦敦保险市场针对开口/预约保单的 Market Reform Contract 或简称 MRC 中有一条排外性的管辖权条文(exclusive jurisdiction clause),其中的用词是:"... each party agrees to submit to the jurisdiction of the Courts of England and Wales."另外,针对个别航次的保单 MAR 91 也有类似的条文:"This insurance shall be subject to the exclusive jurisdiction of the English courts, except as may be expressly provided herein to the contrary."

但在开口/预约保单下签发的保险证明(certificate of insurance)如果使用的是劳合社标准格式的保险证明(Lloyd's certificate of insurance),它的最后部分有加上一条英国法院作为非排外性管辖权条文说:"This insurance is subject to the non-exclusive jurisdiction of the English Courts"。这条非排外性管辖权条文看来是作用不大。

英国法院的管辖会有它的优越之处,针对海上保险(不论是货物还是船舶),英国法律毫无疑问是最详尽与完善,而对英国保险法最熟悉的也就是英国法院。所以在历史上英国法院也是尽量垄断海上保险带来争议的管辖权,但近年来也了解如果想垄断世界上有关海上保险合约的争议是不可能的事。所以在伦敦市场,很早就已经接受一条 US Service of Suit Clause,给美国的受保人在美国法院提出诉讼的选择权。这虽然不是一条排外性管辖权条文,但受保人如果选择去美国起诉就会受到英国法院的尊重。另在海上货物保险的开口/预约保单,其他许多国家的受保人与保险人都在大量的签定保险合约(可一提的就是许多国家都有法律或者实践做法鼓励受保人的货方在当地的保险市场投保第一线的海上货物运输保险),他们不一定会使用英国的 MRC 格式。例如,在本章第 3.3 段已经提到的 Evialis v. S. I. A. T (2003) 2 Lloyd's Rep. 377 先例中,所有有关开口保单的当事人或经纪人都是在意大利,而使用的标准格式也是意大利商会组织所拟定的名为 Polizza Italiana di Assicurazione Merci Trasportate (edizione 1983),写的是意大利文。在该格式的 Article 16,更加有一条管辖权条文说:"The competent court, at the choice of the plaintiff, is exclusively that of the court office of the place in which is located the head office of the insurer or the agency which is in charge of the policy or in whose offices the contract was concluded."

6.2 保险合约没有明示管辖权条文:普通法的地位

已经提到过,针对非欧盟国家的管辖权争议目前在英国还是要根据普通法的地位。在普通法下,根据不少先例,如 The "Eleftheria" (1969) 1 Lloyd's Rep. 237;The

"El Amria" (1981) 2 Lloyd's Rep. 119; The "Bergen" (No. 2) (1997) 2 Lloyd's Rep. 710; Donohue v. Armco Inc (2002) 1 Lloyd's Rep. 425 (HL),一条如 Market Reform Contract 中的英国法院管辖权条文一般都会被支持。英国法院管辖权的基础在普通法下主要是根据"送达"(service)。如果被告在英国法院管辖境内能够被原告送达,这就给了英国法院管辖权的基础。如果被告是一家在英国注册成立的公司(不论他在英国有否实际的业务),原告就可以根据 1985 年《公司法》c. 6 s. 725(1),2006 年《公司法》c. 46 s. 1139,或 Civil Procedure Rule(简称 CPR)送达。一个外国的公司但在英国注册(《11th Company Law Directive 89/666/89》)也可以在境内送达。如果是自然人的被告,只要在英国法院管辖境内能找到,就可以送达。即使自然人的被告只是短暂在英国停留,如在希斯罗机场过境,也会被原告送达后就使英国法院有管辖权进行审理。另是如果在双方的合约中同意了送达的办法(mode of service),这也是完全受到尊重:CPR r 6. 11。这种情况在海上货物保险合约也经常会有,如在 Evialis v. S. I. A. T. (2003) 2 Lloyd's Rep. 377,在有关的保险证明(certificate of insurance)中,就有一条文"Address for Legal Proceedings in UK: W K Webster & Co., 6 Lloyd's Avenue, London EC3N 3AX, UK"。另外,如果涉及了海事纠纷可以在英国法院管辖境内能够成功告船(in rem),把告票送达有关的船舶或姐妹船,这也使得英国法院有管辖权进行审理。

但如果没有办法在英国法院管辖境内送达,因为被告是在外国,这就涉及了原告要向英国法院申请允许把告票送达外国(serve out of jurisdiction):CPR r 6. 36 与 Practice Direction B, para. 3. 1(6)(d)。这是因为这样做在外交上与国际友好会比较敏感,会被视为是干预外国法院的主权,所以是要法院的允许才能这样做。要取得申请,原告是要证明他有一个良好论点的案件(good arguable case),这通常通过案件的事实说服英国法院英国是一个自然的管辖地(natural forum)或是双方同意的管辖地(agreed forum)。反正是原告有一个举证责任说明英国是恰当的审理地点:CPR 6. 37(3)。另外,原告也必须证明他有一个诉因(cause of action),而且有一个合理的机会可以在审理中胜诉(reasonable prospect of success at trial):CPR 6. 37(1)(d)。这方面的案例可参阅:Seaconsar (Far East) Ltd. v. Bank Markazi Jomhouri Islami Iran (1994) AC 438。

6. 2. 1　一方当事人如果违反合约中的明示英国法院排外管辖权条文

如果保险合约的其中一方当事人漠视明示的英国法院管辖权条文,英国法院是会作出止诉禁令(anti - suit injunction),近期这方面涉及海上货物运输的先例有 OT Africa Line Ltd. v. Magic Sportswear Corp (2005) 2 Lloyd's Rep. 170 与 The "Hornbay" (2006) 2 Lloyd's Rep. 44。只会在很特殊的情况下才有可能出现英国法院不支持英国法院管辖权条文。例如一种罕见的情况就是在外国(美国或加拿大)的有管辖权法院已经在审理一个案件并涉及多个当事人,而其中一个当事人的合约是有英国管辖权条文。在这种合并审理(consolidated trial)的案件,显然英国只单独处理一个合约并非是好的做法,就会更愿意让美国法院合并审理。这方面先例有 Bouygues Offshore SA v. Caspian

Shipping Co. (1998) 2 Lloyd's Rep. 461 与 Donohue v. Armco Inc (2002) 1 Lloyd's Rep. 425 (HL)。这种情况反过来看,英国法院也会不支持外国管辖权条文,如在英国法院合并审理的案件中,其中一个当事人说他的合约中是有其他国家的管辖权条文,要求英国法院中止案件审理,就会被拒绝:Citi – March Ltd. v. Neptune Orient Lines Ltd. (1997) 1 Lloyd's Rep. 72; The MC Pearl (1997) 1 Lloyd's Rep. 566; Konkola Coppper Mines plc v. Coromin (2006) 1 Lloyd's Rep. 410。但如果其中一个当事人的合约有一条外国仲裁条文,英国法院才会难以拒绝他要求中止审理的申请,必须承认外国仲裁,因为这涉及了 1958 年《纽约公约》。

6.2.2 一方当事人如果违反合约中的明示外国法院排外管辖权条文

这是另一种情况,双方当事人在保险合约或者其他的合约中约定了一条外国法院排外管辖权条文,但其中一方的当事人选择漠视并在英国法院提出起诉。在这种情况下如果被告反对英国法院的管辖,英国法院就会要考虑是否要中止英国法院的程序。已经在较早的第6段说到,英国法院只会在很少情况下才会支持原告的"违约行为",并拒绝中止(stay)英国法院的程序。在 The "Eleftheria" (1969) 1 Lloyd's Rep. 237 先例,Brandon 大法官说只会在特殊的情况下才拒绝中止英国法院的程序,主要就是考虑在中止后原告被迫去外国法院时会否得不到一个公平的审理(fair trial)。Brandon 大法官提到有以下的考虑:"The principles established by the authorities can, I think, be summarized as follows: (1) Where plaintiffs sue in England in breach of an agreement to refer disputes to a foreign Court, and the defendants apply for a stay, the English Court, assuming the claim to be otherwise within the jurisdiction, is not bound to grant a stay but has a discretion whether to do so or not. (2) The discretion should be exercised by granting a stay unless strong cause for not doing so is shown. (3) The burden of proving such strong cause is on the plaintiffs. (4) In exercising its discretion the Court should take into account all the circumstances of the particular case. (5) In particular, but without prejudice to (6), the following matters, where they arise, may be properly regarded: (a) in what country the evidence on the issues of fact is situated, or more readily available, and the effect of that on the relative convenience and expense of trial as between the English and foreign Courts. (b) Whether the law of the foreign Court applies and, if so, whether it differs from English law in any material respects. (c) With what country either party is connected, and how closely. (d) Whether the defendant's genuinely desire trial in the foreign country, or are only seeking procedural advantages. (e) Whether the plaintiffs would be prejudiced by having to sue in the foreign Court because they would (i) be deprived of security for the claim; (ii) be unable to enforce any judgment obtained; (iii) be faced with a time – bar not applicable in England; or (iv) for political, racial, religious or other reason be unlikely to get a fair trial."

最后只简单地说,上述 Brandon 大法官所讲的多个考虑在今天恐怕已经被收紧。

换言之,英国法院会更加尊重一条双方约定的明示外国法院排外管辖权条文(更不用说是同意一条仲裁条文)。举例说 Brandon 大法官所讲的(e)(iii)考虑原告会否去外国的法院面对时效已届满的抗辩而受到了损害。如果有的话,法院以前会要求被告同意不以时效届满的抗辩交换同意中止英国法院程序。但在 The "Spiliada" (1987) 1 Lloyd's Rep. 1,Goff 勋爵明确表示不再是考虑之一,说:"Now, to take some extreme examples, suppose that the plaintiff allowed the limitation period to elapse in the appropriate jurisdiction, and came here simply because he wanted to take advantage of a more generous time bar applicable in this country; or suppose that it was obvious that the plaintiff should have commenced proceedings in the appropriate jurisdiction, and yet he did not trouble to issue a protective writ there; in cases such as these, I cannot see that the court should hesitate to stay the proceedings in this country, even though the effect would be that the plaintiff's claim would inevitably be defeated by a plea of the time bar in the appropriate jurisdiction."

The "Spiliada"的贵族院先例只是针对自然或适合的管辖地争议(这在下一段会讨论),如果是针对一条明示外国法院排外管辖权条文而中止英国法院程序,估计在这一方面法院应该会更加不理会违反该条文的原告会在外国法院面临时效届满的困境。

6.2.3　自然或适合的管辖地

如果没有明示管辖权条文,英国普通法的默示地位就是找出一个最自然或适合的管辖地(natural or appropriate forum)是对双方当事人最有利与最后能够伸张正义。如果有这样的管辖地,英国法院会自己中止审理,把管辖权让给其他国家的法院。这也是 Forum non conveniens 的说法,其中重要的先例是贵族院的 The "Spiliada" (1987) 1 Lloyd's Rep. 1,另一个是上诉庭先例 Lubbe v. Cape Plc (2000) 1 Lloyd's Rep. 139。可以说,英国法院找出哪个是最自然或适合的管辖地,要针对很多由双方当事人提出的各方面利弊因素,然后在平衡后作出裁量权。其中一个重要因素是针对证据主要的所在地,另一个是与英国法院相比另一个管辖地法院是否可靠(这包括司法公证、法官水平与延误)。如在先例 Lubbe v. Cape Plc 案件是发生在南非,所有的证据都是在南非,除了比较容易取证,代价与在英国法院相比也会是很低。南非法院也被视为是有足够水平对案件作出公平的审理。所以在该先例,最后是判南非比英国更适合。但在 The "Spiliada",贵族院是判与加拿大法院相比,英国法院是更适合的管辖地。其中被视为重要的因素包括证人出庭的方便(其中在该案件专家证人就住在伦敦),以及英国法院已经判过了与当时仍在审理的几个同类案件(另一艘船舶也在审理,名为 Cambridgeshire 轮,同类案件是涉及了加拿大出口的硫磺是否造成了船舱钢板的严重腐蚀),导致英国比起加拿大有更多这方面经验的审理法官、代表律师与专家证人等。这会导致有效率、有水平与更省钱的审理,最终有利双方当事人能够伸张正义。有关这种择地行诉(forum shopping)的国际性案件,笔者在多本其他的书中有提到,如是《海事法》第 5 页,不去重复。只说,如果为了肯定与避免浪费金钱而择地行诉,最好还是有一条明示排外性管辖权条文或是仲裁条文。

6.3 保险合约没有明示管辖权条文:欧盟国家的地位

接下来要讨论的是《Council Regulation (EC) 44/2001》(《EC Judgments Regulation》),这份法律文件是在2000年9月22日通过,主要是针对民商事纠纷的管辖权与判决的承认与执行。该文件是通过《Civil Jurisdiction and Judgments Order 2001》被引入了英国立法,并于2002年3月1日生效。该份法律文件之所以重要是因为由伦敦保险市场签发的海上货物保险合约或保单中的管辖权条款绝大部分都要受这份法律文件的约束。

根据《EC Judgments Regulation》之 Article 2,在一般的保险合约原告是可以在被告的住所地起诉。而根据 Article 3,与保险相关的诉讼原告(受保人或者是保险受益人)也是可以在他自己的住所地起诉。这种规定显然是为了保护原告,他们会是一般的老百姓,所以可让他们在自己的住所地提起诉讼,会有方便、省钱与安心等好处。同样的优待也在 Article 2 中被延伸消费者与雇佣合约的雇员。

这些对保险人作为被告而言,都是强制性的法律条文,但是如果保险合约有明示管辖权条文是允许受保人在其他国家的法院(不论是否是 EC 成员国)提起诉讼,也都是可以承认的。

根据《EC Judgments Regulation》之 Article 2,对上述强制性的法律条文也是有两种例外情况允许订约自由,就是被远洋船舶运输的货物(也就是本书针对的情况)或者是属于"大风险"(large risk)的情况。在这两种例外情况,双方可以同意一条排外性管辖权条文,这就不存在任何强制管辖权了。虽然是这样,管辖权条文的有效性还是要根据《EC Judgments Regulation》之 Article 23(1)来解释。如果合约的一方或多方是欧盟成员国,并且同意了某个欧盟成员国的法院是有管辖权,Article 23(1)就会适用。

因此,如果保险人的住所地是在英国,英国是欧盟的成员国,《EC Judgments Regulation》就会适用在他所签订的保险合约。如果该保险合约的受保人住所地在德国,但明示规定了管辖权是在某个欧盟成员国(如法国或者比利时),该明示管辖权条文也有效。即便该保险人的住所地并非是欧盟成员国(如日本或美国的保险公司),但如果外国保险人在某个欧盟成员国是有分公司或分支机构存在,而恰恰是该分公司或分支机构的运作(如签发了有关的保险合约)导致了纠纷的产生,则该保险人的居住地会被视为是在该欧盟成员国。

总结来说,《EC Judgments Regulation》适用在保险合约的管辖权条文是要满足两个条件:(1)合约的一方是欧盟成员国;(2)该管辖权条文明示约定了某个欧盟成员国的法院有管辖权。对于满足了以上两个条件的管辖权条文,《EC Judgments Regulation》之 Article 23 是这样规定:"Such jurisdiction shall be exclusive unless the parties have agreed otherwise."

在上述介绍过的先例 Evialis v. S. I. A. T (2003) 2 Lloyd's Rep. 377,保险证明(certificate of insurance)上是有这样的一条条文:"Address for legal proceedings in UK:

W K Webster & Co... London, United Kingdom”,该条文本质上与本章第6.9段的US Suit of Service条文相同,也就是接受英国的管辖权。但该条文被英国法院根据Article 23解释为一条非排外性的管辖权(permissive jurisdiction clause)条文,这看来是与第6.1段所介绍的劳合社标准格式的保险证明的non-exclusive jurisdiction条文是一致的。不过Market Reform Contract中的管辖权条文“each party agrees to submit to the jurisdiction of the Courts of England and Wales”,根据Article 23就被认为是英国法院具有排外性管辖权。而根据先例S&W Berisford plc and NGI International Precious Metals Inc. v. New Hampshire Insurance Co. Ltd. (1990) 1 Lloyd's Rep. 454,MAR 91中的管辖权条文“This insurance shall be subject to the exclusive jurisdiction of the English courts, except as may be expressly provided herein to the contrary”,Article 23也被认为是英国法院具有排外性管辖权。

6.4 《EC Judgments Regulation》与《Lugano Convention》的关系

1988年《Lugano Convention》的全称是《Convention on Jurisdiction and the Enforcement of Judgments in Civil and Commercial Matters》(已经有了2007年的新版本,详见本章6.6.2段),它的适用比《EC Judgments Regulation》较为广一些,因为它包括了欧洲自由贸易区的三个成员国:挪威、冰岛和瑞士。该公约通过《Civil Jurisdiction and Judgments Act 1991》在英国生效。其中的规定与适用在所有欧盟国家的《EC Judgments Regulation》并非是在所有方面都相同。在海上货物保险相关的管辖权问题上,除了“大风险”(large risk)例外这一点,两个欧盟公约的大原则都相同。这里有必要说明的是欧盟(European Community)是欧共体(European Union)的前身。另EFTA的成员国挪威、冰岛与瑞士都不是欧盟国家。如果保险合约一方是EC或者EFTA的成员国,而合约中又规定了某EC或者EFTA成员国的法院有管辖权,那么《Lugano Convention》也是有效力的。对于既是欧盟成员国又是《Lugano Convention》成员国的国家(如英国),两个公约会同时生效,这就会出现重复或重合。

例如,在先例Tradigrain SA v. S. I. A. T. S. p. A & Others (2002) 2 Lloyd's Rep. 553,是关于海上货物运输保险,所在地在瑞士日内瓦的原告Tradigrain SA在英国开始了诉讼,而被告是30多家所在地分布在不同欧盟成员国的保险公司(各占不同份额),其中有两家是在英国。有关争议的保险是通过位于德国的保险代理人代表位于意大利的保险公司S. I. A. T. 达成的。该保险合约承保的是在印度的菜油的储存风险(storage risk),合并了协会货物条文(一切险)。其中还有一条汉堡管辖权条文,关于该条文的有效性是要受《Lugano Convention》的约束,因为原告的所在地是瑞士。

6.5 《EC Judgments Regulation》对明示管辖权条文在形式上的要求

与在本章6.1段所针对的普通法下的排外管辖权条文相比,这方面在《EC Judgments Regulation》之Article 23(1)与《Lugano Convention》之Article 17(1)有一些规定,就是明示管辖权条文必须是以书面形式且经过双方同意,如下:“(a) in writing or evidenced in writing; or (b) in a form which accords with practices which the parties have established between themselves; or (c) in international trade or commerce, in a form which accords with a usage of which the parties are or ought to have been aware and which in such trade or commerce is widely known to, and regularly observed by, parties to contracts of the type involved in the particular or commerce concerned."

上述的(c)是英国要求加在原先的1968年《EC Jurisdiction Convention》所欠缺的地方,原因是为了保障英国法院长久以来对国际贸易中大量使用标准格式合约(其中有英国法院管辖权条文)以及习惯性做法下所带来的管辖权。如提单,由于它的可转让性以及通常只有船长代表船东签字,以致即使有一条管辖权条文,也很难证明是双方以文书形式同意,特别是提单转让至无辜第三人的手中。所以加上上述的(c)就可以根据国际贸易的习惯性做法假设双方是同意英国管辖权。这方面的欧共体判例有 Case C-106/95 Mainschiffahrts-Genossenschaft eg v. Les Gravieres Rhenanes (MSG) (1997) All ER (EC) 385 与 Case C-159/97 Trasporti Castelletti Spezizioni International SpA v. Hugo Trumpy SpA (1999) I L Pr 492。

很明显,开口/预约保单如果根据 Market Reform Contract 的标准格式,保险人与受保人是满足了对管辖权条文书面形式的要求。但对于保险证明(这往往是开口保单中不同航次所签发的保险证明,最后流转到收货人的手中)即使合并了 Market Reform Contract,对持有人来讲,针对管辖权条文是否有被有效的合并与满足了文书形式的要求还不是很明朗。在先例 Tradigrain SA v. S. I. A. T. S. p. A & Others (2002) 2 Lloyd's Rep. 553,开口保单下签发的一份保险证明是没有明示提到管辖权,它唯一提到的就是开口保单的号码。而开口保单的管辖权应是规定了汉堡法院有管辖权,因为明示合并了《德国海上保险条例》(German Rules of Marine Insurances 或 ADS)与协会货物条文。这被判定保险证明不能依赖泛泛的合并引进开口保单中的管辖权条文。Colman 大法官跟从了先例 Credit Suisse Financial Products v. Societe Generale d'Enterprises (1997) CLC 168 以及再保险合约中的管辖权合并条文的相关判例 AIG Europe SA v. QBE International Insurance Ltd. (2001) 2 Lloyd's Rep. 268 得出的结论是,合并条文是可以有效合并管辖权条文,但这只有在它清楚写明管辖权条文存在的情况下,而本先例中是没能够满足。Colman 大法官是这样说:"The certificates of insurance issued by Aon(保险经纪人)in respect of each shipment refer to the ADS General Rules of Marine Insurance and to the Special Conditions for Cargo (ADS Cargo 1973/1984). They make no express reference to jurisdiction provisions in the Open Cover. The only specific reference to that contract is the reference number. That clearly does not operate to incorporate the Hamburg jurisdiction clause. Displacement of the jurisdictional rules under the Lugano Convention by agreement between the parties contract is governed by Article 17. Under those provisions the only available basis for incorporation in this case would be an agreement in writing or evidenced in writing under 17(a) for there is no evidence to support a course of dealing under (b) or a form adopted by trade usage under (c). In a very recent decision in AIG Europe SA v. QBE International Insurance Ltd. (3 May 2001) Moore - Bick J. considered the application of Article 17(a) with reference to Estassis Salotti di Colzani Aimo etc v. RUWA Polstereimaschinen Gmbh C - 24/76 [1976] ECR 1831 and the main English decision on Article 17 - Credit Suisse Financial Products v. Societe Generale d' Enterprises [1997] CLC 168 (CA), - as well as the English decisions on incorporation of jurisdiction clauses into contracts of reinsurance, and concluded that, whereas under Article 17(a) general words of incorporation might be effective to incorporate a jurisdiction clause, they would do so only if they clearly and precisely demonstrated the existence of a consensus to that effect in relation to jurisdiction clauses."

看来这里的问题与提单合并租约时有否将租约中的排外性管辖权条文与仲裁条文合并进来是类似的。

6.6 关于管辖权的例外情况

6.6.1 例外情况之一:被远洋船舶运输的货物

与消费者有关的立法,大原则是受保人有权利在他自己的所在地起诉保险人(见上述6.3段)。但是当英国将《EC Jurisdiction Regulation》纳入到自己的法律体系中后,关于海上与航空保险就产生了一些例外情形。以远洋船舶运输的货物而言,这些保险合约的受保人被认为是不需要像普通的消费者那样受到保护,所以如果保险合约中的管辖权条文与大原则背离也是可以允许的。那么合并了协会货物条文并涉及了短暂在岸上储存货物(这方面在本书第十一章有详论)的保险合约是否也可以背离该大原则呢?根据先例 Tradigrain SA v. S. I. A. T. S. p. A & Others (2002) 2 Lloyd's Rep. 553,虽然货物并非在海上运输途中,但保险合约或开口保单中的汉堡管辖权条文是有效的,也就是说,虽然货物不是在海上运输的途中,但只要储存风险是与海上运输有关就可以偏离大原则。而纯粹的仓储风险,除非是满足了大风险的要求,都必须遵守《EC Judgments Regulation》之 Article 3 关于大原则的规定,也就是受保人有权利在他自己的住所地起诉保险人。

6.6.2 例外情况之二:属于"大风险"情况

将《Lugano Convention》Article 12A 与《EC Judgments Regulation》Article 14.5 作比较,会发现前者是没有关于大风险的例外规定。不过在 2007 年 10 月 30 日,欧盟成员国与丹麦以及另外 3 个 EFTA 成员国签订了新的《Lugano Convention》让《Lugano Convention》的相关规定与《EC Judgments Regulation》一致。关于大风险的定义在 Council Directive 73/239/EEC 中是有规定(这在本章第 5.2 段是有介绍):大风险包括了货物运输途中的损坏与损失,而不论是以何种方式运输。另外也包括了财产保险中的火险、爆炸、风暴与盗窃险,只要保单持有人是大的机构(substantial concern)。

6.7 最先起诉的法院(The court first seized)

根据《EC Judgments Regulation》Article 2,在一般的保险合约,原告是可以在被告的住所地起诉。但在较早已经谈到过被远洋船舶运输的货物以及与远洋运输有关的短暂的岸上储存风险是属于例外情况。这样一来，如果有关的保险合约中没有一条明示的管辖权条文，就有可能是不止一个法院拥有管辖权。在这种情况下，从对自己最有利的角度出发，很可能受保人在一个国家的法院提起诉讼，而保险人在另外一个国家也提起诉讼，而不同的国家在何种情况下接受管辖权会有所不同，经常会是两个或两个以上的国家法院都认为自己有管辖权。这种抢夺管辖权的情况肯定是令人不满意的。为了避免这种情况，《EC Judgments Regulation》就规定了如果多个欧盟成员国的法院都有管辖权，那么是要由"快一步"（first seized）的法院来决定，这包括了进行审理或者中止自己的诉讼程序将管辖权让给另一个成员国。

《EC Judgments Regulation》关于多个法院的管辖在 Article 27 与 28 是这样规定：

"Article 27(1) Where proceedings involving the same cause of action and between the same parties are brought in the courts of different Member States, any court other than the court first seised shall of its own motion stay its proceedings until such time as the jurisdiction of the court first seised is established.

Article 27(2) Where the jurisdiction of the court first seised is established, any court other than the court first seised shall decline jurisdiction in favor of that court.

Article 28(1) Where related actions are pending in the courts of different Member States, any court other than the court first seised may stay its proceedings.

Article 28(3) For the purpose of this Article, actions are deemed to be related where they are so closely connected that it is expedient to hear and determine them together to avoid the risk of irreconcible judgments resulting from separate proceedings."

在先例 Evialis v. S. I. A. T (2003) 2 Lloyd's Rep. 377，保险人在意大利开始了针对货损索赔的诉讼程序。受保人根据英国管辖权条文向英国法院申请禁令禁止保险人在意大利提起诉讼程序。根据 Article 27 与 28，英国法院不能作出命令，因为意大利法院是最先接受起诉的法院。事实上，根据先例 Turner v. Grovit (2004) 2 Lloyd's Rep. 169，欧洲法院已经禁止英国法院向其他"快一步"的欧盟成员国法院作出止诉禁令。

这些方面，可以参考笔者《仲裁法——从 1996 年英国仲裁法到国际商务仲裁》第 188 页与《仲裁法——从开庭审理到裁决书的作出与执行》第 252 页的相关内容介绍。

6.8 仲裁

文书仲裁条文在海上货物保险合约中是很少见的，这在船舶保险也是有同样的情况，正如上述曾经介绍 MAR 与 Market Reform Contract 中都有一条排外性的英国法院管辖权条文（exclusive jurisdiction clause），就是双方在保险合约内发生争议后必须去英国法院诉讼。但在再保险合约中，伦敦市场普遍加上文书仲裁条文，导致有争议的话，保险人与再保险人必须通过仲裁去解决争议。他们不能去英国法院，即使英国法院本来是有管辖权（如被告的住所地是在英国或再保险合约是在英国签订）。因为根据 1996 年《英国仲裁法》Section 9(1),英国法院必须中止诉讼程序,让仲裁解决争议。而如果是一方当事人(保险人或者是再保险人)违反仲裁条文在其他的欧盟成员国法院最先提起诉讼,另一方当事人可以去该成员国法院要求中止法院诉讼程序,这是根据 1958 年《纽约公约》,而欧共体成员国可以说都是《纽约公约》的成员国。至于欧共体的法律《EC Judgments Regulation》Article 1 [2] [d]排除公约适用在仲裁,不针对仲裁的原因就是,欧盟成员国都是《纽约公约》的成员国,有了国际公约的约束就不好再用区域性的公约针对。虽然如此,欧盟法院在著名的 The "Front Comor" (2009) 1 Lloyd's Rep. 413 不允许英国法院去对其他欧盟成员国法院作出止诉禁令,迫使有关当事人非去伦敦仲裁不可。有关这方面的情况笔者在《仲裁法——从开庭审理到裁决书的作出与执行》第 257 页有相关介绍。

笔者对这一现象是有点难以理解,就是为什么英国的直接或第一线海上保险喜欢法院的管辖权,但再保险就去仲裁。笔者针对这个问题也曾经向一些专家请教过,包括 Robert Merkin 教授。这一疑点在笔者与汪鹏南教授所著《英国海上保险条款详论》第 402 ~ 406 页有谈到,并谈到在第一线海上保险去英国法院可能会有些比仲裁优越的地方。例如,谈到了英国法院的传统做法是可以下令索赔全损的船东必须先交出全面的船舶文件,拒赔的保险人才需要作出抗辩。[1] 另可以想到的是直接的海上

---

[1] 这种做法在 18 世纪的英国普通法就发展起来了,原因是发生损失的地点是在很远的地方,海上保险人有困难去调查以质疑或者抗拒一个船东或货方的索赔,所以英国法院有了这种做法,希望对保险人的利益作出平衡。随着通讯和交通的发展,保险人的这一困难得到很大解决。加上历史上发生不少保险人以法院这一命令去留难受保人的船东与货方。所以,英国法院不再愿意作出这种命令去要求受保人提供非常广泛的船舶文件。但还是会有这种做法,比较近期涉及的先例有:Probatina Shipping Co. Ltd. v. Sun Insurance Office Ltd. (1973) 2 Lloyd's Rep. 520;The "Star Sea" (2001) UKHL 1。有权在诉讼程序中作出这种命令,也在 CPR Rule 31. 12 与 58. 14(2)。这方面可以节录 Colman 大法官在其 2008 年著的《The Practice and Procedure of the Commercial Court》中第 6 版第 239 页所说:"An application for ship's paper is, like other applications for specific disclosure, made under CPR Part 31. 12, but also receives specific mention in CPR Part 58. 14. The application arises in claims brought by or against insurers on marine policies where the insurers allege that the loss has been caused by the wilful misconduct of the assured. The effect of the order is that the assured is required to give disclosure on oath and is to produce for inspection all the ship's papers. The application may be made at any stage in the proceedings and on such terms as the court thinks fit, including a stay for proceeding, traditionally, it is made once the claimant assured has served his particulars of claim but before service of the defendant insurers' defence. It may be made against a party who claims on a marine policy but who did not operate the vessel nor have possession of or direct control over her, such as a mortgagee, in which case the order imposes a duty to take all reasonable steps to procure disclosure of the ship's papers from the owners or from whichever party may have them. It is not confined to claims under a hull and machinery policy—it may also be made where the claim is advanced under a cargo policy and the insurers propose to reply by way of defence on the allegation that the assured was a party to or aware of the loss of the cargo by wilful misconduct, such as where there is a conspiracy to scuttle the vessel with the cargo on board or to simulate shipment. An order for ship's paper is not available in cases where the carriage was exclusively over land; where, however, it includes but is not confined to land transit an order will be made in an appropriate case even where the loss occurred during the land portion of the transit."

保险经常会涉及多位保险人,各自承保不同的份额。其中在第一章第1段提到的MAR 91的标准格式中有一页是填写Definitive numbers of the Syndicates and proportions,就是将所有保险人以及他们各自的承保份额列出来,并在一开始就规定每个保险人只是为他承保的份额负责(Each Underwriting Member of a syndicate whose definitive number and proportion is set out in the following Table shall be liable only for his own share at his respective Syndicate's proportion)。在Market Reform Contract中,也有类似的规定,如说明保险人的责任是分开而不是连带的(This section provides that the liability of insurer is several not joint and is not re-produced),另也有条文针对保险人各自的承保份额(Basis of written lines)。这都表示如果有了争议,如最常见的拒赔,受保人要同时向多位保险人提出诉讼。这在英国法院是做得到的,因为法院可以下命令将所有保险人都列为共同被告。但仲裁就是没办法解决这种合并审理的问题。其他可能的原因包括第一线保险希望由法院审理就有了公开的先例,可以给以后的案件进行指引;而仲裁就没有建立先例的机会。另可能会有的原因是英国商业法院在传统上一直由水平很高而且对保险业务极为熟悉的大法官来审理,这给了保险人与受保人很大的信心。

6.9 接受美国诉讼条文(USA Service of Suit clause)

该条文已经在英国保险合约内存在了很长时间,虽然各个时期采用的措辞可能有不同。这个现象可以作以下三方面的分析:(1)英国保险的重要性是不容置疑的,因为世界上其他国家的第一线保险为了在全球范围内分散风险就避免不了要去英国保险市场寻求再保险。(2)美国作为全球的经济强国对再保险的需求很大。(3)英国保险市场也知道不能强制所有其他国家都接受英国法院的管辖权与法律。虽然英国人明显对他们的法院与法律感到自豪,而且对其他国家的法院不安心。但这里很久以来只有一个例外,就是英国认为美国法院的判决可以接受。这就带来在英国签订的保险合约,只要涉及美国的受保人或保险人,都会加上一条接受美国诉讼条文。该条文并非是管辖权条文,更加谈不上是一条排外管辖权条文(exclusive jurisdiction clause)。它的作用只是给美国的受保人或保险人多一个选择,就是在起诉伦敦保险人/再保险人时可以不去英国法院而去美国法院。

这种条文的内容在先例Ace Insce v. Zurich (2000) 2 Lloyd's Rep. 423中是有出现:"It is agreed that in the event of the failure of the Underwriters hereon to pay any amount claimed to be due hereunder, the Underwriters hereon at the request of the Insured (or Re-insured), will submit to the jurisdiction of a Court of competent jurisdiction within the United States. Nothing in this Clause constitutes or should be understood to constitute an action in any Court of competent jurisdiction in the United States..."

有关这一个条文,上述先例的Longmore大法官是这样说:

"The service of suit clause outweighs these comparatively minor considerations. Such clauses are well known to insurance practitioners and should be given a proper and sensible construction. It is fairly clear that, if the insured had exercised their option to sue in New York in Armadora Occidental S. A. v. Horace Mann Insurance Co. (1977) 22 Lloyd's Rep. 406, the courts would not have maintained the leave to serve out of the jurisdiction granted to the claimants in that case. The effect of the clause was also considered in the unreported case of Excess Insurance v. Allendale Mutual Insurance Co. (C. A. Mar. 8, 1995). In that case, as in this, reinsurers had sued for a declaration that they were not liable under a reinsurance policy. The reinsured carried on business in Illinois and had their head office in Rhode Island where proceedings were, later than the English proceedings, begun by the reinsured. There was a service of suit clause in virtually identical terms to the clause in this case. Saville J. held that it was a breach of contract for reinsurers to have brought suit in England and that the leave granted to serve out of the jurisdiction should be set aside. The Court of Appeal did not agree with this construction of the clause and held that the underwriters had no obligations at all until they had received a request to submit to a court of competent jurisdiction in the United States. Hobhouse L. J. said:

The function of the first part of this clause is to give rights to the assured which enable him, if he so chooses, to serve the underwriter with process in a United States court of the assured's choice.

Despite his disagreement with Saville J.'s approach, however, he decided (and the other members of the court agreed) that it was 'inevitable' that the court's discretion should be exercised to set aside the leave granted to serve out of the jurisdiction. That was because proceedings had been started properly in Rhode Island:

... as a matter of jurisdiction. That is the effect of the service of suit clause and no one has argued before us to the contrary.

Hobhouse L. J. then made clear that the judge in Rhode Island would consider his own jurisdiction and could decide, if he wished, to stay the proceedings so that they could continue in England or allow them to continue in Rhode Island. But it was a matter entirely for him and it was inappropriate for the English court to give leave to serve out of the jurisdiction.

So here, proceedings have been properly started in Texas. Those proceedings are continuing. The Judge in Texas can make any order he or she thinks fit as to the venue of those proceedings but the leave given by Mr. Justice Thomas to serve ZAIC should be set aside and, other things being equal, there should be a stay of the proceedings against ZIC."。

7. 重要案例的介绍:Evialis v. S. I. A. T

最后,可以把多次提到的先例 Evialis v. S. I. A. T (2003) 2 Lloyd's Rep. 377 所

涉及的案情作稍微详细一点地介绍,因为它涉及了适用法与管辖权的争议,而且有关的当事人都是欧盟国家成员。案情是一家法国公司 Evialis 以 CIF 向一家意大利公司 Ametra 购买了一船的棉花球(cotton pellets),装港是非洲象牙海岸的首都 Abidjan,而卸港就是法国的 Rouen。CIF 卖方 Ametra 所租用的船舶名为 Irene 轮,它在 Rouen 卸货的时候发现货物损坏。在结汇的时候,Ametra 转让或者交出了一份保险证明(certificate of insurance),说明名为 S. I. A. T 的意大利保险公司承保该批货物的一切险。在 Ametra 与 S. I. A. T 之间的开口/预约保单,承保一切险是合并了英国保险市场 1982 年版本的协会货物条文(一切险)(Institute Cargo Clauses [A])。在 Evialis 发现了货物损坏(金额高达 225 万法郎),就通知了 S. I. A. T,并在不久后向 Rouen 法院开始诉讼,并申请法院指定专家核定损失。该专家也在 2001 年 10 月 5 日给出报告说损失是 225 万法郎。到了 2002 年 6 月 21 日,S. I. A. T 在意大利的热那亚法院提起诉讼并要求法院对以下三个方面作出宣告判决:(1) Evialis 的索赔根据《意大利航海法》之 Article 1457 只有 1 年时效,该时效已届满;(2)货物的损坏原因是固有缺陷,这不属于承保的风险;(3) Evialis 没有减少损失,违反了施救责任与义务。

这导致了在 2002 年 10 月 20 日,Evialis 在英国法院开始了诉讼,并要求英国法院判定到底保险人应否作出赔付的争议的管辖权是在英国法院而非是意大利法院。在英国法院 Evialis 也申请了一个止诉禁令(anti - suit injunction),禁止 S. I. A. T 在意大利法院继续诉讼。同时在三天后,Evialis 向热那亚法院申请中止诉讼程序并质疑它的管辖权,根据的理由有:(1) Evialis 是一家法国公司;(2) S. I. A. T 与 Ametra 之间的开口/预约保单是有一条排外管辖权条文(exclusive jurisdiction clause),该条文并没有明确说意大利法院有权管辖,如下:"The competent court at the choice of the plaintiff, is exclusively that of the court office of the place in which is located the head office of the insurer or the agency which is in charge of the policy or in whose offices the contract was concluded."

而双方的争议也涉及了适用法方面,显然,S. I. A. T 认为适用法是意大利法,但 Evialis 就认为是英国法。看来仅是针对索赔时效,两国的法律就已经有很大的不同。

Smith 大法官根据英国当时 1982 年的有关法律(在该方面与上述第 1 段所讲的 2000 年《Financial Services and Markets Act》立法没有区别),判意大利法律是适用法,说:

"However, as I have stated, the insurers say that the contract of insurance is governed by the law of Italy, and that the English law on these questions is not in point. The law applicable to the contract is to be determined under the provisions at section 94B(1) and part 1 of Schedule 3A of the Insurance Companies Act 1982 (which have since been repealed and replaced by the Financial Services & Markets Act 2000 and Regulations thereunder). That is because the contract constituted 'general business', which includes insurance of goods in transit. It covered risks situated in a member state, Italy, that being where the policyholder, Ametra, had their establishment when the contract was entered into: section 96A(3)(d)(ii). Paragraph 1(1) of schedule 3A provided:

'Where the policy holder has his habitual residence or central administration within the territory of the member State where the risk is situated, the law applicable to the contract is the law of that member State.

However, where the law of that member State so allows, the parties may choose the law of another country.'

Accordingly, Italian law would be applicable to the contract unless the parties chose the law of another country. Paragraph 2 of the Schedule provides that any such choice must 'be expressed or demonstrated with reasonable certainty by the terms of the contract or the circumstances of the case'. The essential question, therefore, is whether there was so expressed or demonstrated a choice of English law by the parties, that is to say by Ametra and the insurers. In my judgment, that question is to be determined in accordance with the law of Italy, the law which would be applicable to the contract in the absence of an express choice of law: see Dicey and Morris The Conflict of Laws (13th Ed.) at para 32 – 101. However, I would have reached the same conclusion whether I determined the question by the law of England or that of Italy."

上述对该先例的介绍希望能够更好地说明较早所针对的问题。

第六章　一切险承保风险与局限以及近因原则

协会货物条文（一切险）之第 1 ~ 3 条：承保风险（Risks Covered）[1]

风险

1. 本保险承保保险标的（货物）之损失或损害的一切风险，但不包括下列第 4、5、6 和 7 条规定的除外责任。

共同海损

2. 本保险承保根据运输合约与/或准据法和惯例理算或确定的共同海损和救助费用，其产生是为了避免任何原因造成的损失或与避免任何原因造成的损失有关，但此种原因须不是本保险第 4、5、6 和 7 条除外的危险。

"双方有责碰撞条款"

3. 本保险赔偿受保人就下述承保的风险根据运输合约"双方有责碰撞条款"的责任。在承运人根据该条文出索赔的情况下，受保人同意通知保险人，保险人有权自己承担费用为受保人对此种索赔提出抗辩。

2009 年版本中这一条文在措辞上与 1982 年版本的协会货物条文相比没有作出改变，但由于除外责任有所改变（第 4 ~ 7 条），故保险人的责任范围就实际上有了变化。它基本上就是把这份保险合约承保的风险分三条不同的条文说明。在本章，会针对的只是第 1 条一切险，它针对的是被承保的货物受到实质损失或者损坏（physical loss or damage）。至于承保货物受到非实质损失或者损坏（non - physical loss or damage），也就是上述第 2 条与第 3 条的条文所针对，虽然也被承保，但会在本书第七章进一步解释。

1. 什么是一切险（all risks）

一切险在海上货物运输保险是一个比较新的做法，虽然这种保险已经存在了好几百年的时间。众所周知，以前的货物保险与船舶保险是走在一起的，根据的就是劳合社标准 S. G 保单，会是在很早没有通讯的年代船上货物的所有人也就是船东，或是货物所有人在船上押运并在船舶到达港口后进行贸易。

---

〔1〕 英文条文参见附录三。

劳合社标准 S. G 保单所承保的只是针对性的列明风险(named perils),如海上风险(peril of the sea)、火灾(fire)、外来的暴力盗窃(thieves)、船员的不法行为(barratry)等。除了水险外,也包括一些与战争有关的列明风险,如军舰(men of war)、敌人(enemies)等。这些列明风险包括或不包括些什么情况都有先例针对,并且在 1906 年《英国海上保险法》的附件中给了每一个列明风险权威的解释。

到了第一次世界大战结束后,一切险开始被接受。但一些传统的保险人还是不愿意承保一切险,而一切险的保险通常是以保险经纪人附加条款(broker's clause)的形式承保。到了 1950 年左右,伦敦市场才感觉到有必要把一切险的保险合约规范化,这就在 1951 年首次出现"协会货物条文(一切险)"(Institute Cargo Clause [All Risks])。

有关一切险所承保的范围,最早的先例是 Jacob v Caviller (1902) 7 Com. Cas. 116,该保险合约有一条附加条款说:"The Insurance is against **all risks**, including mortality from any cause, jettison, and washing overboard..."

英国法院判"一切险"(all risk)这一个措辞与劳合社标准 S. G 保单中一连串的列明风险后的总结语"all other perils, losses and misfortunes"是两码事。有了一切险的措辞,就再也不需要加上承保的个别列明风险。

1.1　一切险的承保范围与局限

接下来的介绍先例是 Schloss Bros v Stevens (1908) 2 KB 665,也是一样的判法。Walton 大法官说一切险这一个措辞是承保所有在运输途中发生意外而蒙受的风险("all losses by any **accidental cause** of any kind occurring during the transit")。就这句话而言,有说明风险必须是意外所造成。

再接下来就是著名的贵族院先例 British & Foreign Marine Insurance Company Limited v Gaunt (1921) 2 AC 41,该先例同意 Schloss Bros v Stevens 的判法,并明确规定了一切险的承保范围与不承保的范围。Sumner 勋爵是这样说:"There are, of course, limits to 'all risks'. They are risks and risks insured against. Accordingly the expression does not cover inherent vice or mere wear and tear... it covers a risk, not a certainty; it is something which happens to the subject - matter from without, not the natural behavior of that subject - matter, being what it is, in the circumstances under which it is carried. Nor is it a loss which the assured brings about by his own act, for then he has not merely exposed the goods to the chance of injury, he has injured them himself."

在上述的判决中可看到普通法有一个默示地位就是一切险是不承保一些非意外造成与肯定会发生的风险,以及受保人的货方自己导致的损失。在比较近期的另一个先例 Mayban General Assurance Bhd v. Alstom Power Plants Ltd. (2004) 2 Lloyd's Rep. 609 中,也有同样的说法。Moore - Bick 大法官谈到协会货物条文(一切险)承保的风险十分广泛,但还是有三个后果或限制。一是受保人要证明这个损失是一个意外,而不是肯定会发生的事;二是受保人不需要进一步说明这一个意外到底是怎样的意外与它的本质;三是一切险也不承保自然损耗或固有缺陷,这基本上还是与第一个后果一致。Moore – Bick 大法官说:"The expression 'all risks' is used in policies of insurance as a convenient way of encompassing all insurable risks to which the property in question may be exposed without attempting to identify them individually. The contract nonetheless remains one under which the insurer accepts the risk of loss occurring through the occurrence of some peril acting on the property insured. A number of consequences follow from this. The first is that in order to recover under the policy the insured must prove that the loss was caused by an accident or casualty of some kind. Insurers accept the risk, although the insured must prove a loss by an accident of some kind, it is not necessary for him to go further and establish the exact nature of the accident by which it occurred. The third is that the policy does not cover the insured against loss due to wear and tear or the inherent vice of the thing insured, whether that loss was bound to occur or was fortuitous in the sense that its occurrence depended on the particular circumstances to which the goods happened to be exposed in the course of the voyage."

该先例的判法之后是被上诉庭在先例 Global Process System Inc & Anor v. Syarikat Takaful Malaysia Berhad (2009) EWHC 637 (Comm)推翻(这在第八章4.1段有介绍),但不影响笔者想在这里表达的有关一切险的承保范围与局限的内容。

1.2 一切险的局限:肯定会发生的风险

首先简单介绍一下什么是肯定会发生的风险,马上想到的是一些正常的损耗(ordinary wear and tear),如钢板因腐蚀而破裂。但海上货物运输不像船舶保险,通常承保的时间也就是运输的时间不会很长,估计这种情况很少会出现。另外想到的就是包装不当或不足(improper or insufficient package),因为这是受保人自己导致的损失。在严重的情况下,客观地看是认为在海上运输过程中肯定会出事,而且不必有外来风险导致。正如 F. W Berk v Style & Co. Ltd. (1955) 2 Lloyd's Rep. 382,涉及的货物是袋装硅藻土(Kieselguhr),但包装的纸袋质量很差,结果在卸货的时候因有严重的破裂而需要重新包装,从而产生了施救费用。Sellers 大法官判这笔施救费用不能向保险人在一切险的保险合约中取回,因为"纸袋肯定不能把里面的货物包住"(it could be said to be certain that they could not hold their contents)。

但什么是肯定会发生的损失并不是一个容易作出的结论,所以在现实中也经常带来争议。如在著名的世纪盗窃与鬼船(phantom ship)案例之 The "Salem" (1983) 1 Lloyd's Rep. 342 中,涉及了希腊船东买了"Salem"这艘老龄超级油轮,去在市场出租并揽了一票货,从科威特装20万吨原油去欧洲。但事实上该批骗徒已经与当时实施种族隔离的南非政府(所以受到联合国的禁运)达成买卖协议,把"Salem"船上的一票原油卖给南非。结果在原来的航次半途,船舶绕航去德班把该票原油非法卸下。无辜货方向保险公司提出的索赔中,其中的一个争议就是该票货物在科威特还没有装上船之前,也就是风险还没有开始生效(risks never attach),该票货物的命运就已经是肯定会失去。但上诉庭与贵族院都不接受,认为在那时候还不能肯定说这一世纪盗窃会成功。其中 Kerr 大法官是这样说:"Mr. Hobhouse(保险人的代表大律师) submitted that the proximate cause of the loss of the entire cargo, both of the bulk which was discharged at Durban(南非德班) and of the remainder which went down with the ship, was the fraudulent plan of the conspirators throughout, even before the loading of the cargo.... In substance this submission appears to entail the conclusion that there was already an actual total loss as soon as the cargo was loaded at Mina(在科威特的装港), because the cargo - owners were then already irretrievably deprived of it... I cannot accept this; there was then not yet any irretrievable deprivation or loss."

从 The "Salem"先例看来,在风险开始生效前已经可以肯定一个损失一定会产生的情况会是微乎其微,因为在之后的海上运输中变数太多。例如,有内在缺陷(inherent vice)的货物就已经很难肯定。如一票劣质煤碳,在一个特定的航次中发生自燃几乎是肯定的。但这会有各种变数如不同的船舶装运或在不同的季节运输,或是在某一个航次中所遇到的实际情况如气温比较低,都会导致自燃可能会发生,也可能不会发生。所以,内在缺陷不能被视为肯定的损失,虽然在 British & Foreign Marine Insurance Company Limited v Gaunt (1921) 2 AC 41 案例中说明这也是不承保的。但由于有内在缺陷的货物很多,而且通常也是一种风险(因为不是肯定会发生),所以保险人通常会接受加保,如保险合约中加入"发热、出汗与自燃条文"(HSSC [Heating Sweating and Spontaneous Combustion] Clause): Soya G. mbH. v. White (1983) 1 Lloyd's Rep. 122。

1.3 加保可能会发生的风险的做法

针对一些由于自然损耗造成的货物重量减少的情况,在保险合约中通常会加入"短缺超过 1% 就要赔付"("Covering All Risks, War Risks including shortage in weight but subject to an excess of one per cent of the whole shipment.")的条文:Coven SpA v Hong Kong Chinese Insurance Co. (1999) Lloyd's Rep. IR 565 (CA)。这是假设 1% 损耗以下是肯定的损失,但超过 1% 的损耗就可能是由于一些难以说明/证明的外来因素所导致。

又或是在保险合约中加入"... against all risks of whatsoever nature and/or kind. Average irrespective of percentage. Including blowing of tins. Including inherent vice and hidden defect.":Biddle Sawyer & Co. v Walter Peters (1957) 2 Lloyd's Rep. 339。

但保险人愿意接受承保货物的内在缺陷还是不代表他们愿意承保一个肯定会发生的损失(不论受保人的货方知道与否),否则保费就与货物价值看齐,保险也就没有任何意义。所以这两者之间的分水线在哪里还是经常会带来争议。这有不少的案例如 Dowell & Co. Ltd. v British Dominions General Insurance Co. Ltd. (1955) 2 Lloyd's Rep. 391 与 Soya G. mbH. v. White 等。会在本章第 3 段继续分析这些案例,也另在本书第八章第 4 段有进一步对固有缺陷和保险货物本质所造成的损失的分析，请参阅。

另外一种一切险不承保的是受保人的货方自己导致的损失，一方面这是一般的合约法的默示地位，另一方面是受保人的货方自己导致的损失如包装不足也是肯定会在运输途中产生的损失。这方面也在本书第八章第1段有进一步分析，请参阅。

这些普通法的默示地位在1906年的《英国保险法》中已经有规定，见附录一 Section 55。这样看，根据贵族院的先例 British & Foreign Marine Insurance Company Limited v Gaunt（1921）2 AC 41，保险合约中的用词“一切险”不足以超越1906年《英国海上保险法》Section 55（b）&（c）中的不承保风险，如内在缺陷，虽然立法条文允许订约自由改变该默示地位。

2. 一切险的举证责任

一切险是最普遍被使用的海上货物保险条文，对货方的好处是不需要证明损失是由于什么列明的承保风险所导致，这是与船壳保险（通常只是承保列明风险，特别是伦敦保险市场）最不一样的地方。货方由于不控制海上运输，只是把货物交给承运人或船东，所以要他们对发生的损失举证的确是十分困难或者是不可能的。对保险人而言，由于货方不控制海上运输，所以也不需要担心他们会搞破坏，因此也会愿意承保一切险，不需要受保人的货方在要求赔付时有太多举证的责任。

2.1　列明风险的受保人举证责任先例：The “Popi M”

针对一切险，货方的举证责任很轻微。不像列明风险下受保人有责任根据平衡可能性（balance of probabilities）的原则证明是哪一个列明风险所导致的损失，如果受保人无法做到，如没办法解释的原因（unexplained cause），索赔就不会成功：The “Popi M”（1985）2 Lloyd’s Rep. 1（HL）。相比之下，一切险的保险合约下发生无法解释原因所造成的损失，只要根据平衡可能性的原则应该是意外造成的（发生了不应该发生的事情），但什么原因就不知道，就已经足够要求赔付：Theodorou v Chester（1951）1 Lloyd’s Rep. 204。这里可以简单介绍 The “Popi M”的贵族院先例，说明举证责任的不同分配会带来的不同后果，虽然该先例是船壳保险而不是海上货物保险。在1978年8月5日，Popi M 轮在地中海非常深水的地方沉没，当时天气良好且海上没有风浪。沉没的原因是突然之间有大量海水从船底进入机舱，而最终导致沉没。船东向保险人提出索赔，指称该船舶是由于海上风险或船员疏忽所导致。保险人抗拒的理由就是说船舶的沉没是由于船舶的内在缺陷（如钢板腐烂导致，因为它是一艘老龄船），而针对船员疏忽，保险人指船东没有说到底是什么疏忽导致船舶沉没。因为船东有举证责任说明到底是什么列明风险导致，所以船东依赖专家意见证据，说第一个可能的海上风险就是与没有在海图上标明的水底礁石碰撞，但这很快就连船东自己都否认,因为出事的水域是很多船只航行的惯常通道,并且海水是很深。船东第二个可能的海上风险就是船舶碰上了水中的浮木或者是半浮沉的集装箱,但这种可能性也很快被排除,因为船舶在前行的过程中会用船头把浮木或其他物体向两边推开,顶多也就是船头受损而不会是机舱部位受损。这一来,船东只剩下了第三个可能的海上风险,就是船底的机舱部位是被上浮的潜水艇撞到。这也是可能,船东提供给英国法院的证据就是在过去的10年间此类事故发生了6宗。因为苏联海军会在这海域活动,船东为此还曾经写信去苏联海军询问“你们是否有潜艇撞到我的船”之类,当然苏联对这种军事机密不会理睬。这表示在一审的时候Bingham大法官就要根据双方提供的证据(主要是专家意见证据)决定到底是由于保险人所说的钢板腐烂导致的(等于是自然损耗)或是船舶碰上了潜水艇。Bingham大法官在听取了双方的专家意见后,最终判定不可能是由于钢板腐烂导致的。原因包括金属疲劳导致裂缝需要长时间造成,事前不应该没有任何征兆。上一个航次遇到很坏的天气都没有出问题,在本航次天气状况良好的情况下是不应该出这种问题。而这种大面积的突然进水很快导致船舶沉没应该是由于外来的撞击造成的等。结果Bingham大法官认为是双方提出的两种解释,还是船舶与不知名的潜水艇相撞比较可以接受,说:“although the submission by the plaintiff's that the cause of water entering the vessel was contact by the vessel with a moving submerged object, i. e., a submarine, was inherently improbable, on the balance of probabilities that explanation would be accepted and since such a collision with a submarine fell within the policy cover against perils of the sea, the plaintiffs succeeded against each defendant for his proportionate share of the insured value of the vessel.”

但这案件去了贵族院后被推翻,认为Bingham大法官错误以为他只有两种选择,要么是保险人的解释,要么是船东给的解释。而实际上应该还有第三种选择,也就是正确的选择。这就是在双方都没有办法给出令人满意的解释时,就判是谁有举证责任谁就败诉。Brandon勋爵说:“That third possible solution would have been to say that he was left in doubt as to the proximate cause of the ship's loss, and that, in those circumstances, the shipowners' action should be dismissed on the simple ground that they had not discharged the burden of proof which lay upon them.”

从上述先例就可以看出举证责任的重要性,可以说如果同样的情况在投保一切险的海上货物运输保险,货方只需要证明货物是意外造成了损失或损坏。这应该是很明显,总不能说船舶突然沉没了或是货物被火烧毁或者水湿/浸水还不是意外(accidental)。这一来保险人不想赔,就有举证责任证明该损失是由保险合约内的除外风险(如协会货物条文[一切险]的第6条的战争险)所导致。

2.2　一切险货物保险举证先例:British and Foreign Marine Insurance Co. Ltd. v. Gaunt

有关受保人货方的举证责任,可以介绍著名的先例是贵族院的British and Foreign Marine Insurance Co. Ltd. v. Gaunt (1912) 2 AC 41。案情有关一批羊毛货物,投保的是一切险从阿根廷的 Patagonia 到智利的 Punta Arenas,再直航去欧洲。有一些羊毛在装船之前已经浸水,但浸水的原因没有人知道。诉讼中的争议是到底是不是由一个事故引致该损失的,这就涉及"意外"(accident/fortuity)的问题,因为没有任何意外性的话就不属于保险的范围。贵族院判货方胜诉,理由是浸水本身就不是一个在通常海上运输中可以预见会发生的事情,所以可以推断是由于一些意外事故与不正常的情况所导致。其中 Birkenhead 勋爵说:"The damage proved was such as did not occur and could not be expected to occur in the course of a normal transit. The inference remains, that it was due to some abnormal circumstance, some accident or casualty. We are, of course, to give effect to the rule that the plaintiff must establish his case that he must show that the loss comes within the terms of his policies; but where all risks are covered by the policy and not merely risks of a specified class or classes. The plaintiff discharges his special onus when he has proved that the loss was caused by some event covered by the general expression and he is not bound to go further to prove the exact nature of the accident or casualty which, in fact, occasioned his loss."

2.3 以往海上运输没有发生同类损坏作为证明是意外造成的先例:Noten B. V. v Harding

有些情况比方说水湿(特别是海水)、火烧等,就其损坏的性质而言可以肯定或很可能是意外造成。但有些情况比方说发热、出汗等的内在缺陷,就比较难界定是否由意外造成。然而其中的一种界定办法就是看同样的一种货物在相似的情况下付运是否曾经发生类似的损坏。在 Noten B. V. v. Harding (1990) 2 Lloyd's Rep. 283,涉及的货物是牛皮工业手套,从印度运往荷兰,在卸货的时候该票手套受潮、变色与发霉。有关的保险合约是一切险,但货方向保险人提出索赔时受到抗拒,说损坏是内在缺陷导致,并非在海上运输途中遇到意外所造成。货方以同样货物的以往海上运输并没有或很少发生类似的损坏作为证据,但不被法院所接受,因为没有提供其他航次的资料与证据,所以不知道是否可以作出比较。这表示受保人如果以这种办法举证是"意外"就一定要提供更全面的证据,才有机会成功。上诉庭的 Bingham 大法官这样说:"I accept that if a number of consignments are made in closely comparable conditions, and goods suffer damage on one occasion or a minority of occasions only, it may be possible and right to infer that some fortuitous event has affected the goods on that occasion or those occasions. But it will only be safe to draw that inference if the conditions affecting each consignment are established to be comparable save in respect of the allegedly fortuitous event. In the present case—for reasons entirely understandable, having regard to the way the case developed—the evidential foundation of the argument was never laid. Only containers of gloves shipped during the monsoon season would appear to me to be relevant and in fact it seems that some other shipments—those made during the monsoon season of

1981—did suffer damage. But there was no evidence before the Court to establish the conditions in which either they or any other consignments were shipped and one cannot begin to assess whether the conditions were comparable or not. ”

2.4　保险人以除外风险为由拒赔有举证责任

至于在一切险的保险中，如果保险人拒绝赔付，认为是保险合约中其中的一项或多项列明除外风险适用，这一举证责任是在保险人的头上。这里可以节录 Spinney's v. Royal Insurance (1980) 1 Lloyd's Rep. 406 先例中 Mustill 大法官所说的如下："In my judgment, the insurers cannot bring the clause into play simply by asserting that the loss was excluded by a particular exception, and challenging the insured to prove the contrary. They must produce evidence from which it can reasonably be argued that - (a) a state of affairs existed or an event occurred falling which an exception, and (b) the excepted peril directly or indirectly caused the loss. It is only when an arguable case of this nature is made out that the insured is required to disprove it. ”

3. 无可避免损失之短缺

这一个课题在本章第 1 段有提到过，在这里会进一步解释。经常发生的一些货物短缺，很多时候只是属于一种纸面上的损失(paper loss)。换言之，由于不少货物如原油或大宗货，都会有测量的困难与不准确。这经常导致装港与卸港的测量结果显示货物有短缺，但实际上航次中什么事都没发生过。在一般的货物保险，这种损失不在承保范围内。除了 1906 年《英国海上保险法》之 Section 55(2)(c)说明这种类似损失是不承保之外，普通法也有不少有关的案例。正如 Atkins 勋爵在 De Monchy v. Phoenix Insurance Company of Hartford & Another (1929) 34 Ll. L. Rep. 201 (HL) 中所说："underwriters were insuring against casualties but not of arithmetic. "(保险人承保的是意外损失而不是测算不准确)。

保险市场可以专门加保这种属于无可避免的损失，如正常的泄漏(ordinary leakage)或正常的短量(ordinary loss in weight or volume)，但这样加保也不是万无一失，以下可介绍一些相关的案例。

3.1　货物短缺案例之一：Dodwell & Co. Limited v. British Dominions General Insurance Company Limited

在 Dodwell & Co. Limited v. British Dominions General Insurance Company Limited (1955) 2 Lloyd's Rep. 391 (该先例是在 1918 年 4 月 9 日宣判)先例，涉及了两批桶装油，分别是由两艘不同的船舶从中国运往英国，而途中都发生了泄漏。但这两票货物的保险条文在加保部分都不是完全一样，第一票加保的是泄漏的风险(risk of leakage)，但第二批加保在字面上就广泛得多，措辞为"including risk of leakage from any cause whatever"。结果的判决是在前一票的货物,法院认为承保的只是因为海上运输带来的额外泄漏的风险。根据证据,法院认为5%属于正常泄漏。但该票货最后泄漏是达到了12%,所以保险人只负责赔付5%~12%的差额。但第二票货,由于用字广泛,所以 Bailhache 大法官判保险人需要全部赔付(包括5%),说:"clearly includes all leakage to which these barrels of oil were subjected",所以万变不离其宗,都是应用合约的解释原理来解释保险条文。

3.2 货物短缺案例之二:Maigen & Co. v. National Benefit Assurance Company

在 Maigen & Co. v. National Benefit Assurance Company (1922) 10 Ll. L. Rep. 30 先例中,涉及了将大桶的红葡萄酒从法国的 Beaune 运到伦敦,而保险合约有加保,而且用字广泛说:"leakage and breakage however caused irrespective of percentage"。保险人的争议是大桶不足够坚固使红葡萄酒的泄漏无可避免。但 Grear 大法官不同意,认为这些大桶是足够坚固而泄漏是由于航次中的其他事故导致的。但在最后的判决中还是减除了一些他视为正常的损失(normal loss)。这样看来,Grear 大法官本质还是支持无可避免的损失不需赔付,虽然加保的用词很广泛。

3.3 货物短缺案例之三:Monchy v. Phoenix Insurance Company of Hartford & Another

在 Monchy v. Phoenix Insurance Company of Hartford & Another (1929) 34 Ll. L. Rep. 201(HL)先例中,案情是有关一票松节油(turpentine)从美国佛罗里达运去荷兰鹿特丹,保险是加保了超过1%的泄漏(leakage from any cause in excess of 1%)。证据显示松节油很容易蒸发,可以在没有任何迹象下大量泄漏。受保的货方认为把装货的重量与卸货的重量去比较后,差额超出1%的保险人就要赔付。但保险人抗拒认为实质上没有真正的泄漏,完全是重量计算上的问题。贵族院判是应该有泄漏,而双方如果同意了一个百分比为正常的损失,这是有约束力的。Sumner 勋爵这样说:"when a percentage of normal waste is agreed to, it binds"。

另外 Atkin 勋爵也说:"... it appears to me that much physical loss is on a proper construction of the policy to be taken to be the result of leakage; and for any amount over 1% the assured will recover... There was therefore proved an actual physical loss, and the plaintiffs in the action are entitled to recover the excess over 1% of that actual physical loss."

3.4 货物短缺案例之四:Coven SPA v. Hong Kong Chinese Insurance Co.

在 Coven SPA v. Hong Kong Chinese Insurance Co. (1998) EWCA Civ 1573 先例中,涉及一船的大豆,投保的是一切险条文,但它另加上了一条条文说超过1%的短缺才被承保(Shortage in weight but subject to an excess of 1% in the whole shipment)。结果在航次中,有一批货物的短缺大概有14%,双方接受这个短缺是由于测量上的错误所导致。作为受保人的货方要求保险人赔偿超过1%的短缺,所依据的就是被加上的条文。去了上诉庭,判决结果是货方的要求不被接受。Clarke 大法官认为即使是加上了该条文,它本质上还是要求货物有损失或损坏。Clarke 大法官认为无法接受双方约定保险合约的时候会有任何意图承保一些从来不存在的货物(因为纸面损失就表示这部分货物根本没有装上船),而且货方也无法证明他对这部分货物(从来没有存在过)有可保利益。上诉庭也没有说死对这种纸面损失肯定不能投保,但若投保,显然双方所约定的承保风险恐怕要比现在使用的文字更加清楚才有希望成功。其中,Clarke 大法官所讲可节录如下:“I accept that it would be possible to insure against a measurement error and that there may indeed be commercial reasons why a receiver might want such cover, but it would be a most unusual type of marine cargo cover and clear terms would be required to effect it. This was essentially a marine cargo policy against loss of and damage to cargo. Moreover it provided cover in respect of beans which existed and not in respect of beans which did not exist. The insured would have no insurable interest in such goods as required by clause 11. 1 of the Institute Clauses and the insurance attached from the time the goods left the warehouse or place of storage as provided by clause 8. 1 of those clauses. ”

3. 5 货物发热案例:Soya G. . m. b. H. v. White

另一贵族院先例也显示了货物的损失或损坏必须是可能会在海上运输途中发生的。反之,如果是一定会发生,就根本不是保险了。这一精神也完全适用在协会货物条文一切险。该先例就是 Soya G. mbH. v. White (1983) 1 Lloyd's Rep. 122,案情是有关大豆从印尼以 CIF 价格运去安特卫普与鹿特丹。第一艘船舶“Teviotbank”轮运载的 2000 吨大豆发热并造成损坏。这导致了受保人对接下去的货物运输不敢怠慢,马上去保险市场加保了一种叫“Heating, Sweating and Spontaneous Combustion”(简称 HSSC 险),所针对的就是货物发热、出汗与自燃的风险。由于 1906 年《英国海上保险法》第 55(2)(c)条规定除非保险合约另有规定,否则保险人不承保内在缺陷(也有译为“固有缺陷”)或货物的本身属性造成的损失:“Unless the policy otherwise provides, the insurer is not liable for... inherent vice or nature of the subject - matter insured. ”。这表示即使是保一切险,如货物有发热、出汗与自燃的风险也要加保 HSSC 险。但即使加保了 HSSC 险,还是要求它带来的损失或损坏并不是一定会发生的。在 Soya G. mbH. v. White 案中,继“Teviotbank”后的两个航次,第一批是 5500 吨的大豆,船舶是“Corfu Island”;第二批是 3200 吨大豆,船舶是“Welsh City”。但两批货物都有损坏,原因是货物发热。第一批所带来货物的损坏是 12.5%,第二批是 45%,总共损失金额高达 73 万美元。但保险人拒赔,其中一个最主要的理由就是这些货物在海上运输过程中一定会有这种损坏。根据双方专家证据,如果运输时的大豆水分含量低于某一个百分比的话,就不会发生这些发热的情况;但超出 14% 的话,并且针对有关的航次是 45 天与装货时的温度是 30℃,就一定会在航次中发热。在一审,Lloyd 大法官接受货方/受保人的专家证人所说的,水分含量在 12% ~14%,就是介于灰色地带,即在运输途中可能会发热,也可能不会发热。而 Lloyd 大法官也根据证据(主要是根据一个在装货时的样品证明)判"Corfu Island"与"Welsh City"在装货的时候大豆水分含量低于13%，显示运输途中的发热并不是一定会发生，所以判保险人败诉。第一审的判决受到上诉庭与贵族院的支持。在贵族院 Diplock 勋爵并没有肯定说装货时的大豆水分高到发热现象一定会发生时可否获得赔付，但答案显然是明确的，Diplock 勋爵说："In conclusion I should make it clear that since in your Lordship's House the concurrent findings of fact that the moisture content of the soya beans fell within a grey area was accepted so that deterioration from heat and sweat in the course of the voyage was not inevitable, it has not been necessary for your Lordships to consider whether the insurers would have been liable under HSSC policy if, unknown to the assured, the moisture content of the beans on shipment had been so high as to make such deterioration inevitable. On that question, on which we have heard no argument, I express no opinion."

这一个先例在上诉庭的时候，Donaldson 大法官认为"无可避免的损失"更准确地应被称为"预先知道肯定会发生的损失"，反正在保险的范围外，除非写得十分清楚与文字上根本不可能有另一种解释，否则保险人极不可能愿意承保这些损失。他说：

"Inevitability of loss is not mentioned in s. 55 of the Marine Insurance Act, because it operates at a much more fundamental level than the rule that underwriters are only liable for losses proximately caused by perils insured against. Underwriters can rely upon inevitability of loss, because the whole concept of insurance is about risks, not certainties. In a sense the use of the term 'inevitability' misleads. In practical terms there is as much a risk if the inevitability of a loss is not known as if the loss itself may or may not occur. Overdue ships and cargo can be insured, notwithstanding that the whole basis of the insurance is that their loss may not only be inevitable, but already have occurred. I would therefore prefer to use the term 'known certainty' instead of 'inevitability'. This has to be conjoined with the words 'of the loss or of the particular extent of the loss' to take account of the fact that in some cases the whole loss may be certain, but in others only part.

I regard this defence as stemming from the nature of a contract of insurance, although if the certainty of the loss is known to the assured and not to the underwriter, other defences will be open, e. g. fraud, non-disclosure or, possibly, loss by the act of the assured in knowingly exposing the subject matter to certain loss. However where the certainty of loss is known to both assured and underwriter, as for example is the case with cargoes which always lose some weight or volume in transit, other than that insurance is about risks and not known certainties, it is difficult to see any basis for exemption from liability. **This is not to say that known certain losses cannot be the subject matter of a contract of indemnity; merely that very clear words will be required since it is highly improbable contract for someone to make in the course of his business as an insurance under-**

writer."(加黑的是笔者的强调)

笔者估计通过十分清楚的文字来说明是承保即使是预先知道肯定会发生的损失,保险合约也会是在HSSC条文后多加一句说明:即使是预先知道肯定会发生的货物有发热、出汗与自燃,这也是被承保。

4. 近因(proximate cause)

近因是保险法(甚至是社会上的任何事情)一个非常重要的原则,因为事故导致的损失往往是有一连串的原因所造成,而这些不同的原因往往不是同时发生,而都是有先有后;而不同的原因对造成的损失所起的作用也会很不同:有的原因可能直接导致了损失的发生,而有的原因只是导致了损失的扩大,有的原因可能只是对整个事故起到了很小的作用等。而所有这些原因会是部分属于受保的列明风险(named risks),部分原因则没有说明,有的原因甚至是被明确排除在承保范围的"除外风险"(excluded risks)。而在1906年《英国海上保险法》,在Section 55(1)是规定:"Subject to the provisions of this Act, and unless the policy otherwise provides, the insurer is liable for any loss proximately caused by a peril insured against, but, subject as aforesaid, he is not liable for any loss which is not proximately caused by a peril insured against."

要找出损失的近因,还不只是上述所介绍的到底近因是承保的列明风险或者是除外风险,还涉及了近因到底是哪一个保险合约应该赔付。如水险合约或者是战争险合约,因为它们是分开向不同的保险人投保的。而即使货物投保的是一切险(all risks),也存在这一个问题,因为一切险还是有一连串的除外风险,不论是在1906年《英国海上保险法》中默示的还是在保险合约中明示的(这在第4~7条,在本书第八章详论)。这可以节录Potter大法官在The "Aliza Glacial" (2002) 2 Lloyd's Rep. 421中所说的一段话:"Whenever an argument as to causation arises in respect of rival causes contended for under a policy of insurance, the first task of the Court is to look to see whether one of the causes is plainly the proximate cause of the loss."

要找出近因并不容易。如曾经在一个工业伤亡的案件中,一个人死亡的近因居然把他的出生也列在其中:Coxe v. Employers Liability Assurance (1916) 2 KB 629。显然,没有一个人的出生,就不会有他的死亡,但将出生作为死亡的一个原因太间接也太遥远。再多举一个例子,如果船舶与船上的货物在航次中失踪,原因不明,这会是水险或者战争险的承保范围?显然出事地点是在天气恶劣的水域与出事的时间是在有很多德国潜艇出没的第一次世界大战期间会得出不同的推断与结论。这种情况因为通讯的发达与科技的进步,现在已很少发生,但还是会存在并会带来向保险人索赔的困难,因为无法证明承保的风险是造成损失的近因:The "Popi M" (1985) 2 Lloyd's Rep. 1。

4.1 根据发生时间先后来寻找近因的早期判例

在早期所判的案例,找出损失的近因主要的考虑是在时间方面。也就是时间上越接近损失的原因就越被视为近因,然后看它是否是属于承保的风险。这里可举 Hamilton, Fraser & Co. v. Pandorf & Co. (1887) LR 12 App Cas 518 (HL)。这是一个租约与提单的争议,有关的货物是一船的大米去英国的利物浦。航程中,由于船上的老鼠把一个管道咬了个洞而导致海水涌入把大米浸泡而引起货损。租约中有一条免责条文,说明船东对海上风险免责。这就要弄明白大米损害的近因是什么,因为如果是海上风险(perils of sea),船东免责;如果近因是老鼠,船东就要负责,因为租约中根本没有对老鼠造成的损害免责,甚至还涉及了船舶不适货的问题。

这问题的复杂性可以假设如果是老鼠将大米偷吃造成货损,船东明显不能免责,因为造成损失的原因只有一个,就是老鼠。但如果老鼠将船舶的管道咬了个洞导致海水涌入,就涉及了海上风险,因为海上风险的定义相当广泛,只要是一些海上独有的风险(peculiar to the sea)就包括在内。试想,如果在岸上老鼠将仓库咬了个洞,就不会造成同样的损失。而且,老鼠也不会是船上才有。正如 Esher 勋爵在该先例所说:"But rats do not come from the sea, and are not generated by the sea. They are no more a difficulty on board ship than they are in a warehouse or in a mill."这里也可以换一个角度看,就算是老鼠是造成货损的有效原因(effective cause),但海上风险在时间上是最近的原因(immediate cause)。而在该先例中贵族院判造成货损的近因是海上风险,所以船东免责。在这一个先例中可以看到时间上最接近造成损失的原因会被视为近因,而且也不只是在保险的争议,因为这一先例是租约的纠纷。涉及保险的话,就要从时间上找出最接近损失发生的原因,而且更严格。

这可多举几个以前的先例说明时间上最接近损失发生的原因被视为近因,第一个先例是 Taylor v. Dunbar (1869) LR 4 CP 206。货物是一船的牛肉,由于坏天气导致航次延长而变质,结果被丢到大海里去。法院判保险人不需要赔偿,因为损失的近因是延误(delay),而不是坏天气。而延误根据 1906 年《英国海上保险法》之 Section 55(2)(b)规定:"Unless the policy otherwise provides, the insurer on ship or goods is not liable for any loss proximately caused by delay, although the delay be caused by a peril insured against",所以保险人不用赔付。

第二个先例是 Pink v. Fleming (1890) 25 QBD 396,涉及了一船水果(桔子与柠檬),船舶在半途发生撞船,船舶并没有沉没或对水果造成损坏。但碰撞造成船舶损坏,需要修理才能继续该航次,而修理期间也需要把水果卸到岸上,暂时存放。这延误造成了部分水果的损坏。但上诉庭依从 Taylor v. Dunbar 的判法,认为损失的近因不是撞船而是延误。

第三个先例并非是海上保险:Lawrence v. The Accidental Insurance Company (Ltd) (1880-81) LR 7 QBD 216。这是一个有关人身伤亡的保险合约,承保的就是意外造成的伤亡,不保的就是受保人突然晕倒(fits)。受保人在火车车轨上突然晕倒之后,火车驶过将受保人轧死。法院判保险人要负责,因为突然晕倒并非死亡的直接近因(the proximate and immediate cause of death),火车驶过才是死亡的直接近因。

总结而言,特别是针对保险,以前针对近因主要的强调就是时间的先后。这可节录 Willes 大法官在先例 Ionides v. Universal Marine Insurance Co. (1863) 14 C. B. N. S. 259 说:"The ordinary rule of insurance law is that ... you are not to trouble yourself with distant cause, or to go into a metaphysical distinction between causes efficient and material and causes final; but you are to look exclusively to the proximate and immediate cause of the loss..."

另在 Leyland Shipping v. Norwich Union (1918) AC 350 (HL),在双方代表大律师的争辩中,Leslie Scott 勋爵更明确地说"... according to English law, the last cause only must be regarded and the others rejected, although they contributed to the result."

4.2 根据重要性与有效性来寻找近因的后期先例

将时间上最接近损失的原因作为近因在英国法院有了不同的看法,就是改变为寻找什么是最主要(predominant)与有效(efficient)的原因造成的损失,这是在 Leyland Shipping v. Norwich Union (1918) AC 350 (HL)。案情涉及承保的船舶"Ikaria"在第一次世界大战期间,1915 年的 1 月 30 日,在离目的港法国勒阿弗尔港(Le Havre)还有 25 海里处,被德国潜艇发射的鱼雷击中,并造成严重损坏,第一货舱全部进水,海水也同时进入第二货舱。通过拖船的救助,总算把船舶拖进勒阿弗尔港并挂靠泊位。如果船舶能够在泊位停留并进行修理,船舶可以说是安全。但在第二天,即 1 月 31 日,勒阿弗尔港受到飓风的袭击,导致船舶不断与泊位碰撞。港口当局担心该船舶在泊位处沉没,而该泊位有重要的军事用途,所以命令船舶必须离开去外锚地搁浅或在防波堤抛锚。这最终导致船舶在 2 月 1 日折断,变成全损。船东以海上灾难提出索赔,但贵族院判是战争险而不是水险的保险人负责,因为船舶被鱼雷击中后从来没有脱离严重的风险。贵族院也提到了发生时间上的远近(飓风在近,鱼雷在远)并非决定性的,真正有效与最重要的原因造成最后的损失才算是近因。Shaw 勋爵这样说:

"I will venture to remark that one must be careful not to lay the accent upon the word 'proximate' in such a sense as to lose sight of or destroy altogether the idea of cause itself. The true and the overruling principle is to look at a contract as a whole and to ascertain what the parties to it really meant. What was it which brought about the loss, the event, the calamity, the accident? ...

To treat *proxima causa* as the cause which is nearest in time is out of the question. Causes are spoken of as if they were as distinct from one another as beads in a row or links in a chain, but—if this metaphysical topic has to be referred to – it is not wholly so. The chain of causation is a handy expression, but the figure is inadequate. Causation is not a chain, but a net. At each point influences, forces, events, precedent and simultaneous, meet; and the radiation from each point extends indefinitely. At the point where these various influences meet it is for the judgment as upon a matter of fact to declare which of the causes thus joined at the point of effect was the proximate and which was the remote cause.

What does ‘proximate’ here mean? To treat proximate cause as if it was the cause which is proximate in time is, as I have said, out of the question. The cause which is truly proximate is that which is proximate in efficiency. That efficiency may have been preserved although other causes may meantime have sprung up which have not yet destroyed it, or truly impaired it, and it may culminate in a result of which it still remains the real efficient cause to which the even can be ascribed. ”

Shaw 勋爵接下来也解释了为什么船舶被鱼雷击中才是近因:“In my opinion the real efficient cause of the sinking of this vessel was that she was torpedoed. Where an injury is received by a vessel, it may be fatal or it may be cured: it has to be dealt with. In so dealing with it there may, it is true, be attendant circumstances which may aggravate or possibly precipitate the result, but which are incidents flowing from the injury, or receive from it an operative and disastrous power. The vessel, in short, is all the time in the grip of the casualty. The true and efficient cause never loses its hold. The result is produced, a result attributable in common language to the casualty as a cause, and this result, proximate as well as continuous in its efficiency, properly meets, whether under contract or under the statue, the language of the expression ‘proximately caused’. ”

除了要找出最主要与最有效的原因作为近因外,英国法院还有强调在一连串的事实中找近因,也必须用一个符合普通人的正常思维全面看待(broad common sense view of the whole position)。在 Canada Rice Mills Ltd. v. Union Marine & General Insurance Co. Ltd. (1940) 67 Lloyd's Rep. 549 中 Wright 勋爵是这样说:“Causation is to be understood as the man in the street, and not as either the scientist or the metaphysician, would understand it. Cause here means what a business or seafaring man would taken to be the cause without too microscopic analysis but on a broad view. ”

在 Wayne Tank & Pump v. Employers' Liability (1973) 2 Lloyd's Rep. 237, Denning 勋爵总结说:“Since *Leyland's* case it has been settled in insurance law that the ‘cause’ of a loss is that which is the effective or dominant cause of the occurrence, or, as it is sometimes put, that which is in substance the cause, even though it is more remote in point of time, such cause to be determined by common sense, see Gray v. Barr (1971) 2 Lloyd's Rep., at p. 5. ”

这些改变带来了后来很不一样的判法:P. Samuel & Co. v. Dumas (1924) A. C. 431; 18 Ll. L. Rep. 200,案情涉及了船舶因为船东故意把海阀打开让海水涌进来造成船舶沉没,显然这是一个典型人为凿沉船舶想骗保险金的案件。该案例的原告也不是欺诈的船东(他已经失踪),原告是贷款给船东的无辜方(mortgagee)。原告指称造成船舶全损的近因是海上风险,而船东的恶意行为(willful misconduct)只是遥远的原因。显然从时间上来看这是成立的,因为船东的恶意行为时间上更早,他把海阀打开导致海水涌进时间上比较晚,这可看先例 Hamilton, Fraser & Co. v. Pandorf & Co. (1887) LR 12 App Cas 518 (HL),就可以看到两个案件在事实上的相通之处。但由于法院在 Leyland Shipping v. Norwich Union (1918) AC 350 (HL)针对近因有了不同的强调,再也不强调时间的先后,而是强调主要与有效的原因,所以在先例 P. Samuel &Co. v. Dumas,贵族院判近因是船东的恶意行为(wickedness of man),而 1906 年《英国海上保险法》之 Section 55 (2)(a)说明除非保险合约有明示规定,是不承保受保人的恶意行为。在该先例后直到现在的做法,贷款给船东的人士或银行都会另投保一种名为"贷款人利益保险"(mortgagee interests insurance)的保险,明示约定该保险承保的风险是船东的恶意行为。可以说遇到同样的情况,无辜的银行也不会受到损害。但要作出赔付的是"贷款人利益保险"的保险人,而不是船东所投的船壳险或战争险的保险人。因为这种凿沉船导致船舶全损的近因就是船东的恶意行为而不是其他有效与重要的原因所造成。

在上一段也提到了 Taylor v. Dunbar (1869) LR 4 CP 206 与 Pink v. Fleming (1890) 25 QBD 396 的先例,但在针对如何找出近因有了不同的强调后,估计判法也有了很大不同。这里可以举一个相应不同的看法,虽然它是一个美国先例,名为 Lanasa Fruit Steamship & Importing Co. Inc. v. Universal Insurance Company (The Smaragd) (1938) AMC 1。案情是一船的香蕉腐烂,原因是由于船舶搁浅导致的延误。美国最高院判损失的近因是船舶搁浅,这是承保的风险,而不是延误。美国最高院依从先例 Leyland Shipping v. Norwich Union (1918) AC 350 (HL),而不接受从时间的先后找近因的说法。

4.3　根据不同案件的事实找出近因与大致分类

可以说大部分的保险案件在全面了解事实后,都能客观找出事故与损失的近因。但由于每个案件都会有不同的事实,所以导致有很多这方面的争议都涉及昂贵的诉讼。而且,判决也有一定程度的不稳定,正如《Chalmers Marine Insurance Act 1906》第 9 版第 78 页所说:"though the rule (指近因的说法) is universally admitted, lawyers have never attempted to work out any philosophical theory of cause and effect, and it is probably as well for commerce that they have never made the attempt. The numerous decisions on the rule are rough and ready applications of it to particular facts. As might be expected, many of the decisions are difficult to reconcile. But the apparent inconsistencies may be regarded as depending rather on inferences of fact than on matters of law."

但大致上还是可以把它分为三类如下。

4.3.1　前因造成无可避免损失的案件(inevitable cases)

这一个类别可以这样来解释,就是前后有两个原因造成最后的损失,但第一个原因可以说是致命的一击(death blow),而客观看后来的原因也难以改变最后损失的命运。在这种情况下，很简单是前因就是近因。这一类别可以 Leyland Shipping v. Norwich Union (1918) AC 350 (HL)作为典型的例子，该船舶被水雷击中后，从来没有脱离危险，后来的飓风导致船舶全损，可以说后来飓风的出现并没有太多改变船舶的命运。类似的情况也可以另外一个假设的例子说明，就是该船舶被水雷击中后被拖带到一个港口避难。由于船舶失去动力，所以明知道拖带有危险，特别是该避难港口的航道航行不容易，但没有其他更好的办法处理。结果船舶果然在航道搁浅而造成船底损坏甚至全损，同样的道理就是水雷击中就是整个损失的致命一击。

4.3.2 前因激发或导致后来的原因而造成损失的案件("weakening" cases)

这一类别的前因谈不上是致命一击，甚至不是由它造成最后的损失，但它导致了后来的原因更容易出现或激发了后来的原因，而后来的原因才造成了损失。这种案件要找出近因最不容易，也最富争议性。它也可以以因果链(chain of causation)或因果关系(causation)解释，就是前因被后来的原因打断了因果关系(*novus actus interveniens* 或 intervening act)。这与侵权和违约的因果关系类似：Lloyds TSB General Insurance Holdings Ltd. v. Lloyds Bank Group Insurance Co. Ltd. (2001) Lloyd's Rep. IR 224。显然，在后来出现的原因(通常是人为疏忽或故意行为或其他不平常事情的发生)应该是独立而且程度上比较严重才会导致打断因果关系，变成了后者才是导致损失的近因，而前因只变成了远因。找出近因在侵权的范畴更是重要与复杂，正如 Hart 教授与 Honore 教授所著的《Causation in the law》第 133 页所说："... we are concerned to inquire how far in the law of tort, when causal connection between a wrongful act and harm is an element in responsibility, the decisions of the courts have been controlled by the principle that this connection is negative if the factors required, in addition to the wrongful act, for the production of the harm include a voluntary human action or an abnormal occurrence. Our conclusion is that this principle has been applied over a very wide area of the law of tort, sufficient perhaps to enable us to speak of a traditional doctrine."

这些案件很多，而且判决会有争议性。例如在 Lawrence Aberdein (1821) 5 B & Ald 107，由于船舶在海上遇上风浪，导致船上的货物(牲畜)因受惊吓互相践踏而受伤，判近因是海上风险。另在 Bondrett v. Hentingg (1816) Holt NP 149，涉及了船舶搁浅(这是被承保的海上风险)，但给了沿岸的盗贼机会上船强抢东西，这被判近因是海上风险而不是盗贼。

在财产保险，有案例判空袭期间有人趁机偷东西，判的近因不是空袭而是盗窃行为：Winicofsky v. Army & Navy Insurance (1919) 35 TLR 283。同样的理念下，一场火灾给暴徒抢劫的机会，判的近因是暴徒的不法行为而不是火灾：Marsden v. City & County Insurance (1865) LR 1 CP 232。另在一个建筑物起火并带来爆炸，判是爆炸才是损失的近因：Everett v. London Assurance (1865) 19 CBNS 126, Stanley v. Western Insurance Co. (1868) LR 3 Ex 71, Re Hooley Hill Rubber & Chemical Co. Ltd. (1920) 1 KB 257, Curtis & Harvey (Canada) Ltd. v. North British & Mercantile Insurance Co. (1921) 1 AC 303。

一种情况不明朗的是:船舶搁浅或者碰撞显然是毫无争议的海上风险(perils of sea)原因所导致,是传统与最典型的承保风险。但如果船舶搁浅或碰撞是由于船员疏忽,特别是很严重的疏忽,这会否导致近因变为船员疏忽?照理说海上风险与船员疏忽在目前的船壳保险条文中都属于承保的风险,不必区分。但由于船员疏忽是规定在2003年国际船壳保险条文的2.2.3条,而在2.2条所承保的各项风险是受到但书条文的约束,该但书条文是说"除非此种损失或损害并非由于受保人、船东或管理人克尽职责所致"(provided such loss or damage has not resulted from want of due diligence by the Assured, Owners or Managers)。而2.1条项下承保的海上风险是没有但书条文的约束。所以在有一些案件涉及了船东有否恪尽职责时还是要找出哪一个是导致了损失的近因,因为严重的船员疏忽有可能是船东没有恪尽职责雇用与训练船员。但通常是没有这种争议,因为在1906年《英国海上保险法》之Section 55(2)(a)有规定是在这种情况下,即使海上风险是由船员疏忽所导致也不受影响,说:"The insurer... is liable for any loss proximately caused by a peril insured against, even though the loss would not have happened but for the misconduct or negligence of the master or crew"。1906年的立法有这样规定所受的影响可能是当时的法律理念认为船员疏忽在时间上是远因,搁浅或碰撞是近因。但由于有这样的默示法律地位规定,所以在保险的案件中,就会与租约或者提单的案件得出不同的近因。前者是海上风险,而后者就会是船员疏忽。

还有一种情况也是不明朗的,就是在人身伤亡保险,受害人遇上了事故而带来自然的后果(natural cause)。典型就是受害人遇上了意外,如因车祸被送进了医院而感染了肺炎,这就带来了车祸是近因或者肺炎是近因的问题?如果肺炎导致了该受害人的死亡,可否说肺炎中断了因果链?在大量的案件中,都会判近因就是车祸:Fitton v Accidental Insurance Co. (1864) 17 CBN 122, Isitt v. Passengers Assurance Co. (1889) 22 QBD 504, Mardorf v. Accident Insurance Co. (1903) 1 KB 584, Re Etheringron and Lancashire and Yorkshire Accident Insurance Co. (1909) 1 KB 591, Smith v. Cornhill Insurance (1938) 3 All ER 145, Cawley v. National Employers' Accident (1885) 1 TLR 255。

但如果换了是受害人本身就有一个自然的缺陷,这导致了他遇上意外,这一来到底哪一个是近因呢?例如,体质很容易晕倒的人在突然晕倒后掉到河里被淹死或被火车轧过导致死亡,或者是盲人在过马路的时候被汽车撞倒,到底近因是受害人本身体质上的缺陷还是意外?通常情况下法院会判意外是近因,这些案例有:Winspear v. Accident Insurance (1880) 6 QBD 42, Reynolds v. Accidental Insurance Co. (1870) 22 LT 820, Lawrence v. Accidental Insurance Co. (1882) 7 QBD 216。总的说是涉及人身伤亡的案件,会有感觉好像是法院同情受害人归咎属于承保范围内的意外才是损害的近因,因为受害人在意外才会获得保险的赔付。

4.3.3 前因诱发受保人改变做法并遇到后来的原因造成损失的案件（“state of affairs” cases）

第三种情况是一种前因本身并没有造成任何的损失，只不过是有了这一个前因，诱使（induce）受保人改变主意采取了另外一种行为，而在实施这种行为的过程中，后来的风险出现并导致了损失。在这种情况下，通常都会认定后来风险是损失的近因，因为前因本身没有导致损失，而改变为另一种行为通常被视为中断因果链。举例说，如果一艘船舶在被警告要航行的水域有海盗出没，船东/船长因为害怕而更改航线，结果在新的航线上因为遇到风暴导致全损，则该全损会被认定为是海上风险导致，与海盗风险无关。这判法案件有不少，涉及在世界大战期间改变航线为了逃避敌方军舰或潜艇，但后来遇上了海上风险：The “Coxwold”（1942）AC 691；Moor Line v King and United Kingdom War Risks Association（1920）4 Ll LR 286；British Steamship Co. v. R（1921）1 AC 99；Green v. British Indian Steam Navigation Co.（1921）1 AC 99；Yorkshire Dale SS Co. v. Minister of War Transport（1942）AC 691；Liverpool & London War Risks v. Ocean SS Co.（1948）AC 243。

同样道理，因为担心被捕获而放弃航次导致损失的近因也不能被认定为是捕获。如果是机场被入侵的军队占领，地面上的飞机没有被开走，之后被解放战争中的炮弹击毁，这击毁的近因不能被认定为是最初入侵军队的占领，因为占领与飞机的击毁之间并没有必然的关系。

4.4 以明示条文排除近因原则的适用

近因原则的默示法律地位在上述已经介绍过，但在现实中保险人希望在承保不同的风险时将该近因原则进行扩大或限制，这就只能通过明示条文超越默示地位。举例说，在协会货物保险条文之4.7条，条文是排除核武器的风险。由于保险人惧怕核武器/装置的杀伤力太大与影响深远，所以不希望只是依赖近因原则的默示法律地位，而是说明损失只要是直接或间接由于核武器/装置引起的就被排除在外。而“直接或间接导致”一词可以说是在海上保险中含义最广泛的用词，该条文为：“In no case shall this insurance cover -4.7 loss damage or expense **directly or indirectly caused by or arising from** the use of any weapon or device employing atomic or nuclear fission and/or fusion or other like reaction or radioactive force or matter.”

另一个极端是以明示条文限制近因原则（proximate cause）的适用，即规定只有承保的风险是损失发生的唯一（solely）、绝对（exclusively）与直接（directly）原因的情况下，受保人才可以得到赔偿。这里可以介绍香港的先例 Vastgrand Industrial Ltd. v. Hong Kong and Shanghai Insurance Co. Ltd.（2002）HKEC 494，案情涉及原告投保的保险合约规定是只承保台风与风暴造成的损失，后来有了很大的风暴，导致珠江水位大涨，原告的工厂也因此而被淹没。作为被告的保险人否认自己有责任，并争辩说在洪水前几天，风暴已经减弱。法院的观点是该损失在承保的范围内，并说直接原因不必是最重要的原因，只要是重大的原因造成损失就已经足够。这样看来，这种方法大致是与近因原则是相同的。

在货物保险的条文中还会有其他明示条文试图改变近因原则,但许多在效力上有疑问。这里还存在一个问题就是如果放宽,是要放宽到什么程度?而正如前面介绍过的,一个人的出生也可以说是他死亡的一个间接原因,但这间接要到什么程度才算是合理?不妨先介绍明示条文中最广泛的"直接或间接导致"(directly or indirectly caused by or arising from)一词。这里首先介绍案件:Coxe v. Employers Liability Assurance (1916.) 2 KB 629,案情涉及了一个军官在检阅士兵的时候被火车撞死,因为当时是在"一战"期间,灯火管制导致路轨周围昏暗。有关的保险合约说明是不赔偿军官的死亡,如果死亡是直接或间接由战争引起或导致(This policy does not insure against death... directly or indirectly caused by , arising from, or traceable to ... war...)。在第一审,判近因是战争。在上诉庭,Scrutton 大法官认为有"间接"(indirectly)这一词,所以不能干预仲裁庭的裁决。他也认为无法理解什么才是"间接的近因"(indirect proximate cause),但可以清楚地看到双方想排除近因原则,说:"... the words which I find it impossible to escape from are 'directly or indirectly.' There does not appear to be any authority in which those words have been considered, and I find it impossible to reconcile them with the maxim *causa proxima non remota spectatur*. If it were contended that the result of the words is that the proximate cause, whether direct or indirect, is to be looked at, I should reply that that result does not appear to me to be consistent or intelligible. I am unable to understand what is an indirect proximate cause, and in my judgment the only possible effect which can be given to those words is that the maxim *causa proxima non remota spectatur* is excluded and that a more remote link in the chain of causation is contemplated than the proximate and immediate cause."

但 Scrutton 大法官也感觉到"间接"这一词很难给它一个合理的限制,他提到该军官的出生也可以认为是他死亡的一个间接原因。但他也给了一些指引说:"a more remote link in the chain of causation is contemplated."。而在先例 Spinney's v. Royal Insurance (1980) 1 Lloyd's Rep. 406,Mustill 大法官认为将"间接"应该限制在与损失有关系(connection)的范围,而不是该原因再也不是造成损失的原因而变为历史的一部分(an event ceases to be a cause of the loss, and becomes merely an item of history)。Mustill 大法官比较详细的判词如下:"I now turn to the question whether there was a sufficient causal connection between the operation of the excepted perils and the losses which I have described. The type of connection required is defined by the causation clause, and the mode of proof by the reverse burden clause. The meaning of the former was the subject of citation and argument at the trial. I do not find it necessary to discuss the reported decisions on the meaning of various individual words of the clause, for whatever they may mean on their own, **it is quite clear that the draftsman has gone to great lengths to ensure that the doctrine of proximate cause does not apply. Plainly, there must be some**

limit on the application of the clause, for the chain of causation recedes infinitely into the past. The draftsman must have intended to stop somewhere: and that place must be the point at which an event ceases to be a cause of the loss, and becomes merely an item of history. The draftsman has not explained how that point is to be identified, nor indeed do I believe that words can be found to do so. It is, eventually, a matter of instinct – but an instinct guided by the fact that this is a policy which (unlike others in which similar clauses can be found) expressly insures against violent acts. In essence, the task is to assess whether the particular act of violence simply takes place against the background of a 'warlike' state of affairs, or whether it has itself (even if in a rather remote way) a warlike aspect of its own."(加黑部分是笔者的强调)

另在先例 Oei v. Foster and Eagle Star Insurance Co. Ltd. (1982) 2 Lloyd's Rep. 170,也是类似的判法。最后一提的是《O'May on Marine Insurance》一书中,O'May 律师建议最好避免使用"indirect"一词,因为给间接的因果关系一个合理的限制很困难(in view of the difficulty in setting any reasonable limits to indirect causation)。

另一个用词也会是改变与扩大近因原则"可归因于"(attributable to)或"合理可归因于"(reasonably attributable to),在海上保险也是保险人用在比较严重的风险,所以要更广泛地把它排除在外,这就是受保人的恶意行为(wilful misconduct)。这种恶意行为在海上保险最典型的就是船东恶意凿沉船舶,在岸上保险最典型的就是纵火。把近因原则扩大就可以在受保人做这种事情时,如果有其他原因共同导致或者扩大损失,保险人也有保障可拒赔。这可以节录 2009 年协会货物条文之 4.1 的规定:"In no case shall this insurance cover loss damage or expense **attributable to** wilful misconduct of the Assured.",这与 1906 年《英国海上保险法》之 Section 55(1)(a):"The insurer is not liable for any loss **attributable to** the wilful misconduct of the assured..."对比之下就看到两者都采用了相同的措辞"可归因于"。

《Arnould's Law of Marine Insurance and Average》第 16 版对"attributable"一词的解释如下:"It seems, however, to be clear in principle that wilful misconduct of the assured is a defence not only when it is the proximate cause of loss but also when it is only one of the effective causes of, or factors contributing to a loss. A similar rule appears also to obtain in cases, of the type provided for in section 39(5) of the Marine Insurance Act 1906, where the ship is sent to sea in an unseaworthy state, with the privity of the assured."

从这个意义上说,"可归因于"的意思不必局限在近因,而只要是受保人的恶意行为是导致损失的其中一个有效原因就已经足够。

另外一个用词,不论有没有在前面加上"合理地"(reasonably)应该都是同一个意思。《Arnould's Law of Marine Insurance and Average》关于该词到底有怎样的作用论述如下:"The test for causation under the words 'reasonably attributable to' may be less stringent than the proximate cause test. In principle, it appears that reasonable evidence of a causal link between the specified peril and the loss claimed is sufficient under this part of the clause."

但在 The "Salem" (1982) 1 Lloyd's Rep. 369(CA),上诉庭 Kerr 大法官有不同的看法,认为"可归因于"不能改变近因原则。他这样说:"But I think that these words 'may have been attributable to' are neutral words which cannot be read as intended to alter the well – established principles of causation in this field."。这在 John Dunt 2009 年所著的《Marine Cargo Insurance》第 130 页分析该案例,认为是该案件的情况特殊,并且 Kerr 大法官只是随口讲讲(*obiter*)。John Dunt 的结论还是:"'Attributable to' is wider than proximately caused by and covers the case where the risk is 'a' cause of the loss even where it is only one of the effective causes or factors contributing to the loss."

毕竟,如果是用明示的合约条文改变默示的法律地位就必须说得十分清楚。其实现在什么样的用词可以将近因原则有效地排除还不是很明朗,像"caused by"、"resulting from"、"due to"、"arising from"、"consequences of"这些用词都不足够改变近因的原则。

首先介绍"caused by",Scrutton 大法官在先例 Coxe v. Employers Liability Assurance (1916) 2 KB 629 中说:"They are words which always have been construed as relating to the proximate cause."

接下来介绍"resulting from",上诉庭的 Potter 大法官在先例 Lloyds TSB General Insurance Holdings Ltd. v. Lloyds Bank Group Insurance Co. Ltd. (2002) Lloyd's Rep. IR 113 中说:"In my view the expression 'result from' undoubtedly imparts the notion of causation which, in turn, in all branches of insurance law, involves application of the notion of proximate cause, applied with good sense, so as to give effect to and not to defeat the intention of the parties."

关于"due to"与"arising from",《Arnould's Law of Marine Insurance and Average》,第 16 版在第 938 页这样说:"Words such as 'due to' 'resulting from' 'arising from' in an exceptions clause in a policy have been construed as excluding only those losses proximately caused by the events mentioned."

4.5　同时有多个近因(concurrent causes)

根据严格的近因说法或理论,必须要找出一个造成损失的原因作为有效的近因,而不能有多过一个的原因作为近因。这在一些案件中会带来困难,因为有多过一个原因造成而且很难分得出什么是最重要与最有效的原因。这在 P. Samuel & Co. v. Dumas (1924) 18 Lloyd's Rep. 200 先例,贵族院持不同意见的 Sumner 勋爵也有针对这一个问题说:"Where a loss is caused by two perils operating simultaneously at the time of loss and one is wholly excluded because the policy is warranted free of it, the question is whether it can be denied that the loss was so caused, for if not the warranty operates."

另在 Leyland Shipping v. Norwich Union（1918）AC 350（HL），Wright 勋爵这样说："... where there are two perils both of which are proximate causes of the loss and in an open policy the shipowner could have recovered on either, then, if one of those perils is excepted by the warranty the underwriters are not liable."

但可以说权威性的先例针对两个或以上的近因还是欠缺，直到 Wayne Tank & Pump v. Employers' Liability（1973）2 Lloyd's Rep. 237，在这个有关火灾的先例是工厂里面安置了一个有缺陷与危险的设备，起火是因为在没有人监管的情况下将该设备开动，这涉及了员工的疏忽。这就带来到底是危险设备还是员工疏忽才是近因，前者是保险合约的除外风险，后者是在保险合约承保的范围内。Denning 勋爵在上诉庭认为根据正常思维或是常识（common sense）应该是危险设备，说：

"So I would approach this case by asking which of the two causes was the effective or dominant cause? I should have thought that it was the first cause, the dangerous nature of the installation, and thus within the exception. So that the Employers' Liability were not liable under this policy.

The Judge was much inclined to hold that it was the dangerous installation which was the dominant cause. But he was dissuaded from that view by Mr. Le Quesne（原告代表大律师）, who argued, with his usual persuasiveness, that the act of the man（in switching on the heating tape）was a *novus actus interveniens* which was predominant in effectiveness. It was the cause of the fire. It did not come within the exceptions. So the Employers' Liability were liable.

I must say that I do not care for this emphasis on *novus actus interveniens*. It seems to me to be going back to the old and forsaken test of the latest in time. I would reject *novus actus*. I would ask, as a matter of common sense, what was the effective or dominant cause of the fire? To that question I would answer that it was the dangerous installation of a pipe which was likely to melt under heat. It seems to me that the conduct of the man in switching on the heating tape was just the trigger—the precipitating event—which brought about the disaster. There would have been no trouble whatever if the system had been properly designed and installed.

Seeing that the dangerous installation was the dominant cause, it comes within the exceptions and the Employers' Liability company are not liable on this policy."

Denning 勋爵接下去也说即使在没有办法找出一个单独最有效近因的情况下，危险设备是除外风险而员工疏忽在承保范围内，这样看来保险人可以依赖除外风险。但 Denning 勋爵提到了并没有太多先例针对这一方面的问题，这显示"同时有多个近因"的说法也是近期才发展起来的。Denning 勋爵说："That is enough to decide the case. But I will assume, for the sake of argument, that I am wrong about this: and that there was not one dominant cause, but two causes which were equal or nearly equal in their efficiency in bringing about the damage. One of them is within the general words and would render the insurers liable. The other is within the exception and would exempt them from liability. In such a case it would seem that the insurers can rely on the exception clause. **There is not much authority on it...**"

要强调的是适用"同时有多个近因"的说法，必须是在无法在合理找出单独一个近因的情况下。Potter 大法官在 The "Aliza Glacial" (2002) 2 Lloyd's Rep. 421 一案中说:"It is only when a court is driven to the conclusion of more than one proximate cause, that the concurrent cause rules apply."

在"同时有多个近因"的说法下，可以粗略地分为以下三种情况。

4.5.1 多个近因都属于承保的列明风险

在这种情况下，应该明确不过就是保险人要承担赔付的责任。比方说，船员疏忽造成海上灾难，而两个都是承保的列明风险，保险人显然要负责。

4.5.2 多个近因有一个是承保的列明风险，但其他的既没有说是承保也没有说是排除

在这种情况下，保险人也需要负责。这可节录 Bennett 教授所著的《The Law of Marine Insurance》第二版之 9.22 段所说的话:"Provided the policy covers at least one of the perils qualifying as a proximate cause of the loss and none are expressly excluded, the assured is entitled to recover. The loss is caused by a covered peril and there is nothing in the policy to deny cover."这方面有关的先例是 The "Miss Jay Jay" (1987) 1 Lloyd's Rep. 32，案情涉及一个设计有缺陷的游艇在航行中发生全损。这设计上的缺陷导致该游艇超过一定速度航行时会离开海平面，而设计上没有缺陷的游艇仍会贴着海平面。全损是由它本身的设计缺陷导致的不适航以及坏的天气(虽然并非不正常的坏天气)共同造成，两个都属于有效的近因，因为缺少任何其中的一个原因都不会造成游艇的全损。坏天气是在保险合约承保的范围内，而设计缺陷导致不适航就没有明确说明是承保，但也没有被列明在除外条款内。这是因为该船舶保险是定期保险合约(time policy)，1906 年《英国海上保险法》之 Section39(5)说明定期保险合约是没有对适航的默示保证，只是在船东私谋让不适航的船舶开航的情况下才对不适航导致的损坏不用赔付。显然设计有缺陷导致不适航不是船东的私谋。结果是判保险人要赔付，上诉庭的 Slade 大法官说:

"However, since the instant policy contains no relevant exception relating to loss caused by unseaworthiness of the vessel, different principles apply. The legal position in such a case is stated thus in Halsbury's Laws of England (4th ed.) vol. 25 par. 181 which relates to marine insurance policies:

It seems that there may be more than one proximate (in the sense of effective or direct) cause of a loss. If one of these causes is insured against under the policy and none of the others is expressly excluded from the policy; the assured will be entitled

to recover.

No authority has been cited to us which leads me to suppose that this passage incorrectly states the relevant law relating to marine insurance policies and, in my judgment, it incorporates the principle applicable to the present case. The crucial point is that in the contingencies envisaged in the passage, for the purpose of applying the provisions of the policy and s. 55 of the Act, the loss is treated as proximately caused by the cause insured against, notwithstanding the presence of a concurrent cause not covered by the policy. ”

4.5.3 多个近因有一个是承保的列明风险,另一个是被排除的列明风险

在这种情况下,就更加复杂了,因为要涉及怎样全面解释有关的保险合约。这里涉及承保的列明风险或一切险与排除的风险(明示或默示)之间的冲突,但又必须要给它们都有一定的解释。作为起点,可以说是特别在承保一切险,如果有一条明示的条文针对一些排除的风险,就可以根据两个解释合约的规则说明排除的风险应该超越一切险。第一个解释合约的规则是“假设双方不会约定多余的内容”,因为如果除外风险条文的效力高于一切险条文就给除外条文一定的意思,但如果相反认为除外风险条文的效力低于一切险条文,那么除外风险条文的存在就显得多余。第二个解释合约的规则是“面窄与特别针对一件事的条文超越广泛与一般性的条文”,而显然是列明的排除风险相比承保一切险条文通常是面窄与特别针对。这些合约解释的规则在笔者所著的《合约的解释》一书中有详细介绍,请参阅。

但由于有不同的保险合约与不同的措词/结构,所以会有情况是不允许排除的风险完全否定承保的列明风险,也有情况是判特定排除的风险超越了承保的列明风险。

在前一种情况下,可举第一个先例 The “Lydia Flag” (1998) 2 Lloyd’s Rep. 652。该船在航次中掉了船舵,估计是由于几个月前在干坞进行修理工人拆除检查时的疏忽导致的。有关的保险合约格式是1983年条文协会船壳定期保险条文,其中第6.2.4条有修理人疏忽的列明风险。但该保险合约多加了一个附加保证,说明保险合约在开始生效的时候船舶必须适航,有关条款如下:“11. Warranted that at the inception of this policy the vessel... shall be in a seaworthy condition and thereafter during the valid period of this policy the insured shall exercise due diligence to keep the vessel seaworthy...”

而保险人拒赔的理由是船舶破坏了该适航的承诺性保证条文,因为它的船舵有问题所以不适航。但问题是如果支持保险人的说法,即船舵(或船舶上的其他机件)如果有问题(这问题可以是修理人疏忽造成或其他潜在缺陷造成),显然就是船舶不适航(因为在文字上针对保险生效时的“适航”一词是指“绝对的适航”,在保险生效后才减为“恪尽职责”),就否定了清清楚楚被承保的明示列明风险(不论是修理人疏忽还是潜在缺陷造成船舶不是绝对适航)。毕竟,保险就是为了针对列明风险所导致的损失或损坏,这才是保险合约的主要目的。所以以一条附加承诺性保证条文否定列明风险整体对保险合约的解释就说不通。笔者还可以多加一个解释就是较早提到的第二条解释合约的规则“面窄与特别针对一件事的条文超越广泛与一般性的条

文”,显然列明风险才是面窄与特别针对,相反承诺性保证“保险生效时适航”却是泛泛而谈,因为适航针对的面是非常广泛的。所以在 The “Lydia Flag”案中,Moore - Bick 大法官不同意保险人对保险合约所作出的解释,他说:

“If Mr. Phillips(保险人代表大律师)is right this construction of the policy could lead to some startling results. In this case it is accepted that the loss of the rudder was caused by negligence on the part of the repairers. It could just as well, of course, have been caused by some latent defect in the mechanism securing the rudder to the rudder stock. One would be surprised to find that having taken insurance of this kind and the vessel being unseaworthy by reason of a latent defect at the inception of the policy the owners would be completely without cover if the vessel was lost as a result, for example, of a collision with another vessel for which no fault could be attached to the owners of the vessel simply because there was a latent defect which had not in any way contributed to the casualty. That leads me to wonder whether a sensible construction can be placed on this policy which would not deprive the owners of cover under circumstances of that kind but would still give some meaning to all the clauses of the policy...

In my judgment the only sensible way in which to read these clauses together is in the way suggested by Mr. Butcher(受保人大律师)and in those circumstances I am satisfied that cover is not lost in so far as the vessel may be unseaworthy at the inception of the policy as a result of latent defect or negligence, as in this case, of repairers, provided of course that unseaworthiness has not resulted from want of due diligence on the part of the owners or manager. So as a matter of law, therefore, I reject the construction of the policy suggested by Mr. Phillips.”

另一个同样道理的先例是 IF P&C Insurance Ltd. (Publ) v. Silversea Cruises Ltd. (2004) Lloyd's Rep. IR 696。有关的保险合约是承保旅游船舶船东的估计收益,而其中的一个承保的列明风险是“美国国务院发出建议或警告有关战争风险、武力冲突、民变或恐怖分子行为”(Resulting from a State Department advisory or similar warning by competent authority regarding acts of war, arm conflict, civil commotions or terrorism, whether actual or threatened)。但有关的保险合约也排除了这种风险造成的直接损失。在 2001 年著名的“9 · 11”事件导致纽约国际贸易中心倒塌,使美国的旅游船舶生意大受影响,导致船东向保险人提出索赔。生意大受影响的原因应该是恐怖分子的袭击与美国国务院警告继续有这种恐怖袭击。保险人拒绝赔偿的理由是,恐怖分子袭击不是承保的列明风险,而且是被排除的风险。英国上诉庭不同意保险人的理由,判决:“There is no intention under this policy to exclude loss directly caused by a warning concerning terrorist activities just because it can also be said that the loss was also directly and concurrently caused by the underlying terrorist themselves.”

在后一种情况下,只适用在面比较广的列明风险,而被排除的只是其中的一个小部分,那么这种排除就会被解释为有效或效力更大,因为更有针对性或面更狭窄。否则,等于就是不给这个排除的风险任何的解释,因为这是与全面解释保险合约的精神(就是给双方所定的合约条文都有一个解释,而不是动辄以它们之间有矛盾而否定其中一条)不相配合的。这里有关的先例是 Wayne Tank & Pump Co. Ltd. v. Employer's Liability Assurance Corp Ltd. (1974) QB 57,Cairns 大法官说:"The effect of an exception is to save the insurer from liability for a loss which but for the exception would be covered. The effect of the cover is not to impose on the insurer liability for something which is within the exception."

以 2003 年国际船壳保险条文为例,就有许多情况是列明风险与排除风险起冲突,特别是水险与战争险之间的分别。这里要提到第 29 ~ 31 条说明的首要条款(paramount clause),应该优先解释,这起了很大的帮助。比如说,船员不法行为的承保列明风险是在第 2. 25 条。但在 30. 3 条排除了任何人士出于恶意使用任何武器或引爆爆炸物的风险,而且没有好像第 29. 2 条把船员的不法行为除外。这就导致了船员不法行为的列明风险到底是属于水险还是战争险赔付就有了不稳定。可以说,它主要根据的就是船员不法行为所采用的手段或做法。如果是凿沉船舶或放火,这属于水险(参见 The "Grecia Express" (2002) 2 Lloyd's Rep. 88;North Star Shipping Ltd. v. Sphere Drake Insurance Plc (2005) 2 Lloyd's Rep. 76)。但如果船员不法行为是采用武器或爆炸品,这就属于战争险,或是被第 30. 3 条所排除。这里顺便提及的是 Bennett 教授所著的《The Law of Marine Insurance》第二版第 481 页脚注,其中提到 Colman 大法官在 North Star Shipping Ltd. v. Sphere Drake Insurance Plc 中可能判错,因为他提到该船被恶意引爆不属于战争险,而是涉及了船员的不法行为。

再多举一个例子,就是海盗属于承保的列明风险(第 2. 1. 5 条),而 1906 年《英国海上保险法》对海盗的定义也包括了暴乱分子(rioters)从岸上攻击船舶(who attack the ship from the shore)。但根据第 29. 4 条,把"暴动与民变分子"所造成的损失以首要条款的形式排除。所以,海盗带来的损失属于水险的承保范围,但暴乱分子的海盗行为被排除在水险外。

以上举的例子是主要来自船舶保险而不是货物保险,这是因为船舶保险的有趣先例比较多。笔者在这里只是为了介绍任何合约(也包括了货物保险合约)整体解释的重要性。

5. 总结

协会货物条文(B)与(C)只承保列明风险,这与协会货物条文(A)的承保一切险很不一样。在前者受保人会对货物损失/损坏有举证责任,而如果做不到的话就会面对本章 2. 1 段提到先例 The "Popi M"(1985) 2 Lloyd's Rep. 1 (HL)同样的问题。所以这对货方而言，如果货物在海上运输中途会遇到货损货差（如货物本身原因或外来原因所造成），而近因难以确定或调查举证费用昂贵，就应该尽量投保一切险，即使是要支付比较高昂的保费。相反，如果不会有这种海上运输中不知情货损货差的问题，一有货物的损失或损坏就是公开与明确的近因所导致（如船舶发生严重事故如沉没），才值得投保协会货物条文（B）与（C）以节省保费。但在一切险，由于有默示或明示的除外列明风险，所以找出与证明什么是货物损失的近因还是有必要的。只不过这个举证责任不是在受保人而是在保险人。这表示在一切险，如果发生了比较严重的货损货差，保险人应该尽早作出调查取证。因为将来如果根据除外列明风险而拒赔，举证责任是在保险人。

讲到近因，也就是找出导致损失的有效与重要的原因（可能是一个也有可能是多于一个），这一重要性也不只是在保险，而实际上所有的社会问题也都同样重要。例如，笔者听过这样的讨论，就是一个人从 20 楼跳下，当他经过 10 楼的时候，有人向他开枪把他打死。但该人死亡的近因到底是什么，开枪的人是否有谋杀罪或误杀罪？或是死者在 20 楼跳下的时候死亡的命运已经是不可扭转，正如本章 4. 3. 1 段所说的"前因造成无可避免损失的案件"。笔者也见过一些案例，如一个人买了把木梯，回家后才发现木梯的质量有问题。他本可以把梯子拿回商店调换，但是由于赶工程进度或是他本人嫌麻烦就没有拿去调换。结果在施工过程中从梯子上摔下并受伤。那么他受伤的近因到底是什么，是梯子的质量还是他自己明知质量不好仍旧使用的决定？这种情况是否接近本章 4. 3. 3 段介绍的"前因诱发受保人改变做法并遇到后来的原因造成损失的案件"？

近因的探索还可以涉及更大的社会问题或国家大事，因为必须找出有效与重要的原因才能对症下药。但思考的方法万变不离其宗，就是要找出一个结果的近因就需要全面了解事实，而事实是要根据客观与可靠的证据认定，然后有好的头脑从中找出什么才是有效与主要的原因。

第七章　其他非实质损失方面的承保:共同海损、救助费用、碰撞责任与航程终止

“协会货物条文(一切险)”(Institute Cargo Clauses [A])承保的是一切险,第1条是明确承保货物在海上运输中受到实质损失或损坏(loss of or damage),但该协会条文也承保了其他非实质损失,这种损失基本上就是费用或者金钱的支出。本章就是分析承保的非实质损失是什么,同时请注意“协会货物条文(B)&(C)”(Institute Cargo Clauses [B]&[C])也有同样的条文,只是实质损失或非实质损失(除了共同海损与救助费用)只局限在承保的列明风险所导致,比一切险局限得多。

请参见附录三中有关条文,包括条文2、3与12,其详细介绍分别见以下第2、3、4、5段。

1. 共同海损(General Average)

1.1　背景介绍与英国海上保险法的定义

共同海损的历史非常悠久,比海上保险的历史悠久得多,而这两种制度之间没有必然关系,只是船东与货方在海上保险都会投保产生共同海损的风险,所以造成了两者之间在操作上关系十分密切。共同海损的整个理念来自公平对待所有在同一航程中“同舟共济”的利益方,包括船东与货方(可能有不同的货物属于不同的货方)。在古代,航海是十分冒险的事情,其中由于定位困难以及没有准确的海图,像搁浅这种海难非常容易发生。如果发生这种海难并当场造成了损坏,如船壳破了个洞或掉了个锚,这是船东自己的损失(可称为“单独海损”[particular average]),算他运气不好,其他没有造成损坏的货物没有义务分摊这笔损失。但如果搁浅后怎么样摆脱这个困局就会有几种不同的方法可供选择,一是把船上的部分货物抛入海中以让船舶减轻重量浮起,也有可能是把船舶的部分设备抛入海中以达到同样的目的。一两百年前船舶从帆船变了是机动,还会多一个选择,就是把船舶倒回深水部分,但这样做会造成船底更大的损坏,也会让主机有更大的损耗。还有的选择是雇佣一艘大马力的拖轮把船舶拖去深水,或是安排海上船靠船的货物转运以让搁浅的船舶减载等。选择会涉及牺牲哪一方的利益,毕竟最后能够摆脱困境,脱离危险甚至能够完成航次对大家都有好处。所以就有了共同海损的做法,就是不管谁的利益被牺牲,或是船东支付

了费用(如雇佣拖轮),这被称为共同海损牺牲(general average sacrifice)或共同海损费用(general average expense),最终大家需要根据航次完毕后的实际价值(船舶或货物)的比例分摊。

希望有了这样的解释就很容易明白1906年《英国海上保险法》Section 66,[1]对共同海损的定义以及与海上保险的关系。

在很多有关共同海损的先例中举一个就是Boag v. Standard Marine Insurance Company Ltd. (1937) 57 Lloyd's Rep. 83,案情涉及一艘船舶搁浅后把部分的货物抛进了海里,让船舶最后能够浮起来。结果在分摊计算后,抛下海的货物能够从其他利益方大概取回50%的利益价值。也可以说,即使是没有作出牺牲的货方与船东,实际上也作出了50%的分摊或承受50%的损失。

1.2 共同海损的要素

总结说,共同海损有以下要素:(1)"特殊的牺牲或费用"(extraordinary sacrifice or expenditure);(2)"自愿"(voluntarily),这也代表有一定的选择性;(3)合理作出牺牲或花费;(4)"当时有危险"(in time of peril);(5)该危险不是由要求分摊共同海损一方自己的过错或疏忽所导致,否则其他的利益方向他索赔损失还来不及,怎么轮到他要求其他利益方分摊损失;(6)"为保障财产"(for the purpose of preserving the property);(7)"船货共同风险"(common adventure)。

有关这一课题在笔者《海事法》的第六章有详细介绍,不去重复。

1.3 共同海损分摊的法律

1.3.1 共同海损在卸港宣告与理算

共同海损的分摊是在货物安全到了卸港时才提出的:Chellew v. Royal Commission on the Sugar Supply (1922) 1 KB 12。这也是现实,因为在中途避难港(port of refuge)作出了共同海损牺牲或者费用,如果马上要求获救的利益方分摊根本不现实。例如,船东根本不知道货方最终是谁,因为提单还可能正在流转,也不会有货方到中途港前来提货。这表示船舶离开避难港后,还需要继续去卸港,然后才能向货方提出或宣告共同海损。还有一个现实的考虑就是稍后讲到的船东会强制货方为共同海损分摊提供担保,在普通法下,船东对货物有留置权(lien)。显然船舶也只有在到了最终的卸港货方来要求提货时,船东才可以行使留置权。这在《约克-安特卫普规则》(York-Antwerp Rules)2004年版本也有说明如下:"(1) General average shall be adjusted as regards both loss or contribution upon the basis of values at the time and place when and where the adventure ends..."

而在英国普通法中,Cockburn大法官早在先例Mavro v. Ocean Marine Insurance Co. (1875) LR 10 CP 414中说:"The adjustment must be made at the port of destination, if it be reached, but if the voyage is interrupted by some supervening cause, which

---

[1] 参见本书附录一。

necessitates or justifies its termination at some intermediate place, that place is the proper place of adjustment."

到底航次是将哪里作为目的地需要看船东与货方的协议,这主要就是租约或提单了。当然在订约自由下,他们完全可以再作出改变,如把目的地卸港改为中途避难港。如果在原来的租约中有几个卸港,这也不影响在航次完结后一次作出共同海损的理算。只是在最早卸港卸下的货物不在余下的航次有共同利益,所以在余下的航次如果遇到共同海损的事故,已经卸下的货物是不会分摊的。它需要分摊的只是之前的共同海损牺牲/费用。

1.3.2 对中途花费的共同海损费用作出投保

这种做法就可能带来很多细致的问题,如船舶如果从避难港离开后中途沉没,那岂非船东在避难港所花费的费用就拿不回来了,正如先例 Chellew v. Royal Commission on the Sugar Supply (1922) 1 KB 12。所以如果船东作出了共同海损的花费,由于船舶还没有安全抵达目的地的卸港,就需要为这笔钱投保名为"General Average Disbursement Insurance"的保险。而这笔保费也算是共同海损费用的一部分,可以一并加入投保金额与事后分摊:这方面在《约克－安特卫普规则 2004》Rule XX (b)中说:"The cost of insuring average disbursements shall also be allowed in general average."

这一来,如果航次顺利完成就在卸港作出分摊。但如果不能完成,就是船舶遇上另一个新风险导致船货全损或货物受到损坏而导致货价大跌(这表示由于实际价值大跌会导致货方的分摊相应减少),船东就向保险人取回这笔较早时花费的共同海损费用。伦敦保险市场也有这种保险的标准条文,名为 Average Disbursement Clauses,它所承保的标的在第4条有说明,如下:"This insurance is in respect of general average disbursements and salvage and salvage charges inclusive of costs."而承保的风险就是在第6.1条,如下:"... this insurance covers extinction or reduction of the contributory value of the property and freight at risk..."

1.3.3 共同海损理算的适用法

由于理算与分摊共同海损是在卸港,所以共同海损的适用法与管辖权也是理所当然属于卸港的法律与法院。虽然绝大部分的海事国家包括中国都有自己的法律针对共同海损的原则与理算方法,但它们之间在细节方面有很大差异。所以为了统一做法,国际海事组织(Comite Maritime International,简称 CMI)很早就已经拟定了《约克－安特卫普规则》(York－Antwerp Rules)给国际航运界使用。但不像国际海事组织另一项重要的成果,就是1924年的《海牙规则》(Hague Rules),《约克－安特卫普规则》并没有被提升成为国际公约或被有关国家立法,而一直是民间的一套规则。所以它要能够约束有关当事人,有关的海上运输合约必须规定船东与货方之间的共同海损以《约克－安特卫普规则》作为理算方法,也就是通过订约自由与合约法来约束大家。经过多个版本的修改,最新的是2004年的版本。

在今天能够见得到的提单/海运单格式或租约格式都有这样的一条类似的条文

将《约克－安特卫普规则》合并进来,如 Congenbill 1994 的散装货租约提单格式的第 14 条说:"General Average shall be adjusted, stated and settled in London according to the York Antwerp Rules 1994, or any modification thereof, in respect of all cargo, whether carried on or under deck..."

在海上保险合约,虽然是承保共同海损的分摊,但为了避免保险人面对一些不可以接受的共同海损法律或者规定而要承担不合理的分摊,所以规定了共同海损的理算必须是以航次完结的时候目的地港的有关法律与做法为准,或根据《约克－安特卫普规则》。这可举 2003 年国际船壳保险条文,承保船壳险,它的 8.2 条是"General average shall be adjusted according to the law and practice obtaining at the place where the adventure ends, as if the contract of affreightment so provides the adjustment shall be according to the York－Antwerp Rules."

在协会货物条文(A)(B)(C)的第 2 条对承保共同海损的分摊规定的比船舶保险宽松只是说:"adjusted or determined according to the contract of carriage and/or the governing law and practice",并没有强制要求分摊共同海损的理算必须根据《约克－安特卫普规则》。估计是因为在现实中,海上运输合约的拟定货方通常没有办法抗拒,特别是在班轮运输。所以如果有一家中国的船公司签发的提单规定了要根据《北京共同海损理算规则》在北京理算,但有关的航次不是美国去中国,而是中国去美国。这一来,共同海损的理算既不是根据美国卸港的法律,也不是根据《约克－安特卫普规则》,两者(北京的理算与《约克－安特卫普规则》的理算)之间的理算有差别就会带来争议。所以为了更好地保障没有谈判力量的货方,协会货物条文不要求必须以《约克－安特卫普规则》理算,这与船壳保险不一样。

1.4　共同海损分摊的实际做法

船舶安全抵达卸港,收货人前来提货,船东就可以要求其分摊共同海损。事实上在共同海损事故发生后,船东就会很快委任专业的海损理算师进行理算。但问题是理算要涉及很多的事实认定以及取得有关证据,如船舶与货物在卸港的实际价值是多少。所以,整个理算过程非常漫长而且复杂,一两年很常见。这就带来一个问题,就是当货方在卸货港要求提货时,共同海损的理算可以说是刚起步,根本没有依据可以向货方(或是他背后承保的保险人)要求分摊。因此,在卸港有好几件重要的事情要做,如下。

1.4.1　共同海损契约(General Average Bond)

这就是要求货方签署这份契约,内容是货方同意将来会按照海损理算师的理算结果进行支付,以下可节录劳合社的一份标准契约:

"Lloyd's Average Bond

To...(船东名字)

Owner(s) of the...(船舶名字)

Voyage and date...(航次与日期)

Port of shipment... (装港)

Port of destination/discharge (卸港)

Bill of lading or waybill number(s) (提单号)

Quantity and description of goods (货物数量与规格):______________

In consideration of the delivery to us or to our order, on payment of the freight due, of the goods noted above we agree to pay the proper proportion of any salvage and/or general average and/or special charges which may hereafter be ascertained to be due from the goods or the shippers or owners thereof under an adjustment prepared in accordance with the provisions of the contract of affreightment governing the carriage of the goods or, failing such provisions, in accordance with the law and practice of the place where the common maritime adventure ended and which is payable in respect of the goods by the shippers or owners thereof.

We also agree to:

(i) furnish particulars of the value of the goods, supported by a copy of the commercial invoice rendered to us, or, if there is no such invoice, details of the shipped value and

(ii) make a payment on account of such sum as is duly certified by the average adjusters to be due from the goods and which is payable in respect of the goods by the shippers or owners thereof.

Date... Signature of receiver of goods...

Full name and address..."

要货方签这一个契约除了要取得有关货方的资料以方便以后联系外,还约束货方要分摊共同海损本来就可能会有法律的约束。第一个就是根据卸港的有关法律,已经支持了船东向货方提出共同海损分摊的要求。除了这一法律默示地位外,多数提单或其他海上运输合约还会明确规定货方有责任分摊共同海损。所以这一契约只是重复这一方面的责任,特别是签这份契约的收货人并不是原来的发货人或者承租人,他甚至会是银行。

1.4.2 共同海损担保 (General Average Guarantee)

仅有了共同海损契约与货方将来同意共同海损的理算与分摊,这绝对是不足够的,所以另一个必须有的是货方提供财务的担保。由于还没有理算准确的分摊金额,但作出一个保守与稍微偏高的分摊金额还是可以的,可以这个数字要求货方提供共同海损分摊的担保。

由于大部分的货物都有投保海上运输风险,而协会货物条文也明确是承保共同海损。所以不少情况下共同海损担保是由保险人或保险公司作出的。在大部分的情况下,这些保险人或保险公司都是合法的(如香港与世界其他地方要成立保险公司都必须满足法定的资本要求与受到监管,不应该有太多的"光棍"公司),所以可以被船东接受。伦敦海上保险市场也有这种标准格式,如下:

"Average Guarantee

To: the Owners of the vessel named below and other parties to the adventure as their interests may appear.

VESSEL... from... to...
CASUALTY and DATE...

In consideration of the delivery in due course of the goods specified below to the consignees thereof without collection of a deposit, we, the undersigned insurers, hereby undertake to pay to the shipowners or to the Average Adjusters *, on behalf of the various parties to the adventure as their interest may appear, any contribution to General Average and/or Salvage and/or Special Charges which may hereafter be ascertained to be properly due in respect of the said goods.

We further agree:

(a) to make prompt payment(s) on account of such contribution as may be reasonably and properly due in respect of the said goods, as soon as the same may be certified by the Average Adjusters

(b) to furnish to the said Average Adjusters at their request all information which is available to us relative to the value and condition of the said goods

Port of Loading:（装港）
Port of Discharge:（卸港）
Bill of Lading:（提单编号）
Quantity & description of goods:（货物数量与规格）
Insured Value:（投保金额）
Policy/Ref No. and Premium (if known):（保单编号与保费）

Signature of Insurers...（保险人签名）
Name and Address...（保险人名字与地址）

Telephone No...
Fax No...
Email...
Date...

* The Average Adjusters are:（共同海损理算师名字与地址）"。

1.4.3　共同海损押金(General Average Deposit)

会有情况是货方没有投保(特别是在班轮运输中少量的一批货或是私人物品有

可能发生),这就会要求货方以现金作为押金。这个押金会存放在一个专门开设的船东与货方(可以是他们的代表如海损理算师)的联名账户里。而有关的标准格式也可以节录如下:

"General Average Deposit Receipt

Lloyd's Form

No. . . .

Dated at. . .

Vessel. . . from. . . to. . .

Nature and date of accident. .

RECEIVED from Messrs. . .

The sum of (in words). . .

Deposit on account of General Average and/or Salvage and/or Charges, being. . . percent on. . . provisionally adopted as the contributory value of the following goods, viz:. . .

B/L or Waybill No. . .

. . . Pounds

Signed. . .

For and on behalf of the Trustee(s) or nominated representative

NOTES

For Depositors: If insured you may wish to send this receipt together with the original policy or certificate of insurance to your insurers who, subject to the policy conditions, may be prepared to refund this deposit. If not insured you should notify the Average Adjusters direct of your interest and retain this receipt until the adjustment is issued when any credit balance can be claimed.

For Insurers: When a repayment of this deposit has been made, advise the Average Adjusters and thus assist in final settlement.

NO DUPLICATE OF THIS RECEIPT CAN BE ISSUED.

N. B. The refund, if any, will only be made to the bearer of, and in exchange for, this Receipt, and will be the whole balance of the deposit after satisfying the General Average and/or Salvage and/or Charges, without deduction or set off of any other claims of the Shipowner against the Shipper or Consignee.

The General Average will be adjusted in . . . and the Shipowners have given the necessary instruction to Messrs. . . Average Adjusters.

General Average Deposit Receipt (Lloyd's Form) – Counterfoil

Dated at...

Vessel...

Depositors...

Description of goods... B/L or Waybill No...

Contributory value (provisional)... Amount of deposit..."

这种做法在《约克－安特卫普规则》,1974、1994 与 2004 年版本都有同样的针对,是 Rule XXII,如下:"Where cash deposits have been collected in respect of cargo's liability for general average, salvage or special charges, such deposits shall be paid without any delay into a special account in the joint names of a representative nominated on behalf of the shipowner and a representative nominated on behalf of the depositors in a bank to be approved by both. The sum so deposited, together with accrued interest, if any, shall be held as security for payment to the parties entitled thereto of the general average, salvage or special charges payable by cargo in respect to which the deposits have been collected. Payments on account of refunds of deposits may be made if certified to in writing by the average adjuster. Such deposits and payments or refunds shall be without prejudice to the ultimate liability of the parties."

1.4.4 共同海损的留置权(Lien)

上述的船东要求显然必须要有法律依据作出强制执行,否则很难可以逼货方提供担保或押金。笔者很久以前在海损理算公司工作过,还清楚地记得多年前的一件事,香港一个很小的货方拿了一把刀冲进海损理算师的办公室说:"我已经交了运费,为什么还要交什么共同海损分摊的押金,我听不明白,赶快给我放货!"

这一法律依据就是英国普通法(也是许多其他地方的法律,如美国与香港)非常罕有地给船东一个普通法下的留置权:Simonds v. White (1824) 2 B. &c. 805;Huth v. Lamport (1886) 16 QBD 735。这表示不像滞期费或亏舱费这种只能靠合约赋予留置的权利,船东根本不需要在提单或其他海上运输合约中加入对共同海损分摊的留置权条文。

有关行使留置权,船东必须通知货方他所要求的金额与足够的资料支持这一金额的计算,货方自己可以作出计算。如果货方愿意支付一笔合理的钱或是提供合理金额的担保,但船东还是拒绝放货,这在法律上构成对货物的侵占(conversion of cargo):Anderson Tritton & Co. v. Ocean Steamship Co. (1884) 10 App Cas 107,Huth v. Lamport (1886) 16 QBD 735(有关侵占的问题在本书第十四章 11.3 段有详论)。货方也可以向卸港的法院求助,法院会在货方把船东要求的金额存放在法院作为交换法院命令船东必须马上放货。

船东不能对共同海损分摊索取的金额或是担保狮子大开口,并且必须有根有据,还可以节录 Scrutton 大法官在 Albemarle Supply Co. Ltd. v. Hind & Co. (1928) 1 K. B. 307 有以下权威说法:"A person claiming a lien must either claim it for a definite amount or give the owner particulars from which he himself can calculate the amount for which the lien is due. The owner must then, in the absence of express agreement, tender an amount covering the lien really existing. If he does not, unless excused, he has no answer to a claim of lien. He may be excused from tendering (1) if he has no knowledge or means of knowledge of the right amount; (2) if the person claiming the lien for a wrong cause or amount makes it clear that he will not release the goods unless his full claim is satisfied, and that claim is wrongful. The fact that the claim is made for more than the right amount does not matter unless the claimant give no particulars from which the right amount can be calculated, or makes it clear that he insists on the full amount of the right claimed."

另节录的是 Rose 教授 2005 年《General Average Law and Practice》第二版中 97 页也有提到,如下:"He [指船长] must not demand an unreasonable security, which, if given, will not be upheld, e. g., if it makes the shipowner's adjuster an arbitrator, favors the shipowner in an appeal from an arbitrator, requires cash deposits to be in the joint names of shipowner and arbitrator, or entitles the shipowner to draw on such deposits without the depositor's consent, possibly in full and so beyond the amount for which the depositor is ultimately found to be liable: Huth v. Lamport [1886] 16 QBD 735. See also Brandeis, Goldschmidt & Co. v. Economic Insurance Co. Ltd. [1922] 11 Lloyd's Rep. 42 (in which insurers refused an indemnity for a cash deposit paid to a representative of the shipowner without security); Salvage Association v. Suzuke & Co. Ltd. [1929] 35 Lloyd's Rep. 45."

1.4.5 在中途港放货的情况

会有不少情况是在中途的避难港就会放货,这就会导致在中途港已经要处理共同海损分摊的问题,因为已经发生了共同海损的牺牲或费用。例如:

1. 船舶的损坏再也没办法继续航程去目的地卸港,货方必须在中途港取回货物并自己安排续运到目的地港,这也是本章第 5 段介绍的续运费用。这一来,就代表航次的风险到此已经终止(adventure is terminated)。

2. 货方自己另有安排,如把该票货物在中途港处理掉,再也不必去卸货目的地。至于为什么这样做,可以是货方自己有各种商业理由,他本来中途就准备改变卸货港或者是中途港的市场价格恰好比原来卸货港的高。也可能货物是应季,续运去原来的卸货港已经为时已晚,而正好在卸货港可以及时转售等。这一来,正常情况下,船东没理由阻止货方在中途港取回他的货物而坚持将货物运往原来的卸货港。所以货方与船东会不难达成协议,让货物在中途港卸下。船东应该要求的就是让货方出示全套的正本提单以及肯定运费已经支付掉(一般在 CIF 与 CFR 买卖中都不是问题,因为通常都是运费预付提单)。对这些货物而言,再也不会共同去目的地港(no common adventure),也代表航次的风险到此已经终止(adventure is terminated)。在这里一提的是根据美国与加拿大的法律,货方有法定权利要求船东在中途避难港交出货物,这方面的问题会在不可分割协议与 Bigham 条文再进一步解释(本章之 2.4.6 段有介绍)。

3. 货物还是要按计划续运去目的地的卸货港,但由于在避难港口需要对船舶进行修理(通常是暂时修理)才能续运,而修理是船底或船舵等的水下部分,需要把部分甚至是全部的货物卸下才能进干坞或进行修理。但由于把这些货物卸下在避难港储存,仓储费用很贵,而且在船舶修理好之后再将该货物装上原船舶,也会产生费用,反而是干脆把这批货用其他船舶直接转运去目的地港更经济与直接了当。这一来原船东支付给其他船舶的额外运费也是共同海损费用之一,大家将来分摊,名为替代费用(substituted expenses),因为它替代(减少或避免支付)本来属于共同海损费用的仓储费用,这在《约克 - 安特卫普规则》Rule F 有规定。而另在《Rules of Practice (1997) of The Association of Average Adjusters》Rule F15 更明确说明是如下:"That if a ship be in a port of refuge at which it is practicable to repair her so as to enable her to carry on the whole cargo, but, in order to save expense, the cargo, or a portion of it, be transhipped by another vessel, or otherwise forwarded, then the cost of such transshipment (up to the amount of expense saved) shall be divided in proportion to the saving of expense thereby occasioned to the several parties to the adventure."

这种情况下还有其他的做法,如把损坏的船舶与船上货物一并从避难港拖带到卸港,把货物卸掉之后再进行修理(这是在《Rules of Practice (1997) of The Association of Average Adjusters》Rule F14)。也会是,避难港根本没有仓库可以储存有关的货物,如化学品或者食用油,需要租用另一艘化学品船作为浮动仓库。也可以干脆把货物在中途港以低价出售更划得来,注意这与上面所讲的货方因为自己的商业原因将货物在中途港出售不一样,这里就是船东在取得货方的同意下这样做,目的是为了减少共同海损费用。这是在《Rules of Practice (1997) of The Association of Average Adjusters》Rule F16。

这种可能有的不同选择(因为有了选择才能算是共同海损的费用),最终做法还是要合理,而哪一做法比较省钱显然是判断合理与否的重要方面。

这种船东私下安排的用其他船舶转运并非本章第 5 段所讲的需要由货方保险人承担的续运费用(forwarding charges),因为不涉及航次的受阻或是船东毁约,而只是涉及共同海损事故。毕竟会有情况是船东安排转运(transhipment)根本没办法提前通知货方或提单持有人。

反正在以上第一种与第三种的情况下会带来两种变数,一个变数是要在中途避难港卸下与运走的货物是船上全部货物,这就代表原来的船舶在修完之后也不需要去目的地的卸港。这一来,可以同时加上第三种的情况,本来在卸港才宣告与理算的共同海损就变成要在该中途港进行了。这等于介绍过要在原来卸货港履行的一系列手续,如要货方签订共同海损契约(General Average Bond)与提供共同海损担保(General Average Guarantee)或是押金(deposit)都要在卸货的中途港进行,而理算适用的法律也可能变成了中途港的法律,但现实中绝大部分的情况会根据《约克 - 安特卫普规则》,因为它是被海上货物运输合约所合并的。

第二个变数是这个船舶在修完后还是要去目的地的卸货港,因为船上还有其他货物需要运去原来的卸港。这一来,共同海损的宣告与理算还是要到达原来的卸港才可以开始进行,也只会是进行一次,不可能在中途港另理算一次。这就带来疑问,在中途港卸下转运或处理掉的货物应该怎样分摊共同海损。答案是《约克 - 安特卫普规则》的精神就是尽量把这些货物当作还是在船上,继续去目的地港。

1.4.6 不可分割协议(Non - separation Agreement)与 Bigham 条文

为了把共同海损分摊的权利与责任建立在原来的船舶继续航程去到目的地的卸港的基础上,有一种做法已经存在了上百年。这就是货物在中途避难港卸下来要转运到目的地或以其他办法处理,船长在允许这样做的情况下也会要货方签署一份文件,名为不可分割协议(Non - separation Agreement)。内容就是说货物即使是在中途转运,也把它当成仍在船上,要到原来的目的地港分摊共同海损。

这一份协议如下:

"Non - Separation Agreement

Vessel. . . .

Voyage. . .

Casualty. . .

Non - Separation Agreement (Standard Form)

It is agreed that in the event of the vessel's cargo or part thereof being forwarded to original destination by other vessel, vessels or conveyances, rights and liabilities in general average shall not be affected by such forwarding, it being the intention to place the parties concerned as nearly as possible in the same position as they would have been in the absence of such forwarding and with the adventure continuing by the original vessel for so long as justifiable under the law applicable or under the Contract of Affreightment. (如果船上的货物或者部分货物由其他船舶转运去目的港,大家共同海损的权利与责任不受转运/续运的影响,双方的意图是把大家放在原来的位置,也就是当作没有发生过转运/续运。而整个航次视为根据有关的海上运输合约由原来的船舶继续完成。)

The basis of contribution to general average of the property involved shall be the values on delivery at original destination unless sold or otherwise disposed of short of that destination; but where none of her cargo is carried forward in the vessel she shall contribute on the basis of her actual value on the date she completes discharge of her cargo.（大家分摊共同海损是根据财产到达目的地的卸港的实际价值为准，除非是半途被出售或处理掉。但如果最终还是没有在原来的船舶把货物运到目的地，分摊的价值就要根据原来船舶把货物卸下一天的实际价值为准。）（这句话需要稍作解释，举例说是巴西去中国但半途在南非出事并去了开普敦作为中途避难港，并在该港用其他船舶转运了部分的货物去了中国。该船舶在开普敦修完之后继续前往中国卸港，但半途出了另一次事故，导致船舶再去新加坡作为中途避难港。而在新加坡宣告放弃航次，因为船舶推定全损，租约受阻。换言之，该船舶从来也没有到中国的卸港。这一来，在计算共同海损的分摊时，变成是在新加坡进行而不是中国，而早前转运/续运的货物根据不可分割协议，要按比例分摊的价值也是以在新加坡卸下货物当天的货物实际价值为准。）

Bigham Clause (optional)

It is understood that the amount charged to cargo under this agreement shall not exceed what it would have cost the cargo owners if cargo was delivered to them at... (port of refuge) and forwarded by them to destination.（这一条名为 Bigham 条文，是一条选择性条文，表面的文字是说船东安排转运的费用是不能超过货方自己安排转运/续运的费用。稍候会对本条文进一步解释。）

Signature of Receiver of
Goods or other party giving
security for the General Average...

Full name and address...
Date ... "

上述不可分割协议与 Bigham 条文也已经加入《约克 - 安特卫普规则 2004》的 Rule G(2)特别针对如下："When a ship is at any port or place in circumstances which would give rise to an allowance in general average under the provisions of Rules X and XI, and the cargo or part thereof is forwarded to destination by other means, rights and liabilities in general average shall, subject to cargo interests being notified if practicable, remain as nearly as possible the same as they would have been in the absence of such forwarding, as if the adventure had continued in the original ship for so long as justifiable under the contract of affreightment and the applicable law. The proportion attaching to cargo of the allowances made in general average by reason of applying the third paragraph of this Rule shall not exceed the cost which would have been borne by the owners of cargo if the cargo had been forwarded at their expense."

1.4.6.1　不可分割协议对货方与船东的好处

不可分割协议有这么久的历史，因为它对货方与船东都有好处。对货方的好处就是船舶可以比较快地将货物转运到目的地,而不需要漫长地等待原船舶修妥后再去原来的目的地港。毕竟会有情况是中途港与目的港已经很近,而且转运安排非常容易。如货物是去广州,但船舶出了共同海损的事故而滞留在香港并要进行长达两个月的修理。显然对货方而言船东马上安排转运是一件好事。对船东而言,把货物卸下存在香港的仓库等船舶修理完毕再装运去广州也有好处。最明显的好处就是可以把事故导致的延误损失作为共同海损作出分摊,一部分是货方或它的保险人支付,另一部分是船舶保险人作出的支付。而这也是货物保险唯一赔付延误造成损失的情况,这在协会货物条文(A)(B)(C)中4.5条文的括号内的内容有说明。所以整条4.5条文就是说保险人不负责承保风险带来延误造成的损失、损坏或费用,但第2条文中共同海损造成延误是唯一的例外:"In no case shall this insurance cover loss damage or expense caused by delay, even though the delay be caused by a risk insured against [except expenses payable under Clause 2 above]."

这也是重复了1906年《英国海上保险法》Section 55(2)(b):"Unless the policy otherwise provides, the insurer on ship or goods is not liable for any loss proximately caused by delay, although the delay be caused by a peril insured against."

这里的原因是保险人既然支付共同海损,而共同海损在这种情况下包括了船舶延误的损失,所以保险人通过分摊共同海损费用间接赔付延误损失(至少是部分的延误损失),这也是保险人赔付延误损失的唯一情况。至于什么是船舶的延误损失,显然船员工资与船舶给养的费用就是最典型的,所谓船舶的固定费用(fixed costs)。在《约克-安特卫普规则2004》的Rule XI这样规定:"(a) Wages and maintenance of master, officers and crew reasonably incurred and fuel and stores consumed during the prolongation of the voyage occasioned by a ship entering a port or place of refuge or returning to her port or place of loading shall be allowed as general average when the expenses of entering such port or place are allowable in general average in accordance with Rule X(a). (b) For the purposes of this and the other Rules wages shall include all payments made to or for the benefit of the master, officers and crew, whether such payments be imposed by law upon the shipowners or be made under the terms of articles of employment."

这表示货方签署了不可分割协议,就不会因为在中途避难港把货物卸下后,甚至不再需要去目的地卸港,而共同海损也就到此为止。没有不可分割协议,就表示船舶继续在修理的延误损失,船东就要自己承担了。

有了上述的解释就可以大部分明白Clarke大法官在先例The "Abt Rasha" (2000) 2 Lloyd's Rep. 575所讲如下:

"As the judge observed at page 10, when a vessel is forced to call at a port of refuge, there are obvious attractions in entering into a non-separation agreement from the point of view of both shipowners and cargo-owners. I consider first the benefits of such an agreement without a Bigham clause. The benefit to cargo - owners is that they can promptly recover their cargo in circumstances where substantial delay might otherwise ensue while the shipowners, anxious to earn their freight, store the cargo, carry out repairs and then resume the voyage. In this case it would have involved considerable delay and large storage costs. The freight, which was payable at destination, was of the order USMYM1,800,000.

From the shipowners´point of view, the advantage of entering into a non - separation agreement is that they are able to treat the general average situation as continuing when otherwise it would terminate with the result that they can recover contribution pro rata to value for post - separation expenses which would otherwise fall entirely on them during both the period leading up to repairs and the repair period itself. There is the added attraction of converting some ordinary running expenses, which would be excluded by clause 16 of the Institute Time Clauses, into general average expenditure, which in turn would render them recoverable in part from hull underwriters. As the judge observed (and as appears above), with the benefit of hindsight these attractions were enhanced in the present case given that the total sums involved were in the region of USMYM5 million and the value of the cargo was nearly three times that of the vessel."

1.4.6.2 Bigham 条文

接下来要解释合并在不可分割协议中的 Bigham 条文到底是怎么回事。Bigham 条文 20 世纪 70 年代在美国开始使用,到后来在英国也普遍使用。在 1994 与 2004 年《约克 - 安特卫普规则》的 Rule G(2)也被合并进去。

这里首先要解释的是美国与英国法律的不同之处,就是在美国如果船舶去了中途避难港,货方有权利在同意支付运费下向船东要求交出货物让他处理,包括自己安排续运到目的地港:The "Domingo De Larrinaga" (1928) A. M. C 64。但英国就不这么简单,如上述所讲的,往往要通过船东与货方达成协议才可以这样做。原因很简单,合约既然没有受阻,在避难港修妥之后可以继续航程,要终断合约就需要双方的同意。而更大的考虑就是如果运费是到付,而中途避难港与卸港已经是很近,就没有理由不让船东完成航次赚取运费。英国的法律是货物必须要抵达目的地的卸港,把货物交出给收货人才可以赚取运费:Dakin v. Oxley (1864) 15 C. B. (N. S.) 646。

如在上述提到的先例 The "Abt Rasha" (2000) 2 Lloyd's Rep. 575,该船舶是一艘超级油轮,而油轮是运费到付的情况,所以该船舶待修理完毕后到目的地港可以赚取 180 万美元的运费。即使是船东自己安排另外的船转运去目的地,由于托运人就是原船东,所以可以通过转运的船舶行使留置权把运费拿到手。

这一来,对美国的货方而言,如果海上运输合约是根据英国法的地位,就算被迫让船东安排转运去目的地并把费用作为共同海损,他也不会希望出现一种情况,就是船东转运的费用大大超出他自己安排转运要花的费用,这就带来了 Bigham 条文。该条文的历史在 The "Abt Rasha"有解释:

"The problem in the present case has arisen from the fact that the non - separation agreements included paragraph 3, namely the Bigham clause. The Bigham clause has been introduced into non - separation agreements only comparatively recently. We were told that its name derives from Mr Bigham of Bigham, Englar and Jones, who were the New York lawyers representing the successful consignees in the *Domingo De Larrinaga* [1928] AMC 64. In that case it was held by the United States Federal Court for the Southern District of New York that consignees of damaged cargo, which had been discharged at a port of refuge to permit inspections of the hull, were entitled, on paying full freight, to refuse to have their goods reloaded so that the vessel could be towed to destination and to demand their goods at the port of refuge, even where the shipowners had arranged for towage of ship and cargo to destination.

I am not sure when the Bigham clause was first devised, but the evidence shows that the practice of including it in non - separation agreements was first introduced at the instance of United States cargo underwriters during the 1970s. Again, as the judge put it, the rationale was that, since as a matter of United States law (as demonstrated in the Domingo De Larrinaga) a cargo - owner could insist on taking possession of his cargo at a port of refuge, he should not be in any worse position than if he had done so. The practice was not immediately introduced in England, but the judge said at page 10 that it was probably introduced in the 1980s. He added that it has now become a commonplace, although not invariable, practice to include the Bigham clause in non - separation agreements. The expert evidence shows, however, that it is rare for the cap to be invoked. Indeed one of the experts said that he had never known it happened."

据悉,Bigham 条文带来的问题很少听到过,但其中在先例 The "Abt Rasha"就是有关这一问题的。案情涉及在船东委任的海损理算师所计算的结果下,船舶由于机器故障到了两个南非的避难港口 Durban 与 Port Elizabeth,以及最后把货物转运去鹿特丹的共同海损费用,货方(涉及 30 多万吨的原油)需要分摊 3,61,776.22 美元。但如果货方一早就在避难港口自己安排把这批原油转运,他所要花的费用只是 2,814,349.94美元。所以根据 Bigham 条文,船东在海损理算的时候就会有 787,426.28美元没办法获得分摊。该先例涉及船东向船壳保险人要求赔付这笔钱,因为后者要在保险合约下承担共同海损的费用。

1.4.7 共同海损的减少

共同海损的减少已经有一段时间,不少航运的人士应该都感觉得到。笔者觉得其中造成这一现象的最大原因是以下两个方面。

1.4.7.1 货方拒绝分摊共同海损与质疑船东不试航

1.4.7.1.1 犯错的一方不能提出要求分摊共同海损

很早就已经有说法是犯错的一方所导致的危险情况并产生共同海损,它所作出的牺牲或所花的费用不能要求其他无辜的利益方分摊。这可节录 Watson 勋爵在先例：Strange, Steel & Co. v. A Scott & Co. (1889) 14 App Cas 601 中所讲："He cannot be permitted to claim either recompense for services rendered, or indemnity for losses sustained by him, in the endeavor to rescue property which was imperiled by his own tortuous act, and which it was his duty to save."

这一说法可以适用在货方，如货物的危险性被隐藏，货物被装上了船舶结果在航次中导致了整条船的安全受到威胁而产生共同海损，如去了避难港口，如果在行动中有这些危险货物被牺牲，他的货方不能要求其他的利益方分摊这部分的共同海损：Greenshields, Cowie & Co. v. Stephens & Sons (1908) AC 431（涉及了货物是煤炭，因为自燃发生火灾并部分货物被抛到大海里）。但这种情况很罕见，绝大部分还是涉及了船舶的犯错，以致船东不能向船上货物的货方要求分摊共同海损。例如，在先例 Schloss v. Heriot (1863) 14 CB(NS) 59，船舶不适航，而不适航导致了共同海损，船东被否定要求货方作出分摊。另在 Strange, Steel & Co. v. A Scott & Co. (1889) 14 App Cas 601 与 The "Mary Thomas" (1894) P 108，判是航行疏忽导致的共同海损也是不能要求分摊。在先例 Reardon Smith Line Ltd. v. Black Sea & Baltic General Insurance Co. Ltd. (1938) 60 Lloyd's Rep. 353，如果船舶曾经有不合理绕航，也不能要求分摊共同海损，Wright 勋爵在先例 Hain SS Co. Ltd. v. Tate & Lyle Ltd. (1936) 41 Com Cas 350 中这样说："the casualty and consequent general average loss must be deemed to have been caused by the deviation since it is impossible to say that the casualty would have occurred if there had been no deviation."这方面也可看加拿大的先例 The "Orient Trader" (1973) 2 Lloyd's Rep. 174 (Can SC)。

而这个法律地位是根据两个理论形成的，在 Schloss v. Heriot (1863) 14 CB(NS) 59 先例中有提到：(1)避免绕圈的诉讼(avoid circuity of action)，最后还是原地踏步，造成诉讼费用与时间的浪费；(2)无辜的利益方对犯错的一方要求分摊共同海损可以有一个衡平法的抗辩(equitable defense)。这两个理论，前者看来是在程序方面，后者则主要是在实体方面。例如，如果货方错过了 1924 年《海牙规则》或其他海上运输合约内的时效条文没有向船东及时提出不适航或者不合理绕航的索赔，他还能够以衡平法的抗辩拒绝船东提出的共同海损分摊，因为这有 6 年的时效：Goulandris Bros Ltd. v. B Goldman & Sons Ltd. (1958) 1 QB 74。

这导致了最后在《约克－安特卫普规则》中有了折中的办法。这就是在 1974、1994 与 2004 年版本中的 Rule D，如下："Rights to contribution in general average shall not be affected, though the event which gave rise to the sacrifice or expenditure may have been due to the fault of one of the parties to the adventure; but this shall not prejudice any remedies or defences which may be open against or to that party in respect of that fault."

这一条文的意图应该明确，就是轻微改变英国普通法的地位，即共同海损的宣告、处理与理算还是正常进行，而所有利益方要作出分摊不受影响。但这不影响作出分摊的一方向他认为有过错引起共同海损的另一方提出诉讼与索赔。

1.4.7.1.2 犯错的一方在合约或法律免责是否有不同后果

另一个重要问题是在海上运输合约,特别是提单经常会对一些船东犯的错误或者疏忽免责。特别在1924年《海牙规则》后,几乎所有提单的免责就局限在航行过失导致的货方损失。至于在租约内,由于有订约自由,到底哪些免责还要看个别租约的条文。著名的《金康租约》条文倾向偏袒船东,所以在它的第2条文中把适航的责任也大幅度减轻,可以在不适航情况下免责。这一来,疑问就是免了责的错是否就能被视为"没有错"。这里的看法英国与美国的法律又有很大差异:在英国的先例 The "Carron Park"(1890) 15 PD 203,船东的雇员因为疏忽而没有关上舱盖,导致雨水渗漏,损坏了货方的货物。但由于租约有一条对船东十分广泛的免责条文:"any neglect or default whatsoever of the ... servants of the shipowners ... to be excepted",判是免责的错等于没有错。在这个先例之后,相关与一致判法的案例还有好几个,如 Milburn & Co. v. Jamaican Fruit Importing and Trading Company of London (1900) 2 Q. B. 540, Louis Dreyfus & Co., Ltd. v. Tempus Shipping Company, Ltd. (1931) AC 726 与 The "Makedonia" (1962) 1 Lloyd's Rep. 317。其中在贵族院的先例 Louis Dreyfus & Co., Ltd. v. Tempus Shipping Company, Ltd 中,Atkin 勋爵这样说:"I myself find it difficult to conceive of a fault in this relation which, though not actionable, is yet in some manner so blameworthy as to deprive the party of his right to contribution... The object of the exception is to protect the person committing the act in question from liability for any consequences of it; and this is effectively secured whether it is said that there shall be no duty to avoid doing the act or no obligation to pay any compensation if it is done."

所以根据英国法船东如果是犯错,可以与船东的共同海损权利对冲的只能是货方根据有关的海上运输合约条文或立法可以向船东起诉的索赔(actionable fault)。这也有道理,因为如果在免责的情况下,船东作出共同海损的费用在将来没有办法分摊,就会有危险船东不愿意作出合理的花费。

1.4.7.1.3 美国不同的法律地位与 New Jason Clause

但根据美国的法律,有完全不同的看法。美国法律认为免责条文只是用来作盾牌而不能用来作矛或者剑,而船东向货方要求分摊共同海损是矛或剑的做法。最早的案例就是美国最高院的 The "Irrawaddy" (1898) 171 US 187,接下来的先例是 The "Jason"(1910) 225 US 32 与 The "Strathdon"(1899) 94 Fed Rep. 206。在 The "Jason"中,美国最高院说船东可以合法加上一条条文,说明在对过错或疏忽免责的情况下,货方还是要分摊共同海损。换言之,不能只靠一条免责条文,因为它只起到盾牌的作用。这就导致了另一条标准条文,名为 New Jason Clause,印在几乎所有的海上运输合约中,不论是租约或提单。除非涉及根本不会与美国发生任何关系的航次,共同海损不会在美国理算,如在中国沿海或者长江上的运输。该 New Jason Clause 的全文可节录《金康租约》的第12条,如下:"In General Average to be adjusted in accordance with law and practice of the US, the following clause shall apply : 'In the event of accident, danger, damage or disaster before or after the commencement of the voyage, resulting from any cause whatsoever, whether due to negligence or not, for which, or for the consequence of which, the Owners are not responsible, by statute, contract or otherwise, the cargo shippers, consignees or the owners of the cargo shall contribute with the Owners in General Average to the payment of any sacrifices, losses or expenses of a General Average nature that may be made or incurred and shall pay salvage and special charges incurred in respect of the cargo... "

1.4.7.1.4 船舶不适航导致不能成功要求货方分摊共同海损的先例

在现实中,由于很多共同海损事故都与船东的过错/疏忽有关,特别是在船东有义务恪尽职责(due diligence)令船舶适航:The "Muncaster Castle" (1961) 1 Lloyd's Rep. 57。所以涉及航行疏忽不论是搁浅或者是碰撞,或是船舶机器在航行半途因为潜在缺陷而出现故障(这是发生救助与去避难港口的常见原因)等表面看起来船东可以免责的事项,货方经常会向船东提出船舶不适航的争辩/抗辩(如船舶欠缺最新的海图,船员训练与素质有缺陷,船舶机器的缺陷应该可以在开航前发觉而并非真正的属于潜在缺陷等),因为在1924年《海牙规则》下,船东恪尽职责令船舶适航是其可以享受免责的先决条件。

这种做法除了带来昂贵的诉讼费用外,还会导致船东在聘请了海损理算师之后的理算与分摊最终不能成功向货方要回来。由于船东互保协会是承保船东在违反适航义务导致的货损,同样的道理下,如果是由于船舶不适航导致共同海损应该由货方分摊的部分金额取不回来,也应该是互保协会应该赔付给船东的。至于船舶应该分摊的共同海损,就由船舶保险人赔付。

这种情况很多,令人感觉到船东何必劳民伤财地进行昂贵的共同海损理算,最后还是一场空。

这种被报道的案例很多,可列举一些近期的先例,如下:

1. The "Texas" (1970) 1 Lloyd's Rep. 175 (船舶在开航时货舱有烟由于船长的疏忽/过错没有发现,这等于是不适航而最终导致了火灾,由此产生的共同海损分摊不可以向货方取回)。

2. The "Aga" (1968) 1 Lloyd's Rep. 431 (船舶在开航的时候没有足够的稳定性,船舶不适航,以致在中途船舶发生倾斜,而为了避免翻船,船长令船舶冲滩,由此造成的共同海损货方可以不分摊)。

3. The "Lendoudis Evangelos II"(2001) 2 Lloyd's Rep. 304 (本先例中被判船东并没有违反恪尽职责让船舶适航的义务,所以可以要求货方分摊产生的共同海损。)。

4. The "Fjord Wind" (1999) 1 Lloyd's Rep. 307(船舶在刚刚离开南美装港就发现主机有故障,要折回装港,并发现主机的曲柄轴承[crankpin bearing]断裂并需要长达3个月的修理,船东宣告去意大利的航次受阻而拒绝续运,结果货方要自己安排续运把船上的27,000多吨大豆用另一艘名为Dobrota的船舶转运去目的地港。事后货方向原船东提出索赔,指称船舶开航的时候不适航,而原船舶反索赔共同海损分摊,因为在受阻前就已经产生了少量的共同海损费用。英国法院与上诉庭判船舶开航的时候不适航,有关共同海损的反索赔,Moore - Bick 大法官说:"Following the casualty the owners declared general average and it was common ground that certain costs incurred by the owners in connection with running the vessel were properly to be allowed as general average expenditure. It was also common ground, however, that if the casualty was caused by a breach of contract on the part of the owners, their claim to recover a contribution from cargo interests could not be sustained. In view of the conclusion I have reached on that question it follows, therefore, that the club's claim as assignee [船东互保协会作为受让人] of the owners' right to general average contribution must fail.")。

5. The "Isla Fernandina" (2000) 2 Lloyd's Rep. 15 (船舶从厄瓜多尔装香蕉去利比亚与俄罗斯,中途发生了很多事故,包括船舶搁浅与发电机坏掉。这导致了几方面的争议,其中有关搁浅,Langley 大法官认为有无可争议的证据证明船上的海图与航行设备不符合要求)。

6. The "Kamsar Voyager" (2002) 2 Lloyd's Rep. 57 (船舶在美国路易斯安那装30,000吨大豆去韩国仁川,途中主机冒烟。在主机打开后发现活塞有严重的破裂,之后换上了备用的活塞,但这带来了更严重的损坏,因为备用的活塞不适合该主机。船东宣告共同海损,但货方拒绝分摊,声称船舶没有适用的备件,这构成开航时的不适航。Dean 大法官同意并判船东败诉,说:"The owners have failed to prove that MAN exercised due diligence in and about the supply of the incompatible spare piston. [注意MAN是著名的主机生产商并供应船东零件,但船东没有办法证明MAN已经恪尽职责,在此可以见到适航的责任下放给第三者,即使第三者名气很大也必须举证他没有疏忽] The owners have not satisfied the burden on them under art. III, r. 1 of the Hague Rules of proving the exercise of due diligence to make 'Kamsar Voyage' seaworthy and were responsible for her unseaworthiness at the commencement of the voyage in respect of both the cracked piston in No. 1 unit and the incompatible spare piston on board which was supplied by MAN. It follows that the G. A. expenditure was caused by their actionable fault and they are unable to recover the cargoes' proportion from the defendant insurers under the average guarantees.")。

7. The "Torepo" (2002) 2 Lloyd's Rep. 535(船舶在阿根廷装一船的汽油去厄瓜多尔,船舶可以通过巴拿马运河,但最后决定通过南美洲最南部的合恩角。由于装港没有海图供应,所以安排在半途才通过引水员提供给船舶,但提供的海图不准确。之后船舶搁浅并需要救助,船东事后宣告共同海损。货方事后向船东提出索赔,损失是支付给救助人的救助奖金并要求退还提供了的共同海损担保[理算应该是还没有完成]。Steel 大法官不认为是船舶不适航导致了搁浅,认为海图的偏差并非导致搁浅的原因,真正/主要的原因是航行疏忽,船东可以免责。Steel 大法官说:“The discrepancy between the charts is not of itself the cause of the casualty. If relevant at all [and I doubt whether the discrepancy was really new to pilots who were transiting the channels on numerous occasions], it would not have reasonably called for more than a moment's reflection, once the discrepancy was unearthed, to realize that it had no significance as regards the position of the vessel which was being monitored by parallel indexes, ranges off the coast and times abeam lights and promontories. If the pilot's attention truly was deflected more than momentarily, it was in any event negligent navigation on his part.”)。

8. Sunlight v. Ever Lucky Shipping Company Ltd. (2004) 2 Lloyd's Rep. 174(这是一个新加坡上诉庭的先例,船舶是从西非装一批木材[部分装在甲板]去印度。在航行半途,船舶主机的曲柄箱发生爆炸而失去动力,结果船舶被拖带去南非开普敦。但由于开普敦没办法修理,结果连船带货再被拖带去印度卸港,这一连串的事故导致了共同海损,但货方拒绝分摊,声称船舶是不适航。而船东的抗辩说主机的缺陷属于潜在缺陷。上诉庭同意船舶在开航前是不适航,所以权去要求共同海损的分摊)。

总结而言,在 1924 年《海牙规则》下,船东想向货方要求共同海损分摊也不容易成功,如果真的将来有一天《鹿特丹规则》全面被采用,船东的航行/管船的过错/疏忽的免责被废除,共同海损理算恐怕也会被摆进博物馆了。

最后一提的是由于共同海损不是来自合约法,而是来自一个公平原则,正如 Deering v. Earl of Winchelsea (1787) 2 Bos & Pul 270 (Ex), 274 中,Eyre 大法官所说:“In the case of average there is no contract express or implied, nor any privity in any ordinary sense. This shows that contribution is founded on equality, and established by the law of all nations.”所以,如果船东犯错,他没有权利向其他的货方分摊共同海损,但不代表无辜的货方如果由他的货物作出共同海损的牺牲,他不可以向其他的货方要求分摊。他们之间不存在合约关系,也就是说共同海损不是来自合约法。这一点可以从先例 Strange, Steel & Co. v. A Scott & Co. (1889) 14 App Cas 601 看到。

1.4.7.2 船东自己承担共同海损的费用与 G. A. Absorption Clause 的兴起

首先要说明的是,如果有其中一些货物作出了共同海损的牺牲,船东有责任宣布共同海损让所有利益方作出分摊。否则,船东会要对作出牺牲的货方负责任:Strang v. Scott (1889) 14 App. Cas. 601;Nobel's Explosives v. Rea (1897) 2 Com. Cas. 293。但这种情况今天的共同海损比较少见,较多发生的还是涉及了共同海损费用,如避难港口的费用与拖轮费用。这些费用显然是船东先垫付,所以如果船东选择不提出/宣告共同海损,完全可以这样做。这种情况会出现在船东没有经验与无知。笔者以前就见过共同海损发生后,船东没有这样做。但更多的情况是在船东完全知道的情况下选择不宣告共同海损与作出分摊,尤其是在班轮运输。第一个原因是对班轮与客户的关系有影响,第二个更大的原因就是在经济上不划算。试想一艘集装箱船上经常会有2000/3000个或更多的货主,如果每一个货方都要签一份GA Bond,交押金履行一整套手续,可以说劳民伤财,在共同海损费用不高的情况下肯定得不偿失。之后还需要漫长与昂贵的理算,而海事理算师的收费不见得比海事律师收得便宜,这些收费都被当作共同海损费用一并分摊。所以,举一个简单的例子,共同海损费用是100万港币,但整个理算费用是200万港币,而船舶价值要分摊一半,表示船东最后的分摊是150万港币。显然,船东干脆自己承担100万共同海损费用更加省事。

但要船东自己掏腰包也不会令船东服气,因为不提出与宣告共同海损,除了要承担货方所需要的分摊外,连船舶的分摊部分也是自己承担,但这明明是船舶保险人的责任。所以,船东在船舶保险合约中加上了一条条文,与保险人同意在某一个金额下的共同海损(不少集装箱船舶的金额定在100万美元),船东不需要向货方提出与宣告而由保险人赔付。其中世界上最大的船东组织BIMCO在2002年拟定了一条让船东加在船舶保险合约中的条文,名为:"General Average Absorption Clause",内容如下:

"IMPORTANT NOTICE: This Clause is specifically designed for incorporation into marine insurance policies and should not, under any circumstances, be incorporated into charter parties.(注意本条文只是加在船舶保险合约,而不是加在租约中,因为船东对货方而言应该还是保留选择权是否要宣告共同海损,如装的货物只涉及一个货方而且整船的货物价值高昂,就没有理由不宣告共同海损了。)

1. If the Assured does not claim general average, salvage or special charges from cargo, freight, bunkers, containers or any property not owned by the Assured on board the vessel (hereinafter called "Property Interests"), the Insurers shall pay in full the general average, salvage and special charges up to... % of the insured value of the vessel or USMYM... whichever is the higher. The % of the insured value of the vessel or the USMYM sum agreed under this clause shall not be less than USMYM150,000.(金额是可以根据谈判结果作出改变)

1.1 The Insurers shall also pay the reasonable fees and expenses of the average adjuster for calculating claims under this clause in addition to any payment made under 1. above.

1.2 If the Assured claims under this clause he shall not make any claim for general average, salvage or special charges against the Property Interests.

1.3 Claims under this clause shall be adjusted in accordance with the York - Antwerp Rules 1994, excluding the first paragraph of Rule XX and Rule XXI, relating to commission and interest.

1.4 Claims under this clause shall be payable without application of the deductible.

1.5 Without prejudice to any defences they may have under the terms of the policy the Insurers waive any defences to payment under this clause which would have been available to the Property Interests.

1.6 In respect of payment made under this clause the Insurers waive any rights of subrogation they may have against the Property Interests. This waiver shall not apply where the incident giving rise to such payment is attributable to fault on the part of Property Interests.

1.7 For claims under this clause the vessel shall be deemed to be insured for its full contributory value. ”

这估计导致了在2003年国际船壳保险条文中也加入了一条标准条文——第40条，其中有关的主要部分是：

“40 GENERAL AVERAGE ABSORPTION

40.1 If the Underwriters have expressly agreed in writing and subject to the provisions of Clause 8, the following shall apply in the event of an accident or occurrence giving rise to a general average act under the York – Antwerp Rules 1994 or under the provisions of the general average clause in the contract of affreightment.

40.2 The Assured shall have the option of claiming the total general average, salvage and special charges up to the amount expressly agreed by the Underwriters, without claiming general average, salvage or special charges from cargo, freight, bunkers, containers or any property not owned by the Assured on board the vessel (hereinafter the “Property Interests”)... ”

有兴趣在这方面了解更多的读者可以参阅笔者与汪鹏南教授合著的《英国海上保险条款详论》一书第374页。

1.4.8　共同海损与货物保险之一：对协会货物条文(B)与(C)扩大承保责任

对共同海损的承保，协会货物条文(A)(B)(C)的第2条都说明是承保共同海损与海难救助的费用，只除了由于第4~7条中的除外风险导致的共同海损。众所周知，这些被排除的列明风险包括有受保人的恶意行为、货物包装不足、货物内在缺陷、货方知情的船舶不适航不适货、战争风险、罢工风险等。对共同海损的承保面这么广泛，对协会货物条文(A)承保的是一切险并不奇怪，但对(B)与(C)条文看来太宽松。换言之，即使不是(B)与(C)列明的承保风险所引起的共同海损，只要不是除外风险所引起，保险人都负责赔付。换言之，如果是货物实质的损失与损坏，受保人的货方都必须证明是列明的承保风险造成的才有的赔付，但发生共同海损的分摊就没必要证明了。这里的原因是因为在卸货港时，船东宣布共同海损并需要提供担保才放货，货方与他的保险人在非常局限资料的情况下，很难知道是什么原因造成共同海损，所以现实一点就索性去承保共同海损的分摊。

1.4.9　共同海损与货物保险之二：投保金额比货物需要分摊的价值低的情况

这一问题的了解先要介绍1906年《英国海上保险法》Section 66(4)：“Subject to any express provision in the policy, where the assured has incurred a general average expenditure, he may recover from the insurer in respect of the proportion of the loss which falls upon him; and, in the case of a general average sacrifice, he may recover from the insurer in respect of the whole loss without having enforced his right of contribution from the other parties liable to contribute. ”

另在 Section 73 对这一方面说的更加明确,而且也包括了救助费用,说:“(1) Subject to any express provision in the policy, where the assured has paid, or is liable for, any general average contribution, the measure of indemnity is the full amount of such contribution, if the subject – matter liable to contribution is insured for its full contributory value; but, if such subject – mater be not insured for its full contributory value, or if only part of it be insured, the indemnity payable by the insurer must be reduced in proportion to the under insurance, and where there has been a particular average loss which constitutes a deduction from the contributory value, and for which the insurer is liable, that amount must be deducted from the insured value in order to ascertain what the insurer is liable to contribute. (2) Where the insurer is liable for salvage charges the extent of his liability must be determined on the like principle. ”

这表示英国默示法律地位就是针对共同海损的分摊与救助费用/报酬,保险人负责的只是他承保保险价值的部分。如果货方投保的保险价值比实际货物价格偏低而造成不足额保险(under – insurance),这差额要由货方自己支付。这是因为共同海损的分摊是根据船舶与货物到达目的地港的实际价值,不理会保险合约内的保险价值,毕竟货方可以不投保或投保一个比较保守的金额。在《约克 – 安特卫普规则 2004》,Rule XVII 说明分摊共同海损的货价以卸货时的实际价值为准。这表示两个不同的价值有可能会有偏差,如果保险价值偏高,就不会有不足额保险的问题,保险人要全数赔付共同海损的分摊。但如果保险价值不足额,保险人就根据上述所讲的 1906 年立法地位作出赔付了。举例说,如果保险价值只是分摊共同海损的卸货时实际价值的一半,保险人负责赔付的共同海损分摊也只是赔付一半了。同样道理也适用在救助费用/报酬,这在 Section 73(2)。

这里顺便对 Section 73(1)中最后一句解释一下,用一个假设的例子很容易说明。如果一艘船舶(或一批货物)到达卸港的实际价值是 200 万美元,保险价值只是 100 万美元,这明显是不足额保险。把这个例子稍微作出改变,就是在同一个航次中遇到承保风险造成的单独海损(particular average),反正就是该船舶本身被损坏造成的部分损失,估计需要修理费用高达 120 万美元。这一条破破烂烂的船舶到了卸港,显然实际价值不会是 200 万美元,而应该接近 80 万美元。这一来,以 80 万美元比较保险价值的 100 万美元,表面上看没有不足额保险。但事实上是存在的,只是因为产生了保险人要承保的单独海损与赔付 120 万美元而把这个事实掩盖了。所以要把该 120 万美元修理费加在船舶在卸港的实际价值才看有否不足额保险。

由于协会货物条文(A)(B)(C)没有针对,这就会有危险是货物价值在市场飙升时,共同海损分摊或救助报酬在不足额保险的情况下会造成赔付不足。所以,现在很多时候的货物保险会多加一条附加条文超越这个默示法律地位:"For the purposes of claims for General Average Contributions and Salvage Charges recoverable hereunder the subject – matter insured shall be deemed to be insured for its full contributory value, General Average deposits shall be payable on production of General Average deposit receipts."这就可以避免有这一危险了。

最后一提的是在协会货物条文(A)(B)(C)第16条施救费用,是不会带来不足额保险时按比例赔付的情况。在1906年《英国海上保险法》的Section 78(1)也没有类似共同海损分摊的规定要求施救费用在不足额保险的情况下按保险价值的比例赔付。这也有道理,毕竟保险人额外支付施救费用就是为了鼓励受保人采取一切在他能力范围内的行动与花费,即使施救不成功也可以获得赔付。这一来,如果按比例导致赔付不足,就失去了鼓励的意义。

2. 海上救助(maritime salvage)

2.1　定义

海上救助是海上独有的做法与理念,在岸上没有同样的说法。这是因为以前在海上如果发生了海难或需要帮助,在没有通讯能力与海上没有救援能力的远古年代,只能作出有限的鼓励做法,就是希望路过的船舶伸出援手进行救助,而救助成功就可以获得丰厚的奖金,而且在获救财产(船舶与货物)的价值不足够支付所有债权人,救助奖金是排在非常优先的海事优先权。这种海上救助没有合约关系,是所谓的纯救助(pure salvage)。在许多权威的定义中,可以随意举The"Neptune"(1824)1 Hag. Adm 227先例,Stowell勋爵说:"one who, without any particular relation to the ship in distress, prefers useful service and gives it as a volunteer adventurer without any pre – existing convenant that connected him with the duty of employing himself for the preservation of that ship."

在The"Hestia"(1895)P. 193, Bruce大法官说:"But salvage claims do not rest upon contract. Where property has been salved from sea perils, and the claimants have effected the salvage, or have contributed to the salvage, the law confers upon them the right to be paid salvage reward out of the proceeds of the property which they have been saved or helped to save. No doubt the parties may by contract determine the amount to be paid; but the right to salvage is in no way dependent upon contract, and may exist, and frequently does exist, in the absence of any express contract, or of any circumstances to raise an implied contract."

另在Kennedy & Rose所著的《Law of Salvage》第六版一书中16段说:"A salvage service is a service which confers a benefit by saving or helping to save a recognised subject of salvage when in danger from which it cannot be extricated unaided, if and so far as the rendering of such service is voluntarily in the sense of being attributable neither to a pre-existing obligation nor solely for the interests of the salvor,... the cause of action for which accrues and is complete at the date of the termination of the services."

从这一个定义可见,海难救助需要以下"要件"(ingredients):(1)只针对海上财产(maritime property);(2)该海上财产面临危险(danger);(3)第三者是自愿施救(voluntary),与合约无关;(4)海上财产全部或部分成功救回(success),否则也没有条件给救助人任何奖金。

2.2 纯救助与合约救助

通讯发达且海上救援能力大大加强(这里有许多属于专业救助人,他们有完整的设备与人员,可以随时待命对海上的船舶进行救援,如中国的救捞局),所以纯救助已经很少见到。一般非专业的救援也不值得鼓励,因为很多时候只会帮倒忙。现在的救助往往都变为合约救助,因为专业救助人也不愿意劳师动众带着全套的人员与救援设备赶到遇难船舶时,遇难船舶的船长说"我不需要你自愿施救"而白跑一趟。但如果提前就有了救助合约,船东/船长就不能够毁约。所以今天的不同公司专业救助人就算要抢生意,也不是大家抢了把救助船舶与设备赶去现场,希望比对手早到一步,而是抢先向船东争这一份救助合约。而这一份救助合约最著名的标准合约就是 Lloyd's Open Form 或简称"LOF"。LOF 与纯救助的唯一相同之处就是救助不成功就没有任何报酬,毕竟也没有海上财产被救回可以支付给专业的海上救助人。但如果救助成功(即使只是部分成功),就有了条件作出支付,而这个报酬是根据劳合社对救助有经验的仲裁员(他们都是一些海事法的御用大律师)根据实际救助的各种细节作出他们认为是合理的报酬。这就是著名的"无结果无报酬"(No Cure No Pay)原则。LOF 的最大优点就是报酬的计算是由劳合社的仲裁员作出,被视为有公信力,在绝大部分的情况下被世界上的船舶与货物保险人所接受,毕竟对船东与船长而言,最安全与事后不会受到批评的做法也就是签订 LOF 的救助合约。

2.3 救助与环境保护带来的问题

只在这里顺便一提 20 世纪 60 年代开始,国际上对环境污染的关注开始影响救助。有好几艘著名的大油轮如 Atlantic Empress、Christos Bitos、Amoco Cadiz 等由于政府对油污的担心,拒绝为这些受到损坏的油轮提供救助工作场所,包括拒绝进港避难。例如,在比较近期的 Castor 轮,船上装了 3 万吨汽油与 100 吨燃油,出事后被 6 个国家拒绝进港作为避难港,救助人要求在西班牙附近冲滩以进行救助工作,如把船上的货物轻载,但也被拒绝。这种困境经常导致救助人别无选择,只能把这些油轮连船带货拖到深海然后凿沉,反正在大西洋或者太平洋造成小小油污也不会有人感觉得到,至少不会让单个的国家成为受害者。这导致了遇难的油轮被笑称为"国际麻风病人",到处被人赶,而且就长远而言,污染大西洋与太平洋也不是好事。所以在

1989 年的《国际救助公约》(International Salvage Convention),引进了一个全新的理念,即从好几百年的财产救助(property salvage)变成责任救助(liability salvage),即减少油污责任也可以得到救助报酬。这在公约的两个方面有显示:一是第 13 条之 1(b)说明救助人的技术与努力避免或减少对环境的破坏(the skill and efforts of the salvors in preventing or minimizing damage to the environment)也是作为核算救助报酬的一个考虑。换言之,救助成功会带来一个比以前只考虑财产救济得出来的报酬会更高的结果,也就是所谓的"enhanced reward"。二是第 14 条规定了如果因为环境会受到污染而救助被迫放弃,因此赚不到救助报酬,救助人有权向船东取得一个特别补偿(special compensation)。这一特别补偿的计算办法基本上是根据救助人所作出的花费,然后给一个百分比的增加,如 30% ~100% 不等。而被报道说有记录的最高增加是 65%,这是在 The "Nagasaki Spirit" (1995) 2 Lloyd's Rep. 44 的案例。

显然,在救助不成功的情况之下,这一特别补偿也只有船东负责支付,这是船东互保协会负责赔付的。货方由于全损而什么都没有,根本找不到到底谁是提单持有人。只有在第 13 条"enhanced reward",货方会有可能间接负责保护环境的责任救助。反正在《国际救助公约》Article 13(2)中这样说:"Payment of a reward fixed according to paragraph 1 shall be made by all of the vessel and other property interests in proportion to their respective salved values. However, a State Party may in its national law provide that the payment of a reward has to be made by one of these interests, subject to a right of recourse of this interest against the other interests for their respective shares. Nothing in this article shall prevent any right of defence."

这一方面在《约克 - 安特卫普规则 2004》也有了针对,就是在 Rule VI(b)中这样说:"Salvage payments referred to in paragraph [a] above shall include any salvage remuneration in which the skill and efforts of the salvors in preventing or minimizing damage to the environment such as is referred to in Art. 13 paragraph 1(b) of the International Convention on Salvage 1989 have been taken into account."。换言之,货方与货物保险人也为环境保护作出了部分贡献。

这里的发展还有不少,包括在 1999 年在国际互保协会与国际救助人协会的商讨下,以一个私人的协议形式(Special Compensation P& I Club Clause,简称 SCOPIC)替代复杂、富争议性与涉及了昂贵诉讼与专家意见的特别补偿。SCOPIC 条文已经有了几个版本,包括 1999、2000、2005、2007 年的版本。但这一复杂的问题不需要在本书详论,因为它只关系到船东与他的互保协会。如果想对这方面了解更多,读者可参阅笔者《海事法》第五章。

2.4　救助报酬是否算作共同海损的一部分

接下来要谈的是救助与海上货物运输保险的关系。救助报酬是否可以被视为共同海损的部分?在这一方面英国的法律与世界其他国家的海事法律不一样,不把救助报酬视为共同海损。第一,以纯救助(pure salvage)为例,出于救助人的自愿,这就与共同海损需要船长主动并且有选择性地作出牺牲或花费为船货共同安全/利益就有了根本性的差异。第二,救助很少有这么巧把船舶救到安全地点,而该安全地点恰恰就是目的地的卸港。这表示在中途港,就已经要求船舶与货物分别对救助报酬进行支付,不会等到去目的地的卸港。第三,船舶与货物分别支付救助报酬或提供救助人的担保(因为最后是多少报酬如果大家不能同意就要由有管辖权的法院进行审理),等于是船舶与货物各顾各的,谈不上这笔费用是为了大家共同利益所作出的花费:The"Raisby" (1885) 10 PD 114。除了一些集装箱是有大量的小货主会有不同做法外,不存在船东会愿意掏钱为船上货物提供救助担保。

至于合约救助(contract salvage),也就是签订标准的救助合约 LOF 之后才进行救助,可以说在船长主动签订 LOF 的情况下,就比较接近共同海损,毕竟救助也是为了船舶与货物的共同安全/利益。但由于 LOF 的条文下,救助人有权利向船舶与船上货物分别要求支付报酬,而实际上的做法也是如此,所以根据英国的先例 The "Raisby"还是不能算作共同海损。在先例 Australian Coastal Shipping Commission v. Green (1971) 1 QB 456, Denning 勋爵曾经这样说:"If the tug had rendered salvage services on the usual terms of ' no cure, no pay', the contract would undoubtedly have been a 'general average act'." 而这一说法被 Rose 教授在所著的《General Average Law and Practice》第 2 版第 5 页指是错误。

反而,合约救助下作出的支付或报酬应被视为施救费用(sue and labor),因为是船长或船东为了避免更大的损失主动采取的施救措施。这在海上保险合约都有规定会在赔付了全损后,额外要支付的钱。船壳保险的保险人固然要支付这一笔 LOF 下的救助报酬,因为很明显这属于施救费用;同样道理,货物海上运输保险的保险人也要支付这一笔 LOF 下的货方应该支付的救助报酬。至于不是货方自己作出签订 LOF 的决定,也可以根据一个解释,就是船长以紧急代理人(agent of necessity)的身份代货方签订 LOF。所以货方也是在合约救助下以施救费用向保险人索赔这笔报酬,而不是纯救助的救助费用。

2.5 《约克－安特卫普规则》试图统一这方面法律作出的努力

英国法律与其他国家法律的不同,曾经在《约克－安特卫普规则》1974 年与 1994 年版本作出过努力将其与其他国家统一。这就是以明示条文的形式将救助报酬当作共同海损一起理算。这就是在 Rule VI 所说如下:"Expenditure incurred by the parties to the adventure in the nature of salvage, whether under contract or otherwise, shall be allowed in general average provided that the salvage operations were carried out for the purpose of preserving from peril the property involved in the common maritime adventure."

但到了《约克－安特卫普规则》2004 年版本就有了改变,就是变为英国法的地位,除非船东为船上的货物一并支付救助报酬才有例外。这是在 Rule VI(a)如下:"Salvage, payments, including interest thereon and legal fees associated with such payments, shall lie where they fall and shall not be allowed in General Average, save only that if one party to the salvage shall have paid all or any of the proportion of salvage (including interest and legal fees) due from another party (calculated on the basis of salved values and not General Average contributory values), the unpaid contribution to salvage due from that other party shall be credited in the adjustment to the party that has paid it, and debited to the party on whose behalf the payment was made."

2.6 救助报酬在协会货物条文中的规定

救助报酬不论是被视为共同海损(根据英国以外其他国家的有关法律或是海上运输合约合并的《约克-安特卫普规则》1974 或 1994),或是被视为纯救助报酬/费用,或是被视为合约救助的施救费用,在协会货物条文(A)(B)(C)都有承保,已经解释过,其第 2 条说明是承保共同海损与救助费用(this insurance covers general average and salvage charges),把两种费用加在一起就是避免有时讲不清。这里也可以节录 1906 年《英国海上保险法》针对救助报酬的定义,这在 Section 65(2):"'Salvage charges' means the charges recoverable under maritime law by a salvor **independently of contract**. They do not include the expenses of services in the nature of salvage rendered by the assured or his agents, or any person employed for hire by them, for the purpose of averting a peril insured against. Such expenses, where properly incurred, may be recovered as particular charges or as a general average loss, according to the circumstances under which they were incurred."(加黑部分为笔者的强调)

从以上加黑部分可以看出,救助费用只是指没有合约的救助,也就是纯救助,这笔救助报酬/费用才可以算作救助费用。换言之,协会货物条文(A)(B)(C)第 2 条是只承保共同海损与纯救助产生的费用。而合约救助产生的救助报酬则属于施救费用,在协会货物条文(A)(B)(C)的 16 条有规定承保。

3."双方有责碰撞条文"(Both to Blame Collision Clause)

这作为保险人在协会货物条文(A)(B)(C)承保的非实质损失的风险责任,要进一步了解的话,就必须介绍船舶在海上发生碰撞时的一些责任方面的问题。众所周知,船舶碰撞还是经常会发生并造成对船舶与船上货物的损失或损坏。对本船与船上货物而言,这种损失或损坏显然属于承保的海上风险(peril of the sea),可以从保险人获得赔付。由于协会货物条文(A)(B)(C)都是承保海上风险,所以如果发生船舶碰撞都是可以获得赔付的。在 2009 年的(B)(C)条文更是明确在 1.1.4 条承保的列明风险之一是"collision or contact of vessel craft or conveyance with any external object other than water"。至于(A)条文由于是一切险则根本不需要再个别说明承保哪些海上风险。

但涉及了船舶碰撞,难免的就是船与船之间涉及了侵权的责任。这根据个别案件的事实是碰撞的两条船各自要承担某一些责任是根据他们所负过错的比例。在比较罕见的情况下,如一艘在锚地的船舶被另外一条船撞上,后者要负完全的责任。通常情况下则是两条船舶都有一定程度的责任(both to blame),只不过是过错比例多少的问题。

3.1 管辖权的问题

怎么样分摊碰撞责任通常由有管辖权的法院作出,虽然在比较少的情况下,发生碰撞的两艘船舶会达成协议让有航海经验的仲裁员作出裁决。这里就首先带来对碰撞事故的管辖权的问题,即哪个国家的法院有管辖权进行审理。毕竟很多时候碰撞是发生在公海或一些法律不健全没有外国人愿意打官司的国家的水域(如 The "Vishva Ajay"[1989] 2 Lloyd's Rep. 558 碰撞是发生在印度;The "Po"[1990] 1 Lloyd's Rep. 418 碰撞是发生在巴西的港口 Rio de Janeiro;The "Kapitan Shvetsov"[1998] 1 Lloyd's Rep. 199 碰撞是发生在曼谷)。这就带来船舶碰撞经常会出现的船东、货方或船舶造成人身伤亡的受害者试图选择有利诉讼地点的做法或简称"择地行诉"(forum shopping),即通过"对物诉讼"(in rem action)与"扣船"(arrest of ship)取得管辖权并同时取得诉前担保。在大部分的国家,包括在英国以及受英国法律影响的国家或管辖权地点如新加坡或香港,只要在它们的水域能够把对物诉讼的告票送达到船上就给了当地的法院管辖权。这表示在太平洋公海碰撞的两艘船舶,其中一艘继续航程进了香港水域,就有可能被对方船舶的船东先以对物诉讼的形式使香港法院取得管辖权,并通过扣船取得碰撞损失的担保。也有可能碰撞不是发生在公海而是在新加坡的水域,这一来,在香港被成功对物诉讼就有可能向香港法院申请中止,要求把管辖权让出给新加坡法院,因为新加坡法院才是"自然诉讼地点"(natural forum)。这就涉及哪里才是方便诉讼地点的争议(forum non conveniens),本章对这一个课题也不准备多作介绍,只简单节录 Sheen 大法官在 The "Coral Isis"(1986) 1 Lloyd's Rep. 413 中的评论如下:"It must frequently happen that when such a collision has occurred no court can properly be described as 'the natural forum' or ever 'a natural forum'. The reasons are self evident: the two ships may be registered in different countries; their owners and managers may be companies incorporated in yet other countries; the master and crew may be nationals of still different countries; after the collision the ships may go into repair yards in other countries and remain there until there comes a convenient moment to arrest them and thereby institute proceedings in rem."

但这也不代表船舶碰撞没有自然诉讼地点,特别碰撞是在某个国家的港内:The "Abidin Daver"(1984) 1 Lloyd's Rep. 339。

总结而言,择地行诉在船舶碰撞还是经常会有,因为不同地点的法院管辖会有不同的优点/缺点,其中:

(1)在一些严重的船舶碰撞造成损失或者损坏会导致船舶责任限制(有关责任限制请参阅笔者的《海事法》第二章),但国与国之间会有不同而造成索赔金额的很大差别。责任限制虽然已经有国际公约,也就是 1976 年的《责任限制公约》(Convention Relating to the Limitation of Liability of Owners of Sea - going Ships),但美国就拒绝加入该公约,认为公约责任限制太低。这表示在损失或损坏严重的船舶并认为对方船舶负大部分的责任就会倾向于在美国提起对物诉讼。另可介绍先例 The "Herceg Novi" (1998) 2 Lloyd's Rep. 454,碰撞发生在新加坡水域,但其中一艘船舶在英国提出诉讼,其中一个原因是英国已经是 1976 年《责任限制公约》的成员国,而新加坡还是停留在 1957 年《责任限制公约》。另在 The "Kapitan Shvetsov" (1998) 1 Lloyd's Rep. 199,也是因为适用不同的责任限制公约而产生争议。

(2)还有在其他方面包括在诉讼程序或实体法上的优劣,以及处理这种案件的经验。例如,英国海事法院就是世界上最有经验、所出判决最有说服力而人们也最愿意去的法院,但现在世界著名的港口在英国已经不多,所以要通过对物诉讼或者是扣船取得管辖权已不是那么容易。而相比英国,美国法院值得择地行诉的因素有不少:很多船舶去美国港口;赔偿的金额通常比较高;当地的律师会在一些案件如人身伤亡愿意接受"不成功没有报酬"与即使是败诉也不需要承担胜诉方的诉讼费用;披露方面会更广泛与有可能去集体诉讼等好处。

在现实中,有不少船舶碰撞会通过友好谈判同意哪个国家法院管辖与互相提供担保,这就可以免去择地行诉所带来的法律费用。这通常能够做得到是因为船舶的背后涉及保险人与互保协会,尤其是互保协会的影响力极大,而十多家互保协会大部分都是英国的互保协会。显然他们对英国海事法院有信心与熟悉,所以一涉及谈判同意管辖权,可以说 100% 都会同意英国海事法院管辖。就算有时候他们之间有利益冲突,如涉及责任限制,他们也会达成协议英国海事法院管辖与审理但最终的赔偿是适用其他国家的更高或更低的责任限制额度。这也解释了为什么船舶碰撞的案件无论是发生在公海还是其他国家的水域会有这么多去英国审理。否则,如果只是靠择地行诉,已经提到船舶去英国港口的几率不多,英国海事法院也不会有这么大的影响力。

择地行诉的情况还是有的,毕竟船舶在碰撞责任不涉及互保协会的情况还是有的(如向船壳保险人投保 4/4 的碰撞责任),互保协会之间谈不拢,远洋船舶与小渔船碰撞(后者是没有互保协会)等的情况。

船舶碰撞以诉人的方式替代对物诉讼的情况不多见,毕竟现在很多船舶都是悬挂方便旗。估计不会有人希望碰撞责任去巴拿马或利比里亚法院作出审理。

3.2　碰撞的过错

碰撞过错的分担主要是涉及对事实的认定,而事实的认定就如须谈到众所周知的《国际避碰规则》,最新的版本是 1972 年的《Convention on the International Regulations for Preventing Collisions at Sea》。在《国际避碰规则》有很多细节,在本章不会多讲,其中部分的内容可参阅笔者所著《海事法》的第七章。其中包括什么是适当瞭望,什么是船舶安全速度,怎么样才是恰当的避免碰撞的行动,在航道或狭窄水道的恰当做法等。

只一提的是富有经验的英国海事法院历史悠久的一些对碰撞事实认定的做法：

(1)要求碰撞的当事人尽早单方面向法院递交一份名为“Collision Statement of Case”的文件，这等同于以前名为“Preliminary Act”的文件，内容是把所有有关碰撞的事实作出文书的陈述，如碰船的地点与天气，自己船舶的航行与船速，在什么时候首次看到对方的船舶，向对方船舶作出怎样的指控等。由于这是在不知道对方船舶会作出怎样的陈述与提供怎样的证据前向法院提交的文件，船东就不敢乱写，否则将来显示该文件的陈述被夸大或作假时，提交文件的船东就会一败涂地或是麻烦大了。至于为什么双方船东开始诉讼后很快就可以提交该份文件，这是因为船舶碰撞是很大的事故，双方船东(他的互保协会与船舶保险人)会在事发后马上派律师上船保存证据/录口供，不像一些事故，即使开始诉讼也会是边打官司边调查案情与搜集证据。所以，递交这份文件不是问题。在英国法院这份文件的内容会被视为对事实的承认(admission of facts)。

(2)英国海事法院是针对船舶碰撞是唯一的法院分支，习惯自己聘用中立的专家证人协助法官更加正确地认定涉及专业知识的事实，而其他采取对抗制的英国法院分支没有同样的做法。这些专家一般都是老资格的退休船长，所谓的 Elder Brethren of Trinity House，而他们作为英国海事法院的专家，名为海事评核官(Nautical Assessor)。由于有了法院的独立专家，一般情况下就没有必要让当事人提供自己专家证人的意见：Owners of the Bow Spring v. Owners of the Manzanillo II (2005) 1 Lloyd's Rep. 1。

3.3 碰撞责任的分摊

碰撞责任的分摊就是认定对碰撞的造成是谁的过错，而如果双方都有过错，就是怎样确定比例。这就涉及了一个年代比较悠久的国际公约，名为 1910 年《碰撞公约》(《Collision Convention 1910》)，在英国它于 1911 年通过立法成为《Maritime Convention Act》。它规定了这一根据两艘碰撞船舶的过错比例分摊赔偿责任的做法，措辞如下：“Whereby the fault of two or more vessels damage or loss is caused to one or more of those vessels, to their cargoes or freight or to any property on board, the liability to make good the damage or loss shall be in proportion to the degree in which each vessel was in fault.”

该国际公约其他有关与有趣的地方是：

1. 该国际公约年代比较早却一直没有新的版本出现，在联合国也没有任何修订/改善的提议，而其他的公约如《责任限制公约》已经有了新的版本，这说明该公约经得起时间的考验。

2. 该国际公约也规定了诉讼时效是自碰撞发生之日起 2 年。

3. 本章所讲内容关系最密切的在从节录的条文可以看出，将船与货放在一起当作同一方(same party)。也就是说，如果本船的过错是 30%，就表示对方船舶的过错是

70%。这一来,本船的损失可以向对方船舶索赔与取回70%(假设对方船舶在碰撞中没有受到损失,否则对方的损失也可以向本船取回30%,并把两笔钱对冲),而本船的货物损失或损坏也只能向对方取回70%。再举一个例子,碰撞全部是本船的过错,负100%的责任,就会导致本船与本船上的货物的损失或损坏都不能向对方船舶提出索赔。可以说该国际公约与英国以前的普通法地位是一致的:The "Milan" (1861) Lush. 388,就是把船货视为一家,船舶在碰撞有错,船上的货物也有错。估计从前的实际做法是船货一家,所以传统的海上保险也是以劳合社标准SG保单承保在一起。

(4)要注意的就是该国际公约没有把第三大类受影响的一方扯在一起,就是人身伤亡。涉及人身伤亡,该公约下双方如果都有错就对受害者负共同的连带赔偿责任。Article 4 这样说:"In respect of damages caused by death or personal injuries, the vessels in fault are jointly as well as severally liable to third parties, without prejudice however to the right of the vessel which has paid a larger part than that which, in accordance with the provisions of the first paragraph of this Article, she ought ultimately to bear, to obtain a contribution from the other vessel or vessels in fault."

这等于同岸上"共同侵权人"(joint tort - feasor)的责任制度是一样,受害人可以向任何一个侵权人(即使他的过错与所负的责任只有10%或不等)要回全部的损失,之后共同侵权人之间根据他们的大小过错与责任程度再相互追偿。

(5)另要一提的是海上运输合约(主要是指提单合约)在过去五六十年主要是根据1924年的《海牙规则》,其中的Article 4 (2)(a) 对航海过失免责,只要船舶在开航前船东恪尽职责令船舶适航。在上文所举的例子中,本船负30%的碰撞责任,对方船舶负70%的碰撞责任,则本船上的货方可以根据侵权向对方船舶索赔回来70%,但由于提单合约中的航海过失免责,本船上的货方不可以向本船的船东索赔另外的30%。这表示对本船货方而言,最好的情况是对方船舶负100%的责任,它就可以向对方船舶要回100%的损失。这一贯以来的做法也没有引起很大的反响,因为船舶与货物早已分家,不像百年前船货是一家。这一来,货方照理由是会提出异议,就是没理由把它与船舶扯在一起,在船舶碰撞有过错就会负上同等程度的责任。但估计没有很大反响的原因是货方的碰撞损失反正是有保险人赔付,真正向对方船舶甚至是本船船东(如根据碰撞由于船舶不适航所引致)把损失取回来只是保险人在赔付之后的代位求偿。对保险人而言,他们也接受代位求偿虽然重要,但不会是赔付的钱都可以向第三者要回来。

(6)根据英国的做法,一般货物会等待两艘碰撞船舶的过错比例判决或和解之后,与对方船舶根据这一比例要求作出赔偿,反正货方没有必要与对方船东在过错百分比方面再打官司,花律师费用。唯一要注意的就是货方要小心保护2年的索赔时效。

3.4 美国碰撞法律的不同与对策

但只有一个主要的国家美国不接受这一种其他主要海事国家的做法,也拒绝加入1910年的《碰撞公约》。这导致了美国对碰撞责任与国际上其他国家很不一样,其中包括并没有根据碰撞船舶的过错比例分担赔偿责任,而是简单地依据普通法,或者是其中的一条船承担全部的赔偿责任,或者是两条船平均承担赔偿责任。这一普通法地位直到先例 United States v. Reliable Transfer Co. , Inc 421 US 397 (1975)才被美国最高院改过来,与 1910 年的《碰撞公约》一致,要求船舶按照过错责任的比例承担赔偿责任。美国最高院这样说:"We hold that when two or more parties have contributed by their fault to cause property damage in a maritime collision or stranding, liability for such damage is to be allocated among the parties proportionately to the comparative degree of their fault, and that liability for such damages is to be allocated equally only when the parties are equally at fault or when it is not possible fairly to measure the comparative degree of their fault."

3.4.1 无辜货方规则

但美国法律另一个重要的不同是在无辜货方规则(innocent cargo rule),认为货方与人命伤亡的受害者一样是无辜方,可以向对方船舶作为共同侵权人(joint tort - feasor)索赔回全部的损失。在美国 The "Atlas" (1816) 93 U. S. 302,315 就是判"无辜货方"可以向对方船舶(只要有一点点的过错)索赔并取回全部损失(除了对方船舶申请责任限制或是船价不高才会少赔)。对方船舶不能抗辩说我在这个碰撞中只有一半过错甚至只是 10%,所以只按过错的比例作出赔偿。因为对方船舶面对的是本船上无辜的货方,好像面对无辜的人命伤亡一样,只要有一点点错就要负连带责任(jointly and severally liable)。而在这种侵权的情况下,双方不存在提单合约的关系,《海牙规则》也不会适用。但对方船舶赔付全部损失后,根据 The "Chattahoochee" (1898) 173 U. S. 540,可连同自己的损失一并向本船的船东根据碰撞责任的比例要回应该由本船船东负责的百分比。

这一来,本船的货方或是他背后有代位求偿权的保险人岂非走了后门或是兜了个圈,本船船东间接赔付给自己船上的货方,而在《海牙规则》下,本船船东本来是免责的。这里就带来一个疑问,本船船东可否再向本船上的货方要回他本来是免责的损失?答案是不可以,因为《海牙规则》中的航海过失免责条文只能够用来作货方索赔时的抗辩,而不可以被用作向货方索赔的依据。换言之,免责条文只能用来作盾牌而不能用来作矛或剑。

3.4.2 船东的对策

于是就引出了加在海上运输合约中的"双方有责碰撞条文"(Both to Blame Collision Clause),以这个条文来起到矛或者剑的作用。这一条文可以节录 1994 年金康租约中的第 11 条作为例,如下:

"Both - to - Blame Collision Clause

If the Vessel comes into collision with another vessel as a result of the negligence of the other vessel and any act, neglect or default of the Master, Mariner, Pilot or the servants of the Owners in the navigation or in the management of the Vessel, the owners of the cargo carried hereunder will indemnify the Owners against all loss or liability represents loss of, or damage to, or any claim whatsoever of the owners of said cargo, paid or payable by the other or non - carrying vessel or her owners to the owners of said cargo and set - off, recouped or recovered by the other or non - carrying vessel or her owners as part of their claim against the carrying Vessel or the Owners. The foregoing provisions shall also apply where the owners, operators or those in charge of any vessel or vessels or objects other than, or in addition to , the colliding vessels or objects are at fault in respect of a collision or contact. ”

如果不了解背景,很难看明白该条条文,但一了解了就很容易明白条文的目的。它没有特别针对美国,因为有其他国家可能会跟从美国的无辜货方规则且避免刺激美国,但显然美国才是主要的目标。条文的内容就是说如果发生碰撞,而对方船舶(non - carrying vessel)有过错(不论多少百分比),本船的货方如果向对方船舶索赔货物损失,而对方船舶会将该赔出去的货物损失加进向本船船东的索赔/对冲(而能够加进去显然就是本船要承担碰撞责任的百分比),本船船东根据该条文可以要求本船货方针对他赔给对方船舶的该笔钱(或者是对冲掉的钱)作出补偿。在英国的法律下,这是订约自由,该 Both - to - Blame Collision Clause 完全有效。而该条文最主要就是印在所有的提单合约(以避免有所遗漏),因为《海牙规则》或《海牙 - 维斯比规则》几乎适用于所有的提单。同时该条文也加印在了租约中,因为虽然《海牙规则》或《海牙 - 维斯比规则》不强制适用于租约,但通常租约都会通过首要条文(Clause Paramount)以订约自由的方式把《海牙规则》或《海牙 - 维斯比规则》合并在租约内,所以也需要 Both - to - Blame Collision Clause 的保障。

这一条文第一个保障就是不鼓励本船货方去美国向对方船舶以侵权索赔100%的货损货差,即使对方船舶只有10%或50%不等的过错与责任。而第二个保障就是即使货方这样做了,本船船舶也可以根据提单/租约中的该条文向本船货方再要回他有过错的那个比例。而班轮运输涉及的海上运输合约通常也只有提单,但散装货或者是石油产品的海上运输就经常会涉及租约,即使有提单的存在且涉及了转让给第三者的货方。更会有情况是提单根本没有起到海上运输合约的作用,而只是一份收据,因为货方也是承租人,如在 FOB 买卖的情况下。

最后一提的是即使该提单/租约代表的航次不行走美国,也不代表该条文在海上运输合约就不具有重要性。这是因为船舶碰撞经常会涉及择地行诉(forum shopping),所以在南中国海发生的船舶碰撞,甚至在曼谷港口发生的碰撞,如果碰撞的其中一条船涉及中国远洋公司的船舶,就难保中国远洋公司的一艘姐妹船不会被对方船舶上的“无辜货方”或是人身伤亡的受害方在美国港口择地行诉,对该中国远洋船舶对物诉讼与进行扣押。这表示在南中国海与亚洲营运的船舶也必须确保在它的提单/租约中有这样的一条 Both - to - Blame Collision Clause。

3.4.3 Both - to - Blame Collision Clause 的有效性与作用

但 Both - to - Blame Collision Clause 在美国也不是一帆风顺的,早在 United States

v. Atlantic Mutual Ins. Co. (1952) 1 Lloyd's Rep. 520，美国最高院就已经判该条文违反了美国1893年的《哈特法》(US Harter Act)(1924年《海牙规则》就是以《哈特法》作为蓝本的国际公约)，所以在提单中的Both - to - Blame Collision Clause无效。同样判法的案例也可见The "Frances Hammer" (1975) 1 Lloyd's Rep. 305。但在American Union Transport Inc. v. United States of America 1976 AMC 1480，判是租约中的Both - to - Blame Collision Clause有效，因为租约与提单是不一样，双方在租约是有平等的谈判力量达成。而在美国以外的国家，如英国，更加是明确在租约甚至是提单中的Both - to - Blame Collision Clause都会被视为有效：The "Giacinto Motta"(1977) 2 Lloyd's Rep. 221。

总结而言，在所有的海上运输合约加上Both - to - Blame Collision Clause还是至关重要的，直到可能有一天《鹿特丹规则》全面替代《海牙规则》与《海牙 - 维斯比规则》，因为前者的国际公约没有对航海过失的免责。这表示货方或者他的保险人不需要在美国向碰撞的对方船舶索赔损失，而可以根据海上运输合约向本船船东与他背后的互保协会把全部损失要回来(暂时撇开责任限制的问题)。

而即使有Both - to - Blame Collision Clause写在海上运输合约，也不代表货方或背后的保险人不会去美国向对方船舶择地行诉，因为以下的原因想取巧：(1)可以像人命伤亡的受害方一样，不必等待碰撞责任分摊，已可在美国向对方船舶以侵权索赔全部损失。至于有否这样的机会，主要看对方船舶(或姐妹船)会否去美国港口，以利对物诉讼并扣船取得诉前保全。(2)已经提到过，Both to Blame Collision Clause在美国会被视为违反《哈特法》或《海上运输法》。这一来，货方早向对方船舶在美国法院成功索赔回来的全部损失也就可以落入囊中。(3)在绕这个大圈中，会有律师/当事人不懂，错失良机。例如，本船船东不理解在租约或提单中的Both to Blame Collision Clause的权益，所以没有在事后向本船货方要求补偿。或是有关的租约中有一条乌干达仲裁条文，导致了本船船东了解他自己的权益也在程序上被卡死。(4)还会有其他各种变数，如本船在对方船舶能扣船前已沉没，所以，根本没有提供诉前保全，已是皮包公司。这一来，对方船舶赔了给本船货方全部损失，无法找本船船东要求索赔/对冲，这样整个索赔链中断。另一种情况是本船船东面对对方船舶索赔申请责任限制。有关责任限制以及1976年《责任限制公约》的问题，笔者在《海事法》第二章有详论，请参阅。

3.4.4 有关案例介绍：The "Giacinto Motta"

碰撞船舶其中一船的货方去美国法院取巧，以至于索赔链中断的先例是：The "Giacinto Motta" (1977) 2 Lloyd's Rep. 221，在该先例中船舶Mermaid与Motta由于航行疏忽在公海相撞。双方同意的事实是：Motta轮全损，其船东损失与索赔500,000英镑；Motta轮所运载的货物全损，货方索赔1,350,000英镑(是USMYM 3,353,268.33)。另一艘船舶Mermaid轮部分损坏，其船东损失与索赔250,000英镑。碰撞导致了两套不同的法律诉讼程序开始：在美国，Motta船上所运载货物的货方索赔成功并达致和解取回2,485,880.37美元,被告显然就是Mermaid轮的船东并要作出支付。在英国海事法院,Motta轮与Mermaid轮船东则开始了船舶碰撞的诉讼,它们通过和解同意双方负有同等的过错,也就是各负50%的责任。英国法律下,Mermaid轮的船舶吨位责任限制在845,705英镑,也就是该事故中Mermaid轮船东最多需要支付的金额。而根据《海牙规则》,Motta轮的船东因为航行过错可享有免责不需要对船上的货主负任何的赔偿责任。这些做法可节录Brandon大法官所说,如下:"The present case is a typical example of such forum shopping, in that the cargo - owners, being prevented by the contracts of carriage from recovering any part of their loss from the owners of the Motta (the carrying ship) in any forum, and being entitled under the law of England or of other countries which are parties to the Convention to recover only 50 percent of their loss from the owners of the Mermaid (the non - carrying ship), elected to sue the owners of the Mermaid in the US in order to recover from them alone in that country, if possible, the whole amount of their loss."

这里也需要介绍一下货方在美国的诉讼,因为它先有了结果。这也容易了解,在美国的碰撞法律下,只要是被告有一点点过错就要对无辜受害方负全责的赔偿,就很容易让双方在责任方面达成共识,就算真的要法院作出判决也会很容易与快捷。所以,在美国的诉讼中,估计原告货方与被告Mermaid轮的船东很快就在责任方面达成共识。但是对赔偿金额这方面双方反而有一定的争议,因为索赔金额的USMYM 3,353,268.33超越了船舶责任限制,也就是如果Mermaid轮船东可以成功享有责任限制就可以大大减少赔偿的金额。但美国在责任限制与国际特别是英国的法律不一致,它也没有签署有关的责任限制公约(当时的1957年《责任限制公约》),因为美国觉得这两个国际公约的责任限额都太低。美国不同的法律在笔者的《海事法》第165页有详细介绍。其中提到了根据1851年的《美国责任限制法》允许船东把责任限制在船价加运费,但如果船东对事故"知情"(with privity),这个权利就会被剥夺。而在美国,从20世纪50年代开始,法院就已经对船东限制责任的权利有十分大的敌意,办法就是通过在"知情"方面挑毛病。所以在上诉庭先例Olympia Towing Corp. v. Nebel Towing Co, 419 F. 2d 230 (1969)有说法是:"in the vast majority of cases limitation is denied for one reason or another."显然如果是限制责任的权利被剥夺,被告的船东就要付全部的赔偿责任了。所以,估计是原告货方与被告Mermaid轮的船东用这个筹码在谈判过程中而最终达成了赔偿2,485,880.37美元的协议。被告谈判的筹码就是说:"我可以向法院申请责任限制,就是只要赔索赔金额的一半,因为Mermaid轮的市场价格就是这么多。"而原告的谈判筹码就是说:"如果你申请责任限制,我就会说服法院否定你的权利,你是知道美国法院对这方面的敌意。"结果,显然是双方都作出让步,因为大家心里都没有底,而最终达成了2,485,880.37美元的赔偿。

现在剩下的问题是在英国海事法院,Mermaid轮的船东是否是有权向Motta轮的船东索赔回来他已经支付给 Motta 轮上货方的赔款,以及可以索赔回来多少。假设根据 1894 年《英国商船法》,Mermaid 轮有权享受责任限制,已经向 Motta 轮上的货方支付了赔款,Mermaid 轮船东可否把这笔钱一并考虑并共同分摊英国法律下的责任限制基金。

Motta 轮船东当然反对赔给货方的 2,485,880.37 美元分摊 Mermaid 轮的责任限制基金共 845,705 英镑。因为现在剩下的只有 Motta 轮全损的索赔,共 500,000 英镑。假设是 Mermaid 轮要赔付给 Motta 轮,表示这笔责任限制基金完全足够。但如果允许在美国赔偿货方这笔钱加进来一并计算,Motta 轮可能得到的赔偿就会少得多,如只有责任赔偿基金的 1/4。

法院最终的判决是,根据公平合理的原则,既然是同一个事故就没有理由不让 Mermaid 轮的船东把较早前赔偿给 Motta 轮上货方的钱一并在责任限制基金分摊。但由于只是英国诉讼,所以能够分摊的仅仅限于假设 Motta 轮上货方在英国向 Mermaid 轮提起诉讼并直接向该责任限制基金提出索赔可以成功的部分。而根据英国的碰撞法律,Mottta 轮的货方按照 50:50 的过错比例只可以向 Mermaid 轮的责任限制基金索赔回货损的一半,也就是 2,485,880.37 美元的一半才能加进来一并分摊。Brandon 大法官这样说:"while the owners of the Mermaid are entitled to be given credit, in the distribution of their limitation fund, in respect of the cargo claim, the amount of the credit to be allowed to them cannot exceed the amount of the dividend which would have been receivable by the cargo - owners from such fund if they had brought their claim against it instead of enforcing payment in respect of it in the United States in the way that they did. In calculating what the amount of such dividend would have been, it is necessary to proceed on the basis that the cargo - owners' right of recovery would have been governed by English law as contained in s. 1 of the Act, and that under that law they would only have been entitled to bring a claim against the fund for 50 percent of their loss."

3.5 Both to Blame Collision Clause 与货物保险的关系

接下来就是介绍为什么在协会货物条文的第 3 条承保 Both to Blame Collision Clause 的非实质损失的风险。可以说在介绍了上面的背景知识后就很容易明白,这就是如果在船舶碰撞后,导致船上货物部分损坏或全损,懂行的货物保险人在赔付后行使代位求偿权时肯定有很大的诱因去美国择地行诉,将货损全部要回。这就会带来一连串的后果,包括对方船舶把不应由他负责的碰撞责任比例的货损向本船船东要求索赔/对冲。然后,本船船东就会根据海上运输合约(提单/租约)的 Both to Blame Collision Clause 向货方要求补偿。如果货方抗拒,就根据该海上运输合约中的管辖权条文/仲裁条文逼货方就范。这一来,货方要付出的可能是高达 90% 或 95% 的货损货差补偿(这在对方船舶只需要承担 10% 甚至是 5% 的碰撞责任的情况下)。这一来货方可就惨了,以为向保险人成功获得赔付货物的全损,结果却要补偿给本船的船东,原因是保险人在美国提出索赔。本来,根据英国的法律,保险人因为代位求偿而导致受保人蒙受损失或者不利,有一个默示地位是保险人需要赔付受保人:England & England v. Guardian Insurance Limited (2000) Lloyd's Rep. IR 404。但难保保险人不会提出一些抗辩,如受保人的货方自己不应该在海上运输合约内加入 Both to Blame Collision Clause,这才是货方遭受损失的主因而不是保险人的代位求偿行动。估计这种抗辩应该不大会成功,因为加入一条 Both to Blame Collision Clause 已经在航运界被视为标准与无可避免的做法。但为了明确与令这方面是无可争议,显然最好就是在协会货物条文中加入第 3 条的条文。

4. 续运费用(Forwarding Charges)

这一承保的非实质性损坏的风险涉及两个方面的问题:一是航程终止(loss of adventure),二是施救费用与责任(sue and labor)。以下稍作分析。

4.1 航程终止(loss of adventure)

英国普通法很早就已经有说法是,海上货物运输保险不仅承保了货物在海上运输的途中遭受实质的损失或损坏,也承保货物由于承保的风险导致了航程终止以至于货物不能安全到达保险合约中约定的目的地的风险。这里可举几个年代比较古老的先例来说明,第一个先例是 Barker v. Blake (1809) 9 East 283,Ellenborough 勋爵说:"The prolonged detention of ship and cargo may properly be considered a loss of the voyage and such a loss is... a total loss of the goods."

第二个先例是 Anderson v. Wallis (1813) 2 M&S 247,Ellenborough 勋爵说:"A total loss of cargo may be effected not merely by the destruction of that cargo, but by a total permanent incapacity of the ship to perform the voyage. That is a destruction of the contemplated adventure."

第三个先例是 Rodocanachi v. Elliott (1873) LR 9 CP 649,案情涉及了一票丝绸从日本运往伦敦,投保了平安险(free of particular average),该份保险合约也承保了君主禁止(restraint of princes)的风险,表示战争险也有承保。该票丝绸是在 1870 年法国与普鲁士的战争期间以陆运的方式从马赛运往伦敦。之后德国占领了法国的大部分地区,并包围了巴黎,以致这批货物永远(在事发时的判断)滞留在巴黎,去不了目的地伦敦。该批货物并不会因此而造成物理上的损失或损坏,而且法律地位 1906 年《英国海上保险法》Section 55(2)(b)是保险人不负责赔付延误带来的损失。在区分延误与航程终止时,Bovill 大法官说了这样一段话:"No doubt the goods existed in specie and uninjured. It is equally clear that, in our law, a mere delay or interruption of the voyage will not give the assured a claim against the underwriters, unless such delay is caused by a peril insured against, and the voyage or adventure is thereby altogether frustrated. The question therefore is, whether there has been such a loss in this case."

Bovill 大法官的结论是由于巴黎被德国军队包围而导致货物永远被滞留在巴黎，以致航程终止，这不仅仅是短暂的延误。换言之，对于该票货物航程终止的损失，保险人应该赔付。

第四个先例是 British & Foreign Marine Insurance Company Ltd. v. Samuel Sanday & Co. (1916) AC 650。该先例中，有一票货物是亚麻籽与小麦，从阿根廷的 River Plate 运往德国汉堡，所投保的保险合约承保了君主禁止(restraint of princes)的风险。在该票货物被装上了两艘英国的船舶后，"一战"的爆发使得该批货物不可能由英国船舶运到德国。结果这批货物被卸在了英国的利物浦和格拉斯哥，而受保人将它们提走后已经妥善保管。但受保人仍然向保险人索赔航程终止的损失(a total loss of the adventure)，索赔金额实际上是市场的货价损失，即货物如果可以成功运到德国汉堡的市场价格与在英国卸下价格的差价。注意是市场差价如果只是由于延误，如因为坏天气而航次拖慢了一个月才抵达目的地，这是保险人不负责赔付的风险。该先例判受保人胜诉。Wrenbury 大法官这样说："... where goods are insured at or from one port to another port the insurance is not confined to an indemnity to be paid in case the goods are injured or destroyed, but extends to an indemnity to be paid in case the goods do not reach their destination. This may be variously described as an insurance of the venture, or an insurance of the voyage, or an insurance of the market, as distinguished from an insurance of the goods simply and solely. Goods delivered at the port of destination may be of value very different from their value at the port of loading. The underwriter's obligation is to pay money in the event of the goods failing to arrive at their destination uninjured by any of the perils insured against."

第五个先例是 Rickards v. Forestal Land, Timber and Railways Co. Ltd; Middows v. Robertson Ltd. and Other Cases (1941) 70 Lloyd's Rep. 173 (HL)，案情在下一小段介绍，在这里只节录 Wright 勋爵对海上货物运输保险承保货物损失或损坏外的航程终止有很明确的说法："The primary subject of the insurance is the goods as physical things, but there is superimposed an interest in the safe arrival of the goods... Thus it is sometimes said that the policy on goods covers also loss of market, because the owner is generally shipping them for sale at a profit; but the advantage contemplated may be some other purpose of the assured, as for instance, as raw material or machinery for his factory for use at the destination. I prefer the phrase 'loss of the adventure'. It follows that a policy on goods is in truth one covering a composite interest, the physical things or chattels, against their destruction, damage or deprivation, and also the expected benefit from arrival. The subject-matter may be described as chattels-cum-adventure. It seems to follow inevitably that if the goods are lost the adventure is lost also. If they are damaged and suffer a partial loss the adventure may or may not be lost. But the adventure may be lost even though the goods are neither damaged nor lost nor taken from the assured's possession or control. ”

最后，除了先例外，承保航程终止的风险也在1906年《英国保险法》有所规定。在Section 60 (2)(iii) 有关货物的推定全损说："There is a constructive total loss... In the case of damage to goods, where the cost of repairing the damage and forwarding the goods to their destination would exceed their value on arrival. ”

4.2　航程终止会带来的全损与部分损失

航程终止（不论当时货物是否已经有实质的损坏）会带来全损或部分损失。在货物根本去不了保险合约目的地的情况下，真正全损（actual total loss）就会有可能出现。有关的案例有Anderson v. Wallis (1813) 2 M&S 247，另外还有Arnould's Law of Marine Insurance and Average，2008年第17版之29.45段所列举的先例。在5.1段提到的先例Rodocanachi v. Elliott (1873) LR 9 CP 649与British & Foreign Marine Insurance Company Ltd. v. Samuel Sanday & Co. (1916) AC 650中，货物都是因为战争险而造成真正全损。举一个一切险的例子，如果保险合约中的目的地港因为地震或者是火山爆发根本去不了，导致航程终止。如果在航程终止后该票投保的货物能够出售并取回部分市场的价格，索赔就只局限于市场差价。但有不少货物没有市场出售，如专门为目的地港的某工厂而造的设备，这就明显是一个真正全损。

而推定全损（constructive total loss）会出现在航程终止后，把货物运去保险合约的目的地变得不大可能（unlikely）。这也是1906年《英国海上保险法》，Section 60 (2)(i)的规定推定全损其中的一种情况说："There is a constructive total loss... where the assured is deprived of the possession of his ... goods by a peril insured against, and (a) it is unlikely that he can recover ... goods, as the case may be, or (b) the cost of recovering ... goods, as the case may be, would exceed their value when recovered. "在《英国海上保险法》的同一条中也谈到了(b)的另外一种推定全损，就是避免航程终止的风险所花的费用比货物的价值还要高。这就可以想得到不少情况是一些货物，尤其是价格比较低如矿砂或者是煤炭，如果想办法续运至保险合约中的目的地所要花的钱比货价本身还要高，这也会构成推定全损。

至于什么是部分损失（partial loss），在1906年《英国海上保险法》的Section 71名为Partial loss of goods, merchandise, etc中有针对。但针对赔付尺度（measure of indemnity）主要是在Section 71(3)，如下："Where the whole or any part of the goods or merchandise insured has been delivered damaged at its destination, the measure of indemnity is such proportion of the sum fixed by the policy in the case of a valued policy, or of the insurable value in the case of an unvalued policy, as the difference between the gross sound and damaged values at the place or arrival bears to the gross sound value. "该条文只是针对货物抵达目的地时有实质损坏，赔付尺度是怎么样计算。但Section 71并没有针对航程终止的部分损失，所以协会货物条文就加了一条续运费用条文（forwarding charges）作为在这种情况下的赔付尺度。毕竟在航程终止，但货物没有实质损坏，如

果经济上值得续运去目的地,受保人的损失也只有续运的费用。这一条文还有其他的原因,如施救费用与责任方面,稍后在5.4段会有介绍。

4.3 受阻条文(Frustration Clause)

在5.1段介绍的第四个先例 British & Foreign Marine Insurance Company Ltd. v. Samuel Sanday & Co. (1916) AC 650 令伦敦的保险市场变得很担心,因为在当时世界局势还比较动荡,这种事情还是会出现而且是大规模出现。在1919年4月,F. D. MacKinnon 御用大律师建议说,如果战争险的保险人在类似的情况下不想赔付,可以加入一条受阻条文(Frustration Clause):"Warranted free of any claim based upon loss of, or frustration of, the insured voyage, or adventure, caused by arrests, restraints or detainments of kings, princes or peoples."而该条文在1919年5月1日在市场出现。这一条受阻条文在"协会战争条文(货物)"(Institute War Clauses [Cargo])是在3.7条,而在"协会罢工条文"(Institute Strikes Clauses [Cargo])是在3.8条,这方面请看本书第九章。但注意是在协会货物条文的(A)(B)(C)中承保水险的风险所引起的航程终止所带来的损失,所以在这些条文之中就不会像战争险与罢工险条文一样有一条受阻条文。相反(A)(B)(C)则都有了一条续运费用条文(forwarding charges),而该条文在战争险与罢工险都没有。

有关受阻条文只是作为货物实质损失或损坏的保险,在5.1段提到的第五个先例 Rickards v. Forestal Land, Timber and Railways Co. Ltd; Middows v. Robertson Ltd. and Other Cases (1941) 70 Lloyd's Rep. 173 (HL)中有针对。该先例发生在第二次世界大战,英国受保人的货方把运回英国的货物装在德国船舶上。"二战"一爆发,德国船舶的船长奉命把船舶开回德国。有关的3艘船舶有2艘船舶在半途遇到英国军舰的阻止,结果德国船舶的船长把船舶凿沉造成船上货物的全损。第三艘船舶顺利开回德国并把货物卸下,但显然英国的货方不可能去敌方的德国把货物要回来,所以实际上,3票货物都真正全损。但由于有关的保险合约已经加进了一条受阻条文,这就给了保险人一个拒赔的理由说德国船长奉命把船舶开回德国而不是英国的目的地港,就已经构成了航程终止(loss of adventure)。而由于保单对战争险有一条受阻条文,所以保险合约就终止,他们也不必负责赔付后来发生的全损。这在第一审被接受,但上诉去了上诉庭就被推翻,认为货物实质的损失与损坏才是保险合约最主要针对的风险,其他像施救费用或是共同海损分摊等的只是额外的承保风险,属于次要。MacKinnon 大法官这样说:

"The subject - matter of the contract is, of course, the goods, and they are insured against loss or damage by insured perils. But even if the goods are not so lost or damaged, there is an additional insurance against the loss of the their voyage. The learned Judge considers this to be not an additional risk, but an essential part of it in every case...

I think it is unnecessary to discuss further this elementary misconception as to the nature of a policy upon goods. I would only add that, if the view of the learned Judge were correct, the assured under this policy must have accepted the most fatuous and worthless contract ever made by a sane man. The policy solemnly insures his goods against loss by war perils, and his being thereby deprived of them. But the frustration clause, upon the Judge's reasoning, would in every case of such deprivation that I can imagine make that promise absolutely nugatory."

4.4　施救(sue and labor)费用与责任

货物保险人在航程终止的时候愿意赔付续运费用，除了把它当作一个部分损失的赔付外，也可以把它当作一个施救费用。众所周知，施救费用是一项在赔付了保险标的全损或部分损失之后另外需要赔付的一笔钱，是保险人为了鼓励受保人(在本书就是货方)采取合理行动避免货物的全损或更严重的部分损失，不要因为货物损失或损坏，反正有保险就管他的。而这种采取行动所产生的费用可以得到额外的赔付。所以，在船壳险的保单都会加上一条施救费用条文，以合约条文的方式约束受保人必须合理施救。如在笔者与汪鹏南教授合著的《英国海上保险条款详论》第二版第259页就介绍了2003年国际船舶保险条文第9条的"受保人的(施救)义务"(Duty of the Assured [Sue and Labour])，而受保人显然就是指船东。但在海上货物运输保险，由于货物交给了船舶/承运人，货方通常管不到甚至不会知道出了什么风险。所以在协会货物条文中虽然也有第16条文要求受保人的货方进行施救并承诺赔付有关的施救费用，但唯一或现实属于货方自己主动施救的可能性就出现在航程终止条文，为了鼓励货方采取施救行动，所以加上这一条针对性的续运费用条文。

续运费用被视为施救费用可介绍先例 Wilson Bros Bobbin Co. Ltd. v. Green (1917) 1 KB 860，案情是在一战期间有一批木材装在一条挪威船舶上准备运去英国，但船舶在开航后不久被德国军舰阻止，结果被迫把木材在一个挪威港口 Grimstadt 卸下并被货方安全储存起来。后来，该批木材成功被货方续运去英国目的地港 Garston。而保险方面，货方投保了战争险，而战争险的保单有一条施救费用条文(Sue and Labor Clause)。货方本来向保险人索赔的是推定全损，因为货物储存在 Grimstadt，货方认为不大可能(unlikely)续运到 Garston。但英国高院不同意这个说法，认为不是航程终止的实质/推定全损。这就带来了下一个问题，货方花的金钱把货物储存，最后成功续运到 Garston 能否将该笔费用作为施救费用索赔。英国高院同意，Bray 大法官这样说："If the loss was incurred by the perils insured against, namely, war risk, it covered particular average loss as well as total loss, and it seems to me that there was at all events a danger of a partial loss here. The goods were at Grimstadt, the port of destination was Garston, and the goods could not safely be got to Garston without incurring the expense of storage at Grimstadt and the cost of forwarding and therefore, in my opinion, these were expenses... incurred in endeavoring to avert that loss."

但 Bray 大法官认为货方如果不拖延而是尽早安排续运，除了运费会比较便宜，也可以省下部分的储存费用。所以只判是保险人需要赔付部分的施救费用。这方面实际上在协会货物条文(A)的第12条续运费用条文最后的一句也有明确说明,就是由于受保人的(货方或他的雇员)过错/疏忽等原因造成的费用不赔付。

在这里也可以进一步谈谈施救费用的其他方面,虽然不只是针对续运费用。第一个方面就是到底受保人有没有合理施救或违反施救的义务或责任以合理作为标准,合理当然是法院客观与全面看整个案件之后作出的判断。在 The "Vasso" (1993) 2 Lloyd's Rep. 309,案情涉及了一船的矿砂从南非去中国,船舶中途沉没。保险人指称受保人的货方没有冻结该船船东的保险赔付,导致了保险人取不到诉前保全,这违反了施救责任。Hobhouse 大法官认为受保人没有足够的证据说明该船舶是在伦敦投保以及会在伦敦作出全损的赔付,所以要求货方申请冻结令(freezing injunction 或 Mareva injunction)并不合理,说:"Neither under Section 78 of the 1906 Act, nor under Clause 16 of the Institute Clauses is the assured required to act unreasonably or to undertake any step other than one which could reasonably be expected to result in the avoidance or reduction of the loss."

另在香港上诉庭的 Miruvor Ltd. v. National Insurance Co. Ltd. (2003) 3 HKC 208,涉及了8次去巴拉圭的付运。保险人针对第7次付运的盗窃损失作出拒赔,理由是受保人应该警告他在巴拉圭的代理人有关较早付运的损失并采取预防。香港上诉庭判:"It was not sufficient for the insurers merely to show the failure the assured to take reasonable steps to avert or minimise the loss: they have to go further and show that the measures that had not been taken, would have been the dominant cause for the loss."

如果能够证明受保人违反了施救责任或义务,保险人的救济并非拒赔而只能证明损失并向受保人提出索赔或作出对冲。这方面可举 The "Vasso",Hobhouse 大法官说:"may cause loss to the insurer in which case the insurer will have a claim for damages against the assured in respect of the breach (违反施救责任) in so far as the insurer has been caused loss."

Hobhouse 大法官继续有说:"that a failure to minimise a loss or protect the value to the insurer of his rights of subrogation gives rise to more than a cross – liability of the assured to the insurer in damages and a potential for setting – off that liability against the liability of the insurer under the policy, either in whole or in part. On this the law is clear."

在现实的做法,保险人在收到索赔通知(notice of claims)后一般的做法就是不会表示接不接受,但会加上一个"受保人应该作为一个谨慎的没有投保的货方行事(act as a prudent uninsured)"的要求。这就表示受保人为他自己的利益(因为将来不一定获得赔付)或是协会货物条文下的施救责任或义务下,他都必须合理地行事。在这种情况下,保险人也经常会参与,如他会有更好的渠道把损坏的货物当作"跳楼货"(distressed cargo)出售。对受保人而言,这也是好事,因为令保险人将来更难指称受保人没有合理施救。在这种情况下保险人的参与,是不必害怕被指称是对将来拒赔的弃权,这也是在协会货物条文中加上第17条文的原因。该弃权条文(Waiver

Clause)如下:"Measures taken by the Assured or the Insurers with the object of saving, protecting or recovering the subject - matter insured shall not be considered as a waiver or acceptance of abandonment or otherwise prejudice the rights of either party."

4.5 承保风险带来的续运费用才可以得到赔付

这是一个可以理解的说法,因为如果不是承保风险所导致的航程终止(loss of adventure),就不会是保险人的赔付责任。所以没有理由要保险人负责续运费用,即使因为不续运而造成货物的全损也不关保险人的事。这在协会货物条文(A)(B)(C)的第12条一开始就已经说明"Where, as a result of the operation of a risk covered by this insurance..."

协会货物条文(A)下,因为承保的是一切险,所以如果不是第4~7条列明的除外风险导致的续运费用,保险人都要赔付。而在(B)与(C)条文下,因为承保的只是有限的列明风险,只有有限的列明风险造成的续运费用才可以得到保险人的赔付。

在这一方面就可以带出续运费用条文的前身是为了针对承保平安险(free from particular average 或简称 FPA)。众所周知,平安险是一个比较局限的险种,只有在全损的时候才有的赔付,而部分损失/损坏就没得赔付。对货方的好处显然就是保费应该是低了很多,但通常也只是一些价值比较低,加上货物本身不大会发生部分损失/损坏,只会因为船舶出大事如沉没才会有损失(往往也就是全损)的情况下才会投保平安险,如货物是矿砂。针对平安险就带来一个疑问,就是续运费用或施救费用的产生是否肯定为了避免发生全损而不是为了避免部分损失。这方面的先例有 Great India Peninsular Railway Co. v. Saunders (1861) 1 B&S 41; Booth v. Gair (1863) 33 LJCP 99; Kidston v. Empire Marine Insurance Co. (1866) LR 1 CP 533。在先例 Great India Peninsular Railway Co. v. Saunders 中,涉及一批火车轨的货物从伦敦运去孟买,但由于坏天气而无法继续航程,结果船舶绕航去了英国的普利茅斯避风,之后才把火车轨续运去了孟买。但货方向保险人要求额外运费的赔付败诉,因为法院认为投保的是平安险,而不认为该批货物是全损。续运不是为了去避免全损的风险。所以,为了避免这种争议,在1963年的协会平安险保险条文(Institute Cargo Clauses [FPA] 1/1/63)就加了一条条文明确承保续运费用如下:"...also to pay special charges for landing warehousing and forwarding if incurred at an intermediate port of call or refuge, for which the Underwriters would be liable under the standard form of English Marine Policy with the Institute Cargo Clauses (W.A.) attached."

4.6 航程终止与延误的区别

这是一个很重要的问题,必须能够作出明确的区分,原因是航次的延误即使是承保风险(如坏天气)所带来的损失(不论是实质损失如水果腐烂,或是经济损失如市场差价)保险人是不承保的。这在1906年《英国海上保险法》Section 55(2)(b)有说明,如下:"Unless the policy otherwise provides, the insurer on ship or goods is not liable for any loss proximately caused by delay, although the delay be caused by a peril insured against."

在协会货物条文(A)(B)(C)中,也明确在4.5条说明"In no case shall this insurance cover... loss damage or expense caused by delay, even though the delay be caused by a risk insured against (except expenses payable under Clause 2 above)."

但问题是航程终止(loss of adventure)的风险在绝大部分的情况下涉及延误,因为不存在货物实质的损失或损坏,如较早介绍的先例:Rodocanachi v. Elliott (1873) LR 9 CP 649承保的货物是丝绸与Great India Peninsular Railway Co. v. Saunders (1861) 1 B&S 41中的火车轨,这些货物可能在中途港存放很长时间也不会有实质损坏。

但事实上区分延误与航程终止也不是太困难,因为仅是航程延误(不论是什么原因如坏天气或者是发生海上事故)不会造成航程终止。航程终止只应该发生在受阻(frustration)、毁约(repudiation)与放弃(abandonment)。例如,船东拒绝继续航程去目的地,因为船舶需要长时间修理。不论这种情况是否会构成该航次的受阻,或只是船东的毁约(如修理时间不足够长而构成海上运输合约的受阻或是修理的原因是船舶在开航的时候不适航),这恐怕要将来在诉讼结束后才会有答案,但不能否认的就是航程在当时已经终止。

区分延误与航程终止的主要先例是Wilson Bros Bobbin Co. Ltd. v. Green (1917) 1 KB 860,有关的案情上文已经介绍过,反正保险人的其中一个抗辩就是保险合约排除赔付延误的损失,而该批木材储存在挪威港口Grimstadt的费用与后来续运去英国Garston的费用实是延误的损失,保险人不应该赔。Bray大法官不同意保险人的争辩说:"The claim for the expense of storage and reshipment may be dealt with together, and as to this [保险人代表大律师提出的] first point was that as the claim arose from delay it was excluded by the express terms of the policy. In my opinion that point fails. I do not think the clause excluding all claims arising from delay affected in any way the suing and laboring clause."

这方面的问题对会腐烂的货物(perishable cargoes)特别敏感,会有情况是到底为了避免"航程终止造成全损"而产生的续运/施救费用或是为了避免"延误"会有争议。在一个极端的例子可以说是有关的货物有季节性,如日历,应季商品或是成衣,会发生情况是船舶在中途港出了一个小的事故需要修理10天时间,它们就已经没办法等待,货方需要马上安排续运,搞不好还要以空运的方式续运。这种情况显然费用是来自为了避免延误,而原来的航程根本也没有终止,因为船东没有不打算在修理10天后继续开去目的地。所以,保险人就没有理由赔付这些续运费用。

最后可节录John Dunt的《Marine Cargo Insurance》一书之13.69段有关这方面所说如下:"It is convenient at this point to touch on the position in relation to perishable cargoes where the situation is more complex as there will inevitably be a combination of causes, delay and the peril or risk causing that delay. Clause 4.5 of the revised Institute Cargo

Clauses, and the Marine Insurance Act 1906 section 55 (2)(b), both recognise that, in delay cases, there will be concurrent causes of loss, one delay and the other a peril insured. When there are concurrent causes of a loss, one covered and one excluded, the exclusion will prevail. Where a cargo will deteriorate over time, which applies, more or less, to almost all cargoes, it can always be said that one of the reasons for forwarding the goods is to prevent delay. In those circumstances it may be argued that the delay exclusion will apply to almost all cases of loss of the adventure. **The law, however, is that it is not sufficient for delay to be one of the causes as the requirement is that delay must be a dominant cause at least equal in efficiency to any other competing cause. It may be submitted, therefore, that apart from the cases where goods are time sensitive, or are forwarded for commercial reasons, delay will today rarely be identified as the proximate cause or even a concurrent predominant cause.** "(加黑部分为笔者的强调)

4.7 赔付续运费用的排除情况

最后在协会货物条文(A)第12条明确说明"This Clause 12... shall be subject to the exclusions contained in Clauses 4,5,6 and 7"。至于协会货物条文第4~7条的列明除外风险在本书第八章有详细介绍,请参阅。这些被排除的列明风险包括有受保人的恶意行为、货物包装不足、货物内在缺陷、货方知情的船舶不适航不适货、战争风险、罢工风险等。例如,由于战争风险引起的航程终止,显然不是一切险的水险要负责续运费用。要负责的应该是另外加保的战争险,虽然已经解释过因为战争险的协会条文有一条受阻条文(Frustration Clause)而不会赔付,这等于受保人要自己承担。

其中要重复的是在航运低潮时,如在80年代大量的船东在航次进行中途倒闭以致去不了目的地港。显然,这是一种典型的航程终止(loss of adventure),原因可以算是船东或承运人的毁约(repudiation)。所以在一切险的保险合约下,保险人应该赔付续运费用。这方面也有先例的支持:London & Provincial Leather Processors v. Hudson (1939) 64 Ll. L. Rep. 352; Integrated Container Service Inc. v. British Traders Insurance Co. Ltd. (1984) 1 Lloyd's Rep. 154。London & Provincial Leather Processors v. Hudson先例的法律地位是如果保单中有一切险(all risks)条文,而因为承运人的倒闭不但导致了航次的延误,也导致了货物的损失,这种情况下保险人都要负责赔付。所以,货物续运费用的花费也可以在施救条文下得到赔付的说法应该是站的住脚的。

另在先例 Integrated Container Service Inc. v. British Traders Insurance Co. Ltd. (1984) 1 Lloyd's Rep. 154,案情涉及了一个集装箱租赁公司为他手中的集装箱投保了12个月的全损风险,保险合约中也有一条施救条文。1972年,受保人把一批集装箱租赁给一家名为Oyama的公司用来转租给船公司在远东使用。后来Oyama在1975年倒闭,它也没有为租进来的集装箱投保。这导致了受保人需要在亚洲各个港口去把集装箱运回 Oyama 的堆场(depots)才能收回所有的集装箱,否则就会丢失。这些行动导致费用的产生,受保人就向他投保的全损承保人以施救费用提出索赔。这在第一审与上诉庭获得支持,Everleigh 大法官这样说:

"At the beginning of the rescue operation some of the containers were in active use. Some lay on the quayside. Some were in warehouse. Port dues had been incurred in relation to some and warehouse charges were mounting in relation to others which thus became the subject of a lien for those dues and charges. The [受保人] had submitted details of their expenses to the [保险人] together with supporting invoices and other documents. Those details are set out in a schedule to the points of claim. They consist of payments made in respect of customs and storage charges in order to secure the release of containers; the cost of transshipment to the depot; the cost of removal from the [Oyama's] depots to the [受保人] depots; the traveling expenses of those engaged in the rescue work and legal fees for advice obtained from Japanese lawyers. The [保险人] admitted that the expenses were paid for the purpose of recovery of containers from the various locations referred to in the documents set out in the schedule.

The learned Official Referee (一审法官) accepted the [受保人] contention that the expenditure was necessarily incurred in order to prevent loss or damage to the containers in a situation to which the sue and labour clause of the policy applied."

在该先例中可以看到一切险也是承保倒闭的风险引起的损失,包括施救费用。虽然该保险合约并非协会货物条文(A)或类似的条文,但在上诉庭的争辩中涉及了有关把集装箱从 Oyama 的堆场转运去受保人堆场的费用,上诉庭看来还是把它与本段所讲的续运费用当作一回事,Dillon 大法官这样说:"This policy, however, is not an insurance on a voyage, where it may be justifiable... to claim under a sue and labour clause the expense of forwarding cargo to its contractual destination, even though the voyage had been abandoned at an interim port by the carrier."

已经介绍过这种事故在 80 年代很多而导致了大量损失,因为续运费用通常是不会便宜,搞不好会比原来的运费还要高。保险人也会感觉这种损失有商业损失的味道,就是安排付运的货方(CIF 卖方或者是 FOB 买方)没有谨慎寻找财务状况良好的船东,所以不愿意承担这部分损失的责任,这带来了一条除外风险的明示条文就是 4.6 条如下:

"In no case shall this insurance cover... loss damage or expense caused by insolvency or financial default of the owners managers charterers or operators of the vessel where, at the time of loading of the subject - matter insured on board the vessel, the Assured are aware, or in the ordinary course of business should be aware, that such insolvency or financial default could prevent the normal prosecution of the voyage.

This exclusion shall not apply where the contract of insurance has been assigned to the party claiming hereunder who has bought or agreed to buy the subject – matter insured in good faith under a binding contract. ”

上述第4.6条文的第二段针对的就是不影响无辜的买方，如果受到同样的影响。一个典型的情况会是中国的进口商以CIF或者CFR进口，但航次半途遇到这种情况导致航程终止。船舶虽然不是由中国买方所租用，但后果却要买方承担。因为在买方与卖方一开始就订下的买卖合约，一般海上运输的风险在货物越过船舷后就转移给了买方：Fragano v. Long (1825) 4 B & C 219。而船东的倒闭导致的航程终止，发生在风险转移之后，显然是买方应该承担的风险。这方面还可以节录《Benjamin's Sale of Goods》第六版之19 – 106段所说如下："In The 'Julia' [1949] A. C. 293 Lord Porter said that risk, under a c. i. f contract, 'generally passes on shipment or as from shipment.' The risk is thus commonly separated form property : the seller's obligation to cover the buyer by insurance from shipment is regarded as evidence of agreement to exclude the ordinary rule that risk passes with property. Lord Porter's statement contains two rules. Where the goods are sold and then shipped, the risk passes on shipment; but where they are already afloat at the time of sale it is more apposite to refer to the risk as having passed *as from* shipment. ”

除了风险转移外，还有个现实的问题，就是买方即使知道航次中途出了事故，也没有办法不对卖方支付CIF或者是CFR的货价。很大部分的买卖都是通过信用证进行支付，卖方只要提供给有关银行一套完整与没有不符点的付运单证（其中最重要的就是一套装船提单）就可以获得支付。这是买方根本没有办法阻止的现实情况，所以既然无可避免地支付货价，船东破产而导致航程终止的残局非要由买方来收拾，因为他才是有切身利益的。

顺便一提的是即使是买卖合约不涉及信用证的支付，在CIF或CFR这种属于单证买卖，只要卖方向买方提供付运单证，买方还是不能因为航次中途出了事故而拒绝支付。买方唯一的救济就是向毁约的船东索赔损失（但倒闭了的船东根本赔不起）或是向保险人索赔，而不是与卖方纠缠。这方面可以节录《Benjamin's Sale of Goods》第六版之19 – 077段所说如下："Just as the loss, destruction or enemy seizure of the goods after shipment does not discharge the seller from his obligation to tender documents, so these events do not relieve the buyer form his obligation to pay the price. The remedy of the buyer (if any) in such cases in against the carrier for breach of the contract of carriage, or against the underwriter on the policy of insurance. But the buyer is bound to pay the price on the tender of documents even though he has no claim either against the carrier, because the goods were lost through some cause for which the carrier was not responsible, or against the underwriter because they were lost by a peril not insured against. ”

所以，协会货物条文（A）看来是想对这种无辜蒙受损失的货方如上述所讲CIF或CFR的买方网开一面，说明4.6条文中规定的除外风险在这种情况是不适用的，只要买方在早前已是善意与订下一个有约束性的买卖合约，买下或同意买下这批货物。但如果不是善意或在知道出了事故后才订的合约（或者是倒签），就不包括了。例如，FOB 买方在出了事故后，明知道自己因为第 4.6 条而赔不到续运费用，就找一个友好公司订立一份 CIF 合约，让他作为“无辜”买方向保险人提出索赔。

最后一提的是在这种事故中，会有分不清的情况，如经济状况有问题的船东在中途港口出一点事情就借口扯皮，拒绝继续航程去目的地港，实际上想敲货方一笔钱资助完成航次。这种情况分不清到底是船东毁约（repudiation）或是真正的原因是经济困难（financial default），这就涉及事实的认定，看哪一个才是真正的近因。

5. 案件的介绍

5.1 案情

最后，笔者简单介绍一个实际处理的案件，其中有很多发生的事情都与本章上述所讲的各方面有关联。事件发生在二三年前，涉及一船价值高达 2 亿人民币的菜籽油从南美洲运去中国。该批货物是向著名的国际贸易商以 CFR 价格购买，所以船舶是由该贸易商以卖方的身份租进来的，但货物保险是由中国的买方所购买的，投保的是 PICC 保单的一切险。被租用的船舶是一艘希腊船东拥有的方便旗船，但船龄比较老，而且船舶状况不敢恭维。但这也是 CIF 或者 CFR 买卖的通病，因为风险越过船舷后就转移给了买方，海上运输的风险也就不在卖方。所以除非买卖合约有规定，如约束卖方租用船龄较低或某些船旗的船舶（但这种情况不多），卖方对船舶的状况一般不大关心。关心还是船舶的船期（能否配合备货与付运的日期）以及运费等租约的条件。另要一提的是卖方在菜籽油装船后不久就已经把所有的运费支付给了希腊船东，这也是 CIF 或者 CFR 买卖的惯常做法，因为有了一套预付运费提单才可以结汇。而且，CIF 或 CFR 的货价本身就包含了运费。船东在运费到付的情况下就会更加积极履行整个航次（The “Abt Rasha” (2000) 2 Lloyd’s Rep. 575），而运费预付的情况下该积极性就显然低很多。

该船舶在航次中途的南非开普敦附近，在天气不是很坏的情况下，船舵丢失了。这导致船东需要雇佣拖轮把该船舶拖去开普敦这个中途的避难港口。没了船舵，显然必须修妥才能继续去中国卸港的航程。船舶进了开普敦港不久，船东、船级社与船舶保险人各自所委任的验船师就上船作出检查并在当地作出调查，大约在一二个星期后认为船舶要在开普敦港修理，当地也可以作出修理，而修理的时间大概是 3 个月。

5.2 面对的问题

但问题有以下几点：

1. 船舶是满载，必须把菜籽油全部卸下或者部分卸下才可以进干坞，或者是在港口把船头压下船尾露出水面的情况下才可以修理并安装新的船舵。

2. 船舶估计在开普敦修理，包括等待船舵配件从生产商运到开普敦的时间，估计是3个月。

3. 中国买方希望菜籽油能够尽快运回中国，因为3个月的延误虽然不会令菜籽油变坏，但质量会下降而且会错过当时在中国很高的市场。

4. 船东很快就向货方宣告航次受阻，拒绝在修理船舵后续运去中国港口。这种心态可以理解，因为一大笔的运费已经落入囊中，刚好借这一机会摆脱剩下的租约履行责任。

5. 中国货方通过笔者向希腊船东施压，其中就是让货方代表的验船师上船检查。检查的目的显然就是确认船舶在南美开航时的适航状况，这也是为了将来向船东提出索赔与为了拒绝共同海损费用的分摊作出准备而需要做的调查取证。这方面请看本章第2.4.7.1.1段。船东一度不合作，但笔者以向开普敦法院申请上船检查的命令作为压力，结果逼迫船东就范。

6. 针对向船东提出索赔有关的损失，估计的金额很大，这是因为菜籽油本身的高价值与延误带来的利息损失与市场差价。但影响索赔能够成功到什么地步会有几方面的变数，一是减少船上菜籽油的损失，除了避免进一步的延误，更要避免延误导致的菜籽油损坏。二是该船舶可以根据船舶吨位限制责任，而这样做就会赔偿不足，特别是损失打大。三是船舶抵押给银行，而银行的抵押权比一般的货物索赔优先。但这个保留还是次要，因为船东有互保协会承担责任，恐怕很难把银行扯进来。

7. 该船舶还有另一批属于另一位货方的少量的菜籽油，数量大概是笔者客户所拥有的菜籽油的7%。这里涉及了两位不幸的买方怎样合作处理转运的问题与怎样分摊有关的费用与责任。

5.3　解决的办法与涉及的工作

这就带来以下的一些应对与大量工作：

1. 首先要说服中国的保险公司在一切险的保险合约下，要承担把这批菜籽油从南非开普敦转运到中国卸港的运费。因为希腊船东已经强硬地表示航程终止，而航程终止是承保的范围之一。不论希腊船东是对还是不对，反正租约与提单的受阻或是毁约，都无可避免地涉及了航程终止（loss of adventure）而需要续运/转运去目的地。所以，根据一切险的保险合约下的施救费用条文（Sue and Labour Clause）或/与续运费用条文（Forwarding Charges Clause），中国的保险公司都应该赔给中国的货方。这里涉及了多次的谈判，并需要取得中国法律针对这种情况的专家意见。但最终，中国保险公司只是部分赔偿了中国货方，而笔者觉得不对。有关这一课题请看本章第5段。

2. 在与中国保险公司的交涉中也涉及了保险合约不赔付延误带来的损失，而菜籽油作为一个容易腐烂的货物（perishable cargo），需要尽早转运回中国所涉及的费用被中国保险公司视为延误造成的损失。毕竟中国货方也希望尽早通过转运把菜籽油运回中国。但笔者坚决认为这不是延误的损失，主要或有效的近因是希腊船东拒绝续运造成航程终止(loss of adventure)。这在上述5.6段有介绍。

3. 由于中国保险公司起初的态度并不明朗，笔者代表货方向希腊船东施加压力。这就是逼希腊船东接受航次并没有受阻，他如果拒绝在修理后续运就是违约。笔者以合并进提单中租约内的伦敦仲裁相逼，但希腊船东态度非常强硬，可以说同样的压力加在日本或中国船东身上有更大的可能会管用。背后真正的目的就是如果船东接受租约或提单并没有受阻，为了不毁约，就继续有合约的责任完成航次，因为运费已经落入囊中了。这一来，整个做法就变成共同海损的做法，为了让船舶修理，必须安排菜籽油部分或全部从船上卸下并储存在岸上的油库。但估计这样做费用很高，所以就会以替代费用(substituted expense)的做法另租一艘船舶把整批的菜籽油运回中国。至于转运的运费(300万美元)由希腊船东先支付然后作为共同海损的费用让大家分摊。这方面请看本章的第2.4.5段。

4. 即使希腊船东肯继续航程(事实上他始终拒绝)，但不是通过以替代费用把货物转运的做法，而是存放在开普敦直到修理完毕再重新装上船舶继续航程，这可能不比由中国买方自己尽早安排转运有更大的好处。正如上述2.4.6段解释Bigham Clause的时候所提到，货物可以通过转运早一点到中国，而结果也是如此，笔者只是比航程本来所需要的时间多花了5个星期就将菜籽油运到了中国。而该希腊船东的船舶继续在开普敦停留2个多月后才修理完毕，继续航程要在之后才可以开始。这些延误除了导致市场差价，还有菜籽油的质量可能会受影响(虽然程度不能准确掌握)，更明确的就是避难港口的费用会多产生一大笔，也就是菜籽油的储存费用。这些都是共同海损的费用，中国买方与中国保险公司恐怕要分摊一大部分。

5. 由于菜籽油的价格比船舶的价格高很多，所以在共同海损理算，恐怕也是货方要分摊大部分。但对中国货方的好处是中国保险公司对赔付续运费用有保留，但对赔付共同海损的分摊就不像是有争议的余地。另一个好处就是不需要中国货方麻烦安排转运/续运，因为工作量不少，而且还要预付转运船舶的运费。这些工作是中国保险公司与贸易商的卖方都不肯插手/协助的。

6. 但最后还是中国的货方通过笔者把这整票的菜籽油转运回中国的，这里面涉及复杂与繁重的工作。其中包括：(1)在市场租船(这种适合装菜籽油的船舶不多，特别是在南非开普敦附近，因为那里并非菜籽油的惯常出口地。还有一个困难是中国货方作为承租人在国际市场没有知名度，所以一般船东不愿意出租，需要很大的说服与作出一些保证)。(2)谈判运费与空放奖金(ballast bonus)。(3)谈判其他的租约条文(包括装卸率、滞期费、开普敦装港是以船靠船装货、菜籽油在转运期间的加热等许多技术性/法律性问题)，(4)为中国买方作为承租人向互保协会投保承租人的责任风险。(5)其他许多的所谓租约后期工作(post - fixture work)，包括不断与转运船舶联络，与给予指示，签发提单，委任装卸港代理，与装卸港代理结算，在航次完毕后与转运的船东结算(其中包括滞期费的争议与最后的和解)。(6)租约以外也涉及说服中国保险公司,转运/续运过程继续受到一切险的承保。这总算在不久后得到确认,否则中国的买方还要另外投保或加保以避免夹在当中。当然在笔者看来,转运/续运过程仍然在一切险的承保范围内。

7. 还有其他的麻烦,就是租进来的转运/续运船舶(是一艘挪威船旗船况良好的船舶)到了开普敦并准备马上开始与希腊船东的船舶以“船靠船”的方式将菜籽油转装,与希腊船东说的一切安排突然之间被推翻,显然希腊船东想逼使中国货方放弃将来对他以不适航为由提出索赔。而推翻的理由主要就是针对一些共同海损分摊的手续,包括提供共同海损分摊的担保(General Average Guarantee)。本来中国保险公司已经通过伦敦的代理人向希腊船东作出担保,笔者以为再也不会节外生枝,但后来希腊船东否认曾经接受过这样的安排,而坚持要中国货方提供可以接受共同海损担保,否则将会继续行使对船上菜籽油的留置权。但这表示转运/续运船舶延误在开普敦等待装货,而每天的滞期费是一笔可观的数字。笔者最后通过南非法院作出命令要希腊船东卸货才总算解决问题,但已经带来了一段时间的延误。

8. 还有是已经提到的同一艘船舶有另一批菜籽油属于另外一个中国买方,可以说如果所有上述整套的工作只是把我们自己的货物转运,不理会该少量的货物,那该少量货物几乎无法救回,除了数量少,更重要的是该中国货方也不懂怎样做。结果笔者的客户就跟他们直接联络,最后达成协议,只要他们按比例承担转运运费就替他们安排好。本来笔者还建议客户在谈判时要求另外的中国买方也承担部分,包括笔者的费用以及其他许多的费用如代理费等,认为这样比较公平。笔者还准备了一份协议让客户与另外的中国买方签署。这个协议除了要求按比例承担转运运费外,还包括该批菜籽油的卸货率与怎样承担转运船舶的滞期费,在转运与最后卸货时如果发生货物短缺怎么分摊,替另外的中国买方安排转运不承担任何责任,包括在转运船舶发生货损货差,但不影响他们向该挪威船舶根据提单直接索赔等。

9. 当菜籽油从原来船舶上全部卸下来并顺利从开普敦转运/续运去中国港口,笔者对希腊船东可以说再也没有任何顾忌,而且手中已经搜集了证据能够表面证明船舶在南美装港开航时不适航。但笔者也不急于扣船取得担保,虽然向这种单船船东索赔,取得诉前担保绝对重要。不急的原因是该船舶修理长达3个月的时间,在这个期间船舶无处可逃。而在等待的期间,中国货方也与中国保险公司达成对转运/续运费用最后赔付多少的和解协议。而中国保险公司委任一家英国律师所准备行使代位求偿权向希腊船东索赔损失,这里就存在中国货方是否要参与与怎样分摊律师费的问题。显然,由于中国货方赔不足,所以有部分的转运/续运费用要向希腊船东索赔,而且更要加上的一笔损失是这一事故带来的延误造成的利息与货价损失。由于向希腊船东提出索赔(通过提单合并租约中的伦敦仲裁条文)只能有一个诉因,但这一诉因所要索赔的总金额包括了中国货方与中国保险公司的损失,如各占一半。所以谁作代表与怎样分摊诉讼费用就有了不同看法(这方面在本书第十三章第8段有详细介绍)。一个做法,也是笔者希望的做法,就是笔者代表中国货方向希腊船东提出伦敦仲裁,而索赔的总金额包括了中国货方的利益与中国保险公司的损失。根据英国的法律,中国保险公司代位求偿权限制在他赔付给中国货方的金额,而且他向希腊船东索赔也只能以中国货方的名义。但另一个做法就是伦敦仲裁交给英国保险公司所委任的英国律师所,这样中国货方损失的部分要与中国保险公司的损失一并交出给英国律师所向希腊船东索赔,并且按比例分摊诉讼费用,而笔者只能协助英国律师事务所。至于在开普敦法院向希腊船东的船舶扣船并向他背后的互保协会逼出一份诉前担保,数额是中国货方与中国保险公司利益的总和,这工作必须通过南非的律师,中国保险公司委托的伦敦律师或中国货方委托的笔者都无法代劳。

10. 在犹豫不决时,也就是船舶将修理完毕要开航找下一票生意时,美国华尔街引发的全球金融海啸令该船舶价值在一两个星期内降了2/3,从2000万美元以上降到不到800万美元,这导致了扣船能够取得的诉前担保也不足够赔付中国货方与中国保险公司总共的损失。中国货方大概对已经安全在中国把所有菜籽油收到很高兴,而且当时菜籽油在中国的市场价格相比世界市场不是太差,所以即时决定放弃向希腊船东的索赔。这一来,只剩下中国保险公司根据代位求偿权向船东提出索赔,而笔者的工作显然也必须告一段落。

11. 这是笔者近期很少处理的一个案件(因为笔者主要的工作是全职仲裁员,虽然笔者也多了有能力处理这种案件的助手,可以接受委任),涉及了本章所讲的大部分问题,所以就简单地介绍给大家,让大家看到实务中遇到这样的问题应该怎样处理。希望在看了本章节特别是该案例后能够给中国货方与保险公司的同仁一些启示。

第八章　除外风险

除外责任〔1〕

4　本保险概不承保：

4.1　可归咎于受保人的蓄意恶行的损失、损害或费用。

4.2　保险标的之正常渗漏、正常重量或体积损失、或正常磨损。

4.3　保险标的之包装或准备不足或不当而不能经受所保运送通常的事故所引起的损失、损害或费用，如果此种包装或准备是由受保人或其雇员实施的，或是在本保险责任开始前实施的（在本条文意义上，“包装”应视为包括集装箱内的积载，而受保人的雇员不包括独立承包商）。

4.4　保险标的之固有缺陷或性质引起的损失、损害或费用。

4.5　迟延造成的损失、损害或费用，即使该延迟是由承保风险引起的（但根据上述第2条支付的费用除外）。

4.6　因船舶的所有人、经理人、承租人或经营人的破产或经济困境产生的损失、损害或费用，如果在保险标的装上船舶时，受保人知道或在通常业务过程中应该知道，此种破产或经济困境可能阻止航次的正常执行。

如果保险合约已经转让给根据一个有约束力的合约已经善意购买或同意购买保险标的之根据本保险合约索赔的人，本除外条文对他不适用。

4.7　因使用原子或核裂变和/或聚变或其他类似反应或放射性力量或物质所制造的任何武器或装置直接或间接产生的或引起的损失、损害或费用。

5　5.1　本保险概不承保损失、损害或费用，如其起因于

5.1.1　船舶或驳船不适航或对保险标的之安全运输不适合，如果受保人在保险标的装载其上时对此种不适航或不适合有私谋。

5.1.2　集装箱或托盘对保险标的之安全运输不适合，如果装入或装上发生在本保险责任开始之前，或者是由受保人或其雇员实施的，而且他们在装载时对此种不适合有私谋。

5.2　如果保险合约已经转让给根据一个有约束力的合约已经善意购买或同意购买保险标的之根据本保险合约索赔的人，上述第5.1.1条规定的除外责任对他不适用。

---

〔1〕　见附录三第4～7条（EXCLUSIONS）。

5.3 保险人放弃载运保险标的到目的港的船舶不得违反默示适航保证或适运保证。

6 本保险概不承保损失、损害或费用,如其起因于

6.1 战争、内战、革命、造反、叛乱或由此引起的内乱或任何交战方之间的敌对行为。

6.2 捕获、扣押、扣留、拘禁或羁押(海盗除外)和此种行为引起的后果或进行此种行为的企图。

6.3 被遗弃的水雷、鱼雷、炸弹或其他被遗弃的战争武器。

7 本保险概不承保下列损失、损害或费用

7.1 罢工者、被迫停工工人,或参加工潮、暴动或民变的人员造成者。

7.2 罢工、停工、工潮、暴动或民变造成者。

7.3 恐怖行为造成者,恐怖行为是指任何人的行为,其代表或与任何组织有关联,此种组织诉诸武力或暴力,实施旨在颠覆或影响某政府的行动,不管该政府是否合法成立。

7.4 出于政治、伦理或宗教动机行事的任何人造成者。

协会货物条文(A)1/1/09之第4条是规定一切险不承保的各项风险或情况,包括第4.1条的蓄意恶行,第4.2条的一般性损耗,第4.3条的包装不足或不适带来的损失或损坏,第4.4条的内在缺陷或保险货物的本身性质所造成的损失或损坏,第4.5条的延误造成的损失或损坏,第4.6条的船东、船舶经理人、承租人或船舶营运人的清盘或经济不善带来的损失或损坏,第4.7条的战争武器或核爆炸直接或间接所造成的损失或损坏。第5条是船舶不适航或集装箱不适货。第6条是战争险除外。第7条是关于罢工险和恐怖活动险除外,内容较复杂且对恐怖活动有新的定义。第4条和第5条的修改反映保护善意的买方和保单受让人。

1. 第4.1条:受保人货方之蓄意恶行

协会货物条文(A)1/1/09之4.1条实际上是重复1906年《英国海上保险法》Section 55 (2)的规定,而且在1982年与2009年协会货物条文的文字上没有区别,如果涉及受保人货方的蓄意恶行(wilful misconduct)保险人不会作出赔付。协会货物条文加上这些在英国立法规定了的豁免是因为后者属于默示地位,这一来,在含有明示(第1条)约定承保一切险的保险合约中,解释起来分量不足。但如果把这些一切险中不承保的风险都以明示条文另外规定作为除外风险的话,法律地位就会很明确。

什么叫蓄意恶行在最近的一个案例 Thomas Cook v. Air Malta (1997) 2 Lloyd's Rep. 399 中作出定义,可以节录如下:"What does amount to wilful misconduct? A person willfully misconducts himself if he knows and appreciates that it is misconduct on his part in the circumstances to do or fail to do something and yet (a) intentionally does or fails or omits to do it or (b) persists in the act, failure or omission regardless of the consequences or (c) acts with reckless carelessness, not caring what the results of his carelessness may be. (A person acts with reckless carelessness if, aware of a risk that goods in his care may be lost or damaged, he deliberately goes ahead and takes the risk, when it is unreasonable in all the circumstances for him to do so)."(蓄意恶行第一种情况是故意,第二种情况是不顾后果的玩忽职守,第三种情况是严重的疏忽,如明知某行为会对货物造成风险还执意做并且在当时环境是完全不合理。)

至于较早的先例,如说明蓄意恶行并不等于疏忽或者是不小心,即使是到了十分严重的程度,而是要涉及受保人有意图的、蓄意的而且知道是错误的,才构成蓄意恶行。其中第一个要介绍的先例是 Beresford v. Royal Insurance Co. Ltd. (1938) AC 586,Atkin 勋爵说:"On ordinary principles of insurance law an assured cannot by his own deliberate act cause the event upon which the insurance money is payable. The insurers have not agreed to pay on that happening. The fire assured cannot recover if he intentionally burns down his house, nor a marine assured if he scuttles his ship, nor the life assured if the deliberately ends his owner life. This is not the result of public policy, but of the correct construction of the contract."

另要介绍的先例是 Horabin v. British Overseas Airways Corp (1952) 2 Lloyd's Rep. 450,Barry 大法官说:"Wilful misconduct, to put it most shortly, as it has often been put in the past, is misconduct to which the will is a party, and it is something which is wholly different in kind from mere negligence or carelessness, however gross that negligence or carelessness maybe. I think the first thing for you to remember is that the will must be a party to the misconduct, and not merely a party to the conduct or which complaint is made. Let us take this example: if the pilot of an aircraft knowingly does something which subsequently a jury find amounted to **misconduct, those facts alone do not show that he was guilty of wilful misconduct**. To establish wilful misconduct on the part of this imaginary pilot, it must be shown not only that he knowingly (and in that sense willfully) did the wrongful act, but also that when he did it he was aware that it was a wrongful act—that it is to say that he was aware that he was committing a misconduct. (这里大致上强调说要构成蓄意恶行是一定要有"明知故犯"的情节,仅是严重疏忽或不良行为本身是不足够。) It is of no avail to the plaintiff in this case to establish wilful misconduct unless he can also establish that the wilful misconduct caused the accident."

另一个先例是在 Rustenberg Platinum Mines Ltd. v. South African Airway (1977) 1 Lloyd's Rep. 564 中 Ackner 大法官说:"It is common ground that 'wilful misconduct' is far beyond negligence even gross or culpable negligence, and involves a person doing or omitting to do that which is not negligent but which he knows and appreciates is wrong, and is done or omitted regardless of the consequences, not caring what the result of his carelessness may be."(蓄意恶行是超出了疏忽,甚至是严重或有错的疏忽。蓄意恶行是一个人明知道做或者不做一些事情是错的,但仍然不顾后果,故意做或者不做。)

但对货方而言,由于他不涉及货物的运输,所以很难想象怎会有这种蓄意恶行的情况造成货物的损失或者损坏。这与两三百年前的情况不一样,船舶与货物有可能都是属于同一个人拥有(所以在劳合社标准 S. G 保单就是船货一起承保的),如果船东蓄意恶行,如凿沉船舶,就会是货物的损失也是由于蓄意恶行导致。

显然,海上货物的保险人要以蓄意恶行拒赔是十分不容易的,因为要证明作为受保人的货方的意图不仅是严重的疏忽或者是不小心。所以,有个别情况是把受保人的疏忽或者不小心也要作为一个拒赔的理由的话,就另需要有条文针对,这可举第5.1.2 条,主要针对的是集装箱不适合有关货物的运输,而堆箱的工作是由受保人或者他的雇员负责。在这种情况下,只要他们知道并且私谋(视而不见)有关的集装箱是不适货的话,保险人也不需要赔偿。换言之,在程度上会是达不到蓄意恶行而仅仅是严重的疏忽,毕竟证明意图并不是容易的事。这种情况会有很多,如针对易腐的货物,明知道装载的集装箱不能达到适当的温度,又或者是明知道集装箱有一个洞,可是照样堆货等。

也会有个别情况可以证明受保人的蓄意恶行,如明知道货物有缺陷(包括明知道货物在正常运输中会发生腐烂,如在本书第三章3.7 段所讲的情况),但还是付运。这可节录先例 National Oilwell (UK) Limited v. Davy Offshore Limited (1993) 2 Lloyd's Rep. 582,Colman 大法官说:"When one comes to investigate the particulars of wilful misconduct pleaded by DOL(该先例中的保险人) it is quite clear that they have adequately set out a factual basis upon which a plea of wilful misconduct can be founded. What is pleaded is that NOW (该先例中的受保人) knowingly delivered defective equipment and that it is to be inferred from the pleaded facts that they also knew that such supply was liable to cause substantial loss or damage of the kind pleaded, namely insured loss or damage. If those facts were proved at the trail, wilful misconduct might well be sufficiently established because the court would be entitled to infer either that NOW deliberately caused an insured loss or that they were recklessly indifferent as to whether their conduct brought about such a loss."

即使谈不上是蓄意恶行,也有先例判是受保人自愿的行为(voluntary act)导致了可以预见的损失或损坏,保险人也可以拒绝赔付。原因是受保人自愿的行为导致可以预见的损失或损坏就谈不上是意外事件(fortuitous)。在先例 The "Wondrous" (1991)1 Lloyd's Rep. 400,该船舶租给了伊朗德黑兰的公司在伊朗装一船的糖浆去欧洲,由于没办法提供足够货物而造成严重的延误,导致船舶最后在伊朗的 Bandar Abbas 港停留了1年以上,变成死船才被拖离该港。本来在租约中有滞期费的约定,但承租人没有支付1毛钱。换言之,这一租约对船东来讲是灾难性的后果。期间,由于船东欠下了港口使费,而船东因为与承租人的争议而拒绝支付,这导致船舶根据伊朗法律被海关当局扣留(detain)。该船舶投保了战争与罢工险,承保风险之一就是船舶被扣留(peril of detainment)。但Hobhouse大法官判扣留的近因是船东自己违反了伊朗法律没有支付欠下的港口使费,也提到只是指出有政府当局的扣留并不足够可以要保险人负责赔付,而要进一步证明是意外,说:"... it was still necessary for the claimants to show that the detention was fortuitous. How to characterize the element of fortuity in this context is not easy. If the owners had asked themselves at the time of placing the cover or at the time of making the charter-party whether detention for any substantial period after loading a cargo at Bandar Abbas was to be anticipated or likely to occur in the ordinary course, they would have correctly answered that it was not. But, on the other hand where a situation comes about as a result of the voluntary conduct of the assured, it would not normally be described as fortuitous. It did not happen by chance but by the choice of the assured. Put another way, it would be in the ordinary course that, if the owners of the vessel do not pay the port dues for which they are liable to the port authority in respect of the stay of the vessel in that port (or provide acceptable security), the vessel will not be cleared. For the purposes of the law of insurance, in the absence of an express agreement to the contrary, a policy should not be construed as covering the ordinary consequences of voluntary conduct of the assured arising out of the ordinary incidents of trading; it is not a risk."

这种情况对海上货物运输保险也会有关系,如在协会货物条文(一切险),普通法认为破产倒闭引起的货物损失(不论是被抛弃、留置或拍卖)也是被承保。但如果货物的留置或拍卖是由于受保人的货物自愿行动所引起,如没有支付进口国家的关税,或是支付给承运人运费或其他欠下的款项,最终导致了货物的损失,就会面对先例The"Wondrous"中类似的结果。

2. 第4.2条:正常渗漏、正常的短量或正常磨损

协会货物条文(A)1/1/09之4.2条不承保这种所谓的"风险"就是因为它会是在海上运输途中几乎无可避免或肯定会发生而造成货损货差。有关正常渗漏与正常的短量的先例在本书第六章第3段有详细的介绍,不再重复。只说是这些除外的风险也是在1906年《英国海上保险法》Section 55 (2)(c)有规定。但该立法条文是有这样的字眼"unless the policy otherwise provides",这表示可以通过保险合约的明示条文来改变这种默示的法律地位。而这种做法也经常有,如在本书第六章第3.1、3.2与3.4段中分别介绍的先例:Dodwell & Co. Limited v. British Dominions General Insurance Company Limited (1955) 2 Lloyd's Rep. 391;Maigen & Co. v. National Benefit Assurance Company (1922) 10 Lloyd's. Rep. 30;Coven SPA v. Hong Kong Chinese Insurance Co. (1998) EWCA Civ 1573。这些案例也显示了即使对正常渗漏、正常的短量的风险进行了加保,通常能够被承保的也只是那些有可能发生或不发生的灰色地带(grey area):Soya G. m. b. H. v. White (1983) 1 Lloyd's Rep. 122。而针对肯定会发生的损失,要被承保就要在保险合约中用最清楚明确不会有第二种解释的文字才可以。正如Clarke大法官在先例Coven SpA v. Hong Kong Chinese Insurance Co. (1999) Lloyd's Rep. IR 565 (CA) 所说:"I accept that it would be possible to insure against a measurement error and that there may indeed be commercial reasons why a receiver might want such cover, but it would be a most unusual type of marine cargo cover and clear terms would be required to effect it. This was essentially a marine cargo policy against loss of and damage to cargo..."(Clarke大法官接受是可以针对测量错误造成货物短缺投保,但这会是一种非常不寻常的海上货物运输保险,并且合约条文需要用非常清楚明确的文字。)

测量错误造成货物短缺的情况(paper loss)在很多货物会发生,如原油或重油的海上运输。可以说这种货物或多或少地都会有短量,因为并不是船舱里的每一滴油都可以卸到岸上去。固定航线上的原油运输通常都会有一个固定比例的短量,这甚至会是测量错误,如在装港测量的数字较实际重量高一点,而在卸港测量的数字较实际重量低一点。两者(提单数字与收货数字)一比较就有短量,但实际上短量的货物根本不存在。

但是短量也可能会是其他原因,如卸港当时气温太低、船长没有在到达卸港前把船上原油充分加热,船上油泵问题或船员疏忽等原因,以至于原油不能完全卸下,这种短量就显然是风险了。

至于除外风险的正常磨损,这与货物保险关系非常小,因为海上货物运输的承保期限不会太长。期间不大可能造成正常磨损的损失。正常磨损在海上保险主要是会发生在船舶的定期保险,由于承保的时间比较长,老船就会有正常磨损作为损失的近因。如先例Wadsworth Lighterage & Coaling Company Limited v. Sea Insurance Limited (1929) 34 Lloyd's Rep. 285,案情涉及一艘50年船龄的木制驳船在好天气的情况下沉没。有关海上货物运输保险的案例非常罕见,如果有货物生锈或严重磨损向保险人要求赔付,虽然在短短的海上运输不会造成正常磨损(这是拒赔理由),但保险人会有其他的拒赔理由,如这种情况很可能发生在一些"二手货"或者存放在发货人仓库很长时间才付运的"老货"。而这种情况,是受保人在投保时应该向保险人披露的:Berger and Light Diffusesrs Pty Ltd. v. Pollock (1973) 2 Lloyd's Rep. 442。

3. 第4.3条:包装不足或不适带来的损失或损坏

针对这一方面,先节录1982年协会货物条文第4.3条,以便读者与2009年相应条文(本章开头有节录)可作出比较:"Loss damage or expense caused by insufficiency or unsuitability of packing or preparation of the subject-matter insured (for the purpose of this Clause 4.3 'packing' shall be deemed to include stowage in a container or liftvan but only when such stowage is carried out prior to attachment of this insurance or by the Assured or their servants)."

接下来详细分析该项的除外风险。

3.1　包装是否属于被承保的保险标的

包装通常会被视为保险标的(subject-matter insured),毕竟很多时候保险的标的会有说明货物的包装,如袋装水泥(bagged cement)。所以,如果货物本身没有损坏而只是包装有损坏,保险人也要负责赔偿。在 Brown Bros v. Fleming (1902) 7 Com Cas 245,案情涉及从苏格兰装运一批 228 盒威士忌酒去新加坡,结果威士忌酒本身没有损坏,但包装包括酒的标签与瓶塞都受到损坏。这被判是属于保险标的,Bingham 大法官说:"the straw in which the bottles were packed and the labels upon the bottles [were] part of the subject-matter insured just as [were] the bottles and corks."

包装不被包括在保险标的的情况就是保险合约没有说明,换言之,这还是一个解释保险合约的问题:Vacuum Oil Co. v. Union Insurance Society of Canton Ltd. (1925) 24 Lloyd's Rep. 188。

虽然货物包装通常会被视为保险标的,但要小心的是,如果包装本身有缺陷,这自然变为货物的内在缺陷,就会带来保险人拒赔,而根据就是 1906 年《英国海上保险法》Section 55 (2)(c)的规定,即货物的内在缺陷是不承保的。这里的默示地位可看先例:Berk (FW) & Co. Ltd. v. Style (1956) 1 QB 180;Gee & Garnham Ltd. v. Whittall (1955) 2 Lloyd's Rep. 562;Soya GmbH v. White (1982) 1 Lloyd's Rep. 136 之 149 页。

在 2009 年协会货物条文的本条,可以说只是以明示条文重复说包装如果是不足或者是不适的话就会被排除在 2009 年条文的一切险承保范围外。所以在 1982 年协会货物条文首次有了本条。

3.2　什么是包装与准备

这条文明示说明一切险是不赔付由于不足够或不适合的包装导致的损坏。另也说明不赔付由于对货物不足够或不适合的准备工作所导致的损坏。包装就是给货物加上另外一层,以防止在运输途中因为搬运、碰撞或磨损而导致的货损。

包装是不包括在船舱内装货或堆货,这些作业如果有缺陷的话在一切险条文还是会对损失或者损坏承保的。这里可举 Helicopter Resources Pty Ltd. v. Sun Alliance Australia Ltd. (The Icebird) (1991) 312 MLN, Ormiston 大法官说:"to those steps which are necessary to prepare the cargo for the loading process, not to the very acts which result in the cargo being stowed on board."

但有了集装箱运输之后,如果把货物堆装在一个集装箱内,就有点说不清这到底是属于货物在船舱内堆装还是给货物的包装。如果把集装箱认为就是货物的包装,就会有情况是集装箱有缺陷如漏水。也会是集装箱货物堆装不适当,如堆装不好或是冷藏的温度不够。而上述条文也明确说明把货物堆装在集装箱或卡车也算是包装。更会有复杂的情况是集装箱的堆装由货方/发货人自己处理,也会是在开始付运后由货物代理人处理,特别是在要拼货的情况下。

准备货物付运工作接近包装,但也并非是肉眼看得见的货物包装。例如,为了防止生锈而涂上抑制剂(inhibitor),或是为了防止鱼粉在航次中发生自燃而在付运前作防氧化处理(anti-oxidant treatment)。反正,两种工作没有做好的话都会导致货物在海上运输途中受到损坏。但情况只是在风险开始生效前就已经发生或者这种堆装是由受保人的货方或者是他的雇员所处理。这里可以节录澳大利亚的先例 Helicopter Resources Pty Ltd. v. Sun Alliance Australia Ltd. (The Icebird) (1991) 312 MLN 中, Ormiston 大法官对这两种操作的描述:"The word 'packing' should otherwise be confined to the placing of an outer covering over the cargo or the placing of the cargo in a box or a similar container specifically designed for the transportation of that cargo... The word 'preparation' in sub-clause 4.3 is clearly wider in its connotation but it is also directed to those steps taken to make an item ready for transportation before it is taken and placed on board the vessel, in the course of the process of loading and stowing the cargo. Whereas the word 'packing' may be confined to the placing of goods in some form of outer covering, whether peculiar to the item shipped or of a more general kind, the word 'preparation' contemplates that there may be other acts which may be necessary to prepare cargo for loading and stowing on board a vessel... The removal, adjustment and securing of some mechanical part may be required for an item to be shipped 'in bulk' and there are many and various other ways in which cargo is prepared for transportation without it being packed. But in each case the sub-clause is directed to those acts done before the cargo is loaded and stowed on board."

另有关包装与准备货物作出运输的重要性也在先例 Mayban General Assurance Bhd v. Alstom Power Plants Ltd. (2004) 2 Lloyd's Rep. 609 中有提到,Moore-Bick 大法官这样说:"In many cases the ability of the goods to withstand the incidents of the voyage will depend on the extent to which they are protected by packing."但这被后来的上诉庭在先例 Global Process System Inc & Anor v. Syarikat Takaful Malaysia Berhad (2009) EWHC 367 (Comm)推翻,这在本章4.3段有详细介绍。

3.3 包装或准备的程度

合理的要求就是对货物的包装或准备程度达到应该能够应付将要进行航次中通常可以预见的事情与天气,这也是普通法的地位。这里可以节录 Mayban General Assurance Bhd v. Alstom Power Plants Ltd. (2004) 2 Lloyd's Rep. 609 中,Moore-Bick 大法官这样说:"This is a matter which is expressly covered by clause 4.3 of the Institute Cargo Clauses, but inadequate packing, where packing is required to enable the goods to withstand the ordinary incidents of the voyage, can properly be regarded as an aspect of inherent vice. The insurer is entitled to assume that the goods as presented for shipment are packed in a way that will enable them to withstand the ordinary incidents of carriage and, unless he expressly agrees otherwise, does not accept the risk of loss caused by inadequate packing. For some kinds of goods packing may extend to bracing necessary to prevent the movement of internal parts."

这一普通法默示的地位适用在1982年的协会货物条文,因为1982年的版本没有针对货物包装的程度的明示规定,2009年的协会货物条文则明确说明是要"withstand the ordinary incidents of the insured transit."

3.4　什么时间包装或准备以及由谁操作

绝大部分的情况,甚至是所有通常的情况,货物是在付运前进行包装或准备,这也是在保险合约承保的风险还没有生效前(risks have not yet been attached)。这些操作是由货方或者他的雇员进行,也会是由作为独立第三人的承包商(如货代)进行包装。但保险人不会理会或作出区分,反正包装或准备有缺陷都会被认为是货物的内在缺陷,另也在1982年的条文中第一句说明是不属于承保的范围。

但在集装箱运输普及之后,就在包装方面带来了一个新的课题。已经提到过在集装箱中堆放货物是属于"packing"的一种,而在集装箱中堆放货物也不一定发生在保险合约承保的风险还没有生效前,而堆放的人也不一定是货方或者他的雇员。首先,集装箱的堆放还是会发生在保险合约承保的风险还没有生效前,也就是货方在他自己的仓库中将货物装箱,然后让承运人/货运代理人(freight-forward)将整个集装箱拉走。但也有很多情况是货运代理人把货物从多个货方手中接过来,然后在货运站拼箱。更会有情况是在中国内陆的某个城市如西安或重庆就把货物从货方手中接过来,通过卡车或火车将货物运到深圳或上海后才装箱。可以说在后两种情况,堆装集装箱的时间是在保险合约承保的风险已经生效后。而且,堆装到底是否足够与适当往往也不是受保人的货方的控制。所以对保险人而言,这一方面的问题在一切险是不针对或试图把它排除在承保范围外。保险人所想针对的就是货方在自己的仓库内将货物装箱的问题,正如已经介绍过的在1982年的协会货物条文中保险人是不会关心这些问题的,因为只要是货物包装有缺陷就一律不赔。

这对货方不利的地方是堆装集装箱如果是由第三者如货运代理人或者是独立承包商进行,而且在风险开始生效前,货物出事的话就不能得到赔付。而且在现实中,通常货方是交给独立承包商去操作。这导致一些做法就是以经纪人条文(broker's clause)作为附加条文加保,要是包装或准备工作不是由货方或他的雇员处理,就属于承保的范围。据说,对1982年条文不满意的人士不少,如日本保险市场就拒绝接受,虽然他们一直跟从英国海上货物保险的做法。

这导致了在2009年协会货物条文在这方面的重大改变。将1982年与2009年协会货物条文的相关内容进行对比,就可以发现1982年版本中是说只要损失是由于把货物堆装在集装箱或卡车的操作以及对货物的准备不足够/不适合而造成,则这些损失都不在承保的范围内。而2009年的版本中则规定只有在这些把货物堆装在集装箱或卡车操作是在风险生效前由受保人或其雇员进行的时候,所造成的损失或损坏才不在承保的范围内。在这种情况,保险人的眼中看来是等于货物本身有内在缺陷,所以不愿意承保。

但如果这些操作是由独立第三人的承包商进行,即使有缺陷,所造成的损失也是在承保的范围内。在这一方面,保险人显然是在2009年的版本中作出了让步。而保险人担心的是,作为受保人的货方为了省钱,雇佣一些没有资格与经验不足但却收费便宜的独立承包商操作而增加货损风险。就这种危险而言,保险人唯一的保障就是如果货方一贯有这样的做法,他作为受保人就应该在投保时将这个做法自动披露给保险人,否则后者可以回避保险赔付责任。

在2009年协会货物条文也不会有争议,如在付运前仓库内的堆放集装箱,虽然操作的人是货物代理人或独立承包商,但受到作为受保人的货方控制与指示。这一来,保险人就可能争辩说,此种情况下相当于是由受保人进行的包装与准备的操作。

3.5　什么是有效的近因:包装不足够与海上风险

在运输途中遇到坏天气而造成货损就有可能会带来这方面的争议,即到底货损是由包装不足够导致还是由航次中的海上风险所导致。有时候是哪一个作为有效的近因十分明确,如海上是相对风平浪静而还是发生了货损,显然包装不足才是有效的近因。但如果航次中遇上的天气是相对恶劣,甚至是不可预见的恶劣,但还是不能说死一定造成货损,这种情况下就会产生争议,因为海上风险是承保的范围,而包装缺陷则不属于。在 Mayban General Assurance Bhd v. Alstom Power Plants Ltd. (2004) 2 Lloyd's Rep. 609 中,案情是有关一座大型电力变压器(Electrical Transformer)的海上运输。货物从利物浦运去马来西亚,保险合约是1982年一切险条文,途中由于风浪的影响导致机器的接合处(joint)受到损坏。虽然曾经遇到的风浪是8级风或以上,但在该条航线尤其是在冬天的时候这种风浪是可以预见的。Moore-Bick 大法官说:

"It was not suggested that the damage during the course of the voyage was inevitable, and indeed such evidence as there is a previous successful shipment of similar times of transformers makes it clear that it was not, but it does not follow that the damage was proximately caused by an external fortuitous event. The point is well illustrated by the case of Noten BV v. Harding (1990) 2 Lloyd's Rep. 283 which concerned a consignment of leather glove damaged by moisture that had evaporated from the goods and condensed on the vessel's steelwork before dropping onto them causing them to become mouldy and mildewed. Damages caused in that way was not inevitable, as previous successful shipment of similar goods demonstrated, but when it did occur it was properly to be regarded as having been caused by the nature of the goods themselves rather than by an external cause. The case also provides a useful reminder that issues of causation should normally be determined by applying common sense rather than too refined an analysis.

It was common ground that the immediate cause of the damage to the transformer in the present case was the violent movement of the vessel due to the actions of the wind and sea. These in themselves were certainly events of a fortuitous nature and they were external to the cargo, but were they the real cause of the loss? The action of the winds and waves is, of course, an inevitable incident of any voyage and is therefore a hazard to which all goods carried by sea are necessarily exposed. Goods tendered for shipment must therefore be capable of withstanding the forces that they can ordinarily be expected to encounter in the course of the voyage and these may vary greatly depending on the route and the time of year. In a case such as the present, therefore, the competing causes, namely, perils of the sea and inherent vice, are to a large extent opposite sides of the same coin. **If the conditions encountered by the vessel were more severe than could reasonably have been expected, it is likely that the loss will have been caused by perils of the sea (though even then there might be evidence that the goods would have suffered the same degree of damage under normal conditions). If, however, the conditions encountered by the vessel were no more severe than could reasonably have been expected, the conclusion must be that the real cause of the loss was the inherent inability of the goods to withstand the ordinary incidents of the voyage.**"（这里其实是针对寻找货物损坏的近因，根据常识就可以推理如果航次遇到的天气比合理估计要坏，就有可能这个损失是海上风险造成。但如果航次遇到的天气并不比合理估计坏，就可以得出结论是货损的真正原因是货物内部问题，导致它根本不能承受航次估计会遇到的坏天气。）

至于判决保险人不必赔付，Moore-Bick 大法官说："In the light of the evidence as a whole I am satisfied the loss in the present case was caused by the inability of the transformer to withstand the ordinary conditions of the voyage rather than by the occurrence of conditions which it could not reasonably have been expected to encounter. It follows that the insurers are not liable to indemnify Alstom（受保人）in respect of the damage it suffered."

本条文也很清楚写明不承保的包装本身有缺陷只限制在两种情况：一种情况是由受保人自己或者是他的雇员负责，这里有的可能性就是他自己的疏忽或者是不小心造成。而这也只会发生在 CIF 的发货人，因为他才是卖方而且他才是投保的人。另一种情况是在风险生效前（开始货物运输前，如离开卖方的仓库装上卡车或火车），就已经存在包装本身有缺陷的问题，这就不管包装缺陷是否是由受保人或者他的雇员负责。只在这两种情况下出现包装有缺陷的问题，保险人才不负责赔付。至于还会有什么包装本身有缺陷造成货物损失或损坏，但保险人要作出赔付的情况，笔者可以想到的是，如在海上运输途中遇上事故，导致了船长要对受影响的货物特别处理,如重新包装后才能继续运输到目的地,这一来,如果包装有缺陷而造成新的或更严重的损坏,是被承保的。针对这方面可以举一个案件来说明,它是有关一批包装了的货物二氧化钛(titanium dioxide)。它在岸上的运输终结后,在装上船舶前要在仓库内把它放到货盘(pallet)上,然后再用叉车堆放在集装箱内。但问题出在货盘的木材潮湿,这导致了最后装在密不通风的集装箱内发潮而引起货物的损坏。幸亏这一个把货物放到货盘的工作是货方交由独立承包商负责,他不属于货方的雇员,所以最后获得赔付。但如果这一个把货物放到货盘的工作是在离开仓库前已经做好,特别是由作为受保人的货方自己负责,这样的话就赔不到了。

相比2009年条文,除了把已经过时的"仆人"改为"雇员"外,也在最后的一句话(括号里)说明独立承包商(independent contractors)并不属于受保人的雇员。另在2009年条文,也把1982年条文中的一个模糊的措辞"lift-van"(升降货车)删除。最后一个改变是规定了什么叫"足够"与"合适"的包装,就是包装本身必须足以承受一般被承保的海上运输事故(To withstand the ordinary incidents of the insured transit)。这就表示要看怎样的运输(岸上与海上)与需要一些什么准备,包装就应该达到怎样的程度。这种争议在 Mayban General Assurance Bhd v. Alstom Power Plants Ltd. (2004) 2 Lloyd's Rep. 609 中有针对,Moore-Bick 大法官认为,虽然该损坏不是必然会发生,但如果发生是由于货物本身如包装不足以面对这些一般性的与可以预见的海上运输风险的话,保险人就不需要作出赔付,即使保的是一切险:"In many cases the ability of the goods to withstand the incidents of the voyage will depend on the extent to which they are protected by packing. This is a matter which is expressly covered by Cl. 4.3 of the Institute Cargo Clauses, but inadequate packing, where packing is required to enable the goods to withstand the ordinary incidents of the voyage, can probably be regarded as an aspect of inherent vice. The insurer is entitled to assume that the goods as presented for shipment are packed in a way that will enable them to withstand the ordinary incident of carriage and, unless he expressly agreed otherwise, does not accept the risks of loss caused by inadequate packing. For some kinds of goods packing may extend to bracing necessary to prevent the movement of internal parts."

4. 第4.4条:固有缺陷或保险货物的本质所造成的损失或损坏

这一条在2009年协会货物条文没有作出什么改变,而该明示条文实际上也重复了1906年《英国海上保险法》第55(2)(c)的规定。

4.1 什么是固有缺陷

固有缺陷的定义 Sumner 勋爵在先例 British & Foreign Marine Insurance Company

Ltd. v. Gaunt (1921) 2 AC 41 中这样说:"A loss by inherent vice is one which is proximately caused by the natural behavior of the subject-matter insured, being what it is, in the circumstances in which it was expected to be carried."

另在 Soya GmbH v. White (1983) 1 Lloyd's Rep. 122 中,Diplock 勋爵这样说:"This phrase (generally shortened to 'inherent vice') where it is used in s. 55(2)(c) refers to a peril by which a loss is proximately caused; it is not descriptive of the loss itself. It means the risk of deterioration of the goods shipped as a result of their natural behaviour in the ordinary course of the contemplated voyage without the intervention of any fortuitous external accident or casualty."(固有缺陷造成的损坏近因是货物本身在航次中出现的自然变化,而没有任何外来的意外影响/干预。)

通常而言,"缺陷"是指内部,但带来的后果也就是造成的损坏,经常会有外来的因素促成,如天气:Global Process Systems Inc v. Syarikat Takaful Malaysia Berhad (2009) EWHC 637 (Comm), para. 102。货物固有缺陷的一些典型例子如下:(1)水果腐烂(fruit becoming rotten-internal decomposition);(2)面粉发热(flour heating);(3)酒变酸(wine turning sour);(4)煤的发热与自燃(coal heating and spontaneous combustion);(5)大豆发热(heating of soya bean);(6)鱼褪色(discloration of fish):Albacora SRL v. Westcott & Lawrence Line Ltd. (1966) 2 Lloyd's Rep. 53;(7)堆装在集装箱内的货物受潮(moisture damage carried by container):TM Noten BV v. Harding (1990) 2 Lloyd's Rep. 283。

反正在保险合约没有另外明示规定的情况下,由于固有缺陷或货物本质造成的损失或损坏保险人是不负责赔付的,不论这是肯定会发生的后果(certainty)或是意外的(fortuitous)的后果。这一点 Moore-Bick 大法官在 Mayban General Assurance Bhd v. Alstom Power Plants Ltd. (2004) 2 Lloyd's Rep. 609 中说一切险也不承保货物的固有缺陷,不论是肯定还是意外的("whether that loss was bound to occur or was fortuitous"),但这一说法被后来一个上诉庭判例 Global Process System Inc & Anor v. Syarikat Takaful Malaysia Berhad (2009) EWHC 367 (Comm)认为太广泛,这方面会在稍后 4.3 段详论。

1906 年《英国海上保险法》说明保险合约可以另外同意,毕竟这不涉及非法或是违反公共政策。所以,已经介绍过的 Soya G. m. b. H. v. White (1983) 1 Lloyd's Rep. 122 先例,它涉及了大豆货物投保了 HSSC 险,这就是典型的例子投保固有缺陷或货物本质所造成的损失或损坏。但正如所介绍的那样,即使这样加保,保险人要赔付的也只是意外的损失或损坏,也就是在灰色地带可能发生的货损,而不是肯定会发生的后果,这在本书第六章第 3.5 段有详细介绍。当然,如果不加保的话,就是两种情况都不能获得赔付或会有更大的争议性。

4.2 货物受潮是否是固有缺陷

货物受潮在集装箱运输出现之前就已经常发生,特别是一些货物本身就有水分与容易吸收空气中所含水分的"wet cargo"(如茶叶、烟草、皮革、oil cake 等),如果遇上了高温与潮湿的天气在装港与海上运输途中,就会释放潮气并会与冷空气接触冷凝成水滴滴在货物上造成损坏。这种情况可以在一定程度上避免或减少,如果在堆装货物的时候有足够的垫仓物料,将 wet cargo 与 dry cargo 隔离与航程中好好的通风。有了集装箱运输后,这种问题与船艺已经是过时,但还是会有货物在集装箱内受潮是否是固有缺陷的问题。

受潮是否是属于一个意外风险是有争议,因为潮湿的天气并不能算是意外或者风险。首先要介绍的先例是 Whiting v. New Zealand Insurance Company Ltd. (1932) 44 Lloyd's Rep. 179,案情涉及一票纸制的帽子从日本运去伦敦。这种货物的海上运输已经维持了 20 年都没有什么问题,但后来就开始发生货损,帽子到了伦敦发觉因为受潮而发霉。有关的保险合约所承保的列明风险包括了海上风险(这里应该是咸水)与淡水(这里是指雨水将货物淋湿)。根据提供的证据,英国法院认为是货物在日本装港码头等待装船时受潮,并认为保险人应该赔付。Roche 大法官认为只要受潮是"来自外来原因"(came from an outside source),就应该赔付,说:"Whatever the cause for the mould I am satisfied that it was an external cause. It is suggested that it might have been moist atmosphere. If it was that I think it would not be a matter which would render the [保险人] liable. Moist atmosphere is not an accident or peril that is covered. It is more or less a natural test or incident which the goods have to suffer and which the underwriter has not insured against... I think there was wet on the quay which affected these cases and from the cases went into the goods themselves in the form of moisture. I do not mean in the form of running water. The wet which affected the cases would set up that moist atmosphere which is shown to encourage the growth of this fungus, mould. Moisture of that sort originated in most of the cases through fresh water. Standing in pools on the quay is a peril which is insured against. Accordingly, I hold that the [保险人] are liable for damage occasioned by that cause."

接下去要介绍的先例就是 C. T. Bowring & Co. Ltd. v. Amsterdam London Insurance Co. Ltd. (1930) 36 Lloyd's Rep. 309,案情涉及花生从中国运到欧洲,但在卸货的时候发现货物发热(heating)与受潮(sweating)。有关的货物保险承保由于外来原因所造成的发热与受潮(To pay average and/or damage from sweating and/or heating when resulted from external cause)。受保人的货方在这种列明风险的保险合约是要证明货物的损坏是来自外来原因,但针对发热并不成功,因为英国法院判发热的损坏部分是由于花生本身的原因造成。可是针对受潮部分的货物损坏,英国法院认定受潮是来自船舱出汗(潮气在接触到船舱的钢板后冷凝),这是外来因素。Wright 大法官这样说:"The external cause, to my mind, is the moisture which condenses on the ship's side or on the ship's beams. Where that moisture comes from it is impossible to say. It may come from the moist air which comes down the ventilators in the tropics; it may come from ordinary condensation, precipitation of the moisture in the air, when there are alternations of heat and cold, but wherever it comes from it is moisture; it is water - sweat water it is called sometimes. **It is impossible to trace the original of that sweat water to the goods in question here. In any case, the sweat water has gone, as it were, into the universe on its own, even if it has come from those particular goods that are insured. It has set up a life of its own and has achieved an identity of its own**; and I think it has merited the appellation of an external cause whether the sweat water, which I take it is forming inevitably in every ship on all these voyages, happens to drop on any particular bag or on any of the assured bags. To what extent it happens to drip on those bags is, I think, fortuitous, and a matter of chance (using that word broadly) and a casualty. "(加黑部分是笔者的强调,意思是说导致船舱出汗的潮气来源是没有办法知道的,而就算是来自受保的货物本身,这也再在冷凝后有了自己的生命,再损坏某一些货物就是一个外来的原因。)

货物受潮到了集装箱运输后,就有了先例 TM Noten BV v. Harding (1990) 2 Lloyd's Rep. 283,案情涉及一票货物(工业用皮手套),堆装在集装箱内从印度运往荷兰鹿特丹,但在卸货时发现货物严重受潮与发霉。在一审,认定的事实是潮气来自手套本身,后在集装箱壁上冷凝后落在手套上造成损坏。所以,一审的 Philips 大法官根据先例 C. T. Bowring & Co. Ltd. v. Amsterdam London Insurance Co. Ltd. (1930) 36 Lloyd's Rep. 309 判是外来原因造成货损,而不是手套本身的固有缺陷造成。但这在上诉庭被推翻,其中 Bingham 大法官这样说:"Counsel who appeared for the assured in this appeal accepted that if the damage complained had been caused by excessive moisture in the gloves, but without the intervening process of condensation on the roof of the containers, the position would have been different. But he said it was a crucial fact that the moisture condensed on the container roofs before dropping down on the gloves. I do not for my part think that this answer given by the assured would appeal to the common sense of the business or seafaring man. He would not understand how the water which had caused the damage could be regarded as coming from a source external to the goods, but would on the uncontradicted findings regard the gloves as the obvious and the sole source of the water. He would, I think, regard the suggested distinction based on the intermediate migration of moisture to and condensation of moisture on the roofs of the containers as owning more to the subtlety of the legal mind than to the common sense of the mercantile."

该判决是在很大程度上把集装箱视为是货物的包装,所以集装箱出汗是内部的固有缺陷,这与以前船舱出汗被视为是外来原因不一样。这会对受保人的货方带来一定的危险,就是货物在集装箱受潮的潮气来源如果说不清楚,也证明不了是外来原因,受保人很可能不能够得到赔付。John Dunt 在他 2009 年所著的《Marine Cargo Insurance》一书之 147 页说:"The approach to condensation damage in containers can leave an assured, who has had many successful shipments, without insurance coverage when a combination of unknown fortuitous circumstances, going beyond moist conditions at shipment and cool conditions at discharge, combine to produce damage originating within the goods themselves."

4.3 固有缺陷与坏天气的关系

固有缺陷会与航次中遇到的坏天气有关系,很难分出哪一个才是近因。正如 Waller 大法官在先例 Global Process System Inc & Anor v. Syarikat Takaful Malaysia Berhad (2009) EWHC 637 (Comm)中所讲:"Inherent vice can be a cause even though some outside agency such as the motion of the waves has contributed causally to the loss."

这一来,如果分不出是哪一个才是近因,把坏天气与固有缺陷都视为是共同近因(concurrent causes),前者被承保,后者是除外风险的情况下,保险人还是不需要赔付。这在本书第六章第 4.5 段有介绍,也是 Moore-Bick 大法官在 Mayban General Assurance Bhd v. Alstom Power Plants Ltd. (2004) 2 Lloyd's Rep. 609 中的判法。以下也可以更详尽地谈谈有关的案情,涉及的货物是一座庞大的变压器,投保了一切险,而航次是从英国去鹿特丹(船舶名为 Eliane Trader)然后再转运去马来西亚。但在 Eliane Trader 轮运输的航次,船舶遇上了坏天气,风力是 8 级,海浪高达 6 米,坏天气的时间长达 27 小时。这造成了变压器的损坏需要高达 100 万英镑的修理费用,损坏是由于船舶在坏天气下强烈的摇动而产生张力与压力而导致。受保人索赔,保险人就以固有缺陷为由进行抗辩。根据专家意见与其他证据,Moore-Bick 大法官认定这种超过 24 小时的坏天气在这条航线两年半的时间里才有一次。而船舶不定期的走这段水路,每八年半会遇上一次这样的坏天气。反正是,Moore-Bick 大法官认为这种坏天气不是不可预见的。这一来受到可以预见的坏天气造成的损坏显然就是货物本身的问题。Moore-Bick 大法官是判保险人胜诉,说:"the loss in the present case was caused by the inability of the transformer to withstand the ordinary conditions of the voyage rather than by the occurrence of conditions which it could not reasonably have been expected to encounter."

但这一判决引起了很强烈的不同意见,就是一切险希望承保的风险没有理由局限在完全意想不到的情况,如果是这样一切险就太局限。毕竟,可以预见到但不一定会发生的坏天气本身就是一种风险。另一个不同意见在 Moore-Bick 大法官把货物保险与船舶适航与否的问题扯上关系,就是说如果航次中能够预见的坏天气船舶是不能抵御的话,这就是不适航了。但这种关系是被认为不恰当的。其中可节录 Howard Bennett 教授在 1977 年的《Lloyd's Maritime Law Quarterly》写了一篇很有分量的文章名为《Fortuity in the law of marine insurance》,部分有关内容节录如下:

"It is, with respect, suggested that this analysis falls into error. First, the reference to vessel and cargo indicates that Moore-Bick J was drawing a parallel between the standards expected of a carrier of goods by sea and the limits of cover offered by a marine insurer. It has already been suggested that it is by no means self-evident that such a parallel can be supported. Secondly, assureds do not procure insurance against losses that they consider fanciful. Rather, it is precisely because commercial experience indicates a certain level of probability of a particular type of loss that the reasonable person considers insurance a sensible and prudent investment. If, however, goods have to be fit to withstand reasonably foreseeable perils or the loss will be considered to be proximately caused by the inherent vice of the goods, or at least not by a 'risk' within the meaning of the 'all risks' insuring clause, much of the point of cargo insurance disappears. 'All risks' cover would be confined to loss or damage occasioned only by wholly unusual perils or wholly unusual examples of known perils. 'All risks' insurance would not cover cargo destined for New Orleans against loss or damage caused by a hurricane of no greater force than Hurricane Katrina that so devastated the city and surrounding area in 2005. It would not insure against loss by piracy cargo that was to be shipped through waters notorious for piratical attacks, such as the Straits of Malacca. And what sort of packaging and security would be required to insure cargo against theft on a voyage during which theft was within the reasonable commercial experience?

Insurers know they are being asked to assume risks that might well occur and have the protection of the law of non-disclosure and misrepresentation in reaching their decision on whether to accept the risk and, if so, on what terms. Insurers, of course, enjoy contractual freedom to restrict their liability by reference to the probability of loss occurring. However, the approach to inherent vice adopted in *Mayban* represents a restriction on cover that goes far beyond any logical presumed exclusion of ordinary losses and introduces a starting dichotomy between hull and cargo insurance that does not seem to respond to commercial common sense. Foreseeable events, it is suggested, can still constitute risks within the meaning of an all risks policy and the concept of inherent vice should be confined to losses analogous to ordinary wear and tear emanating from the internal characteristics of the insured property.

The above discussion has focused on the single, prolonged period of heavy weather encountered by the *Eliane Trader*. It may, however, be noted that, on the facts of *Mayban*, 'it would not have been at all unusual for the transformer to be exposed to several similar, albeit briefer, spells of bad weather at various stages of its voyage to the Far East' and the damage could have been caused by two or three such shorter periods of adverse weather. The decision in the case may be justified if such shorter periods of bad weather could be considered so ordinary and natural an incident of the voyage that it would be unusual to complete a voyage without encountering them. An inability to withstand such shorter periods would then qualify as inherent vice even on the narrow view favored in this article."

这方面又有了一个新发展就是先例 Global Process System Inc & Anor v. Syarikat Takaful Malaysia Berhad（2009）EWHC 367（Comm），案情是有关一个自升式钻油台（jack-up oil rig）被当作是货物去装在一条驳船上从美国德州运往马来西亚。它是投保了一切险，但在经过南非的时候，由于金属疲劳而产生裂缝（fatigue crack）加上风浪比较大而导致了自升式钻油台的 4 条支撑腿中 3 条断掉。在一审的时候，Blair 大法官判金属疲劳而产生裂缝很可能是固有缺陷造成，但不是无可避免。Blair 大法官也认为航次中的天气也是可以合理预见，所以损失或损坏的近因应该是固有缺陷造成。这里也顺便一提，就是判法是与 Mayban General Assurance Bhd v. Alstom Power Plants Ltd.（2004）2 Lloyd's Rep. 609 中说一切险不承保货物的固有缺陷，不论是肯定还是意外的（"whether that loss was bound to occur or was fortuitous"）一致。

但在上诉庭是不同意 Moore-Bick 大法官在先例 Mayban General Assurance Bhd v. Alstom Power Plants Ltd.（2004）2 Lloyd's Rep. 609 中一个比较广泛的说法，认为是一个对固有缺陷更狭窄的解释比较适合。其中 Waller 大法官说很大程度受到 Howard Bennett 教授文章的影响，判只有在没有一个承保的风险可说是事故的近因，固有缺陷才会是变了唯一的近因："inherent vice may not be a proximate cause if there is an eventuality or accident from without that causes the loss... It is only if a peril insured against is not a proximate cause that inherent vice can be the sole and proximate cause."

Waller 大法官认为考虑坏天气，必须考虑是否双方都认为在这样一个正常航次中造成该事故的坏天气是一定会发生（bound to occur）。而在这一个案件所认定自升式钻油台的支撑腿断掉航次中的风浪并非是一定会发生，这等于是事故的近因并非是来自故有缺陷。

这上诉庭的决定显然是对保险人不利，他们如果将来希望以固有缺陷作为拒绝赔付的理由，必须要提供给法院充分的证据（包括专家证人）——有关航次中真正遇到的天气与该航次中一般双方都应该理解的天气状况作出比较。保险人要是证明航次不遇到有关的坏天气才是怪事，在这样情况下固有缺陷才会是成为唯一的近因。最后一提的是笔者在写本书时还不知道贵族院最后的判法，因为该先例正上诉去贵族院。

5. 第 4.5 条：延误造成的损失或损坏

协会货物条文（A）1/1/09 之 4.5 条相比之前的条文并没有作出大的改变，除了把由于延误作为"近因"（proximately）一词删除。本来，1982 年条文的说法只是为了跟从 1906 年《英国海上保险法》section 55（2）（b）强调近因与远因的说法，但"近因"一词由于有了不同的强调（以前是强调时间上的最接近的事件是近因，现在是有效与重要的事件是近因，参见本书第六章第 4 段），被认为是带来了一定的困扰，所以在

2009 年条文把“近因”一词删除,但这应该没有什么实质的影响。

延误会带来的损失或损坏,会是实质性的,如一船香蕉因为发生海上事故(碰撞或搁浅),虽然没有对香蕉造成任何损坏,但由于航次的延误而导致一船的香蕉变为全损。这除了香蕉本质的原因,因为天气坏(会是可预见或不可预见的)而导致航次拖长,造成了香蕉的腐烂。还有是延误带来的损失也会在经济方面,市场的差价就是一个典型的例子,但也可以货物是 2010 年的日历或者是记事簿或圣诞节的商品,因为延误而过了季节才到达卸港所造成的损失。特别是今天的集装箱运输带来了很多情况下收货人都会将物料的储备减到很低,而靠的是源源不绝的物流运输与供应。所以遇到延误的话就可能带来很大的经济损失。所以在协会货物条文(A)(B)(C),针对延误的除外责任也是尽可能写得很广泛,以免保险人会面对类似直接或间接的损失或损坏。在很大程度上,这条文也是重复默示的立法地位,就是 1906 年《英国海上保险法》第 55 (2)(b)条如下:“Unless the policy otherwise provides, the insurer on ship or goods is not liable for any loss proximately caused by delay, although the delay be caused by a peril insured against.”

5.1　延误造成的经济损失不赔

海上运输的货物品种很多,有些是很容易受到延误的影响而造成实质性货损,如易腐烂的货物(perishable cargo)。但另一个极端是有些货物根本不会因为延误而造成货损,如钢材、成衣或制成品等。运输的延误会因为市场的变化而给这些货物带来经济的损失,如错过了一个好的市场。还有一些货是属于这两个极端之间的,如烟草会因为延误而带来潮湿。

但可以说对很多货物而言,延误往往造成的是经济上的损失。这里可介绍的先例是 Canada Quebec Superior Court 的案子 Federation Insurance Company of Canada v. Coret Accessories, Inc., and Hirsh (Trading as S. A. Hirsh & Co.) (1968) 2 Lloyd's Rep. 109,案情是有关一批货物(手袋的配件)从西班牙运到加拿大的蒙特利尔,但由于罢工货物卸不下来,准备去美国卸下后转运,但其间货物丢失了。由于这是属于承保风险造成的损失,保险人作出了赔付。在两个月后,该批货物被找回来了,但受保人的货方拒绝接受该批货物,因为该批货物已经过季了,这导致了保险人与货方之间的争议,法院判保险人胜诉,原因是保险合约不负责延误造成的损失。Collins 大法官这样说:“Loss or damage arising from loss of market as well as loss, damage or deterioration arising from delay are specifically excluded. It was delay which caused the loss or damage. There was no obligation to deliver within a specified delay. Consequently as the policy did not cover the event which gave rise to the loss, the defendant has no claim under the policy and the money paid in good faith on a presumed loss must be returned by the defendant.”

同样的说法也可以节录 John Dunt 在《Marine Cargo Insurance》2009 年版之 11.64 段,他举了一个例子,就是船舶因为风浪而延误造成易腐货物变质,或错过市场,但没有受到风浪而造成任何实质损失,也是没的赔付,不论保险合约是否是一切险。他这样说:"However, if a ship is delayed in similar circumstance by a storm and a perishable cargo deteriorates, or there is a loss of market, because of the passage of time and not because of any physical damage directly caused by the storm, then there will be no cover for that loss which will be caused by delay."

在上述情况,易腐货物变质,保险人不必承担责任,是可以从另一个角度进行分析,就是延误在这种情况下是一个主要与有效的原因。遇上风浪,特别是可以预见的风浪,充其量是造成的原因之一。这与发生了一个重大与不能合理预见的事故如搁浅或者碰撞后导致延误并造成易腐货物损坏的情况下分析什么是主要与有效的原因不同。

5.2 延误不影响施救费用

延误在严重的情况时会导致航次的受阻,其结果就不仅是一个航次延误那么简单了。航次受阻也可以被称为是"航程终止"(loss of adventure),往往会涉及受保人的货方需要把该批货物从中途港转运去目的港。这可能会带来金额庞大的施救费用,带来的问题就是这施救费用不可以得到赔付,因为它毕竟是由于延误而产生的,只不过是延误造成了航程的终止。有关这一个课题已在本书第七章之5段有过详论,不再重复。

5.3 保险人赔付延误损失唯一的情况:共同海损

船舶在发生事故后,如果船舶是要开去港口修理,在这修理的期间船东是会因为延误而造成船期的损失,这将也是共同海损的一项分摊内容。该项延误损失一部分是由货方或他的保险人支付,另一部分是由船舶保险人支付。而这也是货物保险唯一赔付延误造成损失的情况,这是在协会货物条文(A)(B)(C)中第4.5条括号内的内容有说明。所以整条4.5条文就是说保险人不负责承保风险带来延误造成的损失、损坏或费用,而第2条中共同海损造成延误是唯一的例外:"In no case shall this insurance cover loss damage or expense caused by delay, even though the delay be caused by a risk insured against [except expenses payable under Clause 2 above]."

6. 第4.6条:船东、船舶经理人、承租人或船舶营运人的破产或经济困境带来的损失或损坏

协会货物条文(A)1/1/09之4.6条作出了重要的改变,先节录1982年协会货物条文第4.6条,以便读者与2009年相应条文(本章开始有节录)可作出比较:"Loss damage or expense arising from insolvency or financial default of the owners managers charterers or operators of the vessel."

6.1 有关风险是否承保的先例:London & Provincial Leather Processors v. Hudson

这一风险在20世纪70年代后期与80年代初航运低潮的时候经常会发生,就是

承运人或船东在收取了运费后,半途发生经济不妥而无法继续该航次,导致了货方或收货人需要安排转运才能把货物运到目的地。显然这会带来延误与额外的费用。延误造成的损失并不是承保的范围,这一点很明确。至于额外的转运费用是否是一切险承保的施救费用却有争议,毕竟这一个损失是属于意外。此外,也有对保险人不利的先例,就是 London & Provincial Leather Processors v. Hudson (1939) 64 Ll. L. REP. 352。该先例的法律地位是如果保险合约中有一切险(all risks)条文,而因为承运人的倒闭不但导致了航次的延迟,也导致了航程终止,这种情况下保险人都要负责赔付。所以,货物转运的花费也可以在施救条文下得到赔付的说法应该是站得住脚的。

这显然是令伦敦保险市场不满意,因为他们的感觉是船东的破产或经济困境是一种商业的风险,是一般保险不愿意承担。而伦敦劳合社规定(Lloyd's Regulations)禁止劳合社去承保经济损失,如生意上的亏本或对手的倒闭。

6.2　1982 年条文作出的明示规定

所以,到了 1982 年条文就加上了这一条第 4.6 条,说到底是保险人不愿意承保这些属于商业上"遇人不淑"的风险。

在过去的 5 ~ 6 年,航运经历了史无前例的好景,所以这一问题好像很遥远。但在 2008 年 10 月份以后,航运市场急转直下,很明显这种风险又会大量出现。这包括船东本身就没有足够的流动资金完成这一航次,如要付钱买燃油或支付船员工资。也会是船东本身还勉强有足够的流动资金,但融资的银行因为自己的政策改变或其他原因决定在航次的中途港(如新加坡)把船舶扣押并通过法院出售。毕竟银行要找一个技术上的船东违约的事件,如船舶市场价格跌得太低而不足作为对银行的担保,是十分容易的事情,所以银行若不再支持某个船东,在航运低潮时对船东是致命打击。

很不幸的是,今天的国际贸易很多时候就是 CIF 或 CFR 买卖,这表示运费基本上在装完货就已经全部被支付。当然,在这种情况下提单通常会是运费预付提单(freight prepaid)。所以在法律上,船东没有办法要求货方或提单持有人再多作出一个运费的支付。这方面的法律地位十分清楚,如在 Cho Yang Shipping v. Coral (1997) 2 Lloyd's Rep. 641 中,上诉庭曾经提到一审的 Hallgarten 大法官说:"The basic commercial function of a 'freight prepaid' clause was to assure the notify party or other consignee that as between himself and the shipowner no liability for freight could be asserted; the expression 'freight prepaid' served in no way to affect the basic liability of the shipper if freight had not in fact been prepaid."

但法律地位是另一回事,在船东山穷水尽时,实在没有钱完成航次,他是不会关心法律的。所以,即使是签发了运费已经预付的提单,船东在航次半途要求多给一笔运费否则就不前往目的地港的情况在航运低迷时是经常会听到的,就像是 The "Alev" (1989) 1 Lloyd's Rep. 138。

由于在散货的海上运输,运费全部要预付的情况实在是太普遍了,导致在航运好景的过去几年里，船东的谈判力量很大，结果在笔者所遇到的FOB买卖，根本不需要签发运费预付提单，但船东仍然不肯依照普通法的地位，就是运费在货物被运到目的地的卸港才需要支付。现在航运市场急转直下，船东是否可以向货方坚持，还是要拭目以待。但要明确的是，即使运费到了目的港才要支付，或者是不涉及航次租约的期租合同，仍然是难以防止这些不幸事情的发生。充其量，运费如果要到目的港才需要支付，即使遇上船东半途因为经济不妥或者是清盘而无法继续航次，货方的损失也少得多。因为可以用省下来的运费替代转运费用，或者是说服融资的银行允许船东完成已经剩下路程不远的航次以赚取运费。

6.3 2009年条文作出的改变

在1982年条文，这些风险造成的损失，是不能获得赔付的。但到了2009年条文，就作出了一定程度的放松，对货方来说是有利的。放松的地方就是不获得赔付只适用在装货时，受保人是知道或参与该业务应该知道，在该航次中会发生船东或者承运人的清盘或者经济不妥。显然，受保人是不需要来一个很详细与昂贵的调查看看船东或者承运人是否经济不妥或面临清盘，所需要的应该就是一个谨慎的商业人士会作出一般性的判断。至于什么是受保人参与该租船业务应该知道的，可以举例说某一个船公司到处宣扬自己会随时清盘或在市场上该船公司被谣传随时会倒闭，但受保人仍然坚持装货。在这种情况下，航次半途如果出现这种风险，保险人有权拒赔。

2009年条文中拟定得不是很好的地方是，它针对的时间是装货的时间（time of loading），而受保人通常是在装货前已经订立了运输合约（不论是租约还是订舱单），如果在那时没有办法合理知道船东或者承运人面临清盘或者经济不妥，而这个消息只是在装货前才暴露出来，受保人就会非常矛盾。原因是合约的一方发生经济不妥甚至是清盘，除非合约有明示规定，并不是另一方可以终断合约的合法理由。这一来，受保人会面临两难处境：装货，出了事故货物保险是不赔的；如果不装货，就会面临船东或者承运人违约的指控以及索赔有关的损失。

至于受保人是谁，可以说在CIF的买卖，通常就是卖方。而在CFR与FOB的买卖，通常就是买方。在FOB的情况下，显然受保人也是安排海上运输的买方。所以如果他租用的船舶半途发生船东清盘或经济不妥，而他又不幸已经在装货时把运费全部支付了，再加上在装货时航运市场上该船东经济困境的消息已经满天飞，这一不幸的FOB买方就会有麻烦了。

但在CIF或CFR的买卖，众所周知通常的做法就是，卖方在装船后取得一套运费预付的提单，就会结汇并交出该套提单给买方的银行。这套提单往往会流转到买方手中，而如果在航次半途船东或者承运人发生清盘或者经济不妥，这到底会怎样影响无辜的买方呢？毕竟，出事的船舶不是他租入或者安排的。而且，有可能卖方在装船时的确也知道了船东或者承运人发生清盘或者经济不妥。但问题是在CIF或者CFR的情况下，卖方对这方面的危险是漠不关心的，因为运输的风险不在他头上，而且他结汇就拿到货款了。针对买方,这可以说是 CIF 或者 CFR 买卖的一个重大的缺陷或不幸。幸亏在 2009 年条文,已经多加上一段说明,这一个除外风险不适用于无辜的买方,因为他根据一个合约(也就是指 CIF 或 CFR 货物买卖合约)买了这一票货物。这种风险在目前航运低迷的情况下是很有可能会发生的,但在 1982 年条文的同一条文只是简单说不赔这种风险,换言之,不存在无辜的提单持有人可以不受影响。2009 年条文有了这一改变,可以说对无辜的买方(特别是大量的中国内地以 CIF 或 CFR 进口的无辜买方)是一个重要与极佳的改变。

7. 第 4.7 条:核战争武器直接或间接所造成的损失或损坏

对核污染(不论是岸上的发电厂或者是核武器)所造成的损失最早涉及一条著名的条文名为 Radioactive Contamination Exclusion Clause(简称 RACE),目的是排除在保险合约内涉及核污染所带来的损失。

最初,该条文的出现是在 1959 年的 12 月,而且最初只涉及岸上风险的保险合约。这就是英国 British Insurance (Atomic Energy) Committee 作出第一版的 RACE 条文,想针对的只是岸上核发电站会带来的风险,而条文也相对简单,说明有关保险合约是不赔付任何损失是由于:"directly or indirectly caused by or contributed to by or arising from ionizing radiations or contamination by radioactivity from any nuclear fuel."

到了 1990 年 10 月 1 日,RACE 条文已经变为以下的版本:

"In no case shall this insurance cover loss damage liability or expense directly or indirectly caused by or contributed to by or arising from

1.1　ionising radiations from or contamination by radioactivity from any nuclear fuel or from any nuclear waste or from the combustion of nuclear fuel

1.2　the radioactive, toxic, explosive or other hazardous or contamining properties of any nuclear installation, reactor or other nuclear assembly or a nuclear component thereof

1.3　any weapon of war employing atomic or nuclear fission and/or fusion or other like reaction or radioactive force or matter."

其中要注意的是第 1.3 条加上了核武器,这是因为在和平的时候(如果在战争的时候保险合约就可以以战争豁免为由不赔付),也会发生这种危险。其中一些事件如在 1996 年 1 月份,一架北约的飞机在西班牙不小心掉了 4 个核弹头的事故。

海上货物保险是在 1982 年的条文(协会货物条文或 Institute Cargo Clause)第 4.7 条首次加入了有关的条文,但只是把 RACE 条文中的最后部分针对核武器加上为:"loss damage or expense arising from the use of any weapon of war employing atomic or nuclear fission and/or fusion or other like reaction or radioactive force or matter."

但要注意的是，它没有把岸上核电厂可能发生的核污染排除在外，大家可能会感到有点不解，如 A. George 在 1968 年的《Lloyd's Maritime Law Quarterly》第 438 页发表的文章《The New Insurance Cargo Clauses》。可能的原因是岸上的核电厂所造成的核污染对于在海上航行船舶所装载的货物通常情况下影响不会大，无须排除。而实际上保险人真正担心的是当核武器在港口或仓储区域发生意外就可能会对大量船舶上或者仓库中的货物造成大面积的污染。这种情况的出现即使是传统的爆炸都会造成灾难性的损失，好像 1944 年发生在孟买港口与 1917 年发生在加拿大哈利法克斯港口的爆炸。而这些爆炸都是一般的商业保险没有能力赔付或不想承保的。

在 2001 年的"9·11"事件后，公众对恐怖主义可能带来的袭击有了新的警觉。其中一个方面就是担心一种"肮脏炸弹"（dirty bomb），它就是一些传统的爆炸设施但加上了放射性的物体，而且外观上看是跟传统的武器不一样。因此在 2002 年 11 月 1 日，RACE 条文就将"武器"一词扩展为"武器或设施"。另也把 RACE 条文扩大至"所有含有放射性危险与污染的物质因为放射性、有毒性、爆炸性而造成的损失"（the radioactive, toxic, explosive or other hazardous or contaminating properties of any radioactive matter）。

此外，也针对了其他的恐怖袭击包括生化武器与电磁袭击，并有了相关的条文将它排除在承保范围外。这就是扩展了的 RACE 条文，全名为 Institute Radioactive Contamination, Chemical, Biological, Bio-Chemical and Electromagnetic Weapons Exclusion Clause, 10/11/2003（简称为 Extended RACE Clause 或 CL370）。措辞如下：

"**This clause shall be paramount and shall override anything contained in this insurance inconsistent therewith**

1 In no case shall this insurance cover loss damage liability or expense directly or indirectly caused by or contributed to by or arising from

1.1　ionising radiations from or contamination by radioactivity from any nuclear fuel or from any nuclear waste or from the combustion of nuclear fuel

1.2　the radioactive, toxic, explosive or other hazardous or contamining properties of any nuclear installation, reactor or other nuclear assembly or a nuclear component thereof

1.3　any weapon or device employing atomic or nuclear fission and/or fusion or other like reaction or radioactive force or matter

1.4　the radioactive, toxic, explosive or other hazardous or contaminating properties of any radioactive matter. The exclusion in this sub-clause does not extend to radioactive isotopes, other than nuclear fuel, when such isotopes are being prepared, carried, stored, or used for commercial, agricultural, medical, scientific or other similar peaceful purposes

1.5　any chemical, biological, bio-chemical, or electromagnetic weapon."

特别要注意的有以下几个方面：

1. 第一句的条文（黑体）说明是该条文是首要条文，当合约中的其他条文（不论是以附加条文的形式还是以其他颜色的文字表示强调）与该条文有矛盾时，该条文具有超越性的效力。

2. 在该条文中用词是“直接或间接导致或源于”（directly or indirectly caused by or contributed to by or arising from），这在保险合约是一个含义最广的措辞，可以避开“近因原则”（proximate cause）。由于本条文所述的风险如果发生，有可能会造成很长时间与很大范围的影响，如在核爆炸发生后引起抢劫或者是大火而造成损失，而抢劫或大火的近因到底是什么有点说不清楚，尤其是与核爆炸发生的时间隔的很远。在“直接或间接导致或源于”的用词下，可以避开近因原则的追究。这方面请看本书第六章第4.4段。

3. 条文1.1与1.2针对的是要排除岸上的核燃料或核废料所造成的污染造成的损失，其实就是最早期的RACE条文想排除的列明风险。

4. 条文1.3是强调除了核武器之外还包括了核装置。

5. 条文1.4将不承保的范围扩大至“所有含有放射性危险与污染的物质因为放射性、有毒性、爆炸性而造成的损失”（the radioactive, toxic, explosive or other hazardous or contaminating properties of any radioactive matter）。但是又明确说明了这些除外是不包括放射性同位素（radioactive isotopes），因为在医学、科学、农业等领域，放射性同位素的使用是非常的广泛。如Las Alamos National Laborartory Newsletter, 10 September 2007, Vol. 8, No. 19 p. 1. 就曾报道说美国有1600万医疗程序有使用核药物（nuclear medicine）；再如家用的烟雾报警器，也使用了镅的同位素。而这些物质在运输与储藏的过程中也会有泄漏的危险，所以有这种和平用途的产品在海上运输并需要投保完全是不应该被排除在承保范围之外，保险人也希望承保并赚取保费。但注意是这方面不包括核燃料的运输与储藏，尽管核燃料也是作为和平用途。

6. 这是新的Extended RACE Clause或CL370，除了核风险外，也将其他的大规模杀伤性武器包括在了列明的除外风险中。其中包括了化学武器（chemical weapon）、生物（biological weapon）、生化武器（bio-chemical weapon）与电磁武器（electromagnetic weapon）。化学武器主要就是一些有毒的武器，而生物武器主要就是一些与细菌有关的武器，在美军攻打伊拉克时很出名的“炭疽夫人”擅长的就属于生化武器范畴。至于电磁武器是利用电磁相互感应的原理，通过自动爆炸装置让电子设备包括电脑大面积的被干扰甚至是停顿。

7. 这一条Extended RACE Clause或CL370现在已经普遍合并在海上货物运输保险合约，即使是一些恐怖袭击威胁不大与警觉性不是很高的地方如亚洲、非洲、拉丁美洲，因为最终还是要在伦敦的保险市场上进行再保，在再保险人的压力之下，保险人与受保人的合约中也都会加上该条文。

最后介绍的是伦敦市场在同时间推出了一种攻击电脑的黑客行为（包括了恶意密码与电脑病毒）的保险条文，名为“Institute Cyber Attack Exclusion Clause, 10/11/2003”，措辞如下：

"1. 1 Subject only to Clause 1. 2 below, in no case shall this insurance cover loss, damage, liability or expense directly or indirectly caused by or contributed to by or arising from the use or operation, as a means for inflicting harm, or any computer, computer system, computer software programme, malicious code, computer virus or process or any other electronic system.

1. 2 Where this clause is endorsed on policies covering risks of war, civil war, revolution, rebellion, insurrection, or civil strife arising therefrom, or any hostile act by or against a belligerent power, or terrorism or any person acting from a political motive, Clause 1. 1 shall not operate to exclude losses (which would otherwise by covered) arising from the use of any computer, computer system or computer software programme or any other electronic system in the launch and/or guidance system and/or firing mechanism of any weapon or missile."

它针对的风险是如果电脑受到黑客的攻击(包括了恶意密码与电脑病毒)会造成大规模的混乱。而目前集装箱的方位追踪主要是通过电脑来操作,混乱会导致集装箱的丢失,或者是集装箱长时间找不到导致里面的货物腐烂而发生损失。这一条条文是意图与 Extended RACE Clause 或 CL370 一并使用在海上货物运输保险中,但估计是对集装箱运输更为重要。其他要注意的有以下两点:(1)它不是作为一条首要条文,表示与保险合约其他条文有矛盾时,解释合约的一般原则是会适用。(2)条文 1. 1 是将攻击电脑的黑客行为(包括了恶意密码与电脑病毒)排除在承保范围之外,但条文 1. 2 却又明确规定了,如果投保的只是战争险(而一般货物运输是以预约/开口保单[open covers]的形式投保,并包括了水险与战争险),由于控制导弹或其他武器点火装置或者引导装置的电脑、电脑网路、软件或其他电子网络被攻击导致导弹偏离目标而造成货物损失仍是在承保的范围内;否则战争保险就失去了意义。

8. 第 5 条:船舶不适航与集装箱不适货除外条文

8.1 针对船舶不适航的法律地位与有关的条文

在 1906 年《英国海上保险法》,Section 39(1)是说明航次保险(这包括了船舶或者货物的航次保险)就会有一个默示保证,是有关的船舶在开航前与开航当时必须是适航,条文如下:"In a voyage policy there is an implied warranty that the commencement of the voyage the ship shall be seaworthy for the purpose of the particular adventure insured."

另针对货物保险还有一个条文是 Section 40(2):"In a voyage policy on goods or other movables there is an implied warranty that at the commencement of the voyage the ship is not only seaworthy as a ship, but also that she is reasonably fit to carry the goods or other movables to the destination contemplated by the policy. ”

这一默示法律地位显示了以下几个重要之处：

1. 首先要明白这里的措辞是要受保人向保险人作出这样的承诺性保证，而在保险法领域承诺性保证是非常严厉的条文，因为1906年的立法中已经说明违反承诺性保证会带来的严重后果。这后果就是一旦违反，保险人就可以自承诺性保证被违反之日起解除保险合约责任（主要是指赔付责任），这是在Section 33(3)，规定如下：“A warranty ... is a condition which must be exactly complied with, whether it be material to the risk or not. If it be not so complied with, then, subject to any express provision in the policy, the insurer is discharged from liability as from the date of the breach of warranty, but without prejudice to any liability incurred by him before that date. ”

举例说，船舶在开航前不适航或不适货就等于违反了这一个默示的承诺性保证，保险人就可以自开航一天解除保险合约责任，再也不必对任何货物的损失作出赔付，即使货物的损失是与开航时的不适航没有任何关系。比如，不适航是舱盖漏水，但实质造成货物损失是火灾，但保险人还是不需要赔付。这就是英国法律的地位，已经详细的在第四章第2段有十分详尽的介绍，不再重复。

2. 这一严厉的法律地位有历史背景，在以前的年代，船舶与货物经常是一家，通常可能是用同一份劳合社标准S. G保单对船舶与货物同时投保。这表示对保险人作出保证船舶在开航前是适航/适货，不论是从船舶或货物的角度都是针对同一个受保人。还有，根据英国的合约法，任何合约的承诺都是一个绝对或严格的承诺。所以受保人对保险人作出适航的保证，没有像《海牙规则》将适航规定为“due diligence”，而将其视为绝对的责任。除了船舶是越来越复杂，这不适航的面会是很广，而且经常能够挑出毛病。

3. 海上保险的受保人都会想办法避免这一严厉的法律地位。针对船舶，船东逃避的办法就是不投保船舶的航次保险而通常投保长达一年的定期保险（time policy）。这种保险是不存在有适航的保证，因为在保险生效时，该船舶可能是在某一航次的中途，甚至刚发生事故，在大海之中也根本谈不上修理，作为受保人的船东是绝对不可能作出适航的保证。这在1906年《英国海上保险法》Section 39(5)也有针对但宽松得多的规定，说：“In a time policy there is no implied warranty that the ship shall be seaworthy at any stage of the adventure, but where, with the privity of the assured, the ship is sent to sea in an unseaworthy state, the insurer is not liable for any loss attributable to unseaworthiness. ”换言之，要求在承保的期间受保人的船东不会在明知道船舶不适航的情况下还是要求开航，如此，保险人是不赔付由于该不适航所造成的损失，即损失是需要与违约有因果关系，这与承诺性保证的违反很不一样。

4. 针对货物保险，不像船舶可以说是非要每一个航次投保不可。即使货物保险是以预约/开口保单（open cover）的形式，本质上还是每一个航次投保。所以就受到1906年立法Section 33(3)的直接影响。加上这些年来在实际的操作中，货方与船东已经根本不可能是一家,货方通常是找陌生的船东承运货物,这样要求货方保证船舶在开航前与开航当时适航是很不现实的。所以,货方逃避适航的严厉法律地位的办法就是在海上货物保险合约里加上明示条文,以超越默示的法律地位。这些明示条文与一直以来的改变会在下一段解释。

8.2　针对不适航的有关条文

以明示条文的方式超越适航的默示法律地位,首先是在1963年的协会货物条文(一切险)(Institute Cargo Clause,简称ICC,All Risks)中采用了一条简称为"Seaworthiness Admitted Clause"(承认适航条文),措辞为:"The seaworthiness of the vessel as between the Assured and Underwriters is hereby admitted."

从文字上看来,就是即使船舶是不适航但保险人与货方之间还是达成共识即船舶适航符合法律的承诺性保证,这里也有保险人对船舶的适航承诺性保证弃权的味道。但显然,这么简单的文字还是不足够且不令人满意的。例如,如果真的是发生货损,而造成的有效原因正是不适航,如舱盖漏水,到底保险人是否应该作出赔付就不明确了。因为保险人只是对适航的承诺性保证作出承认或弃权,但没有进一步说明即使是不适航引起的货损货差也作出赔付。

所以在1982年的条文就带来了改变,规定在第5条,措辞如下:

"5 Unseaworthiness and Unfitness Exclusion Clause

5.1　In no case shall this insurance cover loss damage or expense arising form unseaworthiness of vessel or craft, unfitness of vessel craft conveyance container of liftvan for the safe carriage of the subject-matter insured, where the Assured or their servants are privy to such unseaworthiness or unfitness, at the time the subject-matter insured is loaded therein.

5.2　The Underwriters waive any breach of the implied warranties of seaworthiness of the ship and fitness of the ship to carry the subject-matter insured to destination, unless the Assured or their servants are privy to such unseaworthiness or unfitness."

这里的5.2条文有点类似1963年的协会货物条文中的"Seaworthiness Admitted Clause"(承认适航条文),是说保险人承认船舶是适航或对这一个承诺性保证弃权,除非是受保人或其雇员对船舶的不适航是有私谋(privity)。但在5.1条文说明是如果受保人或其雇员在将货物装船时就知道船舶是不适航,则由于不适航引起的货损货差,保险人是不赔付。也就是说,如果货损是由不适航引起,而受保人或其雇员并没有私谋,则保险人还是要赔付货损的。但这里还是有不明朗之处,因为5.2条文所放弃的默示适航承诺性保证只是在一种情况下不管用,也就是受保人或他的雇员对不适航有私谋。这一来,如果是这例外情况适用,法律默示的地位就是一旦不适航,保险人在保险合约中就解除今后所有的赔付责任。也就是在后来发生的事故造成货损/货差,不论是什么原因造成,货方还是不能得到赔付。这表示在1982年协会货物条文下,举例说如果船舶是因为船员人数不足而不适航,而货方是知道或可以知道,这就变为了是5.2条文的例外情况适用,货方破坏了适航保证,保险赔付责任就解除。事后在航次中遇到意外,如发生火灾或是遇上海盗,与船员不足导致的不适航是毫无关系,但保险人还是可以拒赔。

2009 年协会货物条文相比 1982 年的条文作出了很多有利于货方的改变,如下:(1)在 5.3 条文保险人对受保人在 1906 年立法下默示的船舶适航的承诺性保证是弃权而且是无条件的,不像 1982 年有一个例外(就是受保人或其雇员对船舶的不适航是有私谋)。(2)在 5.1 条文,它是针对了两种不同的情况保险人不赔偿:5.1.1 条文针对的是船舶(驳船)的不适航或不适合有关的航次,并且受保人有私谋;5.1.2 条文针对的不是船舶而是集装箱或其他付运的工具不适合,而且时间上是限制在将货物装上集装箱或其他付运的工具是发生在保险合约承保风险开始或生效前,并且是受保人或其雇员有私谋。

对以上两种不同情况,有以下几个重点可以解释一下:

1. 这两种情况的不适航或者不适货,必须是有效导致货损的原因,保险人才可以拒绝赔付。这与适航的承诺性保证不一样,而适航的默示承诺性保证保险人已经是无条件在 5.3 条文放弃,所以再也没有关系了。

2. 分开的两种不同情况,前者是针对船舶的不适航,它只针对受保人的货方有私谋,而没有包括货方的雇员。这是因为租用或者选择付运的船舶(驳船)是否适航是货方可以知道的。如像船舶的船籍、船名甚至是其他的情况,货方或他的高级管理人员是可以通过公共渠道或与船东的交往中可以知道。受保人的货方对船舶不适航会有私谋的情况在今天的国际货物买卖与海上运输很少会出现,一种情况是货方拥有自己的船队运输他自己的货物,就像 The"Lady Gwendolen"(1965) 1 Lloyd's Rep. 335 先例一样。该船由 Guinness 啤酒公司拥有,船舶装运的就是该公司的啤酒。该船在大雾中发生碰撞,并被发现该船长以前经常在大雾中超速航行,但船东与他的总管没有作出纠正,也没有好好的教育他使用雷达。结果判船东(也是货方)对这种不适航的情况"有错与知情"(actual fault and privity),不允许船东限制赔偿责任。如果涉及海上货物保险,由于该船舶也是货方拥有,就会有危险被指控说他对船长的不适航有私谋而会遭受保险人拒赔了。另一种情况是货方租船,但即使是这种情况,作为承租人也很少会对船舶不适航有私谋。会有个别案件如货方作为期租承租人不小心供应劣质的燃油给船舶,导致半途出事,会有可能出现这种争议。

3. 后者的情况是针对集装箱或其他付运的工具如卡车,往往进行监督的是货方的低层雇员,所以如果是涉及私谋,如看到集装箱有洞知道会漏水但还是把货物堆装进去。相反这种私谋通常不会涉及货方或他的高级管理人员。其他的不适合可以是集装箱肮脏、浸水、冷藏箱的温度不足等情况。在这种情况下导致货物损失或损坏,保险人也可以拒赔,但只是局限在两种情况。一是堆装货物在集装箱内是在运输风险生效前,这通常会是发货人或卖方在自己场地堆装货物进集装箱准备付运的情况。这表示如果他在堆装时发现集装箱不适合,但还是进行堆货,这样的话发生保险人拒赔也很正常。二是堆装货物在集装箱是由作为受保人的货方或他的雇员负责,在这种情况下集装箱如果不适货，并可以知情的话，保险人就可以拒赔。但在这两种情况以外，如作为受保人的货方/卖方把货物交给独立的货代，并任由货代去集装箱集散地堆箱再装上远洋船舶等的做法，由于集装箱不适合安全运载货物而出事的话，就不会影响货方向保险人索赔的权利了。

在这里顺便一提，第4.3条文有关包装不足或不适在1982年条文也针对了集装箱的堆货，但该条文针对的情况是集装箱本身没有不适合的地方，只是在堆货方面没有做好，如因为捆绑不足而导致货物在运输途中发生碰撞与移动。但在本条文并不是针对堆货方面做得怎样，而是针对集装箱是否适合安全运载货物。

4. 至于什么是"私谋"，在笔者的《海事法》一书第二章的3.2段有详细解释，不多讲。简单说就是"知情"(with knowledge)这个不适航的情况以及"熟视无睹"(turn a blind eye)。而知情不必是"真正知情"，"推定知情"(constructive knowledge)已经足够。这不是一个很重的责任，比起疏忽(negligence)或是恪尽职守(due diligence)是较低：The "Eurysthenes" (1976) 2 Lloyd's Rep. 171 (CA); The "Star Sea" (2001) 1 Lloyd's Rep. 389 (HL)。

8.3 无辜受让人不受影响

这是在5.2条文："Exclusion 5.1.1 above shall not apply where the contract of insurance has been assigned to the party claiming hereunder who has bought or agreed to buy the subject-matter insured in good faith under a binding contract."该条文是2009年协会货物条文中新加的，可以说是保险人所作出的一个很重要的让步。有以下几个重点可以解释一下：

1. 第5.2条文说明第5.1条文的除外不影响善意受让了保险合约的第三人。这表示无辜的提单持有人，同时也是保险合约受让人，就不受影响。这种情况经常会在国际货物买卖中发生，如一个典型的CIF买卖，卖方把货物付运后取得了一套提单并在较早时把该票货物的海上运输投保，就会把这些单证(提单加上保险证明或保单)去银行结汇，同时把这些单证转让给买方以取得货款。这表示由于卖方对船舶不适航或者集装箱不适合安全运载货物有私谋的话，造成了货物的损失或损坏，也不会影响无辜买方的索赔权。这不像以前如果遇上这样的情况，无辜买方在向保险人索赔而保险人不必赔付时，他就只能根据买卖合约向卖方提出索赔。应注意的是，在1982年的协会货物条文是没有2009年的第5.2条文，这表示货物如果是包装不足或不适而导致在海上运输途中损坏，在1982年的条文下保险人即使是面对无辜的买方也可以拒赔。

2. 考虑到今天在国际货物买卖中很多是CIF，可以说这是保护无辜受让人或提单持有人的重要条文。

3. 海上保险合约根据1906年《英国海上保险法》Section 50 (3)说明是货物保险合约是可以通过背书或习惯做法(通常就失去交出)转让给买方，让买方作为受让人直接向保险人索赔："A marine policy may be assigned by indorsement thereon or in other

customary manner."

4. 第5.2条文也要求无辜的买方有一个有约束性的买卖合约(binding contract)与善意(in good faith)。这是针对一些通常会发生的情况,即使是在海上风险导致了全损(total loss),但买方还是不能脱身与必须支付货价给卖方(通常是通过信用证)。因为他与卖方有一个有约束性的货物买卖合约,而根据该合约的明示或默示条文,海上运输的风险是在货物装上船就转移给买方。但如果双方并没有一个约束性的合约,如买方在一些情况下可以从货物买卖合约脱身,如船舶的不适航,这就表示买方不能根据这个条文向保险人索赔而是要向卖方索赔。至于不善意,很容易想到一个例子就是受保人的货方自己违反了5.1条文的适航,但事后找一家相熟的公司作为买方订立并倒签一份买卖合约,然后通过该公司扮演一个无辜受让人向保险人索赔,这显然是欠缺善意了。

最后提一下第5.2条文,它说明第5.1条文的除外不影响善意受让了保险合约的第三人。这表示无辜的提单持有人,同时也是保险证明或保单持有人,就不受影响。这种情况经常会在国际货物买卖中发生,如一个典型的CIF买卖,卖方把货物付运后取得了一套提单并较早时把该货物的运输投保,就会把这些单证去银行结汇,同时把这些单证转让给买方以取得货款。这表示由于卖方对船舶不适航或者集装箱不适合安全运载货物有私谋,造成了货物的损失或损坏,也不会影响无辜买方的索赔权。

8.4　保险人对船舶适航与否的第二种控制

除了上述所讲的有关船舶适航与集装箱或其他付运工具的适货问题在2009年协会货物条文有所针对外,但还有第二种情况保险人针对这一方面是作出控制,而且是非常重要。这就是如果针对个别航次的货物运输进行单一投保或更多情况是以预约/开口保单(open cover)的形式投保,往往对将来航次会租用的船舶是没有办法知道,也无从披露。保险人为了控制受保人不会租用在适航方面太差劲的船舶,就通常会在个别航次的保单或预约/开口保单加上一条"协会船级条文"(The Institute Classification Clause),目前采用的是2001年1月1日的版本。在这个条文,所针对的是船舶的标准(standard)、船级(classification)与船龄(age)。

8.4.1　协会船级条文之船级控制

在进一步解释这一条重要的条文,先把有关船级的部分节录如下:

"INSTITUTE CLASSIFICATION CLAUSE 01/01/2001

QUALIFYING VESSELS

1 This insurance and the marine transit rates as agreed in the policy or open cover apply only to cargoes and/or interests carried by mechanically self-propelled vessels of steel construction classed with a Classification Society which is:

1.1　a Member or Associate Member of the International Association of Classification Societies (IACS), or

1.2 a National Flag Society as defined in Clause 4 below, but only where the vessel is engaged exclusively in the coastal trading of that nation (including trading on an inter-island route within an archipelago of which that nation forms part).

Cargoes and/or interests carried by vessels not classed as above must be notified promptly to underwriters for rates and conditions to be agreed. **Should a loss occur prior to such agreement being obtained cover may be provided but only if cover would have been available at a reasonable commercial market rate on reasonable commercial market terms.**"(加黑部分是笔者的强调)。

这里首先要提的是上一个版本的协会船级条文是1997年8月1日版的,在该条文的一开始是讲"这一个保险费率只是适用于那些装运在符合该协会船级条文规定的船上的货物……",原文是"The marine transit rates agreed for this insurance apply only to cargoes and/or interests..."这就带来一个不明朗的地方,如果有关船舶不符合协会船级条文的规定,是否意味着双方约定的保险费率不再适用,需要另达成协议,但货物保险还是适用,期间出了事故保险人还是要赔付,但需要与保险费率的差额作出对冲,还是整个货物保险合约无效。其中有一个新加坡上诉庭的先例是Everbright Commercial Enterprises Pte Ltd. v. AXA Insurance Singapore Pte Ltd. (2001) 2 SLR 316,判是在这种情况下,应该是整个货物保险合约无效。这在2001年版本的协会船级条文,也在一开始把这个地位明确了,就是在"保险费率"之前加上了"本保险"(this insurance),只在以下情况的船舶适用/有效。

而符合2001年版本的协会船级条文对船级规定的情况是分为两类,分别是在1.1条文和1.2条文。在1.1条文,它是规定有关船舶必须入级到一个船级社,而该船级社是国际船级社协会(International Association of Classification Societies,简称IACS)的会员或准会员。可以说世界著名的船级社都是IACS的会员,如劳合社、美国船级社与中国船级社等。在这些船级社入级的船舶是完全符合2001年协会船级条文的船级规定。

在1.2条文,它是对船级要求的一点放松,就是一些非IACS会员的船级社(通常也表示这些船级社的标准会有一定的疑问),入级的船舶也可以被接受但该船舶必须是悬挂与该船级社同一国籍的船旗,而且该船舶只能在该国家的沿岸或岛屿之间航行。举例说,适用在一艘菲律宾船舶,入级菲律宾船级社,并且只在菲律宾的岛屿之间航行。显然这种情况比较狭窄,而且不远航风险也相对比较低,所以保险人可以接受。

但这里也有一个新的发展需要一提,欧盟反垄断机构在过去几年对IACS进行调查,最终在2009年双方达成协议。协议是欧盟反垄断机构给予IACS一段时间的豁免,但IACS也要作出一定程度的让步,就是让本来不被接受的船级社(或本来被驱逐除去的船级社如波兰)回来参与到IACS,而准会员也被取消等。这样一来,会有担忧是整个IACS的船舶安全与适航的标准会一定程度的下降。而且,由于IACS会员数目变得太多而导致协会船级条文对 IACS 会员或准会员的接受失去意义。所以，再过一段时间，等尘埃落定后，看看伦敦保险市场会怎样修改协会船级条文。

8.4.2　协会船级条文之船龄控制

这里把有关船龄的部分节录如下：

"AGE LIMITATION

2 Cargoes and/or interests carried by Qualifying Vessels (as defined above) which exceed the following age limits will be insured on the policy or open cover conditions **subject to an additional premium to be agreed**.

Bulk or combination carriers over 10 years of age or other vessel over 15 years of age unless they:

2.1　have been used for the carriage of general cargo on an established and regular pattern of trading between a range of specified ports, and do not exceed 25 years of age, or

2.2　were constructed as containerships, vehicle carriers or double-skin open-hatch gantry crane vessels (OHGCs) and have been continuously used as such on an established and regular pattern of trading between a range of specified ports, and do not exceed 30 years of age."

显然是针对船舶的适航标准，除了船级外，船龄是另外一个主要的考虑。在这个协会船级条文下，散装货船或油矿两用船是不能超过 10 年的船龄，而其他类型的船舶是不能超过 15 年。但在 2.1 条文，针对班轮，船龄是不能超过 25 年。最后是 2.2 条文中针对的船型，就是集装箱船、运车船或双壳船并且是一直在固定的航线上航行，船龄只要不超过 30 年就可以接受。

需要注意的是，协会船级条文中的船级与船龄的规定都只是针对船舶(vessel)，而装卸港的驳船(craft/barge)是不受协会船级条文的管辖。对后者而言，标准与船龄要根据当地港口的规定。在有些地方的驳船，特别是淡水与没有什么风浪，船龄高达五六十年还是在营运。

8.4.3　"续保"(held cover)

协会船级条文最后的一段说明如果受保人的货方租用或使用的船舶是不符合船级与船龄的规定，是可以续保。这种情况的出现也经常会有，因为作为卖方的货方在付运时会有很多需要关心的地方，如买卖合约与信用证的最后付运日期已经非常接近，但想租用或使用的船舶就找不到，可能只有一艘但不符合协会船级条文的规定。这一来，权衡轻重之下，还是会租用并把货物装上这条船，因为毕竟超龄也只是一二年，不会对风险带来太大的区别，这样的话卖方还是需要续保，即使是加保费也会是有限，甚至是没有。

有关续保这一个重要的课题在第十一章之 7.1 段有详论，请参阅。在这里只重复三个方面，如下：

1. 续保的好处是受保人的货方即使违反了协会船级条文，但他可以通过续保就令保险合约一直生效,而保险人通常除了要求合理加保费外,也必须继续承保与作出赔付。

2. 续保有局限是违反协会船级条文太严重的情况下以至于不可以在保险市场以合理的加保费获得承保(说白了就是没有保险人愿意承保)。这方面的先例有新加坡上诉庭的 Everbright Commercial Enterprises v Axa Insurance Singapore (2001) 2 SLR 316,有关的船舶是没有船级,悬挂的是 Belize 的船旗,它在一个不存在的互保协会说是投保了责任风险等。新加坡法院作出了判决,认为合理的费率在保险市场是找不到的,所以不存在续保。所以,在 2001 年的协会船级条文就加上一条重要的针对续保的条文:只有续保是以合理的保费费率在合理的条件下实现的,在续保前发生的货损才可以得到赔付(Should a loss occur prior to such agreement being obtained cover may be provided but only if cover would have been available at a reasonable commercial market rate on reasonable commercial market terms)。换言之,即使是货方租的船舶不符合协会船级条文,也千万不要租用一艘太离谱的船舶,如没有船级,没有船旗,而且是 50 年船龄的散装船,这种情况下会有保险人愿意承保才怪,而受保人的货方也不存在有续保的权利。

3. 最后一提的是,负责草拟有关条文的伦敦保险市场的 Joint Cargo Committee,针对 2001 年版本中的续保条文曾经作出了以下有关何为合理费率与合理条件的指引:"It was felt that there had been misunderstandings in some quarters as to what was meant by ' held covered ' and that some elaboration would be helpful. Evidence of ' market terms ' would require an exercise to establish what terms might be obtainable in the market place i. e. from a representative sample of underwriters active in the class of underwriting cargo business. The fact that one underwriter might quote for a risk generally regarded as unacceptable by such a representative sample of underwriters, would not be evidence that the risk could be insured at a ' reasonable commercial market ' rate/terms. The collective view of such a sample would represent the market position. "(认为在市场上有对何为"续保"产生误解,需要进一步澄清。有关合理市场条件是需要确定,以什么条件这一个风险可在市场投保。这是要找一些有代表性的保险人,经常在货物保险市场承保。如果只是找到证据证明有一位保险人愿意以某一条件或费率承保这一风险,但其他有代表性的保险人不认为可以接受,这是不能作为证据说明有关的风险可以以合理保费费率与条件投保。必须要是多个有代表性保险人的集体意见才可以当作是市场的地位。)

9 第 6 条:战争除外

由于 1982 年协会货物条文与 2009 年的版本对本条文是一样的措辞,它主要的目的就是把这一个投保一切险的风险分为水险与战争险,换言之,在这份保险合约投保的只是水险,而战争险就根据协会货物条文(一切险)第6条被排除在外。至于货物运输要投保战争险,货方就需要加保,以协会战争条文(货物)(Institute War Clauses [CARGO] 1/1/09)作为保险合约条文,这方面承保的风险会在第九章的第1段与第2段进行介绍。

要了解这一做法,是需要从历史讲起。在船舶保险的最早年代,也就是17世纪初,在劳合社市场,由同一保险合约承保船舶与货物(这也是在英国保险市场雄霸了200多年并是在1906年《英国海上保险法》作为附件一的劳合社标准S. G保单的来由,其中S. G. 是代表Ship & Goods),而且在同一份保险合约承保列明的水险与战争险。S. G. 保险合约承保的风险包括:"the seas, men of war, fire, enemies, pirates, rovers, thieves, jettisons, letters of mart and countermart, surprisals, takings at sea, arrests, restraints, and detainments of all kings, princes, and people, of what nation, condition, or quality soever, barratry of the master and mariners, and of all other perils, losses, and misfortunes, that have or shall come to the hurt, detriment, or damage of the said goods and merchandise, and ship, etc."

而劳合社在船舶与海上货物运输保险的重要性众所周知,由于英国1720年的《Bubble Act》只允许个人的保险人经营业务,这正是劳合社的做法就是以个人名义参与各种保险集团,名为syndicate。该立法造就了劳合社的垄断与崛起,长达100年之久,直至1824年《海上保险法》(Marine Insurance Act)才打破垄断的局面,允许英国保险公司经营海上保险业务。

9.1　战争险与水险的分离

同一保险合约承保水险与战争险的做法在以前是通过列明风险同时包括了水险与战争险,在当时的年代也的确有必要。例如,船舶与所载的货物在大海失踪,在当时通讯欠缺与国际环境并不稳定的情况下是不容易知道该船舶是因为水险还是因为战争险导致失踪,举证责任是在受保人。一并承保的话就无须作出区分,反正保险人难逃要作出全损的赔偿。这一情况到了19世纪才有了改变,在1898年6月15日,劳合社在他的大会中通过决议把水险与战争险分开承保,并要求在海上保险合约的劳合社标准S. G保单中加上一条名为Free of Capture and Seizure Clause,简称FC&S条文,作用是把劳合社标准S. G保单的列明战争险排除,另投保。那么为什么不在原来的保险合约中将"enemies, letters of mart and countermart, surprisals, arrests of all kings, princes, and people"直接删除呢?英国保险行业的人们习惯尊重传统,很少改变以前的用词,只是在有需要的时候加入另外的条文以超越以前的条文。最早版本在1912年8月1日的FC&S条文措辞是:"**Free of Capture, Seizure etc. Clause**

Warranted free of capture seizure and detention, and the consequences thereof or any attempt thereat, piracy excepted, and also from all consequences of hostilities or warlike operations, whether before or after declaration of war."

这一分开承保的改变是来自几个方面的影响，其中一个重要的影响是在 1862 年首先出现了鱼雷与 1893 年法国建造了第一艘潜水艇。鱼雷与潜水艇可以对船舶造成重大的威胁，传统的海上武器（主要就是大炮）与它们不能相提并论。而同时，船舶价格与货物的价格在拿破仑战争后大幅度提高。在 1898 年，还发生过一宗事件，涉及英法争夺苏丹，导致了英法差点发生战争。而在同年代，英国与美国之间的关系也非常紧张。这导致了劳合社十分关心有强大海军力量的英法与美国发生全面战争会带来的严重后果，因为这可能导致劳合社的保险人面对承担不起的经济后果。这种情况后来几乎发生，可显示商业保险市场的局限。就是在 20 世纪 80 年代，来自对美国因为石棉污染为主的再保险赔付导致了英国劳合社的保险人严重亏损，几乎没有能力赔付以至于要破产。在短短的 3 年期间，劳合社保险人亏损了 60 亿英镑，其中在 1990 年，亏损是 29 亿英镑，这是劳合社从来没有过的亏损。而分摊到每个保险人的头上，就是平均每个人在该年年度要承担 10 万英镑。反正这些亏损导致好几个保险人自杀与倒闭，因为大家都是以个人的名义承保承担无限责任。这种恶劣情况到了 1993 年劳合社委任了新的主席与首席执行官并做出了一些基本性的改革，成功地吸收了有限公司的大量资本（corporate capital）才慢慢恢复元气。可见，商业保险市场承受风险的能力还是很有限，如果要承担犹如无底洞似的风险，如“二战”中纳粹德国对英国伦敦轰炸造成的财产损失，就必须由国家或国民自己承担了。

上述的 FC&S 条文带来无数的诉讼，到了 The“Coxwold”(1942) 73 Lloyd's Rep. 1，它的版本已经变得非常复杂，如下：“Warranted free of capture, seizure, arrest, restraint or detainment, and the consequences thereof or of any attempt thereat; also from the consequences of hostilities or warlike operations, whether there be a declaration of war or not; but his warranty shall not exclude collision, contact with any fixed or floating object (other than a mine or torpedo), stranding, heavy weather or fire unless caused directly (and independently or the nature of the voyage or service which the vessel concerned or, in the case of a collision, any other vessel involved therein, is performing) by a hostile act by or against a belligerent power; and for the purpose of this warranty“power”includes any authority maintaining naval, military or air forces in association with a power.”

Coxwold 轮是“二战”期间的一艘商船，装了汽油供应给在挪威的英国军队，它必须加入护航并需要不断根据护航队长的指令调整航向以避开德国潜艇与鱼雷的攻击。显然，该船舶是在参与一种类似战争的行为（warlike operation）是受保人与保险人在诉讼的时候没有争议的。但发生事故时是在下大雨并且能见度不好，再加上灯火管制（所以看不见护航队伍前面的船舶）且灯塔的灯也不亮（导致无法确定船舶方位），这最终导致了 Coxwold 轮搁浅。于是带来一个争议：到底搁浅是水险还是战争险的责任？毕竟在这种情况下，水险的风险也的确大增。结果该先例去了贵族院，把上诉庭的判决推翻，判是属于战争险导致的损失。这一来，伦敦保险市场并不满意，因为在战争期间，可以说是这些船舶都参与类似战争的行为如加入护航，岂非再也不需要投保水险了,等于劳合社也没有生意可做。这导致了 FC&S 条文又要作出修改,修改后的就如上文节录。该条文的复杂是表现在它首先将劳合社标准 S. G 保单中的战争险排除,然后规定这种除外不包括碰撞、搁浅等的水险,只要不是由战争的风险所直接带来的(如被敌方军舰拦腰撞沉)。反正这个 FC&S 条文并不是能看得懂英文的人就看得懂,所以带来很多批评,如在 The"Anita"(1970)2 Lloyd's Rep. 355,Mocatta 大法官也有以下的说法:"It is probably too late to make an effective plea that the traditional methods of insuring against ordinary marine risks and what are usually called war risks should be radically overhauled. The present method, certainly as regards war risks insurance, is tortuous and complex in the extreme. It cannot be beyond the wit of underwriters and those who advise them in this age of law reform to devise more straightforward and easily comprehended terms of cover."

另外,联合国在 1978 年的一份名为 TD/B/C. 4/ISL/27 的 119(4)报告中建议说:"The antiquated Lloyd's S. G. Form should be revised and updated. Specifically, the Perils Clause should be revised to be comprehensible in the modern day context as well as to eliminate war risk terminology. Furthermore, the Perils Clause should be combined with the other appropriate Institute Clause so that the designated risks appear in one unified Risks Clause. Consideration should be given to altering the method of granting insurance coverage from the enumeration of perils method to an all risks grant of coverage minus specific exceptions. Consideration should also be given to facilitating the method of granting war risk insurance. All these reforms are designed to make the insurance coverage easier to understand and to interpret, particularly in view of its international use."

反正是英国保险市场面对这些国际批评也懂得进行适当的调整,也就是在 1982 年推出了新的保险合约格式(Lloyd's Marine Policy,简称 MAR)与有关协会货物条文,完全摒弃了劳合社标准 S. G 保单,也同时摒弃了 FC&S 条文。但本书无意进一步分析与 FC&S 条文有关的先例,这已经变成了历史,这里只是让大家明白发展的来龙去脉。

9.2　对承保战争险作出的局限

把战争险与水险分开承保后,到了 19 世纪 30 年代,保险市场针对承保战争险增加了一连串的限制。这是由于现代战争与武器可以造成的重大破坏,尤其是在人口与财产密集的情况下,首次在 1937 年 4 月 26 日表现出来。当天,德国空军参与西班牙内战,并攻击了没有任何抗御力量的西班牙的历史名城 Guernica。在 3 个小时内,飞机投掷的炸弹与飞机上的机关枪扫射,导致了几乎全城摧毁与大部分民众被屠杀。由于当时的通讯已经比较发达,导致该事件被广泛报道,令世界各国知道该事件的血腥与摧毁性。这也引起了伦敦保险市场的关心,导致他们在第二年,即 1938 年达成一个协议名为"排除战争与内战风险协议"(War and Civil Risks Exclusion Agreement),该协议最新是 1982 年 4 月 1 日的版本。它的目的是排除所有保险与再保险合约中有关战争与内战风险的直接或间接损失的责任。但该协议有例外的情况允许战争险可以承保,这就是在海上保险(不论是货物还是船舶)方面。有关货物在海上的运输是可以投保战争险的,因为风险不集中,只涉及个别船舶上的货物,但受到一个名为“War Risks Waterborne Agreement”的限制。

针对货物的“War Risks Waterborne Agreement”,主要的限制是承保战争险尽量局限在海上运输的时间内,因为毕竟个别船舶的风险不会如岸上的风险那么集中。所以,货物战争险的第5条的运输条文(Transit Clause)比承保水险的(A)、(B)与(C)保险合约的运输条文(以前被称为仓至仓条文)局限,只承保货物装上大船直到卸下的这个期间,而不是整个从仓库到仓库的期间,因为后者涉及了岸上的战争险。

另外的限制是在预约/开口保单(open cover)形式的货物保险,如保险人有权给7天不等的通知就可以中断战争险保险合约关系。需要有这样的一个规定就是因为预约/开口保单作为一个合约时间是会比较长,但期间如果有一些突发的战争风险,再不是原来偏低的保费可以满足,甚至保险人不愿意再承保,就会有问题是他不能说走就走,因为这会涉及毁约。要合法这样做,就必须在订约的时候加上一个条文说是保险人有选择权,在作出通知后就可以脱身。只要是订约自由,这样的约定就应该有效。说到这一方面,也可以一提是由于海盗(特别是索马里海盗)风险的大幅度增加,而在协会货物条文(一切险)内海盗险是属于水险(因为没有被排除),所以伦敦保险市场在2009年也引进了一条类似的条文附加在协会货物条文(一切险)中可让保险人单方面给了通知就脱身。有关条文Cargo Piracy Notice of Cancellation请见稍后9.4段。

另一个限制是在预约/开口保单形式的货物保险会有对责任限制的规定,如“USMYM 1,000,000 any one sending, shipment and/or location”,这里的限制就是不论是水险还是战争险保险人最多赔付1,000,000美元。这尤其是限制了货物同时在一个地点(location)如在装货或卸货的码头同时有受保人几票货物一并受到战争险的摧毁,保险人也限制了赔付责任。

而这种限制也会带来大问题,包括在政治方面。记得在两伊战争时期,当时的萨达姆政权是受到阿拉伯国家与西方国家特别是美国政府的支持向伊朗开战,而战争是需要大量的物资支持。当时的伊拉克是很大程度需要从约旦的港口进口物资,这就需要一个很漫长而且很危险的路上运输才可以将物资运到伊拉克。但由于只有水险才可以是仓库到仓库,而战争险对该段路上运输是不承保,导致了贸易的困难。从而致使伊拉克与其他的阿拉伯国家对伦敦保险市场的强烈不满与抗议,而最终阿拉伯国家自己成立了一个基金承保这段路上的战争风险才让贸易能够顺利进行,否则不论是出口商还是进口商谁都不愿意承担这种巨大而且无法得到保险保障的风险。

9.3 英国政府参与战争险的承保

在1903年英国政府委任了一个委员会看看战争的风险是否可以由商业的保险市场承保,委员会的结论是可以。但在后来的日俄战争,鱼雷所造成的庞大损失显示了伦敦保险市场无法或不愿意承担这种重大的战争风险。结果在1913年英国成立了第二个委员会并为政府在 1914 年 8 月设计了一个计划。其中有关船舶的战争险承保,由英国政府承担 80% 的再保风险。针对货物在海上的战争险承保,就由英国政府成立了一个国家保险办(State Insurance Office)直接承保装在英国船舶上的货物。但对货物的承保是允许商业市场进行竞争,这造成了在第一次世界大战期间,海上货物保险有 70% 是保险市场承保,而只有 30% 以下才是国家保险办承保。往往是风险更大或更严重的才是国家保险办承保,这导致了英国政府在船舶战争险有盈余,但在货物战争险就亏损。

到了第二次世界大战就有了不同的计划,就是英国政府与劳合社保险市场达成了一个君子协议以减少他们之间的竞争。例如,涉及英国港口的航次,商业市场同意会收取比政府更高的保费,但不涉及英国港口的航次,保险市场就可以自由决定保费的高低等。

到了 1952 年,又有了不同的计划,这是通过立法带来了 Marine and Aviation Insurance (War Risks) Act,其内容包括英国政府提供战争险保险,如果船东或货方无法在商业保险市场获得承保,英国政府有权成立一个基金名为"Marine and Aviation Insurance (War Risks) Fund"收保费与作出赔付,通过与英国战争险互保协会的协议提供再保险等安排。

9.4　海盗险的承保

唯一值得一提的是 2009 年协会货物条文之 6.2 条的有关捕获风险条文,在括号中说明不包括海盗(piracy excepted)。换言之,如果船舶与船上的货物被索马里海盗捕获,并最后遭受损失或需要付赎金作为施救费用或共同海损费用才能取回这些货物的话,这不属于战争险范围。但要说明这些海盗险只是在(A)条文才是承保范围,因为保的是一切险。但在(B)条文及(C)条文,这个风险就不被列明承保。由于索马里海盗的猖獗,导致了大量的与海盗有关的索赔,所以在不久前,伦敦保险市场引进了一条名为"Cargo Piracy Notice of Cancellation"的条文附加在一切险的货物保险。条文内容如下:

"Where this insurance covers piracy and/or general average, salvage and sue and labour charges arising from piracy, such cover may be cancelled by insurers giving 7 days notice in writing, cancellation to take effect on the expiry of 7 days (10 days in respect of reinsurance) from midnight of the day on which the notice is issued by insurers.

Insurers agree to reinstate this coverage subject to agreement between insurers and the insured prior to the cancellation taking effect as to any new rate of premium and/or conditions and/or warranties. Such cancellation shall not affect any insurance which has attached before the cancellation takes effect.

If the cancellation is in relation to specific geographical areas, such areas will be clearly defined by insurers in the notice of cancellation."

这个条文是不影响海盗险还是水险所承保,但水险没有像战争险保险合约一样允许保险人可以给出7天的通知,然后再中断战争险的承保。这里的原因是战争的严重性会转眼之间有所变化,所以保险人必须根据订约自由而获得从合约中脱身的机会,即使再承保也可以收取不同的保费或者约定不同的承保条件。而索马里海盗的风险现在也会是瞬息万变,所以要附加这一个条文。照理说,海上货物保险通常只是一个航次,保险期间不会像船舶保险一样多是长达一年。但还是有这个必要的,更何况很多货物保险是以预约/开口保单的形式,保险期间会拖得更长了。

10. 第7条:罢工、暴乱与恐怖行为除外

协会货物条文的1982年版本与2009年版本在本条文本质上基本相同,就是把罢工等风险排除在(A)条文以外,受保人如果有这个需要就另以协会罢工条文(货物)(Institute Strikes Clauses [CARGO])1/1/09投保或者加保。但在2009年条文中,明显就在第7.3条把恐怖行为的风险扩大,特别是他们作出袭击的意图也尽量包罗万象(从1982年只针对政治意图加上意识形态上与宗教上的意图)。这一来,在协会罢工条文(货物)1/1/09也作出相应的修改,如果需要承保的话就可以获得保障。但要注意的是,货物罢工险承保的只是一些实质的损失或损坏,以及为了避免或减少该损失的施救费用,不包括因为罢工或者恐怖行为导致货物运输的延误带来的损失。

恐怖行为的风险在近年来越来越受到重视。本来这一风险主要是针对航空运输的,与船舶关系不大。例如在1960~1970年间,有超过200架民航的飞机被恐怖分子劫持。但在同时间,没有什么船舶受到恐怖行为的影响。可以提出的是意大利船舶Achille Lauro轮在1985年被四个巴勒斯坦恐怖分子劫持。另是在2002年10月6日,一艘名为Limberg轮的法国超级油轮受到了恐怖分子的袭击并造成了船货的损坏。但针对货物而言,它不只是在船舶上,也可以在岸上受到恐怖行为的威胁并造成可能的损坏。如2001年美国的"9·11"事件,类似的恐怖行为如果发生在码头附近,就可以造成很多船舶与运输货物(不论是在船上还是在岸上的货物)的损失或损坏。

首先,可以探讨恐怖行为的定义,根据英国Reinsurance(Acts of Terrorism) Act 1993立法Section 2(2)的定义(立法主要是针对当时的爱尔兰共和军):"In this section 'acts of terrorism' means acts of persons acting on behalf of, or in connection with, any organisation which carriers out activities directed towards the overthrowing or influencing, by force or violence, of Her Majesty's Government in the United Kingdom or any other Government *de jure de facto*."

但这一定义看来只针对为了影响政府的恐怖行为,但没有针对为了威胁民众造成社会不安的恐怖行为。定义也没有追究恐怖行为是为了达成什么意图。最后,这一定义不针对个体的恐怖行为,因为其只是针对代表组织或者和组织相关的个人恐怖行为。

另一定义是在 Prevention of Terrorism(Temporary Provisions) Act, 1989 s. 20(1)中(其主要也是为了针对当时的爱尔兰共和军):"Terrorism means the use of violence for political ends, and includes any use of violence for the purpose of putting the putting the public or any section of the public in fear."

有关恐怖行为与战争的区别,他们的区别在两个先例中有所涉及。第一个是美国的先例 Pan American v. Aetna Casualty (1975) 1 Lloyd's Rep. 77,案情涉及在 1970 年 9 月,巴勒斯坦恐怖分子劫持了四架民航飞机。其中的一架被劫持去了黎巴嫩首都贝鲁特并事后在该机场被炸毁。在事后的泛美航空公司和保险公司的诉讼中,其中提到了美国国务卿向联合国发言并提出有关恐怖行为与战争的分别,说:

"The issue is not war-war between states, civil war, or revolutionary war. The issue is not the strivings of people to achieve self-determination and independence. Rather, it is whether millions of air travelers can continue to fly in safety each year. It is whether a person who receives a letter can open it without the fear of being blown-up. It is whether diplomats can safely carry out their duties. It is whether international meetings—like the Olympic games, like this Assembly—can proceed without the ever-present threat of violence...

Certainly the terrorist acts I have cited are totally unacceptable attacks against the very fabric of international order. They must be universally condemned, whether we consider the cause the terrorists invoke noble or ignoble, legitimate or illegitimate. We must take effective steps to prevent the hijacking of international civil aircraft."

在这个发言中可以挑出几个恐怖行为的特征,如一些不代表政府的政治团体造成故意的暴力,针对没有参与战争的平民与他们的财产,发生恐怖行为的地点是远离战争地点,希望造成宣传的后果。恐怖行为的例子有劫持飞机,邮寄带有爆炸品或化学品的邮件,刺杀外交人士和袭击无辜的运动员等。

在英国受"9·11"事件波及的案例 P&C Insurance Limited (PUBL) v. Silversea Cruises Ltd. (2004) Lloyd's Rep. IR 696 (CA)中,上诉庭也提到了恐怖行为与战争的区别。其中说到"9·11"事件是不会被一般人视为战争行为,战争行为是需要一个明确的对象开战。还有是战争行为有一定的持续性,而不是一个单一的偶然性袭击。Ward 大法官说:"Men of business, the underwriters and the insured, would not have said that 11 September was an 'act of war' but rather that it was terrorist action from extremist groups. To have declared 'war on terror' was a rhetorical response serving only to emphasise that there was no identifiable 'side' against whom the war could be waged. Further, an 'armed conflict' had an air of continuity about it, and what were essentially random attacks did not carry for ordinary businessmen, the sense of present and persisting fighting between military groups which was the hallmark of armed conflict."

而前面已经提到过,在 2009 年的条文中已经把恐怖行为的风险扩大,其中是从原先的袭击意图只是针对政治方面,而现在已经扩大到了意识形态与宗教上的意图。

本来,政治意图已经是一个广泛的术语,但加上了意识形态(ideological)上的意图后可以说是更加广泛。本来这一个词是已经被考虑过但最终没有采用,原因是其过于广泛且无法确定范围,但现在加进了这个条文。至于加上宗教上的意图,应该是更加明确,因为近些年的很多恐怖行为均是基于这种意图。

最后一提的是,这种风险与其他种类的是属于水险的风险也不是这么容易区分的,如暴力盗窃(theft)、恶意行为(malicious act)、海盗(pirates)等。比如说是现在的索马里海盗,也受到一切险的承保。但问题是如果索马里海盗的行为一旦被定义为恐怖行为,如涉及了政治意图或意识形态或宗教上的意图,就会带来严重的后果。其中一个是一切险不再赔付受保人的损失,因为这一条除外条文的规定。还有是船东或货方想给海盗赎金也带来困难,因为目前联合国有公约禁止直接与间接支付金钱给恐怖行为,这是1999年12月9日第54届联合国大会通过的《制止向恐怖主义提供资助的国际公约》禁止直接或间接的支付金钱给恐怖组织。

第九章　协会战争险/罢工险条文(货物)与有关协会货物条文(B)与(C)的承保

1. 协会战争险条文(货物)承保风险

协会战争险条文(货物)中的第1条就是针对所承保的列明风险,而这些列明风险分为三大类,其中第1.1条针对从战争(war)直至叛乱(insurrection)的一连串涉及有暴力的列明风险。而第1.2条针对从捕获(capture)直至羁押(detainment)的一连串不一定涉及暴力的列明风险。而第1.3条就针对一些和平的时候都会面对的,如弃置了的水雷、鱼雷、炸弹、武器等。

1.1　第一类战争险

这条承保由于"战争、内战、革命、造反、叛乱或由于这些原因引起的民变"("*War civil war revolution rebellion insurrection or civil strife arising therefrom, or any hostile act by or against a belligerent power*")所引致的损失。

针对这些列明风险的解释,曾经有个说法用由上至下的阶梯型(ladder)对这一类型的风险作出描述。也就是说,国与国之间的战争是最严重与层次最高的风险,然后到了最低层次的叛乱。这种说法可见Farwell大法官在Republic of Bolivia v. Indemnity Mutual Assurance Co Ltd (1909) 1 KB 785在第801页所说的。但这个说法不被后来的一些著名先例所接受,如Mustill大法官在Spinney's (1948) Ltd v. Royal Insurance Co Ltd (1980) 1 Lloyd's Rep 406中所说的,如下:"reliance was placed on a number of judgments (such as that of Lord Justice Farwell in the Republic of Bolivia case) in which Courts have identified various stages through which civil strife can pass as it becomes progressively worse: the suggestion being that if one can establish an order of ranking with civil war at the top, and if the characteristics of a peril lower down the list can be established, it can safely be assumed that a civil war must possess all these characteristics together with some others. **I have not found this approach very productive. Even if a ranking could be devised, it would not be invariable. In certain instances, some of the steps would be omitted. Furthermore, I am not convinced that all the listed perils lie in a straight line with riot at the bottom and civil war at the top. Some appear to stand rather to one side....**"(Mustill大法官不认为这个说法很有建设性,因为在

不同的情况中会有一些阶段是不会出现的，也会有些情况中这些阶段是相当一致的与不容易区分。）

另外，Rix 大法官在 Kuwait Airways Corp v. Kuwait Insurance Co (No. 1) (1996) 1 Lloyd's Rep 664 中有同样的说法，说："... as to the ladder approach, or as to the approach to the effect that the terms found in pars. (a) to (f) (these are insured perils with (a) war, invasion, foreign enemies, etc to (f) hi-jacking) should be construed so as to permit of no overlap between them, or some of them, I am distrustful of the usefulness of such general maxims, save in limited circumstances... The fact is, that the ladder approach and the no overlap approach may be able to grade a list of perils in a descending or ascending order of gravity, but that is not to say that some terms of greater gravity may not embrace, rather than be distinct from, other terms of lesser gravity; and some terms may be more general, others more specific. The no overlap approach, however seeks to give each peril or groups of perils an exclusive meaning..."（Rix 大法官也不接受这些一般性的说法，除了在一些局限的情况下。这些说法是一个阶梯型，每一个阶段都是独立的，不与其他阶段重叠。但事实上有一些比较严重的阶段会包括一些不那么严重阶段的风险。例如，"造反"就会包括"叛乱"，两者之间很难区分。）

在 Kuwait Airways Corp v. Kuwait Insurance Co 先例中，要区分在该保单中是哪一种战争风险，第 4 条文有关承保科威特航空公司放置在科威特机场的昂贵零件或设备是只有除了承保风险(a)的其他战争风险引致的损失才能获得延伸去承保，有关条文如下："It is noted and agreed that the indemnity provided by this Policy other than Par. (a) of Section 1 is extended to include loss of or damage to Aircraft Spares and equipment which is the property of the Assured or for which they are responsible...."

而承保风险(a)的列明风险有战争、外国侵略、外国敌意行为、内战，等（war, invasion, acts of foreign enemies, hostilities [whether war be declared or not], civil war, rebellion, revolution, insurrection, attempts at usurpation of power.）。显然，针对 1996 年伊拉克侵略科威特而造成的这些损失，保险公司作为被告声称是由承保风险(a)所引起，所以不赔付。但受保人的科威特航空公司说是由延伸被承保风险(c)或(e)所引起，它们分别是："(c) Any act of one or more persons, whether or not agents of a sovereign power, for political or terrorist purposes and whether the loss or damage resulting therefrom is accidental or intentional.（由于政治或恐怖的原因，部分人士不论是否属于主权国家的代理人，意外或故意的行动所造成的损失。）(e) Confiscation, nationalisation, seizure, restraint, detention, appropriation, requisition for title or use by or under the order of any Government (whether civil military or de facto) or public or local authority.（没收、国有化、扣押、拘禁、羁押、征收等根据某些政府的命令。）"

另外介绍的是 National Oil Company of Zimbabwe v. Nicholas Collwyn Sturge (1991) 2 Lloyd's Rep 281，案情涉及一个非法组织名为 Mozambique National Resistance

(Renamo),由于想推翻 Frelimo 政府(莫桑比克解放前线),将莫桑比克的油库炸毁。争议是要看该行为是属于内战、革命、造反、叛乱或民变("loss damage or expense caused by ... civil war, revolution, rebellion, insurrection, or civil strife therefrom ...")还是恐怖行为("Any terrorist or person acting from a political motive"),因为前者的风险被排除在承保范围外,而后者是在承保范围内。非法组织 Renamo 是受到白人政府的支持,推翻 Frelimo 政府。而 Frelimo 在 1974 年从葡萄牙独立的时候就已经掌握了合法政权。Saville 大法官认为这些被排除的战争险的定义在一个商业合约中应该尽量从商业人士的角度看待,而保险人只要证明当时莫桑比克的情况如果已经能够达到叛乱,就不用进一步考虑阶梯中更高的造反或者是内战,因为保险人已经可以拒赔。Saville 大法官这样说:"In the context of a commercial contract such as the policy under discussion, the expressions 'civil war', 'rebellion' and 'insurrection' bear their ordinary business meaning. In this context, 'civil war' means a war with the special characteristic of being civil - ie being internal rather than external - see Spinney's (1948) Ltd v. Royal Insurance Co Ltd (1980) 1 Lloyd's Rep 406. 'Rebellion' and 'insurrection' have somewhat similar meanings to each other. To my mind, each means an organised and violent internal uprising in a country with, as a main purpose, the object of trying to overthrow or supplant the government of their country, though 'insurrection' denotes a lesser degree of organisation and size than 'rebellion' - see Home Insurance v. Davila (1954) 212 F. 2d 731. Underwriters accept that if they cannot establish insurrection then they must necessarily fail on rebellion."

在该先例根据专家证人和其他证据,Saville 大法官接受当时莫桑比克是有一个叛乱(insurrection)。

以下就每一种列明风险进行探讨。

1.1.1 战争(war)

该列明风险针对海上货物运输保险是在 1982 年首次被引入协会货物保险条文。可能由于历史不是太长且这段时间还比较和平,所以对货物的战争保险还没有针对性的先例;但从以前的一些有关先例可以看到其定义。战争一般来说是有两个或更多的主权国家的政权(不论是否受到外国或者是国际社会的承认)参与的武力冲突。"战争"这一词用在商业性的合约,不论是保单还是租约,英国法律都会给它们一个商业性(commercial)与常识性(common sense)的解释,而不会根据一些技术性的解释,如要英国外交部作出承认或参与战争的国家必须公开宣战。

在 Kawasaki Kisen Kabushiki Kaisya v. Batnham Steamship Co Ltd (1939) 63 LLP 155 的先例,涉及中日战争全面爆发前的武力冲突以及双方积极备战,其中可以介绍一些事态的发展,如在 1937 年 8 月 23 日,美国国务卿呼吁中日双方不要以战争解决问题。在 8 月 25 日日本海军封锁中国海岸,不准中国船舶进出,并在 9 月 2 日把封锁延伸到所有的船舶。8 月 30 日中国政府向当时的"联合国"(League of Nations)投诉日本侵略,当时的蒋介石总统要求国际社会插手干预中日间没有宣战的战役(undeclared Sino-Japanese War)。在9月2日,日本外相说在中国的一切行动都是为了逼使中国变得更友好,并说明在中国并没有战事,只是一个重大的武力冲突,而日本愿意随时停止。在9月6日,美国罗斯福总统命令所有在中国的美国人必须马上离开。在9月15日,在当时的"联合国"大会中,中日双方的代表互相指责,其中日本代表指称中国所指的侵略是扭曲事实。至于在 Kawasaki Kisen Kabushiki Kaisya v. Batnham Steamship Co Ltd 先例中,案情是租约中有条文说明如果有战争爆发是涉及日本(注意承租人是日本公司),船东或者承租人有权利可以中断该租约,而船东也是在9月18日向承租人宣告中断该租约。船东的立场显然是在9月18日前中日已经发生战争,而租约内"战争"一词应该给它一般性的解释,而不是技术性的解释。但承租人从英国外交部取得一封信函,说明"在目前的情况下,中国的情况是不确定与混乱的,英国政府是不能说死中国已经发生了战争。"(that the current situation in China is indeterminate and anomalous and His Majesty's Government are not at present prepared to say that in their view a state of war exists.)承租人认为这种是否属于战争的情况最好是由英国政府说了算,毕竟租约的适用法是英国法。而一般人包括法院去解释是否发生战争会根据传言、报纸报道等来判断,就比不上英国政府因为它们会有特别的资料可循。但在仲裁庭、高院与上诉庭都不支持承租人的说法,也不同意"战争"一词会有什么技术性。其中 Greene 大法官这样说:"But I must not be taken as in any sense disagreeing with the further view expressed by the learned Judge, that in the particular context in which the word 'war' is found in this charter-party, that word must be construed, having regard to the general tenor and purpose of the document, in what may be called a commonsense way. If one had asked the owners of this vessel on the relevant date, if this charter-party had never existed, or if one had agreed any shipowner what he thought about the then present position between China and Japan, as to whether or not a war existed, I cannot imagine any commercial person with any common sense answering that question in any other way than that in which the arbitrator has answered it. ... It seems to me that to suggest that within the meaning of this charter-party war had not broken out involving Japan on the relevant date, is to attribute to the parties to it a desire to import into their contract some obscure and uncertain technicalities of international law rather than the common sense of business man."

Mustill 大法官在 Spinney's v. Royal Insurance (1980) 1 Lloyd's Rep. 406 也是有同样的说法,认为在某些情况(如英国与其他国家外交关系的状况,英国是否承认外国的政权,或英国是否与一个外国开战等)的确是英国政府说了算。但有关在保单或其他商业合约中对战争的解释(判断黎巴嫩在1976年的时候是否处于内战的情况)并不是根据英国政府的承认与否。Mustill 大法官认为除非法院满足英国政府对保单中"战争"这一词的解释是与法院的解释完全一致,才会考虑接受英国政府的说法。

Mustill 大法官这样说：

"I did not accept the plaintiffs' application. There are, of course, well-recognized situations in which it is the practice of the Court to consult the Secretary of State, and on which his response is treated as conclusive. There are mainly, if not exclusively, cases in which the state of the United Kingdom's diplomatic relations forms an integral part of the issue in suit. Such cases include those where the issue is whether the United Kingdom recognizes a person as a foreign sovereign, or whether the United Kingdom is at war with a foreign state, or whether the United Kingdom has recognized the existence of a state of belligerency between two foreign nations. By analogy, the Court will consult the executive of a foreign state where the issue is whether that state is at war with another: Dalmia Dairy Industries Ltd v National Bank of Pakistan (1978) 2 Lloyd's Rep 233.

The present case is not in this category. The issue is not whether the events in Lebanon were recognized by the United Kingdom as amounting to a civil war in the sense in which the term is used in Public International Law with the corollary that this country would, if the occasion had arisen, have accorded to the participants the rights and demanded of them the duties appropriate to belligerents. The question here is whether there was a civil war within the meaning of the policy. The two questions are not the same, and a pronouncement by the Secretary of State on own will not suffice to decide the other...

Answering the question would require the Secretary of State to ascertain the meaning of the words used in the policy, and unless the Court could be sure that the Secretary of State and the Court were adopting the same interpretation, the exercise would serve only to confuse..."

接下来介绍的是一个美国上诉庭的先例:Pan American v. Aetna Casualty (1975) 1 Lloyd's Rep 77。案件涉及在 1970 年,泛美航空公司的一架波音 747 飞机从布鲁塞尔开往纽约的时候被两名巴勒斯坦人劫持,先飞去了贝鲁特,最后去了开罗把飞机炸毁。该两名巴勒斯坦人是属于一个名为 Popular Front for the Liberation of Palestine (PFLP)的组织,而他们行动的目的就是惩罚美国政府一直支持以色列对付巴勒斯坦人的行为。由于当时劫持飞机的行为很少出现,所以保险市场还没有特别针对劫持飞机造成的损失,只是在酝酿加入这些条文作为一切险的除外风险。这导致了泛美航空公司向保险人提出索赔,要求赔偿该 747 飞机的损失共达 25,000,000 美元。泛美航空公司投保的是一切险,但有条文排除战争险,只是排除的战争险中没有特别说明飞机被劫持与破坏的情况。所以,保险人为了抗拒赔付,指称有关的事件实际上是战争与其他的列明风险,或民间暴乱(civil commotion)等,而这些都是属于除外条文中的事项。这都被法院拒绝,其中有关战争的列明风险,法院认为是不能延伸至一个政治组织(但并非代表主权国家或受雇于主权国家)故意与暴力地对一些民间的财产造成损失,主要是为了宣传的作用,而且造成损失的地点是远离一些战争地区:

"The term 'war' was defined as an employment of force between governments and the phrase 'warlike operations' could not be extended to include infliction of international violence by political groups (neither employed by nor representing the government) upon civilians and their property at places far removed from the locale or subject of any warfare; and the avowed purpose of the destruction was not coercion and conquest but the striking of spectacular blows for propaganda effect."

1.1.2 内战(civil war)

内战与战争不同的地方在于,内战主要指发生在国家内部而不是对外的战争。这可看 National Oil Company of Zimbabwe v. Nicholas Collwyn Sturge (1991) 2 LLR 281 中 Saville 大法官给内战的定义,如下:"In this context, 'civil war' means a war with the special characteristic of being civil - i. e. being internal rather than external..."

在 Spinney's (1948) Ltd and others v. Royal Insurance Co Ltd (1980) 1 Lloyd's Rep. 406 中,Mustill 大法官认为考虑是否属于内战必须针对三个问题,如下:(1)可否说敌对的双方或多方之间发生冲突?(Can it be said that the conflict was between opposing 'sides'?)(2)敌对各方的目的是什么及他们有什么计划去实现这个目的?(What were the objectives of the"sides", and how did they set about pursuing them?)(3)冲突的程度与它有否影响公共秩序与居民的生命?(What was the scale of the conflict, and of its effect on public order and on the life of the inhabitants?)

该先例的案情是原告在黎巴嫩的贝鲁特开了一间超级市场,并在 1975 年向作为被告的保险人对这些财产投保一切险。一切险也包括了暴动与罢工,但排除了内战、革命、造反、叛乱等战争风险。在 1976 年年初,有一群暴民冲进该超级市场大肆破坏与抢掠,造成损失高达 1,400,000 英镑。原告向被告的保险人提出索赔,但被告拒绝赔偿。而针对内战与造反等,Mustill 大法官认定当时黎巴嫩十分混乱,可以说大家在混战,所以不构成内战,因为没办法去认定有哪些敌对的各方及他们的目的,说:"... there were no 'sides' which could be identified as being engaged in a civil war in the more usual sense of the term, i. e. in a struggle by one side to wrest power from the other; although the fighting in Lebanon was nothing to suggest that by January, 1976, matters had advanced beyond massive civil strife and virtual anarchy to the stage of a civil war; and if the other characteristics of a civil war had been present, there would have been a finding for the defendants on this issue."

顺便一提的是在该先例,被告保险人最终还是胜诉,因为排除了的战争风险还有一项就是民间暴乱,其严重程度变成是一个集体的行动(civil commotion assuming the proportions of or amounting to a popular rising)。Mustill 大法官认为黎巴嫩在 1976 年年初就是处于这种情况,因为民间暴乱不像内战或造反,不需要有推翻现有政府的政治目的。它只需要在暴民之间有一定的凝聚力就已经足够。

1.1.3　革命、造反、叛乱(revolution, rebellion, insurrection)

把这三个战争风险放在一起讲是因为它们有共通点,一般而言有两个要求:(1)涉及有组织的暴力;(2)目的是推翻现有政权并作出替代,即使不是全国范围内的也是在国家的部分地区。这里可以先节录 Mustill 大法官在 Spinney's v. Royal Insurance (1980) 1 Lloyd's Rep. 406 中针对"造反"一词说:"As regard 'rebellion' I adopt the definition in the Oxford English Dictionary (Murray): '... organised resistance to the ruler or government of one's country; insurrection, revolt.' To this I would add that the purpose of the resistance must be to supplant the existing rules or at least to deprive them of authority over part of their territory. The dictionary defines 'insurrections' in a similar manner, but also suggests the notion of an incipient or limited rebellion..."

以上 Mustill 大法官提到"造反"与"叛乱"是同义,只是在程度上不同。至于"造反"与"革命"的区别,有一个说法就是成功的造反就是"革命";而不成功的"造反"就会停留在"造反"或"叛乱"的层次。这可以看到历史上有许多成功的"造反"提升变为革命,如法国大革命、美国大革命、俄罗斯十月革命。

有关它们是同一理念(包括内战)但程度不同,也可以看美国的 Pan American v. Aetna Casualty (1975) 1 Lloyd's Rep 77, Hays 大法官说:"'Insurrection' presents the key issue because 'rebellion,' 'revolution,' and 'civil war' are progressive stages in the development of civil unrest, the most rudimentary form of which is 'insurrection.'"

在 National Oil Company of Zimbabwe v. Nicholas Collwyn Sturge (1991) 2 LLR 281 中 Saville 大法官认为保险人如果证明不了是"叛乱"(而这也是拒赔的理由),也就自动表示没有可能证明严重程度更高的"造反",有关的判词可重复如下:"'Rebellion' and 'insurrection' have somewhat similar meanings to each other. To my mind, each means an organised and violent internal uprising in a country with, as a main purpose, the object of trying to overthrow or supplant the government of that country, though 'insurrection' denotes a lesser degree of organisation and size than 'rebellion'..."

接下来介绍两个比较近期的先例,第一个是特立尼达和多巴哥(Trinidad & Tobago)上诉庭的 Grell-Taurel Ltd v. Caribbean Home Insurance Co Ltd (2002) Lloyd's Rep. IR 655,案情涉及一个组织名为"Muslimeen"把西班牙港的特立尼达和多巴哥警察总部炸毁,并同时攻占议院,杀死了 6 人,并扣留了 16 个人质,其中一个人质是该国的首相。之后,Muslimeen 也攻占了电视台并作出宣布说千里达政府被推翻。在该案例,特立尼达和多巴哥上诉庭接受当时所发生的事实是一场叛乱。

同样判法的另一个先例是斐济群岛最高院判的 Tappoo Holdings Ltd v. Stuchbery (2008) Lloyd's Rep. IR 34。在该先例,是有必要区分到底是"叛乱"(因为保单把这一个风险排除在外)或是"民间暴乱或暴动"(civil commotion or riots)(因为保单承保这一风险)。案情是在 2000 年 5 月 19 日,一位 George Speight 先生与他的同谋武力占领了斐济群岛的议院并把首相与其他的政府官员作为人质。这导致了斐济群岛变得无法无天并开始了暴动，其中受保人拥有的在市区的一个商店被暴徒抢掠与破坏。受保人的争辩是当时的暴力程度不足够构成叛乱，但最高院考虑了其他的先例包括上述英美的先例，判是属于叛乱，说："The cases established that (i) an 'insurrection' was an attempt by force to overthrow the established government, which depended on the objective of those involved, particularly the leaders, but not on their prospect of success; and (ii) the number taking part did not need to be large, and there did not need to be a high level of planning, so that an 'insurrection' could be a loose affair... The number initially involved in the coup and Parliament House was not too small for the enterprise to be characterized as an 'insurrection'. The statements of Mr. George Speight and his confederates at Parliament House ... on 19 May 2000 made their intention to overthrow the established Government ('this is a civil coup') very plain and their actions spoke as loudly as their words."

1.1.3.1 区分"叛乱"与"民间暴乱"的重要性

最后要一提的是针对海上货物运输保险，区分"叛乱"与"民间暴乱"十分重要，而这两种风险不容易区分。首先在2009年协会货物条文（一切险）中，叛乱是被第6.1条文排除，民间暴乱是被第7.1条文排除。而这些被排除的风险如果要投保的话，叛乱是以协会战争险条文（货物）之第1.1条文作出承保，但民间暴乱则是以协会罢工险条文（货物）的第1.1条文作出承保。所以，要区分的第一重要性是在它们属于不同的保单承保，而且作为货方的受保人可能只会是投保其中一种风险。

但另一个更重要的是即使作为货方的受保人把两种风险都投保，也不是万无一失。因为战争险受到Waterborne Agreement的约束（有关Waterborne Agreement请参阅本书第八章9.2段的介绍），不会承保岸上的风险。换言之，战争险只承保货物装上远洋船舶直到货物在卸港卸下这个期间，或者该保单在该船舶到了卸港15天之后（不论有否卸货）就终止。但罢工险不受这个约束，它承保的时间段与一切险一样，是从仓库到仓库，也就是在第5条的运输条文（Transit Clause）。毕竟，货物受到叛乱或民间暴乱这种风险更大可能发生在岸上，而不会发生在大海航行的船舶上。这表示对受保人而言，如果受到损失能够说明是民间暴乱造成的话，这个损失就会得到赔付。

1.1.3.2 如何区分"叛乱"与"民间暴乱"

有关"叛乱"与"民间暴乱"的区分，最详细的解释是在Spinney's v. Royal Insurance (1980) 1 Lloyd's Rep. 406中，Mustill大法官针对以前分得不是很细的先例（主要是Mansfield勋爵在Langdale v. Mason [1780] 2 Park on Ins. 965说民间暴乱与叛乱有关联并属于叛乱的一种）作出以下分析：

"civil commotion connotes something considerably more serious than a mere leaderless mob... The most recent, and most authoritative, discussion of civil commotion is to be found in Levy v. Assicurazioni Generali (1940) 67 LLP 174, where Lord Justice Luxmoore said：'... an insurrection of the people **for general purposes**, though not amounting to rebellion; but it is probably not capable of any very precise definition. The element of turbulence or tumult is essential ... '

... Quite plainly, these cases do not equate civil commotion with rebellion. But is it necessary for there to be an 'insurrection' in the narrower sense, to which I have already alluded: so that the exception does not apply unless the persons engaged in the disturbance have some degree of common purpose to bring down the government? It would be odd if this were so, since the policy already specifically excludes insurrection. But does the language employed by Lord Mansfield nevertheless compel this interpretation? I do not think that it does. My reasons for this opinion are so exactly expressed by the judgment of the Court in Lindsay & Pirie v. The General Accident Fire and Life Assurance Corporation Ltd. (1914) SAR (App. D.) 574, delivered by Mr. Justice Solomon ... :

'... I do not think that he (Lord Mansfield) could possibly have used the word 'insurrection' in its ordinary sense of a rising of the people in open resistance against established authority with the object of supplanting that authority. On the contrary, it would appear from the rest of his language that he used the word in its strictly etymological sense of 'rising', and that the effect of his direction to the jury was that a rising of the people (by which I presume he meant a considerable number of the population), for purposes of general mischief amounted to civil commotion within the sense of the exception to the insurance policy... For the history of the period makes it clear that the Gordon Riots, which began as a rising against Roman Catholics, eventually degenerated into mere destruction and plunder, and that there was never an insurrection with the objection of overthrowing the Government of the country. '

This interpretation of what Lord Mansfield said is consonant with the opinion of Mr. Justice Bucknill, approved by Lord Justice Vaighan Williams, in London and Manchester v. Heath (1913) 3 KB 411that the Gordon Riots involved: **'a general rising up of the people to do terrible things.'**"

最后 Mustill 大法官得出一个结论就是民间暴乱是不必有目的推翻政府,只需要暴民之间有一定的凝聚力就已经足够,说:"I find nothing in the authorities compelling the Court to hold that a civil commotion must involve a revolt against the government, although disturbances must have sufficient cohesion to prevent them from being the work of a mindless mob. Confused and fragmentary as the violence in the Lebannon may appear, this requirement is satisfied, and I hold that in January 1976, and for months before, a state of civil commotion prevalent in Lebannon."

John Dunt 在其2009年版的《Marine Cargo Insurance》中10.40段对民间暴乱的定义也有以下的看法:"'Civil commotions' seems to fill the gap left by the technical meaning given to riot. What an ordinary business person might well consider a riot, could well be civil commotions. It is further submitted that in Clause 1. 1 of the Strike Clauses the phrase ‘strikers, locked-out workmen, or persons taking part in labour disturbance’, should be read together with the words ‘riots or civil commotions’ and contrasted to the excepted perils under Clause 3. 10 beginning with ‘insurrection, or civil strife arising therefrom’. **The key to the covered perils is a state of unrest, starting with a strike, and rising to a civil commotion, but not directed at overthrowing the government** which, by way of contrast, is the determining characteristic of insurrection. ”(加黑部分是笔者的强调)

1.2　第二类战争险

此 1.2 条文承保的是由于“捕获、扣押、扣留、拘禁或羁押”(“Capture seizure arrest restraint or detainment, arising from risks covered under 1. 1 above, and the consequences thereof or any attempt thereat. ”)所引致的损失。

1.2.1　被一切险排除的拘禁或羁押风险比战争险承保的范围广而带来货物被拒绝进口的不承保风险

这主要要注意的是上述第 1.2 条文规定的列明战争风险必须是由第 1.1 条文承保列明战争风险所引致的捕获或扣押等才被承保。这与协会货物条文(一切险)第 6.2 条排除了货物的损失是由于“捕获、扣押、扣留、拘禁或羁押”所造成的后果(6. In no case shall this insurance cover loss damage or expense caused by:6. 2 capture seizure arrest restraint or detainment (piracy excepted), and the consequences thereof or any attempt thereat)相比产生了一个重要的空档,就是一批货物如果被敌对国家捕获或造反的一个组织捕获,这就可以得到赔付,因为这一个风险在协会货物条文一切险被排除后但在协会战争险条文承保;但如果一批货物是因为违反一些国家的进出口规定(即使是莫名其妙或者是不为人知的规定)而被扣留或羁押,这种风险是被协会货物条文一切险在 6.2 条排除后,也并没有在协会战争险条文 1.2 条文承保,因为这种扣留或羁押与第 1.1 条文的列明战争风险无关,所以就不能得到赔付了。以上可以看出,所有一切险排除的风险并非都是战争险承保的范围。

这一来,对一些易腐或者是供食用的货物来说是比较危险的,因为它们受到扣留或羁押导致货物损失的机会较大。例如,肉类会受到口蹄疫的影响、家禽类会受到亚洲禽流感的影响、果仁会受到飞蛾与甲虫的影响、葡萄干会受到茎与梗的影响等。这种案例也有被报道,如英国贵族院的 The“Giannis NK”(1998) 1 Lloyd’s Rep 337。这方面较早被报道的著名先例是一个英国案例:Miller v. The Law Accident Insurance Co (1903) 1 KB 712,案情涉及一批活牛从利物浦运到布鲁诺斯艾利斯,但在卸港检查后说是该批活牛生病而被拒绝进口。之后,阿根廷政府作出一个规定禁止所有英国活牛进口。这导致原来那批被禁运的活牛要转运到乌拉圭的蒙得维的亚以贱价出售。货方的受保人为该批活牛投保,而保单是以前的劳合社标准 S. G 保单,其中包括的列明风险有"捕获、扣押、扣留、拘禁或羁押",而货方也根据这些列明风险向保险人索赔。但英国法院判这些列明风险不包括货物因卫生理由而被当地政府拒绝进口或者作出禁运。

所以,针对易腐货物而且容易被拒绝进口的货物需要另外投保这一个风险,因为目前在一切险的水险保单或是战争险都不承保。这方面可参考本书第三章第3.8段。

1.2.2 加保货物被拒绝进口的风险

这导致了在英国伦敦的保险市场1955年推出了对这种风险的加保,名为"货物被完全拒绝进口的保险条文"(Full Rejection Clause)。这种保险有一些明示的保证,就是货方的受保人必须严格在付运前马上进行检查并取得一份货物良好的证明。另外需要保证有关的货物完全符合付运国家的要求,例如有去熏货(大米往往会有这种要求),或有货物标签与包装符合目的地港的进口要求。

但还会有不清楚的地方就是如果货物是在航次的半途受到损坏而变质或腐烂,结果在卸货港被拒绝进口或扣押,这属于一切险承保的风险还是这一种加保的风险?显然,如果在卸货港被拒绝进口或扣押是由于当地政府的不合理或不当行为而造成,就应该更加明确是属于这一种加保风险所承保的范围。这一点在一个美国先例中明确说明,该先例是 Berns v. Koppinstein Inc (1959) AMC 2455, confirmed on appeal (1960) AMC 1379。案情涉及印度花生进口去纽约,但被美国的有关部门(US Food and Drug Administration)认为货物被飞蛾与甲虫污染。保险人拒绝赔付,认为要求付运前作出检查的明示保证没有被严格遵守。纽约法院的 William B. Herlands 大法官说这种保险承保的不是货物质量变坏,而是政府的行为,不论这一行为是合理还是不合理:"The risk insured by the full rejection insurance was not a deterioration of the quality or loss in quantity (as is the case in the 'all-risk' clause), but an act of the United States Government or Departments thereof, including but not limited to the US Food and Drug Administration, 'for any reason whatsoever'. **The peril insured against** by the rejection insurance was not the presence of a putrid substance but **the act of the Government**. Arbitrary rejection or detention, miscarriage of administrative determination in rejection or detaining was just as fully covered as justified rejection and detention because the Clause refers to 'any reason whatsoever'. The act of the Government was the 'peril', not the condition of the goods. One bug in any bag would have justified rejection under the language of the Food, Drug & Cosmetic Act."

之后,在美国也有相关的案例:Continental Sea Foods Inc v New Hampshire Fire Insurance Company (1964) AMC 196.(案情涉及巴基斯坦冻虾运到美国,但半途腐烂导致在美国被拒绝进口)与 Schwartz & Co v. Hepburn 302 F 2d 576 (1962)。在后一个先例,有"货物被完全拒绝进口的保险条文"的保险与一般的海上货物运输保险不一样,而两种保险如果有矛盾,前者的保险是超越后者。所以,"货物被完全拒绝进口的保险条文”的保险是一种额外的保险，不取决于货物在一般的海上货物运输保险是否获得承保。这表示货物不必在运输半途损坏或者腐烂而导致在卸港被拒绝进口才会被承保，而即使是在卸港被无理拒绝进口，不论是为了保护本地的市场还是对本来应该是可以接受的货物吹毛求疵，都可以在“货物被完全拒绝进口的保险条文”的保险中得到赔付。

到了 1975 年 5 月，伦敦市场推出了另一条大致相同的保险条文，名为“The London Rejection Risks Clauses 1975”。它把承保的范围（针对进口国家拒绝货物或销毁货物）写得更明确，如下：“Subject always to the following conditions and exclusions this policy is extended to cover the risk of rejection or condemnation by the government of the country of import or their agencies or departments during the period of this insurance.”

而承保范围所提及的条件（conditions），就是货物的生产、准备与包装符合出口国家的规定与适合进口，具体文字如下：“It is a condition of this insurance that the interest insured is produced, prepared and packed in accordance with the regulations of the Government or Country of Origin and it is fit for export to the importing country.”

这个条件相当于承诺性保证（promissory warranty），但由于 1906 年《英国海上保险法》之 Section 33(3) 对保险合约中的承诺性保证有过度严厉的规定，即一旦不严格遵守，保险人就自动解除赔付任何损失的责任，即使后来的损失与承诺性保证是否有遵守没有任何关系。所以估计改成条件条文（condition）会对受保人比较公平，虽然作为条件还是十分严格。有关这种条件是否有遵守还是会决定受保人会否得到赔付，这里涉及两个美国先例：SSC International Inc v Cornhill Insurance Company Limited No. 77 Civ 5490 (MP) (SDNY 5 December 1978) 与 Snyder International Inc v Dae Han Fire & Marine Insurance Company Limited (unreported) District Court of Massachusetts, Civ 77-2579-S of 14 September 1981。前一个先例涉及进口冻虾与甲鱼片，判受保人有遵守条件。但在后一个先例涉及葡萄干的茎与梗太长而被拒绝进口，但受保人没办法证明他有遵守条件，即货物符合进口国家美国的要求，所以保险索赔被拒绝。

1.3 第三类战争险

这类战争险承保由于“被遗弃的水雷、鱼雷、炸弹或其他被遗弃的战争武器”（derelict mines, torpedoes, bombs or other derelict weapons of war）所引致的损失。这种列明风险在太平盛世的时候还是会出现，毕竟在真正发生战争的时候是不会遗弃鱼雷或水雷的，而只会是使用。而且这种协会战争险条文（货物）也不是适用在战争特别是大型战争的时候。遗弃的水雷或鱼雷带来的风险在第二次世界大战后特别严重，根据 1958 年美国货物战争险再保交易所（American Cargo War Risk Reinsurance Exchange）发布的报告，“二战”后已经有 446 艘船舶因为遗留下来的水雷爆炸而被损坏或是沉没；而在之前的两年有 250 个漂浮的水雷被过往船只或是岸上的监察站发现。尽管存在的被遗弃的水雷是越来越少，但笔者在几年前还听说过这种事故发生，所以风险仍是存在，就有投保的必要。

顺便一提的是这一连串的列明风险到底是属于水险还是战争险也有点说不清。曾经有先例是 The“Naussau Bay”(1979) 1 Lloyd's Rep 395,涉及挖泥船在疏浚的时候吸入了海床的炸药(是在第二次世界大战后英军抛下的炸弹),导致在吸管部分发生爆炸并最终令船舶沉没。Walton 大法官判这不是战争风险,把炸弹遗弃实际上是一个追求和平的行为,属于水险。这代表在一切险的保险合约中是受到承保的。

所以现在在做法上是先去协会货物条文(一切险)的 6.3 条文把这一连串的列明风险明示排除,然后在协会战争险条文(货物)的 1.3 条文明确加上作为承保的列明风险,这等于改变了 The“Naussau Bay”的默示法律地位。

2. 协会战争险条文(货物)排除的列明风险

协会战争险条文(货物)除外的列明风险与协会货物条文(一切险)中的除外列明风险基本上相同:

协会战争险条文(货物)之 3.1 条文是类似协会货物条文(一切险)之 4.1 条文,排除的是受保人货方之蓄意恶行;协会战争险条文(货物)之 3.2 条文是类似协会货物条文(一切险)之 4.2 条文,排除的是正常的泄漏、正常的重量/体积减少、正常的磨损引起的货物损失;协会战争险条文(货物)之 3.3 条文是类似协会货物条文(一切险)之 4.3 条文,排除的是包装不足或不适带来的损失或损坏;协会战争险条文(货物)之 3.4 条文类似协会货物条文(一切险)之 4.4 条文,排除的是固有缺陷或保险货物的本质所造成的损失或损坏;协会战争险条文(货物)之 3.5 条文类似协会货物条文(一切险)之 4.5 条文,排除的是延误造成的损失或损坏;协会战争险条文(货物)之 3.6 条文类似协会货物条文(一切险)之 4.6 条文,排除的是船东、船舶经理人、承租人或船舶营运人的破产或经济困境带来的损失或损坏;协会战争险条文(货物)之 3.8 条文类似协会货物条文(一切险)之 4.7 条文,排除的是核战争武器直接或间接所造成的损失或损坏。

协会战争险条文(货物)之 4 条文类似协会货物条文(一切险)之 5 条文,排除了受保人知情下的船舶不适航与集装箱不适货造成的损失或损坏。相比之下,协会战争险条文(货物)多出了 3.7 条文是协会货物条文(一切险)所没有的,名为受阻条文(frustration clause)。在本书第七章第 5.3 段已经有介绍,作用是为了使战争保险人不用为续运费用(forwarding charges)负责。部分重复一下,协会货物条文(一切险)是承保了航程终止(loss of the adventure)的风险,即使是货物没有实质性的损坏:British & Foreign Marine Insurance Company, Limited v. Samuel Sanday & Co (1916) 1 AC 650 (HL),Forestal Land, Timber & Railways Company Ltd v. Richards; Middows Ltd v. Robertson and Other Cases (1941) 70 Lloyd's Rep. 173 (HL)。所以这也带来了协会货物条文(一切险)之 12 条文,承保货物转运到目的地的续运费用。这在战争险所导致的航程终止,普通法也有同样的地位,这方面的先例是 British & Foreign Marine Insurance Company, Limited v. Samuel Sanday & Co,案情是有关在"一战"期间,有两艘英国船舶从阿根廷去汉堡,但由于英德宣战而不能继续航程,船上的货物被迫在英国利物浦与格拉斯哥卸下。英国贵族院判这是一个航程终止造成的推定全损,保险人需要赔付货物的损失。保险人为了避免这种会在战争期间大量发生的风险,毕竟一般战争险的保费不会太高就引进了这样的一条受阻条文,明示将其约定为排除在外的列明风险。

但如果航程终止并同时加上了货物的实质损失/损坏,这就不受这一条受阻条文的限制,是可以获得赔的。这是在"二战"期间发生的 Forestal Land, Timber & Railways Company Ltd v. Richards; Middows Ltd v. Robertson and Other Cases,案情涉及了德国船舶装运了英国的货物,在英德宣战后除了导致航程终止,不会继续航行去英国目的地港外,船舶也在德国纳粹政府的命令下被凿沉导致货物全损。这被判是受阻条文并不适用。

最后一提的是在伦敦保险市场也有一条协会条文明为 Institute Additional Expenses Clauses (Cargo-War Risks) 1/7/85,它是超越受阻条文的,为了让货方的受保人可以因为战争险导致航程终止需要把货物转运到目的地港花费的续运费用(forwarding charges)得到加保。但可能因为在和平时期这种风险非常罕见与大家不关心,所以这一个协会条文很少有人使用,本书也就略过不谈了。

3. 协会罢工险条文(货物)

罢工的风险最早在 1912 年与战争险同时在劳合社标准 S. G 保单被一条明示条文排除在外,该条文名为"罢工、暴动与民间暴乱",措辞如下:"**Strikes, Riots and Civil Commotions Clause** Warranted free of loss or damage caused by strikes locked-out workmen or persons taking part in labour disturbances or riots or civil commotions."

再进一步分析之前需要给何为罢工、暴动、民间暴乱这些相关的词语一些定义。

3.1 何谓罢工

先可以介绍立法的定义,这是在英国的《雇佣合约法》(Contracts of Employment Act1963)中:"The cessation of work by a body of persons employed acting in combination, or a concerted refusal under a common understanding of any number of persons employed to continue to work for an employer in consequence of a dispute, done as a means of compelling their employer or any person or body of persons employed, or to aid other employees in compelling their employer or any person or persons employed, to accept or not to accept terms or conditions of or affecting employment."

接下来介绍普通法下的定义与历史的变化。在早年的先例,看来对罢工的定义比较狭窄,只局限在工资的纠纷,估计在那些年代没有什么福利与人权可言。这些先例有 King & Parker (1876) 34 LT 887 与 Stephens v. Harris & Co. (1887) 57 LJQB 203,在后一个先例,Coleridge 大法官判是小工由于害怕霍乱疫症而停工,并不是罢工,说:"When one hears of persons striking, it does not mean a refusal to work because the weather happens to be hot, but a standing out for higher wages."

罢工的定义在接下来的案例就开始比较宽松。在 Williams Brothers (Hull) Ltd v. Naamlooze Vennootschap W H Berghuys Kolenhandel (1915) 21 CC 253,案情是有关一艘中立的荷兰船舶,船员由于害怕德国海军的袭击而拒绝开航离开英国港口,船东希望以罢工作为免责。Sankey 大法官不接受罢工只针对工资,认为可包括工人因为有不满或者忧虑而集体拒绝工作,说:"A strike does not depend on merely upon the question of wages. At the same time, I do not think it would be possible to say the abstention of a workman from mere fear to do a particular thing or perform a particular contract would necessarily constitute a strike. I think the true definition of the word 'strike', which I do not say is exhaustive, is a general concerned refusal by workmen to work in consequence of an alleged grievance."

下一个是 Seebery v. Russian Wood Agency (1934) 50 Lloyd's Rep. 146 先例,案情是俄罗斯列宁格勒的小工拒绝为拉脱维亚(Latvian)的船舶装货,原因是同情与支持拉脱维亚的工会。这案例的特别之处是:(1)与劳资纠纷无关,而这是一直以来对罢工的解释;(2)罢工的港口工人本身没有任何不满,只是为了同情其他类别的工人/工会;(3)罢工只影响装了煤炭的少数船舶,而其他与拉脱维亚无关的船舶/货物装卸正常。MacKinnon 大法官判这也是罢工。MacKinnon 大法官这样说:"... that is the curious incident of this strike, work was going on in this port and ships of many nationalities were being loaded with all due diligence, but the stevedores did not in fact load any cargo on Latvian ships, and it was said that it was a strike in sympathy with some labour grievance of some alleged unions or other workers on or connected with Latvian ships in Latvian and other ports. That was the nature of the strike."

接下来是另一个与 Seebery v. Russian Wood Agency 类似案情的 The "Laga" (1966) 1 Lloyd's Rep. 582 先例,McNair 大法官特别提到罢工的定义应根据时代的改变而作出改变,说:"Strikers in every sense of the word occur today which are not concerned directly with wages. They are concerned, for instance, with working conditions; and so I think one has got to bear in mind that the meaning of the term 'strike' must change with the progress (if that is the right word) if industrial history and it may have a different meaning today from the meaning given to it a century ago."

在该先例中,案情是有关法国南特(Nantes)的港口工人(包括了拖轮船员、领航员、装卸小工等人)拒绝为"Laga"轮卸下一船的煤炭,为了同情与支持当时在罢工的法国煤炭工人。争议是在租约下承租人可否依赖免责/停算装货时间条文内的罢工事项。但 McNair 大法官判是属于罢工。从这里看来罢工的定义自此变得十分广泛了。

最后一提的是 The“New Horizon”(1975) 2 Lloyd's Rep. 314 先例,上诉庭的 Denning 勋爵所作出的定义如下:“I think a strike is a concerted stoppage of work by men with a view to improving their wages or conditions, or giving vent to a grievance or making a protest about something or other, or supporting or sympathizing with other workmen in such endeavour. It is distinct from a stoppage which is brought about by an external event such as a bomb scare or by apprehension of danger.”(罢工是一个集体的停止工作,为了改善他们的工资水平或者工作条件,或者为了不满/忧虑出一口气,或者为了对一些事情作出抗议,或者为了支持/同情其他工人。这与停工是因为外来的事情所导致,如炸弹威胁或者估计有外来危险并不一样。)

3.2 “资方停工”(lock-out)

这个方面的定义在英国几个有关的立法都有提及,如 1978 年《Employment Protection(Consolidation) Act》之 Section 15 (1)和 Schedule 13, 24 段,1982 年《Employment Act》之 Section 20 (1)和 Schedule 2, 7 (1)段与 1992 年《Trade Union an Labour Relations (Consolidation) Act》之 Section 235 (4)。另可节录 John Schofield 在他所著的《Laytime and Demurrage》一书第五版之 4.379 段,如下:“‘Lock-out’ has been defined as the closing of a place of employment or the suspension of work or the refusal by an employer to continue to employ any number of persons employed by him in consequence of a dispute, done with a view to compelling those persons, or to aid another employer in compelling persons employed by him, to accept terms and conditions of or affecting employment. This definition is, however, not comprehensive, for a lock-out may be instituted for purposes other than compelling workers to accept terms and conditions of or relating to employment.”

换言之,资方停工恰恰与罢工相对,都是涉及劳资双方之间的纠纷。罢工是来自工人,资方停工是来自雇佣者把大门关起来不让工人上班。资方停工也可以导致暴力并造成货物的损失或损坏,如工人受到这一刺激而造成暴动或放火烧毁仓库。

3.3 什么是工人骚乱(labour disturbances)

这一个词应该是针对罢工,它与资方停工一样都应该是只局限于劳资之间的纠纷(顶多包括声援其他已经罢工的工人),所以有局限性。如不包括因为炸弹威胁或估计有危险的停工,正如 Denning 勋爵在 The“New Horizon”(1975) 2 Lloyd's Rep. 314 先例所讲。所以在其他相关的合约如租约,除了罢工外也往往加上了工人停工(stoppage of labour)。这里的工人骚乱应该就是好像工人停工扩大罢工以外工人所带来的问题。但由于海上货物保险合约不承保这种罢工风险所带来的间接后果(后详),所以它所用的措辞不是工人停工而是工人骚乱,因为后者才会造成货物的损失或损坏。

3.4 什么是暴动(riots)

针对“暴动”,它的定义在 Field v. Receiver of Metropolitan Police (1907) 2 KB 859

有介绍,即要构成暴动就必须有五个要素:必须至少有三个人以上,大家有一个共同目标,并且为了达成这个目标而准备互相协助,期间不惜使用武力针对任何反对他们的人,而这个武力程度是会令一个有一般性、合理意志与勇气的人士感觉到警戒。(To constitute a riot there must be at least three people engaged in the execution or inception of a common purpose with an intent to help one another, by force if necessary, against any person who may oppose them and in so doing the force or violence must be such as to alarm at least one person of reasonable firmness and courage.)

在美国的 Pan American v. Aetna Casualty (1974) 1 Lloyd's Rep 207,一审的地方法院 Frankel 大法官也给了"暴动"一个类似的定义,如下:"A 'riot' for insurance purposes, is a gathering of three or more persons with a common purpose to do an unlawful act, with overt acts to accomplish that purpose, with an apparent intention and ability to use force if necessary against any person who may oppose them in the execution of their common purpose, and with force or violence displayed in such manner as to deter from opposing them at least one person of reasonable firmness or courage who might otherwise oppose them. A riot exists if three or more persons, with a common object and intent to help one another, use force or violence or threaten force or violence in such a manner to cause alarm."

另外也可以一提的是美国的上诉庭先例 Pan American v. Aetna Casualty (1975) 1 Lloyd's Rep 77 也有很大篇幅提到针对一家波音 747 飞机在开罗被摧毁是否是属于暴动(或其他的除外列明风险)。上诉庭支持一审对暴动的解释,就是暴动必须造成骚动或者混乱(tumult),Hays 大法官说:"Under this formula, a riot occurs when some multitude of individuals gathers and creates a tumult. A substantial weight of authority supports this formulation. It is the definition of riot that most accords to common sense."美国上诉庭也提到了好几个先例,其中一个是 Hartford Fire Insurance Co v. War Eagle Coal Co 295 F. 663 (4th Cir. 1924),涉及 5 个偷偷摸摸的人在夜间放火并判这不是暴动,因为没有造成骚动与混乱,甚至在放火前没有示威(for there was no tumult nor disturbances, nor even a demonstration before the fire)。这显然是一般人接受的定义,就是暴动要对和平造成干预。

但看来在英国的普通法还是给暴动一个比较技术性而不是一般人理解与接受的解释。在 The"Andreas Lemos"(1982)2 Lloyd's Rep 483,案情涉及了船舶是在孟加拉的吉大港锚地等待泊位时,晚上被一批持刀的小偷上船偷东西(包括船舶的缆绳,价值大约 5000 美元),但后来在走的时候被船员发觉,于是小偷就拿出刀指吓船员以利于逃走。由于同类案件很多,所以该先例虽然涉及的金额不大,但还是以"test case"的形式看法律是怎样说。其中要针对的包括这一个损失是否属于海盗或是暴动。Staughton 大法官不认为这是海盗,因为偷偷摸摸不会是海盗的行为。但在本段最主要的还是有关暴动,显然一般人的理解不像是一个暴动,但问题是在他们逃走的时候曾经以武力威吓,所以 Staughton 大法官认为该案中的情况完全符合 Field v. Receiver of Metropolitan Police (1907) 2 KB 859 先例中的五个条件。但之前上船偷偷摸摸地偷东西,由于不涉及任何武力的威吓,就不能算是暴动。只不过由于他们在逃走之前已经将偷来的东西抛给了海上接应他们的小艇,所以在出现暴动之前就已经造成的损失,保险人不用赔付。Staughton 大法官这样说:"If one takes the word in its current and popular meaning, nobody but a Sloane Ranger would say of this casualty: 'It was a riot'. The word today means the sort of civil disturbance which has recently occurred in Brixton, Bristol or Wormwood Scrubs. Mr. Saville (保险人代表大律师) referred me, in this connection, to the case of Pan American v. Aetna Casualty (1974) 1 Lloyd's Rep 207, decided in the United States District Court for the Southern District of New York. There an aircraft had been hijacked and blown up by members of the Popular Front for the Liberation of Palestine. The insurers denied liability on the ground that this was a loss by 'riots', and therefore excluded. District Judge Frankel expressed some forthright criticism of English jurisprudence on this point, and declined to depart from the current and ordinary meaning of the word. That approach attracts considerable sympathy, at any rate from me, and at any rate in theory. But on further examination it cannot be adopted for an English policy of marine insurance.... A riot did occur. But it was not complete until after the loss; the loss was not caused by the riot."

3.5 什么是民间暴乱(civil commotions)

至于"民间暴乱",较早在解释"叛乱"(insurrection)的时候,就已经对民间暴乱与叛乱的不同有过详述。重述如下:有关"叛乱"与"民间暴乱"的区分,最详细的解释是在 Spinney's v. Royal Insurance (1980) 1 Lloyd's Rep. 406 中,Mustill 大法官得出一个结论就是民间暴乱是不必有目的地推翻政府,只需要暴民之间有一定的凝聚力就已经足够,说:"I find nothing in the authorities compelling the Court to hold that a civil commotion must involve a revolt against the government, although disturbances must have sufficient cohesion to prevent them from being the work of a mindless mob. Confused and fragmentary as the violence in the Lebannon may appear, this requirement is satisfied, and I hold that in January 1976, and for months before, a state of civil commotion prevalent in Lebannon."

也另有一个说法比较严重,"民间暴乱"是"暴动"与"内战"的中间阶段。要构成"民间暴乱",就必须有一定程度的"骚动与混乱"(turbulence or tumult),但它不包括一些漫无目的的暴徒行为。

另在 Pan American v. Aetna Casualty (1974) 1 Lloyd's Rep 207,一审的 Frankel 大法官曾经提到双方当事人同意的说法是民间暴乱类似暴动,但涉及更严重程度的骚动(A"civil commotion"for insurance purposes, describes a situation similar to a riot but involving either a more serious disturbance or one that is a part of a broader series of disturbances)。

3.6　协会货物条文对罢工险的排除与加保

在以上对罢工险的定义与解释中可以看出,它与另一个类别的战争险相同之处是都涉及了暴力,而最大的不同就是后者涉及政治目的。但做法上都是一致的,就是以条文把这两种风险从协会货物条文(A)或(B)或(C)排除,让协会货物条文特别是(A)的一切险明确只是承保水险,然后让受保人加保战争险或罢工险。

在协会货物条文(A),排除罢工险的是第7条(注意[B]与[C]条文也是类似写法),可节录如下:

"In no case shall this insurance cover loss damage or expense

7.1　caused by strikers, locked-out workmen, or persons taking part in labour disturbances, riots or civil commotions

7.2　resulting from strikes, lock-outs, labour disturbances, riots or civil commotions

7.3　caused by any act of terrorism being an act of any person acting on behalf of, or in connection with, any organisation which carries out activities directed towards the overthrowing or influencing, by force or violence, of any government whether or not legally constituted

7.4　caused by any person acting from a political, ideological or religious motive."

这里要特别注意的是7.1条与7.2条所排除的是所有是罢工险造成(caused by)或导致(resulting from)的损失、损坏或费用(loss, damage or expense)。但在协会罢工险条文(货物)(Institute Strikes Clauses [Cargo] 1/1/09)所承保的在第1与1.1条只是说:"This insurance covers... loss of or damage to the subject-matter insured caused by 1.1 strikers, locked-out workmen, or persons taking part in labour disturbances, riots or civil commotions."

这里可以注意到的罢工险即使加保,范围也是狭窄得多,因为它保的只是货物的损失与损坏(loss or damage),而不包括费用。另外它也讲明只是由罢工险"造成"(caused by)而没有"导致"(resulting from)一词。

为了更清楚地显示这方面的意图,协会罢工险条文(货物)更在3.7条明确排除:"loss damage or expense arising from the absence shortage or withholding of labour of any description whatsoever resulting from any strike, lockout, labour disturbance, riot or civil commotion."

另外,好像战争险一样,协会罢工险条文(货物)在3.8条有一条受阻条文(Frustration Clause),这好像战争险的3.7条受阻条文一样,是不承保航程终止(loss of the adventure)的风险,正如在本章上述第2段提到的。反正是罢工险好像战争险的加保一样,但与协会货物条文(一切险)不一致,就是它没有包括第12条的货物转运到目的地的续运费用(forwarding charges)。

这一来,就可以很清楚地看到保险人只想承保货物由于罢工所造成的实质损坏,如罢工工人放火把仓库烧毁而导致里面的货物全损，这是保险人要赔付。但由于罢工险所导致的间接损失，如由于工人罢工而货物无人处理，以致受天气影响变坏要花额外费用对货物作出处理，这是不属于承保范围。

这样看来，罢工与暴动或民间暴乱基本上都是一致的，只是暴力程度不一样。而一些属于和平的罢工，在货物保险里面是没有关系的，因为和平的罢工只会造成间接的损失，而不会造成货物的实质损失。

4. 恐怖行动(terrorism)为什么要投保

遭受恐怖行动的风险是在一切险条文的7.2与7.3被排除在承保范围之外，再通过罢工险条文的1.2与1.3可以进行加保。讲到恐怖行动，历史上主要是针对飞机被劫持，而船舶被劫持的恐怖行动相对比较罕见。比较著名的也只有1985年一艘名为Achille Lauro的意大利客轮被4个巴勒斯坦的恐怖分子劫持，但该事件并不涉及货物。而这不代表船上的货物不会受到恐怖行动的威胁，其中最著名的是在2002年10月6日一艘名为Limberg的法国超级油轮被阿尔盖特(Al-Qaeda)恐怖分子用装满炸药的小船引爆而造成船舶以及所装货物的损失与损坏。

4.1　恐怖行动的法律定义以及其与战争风险的区别

首先也是要把什么是恐怖袭击的法律定义讲清楚，这并不容易，尤其是与其他的暴力行动如类似战争的行为(warlike operation)、敌对行为(hostilities)、骚乱(insurrection)作出区分，毕竟这是属于两种不同的险种。这还存在从谁的角度看待，如在一些巴勒斯坦所谓的“恐怖分子”的眼里，他们从事的是类似战争的行为，但在西方国家或者以色列的眼中他们从事的是恐怖行动。

在英国，为了针对爱尔兰共和军的恐怖行动，在1993年有立法名为《Reinsurance (Acts of Terrorism) Act》，定义是在Section 2(2)，如下：“In this section ‘acts of terrorism’ means acts of persons acting on behalf of, or in connection with, any organisation which carries out activities directed towards the overthrowing or influencing, by force or violence, of Her Majesty's Government in the United Kingdom or any other Government *de jure or de facto.*”

由该定义可以看出，英国立法的定义下恐怖行动必须是旨在推翻或影响政权，而且必须是使用暴力造成财产的损失或损坏。还有是恐怖行动不像仅仅一个人的行为就可以构成，而必须是代表或者与某恐怖组织有联系。如果只是有个别人士实施恐怖行动，就可能是属于协会罢工险条文之1.3条。

至于在“二战”之前1937年一个名为《League of Nations Convention for the Prevention and Punishment of Terrorism》的国际公约给的定义是“Acts of terrorism mean criminal acts directed against the state and intended or calculated to create a state of terror in the minds of particular persons, or a group of persons or the general public."

在美国先例 Pan American v. Aetna Casualty (1974) 1 Lloyd's Rep 207 中,法院有区分战争行为、类似战争行为以及恐怖行为。Frankel 大法官引述了美国国务卿有关恐怖行动与战争行为区别的讲话,如下:"This issue is not war - war between states, civil war, or revolutionary war. The issue is not the strivings of people to achieve self-determination and independence. Rather, it is whether millions of air travellers can continue to fly in safety each year. It is whether a person who receives a letter can open it without the fear of being blown-up. It is whether diplomats can safely carry out their duties. It is whether international meetings - like the Olympic games, like this Assembly-can proceed without the ever-present threat of violence."(问题不在战争,这也不是国与国之间战争或是内战,或是革命战争。问题也不在一些人争取自主与独立。事实上,问题是数以百万计的飞机乘客能否继续安全地飞行。问题也是任何人在打开一封邮件的时候会否被炸死。问题也在外交人士能否在安全的情况下履行职责。问题也在国际的会议如奥林匹克运动会或其他国际性会议能否和平举行而不受到暴力的威胁。)

Frankel 大法官总结恐怖行为是不可接受,因为它对国际秩序的攻击,说:"Certainly the terrorist acts I have cited are totally unacceptable attacks against the very fabric of international order. They must be universally condemned, whether we consider the cause the terrorists invoke noble or ignoble, legitimate or illegitimate. We must take effective steps to prevent the hijacking of international civil aircraft."

另有关恐怖行动的定义是在英国的先例 P&C Insurance Limited (PUBL) v. Silversea Cruises Ltd (2004) Lloyd's Rep. IR 696 (CA)中提到,该先例是与"9·11"事件有关的其中一个案例。在针对有关战争或武力冲突(armed conflict)与恐怖行为的区别,Ward 大法官这样说:"Men of business, the underwriters and the insured, would not have said that 11 September was an 'act of war' but rather that it was terrorist action from extremist groups. To have declared 'war on terror' was a rhetorical response serving only to emphasise that there was no identifiable 'side' against whom the war could be waged. Further, an 'armed conflict' had an air of continuity about it, and what were essentially random attacks did not carry for ordinary businessmen, the sense of present and persisting fighting between military groups which was the hallmark of armed conflict."

Rix 大法官虽然原则上表示同意,但他说话比较小心,他说:"the fact that everyone could agree that 9/11 was an example of a terrorist attack does not to my mind itself answer the question of whether it amounted to something more."

总结说根据上述一些先例的说法,恐怖行动的特点应该有以下几点:(1)涉及暴力;(2)背后有政治目的的组织(但通常不代表合法政府);(3)暴力是针对平民与他们的财产;(4)暴力行动是远离战区;(5)恐怖行动不一定有明确的对象,这与战争不一样;(6)武力冲突有延续性的味道,不像恐怖行为只是偶然出现。

4.2 什么是任何人士的行动具有政治、意识形态或者是宗教的目的

接下去谈的是有关罢工险的1.3条有关承保列明风险的任何人士的行动具有政治、意识形态或者是宗教的目的。这一风险显然也是与恐怖行动接近,但较早的时候曾经谈到过英国1993年立法《Reinsurance (Acts of Terrorism) Act》的定义是恐怖行动必须是代表或者与某恐怖组织有联系。所以如果只是有个别人士实施恐怖行动,就是属于协会罢工条文之1.3条,反正也能够被承保。措辞也是非常广泛,只要该行动的人士有政治、意识形态或者是宗教的目的就已经足够,这可以说是包罗万有,也省去区分目的到底是什么的麻烦。这里可举一个涉及意识形态导致恐怖行动的美国案例,名为 Newmarket Investment Corporation v. Fireman's Fund Insurance Company 774 F. Supp. 909 (1991), US District Court Eastern District of Pennsylvania。案情涉及了美国在智利的大使收到匿名电话说是从智利去美国的水果都受到了山埃(cyanide)的污染,作为抗议与警告美国对智利的剥削与智利目前的贫穷。这导致了美国政府暂时中止了智利水果的进口,但最后只发现了两粒葡萄受到污染。反正这带来了受保人也就是该案例原告的损失,他想向保险人索赔,因为他加保了罢工险,其中包括了恐怖行动或意识形态所造成的破坏或恶意行为。该保险名为"Strikes, Riots and Civil Commotions Endorsement",有关内容如下:"Destruction of or damage to the property insured directly caused by vandalism, sabotage or malicious act, which was deemed to encompass the act or acts of one or more persons, whether or not agents of a sovereign power, carried out for terroristic or ideological purposes."结果该案例的陪审团判恐怖行动是造成受保人损失的近因。

4.3 保险人愿意承保恐怖行动的限度之一:不承保岸上

伦敦的保险市场对恐怖行动带来货物的损失或损坏好像上述所讲的法国油轮Limberg是愿意作出承保,所以是包括在协会罢工条文的1.2条与1.3条。但保险人愿意对船舶与船上的货物作出承保并不代表他们不担心在风险集中的情况下,恐怖行动会带来灾难性的损失或损坏,"9·11"事件就是一个最典型的例子。而对海上货物运输的风险如果比较集中的情况通常只会发生在装卸港的仓库或岸上其他的集散地。但恐怖行动的风险是在罢工险投保,而不是在战争险,所以不受 Waterborne Agreement的约束;相反,罢工险的第5条与一切险一样,有一条所谓仓库到仓库的运输条款。所以,好像战争险一样,保险人希望对恐怖行动的承保也局限在海上这一段期间,而不承保岸上的风险。这带来了一条名为JC56的条文,以首要条文的形式附加在协会罢工险条文中,而它的全名是"Termination of Transit Clause (Terrorism) 2009"(JC 2009/056 01/ 01/2009),内容如下:

"This clause shall be paramount and shall override anything contained in this insurance inconsistent therewith.

1 Notwithstanding any provision to the contrary contained in the contract of insurance

or the Clauses referred to therein, it is agreed that in so far as the contract of insurance covers loss of or damage to the subject-matter insured caused by any act of terrorism being an act of any person acting on behalf of, or in connection with, any organization which carries out activities directed towards the overthrowing or influencing, by force or violence, of any government whether or not legally constituted or any person acting for a political, ideological or religious motive, such cover is conditional upon the subject-matter insured being in the ordinary course of transit and, in any event, **SHALL TERMINATE: either**

1.1 as per the transit clauses contained within the contract of insurance, or

1.2 on completion of unloading from the carrying vehicle or other conveyance in or at the final warehouse or place of storage at the destination named in the contract of insurance,

1.3 on completion of unloading from the carrying vehicle or other conveyance in or at any other warehouse or place of storage, whether prior to or at the destination named in the contract of insurance, which the Assured or their employees elect to use either for storage other than in the ordinary course of transit or for allocation or distribution, or

1.4 when the Assured or their employees elect to use any carrying vehicle or other conveyance or any container for storage other than in the ordinary course of transit, or

1.5 in respect of marine transits, on the expiry of 60 days after completion of discharge overside of the subject-matter insured from the oversea vessel at the final port of discharge,

1.6 in respect of air transits, on the expiry of 30 days after unloading the subject-matter insured from the aircraft at the final place of discharge,

whichever shall first occur.

2. If the contract of insurance or the Clauses referred to therein specifically provide cover for inland or other further transits following on from storage, or termination as provided for above, cover will re-attach, and continues during the ordinary course of that transit terminating again in accordance with clause 1."

4.4 保险人愿意承保恐怖行动的限度之二:核武器/装置、生化武器与电磁袭击的恐怖行动

协会罢工险条文之3.9条有排除核武器/装备所带来或导致的直接/间接损失:"In no case shall this insurance cover loss or damage or expense directly or indirectly caused by or arising from the use of any weapon or device employing atomic or nuclear fission and /or other like reaction or radioactive force or matter."这表示恐怖分子(不论是恐怖组织或者是个人行动)提升到使用核武器/装置的情况下是罢工险保险人不承保的。这里的3.9条文没有针对用生化武器与电磁袭击发动的恐怖行动,但应该是

一样的理念。

有关这些大规模杀伤性武器(massive destruction weapon)风险在本书第八章有详论,不再重复。

5. 有关协会货物条文(B)与(C)的承保

本书的第六章已经详尽地分析了协会货物条文(A)的一切险承保范围,但还没有分析协会货物条文(B)与(C),虽然间或有提到。原因非常简单,今天的海上货物运输保险绝大部分都是投保一切险,投保协会货物条文(B)与(C)就非常少见,但也并不是没有,如在 Soya G. m. b. H. v. White (1983) 1 Lloyd's Rep 122 先例。还有就是在再保险,第一线的保险人承保了金额巨大的一切险之后,进行再保险时可能就会投保协会货物条文(B)与(C),而自己承担它们之间差别的风险。

由于笔者不准备花太大篇幅针对协会货物条文(B)与(C),所以就将该课题放在此处与战争险/罢工险一并谈而不另立章节。

协会货物条文(B)与(C)承保的列明风险都是在第1条,可节录如下以更好地显示它们之间的差别,首先节录的是协会货物条文(B):

"Institute Cargo Clause (B)

1 This insurance covers, except as excluded by the provisions of Clause 4,5,6, and 7 below,

1.1 loss of damage to the subject-matter insured reasonably attributable to

1.1.1 fire or explosion

1.1.2 vessel or craft being stranded grounded sunk or capsized

1.1.3 overturning or derailment of land conveyance

1.1.4 collision or contact of vessel craft or conveyance with any external object other than water

1.1.5 discharge of cargo at a port of distress

1.1.6 earthquake volcanic eruption or lightning

1.2 loss of or damage to the subject-matter insured caused by

1.2.1 general average sacrifice

1.2.2 jettison or washing overboard

1.2.3 entry of sea lake or river water into vessel craft hold conveyance container or place of storage

1.3 total loss of any package lost overboard or dropped whilst loading on to, or unloading from, a vessel or craft."

接下来是协会货物条文(C):

"Institute Cargo Clause (C)

1 This insurance covers, except as excluded by the provisions of Clauses 4, 5, 6 and 7 below

1.1　loss of or damage to the subject-matter insured reasonably attributable to

1.1.1　fire or explosion

1.1.2　vessel or craft being stranded grounded sunk or capsized

1.1.3　overturning or derailment of land conveyance

1.1.4　collision or contact of vessel craft or conveyance with any external object other than water

1.1.5　discharge of cargo at a port of distress

1.2　loss of or damage to the subject-matter insured caused by

1.2.1　general average sacrifice

1.2.2　jettison."

从以上的节录就马上可以看到协会货物条文(B)与(C)之间的差别是(C)条文承保的列明风险少了四项,这包括在(B)条文的1.1.6条的地震、火山爆发与闪电(earthquake, volcanic eruption or lightning);1.2.2条的冲入大海(washing overboard);1.2.3条的船舶、驳船、船舱、运输工具、集装箱或储存地点进水(海水、湖水或河水);1.3条的在船舶装卸时整件货物因为掉进大海或跌下的全损。

这些差别会带来怎么样的货物损失与损坏可简单举几个例子。首先针对地震,这种索赔很少有听说,但不是没有。如在1995年的神户大地震就有这种货物损失或损坏的索赔,虽然没有任何有关的案例。更加接近的就是在2004年12月29日发生在泰国的海啸(tsunami),这会对财产造成极大的破坏,包括在海上运输中的货物(不论是对方在码头、仓库或者装在船舶上)。海啸是由海底地震引发的,而协会货物条文(B)的1.1.6条说明只要是地震风险合理引致(reasonably attributable)的货损货差都获得承保,这"合理引致"的措辞显然是为了扩大近因原则(这方面可看第六章第4.4段),所以海啸是应该可以根据明示风险的地震向保险人要求赔付。

至于火山爆发带来的索赔也是很少听说,但是可以想象得到会有这种可能,毕竟海上货物运输保险承保的大部分风险都是在岸上发生的。最后要谈的是闪电,笔者也见过油轮被闪电击中爆炸而导致船货全损的事故。

接下来要谈的是冲入大海的风险,这只会发生在装在甲板的货物。通常是除非习惯性地装在甲板,否则把货物装在甲板是不会获得承保,除非有加保,这里可参见1906年立法的Schedule 1 Rule 17。至于习惯性装在甲板的货物也经常听说在坏天气时被冲入大海,这马上可以想到集装箱与木材。但要注意的是,如果这些货物是因为捆绑不当而被冲入大海就不属于这一列明风险,因为这里又涉及了什么才是最重要与有效的原因(请看第六章第4.2段)。

至于船舶或驳船,集装箱或储存地点进水(海水、湖水或河水),这有一点接近

(但并不雷同)以前在劳合社标准 S. G 保单中承保的海上风险(peril of the sea)。这包括哪一些事故可以节录 Wright 勋爵在 Canada Rice Mills Ltd v. Union Marine & General Insurance Co. Ltd. (1940) 67 Lloyd's Rep. 549 所说以得到一些启发,如下:"Where there is an accidental incursion of sea water into a vessel at a part of the vessel and in a manner where sea water is not expected to enter in the ordinary course of things and there is consequent damage to the thing insured, there is prima facie a loss by perils of the seas. The accident may consist in some negligent act, such as improper opening of a valve, or a hole made in a pipe by mischance, or it may be that sea water is admitted by stress of weather or some like bringing the sea over openings ordinarily not exposed to the sea, or, even without stress of weather, by the vessel heeling over owing to some accident or by the breaking of hatches or other coverings. These are merely a few among many possible incidences in which there may be a fortuitous incursion of sea water. It is the fortuitous entry of the sea water which is the peril of the sea in such cases."

要算是这个列明风险作为货物损失或损坏的近因,进水必须是个意外事故,而且由坏天气所引起,虽然这个坏天气并不需要达到不寻常的程度:请看 Merkin 教授在《Marine Insurance Legislation》第三版之第 114 页。这表示货物被雨水损坏则不属于这一个列明风险承保的范围内。如果这个雨大得很不寻常的话,会否有分别。答案应该是否定的,因为协会货物条文(B)之 1. 2. 3 条说明进水必须是进入船舶、驳船、船舱、运输工具、集装箱或储存地点,但没有说明雨水直接接触到货物而造成的损坏。当然,如果这个雨下得很大而导致了洪水,且洪水流入了集装箱集散地或是货物的仓库,而造成货物的损坏,在这种情况下这一个列明风险是承保的。最后一提的是 1. 2. 3 条是严格地适用近因原则,而不像上一部分的列明风险只需要"合理引致"(reasonably attributable)。所以,货损必须是进水直接导致的,而不包括如船舱出汗导致的货损。这里可以节录 John Dunt 在其 2009 版的《Marine Cargo Insurance》之 9. 33 段所说:"It is submitted that the better view is that the (B) and (C) Clauses visualise immediate contact between the cargo and water which causes damage and not condensation damage."

最后谈一谈协会货物条文(B)之 1. 3 条的在船舶装卸时整件货物因为跌落而造成的全损,这一种风险在以前散货运输的时候经常会有,就是货物在装卸的时候会掉落大海或码头导致全损。可是到了集装箱运输的时代,这种风险已很少见到。另外一提的是这一个列明风险只针对船舶或驳船的装卸,但没有包括岸上运输工具如火车与卡车在装卸时也会出现的这种意外。这里的原因并不是太明确,虽然有一个权威的说法是如果在岸上发生的话举证比较困难:请看 O' May 之《Marine Insurance: Law and Policy》第 183 页。笔者还怀疑另一个原因会否也有关系,就是岸上运输工具的装卸中掉下的货物不像船舶装卸掉下的货物那么容易造成全损。

至于协会货物条文(B)与(C)都承保的列明风险,本书就不多介绍了。针对受保人的货方来讲,这种条文的承保相对较少。还有在协会货物条文(B)与(C)承保的是共同海损与救助费用(第2条)、双方有责碰撞条文(第3条)、续运费用(第12条)与施救费用(第16条)。有关这些非实质性损失方面的承保,在本书第七章有详论,不再重复。一提的是在几个方面:首先根据1906年《英国海上保险法》Section 66(6)是说明在没有明示规定下,保险人不负责共同海损的损失与分摊,除非是为了避免承保的损失。但在协会货物条文(B)与(C),第2条针对共同海损与救助费用,保险人一概支付,不论是为了避免任何除了是明示除外的风险(with the avoidance of loss from any cause accepted those exclude in clauses 4,5,6 and 7 below)。这等于是改变了Section 66(6)的说法,就是不明示承保的风险所导致的共同海损与救助费用也获得承保。这里的原因在本书第七章有介绍,就是航次完毕要马上提供共同海损担保的时候,货方与他的保险人没有办法很快确定共同海损(或救助)是否是承保的列明风险所导致,所以干脆包括在承保范围内。

至于双方有责碰撞条文,协会货物条文(B)与(C)都把船舶碰撞列明为承保风险,所以承保这方面也就理所当然。

最后一提的是续航费用与施救费用,有关的条文就说明必须是承保列明风险所引起的才获得承保。第12条说:"Where, as a result of the operation of a risk covered by this insurance..."而第16条说:"... in respect of loss recoverable hereunder."

第十章　损失的类别：全损、推定全损与部分损坏

1. 损失或损坏

协会货物条文在第 1 条就说明是承保保险标的的损失与损坏。损失(loss)一般是针对失去货物的所有权，如货物被盗窃(theft)。损失也会是针对货物损坏，但受保人对所有权的控制并没有失去，本章稍后会针对这些情况。至于货物的损坏(damage)，这里比较针对的就是实质的损坏导致了货物被摧毁变成全损或者是部分损失。这与"损失"有一点不同，就是损坏是不针对货物的完整无缺，只因为盗窃或其他原因失去所有权。在 1906 年《英国海上保险法》，它针对保险标的全损的定义所用的措辞就是"损坏"，这是在 Section 57(1)："Where the subject-matter insured is destroyed, or so damaged as to cease to be a thing of the kind insured, or where the assured is irretrievably deprived thereof, there is an actual total loss."

损失或损坏对受保人而言，也可以分为两种。第一种就是实质损失或损坏(physical loss or damage)，如货物被盗窃，或者连船带货一起沉没在大海，又或者只是少量的货物因为船舱进水而受到损坏。第二种就是经济损失(financial loss)，这种典型的例子也有很多，如船舶因为天气的原因导致船期延长，晚到卸港以致市场价格下跌导致的损失。其他例子是像共同海损的分摊(因为要分摊的货物没有受到任何实质的损失或损坏)、救助费用等。英国普通法的默示地位是认为海上货物保险根据协会货物条文只针对实质损失或损坏，Clarke 大法官在先例 Coven SPA v. Hong Kong Chinese Insurance Co (1999) Lloyd's Rep IR 565 说："all risks cover applies only to physical loss and damage"。其他有关的先例有 De Monchy v. Phoenix Insurance Company of Hartford (1929) 34 Lloyd's Rep 201, Fuerst Day Lawson Limited v. Orion Insurance Co Ltd (1980) 1 Lloyd's Rep. 656。

1.1　不承保经济损失，除非特别约定

但法律并没有阻止双方在货物保险合约以明确的文字与措辞承保经济损失，所以在协会货物条文，第 2 条针对的是承保共同海损的分摊，第 3 条针对"双方有责碰撞条文"(Both to Blame Clause)，第 12 条针对航次终止(loss of adventure)的续运费用(这些在本书第七章都有介绍)与第 16 条针对施救费用(在第七章第 5.4 段有介绍)，这些都是典型例子，与货物的实质损失或损坏没有关系。

至于其他一些经济损失，如市场下跌甚至是做生意亏本，这种风险是保险人不会了解也不愿意承担，所以不会在协会货物条文或保险合约里面有明确条文针对。

但针对货物保险还会有一种要个别加保的损失或损坏，就是针对假提单的风险。可称为以"Fraudulent Bills of Lading Clause"加保，而承保的风险就是"因为假提单被受保人接受所带来的损失"（loss or damage occasioned through the acceptance by the Assured of fraudulent Bills of Lading）。承保这种风险对保险人是非常危险，因为一旦遇到损失就是全损。而且会经常发生，几乎每家中国的外贸公司都有过类似的经历，而且还在不断发生。鉴于此，保险人在承保类似的风险时，一定要对受保人的业务水平有足够的了解，因为事实上保险人承保的也就是受保人的业务水平。有关这种假提单的风险在笔者的另一本新书《信用证》中会详细介绍，在这里只是简单地说：问题主要出现在 CIF 或 CFR 买卖，因为这种是被称为文件买卖（documentary sale）。这表示买方用成百上千万美元的钞票（通常是通过银行结汇）买回来的不是一船货物而只是一套单证，而其中最重要的文件就是装船提单（shipped bill of lading），提单上标明货物正在某船舶上从装港运往卸港的途中。而事实上，根本没有这票货物在某船舶上，甚至根本没有这艘船舶或者该船前不久才被拆为废铁。要知道，任何单证都可能假造，所以假造一套提单与其他付运单证是很容易的事。难怪这种欺诈，因为容易，不必要任何成本，利润丰厚且通常不会有法律后果（因为在国际层面很难制裁一个外国骗子），所以被称为世界上"最完美"的犯罪（perfect crime）。

本来，如果以 FOB 买货就安全得多，因为买方派的船舶在装港有没有货装上船很快可以知道，而且在货价付出去之前。但问题是买方如果不懂得航运就没有办法以 FOB 进行买卖，因为这涉及了复杂的租船业务。所以导致了发展中国家包括中国大量的进口都是以 CIF 或 CFR 买卖进行。即使是以 CIF 或 CFR 买货，买方还有其他对付假提单风险的做法，而其中最重要的就是调查卖方的背景。如果是与西方一些著名的贸易公司以 CIF 或 CFR 买货，他们可以在谈判订合约等方面非常厉害，但他们就不会做非法的事情，因为假提单是明显属于欺诈的非法行为。但奈何有不少买方为了省钱或不知道渠道，不会愿意掏钱摸对手的底，也不知道在国际的层次上怎样做。所以，简单地说，以假提单欺骗发展中国家这种公司非常容易。

所以如果笔者是保险人，就恐怕并不会在中国推广这种风险的承保业务。但这种保险在其他国家还是有，以下介绍两个有关的美国先例。第一个就是 Chemical Bank v. Affiliated FM Insurance Company（1993）AMC 1743，案情涉及一些银行对一批价值高达 1 亿美元的咖啡为买方提供融资让他购买，而买方就是以这套付运单证作为担保，并且把货物保险合约背书转让给该银行。而保险合约是加保了"Fraudulent Bills of Lading Clause"，说明是承保"loss or damage occasioned through the acceptance by the Assured of fraudulent Bills of Lading"。结果是遇上假提单，根本没有这些咖啡。这些银行作为受保人或受让人向保险公司索赔这笔经济上的损失，保险公司以货物保险合约本质上只针对货物遭受的实质损失或损坏作出抗辩。美国法院判是保险公司败诉，Vincent Broderick 大法官这样说："[保险人] primary argument is that the core purpose of the policies involved was to cover physical goods and merchandise (consisting principally of coffee), against losses on the high seas and related hazards to which shipments of merchandise may be exposed... Certainly the Affiliated policy was basically intended to provide coverage against injuries caused by loss of goods. This does not mean that other clauses included in the policy which by their terms extended beyond this central objective were rendered void."

估计在英国法院也会是同样的判法，虽然笔者没有找到有关的先例。但在美国另一个上诉庭先例 Centennial Insurance Company v. Lithograph Sales (2002) 29 Fed. Appx. 835，判是该先例中有关的"Fraudulent Bills of Lading Clause"，赔的只是实际损失或损坏，经济损失不包括。但该"Fraudulent Bills of Lading Clause"所用的文字比上一个先例文字简短，只是说："loss of or damage to the property insured"。所以，还是订约自由与根据双方订的合约条文作出解释。写法不同就会带来不同解释，这不是以同一个标题说明是"Fraudulent Bills of Lading Clause"就可以解决问题，而要看该条文的实质内容。

1.2 什么是货物的实质损失

在这里是先针对货物的实质损失(physical loss)，而针对货物保险，这主要是受保人对货物的占有权(possession)与控制权(control)的失去。至于货物由于承保风险而招致损失，如货物被大火烧毁或者连船带货沉没，是把这种情况视为实质损坏(physical damage)，这会稍后解释。

受保人对货物失去占有权与控制权的风险可以是货物被第三人非法占有(conversion of cargo)或被第三人抛弃(abandonment of cargo)或是被留置与拍卖(lien and sale)。而针对非法占有，也不必区分到底是刑事行为如盗窃或只是属于民事的侵权。而在一切险，一直以来货物被盗窃的话是获得承保的。这可以介绍在先例 London & Provincial Leather Processes, Ltd v. Hudson (1939) 64 Lloyd's Rep 352，案情是涉及一批货物是毛皮，投保了一切险并延伸"against all and every risk whatsoever, however arising... at and from any port or ports, place or places in Germany and whilst there for not exceeding three months"。保险期间这票货物是在德国公司 A 的手中进行加工，它把部分货物分包给了另外的公司 B。结果 A 破产，B 是 A 的债权人就对他手中有的毛皮行使留置权。A 的破产接管人也拒绝归还受保人的毛皮。受保人就向保险公司提出索赔并最终胜诉。Goddard 大法官说："in English law, we should call conversion, because having a demand made upon them to deliver up the goods they refused to do so and have asserted a right to retain the goods which was bad in law, a right which they had no right to enforce against the goods. Therefore that was a conversion. For my part I am unable to see why, if goods which are insured against all-risks are converted so that the true owner, the assured, is deprived of the possession of the goods, he is any less entitled to recover under the policy than he would be if the goods were stolen. He is deprived of the possession in one case by theft; He is deprived under circumstances which would render the spoliator liable to the criminal law. It is a matter of the state of mind whether there was a felonious mind. **In the case of conversion he is equally deprived of his goods and equally wrongfully deprived, but wrongfully only in the sense that a civil tort is committed and not a criminal wrong.** "

这种货物被第三人侵占的风险针对货物运输保险是非常大,也只有在协会货物条文(A)才被承保,而一些经常出现的情况导致货物损失会是盗窃(theft)、海上被侵占(takings at sea)、欺诈(fraud)、货物所有权转移(transfer of title)、货物被抛弃(abandonment of cargo)、货物被留置或拍卖(lien or sale),以下分别作出解释。

1.2.1　盗窃(theft)

盗窃的法律定义在1906年《英国海上保险法》有规定,是在《Rules for Construction of Policy》之Item 9:"The term "thieves" does not cover clandestine theft or a theft committed by any one of the ship's company, whether crew or passengers."显然,这一个定义不包括偷偷摸摸的小偷,而只是指使用武力的盗窃。偷偷摸摸的小偷英文说法是"pilferage",这种行动的特征是没有人看到小偷的行为,正如Scrutton大法官在Cleveland Twist Drill Company (Great Britain) Limited v. Union Insurance Society of Canton Ltd (1925) 23 Lloyd's Rep 50(CA)所说:"it is one of the particularities of secret theft that you do not see it happen."

但有了一切险的承保,这一传统的分别已经不再重要,因为暴力盗窃或小偷都是属于意外(accidental),正常情况下不应该发生,所以应该是承保。而在协会货物条文(B)&(C)它与以前的"平安险"(Free from Particular Average,简称FPA)与"水渍险"(With Average,简称WA)是不一样,它没有在列明风险中包括盗窃(theft)与小偷(pilferage)。所以,如果货物投保的是(B)&(C)条文,但在运输途中会有这种风险,就必须加保"偷窃与提货不着险"(Theft, Pilferage and Non-delivery,简称TPND)。但估计这种情况不多,因为值得被小偷光顾的货物从价值上来讲应该都是值得投保(A)条文的。TPND的加保,条文措辞如下:"In consideration of an additional premium, it is hereby agreed that this insurance covers loss of or damage to the subject-matter insured caused by theft or pilferage, or by non-delivery of an entire package, subject always to the exclusions contained in this insurance."

最后解释一下"提货不着"(Non-delivery)是针对货物失去了,虽然有提单证明它是装上了船舶,但到了卸货港就交不出货。由于举证责任是在受保人的头上,而他没有办法证明货物是半途被盗窃还是被偷偷摸摸的小偷偷走。所以就一并投保"提货不着"险,反正两种情况都包括。

在美国,由于Atlantic Insurance Co v. Storrow NY Ch 1835的先例判保险合约中"theft"一词是包括了小偷,所以为了与英国的法律地位相同,方便再保险,在涉及美国的货物运输保险就用稍微不同的措辞名为"assailing thieves"来表示是需要暴力的盗窃。

要构成盗窃,Donaldson 大法官在 The"Mandarin Star"(1969) 1 Lloyd's Rep 293 说明必须有四个要件:(1) a change of possession;(2) contrary to will of possessor;(3) without *bona* fide claim of right and;(4) with intent permanently to deprive owner。意思就是说首先是改变了货物的占有,货物的占有变成去到盗窃人的手中;其次是这种改变与原来占有人的意愿相违背;再次是后来的占有人无权主张这种占有;最后是盗窃人永远都不想把货物再归还给原来的占有人。Donaldson 大法官在该先例判是"盗窃"一词是以商业人士的角度看待,但这在后来的先例 Grundy v. Fulton (1981) 2 Lloyd's Rep 666 不被认同,认为"盗窃"一词是以刑事罪的角度看待,Stuart-Smith 大法官这样说:"Mr. Prosser [原告代表大律师] relying on the [Mandarin Star] case, contends that the word ' theft ' in the policy should not be interpreted in the strict sense of criminal law but should be understood as commercial men would understand it... In my view, in this policy with which I am now concerned, theft must be given the same meaning as in the criminal law ... "

1.2.2 海上被侵占(takings at sea)

海上被侵占一直以来的说法是敌人或海盗占有船舶或者货物。这里可以先节录权威的 Halsbury's Laws of England (1st ed.) Vol. 17 para. 870 – 871 的说法:"Seizures and takings at sea include deprivation of possession, whether the seizure or taking was lawful or unlawful, and whether by enemies or pirates."

另在 Gow 著的《Marine Insurance (1896)》之 114 页说:"Taking at sea is commonly expressed in modern commercial language as ' seizure '."而 Templeman 在《Marine Insurance (1903)》第 34 页说:"Surprisals and Takings at Sea, these words require no explanation, being merely another way of expressing ' Capture '."

有关这一种风险,只有(A)条文才承保,这种风险会导致货物实质损失,可以举两个著名的先例说明,而且在今天的航运还是会发生。第一个要介绍的先例是 The "Mandarin Star"(1969) 1 Lloyd's Rep 293,案情涉及了该船舶期租 6 个月给了一家名为"Asia Line"的公司,而在 Asia Line 的指令下,船舶在曼谷装了一船的大豆去日本神户,并签发了运费预付的提单。由于 Asia Line 没有给租金,导致了船东最后把船舶开到了神户后再绕航回去香港,并声称把该批货物留置以支付欠下的租金。显然,船东这样的做法并不正确,即使留置货物,也只能是到了卸港才能行使而不是在航次的半途。该货物运输保险是根据劳合社标准 S. G 保单,其中的列明风险包括盗窃与海上被侵占。在受保人的货方与保险人之间的争议,第一审的 Donaldson 大法官判这不属于海上侵占而属于盗窃。但去了上诉庭,判法被改变过来,判货物的损失是属于海上侵占而不是盗窃,因为认为船东很可能只是诚实地以为他可以行使留置权利,但实际上是错误,而这种情况下不会是盗窃。其中 Denning 勋爵给了海上侵占一个广泛的定义,而不是传统的说法只是局限在海上的捕获(capture)或扣留(seizure)类似的情况,说:"The first risk which we have to consider is 'takings at sea'. Has there been in this case a 'taking at sea'? There is very little authority indeed, even after 400 years, on 'takings at sea'. It includes capture and seizure. But I do not think it is confined to those two. 'Takings at sea' is capable of a wider connotation. That is shown by Rickards v. Forestal Land, Timber and Railways Company, Ltd. [1942] A. C. 50; [1941] 70 Lloyd's Rep 173, in which, at the outbreak of the last war, a German vessel called the 'Minden', instead of proceeding on her normal voyage, put into Rio de Janeiro. On the orders of the German Government, she left Rio and tried to get back to Germany. She was intercepted by a British warship. She was then scuttled by the crew. It was held that the orders of the German Government amounted to 'restraint of princes'. But Lord Wright used words which import that the goods were 'taken', even though they remained on the same ship with the same master. He said: ... What happened here was that the master, being in possession of the goods as a carrier for the assured, seized them in the sense that he ceased to hold them as carrier and changed the character of his possession by taking and controlling them as agent for the German government with the intention and effect of holding them adversely to the assured and applying them to the hostile purposes of his government... The master was actually in possession of the goods throughout. He simply took them from the assured by dealing with them adversely to their interests and throwing off the role of a private carrier in which capacity he had held them... as bailee for the assured... So here it seems to me that the master of the Mandarin Star, on behalf of the owners, changed the character of their possession."

注意 Denning 勋爵的判法与传统说法不一样,他是把船长与船东,本来就已经是货物的托管人,把货物非法侵占(misappropriation of cargo)也包括在"海上被侵占"内。这一判法在后来的 The"Salem"(1983) 1 Lloyd's Rep 342 被贵族院推翻,而事实上 Denning 勋爵在上诉庭也有说他对 Wright 勋爵所说的意思与理解有了偏差。有关 The"Salem"先例的案情在本书第六章的 1.2 段有详细介绍,大致就是船东把一船属于壳牌(Shell)石油公司的 20 万吨原油,本来的目的地是去欧洲,但半途去了南非德班偷偷地把船上的 18 万吨原油卖了给当时实行种族隔离(所以受到阿拉伯国家的禁运)的南非政府。而剩下的大约 2 万吨原油与船舶一起沉没,借此造成污染以掩人耳目。受保人的壳牌石油公司向保险公司根据保险合约的劳合社标准 S. G 保单提出索赔,在第一审胜诉,Mustill 大法官根据 The"Mandarin Star"先例判这是海上被侵占。但这在上诉庭与贵族院被推翻。在上诉庭,法院认为即使是根据 The"Mandarin Star"船东想把货物非法侵占也不会在海上作出这个决定。要么是在装货前就有这个阴谋,也应该是如此。要么是在船舶到了德班把货物卸到岸上的那一个时间,这也不是在海上。而贵族院的 Roskill 勋爵更是判海上被侵占不包括船东非法侵占船上的货物,把货物据为己有。

这些问题到了今天在协会货物条文(A)都不存在,因为都是属于承保风险均可以获得赔偿。即使是船东(或者其他托管人如仓库保管人)把货物侵占(misappropriation of cargo),这也是受到承保。要提到的是与 The"Mandarin Star"与 The"Salem"中的类似的风险在航运不景气的时候还是确实存在的,不论是由于船东的无知乱来,或是像"鬼船"(这个问题在本书第十一章第9段有详论)的这种情况。

顺便要一提的是货物如果被第三人侵占,到底是以哪一个时间为准。这在 Mitsui Marine & Fire Insurance Co & Ors v. Bayview Motors Limited (2003) 1 Lloyd's Rep 131 (CA)的先例有涉及。案情是有关6辆 Toyota 的汽车,在 Santo Domingo 卸下再转运去其他附近的两个小岛,但在卸到由海关控制出入的保税仓库后,在该一切险保险合约的承保期间,海关拒绝放货。但真正决定把这些被侵占的汽车分给其他的官员的时间是在把货物卸下后60天届满之前还是之后就有争议了。这是因为在中途港卸下的话如果60天还不继续运输,就被视为运输风险终止与保单失效(这在本书第十一章第4.1.2.3与4.4段有详述)。这看来关系到保险人在该一切险的保险合约是否需要赔付,而英国上诉庭是认为适用"死亡一击"(death's blow doctrine),就是在保险合约还是有效的时候货物实际上已经是被侵占,这无可避免地导致了货物的全损。Eveleigh 大法官这样说:"Moreover, it did not matter if further loss might occur after the expiration of the policy, for the containers had already been the victims of an insured peril within the policy period. They had received a potential death blow."

1.2.3 欺诈与货物所有权转移(fraudulent loss of cargo)

这种风险经常会面对到底是实质损失(physical loss)还是经济损失(financial loss)的疑问,因为后者的损失保险人不会赔付。简单地说,如果买方(作为骗子)把货物骗到手,从来没有准备向卖方作出支付,这是属于一切险的承保风险,因为受保人的卖方被欺骗而损失了这批货物。但如果买方从卖方取得这票货物的时候并没有不支付或欺诈的意图,而是后来改变主意,这导致卖方收不到货款是一种经济损失。显然作出区分并不容易,特别是一批货物经过多次转卖而导致决定卖方最终向买方收不到货款,该买方是在什么时候有了这种不诚实与不合法的想法。在 Australia & New Zealand Bank v. Colonial and Eagle Wharves Limited (1960) 2 Lloyd's Rep 241,案情涉及仓库保管人占有了一批货物(羊毛)并等待为该批货物提供融资的银行命令怎么样处置(to order of the bank),但被一个骗子把这批货物骗去转售并事后宣布破产。有关的货物保险是承保一切险,McNair 大法官判这是一个欺诈,一切险是要承保,即使该批货物是自动交给骗子,也不改变是承保的风险。

在货物所有权转移的案件,也是有区分实质损失与经济损失的困难。如果在一个买卖合约,卖方把货物所有权转移给买方时,买方就已经有不诚实的想法将来不会支付或是买方在那个时候已经是经济上破产,所以根本不会或不可能将来支付卖方,这是属于一切险承保的风险。但换一个例子是把货物所有权转移的时候,卖方与买方订立的买卖合约是规定交货之后的 3 个月或半年才支付,到了要支付的时候,买方拒绝支付或者发生清盘/倒闭。这就属于经济损失或一种信贷损失(credit loss),是不在承保的范围内。这方面可参考先例 Glencore International A. G. v. Alpina Insurance Company Limited (2004) 1 Lloyd's Rep 111。

1.2.4 货物被抛弃、留置或拍卖(cargo abandoned, liened and sold by court)

在 Integrated Container Service Inc v. British Traders Insurance Co Ltd (1984) 1 Lloyd's Rep 154(该先例在本书第七章 5.7 段有详细介绍),Dillon 大法官就提到:"The policy is against all risks, and I can see no reason why the risk of a lawful sale by a third party should be excluded. The [受保人] effectively lose their containers whether the sale is lawful under a lien—port regulations or a process of judicial execution—or unlawful."

该先例虽然不是货物运输保险,而是为集装箱投保了 12 个月的全损风险,但道理是一样,就是在一切险,如果货物在运输半途被其他人(这包括船东、其他承运人如货代或者仓库保管人)不论是什么原因,抛弃与置之不理,或者是通过留置(不论是合法还是不合法),导致货物最后是被法院拍卖,这种损失在一切险下都可以获得赔付。这当然是不能涉及受保人自己的故意行为(wilful conduct)或自愿的行为(voluntary act),如受保人没有支付给船东合法赚取的运费或滞期费(或者有争议的时候提供给船东担保以交换放货),又或是没有支付给仓库保管人储存费,这导致了第三人对货物的留置并最后导致货物被法院拍卖(这种问题在笔者的《程租合约》第十二章有详论),受保人的这种损失是不可以获得保险人的赔付,因为这是受保人自己的过错或行为所导致,可以说是受保人的蓄意恶行(wilful misconduct)。根据 1906 年《英国海上保险法》Section 55(2)(a),受保人的蓄意恶行导致的货物损失保险人是不需要赔付。另在协会货物条文的 4.1 条又将 1906 年立法的该默示法律地位重述作为一切险的除外风险,这在本书第八章第 1 段有详细介绍,其中也有提到先例 The "Wondrous"(1991)1 Lloyd's Rep 400,请参阅。

但这种情况会是没有受保人的蓄意恶行,而是承运人如货代的过错,没有支付运费或仓库费用给分包的承运人或仓库保管人。这导致了分包的承运人或仓库保管人把货物留置并有可能申请当地法院拍卖。这种情况下,如果受保人有损失,保险人还是应该赔付。这种案件在本章 1.2 段介绍的先例 London & Provincial Leather Processes, Ltd v. Hudson (1939) 64 Lloyd's Rep 352 就有,是分包人 B 留置货物,因为主承包人 A 欠他的钱。虽然货物并非是 A 所拥有,这不影响 B 的留置权,因为 B 是为该货物(毛皮)提供了服务。另外,可参见笔者在《船舶融资与抵押》一书中所提案例 Chellarm v. Butlers (1978) 2 Lloyd's Rep 412。[1]

---

〔1〕 杨良宜:《船舶融资与抵押》,大连海事大学出版社 2003 年版,第 94 页。

1.2.5 船东、船舶管理人/经营人与承租人破产/倒闭(bankruptcy of carrier)

在先例 London & Provincial Leather Processes, Ltd v. Hudson (1939) 64 Lloyd's Rep 352,涉及主承包人 A 的倒闭,但看来并不影响一切险下保险人是要负责有关的货物损失。在 Integrated Container Service Inc. v. British Traders Insurance Co. Ltd. (1984) 1 Lloyd's Rep. 154,也是涉及了租用集装箱的公司倒闭。在倒闭后,虽然承保标的也就是集装箱没有面对实质损害的风险,但看来也不影响受到承保。Everleigh 大法官这样说:"The [受保人] had let on hire their containers to a company that was trading effectively and was in a position to maintain the necessary organization to look after the containers and to perform the duties imposed upon them in the capacity as bailees. When, as a result of their insolvency, they ceased to operate they were no longer bailees capable of taking care of the goods. The containers were effectively abandoned by their custodians. They were consequently exposed to the risk of theft, misuse, enforcement of a lien—in other works to the risk of loss or damage from some cause or another. **We are concerned with a policy which covers all risks. Therefore if the [受保人] have established the existence of a threat of loss or damage, no matter if that threat resulted from the insolvency of the lessee, they are entitled to recover moneys laid out to avert a loss which might result from a variety of reasons.**"

这样看来如果货物保险合约是一切险,普通法认为破产倒闭引起的货物损失(不论是被抛弃、留置或拍卖)也是被承保。这在 John Dunt 的《Marine Cargo Insurance》一书之 8.53 段也有反映,说:"There was some doubt in the market as to whether an all risks cargo policy covered losses arising from insolvency. However, the decision of Goddard LJ in London & Provincial Leather Processes, Ltd v. Hudson held that where the assured was wrongfully deprived of his goods as a result of a conversion there was an all risks loss even if the conversion resulted from the insolvency of the third party to whom the assured had entrusted the goods. It therefore appeared that where insolvency led not merely to delay in the voyage, which would be excluded, but to a loss of the goods or the adventure, that loss would be covered under an all risks policy. Moreover, the expense of forwarding the goods to destination, to avoid a loss of the adventure, was arguably covered under a cargo insurance as sue and labor."

但破产/清盘并不是一个承保风险,因为它本身不会导致保险标的的损失或损坏,正如 Integrated Container Service Inc. v. British Traders Insurance Co. Ltd. (1984) 1 Lloyd's Rep. 154, Dillon 所说:"The insolvency of [the lessee] is not a risk insured against under the policy, since it does not in itself involve any loss or misfortune to, or indeed have any effect on, the containers or other chattels, the subject-matter of the insurance."

这一来,如果出了这种事情,就会存在两个风险所导致的情况。一个风险会是任由货物被抛弃就会有危险因为风吹日晒导致货物损坏(正如Integrated Container Service Inc. v. British Traders Insurance Co. Ltd. (1984) 1 Lloyd's Rep. 154)。这个风险也可以导致货物被分包人因为主承保人的破产/倒闭欠钱而留置货物甚至要通过法院命令拍卖。显然这种损失或损坏是一切险承保的风险。但另一个风险是不承保,就是破产/倒闭的风险。这一来,如果一个是承保的风险,另一个是除外风险,这就需要找出近因了。

但在协会货物条文,针对除外风险的是4.6条,并不广泛,这在本书第八章第6段有介绍。它的第一个局限是只针对船东、船舶管理人、承租人与船舶经营人的破产或倒闭,没有包括岸上运输的承运人或仓库管理人。第二个局限是针对受保人在装货的时候知道这一个破产/倒闭会妨碍航次的正常进行。这种是保险人不容易证明的,而且只适用在受保人就是租船的CIF卖方或FOB买方。第三个局限是这种除外条文不影响无辜的提单持有人,而无辜的提单持有人向保险人提出索赔的在国际贸易还是占多数。

1.3　什么是货物的实质损坏

货物实质损坏的例子也是多不胜数,这包括了石油产品经常会因为船舶本身或者船舶上装运的其他石油产品而遭受污染。实质损坏可以说是导致了货物本质的改变。

但如果只是怀疑,其实是没有实质损坏,保险人是不需要赔付。这里可以举有关的四个先例。第一个先例是Cator & Others v. The Great Western Insurance Co of New York (1873) LR 8 CP 552,案情涉及1700包茶叶,其中450包因为被海水浸泡而损坏,但其余的茶叶是完好。结果良好的茶叶出售价格也受到很大影响,受保人向保险人索赔这一损失。这被法院拒绝,Bovill大法官这样说:"The insurance is against damage to the goods, and not against loss to the assured otherwise than by reason of damage to the goods themselves... The underwriters insure against damage to the goods by the perils insured against; but they do not, in our opinion, insure against damage by prejudice or suspicion, though such prejudice or suspicion be reasonable and be general in fact in business, when there is no damage in fact to the goods themselves; and, if this policy were to be so construed, it would make them insures, not only against direct damage to the goods insured, but against damage to other goods in the same ship affecting the credit and thereby the value of the goods insured, and would create indirect and collateral and consequential liabilities from suspicion and prejudice, which it would be almost impossible for the underwriters to estimate in fixing a premium proportionate to the risk."

第二个先例是Lysaght Ltd v. Coleman (1895) 1 QB 49,案情涉及一批镀锌的铁板运去伦敦。在卸下的时候发觉有部分损坏,保险人对这部分损坏进行了赔付(包括发票价格与最后出售的差价,再加上检查损坏货物的费用)。但保险人拒绝赔付检查没有遭受损坏货物的费用,Rigby大法官表示同意,他说:"It cannot be said that a suspicion of damage entitled [受保人] to incur costs, at the expenses of the underwriters, if no damage had actually taken place; and it that may be said with truth as to the whole cargo, I think it follows that [受保人] could not in this case be entitled to make good this claim against the underwriters in respect of the goods to which there had been no damage."

第三个先例是 Overseas Commodities Ltd v. Style (1958) 1 Lloyd's Rep 546,案情涉及猪肉罐头在海上运输的过程中有一部分损坏,结果没有损坏的罐头也是以很低的价格处理掉。McNair 大法官也是判说海上货物运输保险承保的是货物的实质损坏,完好的货物只是由于人们的怀疑而被低价处理掉导致受保人遭受的损失是不在承保的范围内。

第四个先例是马来西亚的 Boon & Cheah Steel Pipes Sdn. Bhd. v. The Asia Insurance Co Ltd (1975) 1 Lloyd's Rep 452,法院接受了 Mustill 御用大律师的争辩,即对怀疑有损坏的货物作出的检查的费用不可以包括在推定全损的计算中。

2. 货物实质损失或损坏的类别

实质损失或损坏可以归纳为三种:第一种是真正全损(actual total loss);第二种是推定全损(constructive total loss);第三种是部分损失或损坏(particular average loss or partial loss)。

它们的定义在 1906 年《英国保险法》有清楚的规定,以下分别作出介绍。

2.1 真正全损

其中有关真正全损是在 Section 57,如下:"57 Actual total loss (1) Where the subject-matter insured is destroyed, or so damaged as to cease to be a thing of the kind insured, or where the assured is irretrievably deprived thereof, there is an actual total loss. (2) In the case of an actual total loss no notice of abandonment need be given."

在以上的定义中可以得出三种情况会构成真正全损:(1)保险标的的货物被摧毁(destroy);(2)损坏到一个程度以至于再也不是原来投保时的货物;(3)受保人不可扭转地被剥夺了所有权。

2.1.1 保险标的的货物被摧毁

这种情况应该显而易见,如船舶起火导致货物被烧成了灰。但如果货物着火,不过还是保留有原来的形态(original character),可以修复,只是修复费用是货物本身价值的好几倍,重新制造另外的货物反而更便宜,这表示货物并没有被摧毁,不能算是真正全损,而充其量只是一个推定全损:Lohre v. Aitchison (1878) 3 QBD 558, 562; Bell v. Nixon (1816) Holt 423。

有一些货物本质上是没有办法摧毁,如黄金。即使黄金沉没在深水,它也不会被摧毁,只是打捞费用高昂而不值得。这一来,也充其量只是一个推定全损。因为科技是越来越先进,很少有东西是不可以被修复,关键是值不值得的问题。

2.1.2　损坏到一个程度以至于再也不是原来投保时的货物

这种真正全损发生的机会也不是太多,基本上就是投保的货物如水泥(cement)在被海水浸泡后变得更像是混凝土(concrete),从商业角度来讲无法把损坏的货物叫作水泥:Duthrie v. Hilton (1868) LR 4 CP 138。

有关这种真正的全损,最出名的先例是 Asfar & Co v. Blundell (1896) 1 QB 123。有关的货物是枣子(dates),由于运载的船舶沉没而遭到损坏。在船舶浮起来的时候,枣子已经完全失去了原来的形态,变成英国上诉庭形容的"a mass of pulpy matter impregnated with sewage and in a state of fermentation"。虽然枣子不适合食用,但这票货还是以相当好的价格卖给了酒商酿酒。这里就涉及了这批枣子是否是真正全损的争议,毕竟也涉及到底要不要为这批枣子(如果还能算是枣子)支付运费。英国上诉庭判是真正全损,其中 Esher 勋爵这样说:"... is whether, as a matter of business, the nature of the thing has been altered. The nature of a thing is not necessarily altered because the thing itself has been damaged; wheat or rice may be damaged, but may still remain the things dealt with as wheat or rice in business. But if the nature of the thing is altered, and it becomes for business purposes something else, so that it is not dealt with by business people as the thing which it originally was, the question for determination is whether the thing insured, the original article of commerce, has become a total loss. If it is so changed in its nature by the perils of the sea as to become an unmerchantable thing, which no buyer would buy and no honest seller would sell, then there is a total loss."

如果损坏并没有导致货物本身从商业角度看完全变成另一种东西,用途也是不一样,这样也是不属于这一种类的真正全损。例如,在先例 Francis v. Boulton (1895) 65 LJQB 153,货物是一批大米,投保的价格是 450 英镑,但也是因为沉船而被泡在水里面而遭到损坏,之后将大米捞起来晒干以大约 100 英镑出售。而捞起来与晒干的工作也大约花费 65 英镑。但英国法院就判这不是真正全损而只是部分损坏。

最后举一个比较新的先例解释有关这一个问题,先例涉及了船舶而非货物保险,是 The"Shakir III"(1997) 1 Lloyd's Rep 586。案情是有关的船舶没有动力,被拖带去黄埔港拆废船。但在锚地等待的时候因为避风而最后导致搁浅。该船的保险金额是 300 万美元,但要把该船浮起与救助的费用估计最少要 800 万美元,这还没有估计船底可能会有损坏导致船舶更不值钱。还有,在中国内地的海域要进行救助,还要得到当局的批文。这些加起来都是困难重重,但被判是不足以构成该船舶不可挽救地被剥夺。Potter 大法官说:"The undisputed evidence in this respect was to the effect that it was feasible to salvage the vessel subject to accessibility and cost."另外,该船舶能否算是"本质上有了根本的改变"(这也是本小段要针对的问题),由于看来船舶搁浅会有很大的损坏,很可能会在救助时在水底部分断裂为两段,再也不能说它是一艘船舶,而变成一堆废钢。但 Potter 大法官不接受,认为除非船舶真正断裂为两段,否则作为船舶的本质还是没有改变,他说:"... the photographs and the weight of the evidence before me show that it was not in fact in two and still retained its original appearance and character as a single vessel, so that it seems to me that in the course of salvage it would have to be separated into two halves for towage goes more to the economics of salvage than to the question of whether the vessel had lost its essential character. ”

最后要讲的这种真正全损与推定全损很难区分,就是货物损坏有没有到一个程度从商业角度看是原来的形态与本质有了改变。可以说有了争议的话,受保人与保险人都可以找到商业人士作为专家证人支持自己的观点。而法院在很难作出判断的时候也会是倾向接受是推定全损而非是真正全损,所以受保人还是应该及时作出委付通知,因为这是构成推定全损的前提条件。

2.1.3 受保人不可扭转地被剥夺了所有权

不可扭转地被剥夺(irretrievable deprivation)并不需要肯定货物是被剥夺,但可以说这个程度还是要很高,因为它需要与推定全损的"不大可能"(unlikely)可以在合理的时间内要回货物作出区别。

这方面可先介绍 The"Minden"(1942) AC 50,87,Wright 勋爵这样说:"There is a real difference in logic between saying that a future happening is uncertain and saying that it is unlikely. In the former the balance is even; no one can say one way or another. In the later there is some balance against the event. It is true that there is nothing in the Act to show what degree of unlikelihood is required. If on the test of uncertainty the scales are level, and degree of unlikelihood would seem to shift the balance, however slightly; it is not required that the scale should spring up and kick the beam. ”

另可以举船壳保险的著名先例:The"Anita"(1970) 2 Lloyd's Rep 365,案情涉及了该船舶因为走私而被越南海关扣留,并在后来的一个特别成立的军事裁判庭(当时是越战期间)把该船舶充公。在 1967 年 3 月 13 日由保险人委任的一位越南中间人想办法把船舶释放,但被告知是几乎没有希望。该越南中间人的计划是希望作出一个专家报告说明该船舶并不值钱,然后通过这个报告说服越南政府把它公开拍卖。估计不会有其他投标人竞买,所以可以以低价把该船舶买回,其中还要涉及贿赂越南的官员。这一计划即使会成功也需要好几个月的时间。到了 1967 年 8 月 29 日,当受保人的船东向保险人提出索赔要求赔付真正全损的时候,该船舶已经在越南被扣留了 17 个月。最后看来计划还算是成功,因为在 1968 年 5 月 21 日,该船舶通过公开拍卖被买回。Mocatta 大法官针对开始诉讼的一天(因为这就是诉因的一天),认为当时把船舶要回来的希望很渺茫,但还是不能说是不可扭转地被剥夺,说:"It may be true that the order of confiscation divested the plaintiffs of the legal ownership of the vessel as it is the case after condemnation of a ship by a Prize Court. But the test of irretrievable deprivation is clearly far more severe than the test of unlikelihood of recovery of possession and, despite the gloomy prospects for the future as at August 2, 1967, I feel unable to find that the plaintiffs were at that date irretrievably deprived of their vessel. ”

但以前是有先例认为如果保险标的(不论是船舶还是货物)被其他法院出售或拍卖,所有权有了改变,这应该是明显的不可扭转地被剥夺。其中著名的 Cossman v. West (1887) 13 App Cas 160(这一先例不像在 The"Anita"先例中有被提到,表示 Mocatta 大法官不一定有考虑这一先例),案情涉及船长与船员叛变,把船舶凿沉。但该船舶被救助人成功施救并拖到安全地点,之后被海事法院下令拍卖以支付救助奖金。而该船舶最后被修复。英国枢密院认为这是一个真正全损,Sir Barnes Peacock 说:"To constitute a total loss within the meaning of a policy of marine insurance, it is not necessary that a ship should be actually annihilated or destroyed; it may, as in the case of capture and sale upon condemnation, remain in its original state and condition; it may be capable of being repaired if damaged; it may be actually repaired by the purchaser, or it may not even require repairs. If it is lost to the owner by an adverse valid and legal transfer of his right of property and possession to a purchaser by a sale under a decree of a Court of competent jurisdiction in consequence of a peril insured against, it is as much a total loss as if it had been totally annihilated..."

2.1.4 极度轻微的原则(*de minimis* principle)是否适用

法律是有一个说法,对极度轻微的事情就不加考虑,这就带来一个问题是在考虑真正全损的时候会否适用。在先例 Glennie v. London Assurance Co (1814) 2 M & S 371,涉及一批大米受到严重损坏,最后只能以 10% 的原来价值出售,但法院判这只是部分损坏。在另一个先例 Hedburg v. Pearson (1816) 7 Taunt 154,损坏货物只剩下 3% 的价值,法院也拒绝判这是一个真正全损而只是部分损坏。这种判法在货物保险中会有重大影响,因为投保只是局限在全损(total loss only),或者只是投保了平安险(Free from Particular Average)。这样看来,极度轻微的原则在针对真正全损时并没有被适用。

在一个比较近期的马来西亚先例名为 Boon & Cheah v. Asia Insce (1975) 1 Lloyd's Rep 452,受保人的货物是 668 支钢管,要从 Prai 运去 Brunei。运输的办法是把这些钢管装在驳船内由拖船拖带,但半途遇到海上风险而导致大部分的货物掉到海里,只剩下了 12 支。拖船与驳船被迫去了新加坡,在新加坡的检查发现这 12 支钢管也受到了损坏,但最后该 12 支钢管还是运去目的地。受保人于是向保险人提出索赔,指这是一个推定全损或是一个真正全损(在极度轻微的原则适用下)。这里也要说明受保人投保的是平安险(Free from Particular Average),所以如果不能成功索赔全损,就等于保险人完全不用赔付了。在马来西亚的法院,判是受保人败诉。针对推定全损,法院认为受保人没有提供足够的证据说明把货物恢复并续运去目的地会超出货物在目的地的价格。但针对本段的问题,法院认为 12 支钢管还是在程度上代表相当大的价值,所以极度轻微的原则不适用。但也顺便提到如果只是剩下 1 支或 2 支,该原则就会适用了。Shah 大法官这样说:"In my judgment, 12 pipes measuring a total of 360 ft., weighing 36 tons, costing MYM14,400 and insured at MYM16,000, affect far too high a proportion of the whole consignment of 668 pipes to be capable of being dismissed as a matter *de minimis*. It may well be that in the case of a single pipe or two out of the whole assignment, the rule would apply, but I fail to see how it is possible to hold that 12 pipes can be ignored or treated as trifling and to be brushed aside. I find therefore on the facts before me that a consignment of 668 pipes is not totally lost when 12 pipes making it up are not lost. ”

2.2 推定全损

1906 年《英国海上保险法》关于推定全损的条文有不少,因为它涉及受保人怎样才是行使他的权利选择索赔推定全损,这包括了向保险人及时作出委付通知(Notice of Abandonment)。这是 Section 60 至 Section 63[1]。

2.2.1 推定全损的类别

根据 1906 年《英国海上保险法》Section 60, 推定全损总共有六种,可以归纳为四大类。

第一大类是在 Section 60(1),其中涉及了两种推定全损,就是受保人放弃(abandon)货物,因为看来真正全损是无可避免,或者要花费比保险标的价值更高的钱保全。这方面的先例是 The “Lavington Court”(1945) 2 All ER 357,涉及是船壳保险而不是货物保险。另是本章第 3 段也有先例针对这一方面,特别是说明 Section 60(1)的“放弃”(abandon)与 Section 60(2)给保险人的委付通知(Notice of Abandonment)不一样。Section 60 (1)基本上就是假设一个合理的船东或是货方,没有投保任何保险,在遇到这种情况就是真正全损是无可避免或要花更多的钱把船舶或货物保全,他就会放弃了。这就是 Section 62(1)中“abandon”的含义。这种情况在海上货物保险也不大会出现,因为受保人的货方不会是跟在船上亲自看到意外发生与认定真正全损看来是无可避免,所以不去多讲。

第二大类是在 Section 60(2)(i),承保风险剥夺了受保人对货物的占有,原因是取回不大可能(unlikely to recover)或取回要花费的钱比保险标的的货物价值更高。显然第二大类与第一大类的区别之一只是时间先后的问题,但它们都是一种经济上的全损。就是有关的保险标的可以保全(preserve)、修复(repair)或取回(recover),只是经济上不划算而不是做不到。

第三大类是在 Section 60(2)(ii)。针对的是船舶的损坏而不是针对货物,所以在本书中不需要针对。

第四大类是在 Section 60(2)(iii)。针对的是货物受到损坏,而把它修复并续运到目的地是超出了货物抵达后的价值。海上货物保险是要同时考虑续运的费用(这方面在本书第七章第 5 段有详及),这是与船舶损坏的不同之处,因为船舶是不存在要续运去目的地。这里也显示了海上货物运输为什么会有航次终止的风险。这一法律地位看来也是以明示条文重复使之更加明确,这就是在协会货物条文(A)(B)(C)

---

〔1〕 参见附录一。

的第 13 条:“13. No claim for Constructive Total Loss shall be recoverable hereunder unless the subject-matter insured is reasonably abandoned either on account of its actual total loss appearing to be unavoidable or because the cost of recovering, reconditioning and forwarding the subject-matter insured to the destination to which it is insured would exceed its value on arrival. ”

2. 2. 2　推定全损在货物保险

推定全损对船壳保险是非常重要,所以大部分有关的案例都是船壳保险,如 The “Bamburi”(1982) 1 Lloyd's Rep 312 与 Royal Boskalis Westminster NV v. Mountain (1997) LRLR 523。岸上保险是没有推定全损而只有真正全损(Moore v. Evans [1918] AC 185),在 The“Kastor Too”(2004) 2 Lloyd's Rep 119,Rix 大法官说:“Members of the public are, we suspect, familiar with the concept of the writing-off of motor-cars which have suffered an accident causing damage that is not worth repairing. However, it is only marine insurance that formally recognizes the concept of a constructive total loss. Outside marine insurance, the only total loss which is acknowledged is an actual total loss. Marine insurance, however, has two kinds of total loss, actual and constructive. Both are equally total losses. ”

针对海上货物保险,本来是十分复杂的推定全损就变得相对简单。因为受保人的货方在知悉了货物发生严重事故的时候,通常是时间上已经很晚,没有必要再作出委付通知,因为根据 Section 62(7)就是对保险人不会有任何利益的情况下是不需要这样做。但推定全损对船壳保险而言十分重要,如果读者有兴趣可以参阅笔者与汪鹏南教授合著的《英国海上保险条款详论》第二版第 308 页的有关内容。所以针对推定全损绝大部分来自船壳保险。但有关货物推定全损的案件也不能说是没有,其中可以举的例子 The“Minden”(1942)AC 50,案情是货物装在德国船舶上,但“二战”爆发后,德国变成了敌对国,船长奉德国的命令放弃航次开回德国。虽然去德国的航程中会遇上英国舰队的封锁,有可能把这批货物取回。但德国船长奉命在遇上这样的情况时把船舶凿沉,可以说看来真正全损是无可避免。所以法院判这批货物是推定全损。

针对货物推定全损,近期倒是有一个很有趣的先例 Masefield Ag v. Amlin Corporate Member Ltd (2010) EWHC 280 (Comm)。案情关系到货物被索马里海盗连船带货抓去,要求赎金,有否可能被视为真正全损或推定全损。这稍后会在本章第 3 段有详论。

2. 3　部分损失或损坏

部分损失或损坏应该很容易了解,基本上不是全损就是部分损失或损坏。在 1906 年《英国海上保险法》其中有关部分损失或损坏是在 Section 64,如下“64. Particular average loss (1) A particular average loss is a partial loss of the subject-matter insured, caused by a peril insured against, and which is not a general average loss. (2) Expenses incurred by or on behalf of the assured for the safety or preservation of the subject-matter insured, other than general average and salvage charges, are called particular charges. Particular charges are not included in particular average."

事实上,即使是推定全损,本质上还是部分损坏,只是从经济角度来看不值得把损失或损坏的货物修复或取回。所以,对这种通常会是十分严重的部分损失或损坏,1906年《英国海上保险法》给了受保人个选择,就是通过向保险人作出委付通知,就可以索赔推定全损。但如果没有作出这个选择,就仍被视为部分损失或损坏。这在 Section 62(1)说得很清楚,如下:"... where the assured elects to abandon the subject-matter insured to the insurer, he must give notice of abandonment. If he fails to do so the loss can only be treated as a partial loss."(如果受保人选择抛弃保险标的给保险人,他必须作出委付通知。如果他没有这样做,他的损失只能被视为部分损失。)

至于为什么要选择索赔推定全损,而不只是希望索赔部分损失或损坏?它们的区别表面看来是不大,因为索赔部分损失或损坏也可以赔付到最高的保险价值,而这个保险价值也就是推定全损会支付的钱。这里就会涉及其他的原因,如在船舶保险合约,可能会约定了很高的免赔额,如果索赔部分损失或损坏,该免赔额是要扣除,但如果是索赔推定全损,则不需要扣除该免赔额。笔者认为更大的原因是在受保人还是否想继续拥有保险标的,因为作出了委付通知就必须把保险标的抛弃并交给保险人。但如果只停留在部分损失或损坏,这个保险标的修好以后所有权还是受保人的。所以,如果船舶是船东非常珍惜的,不论是从感情上还是从将来的很好市场预期的方面看,船东都会选择索赔部分损失或损坏。但如果市场不好或前景不看好,船价一路下跌而船舶的保险价值又很高,船东会是非常愿意作出委付。针对货物保险,已经介绍过很少会涉及作出委付通知的做法,因为货方了解事故的时候往往已经很晚,而根据 1906 年《英国海上保险法》Section 62(7),就是对保险人不会有任何利益的情况下是不需要这样做,这在本章 2.2.2 段有介绍。但还会有比较罕见的情况出现,如先例 Masefield Ag v. Amlin Corporate Member Ltd (2010) EWHC 280 (Comm),受保人的柴油在船舶被海盗劫持的时候一起被掠走,而在船东与海盗谈判期间,受保人担心柴油的价格下跌,迫不及待向保险人作出委付通知,希望以推定全损索赔保险价值。而的确是在事后,该批柴油去了卸货港鹿特丹出售的价格因为市场下跌少了 700 万美元。而且这 700 万美元以部分损失索赔也是不会成功,因为这是由于延误遇到市场下跌而产生,而该项是海上货物运输保险合约中除外风险之一。所以是否能够索赔推定全损会是至关重要。

3. 有关索马里海盗掠走货物是否全损的先例

3.1　以前海盗捕获的英国法律地位

先要一提的是有关海盗捕获或者扣留是曾经有过一个古老的先例,说这种情况一发生就可以马上构成真正全损,先例是 Dean v. Hornby (1854) 3 El & Bl. 180。案情是有关的船舶投保定期保险,而在受保期间的 1851 年 12 月,该船舶从智利的 Valparaiso 去英国利物浦经过麦哲伦海峡的时候,被海盗捕获。但到了 1852 年 1 月该船舶再度被一艘英国的军舰抢回来并把船舶开回智利的 Valparaiso。之后的 1852 年 4 月该船舶被捕获的消息才传回给英国船东(因为那是通讯困难的年代),船东在 4 月 30 日向保险人作出了委付通知,但保险人拒绝接受委付。该船舶后来被从智利的 Valparaiso 开回去利物浦并且被海事法院判给了海军作为奖赏,反正在那个年代公海上就是抢来抢去。有关船东是否能够向保险人成功以海盗捕获的承保风险索赔全损,英国上诉庭判是可以。Campbell 勋爵说:"I am of opinion that, according to English law, the plaintiffs, in comformity with decided cases, are entitled to judgment. The underwriters undertake for the safety of the ship form April 1851 to April 1852. In December 1851 she is taken by pirate. Then, in fact, a total loss has occurred. After that, she never is restored to the owner; nor have they had an opportunity of regaining possession. They have lost the possession by events over which hey have no control, and therefore are entitled to the indemnity for which they have paid. The cases referred to establish this principle: that if once there has been a total loss by capture, that is construed to be a permanent total loss unless something afterwards occurs by which the assured either has the possession restored, or has the means of obtaining such restoration."

另 Coleridge 大法官也同意如下:"I am of the same opinion. There was a capture by pirates; and, if that were all, there would unquestionably be a total loss..."

该先例后来被当作在海盗把船舶或货物捕获就可以马上被视为真正全损的权威先例。在涉及伊拉克短暂侵略科威特并把科威特航空公司的飞机掠走的先例 Kuwait Airways v. Kuwait Insurance (1996) 1 Lloyd's Rep. 664, Rix 大法官就有以下的说法:"In case of capture, because the intent is from the first to take dominion over a ship, **there is an actual total loss straightaway**, even though there later be a recovery: see Dean v. Homby (1854) 3 El. & Bl. 179 (a case of piratical seizure)."

3.2　索马里海盗的问题

但一二百年前被海盗掠走的船舶或货物与今天索马里的海盗是有很大不同,以前被加勒比海盗掠走的东西在那个年代是没有太大可能再取回来,可以说对受保人而言就构成不可扭转的全损。但今天被索马里海盗掠走的船舶与货物最终都是被放走让受保人取回,当然是在支付了赎金以后。可以说古代与现代海盗的做法是很不一样。

索马里海盗的问题在 2007 年开始出现,问题变得越来越大。根据统计,2007 年到 2008 年 9 月,共有 9 艘船舶被索马里海盗掠走得到赎金后释放。据记录,整个 2008 年度共发生 293 次海盗袭击,而这个数字到了 2009 年前 9 个月就达到 309 次。索马里海盗的典型做法就是在捕获与扣留船舶货物后,就会向船东开出一个赎金的数目,然后双方的代表会进行谈判(很多是在伦敦进行),而谈判成功与在支付赎金后就会释放船舶与货物。索马里海盗是没有任何意图长期或永久占有该船舶与海上的货物,如把船上货物在海盗的巢穴卸下另作处理或出售。整个过程从捕获直到释放通常是 21 ~ 68 天,平均是 37 天。据说到目前为止还没有一宗是船舶被海盗掠走交了赎金后没有被放回的。

3.3 目前索马里海盗捕获的英国法律地位

最近针对索马里海盗,有了一个重要与有趣的先例。这就是货物如果被海盗捕获或者扣留,这是否是真正全损或是推定全损或是部分全损。该先例是 Masefield Ag v. Amlin Corporate Member Ltd (2010) EWHC 280 (Comm)。案情涉及一艘马来西亚的船 Bunga Melati Dua 在 2008 年 8 月 19 日被索马里海盗连船带货抓了去。原告 Masefield 是该船舶上两批柴油的货方,该货物高达 1300 多万美元,通过开口/预约保单(open cover)投保了一切险。到了 2008 年 9 月 18 日,当时船东还是在与索马里海盗谈判有关赎金的问题,货方向保险人作出了委付通知。有说法是柴油的市场价格在下跌,所以货方想借这个机会脱身并把投保金额全部要回。而在 10 天后,马来西亚船东就与海盗谈妥并支付了赎金,船舶与货物也就被释放并继续开往荷兰的鹿特丹。船舶是在 2008 年 10 月 26 日在鹿特丹将货物卸下,但由于市场价格的变化,货方蒙受了 700 万美元的损失(这是在比较推定全损能够成立的情况下保险人支付了保险价值)。

货方并没有索赔部分损失,所以有关的先例也没有针对。但估计是提出 700 万美元作为部分损失也不会成功,因为海盗即使是承保的风险之一,它所导致的延误(delay)与市场价格下跌带来的损失也是属于协会货物条文 4.5 的除外风险。

所以,先例针对的纯粹就是货方在作出委付通知的一天,即 2008 年 9 月 18 日货物是否是真正全损或推定全损。根据英国法律要看的事实就是以当天的情况为准,而不能从事后诸葛亮的角度看。至于在 2008 年 9 月 18 日前后的重要事实可总结如下:(1) 在船舶被索马里海盗掠走的第二天也就是 2008 年 8 月 20 日,其中一个货方(马来西亚公司名为 Carotech Berhad)发出邮件说:船东正在与海盗谈判。(2) 2008 年 8 月 24 日,受保人在公司内部有邮件传播,内容是说海盗已经与船东联系并要求 200 万美元的赎金。而马来西亚政府已经向美国政府求助。虽然该消息是没有被证实的。(3) 2008 年 8 月 26 日,受保人收到船东的邮件,说为了船员的安全与海盗的谈判正在进行。(4) 2008 年 8 月 26 日,Lloyd's List 报刊报道说:"马来西亚政府正在与海盗对话,以确保 39 名船员可以被释放,国家副总理说……"(5) 2008 年 8 月 28 日,船东经纪人 Clarksons 通知受保人说船东正在尽最大的努力确保释放船员。(6) 2008年 8 月 31 日,船东通知船员家属说船员会在 30 ~ 40 天内被释放。(7) 2008 年 9 月 2 日,船东召开新闻发布会证实释放该船舶的谈判还在进行,今年在亚丁湾至少有 30 条船舶被劫持,在所有这些事件中,没有听说船员有被伤害的。(8) 2008 年 9 月 2 日,国际海事组织(ICC International Maritime Bureau)的 Captain Mukundan 在接受采访时说船员被释放前是需要进行 2 ~3 个月的谈判。他说这事不能着急,海盗感兴趣的不是船舶或货物而是钞票。(9) 2008 年 9 月 2 日,船东代表证实有一队人正在与海盗接触,并说海盗要求 200 多万美元才会释放该船舶;而马来西亚军方派出两艘军舰去亚丁湾帮助释放船员。(10) 2008 年 9 月 15 日,Lloyd's List 报刊报道说马来西亚国家安全委员会秘书说与海盗的谈判进展良好,希望最终是好消息。(11) 2008 年 9 月 18 日,受保人的货方向他的保险人作出委付通知。(12) 2008 年 9 月 22 日,Clarksons 告诉受保人的代表说:"与海盗的谈判进展良好。与船上的通信每天都有,根据最近一次的联络,船上所有船员仍旧是安全的。船东会把船员的生命安全放在第一位,接着就是船员、货物与船舶尽快得到释放。为了保护船员及其家人的安全,现在不能够提供关于谈判更详细的信息"。(13) 2008 年 9 月 28 日,船东向海盗支付了 400 万美元的赎金(包括另一艘姊妹船的赎金),船舶/船员与货物在被扣留了 40 多天后被随即释放。(14) 2008 年 10 月 26 日,船舶抵达鹿特丹卸货。

英国法院 Steel 大法官认为在这种情况下不可能有一个真正全损,因为并不是没有办法合法、实际把货物取回来(legally and physically impossible to recover the goods),也不是说把货物取回来所需要的时间比较长,导致货物会全部变坏。他这样说:"It is of note in the present case that the condition of the ship and cargo off Somalia had not deteriorated significantly in the period up to the abandonment to underwriters, the ransom sought whilst large was on a par with sums paid by other owners and represented only a tiny proportion of the overall value but most important of all the cargo-owners had lost only possession and not dominion over (or property in) their goods."

至于推定全损,Steel 大法官认为根据 1906 年《英国海上保险法》Section 60 有两个要求受保人都达不到:(1) The subject matter must be abandoned(保险标的事实上是被抛弃);(2) Because an ATL appears unavoidable(保险标的的真正全损看起来是无可避免)。而在本案例中,根本是从来没有放弃过从索马里海盗的手中把船舶货物取回来,也从来没有是货物真正全损看来是无可避免。

有关货物事实上有否被抛弃,这是与向保险人作出委付通知的"抛弃"有不同之处,这方面在本章 2.2.1 段有解释。正如 Steel 大法官以一个 1945 年的先例作出解释如下:

"In the first place the vessel and its cargo were not abandoned in the relevant sense. What is required is not a notice of abandonment in the sense of Sections 61, 62 and 63 of the Marine Insurance Act but the abandonment of any hope of recovery. The distinction is spelt out in Court Line v R (1945) 78 Ll. L. Rep 390 in the judgment of Lord Justice Scott at pp. 395/396:

'When the ship is spoken of as 'abandoned on account of its actual total loss appearing to be unavoidable,' the word is used in nearly the same sense as when according to the law of salvage the ship is left by master and crew in such a way as to make it a "derelict," which condition confers on salvors a certain but not complete exclusiveness of possession, and a higher measure of compensation for salvage services. But to constitute the ship a 'derelict,' it must have been left (a) with that intention (*animo derelinquendi*) (The John and Jane, 4 C. Rob. 216); (b) with no intention of returning to her; and (c) with no hope of recovering her. Obviously that sense of the word is frequently inappropriate to the second case to which the first sub-section applies, namely, because it could not be preserved from total loss (that is, an economic test) 'without an expenditure which would exceed its value when the expenditure had been incurred.

Another distinction between those two alternative grounds in sub-s. (1) for claiming a constructive total loss is that in the latter case the financial estimate is one which normally would be made by the owner; whereas the forecast of the probability of actual total loss would, at any rate a century ago, nearly always have to be made by the master on the spot; and even in these days of easy and quick wireless communication, the decision would very often devolve on the master. The making of the financial estimate is, of course, merely an exercise of business judgment and discretion. The abandonment which follows after it may be expressed in a letter and not in boats as in the first alternative; or be a mere mental decision by the owner that he will exercise the option which Sect. 61 allows him. There is a somewhat similar contrast between the two alternatives of sub-s. (2) (i) (a) and (b). In Sect. 61 the word "abandonment" seems to import an act on the part of the assured, but in truth it amounts usually to nothing more than his making up his mind to give notice of abandonment to the insurer under Sect. 62 (1), at the peril of losing his right of election under Sect. 61. The legal consequences of a notice of abandonment if accepted by, or established as valid against, the insurer is to pass the property to the underwriter as an abandonment to him under Sect. 61. A valid "abandonment" in Sect. 63 necessarily means an abandonment by the assured to the insurer and passes the property to him. It cannot be the same act as is contemplated by Sect. 60 (1), where the act is done in consequence of an actual total loss appearing unavoidable. That abandonment, for example, by the master and crew leaving the ship with the intention of never returning, etc., may lead up to and justify a subsequent abandonment to the insurer, but the two are wholly different acts, and distinct in kind.'

No such abandonment has occurred. To the contrary the shipowners and the cargo owners had every intention of recovering their property and were fully hopeful of doing so."

有关的先例也有针对向索马里海盗支付赎金是否合法的问题,因为如果这是不合法,就存在一个问题是不能把用不合法的方法将保险标的取回加以考虑来认定是否是一个真正全损。可以举个简单的例子,船舶或货物是根据某国家法律如《海关条例》被充公。但由于某国家贪污腐败,要取回来唯一的希望是贿赂官员。这样的话就不能说货物没有全损,因为谈不上是不可扭转地被剥夺(irretrievable deprivation)或不大可能将货物取回(unlikelihood of recovery of possession),因为还有非法渠道可以尝试。

Steel 大法官判是支付赎金在英国法律基本上是合法,也不违反公共政策。毕竟伦敦保险市场在 2008 年 8 月开始提供"绑架与赎金"的保险(Kidnap & Ransom cover),为船舶与货物受保人提供更多与更明确的保障。所以,总不能把这种做法视为非法。Steel 大法官这样说:"I am wholly unpersuaded that it would be right to categorise the payment as contrary to public policy: i) As already noted the payment of ransom is not illegal as a matter of English law (nor I can assume as a matter of Somali, Swiss or Malaysian law). ii) Circumstances have arisen where legislative action has intervened to make such payments illegal: see e. g. the Ransom Act 1782. The courts should refrain from entering into the same field. iii) So far as harm is concerned it is true that payments of ransom encourage a repetition, the more so if there is insurance cover: the history of Somali piracy is an eloquent demonstration of that. But if the crews of the vessels are to be taken out of harm's way, the only option is to pay the ransom. Diplomatic or military intervention cannot usually be relied upon and failure to pay may put in jeopardy other crews."

总结而言,索马里海盗袭击或掠走船舶与货物虽然是一切险的承保风险之一,但在目前这种操作下,看来是不会构成船舶或货物的实质性真正全损,推定全损或部分损失。但有例外会是:

1. 通常是由船东支付的赎金释放船舶是可以向保险人以施救费用(sue and labour)要求赔付,这在 Steel 大法官的判词中也有涉及,说:"It is also to be noted that payments of a ransom are recoverable as a sue and labour expense: see Royal Boskalis Westminster NV v Mountain [1999] QB 674. Albeit the point was not pursued in argument and left Pill LJ concerned as to whether recovery was repugnant to English notions of legality, the majority's view is a strong indication that the Claimant's position is misconceived: 'The terms in which the duty under section 78(4) is expressed are wide enough on their natural meaning to embrace expenditure necessary to procure the release of a vessel that has been seized and I see no reason of policy or practice why they should not do so. If that is right, then it would be strange indeed if such expenditure did not fall within the sue and labour clause. In my judgment the assumption of the editors of Arnould that payment of a ransom, if not itself illegal, is recoverable as an expense of suing and labouring is well founded'."

2. 如果涉及船上有货物,船东支付的赎金可以被视为共同海损费用(general average expense)。有关这些非实质性损坏的承保在本书第七章第 2 段有介绍。

3. 如果索马里海盗在攻击时造成船舶或货物的损坏或者在扣留时造成损失或者损坏,这是实质性损坏,保险人在一切险应该赔付。

4. 如果将来法律变为支付赎金是非法，就从 Masefield Ag v. Amlin Corporate Member Ltd（2010）EWHC 280（Comm）先例看来，一旦船舶或货物被海盗掠走要求赎金，而支付赎金（即使是非法）也是把船舶或货物取回的唯一可行与安全的做法，成立一个真正全损或一个推定全损的机会就大大增加。这方面并不稳定，一直就有说法是索马里海盗如果涉及恐怖分子组织，支付赎金就变成非法，因为 1999 年 12 月 9 日第 54 届联合国大会通过的《制止向恐怖主义提供资助的国际公约》禁止直接或间接支付金钱给恐怖组织。此外 2010 年年初就有谣言说美国会单方面或者通过联合国安理会把支付给海盗的赎金视为非法，这导致一些国际船东组织如 Chamber of Shipping 大力反对，并发信函给美国国家安全部、交通部、国防部游说这样做的弊端，包括对船员生命安全的威胁、对国际贸易的影响等。总之，这一问题还是会有不断的发展，大家拭目以待。

3.4 美国法律地位

美国政府在 2010 年 4 月 12 日由奥巴马总统签署了有关索马里的行政命令（Executive Order concerning Somali）。该行政命令针对的是在任何美国人士（包括美国法人与他的分公司）占有或控制下的财产或财产利益，其具体内容是不允许资助一些会直接或间接影响索马里的和平、安全与稳定的活动。其中索马里海盗的行为就被指明是属于这种活动。这一行政命令是马上生效，如果违反就会面对美国的惩罚与刑事制裁。换言之，美国的法律现在是与英国不一样，在美国支付索马里海盗赎金是刑事犯罪。针对船舶与海上保险马上想到的就是该行政命令直接影响美国船舶的机会恐怕不会太多，因为挂美国旗的船舶毕竟有限。但如果涉及海上保险，其涉及面就广得多，而且会涉美国人士的机会就大大提高。举例说，船舶在支付了赎金给索马里海盗之后向货方（通过共同海损的做法）要求分摊，或是保险公司再向分保人要求补偿，这就涉及了很多不同的人士。如针对货方，一艘船舶上可能会有上千个不同的货方，这就有可能其中一位或多位是美国人士，他们不能支付共同海损的分摊，因为这会被视为间接资助索马里海盗，是犯法的行为。而货方从保险公司获得共同海损分摊的赔付后，假设该保险公司是一家英国保险公司，也难保该英国保险公司在他的再保安排不涉及美国再保险人。

第十一章　承保风险的开始与结束，航次延误，航次改变

第 8 条：运输条文（Transit Clause）[1]

8. 8.1　除下述第 11 条另有规定外，本保险责任始于保险标（货物）的首次从（在保险合约注明地点的）仓库或存放地点为开始运送而为立即装入或装上运输车辆或其他运输工具而移动之时，在通常运送过程中连续并且终止于

8.1.1　在保险合约中注明目的地从运输车辆或其他运输工具全部卸到最后仓库或存放地点，

8.1.2　在保险合约注明的目的地或之前从运输车辆或其他运输工具全部卸到任何其他仓库或存放地点，其由受保人或其雇员用作通常运送过程以外的存放或分发，或

8.1.3　在受保人或其雇员选择将运输车辆、其他运输工具或集装箱用作通常运送过程以外的存放，或者

8.1.4　保险标的在最后卸港从船舶卸下满 60 天，

以上各项以先发生者为准。

8.2　如果在最后卸港从船舶卸下后，但在本保险终止之前，保险标的（货物）被转运到非本保险承保的目的地，本保险在依然受前述第 8.1.1 条到第 8.1.4 条规定的终止所限制的同时，终止于为向此其他目的地转运而首次移动之时。

8.3　在受保人不能控制的迟延、任何绕航、强制卸货、重装或转载期间，以及船东或承租人行使根据运输合约赋予的自由权产生的任何航海上的变更期间，本保险继续有效（但须受上述第 8.1.1 条到第 8.1.4 条规定的终止和下述第 9 条规定的制约）。

2009 年条文相对 1982 年条文[2]有一定的改变，其中 2009 年条文的承保期限扩展了。

---

〔1〕　英文条文参见附录三。

〔2〕　1982 年相关要文参见附录二。

1. 承保风险的期限:从海上运输伸延到"仓至仓"

这是一条很重要的条文说明保险人承保的期限,而且该条文一向是很具争议的。海上货物运输保险人最早只承保海上运输那段时间的风险,所以以前的劳合社标准 S. G. 保单只规定从哪一个装港开始(at and from)直至在卸港安全从船上卸下并着陆(discharged and safely landed),再加上用小船或驳船把货物运送到远洋船舶的风险(Craft risks)。正如 Byles 大法官在 Lane v Nixon (1866) LR 1 Cp 412 中所说的:"The general rule in the law of insurance, that the policy covers not only the voyage from port to port, but also the transit of the goods to and from the ship."

发展下去是货物保险伸延到整个运输过程,不论是海上还是陆上。这在 1906 年《英国海上保险法》之 Section 2(1)有针对,所以双方可以明示约定把海上风险伸延到陆上的运输,这不会影响该保险在本质上还是海上货物运输保险:Simon Israel v. Sedgwick (1893) 1 QB 303; Kallis (Manufacturers) Ltd v. Success Insurance Ltd (1985) 2 Lloyd's Rep. 8 (PC); Nam Kwong v. China Insce (2002) 2 Lloyd's Rep 591 等先例。有关这几个先例的详细介绍参见本章 6. 3. 3 段。1906 年立法的有关条文是在 Section 2(1):"A contract of marine insurance may, by its express terms, or by usage of trade, be extended so as to protect the assured against losses on inland waters or on any land risk which may be incidental to any sea voyage."

这个最初的做法是根据一条"仓库到仓库条文"(Warehouse to Warehouse Clause),简称"仓至仓条文"。最早的版本是出现在 1912 年的协会货物条文,有关的条文是:"**Warehouse-to-warehouse Clause** Including (subject to the terms of the Policy) all risks covered by this Policy from shippers' or manufacturers' warehouse until on board the vessel, during transshipment if any, and from the vessel whilst on quays wharves or in sheds during the ordinary course of transit until safely deposited in consignees' or other warehouse at destination named in the policy."

仓至仓条文针对不同的货物品种可以作出相应的调整,反正这是订约自由。以植物油为例,在 Tradigrain SA v. S. I. A. T SpA (2002) 2 LLR 553 先例中,显示了相关的条文承保的风险是从装港油柜直到卸港的油柜,如下:"Covering insurance from Loadport Storage Tanks up to Discharge Port Storage Tanks or first port weightbridge."

而到了 1982 年协会货物条文就变成第 8 条的"运输条文"(Transit Clause),保险责任开始是在"从为了开始运送货物而离开仓库或储存地"(This insurance attaches from the time the goods leave the warehouse or place of storage at the place named herein for the commencement of the transit...),而风险终止的时间就不是在货物从运输的船舶卸下与安全着陆的时候,而是伸延到 1982 年条文之第 8. 1. 1 ~ 8. 1. 3 条规定的三

种情况中最早发生者来作为承保风险期限的终止。而到了 2009 年协会货物条文，就进一步向两端伸延了一点点，对受保人更有利，也避免了一些争议。有人为了与以前的“仓至仓条文”相区分，将其简称为“从仓库搁板到车后挡板条文”（from shelf to tailgate），简言之，就是伸延到包括启运出库的装车、发运过程和抵达入库的卸车过程。

有关 1982 年条文中的运输条文（Transit Clause），承保的期限已经是整个运输的过程，只要货物在运送，就受到（A）条文的一切险保障。但有部分作为受保人的货方认为光是运输期间受到保障还是不足够，并寻求对在货方仓库或堆场装货与卸货期间（如在卖方的仓库把货物堆装进集装箱内）会发生的风险进行加保。所以，2009 年条文就作出相应的改变，把承保的时间伸延，包括在货方仓库或堆场装货与卸货的期间。所以在第 8.1 条就从 1982 年条文中的措辞说“从货物离开仓库的时候”（from the time the goods leave the warehouse），变为 2009 年条文的措辞说“为了把货物马上装上运输工具，而在仓库或在储藏的地方首次移动货物”。这样的措辞仍是不承保较早时货物暂时存放在仓库或储存地等待开始运输那段时间的风险，如在那期间仓库发生火灾。

到了今天的集装箱运输，会有情况是在陆上的运输会比海上的运输长得多，但还是可以算是海上货物运输的保险。这里会带来一些微妙的区别。例如，算是海上货物而不是陆上货物运输的保险，1906 年《英国海上保险法》就适用。例如，在本书第十章第 2.2 段有提到海上保险才会有推定全损，但陆上保险就没有。另一个微妙但不能算是太重要的区别是在海上保险，保险人可以向法院申请要求船东披露所有船舶的文件后才需要作出抗辩请求，这一做法在本书第五章第 8.7 段有关仲裁也有提到。虽然这种做法主要是针对船壳保险，但也会对货物保险有关，如保险人怀疑货方与船东有串通把船舶凿沉令货物全损，获取假装把货物付运但实际上没有：British Isles Marine & General Insurance Co Ltd v. Bostandji (1920) 5 Lloyd's Rep 202，Teneria Moderna Franco Espanora v. New Zealand Insurance Co (1924) 1 KB 79。纯粹是陆上运输是没有这种做法：Schloss v. Stevens (1905) 10 Com. Cas. 224。海上运输即使是涉及在陆上运输的阶段发生货损货差，还是可以有这种做法：Harding v. Bussell (1905) 2 KB 83；Leon v. Casey (1932) 2 KB 576。

2. 2009 年协会货物条文中的运输条文中风险的开始

2009 年的相关条文是在 8.1 条，英文是说：“Subject to Clause 11 below, this insurance attachés from the time the subject-matter insured is first moved in the warehouse or at the place of storage (at the place named in the contract of insurance) for the purpose of the **immediate loading** into or onto the **carrying vehicle or other conveyance** for the **com-**

mencement of transit.”本段接下来解释2009年版该条文中特别用词(加黑)的意义及相关普通法判例。

2.1 “马上装上”(immediate loading)的含义

本条文中会有争议的一词是“马上装上”,但这里可以看到保险合约的本意是为了承保货物在运输与在移动过程中的风险,所以要避免一些情况,如在仓库把小部分货物装上车架(trailer)或卡车(truck)就让它停留在那里,其余的货物慢慢在备妥之后才继续装。再举一个例子是货物从货架装上车架或卡车后就开去一个等候的地点停泊,这也不是“马上装上”。应该说协会货物条文的本意是不准备承保在运输前的移动(pre-transit movement)或在运输前的等待(pre-transit waiting)。

“马上”一词是没有规定时间,这表示法律会默示一个合理的时间。但显然保险合约是想把货物从货架装上车架或卡车后马上开始运输,让这些行动连贯在一起。所以,这合理的时间应该是非常短暂。假设货物是在周五的下午被装上了卡车,因为是周末,所以卡车周一的时候才开走,那么周五将该批货物搬上卡车的行为就不属于“马上装上”。这是John Dunt在其2009年版的《Marine Cargo Insurance》中11.22段所持的观点。这表示货物在周五直到卡车开走这段时间,需要加保。但只要货方本来的计划与做法是将货物装上车架或卡车后卡车马上开走,但突然出现不能控制的情况(如仓库去目的地的公路因车祸而突然之间被封闭)导致卡车不能开走,这种情况就另当别论,应该是属于承保的范围。这是因为本来把货物装上并准备马上开走,风险就已经开始生效。之后卡车不能开走,这等于是在运输途中的延误,是由保险合约第8.3条(明示规定运输期间在受保人不能控制的情况下产生延误是属于承保范围)、第9条(如果在受保人不能控制的情况下运输中断的续保)与第10条(改变原来目的地的续保)承保的,这些条文会后详。

2.2 “运输车辆与其他运输装置”的含义

“运输车辆与其他运输装置”(carrying vehicle or other conveyance)的含义到底包括了哪些也可以探讨。很显然,普通的卡车以及专为运输集装箱而设计的车架当然是属于“运输车辆”。而火车或驳船等则是属于“其他运输装置”。至于那些在仓库内使用的叉车或类似装置只有在所搬运的货物是为了马上装上运输工具开始计划的行程才能是属于承保的范围,而如果缺乏了“马上装上运输工具开始计划的行程”这个目的,如叉车只是从一个货架搬到另外一个货架或者是等待的地方,则它们也就不属于承保的范围。

2.3 “开始运输”的含义

“开始运输”(for the commencement of transit)这一用词并不是在2009年的条文中才出现,而是早在1963年的条文中就已经出现,但明白“开始运输”的含义很重要,因为整个保险合约都是为了针对“运输”(transit)的风险。要对这方面了解,就需要参考之前的先例。Roskill大法官在先例Sadler Brothers Company v. Meredith (1963) 2 Lloyd's Rep. 293中就说给何为“运输”一个完全的定义是不可能(an exhaustive definition of transit is impossible),还是要根据每个案件不同的事实来作出决定。

2.3.1 关于“开始运输”一词的美国先例

相关的先例既有美国的也有英国的,就先介绍美国的。在先例 Brammer Corporation and Others v. Holland America Insurance Co 1982 AMC 1548 中,受保人的仓库分为两个区域:生产区域与运输区域。事实上,货物已经从生产区域移动到了运输区域并变为处于承运人的控制之下,承运人为了自己的方便(可能是为了与其他一些货物一并运输)将货物存放在了运输区域一段时间,而恰恰就在这段时间发生了货损。结果法院判在仓库中将货物装上卡车并不足够被视为“运输”(transit),除非是装完之后卡车开出了仓库。而货物虽然是处于承运人的控制之下但仍然存放在仓库中的这段时间是不属于承保的范围。

在另一个美国先例 Kessler Export Corporation v. Reliance Insurance Company of Philadelphia and American Insurance Company of Newark 1962 AMC 2429 中,卡车先是开进了仓库并装上了一部分货物,之后为了继续装货,卡车开到了仓库外面的车道上并将货物全部装上。之后卡车就又倒行回到仓库等待天亮,但不幸在夜里卡车上的货物被偷。主要的争辩就是货物处于承运人的控制之下,这构成了“推定运输”(constructive transit),但受保人的这种争辩最终被法院所拒绝。法院判货物是没有离开仓库,也没有构成运输,无论是真正的还是推定的。

可以说以上两个先例都说明,为了要进行的运输而将货物交给承运人控制,并收到承运人所开的收据是不足以构成“运输”的。的确经常会有情况是承运人提前把货物装上运输工具但只是为了将来才去付运,而这个“将来”会是要等上好几天甚至几个星期。

2.3.2 关于“开始运输”一词的英国先例

2.3.2.1 先例之一:装好货物卡车的暂时停泊

以下介绍英国的先例。在 Sadler Brothers Company v. Meredith (1963) 2 Lloyd's Rep. 293 中,一家为船舶做清洁的公司为他的清洁设备在“商业车辆上的运输”(in transit by commercial vehicles)进行了投保。在出事的时间中,有关的商业车辆是根据警察的指令停在距离该清洁公司仓库 70 码的地方(为了避免阻塞交通),而装在其中一辆车上的设备在清洁工人回办公室取工作表的时候被偷走。保险人争辩说,因为当时汽车是处于停泊状态(parking),所以不是在运输途中。受保人则争辩说,只要这些设备出了仓库的门口,就算还没有被装上所雇佣的商业车辆,都应当是属于在运输途中。Roskill 大法官拒绝了这两种很极端的争辩。在参考与 London Lighterage Clause 有关类似争议的先例 William Soanes Limited v. FE Walker Limited (1946) 79 Ll. L. Rep. 646 与 Kilroy Thompson Limited v. Perkins & Homer Limited (1956) 2 Lloyd's Rep. 49 后,Roskill 大法官认为在该案件中,被偷的清洁设备应该是属于在运输途中,运输的卡车暂时停泊不影响,除非是一个真正的间歇把运输过程打断。他这样说:"... when one is dealing with the transit of goods, anyhow for the purposes of the London Lighterage Clause, and I should have thought the point equally valid when you are dealing with an insurance policy on transit of goods, what one is considering is the goods themselves being in course of transit and not the question of the means of conveyance in which that transit is taking place, be it ship transit and not the question of the means of conveyance in which that transit is taking place, be it ship transit, railway transit, bullock, or whatever it may be; **it is being in motion**. And I think that there one wants to bear in mind that transit has in its nature the element of carriage about it and **the carriage starts not when the movement of the vehicle** in which the carriage is taking place starts, **but when the goods are placed on the vehicle**, and that is what I think Lord Goddard, CJ, had in mind in relation to his barge case when he said it starts from the time when the goods were received on the lighter and thereafter continues, **subject only to the question of a case where you get a really true break or interruption in the carriage**, until such time as the goods arrive at the *terminus ad quem*,... I think here 'transit' means the passage or carriage of goods from one place to another, and **I think the goods were still being carried, and therefore were still in transit from the one place to the other even though the lorry in which they were being carried was temporarily parked**. Obviously an exhaustive definition of transit is impossible, and equally obviously it is undesirable, and certainly I do not propose to attempt one. I am merely concerned with applying the facts of this case as I find them to be to this particular policy."(加黑部分是笔者的强调)。

2009年的协会货物条文规定保险合约是从货物在发货人仓库内第一次移动开始生效,但对货物保险合约而言更核心的是这货物将要从一个地方(发货人的工厂或者仓库)被运到另外一个地方(收货人的仓库)。可以说2009年的条文强调货物的移动(表示货物是在运输途中)多于强调运输工具的移动。有说法是,在这些案件中,是否处于运输途中的关键,是要看货物是否是为了装上船舶或其他运输工具才装上了卡车或者是驳船,而并非只要货物处于承运人的控制之下,该货物就处于运输途中。正如John Dunt的《Marine Cargo Insurance》第232页所说:"the key to 'transit' is in these cases receipt of the goods on to the lorry or lighter, in the sense of them being loaded on board the vehicle or vessel, rather than mere receipt by the carrier."

2.3.2.2 先例之二:Denning勋爵的"运输的附带部分"理论

但也有先例是判当承运人接收了货物,货物就处于运输的途中,该先例是Crow's Transport Ltd v. Phoenix Assurance Company Ltd (1965) 1 Lloyd's Rep. 139 (CA)。货方用自己的卡车将货物运到了卡车承运人(haulier)在伦敦的办公室,以便在那天的晚些时候让承运人运去英国北部。卡车承运人的经理将货物放置在办公室隔壁没有上锁的地下室里,就在该经理外出吃饭的空档货物被盗。在该案中,承运人为货物在运输途中可能产生的风险进行投保(covering the haulier's liability for goods in transit per the Insured's vehicles)，并且加保了货物在运输期间暂时的存放，不论是否在卡车上(The insurance cover extended to the goods whilst temporarily housed during the course of transit whether on or off vehicles)。在第一审的区域法院(County Court)，判是货物没有处于承保期间，因为还没有将货物装上卡车。但在上诉庭，Denning 勋爵以多数意见(Salmon 大法官是有疑问)推翻了一审的判决，并认为该货物是处于承保期间。他这样说："The County Court Judge held that these goods were not in the course of transit. He said:... the course of transit does not begin until some step has been taken by the hauliers towards loading the goods on to one of their own, or sub-contractors', or other hauliers', vehicle... I think that this is too narrow a construction. It seems to me that goods are 'temporarily housed during the course of transit' if they are housed as an incident of the transit, such as when they are temporarily housed for a few hours awaiting loading. [保险人的代表大律师] stressed that it has got to be transit 'per INSURED's VEHICLES'. I agree. But they are in transit per the insured's vehicles when they are awaiting loading in those vehicles. Instances were put in the course of the argument. When you take a parcel to the post office or to a railway station and you hand it over and get a receipt, the goods are in transit from the moment the post office or the railway take them. They are in transit by the post officer or the railway's vehicles, as the case may be, because **from that moment onwards everything that is done is incidental to that transit**. So here it seems to me that from the moment that the plaintiffs accepted these goods from Decca Record Company Ltd [发货人], and took them down the steps, they were there temporarily housed awaiting loading on the plaintiffs' own vehicles. It was an incident of the transit by those vehicles. That seems to me to be 'in transit per [原告的] VEHICLES'."

可以说，Denning 勋爵是把货物存放在承运人办公室的地下仓库并准备于当天的晚些时候装上卡车进行运输视为"运输的附带部分"(incidental to that transit)，所以认为是处于承保期间。至于另一个 Danckwert 大法官是认为发货人用自己的卡车将货物运到承运人的办公室就已经开始了运输，这导致了卡车承运人的经理将货物放置在办公室隔壁没有上锁的地下室里是属于运输途中的暂时存放(temporarily housed during the course of transit)，所以也属于承保范围。但 Salmon 大法官不同意这种解释，因为保险合约是针对卡车承运人运输的风险，用的是承运人的车辆(per the Insured's vehicles)，而用发货人 Decca Record Company Ltd 的卡车明显是不符合这一条。

看来这一上诉庭先例并没有受到业界的普遍认同，认为 Denning 勋爵的判法有些出格。John Dunt 的《Marine Cargo Insurance》第 233 页这样说："With respect, Lord Denning's approach, which does not cite the earlier authorities, takes the concept of 'transit' too far in that it associates 'transit' with the receipt of the goods by the carrier which he described as an 'incident of the transit'. Lord Goddard C. J. in William Soanes Ltd v. FE Walker Ltd held that 'transit' commences from when the goods were 'received on the lighter'. This, it is submitted, means that transit commences when the goods are 'loaded on to the lorry' for early carriage not when the goods are merely received by the haulier for future loading and carriage. The reason why receipt of goods may not be an 'incident of transit' is that it may take place long before loading and transit which would, in practice, be much delay. A haulier or carrier may, for example, store goods temporarily for days, or even weeks, whilst accumulating a suitable groupage load for a container or trailer destined for a European destination and the goods temporarily stored in those circumstances are not in any true sense in 'transit'. It is submitted that the doubts of Salmon L. J. were well founded and the judgment of the County Court Judge more consistent with authority and to be preferred."

2.3.2.3 先例之三:明示条文超越协会货物保险条文8.1

保险合约也是一个合约,可以有订约自由。所以如果想在承运人接收货物的一刻起就当作是承保期间或风险已经开始生效,在双方愿意接受的情况下完全可以作出清楚的明示条文加在保险合约中。接下来的先例可以看到这些相应的增加条文。在 Eurodale Manufacturing Ltd v. Ecclesiastical Insurance Office plc (2003) EWCA Civ 203,原告的运作模式是这样,原告先从供应商那里知道他可以供应多少部手机(货物),然后再接受订单看终端的消费者一共需要多少部,之后再与供应商签订买卖合约。在签完合约之后,就让供应商将手机送到原告租赁的仓库。根据合约,手机的所有权和风险在原告接收货物后就全部转移给他。之后原告会将仓库里的手机再送货给消费者。货物于长周末存放在仓库时被盗。保险合约合并了(incorporate)1982 年的协会货物保险条文,也就是有第 8 条的运输条文。但同时双方同意了一条额外打印上去的"Voyage Clause",是这样规定的:"保险合约从受保人接收投保的货物时生效"(Cover attaches from the time the Assured accept delivery of the insured goods...)。原告争辩说,仓库保管人代他们接收并点算货物就相当于"Voyage Clause"中的"接收"(accept delivery),也就是说从那一刻开始,风险开始生效,一直到把手机送到消费者那里为止。而被告的保险人则抗辩说,该保险是"运输的保险"(transit insurance)",只有在这些手机被分拆成小的包装送货给消费者时,风险才开始生效。

法院最终判是受保人通过他的仓库保管人接收了该批货物,尽管该批货物是处于储存而并非运输过程中,但因为作为附加条文的"Voyage Clause"的效力超越了合并的 1982 年的协会货物保险条文,所以法院判货物于长周末存放在仓库被盗属于在承保期间。

3."正常的运输过程"(ordinary course of transit)的含义

"正常的运输过程"是针对风险开始生效后,也就是开始运输,就会一直对可能产生的风险承保直到去了目的地。但这里就在保险合约里面多加了一个要求就是运输可以是或长或短,也会有情况在半途的时候会有绕行或停留,但只要这是属于正常运输过程中能够预见与是合理或是必须,就不会影响保险合约的承保。加上这一个用词就是为了避免不正常的运输过程,如北京去上海的运输,竟然把卡车绕行到哈尔滨后才去了上海。由于它最终的目的地没有改变,所以 2009 年的协会货物条文的第 10 条也不适用。但如果允许这样做,对保险人很不利,因为承保风险的时间大大增加了。所以有了这个用词就可以保证只是在一个正常的运输中所带来的一些合理或必须的绕行或停留才受到承保。

在英国的保险法,有说法就是受保人不能做任何事情去改变承保风险的本质(nature of risks),但是受保人可以增加承保风险,只要在保单内没有被禁止如通过承诺性保证条文或其他条文禁止:Baxendale v. Harvey (1859) K&N 445;Scottish Coal v. RSA (2008) EWHC (Comm) 880。这一重要的课题在本书第四章第 3.4.1 段有详细介绍,不再重复。而本段与以下会探讨的正是一种受保人改变承保风险本质的做法。

3.1 先例之一:行程根本与原来的运输毫无关系

在先例 SCA (Freight) Limited v. Givson (1974) 2 Lloyd's Rep. 533,案情涉及卡车承运人(haulier)针对在 CMR 公约下(Convention for the International Carriage of Goods by Road)的承运人责任进行了投保。保险合约是承保以受保人的卡车运输货物的过程(whilst in transit per insured's vehicles)并延伸至运输途中的正常期间(whilst in the normal course of transit)。承运人派出两辆卡车运载位于罗马的一批书籍。就在一辆卡车已经装完,而另一辆卡车仍在堆装时,司机们开着装好了的那辆卡车去市中心兜风(joyride)。而就在兜风的途中,发生卡车翻车(overturn),车上的书籍(货物)也被损坏。在该案例中,法院判定至少在货物装上卡车时,运输已经是开始。争论的焦点就是当事故发生时,货物是否算是在运输途中,因为去市中心兜风完全与原来计划的运输没有关系。受保人争辩说,只要运输开始,那之后的所有行程都是在保险合约承保的范围内。Ackner 大法官这样说:"It is well understood that the desire and object of an assured is that the policy shall extend to all such risks as may arise by the venture or operation being carried out in the usual or ordinary manner, and the general words of the policy are intended to be construed so as to conform to the usual and ordinary method of pursuing the venture."

Ackner 大法官是判事故发生时,货物不能算是在运输途中,并对货物不能算是在运输途中的时刻进行了定义,他这样说:"Goods cease to be in transit when they are on a journey which is not in reasonable furtherance of their carriage to their ultimate destination. Obviously a detour which is reasonably necessary to enable a driver to obtain food or rest would be in furtherance of the safe and expeditious carriage of the goods to their ultimate destination. It would be an ordinary incident in the transit of goods by the plaintiff's vehicles. It is a question of degree, as to what is or is not in reasonable furtherance of the carriage of the goods. A deviation which is wholly unrelated to the usual and ordinary method of pursuing the adventure would prevent the goods being 'in transit' within the meaning of the policy."(如果行程根本与原来的运输毫无关系,货物再不能算是在运输途中。显然如果绕行是为了让司机能买些食物或是稍事休息完全可以,也算是正常运输过程的一部分。这里就涉及了程度的问题,什么才算或不算运输的合理部分。如果是毫无关系的绕行,会导致货物不属于保险合约内的正常运输的定义)。

在这里顺便一提就是根据上述的先例,对鬼船(phantom ship)这种风险是不承保,因为虽然作为受保人的货方是无辜(好像本先例的受保人一样),但如果把货物装上鬼船,不诚实的船东由头到尾都是想怎么把这批货物偷掉,从来没有打算去目的地。这表示整个行程与原来打算的运输毫无关系,变为不正常运输,也不在承保范围内。2009 年协会货物条文增加了一条新的条文 10.2 条,在这种情况下不影响承保。这方面会在本章第 9 段谈到该条文时再详细介绍。

3.2 先例之二和三:货物卸下长期存放在码头保税区/仓库(bonded warehouse)[1]是否仍在正常运输过程

接下来另介绍一个同样判法的澳大利亚先例 Verna Trading Pty Ltd v. New India Assurance Co Ltd (1991) 1 VR 129,案情涉及受保人将货物卸下后存放于码头保税区内,因为受保人自己的仓库没有地方,5 周后才开始办理清关手续。但在清关前,货物在保税区内被盗。上诉庭的 Ormiston 大法官在参考了 SCA (Freight) Limited v. Givson 之后,他作出的结论如下:"... the cargo may no longer be in the 'ordinary course' of transit if it is dealt with in a manner inconsistent with the prosecution of the adventure, that is, in a way, or for a purpose which is unrelated to bringing the transit to its expected conclusion by delivery to the defined warehouse or store."

可以看出,该澳大利亚先例是跟从了 SCA (Freight) Limited v. Givson,认为判断货物是否仍是在运输途中要根据个案,看对正常的运输途径是否偏离到一定的程度以至于不能被算作仍是在正常运输途中。

同样的判法也被南非的法院采用:Fedsure General Insurance Ltd v. Carefree Investment Pty Ltd (477/99) [2001] ZASCA 88。在该先例中,装于集装箱内的纤维是从韩国进口去南非东部的德班(Durban),货物在清关前是存放于港口的仓库内,结果被盗。货物是根据 1982 年的协会货物条文进行了投保,其中规定保险合约在货物正常的运输途中(during the ordinary course of transit)一直有效。事实上,受保人将货

---

[1] 保税仓库的所有人可以给海关当局提供担保,这样存放货物在该仓库的货主就可以不必马上付出关税给海关。同时货主可以让潜在的买家到保税仓库检查货物,以决定是否要买。如果货物卖出了,货主才需要付关税;如果没有卖出(如质量太差或者其他原因),则不需要付关税。有时候甚至需要转卖该批货物到其他国家,这样一来货主就不必涉及进口关税。而对于高关税的洋酒或化妆品,能够拖延 2 ~ 3 个月再付关税也会对货主的现金周转有很大帮助。

物存放在港口的仓库内是自己商业上的方便,因为至少在货物存放在港口仓库那段时间不用支付关税,并且他的商业习惯是等到现金流情况比较好的时候才清关。最终法院判这批货物不在正常运输过程中,Howie 大法官这样说:"... a delay or interruption which, objectively viewed, is not part of the usual and ordinary means of effecting transit, and which is occasioned by some **collateral purpose, will disturb the ordinary course of transit**. Accordingly, loss occurring within the period of such delay or interruption will not be covered by the policy... The reason is not that the insurance has come to an end (for it remains in existence), nor that the transit has come to an end (for the journey is not yet finally over) but simply that the insurance pertains to the ordinary course of transit and what is outside the ambit of that course cannot, logically, be within the cover."

3.2.1 "附属目的"的说法

由此延伸出一个附属目的说法(collateral purpose test),如在上述的先例中,受保人的附属目的是自己商业上的方便也就是现金周转,这显然与运输无关。实际上该说法比较近期的应用是在英国的先例 Eurodale Manufacturing Ltd v. Ecclesiastical Insurance Office plc(2003)EWCA Civ 203,该案的案情在上文介绍"运输的开始"时有详细介绍。只讲根据"Voyage Clause"运输是已经开始。将货物暂时存放于仓库,之后配送给终端的消费者并不构成受保人有附属目的。

在应用附属目的说法时,有一问题就是受保人的主观想法是否应该被考虑在内。在 Fedsure General Insurance Ltd v. Carefree Investment Pty Ltd (477/99) [2001] ZASCA 88 中,受保人基于 John Martin of London Ltd v. Russell (1960) 1 Lloyd's Rep. 554 的先例,争辩说他将货物存放于港口仓库的习惯做法不应当被考虑在内,因为这也只不过是他的主观想法。Howie 大法官拒绝了这种争论,他这样说:"And as to the metaphor of a 'shifting cover' dependent solely on intention, there, too, one has no such problem when the question is whether something occurred within the ordinary course of transit. Plainly, subjectivity will be involved in the formation and implementation of a collateral purpose but the impression of a changing cover must disappear on **application of the objective test as** to whether a delay or interruption is or is not part of the usual and ordinary means of effecting transit. The evidence in this matter shows that the theft occurred during a period of transit. In addition, the fact that the goods were in storage at the Container Depot was because the assured had a collateral commercial purpose for leaving them there. It follows that the goods were not stolen 'during the ordinary course of transit' within the meaning of para. 8.1 of the transit clause."

由此可见,附属目的说法在运用上是要通过客观的方法。首先要考虑延误或者中断是否是正常的运输所合理必须的。而这完全是要很客观地看在当时的情况下,运输要怎样才能完成,以及看延误是否在运输途中是合理必须的。如果延误并非是合理必须,那么就可以表面下结论,该受保人当时有附属目的。

3.2.2 受保人主观想法与“Shifting Cover”的说法

上一段提到这一个问题与先例 John Martin of London Ltd v. Russell (1960) 1 Lloyd's Rep. 554。该先例是判受保人的主观想法是不应该被考虑在内，因为人的主观想法很容易改变，这会带来所谓一会儿受到承保一会儿不受到承保，英文即“a shifting cover”。

这方面的说法可节录 John Martin of London Ltd v. Russell (1960) 1 Lloyd's Rep. 554 先例中 Pearson 大法官说：“whose intention is relevant, and at what time is it to be ascertained, and how is it ascertained? There may be a change of intention from time to time; it might be a fluctuating intention; and, of course, the ownership of the goods and the identity of the goods for the purposes of the clause might be changed. There would be, so to speak, a shifting cover, sometimes applied to the goods and sometimes not, and sometimes the goods would be uncovered and sometimes covered, which to my mind is not a reasonably business like interpretation.”

Pearson 大法官也提到了很难证明一个人在想什么，他说在想什么他就在想什么，无论你相不相信，因为他是唯一一个可以就此给出证据的人。

4 承保风险的终止

承保风险终止的确定很重要，因为这个时间点以后发生的损失，保险人再没有责任。如果在这之前没有发生事故，可以说保险人所收取的保费已经是落入囊中。而对受保人来说，清楚地知道何时承保风险已经终止，如果货物仍旧在他手中，他就知道要进行加保。由于货物运输的终止有千变万化的情况，所以在 2009 年的协会货物条文的第 8 条规定了四种承保风险终止的情形，分别规定在第 8.1.1 ~ 8.1.4 条，接下来将对这四种情况逐一进行分析。

4.1 第 8.1.1 条：运输风险终止的第一种情况

4.1.1 “卸下货物”(unloading)的含义

通常情况下，货物被卡车运至目的地后要先从卡车上被卸下，然后用叉车或类似的工具将货物搬入仓库里，在这个过程中哪一个动作的完成代表着保险合约承保风险的终止？在第 8 条的条文中有这样的用词“the completion of unloading”，这应该意味着只有在货物经叉车搬入仓库落定后，“卸下货物”才结束。也就是说，只有在此时，保险人承保的风险才终止。

而“落定”(landing)一词的意思也很讲究，在叉车将货物第一次放于地面上之后就已经是落定，而如果再次用叉车将货物搬起，则这个再次搬起的动作再也不属于承保的范围。

4.1.2 “最终的仓库或存放地点”

什么是“最终的仓库或存放地点”(final warehouse or place of storage)？在协会货

物条文1982年版本以前,有的用词只是“最终的仓库”,“或存放地点”是在1982年的版本中另外加上去的。广义上,有墙有屋檐有门有锁存放货物的地方应该就是仓库。另在先例 Overseas Commodities Ltd v. Style (1958) 1 Lloyd's Rep 546 中也有提到最终的仓库应该起的作用,McNair 大法官说:“In my judgment, on the facts of this case, the final warehouse contemplated by this clause is the final warehouse in this country at which the goods arrived and were made available to the plaintiffs for distribution as part of their stock as importers.”

这看起来很明确,但还是会有不少争议,如它的实体形态。这种争议在 Overseas Commodities Ltd v. Style 与 John Martin of London Ltd v. Russell (1960) 1 Lloyd's Rep. 554 都有被提出。当事人也都有拍照片让法官来从表面判断是否是仓库。为了避免类似的争议才在1982年的条文中加入了“或存放地点”。

4.1.3 运输货棚/区域是否是最终的仓库或存放地点

港口内的简易运输货棚(transit shed)或是运输区域(transit area)是否可以算是最终的仓库或存放地点涉及了好几个先例,就是货物从船上卸下来存放在运输货棚/区域期间发生货损。那么发生的货损是在承保的运输期间,还是货损发生时,承保的风险已经终止?本来应该很明确,“运输货棚”一词本身就代表了暂时性的存放,还有下一步的运输要进行。正如 Pearson 大法官说:“The first and elementary consideration is this. The expression ‘final warehouse’ seems to contemplate that there may be a warehouse which is not final. If one were searching for an example of a non-final warehouse if would be difficult or impossible to find a better example than a transit shed, which is essentially a shed in which goods are temporarily placed pending some further movement to some other place. The word ‘transit’ itself implies its transitory character.”

但经常会出现受保人的货方为了自己的方便/利益,尽量长时间地将货物存放在运输货棚/区域,如为了寻找该批货物的分买方(sub-buyer),或者是已经有了分买方让他自己来运输货棚/区域提货。这无形中延长了保险人承保的期间,增加了承保的风险。

以下举一些有关的先例。

4.1.3.1 先例之一:货物在运输货棚中被大火烧毁

在先例 Westminster Fire Office v. Reliance Marine Insurance Co (1903) TLR 668 中,保险合约有关承保的终止是规定:“... in the event of the goods being temporarily placed upon the quay, it is agreed to hold the same covered while there and until delivered to the export vessel or at any wharf or warehouse within the limits of the port.”该保险合约中虽然没有“最终的仓库”的措辞,但法院最终还是根据保险合约的目的判暂时存放于港口附近的运输货棚中的货物是在承保的范围内。在该先例中,有一票货物是黄麻,从印度的加尔各答(Calcutta)运往英国苏格兰东部港顿提(Dundee)。在4月14日,受保人(也就是收货人)将货物存放在运输货棚内等待称重与分类,并且他也正

在找另外一个买家。不幸的是 4 月 17 日，在还没有找到下一个买家之前，这票黄麻在运输货棚内被大火焚毁。保险人争辩说虽然保险合约是规定承保"暂时存放在码头"（temporarily placed upon the quay）的货物，这表示如果是出口，受保人有计划将货物装上往外运的船舶，或是如果是进口，受保人有计划将货物存放在该港/该城市的其他仓库。而在本案中，受保人并没有计划作两者中的任何一项，所以承保的风险应当是在火灾发生的时候已经终止。而最终法院的判决是保险合约的意图是承保存放于港口范围内仓库内的货物，而如果希望将货物直接转卖的受保人没有将货物卸到仓库里面，将货物暂时存放的货棚的作用就相当于是仓库，而货物也就仍在承保的期间。这样的解释很不利于保险人，而对受保人来讲却是非常有利的。有关该先例的英文总结，可节录 Pearson 大法官所说：

"The ship arrived at Dundee on April 14, 1899; and, in accordance with the practice of the port, some parcels of the jute were landed and were placed in some 'transit sheds' on the quay, in order that they might be sorted and weighed. The consignee had not at that time made up his mind as to the ultimate destination of the jute. He was endeavouring to sell it, but had not yet succeeded in finding a purchaser. According to the by-laws of the port, the jute could not remain in the sheds more than 48 hours; but this rule was not strictly enforced, unless there was pressure by reason of the arrival of a number of ships at the same time. On April 17 a fire took place in the transit sheds, and the jute which was there was seriously damaged. The plaintiff company, with whom the consignee had effected an insurance against fire, paid the amount of the loss. They then took an assignment of the marine policy, and by this action the plaintiffs claimed to recover the amount of the loss from the defendants. The case turned upon the construction of the above-quoted clause in the policy. Mr. Justice Kennedy held that the loss was covered by that clause. The defendants appealed. . . . Lord Justice Vaughan Williams was of opinion that the decision of Mr. Justice Kennedy was right. In his opinion the policy covered the jute at the time when the fire took place. In the circumstances the insured transit was not at an end when the fire happened. His Lordship agreed with the learned Judge that the jute was temporarily placed on the quay at a time when it was open to the consignee to elect what its destination should be.

Lord Justice Romer was of the same opinion. He thought the policy ought to be construed from a business point of view, so as to give effect to it according to the view of business men. The policy was clearly intended to cover something beyond the mere delivery on the quay; the voyage and the risk covered were not ceased when the jute was placed in the transit sheds. The voyage was not to be considered as at an end until the jute had been delivered to an export vessel, or at a wharf or warehouse within the limits of the port. But it appeared to his Lordship that from a business point of view the voyage would end when the jute left the transit sheds. It could not have been the intention that a person who wished his goods to go to a warehouse beyond the limits of the port should be bound first to take them to a warehouse within the limits of the port. That would be absurd."

4.1.3.2 先例之二:货物在运输货棚中生虫

在先例 John Martin of London Ltd v. Russell (1960) 1 Lloyd's Rep. 554,有一票猪油要从芝加哥运往利物浦,投保的是协会货物条文中的一切险,其中是规定:"This insurance... continues until the goods are delivered to the Consignees' or other final warehouse at the destination named in the policy..."猪油在利物浦从船上卸下后被存放在港口码头内的运输货棚内,两天后发现滋生了大批干椰子肉甲虫。保险人拒绝赔付并争辩说,运输货棚就是最终的货舱。另外一种争辩是,如果受保人并没有打算把货物卸到最终的仓库,承保的风险在货物被卸下的那一刻就已经终止。而受保人原来的安排是不会再把货物转运到另外一个仓库,而是由最后的买家自己来运输货棚提货。

受保人的争辩是,从物理形态上来讲,运输货棚不是"仓库",所以承保的风险不能在运输货棚终止。而法院是跟从了先例 Overseas Commodities Ltd v. Style (1958) 1 Lloyd's Rep. 546 拒绝了受保人的这一争辩,理由是本案中的运输货棚看起来很像一个仓库。在此先例之后,该条文被加上了用词"or place of storage",以避免类似的争议并确保无论最终的目的地是否是仓库,承保的风险都已经终止。

受保人的另外争辩是,运输货棚并非最终的仓库。其实,运输货棚的地位在上文的先例 Westminster Fire Office v. Reliance Marine Insurance Co (1903) TLR 668 已经有涉及,并判说运输货棚不构成仓库,在运输货棚内被大火焚毁的货物是在承保的范围内。Pearson 大法官在考虑了该先例后,得出了相同的结论,认为在运输货棚内的货物是在承保的范围内。他这样说:"... in my view, ultimately, as a matter of impression, it is really clear that a transit shed is not a final warehouse. A transit shed, at any rate according to the practice of this port, is the place at which the goods are placed as soon as they are discharged from the ship, and they are then waiting patently to go somewhere else. It is not the final warehouse."

4.1.3.3 先例之三:货物在保税区仓库中被偷

同样的判法在涉及1982年协会货物条文的近期先例 Bayview Motors Ltd v. Mitsui Fire & Marine Ins Co Ltd (2002) 1 Lloyd's Rep. 652;affirmed (2003) 1 Lloyd's Rep. 131 (CA)中也被采用。该先例涉及一批汽车从日本的横滨运往多米尼亚的一个港口(Santo Domingo),并且投保了海上货物运输保险,其中有一条"仓库至仓库"条文,规定承保的风险在货物交给"收货人或者卸到最终仓库或者列明的目的地的其他存储地方"时终止。汽车被卸到了港口内没有围栏的停车场里,这其实是由海关控制出入的保税区(customs compound)。而汽车被海关的关员偷走。一审是判本案中汽车停放的地点不能被视为最终的储存地点。而上诉庭也支持了一审的判法,说:"I think a customs compound is similar to a transit shed: both are "holding" areas （暂时存放区域）. Neither can properly be described as a final place of storage. Goods are not held in a customs compound for storage but for customs purposes."

大意是说海关场院与运输货棚是有相似之处，因为它们都是用来将货物暂时存放的地方，但它们却都不能被视为是最终的储存地点。因为将货物存放于海关场院内的目的并非是为了存放，而是为了通关。

4.1.4 没有"最终的仓库或存放地点"的情况：因为需要将货物转运其他地方

上述提到的先例 Bayview Motors Ltd v. Mitsui Fire & Marine Ins Co Ltd（2002）1 Lloyd's Rep. 652；affirmed（2003）1 Lloyd's Rep. 131（CA）还涉及了另外一点，就是这些汽车（货物）是要从保险合约中规定的卸港，也就是多米尼亚的一个港口（Santo Domingo），另转运去其他的目的地，名为 Turks & Caicos Islands。

这种情况在国际贸易中会很多，将保险合约中列明的卸港作为货物的集散地，货物在从船上卸下后立即就被装上运往周边其他地方的卡车/火车/小船。例如，从美国以 CIF 进口的货物在上海港卸下，随即转运苏州收货人的仓库。这表示从整个运输来看，仓库到仓库是美国的仓库到苏州的仓库，货物在上海既没有存放，也真正只是运输过程的一部分，而上海可以说只是一个"转运港"。但问题是美国卖方投保的保险合约目的地的卸港只是上海，就没有理由要该保险人承担他根本不知道详情的上海到苏州的转运。加上如果买方/分买方对上海到苏州这一段另外投保，就会造成双重保险。最后要提的一个困难是，如果把上海作为承保风险的终止地，也会遇上另外一个困难就是找不到一个"最终的仓库或存放地点"。

在先例 Bayview Motors Ltd v. Mitsui Fire & Marine Ins Co Ltd，就遇到这样的问题。上诉庭的 Tuckey 大法官认为在这种情况下，根本不会有"最终的仓库或存放地点"。如果货物最终要到达的目的地与保险合约中所约定的是一致，1982 年的协会货物条文之 8.1.1 条文才可以适用。但是，如果货物是先到保险合约中的目的地，随即要转运去其他地方，保险合约中列明目的地的仓库或存放地点并非是最终，保险合约也只有在受保人在选择将货物在该目的地存放而不是继续去转运，或是将货物做出分发才会终止。但这还是不包括继续转运的情况，这就要根据该案例的 1982 年的协会货物条文之 8.1.4 条文，就是在如果既没有用于存放也没有用于分发，保险合约是会从船舶上将货物卸下之后的 60 天就终止。Tuckey 大法官这样说：

"Where the final destination of the goods is the destination named in the policy, clause 8.1.1 will operate according to its terms. Cover ceases when the consignee takes delivery or the goods reach their final resting place（warehouse or place of storage）at the destination.

But where goods are intended to go to the destination named in the policy and then on to some other destination I do not think that the clause contemplates that there will be a final warehouse or place of storage at the destination named in the policy. In such a case the warehouse or place of storage is not final and cover will only cease if the assured elects to use it either for storage other than in the course of transit or for allocation or distribution (clause 8. 1. 2), which it is common ground does not apply in our case.

Otherwise cover is extended or up to 60 days by clause (8. 1. 3, now 8. 1. 4 in the revised Clauses). What has been called 'the postscript' to clause 8 has the effect that in such a case coverage is extended for 60 days or 'the commencement of transit is to such other destination' whichever is the sooner."

Tuckey 大法官也有解释这种转运的保险麻烦的地方，就是以上述美国运到上海再转运去苏州作为例子，CIF 的保险合约只承保到上海就终止，而如果分买方把货物从上海转运到苏州，他很有可能也会投保。但通常运输的保险只是在转运开始才生效，这就表示有一个空档的时间没有任何保险作出保障，如果要买方或分买方另外作出投保不容易安排。所以，有了这 60 天的期限，就足够可以在这一个空档作出保障，直到转运开始。Tucky 大法官这样说："This construction makes good commercial sense. In a case like the present the consignee will insure the transhipment. That insurance is likely to attach when the goods leave the warehouse or place of storage at the place named in the policy for the commencement of the transit (see the opening words of clause 8. 1). It would be commercially inconvenient for the consignee to have to arrange separate cover for the period before transhipment and after discharge to the warehouse or storage area in the destination port. It makes sense for the insurers of cargo in its transit to that port to continue cover for a limited time (up to 60 days) until the next stage of the transit starts."

这就导致了 2009 年协会货物条文对针对这种做法的 8. 2 条文作出了更加明确的规定。首先就是节录 1982 年协会货物条文之 8. 2 条："If, after discharge overside from the oversea vessel at the final port of discharge, but prior to termination of this insurance, the goods are to be forwarded to a destination other than to which they are insured hereunder, this insurance, whilst remaining subject to termination as provided for above, shall not extend beyond the commencement of transit to such other destination."

但在 2009 年协会货物条文之 8. 2 条就变为："If, after discharge overside from the oversea vessel at the final port of discharge, but prior to termination of this insurance, the subject-matter insured is to be forwarded to a destination other than that to which it is insured, this insurance, whilst remaining subject to termination as provided in Clauses 8. 1. 1 to 8. 1. 4, shall not extend beyond **the time the subject-matter insured is first moved for the purpose of the** commencement of transit to such other destination."（加黑的部分就是改变的部分）。另在 8. 1. 1 条文，也变为更明确写明就是在该条文，"最终的仓库或存放地点"必须是保险合约中列明的目的地，而在 1982 年条文没有这样的明确说明。

可以说，2009 年协会货物条文的改变除了明确之外，也有针对性并且符合转运的商业要求。这就是根据8.2条,在装运去其他目的地而保险合约没有因为其他原因终止的话,就是转运一开始(first moved for transit)才终止,因为下一份保险合约已开始生效。至于其他原因导致终止,包括像8.1.1条是在转运港把货物卸下在最后的仓库/存放地点(但已经解释过在转运港通常不会有最后仓库/存放地点,所以不会因此而终止)。另外是像8.1.4条就是从船舶上卸下60天的期限,保险合约也就终止。这表示以上述介绍的从美国进口到上海然后转运苏州的例子,只要在上海没有把货物卸下去最后仓库/存放地点,开始转运也没有超过60天的期限,CIF的保险合约就会是一直生效直到上海到苏州的转运开始。

4.2 第8.1.2条:运输风险终止的第二种情况

第二种情况会导致保险合约的终止就是很有可能货物还没有到达保险合约中约定的目的地,但受保人或者他的雇员选择把货物存放,而存放不是正常运输过程所合理必须的,或者为了把货物分发给分买方。因为在这种情况下,由于受保人的选择,可以说运输的过程已经是告一段落,所以保险合约应该终止。这里要探讨的问题就是怎么样构成受保人的选择(election)以及什么构成分发(allocation or distribution)。

先可以介绍有关"选择"的定义,这可节录Goff勋爵在先例The"Kanchenjunga"(1990) 1 Lloyd's Rep 391中所说:"Election itself is a concept which may be relevant in more that one context. In the present case, we are concerned with an election which may arise in the context of a binding contract, when a state of affairs comes into existence in which one party becomes entitled, either under the terms of the contract or by the general law, to exercise a right, and he has to decide whether or not to do so. His decision, being a matter of choice for him, is called in law an election."但有关"分发",就会需要以介绍先例来更清楚地说明。

4.2.1 与"选择"相关的案例介绍

4.2.1.1 先例之一:被判是构成选择的先例

在先例Safadi v. Western Assurance Co (1933) 46 Ll. L. Rep. 140中,有一票货物(棉花与纱线)是从英国曼彻斯特运往叙利亚的大马士革。由于大马士革是一个内陆城市,货物需要经过最近的一个港口名为"Beyrout"转运,在货物从远洋船舶上卸下约40天后,在Beyrout的海关仓库里被大火烧毁。显然,根据货物运输保险合约内的仓库到仓库条文,承保的期限一直到大马士革的仓库。但该保险合约中有一条规定限制了存放在海关仓库的时间只能是30天,有关条文如下:"Manchester to Beyrout and for 30 days in the Customs House and thence to Damascus."所以保险人拒赔,但受保人争辩说那些超过30天的延误他无法控制,而在该保险合约对这种他无法控制的延误是接受的。这种条文在海上货物运输保险都会有,1982年与2009年协会货物条文是在8.3条。

所以,争议的关键就是要认定延误转运是否是受保人无法控制的原因造成或者是受保人因为其他不为人知的私下原因而且作出的选择让货物存放在海关的仓库并超出了30天。这导致双方都提供这方面的证据。受保人提出的证据是叙利亚的罢工/暴动以及去大马士革的铁路运输不安全。这可节录Roche大法官所讲:"At the material time Syria was a territory which was mandated to the government of France, and there were troubles and rebellions going on in Syria against the government of France; and these troubles, which consisted of risings among people called the Jebel Druses, were particularly active in 1926 and 1927. These troubles and risings made the railway unsafe and it is pleaded that there was grave danger in the transit of goods by road and rail from Beyrout to Damascus owing to the unsettled state of Syria following upon revolt of the Jebel Druses in the neighbourhood of Lebanon and Damascus."

但英国法院认定在那个时候暴动已经平息,而铁路运输也并非不安全以至于不能用铁路运输(并认定铁路运输不论是运货物还是乘客每天都在进行),并且这些混乱/危险的情况是在受保人为货物投保时都知道的,而对于这些已经知道的情况是不能说是超出他们控制能力的因素。Roche大法官这样说:"I find with regard to that that these disturbances were at the material time abating; that is to say, they were less severe and less dangerous in the months of March, April and May, 1927, than they had been before and, whilst no doubt there was a certain insecurity about all matters, that insecurity was not in the least such as to prevent the transit of goods from Beyrout to Damascus by train. The railway is 90 miles long. The evidence in this case has been given on both sides by affidavit, but there is uncontradicted evidence from the manager of the railway that both passengers and goods were carried regularly, which I think means daily, and without attack or without successful attack at the hands of the rebels at all material times."

法院最后认定将货物存放在Beyrout港的海关仓库是基于商业目的,因为只要受保人/收货人不将货物从海关运走,他就不需要为该批货物付钱给卖方,也就是可以延长他们的信贷期,而这也变成了受保人/收货人的惯常做法。受保人/收货人的如意算盘其实是这样,如果货物超出30天的存放依然是完好,那么他也就不需要通知保险人,也就不需要为续保(held cover)而多交加保费(additional premium)。如果货物有损坏,他们就可以事后续保,也就是交很少的加保费而获得可能很大的赔偿。所以从整个案件看来,将货物存放于海关仓库内30多天完全是受保人的选择。所以在发生火灾的时候,保险合约承保的风险已经终止。

4.2.1.2 先例之二:被判是构成选择的先例

在Wiggins Teape Australia Pty Ltd v. Baltica Insurance Co. Ltd (1970) 2 NSWR 77,受保人为了自己方便将一批木质纸浆存放在卸港码头的仓库内,法院是判货物已经"不是在正常运输途中"(not in the ordinary course of transit)。并且由于保险合约中有一条"避免延误"条文(这在1982与2009年协会货物条文都是18条),受保人这样做是违反了该项条件(condition)。加上,受保人决定存放在码头仓库是他自己的"选择",所以在发生货损时,保险合约承保的风险已经结束。

4.2.1.3 先例之三:选择与对货物控制权之间关系的先例

下面介绍一个南非的先例 Fedsure General Insurance Ltd v. Carefree Investments (Pty) Ltd (477/99) (2001) 2 ASA 88 (11 September 2001)。案情是一家制衣厂商将纤维装于集装箱内,是从南韩运往南非的德班。该批货物是根据 1982 年协会货物条文(一切险)投保。货物在德班的保税仓库被盗窃,而货物之所以被存放于保税仓库是因为清关要缴纳关税与增值税,但受保人是希望在公司的现金流情况好点的时候再清关。一审时,法院判因为作出选择要将货物继续存放在保税仓库时,受保人并没有取得对货物的完全控制,所以不能算是 8.1.2 条文中的受保人的自愿选择。上诉庭的 Howie 大法官对此表示质疑并推翻一审的判决,他说:"... it seems very much open to question whether, before the election referred to in [8.1.2 of the Transit Clause] can be made, the insured must, as the learned Judge held, have paid the clearance dues and so have obtained control of the goods. There would appear to be no logical reason, when all one is doing in order to store goods is to leave them where they are, for the law to require that one first has to have control before one can use such venue for storage. There would also seem to be scant reason why the necessary election cannot precede the end of such storage and indeed precede the delivery into such storage. On the facts of this case there may well have been termination of the insurance under 8.1.2 but I express no final opinion on that issue."

这段话只是 Howie 大法官随口说说(*obiter*),但说明了受保人在作出协会货物条文 8.1.2 条中的"选择"时并不需要对货物有完全的控制。也就是说,如果在本来属于暂时的存放等待继续运输前,受保人已经是主观打定主意要将货物以存放或分发为目的而不打算继续运输,那么根据 8.1.2 保险合约承保的风险在货物卸下之后就已经终止。

而这里"主观打定主意"(subjective intention)就又会遇到上文第 3.3.1 段在讨论"正常的运输途中"(in the ordinary course of transit)的"附属目的说法"(collateral purpose test)时的困难,就是受保人的主观想法是否应该被考虑在内。根据先例 John Martin of London Ltd v. Russell (1960) 1 Lloyd's Rep. 554,受保人的主观想法不应该被考虑在内,因为人的主观想法很容易改变(a shifting cover),而且很难证明一个人的脑袋在想什么。所以要客观地看受保人的行为,通过他的行为来判断他的意图,也就是他打定了什么主意。这些行为是要证据,通常就是在出事时的当场证据(contemporarneous documentary evidence),如受保人写给仓库的信函(如问准备存放在那里 3 个月收费是多少),或是本来安排好的续运结果通过信函取消掉。

通常情况下,受保人打定主意的时间与货物卸下船舶的时间是不同的。也就是说,打定主意的时间与保险合约终止的时间是不同。而如果在货物卸下前,受保人又改变了主意,选择续运。这在现实中可以是受保人作为卖方与分买方之前有了纠纷,不准备继续运输而需要准备去存放在卸港海关的仓库,也可以作为对分买方施加压力,结果谈判很快有了进展,就选择继续运输去保险合约的目的地,也就是分买方的仓库。这是及时改变了主意或作出选择不把货物存放,承保应该还是有效。

John Dunt 2009 年所著的《Marine Cargo Insurance》第 249 页说:"The timing of the assured's election decision is separate from the termination of the insurance which only occurs on completion of unloading. Thus an election to store the goods outside the 'ordinary course of transit' terminates the insurance when that place of storage is reached and unloading is completed. If the assured changes his mind, and the election to use a warehouse for storage outside the ordinary course of transit is reversed before the goods are unloaded, it is submitted that this would be treated as if that election had never been made. In so far as an irrevocable election could be made before the unloading, for example, by cancelling arrangements for further transit, Clause 8. 1. 2 makes it clear that cover continues until the unloading. Accordingly, the goods will be covered for an accident that occurs during the insured transit before the goods arrive at the non-transit warehouse, albeit that the assured have already elected to use that warehouse **for storage** other than in the ordinary course of transit."(这种情况下可以视为受保人从来没有作出过会导致海上货物运输保险合约终止的选择。如果受保人的决定已经是不可逆转也改变不了地作出选择,比如已经将货物转运去其他地方的运输安排取消,则根据第 8. 1. 2 条,保险合约在货物卸下后终止,也不存在第 8. 1. 4 条的 60 天延期后才终止。所以,即便是受保人已经打定主意要将货物以存放或分发为目的存进仓库,而如果货物是在正常运输途中尚未卸下前发生货损,该货损仍然是在承保的范围内,因为很难证明受保人的主观打定主意,更重要的是在没付诸实施前还可以改变主意。)

4. 2. 2 与"分发"相关的案例介绍

在澳大利亚先例 Leaders Shoes (Aust) Pty Ltd v. Liverpool & London & Globe Insurance Co Ltd (1968) 1 NSWR 279 Supreme Court of New South Wales 中,争议的关键是受保人是否有选择将公路承运人(haulier)的仓库用于分发货物。从表面看来,公路承运人的仓库应该只是属于一个中途站,在该处发生了事故应该是在承保的期限内。在该案中,有一票货物(鞋子)从意大利进口到澳大利亚的悉尼。装鞋子的纸箱被装上了悉尼港内的卡车,之后卡车开往了公路承运人的仓库,就在那天夜里货物被盗。在该批货物中,有一部分箱子的货物是已经找到了分买方,就等第二天送货。因为该批货物的数量特别大,导致了以前的做法就是在悉尼港口内就分发货物给不同分买方不可行。因此,受保人才安排在公路承运人的仓库里进行货物的分发,这其中包括把大箱子打开再个别分发,因为有些分买方买不了整箱的鞋子。

这被法院判是等同于协会货物条文 8. 1. 2 中的"the Assured... elect to use for allocation or distribution"。Macfarlane 大法官说:

"In my opinion there is not any technical or trade meaning of the word 'distribution' and therefore the meaning which is applicable is that derived from the usage of the common man. The Shorter Oxford Dictionary in the relevant sense describes ‘distribution’ as ‘dispersal’ and I cannot think that what was elected by the assured was other than an election that the goods should be dispersed and thereby distributed from the warehouse to the assured's customers.

I must reject the argument... that ‘distribution’ in the present case meant ‘breaking up of the cartons and distributing the contents’. This argument, in my opinion, is unreal in relation to the present transaction. The consignment consisted of cartons of shoes and various of the cartons were intended for different customers. The basis of the distribution among the assured's customers was on the basis of cartons and not on the basis of the contents of cartons."(受保人争辩说,只有将纸箱中的货物拆分才是“distribution”。而Macfarlane大法官拒绝了这种争辩,说类似的大宗交易中,货物是以箱为单位,所以将货物分发给受保人的分买方时也是以箱为单位,而并非是将箱子拆开把一双双的鞋子分发给分买方才算是“distribution”。)

关于分发的时间,Macfarlane大法官这样说:“I am further of the opinion that it is not important that the distribution had not begun or been completed at the time of the theft. The material elements, in my opinion, on the proper construction of this clause are that the insured shall have elected an intention that the goods should be taken to this warehouse and that they should have been delivered thither in pursuance of the intention which had been previously formed that the warehouse should be the place of distribution.”

也就是说,受保人有打定主意与选择去将货物在某仓库分发就足以让保险合约终止。而在这种情况下,没有再改变主意,保险合约承保的风险在货物卸下的那一刻就已经终止,而不是在货物被搬进仓库后。根据第8.1.2条的用词,“the Assured or their employees elect to use either for storage other than in the ordinary course of transit **or for allocation or distribution**”,可以看出只要有选择“**for allocation or distribution**”,都会导致承保的风险终止,而不论是否是“in the ordinary course of transit”。就像在先例Leaders Shoes (Aust) Pty Ltd v. Liverpool中一样,受保人在公路承运人的仓库也应该算是运输途中的一个中间仓库(intermediate warehouse),而且受保人在那里分发货物也没有其他办法,是不得已而为之。按说应该算还在运输途中,但根据8.1.2条文的明确措辞,承保风险已经终止。

4.3 第8.1.3条:运输风险终止的第三种情况

协会货物条文之8.1.3条规定承保的风险会在另一种情况下终止,也就是受保人或他的雇员选择把货物存放在卡车或其他运输工具或集装箱,但不是在正常的运输途中(when the Assured or their employees elect to use any carrying vehicle or other conveyance or any container for storage other than in the ordinary course of transit)。之所以会有这样一条条文是因为保险人担心会有情况是受保人把货物一直存放于运输工具上,从而让承保的期限大大延长。而从表面看来,因为存放是在运输工具上而非在仓库里,会感觉是货物还是在运输过程中。所以,有必要把这种经常出现的情况特别加以说明,是会导致保险合约终止的一种情况。

这方面的先例是 Hepburn v. A Tomlinson (1966) 1 Lloyd's Rep. 309 (HL),案件涉及一批投保了的香烟在运抵了收货人在伦敦的仓库门口后,当天工人已经下班,所以没有将货物卸下。当天夜里发生了盗窃,货物(香烟)被偷走。保险合约规定运输是将在受保人仓库的卸货包括在内,所以法院最后判在货损发生时,货物是在承保期间。这一案例也显示了根据协会货物条文的第 8.1.3 条,保险人根本不愿意承保在正常运输途中受保人为了自己方便(在上述先例就是没有安排加班马上把香烟从卡车上卸下)而选择在这个期间将运输工具用于存放货物,因为这会增加风险。

从第 8.1.3 条的措辞可以看到受保人在"选择"将运输工具用于存放货物时,就会导致承保风险的终止,而并非是"存放"这个实际行动发生时才导致承保风险的终止。但在实践中,两个时间往往是走在一起。因为法院在没有真正发生这一个实际行动,是很难能够判断受保人已经作出明确的选择(manifestation of an election)。这表示受保人之前就打算将运输工具稍后用作存放货物用途,但该意图一直没有显露出来,也不会导致承保风险的终止。承保风险的终止只会发生在运输工具在运输期间变为静止,这是由受保人的选择所导致。这可节录 John Dunt 在其 2009 年版的《Marine Cargo Insurance》中 11.58 段:"The timing of the election calls for special consideration under this Clause. The cover is not terminated on 'unloading', as it is in Clause 8.1.2 [the election to store in warehouse], as the concern is that the goods would not be unloaded but left on the vehicles, or other conveyances, or in a container. This led to the trigger point for termination being the election itself and not the use of vehicles or containers for storage. However, in most cases the two events will be simultaneous. It may be suggested that, in any event, the court is likely to give a purposeful construction to the sub-clause so that it will be the manifestation of the election, most usually by the use of vehicles or containers for storage, that will trigger termination. If this is right, a prior decision to use vehicles for storage, that never manifests itself, would not terminate cover. The goods would remain covered while still moving aboard vehicles that have yet to arrive at the place where their use, once stationary, would be for storage rather than for transit. It is the use of the vehicles for storage, once stationary, that will terminate the risk."

受保人将运输工具或是集装箱用来存放货物而不是用于正常的运输过程可以发生在运输早期,甚至是在运输开始前。如果在运输还没有开始时,如把货物在发货人的仓库就被装上了卡车或是堆装进了集装箱,但没有开始运输,这不影响保险人,因为保险合约承保的风险还没有开始。但会有情况是卡车或集装箱开去仓库附近的另一个地点,然后就停在那里。原因可以是各种各样,如受保人的卖方或者公路承运人受命等待收货人的买方支付货款。这等于是受保人选择将货物用于非正常运输途中的存放,延长了保险人愿意承担的风险。所以这根据第 8.1.3 条也会导致保险合约承保风险的终止,虽然是发生在运输的早期而不是在卸港。这就带来一个经常会发生的问题,就是买方的货款最后还是收到,只不过晚了几天,于是受保人的卖方或者公路承运人继续将卡车开动或把集装箱拉去付运货物。但危险的地方就是由于保险合约已经终止,它不会自动重新生效,而2009年的协会货物条文也没有任何规定,甚至没有续保(held cover)的规定。换言之,这就需要受保人与保险人通过谈判重新订立一个保险合约。而如果当时卡车上或集装箱内的货物没有受到任何损坏,谈判不会有什么问题,顶多就是保费方面。只怕已经出了意外事故导致货物受到损坏,受保人就麻烦了,但又必须披露给保险人。所以,受保人一有需要非正常运输途中的存放,就应该事前与保险人谈判并达成协议。毕竟这是订约自由。

最后一提的是如果延误(如上述的例子就是离开发货人仓库后随即去另一个附近地点等待)是超出了受保人的控制范围,如由于高速公路上发生了车祸或遇上暴风雪导致交通瘫痪,那么根据协会货物条文之8.3条,保险合约承保风险还是会继续有效,不会终止。

4.4　第8.1.4条:运输风险终止的第四种情况

根据协会货物条文之8.1.4条,货物在保险合约中列明的最终卸港从远洋船舶上卸下60天后,保险合约承保风险就会终止。这60天其实是承保的最长期限,除非另去谈判订立新的保险合约。这一条文让保险合约终止,即便是货物尚在正常的运输途中并没有运抵保险合约中列明的最终目的地仓库。在澳大利亚先例 Verna Trading Pty v. Ltd v. New India Assurance Co Ltd (1991) 1 VR 129 中,Ormiston 大法官这样说:"As has been pointed out on a number of occasions, the 60-day period is not to be treated as a generally applicable period of insurance, available to meet the exigencies of the insured. It is merely a maximum period, not even capable of extension pursuant to sub-clause 8.3..."

这60天是保险合约规定的最长期限,即便是出现了8.3条文(后详)超出受保人能够控制的延误(如卸港码头的卡车无法离开因为天气太坏无法继续运输),这60天也不可以延长。这里也没有续保(held cover)的规定,不是说受保人愿意支付合理加保费就肯定可以有承保,但这不表示受保人与保险人不可以谈判达成新的保险合约。所以一发生这种危险,受保人就应该尽快地与保险人达成协议,以免在谈判时发生事故,保险人会打退堂鼓,这是与续保不一样的地方(续保会在本章之7.1段有详论)。

在这里顺便一提的是在战争险,货物在目的地卸港一从船舶卸下,承保风险就终止。这是由于 Waterborne Agreement 的原因,战争险不承保陆上运输。这方面的课题请参阅本书第八章第9.2段的介绍,在这里只为了提醒水险与战争险的承保范围是很不一致的。等于在卸港后陆上的运输,水险还是继续承保直到最后仓库,但战争险的承保就不再有效,而且想加保也没有办法。

5. 有关 8.2 条文需要把货物转运至保险合约注明目的地以外的其他地方

有关这一课题，由于本章在 4.1.3 段已经有了详尽的介绍，所以就没有必要重复。但需要一提的是为了按照协会货物条文的顺序，就应该是介绍完 8.2 条文才能在下一段节介绍 8.3 条文。

6. 有关第 8.3 条的在正常运输途中发生受保人不能控制的事项

6.1　针对航次延误与不合理绕航的法律默示地位

要了解为什么在 1982 年与 2009 年协会货物条文中都有 8.3 条文，就必须先了解英国法律的默示地位有关在正常运输途中发生航次延误、绕航或是事故导致了强制卸货，重装或转载会对海上货物运输保险合约造成什么影响。这默示地位就是在 1906 年《英国海上保险法》中把普通法案例编制为成文法的有关条文，如下：

"第 46 条　绕航（Deviation）

（1）Where a ship, without lawful excuse, deviates from the voyage contemplated by the policy, the insurer is discharged from liability as from the time of deviation, and it is immaterial that the ship may have regained her route before any loss occurs.（当一艘船舶在没有合法原因从保险合约中约定的航次绕航，保险人从绕航一刻开始就解除责任，即使船舶之后重新回到原来的航线后才发生事故，也不影响保险人是解除了责任。至于什么是合法原因可以绕航，这是在第 49 条包括像船长无法控制的情况、为了船舶的安全、为了救人命等。）

（2）There is a deviation from the voyage contemplated by the policy—（a）Where the course of the voyage is specifically designated by the policy, and that course is departed from; or（b）Where the course of the voyage is not specifically designated by the policy, but the usual and customary course is departed from.

（3）The intention to deviate is immaterial; there must be a deviation in fact to discharge the insurer from his liability under the contract.（意图绕航不重要，关键是必须真正发生绕航才可以让保险人解除责任。）

第48条 有关航次延误(Delay in voyage)

In the case of a voyage policy, the adventure insured must be prosecuted throughout its course with reasonable dispatch, and, if without lawful excuse it is not so prosecuted, the insurer is discharged from liability as from the time when the delay became unreasonable.(航次保险中,必须合理速遣,如果没有合法理由不速遣,保险人在发生不合理延误的时候就可以解除责任。)"

6.2 第8.3条所起的作用

在介绍了上述的英国法律默示地位后,就很容易明白协会货物条文第8.3条所起的作用。简单说就是以明示条文超越默示地位。要知道,1906年《英国海上保险法》是没有区分船舶与货物,在远古年代,船舶与货物是一起承保,用的是劳合社标准S. G. 保单。但显然在船舶与货物再也不是一家人的时候,货方对船舶也没有任何影响与控制。所以船舶在航次途中发生不合理绕航或延误,导致了船壳保险(如果是航次保险合约)下,保险人解除赔付责任,这是船东自己的责任。但如果导致货物保险也面对这样的不幸结果,对无辜的货方就非常不公平。而且在今天的做法,船东对船舶的保险都是以12个月不等的定期保险(Time Policy)投保,这些是不受不合理绕航或延误的约束。但货物保险不存在可以这样做,因为就算是以预约/开口保单(open cover),在本质上还是航次保险,因为每票宣告的付运货物都是针对一个特定航次。

所以就有了第8.3条针对受保人的货方在无法控制情况下的不合理绕航或延误,是不影响保险合约的有效性。但注意是必须在受保人无法控制的情况下,而在受保人可以有限度控制,还是需要避免延误。这是在协会货物条文的第18条:"It is a condition of this insurance that the Assured shall act with reasonable dispatch in all circumstances within their control."

这种情况不多,但笔者可以举两个例子。一是在CIF买卖中,卖方也是保险合约的受保人,在船舶接近卸港但他没有收到货款(比如说单证不符以致信用证无法结汇),为了争取时间与买方谈判或另找买方把船上的货物转售,就以承租人向船东作出指示或者要求慢驶甚至停止航行,不能进入卖方认为是无法信任的发展中国家卸港。二是FOB买卖,收货人只是要求船舶慢驶甚至停止航行,因为卸港暂时没有地方存放这批货物或其他原因。反正在这种情况下,作为受保人都有危险,因为这样做也让保险人的保险期限延长。所以必须在做之前与保险人谈判,这也不是续保(held cover)的情况,但只要是没有发生事故前,谈判应该是不会有困难,只是保费增加多少的问题。

6.3 不合理绕航

6.3.1 什么是正常与习惯航线

有关不合理绕航,首先要解释什么是正常与习惯航线(usual and customary route),这也是在1906年《英国海上保险法》Section 46(2)(b)中的措辞。一般而言,这通常是指装卸港之间地理上最直接的航线(direct geographical route):The "Indian

City"（1939）64 Lloyd's Rep 229；Achille Lauro v. Total（1968）2 Lloyd's Rep. 247。

当然，这也会有变化。例如，习惯上去某卸港时先要去另一港口清关或让领航员上船。或是可取道好望角或通过苏伊士运河。又或是，尤其是早期船舶要以大量煤炭作燃料，无法在一漫长航次前装足燃料，需要在中途港加燃料或油水。这一来绕道去中途港并不是不合理绕航。

所以，要证明不是地理上最直接的航线，但仍是正常及习惯航线，是要看每一案件的具体事实与证据，如几乎所有其他同类船舶跑这航次也会这样走。

在这方面，Porter 勋爵在 The"Indian City"（1939）64 Lloyd's Rep. 229 的说法如下："It is the duty of a ship, at any rate when sailing upon an ocean voyage from one port to another, to take the usual route between these two ports. If no evidence be given, that route is presumed to be the direct geographical route, but it may be modified in many cases for navigational or other reasons, and evidence may always be given to show what the usual route is, unless a specific route be prescribed by the charter party or bill of lading... In some cases there may be more than one usual route. It would be difficult to say that a ship sailing from New Zealand to this country［英国］had deviated from her course whether she sailed by the Suez Canal, the Panama Canal, round the Cape of Good Hope or through the Straits of Magellan. Each might, I think, be a usual route. Similarly the exigencies of bunkering may require the vessel to depart from the direct route or at any rate compel her to touch at ports at which, if she were proceeding under sail, it would be unnecessary for her to call."

对班轮的所谓正常及习惯航线，会更不好判断。班轮不像散货船，它从装港直航至卸港的机会是不高，一般会挂靠多个港口。在 Leduc v. Ward（1888）20 QBD 475，它是判发货人知悉班轮不是直航，但这不约束收货人。只要是提单上明示会从装港直航去卸港，收货人即可指控船东不合理绕航。

但问题是，一般只有发货人才会知道班轮的行程航线，去订舱位。幸亏在之后的先例，Evans v. Cunard（1902）18 TLR 374 以及贵族院的 Frenkel v. MacAndrews（1929）AC 545，判是船东可以证明该班轮正常及习惯性的航线，只要提单没明确写明是直航去卸港（proceed directly to the port of delivery）。而在 Evans v. Cunard 写作是"bound for Liverpool"；另在 Frenkel v. MacAndrews 则写作是"with destination Liverpool"；这样的写法并不影响船东举证班轮的一惯正常与习惯航线，不存在不合理绕航。

6.3.2　不合理绕航在提单/租约的严格性

由于 1906 年《英国海上保险法》对不合理绕航的严格对待，就是让海上货物保险人解除赔付的责任，所以在运输合约如租约或者提单，英国法律也作出相应的严格对待。这就是在船舶一不合理绕航后，承租人或者是货方就可以解除责任。如果运费是到付，也有说法是货物安全运抵卸港，船东也不能收取运费：Hain S. S. Co v.

Tate & Lyle (1936) 41 Com. Cas. 350。

这方面可介绍几个权威的说法会更加清楚，第一个先例是在很早以前 Lavabre v. Wilson (1779) 1 Doug. 4th Edn. 284，Mansfield 大法官说："Deviation is not the increase of the risk. If that were so it would only be necessary to give and additional premium. It is that the party contracting has voluntarily submitted another voyage for that which has been insured."（这句话表示了不合理绕航可能改变承保风险本质，这方面的严重性在本书第四章第 3. 4. 1 段有详论。）

第二个先例是 Hain S. S. Co v. Tate & Lyle, Atkin 勋爵说："It is true that the cargo owner may, though very improbably, be uninsured: it is also true that in these days it is not uncommon for marine insurers to hold the assured covered in the case of deviation at a premium to be arranged. But these considerations do not appear to diminish the serious nature of the breach in all the circumstances of sea carriage, and may be balanced by the fact that the ship can and often does take liberties to deviate which prevent the result I have stated."

第三个先例是 The"Sara D"(1989) 2 Lloyd's Rep 277, Lloyd 大法官说："The origin and justification for the rule in deviation cases has always been said to be the need to protect the cargo owner against loss of his insurance cover. So the shipowner assumes the mantle of the insurer, subject only to the exceptions of a common carrier. But with the advent of the held covered clause, this rationale has lost all or much of its force... So I remain of the view that the deviation cases should now be assimilated to the ordinary law of contract..."（这里是说因为船东不合理绕航导致了海上货物运输保险合约被解除，所以法律是要求船东作为货物保险人的替代，再也不能享受运输合约的免责条文，而是要保证货物绝对安全抵达卸港。但由于海上货物保险合约已经有续保条文或类似的条文保护货物受保人，这一理念看来有点过时了，船东不合理绕航的违约应该以一般合约法的法律对待。）

还有，船东没有办法以明示条文允许他可以不合理绕航。针对提单而言，因为有 1924 年《海牙规则》规定船东只能是合理绕航，不能以合约条文减轻责任，所以根本不存在可以这样做。但在租约，是可以享有订约自由。也有先例说明这种条文根据"相悖理论"(repugnancy)的说法，而往往是无效。这在先例 Glynn v. Margetson (1893) AC 351 中，Herschell 勋爵说："... the main object and intent, as I have said, of this charterparty is the carriage of oranges from Malaga to Liverpool. That is the matter with which the shipper is concerned; and it seems to me that it would be to defeat what is the manifest object and intention of such a contract to hold that it was entered into with power to shipowner to proceed anywhere that he pleased, to trade in any manner that he pleased, and to arrive at the port at which the oranges were to be delivered when he pleased."

这一有趣课题，笔者也无意多介绍，反正对货方而言有了第 8. 3 条就根本不必担心船东或承运人不合理绕航与延误，因为保险是根本不会受到影响。但本书还是要作出介绍是因为保险人在赔付了之后，他可以根据代位求偿权向船东作为承运人提出索赔。

6.3.3　不合理绕航与风险还没有生效或开始的区别

这可以介绍先例 Kallis (Manufacturers) Ltd v. Success Insurance Ltd (1985) 2 Lloyd's Rep. 8 (PC)，案情涉及的货物是粗斜纹棉布(denim)的 CIF 买卖，从香港运往塞浦路斯，投保的是 1963 年的协会货物条文的一切险。香港卖家的货物代理人(shipping agent)为了满足买卖合约与信用证的要求，于 1976 年 8 月 3 日签发了一套并不正确的提单，说是把货物在香港装到了 Ta Shun 轮，并且写明卸港是塞浦路斯的 Limassol，而事实上那天该批货物没有被装上船。而在 1976 年 8 月 16 日，这批货物才装上另一艘船舶名为 Ta Hung 轮，但该船舶并不是去塞浦路斯的 Limassol，而是去了台湾的基隆，并把货物卸下，之后再用另一艘船舶 Intellect 轮转运去欧洲。就在 Intellect 轮上，货物被大火焚毁。无辜的买家争辩说，此货损是在保单承保的范围内。而保险人则争辩说保单保的是将该批货物用 Ta Shun 轮从香港运往塞浦路斯，因为该航次从未开始，所以保单承保的风险也从未开始，故货损不在承保的范围内。对这一点，买方回应说是由于仓至仓条文的存在，承保的风险在货物于仓库内第一次移动时已经是开始，至于之后的绕航(deviation)或航次发生改变(variation of adventure)是属于协会货物条文第 8.3 条的规定不在买方控制范围内。一审法院判买方胜诉，上诉庭判保险人胜诉，买方上诉，枢密院最终判保险人胜诉。

枢密院的 Roskill 勋爵认为只有一份属于海上货物运输的虚假提单，而由于货物根本没有装上该提单的 Ta Shun 轮。而货物真正装上船的是 Ta Hung 轮，它所要走的航线根本不是保险合约针对的航线，所以风险根本没有开始。如果风险还没有开始，提单内赋予了承运人必要时改变行程的权利的运输条款与转运条款也变成无关。Roskill 勋爵虽然没有太清楚地针对，但估计这个说法与本章第 3 段提到的鬼船问题相似，因为海上货物保险合约本质上是海上保险，不过后来根据 1906 年《英国海上保险法》Section 2(1)可以将两端的陆上运输风险伸延为“仓至仓”。但如果实际上所走的海上航次根本不是保险合约预计的航次，风险根本就没有生效或开始(attach)。受保人即使是无辜，也不能说短短的从发货人仓库到装港码头的陆上行程风险已经是开始，而之后将装上鬼船或本案例的 Ta Hung 轮说成是超出他控制范围的绕航或转运。有关这方面的先例是 Simon Israel v. Sedgwick (1893) 1 QB 303，案情也是涉及货物装上了不同目的地的船舶。法院拒绝受保人的争辩指货物离开发货人的仓库，承保风险就已经开始生效，装错了船舶只是一个可以续保的绕航，说：“The subject-matter of a marine policy is a marine adventure, which, with respect to cargo, consists of the exposure of the insured cargo to maritime perils, namely the perils consequent on or incidental to the navigation of the seas. A contract of marine insurance may be extended to cover incidental land or inland water transit, but the core subject-matter of the policy remains the designated sea voyage. If the insured cargo never embarks upon that voyage, it never embarks upon the insured adventure."

最后要介绍的有关先例是 Nam Kwong v. China Insce (2002) 2 Lloyd's Rep 591, Stone 大法官说:"The Simon Israel case remained good law and could not be distinguished, he (保险人代表大律师) submitted. The policy in that case incorporated a warehouse to warehouse clause, and included provisions for holding covered in the event of deviation or change of voyage. The Court of Appeal construed the policy as being in substance a marine policy for a defined ocean voyage, to which the inland transits at either end were ancillary. (这句话是说两端的陆上运输只是辅助性) The argument that the loss was covered by reason of the cargo having left the warehouse in the country of shipment on an intended transit to the warehouse at destination was rejected. Similarly in Kallis v. Success, op cit, wherein the successor to the warehouse to warehouse clause, the transit clause, formed part of the cover, the Privy Council approving and following Simon Israel."

这法律地位会带来一个情况就是如果遇上装错船或者鬼船的情况,由于风险从来就没有开始,会导致货物在装船前公路运输途中发生损坏也是没得承保。这是有一点奇怪,正如 Bennett 教授在《The Law of Marine Insurance》第二版之 Para. 17. 12 所说如下:"'Transit Clause' contemplates risk attaching as soon as the goods embark upon the commencement of transit. Where, however, cargo is insured from Port A to Port B, risk does not attach until and unless the carrying vessel sails from Port A bound for Port B with the insured cargo (or at least some of it) on board, even if the policy contains an extension of cover to inland transit incidental to the sea voyage (i. e. warehouse to warehouse). Provided the insured cargo does embark upon the insured sea voyage, "Transit Clause" then backdates the attachment of risk to the commencement of transit. **It would appear to follow that, surprisingly, the ICC do not afford cover against total loss of all cargo prior to commencement of the sea voyage.**"(加黑部分是笔者的强调)

该法律地位在多式联运普遍的今天,可以说是不尽令人满意。因为很多时候,海上的运输过程很可能是只有一小段,而陆上的运输过程则可能是整个过程的很大一部分,并且风险也很可能是不小。

6.4 航次延误

在本章第 6. 1 段已经节录了 1906 年《英国海上保险法》的第 48 条,针对不合理航次延误或没有合理速遣,说明会带来与不合理绕航同样的严重结果,就是保险人可以解除责任。背后的原因可介绍 1906 年立法之前的一些先例。首先,在先例 Hull v. Cooper (1811) 2 Atk 359, Tindal 首席大法官说:"船舶延误抵达是会改变保险人答应承保的风险"(a delay in the arrival of the vessel at the place where the risk is to attach, alters the risk of the insurer)。Tindal 首席大法官解释背后的原因是如下:

"The reason upon which a deviation discharges the insurer, is not that the risk is thereby increased, but because the insured has, without necessity, substituted another voyage for that which was insured, and thereby varied the risk which the underwriter took upon himself. It must be admitted that, if the policy had been effected upon this ship at and from Singapore, the ship then being at Singapore, unreasonable and unjustifiable delay at Singapore would have avoided the policy. Why, but because the voyage, commenced after an unreasonable interval of time, would have become a voyage at a different period of the year, at a more advanced age of the ship, and, in short, a different voyage than if it had been prosecuted with proper and ordinary diligence; that is the risk would have been altered from that which was intended by all parties when the policy was effected.(这里举一个例子,如果承保的是从新加坡开航的航次保险,但该航次在新加坡不合理延误,导致了延误后的开航会面对不同的季节/天气,加上船龄比较老,反正再也不是保险人订立保险合约时约定的费率所愿意承保的风险。这里又是强调了不能改变承保风险的本质。)

But what is the difference with respect to the alteration of the voyage, whether the unreasonable and unjustifiable delay takes place in the course of the ship's voyage to Singapore, or after the ship is at Singapore? The underwriter has as much right to calculate upon the outward voyage ... being performed in a reasonable time and without unnecessary delay, in order that the risk may attach, as he has that the voyage insured shall be commenced within a reasonable time, after the risk had attached. In either case the effect is the same, as to the underwriter, who has another risk substituted instead of that which he has insured against; and in both cases, the alteration is occasioned by the wrongful act of the assured himself."

另一个先例是 De Wolf v. Archangel Maritime Bank & Insurance Co Ltd. (1831) 8 Bing 108, Blackburn 大法官说:"it is not material whether the delay which varies the risk was occasioned by the fault or the misfortune of the assured. In either case the risk is equally varied."(造成延误的原因是否是受保人的过错并不重要,反正是同样改变了承保的风险。这可以想到就算是货方是无辜,不合理延误一样会影响到他对货物的保险。)

这些先例就带来了 1906 年《英国海上保险法》的 Section 48,但这在海上货物运输保险不可以接受,所以就带来了协会货物条文(A)(B)(C)都有 8.3 条去针对航次不合理的延误,只要是受保人无法控制的延误,都不会影响保险合约的有效性。

在这里重复协会货物条文(A)(B)(C)都有 18 条,在可以控制的范围内受保人要避免延误。这种情况不多,除了是大宗货,受保人的货方才会有可能亲自租船,这在一定程度上可以控制船舶的航次履行,部分例子可参见 6.2 段的介绍。

6.5 运输合约条文下允许的强制卸货/重装/转运与航次改变

在强制卸货/重装/转运(forced discharge, reshipment or transhipment)与航次改变

(variation of adventure)的情况，会发生在承保风险的事故后，例如，在中间避难港对受损的船舶进行修理而需要把船舱内的货物强制卸下甚至转运。在这种情况下，本书第七章2.4段有介绍，费用是属于共同海损，而且根据协会货物条文第2条是受到承保。

普通法也有一些案例接受转运合理需要，货物保险合约不会因此中断。例如，在航次中短暂地把货物卸下让船舶进行修理或装配，被认为是可以接受的（参见 Pelly v. Royal Exchange Ass [1755] 1 Burr 341; Brough v. Whitmore [1791] 4 TR 206）。如果航次有必要转运，也有先例判可以接受，即 Tierney v. Etherington (1743) 1 Burr 348 (n)。另是如果原来准备运输的船舶没有办法继续履行（如发生事故或是全损），货物可以让另外一艘船舶继续运输，即 Plantamour v. Staples (1781) 1 TR 611 (n)。虽然在以前的先例还没有充分与清楚地针对千变万化需要转运的情况，但是在1906年《英国海上保险法》第59条就有针对转运的情况规定："Where, by a peril insured against, the voyage is interrupted at an intermediate port of place, under such circumstances as, apart from any special stipulation in the contract of affreightment, to justify the master in landing and re-shipping the goods or other movables, or in transshipping them, and sending them on to their destination, the liability of the insurer continues, notwithstanding the landing or transshipment."

在协会货物条文第8.3条所针对的一些情况，是在海上运输合约给予船东/承运人在他们的自由选择下，可以享有安排强制卸货/重装/转运与航次改变的权利。这种合约条文在许多班轮提单会写得很广泛，而且也不一定会违反《海牙规则》（即使是适用），毕竟《海牙规则》没有明确针对这种情况。但如果要求受保人的货方与班轮船东讨价还价要求改变这种一边倒的条文是不现实，所以就在保险合约明示接受这种情况的发生。显然遇上了这种情况，就至少会带来严重的延误。而且根据普通法，如果航次中途自动改用另外一艘船舶转运，就会被视为不是保险合约所承保的风险。因为货物保险合约虽然一般不说明运载船舶的名字，但一个正常的航次应该只是以一艘船舶进行运输，所以转运就会给保险人机会使他们不需要负责。这里可节录 Francis Rose 教授在《Marine Insurance Law and Practice》一书2004年版的10.85段中所说的如下："Similarly, if goods are to be shipped on board a particular vessel, a voluntary substitution of another vessel *prima facie* has the same effect: as the non-attachment of risk in the case of a voyage policy on a ship sailing to a destination outside the contract, in the unusual case where transit is warehouse-to-warehouse or its equivalent. If the cargo insurance does not specify the ship, nonetheless, the usual course of transit is by a single vessel, so transshipment will in principle discharge the insurer."

所以明示规定货物保险合约不会受到这种情况的影响而被终止，这样对受保人显然比较安全。

以下笔者给一个例子就是这种会出现在班轮提单的所谓自由条文（liberty

clause)是如下:

"Methods and Route of Carriage

(1) The Carrier may at any time and without notice to the Merchant:

(a) use any means of carriage whatsoever,

(b) transfer the Goods from one conveyance to another, including but not limited to transhipping or carrying them on another vessel than that named on the face hereof,

(c) unpack and remove the Goods which have been packed into a Container and forward them in a Container or otherwise.

(d) proceed by any route in his discretion (whether or not the nearest or most direct or customary or advertised route), at any speed, and proceed to or stay at any place or port whatsoever, once or more often and in any order.

(e) load or unload the Goods at any place or port (whether or not such port is named overleaf as the Port of Loading or Port of Discharge) and store the Goods at any such place or port,

(f) comply with any orders or recommendations given by any government or authority, or any person or body acting or purporting to act as or on behalf of such government or authority, or having under the terms of the insurance on the conveyance employed by the Carrier the right to give orders or directions,

(g) permit the vessel to proceed with or without pilots, to tow or be towed, or to be dry-docked.

(2) The liberties set out in Clause 17 (1) may be invoked by the Carrier for any purpose whatsoever, whether or not connected with the Carriage of the Goods, including loading or unloading other goods, bunkering, undergoing repairs, adjusting instruments, picking up or landing any persons, including but not limited to persons involved with the operation or maintenance of the vessel and assisting vessels in all situations. Anything done in accordance with Clause 17(1) or any delay arising therefrom shall be deemed to be within the Contractual Carriage and shall not be a deviation..."

最后一提的是如果在船东行使合约权利强制卸货/重装/转运(forced discharge, reshipment or transhipment)与改变航次(variation of adventure),而期间发生的货损货差在一切险的货物保险下是被承保的。一般如果保险合约是用协会货物条文(B)或者(C),它们之间就会有一点不同。在协会货物条文(B),1.3条有一个列明风险是(C)所没有的,这就是货物在船舶或者小船装卸的时候掉下海或者掉在地上摔坏(total loss of any package lost overboard or dropped whilst unloading on to, or unloading on to, or unloading from, vessel or craft)的所谓"sling damage"。这一在协会货物条文(C)没有被承保的列明风险在今天的班轮运输主要是以集装箱为主估计没有太大的现实影响。这方面在本书第九章的第5段有详论。

7. 第9条:运输合约终止

运输合约的终止 Termination of Contract of Carriage[1]

9 如果由于受保人不能控制的情况,运输合约在其载明的目的地以外的港口或地点终止,或运送在如同上述第8条规定的卸下保险标的前另行终止,那么本保险也按下列规定终止,除非通知了保险人并在本保险有效时提出继续承保的要求,并且受保险人要求的附加保险费的制约

9.1 直至保险标的在此种港口或地点出售并交付,或者除非另有特别约定,直至保险标的到达此种港口或地点满60天,二者以先发生者为准,或者

9.2 如果保险标的在上述60天(或任何约定的延展期间)内被运往保险合约载明的目的地或其他目的地,直至根据上述第8条的规定而终止。

7.1 续保(held cover)

7.1.1 谈判改变保险合约与续保的分别

在解释本条文之前,先讲讲有关续保(held cover)的法律地位。在本条文以及接下去要介绍的第10条有关航次的改变都有明示规定可以续保,而续保是第8条文所没有的。这里会有很大区别,简单说有了续保的明示规定,就算是原来保险合约承保的风险有了偏差,导致了保险合约的终止或者承保风险还没有生效/开始,也因为有了续保,保险人必须要继续作出承保。他通常唯一的权利就是要求合理地加保费,期间保险也不会被终止。但没有续保的明示规定下承保风险本质上有了偏差,就会导致保险合约的终止。虽然在订约自由下,双方可以自由谈判改变订约条文,但不一定谈得拢,也难保保险人想打退堂鼓,就狮子大开口或者干脆就不谈。

2009年协会货物条文希望把续保的法律地位尽量说清楚。这也就是说发生了需要续保的情况,被保人的货方就要尽快通知保险人要求继续承保并支付保险人要求的额外加保费。而在谈判什么是合理额外加保费的期间,如果该货物发生损失或者损坏,虽然双方还没有谈妥,该损失或损坏还是能够获得赔付。换言之,续保可让该保险合约从来都没有终止过。这与一些没有续保保障的情况,如6.1.4中规定的货物从船舶上卸下后最长的期限为60天有很大不同。如果受保人与保险人在谈判期间,这60天届满,原来的保险合约会终止。这显然会令受保人受到压力并作出让步,否则60天届满后货物是没有保险。又如60天届满前发生了事故导致货损,保险人也会终止谈判或狮子大开口。

保险合约有续保的条文主要是针对在普通法或1906年《英国海上保险法》,针对保险合约承保的风险在履行过程中有了偏差,视为改变了保险合约的本质,可以令

---

[1] 英文条文参见附录三。

保险合约马上终止。这一说法或法律地位对保险人太有利,而相对是对受保人不利与太危险。这些偏差包括不合理绕航,不合理延误航次,还有就是装错船的先例 Kallis (Manufacturers) Ltd v. Success Insurance Ltd (1985) 2 Lloyd's Rep. 8 (PC),鬼船有关的先例如 Nam Kwong v. China Insce (2002) 2 Lloyd's Rep 591 与 The"Prestrioka"(2003) 2 Lloyd's Rep 327 等。所以,需要对一些不令人满意但又比较多会发生的情况,特别是受保人不能控制的,以明示条文作出改变。针对受保人不能控制的海上运输中的延误,已在协会货物条文第 8.3 条有针对并在本章第 6.2 段有提到。另一些受保人是能够控制但为了商业的要求(如航次中途的改变,需要去一个不是与原来保险合约一样的目的地),也就以续保条文给受保人一定程度的保障。这里可以节录 Bennett 教授著的《The Law of Marine Insurance》第二版之 Para. 18.111 如下:"Although the doctrine of alteration of risk, as developed by the common law and partially enshrined in the Marine Insurance Act 1906, may be viewed as inflexible and weighted heavily in the insurer's favor, ultimately it serves to provide clear and certain *prima facie* rules and a basis for negotiation of terms relaxing the severity of the default position. The 'held covered' clause is such a term. Under a held covered clause, in the event of a stipulated occurrence, typically one that constitutes an alteration of risk, the insurer's liability is not prospectively discharged. Instead, the assured remains ("is held") covered provided any specified conditions are fulfilled, usually the notification of the event by the assured to the insurer and agreement upon any appropriate additional premium and change of terms."

虽然续保条文对受保人有这么大的保障,它有各种法律默示/明示的限制,受保人必须注意才能让续保条文发挥作用,以下进一步介绍这些限制。

7.1.2 续保的法律地位

续保在本书第八章之 8.4.3 段已经有涉及,以下多补充一些内容,其中多介绍一些有关续保的先例,首先是 Liberian Insurance Agency Inc. v. Mosse (1977) 2 Lloyd's Rep. 560 先例,Donaldson 大法官说:

"I can summaries the application of the held covered clause as follows:(我总结续保条文的地位如下)

(i) The assured seeking the benefit of the clause must give prompt notice to underwriters of his claim to be held covered as soon as he learns of the facts which render it necessary for him to rely upon the clause.(受保人在知道需要续保的事实或情况后,就必须尽快给保险人通知。)

(ii) It is no obstacle to the operation of the clause that it will defeat underwriters' right to avoid the contract for non-disclosure or misdescription.(续保条文不影响保险人发现受保人在订立保险合约时违反披露或有误述去选择让保险合约无效的权利。)

(iii) The assured cannot take advantage of the clause if he has not acted in the utmost good faith.(受保人如果违反了绝对善意是不能享有续保条文的。)

(iv) The clause does not contemplate any alteration in the terms of the insurance other than in respect of premium.（续保条文并没有考虑让保险人改变保险合约条文，只考虑到加保费。这表示保险人不能借这个机会将保险合约中对他不利的其他条文赖掉或改变。）

(v) The clause only applies if the premium to be arranged would be such as could properly be described as a reasonable commercial rate.（续保条文的加保费只是合理加保费。）”

7.1.2.1 什么是尽快给通知？

Donaldson 大法官在上述的先例也对续保的要求分别作出一些重要的解释与要求，如关于受保人怎样才算“尽快给通知”。简单说就是尽快在合理时间内，但什么是合理就要根据不同的情况来定。例如，受保人一知道需要续保的事实（如受保人无法控制的航次半途终止），而当时风险还是在继续（如货物还是完好无缺地存放在中途港），合理的通知时间就会比风险已经终止（如货物已经发生全损）会来得更短。如果货物正处于危险之中会有可能遭受损失或损坏，合理通知时间会是更短甚至要马上作出通知。这里的道理就是让保险人有机会安排再保，而如果太晚，货物已经发生损失，就会导致保险人无法再保。Donaldson 大法官这样说：

“If the assured is to take advantage of the held covered clause he must give notice to underwriters expressly or impliedly seeking cover in accordance with the clause within a reasonable time of learning of the change of voyage or of the omission or error in the description. What time is reasonable will depend upon all the circumstances. Thus if the assured learns the true facts while the risk is still current, a reasonable time will usually be a shorter period than if this occurs when the adventure has already ended. If the assured learns the true facts when the insured property is in the grip of a peril, which is likely to cause loss or damage, a reasonable time will be very short indeed.

It may be objected that it is unfortunate to use the words ‘prompt notice’ when what is meant is notice within a reasonable time. However, in the context of a clause which may impose upon underwriters, and indirectly upon reinsuring underwriters, risks which they have never specifically accepted, I do not think that notice which is other than prompt could ever be said to be given within a reasonable time. In my judgment, the use of the word ‘prompt’ is not only justifiable but also desirable in explanation of the obligation which is implicit in the clause itself.”

较早的时候也有其他的先例可一提，如在 Hood v. West End Motor Car Packing Co (1917) 2 KB 38，案情是有关车子应该装在甲板下面而没有这样做，这需要续保。但受保人在发生了损失后才给保险人续保的通知。这被上诉庭认为是太晚与不合理，Scrutton 大法官这样说：“... the assured could not avail himself of the clause unless within a reasonable time after he knew of the omission or error he gave notice to the underwriters. It is an implied term of the contract that the assured shall give notice to the underwriters within a reasonable time after he knows of the omission or error... the natural tendency of an assured is to wait and see if the matter goes through all right, and only in the case of a loss happening to give notice to the underwriters. In order to meet the tendency the stipulation as to notice is implied. In the present case when the [受保人的代理] knew that the car was being shipped on deck no notice thereof was given to the underwriters until after the loss. That is not within a reasonable time..."

另一个较早的先例是 Thames & Mersey Marine Insurance Co Ltd v. H. T. Van Laun & Co (1917) 2 KB 8，案情涉及了一批活牛从澳大利亚运去中国，但由于目的地港的冰封而要改变航线。当这个消息传到伦敦，受保人过了 10 天后才通知保险人要求续保。在该海上货物运输保险合约，有条文针对绕航可以续保，法院认为受保人有一个默示责任要求合理、尽快甚至是马上通知保险人。在该先例中，这批货物还有是有其他一些在利物浦签发的保单，明确规定了马上给通知，说："notice be given and any additional premium required be agreed **immediately** after receipt of advices."固然续保是合约条文所带来的，解释就要看它所用的文字，在 1982 年与 2009 年的协会货物条文的续保条文（在第 9 与第 10 条）中，所用的文字受保人应该给保险人"**prompt** notice"。该词中文中是"尽快通知"，应该与普通法的地位一致。

最后一提的是一个有趣但不是有关货物保险的续保先例，名为 The"Litsion Pride"(1985) 1 Lloyd's Rep. 437。案情涉及 1982 年的两伊战争期间，该 Litsion Pride 轮装了一船的糖，在波斯湾被伊拉克飞机炮弹击中而导致沉没。当时的波斯湾属于船壳战争险的不许可航区（excluded areas），但可以续保并支付加保费，相关条文如下："(A) This coverage shall extend worldwide, but in the event of a vessel or craft insured hereunder sailing for, deviating towards, or being within the Territorial Waters of any of the Countries or places described in the Current Exclusions as set out below [including any port area that at the date of this notice constitutes part of such a country or place however it may hereafter be described] additional premium shall be paid at the discretion of insurers hereon. (B) Information of such voyage or deviation shall be given to insurers as soon as practicable, and the absence of prior advice shall not affect the cover hereon. In the event of the insured not requiring continuation of coverage for a vessel proceeding into or remaining within an excluded area, he shall so advise insurers hereon before the commencement of such voyage, deviation or period, and it shall be at the insurers' discretion whether and on what terms the insurance shall be reinstated."

在时间上，Litsion Pride 轮是在 1982 年 8 月 2 日开进了波斯湾的不许可航区，而船舶是在 8 月 9 日被导弹击沉。船舶沉没的事故希腊船东是在 8 月 11 日以传真的方式通知了保险经纪人，并让他转告劳合社保险人。保险人的反应是该损失不在承保范围，因为违反了航区保证但没有及时通知与续保（No cover hereunder. Breach of warranty not advised or agreed by underwriters)。但船东反驳,说是保险人早就获得通知船舶要进去波斯湾要求续保,还有船东在 8 月 2 日的一份信函作为证据(估计以信函作出通知就可以把它推到邮递延误造成未能及时送达)。保险人否认他事前获得通知。在高院的审理 Hirst 大法官作出认定是船东为了避免加保费(当时由于波斯湾战争风险很大,所以加保费用非常高,高达 100 万美元一个航次)而作出虚假的证据,说:"The letter was concocted, and the false information invented, in order to deceive the underwriters, in the hope that they would accept that the failure to give notice was an innocent oversight. Whether that failure was innocent or culpable was obviously of the highest materiality to the underwriters in deciding their attitude towards the claim."

所以在该先例,希腊船东败诉,因为他并没有给合理尽快地通知。而且受保人还违反了绝对善意的要求,这是 Donaldson 大法官在 Liberian Insurance Agency Inc. v. Mosse (1977) 2 Lloyd's Rep. 560 所说的第三个要求,这在本章 7. 1. 2 段有介绍。

7. 1. 2. 2　什么是合理加保费?

在先例 Liberian Insurance Agency Inc. v. Mosse (1977) 2 Lloyd's Rep. 560, Donaldson 大法官也讲到续保所需要增加的保费。显然保险人不能借这个机会敲受保人竹杠,如要求保险价值(insured value)的 100% 作为加保费。Donaldson 大法官说加保费应该是按在保险市场能够拿到报价的合理商业费率来确定。Donaldson 大法官这样说:"What then is the limitation which must be implied? In my judgment, the clause only applies if the assured, on the basis of an accurate declaration of all the facts affecting the risk but excluding knowledge of what was to happen in the event, **could have obtained a quotation in the market at a premium which could properly be described as a 'reasonable commercial rate'**. This can be relatively high if the risk is high but it will not be in the same class as, for example, rates of premium for reinsurance cover after a casually has in fact occurred. Still less will it approach 100 per cent of the sum insured."(加黑的部分是笔者的强调,稍候会解释。)

Donaldson 大法官也提到了如果保险人与受保人不能同意,这一增加的保费应该是多少就应该让仲裁员或法院作出决定了。

一般受保人都认为在续保条文下,只要受保人尽早与善意的作出通知,并愿意支付加保费,保险人就非要继续承保不可。而且,在续保还未谈妥之前,如果发生了货损,保险人就有义务赔付。这样认为基本上正确,但还必须满足一默示条件,就是 Donaldson 大法官在上述节录的一段话加黑的部分说要续保的风险可以在保险市场以合理商业保费获得承保。

这一个默示条件在一个香港与新加坡的先例中有所澄清或加以明确。就是有关的船舶被认为适航标准实在是太差劲,根本没有办法在保险市场以一个合理费率获得承保。第一个是香港的先例 Nam Kwong v. China Insce (2002) 2 Lloyd's Rep 591, 有关的船舶没有在一个符合要求的船级社入级,并被法院视为有关的风险没有办法以合理的保费在市场上投保。该先例中货物投保了 1982 年协会货物条文(一切险)。货物是 15,000 吨橄榄油(palm olein),原告 Nam Kwong 也就是受保人从马来西亚购买并准备去北海卸货。装运的船舶名为“Pacifica”,但在马来西亚装了该票货物后就失踪,根本没有去北海,估计该船舶是一艘鬼船。双方其中一个争议涉及了“Pacifica”是否符合保险合约合并了的协会船级条文(Institute Classification Clause),该条文要求船舶不能超龄并且需要在信誉良好的船级社入级,否则就要续保。

另是一个新加坡上诉庭的先例 Everbright Commercial Enterprises v Axa Insurance Singapore (2001) 2 SLR 316,有关的船舶没有船级,悬挂的是 Belize 的船旗,它在一个不存在的互保协会说是投保了责任风险等。新加坡法院达致了同样的判决,认为合理的费率在保险市场找不到。所以,在 2001 年的协会船级条文就加上一个重要的针对续保的条文:只有续保是以合理的保费费率在合理的条件下实现的,在达成续保合议前发生的货损才可以得到赔付。

最后一提的是负责草拟有关条文的伦敦货物保险市场的 Joint Cargo Committee,针对 2001 年版本中的续保条文曾经作出了以下有关何为合理费率与合理条件的指引:“It was felt that there had been misunderstandings in some quarters as to what was meant by ‘held covered’ and that some elaboration would be helpful. Evidence of ‘market terms’ would require an exercise to establish what terms might be obtainable in the market place i. e. from a representative sample of underwriters active in the class of underwriting cargo business. The fact that one underwriter might quote for a risk generally regarded as unacceptable by such a representative sample of underwriters, would not be evidence that the risk could be insured at a ‘reasonable commercial market’ rate/terms. The collective view of such a sample would represent the market position.”(市场上有对何为“续保”产生误解,需要进一步澄清。有关合理市场条件需要确定,以什么条件这一个风险可在市场投保,这是要找一些有代表性的保险人,经常在货物保险市场承保。如果只是找到证据证明有一位保险人愿意以某一条件或费率承保这一风险,但对其他有代表性的保险人不认为可以接受,这不能作为证据说明有关的风险可以以合理保费费率与条件投保。必须要是多个有代表性保险人的集体意见才可以当作市场的地位。)

7.1.2.3　除了合理加保费外,续保能否改变其他条文?

在上述 7.1.2 段有关续保的法律地位,已经提到过 Liberian Insurance Agency Inc. v. Mosse (1977) 2 Lloyd's Rep. 560 先例,Donaldson 大法官就在他意见的第四点说,续保只能收取合理加保费而保险人不可以将保险合约中的其他条文(如免赔额的金额)推倒重来,把一个对保险人不利的合约变成对他有利。这里的原因是续保在原来所承保的航次有了偏差,导致原来的保费不足够,所以要收取加保费,但基础还是根据原来的保险合约条文。Donaldson 大法官这样说:“Accordingly, if the original cover was on all risks' terms, the clause [续保条文] will not affect this. Nor does it contemplate the imposition of or a change in, any excess [绝对免赔额] or franchise [相对免赔额]. It follows that the clause can only be intended to operate if the omission, misdescription or change of voyage is of such a nature that a new premium for a policy on identical terms can be 'arranged'. I understand the word 'arranged' to mean 'agreed or, in default of agreement, fixed by an arbitrator or by the Court'."

这是普通法的默示地位,但已经多次提到过,续保只是合约条文,最终的解释还是要看它的文字与措辞,加上理解它的背景。所以,如果除了加保费以外,续保还需要改变原来的保险合约条文,就需要明确写明,像在2009年协会货物条文,虽然同是续保条文,但可以明确看到第9条与第10条的不同:第9条用词是"subject to an additional premium if required by the Insurers",而第10条用词是"for rates **and terms** to be agreed"。这里估计的原因就是第9条针对海上运输合约在受保人不能控制情况下的终止。这种情况下,把船上货物处理掉,如在中途港转售,或者是安排转运去目的地的卸港,通常只是保险期间有延长,原来承保的风险不会有特别的增加。而第10条针对的是受保人主动作出航次的改变,这原因可能有很多。可能本来的航次是去中国沿海贸易变为去海盗出没的索马里海域,风险会大大的增加。保险人有必要确保能够改变其他保险合约条文,而不仅是收加保费。

7.1.2.4 续保要绝对善意(utmost goodfaith)

Donaldson大法官在7.1.2段Liberian Insurance Agency Inc. v. Mosse (1977) 2 Lloyd's Rep. 560先例的(iii)提到说要绝对善意,这方面有关的先例有Overseas Commodities Ltd v. Style (1958) 1 Lloyd's Rep 546,其中节录McNair大法官所说:"in order to obtain the protection of the 'held covered' clause, the assured must act with the utmost good faith towards the underwriters, this being an obligation which rests upon them throughout the currency of the policy."

绝对善意的其中一个方面是在受保人通知保险人有关续保的情况下,必须提供准确的资料,不能误述(misrepresentation)或不披露(non-disclosure)。这方面也可以节录Donaldson大法官在先例Liberian Ins v. Moses (1977) Lloyd's Rep 560中所说:"In my judgment, the clause only applies if the assured, on the basis of an accurate declaration of all the facts affecting the risk but excluding knowledge of what was to happen in the event, could have obtained a quotation in the market at a premium which could properly be described as 'a reasonable commercial rate'."

至于怎么样才是准确的资料,以The"Litsion Pride"(1985) 1 Lloyd's Rep. 437为例,就应该披露该船舶估计抵达波斯湾战区的大约时间,会在波斯湾停留多久与哪一个是装港或者卸港。因为有了这些资料,保险人才可以考虑再保。Hirst大法官这样说:"Even on a view most favorable to the owners on the facts, it would still have been impossible to acquit them of breach of a duty of utmost good faith, having regard to their culpable failure, which is not disputed, to communicate to the underwriters the facts which they knew well before July 15, such as the E. T. A. in the war zone, the likely duration of the vessel's stay and the nomination of Bandar Khomeini as the discharging port. All these matters were, in my judgment, highly material both in order to enable the underwriters to fix the premium, and to enable them to consider reinsurance."

Hirst 大法官也提到在续保下，受保人不是给了一个通知就足够，而是在后来有什么变化（如船舶抵达波斯湾战区的时间有了改变或停留时间有了改变）也应该提供给保险人，说："Even if Mr. Kentridge［船东代表大律师］were right as a matter of construction that only one single notification was required, it seems to me manifest that, as part of the duty of utmost good faith, it must be incumbent on the insured to include within it all relevant information available to him at the time he gives it; and in any event the self-same duty required the assured to furnish to the insurer any further material information which he acquires subsequent to the initial notice as and when it comes to his knowledge, particularly if it is materially at variance with the information the originally gave."

7.2　第9条：受保人无法控制的运输合约终止

解释了什么是续保，就可以回去简单介绍协会货物条文第9条。它是首次出现在1942年的Institute Cargo Clauses（Wartime Extension）1/5/42，为了针对在第二次世界大战的一些情况，就是有关政府（如船旗国）的命令导致航次半途被终止。反正在这种情况下，受保人的货方无法控制，但他就必须处理在该船舶上的货物，如安排在中途港把该货物出售，或是要转运去其他附近的中途港才能把货物出售，也有可能是转运去保险合约内的目的地卸港。反正在这种情况下，根据本条文就需要续保，以保证货物一直受到承保，直到处理掉。而如果处理的方法是把货物转运，应该协会货物条文第12条的续运费用条文适用，这方面可参阅本书第七章第5段。

8. 第10.1条：航次改变（Change of Voyage）

航次改变 Change of Voyage〔1〕

10.10.1　如果在本保险责任开始后，受保人改变了目的地，受保人应将此情况迅速通知保险人，以便双方重新约定保险费率和条款。

10.2　如果保险标的开始了本保险期待的运送（根据第8.1条），但是受保人或其雇员不知道船舶驶往另一目的港，本保险责任仍应视为从开始此种运送时开始。

2009年条款相对1982年条款〔2〕有一定的改变，以读者可以比较。

发生航次中途要改变目的地以及为什么需要续保，就先要解释1906年《英国海

〔1〕英文条文参见附录三。

〔2〕参见附录二。

上保险法》Section 45。[1]

Section 45 是针对船舶自愿在中途改变航次的目的地就被视为航次改变（change of voyage）。而协会货物条文的第 10 条也是针对这种受保人自愿改变航次的目的地。至于为什么受保人需要这样做，这会是来自千变万化的商业原因，接下来介绍。

在货物保险，都会规定货物的目的地，如中国的上海。至于上海作为目的地是怎样肯定，就是根据有关的货物买卖合约（特别是 CIF 或者 CFR）约定的卸港或者是交货港。但如果在航次的中途目的地有了改变，就可能有了很大的不同风险。这并非是保险人在接受投保时所同意承担的，所以 1906 年立法的默示地位就是保险人可以解除责任（discharge from liability）。而 1982 年条款之第 10 条与 2009 年条款之第 10.1 条作出改变的就是承诺"续保"，即只要货方作出通知并同意增加保费或/与其他保险条件的改变，就不存在保险人解除责任一说。至于要增加多少加保费，就要看改变的目的地与有关的风险了。如从上海改去黄埔港，就像 The"Shakir III"（1997）1 Lloyd's Rep 586 先例一样，风险缩短了，因为航次是从欧洲开始，到黄埔港显然要比去上海要近。但如果目的地是从上海改去俄罗斯海参崴，除了航次加长了外，很可能在当时的季节海参崴的天气也是一个大问题。当然，增加了的风险还是可以通过增加保费作出恰当的对价。至于为什么有这个改变目的地的需要，一种情况就是买方提出要求，就像 The"Shakir III"一样。另一种情况会是卖方结不了汇并加上货物市场下跌而导致买方拒绝接受该批货物，这迫使了卖方要把船上的货物转卖给其他人从而需要改变运输的目的地。还有情况会是有关的货物在卸港被拒绝进港，这可以是政治理由或其他的原因，反正就迫使该批货物要去其他目的地卸货。例如，笔者最近处理的一宗金额庞大的小麦买卖案件，涉及了 4 个航次，每次都是 30,000 吨的小麦从澳大利亚装运去巴基斯坦。但船舶到了巴基斯坦被当局检验后发觉小麦有 Karnal Bunt 的真菌，这导致了该批货物被拒绝进口。结果在延误了 4 个月后，最后以很低的价格转卖给印尼的新买方。可见，如果保险合约不规定可增加保费以续保的话，保险人就会面对严重与根本不能预计的风险（因为承保期限大大延长与多跑了从巴基斯坦去印尼的一个航次）。

其他还有很多商业原因要中途改变航次，如 CIF 买卖，货物由于结不了汇或者被买方拒货或者买方破产而导致受保人的卖方需要改变航次去其他目的地转卖。也会有受保人的收货人由于自己不再需要这票货而且没有地方储存（如一船原油即将抵达中国卸港，但由于用油量比计划偏低而短期内不需要，且没有油库可以在陆上储存），就要将该批浮动货物（floating cargo）转售，而这转售可能会去另一个附近的卸港或是另一个遥远与危险的卸港。

最后一提的就是本条文一开始就讲承保的风险开始后（Where, after attachment of this insurance），受保人自愿改变航次。这表示有关的保险合约针对有关的货物，船

〔1〕 参见附录一。

舶或航次还是不能有错，否则就会令承保风险根本没有开始或者生效，就像 Simon Israel v. Sedgwick（1893）1 QB 303；Kallis（Manufacturers）Ltd v. Success Insurance Ltd（1985）2 Lloyd's Rep. 8（PC）；Nam Kwong v. China Insce（2002）2 Lloyd's Rep 591 等先例（有关这些先例的详细介绍参见本章 6.3.3 段以及本书第四章第 3.4.1 段有关英国法律不允许受保人改变承保风险的本质）。

9. 第 10.2 条：鬼船

2009 年协会货物条文增加了新的 10.2 条，是用来针对"鬼船"（Phantom Ship）的情况，这种情况在 20 世纪 70 年代后期和 80 年代初期非常猖獗。鬼船通常就是一些不值钱的老船，悬挂方便旗，背后的船东是谁根本没有办法查，然后就去租船市场揽货，并对一些价值高而且容易脱手的货物特别感兴趣。之后船舶就根据租约装货，而装了货后根本不是开往签发提单的目的地（显然也不是海上货物运输保险合约中约定的目的地），而是开去另一个可以非法把该批货物脱手的地方。在 70 年代后期，其中一个最热门的地方就是黎巴嫩，因为当地发生战乱，根本没有人可以管这种事情，所以很容易把一些热门的货物以低价出售。这种类似的事件发生得非常频密，据说平均每个星期就有一艘船舶在黎巴嫩非法卸货。而卸货后，该船舶马上改名并改挂另一方便旗，在改头换面后再度去租船市场揽货。其中著名的贵族院先例 The"Siskina"（1978）1 Lloyd's Rep 1 就是类似的案件。另一个世界著名的鬼船案件是 The"Salem"（1983）1 Lloyd's Rep 32，船东把一船属于壳牌（Shell）石油公司的 20 万吨原油，本来的目的地是去欧洲，但半途去了南非偷偷地把原油卖了给当时实行种族隔离（所以受到阿拉伯国家的禁运）的南非政府。

这种鬼船的情况，近十几年来有了减少，原因之一可能是像黎巴嫩在 70 年代的战乱已经平息下来，也没有同样的乱局地区出现可以长期脱手一船的贼赃。另一个原因是航运市场有所复苏。但不表示这种鬼船的情况会消失，而不时还会听到这种案件，其中有报道的就是 The"Prestrioka"（2003）2 Lloyd's Rep 327。

The"Prestrioka"的案情为原告是一批 55,000 吨大米的买方，该批大米总的价格是 150 万英镑。原告向一个泰国的大米出口商以 CIF 价格购入，目的地就是非洲塞内加尔的首都达喀尔。泰国的出口商租用了洪都拉斯船旗的"Prestrioka"轮，并在 1999 年 3 月在泰国 Kohsichang 港装了这批大米。该出口商也同时向泰国的保险公司为该批大米投保了协会货物条文（一切险）。本来如果航次正常的话，应该只需要 32 ~35 天就抵达达喀尔，但该船舶从来没有抵达并且连船带货失踪。原告事后通过国际商会的国际海事局（International Maritime Bureau）的调查认定这是鬼船。原告于是向保险人提出索赔，但保险人拒绝赔付。保险人起初拒赔的理由是船舶不适航，但这是十分牵强的理由，甚至不沾边。但后来保险人成功找到一个该鬼船的缅甸籍的船员，并从他的口中得到了鬼船行踪的一些证据。该鬼船上共有 17 位船员，船长是一位印度人。该缅甸船员从一名印度高级船员的口中得知是要将该批大米运到印度一个港口卸货，最后实际上是在距离孟买港 50 海里的一个港口停泊，但没有卸货，据说是因为没有找到买家。之后船舶继续开往迪拜并最终在迪拜卸了货。而在开往迪拜的航次中，该船舶改了船名，并且船长告知船员该船将在迪拜卸货后拆船。反正这些证据就给了保险人拒赔的理由，就是船舶从来没有去达喀尔的意图，所以根据 1906 年《英国海上保险法》Section 44，承保的风险从来就没有开始。正如 Potter 大法官所说："If the Court determines that, at the time of sailing, vessel and cargo were in truth bound for a *terminus ad quem*（这句拉丁语是指真正想去的目的地）other than that identified in the policy as definitive of the voyage insured, then s. 44 will apply and the risk which *prima facie* attached when the goods left the warehouse will in the event be held not to have attached."

另一个有报道的鬼船先例是 Nam Kwong v. China Insce（2002）2 Lloyd's Rep 591，案情在较早的时候已经介绍过，不再重复。

在鬼船的情况下，无辜受保人失去了保障，因为此种情况下保险人承保的风险根本没有生效/开始。这在 1906 年《英国海上保险法》Section 44 有说明，条文如下："Where the destination is specified by the policy, and the ship, instead of sailing for that destination, sails for another destination, the risk does not attach."

注意是立法的 Section 44 没有针对受保人本人决定船舶开航去一个不同于保险合约中规定的目的地卸港的情况，它只是针对船舶本身去一个不同卸港。这样的措辞就决定了鬼船会给受保人带来的危险。

简单地说，情况就是承保的航次是 A 去 B，但实际上航次还没有开始船舶就决定了是 A 去 C。如果船舶开航时决定是 A 去 B，但半途决定去 C，这才是绕航（deviation）或者是改变航次（change of voyage）。在鬼船的情况下，由于有船东的预谋，显然在一开始就没有打算从 A 去 B（B 是运输合约的目的地卸港），而是决定从 A 去 C（C 是可以非法把货物出售的港口）。这在 Nam Kwong v. China Insce 先例中，Stone 大法官有这样的认定："I therefore find that Pacifica was a 'phantom ship' as popularly so-called—indeed I did not understand the plaintiff to be seriously contending to the contrary. I find further that on the probabilities the owners or operators must in the circumstances have been part of a plan to steal the cargo, and that the intention to steal would have been formed prior to the loading of the cargo."

这一来在鬼船的情况下，承保的风险从来没有开始/生效，正如 Stone 大法官所说如下："A voyage policy is no more than insurance on a particular risk. It is evident that if in actuality the voyage performed is not the voyage described in the policy, then equally clearly it is not the risk that the insurer has bargained to cover. In other words, the scope of the cover from shipment is defined by reference to the voyage so specified, and it is not easy to see why cl. 8 of the ICC[A] should circumvent, or be regarded as circumventing, that situation. The fact that 'all risks' are to be held covered from the time of leaving the warehouse in itself cannot be determinative of insurance cover if the ocean leg of the transit is not that specified in the policy. All risks are held covered if in actuality of transit, of which the specified ocean leg is the major part, takes place as contemplated, and I am unable to see any residual iniquity if cover is regarded as lapsing if in fact the vessel promptly sails for somewhere else."

在鬼船的情况,说是受保人的货方完全无辜也不一定准确,从保险人角度来看,他可以在租船时候小心一点查清楚船东的背景,毕竟鬼船主要出现在租船而不是班轮。但现实是受保人的货方在大部分情况下是控制不了的,因为国际贸易还是以CIF/CFR为主,而受保人的货方往往就是收货人(不论是保险合约通过转让给他或者他在CFR下自己投保),鬼船不是他租的。所以为了改变1906年《英国海上保险法》Section 44的默示地位,2009年协会货物条文10.2条就针对了这种情况,并提供了对无辜的受保人的一些保障。只要是他与他的雇员事前不知道船舶(鬼船)一启航就计划开往另一个目的地,还是被视为承保的风险已经开始/生效。

第十二章　赔付原则与做法

1. 向保险人索赔的时效

保险合约是跟其他的合约或者侵权一样都是受到时效的限制。根据英国 1980 年《Limitation Act 1980》,普通的合约自诉因产生之日起 6 年内可以提起诉讼。针对货物保险是从发生货损那天起算:Chrandris v. Argo Insurance Co Ltd (1963) 2 Lloyd's Rep 65;The"Fanti" and The"Padre Island" (1990) 2 Lloyd's Rep 191;The"Italia Express" (No. 2) (1992) 2 Lloyd's Rep 281。其中在 The"Fanti" and The"Padre Island",贵族院的 Goff 勋爵是这样说:"I also accept that, at common law, the cause of action does not [unless the contract provides otherwise] arise until the indemnified person can show actual loss: see Collinge v. Heywood (1893) 9 Ad. & E. 634. This is, as I understand it, because a promise of indemnity is simply a promise to hold the indemnified person harmless against a specified loss or expense. On this basis, no debt can arise before the loss is suffered or the expense incurred; however, once the loss is suffered or the expense incurred, the indemnifier is in breach of contract for having failed to hold the indemnified person harmless against the relevant loss or expense."

不像租船合约,英国保险市场通常是不会在保险合约中加入明示条文约定比 6 年更短的合约时效(contractual time limit)。但在美国的保险市场,在保险合约条文中加入 1 年的合约时效限制很常见:De Moncy v. Phoenix Insurance Company Hartford and Another (1929) 34 Lloyd's Rep 201。

2. 通知保险人条文

6 年如此长的时效会给保险人带来几个方面的不利:首先是保险人很难预计应该准备多少的保险赔偿金;其次如果受保人只是在时效结束前提出索赔,保险人没有机会参与向第三者索赔的行动。如向船东提出索赔,通常是受到 1924 年《海牙规则》的强制约束,虽然根据协会货物条文(Institute Cargo Clause)第 16.2 条是要求受保人采取所有向第三者(包括承运人或托管人)索赔的行动,以保障保险人在赔付后所拥有的代位求偿权。但毕竟事后质疑受保人采取的行动是否恰当仍是不容易，所以保险合约会有条文要求受保人在发生事故后尽快作出通知，这条文会以赔付的先决条件或一般合约条文的形式出现，这方面可参阅本书第四章第4.4段。这一条通知保险人条文（Notice of claims）并没有写在协会货物条文（不像协会船舶保险条文，如在1/10/1983的版本是在第10.1条，而在1/11/03国际船舶保险条文是在第43.1条），但Lloyd's Marine Policy（MAR 91）与Lloyd's格式的保险证书（certificate of insurance）中就有这一条加黑了的条文如下："In the event of loss or damage which may result in a claim under this Insurance, immediate notice must be given to the Lloyd's Agent at the port or place where the loss or damage is discovered in order that he may examine the goods and issue a survey report."

通知保险人条文的主要作用在Alfred McAlpine plc v BAI（Run-Off）Ltd（1998）2 Lloyd's Rep 694的先例中有解释，Colman大法官说："The obvious purpose of such provision is to enable the insurers to take steps to investigate claims or occurrences which may give rise to claims, in order to minimize their exposure under the policy. They may wish to set in motion independent investigations or cause repair or reinstatement of insured property to be undertaken and, in the case of a liability policy, to take over the defence of claims against the assured or negotiate directly with the third party claimants. Very often it may be in the interests of the insurer under a liability policy to be able to take steps to investigate circumstances which may give rise to a claim against the assured before any such claim has been made against or by the assured under the policy. Under such a policy an insurer may be better able to protect himself if evidence as to the occurrence can be obtained as early as possible, for, if delay occurs, witnesses may disappear and memories may fade and, if a claim is then made, an insurer may be severely prejudiced by having lost the opportunity of defeating or diminishing the third party claim."（让保险人马上进行独立的调查取证，减少将来要赔付的损失。在责任保险接管第三人对受保人的索赔或进行谈判。调查取证越早越好，因为证据的存在与证据的力度会随着时间的过去而消失或减弱。）

这种条文很早在海上货物运输就已经有先例涉及，其中就是上诉庭的D&J Koskas v. The Standard Insurance Company Ltd（1927）27 Lloyd's Rep 59。在该先例，相关条文（保险证明的第11条）用词如下："In case of loss or damage happening to the property insured hereunder, same shall be reported to the representative of the company（see list on back hereof）, or, if there be no such representative at the place, to Lloyd's Agent, as soon as the goods are landed or the loss is known or expected, and in the event of claim arising, all documents in connection therewith are to be submitted for approval."有关货物是皮革，从纽约运去突尼斯，中途货物遇到严重水湿。CIF买方根据转让给他的保险证明向保险人索赔，但通知给的太晚，给通知的时候根本没有办法再对损坏的皮革作出检验。保险人拒绝赔付，指受保人的货方迟延把事故通知最近的劳合社代理人

(Lloyd's Agent),而及时通知是向保险人索赔的先决条件(condition precedent)。但上诉庭不同意,主要的理由就是写的不清楚,没有把这个条文明确说明是先决条件。毕竟,保险人作出承诺赔付损失,如果有什么例外,如晚了通知,就可以不赔付的话,责任是保险人要把这种例外情况写清楚。

看来在海上货物保险的该通知条文只当做是一般性的条文,要提升它,就要在保险合约中加多一句如说明"如果没有及时通知保险人是可以拒赔"。否则如果受保人没有这样做,保险人只能是提出延误通知所带来的损失而不是拒赔。当然,如果受保人没有马上通知(immediately notice)最近的劳合社代理人(在中国大陆据悉劳合社委任的代理人就是外代),没有让他尽快委任检验师作出及时的调查取证与对损坏货物作出检验,就会带来将来保险人即使是赔付也会延误与增加困难,这对受保人也没有什么好处。

另外,迟延通知劳合社代理人也有危险是保险人指称受保人没有合理与及时施救。

这种条文会根据不同的保险人作出调整,例如通知的不是劳合社代理人,而是某一家货物检查公司(surveying company)或是某一家索赔代理(recovery agent)。

针对海上货物保险,估计及时通知保险人不像其他的一些保险合约,如投保责任保险。这种通知条文会加上其他要求,如受保人把知道的有关情况也马上告知保险人。举例说,在涉及专业疏忽责任保险的先例,就有这样的条文:"The Assured shall as a CONDITIIONAL PRECEDENT to their right to be indemnified under this Policy give to the Underwriters notice as soon as possible during the period of this Policy... (a) of any circumstances of which the Assured shall first become aware which may give rise to a claim or loss against them or any of them; (b) of the receipt of notice from any person whether written or oral of any intention to make a claim against them or any of them; (c) of the discovery or reasonable cause for suspicion of dishonesty or fraud on the part of a past or present... employee... Such notice having been given to Underwriters the Assured shall give to the Underwriters as soon as possible full details in writing of the circumstances which may give rise to a claim or loss..."

3. 定值保单与非定值保单

3.1 定值保单与非定值保单的定义

有关定值保单,在1906年《英国保险法》之Section 27有规定如下:"**27. Valued policy** (1) A policy may be either valued or unvalued. (2) A valued policy is a policy which specifies the agreed value of the subject-matter insured. (3) Subject to the provisions of this Act, and in the absence of fraud, the value fixed by the policy is, as between the insurer and assured, conclusive of the insurable value of the subject intended to be insured, whether the loss be total or partial..."

有关非定值保单是在 Section 28,规定如下:"**28. Unvalued policy** An unvalued policy is a policy which does not specify the value of the subject-matter insured, but subject to the limit of the sum insured, leaves the insurable value to be subsequently ascertained, in the manner herein-before specified."

3.2　定值保单与非定值保单的区别

要进一步解释它们之间的区别还要多节录一条 Section 16 :"**16. Measure of insurable value** Subject to any express provision or valuation in the policy, the insurable value of the subject-matter insured must be ascertained as follows:... (3) In insurance on goods or merchandise, the insurable value is the prime cost of the property insured, plus the expenses of and incidental to shipping and the charges of insurance upon the whole: (4) In insurance on any other subject-matter, the insurable value is the amount at the risk of the assured when the policy attaches, plus the charges of insurance."

Section 16 对于非定值保单是非常重要,它规定了非定值保单下怎样计算可保价值(insurable value),也就是作为保险标的的有关货物的成本价格加上运费再加上保险费,注意是它没有包括利润。至于定值保单,它所根据的就是 Section 16 中"Subject to any express provision or valuation in the policy"在保单中明示约定了可保价值,这省得将来要证明并带来争议,这在 Lloyd's Marine Policy 中是称为约定的保险价值(agreed value [if any])。

这一可保价值针对赔付的计算(measure of indemnity)十分重要,不论是涉及了部分损坏的计算,还是代位求偿向第三人索赔成功后在保险人与受保人之间怎样分摊索赔回来的金额,双重保险下受保人的权利等都会受影响。唯一不受影响的就是全损,因为保险人只需要作出投保金额(amount insured 或 sum insured)的赔付。

这里也需要解释的是法律不要求投保时必须要作出足额保险,受保人完全可以为了节省保费或者向不同的保险人分别作出部分投保。所以,1906 年《英国海上保险法》在 Section 81 有针对这样的情况,并规定:"81. Effect of under insurance　Where the assured is insured for an amount less than the insurable value or, in the case of a valued policy, for an amount less than the policy valuation, he is deemed to be his own insurer in respect of the uninsured balance."

如果定值保单中货物的约定价值是 100 美元,但如果只是投保了 80 美元。根据 Section 27(3),保单中约定的 100 美元将会被视为是决定性的。根据 Section 81 如果发生全损,受保人自己是未足额投保部分(即 20 美元)的保险人,所以保险人只需要赔受保人 80 美元。

不论是全损还是部分损失,如何计算受保人应得的保险赔偿,在定值保单的情况下,公式是:

$$\text{足额投保时可以获得的保险赔偿} \times \frac{\text{投保金额(sum insured)}}{\text{保险价值(agreed value)}}$$

在非定值保单的情况下，公式是：

$$\text{足额投保时可以获得的保险赔偿} \times \frac{\text{投保金额(sum insured)}}{\text{可保价值(insurable value)}}$$ [1]

3.3 定值保险的好处

通过以上的解释就可以了解到绝大部分的海上保险，不论是船舶还是货物都是以定值保单进行投保。对受保人而言，双方同意了保险价值就避免了将来要证明保险标的的可投保金额的麻烦：Lidgett v. Secretan (No. 2) (1871) LR6 CP 616,627。另一个好处是受保人可以把他的利润或是其他会面对的费用（如将来发生损坏要购买替代品的费用）也一并加在约定的保险价值内。例如在先例 The "Maira" (No 2) (1986) 2 Lloyd's Rep 12，船舶向银行作出抵押，融资合约内是要求船东对船舶作出投保而保险价值是融资的130%。船价经常由于航运市场大幅波动而在很短的时间内会有很大差别，这在为期一年的定期保险合约非常普遍。不过对货物保险只是一个航次，加上不少货物也没有市场价格，所以这种价格波动通常就会小得多。显然如果是船舶投保了非定值保险，船舶在发生全损后索赔，可投保价值是要以在风险开始时也就是船舶的价值为准："**16. Measure of insurable value** Subject to any express provision or valuation in the policy, the insurable value of the subject-matter insured must be ascertained as follows: (1) In insurance on ship, the insurable value is the value, **at the commencement of the risk**, of the ship, including her outfit, provisions and stores for the officers and crew, money advanced for seamen's wages, and other disbursements (if any) incurred to make the ship fit for the voyage or adventure contemplated by the policy, plus the charges of insurance upon the whole: The insurable value, in the case of a steamship, includes also the machinery, boilers, and coals and engine stores if owned by the assured, and, in the case of a ship engaged in a special trade, the ordinary fittings requisite for that trade."

不过有可能是船价在那个时间点恰好处于低谷，这会导致受保人的船东所得保险赔偿金额还不够赔偿从银行的融资借贷。

在先例 The "Maira" (No. 2) (1986) 2 Lloyd's Rep 12，银行与船东的融资合约中规定船舶要投保船价的130%。在保单更新时，双方同意的保险价值就要高达1200万美元，而当船舶的市场价值只有487.5万美元，但这样的做法也都是合法。从这个先例大家就可以清楚看到定值保单的好处。

定值保单的保险价值只是保险人与受保人之间的协议，所以不影响第三者。例如针对救助奖金或共同海损的分摊，考虑的是有关船舶或货物还是以事发时的市场

---

[1] 如何确定可投保金额要根据1906年《英国海上保险法》Section 16。

价值(如果有市场的话)或实际价值为准。保险合约内的保险价值不加以考虑。

3.4　可以推翻约定保险价值的情况

定值保单中约定的保险价值(agreed value)是决定性的,这表示将来的保险人或受保人都不可以就此再争辩试图推翻这个金额。根据 Section 27(3),唯一可以再这样做的情况就是存在欺诈。欺诈不容易证明,这方面的案例也不多。其中有一个是 Haigh v. de la Cour (1812) 3 Camp 319,案情涉及了受保人的货方提供了一些虚假的发票与提单引诱保险人同意一个保险价值。另一个比较近期的先例是有关船舶保险:The"Game Boy"(2004) 1 Lloyd's Rep 238。案情涉及了保险人指称受保人的船东引诱他同意 180 万美元的保险价值,并提供了一些虚假的文件、二手船买卖合约、船舶检验报告等说明船舶值这个价钱。

针对定值保单中约定保险价值偏高或者太高,保险人除了欺诈的抗辩外(这并不容易),其实还有另一个抗辩就是受保人在投保的时候应该作出自动披露,而没有对重要的情况作出自动披露,保险人就可以回避保险合约中的责任,这是在 1906 年《英国海上保险法》Section 18。[1]

这一个抗辩在先例 The"Dora"(1989) 1 Lloyd's Rep 69 有针对,Phillips 大法官这样说:"The plaintiffs contend that this provision precludes the defendants from challenging the accuracy of the representation made as to the value of *Dora*. The defendatns submit that the provisions of the Act to which s. 27(3) is subject including s. 18 and s. 20. Whether they are right is a question which does not appear to have been directly convassed in any decided case since the passing of the Act. In *Ionides v. Pender* (1874) LR 9 QB 531, where the validity of a valued polciy on goods was in issue, Mr. Justice Blackburn held that it was open to underwriters to rely upon, as material non-disclosure, the over valuation of the goods. In *Slattery v. Manse* [1962] 1 Lloyd's Rep 60, in a claim for total loss of a yacht under a valued policy, which was tried before Mr. Jutice Salmon and jury, Counsel for the plaintiff appears to have conceded that a material misrepresentation as to value, although not made fraudulently, afforded a good defence to the claim. In my judgment that concession was rightly made. Section 18 and 20 of the Marine Insurance Act cover circumstances where underwriters are entitled to avoid the contract of insurance because the assured has broken the obligation of the utmost good faith. It would be a strange result if a term of the contract itself precluded underwriters from impeaching the contract on such grounds. The 1906 Act was a codifying Act and did not alter the law as applied in *Ionides v. Pender*."

在上文节录中提到了先例 Ionides v. Pender (1874) LR 9 QB 531,现在简单介绍一下该先例。在该案中,货物的实际价值或成本(这也算是可保价值)是大约 8000

---

〔1〕 参见附录一 Section 18(1)。

英镑,但投保的保险金额约定 14,000 英镑。其中一部分货物是酒,成本价是 973 英镑,在保险合约中的约定保险价值是 2800 英镑。受保人解释说酒的保险价值约定这么高的原因是酒的利润非常高。而估值过高构成了没有向保险人披露的实质性事实情况。正如上述所讲 Blackburn 大法官说,保险人是可以以受保人没有履行披露义务为由作为抗辩与拒赔理由。

关于估值过高以至于受保人应该向保险人披露的先例还有 Piper v. Royal Exchange Assurance (1932) 44 Lloyd's Rep 103。该先例中受保人是以 1000 英镑的价格买了艘游艇,并以 2000 英镑的保险价值进行投保。在对保险合约进行延期的时候,受保人将保险价值提高到了 2500 英镑。Roche 大法官判是,受保人在最初买游艇的时候出价就过高,也就是说,游艇当时是不值 1000 英镑,所以从乐观的商业角度来看,最初 2000 英镑的保险价值可以接受,因为这是反映了受保人希望将该游艇以差不多的价格转卖的想法。但是在将保险合约续期之前(这等于是订立另一个新的保险合约),受保人就曾多次试图转卖游艇但都没有成功,在这个过程中,受保人就已经清楚知道 2500 英镑是游艇市场价格的 2 倍,所以在将保险合约续期时 2500 英镑的估值过高的程度太过分(excessive),并且应该披露给保险人。

另外,在先例 Gooding v. White (1913) 29 TLR 312 中,保险标的的实质价值仅仅是 2000 英镑,但约定的保险价值是 5000 英镑。Pickford 大法官是判,没有必要看估值过高是否构成保险欺诈,或者估值过高仅仅是对保险标的利润的不合理估计;反正是估值过高已经达到过分的程度,所以不论估值过高的原因是什么,都需要披露给保险人。

由于在现实中约定的保险价值都会比保险标的的市场价格高,这里就存在一个问题,也就是如何确定一条分水线,超过了受保人就应该向保险人披露。这方面在先例 The"Grecia Express"(2002) EWHC 203 (Comm)有指引,案情是涉及了保险人指称管理人在为船舶投保时估值过高太过分,Colman 大法官这样说:"... where the proposed value is consistent with reasonably prudent ship management, the excess over market value cannot be material to the risk, whatever its precise extent. **That which would render the overvaluation material would be the want of any reasonable explanation for the disparity consistent with prudent ship management**. Accordingly, in cases where a reasonable explanation is established the true market value does not have to be disclosed."

另外,Colman 大法官也提到说:"It is only where the disparity [between the agreed and market values] cannot be justified on reasonable commercial grounds that it ought to be disclosed."

由此可以看出,只要保险标的如货物是有合理商业理由可以解释为什么提高约定的保险价值,这就不需要自动作出披露。

3.5 保险价值是保险人要作出赔付的最高金额,即使保险人延误赔付

要强调的就是在定值保单,双方约定的保险价值就是在全损时要赔付的数额。即使保险人处理不当或延误赔付,也不存在受保人的货方可以提出额外的保险合约

索赔。如保险标的是机器,由于晚了赔付保险金而导致生产上的损失,这种损失是不能加在定值保单约定的赔偿金额内。这与美国的地位是不一样:Salamey v. Aetna Casualty and Surety Company (1984) 741 Federal Reporter 2nd series 874。在英国,定值保单约定的赔偿金额相当于合约中的议定赔偿(liquidated damage),只要发生全损,赔了议定赔偿金额也就是全部需要支付的金钱。关于议定赔偿在笔者其他的书籍也有详论,如《装卸时间与滞期费》第592页开始的论述与介绍一些重要的先例如 Suisse Atlantique v. N V Rotterdamsche (1966) 1 Lloyd's Rep. 529,请参阅。

这方面可举先例 The"Italia Express"(No. 2) (1992) 2 Lloyd's Rep 281,Hirst 大法官是说:"I consider that the starting point in this marine insurance case is s. 67 of the Act. In my judgment, this section, together with s. 68 in total loss cases, is conclusively definitive of the extent of the liability of the insurer for loss of the vessel under a valued policy. I am unable to accept Mr. Tomlinson's (受保人的代表大律师) submission that this statutory limitation only applies during the necessarily very brief period of, at most, a day or two between the demand (which, on his theory, for the first time brings into existence the underwriters' primary liability to indemnify the assured under the policy) and the non-payment in immediate response to the demand (which, on his theory, for the first time brings into existence the underwriters' primary liability to indemnify the assured under the policy) and the non-payment in immediate response to the demand (which, on his theory, is the breach giving rise to a claim for damages at large not restricted by the Act). This, in itself, is sufficient to defeat Mr. Tomlinson's argument in marine insurance cases."

显然,保险人在应该赔付的时候不赔付造成延误,受保人可以在延误的期间获得利息。但利息是属于程序法,而不是保险合约的合约赔偿(contractual claim)。

这种争议在岸上的保险合约也经常发生,法律地位对受保人也好不了太多。毕竟是保险人如果延误赔付会给受保人带来不便或对其生意上的干预(如 Sprung v. Royal Insurance [1999] Lloyd's Rep IR 111),或需要在等待赔付损坏车辆赔偿的期间另外租用替代的车辆(Charles Griffin & Co Ltd v. De-La-Haye [1968] 2 Lloyd's Rep 253)等。这也说明了有些受保人在及时得到保险人的赔付后在报纸上刊登感谢信也不是没有理由的。

以下可用《Colinvaux's Law of Insurance in Hong Kong》一书之10.022段中的一句话作总结:"Whatever the position might be in property and other non-marine insurance law, it would seem that there is even less possibility of late payment of a marine claim giving rise to additional damages. In Ventouris v Mountain [1992] 2 Lloyd's Rep 281, the assured claimed from his insurers additional damages by way of distress and hardship, flowing from the failure of the insurers to make prompt payment. Hirst J rejected the claim; and held that the insurer's failure to make payment was immaterial as the insurer was in breach of contract and liable for unliquidated damages as from the date of the casualty, and that damages had to be assessed as at that date. That point aside, there was nothing in the Marine Insurance Ordinance which indicated that any further damages could be recovered."

据闻,英国目前是在研究立法要求保险人必须在合理时间内作出赔付,否则要作出赔偿延误的损失。这一来就等于是改变普通法的地位,而显然立法的主要原因就是为了保护一般受保人不会受到保险人的拖延或刁难。由于这个立法的时间还早,所以笔者无法知道这一最终会成为法律的条文是否会影响海上货物保险或只是局限在保护在英国的消费者。

3.6 海上货物保险通常采用定值保单

海上货物保险基本上都是采用定值保单,受保人与保险人会在保单上面写明保险价值。这一价值就是货物的到岸价格(CIF 价格),再加上 10% 的估计利润。货物的到岸价格一般很容易证明,以 CIF 买卖过程中开出的发票或者买卖合约就可以。至于 FOB 的情况下就会需要提供其他一些运输费用的证明,如租约。至于 10% 的估计利润假设如果货物安全到了目的地,受保人肯定是想要赚钱才会做这个买卖,而合理的利润空间是 10% 。如果货物不能够安全抵达目的地,例如全损,在足额保险的前提下,受保人可以从保险人那里得到 CIF 价格再加上 10% 的利润的保险赔偿。另是,这 10% 的提升除了利润外,也包括了如果发生事故要找替代货物的额外费用。Incoterms 2000 CIF A3 就规定卖方要为货物投保的最小保险金额是 CIF 价格另加 10% 。当然在订约自由的前提下,最终要加多少个百分比的合理利润空间看买卖双方谈判的结果。而这种谈判也只发生在 CIF 买卖,因为是由卖方投保,而货物不能安全抵达目的地承受利润损失的是买方。所以如果买方有更高的估计利润,需要在买卖合约中明确约定卖方需要为 30% 的利润投保,但也可能只要求卖方投保 10% 的利润,剩下 20% 的利润买方自己投保。这方面在本书第三章第 3.6 段已经有针对。

在海上货物保险中,非定值保单的情况极端少见,一种情况会是在开口/预约保单的情况下迟延宣告(在先例 The"Beursgracht"[2002] 1 Lloyd's Rep 574 受保人就是 7 年宣告),双方还没有机会约定保险价值。相关的条文是 1906 年《英国海上保险法》之 Section 29(4)"Unless the policy otherwise provides, where a declaration of value is not made until after notice of loss or arrival, the policy must be treated as an unvalued policy as regards the subject-matter of that declaration."

在先例 Harman v. Kingston (1811) 3 Camp 150,受保人的雇员是作出了一张有关付运的货物的书面宣告,但这宣告被延误递交,直到货物发生损失之后才出示给了保险人。Ellenborough 勋爵说:"where there is an insurance on goods, as may be thereafter declared and valued, this gives the assured a power, by duly declaring and valuing before the loss, to make it a valued policy; but that if the assured do not so declare and value, it is then an open policy, and the interest is a matter of evidence at the trial."

这先例的法律地位也反映在 1906 年《英国海上保险法》Section 29(4)。这就是如果在损失发生前,受保人不论是迟延宣告或是原来宣告的保险价值有错误,都可以作出纠正或补充,令有关的保险合约变为是定值保险。但如果是在损失发生后才宣告保险价值,有关的保险合约就会是非定值保险,就需要根据1906年《英国海上保险法》Section 16通过证据来证明保险标的的可保价值(insurable value),这也是在足额保险的情况下发生全损时保险人要赔付的金额。

4. 货物损失或损坏的赔偿原则

本章接下来介绍的就是货物部分损失或损坏的赔偿原则与计算方法(measure of indemnity)。货物部分损失/损坏分别出现在三种情况:(1)部分货物的全损,如同一票货的10个集装箱有1个掉落海中;(2)货物在损坏的情况下运到目的地;(3)货物由于中途的事故而被迫出售,因为修复然后续运到目的地并不划算。

这三种情况都有不同的赔偿计算方法,其中第一种与第二种是由1906年《英国海上保险法》的有关条文针对,但第三种就没有立法条文针对。

4.1　部分损坏情况之一:部分货物的全损(Total loss of part of the cargo)

4.1.1　定值保单下部分货物的全损保险赔偿的计算

1906年《英国海上保险法》的有关条文如下:"**71. Partial loss of goods, merchandise, etc.** Where there is a partial loss of goods, merchandise or other moveables, the measure of indemnity, subject to any express provision in the policy, is as follows: (1) Where part of the goods, merchandise or other moveables insured by a valued policy is totally lost, the measure of indemnity is **such** proportion of **the sum fixed by the policy** as **the insurable value of the part lost** bears to **the insurable value of the whole**, ascertained as in the case of an unvalued policy."

这条文是有关在定值保险的情况下部分货物发生了全损时,保险赔偿的计算方法。由于保单中只会写明全部货物约定的保险价值(agreed value),而不会写明部分货物约定的保险价值,在部分货物发生全损的情况下,根据Section 71(1),要算出它的约定的保险价值就要先看该全损的部分货物的可保价值(insurable value)占全部货物可保价值的比例,然后用全部货物约定的保险价值乘以该比例算出该部分货物的约定的保险价值。例如,如果一票货90台电脑,CIF价格每台100美元,平均装在三个集装箱内。约定的保险价值是9900美元(包括10%的预期利润)。如果一个集装箱掉落大海导致30台电脑全损,保险赔偿的计算方法是:用30台电脑的可保价值(根据Section 16[3]就是In insurance on goods or merchandise, the insurable value is the prime cost of the property insured, plus the expenses of and incidental to shipping and the charges of insurance upon the whole。在该例子中即30台电脑的CIF价格)3000美元除以全部货物的CIF价格9000美元得出比例1/3;然后用9900美元乘以1/3就得到最终受保人获得的保险赔偿,也就是3300美元。

如果约定的保险价值是另一个金额，如约定的保险价值是 10,350 美元（以 15% 的预期利润投保），这部分全损的 90 台电脑就要赔 3450 美元了。

4.1.2 非定值保单下部分货物的全损保险赔偿的计算

这是规定在 Section 71(2)，如下："Where part of the goods, merchandise, or other moveables insured by an unvalued policy is totally lost, the measure of indemnity is the insurable value of the part lost, ascertained **as in case of total loss.**"

因为 Section71(2) 是提到了"**as in case of total loss**"，而根据 Section 68(2)"Subject to the provisions of this Act and to any express provision in the policy, where there is a total loss of the subject-matter insured ... (2) If the policy be an unvalued policy, the measure of indemnity is the insurable value of the subject-matter insured."

在保险标的全损的情况下，赔偿金额就是保险标的的可保价值，也就是 CIF 价格。非定值保单下部分货物的全损保险赔偿也就是货物的 CIF 价格。在上述所举的例子中如果是非定值保单，保险赔偿就是 3000 美元。

4.1.3 定值保单下不同种类/等级的货物共同投保，部分货物全损时保险赔偿的计算

举例就是 9000 包 3 个不同等级的咖啡被装进了 3 个集装箱，总共约定的保险价值是 99,000 美元。假设装着 300 包最高等级咖啡的集装箱掉落大海。在这种情况下，1906 年《英国海上保险法》Section 72 就会适用。[1]

假设 A 等级每包咖啡的 CIF 价格是 110 美元，B 等级每包咖啡的 CIF 价格是 100 美元，C 等级每包咖啡的 CIF 价格是 90 美元。那么掉落大海咖啡的 CIF 价格（也就是可保价值）就是 33,000 美元，而所有咖啡的 CIF 价格（也就是可投保价值）就是 90,000（110 × 300 + 100 × 300 + 90 × 300）美元。那么 99,000 美元的保险价值在三个等级咖啡中的分配比例将会是：

A 等级 33,000/90,000 = 11/30

B 等级 30,000/90,000 = 10/30

C 等级 27,000/90,000 = 9/30

所以所占的保险价值：

A 等级 99,000 × (11/30) = 36,300

B 等级 99,000 × (10/30) = 33,000

C 等级 99,000 × (9/30) = 29,700

所以 A 等级咖啡的集装箱掉进海里，受保人可以得到的保险赔偿是 36,300 美元。现实当中严格依照 1906 年《英国海上保险法》Section 16(3) 的要求找出货物的成本价格（prime cost）不是很容易。《Rules of Practice of the Association of Average Adjusters》就规定该成本价格可以用发票价格（invoice value）来确定。1906 年《英国海

---

[1] 参见附录一 Section 72(1)。

上保险法》Section 72(2)就规定了另外一种成本价格的确定方法:"Where a valuation has to be apportioned, and particulars of the prime cost of each separate species, quality, or description of goods cannot be ascertained, the division of the valuation may be made **over the net arrived sound values of the different species, qualities, or descriptions of goods.**"而《Rules of Practice of the Association of Average Adjusters》的 Rule E 是规定成本价格可以用,但只有在没有发票价格的情况。

4.2 部分损坏情况之二:货物在有损坏的情况下运到目的地(Cargo delivered damaged at destination)

4.2.1 比例方法计算与直接扣减的区别与法律地位

这种情况在 Section 71 是有规定,如下:"**71. Partial loss of goods, merchandise, etc** Where there is a partial loss of goods, merchandise or other moveables, the measure of indemnity, subject to any express provision in the policy, is as follows:...(3) Where the whole or any part of the goods or merchandise insured has been delivered damaged at its destination, the measure of indemnity is such proportion of the sum fixed by the policy in the case of a valued policy, or of the insurable value in the case of an unvalued policy, as the difference between the **gross** sound and damaged values at the place of arrival bears to the **gross** sound value..."

简单地说,要算出货物在有损坏的情况下运到目的地,受保人可以得到的保险赔偿就要先算出在目的地,货物完好情况下的总价值(gross sound value,简称 GSV)与损坏货物价值(gross damaged value ,简称 GDV)之差占货物完好情况下的总价值的比例,然后用该比例乘以定值保单下的约定保险价值(agreed value,简称 AV),或者是用该比例乘以非定值保单下的可保价值(insurable value,简称 IV)。用公式表示就是:

$$\text{AV 或 IV} \times \frac{(\text{GSV} - \text{GDV})}{\text{GSV}}$$

这种"比例方法"计算保险赔偿金额主要的目的是不想受到货物市场价格波动的影响,因为有许多商品会有市场而且波动幅度很大。在本书第七章也介绍过市场波动产生的损失是非实质性的经济损失,除非是像共同海损费用分摊与续运费用等有明示规定是在承保范围内,保险人对非实质性的经济损失一概不赔。所以,如果仅是赔 GSV 与 GDV 的差额,从表面上看是赔付了受保人的真正损失,但实际上这种方法使得受保人的赔付很大程度上受市场波动的影响。

以下可再举一个简单的例子说明比例方法计算会更容易明白:10,000 吨小麦在海上航行途中被海水损坏,损坏程度是50%。每吨小麦的 CIF 价格是100 美元,小麦的 CIF 总价值就是 100 万美元。被海水浸泡过的小麦最终在目的地以每吨 50 美元的价格被出售,总共是 50 万美元。所以从 CIF 价格的角度看受保人是损失了 **50 万美元**,则保险人赔付的金额就是 50 万美元,这是第一种计算方法。

如果把保险合约中小麦的约定保险价值一并考虑,保险价值是 150 万美元,受保人就会希望保险人赔付给他 **100 万美元**,就是保险价值减去受损小麦出售所得。

如果小麦在当时的市场价格波动很大,就更加会得出另外的损失数字。首先是市场价格上升,连被海水损坏导致受损程度高达 50% 的小麦也可以在目的地以 120 美元每吨出售。这样保险人就只须赔给受保人 **30 万美元**,就是保险价值(150 万美元)减去受损小麦出售所得(120 万美元)。

再换个情况是市场价格大幅度下跌,被海水损坏导致受损程度 50% 的小麦在目的地以 20 美元每吨出售,受保人就会向保险人要求赔付 **130 万美元**,就是保险价值(150 万美元)减去受损小麦出售所得(20 万美元)。

显然在上述四种计算方法下,后两种涉及市场波动带来的影响,这是保险人不想承担的风险,显然不是可以接受的赔偿损失计算方法:Lewis v. Rucker (1761) Burr 1167。

至于第一种的计算方法,问题是纯粹考虑货物的 CIF 价格,但根本没有考虑保险合约的保险价值,看来也是有不可取的地方。毕竟受保人是会根据约定的保险价值高低支付保费,如果纯粹考虑 CIF 价格,受保人多付或少付保费都不会影响最后能够获得的赔付。

至于第二种的计算方法,这是直接扣减,这种计算在先例 Lewis v. Rucker (1761) Burr 1167 是有争议,但最后还没有被英国法院接受。法院支持的是保险人提出的比例方法计算,也就是上述的公式 。

这种按比例方法的计算就能够与保险合约中约定的保险价值(这可能比 CIF 价值高得多,只要这一个差额是有合理的商业原因)联系起来。而 1906 年《英国海上保险法》Section 71(3)的立法也是根据该先例规定要用比例方法计算。

在先例 Lewis v. Rucker (1761) 2 Burr 1167 中,投保的货物是白糖、咖啡还有 indigo(找不到该货物的中文译名),这批货物从 St Thomas 开往汉堡的航次中遭受了海水的浸泡。白糖每桶的保险价值是 30 英镑。被浸泡过的白糖在进一步融化前必须立即卖掉。由于德国有望签订和平条约并有放宽贸易限制的消息传出,白糖的市场价格大幅度下跌到每桶 23 英镑。而被浸泡过的白糖只是卖到了每桶 20 美元。可以看到市场价格的下跌是造成了受保人的货方大部分的损失。而海水造成的损失相对来说是很小,3 英镑除以 30 英镑的保险价值,也就是 10% 的贬值(depreciation)。在受保人向保险人提出诉讼要求赔付的中途,保险人存钱进法院(这一个程序是在法院诉讼中被告愿意支付一定的金额,但原告不接受以致要继续诉讼,被告可以此来保护自己之后的诉讼费用,因为将来法院判决的金额是低于或等于这笔存款的话,原告是要支付之后的所有诉讼费用),数额就是根据以下的公式计算:

$$30\text{ 英镑 (AV)} \times \frac{23\text{ 英镑(GSV)} - 20\text{ 英镑 (GDV)}}{23\text{ 英镑(GSV)}}$$

而这种计算方法是被一群由商人组成的陪审团支持(英国在当时即使在民事或

商事诉讼也是由陪审团认定事实,这种做法已经早有了改变,现在涉及民事或商事诉讼都是由法官进行事实认定与法律判定,只有刑事案件才会由陪审团认定事实)。而这些陪审团成员被 Mansfield 大法官称赞说"understood the question very well and knew more of the subject of it than anybody else present."

而受保人还是争辩,说应该采用直接扣减的方法,也就是用保险价值减去受损货物的出售价值,也就是每桶 30 英镑减去 20 英镑,应该赔偿 10 英磅。他的争辩理由是如果白糖没有被损坏,他就可以等到市场再度上涨才出售。而事实上对运往阿姆斯特丹的白糖,受保人确实是这么做的,并且是后来卖到了每桶 30 英镑甚至更高的价钱。受保人说在汉堡将白糖处理掉是海水浸泡直接导致的,并且海水浸泡也使白糖失去了推迟等待市场回升的可能,所以该损失是由承保的风险导致。乍一听,这种争辩是很有说服力。不过 Mansfield 大法官最终还是认为陪审团的计算方法更可取。他解释说保险人的赔付责任在受损的货物到达与卸到岸上的时候产生,也就是现在根据协会货物条文第 8 条规定当保险期间终止时,计算损失赔偿也应该是以这个时间为准。如果把将来会可能出现的市场价格的变化也考虑在内会是有太多投机性(speculative)与不肯定(uncertain),而且因果关系(causation)也不容易判断。例如,即使白糖市场回升至每桶 30 英镑,但受保人看市场还会继续上涨而继续等待,但随即市场暴跌,这里就涉及了受保人自己的决定在市场投机,导致了因果关系中断。也是这个原因,在用一般合约法的原则计算损失赔偿,如果是有市场的话就根据著名的"违约当天如果有市场的话,就以当天的市场价格为准与合约价格比较"(breach date rule),也是同样的道理。

根据 1906 年《英国海上保险法》Section 71(3)中的措辞"or of the insurable value in the case of an unvalued policy"可以看出,非定值保单下货物在有损坏的情况下运到目的地,计算方法也都相同,只不过定值保单中约定的保险价值是被非定值保单中的可保价值替换,如只是货物在发票中显示的 CIF 价格。

4.2.2 比例方法计算下的"到达价值方法"

在介绍了计算的方法之后,就要对更细节的东西说清楚。在 Section 71(3)中有一个措辞是总价值"gross value"。这在 1906 年《英国海上保险法》Section 71(4)有具体定义。[1]

在这个定义下,总价值代表批发(wholesale)的价格。如果没有批发价格,就以货物的估计价值为准。不论是批发价格或者估计价值,已经产生了的运费、港口卸货费用与港口税收要另外加上,因为不花这些钱是不能把有关的货物运到目的地港。不过要注意的是,根据 Section71(4)中的"beforehand"一词,如果港口税收与费用在后来有了变动(这会影响货物价值),在计算时不予考虑:Johnson v. Seddon (1802) 2 East 581。

---

〔1〕 能见附录一 Section 71(4)。

如果有关的货物是习惯性在存入海关待完税时就出售(sale in bond),该出售价格就被视为总价值。

在现实中,因为有些货物没有市场,或者即使有市场也是非常狭窄,完好货物与有损坏的货物的市场价格是不容易获得或确定。在先例 Whiting v. New Zealand Insurance Company (1932) 44 Lloyd's Rep 179,受保人从神户进口了一种特别类型的巴拿马帽子到伦敦。而其中的部分货物在日本码头等待装船的时候遭受了湿损。当时这些很特别的帽子没有市场,不过法院还是接受受保人提供的证据证明他曾经之前在英国以每打 1 英镑的价钱出售了这些帽子,而可以据此确定完好货物的到达价格。不过值得注意的是,根据先例 Francis v. Boulton (1895) 1 Com Cas 217,有损坏的货物的市场价格可以通过真正的出售取得,而完好货物的市场价格是要根据有损坏的货物出售那天来确定。这两个先例的区别可能就是因为前者货物没有市场,但后者货物有市场造成的。

在实务当中,也许有损坏的货物对受保人来讲还是有用,没有必要出售。这样的话,仅仅为了保险赔偿的计算而将损坏的货物出售确实没必要。而为了出售肯定要产生一些费用。因此在没有现成的市场时,受保人与保险人通常是会对货物的贬值比例(a percentage depreciation)达成和解。并且即使有时是有现成的市场,受保人与保险人也会这样做,从而简化保险赔偿的计算。

Section 71(3)&(4)都仅仅是提到了"goods or merchandise",而不像 Section 71 最开始一句与 Section 71(1)中也包括了"moveables"。而 Section 90 就说明了"moveables"指的是任何可以移动的财产,包括货币、有价证券还有其他的文件但不包括船舶。毫无疑问,即便是货物没有市场或者是没有现成的市场,Section 71(3)中规定计算方法也都适用。因为 Section 75(1)规定了:"**75. General provisions as to measure of indemnity** (1) Where there has been a loss in respect of any subject-matter not expressly provided for in the foregoing provisions of this Act, the measure of indemnity shall be ascertained, as nearly as may be, in accordance with those provisions, in so far as applicable to the particular case."

该 Section 75 是针对保险赔偿计算的一些原则性规定。根据 Section 75(1),不论保险标的的性质是什么,只要可能,都是要根据完好货物与有损坏货物在到达目的地时的价格来计算,这也就是所谓的"到达价值方法"(arrived value approach)。

4.2.3 针对机器或者设备的"协会替换条文"

这会带来另外一个潜在的问题:就是如果保险标的是机器或者设备,某部分或者是某个零件损坏,机器本身因为损坏而贬值的部分会大大超过替换或修理的费用。因此,如果保险标的是机器,保险合约会合并与采用"协会替换条文"(Institute Replacement Clause),而根据该条文,保险赔偿是不应该超过替换或者是修理该部分的费用。并且这样的问题不仅是机器才会有,几乎所有的制成品物件(如电脑、电子产品、技术产品等)都存在同样的问题。而这也就导致了 2008 年 12 月 1 日 Institute Replacement Clause 的修改版本的出台,如下:

"**Institute replacement clause**

In the event of loss of or damage to any part(s) of an insured machine or other manufactured item consisting of more than one part caused by a peril covered by this insurance, **the sum recoverable shall not exceed the cost of replacement or repair of such part(s) plus labor for (re)fitting and carriage costs**. Duty incurred in the provision of replacement or repaired part(s) shall also be recoverable provided that the full duty payable on the insured machine or manufactured item is included in the amount insured.

The total liability of Insurers shall in no event exceed the amount insured of the machine or manufactured item."

该条文所起到的作用就是,保险人在机器或类似的保险标的发生部分货损时可以不受 Section 71(3)中规定的赔偿方法的约束,从而给保险人以保护。同时该条文对基于修理费用的保险索赔也有调整作用。比如,以空运的方式运送备件换下损坏的零件(为了确保损坏更快地得到修理)当然会产生很高昂的运输费用,而这笔费用根据该条文也都不会在保险赔偿的范围内。因为根据协会货物条文 4.5 条,延误带来的损失是不在承保的范围内,那么为了避免延误而产生的费用当然也就不在承保的范围内了。

4.2.4　针对废旧机器/设备的"协会替换条文"

而就在 2008 年 12 月 1 日 Institute Replacement Clause 的修改版本出台的同时,Institute Replacement Clause - Proportional Valuation 也出台供货物保险市场适用。与前者相比,后者措辞上的不同是:"... the sum recoverable shall not exceed such proportion of the cost of replacement or repair of such part(s) as the amount insured bears to **the new cost of the machine or manufactured item**."

举例说明该条款的合理性:保险标的是受保人要处理的废旧机器与/或生产线上的设备,而换上新的零部件的费用可能是大大超过保险标的的处理价格。现实中,不少机器的零部件卖得很贵,这也是生产商赚取最大利润的一种手法。就是原来的机器/设备是很便宜甚至是半卖半送,但之后的零件却狮子大开口,且非买不可,因为有专利保护。这种情况下,由于废旧机器或设备的保险价值会很低,导致保费收入也都会很低,那么保费与换上新的与昂贵的零部件的费用将会非常不成比例。

同时有一种批注是可以加在这两种 Replacement Clause 的货物保险合约内,以适用在保险标的是完全过时的机器(如该机器因为型号陈旧已经是完全停止生产,导致了零部件也不会再生产,使得很难找到相配的零部件,或者即使找到价格也很高)。这个批注是将保险赔偿限制在生产商最后一年生产该被损坏的零部件时的报价单上的价格[manufacturer's list price for the last year of manufacture of the lost or damaged part(s)]。而这个价格是可以根据零售价格指数(retail price index)显示的通胀程度上调。

4.3　部分损坏情况之三:损坏货物中途被迫出售后的损失(salvage losses)

在本书第七章第5段有介绍,由于货物在中途遇到事故而使得航次终止(loss of adventure)(不论当时货物是否有实质的损坏)会带来全损或部分损失。真正全损(actual total loss)在货物根本去不了保险合约目的地的情况下,就会有可能出现。至于推定全损(constructive total loss),情况会是货物的实质性损坏只属于部分损坏(partial loss),但如果将货物中途修复后再续运到目的地的费用是比该货物的到达价值还要高。显然在这种情况下,如果受保人没有投保,他也是不会将受损的货物续运到目的港。

有关这一方面请看本书第七章第5段。这种情况也在协会货物条文第13条有规定:"Constructive Total Loss 13. No claim for Constructive Total Loss shall be recoverable hereunder unless the subject-matter insured is reasonably abandoned either on account of its actual total loss appearing to be unavoidable or because the cost of recovering, reconditioning and forwarding the subject-matter insured to the destination to which it is insured would exceed its value on arrival."

既然是推定全损受保人就需要把部分受损的货物委付/抛弃(abandon)给保险人,这等于是把该货物的所有权交给保险人以换取保险人同意赔付定额保单中的约定保险价值给受保人。这样的话,保险人如果接受委付/抛弃,就会获得受损货物的所有权,并且可以将它在当地或附近安排出售,出售所得金钱是可被称为"损坏货物出售收益"(salvage proceeds),收益肯定是归保险人所有,这等于是代位求偿(subrogation)。

但经常会是保险人不接受委付通知(notice of abandonment),并通常会告诉受保人说"你最好自己作为没有投保的谨慎货方作出合理处理该批受损货物"(to act as a prudent uninsured cargo owner)。这一来,如果有可能这样做,受保人就会在当地将受损的货物出售,以免损失进一步扩大。由于受保人在这样做时,保险人的检验师也在场的话,就很少会有争议说这不是最好的处理方法。之后受保人就可以向保险人提出索赔,而索赔的金额就是约定的保险价值与受保人出售所得的差额,这部分金钱可被称为"损坏货物出售后的损失"(salvage loss)。

这里就带来了一种不协调的情况,而这也是没有办法解决。这发生在货物市场价格上升,而且上升的幅度比货物损坏的程度为大,可以用以下的例子说明。货物可以同样是一批10,000吨小麦,每吨CIF价值是100美元,保险价值是1,100,000美元(CIF价格加上10%的合理利润)。假设是通过货物出售,小麦的受损程度是保险价值的25%,但在目的地市场价格是上升了30%,也就是每吨130美元。这样的话,损坏货物到达目的地后把受损而贬值25%的小麦出售,受保人可以获得975,000美元(10,000吨×130美元×75%)。

而受保人根据保险合约向保险人索赔,根据本章第4.2.1与4.2.2段所介绍的比例方法计算下的"到达价值方法",应该是1,100,000美元(保险价值)×25%(损坏贬值)=27,5000 美元。

这两笔钱加起来,受保人可以获得的总金额是 975,000 美元 + 275,000 美元 = **1,250,000 美元。**

上述是受损货物到达目的地的情况,但如果本章所针对的货物由于中途的事故而被迫出售(salvage losses),根本没有到达目的地,就变为以航次终止的推定全损向保险人索赔。在全损的情况下,由于约定的保险价值被视为议定赔偿金额,所以保险人只需要支付 **1,100,000 美元**。至于受损贬值货物所出售的钱,也就是 975,000 美元,由于保险人赔付了全损,这笔钱根据委付/抛弃的原则是归保险人而不是受保人。

从以上的计算就已经可以看出两种不同计算方法所得出的赔偿金额并不一致,虽然一种情况是货物到达目的地,而另一种情况是货物没有到达目的地。但这仍是属于不协调的情况,毕竟对受保人而言,反正货物受到损坏,但他所能获得保险人的损失赔偿却得出不同的计算结果,而差别纯粹是在航次中途或是到了目的地。在现实中,还会出现航次中途实际上已经非常接近目的地的情况,这就更加显示了不同计算方法出现的差别的不合理。

这里也涉及向船东成功索赔把损失取回来应该怎样在保险人与受保人之间分摊的问题。不论是部分损失或者是全损,保险人都会享有代位求偿权(subrogation)。但代位求偿权的行使只是让保险人向第三人取回他所赔付给受保人的金钱作为最高的标准,而如果第三人赔付的金钱超出了,这部分的钱是要退还给受保人。这一来,在货物由于中途事故而变为推定全损的情况下,而且事故是船舶有责任,保险人在赔付了推定全损后就会以代位求偿权向船东提出索赔。但索赔的金额不会是保险价值的 1,100,000 美元,因为这只是保险人与受保人之间的约定并不约束第三人。准确的索赔金额应该就是该批 10,000 吨小麦完好的情况下抵达目的地的市场价值,也就是由于市场价格上涨了的 1,300,000 美元。这表示保险人根据代位求偿权向船东成功索赔后,只能自己保留 1,100,000 美元,而多出来的 200,000 美元就应该退还给受保人。

一个变数是如果不是以代位求偿权的形式行使向船东提出违约的索赔,而是根据转让(assignment)把向船东的索赔权从受保人转给保险人。这一来,如果成功向船东索赔 1,300,000 美元,这笔钱就会全部归保险人所有。这方面的问题在本书第十三章第 7 段有介绍,不去重复。

5. 绝对免赔额(deductible)与相对免赔额(franchise)

保险人一贯以来对一些微小的损失不愿意作出赔偿,原因有三个:(1)行政费用且麻烦作出调查与赔付,经济上不划算;(2)有一些货物的损失难以决定是什么原因造成,可能承保的风险,但也可能内在缺陷;(3)如果有部分损失,是停留在受保人的头上,这会有间接的作用,希望令受保人小心以避免损失。

上述的三个原因，前两个与海上货物保险的关系比较密切，但第三个应该与海上货物保险关系不大，因为货方很多时候是控制不到海上货物的运输，而这与船舶保险的关系就比较大。

这种做法很早的时候就已经出现在劳合社标准 S. G. 保单，它在最后的部分有一句话名为 Memorandum，内容是"Corn, fish, fruit, flour, and seed are warranted free from average, unless general, or the ship be stranded—sugar, tobacco, hemp, flax, hides and skins are warranted free from average, under five pounds per cent, and all other goods, also the ship and freight, are warranted free from average, under three pounds per cent unless general, or the ship be stranded."

1983 年之后，众所周知劳合社标准 S. G. 保单不再被使用，而 Memorandum 也不再被使用。今天的海上保险合约不论是船舶还是货物，都会有免赔额条款。如在开口/预约保单（open cover）会约定"Deductible:USMYM 500 each and every loss"。这种免赔额都属于一种"绝对免赔额"（台湾称"自负额"），这就是在赔付损失的时候一定要扣除这笔钱，作为受保人自己愿意承担的第一层损失（first layer of loss）。这与 Memorandum 的"相对免赔额"不一样，它是在损失如果超过了相对免赔额就赔付全部的损失，不作任何的扣减。换言之，相对免赔额起到的作用只是在索赔微小的时候节省行政费用。绝对免赔额是 1969 年才正式引入协会船壳保险条款的，此前标准条款规定的是相对免赔额，虽然在当时的实务中也少量存在绝对免赔额的约定。20 世纪 70 年代后，绝对免赔额迅速成为普遍的做法，相对免赔额在海上保险中已十分罕见。

绝对免赔额针对船舶保险是一个相当重要的课题，特别是就近年来有船东接受很高的免赔额以节省保费，这做法接近对部分损失/损坏，部分船东自保。在笔者与汪鹏南教授合著的《英国海上保险条款详论》一书的第二章关于免赔额条款有详细介绍，有兴趣的读者可以参阅。

最后要一提的是如果将来向第三人追偿成功部分的损失，根据著名的贵族院先例 Napier and Ettrick (Lord) v. Kershaw (1993) 1 Lloyd's Rep 197 的"从上到下"的补偿原则（关于该原则在本书第十三章第 13.3 段有详细介绍），将这些钱在受保人与保险人之间分配时，绝对免赔额在优先次序上被放在最后，追偿回来的金钱首先满足的是保险人赔付的部分。

6. 开口/预约保单的赔付限额

货物保险合约除了投保金额（sum insured）作为该保单最高的赔付限制外，另在开口保单/预约保单也有一个赔付限额，针对的就是一个比较大的损失发生在一个地点或者一次的付运，如这样的措辞"MYM1,000,000 any one sending, shipment and/or location"。

这是由于一些国际贸易商会把所有在一个年度的买卖与付运都通过一个开口/预约保单投保,并在每一次付运时向保险人作出宣告(事前或事后)。这一来,保险人会关心的是风险过度集中而导致灾难性的赔付,如在一次付运的货物价值太高,或在有几批不同货物同时集中在同一个装港等待付运,或是有几批货物同时抵达同一个卸港。造成这种情况可以有很多不同的原因,如受保人为了做生意赚钱而做出一个不恰当的调度与安排。也可以是如第十三章第 16.6.4 段中提到的先例 The Niger Co Ltd v. The Guardian Insurance Co Ltd (1920) 4 Lloyd's Rep 320 中因为河水上涨适合河道运输与战争的原因导致找不到船舶及时付运,使得大批货物在装港等待。这种情况对保险人很危险且麻烦,加上保险人通常会再保,如赔付限额 100 万美元其中 80 万美元买了 excess of loss 再保险。

约定这一赔付的限额是可以提高,但开口/预约保单就会要求受保人续保(held covered),也就是发生了这种风险过度集中情况必须马上通知保险人,另支付加保费,可让保险人在市场马上作出选择性再保险(facultative reinsurance)。

这种赔付限额不应该被视为不足额保险(under insurance),针对不足额保险在本书第十三章第 13 段有介绍。这是因为在不足额保险的情况下,赔付会是按比例而不是按足额的损失。这在 1906 年《英国海上保险法》Section 81 :"**EFFECT OF UNDER INSURANCE** Where the assured is insured for an amount less than the insurable value or, in the case of a valued policy, for an amount less than the policy valuation, he is deemed to be his own insurer in respect of the uninsured balance."

但看来还没有这方面的先例,所以只节录 John Dunt 所著的《Marine Cargo Insurance》一书 2009 年版之 15.35 段是说:"This book takes the view that a limit does not create under-insurance as the assured has paid the full premium, or rate on line, and that section 81 should not therefore apply to a partial loss occasioned by the application of a policy limit."显然 John Dunt 先生主要的依据是保险人的保费已经是完全收足,所以就没有道理以不足额保险按比例少一点赔付。

以下可举例怎样计算,首先就是假设开口/预约保单下有 100 万美元的赔付限制:"MYM1,000,000 any one sending, shipment and/or location"。如果有两票不同的货物集中在一起,每票的价值都是 75 万美元。而受保人也为这两票货物支付了足额的保费,或是根据约定的保费费率支付按照实际付运货物价值计算出来的保费(这可称为"rate on line")。

显然,两票货物中任何一票都没有超出 100 万美元的赔付限制,但集中在一起成 150 万就超出了赔付限制。所以如果发生全损,保险人赔付的只是 100 万美元,多出来的 50 万就要受保人自己承担了。

但如果发生的是部分损失而不是全损,而两票货物的总共部分损失是 80 万美元,就会存在争议是保险人应该全数赔付 80 万美元或只是按比例。如果按比例就等于把它视为不足额保险:80 万 ×(100 万/150 万)美元,但根据 John Dunt 的说法,这是不准确的计算,因为不足额保险是往往为了节省保费,但这种开口/预约保单根本不是为了节省保费。

还有就是向第三人追偿/索赔回的钱的分摊问题。这根据著名的贵族院先例 Napier and Ettrick (Lord) v. Kershaw (1993) 1 Lloyd's Rep 197 的"从上到下"的补偿原则(关于该原则在本书第十三章第 13.3 段有详细介绍,也在本章第 5 段有提到过),应该把向第三人取回的钱先赔付给受保人,让他获得损失的全部补偿,剩下来的才给保险人作出扣减。毕竟,保险人在保险合约是对受保人作出了承诺承担在赔付限制内的损失部分(上述例子中的 100 万),就没有理由优先。这方面可继续节录 John Dunt 所著的《Marine Cargo Insurance》一书 2009 年版之 15.35 段是说:"Accordingly, a limit creates a layer and the top-down principle applies with the assured recovering first and any balance being applied to the lower slice of the risk undertaken by the insurers only if the assured has first been fully compensated."

7. 索赔通知

有关索赔通知(Notice of Claims)已经在本书第四章第4.4 段有详论,这里多加一些内容特别是针对海上货物保险。针对这方面保单中会有明示条文作出指引,如在 MAR 91(这在 1983 年替代了劳合社标准 S. G. 保单)与劳合社标准保险证明(在开口保单的每个航次的签发)都有条文规定受保人发现货损货差有马上通知的责任,条文如下:"In the event of loss or damage which may result in a claim under this Insurance, immediate notice must be given to the Lloyd's Agent at the port or place where the loss or damage is discovered in order that he may examine the goods and issue a survey report"。这样要求看来主要的目的就是货损货差发生在海上运输期间的事实保留证据,这是保险人将来为了代位求偿可以向船舶或者承运人索赔的重要证据。当然保险人还有其他的作用,如针对受保人而言就是看看是否在有关的保单中应该作出赔付。毕竟即使是海上货物运输,也不会都是承保一切险,这就变为需要知道有关货损货差所造成的主要原因或近因,看是否属于列名承保风险或是一切险的除外风险。还会有其他的方面,如涉及受保人在投保时没有作出披露或者误述,也会是在出事后检查时才会暴露出来,让保险人知道后可以令保险合约无效。

有关保险合约中的通知要求,可以是有很不同的文字与措辞,特别是在岸上的保险合约。会有一些通知要求说明如果受保人没有及时作出通知,是会被视为违反了先决条件,保险人可以拒绝赔付。也会有一些通知要求把通知的内容也规定得很详细,如通知的内容必须包括什么,可以说受保人面对这种条文都必须要小心。在先例 HLB Kidsons & Ors v. Lloyd's Underwriters (2009) 1 Lloyd's Rep 8,上诉庭 Toulson 大法官说到误导性的通知是无效的通知说:"I would readily accept a proposition that where a policy contains a provision for the insured to notify a circumstance which may give rise to a claim and thereby attach the risk to the policy, it is impliedly incumbent on the insured to see that any such notification is a fair, if summary, presentation of what the insured knows. (This would be consistent with the expert evidence in this case referred to by Rix LJ at para. 63). If the insured chooses to be deliberately misleading or economical with the truth, so that the insurer is not given a fair picture of what the insured knows, I can see a good arguable case for saying that the notification should be treated as invalid."

但针对海上货物条文,上段中引述的 MAR 91 中的条文比较泛泛,没有针对通知的内容,也没有说明它是先决条件。这一来,英国法律地位应该明确是属于一条中间条文,通常只为允许保险人向受保人提出因为延误通知而带来的损失,但不能以受保人违反拒赔。这些方面近期的先例有 Phoenix General Insurance Co of Greece SA v. Halvanon Insurance Co Ltd (1985) 2 Lloyd's Rep 599 与 Travelers Casualty and Surety Co of Canada v. Sun Life Assurance of Canada (UK) Ltd (No. 2) (2007) Lloyd's Rep IR 619。早在先例 D&J Koskas v. The Standard Insurance Company Ltd (1927) 27 Lloyd's Rep 59 (CA),就涉及海上货物保险的保险证明下受保人给保险人损失通知的问题,保险人指称这是属于赔付的先决条件,但上诉庭不同意。

这就带来疑问就是受保人如果违反通知要求可能会带来的结果。在先例 Alfred McAlpine plc v BAI (Run-Off) Ltd (2000) Lloyd's Rep IR 352,上诉庭的 Waller 大法官曾经提到过在极端的情况下,受保人的违约可以被视为毁约(repudiation),让保险人接受并终止保险合约。但在先例 Friends Provident Life & Pensions Ltd v. Sirius International Insurance Corp (2006) Lloyd's Rep IR 45,上诉庭的多数成员不同意 Waller 大法官的说法。该问题的法律地位在先例 Limit No 2 Ltd v. Axa Versicherung AG (2008) Lloyd's Rep IR 330 是被进一步明确,也就是除非在保险合约中明示约定通知要求是先决条件,对通知要求的违反是不构成毁约。但问题是保险人在受保人违反及时作出通知,通常是很难证明有什么实质性的损失,正如 Waller 大法官在先例 Friends Provident 中所说,保险人的损失往往是幻想(illusory)。如果是说保险人因为延误通知而导致了本来会需要负责任的船舶在期间沉没或转售,因此在代位求偿的行动中再也没有机会取得诉前担保。这看来不算幻想或臆猜,但保险人不必需要以延误通知,可以根据受保人没有合理以及及时作出施救行动(这方面请看本书第七章第 5.4 段)所带来的损失向受保人索赔或在赔付时对冲。

8. 向保险人提出索赔的时效

海上货物运输保险通常不会明示索赔时效,这样就会是适用法律的默示地位,1980 年《Limitation Act》规定就是从损失发生之日起 6 年。保护时效的合法的唯一办法就是在有管辖权的法院提起诉讼，或者是开始仲裁（如果保险合约有一条仲裁条文）：Chardris v. Argo Insurance Company, Ltd and Others (1963) Lloyd's Rep 65。6年看起来是很长与充裕，但会有情况是时效届满还没有提起诉讼而导致整个索赔失去。如发生了共同海损，需要很长时间共同海损理算师才可以给出说明货方分摊责任的理算报告。这时货方作为受保人再向保险人索赔时就会有时效届满的危险，所以如果保险人的赔付是拖拖拉拉，受保人就必须尽早提起诉讼以保护诉讼时效。

时效的起算点已经提到就是损失发生的一天，这是因为在这个时候受保人就有了向保险人要求赔付的诉因（cause of action）。针对海上货物运输，损失发生的一天应该是不难确定，通常是在由货方/保险人他们共同委任的检验师对受损货物进行检查并作出关于损失发生时间推定的检验报告中会作出确定。

但在其他的保险合约，有时候对诉因在什么时候产生会有争议，如在责任保险。与海上货物运输保险有密切关系的船东或承运人互保协会，就是一种责任保险。互保协会承保船东面对货方或代位求偿保险人会有的责任，也就是货损货差的责任。而这里就会有疑问就是船东针对互保协会的诉因是在发生货损货差责任时或者是向货方/保险人作出全部赔付时产生。而其中互保协会的做法更加带来混乱，如互保协会的规定通常要求受保人的船东先作出赔付后才可以向互保协会要求补偿，即"paid to be paid"条文（这在本书第三章脚注3中有提到）。但现实做法中，互保协会又往往在出事后不久就提供担保以避免船东的船舶被扣或者是货方采取其他的诉前保全措施。在不少特别是金额大的货损货差索赔，互保协会也往往直接对货方或背后的保险人作出赔付，不会多此一举先要求船东垫付。有关这方面的诉因，Goff勋爵在先例The "Fanti" and The "Padre Island" (1990) 2 Lloyd's Rep 191这样说："I also accept that, at common law, the cause of action does not (unless the contract provides otherwise) arise until the indemnified person can show actual loss: see Collinge v. Heywood, (1839) 9 Ad. & E. 634. This is, as I understand it, because a promise of indemnity is simply a promise to hold the indemnified person harmless against a specified loss or expense. On this basis, no debt can arise before the loss is suffered or the expense incurred, however, once the loss is suffered or the expense incurred, the indemnifier is in breach of contract for having failed to hold the indemnified person harmless against the relevant loss or expense."

另涉及石棉中毒这种案件诉因是在什么时候产生也是很有争议。到底是在受害人为雇主工作暴露在石棉的期间，还是在出现有石棉肺症状的时候，这两者之间会相差十年二十年甚至更长时间。除了计算时效的问题，还会涉及更重要的方面，如哪个雇主的保险人应该负责。这种问题也会出现在财产保险中保险标的有内在缺陷时候，到底是有了内在缺陷时（这就是建造时），或是过了五年十年后内在缺陷被发现时。这些有趣的问题和海上货物运输保险没有太大关系，不去多讲。

9. 举证责任与程度

向保险人提出索赔，受保人有第一步的举证责任证明他的损失是平衡起来较大可能(balance of probability)由于承保的列名风险导致：The"Popi M"(1985) 2 Lloyd's Rep 1。所谓较大可能的标准就是在民事诉讼中采用的标准，也即有等于或大于51%的可能造成。针对一切险，受保人举证责任就轻得多，他只需要证明是发生在承保期间的意外(fortuity)造成了损失：Feurst Day Lawson v. ORION insurance (1980) 1 Lloyd's Rep 656与Global Process System Inc v. Syarikat Takaful Malaysia Berhad (2009) Lloyd's Rep IR 511。有关这方面，在本书第六章有详论，不去重复。只说，在海上货物运输，通常受保人的举证责任都不会太困难，只要是受保人发现发生货损货差后根据保险合约的要求递交损失通知，然后随即作出一个共同检验并得出份检验报告说明货物受损的原因，通常这份检验报告，另加上一份清洁提单说明在装货时货物表面状况良好与数量，就足够作为向保险人提出索赔的证明。麻烦的是在检验报告中的内容对货物受损的原因也说不清楚，甚至作出些对受保人不利的推断，如部分货损是由于内在缺陷引起。

在受保人举证后，如果保险人想拒赔就变为是他的举证责任，要不是证明货损货差是由于除外风险所导致，如较早时候提到的内在缺陷。这在协会货物条文(一切险)4.4条也是属于除外风险。保险人的拒赔也可以根据其他理由如是受保人没有作出实质性披露或者误述(在共同检验的时候发现货物是次品，在投保的时候没有说明)，所以保险人可以令保险合约无效。

不同的保险合约也会有不同的要求，如盗窃险的保险合约就要求受保人报警的证明，至于人命伤亡的保险就需要提供医疗证明。针对这些要求，英国法律是不会有默示条件：Albany Life Assurance Co. v. De Montfort Insurance Co Plc (unrep, 1995)。所以保险人对索赔的受保人有什么证明的要求，都需要明示。

另外，在再保险，由于第一线的保险人经常会与受保人作出和解，不会在所有有争议的索赔都打官司到底。这一来，在和解赔付之后，保险人向再保险人索赔，就会有一定的麻烦证明他实际的损失与和解的合理性。所以，在再保险合约中，经常会加上条文是"follow the settlement"或"follow the fortune"约束再保险人。前者在先例Insurance Company of Africa v. Scor (UK) Reinsurance Co Ltd (1985) 1 Lloyd's Rep 312中有解释，Goff大法官是认为有两个条件向再保险人索赔：(1)索赔属于再保险合约承保的范围(the claim so recognised falls within the risk covered by the policy of reinsurance)；(2) 在第一线的保险人是诚实与采取了所有适合与商业性的步骤达成和解(the insurers acted honestly and took all proper and businesslike steps in making the settlement)。这方面还有近期的贵族院先例Wasa International v. Lexington (2009) 2

Lloyd's Rep 508,由于再保险不是本书的重点,所以不多探讨。

最后一提的是英国也不断有一些先例针对保险人不合理向受保人提出要求损失的证明,提一些刁难性的要求。如在一个涉及火灾保险的先例 Welch v. Royal Exchange Assurance (1939) 1 KB 294,保险合约中有条文要求索赔时需要向保险人提供所有被合理要求的证明与资料(all such proofs and information as may reasonably be required.),但保险人要求受保人提供一些银行账户的资料,受保人拒绝说这些资料与保险索赔无关并拒绝提供。这种做法在英国法院已经受到了一些限制,特别是针对一些人命伤亡的保险。在 Moore v. Woolsey (1854) 8 E & W 243,法院这样说:"all that can be necessary is that proof shall be shown to have been laid before them which reasonable men would be satisfied, and then the inference arises that the proof was to their satisfaction"。较近期的有 Napier v. UNUM Ltd (1996) 2 Lloyd's Rep. 550 与 Widefree v. Brit Insurance (2009) EWHC 3671 (QB)。其中在前者的先例中,法院这样说:"the English cases establish that the insurers' requirements for vouching [what insurers may require as proof of the claim, in the sense of what evidence they can call for no support it] must be reasonable."

最后一提的是笔者听说英国试图立法针对故意在损失证明刁难受保人的保险人,刑事化这种行为。估计即使这样做,应该也是针对一些需要保护的消费者的保险合约,而不会针对国际性的海上货物运输保险。

10. 欺诈性索赔

受保人向保险人提出欺诈性索赔(fraudulent claim)的情况经常会发生,包括在海上货物运输保险。这显然是违反了保险合约的绝对善意原则,但它还有些独特的法律后果,就是保险人可以令保险合约无效,这在本书第二章有详论。有关欺诈性索赔请参见笔者与汪鹏南教授合著的《英国海上保险条款详论》。[1]

笔者最后一提的是在笔者与汪鹏南教授合著的《英国海上保险条款详论》出版后,英国法律又有了新的发展,如最近就有先例名为 Direct Line v. Fox (2009) EWHC 386,涉及了受保人原先的索赔是善意的,而保险人也作出了赔付。但之后受保人以虚假文件想多索赔点,在被发现时受保人撤回他的额外索赔,保险人坚持要把原来作出的赔付也要回来,但最后没有获得法院的支持。看来,虚假索赔也在一定程度上涉及了时间性的问题。

还有在英国与中国香港地区的民事诉讼改革(Civil Justice Reform)后,向保险人提出虚假索赔的还有藐视法院的刑事后果,特别是在一些如人命伤亡的保险。这是

---

〔1〕 杨良宜、汪鹏南:《英国海上保险条款详论》,大连海事大学出版社 2009 年版,第 413 ~419 页。

因为在民事诉讼改革后，向法院提出的索赔请求是要有一个“真实声明”(statement of truth)的确认。如果这与事实相差太远(不仅是提出对自己最有利的索赔[best possible case])，就会有藐视法院的危险。在这之前，向法院作伪证往往是要等到开庭的时候。但现在就在时间上大大提前了，在一开始提出索赔请求时已经会有这个危险。这在 Carol Walton v. Joanne Kirk (2009) EWHC 703 (QB)，案件涉及一位名为 Kirk 的女士，在 2001 年发生了一场交通事故，之后没办法步行多于十步，导致无法工作，并提出诉讼索赔 80 万英镑。责任保险人 Royal Bank Scotland Insurance(RBS)把 2.5 万英镑存进法院以保护诉讼费用，这笔钱也在 21 天内被 Kirk 女士接受了作为和解。这是因为 Kirk 女士被 RBS 委任的私家侦探拍了录像证明她完全有自由行动的能力，导致这个官司打不下去。但在和解后，RBS 向法院申请提出藐视法院的诉讼，因为 Kirk 女士作伪证(for making false statements in documents verified by statements of truth without an honest belief in the truth of the same)。这最后导致 Kirk 女士被法院罚了 2500 英镑，认为情况不至于严重到必须判监。

第十三章　代位求偿权

1. 序言

1.1　代位求偿权与不当得利

代位求偿权(Subrogation)是十分重要的原则,它不只适用在保险,实际上在罗马帝国的时候就已经有这种理念,第三者如果为另一个人偿还了债务,就有了后者的权利向他的债务人要求作出支付。代为求偿权的英文字相等于"替代"(substitution),来自拉丁文的"surrogate"。代位求偿权是适用在许多不同的领域,它可以通过法律的默示地位或明示条文产生,正如 Hoffmann 勋爵在 Banque Financiere de la Cite v. Parc (Battersea) Ltd (1999) 1 AC 221 所说:"Subrogation may arise either from the express or implied agreement of the parties or by operation of law."例如在海上保险,根据 1906 年的《英国海上保险法》之 Section 79,保险人在赔付后就已经有了一个法律默示的代位求偿权。但通常的做法是保险人在赔付后还会要求受保人签发一份代位求偿权协议(这在本章第 11 段有详论),这就表示保险人有了默示与明示的代位求偿权。看来是多此一举的明示代位求偿权除了为了肯定,保险人也往往会在明示的代位求偿协议增加一些与默示地位不一致的要求。例如,明示规定保险人可以以受保人的名义向第三人索赔,即使是还没有作出任何赔付或部分赔付:Arthur Barnett Ltd v. National Insurance Co of New Zealand Ltd (1967) NZLR 874 (NZCA)。或是明示规定保险人向第三人的索赔"是为了他自己的利益"(for its own benefit),这通常表示代位求偿权成功取回的钱比保险人赔付的还要多,可以不必把多出来的部分退还给受保人:请看 J Birds 所著的《Contractual Subrogation in Insurance》(1979) JBL 124,131。

代位求偿权的大原则也是与"不当得利"(unjust enrichment)的说法有密切的关系。在 Banque Financiere de la Cite v. Parc (Battersea) Ltd,Hoffmann 勋爵指代位求偿权是"to describe an equitable remedy to reverse or prevent unjust enrichment which is not based upon any agreement or common intention of the party enriched and the party deprived."

不当得利的说法应该也是近二十年发展起来的。在 Orakpo v. Manson Investments Ltd (1978) AC 95,Diplock 勋爵认为英国法没有一套不当得利的理论(There is no general doctrine of unjust enrichment in English law.)。但现在已经改变了这个说

法,在 Banque Financiere de la Cite v. Parc (Battersea) Ltd 先例已经明确了这套理论,Steyn 勋爵说不当得利的说法是一套独立针对权利与责任的法律(an independent source of rights and obligations),并且与合约法与侵权法并列(ranks next to contract and tort as part of the law of obligations)。

1.2　代位求偿权大原则所适用的领域

涉及代位求偿权的大原则,大致上可以把它分作三个主要的领域,其中第一个也是对本书最重要的领域就是针对保险的代位求偿权,这也是本章要详细介绍。其他两个领域简单一提的第一种是针对债务人 A 欠债权人 B 一笔钱(欠钱的原因可能是来自合约、侵权或不当得利),之后出了一个 C 代 A 把这笔钱支付给了 B,从而解除了 A 的债务责任。C 这样做的原因往往是对同样的一笔债务也有责任。但 A 与 C 之间又没有任何合约的关系关于怎样分摊这笔赔付给 B 的钱。这一来,就会有可能出现一种情况是法律承认 C 有了代位求偿权向 B 要回这笔债务,理据就是假设 C 替代了 B 向 A 索赔。这方面可以简单节录 Michell 与 Watterson 合著的《SUBROGATION Law and Practice》(2007 版)一书之6.03 段,如下:"There are many situations where two parties are liable to a creditor, where one satisfied his own liability to the creditor, and where his payment or other performance also has the effect of discharging the other's liability. In such cases, and whether or not the parties have previously agreed that the performing party should have a contractual indemnity, the law commonly gives him a restitutionary remedy against the other. Depending on the proper distribution of the burden of liability between claimant and defendant, the claimant's primary remedy is a contribution or reimbursement award. In additional, and as a supplementary measure which is capable of supporting either entitlement, the claimant has also commonly been afforded the remedy of subrogation to the paid-off creditor's extinguished rights against the defendant. Such remedies have been made available between various parties, including sureties and principal debtors, co-sureties; sureties and sub-sureties; joint contractors; partners; joint wrongdoers; and several wrongdoers liable for the same damage."

笔者可以信托(trusts)为例。这方面的法律,信托不像是成立一家有限公司,它本身并没有一个法律的身份(legal entity),也不能拥有财产、订立合约与负上法律责任。所以第三人与信托人订立合约,只能被视为他们之间的合约关系。第三人作为债权人如果想对信托下的资产动脑筋,就是根据代位求偿权的大原则,所谓的"creditors of trustees"的说法。

为了更清楚地介绍,笔者不妨介绍一个与国际外贸有关的上诉庭先例,估计可以说明这种问题的复杂性,名为 Niru Battery v. Milestone Trading (2004) EWCA Civ 487。案情涉及 Niru 向 Milestone 购买一票铅锭(lead ingots),并约定以信用证作出支付,而结汇的文件是一份装船提单与 SGS 的检验报告。卖方 Milestone 是向 CAI 贷款资助这一笔交易,并且以该票铅锭的仓库授权证(warehouse warrants)作为担保。但这一来就为 Milestone 带来了一个困境,就是他必须要归还给 CAI 这笔贷款才可以取回仓库授权证,而这笔钱是必须要通过信用证的结汇才会有。结汇是需要一份装船提单,而装船提单是必须把该票铅锭装上船才会有,但没有仓库授权证就没办法从仓库提取装船。反正最后解决办法就是 Milestone 出了一套假的装船提单,并由 CAI 向银行结汇。但事实上该票铅锭已经出售给了第三人,结果就导致了虽然 Niru 的买方支付了货价约 600 万美元,却没有取得货物。在接下来的诉讼,Niru 作为原告被判是胜诉,败诉的是 CAI 与 SGS。CAI 的败诉是根据不当得利,而 SGS 的败诉是根据侵权(因为他疏忽与错误地作出检验报告)。结果 SGS 把这笔 600 万美元的货款赔付给了 Niru。但剩下的问题是 SGS 怎样向 CAI 取回,因为 SGS 的支付也同时解除了 CAI 判决中该负的责任。SGS 向 CAI 提出诉讼时要求把所有赔付给 Niru 的钱要回来,诉因是代位求偿权(subrogation)、扣除(recoupment)(这在本章 2.1 段有介绍)与 1978 年《Civil Liability (Contribution)》中的责任分摊(contribution)。但这里也有微妙的地方,如 1978 年的立法并不适用在一个责任方是因为不当得利,另一个责任方是因为侵权而要负上共同与连带责任。最后上诉庭判 SGS 可以根据代位求偿权向 CAI 把所有的赔付给 Niru 的钱取回来。

代位求偿权大原则的第二个领域是针对债务人 A 欠债权人 B 一笔钱,而在 A 支付之后是可以向 C 要求补偿(indemnity),如根据他们之间的补偿协议或者是责任保险合约。本来根据正常的渠道就是 B 先向 A 追索,等 A 清偿债务以后再向 C 追索,法律不必以代位求偿权或者其他说法作出干预。但会有情况如 A 经济出了问题如倒闭,导致了 B 向 A 追索成功也不会拿到钱,结果让 C 可以逃避补偿 B 的责任。另一种情况会造成不公道的是 C 赔偿给了倒闭/清盘的 A,也会令真正应该得到这笔钱的 B 无法取得,因为他只是其中一个债权人,甚至是无担保的债权人。这种情况可以举一个日常的交通事故为例,A 是一个疏忽的司机,他所驾驶的是他公司的汽车并在执行公务,B 是因 A 的疏忽驾驶而受伤的路人,而 C 是该司机的公司所购买的第三人责任保险人。事故后不久,A 倒闭/清盘。在这种关系下显然 B 可以向 A 提出侵权的索赔并且成功,但最后 C 补偿给 B 的钱会是要在所有债权人之间分摊,A 充其量只是债权人之一。这对其他 B 的债权人,可以说是天上掉下来的钱,并且被认为是属于不当得利。现在已经有立法针对这方面的问题,这就是 1930 年《The Third Parties (Rights against Insurers) Act》。在本书第三章之脚注 3 中,更是提到了该立法有了新版本,就是 2010 年的《Third Parties (Rights against Insurer) Act》。2010 年的立法是允许受害人 B 跳过责任方 A 直接向责任保险人 C 根据保险合约索赔,好像是替代了 A 的合约权利,这就更加接近代位求偿权的大原则了。

1.3 海上保险的代位求偿权大原则的历史

但本章主要还是针对海上保险,特别是货物运输保险的代位求偿权,所以以下要回到这个领域作进一步的探讨。首先节录 1906 年的《英国海上保险法》相关条文如下:

"79. RIGHT OF SUBROGATION

(1) Where the insurer pays for a total loss, either of the whole, or in the case of goods of any apportionable part, of the subject-matter insured, he thereupon becomes entitled to take over the interest of the assured in whatever may remain of the subject-matter so paid for, and he is thereby subrogated to all the rights and remedies of the assured in and in respect of that subject-matter as from the time of the casualty causing the loss. (这是针对全损的情况,保险人有权在赔付全损后有两个权利。一个是委付/抛弃[abandonment]的权利,另一个是代位求偿的权利。)

(2) Subject to the foregoing provisions, where the insurer pays for a partial loss, he acquires no title to the subject-matter insured, or such part of it as may remain, but he is thereupon subrogated to all rights and remedies of the assured in and in respect of the subject-matter insured as from the time of the casualty causing the loss, in so far as the assured has been indemnified, according to this Act, by such payment for the loss. (这是针对部分损失的情况,保险人在赔付后只有一个权利,就是代位求偿的权利。)"

代位求偿权这一理念在英国海上保险法律是首先在 1750 ~ 1850 年之间,Mansfield 勋爵与其他的普通法大法官通过一连串的先例建立来的一个"委付/抛弃权利"(abandonment)的说法。就是保险人在赔付了全损后,有权把保险标的可能还有剩余的价值从保险人接管过来。如在 Roux v. Salvador (1835) 1 Bing (NC) 526, 539 先例,Tindal 首席大法官针对保险人这一个权利这样说:"out of the very nature of the contract of insurance, which is a contract of indemnity only: for the assured would obviously be more than indemnified, unless the underwriter is put into his place as to all the benefit that may be derived from what has been actually saved or recovered from the loss."

到了先例 Simpson v. Thompson (1877) LR 3 App Cas 279 at 284,贵族院首次把"委付/抛弃权利"与"代位求偿权"(subrogation)作出了区分,视为是两种不同但又是十分接近的大原则。Blackburn 勋爵这样说:"Where the owners of an insured ship have claimed or been paid as for a total loss, the property in what remains of the ship, and all rights incident to the property, are transferred to the underwriters as from the time of the disaster in respect of which the total loss is claimed for and paid... **But the right of the assured to recover damages from a third person is not one of those rights which are incident to the property in the ship; it does pass to the underwriters in case of payment for a total loss, but on a different principle**. And on this same principle it does pass to the underwriters who have satisfied a claim for a partial loss, though no property in the ship passes."

接下来在 Castellain v. Preston (1883) LR 11 QBD 380,Brett 大法官就曾给过代位求偿权一个经典的定义如下:"... As between the underwriter and the assured the underwriter is entitled to the advantage of every right of the assured, **whether** such right consists in contract, fulfilled or unfulfilled, or in remedy for tort capable of being insisted on or already insisted on, or in any other right, **whether** by way of condition or otherwise, legal or equitable, which can be, or has been exercised or has accrued, and **whether** such right could or could not be enforced by the insurer in the name of the assured by the exercise or acquiring of which right or condition the loss against which the assured is insured can be, or has been diminished."

这些先例也就是带来了1906年《英国海上保险法》的立法而针对的"委付/抛弃权利"与"代位求偿权"的Section 79。

1.4 其他国家的代位求偿权法律与不同之处

代位求偿权这一理念在许多不同国家的保险法律都有体现,并且其大原则是与英国保险法是一致的,包括美国、加拿大、欧洲大陆的国家、巴西、印度、中国等,但它们在重要的细节上有许多不同。例如,中国与美国的法律就允许保险人在赔付后,以自己的名义向第三人进行代位求偿的诉讼。在先例 Insurance Co of Pennsylvania Ltd v. IBM UK Ltd (1989) Chartered Surveyor Weekly, 12 October,因为是适用纽约的法律,所以就允许保险人以自己的名义提起诉讼。另在一个近期的对国际仲裁十分重要的案例(欧共体法院刚刚在2009年2月10日有了判决),名为The"Front Comor"(2007) 1 Lloyd's Rep 391,涉及意大利承租人拥有的泊位被"Front Comor"挂靠的时候碰坏。之后,承租人向他的保险人索赔并得到赔付,但这不足以补偿他的损失。所以,承租人根据他与船东之间的租约开始了伦敦仲裁(因为租约有伦敦仲裁条文),程序上到双方文书请求的交换。但在那时,意大利保险人行使代位求偿权,根据意大利《民事法典》之Article 1916以自己的名义在意大利法院向船东起诉。这一来,船东向英国法院申请止诉禁令(anti-suit injunction),并获得Colman大法官第一审的支持作出。但后来贵族院把这一个重要的决定交给欧共体法院作最后的决定,就是涉及仲裁而不是法院诉讼,欧共体国家之间可否作出止诉禁令。欧共体法院判是否中止诉讼应由受理案件的法院(本案中是意大利的法院)决定。这重要先例所针对的主要问题与本书无关,所以不详谈,只为了说明代位求偿权不同国家法律的不同之处。

1.5 代位求偿权的合理性与目的

代位求偿权的合理性与目的很简单,而且是分两个方面。第一个方面就是受保人不能在意外中向不同对象取得两次赔偿或补偿,从而得利(the assured should not accumulate recoveries)。这是因为受保人在意外中蒙受损失而经常会有情况是可以根据合约或侵权向第三人索赔损失。但同时,由于受保人为这种意外损失投保,所以也可以向保险人要求补偿。如果没有代位求偿的原则,显然会让受保人有机会取得两次或以上的赔偿,变成他可以有机会从意外事故中得利。这并不公平,也不恰当,因为会增加道德风险,就是受保人有意或无意中希望出事。

第二个方面是法律认为应当作出最后赔偿的一方不是保险人,而是要在合约或者侵权下要负责的责任方或过失方(wrongdoer)。受害人有权向一位以上的责任方提出索赔是经常会有的情况。法律也没有要求受害人必须怎样选择向谁索赔。在现实中,受害人会选择比较容易成功索赔的责任方要求赔付。这一来,如果其中要作出赔付的责任方是保险人,受保人作为受害人也通常倾向向保险人先提出赔付要求,而不会先找负责的第三人(不论是根据合约、侵权或不当得利而要负责)。而这一来,如果没有代位求偿权,就会有机会在保险人赔付后,被视为更加需要负责任的过失方可以脱身,这显然不是好事。

如果没有这两个方面的考虑,就不必支持代位求偿权。在加拿大的最高院先例 Somersall v. Friedman (2002) 3 SCR 109, Iacobucci 大法官这样说:"It is important to keep in mind the underlying objectives of the doctrine of subrogation which are to ensure (i) that the insured received no more and no less than a full indemnity, and (ii) that the loss falls on the person who is legally responsible for causing it... Consequently, if there is no danger of the insured's being overcompensated and the tortfeasor has exhausted his or her capacity to compensate the insured there is no reason to invoke subrogation. Similarly, if the insured enters into a limits agreement or otherwise abandons his or her claim against an impecunious tortfeasor the insurer has lost nothing by his inability to be subrogated."

上述所讲的代位求偿权原则的合理性与目的,就可以理解其他的细节。如代位求偿权只适用在一种补偿性的保险(indemnity insurance),也就是保险人在保险合约中承诺全额或部分补偿受保人的损失。但在另一种可称为是固定金额的保险(sum insurance),没有代位求偿权。这是如人寿保险或意外伤亡保险,出了事后保险人赔付一笔约定的金额后就不存在代位求偿。受保人或他的家属向第三人索赔额外的金额,如果成功也不存在要把索赔金额退还给保险人。毕竟,生命是无价的。这就表示在这种保险,不用担心如前所述第一种方面的考虑,即受保人取得两次赔偿或补偿,从而得利。任命无价就表示向第三人取得比保险人赔付的钱多出 10 倍或是 100 倍,都不能说是受保人得利,甚至是不当得利。

对海上保险而言,不论是船舶还是本书针对的货物运输,都属于补偿性的保险。所以,代位求偿权的原则完全适用。但社会科学总会有例外,这就是在船舶保险经常会有一种所谓的 PPI 保险(Policy Proof Insurance),也就是不需要受保人证明他的实际可保利益(insurable interests),如船东的使费或可赚取的运费。由于英国法律认为这种保险是无效的,属于保险人与受保人之间的君子协定,所以在 PPI 保险赔付之后也不存在保险人有代位求偿权:John Edwards & Co v. Motor Union Insurance Co (1922) 2 KB 249。这又是根据另一个理论否定保险人的代位求偿权。

代位求偿权也可以解释一些现实中可能出现的扯皮现象,就是受保人向保险人要求赔付,但保险人说你应该向对你造成损害的第三人提出索赔,不成功才可以向我要求赔付。这是不能接受的,正确的做法是保险人应该先作出赔付,然后向第三人提出的索赔就变成是保险人的代位求偿权:Collingridge v. Royal Exchange Assurance (1877) 3 QBD 173。已经提到过,受保人想向谁要求赔付是他的选择,受保人甚至可以不向任何人提出要求赔付他的损失，而向自己富有的父亲要。

同样的道理，受害人如果选择先向第三人提出索赔，第三人不能以受害人可以从保险人那里取得部分或全部的赔付为由作出抗辩：Mason v. Sainsbury (1782) 3 Doug 61, Clarke v. Tull t/a Ardington Electrical Services (2002) Lloyd's Rep IR 524。在一个比较近期的先例 Stace & Francis v. Ashby (2001) EWCA Civ 1655，案情涉及受保人拒绝接受保险人的一个部分赔付的和解提议，认为金额不足够。期间，受保人向违约的承建商提出索赔并且成功。但在损失方面，一审法院认为赔偿的金额应该减去保险人所作出的和解提议金额。但去了上诉庭，一审法院的判决被推翻，原因是不应该把保险合约的赔付扯在一起，第三人不能从中得利。

2. 代位求偿的不同情况

在保险法领域，代位求偿涉及了三种不同的情况：(1)如果受保人在保险人赔付之前向第三人已经取得有关损失的一笔金钱，保险人有权向受保人取回或在赔付的时候扣减；(2)如果受保人在保险人赔付之后从第三人取得有关损失的一笔金钱，保险人有权向受保人取回；(3)受保人向第三人可能会有的诉因必须转移给保险人。

在以上的三种情况中，最常见与最复杂的情况就是第一种情况。至于第二种情况，是一种事实的错误(mistake of fact)，就是保险人在不知情的情况下多赔付给受保人，所以根据衡平法的"复原"(restitution)原则可以向受保人取回这笔钱。第三种与第二种情况大致相似，只不过受保人是在保险人赔付后才发生这一情况。根据法律，保险人对受保人从第三人要回的这笔钱是有一个衡平法的留置权(equitable lien)作为有担保的债权人(secured creditor)。

第一种与第二种情况都可以被称为是扣除(recoupment)，接下来先对这一相对比较简单的原则作出介绍。

2.1 情况之一：扣除

扣除(recoupment)主要就是针对保险人在赔付给受保人后，如果发现多赔付了给受保人，就有权要回这多赔付的金额。这个说法本质上就是一种复原(restitution)。多赔付最常见的情况就是受保人从第三人在赔付前或赔付后获得对有关承保损失的部分或全部赔偿，导致受保人再也谈不上有损失，或损失已大大减少。

在 Castellain v. Preston (1883) 11 QBD 380 先例中，判保险人可以享有受保人的所有权利、资助或任何其他的好处，只要是为了减少或者是消除受保人的损失。Brett 大法官这样说：

"The very foundation... of every rule which has been applied to insurance law is this, namely, that the contract of insurance contained in a marine or fire policy is a contract of indemnity, and of indemnity only, and that this contract means that the assured, in case of a loss against which the policy has been made, shall be fully indemnified, but shall never be more than fully indemnified. That is the fundamental principle of insurance, and if ever a proposition is brought forward which is at variance with it, that is to say, which either will prevent the assured from obtaining a full indemnity, or which will give to the assured more than a full indemnity, that proposition must certainly be wrong.

In order to apply the doctrine of subrogation, it seems to me that the full and absolute meaning of the word must be used, that is to say, the insurer must be placed in the position of the assured. Now it seems to me that in order to carry out the fundamental rule of insurance law, this doctrine of subrogation must be carried to the extent which I am now about to endeavor to express, namely, as between the underwriter and the assured the underwriter is entitled to the advantage of every right of the assured, whether such right consists in contract, fulfilled or unfulfilled, or in remedy for tort capable of being insisted on or already insisted on, or in any other right, whether by way of condition or otherwise, legal or equitable, which can be, or has been exercised or has accrued, and whether such right could or could not be enforced by the insurer in the name of the assured by the exercise or acquiring of which right or condition the loss against which the assured is insured can be, or has been diminished."

这是一个十分广泛的说法,但也带来了很大的问题,特别是一些非法律权利(no prior legal entitlement)而获得的资助(voluntary payment)或好处(gift)。举例说,如果受保人的住所被火烧毁,保险人作出赔付,但之后受保人的父母或者子女慷慨地给了他一笔钱作为礼物或者支付他所遭受的损失(不论保险是否能够赔付到),保险人可否根据扣除的原则要求受保人归还?

在《MacGillivray and Partington on Insurance Law》第八版之 1155 段,对扣除原则进行了如下探讨:"The second right(扣除)vested in the insurer by the doctrine of subrogation is to claim from the assured any benefit conferred on the assured by third parties with the aim of compensating the assured for the loss in respect of which the insurer has indemnifies him. The right is usually exercised by an insurer claiming from the assured a sum equivalent to any sum of damages paid to the assured by a third party legally liable for the loss. The right is wider in scope than that, however, and the insurer is entitled to moneys paid to the assured *ex gratia* to diminish his loss **unless intended by the donor to benefit the assured to the exclusion of the insurers.**"

换言之,根据上述的最后一句,即给受保人的金钱、资助或者好处是明确说明不想让保险人获利(to the exclusion of the insurer),也不是为了减少有关的损失(in diminution of the loss),而只是赠送给受保人。这一意图通常最好就是在作出支付给受保人的时候文书说明,就有了证据的保存。这里可介绍一些有关的案例,其中一个是 Burnand v. Rodocanachi (1882) 7 App Cas 333,大致的案情是受保人的货物被美国内战时南联盟巡洋舰毁坏，战争保险人赔付了受保人战争险下的真正全损（actual total loss），但赔付的金额比实际损失少。美国国会在南北战争完结后通过立法支付给受到战争损失的人士（包括受保人）一笔金钱，该笔金钱等值于受保人实际上的损失与保险人作出赔付的差额。问题是，保险人可否根据扣除的原则要求受保人归还该笔金钱。贵族院判不可以，理由是 Hirst 大法官在 Colonia v. Amoco（1997）1 Lloyd's Rep 261 中提到的，即："In Burnand v. Rodocanachi, as the judgments show, the critical factor was the clearly expressed intention of the U. S. Congress to compensate the beneficiaries for their uninsured losses, together with the express exclusion of any claim by the insurers in their own right or that of the assured."

下一个有关的案例是 Merrett v. Capitol Indemnity Corp.（1991）1 Lloyd's Rep 169，Steyn 大法官认为经纪人的支付只是给受保人本人，而再保险人无权要求受保人归还该笔支付，可节录如下："The payment by the brokers was a gift, albeit a gift made for commercial rather than purely disinterested purposes. The contracts of reinsurance are contracts of indemnity. The question is, therefore, whether the payment diminishes the loss. Not every gift to an assured by a broker diminishes his loss. It is a question of fact in each case whether a gift has or has not been paid in diminution of the loss, and if it is established that the payment was intended solely for the benefit of the assured, it has not been paid in diminution of the loss. In that event it must be disregarded in assessing the assured's recoverable loss. These propositions are in my judgment firmly established by Burnand v. Rodocanachi（1882）7 App Cas 333."

最后要介绍的是 Colonia v. Amoco（1997）1 Lloyd's Rep 261 先例，它有不同的判法，保险人要求扣除成功。案情涉及卖方 Amoco 以 FOB 价格卖一船的石脑油给 Astra，Astra 再以 CIF 价格转卖给 ICI。在交货的时候，ICI 发现石脑油受到污染，而污染明确是由于装船前在 Amoco 的管道里面发生。ICI 事后通过保险经纪人要求保险人赔付，Astra 投保的一切险，然后以 CIF 转让给 ICI。同时，ICI 也向 Amoco 索赔。Amoco 最后也同意赔付给 ICI 的损失，大概 810 万美元。而赔付的原因是既有商业上的考虑（Amoco 与 ICI 都是很具规模的公司，并且有商业上的往来），也有 Amoco 自己知道最后责任难逃，虽然他们之间没有直接的买卖合约关系（这表示 Amoco 没有直接对 ICI 的法律责任）。在他们之间的协议中，ICI 把向保险人索赔的权益同时转让给了 Amoco。而之后，Amoco 根据保单向保险人以受让人的身份提出索赔，但保险人的抗辩是受保人（指 ICI）由于得到这笔 810 万美元的金钱的资助或好处，其实是没有真正受到损失。高院与上诉庭判双方意图并不明显显示 Amoco 支付的这笔钱只是为了赠送给 ICI，不让保险人获利。Hirst 大法官这样说：

"It follows that the crucial question is whether, on the construction of the Deeds, and in particular of course the second Deed, it was the intention of Amoco to benefit ICI to the exclusion of the Colonia（原告保险人）.

So far as the second Deed is concerned, the following seem to me to be the cardinal factors:-

1. The recital quoted above expressly records the desire of both parties to 'resolve any disputes that exist or may arise between them as a result of the transactions', and this desire is fulfilled by clause 1.2 under which ICI release and discharge Amoco from 'all claims liabilities obligations and causes of action whatsoever contingent or not contingent, known or unknown, which it now has, had or may have arising out of the transaction'... This to my mind fully vindicates Mr. Thomas'（原告保险人的代表大律师）submission that, irrespective of the question whether there was any direct liability owed by Amoco to ICI, this was a true commercial settlement of any possible claims by the former against the latter.

2. The assignment is expressly qualified by the words 'except to the extent of the insurance underwriter's subrogation rights'. These words must, for the reasons given above, be construed in their wide sense, so as to include Colonia's rights as against ICI to treat Amoco's payment as diminishing (in this case of course actually extinguishing) ICI's loss.

3. This construction is underlined by the last sentence of clause 1.2 which expressly stipulates that the release shall not effect the subrogation rights of the underwriters which they 'have or by virtue of any payment to any person firm or corporation shall acquire' which words are clearly apt to cover Amoco's payment to ICI.

4. The final words of clause 4.1 stipulating that 'no warranty is given express or implied that Amoco will be able to pursue all or any claims' seems to me to show that the parties recognised that Amoco might well not be entitled to pursue their claim against Colonia.

The first Deed, with its provisions for release of ICI's claims against Amoco, and its express reservation of the underwriters' subrogation rights, is fully in line with the second Deed.

Thus, as a matter of pure construction, I am satisfied that the intention demonstrated is not to benefit ICI to the exclusion of Colonia."

这种案件其实也可以从常理得出一定程度的推论,就是受保人如果在赔付前或赔付后向第三人取回一笔钱,而该第三人是商业关系,法院就很难接受这是一份礼物赠送给受保人,并且无意让保险人从中得益。相反,如果第三人是父母子女或好朋友的关系,就很难接受这不是一份赠送给遭遇到不幸的受保人的礼物,而是有意图地让保险人得益从而减少对受保人的赔付。当然,更重要就是看第三人与受保人之间的交往,特别是文书记录,从中找出他们的意图。

2.2 情况之二:向第三人追偿/索赔的代位求偿权

保险人在赔付了受保人之后,可以以受保人的名义起诉造成损失的第三人(如果有的话)是非常重要。由此而索赔回来的钱在实务中被称为追偿款(recoveries),这些钱在保险人平衡支付的保险赔偿金时起到了很大作用。除了向第三人追偿与索赔的权利外,保险人还有另一个相关的权利,这在下一段介绍。

2.3 委付/抛弃与取得保险标的的剩余价值的权利

不论货损是全损还是部分损失,保险人都可以从受保人那里得到代位求偿的权利。如果是全损(不管是真正全损还是推定全损),保险人在赔付后都可以取得保险标的(受保货物)的所有权与它的剩余价值(salvage),而受保人在这种情况下也可以说是把受保货物委付/抛弃(abandon)给了保险人。这一点是在1906年《英国海上保险法》之Section 79(1)有说明,不重复节录。

可以说,不论海上货物运输中发生的是全损还是部分损失,保险人在支付了保险赔偿金之后,都可以从受保人那里得到代位求偿的权利向第三人追偿/索赔。唯一不同的是如果只是部分损失的情况,保险人是不能够取得保险标的的所有权与该保险标的出售的剩余价值(the right to salvage)。

针对全损,代位求偿权(subrogation)与委付/抛弃(abandonment)是两个不同的原则,但经常有混乱,正如Atkin勋爵在先例Glen Line v. Attorney-General (1930) 37 Lloyd's Rep 55 at 61说:"confusion is often caused by not distinguishing the legal rights given by abandonment... from the rights of subrogation"。

针对委付/抛弃与代位求偿权的不同原则,也已经在本章第1.3段有提到Blackburn勋爵在Simpson v. Thomson (1877) LR 3 App Cas 279中的判词,不去重复。

有关这两个不同的原则,稍后会有进一步的分析。它们之间实质后果的不同主要是在委付/抛弃,保险人把委付/抛弃的保险标的出售的剩余价值会有可能比赔付给受保人的钱更多,而保险人由于变成了该保险标的的所有人,是可以获利的。但在代位求偿权,向第三人追偿回来的钱如果超出了保险人赔付的钱是要退还给受保人的。这方面可以节录Mance大法官等著的《Insurance Disputes》第二版之8.70段,针对委付/抛弃情况的,如下:"Accordingly, where for example a car is written off in an accident or where property is stolen and the underwriter has paid a total loss, the underwriter is entitled to take over whatever remains of the car and dispose of it and keep the proceeds or keep any later recovered property. This is so even if the value has increased so that it exceeds the amount paid by the underwriters to settle the total loss claim."

另也要说明的是委付/抛弃与委付通知(Notice of Abandonment)是两码事,委付通知是针对给受保人索赔推定全损的一个选择权,关于这项权利在本书第十章第2.2段有介绍。在岸上的保险,是没有推定全损,所以也不存在给保险人委付通知的做法,但还是在赔付全损后有委付/抛弃的要求。这可节录先例Kaltenbach v. Mackenzie (1878) 3 CPD 467中,Brett大法官说:"I concur in what has been said by Lord Blackburn that abandonment is not peculiar to policies of marine insurance abandonment is part of every contract of indemnity. Whenever, therefore, there is a contract of indemnity and a claim under it for an absolute indemnity, there must be an abandonment on the part of the person claiming indemnity of all his right in respect of that for which he receives indemnity."

最后要提的是,如果在定额保险中受保人为保险标的投的是足额保险,但是后来保险标的在市场价格上涨时发生了损失,如果受保人要向保险人索赔全损(该金额也就是当初投保人约定的保险价值),也要向保险人委付货物的剩余价值(即使是因为市场上涨而变得更值钱)。因为根据1906年《英国海上保险法》之Section 27(3),双方约定的保险价值就是结论性的。

3. 代位求偿权属于衡平法还是合约法

关于代位求偿权的性质,英国法院一直都有讨论。主要有两种说法:一种是源于普通法,认为保险人享有代位求偿权是保险合约中的默示条文(implied term);另外一种是衡平法下的不当得利(unjust enrichment)。

有关衡平法的性质,可介绍在Banque Financiere de la Cite v Par (Battersea Ltd)(1999) AC 221先例中,Hutton勋爵这样说:"the doctrine of subrogation applies in a variety of circumstances where the defendant has been **unjustly enriched** at the expense of the plaintiff, and where **equity** considers that it would be **unconscionable** for the defendant to retain that enrichment. In such a case, as Goff and Jones say, the remedy is fashioned to the facts of the particular case. In the Orakpo v. Manson Investments [1978] AC 95, 104E Lord Diplock stated that some rights by subrogation"appears to defeat classification except as an empirical remedy to prevent a particular kind of unjust enrichment."

另Hoffman勋爵也主张代位求偿权的救济不是当事人合约的意图,他说:"... it is a mistake to regard the availability of subrogation as a remedy to prevent unjust enrichment as turning entirely upon the question of intention, whether common or unilateral. Such an analysis has inevitably to be propped up by presumptions which can verge upon outright fictions, more appropriate to a less developed legal system than we now have ... I think it should be recognised that one is here concerned with a restitutionary remedy and that the appropriate questions are therefore, first, whether the defendant would be enriched at the plaintiff's expense; secondly, whether such enrichment would be unjust; and thirdly, whether there are nevertheless reasons of policy for denying the remedy."

在另一个著名的贵族院先例Napier and Ettrick (Lord) v. Kershaw (1993) 1 Lloyd's Rep 197,在经过常识的分析后也认为代位求偿权是衡平法下的救济,而不是保险合约中的默示条文。

但如果在保险合约中是有一条明示条文针对代位求偿权,这就可能超越了默示的衡平法下的不当得利,对于这一个合约权利的解释就要看有关条文:Bee v. Jenson (No. 2)(2008) Lloyd's Rep. IR 221。

上述的分析看来是纯理论的课题,但在实际的情况中会有非常重大的影响,可以举例来说明。

例子一是如果根据衡平法,在保险人对受保人的索赔作出不合理的拖延或抗拒,他会否在赔付后被否定代位求偿权? 毕竟,衡平法是用来保护无辜方,基本说法或格言就是寻求衡平法救济的一方当事人自己不能有错。这种争议在 England & England v. Guardian Insurance Limited (2000) Lloyd's Rep. IR 404 出现,英国法院认为即使是保险人有不当之处,也不会导致代位求偿权的失去,因为代位求偿本质上属于一个财产的权利,就是保险人对向第三人取回来的金钱有财产权或留置权。

例子二是更加明确与现实,就是受保人发生清盘或破产。这一来,如果向第三人追偿的钱根据代位求偿权是应该归保险人,根据保险合约的默示条文的性质,保险人充其量只是没有担保的债权人之一,最后可能是要不回来多少钱。即使是受保人把向第三人追偿的权利转让给了保险人,也在受保人发生清盘或破产后变为无效:White v. Dobbinson(1844) 14 Sim 273,但如果代位求偿权是属于衡平法就不会有这一问题。

例子三也是明确与现实,就是在衡平法下,如果向第三人追偿回来的钱是在受保人的律师手中,该律师(或其他代理人)就在保险人作出通知后必须把这笔钱交出,因为保险人对这笔钱是有一个衡平法下的财产权利(equitable proprietary right)与留置权。在 Napier and Ettrick (Lord) v. Kershaw (1993) 1 Lloyd's Rep 197,法院作出了一个禁令禁止受保人的律师把向第三人追偿回来的钱支付给受保人,而不理会保险人的索赔。另在先例 England & England v. Guardian Insurance Limited (2000) Lloyd's Rep. IR 404,法院命令第三人赔付的钱是要存放在法院,直到审理有关保险人代位求偿权的争议后才发放。

例子四是在衡平法下,保险人还可以进一步向第三人直接要求把将要赔付的钱交给他。这里可以先节录 Templeman 勋爵说:"In order to protect the rights of the insurer under the doctrine of subrogation, equity considers that the damages payable by the wrongdoer to the insured person are subject to an equitable lien or charge in favour of the insurer."这一进一步的权利会在某些情况下有重要性,就是受保人是在外国,如果第三人赔付给了外国受保人,保险人再向外国受保人或他的律师要求与主张他的衡平法财产权会有难度。这一来,保险人可以早一步向法院申请禁令,以避免第三人在把钱支付给受保人,除非先满足保险人代位求偿权下的索赔。

显然以上的例子所说都只在代位求偿权是衡平法的性质下才可以实现,而如果代位求偿权的性质仅仅是合约的默示条文就无法实现。

4. 保险人必须全数赔付给受保人才会有代位求偿权

这方面英国法很明确与简单,因为《英国海上保险法》Section 79(1)的第一句是说保险人在赔付了完全金额后才可以从受保人那里主张代位求偿权。这也可以通过《英国海上保险法》的结构得到证实:规定代位求偿权的 Section 79、Section 80 与 Section 81 是被共同放在"Rights of Insurer on Payment"的标题下面。

这也说明了为什么在协会货物条文(Institute Cargo Clauses)之 Section 16.2 规定了受保人在还没有被保险人赔付前,要采取适当的行为保护他可能对承运人、托管人或者是其他的第三人的诉讼权利,如在时效之前作出告票或开始仲裁以保护时效(这一课题在下一段会详谈)。由于有可能在那个时候保险人还需要调查才可以作出赔付,所以不存在代位求偿权。任何向第三人追偿的行动必须要通过受保人才能采取,所以最好有一条明示条文强制受保人这样做,否则就是违约。虽然法律也有先例要求不得做一些事情损害保险人在赔付后的代位求偿权,但有明示条文作出针对会更加明确与保险。

要赔付 100% 才会有代位求偿权的先例有:Edwards v. Commercial Union (1922) 2 KB 249;Scottish Union and National Insurance Company v. Davis (1970) 1 Lloyd's Rep. 1。保险人如果不承认责任或者企图扣起部分在保险合约下应该赔偿的钱都不能主张代位求偿权:Scottish Union and National Insurance Company v. Davis。另是在保险人赔付给了保险人之后也可以主张代位求偿权:Assicurazioni General de Trieste v. Empress Assurance Co. Ltd (1970) 2 KB 814。

英国法律不理会的是保险人通过什么办法与做法完全赔付给受保人,主要还是保险人的赔付责任已经全部解除(totally discharged)。有关的先例有 Page v. Scottish Insurance Co (1929) 140 LT 571 (CA);Brown v. Albany Construction Co Ltd (CA, 16 June 1995);Scottish Union & National Insurance Co v. Davis (1970) 1 Lloyd's Rep 1 (CA)。只节录在 Brown v. Albany Construction Co Ltd 先例,上诉庭的 Stuart-Smith 大法官说在该先例下的赔付是:"a perfectly straightforward case where the liability under the policy was discharged in the way which was agreeable to both parties."

如果保险人赔付给受保人的钱是根据一个非法律责任而是优惠的赔付(*ex gratia* payment),这会否让保险人有权主张代位求偿权?这种情况在保险中经常会发生,如受保人有可能违反善意的要求,或者可能破坏了保险合约中的保证条文,又或者受保人没有提供足够的证据证明有关列名风险导致了损失或是损失的具体金额等情况。保险人与受保人如果关系好,或者想避免诉讼,都会考虑优惠的赔付。这一来,保险人如果想主张代位求偿权,最好就在双方的和解协议中明示说明。因为保险人如果想依赖衡平法主张代位求偿权,会在优惠的赔付根本不属于保险合约内的赔付下难以站得住脚。在双方的和解协议,一种做法就是保险人作出的优惠赔付是有条件,条件是受保人必须向第三人提出诉讼,把所有的损失要回来,并在成功后把属于保险人部分的金钱作为信托人事后扣除或退还给保险人:Naumann v. Ford (1985) 2 EGLR 70;Lonrho Export Ltd. v. ECGD (1999) Ch 158, 181。

如果保险人在没有赔付前就以受保人的名义向第三人采取在法院提出索赔，这种不成熟的行动会导致受保人向法院申请把他的名字与诉讼撤销：CPR r 3.4(2)(b)。但保险人可以在事后取得受保人的追认(ratification)，即使追认是在时效已经届满后：Presentationes Musicales SA v. Secunda (1994) Ch 271；The "Frotanorte" (1995) 2 Lloyd's Rep 254；Victoria Teachers' Credit Union v. KPMG (2000) VSCA 23 等。

但英国法的地位与一些其他国家的法律不尽相同。例如在美国，如果保险人只赔付了一部分的钱，就可以保险人与受保人共同的名义向第三人求偿或提出索赔。美国也允许保险人在与受保人达成和解协议后就要求这一个代位求偿权，即使金钱还没有支付。换言之，保险人作出了一个没有条件的支付承诺就会被视为已经作出了支付。至于在中国大陆，据悉也是要求保险人已经作出支付给受保人，才能取得代位求偿权。在中国法院，保险人仅是交出一份代位求偿权表格(通常是一封受保人作出的信函确认已经收到赔偿金额并同意交出对第三人的诉权给保险人)，通常并不足够。中国法院会要求额外的证明是保险人已经作出了赔付，如汇款的证明或是收据。否则，中国法院不允许该索赔被登记。

有这些细节的一个原因估计是根据不同的法律，包括美国(但不是所有的州)与中国的保险人在行使代位求偿权时，可以用他自己的名义向第三人索赔。这表示没有把代位求偿权搞清楚，会存在第三人可能同时受到受保人(根据合约或侵权)与保险人(根据代位求偿)的起诉，面对两次诉讼与作出两次赔付。另一个原因是代位求偿权不像转让(assignment)，在后者有诉权的受保人作为转让人(assignor)必须给第三人(债务人)转让通知与说明转让给谁，才会有一个有效的转让，所以不会有双重诉讼的危险。

5. 保险人在全数赔付给受保人之前所拥有的权利

5.1 受保人有善意与合理保护保险人将来的代位求偿权的默示要求

这一情况是有它困难的地方就是在没有作出全数赔付之前，保险人难以主张他到底有什么权利，除了在保险合约下对受保人是有一个善意与合理保护保险人将来的代位求偿权的默示要求。这可节录一个澳大利亚上诉庭的先例 Sola Basic Australia Ltd v. Morganite Ceramic Pty Ltd (Unreported, 11 May 1989, CA NSW)，说："In every contract of insurance, there is an obligation, implied if not expressed, as between the insurer and the insured that the latter will not do anything to diminish the former's right to subrogation. It does not emerge clearly from the cases what is the source or nature of that obligation. It may be, and I think it is, a term of the contract of insurance which is implied by law... That is to say, the insurer may enjoin any apprehended breach of the stipulation, may subsequently sue for any actual breach in damages, may plead the breach as an defence if the insured claims under the relevant policy of insurance, and may sue for an injunction or damages any third person who induces a breach of that stipulation."

例如,受保人与对损失有责任的第三人达成和解协议,而这一和解协议保险人认为是对他不利的,保险人可以向受保人提出索赔:Commercial Union Assurance Co. v. Lister (1874) LR 9 Ch App 483,West of England Fire Insurance Co. v. Isaacs (1896) 2 QB 377, Horse, Carriage and General Insurance Co v. Petch (1916) 33 TLR 131。但原则上只要受保人与第三人达成一个善意的和解协议(*bona fide* settlement),保险人就通常没有反对的余地,也很难事后证明受到什么损害。有关受保人与第三人达成和解协议并损害保险人,会在本章之 10.3.3 段进一步探讨。

受保人与第三人在出了事故后很快达成和解协议的危险存在,因为他们可能还是有商业上的考虑与关系。笔者记得在很多年之前,中国一家主要的船公司的一艘船舶与另一艘有友好商业关系的新加波船公司的船舶发生严重碰撞,但两家公司的负责人很快就在电话与电文中同意互不追究责任。后来,这带来了保险人包括船东互保协会在这方面的质疑与麻烦。

5.2　保险人对受保人违反默示责任举证的困难

而更困难的是在其他的一些情况,因为这证明受保人非善意或恶意会很困难。如针对采取行动保存将来向第三人索赔的证据,而在海上货物运输经常会有的就是要求船舶所在地法院作出上船检查命令:The"Lady Muriel"(1995) No. 87 (Civil),或是知道第三人企图把财产转移,需要采取行动将有关财产冻结。这种有关程序的行动或不行动,很难会扯得上受保人是善意或者非善意。针对海上货物保险,还有一个大问题就是向第三人的船东提出索赔,经常会面对 1924 年《海牙规则》很短的索赔时效(卸货后的一年),这就存在要求受保人及时采取行动保护时效。但这里的问题比较复杂,因为保护时效必须是在海上运输合约如提单中的准确的管辖地点提起诉讼或开始仲裁才可以有效。举例说,如果提单是有一条伦敦仲裁条文,但受保人却在中国海事法院或日本法院在时效内向船东提出起诉,而没有在时效内开始伦敦仲裁,这等于是没有有效保护时效:Thyssen v. Calypso (2000) 2 Lloyd's Rep. 243。可以说这种事情有时候水平差一点的律师也做不好,更不说是一般货方的受保人,所以很难与受保人的善意或非善意扯上关系。

曾经有先例针对受保人向第三人提出索赔,但保险人不希望受保人这样做的情况。先例名为 AB Exportkredit v New Hampshire Insurance (Unrep, 1988),英国上诉庭判是如果保险合约中没有一条相关的明示条文,保险人是没有权利要求受保人不向第三人提出诉讼。其中 Woolf 大法官认为如果受保人的行动是非常不谨慎(reckless)或是恶意(bad faith),就会不同。

5.3　保险合约加上一条明示条文要求受保人在全数赔付前的责任

因为上述不明确的法律地位,所以海上保险合约都会有一条明示条文针对受保人在获得全部赔付之前应该履行的明示合约责任。这在1993年“国际船壳保险条款”是第9条，该方面在笔者与汪鹏南教授所著的《英国海上保险条款详论》第260页开始有详论，在此不再重复。而针对海上货物保险，在2009年协会货物条文第16条。[1] 有了这一条文但受保人还是没有采取合理的行动，如向第三人在时效届满前提出诉讼，保险人可根据该条文的违约向受保人索赔损失。而如果觉得该救济不足够，保险人会有更大的理据说服有关法院作出禁令/命令要求受保人采取行动。还有一个做法就是保险人尽快把应该赔付的金钱作出支付，然后根据代位求偿权把整个向第三人的诉讼行动接管过来。这一来，保险人喜欢怎样做就怎样做。

5.4 法院对这种明示条文会对保险人严格作出解释

这一条明示条文会带来有争议的情况，在先例 The“Vasso”(1993) 2 Lloyd's Rep 309 中可以显示。案情涉及大约6万吨的铁矿石装在 Vasso 轮前往青岛，但船舶半途沉没导致了货物的全损。保险人在事后与受保人的货方有了争议，保险人指称受保人应及时到法院申请冻结令把船壳保险人会赔付给船东的650万美元冻结，而没有这样做就违反了协会货物条文(一切险)的第16条。但法院不同意，认为只是指责受保人没有采取一些行动并不足够，另外还必须证明一个谨慎合理的受保人，为了自己的利益着想也会采取该行动才足够。Hobhouse 大法官这样说：“Accordingly, on the facts of the present case, the mere failure to apply for a Mareva injunction does not, without more, establish any failure to perform the duty imposed by cl. 16 (or s. 78). The assured, and Mr. Vassiliades their agent, acted reasonably and properly. Mr. Vassiliades conscientiously considered whether or not it was proper to swear an affidavit and apply for a Mareva injunction. He concluded that it was not and underwriters have not proved, or even begun to prove, that he was wrong. On the correct construction of the clause more has to be shown than merely that some step was not taken. Underwriters have to show that the step was a proper one which a reasonable assured, having regard to the interests of himself and the insurers and to the provisions of the policy, should have taken.”

总结说，法院对这种“Duty of Assured”的明示条文会作出对保险人严厉甚至不利的解释，可节录 Svensk Exportkredit v. New Hampshire Insurance Co (Unreported, 30 March 1988, CA) 先例中 Dillon 大法官所说如下：“it cannot be right, where there are difficult tactical decisions to be made, for the insurers to be able to stand on the sidelines and dare (受保人) to take the step that they think reasonable, against the chance that the insurers will be able to say ‘oh well, they should have done something else, so we're let off the hook’: I do not regard that as a commercially viable way of construing this contract.”

---

[1] 参见附录三。

6. 保险人在全数赔付给受保人之后所拥有的权利

根据1906年《英国海上保险法》,保险人在全数赔付之后会有三种权利:代位求偿权(Section 79);在双重保险(double insurance)的情况下,全数赔付的保险人向另外的保险人要求分配的权利(Section 80);在不足额保险(under insurance)的情况下,保险人可以要求受保人分配(Section 81)。在这里先进一步讨论代位求偿权,至于后两种权利稍后会在第14段讨论不足额保险与第17段讨论双重保险。

显然在全数赔付后,保险人有了代位求偿权,可以向对损失有责任的第三人提出索赔,但根据英国法律,原告仍是受保人,这就会带来以下的一些问题:

1. 保险人既然是以受保人的名义向第三人提出索赔,他的权利就局限在受保人可以向第三人主张的权利。如受保人与第三人之间的合约有责任限制或赔偿金额限制,这也影响保险人的代位求偿权。如果第三人对受保人的索赔有权提出对冲,保险人也受到影响。再多给一个例子,就是BIMCO针对海上石油勘探的租船业务所拟定的一些标准格式合约如TOWCON,TOWHIRE与SUPPLYTIME 2005,都有一条名为Knock-for-Knock的条文。这一理念是来自岸上的汽车保险,就是发生了事故,如汽车碰撞,就由各自的保险人赔付,双方不追究责任也不提出诉讼。显然目的是节省有关的行政与诉讼费用,反正发生汽车碰撞,这次你错得多,我错得少,下次就是我错得多,你错得少。对于大型的保险公司来讲就是一笔勾销更划算。这种做法在海上石油勘探的业务中(包括租船业务)也十分普遍,为了节省行政与诉讼费用,不论是承租人与船东谁错多错少,各自的损失由自己的保险人赔付,互相不追究。这一来,显然就是剥夺了保险人在赔付后的代位求偿权。可能保险人会是认为受保人应该在投保之前披露这一事实,但如果这种情况是在海上石油钻探中习惯性或普遍的做法,就有说法是保险人承保这一方面的业务风险应该有所了解,不存在要披露。这在1906年《英国海上保险法》之Section 18(3)(b)有清楚说明不必披露的情况之一:"In the absence of inquiry the following circumstances need not be disclosed, namely:—Any circumstance which is known or presumed to be known to the insurer. The insurer is presumed to know matters of common notoriety or knowledge, and matters which an insurer in the ordinary course of his business, as such, ought to know."(有关这方面在本书第二章第6.2段已有详论。)

2. 如果受保人与第三人在损失后但在保险人全数赔付前达成了和解协议,即使不是善意,对保险人的代位求偿权而言还是有约束力。保险人只有在能够证明该和解协议不是善意并不利影响他的代位求偿权的情况下,才会有权利向受保人索赔损失(这在本章5.1段有提及)。例如在先例West of England Fire Insurance Co. v. Isaacs (1896) 2 QB 377,案情涉及房子受到火灾的损害,火灾保险人赔付给了受保人100英镑的修理费用。但在受保人的租房合约中有规定是房子给火灾损害的话,房东需要修复。但受保人却放弃了要求房东这样做,这导致了保险人事后成功地向受保人要回这100英镑,法院认为受保人剥夺了保险人的代位求偿权。

3. 如果受保人与第三人的合约有一条仲裁条文,保险人的代位求偿权也受到该仲裁条文的约束:Schiffartsgesellschaft Detlef von Appen GmbH v. Wiener Allianz Versicherungs AG (1997) 2 Lloyd's Rep 279;The"Front Comor"(2005) 2 Lloyd's Rep. 257;Starlight Shipping Co v. Taiping Insurance Co (2008) 1 Lloyd's Rep. 230。这一点非常重要且保险人必须小心,因为涉及了海上货物保险行使代位求偿权时经常会遇上这一个问题,因为在最常被使用的CONGENBILL,在1994年的版本首次印上了合并租约仲裁条文的文字,而在租约中十之八九都会是伦敦仲裁。这表示保险人行使代位求偿权向船东提出索赔,不能漠视伦敦仲裁而在中国海事法院提出诉讼。如果保险人这样做,很容易面对英国法院作出的止诉禁令。这进一步也说明了保险人如果将代位求偿权处理得好,也必须熟悉伦敦、香港等主要海事仲裁地点的法律与做法。

4. 如果受保人向第三人索赔的权利已经时效届满,则保险人的代位求偿权也面对时效届满的后果:London Assurance Co v. Johnson (1737) Hardw 269。

5. 保险人向第三人的索赔虽然是真正的原告,但由于名义上是受保人,所以不存在第三人可把保险人扯进来,如向保险人提出要求披露并非是受保人所拥有或控制的文件:James Nelson v. Nelson Line (1906) 2 KB 217。第三人也不能质疑保险人赔付给受保人的钱是少于诉讼中索赔的损失:Bee v. Jenson (No. 2) (2008) Lloyd's Rep. IR 221。

6. 如果受保人在诉讼前或诉讼中发生倒闭而不再存在,保险人也就会失去了他的代位求偿权,除非是保险人想办法恢复受保人公司注册:M H Smith Ltd (Plant Hire) v. Mainwaring (1986) 2 Lloyd's Rep 244 (CA);Re Ballast Plc., Paul Travellers Insurance Co Ltd v. Dargan (2007) Lloyd's Rep. IR 742。这里可以节录Kerr大法官在M H Smith Ltd (Plant Hire) v. Mainwaring先例所说如下:"Alternatively (to subrogation), if the insurer encounters difficulty in persuading the assured to bring the action in respect of the claim for which he has indemnified him, or if he refuses to allow his name to be used, then he can join him in the action in order to compel him to do so, in the same way as the holder of an equitable assignment can bring an action against the debtor or wrongdoer by joining the assignor. If the assignor or, as in this case, the assured is no longer in existence, because the company has been dissolved, then unfortunately for the insurer none of those things can be done by him, since he himself has no cause of action against the wrongdoer. All that he can do, as my Lord has said, ... is to apply to have the company restore to the register."

这表示保险人如果对受保人的经济状况有担忧,但还没有倒闭前,要求受保人向第三人的索赔权利以转让(assignment)的方式替代代位求偿权会是更好的做法,因为这一来就可以允许保险人以自己的名义作为受让人,向第三人提出索赔,再也不受受保人倒闭与不存在的影响。这方面在接下来的第7段会进一步探讨权利转让。

7. 代位求偿权与权利转让

刚提到保险人对受保人的经济状况有担忧,会向受保人取得权利转让(assignment)是更为优胜的做法,这里可以节录 Michell 与 Watterson 合著的《SUBROGATION Law and Practice》(2007 版)一书之 10.63 段:"In M H Smith (Plant Hire) Ltd v. D L Mainwaring (tla Inshore) (1984) 2 Lloyd's Rep 244, an insurer is prevented from bringing subrogated proceedings in the name of an insured company which had been wound up and dissolved. In these circumstances, the insurer might still succeed if it were to obtain an order under the Companies Act 1985, s 651, restoring the company to the register for the purpose of the subrogated proceedings (Cf Re Alan Meek Wagstaff & Co [Ch D 11 December 2000], where an order was made for the benefit of an insurer under the Companies Act 1985, s 653[2B]). However, it would do better to pre-empt the problem, if it can foresee that its insured's liquidation is imminent, by taking an assignment the insured's rights of action."

有关把权利转让的课题在笔者所著的《国际商务游戏规则——英国合约法》第四章第7段有介绍,不多重复。只是说转让分为两种:一是衡平法转让(equitable assignment);二是立法转让(statutory/legal assignment)。

7.1　衡平法转让与立法转让的区别

这两种转让的定义可节录《Chitty on Contracts》第30版19-002段所说有关衡平法转让如下:"If the rights were equitable, the assignee(受让人)could sue in his own name, but it is necessary to make the assignor(转让人)a party to the suit if he retained any interest in the subject matter, for instance if the assignment was not absolute but conditional or by way of charge. ..."

至于立法转让的定义,《Chitty on Contracts》第30版首先在19-006段节录了《Law of Property Act 1925》的 Section 136,然后在19-007段说明立法转让的三个条件并在符合条件后允许受让人以自己的名义向第三人或债务人索赔,不必要扯上转让人,节录如下:"It will be seen that, in order that the section may apply, three conditions must be fulfilled: (1) the assignment must be absolute and not purport to be by way of charge only; (2) it must be in writing under the hand of the assignor; (3) express notice in writing thereof must be given to the debtor or trustee. The general effect of the section is to allow the assignee to sue the debtor in his own name instead of, as previously, having to sue in the name of the assignor and perhaps having to go to a court of equity to compel his joinder in the auction. The section: '... is merely machinery: ... it enables an action to be brought by the assignee in his own name in cases where previously he would have sued in the assignor's name, but only where he could so sue.'"

衡平法转让就必须把转让人扯在同一个诉讼作为共同原告或共同被告(这是看转让人的态度),原因就是要保护债务人,让他把钱支付给受让人或转让人之后就能够将债务一笔勾销,不会有了一个转让而不知道钱应该给谁。需要这样做的主要原因就是转让不够明确,也不够绝对(absolute)。如只是把部分债务转让给受让人,又或者为转让加上一些条件,该条件成立后转让才生效。这都会导致债务人无所适从,需要法院命令将关系搞清楚。至于立法转让的三个条件就是转让必须是清清楚楚,不能附带条件,转让人也必须作出文书转让通知给债务人。这一来,债务人(debtor)所欠钱的对象就从转让人(assignor)变为受让人(assignee),受让人可以自己的名义向债务人索赔。

针对保险合约而言,第三人如船东/承运人如果对货物损失有责任,需要赔偿受保人货方的损失,该船东就变为债务人,而货方就变为转让人。在货方得到保险人的赔付后把索赔权利转让给保险人,保险人就变为受让人。这一诉权属于合约利益,可以自由转让,也不需要得到债务人的同意。会有一些合约,如造船合约中经常加入一条禁止转让合约利益(prohibition of assignment)条文(这在笔者所著的《造船合约》2008年版一书第14章有详论),但这种情况很少会在提单或租约中出现。所以,针对海上货物保险而言,以转让代替代位求偿权通常不会有问题。

针对保险而言,如果转让是因为保险人担心受保人会发生经济问题而倒闭,就要小心在双方同意的转让协议中说明保险人在作出了保险合约中的什么赔付,毕竟在一个开口保单会涉及其他付运的赔付。这就可以避免将来受保人真的倒闭与清盘,不会面对清盘人把转让了但属于代位求偿的钱要回平均分给所有债权人。这在Mance大法官等著的《Insurance Disputes》第二版之8.73段的脚注1这样说:"A liquidator is under a duty to collect in all sums due to the company in liquidation for the benefit of the company's creditors. He will therefore wish to ensure that the assignment is not merely a device to prevent the recovery falling into the general assets of the company for distribution among the creditors. Accordingly, to avoid challenge, the assignment rights are those to which the underwriters would be entitled in accordance with the principles of subrogation."

7.2 代位求偿权与转让的利弊

以下可以总结这两者的利弊:

1. 已经提到过,受保人在诉讼前或诉讼中发生倒闭而不再存在,保险人也就会失去了代位求偿权,因为保险人向第三人的诉讼是以受保人的名义进行:M H Smith (Plant Hire) v. Mainwaring (1986) 2 Lloyd's Rep 244 (CA)。但如果是立法转让,保险人就可以以自己的名义提起诉讼并进行控制,不必受制于受保人的经济状况或存在与否。

2. 如果是转让,成功向第三人索赔后取回来的钱就直接可以支付给保险人,不必通过受保人(即使是保险人有在本章第3段介绍的衡平法下的保障,但还是有一定的麻烦)。而且在转让的情况下,如果取回来的钱比保险人赔付的钱还要多(如在汇率上获利),保险人不必把多余的部分退还给受保人:Lucas Ltd v. Export Credit Guarantee Department (1974) 2 All ER 889。这与代位求偿权不一样,因为代位求偿权下的保险人只能是保留自己赔付给受保人的金额加上利息:Yorkshire Insurance Co. v. Nisbet Shipping Ltd (1962) 2 QB 330。

3. 转让也不同于代位求偿权就是受让人不必支付了完全的金额后才获得。转让在保险人与受保人同意的情况下可以提前作出。虽然在现实中受保人是不会愿意作出转让直到他取得保险合约下的赔付。

4. 还有一个可能的好处是转让只能是利益,如合约利益,而不能是责任。但代位求偿权因为是以受保人的名义向第三人提出索赔,所以会有情况要面对第三人的反索赔。

5. 从以上四点看来,转让比代位求偿权优越。这带来一个说法是转让会全面替代了代位求偿权,在一个有关转让给保险人诉权的先例 The"Columbiana"(1963) 2 Lloyd's Rep. 479,Roskill 大法官说:"It was urged upon me by Mr. Kerr(被告船东的代表大律师)that if this view prevailed, the floodgates - the word is his - would be opened to litigation of a type which the Courts have sought to prevent, because in some cases the underwriters could by assignment recover more than 100 per cent of their loss, whereas by subrogation they could only recover up to 100 per cent of their loss. ..."

但发展下去这种情况并没有发生,在大部分的情况下保险人还是以代位求偿权向第三人追偿,原因在接下来的段节会涉及。

1. 第一个最主要的缺点就是立法转让需将书面的通知给转让人的债务人,这不像代位求偿权保险人赔付了100%的保险金额给受保人就自动拥有向第三人索赔的权利。这一转让的书面通知也不是想象中这么简单,因为保险人与受保人都必须掌握清楚谁是债务人。很多情况下,海上货物保险会涉及的债务人就是提单下的承运人,但要锁定谁是承运人已经是一个大学问,因为他可以是船舶的真正船东,也可以是光船船东,也可以是期租或程租的承运人等。贵族院的 The"Starsin"(2000) 1 Lloyd's Rep. 85 就是这方面典型的案例。还有是海上货物保险的期间不仅是在海上运输的一段时间,在一切险情况下货物受损作出赔付,可能要负上责任的第三人或是债务人更会是仓库所有人、卡车或火车运输公司等。要尽快在赔付给了受保人一段短时间(赔付前受保人不会愿意作出立法转让)把谁是债务人锁定并送达给他转让通知并不是一件容易的事情。这一复杂的问题在本书第十四章第4段有关"谁是承运人"(identity of carrier)会进一步探讨。

2. 另一个缺点是有说法保险人并不愿意以自己的名字作为原告,认为对于声誉有不利影响，虽然笔者对这一点不是太了解，毕竟向第三人提出索赔又不是杀人放火。例如，在《Colinvaux's Law of Insurance in Hong Kong》一书之11.004段有一句说："The fact that the insurer must sue in its own name may result in an welcome publicity. This would appear to be the overriding consideration militating against the widespread use of assignment as an alternative to subrogation."

3. 还有一个比较大的缺点就是今天提单会有不少加上一条仲裁条文，特别是伦敦仲裁，这里就带来一个法律地位还不太清楚的问题。这就是在保险人作出100%赔付之前，会有不少案件是受保人已经开始向船东或承运人采取了一些行动如扣船取得诉前担保，甚至已经开始仲裁。毕竟，这些都是受保人根据协会货物条文第16条要做的事情。这一来，仲裁的两位当事人显然是受保人作为原告，船东或承运人作为被告，根据代位求偿权不需要作出任何变动，唯一就是受保人的背后可能在操作的变为保险人，代表律师本来向受保人作出汇报也变为向保险人作出汇报与要求指示。但一转让，受保人就不能继续作为原告，必须要改为保险人。这就带来不明朗，而法律也不像是太明确。根据The"Felicie"(1990) 2 Lloyd's Rep 21，Phillips大法官认为是有困难，因为仲裁是属于个人的协议。但接下去在The"Jordan Nicolov"(1990) 2 Lloyd's Rep 11，Hobhouse大法官不认为是个问题，只要转让通知除了是给被告的船东或承运人外，还要作出给所有仲裁庭的成员，将来的裁决书会是把原告的名字从受保人变为保险人。看来Hobhouse大法官的立场也受到上诉庭在Schiffartsgesellschaft Detlef von Appen GmbH v. Voest Alpine Trading GmbH (1997) 2 Lloyd's Rep. 279的支持。

4. 还有一个缺点或复杂之处就是有关转让的适用法，根据英国法律，转让的适用法是根据作出转让地点的国家法律。在The"Columbiana"(1963) 2 Lloyd's Rep. 479，判是转让是适用哥伦比亚的法律。据悉，世界上很多国家对于转让的有效性有不同的要求。

7.3　代位求偿权与转让的案例介绍

关于代位求偿权与权利转让的案例有不少，包括以上提到的先例。以下只挑一个作出介绍，其中The"Aiolos"(1983) 2 Lloyd's Rep. 25中有详细的解释，这个先例说明了权利转让的其中一个主要缺点，就是立法权利转让程序的履行是需要作出书面通知给债务人。如果没有书面通知，就变为衡平法转让，则权利的转让人（也就是受保人）必须参加诉讼。这一来，如果受保人倒闭或不合作，保险人就会面对困难。在该先例中，是一票投了保的黄豆被装在Aiolos轮上，结果是货物重量有短少。台湾保险人根据保单予以赔付，并且从受保人那里取得了一张"代位求偿单"(Subrogation Receipt)。可以说受保人通过这张单据已经是把他自己向船东索赔的权利给了保险人。之后保险人就行使保险合约下代位求偿的权利，但错误地以自己的名义在英国海事法院开始了针对船东的诉讼。最开始，船东抗辩指索赔原告只能是受保人，并且英国海事法院基于此理由驳回了保险人的诉讼。上诉时，法院允许保险人将索赔请求中的一句"行使代位求偿的权利"修改为"诉讼权利被转让给了他们",所以是有一个说得通的权利向船东索赔。允许修改就意味着至少这一个诉讼还是能够延续,否则是要根据代位求偿权,重新以受保人名义向船东起诉,就已经过了1924年《海牙规则》的一年时效了。

但是修改的前提条件是保险人必须将受保人(台湾的货方)也作为共同的被告,因为权利的转让人必须参加诉讼(assignors should be before the court)。因为这一转让不符合立法转让的三个条件,其中不存在书面的转让通知给船东。

8. 代位求偿权下谁有权控制向第三人索赔的诉讼

在受保人的损失完全获得赔付后,通常受保人对向第三人索赔的诉讼不会有兴趣继续控制,往往就欢迎保险人把它接管过来。如果诉讼还没有开始,根据代位求偿权的原则,受保人也必须让保险人以他的名义向第三人起诉。但有时候受保人不合作,如拒绝签发授权书,原因会是与第三人还有商业往来或保持友好关系。这一来,为了强制,保险人可以把受保人作为共同被告(另一个被告就是第三人/债务人)提出诉讼:The"Esso Bernicia"(1989) AC 643。也有先例是受保人拒绝这样做或拒绝让保险人接管诉讼,保险人向法院取得命令强制受保人这样做:Commercial Union Assurance Co v. Lister (1874) LR 9 Ch App 483。有关上述做法,在《Colinvaux's Law of Insurance in Hong Kong》一书之11.013段有提到说:"If the assured refuses to lend his name to the proceedings, he may be compelled to do so, ultimately by being joined as co-defendant; this device ensures that the assured is a party to the action so that judgment can be given in his favour, subject of course to the imposition of a charge on the proceeds of the action for the benefit of the insurer."

至于是被告的第三人,他也不能指原告的受保人没有损失,因为保险人已经对他作出全数的赔付,除非合约另有条文改变这一个普通法的地位(这方面请看本章第10段):Bradburn v. Great Western Railway Co (1874) IR 10 Ex. 1;Bovis Construction Ltd v. Eagle Star Insurance Co Ltd (2002) Lloyd's Rep IR 321;Falcon Insurance Co (HK) Ltd v. Cheshire Cat Restaurant & Pub Co Ltd (unrep, DCCJ 5865/2006, [2007] HKEC 2084)。

但是换一种情况是受保人与保险人关于保险赔付达成共识尚需要一定的时间,受保人也会担心万一保险合约下的索赔失败,而再向有责任的第三人(在海上运输就会是船东/承运人)提出索赔就会面对诉讼时效已过,这导致受保人夹在当中处于很被动的地位。所以,受保人会在等待保险人作出赔付的期间通常都会开始针对第三人提出诉讼。毕竟,受保人这样做也是履行他在保险合约下所负的义务。根据先例 The Netherlands Insurance Co Est 1845 Ltd v. Karl Ljungberg & Co AB (1986) 2

Lloyd's Rep 19,2009 年协会货物条文之第 16 条对受保人的此项义务有了更进一步的规定,也就是说,即便保险人拒绝根据保险合约对受保人进行赔付,受保人都有主动的作为义务开始针对第三人的索赔程序。有关这方面,在本章第 5 段有详细的介绍,不再重复。

在 The Netherlands Insurance Co 先例中,有一票货物是胶合板从新加坡运往丹麦,是根据 1963 年的协会货物条文投保一切险,而到达丹麦时货物有损坏。保险人认为该货损不是在承保范围,拒绝赔付,但同时提出要求受保人在不损害(without prejudice to)他们对保险责任否定的前提下,根据受保人义务条款的前身“托管人条款”(the Bailee Clause),受保人是有义务保护诉讼时效以及针对承运人的诉权。英国枢密院最终是判保险人有权作出这样的要求,但是基于保险合约的默示条文受保人可以向保险人要回因此产生的合理诉讼费用。在代位求偿的大原则下,诉讼前的调查取证以及相关的合理诉讼费用都应该算是由保险人补偿的合理花费。

可是受保人对以他自己的名义开始的针对第三人的诉讼程序是否有最终的控制权呢?已经说过,在受保人的损失完全获得赔付后,通常受保人对向第三人索赔的诉讼是不会有兴趣继续控制,往往就欢迎保险人把它接管过来。但经常会有情况是受保人还有部分损失没有获得保险人的赔付,如在不足额保险的情况下,或者不是承保的损失(如延误造成的损失)。这一来,受保人会很想自己继续控制向第三人的诉讼,顶多在成功向第三人取回全部的损失后把保险人已经作出的赔付归还。在先例 Commercial Union Assurance Co v. Lister (1874) LR 9 Ch App 483 中,磨粉机的保险价值是 33,000 英镑,它被煤气爆炸毁坏,而据说煤气爆炸是由于煤气供应商的错误导致。受保人说自己没有投保的损失是 56,000 英镑,据此,受保人没有足额投保。他另外索赔 6000 英镑的利润损失,这也是没有投保的。保险人是愿意赔 33,000 英镑给受保人。但他们担心如果这样做,受保人会接受煤气供应商赔偿没有投保的差额以了结整个诉讼。所以保险人向法院申请禁止令(injunction)与宣告(declaration)有关:(1)保险人也享有受保人的诉权;(2)受保人不能减低诉讼的索赔金额(应是 56,000 + 33,000 英镑);(3)受保人不可以拒绝保险人以受保人的名义起诉。

最终上诉院是判受保人有权控制诉讼的进展,也就是说,受保人才是拥有控制该诉讼程序权利的所有人(*dominus litis*),但唯一的条件他不能减低索赔金额与向第三人追偿回来的钱属于保险人的部分,受保人是以信托人的身份要将该笔钱归还保险人。但该先例主要说明受保人有不得损害保险人代位求偿权的责任与义务。

这方面也可节录 Howard Bennett 教授所著的《The Law of Marine Insurance》第二版之 25.16 段的一段话:“Thus, where the assured is only partly insured, even after payment by the insurer the assured retains the right to control the litigation against the third party, although, where the shortfall results from a deductible, such a clause is likely to be construed as contractually subordinating the assured's interests to those of the insurer.”

总的分析,诉讼第三人的权利本身是属于受保人的,毕竟是以他的名义。即使是受保人根据保险合约得到了保险人的全额赔付,他还是有可能最终要支付诉讼费用,而在败诉时更加要面对被告诉讼费用的索赔,尽管保险人在代位求偿单中是承诺会就此项费用补偿受保人。而且无论如何,受保人都会在法院留下记录,虽然只是民事,但对于有些大公司或是名人来讲,仅是名字被使用就足以引起轩然大波。所以有说法是原则上在所有的案件中,受保人都是向第三人提出诉讼程序的所有人,因为这是他们的诉讼程序。这里可节录 Mance 大法官等著的《Insurance Disputes》第二版之 8.23 段:"Where the insurer has fully indemnified the assured, he can take over the control of the proceedings on his undertaking to indemnify the assured against his costs. However until underwriters have paid the whole of the assured's loss, the assured remains *dominus litis* and is entitled to control the proceedings himself. Accordingly, where the assured has uninsured losses (For example, following a motor accident, the assured may have had a vehicle damage claim settled by his motor insurer and may also have an uninsured loss in respect of personal injuries he has suffered.) or is obliged to pay an excess under the policy he remains *dominus litis*."

另也可节录 Goff 勋爵在 The "Mammoth Pine" (1986) 2 Lloyd's Rep 19 一案中所说的话:"It is first of all desirable to have regard to their setting in the contract of insurance. In this connection, it is to be remembered that, in the event of the insurers paying a claim of an assured for cargo damage under the policy, they would become subrogated to the rights of the assured against the carriers in respect of the relevant damage. If the insurers then wished to enforce such rights against the carriers in legal proceedings, they would be entitled to do so and, although in England they must proceed in the name of the assured, they can do so as *dominus litis*(拉丁文,指保险人以受保人的货方名义去起诉)though only on the basis that they indemnify the assured against costs. For this it follows that, on the appellants' (保险人)submission before the board, the assured(受保人的货方)would be responsible for the costs of litigation commenced under the bailee clause(这条文要求货方向第三者采取合理的法律行动以减少损失,本质与本条款的第 49 条相同)up till the time of payment of the claim by the insurers, but thereafter the cost of litigation would fall on the insurers. This is in itself a somewhat surprising result; and it is not to be forgotten that, under the bailee clause, the obligation on the assured is not merely to commence proceedings but to ensure that all the specified rights are 'properly preserved and exercised'. Costs may therefore be incurred by the assured, in performing their obligations under the clause, not merely in commencing litigation to preserve a time bar but in pursuing litigation so commenced in order to prevent it from lapsing or being otherwise prejudiced by delay; and it is notorious that such costs can, in certain jurisdictions, be by no means insignificant. On the appellants' approach, therefore, it follows that the insurers might have a positive incentive to delay a settlement, thus throwing a greater burden of cost upon the assured; and this would be by virtue of an obligation imposed under the policy which requires the assured to take a course of action which is plainly intended to be for the benefit of the insurers."

9. 共同受保人与代位受偿权的豁免

9.1 不能对共同受保人行使代位求偿权的原因

根据先例 Simpson v. Thomason (1877) LR 3 App Cas 279,保险人不可以通过行使代位求偿权来向受保人索赔。在该先例,涉及同一船公司的姐妹船碰撞,受损的船舶获得赔付后,保险人向另一艘有碰撞责任的船舶提出索赔,但要起诉的是同一船公司或同一受保人。法院判这是不行,而这一问题现在已经有所解决,就是在 2003 年国际船壳保险条款中加入一条姐妹船条文(第 7 条)。

至于在共同受保人的情况下,也有明确的法律说明保险人在赔付了给其中一位受保人后是不会有代位求偿权向另一位有疏忽造成损失的共同受保人提出索赔。支持该说法的一个原因是共同受保人实际上就是只有一个受保人(one assured theory)。但在 Petrofina (UK) Ltd v. Magnaload Ltd (1983) 2 Lloyd's Rep 91,Lloyd 大法官认为更好的解释是循环诉讼(circuity of action),就是大家告来告去,最后还是原地踏步。如保险人向共同受保人提出索赔,而共同受保人作为受保人之一再向同一个保险人要求补偿。这在 National Oilwell (UK) Ltd v. Davy Offshore Ltd (1993) 2 Lloyd's Rep. 582 先例中,受到 Colman 大法官的支持说:"... an insurer cannot exercise rights of subrogation against a co-assured under an insurance on property in which the co-assured has the benefit of cover which protects him against the very loss or damage to the insured property which forms the basis of the claim which underwriters seek to pursue by way of subrogation. The reason why the insurer cannot pursue such a claim is that to do so would be in breach of an implied term in the policy and to that extent the principles of **circuity of action** operate to exclude the claim."

除了循环诉讼的解释外,还有默示条文的说法。这是在 Stone Vickers v. AS (1991) 2 Lloyd's Rep 288,Colman 大法官这样说:"Where a policy is effected on a vessel to be constructed and it is expressed to be for the benefit of sub-contractors as co-assured, if a particular sub-contractor negligently causes loss of or damage to the whole or part of the vessel which has been insured under the policy and the sub-contractor has an insurable interest in the vessel, it is not open to underwriters who have settled the insured shipbuilder' claim to exercise rights of subrogation in respect of the same loss and damage against the co-assured subcontractor. To do so would be completely inconsistent with the insurer's obligation to the co-assured under the policy. The insurer would in effect be causing the assured with whom he had settled to pursue proceedings which if successful would at once cause the co-assured to sustain a loss arising from loss or damage to the very subject-matter of the insurance in which that co-assured has an insurable interest and a right of indemnity under the policy. In my judgment so inconsistent with the insurer's obligation to the co-assured would be the exercise of rights of subrogation in such a case that there must be implied into the contract of insurance a term to give it business efficacy that an insurer will not in such circumstances use rights of subrogation in order to recoup from a co-assured the indemnity which he has paid to the assured. To exercise such rights would be in breach of such a term. In such a case the law recognizes the rights of the co-assured by enabling him to rely on his rights under the policy by way of defence in the proceedings which the insurers have caused to be commenced in breach of their implied obligation under the policy. This is an effective means of enforcing the co-assured's rights and makes it unnecessary for him to join the insurers as third parties in the action. ”

接下来的先例 National Oilwell (UK) Ltd v. Davy Offshore Ltd (1993) 2 Lloyd's Rep. 582，也是以默示条文的解释为保险人不可以通过行使代位求偿权来向共同受保人（co-assureds）索赔，Colman 大法官这样说："The explanation for the insurers' inability to cause one co-assured to sue another co-assured is that in as much as the policy on goods covers all the assureds on an all risks basis for loss and damage, even if caused by their own negligence, any attempt by an insurer after paying the claim of one assured to exercise rights of subrogation against another would in effect involve the insurer seeking to reimburse a loss caused by a peril (loss or damage even if caused by the assured's negligence) against which he had insured for the benefit of the very party against whom he now sought to exercise rights of subrogation. That party could stand in the same position as the principal assured as regards a loss caused by his own breach of contract or negligence. For the insurers who had paid the principal assured to assert that they were now free to exercise rights of subrogation and thereby sue the party at fault would be to subject the co-assured to a liability for loss and damage caused by a peril insured for this benefit... **it is necessary to imply a term into the policy of insurance to avoid this unsatisfactory possibility**... the purported exercise by insurers of rights of subrogation against the co-assured would be in breach of such a term and would accordingly provide the co-assured with a defence to the subrogated claim. ”

以上三种不同说法表面上看来是同一个结果，就是保险人不能以代位求偿权向共同保险人提出索赔。但实际上有区别，首先是只有一个受保人（one assured theory），会带来的后果就是无辜的受保人会受到另一个犯错的共同受保人拖累而赔不到钱。如犯错的程度达到违反了 1906 年《英国海上保险法》Section 55(2)(a)的"蓄意恶行”(wilful misconduct),或是违反了 Section 78(4)的没有采取合理行动减少损失。如果犯错的共同受保人涉及是在投保时不作出实质性披露或误述,或是欺诈,会否影响无辜的受保人问题就更大:Woolcott v. Sun Alliance (1978) 1 Lloyd's Rep 629。如果以循环诉讼(circuity of action)解释,也会在这样的情况下有一定的疑问,就是保险人赔付给了一个无辜的受保人后,再代位求偿向蓄意恶行的共同受保人索赔,该受保人会否可以以循环诉讼作为抗辩。看来,比较有弹性的解释还是以保险合约有默示条文不得向共同受保人作出代位求偿权的索赔,个别案件就是看情况而定,毕竟默示就必须是合理。

9.2 为什么有“共同受保人”

共同受保人(co-assureds)的情况很普遍,他的作用就是作为主要的受保人把相关的公司或人士也扯进来作为共同受保人以获得同一份保险合约的保障。而且变为共同的受保人,即使是相关的公司或人士造成损失,也可以避免保险人在赔付后向他们追偿与索赔。这一做法在 1906 年《英国海上保险法》Section 23(1)被认可,即一份海上保险合约一定要说明受保人或其他人士代理作出投保(The name of the assured, or of some person who effects the insurance on his behalf.)。这方面也可节录 Petrofina (UK) Ltd v. Magnaload Ltd (1983) 2 Lloyd's Rep 91,Lloyd 大法官说:“I would hold that a head contractor ought to be able to insure the entire contract works in his own name and the name of all his sub-contractors, just like a bailee or mortgagee, and that a sub-contractor ought to be able to recover the whole of the loss insured, holding the excess over his own interest in trust for the others.”

所以,在船壳保险,受保人的船东就会有可能把船舶管理公司拖在一起作为共同受保人。这种做法在一些大型的建筑工程包括像造船,由于会涉及许多的分包商与供应商,所以在总承建商或船厂的保险合约中,会把这些类别的有关公司包括在内作为共同受保人。而由于这些分包商与供应商会很多,名字也在订立保险合约的时候无法确定所以会粗略的把所有不知名的分包商与供应商都加进来作为共同受保人。如受保人写为:“ABC 公司 and/or EFG 公司 and/or 分包商 and/or 供应商”。如果漏掉一个想包括在内的共同受保人,就会有麻烦,如在本书第一章第 2.5 段所提到的 The“Jascon 5”(2006) 2 Lloyd's Rep 195,涉及了受保人船东指称保险经纪人漏掉把船厂(新加坡的 Sembawang 船厂)加进来作为共同受保人。

针对海上货物运输保险,伦敦保险市场的开口/预约保单(open covers)是给了何谓受保人一个很广泛的定义,如:“ABC Limited, and/or as agents and/or subsidiaries and/or associated companies and/or whom they may have instructions to insure”。这主要是为了让受保人的贸易商在他的贸易活动中尽量有弹性,如货物在整个海上运输途中的部分路段使用集团子公司的车队/船舶/仓库的情况下,都可以受到保护而不会将来面对保险人的代位求偿的索赔。如果不能给受保人一个很广泛的定义,那么就需要有代位求偿权豁免条款(Waiver of Subrogation Clause)来作为代替,用词如下:

"Insurers waive all rights of subrogation and/or recourse against the Assured and/or subsidiary companies of the Assured engaged in the carriage of and/or storage of the subject-matter insured."重要的是,这一广泛受保人定义也包括 CIF 买方,甚至在 CIF 卖方向保险人宣告时还不知名的 CIF 分买方。针对上述有关受保人的定义,John Dunt 所著的《Marine Cargo Insurance》一书之 3.28 段说:

"This wording not only ensures that all the companies in a group are included as 'Assured' but, more importantly, in the present context, extends the insurance to c. i. f. buyers of a cargo so that the original insured, in this case ABC Limited, acts as 'agent' on behalf of a buyer of the cargo 'for whom they may have instructions to insure'. These arrangements are now reflected in the revised Institute Cargo Clauses in the Benefit of Insurance Clause which provides as follows:

'This insurance covers the Assured which includes the person claiming indemnity either as the person by or on whose behalf the contract of insurance was effected or as an assignee...'

In the light of this provision a c. i. f. buyer from the original assured will now be an 'Assured' not only assignee, but as an assured in his own right falling within the principles set out by Colman J. in National Oilwell (UK) Limited v. Davy Offshore (1993) 2 Lloyd's Rep 582. These principles provide that where the person who makes the insurance has 'express or implied actual authority' to bind a potential co-assured, that will create a binding contract. Evidence of whether the original assured intended to insure the buyer may be provided by reference to the terms of the contract of insurance itself, or by referring to the contract of sale or other admissible material to show what was intended. The insurance wording commonly used in the London market, whereby the original assured acts 'as agent' of the c. i. f. buyer 'for whom they may have instructions to insure' constitutes such evidence. Moreover, a c. i. f. seller normally has actual authority from his buyer to arrange insurance on the goods for the benefit of his buyer who is know or ascertainable at the time the contract is made. The position of a sub-buyer who may not yet exist is less certain but the intention to include such a buyer, being the eventual assignee, is clear and he too should be treated as an 'Assured'."

这表示 CIF 买方向保险人索赔会是既可以作为保险合约或保险证明(certificate of insurance)的受让人,或是共同受保人。大体上他们都不应该有太大区别,因为受让人本来就不会有多于转让人在保险合约下的权利。而作为共同受保人也应该是同样受到保险合约下权利范围的约束,特别是把海上货物保险当作是一份共同保单(joint policy),而不是一份综合保单(composite policy)。有关两种保单的区别在本章 9.5 段有解释。但由于在协会货物保险条文第 5.2 条,针对受保人或他的雇员对相关船舶不适航或集装箱不适货有私谋已经有明示规定不影响无辜的受让人,也就是

CIF 买方或分买方(这在本书第六章 8.3 段有介绍)。看来,作为受让人向保险公司索赔还是有一定的保护。

9.3 共同受保人不受到保障的情况之一

在 National Oilwell (UK) Ltd v. Davy Offshore Ltd (1993) 2 Lloyd's Rep. 582 中,保险合约下的主要受保人是北海油田项目的承包商(DOL),他通过与保险人在保险合约中的约定将分承包商(NOW)也作为了共同受保人,规定如下:"**Other Assureds**: Any other company, firm, person or party (including but not limited to contractors and/or sub-contractors and/or suppliers) with whom the Assured have entered into agreement and/or contracts in connection with the subject matters of this Insurance, and/or any works activities, preparations etc., connected herewith. **The interests of the 'Other Assureds' shall be covered throughout the entire policy period (irrespective of contract period [s]) subject to full coverage as herein, unless specific contracts contain provisions to the contrary, in which event, insurance hereunder for such specific contracts only, shall be limited accordingly**..."

而在分承包商(NOW)与承包商(DOL)的买卖合约中有这样的条文:"The Purchaser shall on behalf of and in the joint names of the Purchaser and ... the Supplier and all sub-contractors insure on an 'All Risks' basis the Work and materials in the course of manufacture **until the time of delivery** in the amount of the Contract Price..."

加黑部分就说明,在主承包商 DOL 与保险人的保险合约(承保海上钻油台的工程的一切险)承保期间规定得很宽泛,是从工程开始直到结束,估计是 18 个月,另加上 2 年的维修保养期间。这一来,如果分承包商也包括在受保人的定义,就表示主承包商 DOL 与所有分承包商的承保期间都是一样。但这显然不是保险人所希望的,因为个别分承包商会是参与工程很短的时间,所以就加了一条上述加黑的文字,说明 DOL 如果与个别的分承包商约定有特定的保险期限,就以该期限为准或限制。而 DOL 与分承包商 NOW 的分包合约中,正是有条文将分承包商的保险期间明确局限到了机器交付主承包商之时。

由此可以看出,分承包商 NOW 被承保的只是这批设备的生产阶段直至交付所产生的损失,也就是说,分承包商 NOW 在将这批设备交付给主承包商 DOL 之后就再也不是共同受保人。而这批设备在水下安装时由于质量缺陷进水而导致损失。分承包商 NOW 起诉主承包商 DOL 想要回他欠下的货款,主承包商 DOL 进行抗辩并提出反索赔。而实际上反索赔是保险人在行使根据保险合约赔付了主承包商 DOL 后向分承包商的代位求偿权。法院判决说保险人有权这样做,因为在发生事故时,分承包商 NOW 已经不是保单下的共同受保人。保单中虽然有明示代位求偿权豁免条款,但这也帮不到分承包商。所以类似的情况下,共同受保人不能认为保单中有一条明示代位求偿权豁免条款自己真的就万事大吉,更为重要的是,要确保自己的受保期间与其他受保人的受保期间一致。

9.4 共同受保人不受到保障的情况之二

在上诉庭先例 Stone Vickers Ltd. v. AS (1992) 2 Lloyd's Rep 578(CA),案情涉及供应商(Stone Vickers)提供给了船厂(AS)一个螺旋桨。AS 与 Stone Vickers 约定为 Stone Vickers 投保有关的造船风险,而事实上 AS 投保了一年半的造船风险(Institute Clauses for Builder's Risks),其中受保人包括了 Stone Vickers,说"Agreed include ... Sub-Contractors as additional co-assured for their respective rights and interests. Without recourse against any Co-assured."该提供的螺旋桨有缺陷,这导致了 AS 向保险人提出要求赔付,保险人也作出了赔付,之后根据代位求偿权向供应商的 Stone Vickers 提出索赔。但 Stone Vickers 就以他是共同受保人作为抗辩,这就涉及了 AS 的造船风险保险合约是否能够把 Stone Vickers 作为共同受保人扯进来。这里涉及 Stone Vickers 能否说成是他与保险人之间的合约关系是合理算是通过 AS 作为代理人。这一问题与提单中的"喜玛拉雅条款"有十分相近之处,有关喜玛拉雅条款在笔者《提单与其他付运单证》一书第 178 页有详细介绍,请参阅。只说,如果船东想根据喜玛拉雅条款让装卸工人也可以享有与他同样的责任限制就必须符合 Reid 勋爵在先例 Midland Silicones v. Scruttons (1961) 2 Lloyd's Rep 365 中所说的四个要求如下:"I can see a possibility of success of the agency argument if (first) the bill of lading makes it clear that the stevedores is intended to be protected by the provisions in it which limit liability, (secondly) the bill of lading makes it clear that the carrier, in addition to contracting for these provisions on his own behalf, is also contracting as agent for the stevedore that these provisions should apply to the stevedore, (thirdly) the carrier has authority from the stevedore to do that, or perhaps later ratification by the stevedore would suffice, and (fourthly) that any difficulties about consideration moving from the stevedore were overcome."

再回到这个先例,上诉庭的 Parker 大法官首先认为是受保人包括了"分承包商"一词是不能无限度包括所有没有被列名也无法确定的人士,而需要给该词合理的范围,说:"... cannot in my judgment mean that all sub-contractors unidentified and incapable of identification at the time were automatically covered. It can only mean that declarations naming or properly describing sub-contractors would be accepted."

基本上 Stone Vickers 如果想成为 AS 与保险人签订的保险合约中的共同受保人,Parker 大法官认为就必须满足四个条件如下:"(a) The policy must make it clear that the sub-contractor is intended to benefit from the provisions in the policy; (b) The policy must make it clear that the main assured, in addition to contracting for the insurance provisions on his own behalf, is also contracting as agent for the sub-contractor that these provisions should apply to the sub-contractor; (c) The main assured must have authority from the sub-contractor to contract on his behalf, although perhaps later ratification by the sub-contractor would suffice; and (d) and difficulty about consideration moving from the sub-contractor would have to be overcome."

而在这一先例中，Parker 大法官认为前两项的要求都没有达到，其余的两项要求就不必再讨论了，说：“I have already concluded that the insurance documents here did not make it clear that Stone Vickers were intended to be protected by its provision. Nor did they make it clear that AS was contracting or purporting to contract both for itself and as agent for Stone Vickers that the insurance should also apply to SV. Indeed in my judgment they made it clear that there was no such intention and that AS were not acting as agent for SV. In those circumstances it is necessary to consider the questions of ratification or consideration.”

9.5 共同受保人不受到保障的情况之三

这里想介绍的情况就是涉及共同受保人的保险合约，可分为两大类。第一类名为共同保单（joint policy），这是针对所有的共同受保人都是对同一种保险利益作出投保，如共同拥有一栋房子或者是一批货物或者一艘船舶。反正在共同保单的情况下，所有的共同受保人在保险合约的命运绑在一起，要么就全部都获得赔付，要么就全部都赔不到，保险人不可以向其中一位受保人主张代位求偿权。

第二类名为综合保单（composite policy），这是共同受保人各自为他们自己的保险利益投保，虽然涉及的是同一份保单。这就会存在保险人在赔付了无辜受保人之后可向有过错的共同受保人主张代位求偿权。例如律师行的合伙人的责任保险就会是一份综合保单，如果其中一位合伙人犯错或欺诈导致其他无辜合伙人要共同承担损失，保险人在赔付后就可以向犯错或欺诈的合伙人追偿。这种综合保单也出现在承建商与分承建商、托管人与委托人、房东与租客等之间的关系。

海上货物保险下的 CIF 卖方与买方看来也是对同一种保险利益作出投保，就是针对该批货物的所有权。但这个保险利益针对不同时段，而不是同一时段。这就带来一个质疑，可否凭借这个原因让无辜的 CIF 买方作为共同受保人（请看本章 9.2 段）不会因为 CIF 卖方的过错导致保险合约无效的影响。也等于是把海上货物保险视为是一种综合保单，保险人在赔付给了无辜 CIF 买方后，可以代位求偿权向犯错的 CIF 卖方追偿/索赔？这可节录 John Dunt 所著的《Marine Cargo Insurance》一书之 8.47 - 8.48 段：

“The question whether the innocent c. i. f. buyer can recover as an assured in his own right, and not as an assignee, depends on whether the cargo policy is joint or composite. Where mortgagor and mortgagee of a ship were insured it was held that the mortgagee's interest was separate, Viscount Cave saying:

‘But in this case there is no difficulty in separating the interest of the mortgagee from that of the owner; and if the mortgagee should recover on the policy, the owner will not be advantaged, as the insurers will be subrogated as against him to the rights of the mortgagee.’

A different interests (mortgagor or mortgagee) were involved that was a composite policy. Where the assured has the same interest, the policy is said to be joint. Under a cargo policy, both seller and buyer have the same interest, ownership of the goods. Their interest is in that sense joint and, on this basis, the c. i. f. buyer's claim as assured under a cargo policy would seem to be tainted with the fraud of the seller. However, the seller and the buyer are not owners of the cargo at the same time. Accordingly, there is much to be said for the view that the innocent buyer should not be prejudiced by the wilful misconduct of the seller. The c. i. f. buyer as assured in his own right has the benefit of a separate contract carved out of the open cover in his favour. The special position of the interest of the c. i. f. buyer may give scope for developing the law in such a way that the position of the non-fraudulent buyer is not affected. There is some support for this approach in the non-marine case of Direct Line Insurance plc v. Khan (2002) Lloyd's Rep IR 364 (CA). In this case Mance L. J allowed leave to appeal, *inter alia* on the basis that the law might be developed in such a way in relation to joint ownership of a house. Although the conventional view of cargo insurance is that the buyer takes subject to the seller's fraud, or wilful misconduct, it is submitted that as a buyer is an assured in his own right there is scope for the development of the law in favour of the innocent c. i. f. buyer either on the basis of a separate contract or a separate interest. If the claim is payable, in theory the insurers could exercise rights of subrogation in the buyer's name against the seller, though in practice this is unlikely to avail them if the seller is a rogue who, as likely as not, has disappeared."

9.6 1999 年《Contract (Rights of Third Parties) Act》

这一立法是在1999年11月11日于英国生效,立法的目的主要是解决部分来自合约相互关系(privity of contract)原则所带来的不合理与困难的情况。这些情况与立法在笔者《国际商务游戏规则——英国合约法》第四章有介绍,请参阅。只说,立法是让第三人直接向合约的一方当事人提出索赔,只要该合约有明示给他合约利益(to confer a benefit)。而被告的合约当事人是不能以第三人并非是合约的一方,无权以该合约条文向他提出索赔作为抗辩。如在人身意外保险,合约中明示了受益方是受保人的侄子,该侄子就可以直接向保险人提出索赔,保险人不能以保险合约的订约方是刚遇到意外事故死亡的受保人为由作为抗辩。

该立法的第三人可以是某一位特定人士,也可以是属于某一类别的人士或只要符合某一种描述的人士。立法的 Section 1(3) 这样说:"The third party must be expressly identified in the contract by name, as a member of a class or as answering a particular description but need not be in existence when the contract is entered into."

这表示在本章9.4段所讲的困难会由于这个立法而有所减轻,如果保险合约中有条文将所有的分承包商、供应商等笼统地都包括在受保人的范围内,在将来是有可能有大量不知名的第三人冒出来根据1999年立法向保险公司索赔与要求享受保险利益。

立法的 Section 1(2)也允许双方在订合约的时候明示规定不让第三人要求享受合约利益。而这种合约条文也常见,已经变了许多合约的特定条文。如在 BIMCO 的 NEWBUILDCON 的标准造船合约格式,就有 48 条的"Third party rights":"Unless expressly identified in this contract, no third parties shall have the right to enforce any terms of this Contract."

但问题在本章 9.2 段有提到在有一些保险合约,如针对大型的建筑工程包括像造船,由于涉及许多的分包商与供应商,所以在总承建商或船厂的保险合约中,会把这些类别的有关公司笼统地包括在内作为共同受保人。由于这些分包商与供应商很多,名字无法在订立保险合约时确定,只能粗略地把所有不知名的分包商与供应商都加进来作为共同受保人。

所以,在这种保险合约,保险人为了保障自己与能够事前就知道谁是共同受保人,会要求每位共同受保人要加进来必须预先向保险人宣告,并由保险人同意:British Telecommunication Plc v. James Thomson & Sons (Engineers) Ltd (1999) 1 WLR 9 (HL, Sc)。

10. 受保人向第三人承诺放弃代位求偿权的情况

这一种情况是发生在受保人自愿或在无知的情况下与要负责人的第三人约定只要有保险人作出赔付,就放弃向他索赔(这部分内容在本章第 5.1 段有涉及)。这显然是一种损害保险人代位求偿权的行为。在订约自由下,措辞还可以是以其他的形式出现,如在合约中说明第三人可以享有受保人在保险合约中的利益(benefit of insurance),但注意受保人并没有把该第三人加在保险合约中作为共同受保人。

10.1 有关先例介绍

这种情况经常出现,如在著名的先例 Canadian Transport Co Ltd v. Court Line Ltd. (1940) AC 934,案情涉及一个期租合约,而船东同意把互保协会的利益让承租人享有,只要是互保协会的规定允许(owners to give time charterers the benefit of the Protection and Indemnity Club insurance so far as club rules allow)。贵族院判是由于船东互保协会的规定并不允许这样做(绝大部分的互保协会规定都规定不允许第三人享有互保协会给船东的利益),这一条文等于没讲。但 Atkin 勋爵有说到,原则上是可以这样规定,毕竟是订约自由,说:"a man may contract with another on the terms that if he is injured by that other then, if he happens to be insured, he will look to the insurers in relief of the wrongdoers."

10.2 《海牙规则》与协会货物条文针对这种情况的规定

这种情况在以前班轮公司有垄断性力量的时候,经常在提单合约中印上一条条文,说明是货物受到损坏,即使船东有责任,但只要是货方有对该批货物投保,货方只能向保险人要求赔付,不得向船东索赔。这种条文在1924年《海牙规则》后,就有了Article III r. 8规定:"Any clause, covenant, or agreement in a contract of carriage relieving the carrier or the ship from liability for loss or damage to, or in connection with, goods arising from negligence, fault, or failure in the duties and obligations provided in this article or lessening such liability otherwise than as provided in this convention, shall be null and void and of no effect. A benefit or insurance in favour of the carrier or similar clause shall be deemed to be a clause relieving the carrier form liability."换言之,在提单加上这种条文也是无效。

为了不让海上运输的船东/承运人(会是海上运输涉及租约,这不受《海牙规则》的约束)与托管人钻空子,1963年的协会货物条文更是有了一条新的第15条,名为"Not to Inure Clause",规定如下:"This insurance shall not inure to the benefit of the carrier or other bailee"。而2009年的协会货物条文措辞如下:"15.2 This insurance... shall not extend to or otherwise benefit the carrier or other bailee."实际上,措辞虽然改变,但意思并没有改变。有了这个条文,如果租约加上一条条文说"shipowners to have the benefit of the cargo insurance so far as the policy allows",就会也是一句空话了。但如果只是"shipowners to have the benefit of the cargo insurance",这就会是货方的受保人剥夺了保险人的代位求偿权。

10.3　受保人放弃代位求偿权的后果

受保人如果与第三人约定放弃代位求偿权,后果会因为约定时段的不同而不同。第一个时段就是在订立保险合约之前,已经在与第三人的合约中作出了这样的约定。第二个时段就是在订立保险合约后但发生损失前。第三个时段是发生损失后但在赔付前。第四个时段就是在保险人作出赔付后。

10.3.1　时段一:在订立保险合约之前,已经在与第三人的合约中作出了这样的约定

这种情况是受保人在投保之前就已经在与第三人的合约中放弃了代位求偿权,或是根本存在不可能行使代位求偿权的情况。这一来,保险人看来唯一的救济就是以受保人没有披露一个实质性的事实,可让保险人回避赔付责任。这里可介绍两个有关的先例。第一个是Tate & Sons v. Hyslop (1885) LR 15 QBD 368,受保人的货方与一艘驳船船东达成协议,船东只在有疏忽的时候才需要负责任,但不必负上共同承运人(common carrier)的严格责任。而有关的保险是有两个不同层次的保费,如果是疏忽才有责任就会收更高的保费,但如果是严格责任就会收较低的保费。由于受保人没有披露只需要驳船船东负疏忽责任的事实,只支付了较低的保费。上诉庭判这是一个应该披露的实质事实(disclosure of material facts),所以保险人可以去回避保单(avoid the policy)。

第二个是比较近期的先例名为:Rich & Co v. Portman (1996) 1 Lloyd's Rep 430,涉及一个著名国际贸易商Marc Rich为他的石油贸易投保一种不常见的险种名为

“滞期费保险”(Demurrage Liability Insurance)。这种保险就是针对 Marc Rich 作为油轮的承租人如果面对船舶在装卸港发生延误产生滞期费的时候作出赔付。这种保险的实质承保范围是用这样的措辞:“This insurance extended in respect of above vessels/trading area only to include all which the assured shall be liable to pay as charters including costs and expenses due to loading/unloading beyond the agreed period. . . ”结果发生了很大的滞期费索赔,但保险人拒付,其中一个理由就是 Marc Rich 在投保时没有披露这些支付给船东的滞期费是不能根据代位求偿权向第三人(如装港的发货人与卸港的 Sumed 管道[经过埃及运油去欧洲的管道]当局)索赔有关的船舶延误,因为他们与 Marc Rich 之间的合约是把船舶延误的责任放在 Marc Rich 的头上。但 Longmore 大法官不接受这一个说法,认为保险人没有提供证明这在这种保险是一个需要披露的实质性事实,说:“But I do not consider underwriters have discharged the onus of showing that in the comparatively new and rarely used market in which demurrage was insured it was material for a prudent underwriter to be informed about either actual or assumed irrecoverability from third parties. What was most material, on my view, was the loss experience. I should add, however, (in case I am wrong about that) that such disclosure as was made was insufficient. The position with NIOC(装港的发货人) was not disclosed at all; the mere disclosure of the Sumed terms(使用 Sumed 管道的条文) without a careful explanation why disclosure was necessary was, in my view, insufficient. ”

可以说,保险人如果以受保人没有作出这方面的披露为由进行抗辩会有一定的困难,原因有:(1)估计法院会对这种技术性的拒赔理由有一定的抗拒。(2)一般而言,降低保险人代位求偿权与剩余价值的事实并非实质性重要,除非是保险人能够证明它会影响保费的高低,如 Tate & Sons v. Hyslop (1885) 15 QBD 368 先例。这方面可节录《Colinvaux's Law of Insurance in Hong Kong》一书之 11. 036 段:“facts which diminish the insurer's rights of subrogation and salvage are prima facie immaterial and are required to be disclosed only where the assured is aware that premium-rating depends upon such rights. ”(3)在 1906 年《英国海上保险法》Section 18(3)(b)是说明承保某一种风险的保险人应该被假设对这方面的业务风险与一般性的资讯有所了解,不存在要披露,受保人可以不必披露。比如说,在本章第 6 段有提到过海上石油钻探的业务经常是 Knock-for-Knock 的约定,就是有了损失就由各自的保险人赔付,双方不追究责任也不提出诉讼。这方面的条文也在涉及海上石油钻探的标准合约格式如 TOWCON, TOWHIRE 与 SUPPLYTIME 2005 中出现。所以,承保有关风险的保险人就应该被假设是知道这一个情况,不能以受保人不披露作为拒赔理由。其他类似的例子更是多不胜数,如海上货物运输的保险人应该知道《海牙规则》会是强制适用在提单合约,而根据《海牙规则》有责任的船东会有责任限制。保险人也应该知道如果货物是以租约进行运输,就会有可能需要接受对船东有利与常见的条文,否则不一定能够顺利租到船。

10.3.2　时段二:在订立保险合约后但发生损失前

在这个时段,如果受保人订立合约放弃向第三人追偿代位求偿权,除非有关的保险合约中有条文禁止受保人这样做,可以说是受保人只要能够有善意的商业理由解释为什么这样做(如不答应这种条文就租不到船舶或做不成有关的生意),保险人不会有什么救济。这里的原因在本书第四章第3.4.1段有提到,就是英国保险法的默示地位只是不允许受保人做任何事情改变承保风险的本质,但是受保人可以增加承保风险,只要在保单内没有被禁止(如通过先决条件或承诺性保证条文禁止):Scottish Coal v. RSA (2008) EWHC (Comm) 880。而受保人向第三人放弃追偿正是一种增加承保风险的做法。

所以在本章10.2段有介绍说协会货物条文就增加了一条新的第15条,名为"Not to Inure Clause",就是以明示条文规定货方不能在这个时段或其他保险期间向第三人(承运人或其他托管人)放弃保险人的代位求偿权。如果受保人这样做,不论有否善意的商业理由,根据该条文保险人是可以向受保人提出索赔。

另可节录《Colinvaux's Law of Insurance in Hong Kong》一书之11.036段:

"There remains the possibility that the assured has entered into an agreement with the third party, exempting the latter from liability, after the inception of the policy but before any loss has occurred. It is clear that, in the absence of any warranty concerning subrogation recoveries, the insurer cannot avoid the policy. **It is also clear that the insurer's contingent subrogation rights come into existence as soon as the policy is entered into**. Consequently, it is possible that the assured might face liability in damages to the insurer for entering into a pre-loss agreement of this nature, at least if there is no *bona fide* commercial reason for such an agreement. It is equally arguable, however, that in this situation there is merely an increase in risk which, in line with general principles, the insurer must bear.

It has been held in Australia that there is no implied obligation on an assured to refrain from entering into an agreement after the policy has incepted which exempts or restricts the third party's liability: State Government Insurance Office (Qld) v. Brisbane Stevedoring Pty Ltd (1969) 123 CLR 228. As was there pointed out, until the contract is made there are no contingent subrogation rights available to the insurers to that it cannot be said that the assured has prejudiced those rights."

10.3.3　时段三:在发生损失后但在赔付前

这一时段可以说还不存在代位求偿权,因为保险人还没有全数赔付。也是因为如此,保险人不容易控制受保人与第三人之间的一些行为,包括是受保人提出索赔或和解的谈判。法律的默示地位是受保人不能作出任何可能损害保险人将来代位求偿权的和解协议:Napier and Ettrick (Lord) v. Kershaw (1993) 1 Lloyd's Rep 197先例中Templeman勋爵所说。如果受保人这样做,就会带来保险人的索赔,如在本章第6段所介绍的先例 West of England Fire Insurance Co. v. Isaacs (1896) 2 QB 377。另在先例 Law Fire Assurance Co v. Oakley (1888) 4 TLR 309 与 Horse, Carriage and General Insurance Co v. Petch (1916) 33 TLR 131,涉及的是受保人投保的是不足额保险,但是与第三人达成了和解协议,而赔偿的钱是受保人不足额保险的部分。这显然属于损害保险人将来代位求偿权的协议,因为保险人也受到该和解协议的约束,不可能再向第三人追偿同一个损失。这种情况估计会有不少,就是受保人以为自己的损失一半向第三人要回来,另一半将来向保险人要回来,但这就会违反了法律的默示地位(这在本章第 5.1 段有介绍这个受保人的默示责任)。

但只要是受保人与第三人达成一个善意的和解协议,并同时考虑受保人自己与受保人的利益(这有点好像是共同海损的理念),法律是允许的:Commercial Union Assurance Co v. Lister (1874) LR 9 Ch App 483;West of England Fire Insurance Co. v. Isaacs (1896) 2 QB 377;Phoenix Assurance Co v Spooner (1905) 2 KB 753;Globe & Rutgers Fire Insurance Co. v. Truedell (1927) 2 DLR 659;Willumsen v. Royal Insurance Co. Ltd 63 DLR (3d) 112 (1975);另有香港先例 Pang Wai Chung v. Hoi Tat Rubber Factory (1992) 2 HKC 447。

这些法律的默示地位是完全可以理解与十分合理,毕竟第三人会作出一个和解的要约,是受保人律师觉得是非常有利(如第三人愿意赔偿 50%,而受保人的律师认为将来胜诉几率不超过 50%),应该马上接受。这一来就没有理由说是受保人不该接受和解协议,毕竟在这种情况下也难以说是该和解是损害了保险人将来的代位求偿权。

10.3.4　时段四:在保险人作出赔付后

在这一时段,保险人可以说是已经有了代位求偿权。但在本章第 8 段有介绍,会有情况受保人作为向第三人索赔的诉讼程序的所有人(*dominus litis*),这往往是受保人自己还有一些没有承保的损失,所以不愿意把诉讼程序的控制权交给保险人。这一来,受保人如果与第三人作出和解协议,正确或最好的办法就是得到保险人的同意。因为根据贵族院的 Napier and Ettrick (Lord) v. Kershaw (1993) 1 Lloyd's Rep 197 先例,保险人在赔付后是对向第三人的索赔的诉讼与取回来的钱有一个"衡平法的押记"(equitable charge)。可以说,受保人就算是与第三人达成一个善意的和解协议,恐怕还是不足够。有关一个和解协议的合理性,法律会有更高的要求,这方面请看最近上诉庭的案件 Siemens Building Technologies FE Ltd v. Supershield (2010) EWCA Civ 7。虽然在这种情况下恐怕保险人向受保人提出索赔(指受保人违反默示条件,损害了他的代位求偿权)也不容易证明有什么损失。这表示会有情况保险人要向法院申请禁令阻止受保人与第三人达成可疑的和解协议,这种行动有可能在上一小段 10.3.3 段的情况也会有需要:John Edwards & Co v. Motor Union Insurance Co Ltd (1922) 2 KB 249, 254-5; Boag v. Standard Marine Insurance (1937) 2 KB 113 (CA) 112;Government Insurance Office (Queensland) v. Brisbane Stevedoring Pty Ltd

(1969) HCA 59, (1969) 123 CLR 228, 241;CSE Aviation Ltd v. Cardale Doors Ltd QBD (Comm Ct) 13 April 2000, [13]。

11. 代位求偿协议

2009 年协会货物条文的 16 条要求受保人"to ensure that all rights against carriers, bailees or other third parties are properly preserved and exercised"。当保险人支付赔偿金额给受保人时,伦敦保险市场的惯例都会要求受保人签一份代位求偿协议(subrogation form or letter of subrogation)。而标准的劳氏代位求偿协议(Subrogation Form)措辞如下:

"I/We acknowledge that by virtue of such payment you are subrogated to all my/our rights and remedies in and in respect of the goods as provided by the law governing the Contract of Insurance and in the case of total loss you are entitled at your option to take over my/our interest in whatever may remain of the goods it being understood that my/our delivery to you of the documents of title relating to the goods shall not be construed as an exercise of such option.

I/We also record that you have authority to use my/our name to the extent necessary effectively to exercise all or any of such rights and remedies; that I/we will furnish you with any assistance you may reasonably require of me/us when exercising such rights and remedies on the understanding that you will indemnify me/us against any liability for costs charges and expenses arising in connection with any proceedings which you may take in my/our name in the exercise of such rights and remedies."

可以看到第一段是 1906 年《英国海上保险法》Section 79 的内容,而第二段则是保险人与受保人之间达成的额外的协议(additional agreement)。根据先例 Edwards v. Motor Union Insurance Co Ltd (1922) 2 KB 249,保险人只有在真正的赔付了受保人以后才享有代位求偿权,如果仅仅是双方达成了代位求偿的协议而并没有真正的支付的话,保险人还是不能享有代位求偿权。根据 1906 年《英国海上保险法》Section 79(1),在全损的情况下,保险人是有选择权取得保险标的的所有权(这一个委付/抛弃的权利在本章 2.2.1 段有详论)。而这里劳氏代位求偿协议第一段是说标的所有权文件的交付并不代表保险人行使了此选择权,这也说明了保险人担心贸然接受该标的后会使他们陷入更大的责任当中,如一批危险品的货物继续在造成污染或是一艘沉没的船舶会被当局要求将残骸移走。

劳氏代位求偿协议的第二段的第一句明示授权保险人以受保人的名义行使代位求偿权,这是英国法律的地位。但接下来的条文就是一些明示条文规定了受保人要作出的各种协助,如向第三人追偿与索赔时作出各种协助,如提供相关的所需要的文件与有关资讯(如与第三人的合约谈判怎样进行,损失发生后与第三人的交流)是最常见的协助。如果向第三人索赔的诉讼要开庭审理,受保人甚至有可能在很长一段时间后还要提供事实证人出庭举证。在一些涉及专业知识的领域,受保人还要提供专业知识上的援助。在这里也明示规定受保人为了协助保险人而产生的费用,保险人承诺对受保人作出补偿与支付。

可以说,劳氏代位求偿协议针对了四个方面:"(i) underwriters are entitled to take over whatever remains in the insured property where underwriters have paid a total loss; (ii) underwriters are entitled to bring proceedings in the name of the assured; (iii) underwriters will provide the assured with an indemnity in respect of the costs and expenses of any recovery action; and (iv) the assured will provide underwriters with assistance in the recovery proceedings. This assistance would include, for example, provision of relevant documents and witness statements or other evidence as required by underwriters."

鉴于代位求偿协议是保险人与受保人之间达成额外的明示协议,在其他方面如果有需要可以详细地规定一些内容。如保险人行使代位求偿权向第三人追偿/索赔的诉讼如果最后失败,就会要受保人作为败诉方承担诉讼费用,包括第三人的诉讼费用。根据劳氏代位求偿协议,有明示规定要保险人补偿与支付给受保人。即使是在默示地位,也会要求保险人在行使代位求偿权时不能损害受保人,如替受保人带来诉讼费用:England & England v. Guardian Insurance Limited (2000) Lloyd's Rep. IR 404。但会有情况这一个承诺并不足够保障受保人,如保险人是家小公司或财力不明的公司,受保人就可以在签发代位求偿协议时要求保险人提供担保,如银行的担保。另一个方面可针对的是向第三人索赔,如果受保人有不足额保险或没有承保的损失,就存在他与保险人之间怎样分配(包括分配诉讼费用与成功取回来的钱)的问题。在Mance 大法官等著的《Insurance Disputes》第二版之 8.30 段是说:"Where the assured has received less than a full indemnity under the policy and recovery of both insured and uninsured losses is pursued against the third party, the strict legal position (in the absence of an agreement to the contrary) is that the assured and the underwriter are taken to have agreed to share the costs of the recovery action on a *pro rata* basis: Duus Brown v. Binning (1906) 11 Com Cas 190. Indeed the costs to be shared extend beyond the strict legal costs and expenses incurred as part of the legal action and may extend to pre-trial investigation and other costs that were reasonably directed to reduce the insured's loss: England & England v. Guardian Insurance Limited (2000) Lloyd's Rep. IR 404. This position can be varied by agreement and this should be recorded in the Subrogation Form."

最后一提的是代位求偿协议本身能否构成有对价的有效合约有疑问,因为它实际上是保险人以支付保险赔偿来换取代位求偿权。但是保险人支付保险赔偿实际上是他在保险合约下的义务与责任,应该说保险人在代位求偿协议下是没有支付任何对价(consideration)。但实践当中,大部分的海上运输货物索赔的和解都涉及了一定程度的妥协与讨价还价，所以也不能肯定说保险人没有付出任何对价。故此，代位求偿协议会在大部分情况被英国法院认为是有效力的。

12. 代位求偿权诉讼在英国法院的程序

在这里可以总结一下在英国法院的程序。可以说英国法院通常不理会这一以受保人名义的诉讼是保险人在背后操纵（除了在受保人败诉后可能产生要支付第三人作为被告的诉讼费用，但受保人倒闭，法院会根据1982年《Supreme Court Act》之Section 51命令保险人作出支付）。以下可节录Michell与Watterson合著的《SUBROGATION Law and Practice》（2007年版）一书之10.183段有关英国法院的一些程序：

"（1）The insured is liable to make standard disclosure of documents as a party to subrogated proceedings under CPR Part 31, but the insurer is not（The 'Frotanorte'［1995］2 Lloyd's Rep 254, 261; Presentationes Musicales SA v. Secunda［1994］Ch 271）. However, it may be that in some cases the insurer could be ordered to make disclosure as a non-party under CPR r 31.17.（披露文件的责任只在受保人，第三人通常不能向保险人要求披露。）

（2）Judgment against the defendant must be entered in the name of the insured, and so defendant must pay the insured in order to obtain discharge（Yorkshire Insurance Co. Ltd v. Nisbet Shipping Co Ltd［1962］2 QB 330, 341; England & England v. Guardian Insurance Ltd［2000］Lloyd's Rep. IR. 404［11］）. Presumably, however, this requirement will be satisfied if the defendant pays another party at the insured's direction, for example, the insurer（William Brandt's Sons & Co. v. Dunlop Rubber Co Ltd［1905］AC 454）.（第三人如果败诉，是要把赔偿的金额支付给受保人才能解除判决的责任，如果直接支付给保险人就需要得到受保人的指示，这等于是转让。）

（3）Costs are awarded to the insured in the event that the action is successful, although they have been incurred at the insurer's direction（R v. Archbishop of Canter bury［1903］1 KB 289［CA］295; Gough v. Toronto and York Rdial Railway Co［1918］42 OLR 415; H Cousins & Co Ltd v. D & C Carriers Ltd［1971］2 QB 230［CA］242; Halliday v. High Performance Pty Ltd［1993］113 ALR 637［HCA］640）. Once awarded, the insurer can recover from the costs from the insured to the extent that their receipt leaves him over-indemnified（Sea Insurance Co. v. Hadden［1884］13 QBD 706［CA］）.（第三人如果败诉是要支付受保人的诉讼费用，如果部分费用是受保人支出，可以取回，但多出的应该退还给保险人。）

（4）Costs are awarded against the insured if the action fails（Morris v. Ford Motor Co［1973］QB 792［CA］800; Wates Construction Ltd v. HGP Greentree Allchurch Evans

Ltd [2005] EWHC 2174 [TCC], [2006] BLR 45: where indemnity costs were awarded following the insured's pursuit of an obviously doomed claim on its insurer's insistence). As discussed previously, the insurer will be obliged to reimburse him under an express or implied term of the policy. If the insured were unable to comply with the costs order, then the court could exercise its jurisdiction under the Supreme Court Act 1981, s 51, to make a costs order against the insurer (CPR r 48.2).(受保人如果败诉是要支付第三人的诉讼费用,受保人可以根据明示或默示的地位向保险人要求补偿取回。如果受保人没有钱支付,法院会有权利要求背后操纵的保险人作出支付。)

(5) If the action is successful, then interest can be awarded on the judgment sum for periods both before and after the insured was indemnified by the insurer, although the insured was not actually out of pocket following the insurer's payment (H Cousins & Co Ltd v. D & C Carriers Ltd [1971] 2 QB 230 [CA]; Metal Box Co Ltd v. Currys Ltd [1988] 1 WLR 175; Clark v. Ardington Electrical Services [2002] EWCA Civ 510, [2003] QB 36 [157]-[162]; The allocation of interest may be the subject of an express clause in the policy: Institute Time Clauses, Hulls [1/1/95] cl 12.4). The insured will keep the interest for the period before, and the insurer will take the interest for the payment after, indemnification, as the insured would otherwise be more than fully indemnified in respect of the later period. Where the insured was under-insured and the whole loss along with interest is recovered in subrogated proceedings, the insured is entitled to a proportionate share of the interest along with the amount of his uninsured loss (Re Miller Gibb & Co. Ltd [1957] 1 WLR 703). The allocation of the interest between the parties may also be the subject of an express clause in the policy (Institute Time Clauses, Hulls [1/1/95] cl 12.4).(这是有关向第三人索赔成功,取得赔偿金包括利息部分在保险人与受保人之间的分配问题。)

(6) Interest can also be awarded on top of a costs order in favour of the insured, even though these costs were paid for by the insurer (Hogan v. Trustees of the Roman Catholic Church for the Archdiocese of Sydney [No. 2] [2006] NSWSC 74 [39]). Again, the insured must account to the insurer for the interest.(这是有关诉讼费用的利息,由于诉讼费用通常是由保险人支付,所以受保人应该归还这笔钱给保险人。)

(7) The fact that an insurer and its insured have previously agreed the amount of the insured's losses between themselves is irrelevant to the calculation of damages payable by the defendant (Brown v. Albany Construction Co Ltd [1995] NPC 100 [CA]: 'the mechanics by which [an insurer chooses to settle its insured's claim] is neither here nor there and is no concern of the third party'; Bee v. Jenson [2006] EWHC 3559 [COMM]: defendant cannot challenge insurer's arrangements to supply insured motorist with replacement vehicle; Crayden's Pharmacy Ltd v. Standard Paving Co [1973] 37 DLR [3d] 167,

168; Verlysdonk v. Premier Petrenas Construction Co Ltd [1987] 60 OR [2d] 65; Grosvenor Fine Art Furniture [1982] Ltd v. Terrie's Plumbing & Heating Ltd [1994] 113 Sask R 105 [Saskatchewan CA] 138-43).（保险人与受保人之间的赔付和解协议或是保险人赔不足因为保险合约中有一个很大的绝对免赔额，这与第三人无关，第三人的赔付还是根据计算损失的大原则，不论是合约或者侵权。）

(8) Nor may the court refer to the terms of such an agreement for purpose of deciding the appropriate track for a subrogated claim by reference to its financial value under CPR r 26.8 (Khiaban v. Beard [2003] EWCA Civ 358; Beaumont Premier Properties Ltd v. Jones [2006] ALL ER [D] 464 [Mar]; Russell v. Wilson The Times, 26 May 1989 [CA]).（法院也是同样态度如上，不理会保险人与受保人之间的协议。）

(9) An insurer sued in its own name cannot counter-claim for damages to which it can only be entitled via subrogation to the insured's rights (Page v. Scottish Insurance Co [1929] 140 LT 571 [CA] 576; Rap Industries Pty Ltd v. Royal Insurance Australia Ltd [1988] 5 ANZ Ins Cas 75,516; Red Sea Insurance Co Ltd v. Bouyges SA [1995] AC 190)."

以上部分内容会在接下来的第 13 段作进一步解释。

13. 向第三人部分成功索赔后赔偿金的分配：一般情况下

这一问题涉及好几个变数与不同情况。最简单的是受保人的损失完全从保险人的赔付中得到赔偿。这一来，代位求偿权下保险人向第三人索赔成功而取回的钱就应该全部属于保险人所有。但这里还会有一定的变数，如第三人的赔偿比保险人赔付受保人的还要高（虽然这种情况不多），原因可能是因为不同货币的汇率有所改变所导致的（Yorkshire Insurance Co v. Nisbet Shipping Co [1962] 2 QB 330），也有可能是保险人赔付给受保人的金额是根据一个和解协议而比起实际损失有所减少。这一来，法律应该很明确，保险人代位求偿只能严格取回他真正赔付的金钱。在先例 Glen Line v. Attorney-General (1930) 6 Com Cas 1,14 Lord Atkin 说："Subrogation will only give the insurer rights up to 20 shillings in the pound."

在先例 Yorkshire Insurance Co v. Nisbet Shipping Co，由于不同货币的汇率改变，受保人的损失本来只是 72,000 英镑，而且保险人已经是全数作出赔付，但后来获得加拿大政府的赔偿。由于加元升值与英镑下跌，加拿大政府的赔偿在兑换成英镑后变成了 126,000 英镑。Diplock 大法官判是根据 1906 年《英国保险法》Section 79，保险人只能取回他所赔付给受保人的金额，而多出来的 54,000 英镑是归受保人。

这里只有一种例外，就是向第三人取回的利息部分（如果向第三人的索赔诉讼可以把利息也取回的情况下)。这是因为利息是要根据受保人与保险人的损失分配,如发生损失后两年才成功向第三人取回这笔利息,而第一年的利息损失是在受保人,但之后保险人作出全部的赔付后,变成第二年的利息损失是在保险人。这一来,向第三人取回这笔利息就要一人一半了,即使是保险人加上这笔利息会取得比他赔付更大的一笔钱。

还有一个变数发生在保险合约有一个绝对免赔额(deductible),可以说针对船舶保险,很多时候都还是金额很大的绝对免赔额。而针对货物保险,开口/预约保单很多时候也是约定一个绝对免赔额。这一来就存在一个情况是,如果向第三人追偿/索赔成功,但金额不足补偿保险人所作出的赔付与受保人自己承担的绝对免赔额,就存在他们之间应该怎样分配的问题。

可以说根据英国法律的默示地位,也就是在 Napier and Ettrick (Lord) v. Kershaw (1993) 1 Lloyd's Rep 197 的先例中判是"由上至下"(top down)的说法下,向第三人取回的钱先是要满足保险人作出的赔付,有剩下来的才是满足受保人自己承担的绝对免赔额。这里的道理就是保险合约中,受保人自己愿意先承担不超过绝对免赔额的损失。但会有情况是保险合约有明示条文针对这种情况下如何在保险人与受保人之间分配,这种情况在海上货物运输保险不常见,也没有在协会货物条文中有针对。但在船舶保险会有规定按比例分配,如在 2003 年国际船舶保险条款,就有 49.4 条文以下的规定:

"49.4 In the event of recoveries from third parties in respect of claims which have been paid in whole or in part under this insurance, such recoveries shall be distributed between the Underwriters and the Assured as follows:

49.4.1 the reasonable costs and expenses incurred in making such recoveries from the third party shall be deducted first and returned to the paying party.

49.4.2 the balance shall be apportioned between the Underwriters and the Assured in the same proportion that the insured losses and uninsured losses bear to the total of the insured and uninsured losses. For the purposes of Clause 49.2 and this Clause 49.4.2, uninsured losses shall mean loss of or damage to the subject-matter insured and any liability or expense which would have been recoverable under this insurance, but for the application of deductible(s) under Clause 15 and the limits of this insurance."

14. 向第三人部分成功索赔后的赔偿金分配:不足额保险与损失未被承保的情况

如果保险人根据保险合约作出全额的赔付,但受保人实际的损失还不足补偿,这种情况经常发生。原因会是受保人投保了不足额保险(under-insurance)。另一种情况会是受保人有其他没有被承保的损失(uninsured loss),如利润损失或是延误损失,这都不是货物保险或其他财产保险所承保的损失类别。

14.1 投保金额少于保险价值的情况

在这种情况下,向第三人成功索赔回来的金钱怎样在保险人与受保人之间分配需要比较复杂的解释。首先,针对受保人投保了不足额保险。这就是在保险合约中同意的保险价值(agreed value),如100万美元。这一来,根据1906年《英国海上保险法》Section 27(3),在没有欺诈的情况下,针对保险人与受保人之间,约定的保险价值就具有结论性,也就是代表保险标的的实际价值(actual value)不能事后再提出异议。而投保不足额保险的情况就是在同意保险价值100万美元的同时,受保人与保险人约定投保金额(amount insured)只是50万美元。至于为什么发生这种情况,可以是受保人自己承担部分风险以节省保费,也可以是受保人希望以不同保险合约向不同的保险人投保部分保险标的的价值。这一来,在英国法律的地位是把受保人视为是共同保险人,在上述的例子下,等于受保人是50%的保险人。这可节录1906年《英国海上保险法》Section 81 如下:"Where the assured is insured for an amount less than the insurable value or, in the case of a valued policy, for an amount less than the policy valuation, he is deemed to be his own insurer in respect of the uninsured balance."

在上述的例子,如果向第三人索赔成功取回的钱也是100万美元(因为保险标的的货物全损),保险人与受保人就可以各自获得50万美元。但如果向第三人取回的钱只是80万美元,由于在不足额保险,保险人与受保人都变成是共同受保人,正确的分配做法就是一人一半,各自获得40万美元了。这一法律地位在一个古老的先例The"Commonwealth"(1907) P 216,案情涉及船舶在碰撞后沉没,有关船舶的保险价值是1350英镑,但船东投保金额只是1000英镑。在后来的碰撞责任诉讼中,对方没有沉没的一艘船舶(估计也是对碰撞要付主要的责任)向法院存入(payment into court)1000英镑作为和解提议与保护进一步诉讼的费用。这一来,就存在这1000英镑怎样在保险人与受保人之间分配,而法院判是双方要平等的按比例分配。保险人就可以取回1000英镑×(1000英镑/1350英镑)=740.74英镑,而剩下的259.26英镑就归受保人。这里要顺便一提的是保险合约中的绝对免赔额并不等于是不足额保险,不能去这样分配:Napier and Ettrick (Lord) v. Kershaw (1993) 1 Lloyd's Rep 197。

14.2 岸上财产保险与海上保险不同的法律地位

注意是岸上的财产保险针对不足额保险并非是与海上保险有同样的法律地位,除非保险合约中有明示条文说明在这种情况下,受保人与保险人是按比例分配有关的损失。这等于以明示条文把受保人在不足额保险视为是共同保险人,把它变得与海上保险地位一致。这种明示条文通常被称为"average clause",而保险合约中的保险价值也会被称为是"subject to average"。这可节录Mance大法官等著的《Insurance Disputes》第二版之8.51段:"However, in the case of non-marine insurance, the assured is not deemed to be his own insurer for the under-insured element, unless there is an average clause in the policy. In fact most property insurances contain an average clause so that the principle found in marine insurance will apply. In the absence of an average clause in a non-marine policy, the assured will be entitled to retain any recovery until he has been fully indemnified."

这一来,针对岸上保险向第三人索赔回来的钱怎样分配还要看保险合约到底有否明示"subject to average"。如果是有明示,这分配就是与上述的例子一样,把受保人视为是共同保险人。但如果是没有明示,或保险合约明示了"not subject to average",在上述例子中,投保金额是 50 万美元,保险价值是 100 万美元,保险人是赔付给受保人 50 万美元,也就是说,受保人还有 50 万美元的损失没有得到补偿。这样,因为是"not subject to average",向第三人索赔取回的80 万美元中就要首先把50 万美元弥补受保人,以让他取得损失的全部补偿,剩下的 30 万美元才是归保险人:Napier and Ettrick (Lord) v. Kershaw (1993) 1 Lloyd's Rep 197 的先例。

14.3 受保人有其他没有被承保的损失的情况

这是不足额保险的另外一种常见情况,就是受保人有其他没有被承保的损失,如已经在本书第十章第 1.1 段所提到的利润损失或是延误损失。也会是,在保单合约中并没有不足额保险,也就是投保金额与保险价值是一致,如都是 100 万美元。但由于市场上涨或其他原因,保险标的的实际价值是在发生全损的时候高达 150 万美元。这一来,向第三人提出索赔,索赔金额显然是 150 万美元而不是 100 万美元,因为保险价值只是保险人与受保人之间的协议,与第三人无关。这一来,如果向第三人的索赔成功,并取回 150 万美元,这在分配时就不会有任何问题,保险人与受保人都会满意。但如果索赔成功,却只取回了 100 万美元,甚至是 80 万美元,怎样分配就有问题。一种分配办法是大家按损失的比例,另一种分配的办法先满足保险人作出的赔付,剩下的(如果有的话)才给受保人。另一种分配的办法先满足受保人,特别是他在发生全损时没有被承保的 50 万美元损失(这也就是所谓的"由上至下"分配原则)。

这方面在贵族院先例 Napier and Ettrick (Lord) v. Kershaw (1993) 1 Lloyd's Rep 197 有一定的解释,就是向第三人索赔取回的钱在分配上是根据不同层次(layer)"由上至下"(top down)分配。但该先例涉及的是再保险人与保险人之间的分配,进一步解释就会涉及再保险的做法。所以,接下来介绍的另一个先例会是更能表达这一"由上至下"的分配原则。先例 Kuwait Airways Corp v. Kuwait Insurance Co SAK (No. 1) (1996) 1 Lloyd's Rep 664,案情涉及 1990 年伊拉克侵略科威特的海湾战争。伊拉克的一个重要的侵略目标是科威特机场,而起初的侵略可谓十分成功与快速,半天不到的时间就已经控制了科威特机场。当时有 15 架属于科威特航空公司(Kuwait Airways Corporation)的民航飞机停泊在科威特机场,全部落入伊拉克军的手中,并在稍后的时间飞去伊拉克。另外,寄存在科威特机场的大批飞机零件也被伊军掠走。之后，科威特航空公司作为受保人向其战争保险人索赔，该保险合约的约定保险价值（agreed value）与投保金额（sum insured）是每架飞机 8000 万美元，15 架就是 12 亿美元。但约定地面损失限额（ground limit）是 3 亿美元，等于 15 架飞机的损失共 12 亿美元只能获得少部分的赔付。该保险合约下，表示飞机在飞行的时候出事，每架就要赔付 8000 万美元。但如果在地面出事，由于很多的飞机在一起导致风险集中，那么就有了一个赔偿的限额，也就是顶多赔 3 亿美元（这等于是海上货物保险的开口/预约保单中的 location limit，在本书第十二章第 6 段有介绍）。但这就表示在这一次事故中，科威特航空公司的损失不能得到完全的赔付。因为科威特航空公司本来向保险人索赔的是 6.92 亿美元的损失，包括飞机与零件，但最终保险人只通过和解支付了 3 亿美元。在赔付之后，由于美国与国际社会的介入，科威特航空公司陆续从伊拉克取回他失去的部分飞机与零件，这就涉及了怎样针对扣除的问题或如何分配这些取回的财产的问题。注意在本先例，科威特航空公司受到的庞大损失并没有完全得到赔付，其中有大部分是没有承保的损失要自己承担。所以，怎样分配就十分重要，而显然贵族院在 Napier and Ettrick（Lord）v. Kershaw 先例中的“由上至下”的计算办法是对科威特航空公司十分有利的，因为优先的就是没有承保的那部分庞大的损失，以保证受保人的所有损失获得赔偿，所以从第三人取回的钱作出分配是属于第一层次（first layer）。相对而言，保险人在保险合约承诺承保受保人的损失，能向第三人取回部分的赔付算是运气，在层次上就没有理由优先于受保人首先获得全数的赔偿，所以只能算是第二层次（second layer）。而如果保险合约中有绝对免赔额，就等于是受保人向保险人同意先自己承担这部分的损失，超出了才需要保险人作出赔付。所以在层次上更加低，是属于第三层次（third layer）。

在 Kuwait Airways Corp v. Kuwait Insurance Co SAK 的一审，Rix 大法官支持“由上至下”的计算办法，这也被上诉庭支持。Rix 大法官作出了以下解释：

“The essential issue there is whether **the value of the recoveries (whatever that should turn out to be), net of application expenses, should be allocated entirely to KAC until they have received a full indemnity for the insured valued** (*sed quaere* the actual value) of the 15 aircrafts lost (the so-called ‘top-down principle’), or whether the net value of those recoveries should be shared proportionately between the parties on the basis of 300/692 parts to the underwriters and 392/692 parts to KAC. If I were wrong in my decision on ‘any one occurrence’, so that KAC were entitled to the full insured value of all 15 aircrafts lost, and to even further sums in respect of spares if I were also wrong in respect of my decisions on the scope of the ground limit and the operative perils, the separate issue of how the recoveries of aircraft and/or spares should be dealt with was not, as I understand it, argued before me. I do not mean thereby that any issue of that kind between the parties has gone by default. It remains to be dealt with, if necessary.

In support of the top-down approach is the decision of the House of Lords in Lord Napier and Ettrick v. Kershaw (1993) 1 Lloyd's Rep 197; (1993) AC 713. It was there decided that an underwriter at Lloyd's who takes out a stop-loss policy to pay for losses within a band of (say) excess of £ 25,000 up to £ 125,000, but loses £ 160,000 on his underwriting and then recovers £ 130,000 from a third party in respect of those losses, holds £ 95,000 for his stop-loss insurer. Although self-insured above £ 125,000, he is entitled to first call on the recoveries in respect of the top slice of his losses, leaving the balance of £ 95,000 for the stop-loss insurer who insures the next slice. Lord Templeman at p. 200, col. 2; p. 731C appears to have considered the top-down approach applicable to competing claims to subrogation in the context of under-insurance or partial insurance or layers of insurance.

Marine insurance was not there in issue. There are oft cited dicta to the effect that the essential principles of subrogation are common to both marine and non-marine polities. It appears nevertheless that the position may well be different in marine insurance: see ss. 79 and 81 of the Marine Insurance Act, 1906 (the"MIA"), Goff & Jones, The Law of Restitution, (4th ed.) (1993) at pp. 610-611, and The"Commonwealth", [1907], where a vessel insured for £ 1000 under a policy which stated her value to be £ 1350 was sunk as a result of a collision, the insurers paid £ 1000, and were held entitled to a share in the sum of £ 1000 (with accruing interest) paid into Court by the owners of the colliding vessel, in the proportion of 1000/1350 as against the 350/1350 payable to the assured.

It seems to me, however, that KAC are entitled to the benefit of the top-down principle: either because it is the principle which most closely confirms to the underlying rationale of subrogation; or because any variation from that principle is confined to marine insurance."

15. 向第三人部分成功索赔后的赔偿金分配：为货物增值部分而加保的情况

在一个国际货物买卖，如果是以 CIF 的价格，就是由卖方作出投保。通常，买方会在买卖合约内规定卖方投保的责任与范围，如要求投保一切险与战争/罢工险，保险人必须是一些有信誉的保险公司等。其中会包括投保金额，这通常会是 CIF 价格另加上 10% 的估计利润。但在有关货物的估计利润高的时候也会要求加上 25%，虽然买方通常不会这样要求卖方，避免让他知道自己赚取过高的利润。如果确实有很高的利润，CIF 买方也喜欢自己作出投保。

另会有不少货物，特别是商品(commodity)会面对市场价格的波动。毕竟在签订了买卖合约直到把货物付运并运到目的地港的时间可能有好几个月。这一来,这票货物的市场价格完全可能升了一倍(或贬值到一半)。在这种情况下,买方就会感觉通过卖方转让过来的保险合约/保险证明(certificate of insurance)所投保的金额不足以保障。毕竟,在货物发生全损的时候,买方就要去市场以升值一倍的价钱购买另一票同样的货物。买方就会可能投保另一份保险合约,投保金额是升值的市场价格与原来 CIF 价格的差别,这种保险可称为增值保险。

为了方便起见,可以把 CIF 中卖方投保的保险称为主保险(primary insurance),而买方为增加的价值所投的保险称为增值保险(increased value insurance)。由于这种情况的存在,就会导致另外一个难题,那就是如果开始针对第三人的诉讼,最后确实是索赔成功,取回部分的赔付,就索赔得来的钱两个保险人之间应该怎么分配。先例 Boag v. Standard Marine Insurance Company Ltd (1937) 57 Ll. L. Rep. 83 就遇到了这种情况。

在该先例中,货方的货物在他的 CIF 发票上显示的价格是 635 英镑,但由于市场价格上涨,该批货物在卸货港的价格是 1043 英镑。减去关税、装卸费、港口使用费等各种开支后,该批货物的净价值是 899 英镑。在 1934 年 9 月 19 日,货方向 Standard Insurance 以货物的总价值 685 英镑投保。而在 1934 年 9 月 28 日,货方通过宣告向另一个保险人 Lloyd's Insurance 就货物增加的价值 215 英镑投保,因为早在 1934 年 9 月 5 日该保险人就已经向货方签发了一份额度为 5000 英镑的浮动增值保单(floating policy)。而船东的船舶是在 1934 年 9 月 27 日搁浅,为了让船舶轻载去起浮,货方的货物被抛进了海里造成全损,这显然是共同海损的牺牲,其他得益方是要作出共同海损的分摊。针对货方而言,保险人是先要赔付货物的全损,至于将来从其他得益方取回的共同海损分摊,这只是属于代位求偿权,归保险人所有。之后 Standard Insurance 于 1934 年 11 月 5 日按照货物全损赔付了货方,而货方也在 1934 年 11 月 3 日向 Standard Insurance 递交了签署的代位求偿协议。货方同时也向 Lloyd's Insurance 就增值部分提出全损索赔,Lloyd's Insurance 也是作出了赔付,1934 年 12 月 14 日货方也向该保险人递交了签署的代位求偿协议。在共同海损的理算,得出的结果是其他得益方(其中包括船舶)要作出的分摊与支付给牺牲货物的货方 532 英镑,而这些钱是被海损理算人作为信托人所持有,等待法院的判决。Standard Insurance 提出的索赔是认为根据代位求偿协议他应该可以得到全部的 532 英镑,毕竟他赔付了 685 英镑。而 Lloyd's Insurance 则提出索赔认为两份保险合约应该是按照比例分配这 532 英镑,归他的也就是 215 英镑(Lloyd's Insurance 赔付的全损)除以 900 英镑(215 + 685)(两份保单加起来的总数)再乘以 532 英镑。这得出来的英镑是 127 英镑,这笔钱应该分配给他。

但英国一审法院是判 Standard Insurance 有权得到全部的 532 英镑,上诉庭维持了此判决。这等于是 Lloyd's Insurance 作为增值保险人一分钱也分不到。

一审的 Romer 大法官认为根据 1906 年《英国海上保险法》之 Section 79,如果保险人支付了赔偿金,那么从造成货损的事故发生时起(from the time of the casualty causing the loss),保险标的的所有权利(包括了向第三人索赔的诉权,收取共同海损分摊,保险标的的剩余价值)都由保险人代位。而搁浅是发生在9月27日,而受保人是在不知情的情况下(显然在那个年代通讯并不太发达)于9月28日才向Lloyd's Insurance进行了宣告,也就是说,那时增值保险才成立。所以,Standards Insurance的代位权利在增值保险成立前就已经成了既定事实(crystalised)。

而上诉庭的Wright大法官更广泛的肯定了Standards Insurance的完全的代位权利,他这样说:

"[Section 79 of the Marine Insurance Act 1906:—

(1) Where the insurer pays for a total loss, either of the whole, or in the case of goods of any apportionable part, of the subject-matter insured, he thereupon becomes entitled to take over the interest of the assured in whatever may remain of the subject-matter so paid for, and he is thereby **subrogated to all the rights and remedies of the assured in and in respect of that subject-matter as from the time of the casualty causing the loss**.

Those words merely give effect to a well-recognised law, subject to one point, which is, however, not here material, applying to subrogation: 'Subrogated to **all** the rights and remedies of the assured in and in respect of that subject-matter as from the time of the casualty causing the loss.' The result is that it is an integral condition of this policy that the Standard Marine Company has a **contingent** right of subrogation which attaches and which vests in them at the moment when the policy is effected. It is contingent in the sense that the state of affairs postulated may never arise, but the contingent right is there, and here the **contingency** has arisen, and the right vested as a contingency has become an effective right...

Mr. Miller's (增值保险人的代表大律师) main argument appears to have been based upon the letters of subrogation. He claims that because the goods-owners have assigned to the Lloyd's underwriters a share of the salvage, that share has been properly vested in the Lloyd's underwriters, and on that ground they are entitled to succeed in their claim here; but it seems to me that if that were done, the effect of it would be that the rights of the Standard Marine Company to subrogation in the sense which I have explained would be prejudiced if they are entitled, as I think they are, to the whole of the rights and remedies of the assured. **Any attempt by the assured to dispose of the value of those rights and remedies in any other direction, whether to increased value underwriter or to anyone else, would, to my mind, either be futile, or, if in fact the rights of the Standard Marine Company were affected, would entitle the Standard Marine Company to bring an action against the goods-owners to recover from them to the extent**

that their valuable rights of subrogation had been prejudiced, I need not refer to authorities for that, because that has long been established."(加黑部分是笔者的强调)

那么双重保险理论(这一个课题稍后在第 17 段介绍,它针对是在两份保险合约承保的是同一风险,而投保的金额是超出了保险标的本身的价值,这一来,英国法律要求两份保险合约的保险人分配[contribute],而不是让受保人从两份保险合约中赚取比损失更多的钱)是否可以帮到 Lloyd's Insurance 呢? 关于这个问题,Wright 大法官这样说:"**Now, the position would have been different if this had been a case of double insurance under Section 32 of the Act, but Mr. Miller** [增值保险人的代表律师] **has very fairly pointed out that it cannot be so regarded**, and I need not trouble any further about that. In the case of double insurance, obviously, as the two sets of underwriters have to share the burden, they would be entitled to the proportionate benefit of any sums which went in reduction of the burden, and they would share both the amount of the indemnity which had to be paid, and against that they would be entitled to share the salvage in regard to which they were entitled to be subrogated in reduction of that indemnity. There is no such question here. **The case here is that of a subsequent and subsidiary insurance, an increased value insurance, which is effected by way of supplement for the goods-owners' convenience in order to make up what he regards as the full value over and above the first insurance. The first insurance is on the whole of the subject-matter, and is on the subject-matter for its full value for purposes of that policy, and as between the goods-owners and the underwriters of that policy. As that is so, they are entitled to the full rights of the subrogation.**"(这基本上是分析增值保险与双重保险的不同之处,增值保险只是一个事后与辅助性的保险,作用是投保货物的全部价值,因为第一个保险的投保金额不足。)

事实上,在该先例的增值保险合约中有一条协会按比例分配条文(a *pro rata* Institute Clause),即是把代位求偿得来的利益按比例在不同保险合约中分配。但 CIF 卖方投保主货物保险合约(primary insurance)中是没有,所以没有理据把增值保险合约中的某条文移植在主货物保险合约中,而法院也不愿意默示。但显然是如果主货物保险合约中真的有同样的分配条文,情况就会很不同。Wright 大法官这样说:"It is perfectly clear that if the Standard Marine policy had contained a clause analogous to which I have read from the f. . p. a fire clauses in the Lloyd's policy, there would have been an express vesting of such a right in the goods-owners, and the matter could have been worked out in accordance with that intention **on businesslike lines** by increasing the total valuation under both policies to the valuation of the two policies taken together."

伦敦保险市场对该先例的判决是非常的不满意,也认为先例 Boag v. Standard Marine Insurance Company Ltd 没有在某些方面给出清楚的答案,如第二份的增值保险如果是在发生全损之前就已经成立或生效,又会怎样分配? 因此伦敦保险市场决定加入一条标准条文在 1982 年的协会货物条文，以保证主保险合约不会漏掉这一条类似协会按比例分配条文（一般增值保险不会有遗漏），这就可以按照 Wright 大法官所说的两份不同的前后保险合约可以“on businesslike lines”作出分摊。而在 2009 年的协会货物条文中该增值保险条文（Increased Value Clause）内容是没有实质的改变，是第 14 条。[1]

第 14.1 条的大意就是，如果受保人投保了主货物保险之后对保险标的的货物又投保了增值保险，那么货物的价值被视为提高至主货物保险与增值保险下投保金额的总和，货物保险承保的责任比例是与货物保险下的投保金额所占两者金额总和的比例相同。它最后的一句也规定了受保人向保险人提供证据证明所有其他的保险合约（包括主货物保险合约与增值保险）。

由此可见，增值保险条文已经变成了协会货物条文中的一部分。这样，对保险人向第三人索赔回来的追偿款（recoveries）而言，如果受保人也确实投保了增值保险，并且在主货物保险合约与增值保险合约中都有类似第 14 条的条文，那么增值保险的保险人是有合约权利按比例分得索赔成功的钱，而货物保险的保险人也确实是有这样的义务给予增值保险人该部分钱。

16. 对保险标的剩余价值的权利（the right to salvage）

在海上货物保险中，“salvage”一词与海上救助的“salvage”一词的含义并不相同，前者是指损坏了的货物。而“right to salvage”则是指保险人对损坏货物的所有权并取得其剩余价值的权利，已经在本章第 2.2 段有介绍，本小段再补充一些内容。这一说法与代位求偿权以及不能让受保人在事故中赚取比真正损失更大的好处有密切的关系，在 1906 年《英国海上保险法》Section 63 (1) 对委付/抛弃（abandonment）也有以下的规定：“Where there is a valid abandonment the insurer is entitled to take over the interest of the assured in whatever may remain of the subject-matter, and all proprietary rights incidental thereto.”

在实践中，保险人通常都会有担心，如果自己接手（take over）保险标的，会在某些特定的情况下招致更大的责任，如危险货物可能正在或将会污染港口/码头，或是更大的灾难就在眼前。毕竟，保险人对发生事故的保险标的的所知道的情况不多，比受保人知道得更少。所以如果受保人愿意作出委付与放弃保险标的，贸然接手是危险的事。

针对委付/抛弃，1906 年《英国海上保险法》Section 63 (1) 明确规定保险人只是有权利（is entitled to），而并非是有义务或责任（is obliged to）接手保险标的的财产权

[1] 参见附录三。

以及作为所有人,并承担相关的责任。很多时候,保险人即使愿意作出全损的赔付,也会明确说明他不行使有关的权利接受委付/抛弃,以免引起误会。如在先例 The "Martin P"(2004) 1 Lloyd's Rep 389,虽然是有关船舶而不是货物的保险标的,道理是一样。Siberry 大法官在第 77 段说:"Initially, Wellington (船舶保险人) did not accept that the vessel was a CTL. However, on Feb 10, 2000 Wellington agreed to the settlement of the claim as for a CTL, but on the basis that they did not accept abandonment of the vessel to them."

针对海上货物保险,实践中通常的做法是,保险人的检验师(surveyor)会连同受保人以及受保人聘请的检验师一起讨论保险标的的剩余价值最多可能是多少,什么是最好的方法作出处置,如出售。而如果损坏的货物还有剩余价值,保险公司以及有国际联系的贸易商(如果他是受保人)应该会知道哪些公司会对该损坏的货物有兴趣,以安排"salvage sale"。反正,能够取回来的剩余价值就可以作为扣减,不论是在赔付全损给受保人之前或者之后。

有时候,在保险人支付受保人全损后很多年,货物才会被挽救回来(recover),如从海底捞上岸,也有可能是很多年后保险人才有机会向第三人代位求偿权的索赔成功。在美国的 Columbus-America Discovery Group v. Atlantic Mutual Insurance Company (1992) AMC, United States Court of Appeals, Fourth Circuit 就是一个很好的例子。在该先例中,1857 年 9 月 12 日,装在 Central America 轮上的黄金是沉没在美国西弗吉尼亚首府查尔斯顿东 160 英里的海域,这批货物的英国与美国保险人是赔付了 100 万美元的全损。130 年后打捞成功,他们都主张对这批打捞上来价值 10 亿美元的黄金的所有权。美国法院判如果保险人能够提供可被接纳的证据证明他们对黄金的所有权,就可以索赔成功。最终黄金价值的 90% 是作为奖金被判给了打捞人。不过即便这样,剩下的 1 亿美元归保险人也是一笔不小的金钱,至少比当时赔偿的 100 万美元多得多。但已经在本章第 2. 2 段提到过委付/抛弃不像代位求偿权,前者是不必以在赔付的钱为最高限额。

这种情况比较近期一点的先例是 The "Evia" (1982) 2 Lloyd's Rep 307, The "Wenjiang" (1983) 1 Lloyd's Rep 400; The "Lucille" (1983) 1 Lloyd's Rep 387; The "Chrysalis" (1983) 1 Lloyd's Rep 503 等一连串的著名先例。在这些先例中,涉及的是 20 世纪 70 年代两伊战争的爆发导致好几十艘船舶被困在沙特阿拉伯河(Shatt-al-Arab)。船舶保险人是赔付了推定全损。不过之后两伊战争结束,船舶可以离开,有部分保险人以委付/抛弃的说法主张了所有权,出售了这些船舶并赚了钱。

这就说明一个问题,除非某些保险标的真的负上了很大的责任且所有人不会有好处,保险人对一些有剩余价值的保险标的还是不要轻易明示拒绝委付/抛弃(好像先例 The "Martin P" [2004] 1 Lloyd's Rep 389),说不定后来会有转机。

17. 双重保险

17.1 双重保险出现在海上货物保险主要情况的介绍

双重保险(Double Insurance)是指两份以上保险合约对同一个受保人承保相同保险标的的同一种风险。这里可以节录 Mansfield 勋爵在 Godin v. London Assurance Co (1758) 1 Burr 489 中给双重保险的定义说:"A double insurance is where the same man is to receive two sums instead of one, or the same sum twice over, for the same loss, by reason of his having two insurances upon the same goods or the same ship."

双重保险会在同一事故中对受保人作出比实际损失更大的赔付,而两份或多份保险合约投保的金额加起来是超出了保险标的的可保价值(insurable value)或是实际价值(actual value)。换言之,如果这两份或以上的保险合约都作出赔付,受保人就会从事故中赚钱,这显然不是一件好事。正如 Saville 大法官在 Napier and Ettrick (Lord) v. Kershaw (1993) 1 Lloyd's Rep 10 中所说:"... that the assured, in case of a loss against which the policy has been made, shall be fully indemnified, but shall never be more than fully indemnified... if ever a proposition is brought forward which is at variance with it, that is to say, which either will prevent the assured from obtaining a fully indemnity, or which will give to the assured more than a fully indemnity, that proposition must certainly be wrong."(受保人遇到承保风险所造成的损失应该获得全面的补偿,但也不应该获得比全面补偿更多的好处。所以,任何的说法阻止受保人获得全面补偿或给受保人获得全面补偿更大的好处,这种说法肯定是错的。)

在现实中,双重保险发生会是由于意外所产生;也会是由于法律(如汽车的第三人保险,一个保险合约跟车,一个保险合约跟人);也会是由于受保人刻意这样做,如对第一份保险合约不放心,甚至怕保险人破产;更会是受保人的不诚实行为向不同保险人投保远超出保险标的实际价值,在发生意外的时候企图赚大钱。在英国法律,不禁止双重保险。但这就带来很多的问题与一些做法,如在不让受保人获得比全面补偿更大的好处的大前提下,不同保险人之间应该怎样分摊对受保人的赔付。

在海上货物保险相比岸上的保险,双重保险的情况比较少。但还是会出现,如对同一票货与同一个航次,CIF 卖方已经投了保并把保险合约转让给买方。但买方由于对卖方投保的保险公司不放心(如一家印尼的小型保险公司),所以自己向熟悉的保险人再投保一次。双重保险也会发生在两种不同性质的保险合约,因为他们都有承保同一风险,如存储在仓库中的货物是被投保了火灾险,不过海上保险合约(marine policy)也会延伸承保存储在仓库中的货物。这种情况发生在 Australian Agricultural Company v. Saunders (1874 - 75) LR 10 CP 668。在该先例中有一批羊毛是投保了火灾险,是说承保"on station, or in transit to Sydney by land only, or in any shed or store, or any wharf in Sydney, until placed on ship"的风险。羊毛是在搬运小工的仓库里被大火烧毁,而这些搬运小工是船东的代理人。火灾险的保险人争辩说,因为货物已经被船东接受要运去英国,所以在火灾发生的时候货物是在运输途中(in transit)所以是处在海上保险合约的承保期间。但这种争辩是被 Blackburn 大法官拒绝,他判是海上保险合约是不承保储存在岸上仓库中的羊毛。可以说该先例中,火灾保险人是承担了全部的赔付责任,海上保险的保险人则是没有责任。

还有一种会出现双重保险的情况是公路承运人(haulier)或者仓库所有人(warehouse keeper),他们作为托管人会为货物投保,这投保可能是以协会货物条文(一切险)进行,而不仅仅是投保他们作为托管人的责任险。有关这一种比较特殊的做法,在本书第三章之 3.3 段已经有过介绍,请参阅。同样是船东作为承运人就比较少会有这种做法,因为船东是一直以来向互保协会投保他作为托管人对船上这批货所负的责任。这一来,如果公路承运人与仓库所有人在发生全损的时候,是可以向保险人提出索赔,即使他对货物的损失没有任何责任,他也不是这票货物的所有人。这是一个受保人必须对保险标的有可保利益条件下一个奇怪的现象,但法律要求他把向保险人要回的这笔钱作为真正货物所有人的信托人持有,需要归还(当然在扣除了应收的费用后,因为如果货物没有损坏,因为货物所有人没有支付相关费用,可以就货物有留置权)。这一来,如果货物所有人自己也有投保,就会构成双重保险的情况。这也表示货物如果是在公路运输或者在仓库里发生损失,保险人就要留心是否是有双重保险,因为存在可能性要其他的保险人分摊赔付。

这可以节录贵族院的先例 A Tomlinson (Hauliers) Ltd v. Hepburn (1966) 1 Lloyd's Rep 309,案情涉及一家公路承运人为一批烟草投保一切险,货物在运输时被偷,但承运人没有责任。保险人拒绝赔付,认为保险合约真正希望承保的只是承运人的责任。加上承运人对这票货物没有所有权,也没有保险利益。但在贵族院,判是保险人败诉。其中依赖了几个重要的先例,其中一个是 Waters and Steel v. Monarch Fire and Life Assurance Company (1856) 5 E & B 870,Campbell 勋爵说:"... I think that a person entrusted with goods can insure them without orders from the owner, and even without informing him that there was such a policy. It would be most inconvenient in business if a wharfinger could not, at his own cost, keep up a floating policy for the benefit of all who might become his customers... as the property is wholly destroyed, the value of the whole must be made good, not merely the particular interest of the plaintiff. They will be entitled to apply so much to cover their own interest, and will be trustees for the owners as to the rest. The authorities are clear that an assurance made without orders may be ratified by the owners of the property, and then the assurers become trustees for them..."

在贵族院的先例,Reid 勋爵判说:"A bailee can, if he chooses, merely insure to cover his own loss or personal liability to the owner of the goods either at common law or under contract and if he does that of course he can recover no more under the policy than sufficient to make good his own personal loss or liability. But equally he can if he chooses insure up to his full insurable interest—up to the full value of the goods entrusted to him. And if he does that he can recover the value of the goods though he has suffered no personal loss at all. But in that case the laws will require him to account to the owner of the goods who has suffered the loss... The fact that a bailee has an insurable interest beyond his own personal loss if the goods are destroyed has never been regarded as in any way inconsistent with the overriding principle that insurance of goods is a contract of indemnity."

17.2　双重保险的要求

1906 年《英国海上保险法》关于双重保险在 Section 32。[1]

进一步介绍双重保险，是介绍什么原因才会造成这种情况。

17.2.1　要求之一：同一个受保人（the same assured）

双重保险的第一个要求是同一个受保人针对同种风险：Godin v. London Assurance Co（1758）1 Burr 489；Petrofina（UK）v. Magnaload Ltd（1984）QB 127；Black Sea & Baltic General Insurance Co Ltd v. Baker（1996）LRLR 353。如果是不同的受保人，如货方为一批货物投保，但另一个受保人如承运人或者托管人为同一批货物投保他可能会有的责任，这不算是双重保险：Black Sea & Baltic General Insurance Co Ltd v. Baker（1996）LRLR 353。双重保险也可以发生在不同的受保人，但一份保险合约的受保人只是作为代理人的身份，而背后实际上是同一人。在 Godin v. London Assurance Co（1758）1 Burr 489，Mansfield 勋爵说："... if the same man really, and for his own proper account, insures the same goods doubly, though both insurances be not made in his own name, but one or both of them in the name of another person, yet that is just the same thing, for the same person is to have the benefit of both policies."

17.2.2　要求之二：同一个保险标的（the same subject matter）

双重保险的第二个要求就是两份以上的保险合约都是针对同一个保险标的。这里可以是一个保险合约只针对特定的保险标的，但另一个针对的保险标的是比较广泛，但后者必须包括了前者。这种争议在先例 Boag v. Economic Insurance Company, Ltd（1954）2 Lloyd's Rep 581 中出现，损失的货物是一批烟草，它已经被装上了卡车准备运去伦敦的码头并准备装上远洋船舶运往澳大利亚给 FOB 的买方。但卡车在受保人工厂停车的地点遇上火灾并把货物烧毁。原告是承保海上运输一切险的保险人，他在赔付了受保人之后向受保人工厂投保了另一份的火灾与盗窃险的保险合约，要求分摊，认为是双重保险的情况。该火灾与盗窃险所承保的保险标的很广泛，基本上包括了受保人工厂的商业存货（stock-in-trade），有关条文是"On stock and material in trade, the property of the insured or held by them in trust or on commission for which they are responsible."英国法院判是该批烟草的货物并非是火灾与盗窃险的商业存

---

〔1〕 见附录一。

货,所以不存在双重保险。

17.2.3　要求之三:同一样保险利益(the same interest)

双重保险还涉及两份保险合约都针对同样的保险利益。这里可节录 Mance 大法官等著的《Insurance Disputes》第二版之 9.11 段:"Where policies are effected to cover different interests there is no double insurance but the principles of subrogation may apply. The distinction is illustrated by the case of a bailee who may insure his full insurable interest up to the value of the goods themselves or, alternatively, his personal liability to the owner of the goods either at common law or under contract. In the first case, where the bailee insures the goods, and likewise the goods-owner also insures the goods, there is double insurance: in the second case, where the bailee insures his liability there is no double insurance and subrogation arises."

这表示货方为他的一批货物投保,但作为他的代理人或托管人也为同一批货物投保(请看本章 17.1 段),这是双重保险。如果他的代理人也是该批货物的托管人,为他的托管人责任投保,这就涉及了不同的保险利益,就不算是双重保险。在后者的情况,只在托管人有责任的时候才需要作出赔付,而这个赔付也往往是支付给货方的海上货物运输的保险人,作为代位求偿权的索赔或扣减。

另在本章第 15 段所介绍的增值保险不等于是双重保险也应该是这一个理由,因为虽然是同一个受保人、同一样保险标的与同样的承保风险,但并非是同样的保险利益。增值保险只针对货物在运输期间增值的部分。

17.2.4　要求之四:同样的承保风险(the same risk)

双重保险也要针对同样的承保风险,正如《MaGillivray & Parkington on Insurance Law》一书第 9 版 23-4 段说:"no double insurance unless at least a substantial part of the same risk is covered by both insurance",依据的是先例 Australian Agricultural Co. v. Saunders (1874-75) LR 10 CP 668。

在先例 Bovis Construction Ltd v. Commercial Union Insurance Co. Plc (2001) 1 Lloyd's Rep 416, Steel 大法官说:"As I understood it, the answer advanced on behalf of Bovis was that there was no double insurance because the cover furnished by the two policies was not co-extensive. But this is not to the point. The right to contribution as between insurers exists where more than one policy covers the risk that has given rise to the claim: see Albion Insurance Co Ltd v. Government Insurance Office of N. S. W (1969) CLR 342."

Albion Insurance Co Ltd 是澳大利亚先例,不同性质或者目的的保险合约并不重要,重要的是两份保险合约都针对同一个风险造成的损失,这就会构成双重保险,受保人的损失要在保险人之间分摊。

17.3　双重保险下受保人的权利与地位

双重保险受保人可能会面对一个保险人的拒赔,理由就是他应该先向双重保险下其他的保险人要求赔付。这种拒赔理由是在英国法下完全站不住脚,因为在1906年《英国海上保险法》Section 32(2)(a)受保人完全有权向双重保险下的任何一位保险人要求赔付。毕竟双重保险早期出现的原因是由于保险人怕第一份保险合约的保险人经济不稳,故作出另一份同样的保险合约。这一来,他完全可以选择他所认为可以容易并快速作出赔付的保险人进行索赔。除了在1906年《英国海上保险法》的有关条文外,也可以节录Mansfield勋爵在Godin v. London Assurance Co (1758) 1 Burr 489所说:"Where a man makes a double insurance of the same thing, in such a manner that he can clearly recover, against several insurers in distinct policies, a double satisfaction, the law certainly says that he ought not the recover doubly for the same loss, but be content with one single satisfaction for it."

受保人不能选择任何一位的保险人进行索赔全部损失的情况就是在有关的保险合约中都有一条明示条文,通常命名为"non-contribution clause"或"ratable proportion clause"。这种条文会有很多不同的措辞,毕竟是订约自由,在下一小段会有介绍。

17.4 双重保险下保险人的危险与应对办法

双重保险会对保险人带来一个很大的危险,就是受保人可以在背后作出双重保险,并在发生事故时分别向不同的保险人提出索赔并赚取一大笔。由于英国法律是允许双重保险,而且并不要求受保人在投保的时候披露这一事实(如已经有了一个同样的保险合约,这在本书第二章之5.3段有介绍):Mathie v. Argonaut Marine Insurance Co (1925) 21 Ll. L. Rep. 145。所以保险人在保险合约中会以各种明示条文控制,包括像明示要求受保人披露其他可能存在的同样的保险合约;要求受保人保证不会在保险期限内投保其他同样的保险合约,除非获得保险人的批准(Australian Agriculture Co v. Saunders [1875] LR 10 CP 668);在保险合约中加入"non-contribution clause"或"ratable proportion clause"等。

17.4.1 "non-contribution clause"与"ratable proportion clause"的作用

其中"non-contribution clause"的先例有Steelclad Ltd v. Iron Trader Mutual Insurance Co Ltd (1984) SLT 304,这种条文是说明先要向其他的保险人索赔损失,只在其他保险人赔不足的情况下(如另一份双重保险有一个赔偿限额),才会作出赔付,把这一份保险变成一份本质上的excess loss或stop loss的保险,说:"This insurance does not cover any loss damage or expense which... is insured or would, but for the existence of this policy, be insured by any other policy or policies except in respect of any excess beyond the amount which would have been payable under such other policy or policies had this insurance not been affected."

至于"ratable proportion clause",一种常见的版本在先例Commercial Union Assurance Co Ltd v. Hayden (1977) 1 Lloyd's Rep 1可见到,有关保险合约中有一条"ratable proportion clause",如下:"If at the time of any claim arising under this section there shall be any other insurance covering the same risk or any part thereof the Company shall not be liable for more than its ratable proportion thereof."

上述的条文经常在岸上保险合约中出现,但不多在海上货物保险合约中出现,其中协会货物条文就没有。但这不表示海上货物保险不会遇到相关问题的困扰,如在稍后会在第 17.6.4 段介绍的 The Niger Co Ltd v. The Guardian Insurance Co Ltd (1920) 4 Lloyd's Rep 320。

17.4.2　两份保险合约都有"non-contribution clause"等的情况

在双重保险下,根据合约的解释,如果一份保险合约有一条"non-contribution clause",但另一份保险合约中没有,受保人就只能向后者的保险人索赔。但如果两份保险合约都有一条"non-contribution clause"(这种情况在岸上保险是很常见的),英国法律目前的看法是两个保险合约中的"non-contribution clause"相互抵消,两份保险合约下的保险人对受保人的损失都有赔付的连带责任。这背后的大原则就是既不应该让受保人投保之后无法获得赔付,也不应该让他从中获利。正如 Mance 大法官等著的《Insurance Disputes》第二版之 9.24 段:"In the more usual situation where two concurrent policies of insurance cover the same risk and each contains a non-contribution clause, excluding liability in the event of the risk being covered by another policy, a literal approach might suggest that the insurance under both policies fails, with the loss covered nowhere, but this absurd result has been avoided by constructing the clause so that they may cancel each other out. This principle of construction, which has been much followed, was stated by Rowlatt J in *Weddell v. Road Transport and General Insurance Co.* Ltd as follows: '... the reasonable construction is to exclude from the category of co-existing cover any cover which is expressed to be itself cancelled by such co-existence, and to hold in such cases that both companies are liable.'"

如果在双重保险下,一份保险合约有一条"non-contribution clause",但另一份保险合约有一条"ratable proportion clause",就曾经有先例判这两条条文本质上无法区分,所以两个不同的保险人都要按比例负责:Austin v. Zurich General Accident and Liability Insurance Companies (1994) 2 All ER 243。

反正这些都是根据保险合约的条文的文字作出合理的解释,特别考虑到保险大原则是为了赔付给受保人,只是不能让他从中赚取利益,正如 Saville 大法官在 Napier and Ettrick (Lord) v. Kershaw (1993) 1 Lloyd's Rep 10 中所说。

如果保险人根据本章第 17.4 段作出了全部损失的赔付给受保人后,如果存在双重保险,英国法律就允许首先赔付的保险人有权向双重保险的其他保险人要求分摊,这在下一小段会进一步介绍。

17.5　双重保险下保险人的分摊

这方面在 1906 年《英国海上保险法》Section 80 关于"right of contribution"已经在本章一开始就已经节录,不去重复。它规定了双重保险导致了投保金额超出了保险标的的实际价值与同意的保险价值,不同的保险人就按照比例分摊,对受保人的损失作出完全的赔付，但不让受保人多赚。

Section 80(2)也说明了其中的某位保险人向受保人的赔付超过了他应该负的份额，他是可以要求其他的保险人分摊的。实际上很多双重保险的诉讼都是发生在保险人之间，与受保人无关，因为他早已经得到了其中一家保险公司的全部赔付。

这方面也可节录 Sickness and Accident Insurance Association Ltd v. General Accident Assurance Corporation Ltd (1892) Sess. Cas. R. 977，Ordinary 勋爵这样说："In Marine Insurance a rule which has long been recognised is that when the insured has recovered to the full extent of his loss under one policy, the insurer under that policy can recover from the underwriters who have insured the same interest against the same risks a ratable sum by way of contribution. The foundation for the rule is that a contract of Marine Insurance is one of indemnity and that the insured, whatever the amount of his insurance or the number of the underwriters with whom he has contracted, can never recover more than is required to indemnify him. The different policies being all with the same person, and against the same risk, are therefore regarded as truly one insurance and if one of the underwriters is compelled to meet the whole claim, he is entitled to contribution form the other underwriters, just as a surety or cautioner who pays the whole debt is entitled to claim ratable relief against this co-sureties or co-cautioners. There is no reason in principle, in my opinion, why the same rule should not be applied to other classes of insurance which are also contracts of indemnity, and this has been recognised by high authority in cases of fire insurance."

17.5.1 保险人之间的分摊要注意的方面

保险人之间的分摊是一件复杂的事情，这可节录 Mance 大法官等著的《Insurance Disputes》第二版之 9.36 段所说如下："... the insurer should consider the respective liabilities to the person insured under the separate contracts of insurance as this will determine the right to contribution which is to be assessed at the date at which contribution is sought rather than the date of the loss or casualty. This will first involve a consideration of policy validity and coverage, in particular any contractual conditions precedent, such as provisions as to notice. It will also involve a consideration of the impact of non-contribution and ratable contribution clauses. Where the first policy contains a non-contribution clause and the other does not, the first insurer may be entitled to decline payment unless the other policy also contains such a clause and the clauses cancel out. Where the first policy contains a ratable contribution clause the first insurer may be entitled to limit his indemnity to a ratable proportion of the loss, and any payment in excess of that amount will be considered voluntary and not recoverable by way of contribution from the other insurer."

17.5.2 保险人之间分摊的计算办法

此外，针对保险人之间分摊的计算办法，目前的法律还不明确，事实上英国法律上百年来都没有说明保险人之间应该怎样在不同情况下作出分摊。其中最重要的是双重保险的不同定额保险合约中都会有个别不同的投保金额(amount insured),这也是保险合约中保险人要赔付的最高赔付责任(limit of liability)。这规定的作用就是在一些金额巨大的保险索赔中,保险人的赔付责任受到限制就不会变成无穷无尽而把保险人拖垮。而这个投保金额与收取保费的高低有很大关系。这一来,在分摊方面就已经会带来很多不同的看法。如投保金额较高的保险人是否要承担更大比例的赔付?另是,如果在损失金额是高于一份保险合约的最高赔付责任而低于另一份保险合约的最高赔付责任的情况下应该怎样分摊?以下将会进一步介绍分摊的计算方法。

基本上伦敦保险市场(针对海上或岸上保险)发展出来有三种:(1)最高责任(maximum liability);(2)独立责任(independent liability);(3)共同责任(common liability)。

17.5.2.1　分摊的计算办法:最高责任与独立责任

最高责任是先计算出不同保险合约中约定的最高赔付责任金额占全部保险合约中最高赔付金额总合的比例,然后再用该比例乘以受保人获得的实际赔偿金额,得出的数额就是不同的保险人应该分摊的金额。

独立责任的计算则是看每份保险合约下保险人应该承担的赔付金额占全部保险合约应该赔付的金额总和的比例,然后用该比例乘以受保人的实际获赔金额得出每个保险人应该分摊的赔付金额。

举个例子,受保人与A保险公司的保险合约中约定的最高赔付责任是5万美元,而与B保险公司的保险合约中约定的最高赔付责任是10万美元,假设受保人在发生事故后应该获得的赔付金额分别为2.5万美元与7.5万美元的两种情况。注意区分两种不同的情况:2.5万美元是低于任何一份保险合约的最高赔付责任金额的,而7.5万美元则是超过A保险公司最高赔付责任金额而低于B公司的最高赔付责任金额。

用最高责任的算法是:

2.5万是受保人的损失时的计算方法

A保险公司

$$\frac{5}{10+5}\times 2.5 = 0.8333 \text{ 万}$$

B保险公司

$$\frac{10}{10+5}\times 2.5 = 1.6667 \text{ 万}$$

7.5万是受保人的损失时的计算方法

A保险公司

$$\frac{5}{10+5}\times 7.5 = 2.5 \text{ 万}$$

B保险公司

$$\frac{10}{10+5}\times 7.5 = 5 \text{ 万}$$

用独立责任的算法是:

2.5 万是受保人的损失时的计算方法

A 保险公司

$$\frac{2.5^{*}}{2.5^{*}+2.5^{**}}\times 2.5=1.25\text{ 万}$$

B 保险公司

$$\frac{2.5^{**}}{2.5^{*}+2.5^{**}}\times 2.5=1.25\text{ 万}$$

7.5 万是受保人的损失时的计算方法

A 保险公司

$$\frac{5^{*}}{5^{*}+7.5^{**}}\times 7.5=3\text{ 万}$$

B 保险公司

$$\frac{7.5^{**}}{5^{*}+7.5^{**}}\times 7.5=4.5\text{ 万}$$

* 根据 A 公司保单应该赔付的金额(限制在最高赔付金额也就是投保金额)

** 根据 B 公司保单应该赔付的金额

其中首先涉及了分摊的计算办法是上诉庭先例 Commercial Union Assurance Co Ltd v. Hayden (1977) 1 Lloyd's Rep. 1,案情是涉及双重保险,一个保险的保险人是 Commercial Union Assurance Co Ltd,而保险合约的最高赔付金额或投保金额是 10 万英镑。另一个保险的保险人是劳合社包括 Hayden 先生,最高赔付金额是 1 万英镑。受保人的 Cartright 发生了事故并向 Commercial Union Assurance Co Ltd 提出索赔,双方达成和解并赔付给了受保人 4425.45 英镑。之后 Commercial Union Assurance Co Ltd 向 Hayden 先生等要求分摊,问题是应该怎样计算。Hayden 先生等认为是应该根据最高责任(maximum liability),这就是把两份保险合约的最高责任加起来,然后按比例分摊损失的赔付。在计算上就等于 Commercial Union Assurance Co Ltd 要赔付 4425.45 英镑的 100,000/110,000,而 Hayden 先生等则只需要负责 4425.45 英镑的 10,000/110,000。但 Commercial Union Assurance Co Ltd 认为应该根据独立责任(independent liability),而既然赔付的钱都低于两份不同保险合约的最高赔付金额,就大家各付一半。英国上诉庭认为是独立责任的计算办法比较恰当,因为在 Commercial Union Assurance Co Ltd 订立保险合约时没有想到会有双重保险,如果在事后扯上其他的保险人按最高责任分摊是不恰当的。特别是该先例涉及的一个责任保险,会有情况是其中一个责任保险合约(如船东互保协会或是岸上汽车的第三人保险)是没有最高赔付限额(unlimited liability)或投保金额,就根本没有办法按照最高责任计算。上诉庭的 Cairns 大法官这样说:"The issue being on of construction and the language being, as it seems to me, equally capable of either suggested meaning, I asked myself which meaning is that more likely to be intended by reasonable business men. The document to be construed are policies, the parties to each of which are an assured and an insurer. It is not to be supposed that when either policy is issued the insurer knows that there is, or is going to be, another policy covering the same risk. Each limit of liability and each premium may be taken to be fixed without knowledge of the limit under any other policy that may have been, or going to be, issued... The independent liability basis is much more realistic in its results. In the case of these two policies, any loss up to Pds. 10,000 would be shared equally, and it is only with larger losses that the proportion of the Commercial Union's share to Lloyd's share steadily increases until with a loss of Pds. 110,000 or more, ten-elevenths of the liability fails on Commercial Union..."

虽然在上述的先例主要是针对责任保险合约的分摊,但有说法是独立责任也适用在财产保险,因为比较公平。但目前英国法律地位并不明朗,也没有有关的先例。这可以节录 Mance 大法官等著的《Insurance Disputes》第二版之 9.42 段的脚注 1 中所说:"In the absence of many authorities the position is unclear... There is a school of thought which believes that the independent liability approach provides a fairer result between contributing insurers and that this approach ought to be applied to both property and liability policies (see MacGillivray & Parkington on Insurance Law, 9th edn at para. 23-50)..."

但 Mance 大法官等著的《Insurance Disputes》第二版之 9.42 段同时说:"The position would therefore appear in law to be the following: (1) In property insurance the usual basis for contribution is the maximum liability basis except where the policies contain pro rata average clause (which are now almost universal except in domestic policies) when the independent liability basis is used. (2) In liability insurance where the policies are unlimited, as in motor insurance, the insurers contribute equally. (3) In liability insurance, where the policy liabilities are limited, the basis for contribution is the independent liability method."

另要注意的是 Mance 大法官等著的《Insurance Disputes》第二版是针对所有的保险类别,特别是岸上的保险。至于海上货物保险的地位,本章第 17.5.3 段介绍。

17.5.2.2　分摊的计算办法:共同责任

共同责任的计算方法实际上是综合了最高责任与独立责任两种计算办法。它先找出最低的最高赔付责任金额或投保金额,这笔钱先要在不同的保险人之间平均分摊。然后多出来的金额就完全要最高赔付责任金额,即投保金额更高的保险人承担。

这方面有一个比较近期的先例 O'Kane v. Jones (2005) Lloyd's Rep. IR 174,它涉及一个船壳保险的双重保险。第一个保险合约投保的金额是 250 万美元,也就是赔付责任的最高限额是 250 万美元。第二个保险投保的金额是 500 万美元。船舶发生全损,这就存在两个保险人之间怎样分摊的问题。根据最高责任与独立责任的计算方法得出的结果都一样,就是 1∶2 的比例。但双方曾经提到了以共同责任的计算办法,这就带来不一样的后果。因为首先的 250 万美元是要两位保险人,等于是各赔 125 万美元。但之后多出的 250 万美元就全部要第二个保险人支付,第二个保险人总共要赔 375 万美元。Siberry 大法官认为共同责任的计算办法不符合 1906 年《英国海上保险法》中 Section 80 (1)的文字,该立法条文是说"to contribute ratably to the loss in proportion to the amount for which he is liable under his contract."这些文字比较适合最高责任与独立责任的计算办法。

17.5.3　海上货物保险在双重保险下的分摊计算办法

针对海上货物保险,双重保险最常出现在本章第 17.1 段所讲的公路承运人

(haulier)或者仓库所有人(warehouse keeper)作为托管人为货物投保与货方自己也作出了海上货物运输保险的投保的情况,英国法律对这一问题的看法是两个保险人之间的分摊应该是以独立责任(independent liability)的计算办法。这里可节录 John Dunt 所著的《Marine Cargo Insurance》一书之 16.45 段,如下:"Where double insurance arises due to storage risks being insured in a warehouse by both property insurers and by cargo insurers a situation may arise where there is a sum insured under a non-marine property policy and a marine policy with an agreed insured value. It is submitted that the most appropriate way of approaching this type of situation is on the 'independent liability' approach and that this best reflects the admittedly ambiguous word 'liability' in section 80(1) of the Act. It was also the approach adopted by the Court of Appeal in *Commercial Union Assurance Co Ltd v Hayden*, although that was a liability insurance case that left open the position regarding property insurance."

另是在香港一宗有关双重保险争议的案例 Tai Ping Insurance Co. v. Tugu Insurance Co. Ltd (2001) 2 HKC 401 中也同样适用了独立责任计算方法。该案例中货物所有人将货物(水貂皮)交给东莞的一家工厂进行加工与制作,后者以托管人的身份持有货物。两方都为该批货物投保,货物所有人向本案的原告太平保险公司投保了海上货物运输保险,最高保赔额为 150 万港币。而东莞的工厂则向被告 Tugu 保险公司投保了货物运输险(Goods in Transit Policy),最高保赔额为 400 万港币。之后,该批货物在从东莞途经文锦渡口岸运往香港的途中被歹徒劫走。太平保险公司在赔付给了货物所有人 1,492,500 港币之后,根据货物投保双重保险而向被告的保险公司要求分摊该笔赔付金额。Stone 大法官在判决如何分摊该笔赔付金额时就采用了独立责任的计算办法。

另一种也是经常在海上货物运输中发生双重保险的情况,是在两个保险人都是承保了海上货物运输的定额保险(如在 CIF 卖方与买方都为同一批货物投保,不论是由于他们之间的误解还是由于 CIF 买方担心第一份保险合约赔付会有问题),这一来,伦敦市场通常是以共同责任(common liability)的计算办法(虽然已经提到过在 O'Kane v. Jones [2005] Lloyd's Rep. IR 174 先例,Siberry 大法官认为共同责任的计算办法不符合 1906 年《英国保险法》中 Section 80 [1]),并估计会继续这样计算。这里可节录 John Dunt 所著的《Marine Cargo Insurance》一书之 16.46 段,如下:"Where double insurance arises because there has been a misunderstanding as to the terms of trade, and both buyer and seller insure the cargo, the likelihood is that both insurers will insure the cargo for the c. i. f. invoice value plus 10%. Clearly, if both insurers have insured the cargo for exactly the same amount they must share equally in any loss. However, where the two insurers have insured for different agreed values, it is submitted that the most sensible way to proceed is on the 'common liability' basis. This requires that the two insurers share the risk up to the agreed value common to each policy and that the insurer for the higher value bears the whole of the balance of the loss. For example, let us assume the seller insures the cargo for a c. i. f. value of £ 10,000 plus 10% , an insured value of £ 11,000, and the buyer mistakenly also insures, but for £ 15,000. In the case of a total loss the seller's insurance would pay 50% of the common amount of £ 11,000 (i. e. , £ 5500) and the buyer's insurers would equally pay £ 5500, for this is double insurance for that common 'layer' making up the £ 11,000. the buyer's insurers having insured a further layer of £ 4000 up to £ 15,000 must pay the £ 4000 excess over the seller's policy. *O'May* records that this method is often adopted in practice in marine cargo insurance in the context of two cargo insurances, both being valued policies. This is the most appropriate method in such a case because of the rule that the agreed value is 'conclusive' under section 27(3) of the Marine Insurance Act 1906. In case of apportionment in relation to subrogated recoveries under valued policies the courts have applied that rule rigorously. It is submitted that the same rule should apply to cases of apportionment between insurers where both policies are valued policies. However, the decision in The Martin P, a hull and machinery case, rejects the common liability method in relation to valued property insurance policies as being inconsistent with the words of section 80(1) of the 1906 Act. This, as we have seen, requires the insurer to contribute 'ratably to the loss in proportion to the amount for which he is liable under his contract'. However, the 'loss' for the insurer of a valued marine cargo insurance contract can never be more than the 'conclusive' agreed value of the goods under section 27(3) of the Act. The only 'loss' therefore which contributes double insurance where there are two agreed value policies is where the values are common. The overlapping of the policies is limited by the conclusive agreed amount of the lower-valued policy and the logic of this approach is that the calculation should therefore be made as in the example set out above. However, the law in The Martin P is that either the maximum or the independent liability method should apply. In practice cargo insurers will presumably continue to apportion contribution on the common liability basis where the double insurance arises in relation to two policies with agreed cargo values."

17.5.4 海上货物保险在双重保险下涉及"non-contribution clause"的情况

在本章之17.4.1段提到协会货物条文或海上货物保险没有一条non-contribution clause,但这种条文在岸上保险(如火险或盗窃险)就通常会有。这在发生双重保险时就会导致海上货物保险的保险人承担了绝大部分的责任,而火灾保险合约有这一条文的保险人的责任相对很轻(当然还要看该non-contribution clause到底是怎样写法):The Niger Co Ltd v. The Guardian Insurance Co Ltd (1920) 4 Lloyd's Rep 320。在该著名的先例中,原告在非洲尼日利亚的Burutu的一个货物集散地发生了一场灾难性的大火。该集散地位于尼日尔河三角洲地带,从尼日尔河上游运下来的货物全部集中在该集散地然后再一起运往英国。Niger河在一年中的8月至11月的期间由于河水上涨适合河道运输，导致有大批的货物储存在 Burutu 等待付运，令保险人的风险大大增加与集中。由于受保人无法将聚集的货物及时付运，火灾导致了超过 750,000 英镑的损失。原告最初的时候是起诉他们的火灾保险人，只是在后来的时候才将承保海上货物保险的保险人也列为了共同被告。在火灾保单中是有一条标准条款"Marine Insurance Clause"（也可以被称为 non-contribution clause）："This insurance does not cover any loss or damage to property which at the time of the happening of such loss or damage is insured by or would but for the existence of this policy be insured by any Marine Policy or Policies except in respect of any excess beyond the amount which would have been payable under the Marine Policy or Policies had this insurance not been effective."

根据该条文，火灾保险人是只赔付海上货物保险的保险人不赔付的部分。正是由于该条文的存在，该先例中，火灾保险人几乎把所有的火灾损失都转嫁给了海上货物保险的保险人。

而在协会货物条文中没有类似的"Marine Insurance Clause"。这等于是火灾保险合约中把主要赔付的责任推了给海上货物保险的保险人，但海上货物保险合约却没有这样类似的条文。这样火灾保险人只有在受保人的损失超过了一定的额度后，他们才有责任赔付超出的部分，就如 excess of loss 的保险一样。如果海上货物保险合约也有一条类似的条文，这就会好像本章在 17.4.2 段所介绍的英国目前的法律地位是两个保险合约中的"non-contribution clause"相互抵消。

18. 不同管辖权的不同法律

英国这一法律地位就根据共同担保人（co-sureties）的衡平分摊原则（equitable doctrine of contribution），所以两个要分摊的保险人之间不需要合约关系，更加不会有侵权的关系。在 American Surety Company of New York v. Wrightson（1910）16 Com. Cas. 37 at 49，Hamilton 大法官说："As contribution between co-insurers depends not upon contract, but upon equity, the law governing the matter must be the law of the tribunal to which the party who is required to do equity is subject, and not the law of the country in which the party seeking to have equity done to him is domiciled, or the law of the country which governs the contract under which the suppliant seeking equity from the other party becomes in his turn liable to the assured."

但其他国家的法律不一定是根据这一原则，如在 Halsbury's Laws of England, 2003 re-issue 中就有提到欧洲一些国家的法律是规定受保人要先向第一份签订的保险合约中的保险人索赔，如果赔付不足再向第二份签订的保险合约中的保险人索赔。所以他们之间不存在分摊的做法。另在美国的保险市场，很多保险合约也有一条类似的条文否定分摊的做法，如下："If an interest insured hereunder is covered by other insurance which attached prior to the coverage provided by this Policy, then this Company shall be liable only for the amount in excess of such prior insurance, the Company to return to the Assured premium equivalent to the cost of the prior insurance at this Company's rates."

由于海上货物保险经常会涉及不同国家的保险人,这表示什么国家的法院管辖会是很重要。例如,如果存在双重保险,中国的保险公司赔付给了受保人之后想要向其他保险人要求分摊,而分摊是一种比较有利的做法,就应该想办法去英国法院寻求救济。毕竟在这种情况下,保险人之间是不会有仲裁协议或其他协议必须适用某一国家的法律。

19. 赔付的保险人作出自愿的支付不能向其他保险人要求分摊

还有保险人如果在他的保险合约中有一条"ratable proportion clause"下还是把所有的损失赔付给了受保人,而不是按照比例赔付。这多赔付的部分被视为一种自愿的支付,不存在可向双重保险的其他保险人要求分摊。这英国法律的地位可参见:Legal & General Assurance Society Ltd v. Drake Insurance Co. Ltd (1992) 1 All ER 283; Bovis Construction Ltd v. Commercial Union Insurance Co. Plc (2001) 1 Lloyd's Rep 416;Drake Insurance plc v. Provident Insurance Plc (2003) All ER (D) 02 (Feb)。但澳大利亚的法律对这方面是有不同的看法:Compensation Services (NSW) Ltd v. QBE Insurance Ltd (2001) NSWCA 267。

20. 事后作出分摊的保险人没有代位求偿权

事后被第一个要求作出分摊的保险人没有代位求偿权(这也包括了委付/抛弃的权利),这一点是在 Speno Rail Maintenance Australia Pty Ltd v. Metals & Minerals Insurance Pte Ltd (2009) 253 ALR 364 先例。该澳大利亚的先例判向第三人索赔的代位求偿权只属于第一个保险人所有。毕竟受保人会签署代位求偿协议(letter of subrogation)也只会给第一个保险人。

21. 双重保险能否把保费退还

这一方面在 1906 年《英国海上保险法》有针对,在 Section 84(3)(f)是在双重保险的情况下可以退还保费，但有一些例外的情况。第一种情况是如果两个保险合约是在不同时间投保，而第一个保险合约是在任何时间都承担所有的风险（if the policies are effected at different times, and any earlier policy has at any time bore the entire risk...）。看来受保人明知道已经有了第一个保险（如由 CIF 卖方投保的），但由于 CIF 买方不放心怕保险人破产而再投保从而造成双重保险，这是不可以退还保费的。第二种情况是如果在其中一份保险合约已经作出了赔付，该保险合约也不存在退还保费（if a claim has been paid on the policy in respect of the full sum insured thereby, no premium is returnable in respect of that policy）。第三种也是最后一种情况是在受保人知道的情况下造成双重保险，也不存在退还保费（这种情况可以与较早介绍的由于 CIF 买方不放心与害怕保险人破产而再投保从而造成双重保险一致）。看来退还保费只是局限在一些无辜的误解中所造成的双重保险。

第十四章　向船舶/承运人索赔的处理

1. 序言

在本书第12章谈到受保人的施救责任与第13章谈到保险人代位求偿的重要性，都显示了受保人的货方与保险人必须知道怎么样做才可能对货损货差有责任的第三人保障索赔的权利。在海上货物运输，这第三人通常就是指承运人，往往是指船东，但不一定。承运人会是期租承租人，也会是光船承租人。另外还会有千变万化的情况出现，如对货损货差有责任的第三人会是船舶上某些危险货物的货方，是他的货物殃及其他货物而造成货损货差。在多式联运中，对货损货差有责任的第三人也可能是岸上的公路承运人、铁路承运人或者是仓库保管人。

成功处理整个索赔会涉及很多的细节与技巧，一般作为货方的受保人或者是保险人是有他们的本行业务，没必要全面掌握。通常，涉及了货损货差的索赔最终要通过有管辖权的法院或仲裁解决，受保人/保险人都会委任这方面有水平的代表律师或索赔代理人（在后者的情况，就是保险人委任索赔代理人依据代位求偿权向船舶/承运人索赔的货损货差，近期的先例 Dolphin Maritime v. Sveriges Angfartygs Assurans [2009] 2 Lloyd's Rep 123）。但这里也不表示受保人或者保险人可以对这方面的知识与做法一无所知，因为往往初期做法还是要靠货方自己处理，如在卸港一发现货损货差，受保人应该怎样做才不会被视为没有放弃对会要承担赔付责任的承运人索赔的权利，并有尽到货物保险合约下的施救责任。另是，即使委任了律师或索赔代理人，在索赔案件处理中要作出重大与明智决定的还是受保人与保险人自己。还有受保人与保险人面对他们委任的代表律师或索赔代理人，他们之间也经常出现严重的利益冲突。委任方如果没有一定的知识就很容易受到摆布或误导，甚至一开始就没水平作出判断委任的律师或索赔代理人是否有水平。

虽然保险合约中会有明示条文作出一定的有关受保人在面临货损货差的指引，如在 MAR 91 与劳合社标准保险证明（在开口保单的每个航次的签发）都有条文规定受保人发现货损货差有马上作出通知的责任，条文如下："In the event of loss or damage which may result in a claim under this Insurance, immediate notice must be given to the Lloyd's Agent at the port or place where the loss or damage is discovered in order that he may examine the goods and issue a survey report."

但即使受保人完全按照该条文做并通过最近的劳合社代理人安排了检验,这也只能针对一个重要方面,就是为货损货差发生在运输期间的事实保留了优质的证据。这离最终的成功索赔还很远。例如,如何保护索赔的时效?针对保险合约,由于通常是没有明示的时效条文,所以根据法律默示地位也就是1980年《Limitation Act》,时效是从诉因产生的一天起6年。但针对海上运输,由于有《海牙规则》(这在英国的立法是1924年《海上货物运输法》)或《海牙—维斯比规则》(这在英国的立法是1971年的《海上货物运输法》)的强制性规定,向船舶/承运人索赔的时效就会是短得多,只是在交货或是应该交货(这是针对货物根本没有到达卸港的情况,如船舶在半途发生严重事故)的一天起1年。这一来,会有不少情况需要受保人自己采取行动有效保护向船舶或者承运人提起诉讼的1年时效。笔者听过受保人过了1年时效后才向保险人提出索赔,虽然保险合约时效还没有过,但如果受保人没有采取任何行动保护时效,保险人就可以根据受保人没有尽到施救责任拒赔或者说是造成损失可对冲赔付。另一种更常见的情况是保险人拒赔或者拖拖拉拉,导致受保人不知道自己最后会不会获得赔付。这一来,受保人为了自己的利益(因为最终保险人可能是不会赔付),也需要确保向船舶或者承运人索赔的权利不受损害或放弃。

或者说,受保人也没必要知道这些细节与技巧,大可以一早委任代表律师。但问题就是受保人如果对这方面的知识与做法一无所知,他往往连应该委任什么律师也掌握不了。在现实中,委任不恰当与水平不足的律师比比皆是,但由于委任方水平不足,根本区分不了。而如果是委任了称职的律师,也会因为他们收费高昂,受保人也通常不会舍得一早作出委任。另在向船东或承运人提出索赔的诉讼中,往往会有很多机会可达成和解,事实上大部分的货损货差案件都是和解掉。至于和解是否对自己有利,这里涉及了对案件事实的知己知彼,对诉讼风险的认识,以及谈判技巧。最终是否接受和解方案,不是代表律师可以决定,这往往就是货方自己或代位求偿后把案件接过来的保险人的决定。这里是如果轻重掌握得好,又是要求受保人与保险人必须一定程度的水平。所以说到底如果要把这件复杂的事情做好,节省费用,受保人与保险人都必须要有一定程度的认识。特别一提的就是在应付索赔方面,船舶/承运人都会十分懂行与机灵。加上他们通常是有互保协会在后面提供意见或者直接处理,所以针对货损货差的索赔受保人与保险人通常难逃要与世界上最厉害的对手打交道。

在本章的第一部分,笔者只打算简单介绍有关货损货差向船东/承运人根据海上运输合约(主要是指提单合约)索赔的几个要点。毕竟,笔者已经另有一本多达700多页的《提单及其他付运单证》,也就不再重复。但在该书并没有详尽介绍的根据侵权或托管等非运输合约诉因的货损货差索赔,也会在本章第二部分涉及。最后在第三部分,笔者会简单介绍多式联运的货损货差索赔,这种涉及集装箱运输并非传统提单合约所涉及的港口到港口的海上运输。所以,受保人的货方与代位求偿的保险人也有必要了解这方面的法律。

Ⅰ. 第一部分:海上运输合约的货损货差索赔

这里要针对的几个重点主要是根据提单合约向承运人提出索赔货损货差的前期,也就是受保人或保险人最需要了解的方面,以免走错路。它们包括:(1)在哪里提出诉讼以保护1年时效;(2)受保人自己是否有诉权(title to sue);(3)谁是承运人(identity of carrier);(4)《海牙规则》或者其他强制性法律是否适用;(5)证明受保人的损失;(6)证明承运人的责任。

以下逐项作出分析。顺便一提,以下的段节,受保人将被称为货方,因为针对的是与船舶与承运人之间的关系,受保人虽然是与货方指的是同一个人,但这个称呼有点不恰当。也不妨在开始的时候介绍一下不同身份的相关人士。首先是对货物有利益的相关人士,可被统称为"货方"(cargo owner),可以是在不同的情况下被称为"发货人"(shipper),"委托人"(consignor),"承租人"(charterer),"提单持有人"(holder/processor of Bill of Lading),"被背书人"(endorsee),"收货人"(consignee),"实际收货人"(receiver)。至于"船方"可以是指"承运人"(carrier),"船东"(shipowner)或"船舶"(vessel)。

以下逐一作较详细的介绍:

1. "发货人"(shipper):通常指把货物交付用以付运的人士,他往往也是与承运人订立运输合约,并在提单中被列名为发货人。根据《海牙—维斯比规则》之Article III,如果发货人提出要求,承运人必须针对装上船舶的货物签发提单。

2. "托运人"(consignor):通常指在货物装上船舶前对货物享有占有权的人士,通常就是该货物的发货人。但会有变化,如一个FOB的卖方会以FOB买方的代理人身份订立运输合约。

3. "承租人"(charterer):通常指租用船舶的人士,但会是与货物有利益关系,这往往指程租合约(voyage charterparty)的承租人。如在CIF或者CFR买卖下,货物的卖方租船,把出售的货物付运。或是在FOB买卖下,货物的买方租船并把船舶派去装港装货。但现在还有很多的租约是期租而不是程租,期租不像程租,并不属于一个货物运输合约,只是对船舶有使用权。很多时候,期租合约的承租人会以二船东的身份营运船舶,所以身份是接近船方而不是货方。但现在会有情况是对货物有利益的相关人士,如CIF卖方或FOB买方以一个TCT(time-charter-trip)的期租方式租用一个航次,这一来承租人就比较接近货方而远离船方了。还有第三种承租人就是光租租约(bareboat charterparty),这种承租人可被称为光租承租人。这种租约与期租不一样的地方就是期租只涉及船舶使用权,但谈不上占有船舶。但光租合约涉及了对船舶的占用,而占用的权利是表现在船舶的船长是由光租承运人雇佣的。所以,光租承租人十分明确属于船方,与货方没有任何关系,因此往往被称为光租船东。

4. "提单持有人"(holder/processor of Bill of Lading):指1992年的《海上货物运输

法》下的提单持有人或占有人。

5. “被背书人”(endorsee):指一份提单背书以及交出的对象。

6. “收货人”(consignee):该人士是在海上运输合约中,通常也就是一份提单中,说明在卸港应该把货物交付的人士。

7. “实际收货人”(receiver):在卸港或在其他港口实际把货物交付的人士。该人士在通常情况下也就是收货人、提单持有人与被背书人。

8. “承运人”(carrier):指与货方订立运输合约的人士,不论他是否真正拥有或占有有关运输的船舶。换言之,提单合约的承运人可以是真正的原船东、期租承租人(以二船东的名义作为承运人)或是光租承租人。

9. “船东”(shipowner):可以指真正的原船东,一般在船舶登记的国家就可以很容易查出。船东也可以是光租承租人/光租船东(demise charterer/demise owner)。

10. “船舶”(vessel):由于海上货物运输的索赔会涉及对物诉讼,那么船舶在对物诉讼(in rem action)下就变成相关的对象。

2. 需要了解的情况之一:在哪里提出诉讼以保护1年时效

首先,《海牙规则》的1年时效必须较早进行保护,否则一旦时效过去,再好的案件也是一场空。能够保护1年时效,就必须在有管辖权的法院或者仲裁庭开始诉讼。一旦这样做,就算诉讼还需要一段较长的时间才能审理完结,时效问题也已经无关。

虽然双方(货方与承运人)可以同意延长时效,但小心是精明的船东或承运人,以及背后的互保协会会加上附带条件,这就会导致双方实际上是没有达成无条件的约定延长时效:The“August Leonhardt”(1985) 2 Lloyd's Rep 28。

有关及时提起诉讼保护时效,关键要注意的地方有好几个。这里可节录Aikens大法官著的《Bills of Lading》2006年版之10.169-10.170:

“**10.169** In order to prevent the time bar accruing, a ‘competent’ suit must be brought within the one-year period. The suit must be ‘competent’ in various senses. **First**, it must be brought by a competent claimant (that is, a party with title to sue) and against the correct defendant (that is, the carrier or ship), although a misdescription of the ‘correct’ party will not invalidate the suit. **Secondly, the suit must be in a competent court or before a competent tribunal. For this purpose the fact that a court has jurisdiction does not suffice if the proceedings before it were brought in breach of an exclusive jurisdiction clause or arbitration agreement. However, the ‘suit’ does not have to be the action in which liability is ultimately decided if the other criteria for**

validity of the suit are fulfilled.

10.170 If such a 'competent' suit is brought within the one-year period it will prevent the time bar operating. However, if the proceedings are subsequently struck out, for example, for want of prosecution, or abandoned, they cannot be relied upon to prevent subsequent new proceedings being time barred. The same may not be the case for proceedings properly brought but stayed, for example, on grounds of *forum non conveniens*: The 'Nordglimt' [1987] 2 Lloyd's Rep 470."

上述的10.169段是说明了两个重点,第一个就是诉讼必须由称职并且有诉权的原告提起,这会在下一段重点介绍。另诉讼的对象被告必须是准确的船舶或者承运人,这也会在后一段重点介绍。在这里只是针对第二个重点,笔者把上述节录加黑的部分。诉讼必须在有管辖权的法院或者仲裁庭提起,如承运人的住所地法院或是扣船地点法院。但在这种情况下,如果提单或租约中是有一条排外性管辖权条文(exclusive jurisdiction clause)规定了其他国家的法院有管辖权,或是有一条仲裁条文,就算是货方在承运人的住所地法院或扣船地点法院提起了诉讼,也不足以保护诉讼时效。

这方面有关的案例有 The"Havhelt"(1993) 1 Lloyd's Rep 523; The"Markos N"(2000) 2 Lloyd's Rep 243。笔者讲讲 The"Markos N"以便大家对这个问题有更好的认识,该先例涉及了一批钢材从俄罗斯运去美国,但在卸港卸下后发觉有货损。货方在美国法院向船东提出起诉,该诉讼是在1年的时效内提起的。但之后在提出抗辩前,船东向美国法院申请中止法院程序,因为有关的运输合约(提单)中有一条伦敦仲裁条文。由于美国是《纽约公约》的签约国,美国是必须遵守公约下的义务中止在美国法院的诉讼程序。这导致货方赶紧委任仲裁员,但已经过了1年时效。双方的争议是这1年时效有否被美国法院(有管辖权的法院)的诉讼程序保护了,导致后来的伦敦仲裁不存在时效已过的问题。在英国法院,Steel大法官判是美国的诉讼程序是没有能够保护时效,否则会带来可笑的后果,就是货方在世界任何一个地方扣船,然后在该地法院起诉就可以保护时效。而即使是争议的最后审理是在另外一个法院(因为提单中约定而享有排外性管辖权)或者是仲裁庭(因为提单中约定了仲裁解决争议)也可以慢慢开始,因为再也不存在时效已过的问题。Steel大法官这样说:

"There can be no doubt that the first proposition is of breathtaking proportions. It would mean, for instance, that if the claimants in the present case had instituted proceedings *in rem* in any jurisdiction in the world which was a party to the 1952 Convention on Arrest of Ships, or otherwise recognized jurisdiction *in rem* for cargo claims, regardless of whether the vessel was in the jurisdiction at the time, let alone whether, following arrest the proceedings were later stayed in the fact of an arbitration clause, those proceedings would remain a suit for the purpose of art. III, r. 6.

This is not just a surprising proposition. It gives rise to absurd results. The mere institution of proceedings in any Court with jurisdiction in principle, regardless of whether service of those proceedings could in fact be effected and even regardless of any contractual commitment to use another forum, would prevent the shipowner from being discharged from liability by reason of the passage of time and allow the claimant to institute proceedings in an appropriate contractual forum at any time thereafter, immune from any time bar threat (at least so far as English jurisdiction is concerned given the provision of s. 39 of the Limitation Act, 1980)."

2.1 提单合并租约中的仲裁条文所带来的时效问题

这种法律地位对中国的货方以及拥有代位求偿的保险公司而言非常危险,因为通常他们会在中国卸港的法院扣船并起诉,根本不理会提单中的仲裁条文。但今天很多提单,如被普遍使用的 Congenbill 1994,都会合并伦敦仲裁条文。这在英国法律被视为完全有效,虽然在中国法律地位还不完全明朗。在中国人民大学夏晓虹女士的博士论文《纽约公约在中国的适用问题研究》中,她在第 96 页关于这个问题的结论是"中国法院对提单仲裁条款、租约并入提单仲裁条款的问题已形成一定倾向性的做法,即:第一,对未经当事人平等协商的提单仲裁条款不予承认。第二,租约并入提单仲裁条款必须是明示并入,要求并入条款必须把仲裁或类似字样在提单的正面表示出来,而被并入的租约及其仲裁条款也必须是可以确定和可执行的,只有这样,该租约并入提单的仲裁条款才有效且能够约束提单持有人"。关于这个结论,她给了这样的注脚:最高人民法院《关于人民法院处理涉外仲裁及外国仲裁案件的若干规定(2003 年 11 月 31 日征求意见稿)》第 30 条为:"具备以下条件,应认定租约中的仲裁条款并入提单,对提单持有人具有约束力:(一)在提单正面明示租约中的仲裁条款并入该提单;(二)被并入的仲裁条款为有效仲裁条款。"[1] 但该条文未在正式的《仲裁法解释》中出现。

不论中国的法律明朗与否或者是完全否定合并的租约中伦敦仲裁条文的效力,英国或者是美国的法院都不会理会。特别是在英国法院他们会大力保护伦敦仲裁并往往会对中国货方或是中国保险人作出止诉禁令(anti-suit injunction),并鼓励船东或者承运人尽量推进伦敦仲裁,抢在中国法院的前面作出裁决书并执行。这里可以举先例 The"Alexandros T"(2008) 1 Lloyd's Rep 230,案情涉及了该船舶从巴西运一船矿砂去中国,途中船舶沉没而造成货物的全损。中国太平保险公司赔付了提单持有人后在 2007 年 3 月 27 日在中国武汉法院根据代位求偿权向船东起诉要求赔偿 5,250,000美元。但在该航次有签发提单,该提单合并了租约的伦敦仲裁条文,船东也在 2007 年 6 月 16 日开始了伦敦仲裁,并向英国法院申请止诉禁令。另在先例 The "Joanna V"(2003) 2 Lloyd's Rep 617 中,案情也是类似,只不过保险公司变为人保,中

〔1〕 沈德咏、万鄂湘主编,最高人民法院研究室、民事审判第四庭编著:《最高人民法院仲裁法司法解释的理解与适用》,人民法院出版社 2007 年版,第 372 页。

国的法院是宁波海事法院。可以说在这些案件中,中方都很难对抗英国法院与伦敦仲裁。

欧共体法院在先例 The "Front Comor" (2009) 1 Lloyd's Rep 413 中判决英国法院不能为了保护伦敦仲裁向其他欧共体成员国作出止诉禁令,英国法院没有办法,除非英国退出欧共体。但针对中国等其他非欧共体成员国,为了保护伦敦仲裁,英国法院不会有任何犹豫作出止诉禁令。

在笔者所著的《仲裁法——从开庭审理到裁决书的作出与执行》,其中在第 248 ~ 249 页曾经提到过这方面新的发展,就是有关《鹿特丹规则》可能会带来的变化请参阅。

笔者曾经针对这方面请教过一些英国法律界的权威人士,即使《鹿特丹规则》最终在全球范围内生效,而中国也加入该国际公约,中国货方或是代位求偿的保险人根据该公约或者中国立法下在中国卸货地点法院向船东或承运人起诉,英国法院会否以提单有合并伦敦仲裁条文作为理由向中国货方或保险人作出止诉禁令,不理会在中国法院起诉的权利是从国际公约而来。笔者没有得到确实的回复,就是英国法院不会作出止诉禁令。看来,这方面的解决办法还是要中国国力强大后而且中国法院敢向有关人士作出"反止诉禁令"(anti-anti-suit injunction),强制当事人必须在中国法院继续审理,否则是藐视中国法院,这会导致最终只能通过政治上的角力才可以解决。

接下来谈另外的问题就是如果诉讼及时在有管辖权与最后作出审理的法院开始,显然是可以保护时效,但细节的问题还是很多。其中在上述节录的 Aikens 大法官著的《Bill of Lading》2006 年版 10. 170 段,就提到了一种危险就是在及时提起的诉讼中,如果原告的受保人/货方或是代位求偿的保险人怠慢推进诉讼(want of prosecution)而导致诉讼被法院或者仲裁庭撤销,后果也是时效没有受到保护而导致可能是强而有力的索赔无法进行。有关这方面在笔者《仲裁法——从开庭审理到裁决书的作出与执行》第 457 ~ 458 页有介绍,不去重复。在今天不断强调仲裁必须从速的情况下,受保人或者保险人如果延误或迟迟不作出决定推进(这种问题经常对中方的原告会发生),就会有更大危险被撤销。

2.2　方便管辖权原则(*forum non conveniens*)

在国际性的争议中,如果有关的合约中对管辖权没有明确约定,在本书第三章 8. 8 段提到过会有多个国家的法院都会有管辖权(管辖权来自各种理由,如扣船地点、被告住所地、合约签订地、合约履行地、合并审理等)。如果有这方面的争议,英国的法院在这种情况下会找出哪一个是最自然或合适的管辖地(natural or appropriate forum)以对双方当事人最有利与最后能够伸张正义。如果有这样的管辖地,英国法院会自己中止审理把管辖权让给其他国家的法院。这是 *Forum non conveniens* 的说法。这里就带来了货损货差 1 年索赔时效的问题。比如,货方或代位求偿的保险人在英国港口扣押了有关的船舶或她的姊妹船,除了取到诉前担保的好处外也让英国法院获得了管辖权。这些行动都发生在1年的索赔时效内,可以说是已经作出了保护。但随后船东想说服法院另有一个更自然或合适的管辖地,如中国,因为造成货损货差的航次是从青岛去广州,船舶是悬挂中国旗,而且有很多事实上的争议是发生在中国,所以证据多数在中国,所以与英国法院相比,中国法院才是更适合的管辖法院,因为大量的证据是只有在中国才可以获得并且代价相对较低。再假设英国法院同意并中止了英国法院的诉讼程序,让受保人或保险人去中国法院起诉。但这就带来个大问题就是经过这一番的折腾受保人再到中国法院起诉,1年的时效已经过了。所以,以前的做法就是被中止的原告会马上要求英国法院加一个中止的条件,就是被告不能在另一个法院以时效已过作为抗辩。由于中止与否涉及了法院的裁量权,所以被告往往也必须同意,这等于同意延长1年时效。但英国法院现在开始有了变化,不一定愿意加这一条件。是否加就要看个别的案件。例如,在上述的例子中认为受保人或保险人应该可以合理见到中国法院才是最自然或合适的管辖地,而且中国法院也可以作出些保护时效的措施,但不这样做,英国法院在中止时就不一定肯加上中止的条件。这也表示整个索赔可能就无法进行了。至于什么是可以保护时效的措施就要看不同国家法院的规定,如在英国法院就往往可以出一张告票,这就足够保护了。但不马上送达与推进法院的程序,就表示这张告票只是为了保护时效,以前是被称为"protective writ"。但如果在最自然或合适的管辖地并不明显时,或者即使明显也没有措施保护时效,英国法院在这种情况下作出中止命令,会是更愿意加上中止的条件。这方面可节录Goff勋爵在贵族院先例的The"Spiliada"(1987) 1 Lloyd's Rep 1中在针对中止与否的考虑时必须对双方当事人最有利与最后能够伸张正义,所说如下:

"But the underlying principle requires that regard must be had to the interests of all the parties and the ends of justice; and these considerations may lead to a different conclusion in other cases. For example, it would not, I think, normally be wrong to allow a plaintiff to keep the benefit of security obtained by commencing proceedings here, while at the same time granting a stay of proceedings in this country to enable the action to proceed in the appropriate forum. Such a conclusion is, I understand, consistent with the manner in which the process of *saisie conservatoire* is applied in civil law countries; and cf. s. 26 of the Civil Jurisdiction and Judgments Act, 1982, now happily in force. Again, take the example of cases concerned with time bars. Here a special problem arises from the fact that, in English law, limitation is classified as a procedural rather than as a substantive matter. Let me consider how the principle of *forum non conveniens* should be applied in a case in which the plaintiff has started proceedings in England where his claim was not time barred, but there is some other jurisdiction which, in the opinion of the Court, is clearly more appropriate for the trial of the action, but where the plaintiff has not commenced proceedings and where his claim is now time barred. Now, to take some extreme examples, suppose that the plaintiff allowed the limitation period to elapse in the appropriate jurisdiction, and came here simply because he wanted to take advantage of a more generous time bar applicable in this country; or suppose that it was obvious that the plaintiff should have commenced proceedings in the appropriate jurisdiction, and yet he did not trouble to issue a protective writ there; in cases such as these, I cannot see that the Court should hesitate to stay the proceedings in this country, even though the effect would be that the plaintiff's claim would inevitably be defeated by a plea of the time bar in the appropriate jurisdiction. Indeed a strong theoretical argument can be advanced for the proposition that, if there is another clearly more appropriate form for the trial of the action, a stay should generally be granted even though the plaintiff's action would be time barred there. **But, in my opinion, this is a case where practical justice should be done**. And practical justice demands that, if the Court considers that the plaintiff acted reasonably in commencing proceedings in this country, and that, although it appears that (putting on one side the time bar point) the appropriate forum for the trial of the action is elsewhere than England, the plaintiff did not act unreasonably in failing to commence proceedings (for example, by issuing a protective writ) in that jurisdiction within the limitation period applicable there, it would not, I think be just to deprive the plaintiff of the benefit of having started proceedings within the limitation period applicable in this country. The approach is consistent with that of Mr. Justice Sheen in The Blue Wave, [1982] 1 Lloyd's Rep 151. It is not to be forgotten that, by making its jurisdiction available to the plaintiff—even the discretionary jurisdiction under R. S. C. O. 11—the Courts of this country have provided the plaintiff with an opportunity to start proceedings here; accordingly, if justice demands, the Court should not deprive the plaintiff of the benefit of having complied with the time bar in this country. Furthermore, as the applicable principles become more clearly established and better know, it will, I suspect, become increasingly difficult for plaintiffs to prove lack of negligence in this respect. The fact that the Court has been asked to exercise its discretion under R. S. C., O. 11, rather than that the plaintiff has served proceedings upon the defendant in this country as of right, is, I consider, only relevant to consideration of the plaintiff's conduct in failing to save the time bar in the other relevant alternative jurisdiction. The appropriate order, where the application of the time bar in the foreign jurisdiction is dependent upon its invocation by the defendant, may well be to make it a condition of the grant of a stay or the exercise of discretion against giving leave to serve out of the jurisdiction, that the defendant should waive the time bar in the foreign jurisdiction; this is apparently the practice in the United States of America."

在同样的课题下,也可介绍先例 The"Nordglimt"(1987) Lloyd's Rep 470,案情是涉及一批大麦从比利时安特卫普去 Jeddah,货物在卸下的时候发觉有损坏。在 1 年索赔时效快将届满时,货方(或是保险人)在比利时法院起诉船东,而比利时法院有管辖权。但由于这是诉人的诉讼,所以不存在诉前担保。通常如果原告想去取得担保,要采取其他的行动,如申请冻结令(Mareva injunction 或者现在称为 freezing injunction)。由于这是海事索赔,想取得诉前担保还有更容易的做法就是扣船。结果几个月后,货方(或是保险人)在英国港口成功把告船告票送达去船东的另一艘姊妹船,并成功扣船取得诉前担保。又过了不久,船东就向英国法院要求把告船告票撤销,主要的原因是1年的索赔时效已过,所以再也没有可在英国法院起诉的诉因。而英国法律不理会其他国家法院已经采取了保护时效的诉讼行动:The"Havhelt"(1993) 1 Lloyd's Rep 523; The"Markos N"(2000) 2 Lloyd's Rep 243。但在英国高院Hobhouse 大法官不同意,他说:"The proceedings in Belgium were competent and brought in time by a party with a title to sue. The carrier was accordingly not discharged from liability. The liability which is the subject matter of the present action in England accordingly continues to exist upon the true construction of the bill of lading and the legislation to which it is subject. The carrier is thus unable to assert the fact, namely that suit has not been brought within the relevant period, which is necessary to support his allegation that he has been discharged from liability. The defendants' case therefore that the plaintiffs have no subsisting cause of action upon which they can sue in the present proceedings must fail... Accordingly I hold that the proceedings *in personam* is Belgium, having been started in Belgium within time and it being accepted that both the parties and the Court were competent, the defendants' liability has not been discharged under art. III, r. 6 and this ground of objection to the arrest of Nordglimt in the present proceedings must fail."

2.3 时效届满后才加上的新诉因

诉因是指存在的事实情况可允许一方当事人向另外的当事人提起诉讼,要求法律救济。这可节录先例 Letant v. Cooper (1964) 2 Lloyd's Rep 339,Diplock 大法官这样说:"A cause of action is simply a factual situation the existence of which entitles one person to obtain from the Court a remedy against another person."。取决不同的事实情况,就会带来不同的诉因。如事实上双方是有合约关系,带来的诉因就会是根据有关合约的违约诉因。但如果双方没有合约关系,但事实存在对方有疏忽,带来的诉因就会对方的侵权诉因。由于在起诉的时候,存在的事实情况原告还没有全部掌握,所以漏了一些诉因。这在后来如在文件披露后发觉有新的诉因再补充,补充的做法往往就是修改原来的索赔请求。但这里带来的危险就是想作出补充时,新的诉因被指时效已经届满。所以,为了小心,原告会在提起诉讼的时候,根据所知道的事实情况,尽可能把所有诉因都列明。在一般的货损货差索赔,列明的诉因是"违约、侵权与托管"(breach of contract, tort and bailment),以求不会漏掉某个诉因。在 The"Kapetan Markos"(1986) 1 Lloyd's Rep 211 中,案情涉及了一船257,000吨原油从科威特通过Sumed 管道运往西班牙,途中发生爆炸产生救助。在1年时效内提出的诉因只是在侵权或者违反责任(tort or breach of duty)。在1年时效届满后,货方的原告才提出新的诉因,包括违约而合约就是指提单。上诉庭允许这样做认为应该宽松解释《海牙规则》的时效,Parker 大法官这样说:"We shall assume, but without deciding, that the making of a claim for the salvage moneys in tort constitutes the raising of an additional cause of action, but in our judgment to hold that on that ground the defendants are discharged from liability would be either to allow the old forms of action to rule as from their graves (as to which see per Lord Justice Diplock in Letang v. Cooper [1964] 2 Lloyd's Rep 339; and Lord Denning, M. R., in In re Vandervell's Trusts [1974] 1 Ch. 269 at p. 321) or to adopt a construction of an international provision which creates a substantive discharge of liability dependent on the incidents of procedural rules in one particular country. Neither is acceptable. The tortuous claim is not barred. Turning to the contractual claims (apart from the charter-party claim which no longer arises)... From first to last the plaintiffs have set up carriage by sea under a contract of carriage by sea under a bill of lading incorporating the Hague Rules, breach of such rules and resulting damage. To hold suit was not brought within a year in respect of breaches of such rules would in our judgment be an abuse of language. It plainly was."

3. 需要了解的情况之二:受保人自己是否有诉权

这个题目在笔者《提单及其他付运单证》第三章有关运输合约谁是其中的合约方里面有详细针对,不去重复。只是在这里将重点再解释一下。在货损货差的索赔,绝大部分所根据的诉因都是看船舶或者承运人是否违反运输合约(主要就是提单)。虽然侵权或托管的诉因也会加上作为替代性(alternative)诉因,但通常货方要证明船舶或者承运人在运输期间的疏忽造成货损货差时货方拥有货物的所有权也不是太容易。这一问题稍后会进一步介绍。

而根据提单合约,因为在很多种情况下,《海牙规则》或类似的强制性法律会适用,通常会对货方更为有利。如要求船舶或者承运人有恪尽职责令船舶适航后,才可以依赖相对有限的免责。

但根据提单合约作为主要的诉因,就无可避免带来了英国法律下合约相互关系(privity of contract)所带来的困难。这就是作为货方向船舶或者承运人提起诉讼,他首先就要证明他是合约的一方,即他有诉权。如果他不是合约的一方或是他没有诉权,他就没有合法的权利(*locus standi*)起诉船东或者承运人。

一般合约明确谁是订约的双方都不会是困难,他们会在谈判后将合约内容明确下来,合约会把订约方的名字记录下来。虽然仍会有情况带来争议,如一方说在谈判的时候清楚说明他只是代理人并在有关的合约中有条文显示了该订约意图,但这种例外情况毕竟是少数。

提单合约就很不一样,由于它的作用就是可以转让,以方便货物在一个漫长的航次中可以转售,所以一直以来就有很大问题。事实上在英国法律第一个以立法改变普通法的合约相互关系就是提单,也就是1855年《英国提单法》。这里的问题是可通过简单的国际贸易例子说明,就是德国的卖方A出售货物给中国的买方B,由于涉及海上运输,所以在CIF买卖下可以说是离不开由A出面安排付运,A与承运人C签订运输合约(这可以是租约或者是班轮运输的订舱单)。即使不是CIF买卖而是FOB,也会有做法是B委托A安排付运。反正到了这个阶段已经是有了两个不同的合约,它们涉及了不同的订约方,也只有他们之间可以根据违约向对方提出索赔损失。显然,B与C没有直接合约关系,他们之间的诉因只能是侵权或托管。在该批货物装上船之后,C在A的要求下会签发一套提单。之后A会把这套提单交给B以换取货款的支付,而如果是涉及信用证就是拿这套提单去结汇。反正货物最后到了中国卸港,B向C提货并交出正本提单是不成问题,因为根据习惯做法已经在Lickbarrow v. Mason (1793) 2 H. Black. 211 (H. L.)中作出了判决提单是物权的凭证(document of title)。但问题是B如果发觉C交给他的货物有损坏,而且货损的本质很明显是船舶不妥造成,B怎样寻求救济。显然,B就是受害者(因为他支付给A的货款是基于良好的货物品质),但他根据合约找不到对象去索赔。B不能在买卖合约向A索赔,因为在CIF或FOB买卖,通常货物在越过船舷后风险就转移给买方。B也不能在普通法下根据运输合约向C索赔,因为他不是合约方。B或者可以要求A去向C索赔,因为A是合约方而且C明显是违约。但即使A肯帮忙,也马上会面对C的抗辩,就是即使C有违约,A因为收到了货款也没有损失,另也不会要对B承担合约责任。这一方面虽然是英国法院在Dunlop v. Lambert (1839) 6 Cl & F 68中有了一个说法,就是A可以替B向C索赔B的实际损失,因为A与C订立运输合约时双方都知道这份提单最终是为了B,这说法是"(A) is entitled to recover by way of damages for breach of contract the actual loss sustained by those for whose benefit the contract is entered into."但整个做法还是困难重重,因为B不容易取得A的协助帮忙向C提出索赔。这也在The"Albazero"(1976) 2 Lloyd's Rep. 467中有提到,Diplock勋爵中这样说:"The only way in which I find it possible to rationalize the rule in Dunlop v. Lambert so that it may fit into the pattern of the English law is to treat it as an application of the principle, accepted also in relation to policies of insurance upon goods, that in a commercial contract concerning goods where it is in the contemplation of the parties that the proprietary interests in the goods may be transferred from one owner to another after the contract has been entered into and before the breach which causes loss or damage to the goods, an original party to the contract, if such be the intention of them both, is to be treated in law as having entered into the contract for the benefit of all persons who have or may acquire an interest in the goods before they are lost or damaged, and is entitled to recover by way of damages for breach of contract the actual loss sustained by those for whose benefit the contract is entered into."

当然,B 还有个合约会可依赖,这就是与保险人 D 的保险合约。但这还是不解决上述的问题,就是 D 在赔付后也会要求代位求偿向 C 索赔。但 D 的权利是不会大于 B 的,所以还是会面对 C 同样的抗辩。

3.1　1855 年《提单法》与它带来有关诉权的问题

1855 年《提单法》就是简单地规定提单下的明示收货人或是背书受让人,就可被当作原来与承运人订立提单合约的当事人,并可以享有向承运人索赔的诉权,但也要承担提单内对承运人的责任。原文为:"Every consignee of goods named in a bill of lading, and every endorsee of a bill of loading to whom the property in the goods therein mentioned shall pass, upon or by reason of such consignment or endorsement, shall have transferred to and vested in him all rights of suit, and be subject to the same liabilities in respect of such goods as if the contract contained in a bill of lading had been made with himself."

这立法的做法有点像合约的变更(novation),就是把订约方作出变动。但合约变更需要大家同意,在 1855 年《提单法》就不需要大家同意,所以有说法是属于强制性的合约变更。但由于该立法在措辞上有它的局限性,就是把提单的转让或者流通去同时与货物所有权转让扯在一起。具体措辞就是"to whom the property in the goods therein mentioned shall pass, upon or by reason of such consignment or endorsement",但在国际贸易中并非都是这样的情况,如把提单背书给银行就不会是为了转让货物所有权,只是为了给银行作为担保。

这导致在 20 世纪 80 年代后期出现了大量的案例涉及被告的船舶或者承运人以货方(或者背后的保险人)没有诉权成功抗辩而不必作出赔偿。这些问题因为有了新的 1992 年《海上货物运输法》替代了 1855 年的《提单法》而已经是过时,所以不多解释,有兴趣的读者可以看笔者的《提单及其他付运单证》一书,其中第 220 页有提到:"总之,20 世纪 80 年代有不少这种案例,也有不少是船东/承运人成功以'title to sue'抗辩收货人索赔的例子,即使是船东违约的责任明确得不能再明确,例如是不适航(The "Kapetan Markos NL"),或是错签发提单(The "Aliakmon"),或是无单放货(The "Future Express"),收货人的索赔最终还是一场空,就是因为没有'title to sue'。比方是:The "San Nicholas" (1976) 1 Lloyd's Rep 8; The "Albazero" (1976) 2 Lloyd's Rep 467; The "Elafi" (1981) 2 Lloyd's Rep 679; The "Sevonia Team" (1983) 2 Lloyd's Rep 640; The "Elli 2" (1985) 1 Lloyd's Rep 107; The "Kelo" (1985) 2 Lloyd's Rep 85; The "Kapetan Markos" (1987) 2 Lloyd's Rep 321; The "Aliakmon" (1986) 2 Lloyd's Rep 1; The "Aramis" (1989) 1 Lloyd's Rep 213; The "Delfini" (1990) 1 Lloyd's Rep 252; The "Filiatra Legacy" (1991) 2 Lloyd's Rep 337; The "Future Express" (1992) 2 Lloyd's Rep 79。

可以总结在80年代后期出现对货方或代位求偿的保险人十分不利的发展，主要的原因是：

1. 法院对1855年《提单法》的解释变得严格，也就是货物所有权的转移是伴随着提单的背书进行的：The“Delfini”(1990) 1 Lloyd's Rep 252。

2. 一种常见的情况就是越来越多的船舶比提单的流转更早抵达卸港，导致了大量无单放货的情况。这表示实质货物的所有权转移是根据保函而不是根据提单，提单在交货后的背书也不会与货物所有权的转移扯上关系：The“Delfini”(1990) 1 Lloyd's Rep 252。

3. 散装货在海上运输无法分开，所以在同一批货属于几个不同收货人的情况下，货物只能在卸港分开后才能转移所有权，与较早时提单的背书没有关系：The“Aramis”(1989) 1 Lloyd's Rep 213。这个问题在1995年《货物销售法》作出了改变，多加上了 Section 20(A)才获得解决。

4. 会有情况是海上运输的风险在买方或收货人，但运输期间与提单背书的时候货物所有权一直不转移：The“Aliakmon”(1986) 2 Lloyd's Rep 1。该贵族院先例涉及韩国的卖方以 CIF 把一船钢材卖给英国买方，但由于买方无法即时转售，买方无法按买卖合约准时支付货款给卖方。这导致了双方谈判找出解决方案。就是约定去把提单交出给买方，让买方在英国卸港 Immingham 向船长提取货物，并把货物存放在仓库中等待卖方的进一步指令。而在这段时间内，买方努力找分买方，而卖方也会尽力帮助尽快把这批货物转售。结果也是按该解决方案做，其中也涉及了韩国卖方向英国买方采取法律行动要求货价的余下金额，但最后双方达成和解。这是因为该批钢材涉及了货损货差，这货损货差部分是在装货前部分发生在运输期间。英国买方，也就是收货人在事后向船东提出索赔，也在1年的索赔时效内。但船东以英国买方没有“title to sue”成功抗辩，因为提单背书与转让货物所有权根本不走在一起。

5. 船东与互保协会也知道了攻击货方的诉权可以取巧而且比较容易击退货损货差，所以经常出现挑剔的要求货方对整个货物买卖的过程进行披露。

3.2 侵权的诉权问题

在这里也可以介绍有关侵权(tort)的诉权(title to sue)的问题，这里就涉及了作为货物托管人的承运人到底对哪一类的人士有谨慎的责任(duty of care)以避免损失。也是这一类的人士在发生货损货差的时候以侵权向承运人提出侵权的诉讼与索赔。这方面可节录 The“Aliakmon”(1986) 2 Lloyd's Rep 1 的相关判词如下：“in order to enable a person to claim in negligence for loss caused to him by reason of loss of or damage to property, he must have had either the legal ownership of or a possessory title to the property concerned at the time when the loss or damage occurred, and it is not enough for him to have only had contractual rights in relation to such property which have been adversely affected by the loss of or damage to it.”

这显然会带来一定的困难，第一就是货方在不少情况下不会知道什么时候发生货损货差。就算能够知道，由于提单的流转，在货损货差发生的时刻，真正受到损失的收货人（因为海上运输的风险通常货物一装上船就转移给他）不一定就是承运人有谨慎责任的人士。这里还有很多其他变数不容易处理，就是侵权的疏忽发生的一天并非是造成损失的一天，换言之，最后的损失是经过一段时间才造成的（progressive damage）。显然，会有情况是疏忽与损失走在一起，例如承运人的装卸工人不小心将货物摔在地上造成损坏。再举一个好的例子就是无单放货，而侵权除了疏忽也包括了侵占（conversion），所以承运人侵权的一刻也就是造成损失的一刻。但现在举经过一段时间才造成损失的例子，The "Starsin" [2003] UKHL 12 就是典型。它涉及了堆装时候的疏忽，但这不会马上造成货物损失而是逐步在航次的中途，这里可以由专家作出推断。但问题是侵权责任到底是指哪一天，是有疏忽的一天还是造成损失的一天。要知道在这两个不同时间，货物的所有权就会随着提单的流转而从卖方手中到了买方手中。在该先例的高院与上诉庭判是以造成损失的一天为准，这也表示要承担海上运输风险的买方或收货人是有诉权的，即使承运人的疏忽是发生在他拥有货物所有权之前。这里可以节录 Aikens 大法官著的《Bills of Lading》2006 年版之 9.25 段所说如下："Thus, a party who acquires title to the goods after the negligence occurs but before it occasions damage may sue. In one sense this may be said to reflect a principle that a duty of care is owed not only to actual owners but to future owners in respect (in either case) of loss suffered in their capacity as owners. But it is really only an application of the rule that the cause of action in negligence is only complete when damage occurs."

以侵权向承运人索赔货损货差还有其他的问题，如侵权通常能索赔经济的损失，这不像是合约。但由于本段主要针对提单合约诉权的问题，所以就先不多讲。

货方/保险人会需要以侵权提出货损货差的索赔还是会有，如索赔的对象不是承运人而是其他第三人，如疏忽的小工，其他向船舶/承运人提供服务的承包商（如提供装卸驳船、浮吊或岸上重吊，但因为维修保养不到位发生事故而造成货损），港口当局（如命令船舶去不安全的地方），货物检验师，仓库保管人（货物在储存过程中失窃）等。在上述的各类人士中，也只有仓库保管人除了有侵权的责任外还有托管人的责任。

如果船舶是装了 A 的货物，但该船舶被期租承租人命令去了不安全的港口并造成货物的损坏。如果该命令是有疏忽，在满足了可预见性与因果关系的考验后，A 可以侵权向该期租承租人提出索赔。这在 Aikens 大法官著的《Bills of Lading》2006 年版第 190 页的脚注 76 提到这种情况在原则上讲得通，但还不知道有这方面的先例。

3.3 1992 年的《海上货物运输法》替代 1855 年《提单法》

这些诉权的问题加上新的发展如有除了提单外其他类型的付运单证使英国有了新的立法去取代 1855 年《提单法》，新的立法就是 1992 年的《海上货物运输法》。该立法的 Section 2 说明有三种货方可以违约的诉因向承运人直接提起诉讼：（1）可转让提单（transferable bill of lading）的合法持有人；（2）在有关的时间内海运单（sea waybill)或者记名提单(straight bill of lading)被明示的收货人;(3)被承运人以一份交货单(delivery order)作出承诺交货给他的人士。

要对这1992年立法有进一步的理解,以下可以先对各种不同名称的付运单证作一些简单的介绍。

3.3.1 租约/订舱单(charter-party/booking note)

租约的定义在《Halsbury's Law》para 1141 定义如下:"a contract whereby an entire vessel or some principal part of her may be used or employed by the charterer for a voyage or series of voyage or for a period of time."

租约(特别是航次租约)虽然是一份海上货物运输合约,它与另一份经常走在一起的海上货物运输合约的提单主要有两个不同之处:(1)租约不是一份货物收据,因为在签订租约时根本还不会有货物装上船舶,这与提单的签发很不一样;(2)租约不是物权凭证,不能够流转。也是这些原因,导致了1855年《提单法》只针对提单但不针对租约。换言之,如果租约要去作出变更(novation),必须是所有有关当事人同意,不会有法律的强制。也可以说,船东与承租人作为租约的订约方,他们之间永远是有诉权去针对对方。另在1924年《海牙规则》也只是针对提单而且明确说明是不适用在租约。这表示租约是有完全的订约自由,责任方面是完全可以不受《海牙规则》的约束。

在同样的原因下,1992年《海上货物运输法》也不针对这种付运单证。

租约通常涉及大宗货,因为租约一般都是租整条船。典型的情况是CIF卖方在货物要付运之前去航运市场找艘船型、航期与地点都配合的船舶,然后与船东进行谈判包括运费等方面,在最终达成协议就有了份租约。如果是FOB买卖,找适合船舶并订立租约的是FOB的买方。提单还是会在装货后签发,毕竟是CIF或FOB都需要有这套单证以利在海上运输期间把货物以提单的形式转售。

接下来介绍订舱单,相比租约两者有很多相似之处,但使用在不同类型的海上运输。租约涉及大宗货,订舱单则一般是货物数量较少适用于班轮运输。今天的集装箱船舶,动辄好几千个集装箱分别由上千个不同的发货人,船东/承运人不会与他们个别谈判并签订租约。通常的做法就是由发货人向船东/承运人以订舱单的形式,作为约束大家提供货物装船与提供运输的依据。订舱单本来不会有细致的海上运输条文,但会说明是以稍后签发的班轮提单条文为准。有关订舱单的定义,可节录Aikens大法官著的《Bills of Lading》2006年版之2.35段所说如下:"The term 'booking note' is a loose one which may cover a number of different types of contract. Some, such as the common 'Conline' form, are contracts of carriage and incorporate terms which are appropriate for a bill of lading (and even refer to 'this Bill of Lading') but are not bills of lading. They provide for the terms to be superseded on the issue of a bill of lading. Others may be much simplier and may be contracts for carriage rather than contracts of carriage. In the former case the obligation is to procure or arrange carriage and the prime function of the note is to record the booking of space aboard the (or a) vessel. The relationship between such contracts and bills of lading subsequently issued is of some complexity and is discussed in Chapter 7."

与租约一样，订舱单并不是1924年《海牙规则》，1855年《提单法》与1992年《海上货物运输法》针对的单证。

3.3.2　大副收据(mate's receipt)

这份文件通常是由监督装货的船舶大副，在货物装上船之后，向发货人签发一份收据。收据中会说明装上船舶的货物数量与表面状况。之后在船东或承运人签发了提单，发货人要把大副收据退还以交换这套提单。大副收据本身并非一个货权的凭证，也不存在可以转售。而且，大副收据也不是有关公约与立法中所针对的单证，如1924年《海牙规则》，1855年《提单法》或是1992年的《海上货物运输法》。这方面可节录Aikens大法官著的《Bills of Lading》2006年版之2.12-2.14段所说如下："A particular and important species of receipt is a mate's receipt. In many instances the carrier will, when first taking possession of the goods, issue a mate's receipt in respect of the goods. As the name implies, the document was, historically, issued by the ship's mate, who would have evidenced the reception of the goods on board the vessel and then issued a mate's receipt to acknowledge that fact. A mate's receipt is generally exchanged for the bill of lading and charterparties frequently require that bills of lading issued are 'in conformity with' the mate's receipts. In legal terms a mate's receipt 'Is not ordinarily anything more than evidence that the goods have been received on board.' Depending on the terms of the mate's receipt the document may be evidence of the condition of the goods when received. It is not necessarily evidence of a contract of carriage (although it may be), but it is evidence of a bailment which may be on express or implied terms. It is not negotiable or a document of title, except in particular circumstances such as by custom of a port or trade."

3.3.3　可转让提单(transferable bill of lading)

可转让提单是最常见的付运单证，可转让与可流通(negotiable)基本上是同样的意思。这种提单作为物权凭证可让货物所有人通过把这套提单背书(endorsement)与交出(delivery)给买方就把该批还在船上运输的货物的所有权转售。这里可以节录Devlin勋爵在先例Kum v. Wah Tat Bank (1971) 1 Lloyd's Rep 439中所说："It is well settled that 'Negotiable', when used in relation to a bill of lading, means simply transferable. A negotiable bill of lading is not negotiable in the strict sense; it cannot, as can be done by the negotiation of a bill of exchange, give to the transferee a better title than the transferor has got, but it can by endorsement and delivery give as good title. But it has never been settled whether delivery of a non-negotiable bill of lading transfers title or possession at all. The bill of lading obtains its symbolic quality from the custom found in Lickbarrow v. mason and that is a custom which makes bills of lading 'negotiable and transferable' by endorsement and delivery or transmission."

可转让提单分为两种，一种是持有人提单（bearer's bill），另一种是指令提单（order bill）。这主要是看在提单中收货人的一栏是怎样写法。持有人提单 Aikens 大法官著的《Bills of Lading》2006 年版之 2.41 段所说如下："A bearer bill requires the carrier to deliver to the bearer (or holder) without the requirement that the bearer is a named consignee or indorsee. A bill of lading made out simply 'to order' may be described as a bearer bill, although, as this will usually be issued to the shipper, it may be descried as a shipper's bill. A bearer bill is a document of title. It may be converted into another type of bill by indorsement by the holder, so an indorsement of 'to X or order' by the holder converts it into an order bill."

最明显的持有人提单就是在提单的收获人一栏写上"bearer"，他的好处就是谁持有这套提单谁就有权要求承运人交货给他，所以转手或转售十分容易，连背书也不需要。但它的风险就是这套提单如果因为丢失或失窃等原因转到非法持有人手中，所有现实中签发持有人提单的情况不多。在上一段的节录也可以看到，这套持有人提单也可以通过背书将它给 X 或者他指令的人士，把持有人提单变为指令提单。这样看来，这两种提单的分别也不是很大。

另一种指令提单 Aikens 大法官著的《Bills of Lading》2006 年版之 2.42 段所说如下："As stated above an order bill is one where the consignee is described either as 'to order', or 'X or order', or 'to the order of X'. A common formula for the naming of a consignee is 'to X or his order', or 'to X or his assigns' and this wording also constitutes an order bill. It appears that there is no difference for this purpose between 'to X or order' and 'to X or assigns' and an order bill includes one where the consignee is simply a named person but other parts of the bill indicate a requirement to deliver to his order and/or or assignees."

指令提单通常是指发货人的指令（to shipper's order），因为货物是来自发货人，所以最后船舶或者承运人要把货物交给谁是要听从发货人的指令。而让船舶或者承运人知道发货人到底是指令谁接收货物，就是通过提单的背书，例如背书给 Y。但也会有一种叫作空白背书（endorsement in blank），就是不说明给谁，这也会令一份指令提单变为持有人提单。指令提单也会有其他的变化，如在收货人一栏写上收货人的指令（to consignee's order）或是某一家银行的指令（to bank's order）。这一来提单如果是写明收货人的指令，但后来发生了争议如收货人拒货或倒闭，找他背书作出指令就会有困难。总结就是指令提单还是在外贸与航运之中最常见与最典型的付运单证，也是国际公约或者立法中所针对的付运单证，如 1924 年的《海牙规则》，英国 1971 年《海上货物运输法》（这是《维斯比规则》在英国的立法）与英国 1992 年《海上货物运输法》（这是替代 1855 年的《提单法》）。此外，信用证规则 UCP 中也是针对指令提单。

3.3.4 记名提单（straight bill of lading）

记名提单与指示提单有很大的不同，就是这份付运文件不能转让或是不流通。

事实上,比较正规的做法就是用图章在提单的正面印上"Non-negotiable"。另外的重要之处就是在收货人栏写明谁是收货人。这一来,做法上有点好像是邮寄包裹,写明收件人的名称与地址。如果说记名提单还是有物权凭证的作用(document of title),也是十分局限,基本上就是通过这种做法把货物从发货人转移给收货人。大概也是这个原因,英国贵族院在 The"Rafaela S"(2005) 1 Lloyd's Rep 347 中判是收货人提货还是需要交出正本的记名提单,否则船舶或承运人可以拒绝交货。有关记名提单 Aikens 大法官著的《Bills of Lading》2006 年版之 2.44-2.45 段所说如下:"A common modern form of document is one where the consignee is a named party, but without any reference to 'to order'. This evidences a contractual obligation on the carrier to deliver to that named party (only), subject to any redirection by the shipper. Any purported endorsement or transfer to other parties is of no effect on the carrier. Such a bill is frequently described as a 'straight' bill, and this terminology will be adopted here, although it is potentially misleading. A straight bill of lading is not negotiable and is not transferable in the normal sense of permitting an indefinite number of transfers. However, as pointed out in The"Rafaela S"(2005) 1 Lloyd's Rep 347 the use of such a bill of lading does or may envisage a transfer of it from shipper to the named consignee. The controversial question as to whether a straight bill is a document of title is discussed in Chapter 6."

3.3.5 海运单(sea waybill)

海运单与记名提单看来是非常接近,就是把收货人的名字明确写清楚,让船舶或者承运人到了卸港的时候把货交给他。海运单也是不可流通的付运文件。这样看来海运单更加接近邮寄包裹或空运时的空运单。这里可以节录在通过 1992 年《海上货物运输法》时的法律专员报告(Law Com. No. 196, Scot. Law Com. 130)对海运单的定义,如下:"A sea waybill is a document which contains or evidences an undertaking by the carrier to the shipper to deliver to the person who is for the time being identified as being entitled to delivery. Sea waybills are broadly similar to 'straight' bills of lading... A sea waybill is a receipt for the goods, but it is non-transferable and is not a document of title... The main advantage of the sea waybill is that, unlike a bill of lading, it does not have to be transmited to the consignee in order for the goods to be surrendered by the carrier on arrival. It also has the advantage that the shipper can vary his delivery instructions out to the carrier at any time during transit."

如果要挑出海运单与记名提单的分别大概是海运单不是物权凭证(即使有限),因为它根本连把有关的货物所有权转让给记名的收货人也做不到。在 The"Rafaela S"(2005) 1 Lloyd's Rep 347 中,Steyn 勋爵讲到了两种付运单证的区别说:"In the hands of the named consignee the straight bill of lading is his document of title. On the other hand, a sea waybill is never a document of title. No trader, insurer or banker would assimilate the two. The differences between the documents include the fact that a straight bill of lading contains the standard terms of the carrier on the reverse side of the document but a sea waybill is blank and straight bills of lading are invariably issued in set of three and waybills not. Except for the fact that a straight bill of lading is only transferable to a named consignee and not generally, a straight bill of lading shares all the principal characteristics of a bill of lading as already described."

另一个分别是海运单根本没有在1924年《海牙规则》或1855年《提单法》被提到。毕竟海运单是比较近期才出现的单证。但在1992年《海上货物运输法》以及实际作用不大的《汉堡规则》有针对这种付运单证。在1992年的立法，"有关的时间内"海运单(或者记名提单)中被明示为收货人的一方就对货损货差有诉权或是与船舶/承运人有运输合约的关系。这是因为原来与船舶/承运人订立运输合约的发货人是可以在运输期间改变海运单的收货人。所以船舶在海上发生碰撞或者大火时造成货损货差，根本到不了卸港，在那时海运单的记名收货人是有诉权的。

海运单在今天是班轮运输经常会见到的付运单证，其中主要原因是现在有很多跨国公司会在国际性运营时，A国的托运人(如中国的某工厂)与B国的收货人(如美国某分销商)属于同一个集团或是关联公司。所以不存在传统的做法就是通过提单让货物在海上运输期间把所有权流转/转售或者用信用证支付货款等问题。这一来，用海运单作为付运单证可以更简单地操作，避免像指令提单在流转时带来的贸易风险，也可以避免提单流转的延误导致需要在卸港提供担保以求无单放货。

3.3.6 交货单(delivery order)

交货单通常是由船东或是承运人签发，让该交货单的持有人或是交货单中的记名买方向船长或者有关货物的托管人(如仓库保管人)出示后可提取交货单里所针对的货物。交货单本身有对船长或者有关货物的托管人指示放货的作用，也有对持有人或是买方作出交货的承诺。交货单的定义可节录Waren Import Gesellschaft Krohn & Co. v. International Graanhandel Thegra N. V. (1975) 1 Lloyd's Rep 146，Kerr大法官这样说："I do not think that it is necessary or desirable to attempt to define 'ship's delivery orders' exhaustively. They must, however, in my judgment, be documents issued by or on behalf of shipowners while the goods are in their possession or at least under their control and containing some form of undertaking that they will be delivered to the buyers (or perhaps to the bearer) on presentation of the documents. If they contain such an undertaking, then it appears to me to be irrelevant whether the documents were originally issued by the shipowners or their agents, or whether they began their life by being addressed to the shipowners or their agents with instructions to deliver to the buyers followed by a reissue of the documents by the shipowner or their agents incorporating such an undertaking."

交货单在实际的业务中会在一种情况下被使用，就是一船的散装货如玉米，在装港只出了一套提单，这套提单经过流转后到了卸港的买方。如果买方想再把这批货物分销给几个不同的分买方，一种做法是以提单向船长提货后再在岸上分销。但这样会产生费用或麻烦，如要租用仓库放置这票玉米。比较好的办法是要求分买方直接向船长提取他们所购买的货物数量，但问题是只有一套提单包括了所有的数量，无法流转给其中任何一位分买方。买方固然可以找作出提单的船东/承运人，要求交换多几套货物数量较少的提单，但这需要时间与麻烦的工作。所以简单的做法是把原来的提单也就是整船货物交出给船东/承运人，并要求签发几份不同的交货单，只要总的货物数量与本来一套提单的数量一致。

交货单比起提单有两个缺点：第一它不是可以流转的物权凭证，除非是持有人的交货单。另一个更重要的缺点，也就是针对本章的内容而言，就是它不能把运输合约中的诉权转让给最后向船长提货的分买方。换言之，1855 年《提单法》没有包括这种付运单证，所以不存在强制的合约变更。这表示分买方真正向船长提货的时候如果发现货损货差是不能直接向船舶/承运人起诉的。该问题可以说也是在 1992 年《海上货物运输法》有了解决。

3.3.7　1992 年《海上货物运输法》总结

介绍了以上各种付运单证，就可以更容易明白 1992 年《海上货物运输法》与诉权的关系。这就是通过 1992 年立法去强制运输合约的变更，让本来不是订约方的收货人可以根据有关的运输合约向承运人提出货损货差的索赔。1992 年立法比起同样作用的 1855 年《提单法》大大扩大了适用范围，因为它是针对海运单与交货单，这些付运单证都是在 1855 年那个年代很少甚至是没有人使用的。这一来，根据海运单或交货单向船长提取货物时，如果发生货损货差就可以直接向承运人提出索赔。

至于提单，这本来是在 1855 年《提单法》重点针对的付运文件，到了 1992 年立法，就扩大到所有的提单合法持有人，不再理会在背书把提单转让的时候是否是为了转让货物所有权。“合法持有人”就显然是有更广泛的针对对象，基本上只要不是以盗窃、欺诈或是暴力取得这套提单，都会算是合法持有人。在 1992 年《海上货物运输法》，Section 5(2) 是有列举合法持有人的类别。它强调该套提单是善意(good faith)取得。

3.4　提单合法持有人与货物保险人必须小心的危险品责任

但提单合法持有人还是要小心，因为运输合约的强制性转让会带来权利(诉权)但也会带来合约责任。本来，任何的合约都会有权利也会有责任，但提单不像其他的合约会是大家订约时双方都会也可以估计到将来他的责任到什么程度。而针对海上运输，货方最可怕的责任就是货物潜在的危险导致了船舶发生重大事故，而这种案件也不断地在出现。例如在笔者《提单与其他付运单证》第 226 ~ 234 页介绍了有关先例 The“Aegean Sea”(1998) 2 Lloyd's Rep 39 与 The“Berge Sisar”(1998) 2 Lloyd's Rep 475。这方面特别危险的是今天这种类型的货物品种越来越多，数量可以少至只有一桶或者一个集装箱也可以多至整船，都会足够把整条船摧毁并造成无数的伤亡与环境污染。而针对法律方面，英国法律很明确给危险品非常广泛的定义，而且是属于严格责任，就算是货方没有疏忽或者是不知情也不可以减轻责任，这方面可参阅贵族院先例 The"Giannis NK"(1998) 1 Lloyd's Rep 337。

针对危险品的责任，发货人要承担责任是无可逃避，毕竟是他把危险品装上船舶并造成重大事故。但针对收货人，他们也会有情况就是与承运人订立运输合约的一方，并把危险品装上船舶。如 FOB 买卖，发货人是以买方（收货人）的代理人身份订舱位或租船。也会是，买方通过货代安排危险品的付运。如果在发货人与买方的关系搞不清楚的时候甚至会有可能被法院视为是大家都对船舶要负责，毕竟合约并不一定只能有两方当事人。在先例 The"Athanasia Comninos"(1990) 1 Lloyd's Rep 277 中，涉及了三艘船舶所装的低质煤炭由于挥发易燃气体而爆炸，造成船舶严重损坏、人身伤亡与共同海损等损失。其中的争议是谁要负责，到底是在提单内名为发货人的 Devco，或者提单内名为收货人的 FOB 买方 CEGB。Mustill 大法官这样说："As regards Devco, there is in my view no room for doubt. They were shippers of the goods, and were named as such in the bill of lading, without qualification. It was argued on their behalf that it was in fact CEGB who were the participants in the contract of carriage. To my mind the position of CEGB has no bearing on the potential liability of Devco. To show that CEGB were principals would not relieve Devco from liability, but would entail that both parties were principals vis-ὰ-vis the plaintiffs. The only circumstance which would discharge Devco would be proof that they were named as participants in the contract without their consent... The original documents were routed to Devco, their designation as shippers, which is not surprising, since that is what they were. It seems to me quite plain that Devco were bound by the contract contained in the bill of lading."

这表示根据 1992 年《海上货物运输法》，提单的合法持有人有必要小心这强制性的合约变更。根据 1992 年立法，Section 3(1) 只是在三种情况下才会对海运单、交货单或提单的持有人强加合约的责任，就是他们向承运人要求或提取货物，或向承运人提出索赔（如船舶在航次半途沉没而导致货物全损）。这样立法就反是为了保护指令提单中曾经被背书的人士（这可能包括银行或其他中间商），不会被船东/承运人指他们有提单合约责任提出索赔，如船舶在航次中途沉没是由于货物是危险品爆炸导致的。这也表示如果有关货物是危险品或是据闻船舶出大事但原因不明，有关的指令提单或持有人提单，特别是涉及银行或是大的贸易公司（表示他们赔得起钱）就要小心不要自己贸然向承运人提出交货要求或向他索赔。如果是记名提单，好像中化集团这种公司经常运载危险品的大公司，最好再把单证背书给集团内部的小公司，通过公司结构局限潜在的庞大甚至是无限责任。这里可节录 Aikens 大法官著的《Bills of Lading》2006 年版之 10.331："If a person obtains rights of suit against a carrier by virtue of the provisions of section 2 of the Carriage of Goods by Sea Act 1992, then it is possible for that person to become liable to the carrier under the bill of lading contract 'as if he had been a party to that contract': section 3 (1). But before the person who has vested rights of suit can become liable under the bill of lading contract, he must have committed one or other of the actions set out in section 3(1)(a), (b) or (c). If a person who has vested in him rights of suit does commit one or other of those acts then he can become liable to the carrier under the indemnity provisions of Article IV rule 6. However, it also appears that the shipper will remain liable by virtue of section 3(3). Thus, the carrier has a choice as to whom he can sue."

这小心的责任就是连代位求偿权下的保险人也必须有，这是因为保险人在赔付了货方之后，以为可以根据代位求偿向承运人索赔。由于英国法下保险人必须是以受保人的名义向承运人采取行动，所以容易有错觉就是即使有反索赔，保险人也不怕，因为反索赔即使成功，赔付的责任也只是在受保人。

3.5　1992 年《海上货物运输法》下不能得到救济的收货人或货方

1992 年立法虽然看来已经是尽量扩大范围让实际收货人也就是蒙受损失的货方可以起诉承运人，但还是有些货方没有在 1992 年立法的范围内以至于不能得到救济。这种例子不多但还是有，一种是货方作出的交货单。因为不是由船东/承运人所作出，所以不属于 1992 年立法 Section 1(1)(c)中的"any ship's delivery order"。这种交货单是由原来的货方把货物分销后所作出的交货单，让这些分买方向这些仓库或者船舶提货，这种可以称为"trader's delivery order"。在这种情况下，收货人的分买方还是会在提货时发现货损货差并蒙受损失，并且是估计船舶/承运人有责任，但可惜就不一定有运输合约的诉权。

另一种例子是提单的收货人一栏是写为"A 银行或者 A 银行的指令"(A's bank or order)，但 A 银行没有背书就交了给收货人向船舶提货，而船长也放了货。这一来该实际的收货人就不能算是 1992 年立法下的合法持有人，蒙受货损货差的损失也是不能直接根据提单去起诉承运人。

这一来，这些蒙受损失的收货人向船舶/承运人提出索赔只能根据侵权或者是托管的诉因。虽然没有 1992 年《海上货物运输法》的帮助，在普通法下也会有两种说法或者情况，这些收货人可以运输合约的关系提出索赔。这普通法的两种说法是默示合约(implied contract)与双方当事人在订约时都知道合约利益最终是为了第三者的利益(contract for the benefit of third party)。有关默示合约的先例是 Brandt v. Liverpool Brazil & River Plate Steam Navigation Co Ltd (1923) All ER Rep 656 (CA)。

但有关这两个普通法的说法，也是有局限性的。如默示合约，就是指承运人与收货人之间的行为显示了他们之间默示有运输合约存在。例如，收货人把欠下承运人的运费或滞期费支付后承运人就把货物交给收货人，这就可以成立默示合约，而双方之间也有构成合约的对价。但如果纯粹是承运人把货物交给收货人，这就很难说是收货人给了什么对价，默示合约的说法也就无法成立。

另是双方当事人在订约时都知道合约利益最终是为了第三者，而第三者就是指收货人。这还是没有解决收货人与承运人之间是没有运输合约的关系，只不过是让遭受损失的收货人可以通过与承运人订立运输合约关系的发货人代他索赔损失。这里的局限在较早已经提到过说:“这一方面虽然是英国法院在 Dunlop v. Lambert (1839) 6 CI & F 68 中有了一个说法,就是 A 可以替 B 向 C 索赔 B 的实际损失,因为 A 与 C 订立运输合约的时候双方都知道这份提单最终是为了 B,这说法是‘(A) is entitled to recover by way of damages for breach of contract the actual loss sustained by those for whose benefit the contract is entered into.’但整个做法还是困难重重,因为 B 是不容易取得 A 的协助去帮忙向 C 提出索赔。”

除了收货人,发货人也会有情况需要向船舶/承运人索赔货损或其他损失。通常发货人与承运人之间有运输合约,不论是通过提单还是订舱单/托单(booking note)的形式,所以发货人肯定有诉权。但 FOB 买卖中是买方自己安排海上运输,这导致卖方与承运人之间没有合约关系也没有诉权。这一来如果承运人的疏忽造成卖方的损失,卖方的合约诉权就得不到保障:Pyrene Co Ltd v. Scindia Steam Navigation Co Ltd (1954) 1 Lloyd's Rep 321。该先例不是涉及货方的诉权,但道理一样,就是货方与承运人之间到底有没有运输合约的关系。案情涉及了卖方与买方达成了 FOB London 的货物买卖协议,而在装货的时候,在货物越过船舷之前挂在船舶吊杆上的货物因为承运人疏忽而摔下并造成损坏。根据买卖合约,风险还没有转移,所以蒙受损失的是卖方/发货人而不是买方。但问题是有关的海上运输是由买方作出安排,所以卖方与承运人之间是没有运输合约的关系。本来,由于疏忽是十分明显,承运人承认责任并作出赔偿。但有没有运输合约对货损的赔付影响大,因为根据《海牙规则》承运人可以享有责任限制。但如果卖方只能是根据侵权向承运人索赔就不存在《海牙规则》的适用。最终高院判是卖方是买方与承运人签订运输合约的受益人,而卖方作为收益人是要受到运输合约中条文的限制。另外大家也预期了提单在装完货之后会签发,所以《海牙规则》适用,在高院的判词中这样说:“In brief, I think the inference irresistible that it was the intention of al three parties that the seller should participate in the contract of affreightment so far as it affected him. If it were intended that he should be a party to the whole of the contract his position would be that of an undisclosed principal and the ordinary law of agency would apply. But that is obviously not intended; he could not, for example, be sued for the freight. **This is the sort of situation that is covered by the wider principle: the third party takes those benefits of the contract which appertain to his interest therein, but takes them, of course, subject to whatever qualifications with regard to them the contract imposes.** It is argued that it is not reasonable to suppose that the seller would submit to the terms of a contract whose detail he does not know and which might not give him the sort of protection of which he would approve. I do not think that as a matter of business this is so. Most people board a bus or train without considering what protection they will get in the event of an accident. I see nothing unreasonably imprudent in a seller assuming that the buyer, whose stake in the contract is greater than his, would have obtained whatever terms are usual in the trade; if he were legally minded enough to inquire what they were, the answer would be that by statutory requirement the contract was governed by the Hague Rules."

4. 需要了解的情况之三:谁是承运人

要正确处理货方或代位求偿权下的保险人的诉权问题,其中一个重要问题就是要看运输合约的另一方,就是该合约下的承运人到底是谁(identity of carrier)。如果签发有提单,在善意第三人持有提单的情况下,当然指的就是提单下的承运人。表面看来,这问题很简单与明确,既然是船舶运输,承运人应该就是船东。但事实上这个问题非常复杂,复杂程度恐怕比上一小段所针对的货方诉权问题还要复杂,毕竟1992年《海上货物运输法》已经是很大程度解决了诉权的问题。但谁是承运人还没有办法以这种方式解决。这里的大前提就是订约自由,也就是说谁愿意作为运输合约下的承运人承担该合约的责任,是完全没有办法强制的。这一来,只要运输合约明确了是原船东自己作为承运人,有诉权的货方或代位求偿权下的保险人要作为索赔对象的,显然也是原船东。也不愁他赔不起,因为他拥有昂贵的船舶另外还有背后的船东互保协会。这种情况在"二战"前是很常见,货方或代位的保险人索赔货损货差可以诉船东(*in personam*)也可以诉船(*in rem*)。并且通过诉船与扣船获得诉前担保,也往往能够逼使船东出面应诉,让接下来的诉讼变为货方与船东之间的诉人诉讼。

4.1　租约提单下承运人的确定

但到了"二战"之后,航运业务有了变化,就是多了很多租约特别是期租合约而不是"二战"前的航次租约。举例说原船东A把船舶出租给B,而出租的方式是光船租约(demise charter),或是期租合约(time charter),这些合约根本不是货物运输合约。之后,B把该船舶营运,并以光船船东的身份或二船东的身份与C的货方签订运输合约。这一来,承运人应该就是B,C如果把有关的提单背书转让给收货人D,航次中发生货损货差,D如果贸然向原船东的A提出索赔(通常通过诉船/扣船把原船东扯进来),就会把承运人的对象彻底搞错。在发觉索赔对象错误后(往往是在船东作出抗辩才发觉),如果1年的时效已经过去就无法挽回。

或说,D怎么会找不到到底应该向谁索赔的资料?答案是经常没有办法知道,因为A与B的租约并不是公开的资料,D根本无法知道。D在确定谁是承运人时唯一可以参考的就是一份提单,这提单往往是些标准的格式如大宗货物提单经常会是Congenbill。能够在里面找到有关承运人的资料通常只是船舶名字以及提单的签字(通常就是船长的签字或者是船舶代理人的签字)。有诉权的货方通常的假设就是船舶船东是承运人,这在今天根据船舶名字找出船东是很容易,这就可以让货方以诉人(*in personam*)的形式起诉船东。或是更加普遍的做法就是以对物诉讼(*in rem*)的形式起诉船舶并同时扣船以提供诉前担保。上述诉人的做法正是假设船东就是承运人,但现实中很多情况是不对。船东在稍后抗辩的时候就会指出他不是承运人,因为船舶已经光租给了 B,而提单上的船长签字只约束 B,因为在光船租约下是 B 雇佣该船长,与原船东的 A 无关。

这导致了对物诉讼的告票中,有经验的海事律师在起诉的时候都会将可能成为被告的人尽量罗列,特别是船东与光租承租人。否则在 1 年时效内作出的告票如果只针对船东,过了时效后才知道有光租承租人就来不及作出补救了。在成功告船与扣船的时候,即使船东愿意提供担保放船,货方也必须要船东明确该船舶是否被光租出去。如果船东明确说没有光船租约,货方就可以安心继续向船东起诉,并接受船东所提供的诉前担保。但如果有光船租约,货方就要坚持以光船船东的名义提供担保才能放船。并且能够在继续的诉讼中知道承运人实际上是光船船东。这些做法都是为了明确谁是正确的被告。

一份提单如果是船长或船长授权签字,当船长是原船东的雇员,显然船长的签字是约束原船东并能够很大程度上明确承运人就是原船东。但是,如果船舶是被光租出去,这样船长就是光租承租人的雇员就不能约束原船东了。

在介绍了光船租约的问题后,期租合约会带来同样甚至是更大的问题。这里的起点就是假设订约双方的意图,货方显然是愿意与原船东订立运输合约而不愿与期租承租人(虽然对外宣称是承运人)打交道,因为期租承租人这种营运人(operator)经常没有资产。但这只是假设,如果提单写得很清楚承运人就是期租承租人或签字就是他自己的名字,这还是不能扭曲。这表示在解释提单中谁是承运人,通常是解释为原船东,因为这会是比较合理的解释。其中,提单(特别是租约提单)内船长的签字以及有否说明是谁的授权下签字是解释合约时一个关键的考虑因素。这里可节录 Aikens 大法官著的《Bills of Lading》2006 年版之 7.60 – 7.61:

"The classic bill of lading provides a 'signature box' as well as printed and typed terms which may provide for the identity of the carrier, and the cases illustrate the difficulties where different provisions point towards different conclusions.

A line of authority culminating in The 'Rewia' (1991) 2 Lloyd's Rep 325 has established that a bill of lading signed by or on behalf of a master cannot be a charterers' bill unless the contract was made with the charterers alone and the person singing had authority to sign and did sign on behalf of the charterers and not the owners. The master may be held to be acting on behalf of the owners for purposes of signature of bills of lading despite a provision in the charter specifying that he signed bills as agent of the charterer: Manchester Trust v. Furness (1895) 2 QB 539. While the terms of a charter may confer actual authority on a charterer to sign bills on the owner's behalf, they cannot generally create apparent authority vis-ὰ-vis a third party independent of the charterer, as the charter cannot constitute 'holding out' to that party."

4.2 班轮或标准格式提单下承运人的确定

如果不是涉及简单的租约提单(如 Congenbill),而是班轮或标准格式提单,解释起来就会更加复杂。因为这种提单通常都会有印本条文(printed clause),如把班轮公司或营运人的名字印在提单正面,并有联络方法,这会误导货方/保险人以他作为对象提出索赔,而忽略了他不一定是该提单下的承运人,而是他期租船舶的原船东才是承运人。另外经常有的印本条文也包括了对承运人的定义(definition of carrier)、光船条文(demise clause)等。在订约自由下,条文怎么写都可以,而这一问题也不是《海牙规则》或《海牙—维斯比规则》能管的范围。反正这种条文特别是光船条文通常是想把承运人局限指原船东而并非提单抬头的班轮公司或营运人。这也有历史原因,就是早期责任限制(直到1957年《责任限制公约》)只适用于原船东,而不适用于承租人。所以为了防止在大的货损货差向承租人直接提出没有限制的索赔,倒不如先让原船东出面将可能有的赔付责任进行限制。这方面请看笔者所著的《海事法》第二章。

由于这些印本条文与提单的签字等各方面经常出现矛盾,这表示有印本条文的提单要正确与全面解释谁是承运人不是件容易的事情,这也带来大量的案例:The "Venezuela"(1980) 1 Lloyd's Rep 393, The "Ines"(1995) 2 Lloyd's Rep. 144, Maritrop Trading Corporation and Others v. Guangzhou Ocean Shipping Company (unreported, 11 December 1997), The "Hector" (1998) 2 Lloyd's Rep 287, The "Flecha" (1999) 1 Lloyd's Rep 612 (被 The "Starsin" 所推翻)。

4.3 目前贵族院关于承运人确定的最权威先例:The "Starsin"

接下来只介绍近期的贵族院先例 The "Starsin" [2003] UKHL 12,有关的案情是船舶涉及了期租承租人 CPS,提单是由 CPS 的港口代理人签发,并且把 CPS 在签字栏注明是承运人。但提单背面有印本条文,其中包括了承运人定义条文与光船条文,说明原船东才是提单的订约方或承运人。在上诉庭,多数意见判该提单的承运人就是原船东,这等于给了背面印本条文更大的分量。其中 Andrew Morritt 大法官这样说:"The signature box is part of the bill of lading. The normal rule whereby greater importance is attributed to specific provisions, including the signature box, put into a standard form is qualified by and to the extent that clause 35 of the standard conditions is applicable."

这在贵族院被一致推翻并强调主要的解释应该看提单的正面而不是藏在后面小字书写的印本条文,而正面最重要的签字一栏。换言之,贵族院判这份是 CPS 的提单,承运人就是他。但这一重要先例也受到质疑,虽然它是目前的英国法律地位,不论市场的反应如何。Aikens 大法官著的《Bills of Lading》2006 年版之 7.69 段就提出了五点质疑,说:

"There are aspects of the speeches in The Starsin on this issue which may not meet with universal approval and it is suggested that the only analysis which proceeds on conventional lines is that of Lord Hobhouse, who emphasised that great weight was to be given to the content of the signature on this bill. For example:

(1) Reference was rightly made to the need of certainty but it is questionable how far the underlying theme of the judgments promotes this. On the contrary it might be said to invite expert evidence as to market understanding on an issue where, as was pointed out in the case, the parties want to be able to ascertain quickly and easily what the position is.

(2) Despite the repeated deference paid to the needs of the commercial community, it is doubtful whether the judgments do reflect real commercial concerns. There was no evidence of market practice (or factual matrix) before the courts, and Lords of Appeal in Ordinary are perhaps not best placed to take judicial notice of it.

(3) The emphasis on the 'front' of a bill of lading is arguably overstated. Commercial men with even an elementary knowledge of bills of lading know that these will contain contractual terms of importance which cannot be fitted on the front. The distinction between the two sides of a piece of paper is in modern times perhaps artificial.(提单毕竟只有一张纸与正反两面,如果只对正面作出重点解释,会否太片面?毕竟在今天的商业文件,会有很多页数,解释起来还是要看整份文件的内容给它综合的解释)

(4) A factor which undoubtedly influenced their Lordships was the content of UCP 500, and in particular the stipulation in Article 23 (a) that a bill of lading must appear 'on its face to indicate the name of the carrier.' As hinted at in Lord Hobhouse's judgment there is an element of the tail wagging the dog in placing reliance on the UCP, as the identity of contracting parties cannot be influenced by the definitions, for banking purposes, of a bill of lading. Traditionally bills of lading do not reveal the identity of the carrier (other than that it is often whoever owns the ship) and this is likely to be of indifference to bankers, at whom UCP 500 is aimed, and who are interested in the bill of lading as a document of title rather than as a contract.(贵族院在该先例中非常重视商业的做法,其中就是强调了信用证在UCP500中规定只是看提单的正面,而不理会背面的条文。但货方与承运人之间复杂的关系以银行在UCP500下针对信用证简单的做法作为依据是否会本末倒置?)

(5) Apart from a cursory reference to the problem by Lord Hobhouse the judgment fails to address the problems posed by the propositions first, that the bill of lading is only evidence of an existing contract (by definition between ascertainable parties) and, secondly, that a contract is only concluded if both the 'putative' carrier is authorised to contract and the counterparty has agreed to contract with him as such. This objection may justifiably said to be an over legalistic one which the commercial community would rather avoid, and certainly the idea that every such dispute requires extensive factual and expert evidence to resolve it, rather than questions of construction, is unwelcome."

但不论怎么说,The"Starsin"是目前这方面最重要的先例,所以可总结说如果货方或者代位求偿的保险人要根据提单找出承运人,他主要是看提单的正面,其中最重要的就是签字。另外可能对承运人有提示的是看提单有否印上某公司的名字(如中远的提单)以及船名。只是在比较罕见的例子,提单正面对承运人的提示实在是太含糊与太矛盾,才会看提单背面的印本条文。

所以在以上的说法中,在一份中远提单,如果船舶是中远的船舶,而签字是船长签字甚至加上了批注"代表船东"(for owners),就很明显承运人是中远。再举一个例子也是份中远提单,但船舶并非是中远的船舶,签字是中远代理并批注"代表中远"(for COSCO),这看来也会显示承运人是中远。但再举个变化,就是上述情况下签字不是中远代理而是船长并加上批注"代表船东",这样看来承运人并非中远,因为中远并不拥有提单上注明的船舶。为什么使用中远提单有可能被其他人盗用,也有可能中远只是期租进来该船舶营运。反正提单的承运人就是该船舶的原船东。这里还会有变化,就是船舶被期租给了中远,之后又被中远期租给了中海,中海去营运。如果船长在提单上签字,并注明是"代表承租人"(for charterer),但没有说明承租人是谁。这样一来由于提单是中远提单,很有可能是中远被认定为承运人而不是中海。

上述都没有肯定的先例,只是笔者根据贵族院先例 The"Starsin"作出的一些判断,希望有助于中国读者更容易理解。

以上所针对的是合约承运人(contractual carrier),毕竟本章所涉及的就是运输合约的诉权。但还有一种承运人名为实际承运人(actual carrier)。这种情况最常见的就是涉及转运,而一程船的船东签发了提单,该提单下他是合约承运人。但在航次半途以二程船转运去卸港,而货损货差就发生在二程船的运输中,如船舶沉没。这一来,该提单的收货人显然可以向一程船提出索赔,因为后者是合约承运人。但如果收货人是想向二程船的实际承运人提出索赔,根据手中合法持有的提单以合约起诉,显然不对。但收货人可以根据侵权或/与托管作为诉因向二程船索赔,这会有好处也会有坏处,较早的时候已经解释过。这也会有实际的商业要求,如合约承运人因为经济困难而倒闭,但实际承运人仍是一家实力雄厚的公司。根据先例 The"K H Enterprise"(1994) 1 Lloyd's Rep 593,带来一个有条件分托管(sub-bailment on terms)的说法。这表示实际承运人虽然不是合约方,但由于收货人与合约承运人的提单合约预期了转运,所以实际承运人虽然没有合约关系,但可以根据提单内的规定(主要是《海牙规则》)作出抗辩,如航海与管船疏忽的免责、1 年时效与责任限制等。

5. 需要了解的情况之四:《海牙规则》或者其他强制性法律是否适用

针对货损货差的索赔,对货方或者代位求偿的保险人很需要知道的就是有关的提单是否强制适用《海牙规则》或《海牙—维斯比规则》,毕竟在这规则下有很多重要规定是必须要做到的如 1 年时效。毕竟针对这方面,世界上有很多不同的强制性法律,如中国的《海商法》,小部分的国家是《汉堡规则》,将来可能还会有《鹿特丹规则》。在没有强制性法律适用的情况下,就会涉及订约自由,看看提单合约到底有哪些明示的规定。会有不少提单格式包括 Congenbill,会明示规定一条名为"首要条文"(clause paramount),内容就是合并《海牙规则》或《海牙—维斯比规则》。

在英国法律的地位,本书第三章已经介绍过针对合约的实体法,如果双方没有明确的适用法条文规定,英国现在的默示地位规定在 1990 年的《英国合约法(实体法适用)》(Contracts (Applicable Law) Act of 1990),根据《罗马公约》(Rome Convention),这表示有关的提单下的运输与英国有密切关系才会适用《海牙—维斯比规则》。因为英国是签约国,这方面的立法是 1971 年《海上货物运输法》。但英国在这方面的法律冲突与其他合约有些不一样,这就是在贵族院的先例 The"Morviken"(1983) Lloyd's Rep 1。在该先例,贵族院判是《海牙规则》或《海牙—维斯比规则》规则是否适用要看该公约本身的规定,这些规定在四种情况是会强制适用:(1)提单是在该公约的缔约国签发;(2)航次是从公约的缔约国开始;(3)提单明示合并某个国家的立法是依据《海牙规则》或《海牙—维斯比规则》,如合并美国 1936 年《海上货物运输法》;(4)提单内有一条首要条文。这一来,表示去英国法院审理的货损货差案件,会绝大部分都强制适用《海牙规则》或《海牙—维斯比规则》,即使是有关的航次与英国没有任何关系,也谈不上是 1971 年英国《海上货物运输法》的强制适用。

本来,The"Morviken"先例的判决是在 1990 年的《英国合约法(实体法适用)》生效前作出的,应该被 1990 年立法超越或替代,但实际上并没有。这方面可以节录《Southampton on Shipping Law 2008》一书之 107—108 页所说如下:"Ever since the decision of the House of Lords decision in The Morviken (1983) 1 Lloyd's Rep 1, however, a decision made before the 1990 Act but which has, perhaps rather surprisingly, stood since then, the English position regarding the law applicable in particular to cargo claims has been rather special. In summary, rather than following the usual conflicts path of first finding out which national law applies (through the conflicts rules contained in the Contracts [Applicable Law] Act 1990) and then, if English law applies, finding out which part of English law applies to the particular dispute (e. g. the Carriage of Goods by Sea Act 1971), the courts will use the 1971 Act itself to decide whether the English Carriage regime applies to the cargo claim. In other words, the conflict rules used for cargo claims are contained in the Carriage of Goods by Sea Act 1971 rather than in the Contracts (Applicable Law) Act 1990. The effect if that if any one of a number of triggers (这就是指上述介绍的四种情况) in the 1971 Act is triggered, then the Hague-Visby Rules will apply, even without an express choice of law clause saying so, and indeed (as was the case in The Morviken itself), in the teeth of an express choice of law clause choosing some other regime.”

该法律地位可以举简单的例子说明，就是一船货物从日本或者新加坡去中国并发生货损货差，由于日本或者新加坡是《海牙—维斯比规则》签约国，所以案件在英国审理（通过扣船获得管辖权或是提单有英国法院的排外管辖权条文）的话就会根据《海牙—维斯比规则》，即使英国与这一个航次没有关系。

6. 需要了解的情况之五：证明货方的损失

证明货方的损失是货方或者代位求偿保险人的责任，这里涉及两个重要方面的举证责任：一是针对货物装上船舶的时间，货物是表面状况良好以及它的数量或者重量。二是针对货物从船舶卸下时，货物的表面状况是否同样良好与它在数量或者重量是否一致（除了是正常损耗）。它针对货物表面状况良好或不良好的原因是如果表面看不到的缺陷，属于固有缺陷，船舶/承运人不论是根据《海牙规则》或《海牙—维斯比规则》都可以免责。

第一方面的证明就是来自一份清洁提单，而根据《海牙—维斯比规则》Article III rule 4，如果该份提单是转让给了无辜第三人，也就是收货人，提单上对货物的陈述就是结论性的证据（conclusive evidence）。看来在贵族院先例 The“Rafaela S”（2005）1 Lloyd's Rep 347 的判决下，一份记名提单（straight bill of lading）下记名收货人也应该可以在索赔时指称这份提单是结论性的证据。但说不通的地方总还是有，就是一份看来与记名提单性质上是差不多的海运单（sea waybill），由于《海牙—维斯比规则》不适用，就不能让收货人依赖海运单对货物的陈述是结论性。

提单对货物的陈述是否是结论性或只是表面性（*prima facie*）的证据主要的分别就是后者可以用其他的证据推翻，其中一个好的理由就是该提单对货物的陈述有偏差，而这样写是在没有承运人的授权的情况下作出的：Grant v. Norway （1851） 10 CB 665。

如果提单的合法持有人所持的是清洁提单，可以说是对货物表面状况良好已经是犹如拍了快照（snapshot）不能推翻。至于提单上货物的数量与重量，如陈述为 2 万吨玉米，这表面看来也是有这个数量的玉米装上船舶。但一般提单的格式中经常印有“重量不知”（weight unknown）或是“据说是 2 万吨”（said to weigh 20,000 tons），这样看来就谈不上是针对货物数量或者重量拍了快照。看来，发货人的做法就是在他准备一份提单让船长签字时，让他把该批注删除。而根据《海牙—维斯比规则》Article 3(3)，除非是承运人或者船长有合理理由怀疑装船货物的重量，或是没有合理的办法检查，他们必须签发该份有货物数量或重量的提单。但现实中会这样做的发货人不多，这就带来需要了解英国法律的地位就是承认这种对货物数量或重量的批注的有效性，最终导致提单持有人在货物短缺的索赔会受到影响，因为提单上的 2 万吨数量并不是结论性:New Chinese Co v. Ocean S. S. Co (1917) 2 KB 664; Canada and Dominion Sugar v. Canadian National (1946) 80 Lloyd's Rep 13; Attorney-General of Ceylon v. Scindia SS Co. Ltd (1961) 2 Lloyd's Rep 173; The "Herroe" and "Askoe" (1986) 2 Lloyd's Rep 281; The "Esmeralda" (1988) 1 Lloyd's Rep 206; The "Atlas" (1996) 1 Lloyd's Rep. 642; The "River Gurara" (1998) 1 Lloyd's Rep 225; The "Mata K" (1998) 2 Lloyd's Rep 614。对该方面有兴趣的读者还可以参阅笔者《提单及其他付运单证》第607~614页。

以上介绍了第一方面的证明,现在介绍第二方面的证明也就是货物在卸下时的快照。这快照就是代表货物在卸下发现货损后的第一时间由船长与货方(也可能是货方的保险人)进行联合检验(joint survey)并作出就货损原因与程度的联合检验报告。如果没有进行联合检验与向船舶/承运人通知货损货差,根据《海牙—维斯比规则》,将被视为交付的货物符合提单上陈述的表面证据,这是在 Article III (6):"Unless notice of loss or damage and the general nature of such loss or damage be given in writing to the carrier or his agent at the port of discharge before or at the time of removal of the goods into the custody of the person entitled to delivery thereof under the contract of carriage, or, if the loss or damage be not apparent, within three days, such removal shall be prima facie evidence of the delivery by the carrier of the goods as described in the bill of lading. The notice in writing need not be given if the state of the goods has, at the time of their receipt, been the subject of joint survey or inspection."

装船提单与联合检验报告缺一不可,否则就证明不了货损货差发生在船舶运输途中,船舶/承运人有必要承担责任。

7. 需要了解的情况之六:证明承运人的责任

由于本书是针对海上货物运输保险,不是针对货损货差的责任与索赔等方面,所以不细谈这方面的内容。毕竟,到了处理货损货差的责任,不论是在英国法院或者是香港/伦敦仲裁,这一个阶段通常不是货方/保险人在处理而是委任了代表律师或者是索赔代理人,所以不必在这里作为重点介绍。

只说这方面其中针对最多的书是笔者的《提单及其他付运单证》,其中第五章涉及了提单下货损货差责任的处理,包括货方与船方各自要举证的方面。也详细介绍了证明的步骤:第一步——货方证明货损货差发生在承运人在海牙规则下要负责的期间;第二步——船东/承运人证明造成货损货差的原因;第三步——船东/承运人证明船舶适航;第四步——船东/承运人证明免责;第五步——货方证明承运人没有妥善与谨慎装卸、堆放与照看货物;第六步——双方对其他有关方面的争辩(包括非法/不合理绕航、索赔时效、单位/单位责任限制)。

另外，针对货损货差责任的处理，也不仅是了解《海牙规则》与《海牙—维斯比规则》，虽然这些最常见与最重要，因为是强制适用于提单。而提单也就是货方与承运人之间最主要的运输合约关系。但在比较少的情况下也会有其他的运输合约关系，如租约或者海运单的合约关系，虽然在这种运输合约中，也经常会加上首要条文合并《海牙规则》或者《海牙—维斯比规则》。但以租约为例，由于有完全的订约自由，所以也不一定会这样做。好像著名的金康租约，它的标准格式就不会有首要条文，也不鼓励这样做，因为金康租约的第 2 条比《海牙规则》或《海牙—维斯比规则》对船东更有利。至于租约在怎样的情况下会变为货方与船东/承运人之间的运输合约而非提单，可以马上想到的情况就是 FOB 买方以自己的名义以航次租约租船，虽然提单还是在装港签发给了发货人并通过背书最后转让给了 FOB 买方，但提单在他的手中只能是一份收据，无法也从来没有意图替代或超越他们之间订立的租约。这方面可节录 Denning 勋爵在先例 The"Dunelmia"(1969) 2 Lloyd's Rep 476 中所说："... in a case such as this the relations between shipowner and charterer are governed by the charter-party. Even though the charterer is not the shipper and takes as indorsee of a bill of lading, nevertheless their relations are governed by the charter, at any rate when the master is only authorised to sign bills of lading without prejudice to the charter."

Ⅱ．第二部分：以运输合约关系以外的货损货差索赔：侵权与托管

8. 序言

以上介绍的情况基本上都是以运输合约关系特别是以提单合约关系的货损货差的索赔，但会有情况是货方或行使代位求偿权的保险人需要以合约关系以外的诉因(cause of action)向承运人提出货损货差的索赔。这样做主要的原因就是受到损害的货方或收货人无法满足他与承运人之间有一个运输合约的关系，所以以提单合约或《海牙—维斯比规则》起诉往往会因为没有诉权而失败告终。大量相关的案例在本章第 3.1 段有介绍，这是因为 1855 年《提单法》的缺陷所导致货方或者收货人没有提单合约下的诉权。这一问题随着 1992 年的《海上货物运输法》基本上解决了，但这并不表示以合约关系以外的货损货差索赔有所减少，因为有了另一种情况出现。越来越多的期租承租人以二船东的身份揽货，并订立海上货物运输合约并说明是承运人，那么在提单合约下诉权的对象就是二船东而不是原船东。

但问题是该二船东往往是皮包公司或者是没有资产的公司，因此货方或者保险人往往都会盯住原船东或者是船舶。但是货方或保险人与原船东是没有合约关系的，这样就出现了合约关系以外的货损货差索赔，这时取得诉前担保或者扣船就显得至关重要了。

另一个较次要的原因就是以合约关系以外的货损货差索赔是想回避《海牙规则》或者《海牙—维斯比规则》下的一些局限,如 1 年的时效、航行疏忽的免责与货物单位责任限制。在《海牙—维斯比规则》之 Article Ⅳ(1)加上了一条条文说明承运人不论是以合约还是以侵权作为诉因都不影响承运人可以限制的责任(“The defences and limits of liability provided for in these Rules shall apply in any action against the carrier in respect of loss or damage to goods covered by a contract of carriage whether the action be founded in contract or in tort.”),但该条文是管不了并非提单合约下承运人的其他属于船方的人士。如二程船的船舶与船东、装卸小工、检验师等。

这一来,为了避免承担非合约关系的责任,并希望把这些其他属于船方的人士扯进来享受《海牙规则》或者《海牙—维斯比规则》的保护,承运人就会以各种做法与说法把他们纳入合约关系内。这种做法与说法有“喜马拉雅条文”(Himalaya Clause)、代理关系(agency)、默示合约(implied contract)或有条件的分托管(sub-bailment on term)等。

9. 侵权与提单合约作为诉因的不同之处

作为非合约关系索赔货损货差主要是根据侵权,它与提单合约有很大不同,但他们各有千秋,以哪一种提起诉讼都有好与不好的时候。不过基本上它们之间的差别主要是源于提单合约是强制适用《海牙规则》或者《海牙—维斯比规则》。这一来,《海牙—维斯比规则》对提出索赔的货方有利的地方有好几点是非常重要的,如:

1. 它明确把证明船舶在开航前适航责任与航次中途发生货损货差的举证责任加在承运人的头上。换言之,如果承运人自己也不知道什么原因导致航次中途发生货损货差,它还是要负责任的。

2.《海牙规则》与《海牙—维斯比规则》针对开航前承运人的责任要求“恪尽职责”(due diligence),这在 The“Muncaster Castle”(1961) 1 Lloyd's Rep 57 中被贵族院明确为所有被承运人雇用的独立承包商都不能有过错导致船舶在开航前不适航。但在普通法下,侵权的疏忽不会延伸到雇主所雇用的独立承包商,换言之,这些独立承包商的疏忽不必要雇主负责:《Clerk & Lindsell on Torts》(19 edn, Sweet & Maxwell, 2005)。在该权威书籍的 6-52 段这样说:“**If the employer has employed an independent contractor to do work on his behalf the general rule is that the employer is not responsible for any tort committed by the contractor in the course of the execution of the work** and in this respect the employees of the contractor, whilst acting as such, stand in the same position as their employer, so that the employer of the contractor is not liable for the torts committed by the contractor's employees. Of course, even though the damage complained of may have been caused by the wrongful act or omission of an independent contractor or his employee, it may also be attributable to the negligence or other personal fault of the employer. If, for example, he has negligently selected an incompetent contractor, or has employed an insufficient number of men, or has himself so interfered with the manner of carrying out the work that damage results, he will himself have committed a tort for which he can be held liable. Again if the employer has authorised or ratified the independent contractor's tort then, on normal principles, he will be jointly liable for that tort. So in Ellis v. Sheffield Gas Consumer's Co (1853) 2 E. &B 767, where a gas company which had no statutory powers to take up the streets for the purpose of laying their pipes for them, and where the contractor's employees, having laid their pipes, insufficiently reinstated the surface thus causing damage, the gas company was held liable. As Erle J. stated: 'The cause of accident was the very thing done in pursuance of the specific directions of the defendants contained in their contract'."

3. 在侵权下,承运人不大可能会对纯经济损失承担责任,如损失只是在货物延误到港而导致市场的损失。除非是货方曾经有依赖(rely)承运人作出过不准确的陈述所导致的纯经济损失,但这种情况很少会有:Commissioners of Customs and Excise v Barclays Bank (2006) 2 Lloyd's Rep 327。有关侵权不接受纯经济损失的索赔,主要还是英国法律的政策考虑,就是避免侵权索赔的范围无限扩大,因为纯经济损失可以延伸很远。这可以节录 Fraser 勋爵在 The"Mineral Transporter"(1985) 2 Lloyd's 303 中所说如下:"some limit or control mechanism had to be imposed upon the liability of a wrongdoer towards those who had suffered economic damage in consequence of his negligence; the policy of imposing such a limit was consistent with the policy of limiting the liability of ships and aircraft in maritime and aviation law by statute and by international agreement ..."

但针对合约,就没有这一局限,事实上很大部分的合约索赔都是纯经济损失,如货物因为船舶不合理绕航或延误而导致了有关货物市场下跌,而替货方或收货人带来损失(loss of market),就在运输合约的范畴内可以向船东或承运人提出索赔:The "Heron II"(1967) 2 Lloyd's Rep 457。

《海牙—维斯比规则》对提出索赔的货方不利的地方也有,如下:(1)《海牙—维斯比规则》下只有1年的时效,相对于侵权下的索赔有6年时效短很多,所以当1年时效过后就只能依赖侵权来进行索赔了。(2)《海牙—维斯比规则》下的货物单位责任限制,但侵权就没有这个限制,恐怕唯一的限制就是船舶的吨位责任限制,在只会在发生很大的货损货差索赔的时候才会有关系。这一来,如果比较昂贵的货物受到损坏,由于单位责任限制的适用而赔少了,货方就会有很大的诱因找一个非承运人的对象,如装卸小工,以侵权提出索赔:Midlands & Silicones v Scruttons (1961) 2 Lloyd's Rep 365。(3)根据《海牙—维斯比规则》承运人可以对航行疏忽或过错(negligence or error in navigation)免责,而这通常是带来重大货损货差的主要原因。所以当发生沉船、搁浅、碰撞等严重事故所导致货损货差索赔,货方如果成功以侵权索赔,就可以回避这一个免责。如向肇事的二程船船东提出索赔,因为他不是货方手中提单的承运人。

10. 英国法律对这方面的看法与政策

英国法院对这种做法如果涉及取巧经常会表示强烈的反感,这涉及两个原因:一是大家好不容易有了国际公约的《海牙规则》与《海牙—维斯比规则》协调船方与货方在海上运输遇到风险导致货损货差的责任分摊,就不能太轻易允许取巧来回避。二是在一连串的合约关系下,最公平与最正常的责任追究就是一个合约一个合约地追究下去,而每个合约有不同的约定,但这是他们之间所愿意接受的。如 A 与 B,B 与 C 之间的两个合约链,A 有了损失告 B,B 有了赔付责任后再找 C 要求补偿。如果在 B 与 C 的合约之间,C 不需要对他的疏忽负责,B 就要自己承担损失了,因为两个合约的有关条文不尽相同。但如果 A 跳过 B 直接以侵权向 C 的疏忽提出索赔(不必理会合约下的疏忽免责),就把整个合约链打断了。

涉及海上货物运输,这一合约链更加复杂。假设 A 是发货人,B 是提单承运人,而 C 是 B 的独立承包商(他可以是装卸小工、仓库所有人、二程船的船东与其他承包与协助整个运输过程的第三人)。但随着提单的转让与流转,提单持有人变了是 D,他也是收货人并且面对货损货差的损失。虽然他们之间都有合约关系,但条文与责任分摊都不一样,这就提供机会给 D 可能有几个选择。一个可能性不大的选择就是以他与 A 的合约(这应该是买卖合约)向 A 提出索赔,但一般而言法律的默示地位是货物装船后风险转移到买方头上,但说不定会有千变万化的明示条文有不同的规定,如说明卖方保证货物安全抵达卸港。一个可能性最大的选择就是 D 向 B 以他们之间的合约(这应该是提单合约)提出索赔,而他们之间的合约关系是来自 1992 年《海上货物运输法》。但如果面对一些困难或不满意之处,如 1 年的时效已经届满,由于单位责任限制而赔不足,《海牙—维斯比规则》下的免责条文,甚至是 B 只是一个光棍公司或者他唯一拥有的一艘船舶在能够取得诉前担保前沉没或转售而导致不值得向他起诉,D 就会考虑选择向 C 提出索赔。但显然在 D 与 C 之间没有任何直接关系,他们只是被一连串的合约串在一起。所以,D 向 C 提起的索赔只能是侵权等非合约关系的诉因。这一来,又回到了合约与侵权关系之间有很大的不同,有机会被取巧,以及本段一开始提出的两个原因导致英国法院对这种做法有敌意。以下进一步谈谈英国法院反感的原因。

10.1 英国法院对以侵权绕过合约关系反感的原因之一:打乱《海牙规则》与《海牙—维斯比规则》达成的平衡利益

针对上述第一个原因,可节录一些英国法院重要的有关说法。首先是 Denning 勋爵在 Midlands & Silicones v Scruttons (1961) 2 Lloyd's Rep 365 中所说的,如下:"My

Lords, I have dealt with this case at some length because it is the first case ever recorded in English books where the owner of goods has sued a stevedore for negligence. If the owner can, by so doing, escape the exceptions in the contract of carriage and the limitations in the Hague Rules, it will expose a serious gap in our commercial law. It has great potentialities too. If you can sue the stevedore for his negligence in unloading, why should you not sue the master and officers of the ship for their negligence in the navigation or management of the ship? No longer need you worry about the limitation to 100 Pounds or 200 Pounds a package. You can recover the value of the most precious package without disclosing its nature or value beforehand. No longer need you worry about bringing an action within one year. You can bring it within six years. Nor are the potentialities limited to carriage by sea. They can be profitably extended to carriage by air and by road and rail. You have only to sue the servants of the carrier for negligence and you can get round all the exceptions and limitations that have hitherto been devised. No doubt the carrying company will stand behind its servants. It will foot the bill, as any good employer would, for the sake of good relations. But when you find that the carrying company has, in the long run, to pay for the damage, you see at once that you have turned the flank of the Hague Rules (for carriage by sea) and the Warsaw Convention (for carriage by air). The exceptions and limitations which are there so clearly given to the 'carrier' do not avail his servants and agents when they are sued. By suing them, the goods owner of risks as hitherto covered by insurance."

上诉庭的 Saville 大法官在 The"Nicholas H"(1994) 1 Lloyd's Rep 492 中有相似的判法,如下:"I am not persuaded by such a proposition. The Hague Rules (and their successor the Hague-Visby Rules) form an internationally recognized code adjusting the rights and duties existing between shipowners and those shipping goods under bills of lading. As Sir John Donaldson, M. R., said in The Aliakmon (1985) 1 Lloyd's Rep 199 at p. 206; (1985) 1 Q. B. 350 at p. 368, the rules create an intricate blend of responsibilities and liabilities, rights and immunities, limitations on the amount of damages recoverable, time bars, evidential provisions, indemnities and liberties, all in relation to the carriage of goods under bills of lading. The proposition advanced by Mr. Gross(货方代表律师)would add an identical or virtually identical duty owed by the classification society (被告的日本船级社)to that owed by the shipowners, but without any of these balancing factors, which are internationally recognized and accepted. I do not regard that as a just, fair or reasonable proposition. Of course such a duty would give the cargo-owners another defendant, which would be very useful if the compensation recoverable from the shipowners was insufficient through lack of funds or if their insurers were not obliged to pay, but as the Vice-Chancellor pointed out in Gran Gelato Ltd v Richcliff Ltd (1992) Ch 560 at 571, that those with whom one deals may become insolvent is an ordinary risk of everyday life."

在 The“Nicholas H”先例中，涉及了货方因为向船东索赔受到了船舶吨位责任限制的影响，所以把赔不足的损失金额向船东的日本船级社以侵权的疏忽提出索赔，指控日本船级社因为检查有疏忽让不适航的船舶开航而导致船货全损。在贵族院其中举了一个例子说明有关《海牙规则》与《海牙—维斯比规则》和侵权不一致的地方并会造成不公平就是在前者的规则中，只强加在船东一个在开航前的责任就是保证船舶适航，但在航次半途就没有这个责任。如果船级社是在装港疏忽检查，看来船级社的责任与船东在《海牙规则》与《海牙—维斯比规则》下的责任相一致。但如果船级社是在航次的中途港疏忽检查，并需要承担船舶适航的责任，那岂非船级社的责任比船东作为承运人的责任更大了？这一点在上面节录的 Saville 法官所说的话中有显示。

10.2　英国法院对以侵权绕过合约关系反感的原因之二：侵权应该以有关合约条文作出限制

英国法律承认有一个并存的责任（concurrent liability），就是在有些情况下可以同时存在合约与侵权的责任。但这经常会带来困难，因为合约的基础是严格责任但完全允许订约自由，所以经常会有条文把合约双方的责任减低，如疏忽的一方也不必负责，或即使要负责赔偿金额也是被限制。这都会导致受害方根据并存责任以侵权向疏忽的一方提出索赔，并借此回避合约对受害方不利的条文。可以说是英国法院对这种取巧的做法不满意，如先例 Tai Hing v. Liu Chong Hing Bank（1985）2 Lloyd's Rep 313，Scarman 勋爵在第 321 页说：“Their Lordship do not believe that there is anything to the advantage of the law's development in searching for a liability in tort where the parties are in a contractual relationship. This is particularly so in a commercial relationship. Though it is possible as a matter of legal semantics to conduct an analysis of the rights and duties inherent in some contractual relationships including that of banker and customer either as a matter of contact law when the question will be what, if any, terms are to be implied or as a matter of tort law when the task will be to identify a duty arising form the proximity and character of the relationship between the parties, their Lordships believe it to be correct in principle and necessary for the avoidance of confusion in the law to adhere to the contractual analysis: on principle because it is a relationship in which the parties have, subject to a few exceptions, the right to determine their obligations to each other, and for the avoidance of confusion because different consequences do follow according to whether liability arises from contract or tort, e. g. in the limitation of action.”

Scarman 勋爵接着说，合约的规定应是主导，不得以侵权之诉来改变：“Their Lordship do not, however, accept that the parties'/mutual obligations in tort can be any greater than those to be found expressly or by necessary implication in their contract... the respondent banks cannot rely on the law of tort to provide them with greater protection than that for which they have contracted.”

针对提单合约的承运人与货方/收货人,这一方面的问题已经在很大程度上得到解决。为此在1971年的《海牙—维斯比规则》,对《海牙规则》的Article 4多加了如下一句:"The defences and limits of liability provided for in this Convention shall apply in any action against the carrier in respect of loss or damage to goods covered by a contract of carriage whether the action be founded in contract or in tort."

但这还是不解决涉及第三方(但他也是根据一连串合约被串联起来的)的情况,如在较早前所介绍的A是发货人,B是提单承运人,而C是B的独立承包商(他可以是装卸小工、仓库所有人、二程船的船东与其他承包与协助整个运输过程的第三人),而D是随着提单的转让与流转成为了最终的提单持有人。这一来,如果D以侵权向C提出索赔,这是《海牙—维斯比规则》也管不了的,而他们之间明显没有合约关系。

就岸上的建筑或工程合约而言,已经有这样的判法。如果A的雇主绕过B的承包商向C的分承包商直接以侵权作出起诉,被视为C对A的谨慎责任(duty of care)必须受到B与A之间的合约条文的限制。这方面的先例有:Co-operative Retail Services Ltd v Taylor Young Partnership (2000) 74 Con. L. R 12, cf ;British Telecommunications plc v James Thomson & Sons (Engineers) Ltd (1999) 1 WLR 9;Norwich City Council v Harvey (1989) 1 WLR 828。

至于在货物运输,虽然曾经有一个贵族院的先例Junior Books v. Veitchi (1983) 1 AC 520也有同样的判决,就是侵权下的谨慎责任必须受到有关合约条文的限制。但看来法律地位还不太明确,这可节录Aikens大法官著的《Bills of Lading》2006年版之9.26段所说的如下:"If a contractual 'chain' exists from A through B to C, this may be a reason for not imposing a duty of care on C in relation to damage to goods owned by A. This analysis has been relied on more in cases where there has been a claim for 'pure' economic loss rather than physical loss and damage. The rationale is that the 'usual procedure' is for claims to be passed up and down the contractual chain, so that to construct a duty of care in tort between those who arte not in a direct contractual relationship will subvert the parties' contractual arrangements and will be unjust. The leading case supporting the restriction of a duty of care, owed by C to A by reference to contractual terms between A and B is the House of Lords decision in Junior Books v Veitchi. Although it has never been expressly overruled, this case has however met with almost universal disapproval. In The Aliakmon Lord Brandon (who had dissented in Junior Books) expressly disapproved, in a carriage of goods context, the approach of Lord Roskill in that case. Carver suggests, when considering C's duty to A, that a term in a contract between B and C is more likely to be relevant, as C is a party and it may provide what he has do so, than one in a contract between A and B, but either contract might, depending on the facts, be relevant to qualification of a duty of care."

10.3 部分解决办法:“喜马拉雅条文”与“有条件分托管”

10.3.1 “喜马拉雅条文”(Himalaya Clause)

针对上述的问题,也有了一些解决的办法。第一种就是商业性的解决办法,在A与B的合约中加上一条“喜马拉雅条文”,就是把承运人B的所有分承包商C(如装卸小工、船员或仓库所有人)都加进说明他们也可以享有合约的权利或责任。“喜马拉雅条文”如果写得好,还会加上一条文说明A如果以侵权向C索赔(这是B无法阻止A的),即使成功,超出了合约的部分也要退换给B。文字上可以如下:“The Merchant undertakes that no claim... shall be made against any servant or agent or sub-contractor of Carrier which imposes or attempts to impose upon any of them... any liability whatsoever in connection with the goods and, if any such claim... shall nevertheless be made, to indemnify the Carrier against all consequences thereof...”

但“喜马拉雅条文”作为合约条文总免不了有局限,如条文写得不明确或者不广泛。其中在Midlands & Silicones v Scruttons (1961) 2 Lloyd's Rep 365中提到一条有效的“喜马拉雅条文”必须满足以下四点要求:(1)提单应该清楚写明小工等人可受提单条款保障,这一般不成问题。(2)提单应清楚写明船东是以代理身份替小工等人订约,把提单免责等条款延伸给他们,这一般也不成问题,只要写清楚。(3)船东作为代理,是有小工等人的授权订这提单合约。如果发生提单签发的时候还没有授权,如卸港小工仍未找好,何来授权?但应仍可事后追认(ratification)。有时会看到在不同的事实情况下,会有争论,如小工是由港口当局指定,而这一点上也确是常有争辩。(4)小工等人要有约因给货方才会有有效合约,这一点已在The“Eurymedon”(1974) 1 Lloyd's Rep 534一先例中被解释了。本来在订约时(签发提单),卸港小工是谈不上有何约因或对价给货方的。但贵族院说,提单订约时只是单方面合约(unilateral contract),它在卸港小工提供服务时(这是约因)变为双方(小工与货方)的全面合约(full contract)。

有关“喜马拉雅条文”,可参阅笔者所著的《国际商务游戏规则——英国合约法》第四章之第5节。

10.3.2 “有条件分托管”(sub-bailment on terms)

接下来要解释有条件分托管之前,首先要讲什么是托管(bailment)。托管最重要的就是对货物的占有。一有了这一占有权,托管人就在托管期间对货物有了一个合理谨慎照顾的责任(reasonable or due care),可以说它是与侵权要对第三人有一个谨慎责任(duty of care)基本上是一致的。但托管有几个不同的种类,如收费的托管(bailment for reward)与免费的托管(gratuitous bailment),它们分别会有不同程度地谨慎照顾托管的货物或者财产。在免费甚至是非自愿的托管一个简单的例子就是笔者在餐馆吃饭留下了一把雨伞,那么该餐馆就对笔者的雨伞有一个谨慎照顾的托管责任直到笔者把雨伞取回。但在本段所要介绍的是一种收费与有条件托管(bailment on term),这也是货物运输中最常见的情况,就是货物交给每一个托管人(不论是提单承运人、仓库所有人、二船东或其他不同方式联运的实际承运人)，都会有一个合约约束订约双方的权利与责任。所以，A 把货物交给 B 作为承运人与托管人，双方的合约是提单，托管的条件应该就是《海牙规则》与《海牙—维斯比规则》所规定的，这一个关系应该不难理解。但如果 B 与 C 的分承包商订立另一个合约，并把货物交出给 C 作为托管人，履行全程运输中的一部分。而在期间 C 发生了疏忽导致货物损坏，这就会带来 A 以侵权作为诉因向 C 提出索赔的可能。有条件分托管这一法律地位就是让 C 可以 A 与 B 之间的合约条文作为抗辩，因为 A 授权 B 分包(sub-contract)，所以应该受到 C 与 B 之间合约条文的约束。说实在，其中的道理与上一小段分析的一样。

这一有条件分托管的法律地位来自贵族院的一个先例 The"Pioneer Container"(1994) 1 Lloyd's Rep 593。有关的案情可参见笔者所著的《国际商务游戏规则——英国合约法》第四章之第 5.7 节相关部分。[1]

最后一提的是还有其他一些比较局限的说法，如代理人或默示合约。代理人的说法就是 B 作为 A 的代理人与 C 订立合约，这就允许 A 以合约关系向 C 索赔货损货差，但这里并非侵权的诉因。至于默示合约的说法是 B 与 C 之间打交道会有情况被视为达成一个默示的合约。但这种说法都有它的局限，如代理人而不是合约方就必须在合约中能够显示这种代理关系，而如果是默示合约就必须 A 与 C 之间都会有一些构成合约的必要条件，如双方都有订约意图与对价/约因。最后要提到英国一个非常重要的立法就是 1999 年《Contracts (Rights of Third Parties) Act》，该立法在笔者所著的《国际商务游戏规则——英国合约法》一书第四章 4.3.5 段有详论，不多介绍。

11. 合约关系以外的货损货差索赔的不同诉因

如果货方或是代位求偿的保险人向承运人提出货损货差的索赔，而且不是依据任何运输合约(主要是提单)的关系，基本的诉因是分为三大类：第一类也是最常见的就是侵权中的疏忽(negligence)。第二类是承运人作为托管人违反了谨慎照顾的托管责任(breach duty as bailee)。第三类也是侵权，指承运人错误干预货物(wrongful interference with cargo)。以下将会对这三种类别的诉因作出分析以及它们各自的要求与局限，如它们也是有诉权的问题，即什么人才能以它作为诉因向承运人提出索赔。

11.1　类别之一：疏忽(negligence)

疏忽是侵权的一个主要诉因，而疏忽的发生会在两种情况下。一是疏忽的一方与受害的一方就相关的争议有同步的合约关系(concurrent contractual relationship)，

[1]　杨良宜：《国际商务游戏规则——英国合约法》，中国政法大学出版社 2000 年版。

这一来法律已经很明确他们之间的争议，包括他们的权利与责任，都是由合约所主导，任何一方不能以索赔的诉因改为侵权或者托管回避合约的规定：Tai Hing v. Liu Chong Hing Bank（1985）2 Lloyd's Rep 313；China & South Sea Bank v. Tan（1990）1 A. C. 536。但本段探讨的是第二种情况，也就是疏忽一方与受害一方没有同步合约关系，他们之间只能是以侵权作为诉因。

侵权是要求所有的人都有一个谨慎责任（duty of care）避免无辜第三人受到损害，这一责任在著名的Donoghue v. Stevenson（1932）A. C. 562先例中得到确立。特别是在法院考虑应否强加这一谨慎责任在某一类人士，会考虑关系是否接近（proximity），这也就是Atkin勋爵在上述先例中提到的“邻居”（neighbor）原则。另一个考虑就是第三人受到损害是否可以预见（foreseeable）。再一个重要的考虑是强加这一谨慎责任从整体上看是否合理与公平（reasonable and just）。

这里不是详细介绍这一方面的法律，毕竟侵权法也是非常复杂，可见《Clerk & Lindsell on Torts》等的权威书籍。但笔者不妨简单介绍一下为什么要有以上的构成要件。针对“邻居”原则，主要是为了避免侵权被任何人作为诉因无限制扩大。如司机开车对路人负有谨慎责任，如果因为司机疏忽驾驶而撞伤路人，这就是一个典型的路人对司机的侵权之诉，而司机与路人的“邻居”关系也是非常明确的。但是因为路人被撞伤，他的家人受到影响而蒙受损失，如他的太太因为要照顾他而被迫辞职，他的工作单位因为他的受伤而蒙受损失等。这时他的太太与他的工作单位与司机就没有“邻居”的关系而不能享有以侵权作为诉因起诉司机的权利。针对本章所探讨的海上货物运输，可以说是作为托管人或者分托管人等参与有关运输过程的人士（不论是装卸小工、仓库所有人、二程船船东等），他们与货方的关系密切，“邻居”原则的满足是不会有问题的。

至于第二个构成要件的损害是否可以预见，也是为了局限侵权赔偿的范围。换言之，这一个避免无辜第三人受到损害的谨慎责任只是针对某些损害（specific category of loss）。在较早前就已经谈到过侵权作为诉因不包括纯经济损失（pure economic loss），而只能是实际损失（physical loss or damage）。针对海上货物运输，典型的实际损失包括了火灾，货物被淡水或者海水浸泡，温度太高或太低造成货物品质损坏，货物在高处坠落损坏，货物堆装不妥而被压坏等。如果货物的所有权被永久剥夺，如货物被盗或是误交给其他人，这也算是一个实际损失：East West Corpn v. DKBS（2003）Q. B. 1509。还会有情况是一些货物如钢材在装卸过程中不慎掉落入海，虽然它本身不会因入海而受损但将其打捞起来的费用大大高于它本身的价值，不会有人做而变成实际损失，这就类似于船舶保险的推定全损（constructive total loss）。显然，疏忽造成了这种损失属于可以预见，所以侵权的法律是强加谨慎责任去避免造成这种损失。

但在贵族院的The“Nicholas H”（1996）A. C. 211先例中，还首次提出了实际损失可以分为直接（direct）与间接（indirect），而谨慎责任主要是针对避免直接的实际损失。该先例在本章 10.1 段有简单介绍案情，就是货方以侵权起诉日本船级社，(NKK)因为其检查疏忽让不适航的船舶开航而导致船货全损。贵族院的 Steyn 勋爵这样说："Counsel for the cargo owners argued that the present case involved the infliction of direct physical loss. At first glance the issue of directness may seem a matter of terminology rather than substance. In truth it is a material factor. The law more readily attaches the consequences of actionable negligence to directly inflicted physical loss than to indirectly inflicted physical loss. For example, if the N. K. K. surveyor had carelessly dropped a lighted cigarette into a cargo hold known to contain a combustible cargo, thereby causing an explosion and the loss of the vessel and cargo, the assertion that the classification society was in breach of a duty of care might have been a strong one. That would be a paradigm case of directly inflicted physical loss... The role of the N. K. K. was a subsidiary one. In my view the carelessness of the N. K. K. surveyor did not involve the direct infliction of physical damage in the relevant sense. That by no means concludes the answer to the general question. But it does introduce the right perspective on one aspect of this case."

但看来直接或者间接的实际损失在英国法律还没有太明确，这可以节录 Aikens 大法官著的《Bills of Lading》2006 年版之 9.12 段所说如下："The nature and relevance of the distinction between direct and indirect physical loss has yet to be fully explored in the courts, but what was perceived by Lord Steyn 'at first glance' has much to commend it....."。而在解释直接与间接实际损失的脚注中进一步说："Although the difficulties with the concept are touched upon in *Perrett v. Collins* (1998) 2 Lloyd's Rep. 255, a personal injury case. That case is in itself not without difficulty: for e. g., Hobhouse L. J.'s suggestion that the reasoning in *The Nicholas H* 'was essentially directed to considerations relevant to economic loss' (p. 264) is, with respect, not an accurate assessment of the issues in the case, where, throughout, the classification society accepted it was a case of physical damage."

在贵族院的 The"Nicholas H"(1996) A. C. 211 中，主要判 NKK 针对货方没有这一个谨慎责任还是根据另一个重要的考虑是从整体上看不是合理与公平(reasonable and just)，所以不强加给日本船级社一个侵权疏忽的责任。

11.1.1　针对侵权的疏忽：谁有诉权？

这一类别的诉因对于海上货物运输的参与方来说是非常重要的，所以还要针对其他的方面探讨，其中之一就是谁有诉权。这方面可以节录贵族院重要的先例 The "Aliakmon"(1986) 2 Lloyd's Rep 1 中所说："in order to enable a person to claim in negligence for loss caused to him by reason of loss of or damage to property, he must have had either the legal ownership of or a possessory title to the property concerned at the time when the loss or damage occurred, and it is not enough for him to have only had contractual rights in relation to such property which have been adversely affected by the loss of or damage to it. ”

简单解释以上原则就是在货物/财产发生损失或者损害时，对货物/财产享有合法所有权（legal ownership）或者占有权（possessory title）的人士才能拥有诉权。这可以租船为例来讲，就是两艘船舶发生碰撞，碰撞是由于 A 船的疏忽而导致，造成无辜 B 船的损失。显然 B 可以侵权向 A 提出索赔损失，而由于双方没有合约的关系也不会存在《海牙—维斯比规则》下航行疏忽可以免责。B 包括 B 船的原船东，因为他是 B 船的合法所有权人，他可向 A 船索赔因为他的航行疏忽而造成的 B 船的实际损失并加上由此带来的经济损失，如船舶因为需要修理带来的延误。如果碰撞未给 B 船造成实际损失（这看来是不大可能，因为碰撞总会造成实际损失，总不会连油漆也不刮掉一些），但由于港口当局对事故调查而延误船舶开航进而导致船舶错过租约的销约期，这样一来，错过销约期的损失是纯经济损失，无法以侵权下的疏忽作为诉因向 A 船索赔。

至于 B 船上的货物，它的合法所有权人（也就是货方如当时的提单持有人），如果因为碰撞而造成货损货差，他也可以侵权直接向 A 船提出索赔。但如果 B 船是出租，承租人的损失就值得进一步分析了。首先假设 B 船是光租给 C 的光租承租人（demise charterer），由于光租涉及了占有船舶，所以 C 的实际损失加上经济损失，他可以侵权向 A 提出索赔。但如果这不是光租，C 只是一个期租承租人（time charterer），这样就比较尴尬了。因为期租承租人并不占有船舶，只是拥有船舶的使用权，加上期租承租人显然不是船舶的合法所有权人。换言之，期租承租人即使在碰撞中受到损害，他都不能以侵权的诉因向 A 船提出索赔。加上期租承租人通常的损失是纯经济损失，如没有办法在市场高涨的时候营运而蒙受利润损失，因为 B 船需要长时间修理。这类先例有 Chargeurs Reunis Compagnie Francaise de Navigation a Vapeur v. English & American Shipping Co.，（1921）9 Lloyd's Rep. 464；The“World Harmony”（1965）1 Lloyd's Rep. 244 与 The“Mineral Transporter”（1985）2 Lloyd's 303。其中在 The“Mineral Transporter”，枢密院的 Fraser 勋爵这样说：“This issue is one of fundamental importance in maritime law and in the law of negligence generally. There is a long line of authority in the United Kingdom for the proposition that a time charterer is not entitled to recover for pecuniary loss caused by damage by a third party to the chartered vessel. The reason is that a time charterer has no proprietary or possessory right in the chartered vessel; his only right in relation vessel is contractual...”

以下对有诉权的合法所有权人与占有权人进一步探讨。

11.1.1.1 合法所有权人（legal ownership）

涉及海上货物运输，货物或财产的合法所有权人通常也拥有占有权（possessory right）或马上占有的权利（immediate possessory right），所以他们有诉权，可以向侵权人提出索赔损失是没有问题的。

在海上货物运输谁是货物的合法所有权人（legal ownership）也是值得探讨的。

如在 CIF 或 CFR 的买卖中,在货物越过船舷时风险也转移给买方或收货人,但是在实际发生货损货差时,由于代表货物所有权的提单还没有背书与交出给收货人,这代表收货人不能以货物的合法所有权人的身份以侵权向船舶或承运人索赔。但在正常的情况下,收货人根本不需要以侵权向船舶或承运人索赔,因为在他合法持有提单后,可以根据 1992 年《海上货物运输法》以提单合约的关系向承运人提出索赔。而如果提单一直没有交出给收货人(如提单有不符点而无法结汇),这等于货物在航次中的风险并没有转移给收货人,而是在持有提单的发货人。所以也不存在收货人需要以侵权向船舶或承运人索赔,因为货损货差的真正损失也不在收货人。这方面可节录 Brandon 勋爵在 The"Aliakmon"(1986) 2 Lloyd's Rep 1 中所说:

"My Lords, under the usual kind of c. i. f. or c. and f. (或是现在所称的 CFR) contract of sale, the risk in the goods passes from the seller to the buyer on shipment, as is exemplified by the obligation of the buyer to take up and pay for the shipping documents even though the goods may already have suffered damage or loss during their carriage by sea. The property in the goods, however, does not pass until the buyer takes up and pays for the shipping documents. Those include a bill of lading relating to the goods which has been endorsed by the seller in favour of the buyer. By acquiring the bill of lading so endorsed the buyer becomes a person to whom the property in the goods has passed upon or by reason of such endorsement, and so, by virtue of section 1 of the Bills of Lading Act 1855(该法已经被 1992 年《海上货物运输法》所取代), has vested in him all the rights of suit, and is subject to the same liabilities in respect of the goods, as if the contract contained in the bill of lading had been made with him.

In terms of the present case this means that, if the buyers had completed the c. and f. contract in the manner intended, they would have been entitled to sue the shipowners for the damage to the goods in contract under the bill of lading, and no question of any separate duty of care in tort would have arisen. . . . "

另一种情况就是所谓的"公平所有权"(equitable ownership)或公平权益,这主要是区分与合法所有权或合法权益的不同。举例说在一个有限公司,他名下所有的财产合法所有权人都属于该有限公司,而公司的股东即使是大股东甚至是享有 100% 股权的股东,他对这些财产也只是有一个公平权益。在海上货物运输,以前经常会出现的情况是运送不可分割的大宗货物(indivisable bulk),如一船两万吨的玉米分别属于三个不同的收货人。根据英国《货物销售法》,针对种类货物,其所有权转移的前提是货物已经被独立分开并以各种标识明确表明是某一买卖合同项下的货物。这样一来,直到货物安全抵达卸港并区分开为三个买卖合同项下的货物,货物的合法所有权才会转移给个别收货人。在这之前,即使收货人取得代表货物所有权的提单,但都不能被视为是合法的所有权人,而只能是公平所有权人。这一问题已经在 1995 年对《货物销售法》的修改而得到解决,在这里只是为了介绍这一个不同之处,就是在以前的立法下,发货人一直属于合法所有权人,直到大宗货能够归于(appropriate)个别的合同。而收货人即使是已经支付了货款也只能是作为公平所有权人,直到卸港把货物分开后才变为合法所有权人。而作为公平所有权人并非对货物占有,不能以侵权向船舶或承运人提出索赔,这是 Brandon 勋爵在 The"Aliakmon"中所说如下:"In my view, the first proposition cannot be supported. There may be cases where a person who is the equitable owner of certain goods has also a possessory title to them. In such a case he is entitled, by virtue of his possessory title rather than his equitable ownership, to sue in tort for negligence anyone whose want of care has caused loss of or damage to the goods without joining the legal owner as a party to the action: see for instance Healey v. Healey [1915] 1 K. B. 938. If, however, the person is the equitable owner of the goods and no more, then he must join the legal owner as a party to the action, either as co-plaintiff if he is willing or as co-defendant if he is not. This has always been the law in the field of equitable ownership of land and I see no reason why it should not also be so in the field of equitable ownership of goods."

与本段的第一段有所不同的是所有权人如果对他的货物或者财产没有占有权,也没有马上可以占有的权利(但这是相对如货物是在其代理人的手中,如果需要可以马上取回,这是有马上占有权),他对实际损失的诉权还会有其他的变化,如有关的货物或者财产被质押(pledge),而在这一期间因为第三人的侵权造成损坏。这一来,向第三人索赔的诉权主要还是在质权人(pledgee),他并非实际拥有损坏的货物或财产,他只拥有占有权。而质押人(pledgor)所能向第三人索赔的只是一种所谓"暂时或永久被剥夺了复归权益"(deprivation either temporarily or permanently of the benefit of his reversionary interest)。这是指一些情况就是在质押期届满应该把货物或者财产归还给所有人或质押人时,这些损坏还是没有或者无法弥补,导致所有人或质押人有真正的损失:HSBC Rail (UK) Ltd v. Network Rail Infrastructure Ltd (2006) 1 Lloyd's Rep. 358。这种情况也适用在光船租约(bareboat or demise charterparty),原船东由于对船舶没有占有权或马上可以占有的权利,也会受到同样的局限。显然在这种情况下,能够向侵权人索赔损失局限得多了。恰当的索赔还是应该由光船承租人作为对船舶有占有权向侵权人提出索赔。

11.1.1.2　占有权人(possessory title)

首先要说明的就是占有权人可以向第三人的侵权索赔所有的实际损失,即使他本人并没有遭受损失。这一点与货物或者财产的所有权人不一样,所有权人必须证明他真正的损失才能向第三人索赔。占有权人如果本人没有损失(如根据他与所有权人的合约不必要为损坏负责,也无须把损坏修好之后才交还给所有权人),他成功向第三人的侵权人索赔是要把取回来的钱退还给所有权人。这被视为索赔损失必须是除了证明被告有责任外,还必须证明原告有真正损失的一个例外情况,在本章较早时也提到过另一种例外情况,即在第 3 段中的 Dunlop v. Lambert (1839) 6 Cl & F 68

与 The"Albazero"(1976) 2 Lloyd's Rep. 467 先例。这里是可以节录上诉庭的 Longmore 大法官在 HSBC Rail (UK) Ltd v. Network Rail Infrastructure Ltd (2006) 1 Lloyd's Rep. 358 先例中所讲：

"It is trite law that a claimant cannot sue in negligence unless he has suffered damage and can then only recover to the extent that he has been damnified(这就是上述所讲的所有权人必须证明他有真正的损失才能以侵权提出索赔). Apart from well-established exceptions (like that of the bailee as settled in The Winkfield [1902] P 42) he can recover only for loss that he has suffered not for loss that somebody else has suffered. The appropriate measure of damage is:

'that sum of money which will put the party who has been injured, or who has suffered, in the same position as he would have been in if he had not sustained the wrong for which he is now getting his compensation or reparation': see Livingstone v Rawyards Coal Co (1880) 5 App Cas 25, 39, per Lord Blackburn.

If one ignores insurance for the moment, the position in the present case is that HSBC has been paid the full value of the carriages which were beyond repair and the repairable carriages have been repaired. In these circumstances whatever may have been the position shortly after the derailment occurred HSBC is now not out of pocket in any way and, on ordinary principles, has suffered no loss and can make no recovery.

It is true that there are exceptions to this principle. Most of the exceptions occur in the law of contract in cases in which the contract (although not a contract of agency) can be regarded as a contract made for the benefit of persons other than the contracting party. These exceptions are considered by Lord Diplock in his speech in The Albazero [1977] AC 774, 846-847 in which he said, however, that the particular exception he was considering (viz the right of a consignor to recover damages from the carrier even when he had been paid for the goods) should not be"extended beyond what is justified by its rationale". Even fewer exceptions in a mercantile context exist in tort; the primary exception is that of The Winkfield which decided that a bailee in possession, or with the immediate right to possession, can sue for the full value of the goods, even if he is not liable to the true owner.

But HSBC(本案中的原告)can cite no authority in support of their proposition that a goods-owner without possession, or the immediate right to possession, can recover the value of the goods even where he has been compensated by his bailee. In both The Charlotte [1908] P 206 and Obestain Inc v National Mineral Development Corpn Ltd [1987] 1 Lloyd's Rep 465 the claimants were goods-owners with the right to possession at the time of the loss. It was held that they could recover the value of the goods even though they had been paid by the persons to whom the goods had been sold. Normally of course ownership carries with it the right to possession and thus the right to sue for full value but Hobhouse J put the law correctly in the latter case when he said, at p 468:

'It has long been settled law that the owner of goods is entitled to sue and recover damages in respect of loss or damage to those goods. The only qualification is that, if he is suing in tort, his claim may be defeated if his title was a bare proprietary one and did not include any right to possession of the goods.'"

在该先例中,案情涉及了 HSBC 是有关财产的所有权人,但该财产被 HSBC 质押并在质押期间受到损坏,本来质权人可以向被告提出索赔,但在他们之间有关的协议中有一条赔偿责任限制的条文会适用。这一来,HSBC 希望以所有权人的名义向侵权人的被告提出索赔,想避开责任限制条文的适用,但在高院与上诉庭都败诉。其中高院的 Steel 大法官对财产没有占有权的所有权人的诉权作出以下总结:"(1) a lessor or bailor of chattels, who was not entitled to possession during the term of the lease, could only sue for damage to his reversionary interest; (2) damage was essential to the tort of negligence and that unless there was damage to the reversionary interest no action would lie; (3) there could be no damage to the reversionary interest unless there was permanent damage to the chattel; (4) any damage which could not be remedied would constitute permanent damage; (5) any damage which could be remedied but was not going to be remedied would likewise constitute such permanent damage; (6) where the subject of complaint is remedied or renewed during the term, the lessor or bailor cannot sue; (7) on the facts, the carriages had been repaired or HSBC had been compensated for their value so no cause of action accrued and HSBC could not, therefore, recover; (8) the fact that the source of the repair and compensation was insurance monies made no difference to that conclusion."

占有权通常就是指对货物有实际的占有。显然,作为托管人(实际承运人或仓库所有人等)或分托管人都会在不同时间实际占有货物,占有权人也可以通过他的代理人占有货物,但如果是通过独立承包商占有就不足够。

这里可介绍 Transcontainer v Custodian Security (1988) 1 Lloyd's Rep 128 先例,案情是关于一家英国进口商名为 Duty Free 从法国进口了 400 箱白兰地酒,并委托了一家名为 Transcontainer 的公司安排运输,而 Transcontainer 又把该运输在英国的部分分包给一家名为 Crossland 公司。整个运输环节开始是以 Duty Free 作为发货人把 400 箱白兰地酒装进集装箱,并交给 Transcontainer 在法国当地的一家拖曳公司将其拖到火车上再交给 French Railway,由 French Railway 运到法国加来港口,最后由 Townsend Thoresen 的船公司运到英国的多佛港。在多佛港是由 Crossland 将集装箱拖到码头的停驿站而并非目的地的 Feltham,码头停驿站是由 Central Electricity Board 拥有并由 Custodian Security 负责 24 小时保安。但第二天一早运载白兰地的卡车与其装载的集装箱被发现不见了,直到 3 天后卡车才被发现,但集装箱里装载的白兰地已经被偷走。Transcontainer 根据与 Duty Free 之间的运输合约把 400 箱白兰地的损失赔付给 Duty Free。之后,Transcontainer 并非与 Crossland 的合约关系起诉 Crossland,而是以侵权为诉因直接起诉疏忽行为的 Custodian Security,因为他就是负责码头停驿站的保安事宜。这样直接告 Custodian Security 其中的好处是跳过了几重的合约关系,如 Transcontainer 与 Crossland 以及 Crossland 可能与 Central Electricity Board 的关系,最后是 Central Electricity Board 与 Custodian Security 的合约关系。Transcontainer 指控说当白兰地酒储存在码头停驿站的时候 Custodian Security 要对白兰地酒尽一切托管人的合理谨慎看管的责任,而 Custodian Security 违背了这一个责任。

在一审法院,Boreham 大法官判 Transcontainer 败诉。Boreham 大法官认定 Custodian Security 确实没有尽到合理谨慎看管白兰地酒的责任而导致白兰地酒的丢失。但是 Transcontainer 必须对这票白兰地酒有占有权(因为他不会是白兰地酒的合法所有权人),否则没有侵权的诉权。这里证明 Transcontainer 有占有权有几个困难:一是在被偷走时实际占有这票白兰地酒的是 Crossland 或是 Central Electricity Board,但他们都不是 Transcontainer 的代理人而是独立承包商,所以 Transcontainer 没办法说是通过其代理人推定占有(constructive possess)这票白兰地酒。这可节录上诉庭的 Slade 大法官所说的如下:"We have been told that, at a much earlier stage in the hearing, before all the evidence had been called, Custodian's Counsel, Mr Janathan Harvie, had expressly accepted that, if Crossland was properly to be regarded as Transcontainer's agent, then at the material time Transcontainer had possession of the goods. However, his contention was that Crossland was not an agent but an independent subcontractor."

另一个困难是 Transcontainer 希望能够接受他是白兰地酒的托管人(bailee),并由他把白兰地酒的占有权转交给 Crossland 作为分托管人(sub-bailee)。作为托管人,就表示占有权的存在。Slade 大法官有以下的说法:"The obvious difficulty facing Transcontainer in this context is that Transcontainer did not have physical control of the goods at the time of the theft and, indeed, had never had physical control of them. In the Court below Transcontainer's Counsel, Mr. Brunner, sought to meet this difficulty by presenting their case throughout on the basis that (a) Transcontainer were bailees of the goods, and (b) it necessarily followed from this that Transcontainer had possession of them."

但这里的困难是 Transcontainer 从来没有占有过这票白兰地酒,而是直接由 Crossland 在多佛港提货然后被偷走。不存在 Transcontainer 占有后才交出给 Crossland 作为分托管人占有。这种情况下,Transcontainer 可被称为 quasi-bailee,但不能算是真正的托管人。这一个法律地位也可举 Metaalhandel v. Ardfields & Jones (1988) 1 Lloyd's Rep. 197,案情涉及了 Metaalhandel 与 Ardfields 的仓库所有人同意把前者的货物寄存在他的仓库里,但由于 Ardfields 的仓库不够位置摆放,遂要求第二被告 Jones 直接把货物存放在他的仓库里。"Ardfields were never in possession of the goods: it was Jones who collected them on Jan. 26 and thereafter stored them at their warehouse at Ashford. I seems to me, on the authorities, that Ardfields were therefore never bailees. This affects the onus of proof ..."所以最后在高院与上诉庭,Transcontainer 因为没有诉权

而无法向疏忽的 Custodian Security 取得补偿。

另一提的是,货物的质权人(pledgee)有足够的权利以侵权的诉因起诉:The Future Express (1993) 2 Lloyd's Rep 542。这方面已经在较早时包括上一小段有详细的介绍。

11.2 类别之二:违反了谨慎照顾的托管责任(breach duty as bailee)

托管人的责任在货物运输通常是根据托管的条件合理谨慎看管货物,并在托管完结时或在委托人提出要求交还的时候交还给委托人。这一责任与侵权的疏忽有一些微妙的差别,就是在侵权下,有一个谨慎责任不对货物造成损坏。但托管的责任还涉及了保护受委托的货物不让它受损失或灭失。

在普通法下,是由委托人证明货物在托管期间发生了损坏或损失。之后是由托管人去证明这损坏或损失不是他的过错所造成。但如果委托人与托管人之间有合约关系,就会受到有关条文的约束。例如,承运人作为货物的托管人可以依赖《海牙规则》或《海牙—维斯比规则》的免责条文作为抗辩。

针对托管,经常会出现的争议就是指称托管人没有足够谨慎看管货物(inadequate care of cargo)与没有获得授权处理货物(unauthorized dealing)。在后者的情况,一个严重的例子就是把货物装在一个没有授权与不合适的地方,如舱内货装在甲板。这会带来严重的后果,如托管人会被剥夺合约的免责条文的保护并需要严格对货物损失负责:Lilley v Doubleday (1880-81) LR 7 QBD 510;Edwards v Newland (1950) 2 KB 534;The Kapetan Petko Voivoda (2003) 2 Lloyd's Rep 1。

另一个也是严重的例子,就是在没有授权下把货物转交给分承包商或分托管人(如在没有授权的允许下用二程船运载货物)。在这种情况下,没有授权的托管人要对分托管人的疏忽造成货物损失负责,这可节录 Metaalhandel v Ardfields (1988) 1 Lloyd's Rep 197 中 Gatehouse 大法官所说的如下:"I was referred to several authorities and to Palmer on Bailment, where all those authorities are examined. In particular the text of Palmer, from pp. 829-831, deals with the obligations to the bailor of the bailee who enters into an authorised sub-bailment. The better view, says the learned author, is that the bailee is liable for the negligence of the sub-bailee, citing BRS Ltd v Arthur Crutchley Ltd (1968) 1 Lloyd's Rep 271; (1968) 1 All ER 811 and Morris v CW Martin & Sons Ltd (1965) 2 Lloyd's Rep 63; (19660 1 QB 716."

在上述两种没有获得授权处理货物的严重违反托管的条件,在 Aikens 大法官所著的《Bills of Lading》2006 年版之 9.51 段有提到,并可节录如下:"The two most common examples of the latter are parting with possession to a sub-contractor or sub-bailee (for example by transhipment) and storing the goods in unauthorised place (such as on deck). Although liability in such circumstances will depend on the terms of the bailment, the bailee may be either deprived of contractual exceptions on the basis that he has gone outside 'the four corners of the contract' and so render himself strictly liable for the loss and damage, thus losing the benefit of exemptions he might have if he had merely taken inadequate care of the cargo."

但即使是在授权下把货物转交给分承包商或分托管人(这种情况在今天的多式联运中经常发生),货物因分托管人的疏忽造成货物损失,托管人还是要对委托人负责。所以有一个说法是托管人对货物谨慎照顾的托管责任是不能下放的(non-delegable)。因为托管人即使是能够获得授权下放他对合约的履行,但他也不能下放他的责任。这也是在 Metaalhandel v Ardfields 先例中有说明的,如下:"Palmer concludes that the position of the quasi-bailee is the same as that of a true bailee, namely, that he is answerable for the faults of his sub-contractor because, although he is entitled to delegate performance, he cannot delegate his responsibility."

根据托管(bailment)向违反了谨慎照顾的托管责任的托管人(bailee)索赔,诉权是在委托人(bailor)。如果涉及一连串的分托管,通常有诉权的是原委托人(head bailor)。但每一个中间的委托人向下一个托管人也有诉权索赔他实际的损失。

11.3　类别之三:承运人错误干预货物(wrongful interference with cargo)

这个新的诉因实际是根据《Torts (Interference with Goods) Act 1977》(或简称"TIGA")的立法,它主要是针对货方的货物或者所有权人的财产受到第三人的错误干预,例如把它侵占或不合法使用。立法的原因主要是在过去 150 年的普通法把这一方面的法律变得非常混乱与复杂,它涉及几种不同的侵权,而且经常会出现重复。这些不同的侵权包括:"非法侵入"(tresspass);"非法侵占"(conversion);"非法占有"(detinue);"复归损失"(reversionary injury)。举一个例子来说明它们之间的重复与细微的不同情况就会造成不同的诉因:如果 A 非法潜入 B 的车子,这就构成非法侵入。如果接下来 A 把该车子偷走,这就构成了非法侵入与非法侵占。如果 B 的车子属于有条件的买卖(conditional sale)或租购(hire purchase),涉及了一家财务公司的 C,这对 A 而言就造成对 C 的复归损失。也会有情况发生就是 A 干预 B 的财产但其间没有构成非法侵入、非法侵占、非法占有与复归损失。这一来,A 也不构成任何侵权的行为。在 British Economic Lamp Co v. Empire, Mile End (1913) 29 TLR 386 中,被告的房东拒绝让原告进入取回他的财产(如原告在搬走的时候留下的财产),这被判是被告不构成侵权。

11.3.1　有关侵权与非法占有等的立法

在英国普通法,有不少案例开始把非法侵占逐步扩大适用在许多不同的情况,由于非法侵占是与非法占有这个概念非常接近,所以"非法占有"(detinue)这一概念在普通法开始式微。简单介绍这两种概念的不同之处:非法占有与侵占的区别在于前者先是合法持有货物或者财产(多数是在托管的关系下),而后在所有权人向其要求归还货物或财产的时候而不予归还或者将货物或者财产损坏或丢失。另是非法占有被视为对物(*in rem*)的诉讼(因为非法占有通常代表财产还在,法院可以下令归还),但非法侵占是属于对人(*in personam*)的诉讼(因为非法侵占通常代表财产已经失去,救济往往只能是向侵权人索赔金钱损失）。还有，在普通法下的损失计算也不同。这可以节录 General and Finance Facilities Ltd v Cook Cars (Romford) Ltd (1963) 1 WLR 644 先例中，Diplock 大法官说：

"There are important distinctions between a cause of action in conversion and a cause of action in detinue. The former is a single wrongful act and the cause of action accrues at the date of conversion; the latter is a continuing cause of action which accrues at the date of the wrongful refusal to deliver up the goods and continues until delivery up of the goods or judgment in the action for detinue.

The action in conversion is a purely personal action and results in a judgment for pecuniary damages only. The judgment is for a single sum of which the measure is generally the value of the chattel at the date of the conversion together with any consequential damage flowing from the conversion and not too remote to be recoverable in law...

On the other hand the action in detinue partakes of the nature of an action *in rem* in which the plaintiff seeks specific restitution of his chattel. At common law it resulted in a judgment for delivery up of the chattel or payment of its value as assessed, and for payment of damages for its detention..."

这导致了在 1971 年，英国的法律改革小组建议把有关的法律概念合理化与简化，由此产生了 1977 年的 TIGA 的立法。在 TIGA，Section 1 创造出了一个新的侵权诉因名为对财产的错误干预（wrongful interference with goods），而这是包括了非法侵占（conversion）、非法侵入财产（trespass to goods）、由疏忽导致对财产或附加其上的利益的损害（negligence so far at it results in damage to goods or to an interest in goods.）、任何其他侵权行为对于财产或附加其上的利益的损害（any other tort so far as it results in damage to goods or to an interest in goods）。注意是以上四种并没有包括非法占有（detinue），因为在该立法中，非法占有的概念被废除。另一提的是香港还没有这方面的立法，所以还要以英国普通法的地位为准。

11.3.2　侵权与非法占有是严格或绝对责任

非法侵占在历史上一直被视为是严格或绝对责任，这里带来的危险就是参与处理被非法侵占的货物但却不知内情的无辜第三方会受到牵连而负责，如在 Hardman v. Booth (1863) 1 H. & C. 803 先例中负责拍卖被侵占货物的拍卖行。Diplock 勋爵在 Marfani & Co. Ltd v. Midland Bank Ltd (1968) 1 WLR 956 中所说：

"... one of the consequences of the historic origin of the tort of conversion and its application to negotiate instruments as 'goods' is that the tort at common law is one of strict liability in which the moral concept of fault in the sense of either knowledge by the doer of an act that it is likely to cause injury loss or damage to another, or lack of reasonable care to avoid causing injury, loss or damage to another, plays no part.

At common law, one's duty to one's neighbour who is the owner, or entitled to possession, of any goods is to refrain from doing any voluntary act in relation to his goods which is a usurpation of his proprietary or possessory rights in them. Subject to some exceptions which are irrelevant for the purposes of the present case, it matters not that the doer of the act of usurpation did not know, and could not by the exercise of reasonable care have known, of his neighbour's interest in the goods. The duty is absolute; he acts at his peril."

以上所讲的严格或绝对责任在普通法或是 TIGA 以及其他的立法中有许多例外的情况。这包括是:代理人不知道也无意改变财产的所有权、托管人按照委托人的命令行事、非自愿的托管人、被告能够显示他或者他的委托人有一个更好的权利、禁止翻供等。至于立法的例外包括为了保护银行的 1957 年的《支票法》Section 4,保护清盘人的 1986 年《破产法》Section 234(3)与 Section 307(4),保护典当行的 1974 年《消费者信用法》之 Section 117。关于这些例外情况可以不必承担严格或绝对责任,本书不再多讲,详情请参阅 Clerk & Lindsell on Torts(19 edn., Sweet & Maxwell, 2005),从 17-70 段开始。

11.3.3 TIGA 的三种救济

在 TIGA 下,错误干预货物会带来 Section 3 所列明的三种救济的其中一种,如下:(1) 法院作出命令要求把非法侵占的货物归还并且以金钱赔偿间接损失(an order for delivery of the goods, and for payment of any consequential damages);(2) 法院作出命令要求把非法侵占的货物归还,但给被告有一个选择就是以赔偿货物价格与间接损失来代替归还货物(an order for delivery of the goods, but giving the defendant the alternative of paying damages by reference to the value of the goods, together in either alternative with payment of any consequential damages);(3) 损失赔偿(damages)。

上述救济(1)不允许被告有赔偿货物价格的选择,而是必须要归还侵占的货物。但是否会作出这种命令则纯粹是法院的裁量权,这表示在一些情况如货物可以在市场买到,金钱的赔偿就已经足够,法院就不会作出归还货物的命令。至于救济(2)与(3)是可以让原告选择。其中救济(3)是不再要求归还货物而只要求金钱赔偿。这赔偿分两个部分,第一部分是货物的价值,第二部分是间接损失。这间接损失只要不是太不可预见或遥远,都可以包括在内。这在《Clerk & Lindsell on Torts》(19 edn, Sweet & Maxwell, 2005)有提到这间接损失是包括像被侵占货物或财产可赚取的利润损失:Bodley v. Reynolds (1846) 8 QB 779;失去了买家:Williams v. Peel River Land Co. (1886) 55 LT 689,Oakley v. Lyster (1931) 1 KB 148;货物被侵占直到法院作出判决期间的货物价格上涨:The "Playa Larga" (1983) 2 Lloyd's Rep. 171;货物或财产被侵占所带来的不便:Carlisly v. Chief Constable, RUC (1988) 9 NIJB 1;货物或财产被侵占所带来的精神痛苦:Grahan v. Voigt (1989) 89 ALR 11;Trafigura Beheer BV and another v. Mediterranean Shipping Company SA (2007) EWHC 944 (Comm)等等。在《Clerk & Lindsell on Torts》第 17-103 段其中部分可以节录如下:"The claimant may recover all such damages as are the natural and direct result of the conversion, for example the cost of hiring a replacement, loss of profits to be made from the chattel, or the loss of a purchaser for it, or (where appropriate) a rise in value between the time of conversion and the time of judgment. However, the mere capacity for profitable use is normally reckoned as included in the capital value of a chattel; where it is, the loss of such use is not a separate head of damage, for if so the claimant would, *pro tanto*, recover twice over. Consequential losses may in addition encompass non-pecuniary interests, such as inconvenience and distress at being deprived of one's property. To be recoverable a given head of consequential damage must have been reasonably foreseeable to the hypothetical converter at the time of conversion, except it seems where the converter knew he was acting wrongly."

这里只介绍最近2007年的先例 Trafigura Beheer BV and another v. Mediterranean Shipping Company SA (2007) EWHC 944 (Comm),案情涉及了几个集装箱的 copper cathodes 货物被第三人伪造报关单与提单提走,导致在上海卸港的真正电子提单持有人无法从承运人 MSC 那里提到货物。后来,提单持有人向承运人在英国法院提出诉讼,因为有关的提单合约是有英国法院的管辖权条文。MSC 虽然也是受害者,但由于侵占货物是严格或绝对责任,所以承认了侵占的责任。双方的争议是针对其他方面,与本段有关的就是根据1977年 TIGA 的的救济办法与损失计算。由于在英国法院作出判决的时候被侵占的货物是在上海,并且已经在上海海事法院等待判决如何处理,所以英国法院不愿意给予 TIGA 下的第一种救济,也就是不愿意判令归还货物,只能以损失赔偿真正的提单持有人/原告。首先是有关被侵占货物的价格,这在 TIGA 第二种救济是说明要参考货物价格(by reference to the value of the goods),这被判是可以依照在货物被侵占的一天或者任何其他日子的货物价格。在该先例中,由于被侵占货物最后被怎么样处理很不肯定,恐怕一直要到上海海事法院作出判决后才会明朗。所以法院判是以英国法院判决的一天为准认定被侵占货物价格。

另外,第二种救济也说明可以加上所有的间接损失(any consequential damages)。这被判是必须能够合理预见(reasonably foreseeable),而不仅指一些因为货物被侵占所直接与自然带来的损失(directly and naturally flows from the conversion)。而在这一先例中,其中一项重要的间接损失是原告因为这票货被侵占而遭受对冲合约(hedging contract)的损失。法院判在集装箱的运输,承运人不会理会集装箱里面到底是什么货物,所以对冲损失并非可以合理预见。所以不能在 TIGA 下把这笔损失取回来。

以上只是很粗略的介绍,因为 TIGA 与有关的侵权不是本书要针对的内容。另一提的是货物在运输与转手过程中被侵占的问题,笔者在所著的其他书中也有详及,其中也有比较更详细的介绍1977年的 TIGA 立法。[1]

---

〔1〕 具体可参见杨良宜:《国际货物买卖》,中国政法大学出版社1999年版,第七章;杨良宜:《提单及其他付运单证》,中国政法大学出版社2001年版,第二章第5段。

11.3.4 针对海上货物运输以 TIGA 作为诉因的情况

以下转去介绍与本书有关的方面。首先,针对海上货物运输,以 TIGA 作为诉因的货损货差索赔包括:

1. Misdelivery:这种违反 TIGA 最常见的情况就是无单交货(正如先例 Trafigura Beheer BV and another v. Mediterranean Shipping Company SA (2007) EWHC 944 (Comm)),但也可以包括其他的情况。如经常会有船东或者承运人声称去留置货物,因为还欠下运费或滞期费。如果船东或者承运人提出这一要求不正确(如提单已经注明是运费已付或是对滞期费的要求是狮子大开口等),都会带来货方以 TIGA 采取诉讼行动(并会加上侵权与托管的诉因,因为都有关系)。如根据 TIGA 要求法院对船东或承运人下命令将货物归还。

2. Sale or disposal:这是针对一种情况就是托管人在没有授权下把货物出售或是处理掉:Howard E. Perry v. British Railways Board (1980) 1 WLR 1375。针对海上货物运输会有例外情况,如承运人/托管人可以把危险货物在航次中途卸下或销毁,这是根据《海牙规则》或《海牙—维斯比规则》Article 4(6)。承运人/托管人也可以在一些属于共同海损的情况下把货物抛落大海。另是在货物估计是不能安全运往卸港,如易腐货物,承运人/托管人可以作为紧急代理人在没有授权的情况下在中途避难港把货物出售。另一种情况可让承运人/托管人在没有授权下把货物出售是委托人拒绝取货,如货物有一点点损坏,委托人作出过激的反应,这在 TIGA Section 13 也有针对。

3. Theft and misappropriation:这些包括承运人/托管人将货物盗走或是非法处置,在海上货物运输会有很多种不同的形式出现。这可以是小偷小摸,如船员把贵重的货物偷走,这在使用集装箱运输之前是经常发生的。或是船东自己偷取货物,如在燃油价格上涨,所以经常听说油轮船东在装运燃油或者原油时,把船舱的货物转移去燃油柜:The "Captain Gregos" (1990) 1 Lloyd's Rep. 310。船东还可以是汪洋大盗或世纪诈骗犯,如把价值高达 5600 万美元的 20 万吨原油中途偷走并非法转卖给南非政府的 The Shell International Petroleum Co Ltd v. Gibbs (1983) 1 Lloyd's Rep. 342。

4. Wrongful retention:这些包括承运人/托管人到了卸港时拒绝交出货物,通常的理由就是留置货物,因为欠下运费或者滞期费等。但如果并没有欠下或是船东乱敲竹杠,这就会是一种错误的扣押货物。如经常会发生倒闭或是欺诈的期租承租人签发了运费已付的提单,但没有把收到的运费按时支付租金给船东,导致船东在卸港甚至还没有抵达卸港就"留置"货物,要求支付运费。这显然就是一种典型的错误扣押货物,在英国法下是受到 TIGA 的管制。这种案件很多,包括像 The "Mandarin Star" (1969) 1 Lloyd's Rep. 293;The "Alev" (1989) 1 Lloyd's Rep. 138 与 Cho Yang Shipping v. Coral (UK) (1997) 2 Lloyd's Rep. 641。

5. Breach of duty as bailee:这是针对托管人违反他的责任,这些责任包括合理谨慎照顾托管的货物以及在要求下或是在托管协议下交还给委托人。此外,托管人也不能在没有授权下处理受托管的货物,如把货物转交给分托管人(转运)。错误干预货物只针对托管人违反合约所造成的货物损失或者毁灭(loss or destruction),而不针对一般的货损。

根据这个错误干预货物的诉因索赔,相比侵权或者违反谨慎照顾货物的托管责任,表面看来是重复(overlap)。但是有一点区别,就是会有情况需要向第三人提出索赔,但他既不是一个托管人,或者是一个分托管人,而他也不存在有任何的疏忽。这一来,就只能以 TIGA 向该第三人起诉了。这可以节录 Aikens 大法官著的《Bills of Lading》2006 年版之 9.84 段,如下:"An advantage of a claim framed in wrongful interference with goods is that, unlike claims in bailment or negligence, it may in some circumstances be made against a party who is not a bailee and who had not acted negligently (or fraudulently). However, the most frequent situations in which wrongful interference with goods is relevant (for present purpose) are when the carrier either delivers goods to the wrong party, or steals it himself."

有诉权的人士在错误干预的时候必须对货物有真正占有权或马上占有的权利,这也可以节录 Aikens 大法官著的《Bills of Lading》2006 年版之 9.85/9.87 段:

"An action for wrongful interference with goods can be brought if and only if the claimant has at the time of the wrongful interference with goods, either actual possession or the immediate right to possession of the goods concerned.

In The"Future Express"(1993) 2 Lloyd's Rep. 542, under complex arrangements made between the buyer and seller of goods, presentation of the bills of lading, made out to order of the buyer's bank (the claimant), was delayed until long after the goods had been discharged under a letter of indemnity provided by the seller to the carrier and they had been delivered (but not to the bank's order). The claimant paid the seller on eventual presentation of documents and sued the carrier for delivery other than against the bill of lading. The action failed, the court concluding that although it was the original intention of the parties that the claimant should become a pledgee of the goods, which would have given it necessary title sufficient to sue, it never did so; nor did it acquire any other security rights in the goods, and thus had no title to sue.

This illustrates a potential limitation on a bank's security rights given the increased prevalence of discharge against letters of indemnity prior to negotiation of documents. However, under COSCO 1992 a bank will generally have a right to sue the carrier in contract once it becomes holder of the bill, even if this is after discharge ..."

针对一般性国际货物买卖的货物所有权人,如持有提单的收货人,他通常也同时拥有占有权或者马上占有的权利。所以在发生承运人/托管人对货物错误干预的时候(如拒绝交货或无单放货等),他有诉权应该是没有疑问的。

Ⅲ. 第三部分：多式联运与全程运输

12. 序言

传统的提单合约涉及海上运输，针对的是港口对港口运输，这一方面已经在本章第一部分有所涉及。这种运输今天主要是针对大宗货（不论是干货或者是湿货），而针对非大宗货也就是以前的杂货，今天都变成集装箱运输。以集装箱运输，由于集装箱容易从一种运输方式转成另一种运输方式，这就提供了机会与方便让承运人提供一站式（one stop shop）的运输服务，可以从发货人的工厂或仓库（这可能是远离一个港口，如一个内陆的城市）提货后安排运输送达给收货人的工厂或仓库。在这种运输中，会涉及多种方式的运输，包括海上、航空、陆上（如火车、卡车等）。而提供这种一站式运输服务的承运人往往不再是传统的船东，而他们与提供运输船舶的船东之间的合约关系也不是传统的租约，而是各式各样的联营合约（pooling agreement）或箱位租约（slot/space charter）等。这种承运人可被称为是"无船承运人"（Non Vessel Owning Common Carriers，简称 NVOCC），他们也可以被称为"多式联运经营人"（multi transport operator，简称 MTO）或"无船多式联运承运人"（Non-Vessel Owning Multi Transport Operator，简称 NVMTO）。提供一站式的运输服务也可以发货代理人的身份安排多式联运，这种人可被称为是货代（freight forwarder）。

NVOCC 或 NVMTO 的承运人是以他自己的名义与发货人订立运输合约，并承担合约内的履约责任。这种运输合约可以有几种不同的名称，如 combined transport bills of lading，multi-modal bills of lading 等，可在以下把这种运输合约统称为 multi-stage bill，简称 MSB。这种经常使用的 MSB 也有一些提供给使用者方便的标准格式，如 BIMCO 出的 Combiconbill 1995，Multidoc 95 与 Conline 2000，这些格式都可在 BIMCO 的网站找到：http://www. bimco. dk。另可包括在 MSB 内的是全程运输提单（through bills of lading），这是针对一些需要用另一艘船舶转运的海上运输。但所涉及的只是海上运输的一种方式，所以不能算是多式联运，虽然这种提单也会涉及同样的问题。至于货代会签发的运输单证可被称为"货代单"（house bill），其中可细分为"service bill"，"groupage bill"，"feeder bill"等。

13. MSB 与传统提单合约的不同之处与责任的判定

这种 MSB 虽然也被称为是提单，但它与传统海上运输的提单合约相比在部分重要的内容上很不一样，集装箱运输的货物相比传统提单合约在要求上也不一样。其中一个方面就是这种货物很少会需要在运输的途中转卖。这与大宗货物的海上运输很不一样,至今还是有部分商品如石油或石油产品在海上运输时以提单的背书与交出进行转卖。这一来,集装箱运输并不很需要传统提单作为物权凭证(document of title)。事实上越来越多的集装箱运输在今天已经弃用提单而采用不可转让的海运单了。

在合约内容方面,MSB 都会有明示条文说明提供的运输与承担的责任只是从港口至港口,但会另有条文说明在安排下一程的运输,承运人是以代理人的身份作出安排。也会有明示条文说明在不同方式的运输会有不同的责任。另也会有明示条文规定说明货物在承运人的托管下,承运人才有责任。双方有了争议,英国法律主要还是看 MSB 的默示与明示条文作出整体的解释,以下段节可以举几个有关的先例说明这种作出判决的方法。顺便一提的是,解释合约的大原则请看笔者《合约的解释》一书。

13.1 根据 MSB 不同明示责任条文作出解释的案例之一:Princes Buitoni v. Hapag-Lloyd

说明在不同方式的运输会有不同的责任的条文可介绍 Princes Buitoni v Hapag-Lloyd (1991) 2 Lloyd's Rep 383,有关的 MSB 第 2b 条文这样规定:"During road-carriage in Europe according to the Convention on Carriage of goods by road, dated May 19 1957 (CMR)..."。案情涉及一个从温哥华运往英国 Felixstowe 的集装箱在从 Felixstowe 运往利物浦的途中丢失,有关责任方面到底 CMR 的公路货物运输公约是否适用,因为这涉及责任限制。根据公约本身,它只适用在欧洲两个不同国家的公路运输。但在这一案件,涉及的只是一个国家(即英国)。在上诉庭,判是 CMR 适用,因为这纯粹是解释 MSB 的有关合约条文,说明只要损失发生"在欧洲的公路运输"(During road-carriage in Europe),而英国是属于欧洲的一部分。如果是要完全依照 CMR 只适用在欧洲两个不同国家的公路运输,条文就需要写作:"Road-carriage in Europe between two different countries in Europe"。

13.2 根据 MSB 不同明示责任条文作出解释的案例之二:The"Ines"

至于说明货物在承运人的控制下承运人才有责任的条文可介绍 The"Ines" (1995) 2 Lloyd's Rep 144 先例。有关的运输是一批电话以集装箱运输从香港去安特卫普,然后转运去俄罗斯的圣彼得堡,但结果货物是在圣彼得堡因为无单放货而失去。有关提单中的一些明示条文可节录如下:

"3. PERIOD OF RESPONSIBILITY Goods in the custody of the Carrier or his agent... before loading and after discharge... are in such custody at the sole risk of the owners of the goods and thus the carrier has no responsibility whatsoever for the goods prior to the loading on and subsequent to the discharge from the ocean vessel...

5. FORWARDING, SUBSTITUTE OF VESSEL THROUGH CARGO AND TRANSSHIPMENT... The carrier to be at liberty to... store the goods... on shore...

The responsibility of the carrier shall be limited to the part of the transport performed by him in a vessel under his management and no claim will be acknowledged by the carrier for damage or loss arising during any other part of the transport...

19. RESPONSIBILITY when joint service The Contract evidenced by this Bill of Lading is between the Shipper and the Owner of the Ocean vessel named herein... and it is therefore agreed that the said shipowner only shall be liable for any loss, damage... arising or resulting... ”

Clarke 大法官在分析有关先例后否定这免责条款可在无单放货方面保障船东，说：“one of the key provisions of the bill of lading, so far as the shipper is concerned, is the promise not to deliver the cargo other than in return for an original bill of lading. That principle protects the shipper from fraud. It also protects the shipowner. The parties would not in my judgment be likely to have contracted out of it. Thus clear words would be required for them to be held to have done so. The clause should be construed so as to enable effect to be given to one of the main objects and intents of the contracts, namely that the goods would only be delivered to the holder of an original bill of lading. The question is thus whether the words in any of the clauses relied upon are sufficient to excuse misdelivery of the goods after discharge. In my judgment they are not. Clause 3... That clause seems to me not be concerned with loss of or damage to the goods and may well include the case where the goods are stolen, but it is not concerned with misdelivery... ”

13.3　根据 MSB 不同明示责任条文作出解释的案例之三：Finagra v. O. T. Africa Line

MSB 会明示规定如果在多式联运中发生货损货差，如果无法确定是在哪一程的运输中发生，责任就如何针对，但如果可以确定货损到底是在哪一程运输中发生，就会根据不同运输方式而有不同的针对。在先例 Finagra v. O. T. Africa Line (1998) 2 Lloyd’s Rep 622，案情涉及了一票的可可豆通过海上运输从尼日利亚的 Lagos 到荷兰的鹿特丹，再通过公路运输至最终的目的地阿姆斯特丹。在有关的 MSB，它的第 5 条有关承运人责任是说明了“除非提单另有规定”(save the bill of lading otherwise provides)，货损货差的责任在没有办法确定是在哪一程运输中发生就适用《海牙规则》。但如果可以决定，根据好几个不同的国际公约/规定作出不同的针对，说：

“(a) if Carriage by sea, the Hague Rules contained in the International Convention for the unification of certain rules relating to Bills of Lading dated 25th August 1924 to apply. Where compulsorily applicable by any national law the Hague Rules as amended by the protocol signed at Brussels 23rd February 1968 the so called Hague Visby Rules to apply.

(b) If Carriage by road, by the Convention on the Contract for the International Carriage of Goods by Road, dated 19th May 1956 (CMR)

(c) If Carriage by rail, by the International Agreement on Railway Transport, dated 26th February 1961 (CIM)

(d) If Carriage by air, by the Convention for the unification of certain Rules relating to International Carriage by Air, signed Warsaw 12th October 1929, as thereafter amended."

此外,它还有另外的一条时效条文要求在交货后9个月提起诉讼,否则承运人再也没有责任。在该先例,货方是在交货的9个月后才提起诉讼索赔货损货差。这就带来一个矛盾,如果《海牙规则》根据提单合约的合并是适用的情况下,它的1年时效与另外条文的9个月时效哪个效力更高,因为这会马上决定索赔的生死。Rix大法官的判决,也是对提单合约的不同条文作出解释如下:

1.《海牙规则》或《海牙—维斯比规则》如果是根据当地立法强制适用,根据Article III(8)承运人是不能够通过合约条文减轻责任(而缩短索赔时效是其中一种),所以9个月的时效约定是无效的。但如果《海牙规则》只是被当事人合并在提单合约中,Article III(8)就不是决定性。毕竟,独立成为一个条文的9个月的时效更有针对性,但合并的《海牙规则》只是泛泛,而Article III(8)只是《海牙规则》的其中一条。Rix大法官这样说:"(1) The presence of a repugnancy clause, whether the clause inherent in the rules in the form of art. III, r. 8, a fortiori a separate repugnancy clause in the contract itself, will always be relevant: but neither its presence, nor its absence is necessarily decisive. A specifically negotiated clause is likely to take precedence over the merely incorporated: Metalfer v. Pan Ocean, The Askin. This is an aspect of the maxim—as Lord Justice Staughton commented in Sabah Flour v. Comfez (1988) 2 Lloyd's Rep 18 at p. 20: 'sometimes enshrined in Latin'—that the general does not derogate from the special."

2. 针对多式联运,提单条文还在不同运输方法中产生货损货差责任在一开始说明"除非提单另有规定"(save the bill of lading otherwise provides),这表示《海牙规则》如果只是有合约条文的效力下,再不能算是首要条文超越其他的条文(包括9个月的索赔时效)。Rix大法官这样说:"There remains the repugnancy clause in art. III, r. 8 itself, but the express proviso 'save as is otherwise provided in this Bill of Lading' indicates that the incorporation of the Hague Rules (or other Conventions) is not to be paramount, but that on the contrary inconsistent provisions in the bill are to have priority: see Holland Colombo Trading Society Ltd v. Alawdeen (1954) 2 Lloyd's Rep 45 at p 53, where almost identical language (unless otherwise provided in the bill of lading) was held to mean that the provisions of the bill prevailed over the Hague Rules in case of conflict."

3. Rix大法官也提到,即使两条条文互相有矛盾,但在大部分的情况下,还是可以协调并给两条条文都有一定的解释。但针对时效条文,这是有要求写得特别清楚明确。而如果本先例是有矛盾而且没办法协调,就应该以时效较长的条文为准。Rix大法官这样说:"(6) More commonly, if the conflicting clauses can live together, then the Courts should seek to give effect to both of them, as in Sabah Flour. (7) Finally, clear words are required for a time bar, so that in a case of doubt or ambiguity the conflict must

be resolved in favor of the longer time limit: Sabah Flour at p. 20, citing and applying Mr. Justice Donaldson in Bunge S. A. v. Deutsche Conti-Handelsgesellschaft m. b. H. (1980) 1 Lloyd's Rep 352 at p. 358."

总的而言,Rix 大法官判的是索赔时效还没有届满。

13.4　根据 MSB 不同明示责任条文作出解释的案例之四:The"OOCL Bravery"

在先例 The"OOCL Bravery"(2000) 1 Lloyd's Rep 394,涉及了美国 1936 年《海上货物运输法》(这是美国对《海牙规则》的立法)与 CMR 之间的冲突。虽然 CMR 是欧洲适用的公约,但该先例是由美国法院根据 MSB 中明示条文作出的解释。该案件涉及了 OOCL 作为承运人把一集装箱的自行车与零部件从美国威斯康星州的工厂运去荷兰的收货人仓库。OOCL 在提取了这批货物后签发了一份 MSB 给货方的 Trek。这批货物之后通过陆上运输至加拿大的蒙特利尔并且被装上集装箱船 OOCL Bravery。船舶到了安特卫普,该集装箱被卸下给 OOCL 的分包人 DeBock 运输公司去安排公路的运输。而事实上,DeBock 把实际的公路运输又分包给了名为 Groeninghe 的卡车公司。但该卡车公司所雇用的卡车司机为了自己的方便,把卡车连同货物停泊在他家附近过夜准备第二天开走。显然这是极端危险与不负责的行为,因为根本没有任何防止盗窃的措施。结果卡车与集装箱在第二天发现已经被盗。在卡车司机报警之后,最终把卡车找回来,但集装箱内的货物就不翼而飞,这导致了货方大约 135 万美元的损失。Trek 最后是能够从保险人的 Hartfort 公司得到全数的赔付,而这一案例就是 Harfort 以自己的名义向 OOCL 提出代位求偿权的索赔。

在责任方面,OOCL 是根本没有可以抗辩的余地,所以真正的争议是在美国《海上货物运输法》或是 CMR 适用。这是因为这两个法规涉及了不同的赔偿责任限制,美国《海上货物运输法》是限制在每个货运单位 500 美元,而该集装箱涉及了 301 架自行车,其中只有 29 架最终被找回。这表示总共的赔付金额可以被限制在 13.6 万美元。但在 CMR,赔偿责任限制是根据损失货物的重量(kg)乘以 8.33 特别提款权(special drawing right)来计算,由此得出的赔付金额是 51,086.89 美元。

接下去节录有关 MSB 的有争议条文,首先是最重要的一条首要条文合并了美国《海上货物运输法》,如下:"23) Clause Paramount. All carriage under this Bill of Lading to or from the United States of America shall have effect subject to the provisions of COGSA which shall be deemed to be incorporated herein... ***Except as otherwise provided herein COGSA***... shall govern the Goods before loading on board and ***after discharge*** from the vessel and while subject to this Bill of Lading."(加黑部分就是强调该明示条文说明是除非另有条文针对,否则美国《海上货物运输法》是适用在货物从船舶卸下后的责任。但注意它没有明确规定 CMR 的适用。)

另一条有关的条文是 MSB:"4)... With respect to all other transportation the Carrier agrees to procure transportation of the Goods for and on behalf of the Merchant in accordance with its tariff(s) and those of Participating Carriers and without waiver of any defenses or exemptions provided by law, if applicable, from the Place of Receipt to the Place of Delivery, and it shall have the right at its discretion to use any mode of transport in addition to the named Vessels, or their substitutes and to arrange participation by other Carriers to accomplish such transportation. ***Each stage of the transport shall be governed according to any law and tariffs applicable to such stage.*** The care, custody and carriage of the Goods during any period in which a Participating Carrier or its contractor or agent is in possession of the Goods shall be the sole responsibility of the Participating Carrier and not the Carrier."

OOCL 的争辩就是在货物被盗时，CMR 应该是当地适用的法律（因为从比利时到荷兰的运输该公约是强制适用），虽然在美国不适用。而且根据 MSB 的第 4 条，OOCL 只是作为货方代理人安排卡车公司的运输。而即使 OOCL 还是有责任，责任限制也应只是根据 CMR。

但美国法院不接受，认为 MSB 的第 23 条是明确说明美国《海上货物运输法》适用。而在该法律下有著名的条文是"禁止承运人通过合约减轻或排除责任"这是在《海牙规则》的 Article III, 8。这一来，MSB 的第 4 条就属于是违反了《海牙规则》的 Article III, 8 而变得无效。至于 CMR，它的不适用是 OOCL 没有在 MSB 中明确规定的，说："I cannot permit the defendants to take advantage of the lower CMR liability limit when the shipper was not provided with a fair opportunity to declare references to the CMR IN (a) the bill of lading or (b) the August, 1996 contract between Trek and defendants. The only contract that incorporates the CMR is the April, 1995 sub-contracting agreement between the defendants and DeBock; Trek was not a party to it, and hence it is not binding on the plaintiff. Where a separate carrier transports goods from the port of discharge to the designated place of delivery, this does not constitute an independent contract for the overland portion of the trip. Instead, such carriage is governed by the incorporated COGSA provisions of the bill of lading."

14. 没有生效的《联合国国际货物多式联运公约》与 MSB 带来的法律问题

集装箱运输发展迅速，这是指商业方面，但在法律方面并没有跟上，也谈不上有国际公约的针对（《联合国国际货物多式联运公约》[United Nations Convention on International Multimodal Transport of Goods, 1980] 于 1980 年 5 月 24 日在日内瓦召开的联合国贸易和发展会议全权代表会上通过，但至今未能生效，据说一个原因是在海上运输的部分引进了不受西方国家欢迎的《汉堡规则》。）目前就英国法而言，针对多式联运带来的争议主要还是对合约的解释（也就是对 MSB 各条文的解释），而且英国法律是完全允许 MSB 有订约自由。相比传统的海上运输就加上了复杂的问题，即在整个运输涉及了一连串的分包商、分分包商、代理人等。还有就是整个运输涉及不同方式时会有当地的法律或者是国际公约的约束或者与 MSB 明示条文之间的协调。当然还少不了的是总会有人在某些情况下希望绕过合约关系以侵权作为诉因。以下的段节会针对这三方面的讨论:(1)在 MSB,谁有诉权与谁是索赔的对象,特别是在不同方式的运输下;(2)MSB 能否在普通法下,1971 年《海上货物运输法》(《海牙—维斯比规则》)与 1992 年《海上货物运输法》下被视为一份提单;(3)在发生货损货差,有哪些法律或公约针对多式联运承运人的责任。

15. 谁有诉权与谁是索赔的对象

在多式联运,经常会涉及好几位的不同承运人,他们会涉及公路运输、铁路运输、二程船运输等。他们之间都会有不同的运输合约串连起来。这一来,如果在不同承运人运输与托管货物期间发生货损货差,有诉权的货方或有代位求偿权的保险人就要准确找出谁是索赔的对象。显然,如果涉及有关货物的全程运输是由一个财雄势大的 NVOCC 签发一份 MSB,货方/保险人就可以向他提出索赔。双方作为有关运输合约的订约方,加上 MSB 很少会出现在运输中途转卖,所以诉权与索赔对象一般都不会成问题。但问题是在多式联运,经常是货损货差发生在 NVOCC 或他的代理人并不占有货物的期间,换言之,货物已经交给其他方式的承运人继续运输。本来在本章较早时已经介绍过,该 NVOCC 根据英国法律的默示地位是即使有权把运输合约的履行转交给其他承运人履行,也不代表可以同时把在履行途中的疏忽或过错的责任一并转移或赖掉(正如在 Metaalhandel v. Ardfields & Jones (1988) 1 Lloyd's Rep. 197 先例所说的:“... although he is entitled to delegate performance, he cannot delegate his responsibility.”

但这一默示地位经常被明示条文所超越,就是在 MSB 通常会有条文说明货物不在合约承运人或 NVOCC 的占有或控制下是不必负责的,正如 The“Ines”(1995) 2 Lloyd's Rep 144 先例。在这里也可以顺便一提英国法律的默示地位是不能接受合约承运人在没有授权的情况下,安排转运(除了已经谈到的一些特殊情况如共同海损或是紧急代理人)。如果合约承运人这样做,会带来严重的后果,好像船舶在航次中不能不合理绕航一样。这是因为合约承运人已经不在履行有关的运输合约范围内(outside the four corners of the contract),所以会失去所有的合约免责或者是限制责任条文,正如 Brandon 大法官在 The“Berkshire”(1974) 1 Lloyd's Rep 185 所说的,如下:“by discharging the goods at Jeddah and transshipping them into another ship not owned or operated by them the shipowners made a fundamental departure from the method of performing the contract contemplated by the parties at the time it was made, and the shipowners were therefore prevented from relying on the exception in cl. 1 of the bill of lading.”

但这一方面也不会有问题，因为在绝大部分的 MSB 都会有广泛的授权给合约承运人或 NVOCC 安排转运或分包，正如 The"Ines"先例中 MSB 中的第 5 条文（请看以上第 13.2 段节录的部分）。

根据以上的分析，显示了货方/保险人会有必要避开有关运输合约向 NVOCC 索赔货损货差，因为成功机会不大或者是没有。退而求其次的就是直接向疏忽造成货损货差的公路承运人或铁路承运人等索赔。至于是否是他们的疏忽造成货损货差，有些情况是十分明确的，如集装箱是在他的占有或托管期间被盗窃或发生意外的。如果货方/保险人是以非合约的关系如侵权的疏忽或错误干预货物，或是违反了谨慎照顾的托管责任，就会面对在本章第二部分所介绍的各种问题，笔者不再重复。这里也会涉及这些被告的公路运输人或铁路运输人或二程船等可否去依赖不同运输合约条文作出抗辩，如本章第 10.3 段介绍的在 MSB 内有一条"喜马拉雅条文"（Himalaya Clause）与有条件的分托管（sub-bailment on term）等。

另一重要的合约关系在多式联运要搞清楚的就是如果在一份 MSB 下向 NVOCC 或货代提出索赔，也要把索赔对象搞清楚。讲到货代，通常的理解是只作为代理人替货方代理全程运输。这在被广泛使用的 FIATA bills 是这样规定的："It must be clearly understood that a forwarding agent is not a carrier; he does not obtain the possession of the goods; he does not undertake the delivery of them at the other end unless prevented by some expected cause of loss or something which affords an excuse. All that he does is to act as agent for the owner of the goods to make arrangement with the people who do carry—steamships, railways, and so on—and to make arrangement so far as are necessary for the intermediate steps between the ship and the rail, the Customs or anything else..."

但货代本身的一个名称并不代表太多的内容，他与货方/发货人的合约关系可以只是一个代理人：The"Maheno"(1977) 1 Lloyd's Rep 82，也可以是作为一个当事人包揽运输：Sonicare v EAFT (1997) 2 Lloyd's Rep 48，也可以作为一个承运人：Center Optical v JTSC (2001) 2 Lloyd's Rep 678。

显然，如果只是一份代理协议，这就不会是一份运输合约或海上运输合约。有关的货代只有作为一个代理人的责任，这包括在行动上要尽合理的职责（act with reasonable diligence），如选择适合的实际承运人：Cliffe v Hull & Netherlands Steamship Company (1921) 6 Ll. L. Rep 136。此外，他也有责任保护委托人货方的利益，特别是针对承运人：Marbrook Freight v K. M. I (London) Ltd (1979) 2 Lloyd's Rep 341。

16. 怎样认定是代理人还是合约承运人

在一份 MSB，到底一位货代是代理人还是合约承运人，经常会出现争议。一个简单的答案就是看有关的明示条文并了解订约时的语境（factual matrix）来解释，而由于在订约自由下什么样的条文都会有，加上不同案件的事实千变万化，所以很难绝对。可以说，到底与承运人订约是以代理人身份还是当事人身份还是要看事实(question of fact)：TICC Ltd v COSCO (UK) Ltd (2001) 1 EWCA Civ 1862。但简单地说，考虑是代理人还是承运人，有两个方面的事实认定非常重要：(1)代理人或者承运人的收费到底是一笔固定金额还是佣金；(2)订约前该货代有否声称他是承运人还是只是一位代理人。

在上述的(1)，如果货代收取一笔固定金额，就显示他或赚或亏，这不是一个代理人会做的事。在 Center Optical v JTSC，香港法院判有关的货代必须对一份货代单负责，不能辩称为代理人，因为有各种理由，如货代单的签字并没有加上批注。另一个重要原因是该货代在运费中赚了钱，这并不是代理人应该做的。

这种情况有时候不容易认定，如在 Cho Yang Shipping v Coral (1997) 2 Lloyd's Rep 641 中，该案例虽然不涉及多式联运，但道理是一样的。案情是原告的船东 C 向被告的货方 D 索取运费。由于 D 在提单内被命名为发货人，所以从提单的表面来看 D 是要对运费负责的，这也是第一审的判决。

事实上，D 是把货物的运输委托给 N，而 N 分包给 I，而 I 再分包给 E，E 就是船东 C 的代理人，并签发提单。D 把运费支付给 N，而 N 也把运费支付给 I。但 I 没有支付运费给代理人的 E 或者船东的 C，所以导致 C 直接根据提单向 D 要求这笔运费。而 D 由于已经支付运费给 M，肯定不会再支付一次给 C，即使从提单的表面看来他会是有支付的责任。但这一审的判决被上诉庭推翻，判 D 不必对运费负责，其中 Hobhouse 大法官这样说："In my judgment the Judge came to the wrong conclusion and asked himself the wrong question. He did not ask himself whether it was to be inferred that D had agreed to pay freight to the Plaintiffs. He did not take adequate account of the fact that the bill of lading is only evidence of the contract between the shipper and the carrier which has been made before the goods were shipped nor of what terms and what agreement were to be inferred from what had happened prior to shipment. He asked himself the question whether there was anything in the bill of lading to preclude liability. He should have asked whether having regard to the facts of this particular shipment it is to be inferred that D were undertaking to the Plaintiffs that they would pay freight to them. In a situation such as that which occurred in this case the question can only be answered by looking at all the relevant evidence not just the fact that D owned the sugar at the time it was shipped and were named as the shippers in the bill of lading. As I have explained earlier in this judgment it is correct that the inference that the shipper is agreeing to pay the freight is the usual inference but it is not a necessary inference and a different inference may in a particular case be appropriate. Here the C and E had their own agreement with I as principals and extended credit to them. Whatever agreement D had made about freight with N was unknown to C and E. E never agreed or attempted to agree any freight with D or N."

看来，上诉庭并没有不同一审的判决，就是 D 的确是提单合约的订约方，但他没有提单合约下对运费的责任。

除了货方/发货人与货代或 NVOCC 的 MSB 之外，还有下一份与其他实际承运人的运输合约如何约定也十分重要。在多式联运，经常会出现多份运输合约或是提单。在安排全程运输时，也经常会有货代在这种运输合约中把自己或他的代理人写作发货人或者收货人。这一来，在这些与其他实际承运人的运输合约中，货方就因为不是合约一方而没有这方面的诉权。但请参阅 Coli v Merzario（2002）1 Lloyd's Rep 608 的例外先例。

17. MSB 能否被视为一份提单

MSB 是否被视为一份真正的提单，特别在是否适用 1971 年《海上货物运输法》与 1992 年《海上货物运输法》上，目前在英国法律下没有太多权威解释。这会有重要的关系，如 1992 年立法不适用的话，就不存在订约的发货人可以把运输合约转让给收货人，并把向承运人索赔的诉权转交给他。

MSB 在两个方面会有问题：一是 MSB 会被视为不是一份海上运输合约；二是 MSB 不能作为物权凭证，因为不能背书与交出，把代表有关货物的所有权或/与占有权转让给第三者。在 Carver on Charterparty, paras 8－078 to 8－079 有说明 MSB 不能作为物权凭证的四个原因：（1）MSB 是以一种不可转让（non-negotiable）的格式；（2）MSB不一定由承运人所签发，经常会有疑问是一份 MSB 从表面看来的承运人到底是代理人身份还是承运人身份，如由货代作为代理人签发；（3）它所针对的运输并不仅是海上运输；（4）它往往不是针对货物付运（shipped bill），而只是针对收到货物。

针对这些问题，可分几个方面来考虑。首先是在普通法，这在 Aikens 大法官著的《Bills of Lading》2006 年版之 11.48 段认为在普通法下没有理由 MSB 不能被视为物权凭证与一份提单，他这么说："For the reasons given above, there is no reason why in principle MSBs cannot be documents of title and otherwise qualify as bills of lading under common law."至于该书怎样根据原因得出该结论，由于内容较多笔者在此不作节录。但在此强调的只是 Aikens 大法官个人的看法，还没有先例作支持。

下一个方面的考虑是 1971 年《海上货物运输法》是否强制适用于 MSB，这是因为该立法的 Section 1(4) 与《海牙—维斯比规则》的 Article II 都明确写明是"海上货物运输合约"（contract of carriage of goods by sea）。但多式联运只是部分的运输涉及海上运输，甚至只是很小的一段。固然，如果是适用，也只能强制适用在海上运输的一段，除非 MSB 另有明示规定。在这一方面 Aikens 大法官著的《Bills of Lading》2006 年版之 11.44 段这样说："... Again it is submitted that a broad interpretation of the concept of contract for the carriage of goods by sea, within the meaning of COGSA, Section 1

(4) and Article II of the Rules, is appropriate. Otherwise the Hague Rules protection will be lost simply on account of the inclusion of a section of land or air carriage in the scope of the contract. In any event, the Hague Rules (by Article I [e] and III. 2) restrict the operation of the Rules to the sea part of the carriage."

再接下去的考虑是1992年的《海上货物运输法》,这方面也可以节录Aikens大法官著的《Bills of Lading》2006年版之11.41-11.43段,其中可以看到没有太多有关的先例以及只是属于Aikens大法官与其他共同作者的看法。内容如下:

"11.41 A bill which is not negotiable cannot, by definition (see section 1[2]) be a bill of lading for the purpose of COGSA 1992. The Act is silent as to what is otherwise meant by 'bill of lading', but if this includes a requirement of evidencing a contract for carriage of goods by sea only, then even a negotiable multimodal bill would not comply with the statutory requirement.

11.42 It can be argued that an MSB, or at least a combined transport bill, cannot be a seawaybill either, because this is defined statutorily (in section 1[3] of COGSA 1992) by reference to a contract for the carriage of goods by sea, and MSBs which cover a non-sea element do not comply. Although this is the view taken by Carver, it is suggested that this is an over technical approach which would provide an unnecessary obstacle to the transfer of rights of suit.

11.43 If an MSB is not a contract for carriage of goods by sea for the purpose of COGSA 1992, it is presumably also not one for the purpose of the Contracts (Rights against Third Parties) Act 1999, in which case even if the consignee cannot gain rights of suit under the former he may do so under the latter."

18. 在发生货损货差时有哪些法律或公约针对多式联运承运人的责任

较早时已经提及在发生货损货差时,最重要的还是要看运输合约或MSB的条文,因为英国法下还是允许订约自由。但多式联运也会涉及一些国际以及地区性的公约,这包括:(1)涉及海上运输的《海牙规则》与《海牙—维斯比规则》,甚至是1980年的《汉堡规则》;(2)在欧洲的公路运输,《公路货物运输法》(法文为"Convention pour Merchandise par Route",简称CMR)会适用,这也是在英国立的法,即1965年的《Carriage of goods by Road Act》;(3)针对铁路运输的是《CIM公约》(法文为"Regles uniformes concernant le contrat de transport intenationale ferroviale des voyageurs et des bagages");(4)针对航空运输的《华沙公约》(《Warsaw Convention》),这也在英国立的法,即1961年的《Carriage by Air Act》。

这些公约之间在多程运输的协调上也带来许多困难。举例说，CMR 的适用虽然是针对公路运输，但也包括其中的一段是海上、空中运输的全程运输，但大前提是货物仍然是在拖车（trailer）或车架上。注意是货物在集装箱内就不属于货物是在拖车或车架上。这是 CMR 的 Article 2"Where the vehicle containing the goods is carried over part of the journey by sea, rail, inland waterways or air, and ... the goods are not unloaded from the vehicle, this Convention shall nevertheless apply to the whole of the carriage."

这种重叠的公约或者法律带来了先例 Thermo Engineers v. Ferrymasters (1981) 1 Lloyd's Rep 200，案情涉及卡车上的货物在装上滚装船舶的时候被碰坏（货物是一座热转换器）。双方的争议主要是《海牙规则》或者是 CMR 适用，因为在责任方面（CMR 的 Article 3 是要公路承运人承担分包商的疏忽或者过错）与损失赔偿等方面都与《海牙规则》不一样。虽然 CMR 是可以包括海上运输，但它在 Article 2(4)也说明了一些例外的情况，但是构成例外情况需要同时满足以下三个条件："(a) the damage etc. occurred during the carriage by the other means of transport. (b) the damage etc. was not caused by an act or omission of the carrier by road, and (c) the damage etc. was caused by some event which could only have occurred in the course of and by reason of the carriage by that other means of transport."

其实也即只有：(1)货物损失是发生在非公路运输的途中；(2)损失不是因为公路运输中的行为或疏忽导致；(3)损失只能够是由于非公路运输途中的事故导致，如船舶沉没或者搁浅。

Neill 大法官最终这样判定："It will be remembered that the damage occurred at the moment when the upper part of the exchanger struck the deckhead of the lower'tween deck of Orion (船名). Mr. Aikens argued that at that moment the carriage by sea had not yet begun, and that it was only when the effective means of carriage had ceased to be by the wheels of the trailer, and the trailer and its load were secured in the ship, that the carriage by road could be said to have ceased. Mr. Mance, on the other hand, argued that carriage by sea includes the operation of loading. He referred me to The Hague Rules and the decision of Mr. Justice Devlin in Pyrene Co. Ltd. V. Scindia Navigation Co. Ltd. (1954) 1 Lloyd's Rep 321.

With respect, I am unable to accept Mr. Aikens' argument that the road transport continued until the trailer and its load were secured in the ship. There is force in Mr. Mance's submission that CMR was intended to fit in with other conventions, and I incline to the view that as a general rule the first condition of art. 2 will be satisfied where it is proved that sea carriage as understood in The Hague Rules has begun. I recognize, however, that there may be cases where the exact line between two successive means of transport will be difficult to draw. I must concern myself with the facts of the present case. ***Here I am satisfied that the damage occurred during the carriage by the other means of transport.*** At the relevant time the loading was well advanced, and, as can be seen from the sketch plan drawn by Mr. Clarke the trailer had already passed across the outboard ramp and across the line of stern.

... Looking at all these circumstances, I do not see that Ferrymasters or the dock company, in any capacity other than as stevedores, were in breach of any duty of care, or that any act or omission of these companies, as persons involved in the carriage by road, caused the damage. The damage was caused by those directly involved in the loading.

... One is concerned to consider not whether the loss or damage could only have occurred in the course of the other means of transport but whether the event could only have so occurred. It seems to me that any adequate description of the relevant events in this case would have to include a statement to the effect that a collision with the bulkhead of a ship had taken place in the course of loading the ship. **Such an event could only have occurred in the course of, and by reason of, the carriage by sea**. I therefore consider that the third condition is satisfied."

可以看到 Neill 大法官认为以上三个条件都得到了满足,所以是属于 CMR 的例外情况而不适用。

案 例 目 录

附录一

Marine Insurance Act 1906

Contents

An Act to codify the Law relating to Marine Insurance.

[21st December 1906]

Annotations:

Modifications etc. (not altering text)

C1This Act is not necessarily in the form in which it has effect in Northern Ireland

C2Act extended by S. I. 1972/971, art. 4, Sch. 15

Marine Insurance

1. Marine insurance defined

A contract of marine insurance is a contract whereby the insurer undertakes to indemnify the assured, in manner and to the extent thereby agreed, against marine losses, that is to say, the losses incident to marine adventure.

2. Mixed sea and land risks

(1) A contract of marine insurance may, by its express terms, or by usage of trade, be extended so as to protect the assured against losses on inland waters or on any land risk which may be incidental to any sea voyage.

(2) Where a ship in course of building, or the launch of a ship, or any adventure analogous to a marine adventure, is covered by a policy in the form of a marine policy, the provisions of this Act, in so far as applicable, shall apply thereto; but, except as by this section provided, nothing in this Act shall alter or affect any rule of law applicable to any contract of insurance other than a contract of marine insurance as by this Act defined.

3. Marine adventure and maritime perils defined

(1) Subject to the provisions of this Act, every lawful marine adventure may be the subject of a contract of marine insurance.

(2) In particular there is a marine adventure where—

(a) Any ship goods or other moveables are exposed to maritime perils. Such property is in this Act referred to as "insurable property";

(b) The earning or acquisition of any freight, passage money, commission, profit, or other pecuniary benefit, or the security for any advances, loan, or disbursements, is endangered by the exposure of insurable property to maritime perils;

(c) Any liability to a third party may be incurred by the owner of, or other person interested in or responsible for, insurable property, by reason of maritime perils.

"Maritime perils" means the perils consequent on, or incidental to, the navigation of the sea, that is to say, perils of the seas, fire, war perils, pirates, rovers, thieves, captures, seisures, restraints, and detainments of princes and peoples, jettisons, barratry, and any other perils, either of the like kind or which may be designated by the policy.

Insurable Interest

4. Avoidance of wagering or gaming contracts

(1) Every contract of marine insurance by way of gaming or wagering is void.

(2) A contract of marine insurance is deemed to be a gaming or wagering contract—

(a) Where the assured has not an insurable interest as defined by this Act, and the contract is entered into with no expectation of acquiring such an interest; or

(b) Where the policy is made "interest or no interest," or "without further proof of interest than the policy itself," or "without benefit of salvage to the insurer," or subject to any other like term:

Provided that, where there is no possibility of salvage, a policy may be effected without benefit of salvage to the insurer.

5. Insurable interest defined

(1) Subject to the provisions of this Act, every person has an insurable interest who is interested in a marine adventure.

(2) In particular a person is interested in a marine adventure where he stands in any legal or equitable relation to the adventure or to any insurable property at risk therein, in consequence of which he may benefit by the safety or due arrival of insurable property, or may be prejudiced by its loss, or by damage thereto, or by the detention thereof, or may incur liability in respect thereof.

6. When interest must attach

(1) The assured must be interested in the subject-matter insured at the time of the loss though he need not be interested when the insurance is effected:

Provided that where the subject-matter is insured "lost or not lost," the assured may recover although he may not have acquired his interest until after the loss, unless at the time of effecting the contract of insurance the assured was aware of the loss, and the insurer was not.

(2) Where the assured has no interest at the time of the loss, he cannot acquire interest by any act or election after he is aware of the loss.

7. Defeasible or contingent interest

(1) A defeasible interest is insurable, as also is a contingent interest.

(2) In particular, where the buyer of goods has insured them, he has an insurable interest, notwithstanding that he might, at his election, have rejected the goods, or have treated them as at the seller's risk, by reason of the latter's delay in making delivery or otherwise.

8. Partial interest

A partial interest of any nature is insurable.

9. Re-insurance

(1) The insurer under a contract of marine insurance has an insurable interest in his risk, and may re-insure in respect of it.

(2) Unless the policy otherwise provides, the original assured has no right or interest in respect of such re-insurance.

10. Bottomry

The lender of money on bottomry or respondentia has an insurable interest in respect of the loan.

11. Master's and seamen's wages

The master or any member of the crew of a ship has an insurable interest in respect of his wages.

12. Advance freight

In the case of advance freight, the person advancing the freight has an insurable interest, in so far as such freight is not repayable in case of loss.

13. Charges of insurance

The assured has an insurable interest in the charges of any insurance which he may effect.

14. Quantum of interest

(1) Where the subject-matter insured is mortgaged, the mortgagor has an insurable interest in the full value thereof, and the mortgagee has an insurable interest in respect of any sum due or to become due under the mortgage.

(2) A mortgagee, consignee, or other person having an interest in the subject-matter insured may insure on behalf and for the benefit of other persons interested as well as for his own benefit.

(3) The owner of insurable property has an insurable interest in respect of the full value thereof, notwithstanding that some third person may have agreed, or be liable, to indemnify him in case of loss.

15. Assignment of interest

Where the assured assigns or otherwise parts with his interest in the subject-matter insured, he does not thereby transfer to the assignee his rights under the contract of insurance, unless there be an express or implied agreement with the assignee to that effect.

But the provisions of this section do not affect a transmission of interest by operation of law.

Insurable Value

16. Measure of insurable value

Subject to any express provision or valuation in the policy, the insurable value of the subject-matter insured must be ascertained as follows:—

(1) In insurance on ship, the insurable value is the value, at the commencement of the risk, of the ship, including her outfit, provisions and stores for the officers and crew, money advanced for seamen's wages, and other disbursements (if any) incurred to make the ship fit for the voyage or adventure contemplated by the policy, plus the charges of insurance upon the whole: The insurable value, in the case of a steamship, includes also the machinery, boilers, and coals and engine stores if owned by the assured, and, in the case of a ship engaged in a special trade, the ordinary fittings requisite for that trade;

(2) In insurance on freight, whether paid in advance or otherwise, the insurable value is the gross amount of the freight at the risk of the assured, plus the charges of insurance;

(3) In insurance on goods or merchandise, the insurable value is the prime cost of the property insured, plus the expenses of and incidental to shipping and the charges of insurance upon the whole;

(4) In insurance on any other subject-matter, the insurable value is the amount at the risk of the assured when the policy attaches, plus the charges of insurance.

Disclosure and Representations

17. Insurance is uberrimæ fidei

A contract of marine insurance is a contract based upon the utmost good faith, and, if the utmost good faith be not observed by either party, the contract may be avoided by the other party.

18. Disclosure by assured

(1) Subject to the provisions of this section, the assured must disclose to the insurer, before the contract is concluded, every material circumstance which is known to the assured, and the assured is

deemed to know every circumstance which, in the ordinary course of business, ought to be known by him. If the assured fails to make such disclosure, the insurer may avoid the contract.

(2) Every circumstance is material which would influence the judgment of a prudent insurer in fixing the premium, or determining whether he will take the risk.

(3) In the absence of inquiry the following circumstances need not be disclosed, namely:—

(a) Any circumstance which diminishes the risk;

(b) Any circumstance which is known or presumed to be known to the insurer. The insurer is presumed to know matters of common notoriety or knowledge, and matters which an insurer in the ordinary course of his business, as such, ought to know;

(c) Any circumstance as to which information is waived by the insurer;

(d) Any circumstance which it is superfluous to disclose by reason of any express or implied warranty.

(4) Whether any particular circumstance, which is not disclosed, be material or not is, in each case, a question of fact.

(5) The term "circumstance" includes any communication made to, or information received by, the assured.

19. Disclosure by agent effecting insurance

Subject to the provisions of the preceding section as to circumstances which need not be disclosed, where an insurance is effected for the assured by an agent, the agent must disclose to the insurer—

(a) Every material circumstance which is known to himself, and an agent to insure is deemed to know every circumstance which in the ordinary course of business ought to be known by, or to have been communicated to, him; and

(b) Every material circumstance which the assured is bound to disclose, unless it come to his knowledge too late to communicate it to the agent.

20. Representations pending negotiation of contract

(1) Every material representation made by the assured or his agent to the insurer during the negotiations for the contract, and before the contract is concluded, must be true. If it be untrue the insurer may avoid the contract.

(2) A representation is material which would influence the judgment of a prudent insurer in fixing the premium, or determining whether he will take the risk.

(3) A representation may be either a representation as to a matter of fact, or as to a matter of expectation or belief.

(4) A representation as to a matter of fact is true, if it be substantially correct, that is to say, if the difference between what is represented and what is actually correct would not be considered material by a prudent insurer.

(5) A representation as to a matter of expectation or belief is true if it be made in good faith.

(6) A representation may be withdrawn or corrected before the contract is concluded.

(7) Whether a particular representation be material or not is, in each case, a question of fact.

21. When contract is deemed to be concluded

A contract of marine insurance is deemed to be concluded when the proposal of the assured is accepted by the insurer, whether the policy be then issued or not; and, for the purpose of showing when the proposal was accepted, reference may be made to the slip or covering note or other customary memorandum of the contract. . . F1

Annotations:

Amendments (Textual)

F1 Words repealed as to instruments made or executed after 1. 8. 1959 by Finance Act 1959 (c. 58), Sch. 8 Pt. II

The Policy

22. Contract must be embodied in policy

Subject to the provisions of any statute, a contract of marine insurance is inadmissible in evidence unless it is embodied in a marine policy in accordance with this Act. The policy may be executed and issued either at the time when the contract is concluded, or afterwards.

Annotations:

Modifications etc. (not altering text)

C1S. 22 excluded by Marine and Aviation Insurance (War Risks) Act 1952 (c. 57), s. 7(1) and Finance Act 1959 (c. 58), s. 30(6)(7)

23. What policy must specify

A marine policy must specify—

(1) The name of the assured, or of some person who effects the insurance on his behalf:

(2)—(5). F1

Annotations:

Amendments (Textual)

F1S. 23(2) - (5) repealed as to instruments made or executed after 1. 8. 1959 by Finance Act 1959 (c. 58), Sch. 8 Pt. II

24. Signature of insurer

(1) A marine policy must be signed by or on behalf of the insurer, provided that in the case of a corporation the corporate seal may be sufficient, but nothing in this section shall be construed as requiring the subscription of a corporation to be under seal.

(2) Where a policy is subscribed by or on behalf of two or more insurers, each subscription, unless the contrary be expressed, constitutes a distinct contract with the assured.

25. Voyage and time policies

(1) Where the contract is to insure the subject-matter "at and from," or from one place to another or others, the policy is called a "voyage policy," and where the contract is to insure the subject-matter for a definite period of time the policy is called a "time policy." A contract for both voyage and time may be included in the same policy.

(2). F1

Annotations:

Amendments (Textual)

F1S. 25(2) repealed as to instruments made or executed after 1. 8. 1959 by Finance Act 1959 (c. 58), Sch. 8 Pt. II

26. Designation of subject-matter

(1) The subject-matter insured must be designated in a marine policy with reasonable certainty.

(2) The nature and extent of the interest of the assured in the subject-matter insured need not be specified in the policy.

(3) Where the policy designates the subject-matter insured in general terms, it shall be construed to apply to the interest intended by the assured to be covered.

(4) In the application of this section regard shall be had to any usage regulating the designation of the subject-matter insured.

27. Valued policy

(1) A policy may be either valued or unvalued.

(2) A valued policy is a policy which specifies the agreed value of the subject-matter insured.

(3) Subject to the provisions of this Act, and in the absence of fraud, the value fixed by the policy is, as between the insurer and assured, conclusive of the insurable value of the subject intended to be insured, whether the loss be total or partial.

(4) Unless the policy otherwise provides, the value fixed by the policy is not conclusive for the purpose of determining whether there has been a constructive total loss.

28. Unvalued policy

An unvalued policy is a policy which does not specify the value of the subject-matter insured, but, subject to the limit of the sum insured, leaves the insurable value to be subsequently ascertained, in the manner herein-before specified.

29. Floating policy by ship or ships

(1) A floating policy is a policy which describes the insurance in general terms, and leaves the name of the ship or ships and other particulars to be defined by subsequent declaration.

(2) The subsequent declaration or declarations may be made by indorsement on the policy, or in other customary manner.

(3) Unless the policy otherwise provides, the declarations must be made in the order of dispatch or shipment. They must, in the case of goods, comprise all consignments within the terms of the policy, and the value of the goods or other property must be honestly stated, but an omission or erroneous declaration may be rectified even after loss or arrival, provided the omission or declaration was made in good faith.

(4) Unless the policy otherwise provides, where a declaration of value is not made until after notice of loss or arrival, the policy must be treated as an unvalued policy as regards the subject-matter of that declaration.

30. Construction of terms in policy

(1) A policy may be in the form in the First Schedule to this Act.

(2) Subject to the provisions of this Act, and unless the context of the policy otherwise requires, the terms and expressions mentioned in the First Schedule to this Act shall be construed as having the

scope and meaning in that schedule assigned to them.

31. Premium to be arranged

(1) Where an insurance is effected at a premium to be arranged, and no arrangement is made, a reasonable premium is payable.

(2) Where an insurance is effected on the terms that an additional premium is to be arranged in a given event, and that event happens but no arrangement is made, then a reasonable additional premium is payable.

Double Insurance

32. Double insurance

(1) Where two or more policies are effected by or on behalf of the assured on the same adventure and interest or any part thereof, and the sums insured exceed the indemnity allowed by this Act, the assured is said to be over-insured by double insurance.

(2) Where the assured is over-insured by double insurance—

(a) The assured, unless the policy otherwise provides, may claim payment from the insurers in such order as he may think fit, provided that he is not entitled to receive any sum in excess of the indemnity allowed by this Act;

(b) Where the policy under which the assured claims is a valued policy, the assured must give credit as against the valuation for any sum received by him under any other policy without regard to the actual value of the subject-matter insured;

(c) Where the policy under which the assured claims is an unvalued policy he must give credit, as against the full insurable value, for any sum received by him under any other policy;

(d) Where the assured receives any sum in excess of the indemnity allowed by this Act, he is deemed to hold such sum in trust for the insurers, according to their right of contribution among themselves.

Warranties, &c

33. Nature of warranty

(1) A warranty, in the following sections relating to warranties, means a promissory warranty, that is to say, a warranty by which the assured undertakes that some particular thing shall or shall not be done, or that some condition shall be fulfilled, or whereby he affirms or negatives the existence of a particular state of facts.

(2) A warranty may be express or implied.

(3) A warranty, as above defined, is a condition which must be exactly complied with, whether it be material to the risk or not. If it be not so complied with, then, subject to any express provision in the policy, the insurer is discharged from liability as from the date of the breach of warranty, but without prejudice to any liability incurred by him before that date.

34. When breach of warranty excused

(1) Non-compliance with a warranty is excused when, by reason of a change of circumstances, the warranty ceases to be applicable to the circumstances of the contract, or when compliance with the

warranty is rendered unlawful by any subsequent law.

(2) Where a warranty is broken, the assured cannot avail himself of the defence that the breach has been remedied, and the warranty complied with, before loss.

(3) A breach of warranty may be waived by the insurer.

35. Express warranties

(1) An express warranty may be in any form of words from which the intention to warrant is to be inferred.

(2) An express warranty must be included in, or written upon, the policy, or must be contained in some document incorporated by reference into the policy.

(3) An express warranty does not exclude an implied warranty, unless it be inconsistent therewith.

36. Warranty of neutrality

(1) Where insurable property, whether ship or goods, is expressly warranted neutral, there is an implied condition that the property shall have a neutral character at the commencement of the risk, and that, so far as the assured can control the matter, its neutral character shall be preserved during the risk.

(2) Where a ship is expressly warranted "neutral" there is also an implied condition that, so far as the assured can control the matter, she shall be properly documented, that is to say, that she shall carry the necessary papers to establish her neutrality, and that she shall not falsify or suppress her papers, or use simulated papers. If any loss occurs through breach of this condition, the insurer may avoid the contract.

37. No implied warranty of nationality

There is no implied warranty as to the nationality of a ship, or that her nationality shall not be changed during the risk.

38. Warranty of good safety

Where the subject-matter insured is warranted "well" or "in good safety" on a particular day, it is sufficient if it be safe at any time during that day.

39. Warranty of seaworthiness of ship

(1) In a voyage policy there is an implied warranty that at the commencement of the voyage the ship shall be seaworthy for the purpose of the particular adventure insured.

(2) Where the policy attaches while the ship is in port, there is also an implied warranty that she shall, at the commencement of the risk, be reasonably fit to encounter the ordinary perils of the port.

(3) Where the policy relates to a voyage which is performed in different stages, during which the ship requires different kinds of or further preparation or equipment, there is an implied warranty that at the commencement of each stage the ship is seaworthy in respect of such preparation or equipment for the purposes of that stage.

(4) A ship is deemed to be seaworthy when she is reasonably fit in all respects to encounter the ordinary perils of the seas of the adventure insured.

(5) In a time policy there is no implied warranty that the ship shall be seaworthy at any stage of the adventure, but where, with the privity of the assured, the ship is sent to sea in an unseaworthy

state, the insurer is not liable for any loss attributable to unseaworthiness.

40. No implied warranty that goods are seaworthy

(1) In a policy on goods or other moveables there is no implied warranty that the goods or moveables are seaworthy.

(2) In a voyage policy on goods or other moveables there is an implied warranty that at the commencement of the voyage the ship is not only seaworthy as a ship, but also that she is reasonably fit to carry the goods or other moveables to the destination contemplated by the policy.

41. Warranty of legality

There is an implied warranty that the adventure insured is a lawful one, and that, so far as the assured can control the matter, the adventure shall be carried out in a lawful manner.

The Voyage

42. Implied condition as to commencement of risk

(1) Where the subject-matter is insured by a voyage policy "at and from" or "from" a particular place, it is not necessary that the ship should be at that place when the contract is concluded, but there is an implied condition that the adventure shall be commenced within a reasonable time, and that if the adventure be not so commenced the insurer may avoid the contract.

(2) The implied condition may be negatived by showing that the delay was caused by circumstances known to the insurer before the contract was concluded, or by showing that he waived the condition.

43. Alteration of port of departure

Where the place of departure is specified by the policy, and the ship instead of sailing from that place sails from any other place, the risk does not attach.

44. Sailing for different destination

Where the destination is specified in the policy, and the ship, instead of sailing for that destination, sails for any other destination, the risk does not attach.

45. Change of voyage

(1) Where, after the commencement of the risk, the destination of the ship is voluntarily changed from the destination contemplated by the policy, there is said to be a change of voyage.

(2) Unless the policy otherwise provides, where there is a change of voyage, the insurer is discharged from liability as from the time of change, that is to say, as from the time when the determination to change it is manifested; and it is immaterial that the ship may not in fact have left the course of voyage contemplated by the policy when the loss occurs.

46. Deviation

(1) Where a ship, without lawful excuse, deviates from the voyage contemplated by the policy, the insurer is discharged from liability as from the time of deviation, and it is immaterial that the ship may have regained her route before any loss occurs.

(2) There is a deviation from the voyage contemplated by the policy—

(a) Where the course of the voyage is specifically designated by the policy, and that course is departed from; or

(b) Where the course of the voyage is not specifically designated by the policy, but the usual and customary course is departed from.

(3) The intention to deviate is immaterial; there must be a deviation in fact to discharge the insurer from his liability under the contract.

47. Several ports of discharge

(1) Where several ports of discharge are specified by the policy, the ship may proceed to all or any of them, but, in the absence of any usage or sufficient cause to the contrary, she must proceed to them, or such of them as she goes to, in the order designated by the policy. If she does not there is a deviation.

(2) Where the policy is to "ports of discharge," within a given area, which are not named, the ship must, in the absence of any usage or sufficient cause to the contrary, proceed to them, or such of them as she goes to, in their geographical order. If she does not there is a deviation.

48. Delay in voyage

In the case of a voyage policy, the adventure insured must be prosecuted throughout its course with reasonable dispatch, and, if without lawful excuse it is not so prosecuted, the insurer is discharged from liability as from the time when the delay became unreasonable.

49. Excuses for deviation or delay

(1) Deviation or delay in prosecuting the voyage contemplated by the policy is excused—

(a) Where authorised by any special term in the policy; or

(b) Where caused by circumstances beyond the control of the master and his employer; or

(c) Where reasonably necessary in order to comply with an express or implied warranty; or

(d) Where reasonably necessary for the safety of the ship or subject-matter insured; or

(e) For the purpose of saving human life, or aiding a ship in distress where human life may be in danger; or

(f) Where reasonably necessary for the purpose of obtaining medical or surgical aid for any person on board the ship; or

(g) Where caused by the barratrous conduct of the master or crew, if barratry be one of the perils insured against.

(2) When the cause excusing the deviation or delay ceases to operate, the ship must resume her course, and prosecute her voyage, with reasonable dispatch.

Assignment of Policy

50. When and how policy is assignable

(1) A marine policy is assignable unless it contains terms expressly prohibiting assignment. It may be assigned either before or after loss.

(2) Where a marine policy has been assigned so as to pass the beneficial interest in such policy, the assignee of the policy is entitled to sue thereon in his own name; and the defendant is entitled to make any defence arising out of the contract which he would have been entitled to make if the action had been brought in the name of the person by or on behalf of whom the policy was effected.

(3) A marine policy may be assigned byindorsement thereon or in other customary manner.

51. Assured who has no interest cannot assign

Where the assured has parted with or lost his interest in the subject-matter insured, and has not, before or at the time of so doing, expressly or impliedly agreed to assign the policy, any subsequent assignment of the policy is inoperative:

Provided that nothing in this section affects the assignment of a policy after loss.

The Premium

52. When premium payable

Unless otherwise agreed, the duty of the assured or his agent to pay the premium, and the duty of the insurer to issue the policy to the assured or his agent, are concurrent conditions, and the insurer is not bound to issue the policy until payment or tender of the premium.

53. Policy effected through broker

(1) Unless otherwise agreed, where a marine policy is effected on behalf of the assured by a broker, the broker is directly responsible to the insurer for the premium, and the insurer is directly responsible to the assured for the amount which may be payable in respect of losses, or in respect of returnable premium.

(2) Unless otherwise agreed, the broker has, as against the assured, a lien upon the policy for the amount of the premium and his charges in respect of effecting the policy; and, where he has dealt with the person who employs him as a principal, he has also a lien on the policy in respect of any balance on any insurance account which may be due to him from such person, unless when the debt was incurred he had reason to believe that such person was only an agent.

54. Effect of receipt on policy

Where a marine policy effected on behalf of the assured by a broker acknowledges the receipt of the premium, such acknowledgement is, in the absence of fraud, conclusive as between the insurer and the assured, but not as between the insurer and broker.

Loss and Abandonment

55. Included and excluded losses

(1) Subject to the provisions of this Act, and unless the policy otherwise provides, the insurer is liable for any loss proximately caused by a peril insured against, but, subject as aforesaid, he is not liable for any loss which is not proximately caused by a peril insured against.

(2) In particular—

(a) The insurer is not liable for any loss attributable to the wilful misconduct of the assured, but, unless the policy otherwise provides, he is liable for any loss proximately caused by a peril insured against, even though the loss would not have happened but for the misconduct or negligence of the master or crew;

(b) Unless the policy otherwise provides, the insurer on ship or goods is not liable for any loss proximately caused by delay, although the delay be caused by a peril insured against;

(c) Unless the policy otherwise provides, the insurer is not liable for ordinary wear and tear, ordinary leakage and breakage, inherent vice or nature of the subject-matter insured, or for any loss proximately caused by rats or vermin, or for any injury to machinery not proximately caused by maritime perils.

56. Partial and total loss

(1) A loss may be either total or partial. Any loss other than a total loss, as hereinafter defined, is a partial loss.

(2) A total loss may be either an actual total loss, or a constructive total loss.

(3) Unless a different intention appears from the terms of the policy, an insurance against total loss includes a constructive, as well as an actual, total loss.

(4) Where the assured brings an action for a total loss and the evidence proves only a partial loss, he may, unless the policy otherwise provides, recover for a partial loss.

(5) Where goods reach their destination in specie, but by reason of obliteration of marks, or otherwise, they are incapable of identification, the loss, if any, is partial, and not total.

57. Actual total loss

(1) Where the subject-matter insured is destroyed, or so damaged as to cease to be a thing of the kind insured, or where the assured is irretrievably deprived thereof, there is an actual total loss.

(2) In the case of an actual total loss no notice of abandonment need be given.

58. Missing ship

Where the ship concerned in the adventure is missing, and after the lapse of a reasonable time no news of her has been received, an actual total loss may be presumed.

59. Effect of transhipment, &c

Where, by a peril insured against, the voyage is interrupted at an intermediate port or place, under such circumstances as, apart from any special stipulation in the contract of affreightment, to justify the master in landing and reshipping the goods or other moveables, or in transhipping them, and sending them on to their destination, the liability of the insurer continues, notwithstanding the landing or transhipment.

60. Constructive total loss defined

(1) Subject to any express provision in the policy, there is a constructive total loss where the subject-matter insured is reasonably abandoned on account of its actual total loss appearing to be unavoidable, or because it could not be preserved from actual total loss without an expenditure which would exceed its value when the expenditure had been incurred.

(2) In particular, there is a constructive total loss—

(i) Where the assured is deprived of the possession of his ship or goods by a peril insured against, and (a) it is unlikely that he can recover the ship or goods, as the case may be, or (b) the cost of recovering the ship or goods, as the case may be, would exceed their value when recovered; or

(ii) In the case of damage to a ship, where she is so damaged by a peril insured against that the cost of repairing the damage would exceed the value of the ship when repaired.

In estimating the cost of repairs, no deduction is to be made in respect of general average contributions to those repairs payable by other interests, but account is to be taken of the expense of future salvage operations and of any future general average contributions to which the ship would be liable if repaired; or

(iii) In the case of damage to goods, where the cost of repairing the damage and forwarding the goods to their destination would exceed their value on arrival.

61. Effect of constructive total loss

Where there is a constructive total loss the assured may either treat the loss as a partial loss, or abandon the subject-matter insured to the insurer and treat the loss as if it were an actual total loss.

62. Notice of abandonment

(1) Subject to the provisions of this section, where the assured elects to abandon the subject-matter insured to the insurer, he must give notice of abandonment. If he fails to do so the loss can only be treated as a partial loss.

(2) Notice of abandonment may be given in writing, or by word of mouth, or partly in writing and partly by word of mouth, and may be given in any terms which indicate the intention of the assured to abandon his insured interest in the subject-matter insured unconditionally to the insurer.

(3) Notice of abandonment must be given with reasonable diligence after the receipt of reliable information of the loss, but where the information is of a doubtful character the assured is entitled to a reasonable time to make inquiry.

(4) Where notice of abandonment is properly given, the rights of the assured are not prejudiced by the fact that the insurer refuses to accept the abandonment.

(5) The acceptance of an abandonment may be either express or implied from the conduct of the insurer. The mere silence of the insurer after notice is not an acceptance.

(6) Where notice of abandonment is accepted the abandonment is irrevocable. The acceptance of the notice conclusively admits liability for the loss and the sufficiency of the notice.

(7) Notice of abandonment is unnecessary where, at the time when the assured receives information of the loss, there would be no possibility of benefit to the insurer if notice were given to him.

(8) Notice of abandonment may be waived by the insurer.

(9) Where an insurer has re-insured his risk, no notice of abandonment need be given by him.

63. Effect of abandonment

(1) Where there is a valid abandonment the insurer is entitled to take over the interest of the assured in whatever may remain of the subject-matter insured, and all proprietary rights incidental thereto.

(2) Upon the abandonment of a ship, the insurer thereof is entitled to any freight in course of being earned, and which is earned by her subsequent to the casualty causing the loss, less the expenses of earning it incurred after the casualty; and, where the ship is carrying the owner's goods, the insurer is entitled to a reasonable remuneration for the carriage of them subsequent to the casualty causing the loss.

Partial Losses (including Salvage and General Average and Particular Charges)

64. Particular average loss

(1) A particular average loss is a partial loss of the subject-matter insured, caused by a peril insured against, and which is not a general average loss.

(2) Expenses incurred by or on behalf of the assured for the safety or preservation of the subject-matter insured, other than general average and salvage charges, are called particular charges. Parti-

cular charges are not included in particular average.

65. Salvage charges

(1) Subject to any express provision in the policy, salvage charges incurred in preventing a loss by perils insured against may be recovered as a loss by those perils.

(2) "Salvage charges" means the charges recoverable under maritime law by a salvor independently of contract. They do not include the expenses of services in the nature of salvage rendered by the assured or his agents, or any person employed for hire by them, for the purpose of averting a peril insured against. Such expenses, where properly incurred, may be recovered as particular charges or as a general average loss, according to the circumstances under which they were incurred.

66. General average loss

(1) A general average loss is a loss caused by or directly consequential on a general average act. It includes a general average expenditure as well as a general average sacrifice.

(2) There is a general average act where any extraordinary sacrifice or expenditure is voluntarily and reasonably made or incurred in time of peril for the purpose of preserving the property imperilled in the common adventure.

(3) Where there is a general average loss, the party on whom it falls is entitled, subject to the conditions imposed by maritime law, to a rateable contribution from the other parties interested, and such contribution is called a general average contribution.

(4) Subject to any express provision in the policy, where the assured has incurred a general average expenditure, he may recover from the insurer in respect of the proportion of the loss which falls upon him; and, in the case of a general average sacrifice, he may recover from the insurer in respect of the whole loss without having enforced his right of contribution from the other parties liable to contribute.

(5) Subject to any express provision in the policy, where the assured has paid, or is liable to pay, a general average contribution in respect of the subject insured, he may recover therefor from the insurer.

(6) In the absence of express stipulation, the insurer is not liable for any general average loss or contribution where the loss was not incurred for the purpose of avoiding, or in connexion with the avoidance of, a peril insured against.

(7) Where ship, freight, and cargo, or any two of those interests, are owned by the same assured, the liability of the insurer in respect of general average losses or contributions is to be determined as if those subjects were owned by different persons.

Measure of Indemnity

67. Extent of liability of insurer for loss

(1) The sum which the assured can recover in respect of a loss on a policy by which he is insured, in the case of an unvalued policy to the full extent of the insurable value, or, in the case of a valued policy to the full extent of the value fixed by the policy is called the measure of indemnity.

(2) Where there is a loss recoverable under the policy, the insurer, or each insurer if there be more than one, is liable for such proportion of the measure of indemnity as the amount of his subscrip-

tion bears to the value fixed by the policy in the case of a valued policy, or to the insurable value in the case of an unvalued policy.

68. Total loss

Subject to the provisions of this Act and to any express provision in the policy, where there is a total loss of the subject-matter insured,—

(1) If the policy be a valued policy, the measure of indemnity is the sum fixed by the policy:

(2) If the policy be an unvalued policy, the measure of indemnity is the insurable value of the subject-matter insured.

69. Partial loss of ship

Where a ship is damaged, but is not totally lost, the measure of indemnity, subject to any express provision in the policy, is as follows:—

(1) Where the ship has been repaired, the assured is entitled to the reasonable cost of the repairs, less the customary deductions, but not exceeding the sum insured in respect of any one casualty;

(2) Where the ship has been only partially repaired, the assured is entitled to the reasonable cost of such repairs, computed as above, and also to be indemnified for the reasonable depreciation, if any, arising from the unrepaired damage, provided that the aggregate amount shall not exceed the cost of repairing the whole damage, computed as above;

(3) Where the ship has not been repaired, and has not been sold in her damaged state during the risk, the assured is entitled to be indemnified for the reasonable depreciation arising from the unrepaired damage, but not exceeding the reasonable cost of repairing such damage, computed as above.

70. Partial loss of freight

Subject to any express provision in the policy, where there is a partial loss of freight, the measure of indemnity is such proportion of the sum fixed by the policy in the case of a valued policy, or of the insurable value in the case of an unvalued policy, as the proportion of freight lost by the assured bears to the whole freight at the risk of the assured under the policy.

71. Partial loss of goods, merchandise, &c

Where there is a partial loss of goods, merchandise, or other moveables, the measure of indemnity, subject to any express provision in the policy, is as follows:—

(1) Where part of the goods, merchandise or other moveables insured by a valued policy is totally lost, the measure of indemnity is such proportion of the sum fixed by the policy as the insurable value of the part lost bears to the insurable value of the whole, ascertained as in the case of an unvalued policy;

(2) Where part of the goods, merchandise, or other moveables insured by an unvalued policy is totally lost, the measure of indemnity is the insurable value of the part lost, ascertained as in case of total loss;

(3) Where the whole or any part of the goods or merchandise insured has been delivered damaged at its destination, the measure of indemnity is such proportion of the sum fixed by the policy in the case of a valued policy, or of the insurable value in the case of an unvalued policy, as the difference be-

tween the gross sound and damaged values at the place of arrival bears to the gross sound value;

(4) "Gross value" means the wholesale price, or, if there be no such price, the estimated value, with, in either case, freight, landing charges, and duty paid beforehand; provided that, in the case of goods or merchandise customarily sold in bond, the bonded price is deemed to be the gross value. "Gross proceeds" means the actual price obtained at a sale where all charges on sale are paid by the sellers.

72. Apportionment of valuation

(1) Where different species of property are insured under a single valuation, the valuation must be apportioned over the different species in proportion to their respective insurable values, as in the case of an unvalued policy. The insured value of any part of a species is such proportion of the total insured value of the same as the insurable value of the part bears to the insurable value of the whole, ascertained in both cases as provided by this Act.

(2) Where a valuation has to be apportioned, and particulars of the prime cost of each separate species, quality, or description of goods cannot be ascertained, the division of the valuation may be made over the net arrived sound values of the different species, qualities, or descriptions of goods.

73. General average contributions and salvage charges

(1) Subject to any express provision in the policy, where the assured has paid, or is liable for, any general average contribution, the measure of indemnity is the full amount of such contribution, if the subject-matter liable to contribution is insured for its full contributory value; but, if such subject-matter be not insured for its full contributory value, or if only part of it be insured, the indemnity payable by the insurer must be reduced in proportion to the under insurance, and where there has been a particular average loss which constitutes a deduction from the contributory value, and for which the insurer is liable, that amount must be deducted from the insured value in order to ascertain what the insurer is liable to contribute.

(2) Where the insurer is liable for salvage charges the extent of his liability must be determined on the like principle.

74. Liabilities to third parties

Where the assured has effected an insurance in express terms against any liability to a third party, the measure of indemnity, subject to any express provision in the policy, is the amount paid or payable by him to such third party in respect of such liability.

75. General provisions as to measure of indemnity

(1) Where there has been a loss in respect of any subject-matter not expressly provided for in the foregoing provisions of this Act, the measure of indemnity shall be ascertained, as nearly as may be, in accordance with those provisions, in so far as applicable to the particular case.

(2) Nothing in the provisions of this Act relating to the measure of indemnity shall affect the rules relating to double insurance, or prohibit the insurer from disproving interest wholly or in part, or from showing that at the time of the loss the whole or any part of the subject-matter insured was not at risk under the policy.

76. Particular average warranties

(1) Where the subject-matter insured is warranted free from particular average, the assured can-

not recover for a loss of part, other than a loss incurred by a general average sacrifice, unless the contract contained in the policy be apportionable; but, if the contract be apportionable, the assured may recover for a total loss of any apportionable part.

(2) Where the subject-matter insured is warranted free from particular average, either wholly or under a certain percentage, the insurer is nevertheless liable for salvage charges, and for particular charges and other expenses properly incurred pursuant to the provisions of the suing and labouring clause in order to avert a loss insured against.

(3) Unless the policy otherwise provides, where the subject-matter insured is warranted free from particular average under a specified percentage, a general average loss cannot be added to a particular average loss to make up the specified percentage.

(4) For the purpose of ascertaining whether the specified percentage has been reached, regard shall be had only to the actual loss suffered by the subject-matter insured. Particular charges and the expenses of and incidental to ascertaining and proving the loss must be excluded.

77. Successive losses

(1) Unless the policy otherwise provides, and subject to the provisions of this Act, the insurer is liable for successive losses, even though the total amount of such losses may exceed the sum insured.

(2) Where, under the same policy, a partial loss, which has not been repaired or otherwise made good, is followed by a total loss, the assured can only recover in respect of the total loss:

Provided that nothing in this section shall affect the liability of the insurer under the suing and labouring clause.

78. Suing and labouring clause

(1) Where the policy contains a suing and labouring clause, the engagement thereby entered into is deemed to be supplementary to the contract of insurance, and the assured may recover from the insurer any expenses properly incurred pursuant to the clause, notwithstanding that the insurer may have paid for a total loss, or that the subject-matter may have been warranted free from particular average, either wholly or under a certain percentage.

(2) General average losses and contributions and salvage charges, as defined by this Act, are not recoverable under the suing and labouring clause.

(3) Expenses incurred for the purpose of averting or diminishing any loss not covered by the policy are not recoverable under the suing and labouring clause.

(4) It is the duty of the assured and his agents, in all cases, to take such measures as may be reasonable for the purpose of averting or minimising a loss.

Rights of Insurer on Payment

79. Right of subrogation

(1) Where the insurer pays for a total loss, either of the whole, or in the case of goods of any apportionable part, of the subject-matter insured, he thereupon becomes entitled to take over the interest of the assured in whatever may remain of the subject-matter so paid for, and he is thereby subrogated to all the rights and remedies of the assured in and in respect of that subject-matter as from the time of the casualty causing the loss.

(2) Subject to the foregoing provisions, where the insurer pays for a partial loss, he acquires no title to the subject-matter insured, or such part of it as may remain, but he is thereupon subrogated to all rights and remedies of the assured in and in respect of the subject-matter insured as from the time of the casualty causing the loss, in so far as the assured has been indemnified, according to this Act, by such payment for the loss.

80. Right of contribution

(1) Where the assured is over-insured by double insurance, each insurer is bound, as between himself and the other insurers, to contribute rateably to the loss in proportion to the amount for which he is liable under his contract.

(2) If any insurer pays more than his proportion of the loss, he is entitled to maintain an action for contribution against the other insurers, and is entitled to the like remedies as a surety who has paid more than his proportion of the debt.

81. Effect of under insurance

Where the assured is insured for an amount less than the insurable value or, in the case of a valued policy, for an amount less than the policy valuation, he is deemed to be his own insurer in respect of the uninsured balance.

Return of Premium

82. Enforcement of return

Where the premium or a proportionate part thereof is, by this Act, declared to be returnable,—

(a) If already paid, it may be recovered by the assured from the insurer; and

(b) If unpaid, it may be retained by the assured or his agent.

83. Return by agreement

Where the policy contains a stipulation for the return of the premium, or a proportionate part thereof, on the happening of a certain event, and that event happens, the premium, or, as the case may be, the proportionate part thereof, is thereupon returnable to the assured.

84. Return for failure of consideration

(1) Where the consideration for the payment of the premium totally fails, and there has been no fraud or illegality on the part of the assured or his agents, the premium is thereupon returnable to the assured.

(2) Where the consideration for the payment of the premium is apportionable and there is a total failure of any apportionable part of the consideration, a proportionate part of the premium is, under the like conditions, thereupon returnable to the assured. (3) In particular—

(a) Where the policy is void, or is avoided by the insurer as from the commencement of the risk, the premium is returnable, provided that there has been no fraud or illegality on the part of the assured; but if the risk is not apportionable, and has once attached, the premium is not returnable;

(b) Where the subject-matter insured, or part thereof, has never been imperilled, the premium, or, as the case may be, a proportionate part thereof, is returnable;

Provided that where the subject-matter has been insured "lost or not lost" and has arrived in safety at the time when the contract is concluded, the premium is not returnable unless, at such time, the insurer knew of the safe arrival;

(c) Where the assured has no insurable interest throughout the currency of the risk, the premium is returnable, provided that this rule does not apply to a policy effected by way of gaming or wagering;

(d) Where the assured has a defeasible interest which is terminated during the currency of the risk, the premium is not returnable;

(e) Where the assured has over-insured under an unvalued policy, a proportionate part of the premium is returnable;

(f) Subject to the foregoing provisions, where the assured has over-insured by double insurance, a proportionate part of the several premiums is returnable:

Provided that, if the policies are effected at different times, and any earlier policy has at any time borne the entire risk, or if a claim has been paid on the policy in respect of the full sum insured thereby, no premium is returnable in respect of that policy, and when the double insurance is effected knowingly by the assured no premium is returnable.

Mutual Insurance

85. Modification of Act in case of mutual insurance

(1) Where two or more persons mutually agree to insure each other against marine losses there is said to be a mutual insurance.

(2) The provisions of this Act relating to the premium do not apply to mutual insurance, but a guarantee, or such other arrangement as may be agreed upon, may be substituted for the premium.

(3) The provisions of this Act, in so far as they may be modified by the agreement of the parties, may in the case of mutual insurance be modified by the terms of the policies issued by the association, or by the rules and regulations of the association.

(4) Subject to the exceptions mentioned in this section, the provisions of this Act apply to a mutual insurance.

Supplemental

86. Ratification by assured

Where a contract of marine insurance is in good faith effected by one person on behalf of another, the person on whose behalf it is effected may ratify the contract even after he is aware of a loss.

87. Implied obligations varied by agreement or usage

(1) Where any right, duty, or liability would arise under a contract of marine insurance by implication of law, it may be negatived or varied by express agreement, or by usage, if the usage be such as to bind both parties to the contract.

(2) The provisions of this section extend to any right, duty, or liability declared by this Act which may be lawfully modified by agreement.

88. Reasonable time, &c. a question of fact

Where by this Act any reference is made to reasonable time, reasonable premium, or reasonable diligence, the question what is reasonable is a question of fact.

89. Slip as evidence

Where there is a duly stamped policy, reference may be made, as heretofore, to the slip or covering note, in any legal proceeding.

90. Interpretation of terms

In this Act, unless the context or subject-matter otherwise requires,—

"Action" includes counter-claim and set off:

"Freight" includes the profit derivable by a shipowner from the employment of his ship to carry his own goods or moveables, as well as freight payable by a third party, but does not include passage money:

"Moveables" means any moveable tangible property, other than the ship, and includes money, valuable securities, and other documents:

"Policy" means a marine policy.

91. Savings

(1) Nothing in this Act, or in any repeal effected thereby, shall affect—

(a) The provisions of the M1Stamp Act 1891, or any enactment for the time being in force relating to the revenue;

(b) The provisions of the M2Companies Act 1862, or any enactment amending or substituted for the same;

(c) The provisions of any statute not expressly repealed by this Act.

(2) The rules of the common law including the law merchant, save in so far as they are inconsistent with the express provisions of this Act, shall continue to apply to contracts of marine insurance.

Annotations:

Marginal Citations

M11891 c. 39.

M21862 c. 89.

92, 93. . . . . F1

Annotations:

Amendments (Textual)

F1Ss. 92, 93, Sch. 2 repealed by Statute Law Revision Act 1927 (c. 42)

94. Short title

This Act may be cited as the Marine Insurance Act 1906.

FIRST SCHEDULE

Form of Policy

Lloyd's S. G. policy Be it known that as well in own name as for and in the name and names of all and every other person or persons to whom the same doth, may, or shall appertain, in part or in all doth make assurance and cause and them, and every of them, to be insured lost or not lost, at and from

Upon any kind of goods and merchandises, and also upon the body, tackle, apparel, ordnance, munition, artillery, boat, and other furniture, of and in the good ship or vessel called the whereof is master under God, for this present voyage, or whosoever else shall go for master in the said ship, or by whatsoever other name or names the said ship, or the master thereof, is or shall be named or called; beginning the adventure upon the said goods and merchandises from the loading thereof aboard the said ship.

upon the said ship, &c.

and so shall continue and endure, during her abode there, upon the said ship, &c. And further, until the said ship, with all her ordnance, tackle, apparel, &c., and goods and merchandises whatsoever shall be arrived at

upon the said ship, &c., until she hath moored at anchor twenty-four hours in good safety; and upon the goods and merchandises, until the same be there discharged and safely landed. And it shall be lawful for the said ship, &c., in this voyage, to proceed and sail to and touch and stay at any ports or places whatsoever.

without prejudice to this insurance. The said ship, &c., goods and merchandises, &c., for so much as concerns the assured by agreement between the assured and assurers in this policy, are and shall be valued at

Touching the adventures and perils which we the assurers are contented to bear and do take upon us in this voyage: they are of the seas, men of war, fire, enemies, pirates, rovers, thieves, jettisons, letters of mart and countermart, surprisals, takings at sea, arrests, restraints, and detainments of all kings, princes, and people, of what nation, condition, or quality soever, barratry of the master and mariners, and of all other perils, losses, and misfortunes, that have or shall come to the hurt, detriment, or damage of the said goods and merchandises, and ship, &c., or any part thereof. And in case of any loss or misfortune it shall be lawful to the assured, their factors, servants and assigns, to sue, labour, and travel for, in and about the defence, safeguards, and recovery of the said goods and merchandises, and ship, &c., or any part thereof, without prejudice to this insurance; to the charges whereof we, the assurers, will contribute each one according to the rate and quantity of his sum herein assuredAnd it is especially declared and agreed that no acts of the insurer or insured in recovering, saving, or preserving the property insured shall be considered as a waiver, or acceptance of abandonment. And it is agreed by us, the insurers, that this writing or policy of assurance shall be of as much force and effect as the surest writing or policy of assurance heretofore made in Lombard Street, or in the Royal Exchange, or elsewhere in London. And so we, the assurers, are contented, and do hereby promise and bind ourselves, each one for his own part, our heirs, executors, and goods to the assured, their executors, administrators, and assigns, for the true performance of the premises, confessing ourselves paid the consideration due unto us for this assurance by the assured, at and after the rate of

In Witness whereof we, the assurers, have subscribed our names and sums assured in London.

N. B. —Corn, fish, salt, fruit, flour, and seed are warranted free from average, unless general, or the ship be stranded—sugar, tobacco, hemp, flax, hides and skins are warranted free from average, under five pounds per cent., and all other goods, also the ship and freight, are warranted free from average, under three pounds per cent. unless general, or the ship be stranded.

Rules for Construction of Policy

The following are the rules referred to by this Act for the construction of a policy in the above or other like form, where the context does not otherwise require:—

Lost or not lost 1

Where the subject-matter is insured "lost or not lost," and the loss has occurred before the contract is concluded, the risk attaches unless, at such time the assured was aware of the loss, and the insurer was not.

From 2

Where the subject-matter is insured "from" a particular place, the risk does not attach until the ship starts on the voyage insured.

At and from 3

(a) Where a ship is insured "at and from" a particular place, and she is at that place in good safety when the contract is concluded, the risk attaches immediately.

(b) If she be not at that place when the contract is concluded, the risk attaches as soon as she arrives there in good safety, and, unless the policy otherwise provides, it is immaterial that she is covered by another policy for a specified time after arrival.

(c) Where chartered freight is insured "at and from" a particular place, and the ship is at that place in good safety when the contract is concluded the risk attaches immediately. If she be not there when the contract is concluded, the risk attaches as soon as she arrives there in good safety.

(d) Where freight, other than chartered freight, is payable without special conditions and is insured "at and from" a particular place, the risk attaches pro rata as the goods or merchandise are shipped; provided that if there be cargo in readiness which belongs to the shipowner, or which some other person has contracted with him to ship, the risk attaches as soon as the ship is ready to receive such cargo.

From the loading thereof 4

Where goods or other moveables are insured "from the loading thereof," the risk does not attach until such goods or moveables are actually on board, and the insurer is not liable for them while in transit from the shore to the ship.

Safely landed 5

Where the risk on goods or other moveables continues until they are "safely landed," they must be landed in the customary manner and within a reasonable time after arrival at the port of discharge, and if they are not so landed the risk ceases.

Touch and stay 6

In the absence of any further licence or usage, the liberty to touch and stay "at any port or place whatsoever" does not authorise the ship to depart from the course of her voyage from the port of departure to the port of destination.

Perils of the seas 7

The term "perils of the seas" refers only to fortuitous accidents or casualties of the seas. It does not include the ordinary action of the winds and waves.

Pirates 8

The term "pirates" includes passengers who mutiny and rioters who attack the ship from the shore.

Annotations:

Modifications etc. (not altering text)

C1Sch. 1 rules 8, 10 amended by Public Order Act 1986 (c. 64, SIF 39:2), s. 10(2)

Thieves 9

The term "thieves" does not cover clandestine theft or a theft committed by any one of the ship's company, whether crew or passengers.

Restraint of princes 10

The term "arrests, &c., of kings, princes, and people" refers to political or executive acts, and does not include a loss caused by riot or by ordinary judicial process.

Annotations:

Modifications etc. (not altering text)

C1Sch. 1 rules 8, 10 amended by Public Order Act 1986 (c. 64, SIF 39:2), s. 10(2)

Barratry 11

The term "barratry" includes every wrongful act wilfully committed by the master or crew to the prejudice of the owner, or, as the case may be, the charterer.

All other perils 12

The term "all other perils" includes only perils similar in kind to the perils specifically mentioned in the policy.

Average unless general 13

The term "average unless general" means a partial loss of the subject-matter insured other than a general average loss, and does not include "particular charges."

Stranded 14

Where the ship has stranded, the insurer is liable for the excepted losses, although the loss is not attributable to the stranding, provided that when the stranding takes place the risk has attached and, if the policy be on goods, that the damaged goods are on board.

Ship 15

The term "ship" includes the hull, materials and outfit, stores and provisions for the officers and crew, and, in the case of vessels engaged in a special trade, the ordinary fittings requisite for the trade, and also, in the case of a steamship, the machinery, boilers, and coals and engine stores, if owned by the assured.

Freight 16

The term "freight" includes the profit derivable by a shipowner from the employment of his ship to carry his own goods or moveables, as well as freight payable by a third party, but does not include passage money.

Goods 17

The term "goods" means goods in the nature of merchandise, and does not include personal effects or provisions and stores for use on board.

In the absence of any usage to the contrary, deck cargo and living animals must be insured specifically, and not under the general denomination of goods.

SECOND SCHEDULE

.... F1

Annotations:

Amendments (Textual)

F1Ss. 92, 93, Sch. 2 repealed by Statute Law Revision Act 1927 (c. 42)

附录二

INSTITUTE CARGO CLAUSES(A)
1/1/82

RISKS COVERED

1. Risks Clause

1. This insurance covers all risks of loss of or damage to the subject-matter insured except as provided in Clauses 4, 5 6 and 7 below.

2. General Average Clause

2. This insurance covers general average and salvage charges, adjusted or determined according to the contract of affreightment and/or the governing law and practice, incurred to avoid or in connection with the avoidance of loss from any cause except those excluded in Clauses 4, 5 6 and 7 or elsewhere in this insurance.

3. "Both to Blame Collision" Clause

3. This insurance is extended to indemnify the Assured against such proportion of liability under the contract of affreightment "Both to Blame Collision" Clause as is in respect of a loss recoverable hereunder. In the event of any claim by shipowners under the said Clause the Assured agree to notify the Underwriters who shall have the right, at their own cost and expense, to defend the Assured against such claim.

EXCLUSIONS

4. General Exclusion Clause

4 In no case shall this insurance cover

4.1 loss damage or expense attributable to wilful misconduct of the Assured

4.2 ordinary leakage, ordinary loss in weight or volume, or ordinary wear and tear of the subject-matter insured

4.3 loss damage or expense caused by insufficiency or unsuitability of packing or preparation of the subject-matter insured (for the purpose of this Clause 4.3 "packing" shall be deemed to include stowage in a container or liftvan but only when such stowage is carried out prior to attachment of this insurance or by the Assured or their servants)

4.4 loss damage or expense caused by inherent vice or nature of the subject-matter insured

4.5 loss damage or expense proximately caused by delay, even though the delay be caused by a risk insured against (except expenses payable under Clause 2 above)

4.6 loss damage or expense arising from insolvency or financial default of the owners managers charterers or operators of the vessel.

4.7 loss damage or expense arising from the use of any weapon of war employing atomic or nuclear fission and/or fusion or other like reaction or radioactive force or matter.

5. Unseaworthiness and Unfitness Exclusion Clause

5.1 In no case shall this insurance cover loss damage or expense arising from, Unseaworthiness of vessel or craft, Unfitness of vessel craft conveyance container or liftvan for the safe carriage of the subject-matter insured, Where the Assured or their servants are privy to such unseaworthiness or unfitness, at the time the subject-matter insured is loaded therein.

5.2 The Underwriters waive any breach of the implied warranties of seaworthiness of the ship and fitness of the ship to carry the subject-matter insured to destination, unless the Assured or their servants are privy to such unseaworthiness or unfitness.

6. War Exclusion Clause

6. In no case shall this insurance cover loss damage or expense caused by

6.1 war civil war revolution rebellion insurrection, or civil strife arising therefrom, or any hostile act by or against a belligerent power

6.2 capture seizure arrest restraint or detainment (piracy excepted), and the consequences thereof or any attempt thereat

6.3 derelict mines torpedoes bombs or other derelict weapons of war.

7. Strikes Exclusion Clause

7. In no case shall this insurance cover loss damage or expense

7.1 caused by strikers, locked-out workmen, or persons taking part in labour disturbances, riots or civil commotions

7.2 resulting from strikes, lock-outs, labour disturbances, riots or civil commotions

7.3 caused by any terrorist or any person acting from a political motive.

DURATION

8. Transit Clause

8.1 This insurance attaches from the time the goods leave the warehouse or place of storage at the place named herein for the commencement of the transit, continues during the ordinary course of transit and terminates either

8.1.1 on delivery to the Consignees' or other final warehouse or place of storage at the destination named herein,

8.1.2 on delivery to any other warehouse or place of storage, whether prior to or at the destination named herein, which the Assured elect to use either

8.1.2.1 for storage other than in the ordinary course of transit or

8.1.2.2 for allocation or distribution, or

8.1.3 on the expiry of 60 days after completion of discharge overside of the goods hereby insured from the oversea vessel at the final port of discharge,

whichever shall first occur.

8.2 If, after discharge overside from the oversea vessel at the final port of discharge, but prior to termination of this insurance, the goods are to be forwarded to a destination other than that to which they are insured hereunder, this insurance, whilst remaining subject to termination as provided for above, shall not extend beyond the commencement of transit to such other destination.

8.3 This insurance shall remain in force (subject to termination as provided for above and to the provisions of Clause 9 below) during delay beyond the control of the Assured, any deviation, forced discharge, reshipment or transhipment and during any variation of the adventure arising from the exercise of a liberty granted to shipowners or charterers under the contract of affreightment.

9. Termination of Contract of Carriage

9. If owing to circumstances beyond the control of the Assured either the contract of carriage is terminated at a port or place other than the destination named therein or the transit is otherwise terminated before delivery of the subject-matter insured as provided for in Clause 8 above, then this insurance shall also terminate unless prompt notice is given to the Insurers and continuation of cover is requested when this insurance shall remain in force, subject to an additional premium if required by the Insurers, either

9. 1 until the subject-matter insured is sold and delivered at such port or place, or, unless otherwise specially agreed, until the expiry of 60 days after arrival of the subject-matter insured at such port or place, whichever shall first occur, or

9. 2 if the subject-matter insured is forwarded within the said period of 60 days (or any agreed extension thereof) to the destination named herein or to any other destination, until terminated in accordance with the provisions of Clause 8 above.

10. Change of Voyage Clause

10. Where, after attachment of this insurance, the destination is changed by the Assured, held covered at a premium and on conditions to be arranged subject to prompt notice being given to the Underwriters.

CLAIMS

11. Insurable Interest

11. 1 In order to recover under this insurance the Assured must have an insurable interest in the subject-matter insured at the time of the loss.

11. 2 Subject to Clause 11. 1 above, the Assured shall be entitled to recover for insured loss occurring during the period covered by this insurance, notwithstanding that the loss occurred before the contract of insurance was concluded, unless the Assured were aware of the loss and the insurers were not.

12. Forwarding Charges Clause

12. Where, as a result of the operation of a risk covered by this insurance, the insured transit is terminated at a port or place other than that to which the subject-matter is covered under this insurance, the Underwriters will reimburse the Assured for any extra charges properly and reasonably incurred in unloading storing and forwarding the subject-matter to the destination to which it is insured hereunder.

This Clause 12, which does not apply to general average or salvage charges, shall be subject to the exclusions contained in Clauses 4, 5, 6 and 7 above, and shall not include charges arising from the fault negligence insolvency or financial default of the Assured or their servants.

13. Constructive Total Loss Clause

13. No claim for Constructive Total Loss shall be recoverable hereunder unless the subject-matter insured is reasonably abandoned either on account of its actual total loss appearing to be unavoidable or because the cost of recovering, reconditioning and forwarding the subject-matter insured to the des-

tination to which it is insured would exceed its value on arrival.

14. Increased Value Clause

14.1 If any increased Value insurance is effected by the Assured on the subject-matter insured under this insurance the agreed value of the subject-matter insured shall be deemed to be increased to the total amount insured herein and all Increased Value insurances covering the loss, and liability under this insurance shall be in such proportion as the sum insured under this insurance bears to such total amount insured.

In the event of claim the Assured shall provide the Insurers with evidence of the amounts insured under all other insurances.

14.2 Where this insurance is on Increased Value the following clause shall apply:

The agreed value of the subject matter insured shall be deemed to be equal to the total amount insured under the primary insurance and all Increased Value insurances covering the loss and effected on the subject-matter insured by the Assured, and liability under this insurance shall be in such proportion as the sum insured under this insurance bears to such total amount insured.

In the event of claim the Assured shall provide the Insurers with evidence of the amounts insured under all other insurances.

BENEFIT OF INSURANCE

15. Not to Insure Clause

15. This insurance shall not inure to the benefit of the carrier or other bailee.

MINIMISING LOSSES

16. Duty of Assured Clause

16. It is the duty of the Assured and their servants and agents in respect of loss recoverable hereunder

16.1 to take such measures as may be reasonable for the purpose of averting or minimising such loss, and

16.2 to ensure that all rights against carriers, bailees or other third parties are properly preserved and exercised

and the Underwriters will, in addition to any loss recoverable hereunder, reimburse the Assured for any charges properly and reasonably incurred in pursuance of these duties.

17. Waiver Clause

17. Measures taken by the Assured or the Underwriters with the object of saving, protecting or recovering the subject-matter insured shall not be considered as a waiver or acceptance of abandonment or otherwise prejudice the rights of either party.

AVOIDANCE OF DELAY

18. Reasonable Dispatch Clause

18. It is a condition of this insurance that the Assured shall act with reasonable despatch in all

circumstances within their control.

LAW AND PRACTICE

19. English Law and Practice Clause

19. This insurance is subject to English law and practice

POSE NOTE

Note- It is necessary for the Assured when they become aware of an event which is" held covered" under this insurance to give prompt notice to the Underwriters and the right to such cover is dependent upon compliance with this obligation.

附录三

INSTITUTE CARGO CLAUSES(A)

1/1/09

RISKS COVERED

Risks

1. This insurance covers all risks of loss of or damage to the subject-matter insured except as excluded by the provisions of Clauses 4, 5 6 and 7 below.

General Average

2. This insurance covers general average and salvage charges, adjusted or determined according to the contract of affreightment and/or the governing law and practice, incurred to avoid or in connection with the avoidance of loss from any cause except those excluded in Clauses 4, 5, 6 and 7 below.

"Both to Blame Collision Clause"

3. This insurance indemnifies the Assured, in respect of any risk insured herein, against liability incurred under any Both to Blame Collision Clause in the contract of carriage. In the event of any claim by carriers under the said Clause, the Assured agree to notify the insurers who shall have the right, at their own cost and expense, to defend the Assured against such claim.

EXCLUSIONS

4. In no case shall this insurance cover

4.1 loss damage or expense attributable to wilful misconduct of the Assured

4.2 ordinary leakage, ordinary loss in weight or volume, or ordinary wear and tear of the subject-matter insured

4.3 loss damage or expense caused by insufficiency or unsuitability of packing or preparation of the subject-matter insured to withstand the ordinary incidents of the insured transit where such packing or preparation is carried out by the Assured or their employees or prior to the attachment of this insurance (for the purpose of these Clauses "packing" shall be deemed to include stowage in a container and "employees" shall not include independent contractors)

4.4 loss damage or expense caused by inherent vice or nature of the subject-matter insured.

4.5 loss damage or expense caused by delay, even though the delay be caused by a risk insured against (except expenses payable under Clause 2 above).

4.6 loss damage or expense caused by insolvency or financial default of the owners managers charterers or operators of the vessel where, at the time of loading of the subject-matter insured on board the vessel, the Assured are aware, or in the ordinary course of business should be aware, that such insolvency or financial default could prevent the normal prosecution of the voyage.

This exclusion shall not apply where the contract of insurance has been assigned to the party claiming hereunder who has bought or agreed to buy the subject-matter insured in good faith under a binding contract.

4.7 loss damage or expense directly or indirectly caused by or arising from the use of any weapon or device employing atomic or nuclear fission and/or fusion or other like reaction or radioactive force or matter.

5. 1 In no case shall this insurance cover loss damage or expense arising from

5. 1. 1 unseaworthiness of vessel or craft or unfitness of vessel or craft for the safe carriage of the subject-matter insured, where the Assured are privy to such unseaworthiness or unfitness, at the time the subject-matter insured is loaded therein

5. 1. 2 unfitness of container or conveyance for the safe carriage of the subject-matter insured, where loading therein or thereon is carried out prior to attachment of this insurance or by the Assured or their employees and they are privy to such unfitness at the time of loading.

5. 2 Exclusion 5. 1. 1 above shall not apply where the contract of insurance has been assigned to the party claiming hereunder who has bought or agreed to buy the subject-matter insured in good faith under a binding contract.

5. 3 The Insurers waive any breach of the implied warranties of seaworthiness of the ship and fitness of the ship to carry the subject-matter insured to destination.

6. In no case shall this insurance cover loss damage or expense caused by

6. 1 war civil war revolution rebellion insurrection, or civil strife arising therefrom, or any hostile act by or against a belligerent power

6. 2 capture seizure arrest restraint or detainment (piracy excepted), and the consequences thereof or any attempt thereat

6. 3 derelict mines torpedoes bombs or other derelict weapons of war.

7. In no case shall this insurance cover loss damage or expense

7. 1 caused by strikers, locked-out workmen, or persons taking part in labour disturbances, riots or civil commotions

7. 2 resulting from strikes, lock-outs, labour disturbances, riots or civil commotions

7. 3 caused by any act of terrorism being an act of any person acting on behalf of, or in connection with, any organisation which carries out activities directed towards the overthrowing or influencing, by force or violence, of any government whether or not legally constituted

7. 4 caused by any person acting from a political, ideological or religious motive.

DURATION

Transit Clause

8. 1 Subject to Clause 11 below, this insurance attaches from the time the subject-matter insured is first moved in the warehouse or at the place of storage (at the place named in the contract of insurance) for the purpose of the immediate loading into or onto the carrying vehicle or other conveyance for the commencement of transit, continues during the ordinary course of transit and terminates either

8. 1. 1 on completion of unloading from the carrying vehicle or other conveyance in or at the final warehouse or place of storage at the destination named in the contract of insurance,

8. 1. 2 on completion of unloading from the carrying vehicle or other conveyance in or at any other warehouse or place of storage, whether prior to or at the destination named in the contract of insurance, which the Assured or their employees elect to use either for storage other than in the ordinary

course of transit or for allocation or distribution, or

8. 1. 3 when the Assured or their employees elect to use any carrying vehicle or other conveyance or any container for storage other than in the ordinary course of transit or

8. 1. 4 on the expiry of 60 days after completion of discharge overside of the subject-matter insured from the oversea vessel at the final port of discharge,

whichever shall first occur.

8. 2 If, after discharge overside from the oversea vessel at the final port of discharge, but prior to termination of this insurance, the subject-matter insured is to be forwarded to a destination other than that to which it is insured, this insurance, whilst remaining subject to termination as provided in Clauses 8. 1. 1 to 8. 1. 4, shall not extend beyond the time the subject-matter insured is first moved for the purpose of the commencement of transit to such other destination.

8. 3 This insurance shall remain in force (subject to termination as provided for in Clauses 8. 1. 1 to 8. 1. 4 above and to the provisions of Clause 9 below) during delay beyond the control of the Assured, any deviation, forced discharge, reshipment or transhipment and during any variation of the adventure arising from the exercise of a liberty granted to carriers under the contract of carriage.

Termination of Contract of Carriage

9. If owing to circumstances beyond the control of the Assured either the contract of carriage is terminated at a port or place other than the destination named therein or the transit is otherwise terminated before unloading of the subject-matter insured as provided for in Clause 8 above, then this insurance shall also terminate unless prompt notice is given to the Insurers and continuation of cover is requested when this insurance shall remain in force, subject to an additional premium if required by the Insurers, either

9. 1 until the subject-matter insured is sold and delivered at such port or place, or, unless otherwise specially agreed, until the expiry of 60 days after arrival of the subject-matter insured at such port or place, whichever shall first occur, or

9. 2 if the subject-matter insured is forwarded within the said period of 60 days (or any agreed extension thereof) to the destination named in the contract of insurance or to any other destination, until terminated in accordance with the provisions of Clause 8 above.

Change of Voyage

10. 1 Where, after attachment of this insurance, the destination is changed by the Assured, this must be notified promptly to insurers for rates and terms to be agreed. Should a loss occur prior to such agreement being obtained cover may be provided but only if cover would have been available at a reasonable commercial market rate on reasonable market terms.

10. 2 Where the subject-matter insured commences the transit contemplated by this insurance (in accordance with Clause 8. 1), but, without the knowledge of the Assured or their employees the ship sails for another destination, this insurance will nevertheless be deemed to have attached at commencement of such transit.

CLAIMS

Insurable Interest

11. 1 In order to recover under this insurance the Assured must have an insurable interest in

the subject-matter insured at the time of the loss.

11. 2 Subject to Clause 11. 1 above, the Assured shall be entitled to recover for insured loss occurring during the period covered by this insurance, notwithstanding that the loss occurred before the contract of insurance was concluded, unless the Assured were aware of the loss and the insurers were not.

Forwarding Charges

12. Where, as a result of the operation of a risk covered by this insurance, the insured transit is terminated at a port or place other than that to which the subject-matter insured is covered under this insurance, the insurers will reimburse the Assured for any extra charges properly and reasonably incurred in unloading storing and forwarding the subject-matter insured to the destination to which it is insured.

This Clause 12, which does not apply to general average or salvage charges, shall be subject to the exclusions contained in Clauses 4, 5, 6 and 7 above, and shall not include charges arising from the fault negligence insolvency or financial default of the Assured or their employees.

Constructive Total Loss

13. No claim for Constructive Total Loss shall be recoverable hereunder unless the subject-matter insured is reasonably abandoned either on account of its actual total loss appearing to be unavoidable or because the cost of recovering, reconditioning and forwarding the subject-matter insured to the destination to which it is insured would exceed its value on arrival.

Increased Value

14. 1 If any increased Value insurance is effected by the Assured on the subject-matter insured under this insurance the agreed value of the subject-matter insured shall be deemed to be increased to the total amount insured under this insurance and all Increased Value insurances covering the loss, and liability under this insurance shall be in such proportion as the sum insured under this insurance bears to such total amount insured.

In the event of claim the Assured shall provide the Insurers with evidence of the amounts insured under all other insurances.

14. 2 Where this insurance is on Increased Value the following clause shall apply:

The agreed value of the subject matter insured shall be deemed to be equal to the total amount insured under the primary insurance and all Increased Value insurances covering the loss and effected on the subject-matter insured by the Assured, and liability under this insurance shall be in such proportion as the sum insured under this insurance bears to such total amount insured.

In the event of claim the Assured shall provide the Insurers with evidence of the amounts insured under all other insurances.

BENEFIT OF INSURANCE

15. This insurance

15. 1 covers the Assured which includes the person claiming indemnity either as the person by or on whose behalf the contract of insurance was effected or as an assignee,

15. 2 shall not extend to or otherwise benefit the carrier or other bailee.

MINIMISING LOSSES

Duty of Assured

16 It is the duty of the Assured and their employees and agents in respect of loss recoverable hereunder

16. 1 to take such measures as may be reasonable for the purpose of averting or minimising such loss, and

16. 2 to ensure that all rights against carriers, bailees or other third parties are properly preserved and exercised,

and the Insurers will, in addition to any loss recoverable hereunder, reimburse the Assured for any charges properly and reasonably incurred in pursuance of these duties.

Waiver

17. Measures taken by the Assured or the Insurers with the object of saving, protecting or recovering the subject-matter insured shall not be considered as a waiver or acceptance.

AVOIDANCE OF DELAY

18. It is a condition of this insurance that the Assured shall act with reasonable despatch in all circumstances within their control.

LAW AND PRACTICE

19. This insurance is subject to English law and practice

NOTE: Where a continuation of cover is requested under Clause 9, or a change of destination is notified under Clause 10, there is an obligation to give prompt notice to the Insurers and the right to such cover is dependent upon compliance with this obligation

附录四

INSTITUTE WAR CLAUSES (CARGO)
1/1/09

RISKS COVERED

Risks

1. This insurance covers, except as excluded by the provisions of Clauses 3 and 4 below, loss of or damage to the subject-matter insured caused by

1.1 war civil war revolution rebellion insurrection, or civil strife arising therefrom, or any hostile act by or against a belligerent power

1.2 capture seizure arrest restraint or detainment, arising from risks covered under 1.1 above, and the consequences thereof or any attempt thereat

1.3 derelict mines torpedoes bombs or other derelict weapons of war.

General Average

2. This insurance covers general average and salvage charges, adjusted or determined according to the contract of carriage and/or the governing law and practice, incurred to avoid or in connection with the avoidance of loss from a risk covered under these Clauses.

EXCLUSIONS

3. In no case shall this insurance cover

3.1 loss damage or expense attributable to wilful misconduct of the Assured

3.2 ordinary leakage, ordinary loss in weight or volume, or ordinary wear and tear of the subject-matter insured

3.3 loss damage or expense caused by insufficiency or unsuitability of packing or preparation of the subject-matter insured to withstand the ordinary incidents of the insured transit where such packing or preparation is carried out by the Assured or their employees or prior to the attachment of this insurance (for the purpose of these Clauses "packing" shall be deemed to include stowage in a container and "employees" shall not include independent contractors)

3.4 loss damage or expense caused by inherent vice or nature of the subject-matter insured

3.5 loss damage or expense caused by delay, even though the delay be caused by a risk insured against (except expenses payable under Clause 2 above)

3.6 loss damage or expense caused by insolvency or financial default of the owners managers charterers or operators of the vessel where, at the time of loading of the subject-matter insured on board the vessel, the Assured are aware, or in the ordinary course of business should be aware, that such insolvency or financial default could prevent the normal prosecution of the voyage This exclusion shall not apply where the contract of insurance has been assigned to the party claiming

hereunder who has bought or agreed to buy the subject-matter insured in good faith under a binding contract

3.7 any claim based upon loss of or frustration of the voyage or adventure

3. 8 loss damage or expense directly or indirectly caused by or arising from any hostile use of any weapon or device employing atomic or nuclear fission and/or fusion or other like reaction or radioactive force or matter.

4. 4. 1 In no case shall this insurance cover loss damage or expense arising from

4. 1. 1 unseaworthiness of vessel or craft or unfitness of vessel or craft for the safe carriage of the subject-matter insured, where the Assured are privy to such unseaworthiness or unfitness, at the time the subject-matter insured is loaded therein

4. 1. 2 unfitness of container or conveyance for the safe carriage of the subject-matter insured, where loading therein or thereon is carried out prior to attachment of this insurance or by the Assured or their employees and they are privy to such unfitness at the time of loading.

4. 2 Exclusion 4. 1. 1 above shall not apply where the contract of insurance has been assigned to the party claiming hereunder who has bought or agreed to buy the subject-matter insured in good faith under a binding contract.

4. 3 The Insurers waive any breach of the implied warranties of seaworthiness of the ship and fitness of the ship to carry the subject-matter insured to destination.

DURATION

Transit Clause

5. 5. 1 This insurance

5. 1. 1 attaches only as the subject-matter insured and as to any part as that part is loaded on an oversea vessel and

5. 1. 2 terminates, subject to 5. 2 and 5. 3 below, either as the subject-matter insured and as to any part as that part is discharged from an oversea vessel at the final port or place of discharge, or

on expiry of 15 days counting from midnight of the day of arrival of the vessel at the final port or place of discharge,

whichever shall first occur;

nevertheless,

subject to prompt notice to the Insurers and to an additional premium, such insurance

5. 1. 3 reattaches when, without having discharged the subject-matter insured at the final port or place of discharge, the vessel sails therefrom, and

5. 1. 4 terminates, subject to 5. 2 and 5. 3 below, either as the subject-matter insured and as to any part as that part is thereafter discharged from the vessel at the final (or substituted) port or place of discharge, or on expiry of 15 days counting from midnight of the day of re-arrival of the vessel at the final port or place of discharge or arrival of the vessel at a substituted port or place of discharge, whichever shall first occur.

5. 2 If during the insured voyage the oversea vessel arrives at an intermediate port or place to discharge the subject-matter insured for on-carriage by oversea vessel or by aircraft, or the subject-matter insured is discharged from the vessel at a port or place of refuge, then, subject to 5. 3 below and to an additional premium if required, this insurance continues until the expiry of 15 days counting from midnight of the day of arrival of the vessel at such port or place, but thereafter reattaches as the

subject-matter insured and as to any part as that part is loaded on an on-carrying oversea vessel or aircraft. During the period of 15 days the insurance remains in force after discharge only whilst the subject-matter insured and as to any part as that part is at such port or place. If the subject-matter insured is oncarried within the said period of 15 days or if the insurance reattaches as provided in this Clause 5. 2

5. 2. 1 where the on-carriage is by oversea vessel this insurance continues subject to the terms of these Clauses, or

5. 2. 2 where the on-carriage is by aircraft, the current Institute War Clauses (Air Cargo) (excluding sendings by Post) shall be deemed to form part of the contract of insurance and shall apply to the on-carriage by air.

5. 3 If the voyage in the contract of carriage is terminated at a port or place other than the destination agreed therein, such port or place shall be deemed the final port of discharge and this insurance terminates in accordance with 5. 1. 2. If the subject-matter insured is subsequently reshipped to the original or any other destination, then provided notice is given to the Insurers before the commencement of such further transit and subject to an additional premium, this insurance reattaches

5. 3. 1 in the case of the subject-matter insured having been discharged, as the subject-matter insured and as to any part as that part is loaded on the on-carrying vessel for the voyage;

5. 3. 2 in the case of the subject-matter not having been discharged, when the vessel sails from such deemed final port of discharge;

thereafter this insurance terminates in accordance with 5. 1. 4.

5. 4 The insurance against the risks of mines and derelict torpedoes, floating or submerged, is extended whilst the subject-matter insured or any part thereof is on craft whilst in transit to or from the oversea vessel, but in no case beyond the expiry of 60 days after discharge from the oversea vessel unless otherwise specially agreed by the Insurers.

5. 5 Subject to prompt notice to Insurers, and to an additional premium if required, this insurance shall remain in force within the provisions of these Clauses during any deviation, or any variation of the adventure arising from the exercise of a liberty granted to carriers under the contract of carriage.

(For the purpose of Clause 5)

"arrival" shall be deemed to mean that the vessel is anchored, moored or otherwise secured at a berth or place within the Harbour Authority area. If such a berth or place is not available, arrival is deemed to have occurred when the vessel first anchors, moors or otherwise secures either at or off the intended port or place of discharge

"oversea vessel" shall be deemed to mean a vessel carrying the subject-matter from one port or place to another where such voyage involves a sea passage by that vessel)

Change of Voyage

6. 6. 1 Where, after attachment of this insurance, the destination is changed by the Assured, this must be notified promptly to Insurers for rates and terms to be agreed. Should a loss occur prior to such agreement being obtained cover may be provided but only if cover would have been available at a reasonable commercial market rate on reasonable market terms.

6. 2 Where the subject-matter insured commences the transit contemplated by this insurance

(in accordance with Clause 5. 1), but, without the knowledge of the Assured or their employees the ship sails for another destination, this insurance will nevertheless be deemed to have attached at commencement of such transit.

7. Anything contained in this contract which is inconsistent with Clauses 3. 7, 3. 8 or 5 shall, to the extent of such inconsistency, be null and void.

CLAIMS

Insurable Interest

8. 8. 1 In order to recover under this insurance the Assured must have an insurable interest in the subjectmatter insured at the time of the loss.

8. 2 Subject to Clause 8. 1 above, the Assured shall be entitled to recover for insured loss occurring during the period covered by this insurance, notwithstanding that the loss occurred before the contract of insurance was concluded, unless the Assured were aware of the loss and the Insurers were not.

Increased Value

9. 9. 1 If any Increased Value insurance is effected by the Assured on the subject-matter insured under this insurance the agreed value of the subject-matter insured shall be deemed to be increased to the total amount insured under this insurance and all Increased Value insurances covering the loss, and liability under this insurance shall be in such proportion as the sum insured under this insurance bears to such total amount insured.

In the event of claim the Assured shall provide the Insurers with evidence of the amounts insured under all other insurances.

9. 2 Where this insurance is on Increased Value the following clause shall apply:

The agreed value of the subject-matter insured shall be deemed to be equal to the total amount insured under the primary insurance and all Increased Value insurances covering the loss and effected on the subject-matter insured by the Assured, and liability under this insurance shall be in such proportion as the sum insured under this insurance bears to such total amount insured.

In the event of claim the Assured shall provide the Insurers with evidence of the amounts insured under all other insurances.

BENEFIT OF INSURANCE

10. This insurance

10. 1 covers the Assured which includes the person claiming indemnity either as the person by or on whose behalf the contract of insurance was effected or as an assignee,

10. 2 shall not extend to or otherwise benefit the carrier or other bailee.

MINIMISING LOSSES

Duty of Assured

11. It is the duty of the Assured and their employees and agents in respect of loss recoverable hereunder

11.1 to take such measures as may be reasonable for the purpose of averting or minimising such loss, and

11.2 to ensure that all rights against carriers, bailees or other third parties are properly preserved and exercised

and the Insurers will, in addition to any loss recoverable hereunder, reimburse the Assured for any charges properly and reasonably incurred in pursuance of these duties.

Waiver

12. Measures taken by the Assured or the Insurers with the object of saving, protecting or recovering the subject-matter insured shall not be considered as a waiver or acceptance of abandonment or otherwise prejudice the rights of either party.

AVOIDANCE OF DELAY

13. It is a condition of this insurance that the Assured shall act with reasonable despatch in all circumstances within their control.

LAW AND PRACTICE

14. This insurance is subject to English law and practice.

NOTE: Where a reattachment of cover is requested under Clause 5, or a change of destination is notified under Clause 6, there is an obligation to give prompt notice to the Insurers and the right to such cover is dependent upon compliance with this obligation.

附录五

INSTITUTE STRIKES CLAUSES (CARGO) 1/1/09

RISKS COVERED

Risks

1. This insurance covers, except as excluded by the provisions of Clauses 3 and 4 below, loss of or damage to the subject-matter insured caused by

1.1 strikers, locked-out workmen, or persons taking part in labour disturbances, riots or civil commotions

1.2 any act of terrorism being an act of any person acting on behalf of, or in connection with, any organisation which carries out activities directed towards the overthrowing or influencing, by force or violence, of any government whether or not legally constituted

1.3 any person acting from a political, ideological or religious motive.

General Average

2. This insurance covers general average and salvage charges, adjusted or determined according to the contract of carriage and/or the governing law and practice, incurred to avoid or in connection with the avoidance of loss from a risk covered under these Clauses.

EXCLUSIONS

3. In no case shall this insurance cover

3.1 loss damage or expense attributable to wilful misconduct of the Assured

3.2 ordinary leakage, ordinary loss in weight or volume, or ordinary wear and tear of the subject-matter insured

3.3 loss damage or expense caused by insufficiency or unsuitability of packing or preparation of the subjectmatter insured to withstand the ordinary incidents of the insured transit where such packing or preparation is carried out by the Assured or their employees or prior to the attachment of this insurance (for the purpose of this Clause 3.3 "packing" shall be deemed to include stowage in a container and "employees" shall not include independent contractors)

3.4 loss damage or expense caused by inherent vice or nature of the subject-matter insured

3.5 loss damage or expense caused by delay, even though the delay be caused by a risk insured against

(except expenses payable under Clause 2 above)

3.6 loss damage or expense caused by insolvency or financial default of the owners managers charterers or operators of the vessel where, at the time of loading of the subject-matter insured on board the vessel, the Assured are aware, or in the ordinary course of business should be aware, that such insolvency or financial default could prevent the normal prosecution of the voyage

This exclusion shall not apply where the contract of insurance has been assigned to the party claiming hereunder who has bought or agreed to buy the subject-matter insured in good faith under a binding contract

3. 7 loss damage or expense arising from the absence shortage or withholding of labour of any description whatsoever resulting from any strike, lockout, labour disturbance, riot or civil commotion

3. 8 any claim based upon loss of or frustration of the voyage or adventure

3. 9 loss damage or expense directly or indirectly caused by or arising from the use of any weapon or device employing atomic or nuclear fission and/or fusion or other like reaction or radioactive force or matter

3. 10 loss damage or expense caused by war civil war revolution rebellion insurrection, or civil strife arising therefrom, or any hostile act by or against a belligerent power.

4. 1 In no case shall this insurance cover loss damage or expense arising from

4. 1. 1 unseaworthiness of vessel or craft or unfitness of vessel or craft for the safe carriage of the subject-matter insured, where the Assured are privy to such unseaworthiness or unfitness, at the time the subject-matter insured is loaded therein

4. 1. 2 unfitness of container or conveyance for the safe carriage of the subject-matter insured, where loading therein or thereon is carried out prior to attachment of this insurance or by the Assured or their employees and they are privy to such unfitness at the time of loading.

4. 2 Exclusion 4. 1. 1 above shall not apply where the contract of insurance has been assigned to the party claiming hereunder who has bought or agreed to buy the subject-matter insured in good faith under a binding contract.

4. 3 The Insurers waive any breach of the implied warranties of seaworthiness of the ship and fitness of the ship to carry the subject-matter insured to destination.

DURATION

Transit Clause

5. 1 Subject to Clause 8 below, this insurance attaches from the time the subject-matter insured is first moved in the warehouse or at the place of storage (at the place named in the contract of insurance) for the purpose of the immediate loading into or onto the carrying vehicle or other conveyance for the commencement of transit, continues during the ordinary course of transit and terminates either

5. 1. 1 on completion of unloading from the carrying vehicle or other conveyance in or at the final warehouse or place of storage at the destination named in the contract of insurance,

5. 1. 2 on completion of unloading from the carrying vehicle or other conveyance in or at any other warehouse or place of storage, whether prior to or at the destination named in the contract of insurance, which the Assured or their employees elect to use either for storage other than in the ordinary course of transit or for allocation or distribution, or

5. 1. 3 when the Assured or their employees elect to use any carrying vehicle or other conveyance or any container for storage other than in the ordinary course of transit or

5. 1. 4 on the expiry of 60 days after completion of discharge overside of the subject-matter insured from the oversea vessel at the final port of discharge, whichever shall first occur.

5. 2 If, after discharge overside from the oversea vessel at the final port of discharge, but prior to termination of this insurance, the subject-matter insured is to be forwarded to a destination other

than that to which it is insured, this insurance, whilst remaining subject to termination as provided in Clauses 5. 1. 1 to 5. 1. 4, shall not extend beyond the time the subject-matter insured is first moved for the purpose of the commencement of transit to such other destination.

5. 3 This insurance shall remain in force (subject to termination as provided for in Clauses 5. 1. 1 to 5. 1. 4 above and to the provisions of Clause 6 below) during delay beyond the control of the Assured, any deviation, forced discharge, reshipment or transhipment and during any variation of the adventure arising from the exercise of a liberty granted to carriers under the contract of carriage.

Termination of Contract of Carriage

6. If owing to circumstances beyond the control of the Assured either the contract of carriage is terminated at a port or place other than the destination named therein or the transit is otherwise terminated before unloading of the subject-matter insured as provided for in Clause 5 above, then this insurance shall also terminate unless prompt notice is given to the Insurers and continuation of cover is requested when this insurance shall remain in force, subject to an additional premium if required by the Insurers, either

6. 1 until the subject-matter insured is sold and delivered at such port or place, or, unless otherwise specially agreed, until the expiry of 60 days after arrival of the subject-matter insured at such port or place, whichever shall first occur, or

6. 2 if the subject-matter insured is forwarded within the said period of 60 days (or any agreed extension thereof) to the destination named in the contract of insurance or to any other destination, until terminated in accordance with the provisions of Clause 5 above.

Change of Voyage

7. 7. 1 Where, after attachment of this insurance, the destination is changed by the Assured, this must be notified promptly to Insurers for rates and terms to be agreed. Should a loss occur prior to such agreement being obtained cover may be provided but only if cover would have been available at a reasonable commercial market rate on reasonable market terms.

7. 2 Where the subject-matter insured commences the transit contemplated by this insurance (in accordance with Clause 5. 1), but, without the knowledge of the Assured or their employees the ship sails for another destination, this insurance will nevertheless be deemed to have attached at commencement of such transit.

CLAIMS

Insurable Interest

8. 8. 1 In order to recover under this insurance the Assured must have an insurable interest in the subjectmatter insured at the time of the loss.

8. 2 Subject to Clause 8. 1 above, the Assured shall be entitled to recover for insured loss occurring during the period covered by this insurance, notwithstanding that the loss occurred before the contract of insurance was concluded, unless the Assured were aware of the loss and the Insurers were not.

Increased Value

9. 9. 1 If any Increased Value insurance is effected by the Assured on the subject-matter in-

sured under this insurance the agreed value of the subject-matter insured shall be deemed to be increased to the total amount insured under this insurance and all Increased Value insurances covering the loss, and liability under this insurance shall be in such proportion as the sum insured under this insurance bears to such total amount insured.

In the event of claim the Assured shall provide the Insurers with evidence of the amounts insured under all other insurances.

9. 2 Where this insurance is on Increased Value the following clause shall apply:

The agreed value of the subject-matter insured shall be deemed to be equal to the total amount

insured under the primary insurance and all Increased Value insurances covering the loss and effected on the subject-matter insured by the Assured, and liability under this insurance shall be in such proportion as the sum insured under this insurance bears to such total amount insured.

In the event of claim the Assured shall provide the Insurers with evidence of the amounts insured under all other insurances.

BENEFIT OF INSURANCE

10. This insurance

10. 1 covers the Assured which includes the person claiming indemnity either as the person by or on whose behalf the contract of insurance was effected or as an assignee,

10. 2 shall not extend to or otherwise benefit the carrier or other bailee.

MINIMISING LOSSES

Duty of Assured

11. It is the duty of the Assured and their employees and agents in respect of loss recoverable hereunder

11. 1 to take such measures as may be reasonable for the purpose of averting or minimising such loss, and

11. 2 to ensure that all rights against carriers, bailees or other third parties are properly preserved and exercised

and the Insurers will, in addition to any loss recoverable hereunder, reimburse the Assured for any charges properly and reasonably incurred in pursuance of these duties.

Waiver

12. Measures taken by the Assured or the Insurers with the object of saving, protecting or recovering the subjectmatter insured shall not be considered as a waiver or acceptance of abandonment or otherwise prejudice the rights of either party.

AVOIDANCE OF DELAY

13. It is a condition of this insurance that the Assured shall act with reasonable despatch in all circumstances within their control.

LAW AND PRACTICE

14. This insurance is subject to English law and practice.

NOTE: Where a continuation of cover is requested under Clause 6, or a change of destination is notified under Clause 7, there is an obligation to give prompt notice to the Insurers and the right to such cover is dependent upon compliance with this obligation.

图书在版编目(CIP)数据

海上货物保险/杨良宜著. —北京:法律出版社,2010.10(2020.1 重印)
(研究生教学书系)
ISBN 978 -7 -5118 -1228 -5

Ⅰ.①海… Ⅱ.①杨… Ⅲ.①海上运输:货物运输—运输保险—研究生—教材 Ⅳ.①F840.63

中国版本图书馆 CIP 数据核字(2010)第 185130 号

海上货物保险
HAISHANG HUOWU BAOXIAN

杨良宜 著

责任编辑 吴 昉
装帧设计 乔智炜

编辑统筹 法律教育出版分社
出版 法律出版社
总发行 中国法律图书有限公司
经销 新华书店
印刷 北京玺诚印务有限公司
责任印制 沙 磊

开本 720 毫米×960 毫米 1/16
印张 42
字数 845 千
版本 2010 年 10 月第 1 版
印次 2020 年 1 月第 6 次印刷

法律出版社/北京市丰台区莲花池西里 7 号(100073)
网址/www. lawpress. com. cn
投稿邮箱/info@ lawpress. com. cn
举报维权邮箱/jbwq@ lawpress. com. cn
销售热线/400 -660 -8393
咨询电话/010 -63939796

中国法律图书有限公司/北京市丰台区莲花池西里 7 号(100073)
全国各地中法图分、子公司销售电话:
统一销售客服/400 -660 -8393/6393
第一法律书店/010 -83938432/8433
西安分公司/029 -85330678
重庆分公司/023 -67453036
上海分公司/021 -62071639/1636
深圳分公司/0755 -83072995

书号:ISBN 978 -7 -5118 -1228 -5
定价:82.00 元